CALIFORNIA
HIKING

The Complete Guide to
1,000 of the Best Hikes in the Golden State

by Tom Stienstra
and Ann Marie Brown

BOOKS BUILDING COMMUNITY™

ISBN 1-57354-022-6

52095

9 781573 540223

>   Foghorn Press
>   Rights Department
>   555 DeHaro Street, Suite 220
>   San Francisco, CA 94107
>   foghorn@well.com

To order individual books, please call Foghorn Press: 1-800-FOGHORN
(364-4676) or (415) 241-9550. Foghorn Press titles are distributed
to the book trade by Publishers Group West, based in Emeryville,
California. To contact your local sales representative, call 1-800-788-3123.

Library of Congress ISSN Data:
April 1997
California Hiking
The Complete Guide to 1,000 of the Best Hikes in the Golden State
Third Edition
ISSN: 1078-960X

The Foghorn Press Commitment
Foghorn Press is committed to the preservation of the environment.
We promote Leave No Trace principles in our guidebooks. Additionally,
our books are printed with soy-based inks on 50 percent recycled paper.

Printed in the United States of America

Introduction

Many of our friends were horror-stricken when they first heard we were writing this book. After all, wouldn't it mean that all their secret, favorite trails would be revealed to all? Well, it turns out that now our friends are elated instead. Like so many people, they are discovering it is difficult to imagine how many wonderful hikes are available in the state of California.

With that in mind, we hope *California Hiking* will quickly become your hiking bible, a guide to California's 1,000 best hikes, including hundreds of little-known spots in all regions of the state.

In this edition, you'll find 500 completely new trails in Southern California, Yosemite, and Tahoe. The rest of the trails have been completely revised and updated to provide the most up-to-date information available.

California Hiking features 350 hikes within 90 minutes of both San Francisco and Los Angeles, along with an additional 650 sprinkled across the state, including California's most remote areas. The hikes detail the most beautiful regions across 20 million acres of national forest, 18.5 million acres of land managed by the Bureau of Land Management, 100 state parks, 53 federal wilderness areas, 12 national parks, and dozens of regional and county parks.

The book also features a hiker-friendly format and easy-to-use map grid system. It assures that any reader will be able to find the location of a quality hike in virtually any area in less than 10 seconds. Each listing includes snapshot ratings for trail beauty and difficulty, as well as the estimated length and time required for each walk. In addition, precise, easy-to-follow directions to each trailhead are provided, along with any special trail rules, information about permits, maps, and phone contacts, and a detailed description of each hike. There are 58 detailed maps, and a 29-page index for cross-referencing.

We've included a wide variety of hikes, ranging from 10-minute walks to lookouts and waterfalls, to week-long trips into remote backcountry. Many of the featured hikes range in length from one to three hours, perfect for most people looking for an afternoon of peace. We've also included every section of the Pacific Crest Trail in California, covering more than 1,700 trail miles.

The outdoors is good for the soul, and hiking can cleanse the body and mind. Our best advice is to go for it—and don't be surprised if we see you on the trail.

—Tom Stienstra and Ann Marie Brown

California Hiking Chapter Reference Map

California Hiking

The Complete Guide to 1,000 of the
Best Hikes in the Golden State

Contents

Northern California

Central California

Featured Areas in Central California (map grids F1–H8) (see shaded pages) .... *page* 381

Southern California

Featured Areas in Southern California (map grids I2–J8) (see shaded pages) .... *page* 557

How to Use This Book

California Hiking is divided into three sections: Northern, Central, and Southern California. These sections are further divided into grids with maps that show where each trailhead is located.

For Northern California trails:
see pages 4–380 (maps AØ–E5)

For Central California trails:
see pages 384–556 (maps F1–H8)

For Southern California trails:
see pages 560–651 (maps I2–J8)

You can search for the perfect hike in two ways:

1. If you know the name of the specific trail you'd like to hike, or the name of the surrounding geographical area (town, national park, national forest, state park, lake, river, etc.), look it up in the index beginning on page 657 and turn to the corresponding page.

2. If you want to find out about hiking possibilities in a particular part of the state, use the state map on page *iv* or on the last page of this book. Find the zone where you'd like to hike (such as AØ in Northern California or I2 in Southern California), then turn to the corresponding pages. For greater detail on a particular region, turn to the "Featured Areas" shaded pages for Northern California (pages 1–3), Central California (pages 381–383), and Southern California (pages 557–559).

The San Francisco Bay Area has been divided even further into four smaller maps, due to the concentration of trails in that area. You will find Marin County on pages 216–249, the San Francisco Peninsula on pages 250–269, the East Bay Area on pages 270–293, and the South Bay Area on pages 294–319.

See the bottom of every page for a reference to corresponding maps.

What the Ratings Mean
Every trail in this book has been rated on a scale of 1 to 10 for its overall appeal, and on a scale of 1 to 5 for difficulty.

The overall rating is based largely on scenic beauty, but it also takes into account how crowded the trail is and whether or not you'll hear the noise of nearby civilization.

The difficulty rating is based on the steepness of the trail and how difficult it is to traverse. A flat, open, clearly marked trail is rated 🥾, while a cross-country scramble with huge elevation gains is rated 🥾.

Hiking the Pacific Crest Trail (PCT) and the John Muir Trail (JMT)
In addition to describing 1,000 individual hikes, this book features the entire 1,700 miles of the Pacific Crest Trail (PCT) in California and the 211-mile John Muir Trail (JMT). The PCT is split into 48 sections throughout *California Hiking* and can be found in chapters A1, B1, B2, B3, C3, D3, D4, E4, F5, G5, H4, H5, I5, I6, and J6. The JMT is broken into four sections in this book and can be found in chapters E4 and F5.

Overall Rating

🥾1 🥾2 🥾3 🥾4 🥾5 🥾6 🥾7 🥾8 🥾9 🥾10

Poor .... Fair .... Great

Difficulty

🥾1   🥾2   🥾3   🥾4   🥾5

A stroll .... Moderate .... A real butt-kicker!

The 48 PCT sections are arranged in chapters according to the location of their major trailheads. PCT sections can be easily found on the maps, in the regional tables of contents (pages 2, 382, and 558), and in the chapters, since they are always referred to by the initials PCT.

Because the PCT is usually hiked from south to north, you will find the first section (PCT-1) in chapter J6 and the last section (PCT-48) in chapter A1. The segments are grouped together at the end of the chapters in which they appear.

Trail Names, Distances, and Times

Each trail in this book has a number, name, and mileage listing and the approximate amount of time needed to complete the hike. The trail's number allows you to find it easily on the corresponding chapter map. The trail name is either the actual name of the trail (as listed on signposts and maps) or a name we gave to a series of connected trails or a loop trail. In these cases, the trail name is taken from the major destination or focal point of the hike. All mileages and approximate times refer to round-trip travel, unless the route is specifically noted as one way. In the case of one-way hikes, a car shuttle is advised.

Fees and Permits

As of May 1997, a major change has been made in the fee status of national forests across the country. Some United States Forest Service lands that were previously free to the public are now subject to use fees. In California, only six national forests have so far been affected: Angeles, Cleveland, Los Padres, San Bernardino, Shasta-Trinity, and Lake Tahoe Basin Management Unit.

In the four Southern California national forests (Angeles, Cleveland, Los Padres, and San Bernardino), fees are collected through the sale of a national forest recreation pass. The pass can be purchased for day use ($5 per day), or on a yearly basis ($30 per year). If your vehicle is parked on Forest Service land in any of these four forests, it must display a national forest recreation pass. (A pass is not required to drive through the national forests, only to park.) The same pass is good for travel anywhere in Angeles, Cleveland, Los Padres, and San Bernardino National Forests.

In Shasta-Trinity National Forest and Lake Tahoe Basin Management Unit, fees are charged only at certain sites. Visitors can pay at individual sites for day use or purchase an annual recreation pass for $30. In addition, a fee is now charged at the Mono Lake Visitor Center in Inyo National Forest.

Recreation passes for all six national forests will be available at any United States Forest Service ranger station.

Wheelchair Users

We have designated a list of user groups for each trail; under this category, we have attempted to list as much information about wheelchair facilities and access as possible. A complete list of wheelchair-accessible hikes can be found in the index on page 684. Since definitions of wheelchair accessibility and facilities vary, please call the contact number to ensure that your particular needs will be met.

Maps

For every trail in *California Hiking*, we provide the names of the USGS (United States Geologic Survey) topographic maps that feature the trail. These maps are sold by major sporting goods stores, outdoor retailers, and the USGS. To order maps from the USGS or to request a catalog of their maps, write to:

United States Geologic Survey
Western Distribution Branch
Box 25286, Federal Center
Denver, CO 80225

Each map listed in this book is sized at 7.5 minutes and costs $4, plus a $3.50 handling fee per order, no matter how many maps you order. You may order maps by phone or fax using a credit card. To reach the USGS, phone (800) 435-7627, or fax (303) 202-4693.

A private company called Map Link also carries a complete line of USGS topographic maps for California. While these maps cost slightly more than ordering them directly from the USGS, Map Link provides a good option if the USGS is out of stock. To reach Map Link, phone (805) 692-6777 or write to:

Map Link
30 South La Patera Lane, #5
Santa Barbara, CA 93117

Northern California

Featured Areas .... *pages* 2–3

Featured Areas .... *pages* 2–3

Overall Rating

| 1 | 2 | 3 | 4 | 5 | 6 | 7 | 8 | 9 | 10 |

Poor .... Fair .... Great

Difficulty

| 1 | 2 | 3 | 4 | 5 |

A stroll .... Moderate ...... A real butt-kicker!

Featured Areas in Northern California

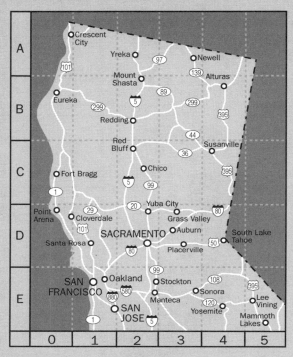

Map A0

Adjoining Maps: East: A1 ...... *page* 16
South: B0 46

Northern California Map .... *page* 2

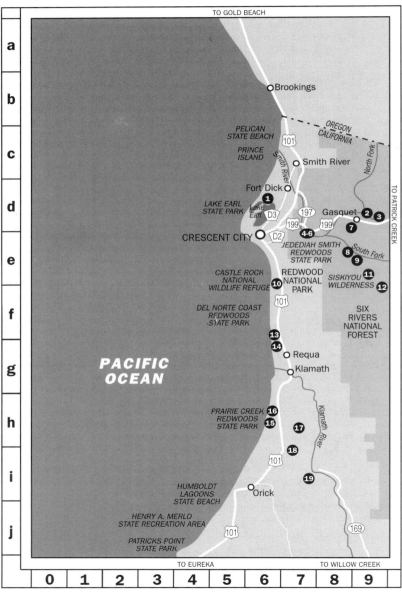

TO GOLD BEACH

Brookings

PELICAN
STATE BEACH   101

OREGON
CALIFORNIA

PRINCE
ISLAND

Smith River   North Fork

Smith River

Fort Dick   O

1

LAKE EARL
STATE PARK   Lake
Earl   D3   197   Gasquet   **2** **3**

199   199   **7**

CRESCENT CITY   D2   **4-6**

JEDEDIAH SMITH
REDWOODS
STATE PARK   South Fork   **8**
9

CASTLE ROCK
NATIONAL
WILDLIFE REFUGE   **10**   REDWOOD
NATIONAL
PARK   SISKIYOU
WILDERNESS   **11**
12

DEL NORTE COAST
REDWOODS
STATE PARK   101

SIX
RIVERS
NATIONAL
FOREST

13
14   Requa

PACIFIC
OCEAN   Klamath

PRAIRIE CREEK   **16**
REDWOODS   **15**
STATE PARK   **17**

Klamath River

18

101

19

HUMBOLDT
LAGOONS
STATE BEACH   Orick

HENRY A. MERLO
STATE RECREATION AREA   101

PATRICKS POINT
STATE PARK   169

TO EUREKA   TO WILLOW CREEK

TO PATRICK CREEK

A
B
C
D
E
0 1 2 3 4 5

Chapter AØ features:

❶ Pelican Bay Sand Dunes

2.5 mi/1.0 hr

Location: On the coast of Del Norte County north of Crescent City; map AØ, grid d6.

User groups: Hikers, dogs, and horses. No mountain bikes. No wheelchair facilities.

Permits: No permits are required. Parking and access are free.

Directions: From Crescent City, drive nine miles north on U.S. 101 and turn west on Lake Earl Drive (County Road D3). Drive 1.5 miles southwest, turn west on Morehead Road, and drive to Lower Lake Road. Turn right and drive a short distance north, then turn west on Kellogg Road and drive to the parking lot at the end of the road.

For trail and walk-in beach access, in Crescent City, turn northwest on Northcrest Drive and drive 1.5 miles to Old Mill Road. Turn west (left) on Old Mill Road and drive three miles to Sand Hill Road. For the state park trailhead, turn left at Sand Hill Road and drive a quarter of a mile to the trail entrance. For Fish and Game trail and walk-in beach access, drive on Old Mill Road to the locked gate at the road's end (about 100 yards past the Sand Hill Road turnoff).

Maps: For a free brochure and map, write to Del Norte County Parks at the address below. To obtain topographic maps of the area, ask for Crescent City and Smith River from the USGS.

Contact: Del Norte County Parks, 840 Ninth Street, Crescent City, CA 95531; (707) 464-7230 or fax (707) 465-1783.

Trail notes: The Pelican Bay Sand Dunes seem to sweep on forever, spanning more than 10 miles from the edge of Lake Earl on south along the Pacific Ocean, reaching nearly all the way to Crescent City. After parking and heading south on the beachfront, you can walk for five minutes or five hours—take your pick. Either way, you get a walk where you feel like a solitary speck against the enormous backdrop of untouched sand dunes and ocean. Only rarely will you see other people. The area is known by several names, including Fort Dick Beach, Kellogg Beach, and Pelican Bay Sand Dunes, but by any name, it's a good place to escape to nothing but wide-open beach for miles.

❷ Stoney Creek Trail

1.6 mi/0.75 hrs

Location: In Smith River National Recreation Area northeast of Crescent City; map AØ, grid d9.

User groups: Hikers and dogs. No horses or mountain bikes. No wheelchair facilities.

Permits: Campfire permits are required. Parking and access are free.

Directions: From Crescent City, drive north on U.S. 101 for three miles, then turn east on U.S. 199 and drive 14 miles to Gasquet. Turn left on Middle Fork/Gasquet Road and drive about 100 feet, then turn right on North Fork Road and drive one mile. Turn right on Stoney Creek Road and drive a short distance to the trailhead.

Maps: For a free brochure and hiking guide,

write to Smith River National Recreation Area at the address below. For a map of Six Rivers National Forest, send $4 to USDA-Forest Service, 630 Sansome Street, San Francisco, CA 94111. To obtain a topographic map of the area, ask for Gasquet from the USGS.

Contact: Smith River National Recreation Area, P.O. Box 228, Gasquet, CA 95543; (707) 457-3131 or fax (707) 457-3794.

Trail notes: This easy walk in an unblemished river setting will take you to the mouth of Stoney Creek, right where it pours into the North Fork Smith River. It's the kind of special place where you just sit and listen to the flow of moving water as it gurgles and pops its way over stones smoothed by years of river flows. The hike is easy, with a few ups and downs, as it follows a bluff adjacent to the North Fork Smith, a designated Wild and Scenic River, then is routed right out to the mouth of Stoney Creek. You're surrounded by woods and water.

❸ Elk Camp Ridge Trail

7.5–19.0 mi/
3.5 hrs–2.0 days

Location: In Smith River National Recreation Area northeast of Crescent City; map AØ, grid d9.

User groups: Hikers, dogs, horses, and mountain bikes. No wheelchair facilities.

Permits: No permits are required. Parking and access are free.

Directions: From Crescent City, drive north on U.S. 101 for three miles, then turn east on U.S. 199 and drive 14 miles to Gasquet. Turn left on Middle Fork/Gasquet Road and drive 100 feet, then bear right as the road forks. Drive one-half mile, then turn right on Old Gasquet Toll Road (County Road 314). Drive 2.3 miles, turn left at the sign for the trailhead, and drive one steep, rough mile to the trailhead.

Maps: For a free brochure and hiking guide, write to the Smith River National Recreation Area at the address below. For a map of Six Rivers National Forest, send $4 to USDA-Forest Service, 630 Sansome Street, San Francisco, CA 94111. To obtain topographic maps of the area, ask for Gasquet and High Plateau Mountain from the USGS.

Contact: Smith River National Recreation Area, P.O. Box 228, Gasquet, CA 95543; (707) 457-3131 or fax (707) 457-3794.

Trail notes: This trail is like a walk through history. It was originally part of a pack trail between Crescent City and the gold mines in southern Oregon, and the memories of the old days can shadow your hike much of the way. The trailhead is at 1,200 feet, but the route climbs right up to the ridge, reaching more than 3,000 feet. Once you reach the ridge, there are excellent views of surrounding peaks (Preston Peak is the big one) and the Smith River Canyon. You may also notice that much of the vegetation along the trail is stunted, a result of the high mineral content in serpentine rocks. The trail keeps climbing and ends at 3,400 feet. From start to finish, the trail continues for 9.5 miles, though almost nobody makes the entire trip. Since most of the route traces a ridgeline, there are no suitable camping areas.

❹ Stout Grove Trail

0.25 mi/0.5 hr

Location: In Jedediah Smith Redwoods State Park northeast of Crescent City; map AØ, grid e7.

User groups: Hikers and wheelchairs. No dogs, horses or mountain bikes. For those who want closer vehicular access, call the park at (707) 464-6101, extension 5112 or 5101, to receive the key to the gate.

Permits: No permits are required. Parking and access are free.

Directions: From Crescent City, drive about three miles north on U.S. 101, then turn east on U.S. 199. Drive about 10 miles (past the formal entrance to Jedediah Smith Redwoods State Park) to Hiouchi. Just past Hiouchi, turn right on South Fork Road (County Road 427) and cross two bridges. At a junction, turn right on Howland Hill Road and drive about two miles to a small parking area on the right and the signed trailhead.

Maps: For a free trail map, write to Jedediah Smith Redwoods State Park at the address below. To obtain a topographic map of the area, ask for Hiouchi from the USGS.

Contact: Jedediah Smith Redwoods State Park, 1375 Elk Valley Road, Crescent City, CA 95531;

(707) 464-6101, extension 5101, (707) 445-6547, or fax (707) 464-7722.

Trail notes: Visiting giant old redwood trees can affect people for a long time. The Stout Tree, the largest redwood in Jedediah Smith Redwoods State Park, is the attraction on this hike. It is so old that it can make your stay on Earth seem mighty brief. The wide, level trail is a 10-minute walk that takes an easy course to the Stout Grove, and then on to the Stout Tree. The giant Stout Tree is protected by a short wood fence, a favorite spot for photographs. Most people take longer than 10 minutes, of course, because they're not used to seeing anything this size, and they take their time absorbing the surroundings. The latter includes the Smith River, located a few minute's walk beyond the Stout Tree. A trail once started here that ran alongside the river, but it was washed out by erosion from flood waters.

❺ Boy Scout Tree Trail

2.8 mi/2.0 hrs

Location: In Jedediah Smith Redwoods State Park northeast of Crescent City; map AØ, grid e7.

User groups: Hikers only. No dogs, horses or mountain bikes. No wheelchair facilities.

Permits: No permits are required. Parking and access are free.

Directions: From Crescent City, drive about three miles north on U.S. 101, then turn east on U.S. 199. Drive about 10 miles (past the formal entrance to Jedediah Smith Redwoods State Park) to Hiouchi. Just past Hiouchi, turn right on South Fork Road (County Road 427) and cross two bridges. At a junction, turn right on Howland Hill Road and drive about five miles to a small parking area and the signed trailhead on the right side of the road.

Maps: For a free trail map, write to Jedediah Smith Redwoods State Park at the address below. To obtain a topographic map of the area, ask for Hiouchi from the USGS.

Contact: Jedediah Smith Redwoods State Park, 1375 Elk Valley Road, Crescent City, CA 95531; (707) 464-6101, extension 5101, (707) 445-6547, or fax (707) 464-7722.

Trail notes: This is the kind of place where a nature lover can find religion, where the beauty is pure and untouched. The trail is a soft dirt path, often sprinkled with redwood needles, that allows hikers to penetrate deep into an old-growth redwood forest, complete with a giant fern understory and high-limbed canopy. The centerpiece is the Boy Scout Tree, the largest tree in the forest here, but what you will remember the most is the pristine serenity of a forest of old redwoods.

This is an easy hike, nearly flat with only small hills, yet extremely rewarding. Just walk into the forest, then a few hours later, walk out. Those two hours in between can change how you feel about the world. A bonus known to relatively few is available if you continue your hike for 3.5 miles, one-way, to the 40-foot free-falling waterfall, making for a seven-mile round-trip hike.

❻ Craig's Creek Trail

7.4 mi/4.25 hrs

Location: In Smith River National Recreation Area northeast of Crescent City; map AØ, grid e7.

User groups: Hikers, dogs, horses, and mountain bikes. No wheelchair facilities.

Permits: No permits are required. Parking and access are free.

Directions: From Crescent City, drive north on U.S. 101 for three miles, then turn east on U.S. 199 and drive seven miles. Just past Hiouchi, turn right on South Fork Road (County Road 427) and drive approximately one-third of a mile. Park in the boat access facility area.

Maps: For a free brochure and hiking guide, write to Smith River National Recreation Area at the address below. For a map of Six Rivers National Forest, send $4 to USDA-Forest Service, 630 Sansome Street, San Francisco, CA 94111. To obtain a topographic map of the area, ask for Hiouchi from the USGS.

Contact: Smith River National Recreation Area, P.O. Box 228, Gasquet, CA 95543; (707) 457-3131 or fax (707) 457-3794.

Trail notes: An old miners' pack route, vintage 1800s style, has been converted into this hiking trail, an obscure path that is overlooked by most visitors. It starts along the South Fork Smith

River, then loops up the slopes of Craig's Creek Mountain, then back down to the river, ending where Craig's Creek enters the South Fork. In the process, it rises above the river and passes through forest, including old-growth redwoods and Douglas fir. Because of the contour of the mountain, the hike includes a good climb but then descends. The starting and ending elevations are the same, 200 feet. Most of the time you can have the entire trail to yourself. The South Fork Smith, a clear, free-flowing stream that drains a huge expanse of the Siskiyou Wilderness, is very pretty here.

❼ French Hill Trail

5.4 mi/3.25 hrs

Location: In Smith River National Recreation Area northeast of Crescent City; map AØ, grid e8.

User groups: Hikers, dogs, horses, and mountain bikes. No wheelchair facilities.

Permits: No permits are required. Parking and access are free.

Directions: From Crescent City, drive north on U.S. 101 for three miles, then turn east on U.S. 199 and drive 14 miles to Gasquet. Park at the Gasquet Ranger Station. The trail is located directly across the highway.

Maps: For a free brochure and hiking guide, write to Smith River National Recreation Area at the address below. For a map of Six Rivers National Forest, send $4 to USDA-Forest Service, 630 Sansome Street, San Francisco, CA 94111. To obtain a topographic map of the area, ask for Gasquet from the USGS.

Contact: Smith River National Recreation Area, P.O. Box 228, Gasquet, CA 95543; (707) 457-3131 or fax (707) 457-3794.

Trail notes: This trail was created originally as a route to transport supplies to build the Camp Six fire lookout station. Well, the lookout has been retired, but they left a high-tech automatic rain gauge in its place. In 1983, this rain gauge documented the most rain ever recorded in the continental U.S. for one season, 257 inches. In the dry season (there really is one up here, believe it or not), the hike to this spot provides a 1,600-foot climb, from a trailhead elevation of 400 feet to the lookout summit of 2,000 feet. It

passes through old-growth Douglas fir and sugar pines, a forest that has thrived from getting so much moisture. The appeal of this hike is to visit such a historic site, the wettest place in California. Otherwise the beauty and quality of the trail are poor to fair compared to that of other nearby areas.

❽ McClendon Ford Trail

2.0 mi/1.5 hr

Location: In Smith River National Recreation Area east of Crescent City; map AØ, grid e8.

User groups: Hikers, dogs, horses, and mountain bikes. No wheelchair facilities.

Permits: No permits are required. Parking and access are free.

Directions: From Crescent City, drive north on U.S. 101 for three miles, then turn east on U.S. 199 and drive seven miles. Just past Hiouchi, turn right on South Fork Road (County Road 427) and drive 14 miles, then turn right on Forest Service Road 15. Drive three more miles to a sign indicating the trailhead, then turn left and drive two miles.

Maps: For a free brochure and hiking guide, write to Smith River National Recreation Area at the address below. For a map of Six Rivers National Forest, send $4 to USDA-Forest Service, 630 Sansome Street, San Francisco, CA 94111. To obtain a topographic map of the area, ask for Ship Mountain from the USGS.

Contact: Smith River National Recreation Area, P.O. Box 228, Gasquet, CA 95543; (707) 457-3131 or fax (707) 457-3794.

Trail notes: This is a perfect trail for a hot summer day, complete with a swimming hole. It's an easy hike through a large forest of Douglas fir. The trail crosses Horse Creek, a small tributary, and then is routed out to a pretty beach on the South Fork Smith River. The starting elevation is 1,000 feet, and the ending elevation is 200 feet. Get the idea? Right, this trail follows an easy descent down to the river, taking about 45 minutes to get there. The swimming hole on the river is secluded and out of the way of most vacationers, so most often you have the place completely to yourself. Note: This is also the trailhead for the South Kelsey Trail. If you are unfamiliar with the area, be sure to have a map of Six Rivers National Forest to reach the trailhead.

⑨ Gunbarrel Trail

2.4 mi/1.75 hrs

Location: In Smith River National Recreation Area east of Crescent City; map AØ, grid e8.

User groups: Hikers, dogs, horses, and mountain bikes. No wheelchair facilities.

Permits: No permits are required. Parking and access are free.

Directions: From Crescent City, turn east on U.S. 199 and drive 25 miles. Turn right on Little Jones Creek Road (Forest Service Highway 16) and drive south 9.6 miles. When the road forks, drive straight ahead on Forest Service Road 16N02 for 4.8 miles, then turn left on Forest Service Road 16N18 (gated and closed in the wet season, October through January) and drive five miles. Bear left on Forest Service Road 15N34 and continue on this road for approximately 1.2 miles. Park at the end of the road. The trailhead is on the left.

Maps: For a free brochure and hiking guide, write to Smith River National Recreation Area at the address below. For a map of Six Rivers National Forest, send $4 to USDA-Forest Service, 630 Sansome Street, San Francisco, CA 94111. To obtain a topographic map of the area, ask for Ship Mountain from the USGS.

Contact: Smith River National Recreation Area, P.O. Box 228, Gasquet, CA 95543; (707) 457-3131 or fax (707) 457-3794.

Trail notes: Now just a minute, here. Do you really want to try this hike? If so, get your ambitions in clear focus, and if you like what you see, then go for it, because your reward will be complete peace and solitude. But it comes with a price: a terrible, long, and circuitous drive to reach the trailhead, two hours from the Gasquet Ranger Station. Then the hike itself demands a steep climb on the return trip, a 1,200-foot elevation gain over little more than a mile.

This trail starts at a ridgeline at 2,500 feet, then dives down the canyon all the way to the South Fork Smith River, where it junctions with the South Kelsey Trail. This is a beautiful spot, where the water is pure and the people nil. Alas, the return is the killer, a demanding climb, and that is why few people make this round-trip.

⑩ Coastal Trail (Last Chance Section)

14 mi/8.0 hrs

Location: In Del Norte Redwoods State Park south of Crescent City; map AØ, grid f6.

User groups: Hikers only. No dogs, horses, or mountain bikes. No wheelchair facilities.

Permits: No permits are required. Parking and access are free.

Directions: From Crescent City, drive south on U.S. 101 for about 2.5 miles. At milepost 23.03, turn west on Enderts Beach Road. Continue on this road for 2.5 miles to the trailhead at the end of the road.

Maps: For a trail guide, send $1.50 (includes tax and mailing) to Redwood National and State Park Headquarters at the address below. To obtain a topographic map of the area, ask for Sister Rocks from the USGS.

Contact: Redwood National and State Park Headquarters, 1111 Second Street, Crescent City, CA 95531; (707) 464-6101, extension 5101, or fax (707) 441-5737.

Trail notes: You get a little bit of heaven and a little bit of hell on this hike. It's one of the feature trips on the Del Norte coast, coursing through a virgin forest and meadows with beautiful wildflowers (in the spring), and granting great coastal views in several spots. The trail starts along the coast, then veers up sharply into dense old-growth forest. That's the heaven. The hell starts when you begin the difficult and steep climb, a gain of 1,400 feet. It doesn't stop there. Ever wonder why the trees are so big? You're likely to find out that it's because they are dripping with moisture, with heavy rain in the winter and ponderous fog in summer. There's more. Wood ticks flourish here, and it's a good idea to wear your socks outside the legs of your pants, to keep the ticks off your legs and also to make them easily visible should they climb aboard for the ride. Like many coastal hikes, hitting good weather is the key.

⓫ South Kelsey Trail

32.2 mi/3.0 days

Location: In Smith River National Recreation Area east of Crescent City; map AØ, grid f9.

User groups: Hikers, dogs, and horses. Mountain bikes are permitted only to the wilderness boundary. No wheelchair facilities.

Permits: No permits are required. Parking and access are free.

Directions: From Crescent City, drive north on U.S. 101 for three miles, then turn east on U.S. 199 and drive seven miles. Just past Hiouchi, turn right on South Fork Road (County Road 427) and drive 14 miles, then turn right at an unsigned road junction. Drive three miles to a sign indicating the trailhead, then turn left and drive two miles.

Maps: For a free brochure and hiking guide, write to Smith River National Recreation Area at the address below. For a map of Six Rivers National Forest, send $4 to USDA-Forest Service, 630 Sansome Street, San Francisco, CA 94111. To obtain a topographic map of the area, ask for Summit Valley from the USGS.

Contact: Smith River National Recreation Area, P.O. Box 228, Gasquet, CA 95543; (707) 457-3131 or fax (707) 457-3794.

Trail notes: Back before cars, trains, and planes, the Kelsey Trail spanned 200 miles from Crescent City eastward to Fort Jones near Yreka. It was built in the mid-1800s by Chinese laborers as a mule train route. Today it has a different purpose, with different sections providing excellent backpacking circuits. The trailhead is near Horse Creek on the South Fork Smith River at a 1,200-foot elevation. The trail initially drops down along the South Fork and continues south for seven miles. There are a few camps here along the river, including one with a makeshift roof, which is like finding heaven during a heavy rain storm. The trail then rises up above the river, climbing all the way for six miles to Baldy Peak and spectacular views. Another 3.1 miles will get you to your destination, Harrington Lake in Klamath National Forest, set at 5,775 feet. With so much "up" going in, take heart that at least the return trip will be mainly downhill. The trailhead also provides access to the McClendon Ford Trail. Other maintained sections of the Kelsey Trail are

noted in the Marble Mountain Wilderness (see chapter A1).

⓬ Summit Valley Trail

16.2 mi/2.0 days

Location: In Smith River National Recreation Area east of Crescent City; map AØ, grid f9.

User groups: Hikers, dogs, and horses. Mountain bikes are permitted only to the wilderness boundary. No wheelchair facilities.

Permits: No permits are required. Parking and access are free.

Directions: From Crescent City, drive north on U.S. 101 for three miles, then turn east on U.S. 199 and drive seven miles. Just past Hiouchi, turn right on South Fork Road (County Road 427) and drive 14 miles, then turn right on Forest Service Road 15. Drive five miles to the trailhead on the left. Park on the side of the road.

Maps: For a free brochure and hiking guide, write to Smith River National Recreation Area at the address below. For a map of Six Rivers National Forest, send $4 to USDA-Forest Service, 630 Sansome Street, San Francisco, CA 94111. To obtain a topographic map of the area, ask for Summit Valley from the USGS.

Contact: Smith River National Recreation Area, P.O. Box 228, Gasquet, CA 95543; (707) 457-3131 or fax (707) 457-3794.

Trail notes: This hike is best taken in the early summer, when the wildflowers are blooming, the Smith River is running with fresh, ample flows, and the temperatures are not too warm. The latter becomes a factor on the return trip, which is a killer climb. The trailhead is set on a ridge at 4,600 feet, with the first mile of the hike on an old jeep road. It travels through meadows where the wildflowers are spectacular in early summer. But then the trail drops, plunging down into a canyon, landing you along the South Fork Smith River at Elkhorn Bar, a beautiful spot at an elevation of 1,160 feet. Here it junctions with the South Kelsey Trail, where you'll find a few primitive campsites along the river. Well, when it comes to hiking, what goes down must come up, and you got it, the return trip is a death march, a 3,500-foot climb over the span of eight miles. Your car waiting at the trailhead never looked so good. This trip can be lengthened easily by junctioning with the South Kelsey Trail.

⑬ Yurok Loop

1.0 mi/0.5 hr

Location: In Redwood National and State Park south of Crescent City; map AØ, grid g6.

User groups: Hikers and partial wheelchair access. No dogs, horses, or mountain bikes.

Permits: No permits are required. Parking and access are free.

Directions: From Crescent City, drive south on U.S. 101 for approximately 14 miles. Turn right at the sign for the Lagoon Creek Parking Area and park there. The trailhead is adjacent to the parking lot.

Maps: For a trail guide, send $1.50 (includes tax and mailing) to Redwood National and State Park Headquarters at the address below. To obtain a topographic map of the area, ask for Requa from the USGS.

Contact: Redwood National and State Park Headquarters, 1111 Second Street, Crescent City, CA 95531; (707) 488-3461, (707) 464-6101, or fax (707) 464-7722.

Trail notes: The Yurok Loop is a great, short loop hike in Redwood National and State Park that starts right next to pretty Lagoon Creek Pond. But wait just a minute: the large trail sign located adjacent to the parking lot is one of the most misleading ever posted. The sign shows the trail looping around the lagoon, which it doesn't. Here's the deal: from the trailhead, it's a 10-minute walk above a beautiful beach with lots of driftwood and a gentle climb to a great coastal overlook. From here, you can scan miles of ocean and many rocky stacks. After enjoying the view, head south, and when you reach a junction, turn left and enter a forest, where the trail burrows almost like a tunnel and heads gently downhill. It then emerges from the forest and leads back to the parking lot, a delightful and easy walk that makes for a perfect break for highway drivers.

Special note: The Hidden Beach section of the Coastal Trail (see the following trail) junctions with this trail.

⑭ Coastal Trail (Hidden Beach Section)

8.0 mi/5.0 hrs

Location: In Redwood National Park south of Crescent City; map AØ, grid g6.

User groups: Hikers and partial wheelchair access. No dogs, horses, or mountain bikes.

Permits: No permits are required. Parking and access are free.

Directions: From Eureka, drive north on U.S. 101 for about 60 miles to the Klamath River. Turn west on Requa Road and drive 2.5 miles to the Klamath Overlook. The trailhead is at the south end of the parking area.

Maps: For a trail guide, send $1.50 (includes tax and mailing) to Redwood National and State Park Headquarters at the address below. To obtain a topographic map of the area, ask for Requa from the USGS.

Contact: Redwood National and State Park Headquarters, 1111 Second Street, Crescent City, CA 95531; (707) 488-3461, (707) 464-6101, or fax (707) 464-7722.

Trail notes: One of the greatest lookouts anywhere in the hemisphere is available at the Klamath Overlook, where you can scan the vast, ocean-blue horizon and actually see the curvature of the earth. To get it requires a 2,000-foot climb, a steep and demanding hike for most. It's the highlight of a stellar section of the Coastal Trail, which follows along coastal bluffs and rocky cliffs, with sweeping views of the ocean, and ultimately, of Hidden Beach. This trail is an excellent place to see the spouts of passing whales in winter and early spring. Pray for a clear day.

⑮ Coastal Trail (Fern Canyon/Ossagon Section)

5.4 mi/3.0 hrs

Location: In Prairie Creek Redwoods State Park south of Klamath; map AØ, grid h6.

User groups: Hikers and mountain bikes. No dogs or horses. No wheelchair facilities.

Permits: No permits are required. There is a state park day-use fee of $5 per vehicle.

Directions: From Eureka, drive north on U.S. 101 for 41 miles to Orick. Drive north for three miles to Davison Road. Turn west on Davison Road and drive eight miles to the Fern Canyon Trail. No trailers or RVs are permitted.

Maps: Trail maps are available at the park visitors center for a nominal charge. A free state parks guide can be obtained by calling (707) 445-6547. To obtain a topographic map of the area, ask for Fern Canyon from the USGS.

Contact: Prairie Creek Redwoods State Park, Orick, CA 95555; (707) 488-2171, (707) 445-6547, or fax (707) 464-7722.

Trail notes: This is a great hike, once one of the best coastal hikes anywhere. There is a good chance of seeing Roosevelt elk (Prairie Creek Redwoods State Park is loaded with them), Fern Canyon (see the following hike), a dense forest (quiet and pretty), and a series of hidden waterfalls, not to mention easy access to a huge, spotless beach (not a single piece of litter). In addition, there is a great trail camp about three miles in. From the parking area, start by crossing a shallow stream, and then take the near-level walk on the trail north as far as your heart desires. Most visitors enjoy the waterfalls and the beach, stopping for a picnic before returning. Elk are common here, and while they are accustomed to seeing people, be sure to give them plenty of room anyway. The only downer here are the mountain bikes. This trail is often wet and soft, so bike tires often damage the trail by leaving tire furrows, and they just plain go too fast for such a pristine spot.

⑯ Fern Canyon Loop Trail

0.8 mi/0.5 hr

Location: In Prairie Creek Redwoods State Park south of Klamath; map AØ, grid h6.

User groups: Hikers only. No dogs, horses or mountain bikes. No wheelchair facilities.

Permits: No permits are required. There is a state park day-use fee of $5 per vehicle.

Directions: From Eureka, drive north on U.S. 101 for 41 miles to Orick. Drive north for three miles to Davison Road. Turn west on Davison Road and drive eight miles to the Fern Canyon Trail. No trailers or RVs are permitted.

Maps: Trail maps are available at the park visitors center for a nominal charge. A free state parks guide can be obtained by calling (707) 445-6547. To obtain a topographic map of the area, ask for Fern Canyon from the USGS.

Contact: Prairie Creek Redwoods State Park, Orick, CA 95555; (707) 488-2171, (707) 445-6547, or fax (707) 464-7722.

Trail notes: The Fern Canyon Loop might just be the most inspiring short hike in California. When you walk along the bottom of Fern Canyon, you'll be surrounded on each side by 50-foot-high walls covered with giant ferns, a dramatic setting that isn't duplicated anywhere in the state. Also adding to the beauty is a small waterfall, pouring in through a chasm in the wall in the canyon and gushing into Home Creek. But it is Home Creek, which runs through the bottom of the canyon, that can cause the one serious problem here. In winter, this creek can flood, making the trail impassable. Although bridges are provided from May through September, always wear waterproof footwear—you often have to hop back and forth across the stream in order to reach the back of the canyon. At the end of the canyon, turn left and climb up the trail to the canyon rim, and then continue through the forest back to the trailhead. A bonus is the adjacent beach, wide-open and spanning for miles. Note that this trail is well known and recommended by many, so it can get a lot of use during the summer months.

⑰ Lost Man Creek Trail

2.0 mi/1.0 hr

Location: In Redwood National Park south of Klamath; map AØ, grid h7.

User groups: Hikers and partial wheelchair access. No dogs, horses, or mountain bikes.

Permits: No permits are required. Parking and access are free.

Directions: From Eureka, drive north on U.S. 101 for 41 miles to Orick. Continue north for 3.5 miles, just past Davison Road, to Lost Man Creek Road. Turn right and drive to the parking area and trailhead. Trailers and RVs are not permitted on Lost Man Creek Road.

Maps: For a trail guide, send $1.50 to Redwood

National and State Park Headquarters (includes tax and mailing) at the address below. To obtain a topographic map of the area, ask for Orick from the USGS.

Contact: Redwood National and State Park Headquarters, 1111 Second Street, Crescent City, CA 95531; (707) 464-6101 or fax (707) 464-7722.

Trail notes: Lost Man Creek is very pretty, with many rock pools and lots of lush vegetation. It's also a destination that is easy to reach. The trail heads southeast, climbing moderately and then nearly leveling out along the creek. Bring your camera, because it is rare to reach such a natural, pristine setting with such a short walk. While the two-mile round-trip is as far as most hikers take it, the trail actually continues on for 10 miles, all the way back down to Bald Hills Road. But only the deranged make the 20-mile round-trip—it's so steep that you'll be howling like a lone wolf baying at the moon.

⑱ Redwood Creek Trail

17.0 mi/1.0 day

Location: In Redwood National Park south of Klamath; map AØ, grid i7.

User groups: Hikers only. No dogs, horses, or mountain bikes. No wheelchair facilities.

Permits: No permits are required. Parking and access are free.

Directions: From Eureka, drive north on U.S. 101 for approximately 41 miles to Orick. About a quarter of a mile north of Orick, turn right on Bald Hills Road. Drive half a mile to the parking area and trailhead.

Maps: For a trail guide, send $1.50 (includes tax and mailing) to Redwood National and State Park Headquarters at the address below. To obtain a topographic map of the area, ask for Orick from the USGS.

Contact: Redwood National and State Park Headquarters, 1111 Second Street, Crescent City, CA 95531; (707) 464-6101 or fax (707) 464-7722.

Trail notes: The Redwood Creek Trail has become a feature hike in Redwood National Park. Though most visitors cut the trip short, it still provides exceptional beauty even in short pieces, with a chance to see elk near the parking area. The trail is routed along Redwood Creek, a pretty stream that flows out to sea near Orick. As you hike into the interior, you'll notice the diversity of the forest, with spruce, alder, redwoods, and maples, and lush fern beds in some areas. Stinging nettle are also abundant here, so stay on the trail. The stream attracts a diversity of wildlife, with ducks, herons, and hawks the most common sightings, and ruffed grouse and eagles occasionally seen. In the summer, the first mile or two of the trail can be quite crowded, but just keep on going. The farther you go, the fewer people you'll see. Note that during the winter, the creek can flood the trail in some areas, making it impassable.

⑲ Tall Trees Trail

2.5 mi/1.5 hrs

Location: In Redwood National Park south of Klamath; map AØ, grid i7.

User groups: Hikers only. No dogs, horses, or mountain bikes. No wheelchair facilities.

Permits: A permit is required if you want to drive to the trailhead, with only a limited number of cars allowed per day. Permits are free and can be obtained at the Redwood Information Center (see directions below). In the summer months, it's advisable to arrive as early as possible; permits usually run out by 10 A.M.

Directions: From Eureka, drive north on U.S. 101 for 40 miles. About one mile before reaching Orick, stop at the Redwood Information Center. (Here you secure a permit number, which is actually a gate combination number you'll need.) Drive north on U.S. 101 through Orick. About a quarter of a mile north of Orick, turn right on Bald Hills Road (look for the "Tall Tree Access" sign) and drive seven miles to a locked gate. Open the gate, drive through, close and lock the gate, then drive six miles down the gravel road to the trailhead. No RVs or trailers are permitted.

Maps: For a trail guide, send $1.50 (includes tax and mailing) to Redwood National and State Park Headquarters at the address below. To obtain a topographic map of the area, ask for Orick from the USGS.

Contact: Redwood National and State Park

Headquarters, 1111 Second Street, Crescent City, CA 95531; (707) 464-6101 or fax (707) 464-7722.

Trail notes: This hike is routed into a grove of tall and ancient redwoods of cathedral-like beauty, with the trail shaded and surrounded by a lush fern understory. Your mission here is to reach Tall Trees Grove, home of the park's tallest tree, 367 feet high and an estimated 600 years old. Hey, some say this is the tallest tree in the world, but that claim usually sets off a debate. In the summer, the Tall Trees Trail is extremely popular, with visitors from all over the U.S. arriving to see the giant old-growth redwoods. The hike to the grove is just over a mile, and if you want to extend the adventure, you can return on the Redwood Creek Trail, or head off on the Emerald Ridge Loop.

Special note: One word of caution: although there are typically high numbers of people on this trail, resist the urge to trek off-trail. There's a lot of poison oak that is sure to get you if you do.

Leave No Trace Tips

Plan Ahead and Prepare

Learn about the regulations and special concerns of the area you are visiting.

Visit the backcountry in small groups.

Avoid popular areas during peak-use periods.

Choose equipment and clothing in subdued colors.

Pack food in reusable containers.

Map A1

Adjoining Maps: East: A2 ...... *page 32*   West: AØ 4
South: B1 54

Northern California Map .... *page 2*

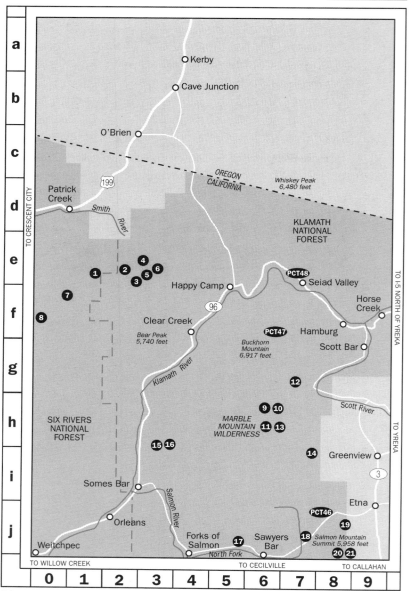

Chapter A1 features:

❶ Doe Flat Trail

3.0 mi/1.5 hrs

Location: In Smith River National Recreation Area east of Crescent City; map A1, grid e1.

User groups: Hikers, dogs, and horses. No mountain bikes. No wheelchair facilities.

Permits: A permit is required only for hikers planning to camp in the wilderness. Contact Smith River National Recreation Area to obtain a free permit. Parking and access are free.

Directions: From Crescent City, drive north on U.S. 101 for three miles. Turn east on U.S. 199 and drive 25 miles. Turn right on Little Jones Creek Road/Forest Service Road 16 and drive south 9.6 miles. When the road forks, bear sharply left on Forest Service Road 16N02 and drive five miles to the trailhead at the end of the road.

Maps: For a free brochure and hiking guide, write to Smith River National Recreation Area at the address below. For a map of Klamath National Forest, send $4 to USDA-Forest Service, 630 Sansome Street, San Francisco, CA 94111. To obtain a topographic map of the area, ask for Devil's Punchbowl from the USGS.

Contact: Smith River National Recreation Area, P.O. Box 228, Gasquet, CA 95543; (707) 457-3131 or fax (707) 457-3794.

Trail notes: Doe Flat is the best backpacking

jump-off point for the Siskiyou Wilderness, and as long as you know that, you'll have all the motivation you need for the trip. There are several excellent destinations from Doe Flat, including Buck Lake, Clear Creek, and Wilderness Falls; all are detailed in the following trips. But hiking to Doe Flat is hardly inspirational. It requires a 1.5-mile jaunt on a closed road to get there, leaving Bear Basin and topping Siskiyou Pass, then cruising down to the Doe Flat Camp. The trail follows an old mining road along Doe Creek to an old mine site, reaching a good camping area at Doe Flat. The area is well wooded, with some huge Jeffrey pines and cedars. For late arrivals, a bonus is the small primitive camping area at the trailhead with three campsites and a vault toilet.

❷ Buck Lake Trail

4.5 mi/2.5 hrs

Location: In the Siskiyou Wilderness east of Crescent City; map A1, grid e2.

User groups: Hikers, dogs, and horses. No mountain bikes. No wheelchair facilities.

Permits: A permit is required only for hikers planning to camp in the wilderness. Contact Smith River National Recreation Area to obtain a free permit. Parking and access are free.

Directions: From Crescent City, drive north on U.S. 101 for three miles. Turn east on U.S. 199 and drive 25 miles. Turn right on Little Jones Creek Road/Forest Service Road 16 and drive south 9.6 miles. When the road forks, bear sharply left on Forest Service Road 16N02 and drive five miles to the trailhead at the end of the road. Hike east on Doe Flat Trail for one mile to reach the Buck Lake Trail.

Maps: For a free brochure and hiking guide, write to Smith River National Recreation Area at the address below. For a map of Klamath National Forest, send $4 to USDA-Forest Service, 630 Sansome Street, San Francisco, CA 94111. To obtain a topographic map of the area, ask for Devil's Punchbowl from the USGS.

Contact: Smith River National Recreation Area, P.O. Box 228, Gasquet, CA 95543; (707) 457-3131 or fax (707) 457-3794.

Trail notes: The first time we saw Buck Lake, it was Memorial Day weekend, as well as the opening day of trout season, and there were so many rising brook trout that all the dimples on the lake surface looked like rain drops. Set in the heart of a wilderness forest setting at an elevation of 4,300 feet, Buck Lake is a little, crystal-pure lake surrounded by old-growth firs. From Doe Flat, it's an easy three-quarter-mile hike. There are plenty of deer and bear in the area, and the brook trout are abundant, though small, at the lake. From Doe Flat to Buck Lake, you'll cross through beautiful meadows and forest, including Douglas, white, and red firs, along with some maples. In the fall, the changing colors of the maples add a pretty touch to the trip.

❸ Devil's Punchbowl

13.0 mi/2.0 days

Location: In the Siskiyou Wilderness east of Crescent City; map A1, grid e2.

User groups: Hikers only. No dogs, horses, or mountain bikes. No wheelchair facilities.

Permits: A permit is required only for hikers planning to camp in the wilderness. Contact Smith River National Recreation Area to obtain a free permit. Parking and access are free.

Directions: From Crescent City, drive north on U.S. 101 for three miles. Turn east on U.S. 199

and drive 25 miles. Turn right on Little Jones Creek Road/Forest Service Road 16 and drive south 9.6 miles. When the road forks, bear sharply left on Forest Service Road 16N02 and drive five miles to the trailhead at the end of the road. Follow the Doe Flat Trail for three miles to reach the trailhead.

Maps: For a free brochure and hiking guide, write to Smith River National Recreation Area at the address below. For a map of Klamath National Forest, send $4 to USDA-Forest Service, 630 Sansome Street, San Francisco, CA 94111. To obtain a topographic map of the area, ask for Devil's Punchbowl from the USGS.

Contact: Klamath National Forest, Happy Camp Ranger District, P.O. Box 377, Happy Camp, CA 96039; (916) 493-2243 or fax (916) 493-2212. Smith River National Recreation Area, P.O. Box 228, Gasquet, CA 95543; (707) 457-3131 or fax (707) 457-3794.

Trail notes: You'll be wondering if you're afflicted with a hex or a charm when you take the trip to Devil's Punchbowl. The hex? The trail includes a climb with about a hundred switchbacks, an endless up, up, and up that'll have you wheezing like a donkey low on hay. The charm? The sight of the lake first coming into view will enchant you. It's small but pristine, set in a mountain granite bowl, framed by an imposing back wall—a shrine. To make this trip, start by hiking past Doe Flat, continuing a short way along Doe Creek. Just after the trail passes a little dirt mound, look for a right turn across Doe Creek. The turn is signed "Devil's Punchbowl," but the sign is occasionally stolen. In that case, be alert for the trail on the right side of Doe Creek. From here you start the first of 100 switchbacks up Bear Mountain, a long, forbidding butt-kicker. When you finally top the ridge, the route crosses Devil's Creek and leaves the forest behind, crossing bare granite domes, the trail marked only by small stacks of rocks. You then cross a rise, and the beautiful gem-like lake awaits. This place is something of a legend, but is visited only by those willing to pay the price of the terrible climb to reach it.

Special note: The entire region surrounding Devil's Punchbowl consists of sheets of bare granite. The few campsites here are merely small, flat sleeping spaces on rock. There is no firewood available, so bring a backpacking stove for cooking. Bring Zip-Loc bags to carry out all refuse, including human waste.

❹ Young's Valley Trail

8.0 mi/3.5 hrs

Location: In the Siskiyou Wilderness east of Crescent City; map A1, grid e3.

User groups: Hikers and horses. No dogs or mountain bikes. No wheelchair facilities.

Permits: A permit is required only for hikers planning to camp in the wilderness. Contact Smith River National Recreation Area to obtain a free permit. Parking and access are free.

Directions: From Crescent City, drive north on U.S. 101 for three miles, turn east on U.S. 199 and drive 32 miles. Turn right on Forest Service Road 18N07 and drive about five miles. Drive on Forest Service Road 18N07 as it veers right and twists its way about 10 miles past Sanger Lake and beyond to the end of the road and the trailhead. The last mile is very rough.

Maps: For a free brochure and hiking guide, write to Smith River National Recreation Area at the address below. For a map of Klamath National Forest, send $4 to USDA-Forest Service, 630 Sansome Street, San Francisco, CA 94111. To obtain a topographic map of the area, ask for Devil's Punchbowl from the USGS.

Contact: Klamath National Forest, Happy Camp Ranger District, P.O. Box 377, Happy Camp, CA 96039; (916) 493-2243 or fax (916) 493-2212. Smith River National Recreation Area, P.O. Box 228, Gasquet, CA 95543; (707) 457-3131 or fax (707) 457-3794.

Trail notes: The four-mile trip from Young's Valley down Clear Creek to Young's Meadow is one of the greatest and easiest trips in Northern California. Young's Meadow, set on the western slope of Preston Peak at an elevation of 4,500 feet, is very pretty and makes an excellent picnic area and campsite.

The hike features a 600-foot descent into the canyon and to Clear Creek. From here, the ambitious can take this trip further, much further. The Young's Valley Trail is a great first leg of a multi-day trip, ultimately heading either far-

ther down Clear Creek to Wilderness Falls, an awesome setting (see the following hike), or to Rattlesnake Meadows on the slopes of Preston Peak, a short but rugged climb.

❺ Wilderness Falls

18.0 mi/2.0 days

Location: In the Siskiyou Wilderness east of Crescent City; map A1, grid e3.

User groups: Hikers only. No dogs, horses, or mountain bikes. No wheelchair facilities.

Permits: A permit is required only for hikers planning to camp in the wilderness. Contact Klamath National Forest to obtain a free wilderness permit. Parking and access are free.

Directions: From Crescent City, drive north on U.S. 101 for three miles. Turn east on U.S. 199 and drive 32 miles. Turn right on Forest Service Road 18N07 and drive about five miles. Continue on Forest Service Road 18N07 as it veers right and twists its way about 10 miles past Sanger Lake and beyond to the end of the road and the trailhead. The last mile is very rough.

Maps: For a map of Klamath National Forest, send $4 to USDA-Forest Service, 630 Sansome Street, San Francisco, CA 94111. To obtain a topographic map of the area, ask for Devil's Punchbowl from the USGS.

Contact: Klamath National Forest, Happy Camp Ranger District, P.O. Box 377, Happy Camp, CA 96039; (916) 493-2243 or fax (916) 493-2212. Smith River National Recreation Area, P.O. Box 228, Gasquet, CA 95543; (907) 457-3131 or fax (707) 457-3794.

Trail notes: Wilderness Falls is one of the great secrets of northwestern California, a true hidden jewel, dramatic and pure, and not only untouched, but largely unseen. This bubbling tower of water created by Clear Creek first crashes down about 35 feet into a boulder, then pounds its way down into a foaming pool 100 feet across.

Our recommended route is to start on the Clear Creek National Recreation Trail out of Young's Valley (see previous hike). Follow the Clear Creek Trail for about seven miles to the waterfall, featuring a 600-foot descent to the stream, then a gentle descent the rest of the way. There is an excellent campsite about a quarter of a mile upstream from the falls. It's an easy hike to the waterfall, but the trip back is up all the way, and is best started very early in the morning, when the temperature is the coolest.

Wilderness Falls can also be accessed out of Doe Flat (see hike number 1), but this trail includes a wet, cold, and slippery ford of Clear Creek.

⑥ Preston Peak

16.0 mi/2.0 days

Location: In the Siskiyou Wilderness east of Crescent City; map A1, grid e3.

User groups: Hikers only. No dogs, horses, or mountain bikes. No wheelchair facilities.

Permits: A campfire permit is required. Parking and access are free.

Directions: From Crescent City, drive north on U.S. 101 for three miles. Turn east on U.S. 199 and drive 32 miles. Turn right on Forest Service Road 18N07 and drive about five miles. Continue on Forest Service Road 18N07 as it veers right and twists its way about 10 miles past Sanger Lake and beyond to the end of the road and the trailhead. The last mile is very rough.

Maps: For a map of Klamath National Forest, send $4 to USDA-Forest Service, 630 Sansome Street, San Francisco, CA 94111. A map of the Marble Mountain Wilderness can also be purchased for $4. To obtain a topographic map of the area, ask for Devil's Punchbowl from the USGS.

Contact: Klamath National Forest, Happy Camp Ranger District, P.O. Box 377, Happy Camp, CA 96039; (916) 493-2243 or fax (916) 493-2212.

Trail notes: Only mountaineers need sign up for this trip. The last mile to reach the summit of Preston Peak is steep, rough, and primitive, and with no marked trail, you must have the ability to scramble cross-country and recognize a dangerous spot when you see it. That done, you'll gain the top—7,309 feet and by far the highest spot in the region—with wondrous surrounding views. Even Mount Shasta way off to the southeast comes clearly into view, along with the famous peaks in the Trinity Alps and Marble Mountain Wilderness. The most common route to climb Preston Peak is to hike the Young's Val-

ley Trail to Young's Meadow (an easy two miles), head down the Clear Creek Trail (another easy mile), and then turn east on the Rattlesnake Meadow Trail (about two very steep, rough, and primitive miles). At the end of the Rattlesnake Meadow Trail, hikers must go cross-country for another mile or so to Preston Peak. The last mile is a scramble.

Special note: Always stay off this mountain in wet weather because the route is very slippery, and always avoid routes that cross through loose shale, which can be extremely dangerous. A fall here can be life threatening.

⑦ Island Lake Trail

8.0 mi/2.0 days

Location: In Smith River National Recreation Area east of Crescent City; map A1, grid f0.

User groups: Hikers, dogs, and horses. No mountain bikes. No wheelchair facilities.

Permits: A campfire permit is required. Parking and access are free.

Directions: From Crescent City, drive north on U.S. 101 for three miles, then turn east on U.S. 199 and drive 25 miles. Turn right on Little Jones Creek Road/Forest Service Road 16 and drive south 9.6 miles. When the road forks, continue straight on Forest Service Road 16N02 and drive 2.5 miles, turn left on Forest Service Road 16N28, and drive two miles east to the trailhead at the end of the road. Note: Forest Service Road 16N28 is very rough, gated, often impassable, and therefore closed, in the rainy season (October through June); call Smith River National Recreation Area before planning a trip.

Maps: For a free brochure and hiking guide, write to Smith River National Recreation Area at the address below. For a map of Klamath National Forest, send $4 to USDA-Forest Service, 630 Sansome Street, San Francisco, CA 94111. To obtain a topographic map of the area, ask for Devil's Punchbowl from the USGS.

Contact: Klamath National Forest, Happy Camp Ranger District, P.O. Box 377, Happy Camp, CA 96039; (916) 493-2243 or fax (916) 493-2212. Smith River National Recreation Area, P.O. Box 228, Gasquet, CA 95543; (707) 457-3131 or fax (707) 457-3794.

Trail notes: Island Lake is a mountain bowl framed by the back wall of Jedediah Mountain, a wild, primitive area where threatened spotted owls are more common than hikers. The trailhead is at Little Bear Basin, and after making the quick walk past a clear-cut down to the south fork of the Smith River, you'll enter the untouched Siskiyou Wilderness. Enjoy the stream, because the hike that follows is anything but enjoyable. The trail is routed along a mountain spine, climbing up, up, and up for what seems like an endless three miles. It finally tops a ridge and turns around a bend, where little Island Lake comes into view.

There are two excellent camps at the lake, set in trees near the lake's shore. The trout are eager to bite, but most are very small, dinker-sized brook trout. A great afternoon side trip is to hike the rim around the lake, most easily done in a counterclockwise direction, claiming the top of Jedediah Mountain, a perfect picnic site and a great lookout.

❽ Baldy Peak Trail

10.4 mi/2.0 days

Location: In the Siskiyou Wilderness east of Crescent City; map A1, grid f0.

User groups: Hikers, dogs, and horses. No mountain bikes. No wheelchair facilities.

Permits: A campfire permit is required. Parking and access are free.

Directions: This trailhead can be reached only by hiking the Gunbarrel Trail (see chapter AØ). From Crescent City, drive north on U.S. 101 for three miles, then turn east on U.S. 199 and drive 25 miles. Turn right on Little Jones Creek Road/Forest Service Road 16 and drive south 9.6 miles. When the road forks, bear sharply left on Forest Service Road 16N02 for 4.8 miles, then turn left on Forest Service Road 16N18 and drive five miles. Bear left on Forest Service Road 15N34 and drive 1.2 miles. Park at the end of the road. The trailhead is on the left. Hike the Gunbarrel Trail for 1.2 miles to reach the Baldy Peak section of the South Kelsey Trail.

Maps: For a free brochure and hiking guide, write to Smith River National Recreation Area at the address below. For a map of Klamath Na-

tional Forest, send $4 to USDA-Forest Service, 630 Sansome Street, San Francisco, CA 94111. To obtain a topographic map of the area, ask for Prescott Mountain from the USGS.

Contact: Klamath National Forest, Happy Camp Ranger District, P.O. Box 377, Happy Camp, CA 96039; (916) 493-2243 or fax (916) 493-2212. Smith River National Recreation Area, P.O. Box 228, Gasquet, CA 95543; (707) 457-3131 or fax (707) 457-3794.

Trail notes: The route to Baldy Peak is actually a section of the South Kelsey Trail (see chapter AØ), the historic route that once spanned from Crescent City east all the way through the Marble Mountain Wilderness to Fort Jones. This part of it is an excellent trip, and if you get caught in the rain, a bonus is that the Bear Wallow Shelter (not much more than a roof) is available just beyond the summit. The trip starts on the Gunbarrel Trail (see chapter AØ), which extends for 1.25 miles to the junction with the Kelsey Trail. From there, it's four miles to Baldy Peak at 5,775 feet. The views are outstanding, especially Preston Peak (at 7,309 feet) to the north, the most impressive feature in this wild landscape.

An option for those with plenty of time and endurance is to continue east on the Kelsey Trail, which extends about 12 miles further to Red Hill (5,642 feet), Bear Peak (5,740 feet), and nearby Bear Lake. The latter has an excellent campsite.

❾ Paradise Lake Trail

4.0 mi/2.75 hrs

Location: In the Marble Mountain Wilderness west of Yreka; map A1, grid h6.

User groups: Hikers, dogs, and horses. No mountain bikes. No wheelchair facilities.

Permits: A campfire permit is required only for hikers planning to camp in the wilderness. Contact Klamath National Forest to obtain a free permit. Parking and access are free.

Directions: From Interstate 5 at Yreka, take the Highway 3/Fort Jones exit and drive 16.5 miles to Fort Jones. Turn right on Scott River Road and drive 18 miles to the turnoff for Indian Scotty Campground. Turn left and cross the concrete bridge, then bear left and drive about five miles on Forest Service Road 43N45. Turn right on an unmarked Forest Service Road and follow the signs indicating the Paradise Lake Trailhead for about six miles. The trailhead is at the wilderness border.

Maps: A trail information sheet can be obtained by contacting the Scott River Ranger District at the address below. For a map of Klamath National Forest, send $4 to USDA-Forest Service, 630 Sansome Street, San Francisco, CA 94111. A map of the Marble Mountain Wilderness can also be purchased for $4. To obtain topographic maps of the area, ask for Scott Bar and Marble Mountain from the USGS.

Contact: Klamath National Forest, Scott River Ranger District, 11263 North Highway 3, Fort Jones, CA 96032; (916) 468-5351 or fax (916) 468-5654.

Trail notes: Paradise Lake, set at an elevation of 5,920 feet, is the easiest to reach of the 79 lakes in the Marble Mountain Wilderness. The pretty hike is short enough for a day trip, and it has good lakeside campgrounds if you want to turn your trip into an overnighter. There are also some excellent side trips, including climbing Kings Castle (see the following hike), which tops the mountain rim on the back side of the lake.

From the trailhead at 4,880 feet, the route quickly enters a designated wilderness, then climbs for nearly two miles, steeply in some areas, and switches back and forth through an old, untouched forest. It then emerges from the trees and rises to a saddle, and on the other side is Paradise Lake, sitting in a mountain pocket, emerald-green and peaceful. Paradise is a mostly shallow lake with few trout, but it does have one deep area. Because the hike to the lake only takes two hours, there are usually campers here all summer long. When we visited, there was a strange religious ceremony of some kind going on in which about 50 people had hiked in, formed a circle, and started chanting. We climbed Kings Castle to get well out of earshot and reclaim our own sense of peace.

⑩ Kings Castle Trail

5.5 mi/5.0 hrs

Location: In the Marble Mountain Wilderness west of Yreka; map A1, grid h6.

User groups: Hikers, dogs, and horses, though dogs and horses are not advised because of the rough terrain. No mountain bikes. No wheelchair facilities.

Permits: A campfire permit is required only for hikers planning to camp in the wilderness. Contact Klamath National Forest to obtain a free permit. Parking and access are free.

Directions: From Interstate 5 at Yreka, take the Highway 3/Fort Jones exit and drive 16.5 miles to Fort Jones. Turn right on Scott River Road and drive 18 miles to the turnoff for Indian Scotty Campground. Turn left and cross the concrete bridge, then bear left and drive about five miles on Forest Service Road 43N45. Turn right on an unmarked Forest Service Road and follow the signs indicating the Paradise Lake Trailhead for about six miles. The trailhead is at the wilderness border. Hike 1.9 miles to Paradise Lake, then bear right and continue another half a mile to Kings Castle.

Maps: A trail information sheet can be obtained by contacting the Scott River Ranger District at the address below. For a map of Klamath National Forest, send $4 to USDA-Forest Service, 630 Sansome Street, San Francisco, CA 94111. A map of the Marble Mountain Wilderness can also be purchased for $4. To obtain topographic maps of the area, ask for Scott Bar and Marble Mountain from the USGS.

Contact: Klamath National Forest, Scott River Ranger District, 11263 North Highway 3, Fort Jones, CA 96032; (916) 468-5351 or fax (916) 468-5654.

Trail notes: Kings Castle is the imposing perch that sits on the back side of Paradise Lake, a half-mile climb that tops out at the summit at 7,405 feet. It's a great hike with unforgettable views, looking down at little Paradise Lake as well as far beyond to Northern California's most famous mountain peaks. From the trailhead of Paradise Lake Trail, you make the 1,040-foot climb up to Paradise Lake. From there, the trail crosses the lake's inlet on the left side, then laterals across the side wall toward the peak, eventually switching back and forth to gain the rim behind the lake. The trail then loops and climbs the back side of Kings Castle, a special trip every step of the way, a climb of 2,525 feet from the trailhead.

On our first visit here, we missed the trail and wound up scrambling cross-country style for hours right up to the face of Kings Castle. When we finally gained the summit, we looked at each other, smiling, silently congratulating ourselves for being such rugged mountaineers. Right then, two Girl Scouts suddenly arrived from the other side, cheerful and bouncy, scarcely breathing hard. "How'd you get up here?" I asked. "We took the trail," one of them answered. We just stood there. There's a trail? What trail?

⑪ Marble Mountain Rim

16.0 mi/2.0 days

Location: In the Marble Mountain Wilderness west of Yreka; map A1, grid h6.

User groups: Hikers, dogs, and horses, though dogs and horses are not advised because of the rough terrain. No mountain bikes. No wheelchair facilities.

Permits: A campfire permit is required only for hikers planning to camp in the wilderness. Contact Klamath National Forest to obtain a free permit. Parking and access are free.

Directions: From Interstate 5 at Yreka, take the Highway 3/Fort Jones exit and drive 16.5 miles to Fort Jones. Turn right on Scott River Road and drive 18 miles to the turnoff for Indian Scotty Campground. Turn left and cross the concrete bridge, then bear left and drive about five miles on Forest Service Road 43N45. Look for the sign indicating the Lovers Camp Trailhead. Drive two miles to the trailhead.

Maps: A trail information sheet can be obtained by contacting the Scott River Ranger District at the address below. For a map of Klamath National Forest, send $4 to USDA-Forest Service, 630 Sansome Street, San Francisco, CA 94111. A map of the Marble Mountain Wilderness can also be purchased for $4. To obtain a topographic map of the area, ask for Marble Mountain from the USGS.

Contact: Klamath National Forest, Scott River Ranger District, 11263 North Highway 3, Fort Jones, CA 96032; (916) 468-5351 or fax (916) 468-5654.

Trail notes: Marble isn't usually thought of as a precious stone, but it's gem-like for hikers on

this trail. With Marble Valley nearby, climbing the Marble Mountain Rim can make for a perfect weekend trip and can easily be extended into a longer one. The trailhead at Lovers Camp is probably the most popular in the entire wilderness, especially for packers going by horse (corrals are available at the trailhead). The route heads up Canyon Creek, a moderate climb, then intersects with the Pacific Crest Trail at Marble Valley. This area is very scenic, with lots of deer and wild orchids. Turn right and the trail crosses Marble Mountain itself, and once you've arrived, a side trip to the Marble Rim is mandatory. The views are stunning, sweeping in both directions, with steep drop-offs adding to the quiet drama. The rock itself is unlike anything else in Northern California, a mix of black, red, and tan marble, something you'll never forget.

⑫ Kelsey Creek Trail

18.0 mi/2.0 days

Location: In the Marble Mountain Wilderness west of Yreka; map A1, grid h6.

User groups: Hikers, dogs, and horses. No mountain bikes. No wheelchair facilities.

Permits: A campfire permit is required only for hikers planning to camp in the wilderness. Contact Klamath National Forest to obtain a free permit. Parking and access are free.

Directions: From Interstate 5 at Yreka, take the Highway 3/Fort Jones exit and drive 16.5 miles to Fort Jones. Turn right on Scott River Road and drive 16.8 miles to the Scott River Bridge. Cross it, then turn left immediately and follow the road for three-tenths of a mile. Bear right on another dirt road and drive a quarter of a mile to the trailhead.

Maps: A trail information sheet can be obtained by contacting the Scott River Ranger District at the address below. For a map of Klamath National Forest, send $4 to USDA-Forest Service, 630 Sansome Street, San Francisco, CA 94111. A map of the Marble Mountain Wilderness can also be purchased for $4. To obtain topographic maps of the area, ask for Scott Bar and Grider Valley from the USGS.

Contact: Klamath National Forest, Scott River Ranger District, 11263 North Highway 3, Fort

Jones, CA 96032; (916) 468-5351 or fax (916) 468-5654.

Trail notes: The Kelsey Creek Trail offers many miles of beautiful streamside travel, with the Paradise Lake Basin as the intended destination for most hikers on this route. The trailhead is set near the confluence of Kelsey Creek and the Scott River, and from there, the trail follows upstream along Kelsey Creek. Wildflowers are abundant in the meadows. After four miles, you'll reach Maple Falls, the prettiest waterfall in the region. The trail continues up the canyon, finally rising to intersect with the Pacific Crest Trail just below Red Rock. From this junction, you have many options. The closest lake is secluded Bear Lake, a pretty spot but alas with some tules and mosquitoes. To reach it from the junction requires a short but steep drop down into the basin to the immediate west.

⑬ Sky High Lakes

14.0 mi/2.0 days

Location: In the Marble Mountain Wilderness west of Yreka; map A1, grid h6.

User groups: Hikers, dogs, and horses. No mountain bikes. No wheelchair facilities.

Permits: A campfire permit is required only for hikers planning to camp in the wilderness. Contact Klamath National Forest to obtain a free permit. Parking and access are free.

Directions: From Interstate 5 at Yreka, take the Highway 3/Fort Jones exit and drive 16.5 miles to Fort Jones. Turn right on Scott River Road and drive 18 miles to the turnoff for Indian Scotty Campground. Turn left and cross the concrete bridge, then bear left and drive about five miles on Forest Service Road 43N45. Look for the sign indicating the Lovers Camp Trailhead. Drive two miles to the trailhead.

Maps: A trail information sheet can be obtained by contacting the Scott River Ranger District at the address below. For a map of Klamath National Forest, send $4 to USDA-Forest Service, 630 Sansome Street, San Francisco, CA 94111. A map of the Marble Mountain Wilderness can also be purchased for $4. To obtain a topographic map of the area, ask for Marble Mountain from the USGS.

Contact: Klamath National Forest, Scott River Ranger District, 11263 North Highway 3, Fort Jones, CA 96032; (916) 468-5351 or fax (916) 468-5654.

Trail notes: The Sky High Lakes make for a great, easy overnighter, hiking seven miles each day, or an inspired one-day in-and-outer. The trip starts at Lovers Camp, one of two trails at this trailhead (the other leads to Marble Mountain). For this trip, take the trail out of Lovers Camp on the left, which follows along Red Rock Creek in the Red Rock Valley. Near the crest, you'll reach Shadow Lake, the first of a half-dozen lakes that are sprinkled about the basin. Lower Sky High Lake and Frying Pan Lake are our favorites for swimming and fishing. The trail hooks up with the Pacific Crest Trail at each end of the Sky High Lakes, making a loop trip possible. The trip can also easily be extended for a week or longer in either direction on the Pacific Crest Trail, with many lakeside camps available along the way.

⑭ Shackleford Creek Trail

13.0 mi/2.0 days

Location: In the Marble Mountain Wilderness west of Yreka; map A1, grid h7.

User groups: Hikers, dogs, and horses. No mountain bikes. No wheelchair facilities.

Permits: A campfire permit is required only for hikers planning to camp in the wilderness. Contact Klamath National Forest to obtain a free permit. Parking and access are free.

Directions: From Interstate 5 at Yreka, take the Highway 3/Fort Jones exit and drive 16.5 miles to Fort Jones. Turn right on Scott River Road and drive seven miles, then turn left on Quartz Valley Road and drive about four miles to the sign for Shackleford Trailhead. Turn right and drive to the trailhead at the end of the road.

Maps: A trail information sheet can be obtained by contacting the Scott River Ranger District at the address below. For a map of Klamath National Forest, send $4 to USDA-Forest Service, 630 Sansome Street, San Francisco, CA 94111. A map of the Marble Mountain Wilderness can also be purchased for $4. To obtain a topographic map of the area, ask for Boulder Peak from the USGS.

Contact: Klamath National Forest, Scott River

Ranger District, 11263 North Highway 3, Fort Jones, CA 96032; (916) 468-5351 or fax (916) 468-5654.

Trail notes: Campbell, Cliff, and Summit Lakes are three of the prettiest lakes in the Marble Mountain Wilderness. The ease of reaching them on the Shackleford Trail (only 5.5 miles to Campbell Lake) makes them a popular destination all summer long. The trail is routed up Shackleford Creek to a basin set just below the Pacific Crest Trail. Here you'll find a series of small mountain lakes. In addition to these three largest lakes, there are also little Gem, Jewel, and Angel Lakes. Visiting all of them can make for a great day of adventuring. A bonus is that the trip can be extended by hiking up the rim to the Pacific Crest Trail, then turning right and marching three miles to the Sky High Lakes.

⑮ Haypress Meadows Trailhead

20.0 mi/2.0 days

Location: In the Marble Mountain Wilderness near Somes Bar; map A1, grid i3.

User groups: Hikers, dogs, and horses. No mountain bikes. No wheelchair facilities.

Permits: A campfire permit is required only for hikers planning to camp in the wilderness. Contact Klamath National Forest to obtain a free permit. Parking and access are free.

Directions: From Interstate 5 at Yreka, take the Highway 3/Fort Jones exit and drive 28 miles to Etna. Turn west on Sawyers Bar Road and drive about 35 miles to Forks of Salmon. Turn west on Salmon River Road and drive about 20 miles to a sign indicating Camp 3 and Wilderness Trails (located a quarter of a mile east of Somes Bar). Turn right and drive eight miles to the trailhead at Camp 4.

Maps: A trail information sheet can be obtained by contacting the Ukonom Ranger District at the address below. For a map of Klamath National Forest, send $4 to USDA-Forest Service, 630 Sansome Street, San Francisco, CA 94111. A map of the Marble Mountain Wilderness can also be purchased for $4. To obtain a topographic map of the area, ask for Somes Bar from the USGS.

Contact: Klamath National Forest, Ukonom Ranger District, P.O. Drawer 140, Orleans, CA 95556; (916) 627-3291 or fax (916) 627-3401.

Trail notes: If it's possible to love something to death, then One Mile Lake and the Cuddihy Lakes basin are in for such a fate. This area is perfect for backpacking, with beauty, lookouts, and good trail access, but heavy use may force the Forest Service to close it off to overnighters. If you go, plan on no more than one night in this area before moving on, and don't plan on having the place to yourself. After parking at the trailhead at 4,500 feet, the first two miles of trail lead up and across a fir-covered slope of a small peak (a little butt-kicker of a climb). Then the trail descends into Haypress Meadows, a major junction. Turn right and head up Sandy Ridge, a long, steady climb, and plan to top the ridge and then camp at Monument Lake, Meteor Lake, One Mile Lake, or Cuddihy Lakes. The view from Sandy Ridge is a sweeping lookout of the Marble Mountains to the east and the Siskiyous to the west, with mountain-top glimpses of Mount Shasta and the Marble Rim. Be aware that there are a ton of bears at the Cuddihy Lakes, 40 in a 10-square-mile area according to a study by the Department of Fish and Game.

⑯ Spirit Lake Trail

34.0 mi/4.0 days

Location: In the Marble Mountain Wilderness near Somes Bar; map A1, grid i3.

User groups: Hikers, dogs, and horses. No mountain bikes. No wheelchair facilities.

Permits: A campfire permit is required for hikers planning to camp in the wilderness. Contact Klamath National Forest to obtain a free permit. Parking and access are free.

Directions: From Interstate 5 at Yreka, take the Highway 3/Fort Jones exit and drive 28 miles southwest to Etna. Turn west on Sawyers Bar Road and drive about 35 miles to Forks of Salmon. Turn west on Salmon River Road and drive about 20 miles to a sign indicating Camp 3 and Wilderness Trails (located a quarter of a mile east of Somes Bar). Turn right and drive eight miles to the trailhead at Camp 4.

Maps: A trail information sheet can be obtained by contacting the Happy Camp Ranger District at the address below. For a map of Klamath National Forest, send $4 to USDA-Forest Service, 630 Sansome Street, San Francisco, CA 94111. A map of the Marble Mountain Wilderness can also be purchased for $4. To obtain topographic maps of the area, ask for Somes Bar and Marble Mountain from the USGS.

Contact: Klamath National Forest, Happy Camp Ranger District, P.O. Box 377, Happy Camp, CA 96039; (916) 493-2243 or fax (916) 493-2212.

Trail notes: We've hiked to hundreds and hundreds of mountain lakes, and Spirit Lake is one of the prettiest we've ever seen. It sits at the bottom of a mountain bowl, completely encircled by old-growth trees, with a few campsites set at lakeside. The abundance of wildlife can be remarkable. The far side of the lake is a major deer migration route, an osprey makes regular trips to pluck trout out of the lake for dinner, and the fishing is quite good, especially early in the summer.

Spirit Lake can be the feature destination for a week-long backpack loop, heading out on the Haypress Meadows Trail, up to Sandy Ridge, and then out to the lake, about 17 miles one way. Most hikers will stop for the night at One Mile or the Cuddihy Lakes on the way out, and that is why those two areas get so much use. Spirit Lake is best visited during the first week of June, when the nights are still cold, the people are few, and the area abounds with fish and deer.

⓱ Little North Fork Trailhead

16.0 mi/2.0 days

Location: In the Marble Mountain Wilderness near Sawyers Bar; map A1, grid j5.

User groups: Hikers, dogs, and horses. No mountain bikes. No wheelchair facilities.

Permits: A campfire permit is required for hikers planning to camp in the wilderness. Contact Klamath National Forest to obtain a free permit. Parking and access are free.

Directions: From Interstate 5 at Yreka, take the Highway 3/Fort Jones exit and drive southwest 28 miles to Etna. Turn west on Sawyers Bar Road and drive about 25 miles to the town of Sawyers Bar. Continue west on the same road for four

miles to Little North Fork Road (Forest Service Road 40N51). Turn right (north) here and drive half a mile to the trailhead.

Maps: A trail information sheet can be obtained by contacting the Salmon River Ranger District at the address below. For a map of Klamath National Forest, send $4 to USDA-Forest Service, 630 Sansome Street, San Francisco, CA 94111. A map of the Marble Mountain Wilderness can also be purchased for $4. To obtain a topographic map of the area, ask for Sawyers Bar from the USGS.

Contact: Klamath National Forest, Salmon River Ranger District, P.O. Box 280, Etna, CA 96027; (916) 467-5757.

Trail notes: Your destination options from this great trailhead? There are many: Chimney Rock, Clear Lake, Lily Lake, and Chimney Rock Lake. This makes for an excellent trip, providing you don't mind the long grind of a climb to reach the lakes. Like a lot of trails on the edge of the wilderness, this one starts with a long climb out of a river canyon. From the Little North Fork Trailhead, you start by climbing out toward Chimney Rock, grunting out a rise of about 4,000 feet as you depart the river lowlands and gain access to the Marble Mountain Wilderness. It's about an eight-mile trip to Clear Lake, a good first day's destination. While you can simply return the next day, most people will take several days to venture deeper into the wilderness, with 13 lakes and 20 miles of stream in the Abbotts Upper Cabin and English Peak areas.

⓲ Mule Bridge Trailhead

28.0 mi/3.0 days

Location: In the Marble Mountain Wilderness west of Etna; map A1, grid j7.

User groups: Hikers, dogs, and horses. No mountain bikes. No wheelchair facilities.

Permits: A campfire permit is required for hikers planning to camp in the wilderness. Contact Klamath National Forest to obtain a free permit.

Directions: From Interstate 5 at Yreka, take the Highway 3/Fort Jones exit and drive southwest 28 miles to Etna. Turn west on Etna-Somes Bar Road (Main Street in town) and drive 21 miles to Idlewild Campground. As you enter the campground, take the left fork in the road and continue two miles to the trailhead.

Maps: A trail information sheet can be obtained by contacting the Salmon River Ranger District at the address below. For a map of Klamath National Forest, send $4 to USDA-Forest Service, 630 Sansome Street, San Francisco, CA 94111. A map of the Marble Mountain Wilderness can also be purchased for $4. To obtain a topographic map of the area, ask for Sawyers Bar from the USGS.

Contact: Klamath National Forest, Salmon River Ranger District, P.O. Box 280, Etna, CA 96027; (916) 467-5757 or fax (916) 468-5654.

Trail notes: The trailhead at Idlewild Campground is set alongside the Salmon River, and once you've tightened your backpack, get ready for a long, endless climb up the river drainage. The trail follows along the Salmon River all the way up to its headwaters, gaining about 3,500 feet in the process. Plan on climbing for nearly 14 or 15 miles up along the river until you start reaching the higher country with many lakeside camps. The trail forks eight miles from the trailhead, with the right hand fork leading to Shelly Meadows and the Pacific Crest Trail. The main trail continues north for access to upper Abbotts Camp and many lakes in the upper drainage. This trail ties in with the Little North Fork Trail near Hancock Lake. The prettiest glacial-formed lakes in this region are Shelly Lake (14 miles), Osprey Lake (14 miles), and Bug Lake (14 miles), with good campsites available at Cabin Gulch (12 miles, 6,000 feet), Grants Meadow (14 miles, 6,200 feet), and Shelly Meadows (15 miles, 6,300 feet).

⑲ Taylor Lake Trail

1.0 mi/0.5 hrs

Location: From Etna Summit into the Russian Wilderness west of Etna; map A1, grid j8.

User groups: Hikers, dogs, horses, and wheelchairs. No mountain bikes.

Permits: A campfire permit is required only for hikers planning to camp in the wilderness. Contact Klamath National Forest to obtain a free permit. Parking and access are free.

Directions: From Interstate 5 at Yreka, take the Highway 3/Fort Jones exit and drive 28 miles southwest to Etna. Turn west on Etna-Somes Bar Road (Main Street in town) and drive 10.25 miles. Turn left on a signed access road just past Etna Summit and continue to the trailhead.

Maps: A trail information sheet can be obtained by contacting the Salmon River Ranger District at the address below. For a map of Klamath National Forest, send $4 to USDA-Forest Service, 630 Sansome Street, San Francisco, CA 94111. A map of the Marble Mountain Wilderness can also be purchased for $4. To obtain a topographic map of the area, ask for Eaton Peak from the USGS.

Contact: Klamath National Forest, Salmon River Ranger District, P.O. Box 280, Etna, CA 96027; (916) 467-5757 or fax (916) 468-5654.

Trail notes: Taylor Lake is proof that wilderness-like lakes can be accessible by a wheelchair. The trail is hard-packed dirt and wheelchair accessible, though wheelchairs with wide wheels are recommended. For those with boots instead of wheels, it's about a 10-minute walk to Taylor Lake, a long, narrow lake set on the northern end of the Russian Wilderness. Trout fishing is often very good here, and the walk is short enough so you can bring along a small raft or float tube.

For a side trip option, the Pacific Crest Trail runs east just above the lake, although the most direct access in the area for the PCT is at nearby Etna Summit. The only downer here is that occasionally the Forest Service permits cows to graze, and they stomp the grass at the far end of the lake and sometimes even walk in the shallows.

⑳ Big Blue Lake

6.0 mi/4.5 hrs

Location: In the Russian Wilderness west of Etna; map A1, grid j8.

User groups: Hikers only. No dogs, horses, or mountain bikes. No wheelchair facilities.

Permits: A campfire permit is required only for hikers planning to camp in the wilderness. Contact Klamath National Forest to obtain a free permit. Parking and access are free.

Directions: From Interstate 5 at Yreka, take the Highway 3/Fort Jones exit and drive 28 miles southwest to Etna. Turn west on Etna-Somes Bar Road (Main Street in town) and drive 20 miles. Just before the Salmon River Bridge, turn left on

Forest Service Road 40N54 and continue eight miles to the Music Creek Trailhead.

Maps: A trail information sheet can be obtained by contacting the Salmon River Ranger District at the address below. For a map of Klamath National Forest, send $4 to USDA-Forest Service, 630 Sansome Street, San Francisco, CA 94111. A map of the Marble Mountain Wilderness can also be purchased for $4. To obtain a topographic map of the area, ask for Sawyers Bar from the USGS.

Contact: Klamath National Forest, Salmon River Ranger District, P.O. Box 280, Etna, CA 96027; (916) 467-5757 or fax (916) 468-5654.

Trail notes: There are no trails to Big Blue Lake, and right off, that stops most people from even considering the trip. But if you're willing to scramble a bit, both up along a ridgeline and then down into a granite mountain bowl, your reward is a gorgeous lake, one of the prettiest in Northern California. There are just two camps at the lake, one mosquito-infested site along the northern shore, and another secluded, bugless camp near the outlet, with the lake just out of view.

After parking at the Music Creek Trailhead, you start the trip by hiking up a moderate grade, climbing about a mile and junctioning with the Pacific Crest Trail. Turn left and hike on the PCT for less than a mile, climbing as you go. When you reach a saddle in the mountain, don't continue down the other side on the trail, but instead turn left and leave the trail, traversing across the mountain slope to Big Blue. After about an hour, you'll arrive at the rim above the lake. From here you can drop down, and by following the tree line and scrambling across huge granite boulders, you can work your way down to the lake's shore. This last scramble is most easily accomplished in a counterclockwise direction in the mountain bowl around the lake. It's a bit tricky, but it's a do-able scamper for mountaineers in excellent physical condition.

㉑ Statue Lake

6.0 mi/4.0 hrs

Location: In the Russian Wilderness west of Etna; map A1, grid j8.

User groups: Hikers only. No dogs, horses, or mountain bikes. No wheelchair facilities.

Permits: A campfire permit is required only for hikers planning to camp in the wilderness. Contact Klamath National Forest to obtain a free permit. Parking and access are free.

Directions: From Interstate 5 at Yreka, take the Highway 3/Fort Jones exit and drive 28 miles southwest to Etna. Turn west on Etna-Somes Bar Road (Main Street in town) and drive 20 miles. Just before the Salmon River Bridge, turn left on Forest Service Road 40N54 and drive eight miles to the Music Creek Trailhead.

Maps: A trail information sheet can be obtained by contacting the Salmon River Ranger District at the address below. For a map of Klamath National Forest, send $4 to USDA-Forest Service, 630 Sansome Street, San Francisco, CA 94111. A map of the Marble Mountain Wilderness can also be purchased for $4. To obtain a topographic map of the area, ask for Sawyers Bar from the USGS.

Contact: Klamath National Forest, Salmon River Ranger District, P.O. Box 280, Etna, CA 96027; (916) 467-5757 or fax (916) 468-5654.

Trail notes: Statue Lake earned its name from the one-of-a-kind granite sculptures that frame the back wall of the lake. When you first arrive at the small lake, it's a wondrous yet solemn sight, one of nature's mountain temples. Some of the granite outcrops look like fingers that have been sculpted with a giant chisel. There is a small, primitive campsite on a granite bluff, from which you can often see small brook trout in the lake rising to feed.

After parking at the Music Creek Trailhead, start the trip by hiking up a moderate grade, climbing about a mile, and junctioning with the Pacific Crest Trail. Turn right and hike on the PCT for about 1.5 miles, an easy walk in the forest. When you reach a small spring creek, stop and fill up your canteens, then leave the trail and head uphill. It's about a 30-minute hike crosscountry to the lake, the last 10 minutes over a large field of boulders.

Pacific Crest Trail (PCT) Section Overview

92.0 mi. one way/8.0 days

Trail sections extend from Etna Summit north through the Marble Mountains to Seiad Valley on Highway 96, then onward to the Rogue Wilderness in southern Oregon.

This stretch of the Pacific Crest Trail includes some of its most and least popular sections in Northern California. The Etna Trailhead is an excellent jumpoff, once you get past the first few miles of dry, often hot terrain. It heads directly into the Marble Mountain Wilderness, crossing through Marble Valley, past Marble Mountain itself, then onward past Paradise Lake to the northern sections of the wilderness. Most of the trail here is above tree line, with outstanding lookouts at several points, including a great vista from Marble Rim. As you head north, the trail becomes less and less traveled, eventually leaving the Marbles and descending along Grider Creek to the Klamath River town of Seiad Valley. From here, the trail is routed 34 miles north into Oregon. That section of the trail starts with a steep five-mile climb to Upper Devil's Peak, which keeps most day hikers off the route. For more specific information on major trail sections in this zone of the PCT, see the following three hikes in this chapter.

PCT-46 Etna Summit to Grider Creek

49.0 mi. one way/4.0 days

Location: From Etna Summit north into the Marble Mountain Wilderness west of Etna; map A1, grid j8.

User groups: Hikers, dogs, and horses. No mountain bikes. No wheelchair facilities.

Permits: A campfire permit is required only for hikers planning to camp in the wilderness. Contact Klamath National Forest to obtain a free permit. Parking and access are free.

Directions: From Interstate 5 at Yreka, take the Highway 3/Fort Jones exit and drive 28 miles to Etna. Turn west on Etna-Somes Bar Road (Main Street in town) and drive 10.5 miles to Etna Summit. The parking area is on the right.

Maps: A trail information sheet can be obtained by contacting the Salmon River Ranger District at the address below. For a map of Klamath National Forest, send $4 to USDA-Forest Service, 630 Sansome Street, San Francisco, CA 94111. A map of the Marble Mountain Wilderness can also be purchased for $4. To obtain a topographic map of the area, ask for Eaton Peak from the USGS.

Contact: Klamath National Forest, Salmon River Ranger District, P.O. Box 280, Etna, CA 96027; (916) 467-5757 or fax (916) 468-5654.

Trail notes: The Etna Summit is one of the major access points for the Pacific Crest Trail in Northern California. There is a good, safe parking area (good views from here, too), and at an elevation of 5,492 feet, you don't have to start your hike with a wicked climb, like what is demanded at so many other wilderness trailheads. From Etna Summit, the trail starts by crossing rugged, dry country which is best dealt with in the morning, reaching Shelly Lake about eight miles in. The campground at Shelly Meadows is a good first-night stopover. From there, an excellent second-day destination is the Marble Valley, about another 10 miles north, camping in the Sky High Lakes Basin. The next 20 miles of trail cross through and out of the Marble Mountains. You'll pass Marble Mountain (a side trip to Marble Rim is mandatory), Paradise Lake, and Kings Castle; many visitors will make camp at Paradise Lake. From there, the trail follows Big Ridge to Buckhorn Mountain (6,908 feet), continues past Huckleberry Mountain (6,303 feet), and then drops down to the headwaters of Grider Creek, the next major trailhead access point.

PCT-47 Grider Creek to Seiad Valley

7.0 mi. one way/1.0 day

Location: In Klamath National Forest, southeast of Happy Camp to the Grider Creek Trailhead; map A1, grid f6.

User groups: Hikers, dogs, and horses. No mountain bikes. No wheelchair facilities.

Permits: A campfire permit is required. Parking and access are free.

Directions: From Interstate 5 north of Yreka, turn west on Highway 96 and drive approximately 40 miles to Walker Creek/Grider Creek Road. Turn left on Walker Creek Road and drive about 50 feet, then turn right on Grider Creek and drive to the trailhead.

Maps: A trail information sheet can be obtained by contacting the Scott River Ranger District at the address below. For a map of Klamath National Forest, send $4 to USDA-Forest Service, 630 Sansome Street, San Francisco, CA 94111. To obtain a topographic map of the area, ask for Seiad Valley from the USGS.

Contact: Klamath National Forest, Happy Camp Ranger District, P.O. Box 377, Happy Camp, CA 96039; (916) 493-2243 or fax (916) 493-2212.

Trail notes: The Pacific Crest Trail provides a good access point at the headwaters of Grider Creek, though most hikers use it in order to head south into the Marble Mountain Wilderness, not north. Heading north, it's about a 12-mile trip to the town of Seiad Valley on Highway 96, an excellent place for PCT hikers to pick up a food stash and dump garbage. The trail here follows Grider Creek, an easy descent northward as the stream pours toward the Klamath River. A good Forest Service campground (Grider Creek Camp) is available about three miles before reaching Seiad Valley.

Trail notes: Not many people hike this section of the Pacific Crest Trail, the northernmost segment in California. But it's a great chunk of trail, whether for a day hike or for the whole duration, all the way to Wards Fork Gap on the edge of the Rogue Wilderness in southern Oregon. The ambitious few will head up from the trailhead to the junction of the Boundary National Recreation Trail, a seven-mile trip one way. The first five miles are a steep climb out of the Klamath River Valley, rising to Upper Devil's Peak, elevation 6,040 feet.

This hike marks the final steps of the 1,700-mile Pacific Crest Trail in California, an epic journey for all, but always classic, even if only sections are enjoyed.

PCT-48 Seiad Valley to Oregon Border

36.0 mi. one way/3.0 days

Location: In Klamath National Forest, from Seiad Valley to the Siskiyou Mountains; map A1, grid e7.

User groups: Hikers, dogs, and horses. No mountain bikes. No wheelchair facilities.

Permits: No permits are required. Parking and access are free.

Directions: From Interstate 5 north of Yreka, turn west on Highway 96 and drive approximately 40 miles to the town of Seiad Valley. Continue one more mile west on Highway 96 to the trailhead on the north side. Parking is minimal; park across the highway.

Maps: A trail information sheet can be obtained by contacting the Oak Knoll Ranger District at the address below. For a map of Klamath National Forest, send $4 to USDA-Forest Service, 630 Sansome Street, San Francisco, CA 94111. To obtain a topographic map of the area, ask for Seiad Valley from the USGS.

Contact: Klamath National Forest, Oak Knoll Ranger District, 22541 Highway 96, Klamath River, CA 96050; (916) 465-2241.

Leave No Trace Tips

Travel and Camp with Care

On the trail:

Stay on designated trails. Walk single file in the middle of the path.

Do not take shortcuts on switchbacks.

When traveling cross-country where there are no trails,
follow animal trails or spread out your group so no new routes are
created. Walk along the most durable surfaces available,
such as rock, gravel, dry grasses, or snow.

Use a map and compass to eliminate
the need for rock cairns, tree scars, or ribbons.

If you encounter pack animals, step to the downhill side
of the trail and speak softly to avoid startling them.

At camp:

Choose an established, legal site that will not be damaged by your stay.

Restrict activities to areas where vegetation is compacted or absent.

Keep pollutants out of the water by camping at least 200 feet
(about 70 adult steps) from lakes and streams.

Control pets at all times, or leave them at home
with a sitter. Remove dog feces.

Map A2

Adjoining Maps: East: A1 ...... *page* 16   West: A3 36
                        South: B2 66

Northern California Map .... *page* 2

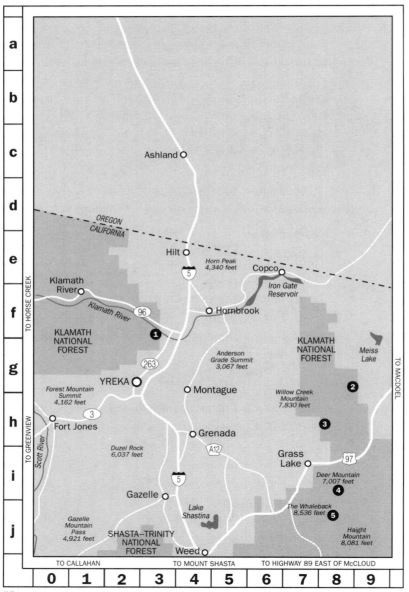

Chapter A2 features:

❶ Tree of Heaven Trail

3.5 mi/2.0 hrs

Location: On the Klamath River in Klamath National Forest northwest of Yreka; map A2, grid f3.

User groups: Hikers, dogs, horses, and mountain bikes. No wheelchair facilities.

Permits: No permits are required. Parking and access are free.

Directions: From Yreka, drive 10 miles north on Interstate 5 to the Highway 96 exit. Turn west on Highway 96 and drive about five miles. Look for the Tree of Heaven Campground on the left. The trailhead is located at the west end of the campground.

Maps: A trail guide can be obtained by contacting the Oak Knoll Ranger District at the address below. For a map of Klamath National Forest, send $4 to USDA-Forest Service, 630 Sansome Street, San Francisco, CA 94111. To obtain a topographic map of the area, ask for Badger Mountain from the USGS.

Contact: Klamath National Forest, Oak Knoll Ranger District, 22541 Highway 96, Klamath River, CA 96050; (916) 465-2241 or fax (916) 465-2237.

Trail notes: The trail out of the Tree of Heaven Campground is one of the best streamside trails anywhere along the Klamath River. Heading downstream along the Klamath, it's a level path that sometimes probes through heavy vegetation, and other times offers direct river access. The fall is an excellent time for berry picking. The trail ends at a good fishing access spot, though the fishing is poor during the prime camping/hiking/vacation season. Salmon start arriving in September in this area, steelhead in November and December. The Tree of Heaven River access is also a good take-out point for rafters and drift boaters after making the all-day run down from Iron Canyon Dam.

❷ Juanita Lake Trail

1.75 mi/1.0 hrs

Location: In Klamath National Forest east of Yreka; map A2, grid g8.

User groups: Hikers and dogs. No mountain bikes or horses. The fishing piers are wheelchair accessible.

Permits: No permits are required. Parking and access are free.

Directions: From Interstate 5 at Weed, take the Weed/College exit in Siskiyous and drive north through town to the Highway 97 turnoff. Drive about 35 miles northeast, then turn left on Ball Mountain Road and drive two miles. Turn right at the sign for Juanita Lake and drive about three miles to the lake, following the signs all the way. The trailhead is near the boat dock at the campground.

Maps: A trail guide can be obtained by contacting the Goosenest Ranger District at the address below. For a map of Klamath National Forest, send $4 to USDA-Forest Service, 630 Sansome Street, San Francisco, CA 94111. To obtain a topographic map of the area, ask for Panther Rock from the USGS.

Contact: Klamath National Forest, Goosenest Ranger District, 37805 Highway 97, Macdoel, CA 96058; (916) 398-4391 or fax (916) 398-4599.

Trail notes: Not many people know about Juanita Lake, including many Siskiyou County residents, but when they find out, they often will take this easy loop trail around the lake to get a feel for the place. The lake is set in a mixed conifer forest, though few trees here are large, and wildlife in the area includes osprey and bald eagles. In the last hour of light during summer, both osprey and eagles occasionally make a fishing trip at the lake. Juanita Lake is a small lake that provides lakeside camping and fishing for brook trout—it's stocked with 2,000 per year. The small fishing piers are wheelchair accessible.

A good side trip is driving on the Forest Service Road up to Ball Mountain, located about two miles southwest of the lake, for great views of Mount Shasta from the 7,786-foot summit.

❸ Goosenest

4.0 mi/2.75 hrs

Location: In Klamath National Forest north of Mount Shasta; map A2, grid h7.

User groups: Hikers, dogs, horses, and mountain bikes. No wheelchair facilities.

Permits: No permits are required. Parking and access are free.

Directions: From Interstate 5 at Weed, take the Weed/College exit in Siskiyous and drive north through town to the Highway 97 turnoff. Turn right on Highway 97 and drive about 25 miles northeast. About three-quarters of a mile past the Tennant turnoff, turn left on Forest Service Road 46N10 and drive about seven miles to a junction of dirt roads. Here, turn left on County Road 7K007 and drive one mile, then turn left again on Forest Service Road 45N22 and drive six miles. Turn right on Forest Service Road 45N72Y and drive 2.5 miles to the trailhead at the base of the mountain.

Maps: A trail guide can be obtained by contacting the Goosenest Ranger District at the address below. For a map of Klamath National Forest, send $4 to USDA-Forest Service, 630 Sansome Street, San Francisco, CA 94111. To obtain a topographic map of the area, ask for Grass Lake from the USGS.

Contact: Klamath National Forest, Goosenest Ranger District, 37805 Highway 97, Macdoel, CA 96058; (916) 398-4391 or fax (916) 398-4599.

Trail notes: This is a short, steep trail that peaks out at the top of Goosenest at an elevation of 8,280 feet. The surrounding views are extraordinary, especially looking south at Mount Shasta. But looking east is also memorable, toward the high prairie country around Meiss Lake and the Butte Valley Wildlife Area, as well as to the west of the little Shasta Valley. Despite the great views, the trail gets very little use, even in the summer months. Most local residents are not aware that the trailhead access is located

fairly near the top of the mountain. The surrounding forest is primarily hemlock and red fir.

❹ Deer Mountain

4.0 mi/2.25 hrs

Location: In Klamath National Forest north of Mount Shasta; map A2, grid i8.

User groups: Hikers, dogs, horses, and mountain bikes. No wheelchair facilities.

Permits: No permits are required. Parking and access are free.

Directions: From Interstate 5 at Weed, take the Weed/College exit in Siskiyous and drive north through town to the Highway 97 turnoff. Turn right on Highway 97 and drive about 15 miles. Turn right on Deer Mountain Road/Forest Service Road 42N12/Forest Service Road 19 and drive four miles to Deer Mountain Snowmobile Park. Turn left on Forest Service Road 44N23 and drive about two miles. There is no designated trailhead; park off the road and hike cross-country to the mountain top. Forest Service Road 43N69 loops around the base of the mountain; you may also hike from anywhere along that road.

Maps: A trail guide can be obtained by contacting the Goosenest Ranger District at the address below. For a map of Klamath National Forest, send $4 to USDA-Forest Service, 630 Sansome Street, San Francisco, CA 94111. To obtain a topographic map of the area, ask for the Whaleback from the USGS.

Contact: Klamath National Forest, Goosenest Ranger District, 37805 Highway 97, Macdoel, CA 96058; (916) 398-4391 or fax (916) 398-4599.

Trail notes: Deer Mountain is the second of a line of small peaks set on the north side of Mount Shasta that extend all the way to the Medicine Lake wildlands. Looking north from Shasta, the first peak is the Whaleback, at an elevation of 8,528 feet, and the second is Deer Mountain, at 7,006 feet. Starting elevation at the parking area is 6,200 feet, and from here, you climb 800 feet through forest consisting of various pines and firs to gain the summit. This route gets very little use, even though it's easy to reach and the destination is a mountaintop. Most out-of-towners visiting this area are attracted to the trails on Mount Shasta instead, and most locals just plain overlook it.

❺ The Whaleback

3.0 mi/2.5 hrs

Location: In Klamath National Forest north of Mount Shasta; map A2, grid i8.

User groups: Hikers, dogs, horses, and mountain bikes. No wheelchair facilities.

Permits: No permits are required. Parking and access are free.

Directions: From Interstate 5 at Weed, take the Weed/College exit in Siskiyous and drive north through town to the Highway 97 turnoff. Turn right on Highway 97 and drive about 15 miles, then turn right on Deer Mountain Road and drive four miles to Deer Mountain Snowmobile Park. Drive about three miles east on Deer Mountain Road/Forest Service Road 19/Forest Service Road 42N12. Turn right on Forest Service Road 42N24 and drive three miles to a gate. Park and hike in. There is no designated trail; you must hike cross-country from the road. The peak is about 1.5 miles from the gate.

Maps: A trail guide can be obtained by contacting the Goosenest Ranger District at the address below. For a map of Klamath National Forest, send $4 to USDA-Forest Service, 630 Sansome Street, San Francisco, CA 94111. To obtain a topographic map of the area, ask for the Whaleback from the USGS.

Contact: Klamath National Forest, Goosenest Ranger District, 37805 Highway 97, Macdoel, CA 96058; (916) 398-4391 or fax (916) 398-4599.

Trail notes: When you pass Mount Shasta driving north on Interstate 5, you'll see this large hump-like mountain that sits directly north of Shasta. It looks like a huge volcanic bump that was born when Shasta was active. This is the Whaleback, 8,528 feet high, providing an excellent hike with a surprise reward at the top. That surprise is a large crater. The Whaleback Summit is actually a volcanic cindercone with a collapsed center. This interesting geology, along with the unsurpassed view of Mount Shasta to the south, makes this a first-rate hike. Yet almost nobody tries it, most likely because they don't realize how near you can drive to the top, or because there is no formal trail. After parking at the gate, you just hike cross-country style up to the rim, steep all the way. The 1.5-mile hike is a scramble only in a few places. In the process, you'll climb 1,100 feet, from a starting elevation of 7,400 feet to Whaleback Rim.

Map A3

Adjoining Maps: East: A4 ...... *page* 42   West: A2 32
South: B3 86

Northern California Map .... *page* 2

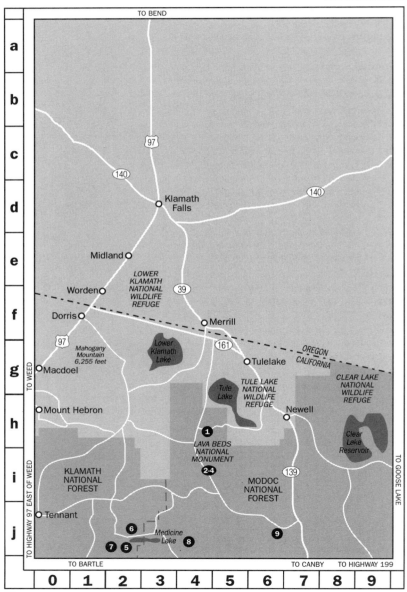

Chapter A3 features:

❶ Captain Jack's Stronghold

1.5 mi/1.5 hrs

Location: In Lava Beds National Monument south of Klamath Wildlife Refuge; map A3, grid h4.

User groups: Hikers only. No dogs, horses, or mountain bikes. The trail is partially wheelchair accessible.

Permits: No permits are required. A $4 park entrance fee is charged.

Directions: From Interstate 5 at Redding, drive east on Highway 299 for 133 miles to Canby. Turn north on Highway 139 and drive 20 miles, then turn west on Lava Beds National Monument Road and follow the signs to the entrance. Drive about 3.5 miles to the visitors center, then head north another 10 miles on the main monument road (unnamed). Turn east on the access road to the trailhead at Captain Jack's Stronghold.

Maps: A free brochure is available by contacting Lava Beds National Monument at the address below. To obtain a topographic map of the area, ask for Captain Jack's Stronghold from the USGS.

Contact: Lava Beds National Monument, P.O. Box 867, Tulelake, CA 96134; (916) 667-2282, (916) 667-2231, or fax (916) 667-2737.

Trail notes: Captain Jack was a Modoc warrior who fought U.S. troops attempting to relocate Native Americans off their historical lands and onto a reservation. Eventually in 1873, Captain Jack was captured and hanged, and this site was later named for him. Captain Jack's Stronghold provides a good introduction to the Lava Beds National Monument. It's an easy walk across volcanic fields, with lots of trenches, dips, and rocks. From this trailhead, there are actually two loop trails available, including a shorter route that is just half a mile long. The general terrain is level, with a trailhead elevation of 4,047 feet and a high point of 4,080 feet, but when you hike it, you'll find that the trail is anything but flat. Note that during the winter, this is an outstanding area to see mule deer. Many of the famous photographs of big bucks in California were taken in this area. The wildlife viewing is best at the onset of winter, after the first inch or two of snow has fallen. In addition, a good nearby side trip is Tule Lake, a favorite wintering area for waterfowl and bald eagles.

❷ Whitney Butte Trail

6.8 mi/4.0 hrs

Location: In Lava Beds National Monument south of Klamath Wildlife Refuge; map A3, grid i4.

User groups: Hikers and horses. No dogs or mountain bikes. No wheelchair facilities.

Permits: No permits are required. A $4 park entrance fee is charged.

Directions: From Interstate 5 at Redding, drive east on Highway 299 for 133 miles to Canby. Turn north on Highway 139 and drive 20 miles, then turn west on Lava Beds National Monument Road and follow the signs to the entrance. Drive about 3.5 miles to the visitors center, then drive another two miles north on the monument main road (unnamed) to the turnoff for Merrill Cave. The trailhead is at the end of the road.

Maps: A free brochure is available by contacting Lava Beds National Monument at the address below. To obtain a topographic map of the area, ask for Schonchin Butte from the USGS.

Contact: Lava Beds National Monument, P.O. Box 867, Tulelake, CA 96134; (916) 667-2282, (916) 667-2231, or fax (916) 667-2737.

Trail notes: The Whitney Butte Trail is one of three wilderness trails in Lava Beds National

Monument, and for many, it's the best of the lot. From the trailhead at Merrill Cave, set at 4,880 feet, the trail heads west for 3.4 miles, skirting the northern flank of Whitney Butte (5,004 feet) and ending at the edge of the Callahan Lava Flow on the park's southwest boundary. This area bears a resemblance to the surface of the moon, and skilled photographers who know how to use sunlight to their advantage can take black-and-white pictures that can fool most people.

❸ Thomas Wright Trail

2.2 mi/1.0 hr

Location: In Lava Beds National Monument south of Klamath Wildlife Refuge; map A3, grid i4.

User groups: Hikers only. No dogs, horses, or mountain bikes. No wheelchair facilities.

Permits: No permits are required. A $4 park entrance fee is charged.

Directions: From Interstate 5 at Redding, drive east on Highway 299 for 133 miles to Canby. Turn north on Highway 139 and drive 20 miles, then turn west on Lava Beds National Monument Road and follow the signs to the entrance. Drive about 3.5 miles to the visitors center, then another five miles to the trailhead on the right.

Maps: A free brochure is available by contacting Lava Beds National Monument at the address below. To obtain a topographic map of the area, ask for Captain Jack's Stronghold from the USGS.

Contact: Lava Beds National Monument, P.O. Box 867, Tulelake, CA 96134; (916) 667-2282, (916) 667-2231, or fax (916) 667-2737.

Trail notes: If you sense ghosts shadowing your footsteps, well, it won't be the first time. Some say this area is haunted by the ghosts of Modoc Indians, who fought troops in several violent battles for custody of the land. While the Modoc warriors eventually lost that war, some say they actually won in the long run, since their spirits haunt modern-day visitors. At the end of the trail, there are interpretive signs that explain the Thomas Wright battlefield site. For an excellent side trip from here, continue off-trail, clambering up to the Hardin Butte, a 130-foot climb, for a view. The butte sits on the western edge of the huge Schonchin Lava Flow.

❹ Schonchin Butte Trail

1.5 mi/1.0 hr

Location: In Lava Beds National Monument south of Klamath Wildlife Refuge; map A3, grid i4.

User groups: Hikers only. No dogs, horses, or mountain bikes. No wheelchair facilities.

Permits: No permits are required. A $4 park entrance fee is charged.

Directions: From Interstate 5 at Redding, drive east on Highway 299 for 133 miles to Canby. Turn north on Highway 139 and drive 20 miles, then turn west on Lava Beds National Monument Road and follow the signs to the park entrance. Drive 3.5 miles to the visitors center, then another 2.5 miles north on the monument main road (unnamed). Turn right at the sign for Schonchin Butte and drive about one mile on an unpaved road to the trailhead.

Maps: A free brochure is available by contacting Lava Beds National Monument at the address below. To obtain a topographic map of the area, ask for Schonchin Butte from the USGS.

Contact: Lava Beds National Monument, P.O. Box 867, Tulelake, CA 96134; (916) 667-2282, (916) 667-2231, or fax (916) 667-2737.

Trail notes: This is a short hike, but for many it's a butt-kicker. A portion of it is quite steep— steep enough to get most folks wheezing like old coal-powered locomotives. That's true even though the trail climbs just 250 feet, from a trailhead elevation of 5,000 feet to the lookout at 5,253 feet. Schonchin Butte has an old fire lookout, and, of course, the views are spectacular, especially of the Schonchin Lava Flow to the northeast. Because of the close proximity to the visitors center, as well as the short distance involved, many visitors make the tromp to the top.

❺ Medicine Lake Loop

4.5 mi/2.5 hrs

Location: In Modoc National Forest northeast of Mount Shasta; map A3, grid j2.

User groups: Hikers, dogs, horses, and mountain bikes. There are wheelchair facilities at the swim beach and the boat ramp.

Permits: No permits are required. Parking and access are free unless you're camping.

Directions: From Redding, turn north on Interstate 5 and drive 56 miles. Take the McCloud-Reno exit and drive 29 miles east on Highway 89 to Bartle. Just past Bartle, turn northeast on Powder Hill Road (Forest Service Road 49) and drive 31 miles to Medicine Lake Road. Drive on Medicine Lake Road to the lake.

Maps: A free brochure on the Medicine Lake Highlands is available by contacting the Doublehead Ranger District at the address below. For a map of Modoc National Forest, send $4 to USDA-Forest Service, 630 Sansome Street, San Francisco, CA 94111. To obtain a topographic map of the area, ask for Medicine Lake from the USGS.

Contact: Modoc National Forest, Doublehead Ranger District, P.O. Box 369, Tulelake, CA 96134; (916) 667-2246 or fax (916) 667-4808.

Trail notes: When you stand on the shore of Medicine Lake, it might be difficult to believe that this was once the center of a volcano. The old caldera is now filled with water and circled by conifers, and the lake is clear and crisp. Set at 6,700 feet, it's a unique and popular destination for camping, boating, and fishing. At some point in their stay, most campers will take a morning or afternoon to walk around the lake. While there is no specific trail, the route is clear enough. There is a sense of timeless history here. Although its geology is comparable to Crater Lake in Oregon, Medicine Lake is neither as deep nor as blue. But a bonus here is the good shore-fishing for large brook trout, often in the 12- to 14-inch class, buoyed by the largest stocks of trout of any lake in the region (30,000 per year). There are also many excellent nearby side trips, including ice caves (along the access road on the way in), a great mountain-top lookout from Little Mount Hoffman just west of the lake, and nearby little Bullseye and Blanche Lakes.

---

❻ Medicine Lake Glass Flow

2.0 mi/2.0 hrs

Location: In Modoc National Forest north of Medicine Lake; map A3, grid j3.

User groups: Hikers and dogs. The terrain is not suitable for mountain bikes or horses. No wheelchair facilities.

Permits: No permits are required. Parking and access are free.

Directions: From Redding, turn north on Interstate 5 and drive 56 miles. Take the McCloud-Reno exit and drive 29 miles east on Highway 89 to Bartle. Just past Bartle, turn northeast on Powder Hill Road (Forest Service Road 49) and drive about 33.5 miles (2.5 miles past the Medicine Lake turnoff). The glass flow is located just off the road on the left; park and go in.

Maps: A free brochure on the Medicine Lake Highlands is available by contacting the Doublehead Ranger District at the address below. For a map of Modoc National Forest, send $4 to USDA-Forest Service, 630 Sansome Street, San Francisco, CA 94111. To obtain a topographic map of the area, ask for Medicine Lake from the USGS.

Contact: Modoc National Forest, Doublehead Ranger District, P.O. Box 369, Tulelake, CA 96134; (916) 667-2246 or fax (916) 667-4808.

Trail notes: The Medicine Lake Glass Flow covers 570 acres but has no designated trails. You can explore in any direction you wish, investigating the ancient, dull, stony-gray dacite, which runs 50 to 150 feet deep. This is part of the Medicine Lake Highlands, located just a mile north of Medicine Lake, where "rocks that float and mountains of glass" (poetic description from Forest Service geologists) resemble the surface of the moon. That is why this area was selected by the Manned Spacecraft Center in 1965 for study by astronauts preparing for the first manned trip to the moon. Most people will just poke around for an hour or two, take a few pictures, and leave saying they've never seen anything like it.

---

❼ Little Mount Hoffman

0.25 mi/0.25 hr

Location: In Modoc National Forest north of Medicine Lake; map A3, grid j3.

User groups: Hikers, dogs, horses, and mountain bikes. No wheelchair facilities.

Permits: No permits are required. Parking and access are free.

Directions: From Redding, turn north on Interstate 5 and drive 56 miles. Take the McCloud-Reno exit and drive 29 miles east on Highway 89 to Bartle. Just past Bartle, turn northeast on Powder Hill Road (Forest Service Road 49) and drive 31 miles to Medicine Lake Road. Turn left and drive to Headquarters Campground on the west side of the lake. You can park and hike in from here. In the summer, the road to the summit is accessible by car.

Maps: A free brochure on the Medicine Lake Highlands is available by contacting the Doublehead Ranger District at the address below. For a map of Modoc National Forest, send $4 to USDA-Forest Service, 630 Sansome Street, San Francisco, CA 94111. To obtain a topographic map of the area, ask for Medicine Lake from the USGS.

Contact: Modoc National Forest, Doublehead Ranger District, P.O. Box 369, Tulelake, CA 96134; (916) 667-2246 or fax (916) 667-4808.

Trail notes: At an impressive 7,309 feet, Mount Hoffman is one of the great spots to take pictures in Northern California, and you get world-class views without a difficult hike. Looking north, you get a sweeping view of Lava Beds National Monument and beyond to Mount McLaughlin in Oregon. To the east is Big Glass Mountain and to the south is Lassen Peak. To the west, of course, is Mount Shasta, the most dramatic photo opportunity available here. The summit is easy to reach in the summer, with a road going eight miles right to the top; from there you can walk around the top, enjoying the views in all directions. There is an old Forest Service lookout station here that is used only rarely during thunderstorms, from which spotters will scan the territory for lightning strikes and the start of forest fires.

❽ Glass Mountain

2.5 mi/1.5 hrs

Location: In Modoc National Forest east of Medicine Lake; map A3, grid j3.

User groups: Hikers and dogs. The terrain is not suitable for horses or mountain bikes. No wheelchair facilities.

Permits: No permits are required. Parking and access are free.

Directions: From Redding, turn north on Interstate 5 and drive 56 miles. Take the McCloud-Reno exit and drive 29 miles east on Highway 89 to Bartle. Just past Bartle, turn northeast on Powder Hill Road (Forest Service Road 49) and drive about 29 miles. Turn right on Forest Service Road 97 and drive about six miles, then turn north on Forest Service Road 43N99 and drive to the southern border of Glass Mountain.

Maps: A free brochure on the Medicine Lake Highlands is available by contacting the Doublehead Ranger District at the address below. For a map of Modoc National Forest, send $4 to USDA-Forest Service, 630 Sansome Street, San Francisco, CA 94111. To obtain a topographic map of the area, ask for Medicine Lake from the USGS.

Contact: Modoc National Forest, Doublehead Ranger District, P.O. Box 369, Tulelake, CA 96134; (916) 667-2246 or fax (916) 667-4808.

Trail notes: Glass Mountain, a glass flow that covers 4,210 acres, is one of the most unusual settings in the Medicine Lake Highlands. It was created when glassy dacite and rhyolitic obsidian flowed from the same volcanic vent without mixing, creating a present-day phenomenon that exhibits no modification from weather, erosion, or vegetation. There are no designated trails on Glass Mountain, so visitors just wander about, inspecting the geologic curiosities as they go. Take care to stay clear of the obsidian, which can have arrowhead-sharp edges and be quite slippery. Don't walk on it and don't handle it. Instead, be sure to stay on the gray-colored dacite.

❾ Timber Mountain

0.5 mi/1.0 hr

Location: In Modoc National Forest near Highway 139 California border check station; map A3, grid j6.

User groups: Hikers, dogs, horses, and mountain bikes. The lookout is partially wheelchair accessible, but the trails are not.

Permits: No permits are required. Parking and access are free.

Directions: From Interstate 5 at Redding, drive east on Highway 299 for 133 miles to Canby. Turn north on Highway 139 and drive 20 miles, then turn west on Forest Service Road 97 and drive about a mile. Turn south on County Road 97A and drive 1.5 miles, then drive south on Forest Service Road 44N19 for about three miles to the base of the mountain. The road continues to the summit, where there is a Forest Service lookout.

Maps: For a map of Modoc National Forest, send $4 to USDA-Forest Service, 630 Sansome Street, San Francisco, CA 94111. To obtain a topographic map of the area, ask for Perez from the USGS.

Contact: Modoc National Forest, Doublehead Ranger District, P.O. Box 369, Tulelake, CA 96134; (916) 667-2246 or fax (916) 667-4808.

Trail notes: When it comes to seeing wildlife, timing is everything. You can make this trip to Timber Mountain in the summer and wonder how it ever earned such a high rating in this book. After all, from the lookout at 5,086 feet, the view is quite nice of the high Modoc plateau country, but hey, a 9? Make this trip in December and you'll see why. In three hours, we saw about 400 deer, including dozens of big mule deer bucks with giant racks. What happens, you see, is that when the cold weather starts (long after the deer season has ended), the herd migrates out of Oregon and arrives in this area for winter. In turn, what you do is make the drive to the summit, park near the Forest Service lookout, then prepare for some fun. You creep to the summit rim, then peer over the side and down the mountain slope, scanning with binoculars. Small groups of 10 to 15 deer seem to be everywhere. That is how you spend your time here, creeping to the edge, peering over the tops of rocks, spotting and stalking, maybe taking a few photographs with a telephoto lens. It can be the best place to see deer in California.

Special Note: In 1993, 1,500 acres were burned in this area, but the summit was not affected.

Map A4

Adjoining Maps: West: A3 ..... *page* 36
South: B4 100

Northern California Map .... *page* 2

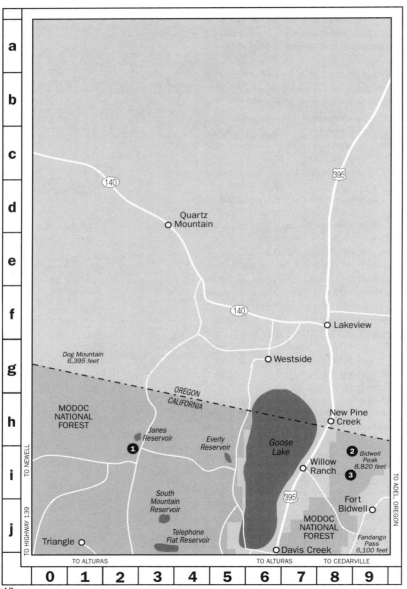

❶ Janes Reservoir

1.0 mi/0.75 hr

Location: In Modoc National Forest north of Alturas; map A4, grid i2.

User groups: Hikers, dogs, horses, and mountain bikes. No wheelchair facilities.

Permits: No permits are required. Parking and access are free.

Directions: From Interstate 5 at Redding, turn east on Highway 299 and drive about 144 miles (17 miles past Canby). Turn left on Crowder Flat Road and continue approximately 30 miles to the reservoir.

Maps: For a map of Modoc National Forest, send $4 to USDA-Forest Service, 630 Sansome Street, San Francisco, CA 94111. To obtain a topographic map of the area, ask for South Mountain from the USGS.

Contact: Modoc National Forest, Devil's Garden Ranger District, 800 West 12th Street, Alturas, CA 96101; phone or fax (916) 233-5811.

Trail notes: A dirt road leads from the southwest corner of Janes Reservoir to Huffman Butte, about a two-mile drive (if your car can't handle the road, you can hike it). The best strategy is to park at the base of the butte, then make the easy climb to the top of it. The reward is a nice view of the lake and the surrounding stark terrain.

This is sagebrush country, the high plateau land of Modoc country. You're likely to see cattle, possibly wild mustangs, and with the number of wetlands in the area, lots of waterfowl, particularly Canada geese. However, you're unlikely to see people. Even though it's very remote for a drive-to area, a bonus is that there are a number of side trips possible to other lakes. The best are the Alphabet Lakes (Reservoir C has the best trout fishing) and Big Sage Reservoir on Crowder Flat Road.

❷ Lily Lake to Cave Lake

0.5 mi/0.5 hr

Location: In Modoc National Forest east of Goose Lake; map A4, grid i8.

User groups: Hikers, dogs, horses, and mountain bikes. No wheelchair facilities.

Permits: No permits are required. Parking and access are free.

Directions: From Interstate 5 at Redding, turn east on Highway 299 and drive approximately 146 miles to Alturas. Turn north on U.S. 395 and drive 40 miles to the town of New Pine Creek (on the Oregon/California border). Turn right on Forest Service Road 2 and drive 5.5 miles east to the lake.

Maps: For a map of Modoc National Forest, send $4 to USDA-Forest Service, 630 Sansome Street, San Francisco, CA 94111. To obtain a topographic map of the area, ask for Mount Bidwell from the USGS.

Contact: Modoc National Forest, Warner Mountain Ranger District, P.O. Box 220, Cedarville, CA 96104; phone or fax (916) 279-6116.

Trail notes: While there are no designated trails, the quarter-mile walk from the campground at Lily Lake over to Cave Lake is an easy and rewarding trip. The surroundings at Lily Lake are quite beautiful—mostly forest with few humans around, and pretty little flowers blooming in the lily pads along the shallow eastern shore of the lake. As you walk to Cave Lake, the surroundings quickly change. This lake is also small, but with a barren shoreline, the trees placed well back from the water. There's a great contrast between the two lakes. A bonus is decent fishing for rainbow trout at Lily Lake and brook trout at Cave Lake. A good side trip is making the short walk over to the headwaters of Pine Creek, a small but pretty stream that is overlooked by most visitors.

❸ Hi Grade National Recreation Trail

1.1 mi/0.5 hr

Location: In Modoc National Forest east of Goose Lake; map A4, grid i8.

User groups: Hikers, dogs, horses, and mountain bikes. No wheelchair facilities.

Permits: No permits are required. Parking and access are free.

Directions: From Interstate 5 at Redding, turn east on Highway 299 and drive 146 miles to Alturas. Turn north on U.S. 395 and drive about 35 miles. Turn right on Forest Service Road 9 and drive 4.5 miles. At the Buck Creek Ranger Station, turn left on Forest Service Road 47N72 and drive about six miles to the trailhead. Four-wheel-drive vehicles are required.

Maps: For a map of Modoc National Forest, send $4 to USDA-Forest Service, 630 Sansome Street, San Francisco, CA 94111. To obtain topographic maps of the area, ask for Mount Bidwell and Willow Ranch from the USGS.

Contact: Modoc National Forest, Warner Mountain Ranger District, P.O. Box 220, Cedarville, CA 96104; phone or fax (916) 279-6116.

Trail notes: This trail is actually 5.5 miles long, but only 1.1 miles are specifically designed for hiking. The remainder of this trail is designated for four-wheel-drive use, one of the only national four-wheel-drive trails in the state. Of course, you can still hike all of it, but it's better to use four-wheeling to get out there, then hike the final mile to get way out there. As you go, watch for signs of old, abandoned mining operations, because gold was discovered here. They never found enough to cause any outpouring of goldminers, though, and the result is a very sparsely populated county, with this area being abandoned completely. The surrounding habitat is a mix of high desert and timber, though the trees tend to be small.

A good side trip from the nearby Buck Creek Ranger Station is to Fandango Pass, with nice views to the east of Surprise Valley and the Nevada Mountains. This is where a group of immigrants arrived, topped the ridge, looked west and saw Goose Lake, and shouted, "Ah ha, the Pacific Ocean! We have arrived!" So they started dancing the Fandango, but alas, as lore has it, got massacred by marauding Indians. That's how the mountain pass got its name.

Leave No Trace Tips

Pack It In and Pack It Out

Take everything you bring into the wild back out with you.

Protect wildlife and your food by storing rations securely.
Pick up all spilled foods.

Use toilet paper or wipes sparingly; pack them out.

Inspect your campsite for trash and any evidence of your stay.
Pack out all trash—even if it's not yours!

Map BØ

Adjoining Maps: East: B1 ...... *page* 54
North: AØ 4   South: CØ 106

Northern California Map .... *page* 2

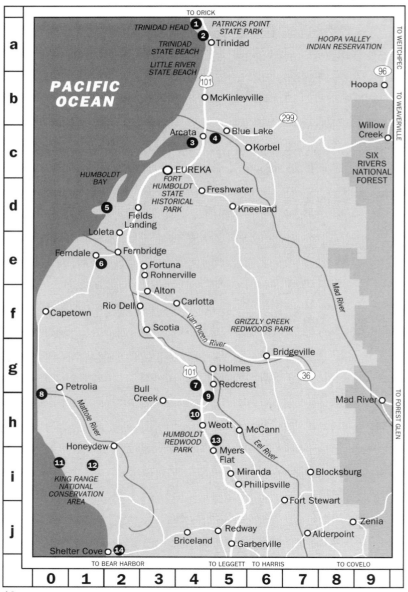

TO ORICK

TRINIDAD HEAD ❶
PATRICKS POINT
STATE PARK
❷ ○ Trinidad
TRINIDAD
STATE BEACH
HOOPA VALLEY
INDIAN RESERVATION

a

LITTLE RIVER
STATE BEACH

**PACIFIC
OCEAN**

[101]

Hoopa ○

96

○ McKinleyville

b

299

Willow
Creek ○

○ Blue Lake

Arcata ○
❸   ❹
○ Korbel

c

SIX
RIVERS
NATIONAL
FOREST

HUMBOLDT
BAY

○ **EUREKA**
FORT
HUMBOLDT
STATE
HISTORICAL
PARK

○ Freshwater

○ Kneeland

d

❺
Fields
Landing

Loleta ○

Ferndale ○ ○ Fernbridge
❻

e

○ Fortuna
○ Rohnerville

○ Alton

○Capetown

Rio Dell ○

○ Carlotta

Mad River

f

GRIZZLY CREEK
REDWOODS PARK

○ Scotia

Van Duzen River

○ Bridgeville

g

[101]

○ Holmes

36

Petrolia ○
❽

Bull
Creek ○

❼ ○ Redcrest
❾

Mad River ○

h

❿
○ Weott
○ McCann
HUMBOLDT
REDWOOD
PARK

Mattole River

Honeydew ○

⓭
○ Myers
Flat

Eel River

TO FOREST GLEN

i

⓫   ⓬

KING RANGE
NATIONAL
CONSERVATION
AREA

○ Miranda
○ Phillipsville

○ Blocksburg

○ Fort Stewart

○ Zenia

j

Shelter Cove ○ ⓮

Briceland ○

○ Redway
○ Garberville

○ Alderpoint

TO BEAR HARBOR   TO LEGGETT   TO HARRIS   TO COVELO

TO WEITCHPEC
TO WEAVERVILLE

0 1 2 3 4 5 6 7 8 9

Chapter BØ features:

❶ Rim Loop Trail

3.0 mi/2.5 hrs

Location: At Patrick's Point State Park north of Eureka; map BØ, grid a4.

User groups: Hikers only. No dogs, horses, or mountain bikes. Partial wheelchair access is available.

Permits: No permits are required. A state park day-use fee of $5 per car is charged.

Directions: From Eureka on U.S. 101, drive about 25 miles north to Trinidad, then continue for five miles to the Patrick's Point State Park signed turnoff. Take that turnoff, and at the stop sign, turn left and drive about one mile to the entrance station. Continue to the Agate Beach parking area.

Maps: For a park map and brochure, send a self-addressed stamped envelope and a check or money order for $1 to Patrick's Point State Park at the address below. To obtain a topographic map of the area, ask for Trinidad from the USGS.

Contact: Patrick's Point State Park, 4150 Patrick's Point Drive, Trinidad, CA 95570; (707) 677-3570 or call California State Parks at (707) 445-6547.

Trail notes: Patrick's Point State Park is set on a coastal headland lush with ferns, spruce, and wildflowers, and bordered by the Pacific, where you can go tidepool hopping or whale watching. That means with this trail you get the best of two different worlds. At times it tunnels through thick vegetation, while at other times it opens up to sweeping ocean views. Along the way there are several spur tails that provide access to many feature areas, including Mussel Rocks, Wedding Rock, Agate Beach, Lookout Rock, Abalone Point, and Palmer's Point. The views are sensational at every one of these spots. The spur trails, while short (they add just 1.5 miles to the hike), will make this a two- to three-hour trip, since you just won't want to rush through it. In addition, the Octopus Tree Trail provides a short hike that starts just across from the northern end of the Rim Loop Trail. This bonus trail provides a chance to see many of these peculiar trees with their roots straddling downed logs.

The only downers here are the fog and the heavy out-of-state tourist traffic, both common during the summer.

Special note: The best wheelchair-accessible section of the Rim Trail is from Wedding Rock to Patrick's Point; visitors must park at the Wedding Rock parking area to access it.

❷ Tsurai Loop

1.5 mi/1.0 hr

Location: On Trinidad Head on the Humboldt coast north of Eureka; map BØ, grid a4.

User groups: Hikers and dogs. No horses or mountain bikes. No wheelchair facilities.

Permits: No permits are required. Parking and access are free.

Directions: From Eureka on U.S. 101, drive about 25 miles north to Trinidad. Take the Trinidad exit, turn left at the stop sign, and drive under the U.S. 101 overpass to Main Street. Drive on Main Street to Trinity Street. Turn left and drive to the end of the road. Turn right on Edwards Street and drive to the parking area.

Maps: For free maps and brochures, contact the Trinidad Chamber of Commerce at P.O. Box 356, Trinidad, CA 95570; (707) 677-3448. To obtain a topographic map of the area, ask for Trinidad from the USGS.

Contact: For general information, contact Axel Lindgren at P.O. Box 62, Trinidad, CA 95570; (707) 677-3473.

Trail notes: The Tsurai Loop is a great, easy walk with coastal vistas, unique terrain, and a nearby restaurant. The views are of the rocky Trinidad Harbor and coast, with benches available along the way to sit and watch for the "puff-of-smoke" spouts on the ocean surface from migrating whales. The terrain includes the 300-foot miniature mountain at Trinidad Head, the pretty beachfront to the north of the Head area, and the Trinidad Pier. The restaurant? It's called Seascape, and you can get a crab/shrimp omelette (in season) for breakfast here that'll have your mouth watering every time you start driving north of Eureka on Highway 101. If there's a waiting line at the restaurant, don't hesitate to queue up.

❸ Sanctuary Trail

2.0 mi/1.0 hr

Location: In Arcata Marsh and Wildlife Sanctuary on the northern edge of Humboldt Bay; map BØ, grid c4.

User groups: Hikers, wheelchairs, and dogs. No horses or mountain bikes.

Permits: No permits are required. Parking and access are free.

Directions: From Eureka on U.S. 101, drive five miles north to Arcata. Take the Samoa Boulevard exit and drive west on Samoa Boulevard to I Street. Turn left (south) and continue to the parking area.

Maps: For a free, detailed trail map, contact the City of Arcata at the address below, and ask for the Marsh and Wildlife Sanctuary Trail map. To obtain a topographic map of the area, ask for Arcata South from the USGS.

Contact: City of Arcata, Environmental Services Department, 736 F Street, Arcata, CA 95521; (707) 822-8184 or fax (707) 822-8018.

Trail notes: The 154-acre Arcata Marsh is the most popular birdwatching area in Northern California, and it's best explored by walking the Sanctuary Trail. Set on a levee above the marsh, the trail is short, flat, and routed in a loop for

perfect viewing possibilities. Several wooden photography blinds are available on the route, where you can hide yourself to take pictures of the birds. The setting is unique, with the coast, saltwater bay, brackish water marsh, pond, foothills, and streams all nearby. This diversity means an outstanding variety of species are attracted to the area, with sightings often including belted kingfishers, ospreys, peregrine falcons, black phoebes, and song and savannah sparrows. In other words, birds from nearly all habitat types are represented, which explains why the Audubon Society gives guided tours regularly. A lot of people drive here to eat a picnic lunch, and just like Pavlov's dog hearing the bell, tons of birds show up in the parking lot daily at noon for handouts.

Also of interest is the Arcata Marsh Interpretive Center, located at the southwest corner of the parking area. Exhibits explore the development of this marsh from its origins as Arcata's garbage dump to part of the city's wastewater treatment system.

❹ Redwood Loop

6.2 mi/3.0 hrs

Location: In Arcata Redwood Park in the Arcata foothills; map BØ, grid c5.

User groups: Hikers, dogs, horses, and mountain bikes. Certain sections of the trail are off-limits to horses and mountain bikes; check the trail map for details. No wheelchair facilities.

Permits: No permits are required. Parking and access are free.

Directions: From Eureka, drive north on U.S. 101 to Arcata. Take the 14th Street exit and drive about one mile east into the parking area at the end of the road. Look for the "Redwood Park Trails" sign. Bikers and equestrians should use the Meadow Trailhead, located where 14th Street enters the park.

Maps: For a free, detailed trail map, contact the City of Arcata at the address below, and ask for the Community Forest Trail map. A free mountain bike trail map is also available. To obtain topographic maps of the area, ask for Arcata North and Arcata South from the USGS.

Contact: City of Arcata, Environmental Services Department, 736 F Street, Arcata, CA 95521; (707) 822-8184 or fax (707) 822-8018.

Trail notes: The Arcata Redwoods provide a respite for students at nearby Humboldt State or locals who want to wander amidst a beautiful second-growth forest. A network of trails covering about 10 miles in all is available, and the Redwood Loop is devised by connecting several of them. For newcomers, a map is an absolute necessity.

Start at the sign noting Redwood Park Trail (mountain bikes are not allowed at this trailhead), and take the Nature Trail, which will take you by many huge stumps, a small creek, and a forest of redwoods and spruce. The complete route features a 1,200-foot elevation gain and then loss, making for a steep trail both on the way up and on the way down. On weekends, kamikaze mountain bikers tearing downhill can turn this hike into an extremely unpleasant experience.

❺ Table Bluff County Park

1–9 mi/1.0 day

Location: On the Humboldt coast on the southern edge of Humboldt Bay south of Eureka; map BØ, grid d2.

User groups: Hikers and dogs. No horses or mountain bikes. No wheelchair facilities.

Permits: No permits are required. Parking and access are free.

Directions: From Eureka, drive south on U.S. 101 approximately 7.5 miles to the Hookton Road exit. Turn west and drive about five miles to Table Bluff County Park. Drive three-tenths of a mile and park at the base of Table Bluff.

Maps: To obtain a topographic map of the area, ask for Tyee City from the USGS.

Contact: Humboldt County Parks Department, 1106 Second Street, Eureka, CA 95501; (707) 445-7652 or fax (707) 445-7409.

Trail notes: You can walk as little or as much as you desire on this great coastal beach. The nine-mile length is the maximum round-trip distance, but there's no developed trail. You can meander south on the sand dunes, best walked at low tides near the water line, where the sand is firmest. The route continues south along a sand spit, with the Eel River Lagoon on one side and the Pacific Ocean on the other. It extends to the Eel River Wildlife Area and all the way to the mouth of the Eel River, for a total of 4.5 miles one-way. Very few people make the entire trip. One reason is that the north wind is common here in the afternoon, and on the trip back, it will be in your face.

❻ Russ City Park Double Loop

2.2 mi/2.0 hrs

Location: In Russ City Park in Ferndale south of Eureka; map BØ, grid e2.

User groups: Hikers and dogs. No horses or mountain bikes. No wheelchair facilities.

Permits: No permits are required. Parking and access are free.

Directions: From Eureka, drive south on U.S. 101 about 11 miles. Take the Ferndale/Fernbridge exit and drive straight about three-quarters of a mile. Turn right at Fernbridge and drive five miles west through town. Turn left on Ocean Street and drive three-quarters of a mile to the park on the right.

Maps: A free map and brochure can be obtained by contacting the City of Ferndale at the address below. To obtain a topographic map of the area, ask for Ferndale from the USGS.

Contact: City of Ferndale, P.O. Box 238, Ferndale, CA 95536; (707) 786-4224 or fax (707) 441-5737.

Trail notes: Russ City Park is Humboldt County's backyard wilderness. Covering just 105 acres, the park has been retained in its primitive state for wildlife, birds, and hikers. Though there's no posted, official name to the route we recommend, we call the trail "Double Loop" because it's set in the shape of a figure eight, which is quite rare. The trail includes a climb up Lytel Ridge, passing Francis Creek, with sections routed amid heavy fern beds and large firs, and offering views of a small pond and the Eel River flood plain. While the trip is relatively short and easy enough, the terrain is steep in spots and the trail is challenging, complete with switchbacks. Heavy fog or rain can make it slippery here. Since it's a city park, Russ is little known by outsiders and can provide quiet, secluded hiking.

❼ 5 Allens' Trail

1.5 mi/1.5 hrs

Location: In Humboldt Redwoods State Park south of Eureka; map BØ, grid g4.

User groups: Hikers only. No dogs, horses, or mountain bikes. No wheelchair facilities.

Permits: No permits are required. Parking and access are free.

Directions: From Eureka, drive south on U.S. 101, turn left at the Redcrest exit, driving under the overpass, and continue about half a mile. Turn right on the Avenue of the Giants. Drive south about three miles, past High Rock Conservation Camp to the 5 Allens' Trailhead parking lot on the left.

For an alternate route, from Garberville on U.S. 101, take the Founders Tree/Rockefeller Forest exit north, turn right and drive about 200 yards. Turn left on Avenue of the Giants, cross over the South Fork of the Eel River, and then bear right at the intersection in order to stay on Avenue of the Giants. Drive a short distance to the 5 Allens' Trailhead parking lot.

Maps: A map and trail guide can be obtained by sending a self-addressed, stamped envelope and a check or money order for $1 to Humboldt Redwoods State Park at the address below. To obtain a topographic map of the area, ask for Weott from the USGS.

Contact: Humboldt Redwoods State Park, P.O. Box 100, Weott, CA 95571; (707) 946-2409, (707) 445-6547, or fax (707) 441-5737.

Trail notes: The 5 Allens' Trail will provide a lasting impression of Humboldt Redwoods State Park for one reason: if you're unprepared, the trail is something of a butt-kicker. Ah, but it's also very short, and well worth the effort in exchange for quiet wonders.

From the trailhead near the Eel River, walk under the highway and then start the climb. Up, up, and up it goes, ascending 1,200 feet over the course of just three-quarters of a mile. In the process, the trail passes through a forest of mixed conifers, the tree canopy providing needed shade in the summer. Even though the hike is quite short, few people make it to the end. But if you want a quiet, peaceful spot—and are willing to pay to get it—you'll find it at the end.

A great short side trip from the trailhead is to hike north instead along the Eel River to High Rock, one of the better shoreline fishing spots for steelhead during the winter migrations.

❽ Lost Coast Trail

25.0 mi. one way/3.0 days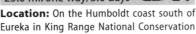

Location: On the Humboldt coast south of Eureka in King Range National Conservation Area; map BØ, grid h0.

User groups: Hikers, dogs, horses, and mountain bikes. No wheelchair facilities.

Permits: Day-use permits are required for organized groups only. A free campfire permit is required for overnight stays, and can be obtained at any Bureau of Land Management office, Forest Service office, or state fire department.

Directions: From Eureka, drive south on U.S. 101 about 59 miles to Redway. Take the South Fork-Honeydew exit and turn west on Wilder Ridge Road. Drive 23 miles to Honeydew, turn right on Mattole Road, and drive 14 miles to Lighthouse Road. Turn left and follow the road to its end. The trailhead is just past Mattole Campground.

Maps: A free map and brochure can be obtained by contacting the Bureau of Land Management at the address below. Specify the King Range Conservation Area map. To obtain topographic maps of the area, ask for Petrolia, Cooskie Creek, Shubrick Peak, and Shelter Cove from the USGS.

Contact: Bureau of Land Management, Arcata Resource Area, 1695 Heindon Road, Arcata, CA 95521; (707) 825-2300 or fax (707) 825-2301.

Trail notes: The Lost Coast and the people who live there seem to be in a different orbit than the rest of California, and that's exactly why visitors make the trip up here. It's called the "Lost Coast" because of the way nature has isolated the area, shielded on all sides by natural boundaries. For a first visit, a great day hike is to take the abandoned jeep trail from the campground at Lighthouse Road and head south three miles to the Punta Gorda Lighthouse. You'll get a glimpse of the greatness here, and probably the inspiration to continue on the Lost Coast Trail, one of California's greatest weekend trips. Set primarily on bluffs and beach, the trail spans 25 miles from the mouth of the Mattole River south to Shelter Cove. In the process it traces some of California's most remote portions of coastline. With two vehicles, one parked at each end of the trail, you can set up your own shuttle, then hike the trail one way. (A shuttle service is available; phone Shelter Cove Campground at (707) 986-7474.) It's better done from north to south, due to winds out of the north; you want them at your back, not in your face. Firm-fitting, waterproof boots with good gripping soles are a necessity: firm-fitting because some of the walking is in soft sand; waterproof because there are several small creek crossings; and good-gripping because some scrambling over wet boulders is required.

Special note: Some parts of the Lost Coast Trail are impassable during high tides. Watch for ticks and take a tide table. Be cautious, too; this is an extremely isolated area.

⑨ Founders Grove Nature Trail

0.5 mi/0.5 hr

Location: In Humboldt Redwoods State Park south of Eureka; map BØ, grid h4.

User groups: Hikers and wheelchairs, though the trail is a bit uneven. No dogs, horses, or mountain bikes.

Permits: No permits are required. Parking and access are free.

Directions: From Garberville, drive north on U.S. 101 about 20 miles. Take the Founder Tree/Rockefeller Forest exit to the Avenue of the Giants. Drive 100 yards across Avenue of the Giants to the Founders Grove Parking Area/Trailhead.

Maps: A map and trail guide can be obtained by sending a self-addressed, stamped envelope and a check or money order for $1 to Humboldt Redwoods State Park at the address below. To obtain a topographic map of the area, ask for Weott from the USGS.

Contact: Humboldt Redwoods State Park, P.O. Box 100, Weott, CA 95571; (707) 946-2409, (707) 445-6547, or fax (707) 441-5737.

Trail notes: Humboldt Redwoods State Park has nearly 100 miles of trails, but it's the little half-mile Founders Grove Nature Trail that provides the shortest and most easily-accessible walk in the park. This trail also gives you the quickest payoff, which explains why it's the most popular hike in Humboldt Redwoods. The trail's location near U.S. 101 makes it easy to reach. At the trailhead, you'll find a small box with brochures describing each element of the self-guided nature trail. Your destination is the Dyerville Giant, the tallest tree in the park, but all the while you'll be surrounded by old-growth redwoods, a great reward for such a small physical investment.

⑩ Bull Creek Flats

9.0 mi/5.25 hrs

Location: In Humboldt Redwoods State Park south of Eureka; map BØ, grid h4.

User groups: Hikers only. No dogs, horses, or mountain bikes. No wheelchair facilities.

Permits: No permits are required. Parking and access are free.

Directions: From Garberville, drive north on U.S. 101 about 20 miles. Take the Founder Tree/Rockefeller Forest exit and drive 1.3 miles on Mattole Road to the trailhead.

Maps: A map and trail guide can be obtained by sending a self-addressed, stamped envelope and a check or money order for $1 to Humboldt Redwoods State Park at the address below. To obtain a topographic map of the area, ask for Weott from the USGS.

Contact: Humboldt Redwoods State Park, P.O. Box 100, Weott, CA 95571; (707) 946-2409, (707) 445-6547, or fax (707) 441-5737.

Trail notes: This trail offers a streamside walk, complete with giant redwoods and a babbling brook. Starting at the trailhead at Bull Creek Flats (a short walk to the Federation Grove), the trail heads west along Bull Creek, an easy but steady grade as you hike upstream. All the while you're surrounded by forest, both redwoods and fir in a variety of mixes. The feature of the route is the Big Tree Area, which you'll reach after four miles of hiking. There are many redwoods here that range five to ten feet in diameter, not to mention the Flat Iron Tree, a huge leaning redwood that grew in strange dimensions in order to support itself. On the broad side, the Flat Iron Tree measures more than 15 feet. After the trail passes the Big Tree Area, it's routed to the mouth of Albee Creek, ending at Mattole Road. The trailhead here, by the way, provides a shorter hike of about a mile to the Flat Iron Tree in the Big Tree Area.

⑪ Spanish Ridge Trail

6.0 mi/3.5 hrs

Location: In King Range National Conservation Area south of Eureka; map BØ, grid i1.

User groups: Hikers, dogs, and horses. No mountain bikes. No wheelchair facilities.

Permits: No permits are required. Parking and access are free.

Directions: From Eureka, drive south on U.S. 101, take the South Fork-Honeydew exit, and turn south on Wilder Ridge Road. Drive about one mile, then turn west on Smith-Etter Road. (Note: This primitive, four-wheel-drive road is closed from November 1 to March 31.) Drive about 10 miles. Turn northwest on Telegraph Ridge Road and drive eight miles to the trailhead gate. When the gate is locked, it's a two-mile walk from here to the trailhead. In summer, the gate is open and it's possible to drive the two miles.

Maps: A free map and brochure can be obtained by contacting the Bureau of Land Management at the address below; ask for the King Range Conservation Area map. To obtain topographic maps of the area, ask for Cooskie Creek and Shubrick Peak from the USGS.

Contact: Bureau of Land Management, Arcata Resource Area, 1695 Heindon Road, Arcata, CA 95521; (707) 825-2300 or fax (707) 825-2301.

Trail notes: In just three fast miles of walking downhill, the Spanish Ridge Trail gives you access to some of the most remote sections of the California coast. Alas, there's a catch, and with this trail it comes on the return trip. What goes down, as all hikers know, must later go up. From the Spanish Ridge Trailhead, the trail descends 2,000 feet in three miles en route to the coast. Know what that means? Right. Going back, it climbs 2,000 feet in three miles, and unless you can get a helicopter ride back, you're looking at some serious grunt work. But it's worth it. The King Range is very rugged, primi-

tive, and isolated. Thanks to that bumpy access road and the 2,000-foot climb on the return trip, it's rare to see other people here.

⑫ King Crest Trail

10.0 mi/6.5 hrs

Location: In King Range National Conservation Area south of Eureka; map BØ, grid i1.

User groups: Hikers, dogs, horses, and mountain bikes. No wheelchair facilities.

Permits: No permits are required. Parking and access are free.

Directions: From Eureka, drive south on U.S. 101, take the South Fork-Honeydew exit, and turn south on Wilder Ridge Road. Drive about one mile, then turn west on Smith-Etter Road. (Note: This primitive, four-wheel-drive road is closed from November 1 to March 31.) Drive six miles to the trailhead.

Maps: A free map and brochure can be obtained by contacting the Bureau of Land Management at the address below; ask for the King Range Conservation Area map. To obtain a topographic map of the area, ask for Shubrick Peak from the USGS.

Contact: Bureau of Land Management, Arcata Resource Area, 1695 Heindon Road, Arcata, CA 95521; (707) 825-2300 or fax (707) 825-2301.

Trail notes: King's Peak is one of the most prized destinations in the King Range. At 4,087 feet, it's the highest point on the Northern California coast, and from it, you get a view that can make you feel like you're perched on top of the world. The ocean seems to stretch on forever to the west, and on a perfect day, you can make out the top of Mount Lassen to the east behind the ridgeline of the Yolla Bolly Wilderness.

Reaching King's Peak requires a five-mile hike from the trailhead on Smith-Etter Road, and in the process you climb some 2,200 feet in elevation. Making the trip on a clear day is an absolute necessity, since paying the price of the climb is buffered by the reward of the sweeping views. Trail signs are poor and water supplies at trail camps are from dubious sources, so it's also essential to have a good map and a double canteen water supply. The entire King Crest Trail extends 16 miles one way, starting from the trailhead listed in this hike to King Crest; then it descends 10.5 miles to the beach. That makes a one way overnight trip with a shuttle vehicle at the end of the trail an ideal alternative.

⑬ Williams Grove Trail

3.5 mi/2.0 hrs

Location: In Humboldt Redwoods State Park south of Eureka; map BØ, grid h5.

User groups: Hikers only. No dogs, horses, or mountain bikes. No wheelchair facilities.

Permits: No permits are required. Parking and access are free.

Directions: From Garberville on U.S. 101, drive north to the Myers Flat exit. Turn right on Avenue of the Giants and drive about one mile north to the Williams Grove parking area or to the Hidden Springs Campground (reservations advised).

Maps: A map and trail guide can be obtained by sending a self-addressed, stamped envelope and a check or money order for $1 to Humboldt Redwoods State Park at the address below. To obtain topographic maps of the area, ask for Weott and Myers Flat from the USGS.

Contact: Humboldt Redwoods State Park, P.O. Box 100, Weott, CA 95571; (707) 946-2409, (707) 445-6547, or fax (707) 441-5737.

Trail notes: This trail makes an ideal, easy trip for campers staying at the Hidden Springs Campground in Humboldt Redwoods State Park. The camp itself is set in forest just above a big bend in the South Fork Eel River, with the trailhead on the southwest side of the camp. The trail starts out nearly flat out of camp, then turns right and laterals adjacent to the highway. It's easy walking all the way amid redwoods both young and old. Then the trail crosses under the highway and over the river on a bridge (only in summer) to Williams Grove, which has a picnic area and rest rooms. Williams Grove Picnic Area can also be reached by car, and then used as a trailhead to hike this route in reverse.

⑭ Chemise Mountain Trail

3 mi/1.0 hrs

Location: In King Range National Conservation Area south of Shelter Cove; map BØ, grid j2.

User groups: Hikers, dogs, horses, and mountain bikes. There are no wheelchair facilities on the trails, but wheelchair-accessible facilities are available in nearby campgrounds.

Permits: No day-use permits are required. A campfire permit is required if you plan to stay overnight. A free permit can be obtained at any Bureau of Land Management office, Forest Service office, or state fire department.

Directions: From Eureka, drive south on U.S. 101 about 60 miles to Garberville. Turn west on Briceland/Shelter Cove Road and drive about 18 miles, then turn left on Shelter Cove Road and drive five miles. Turn left on Chemise Mountain Road and drive a quarter of a mile to the trailhead at Nadelos Campground. You can also go another mile up the road to Wailaki Campground and start there.

Maps: A free map and brochure can be obtained by contacting the Bureau of Land Management at the address below; ask for the King Range Conservation Area map. To obtain a topographic map of the area, ask for Shelter Cove from the USGS.

Contact: Bureau of Land Management, Arcata Resource Area, 1695 Heindon Road, Arcata, CA 95521; (707) 825-2300 or fax (707) 825-2301.

Trail notes: Most visitors to the King Range yearn to climb King's Peak, but just can't gather the time, initiative, or energy for such a demanding excursion. The Chemise Mountain Trail largely solves that problem. It has many of the qualities of the King Crest Trail, including a great view, yet without many of the demands, especially the time required. It's only a 1.5-mile climb from the Wailaki Recreation Site to Chemise Mountain, starting from a trailhead elevation of 2,000 feet to the summit at 2,598 feet. So even though the climb is steep, the end of the tunnel is always in sight, along with the great views. The ridgeline of the Yolla Bolly Wilderness is the eastern horizon, a sweeping expanse of ocean is off to the west, and to the south is a deep canyon and several remote coastal ridges. Since much of the vegetation near the summit is brush, nothing blocks the great views. Way out here, it can seem like there isn't another person in the world.

Map B1

Adjoining Maps: East: B2 ...... *page* 66   West: BØ 46
North: A1 16   South: C1 116

Northern California Map .... *page* 2

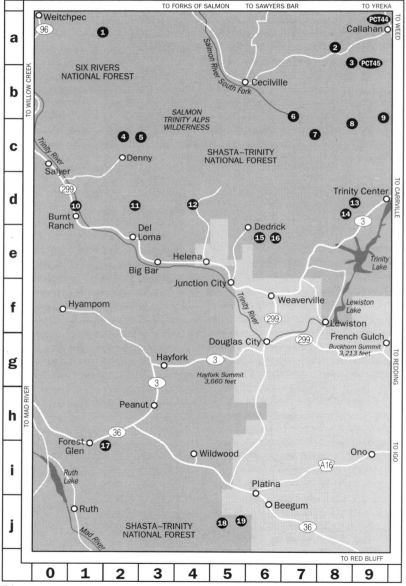

TO FORKS OF SALMON   TO SAWYERS BAR   TO YREKA

a

Weitchpec
96
SIX RIVERS
NATIONAL FOREST

PCT44
Callahan

b

TO WILLOW CREEK
Salmon River South Fork
Cecilville

PCT45

c

SALMON
TRINITY ALPS
WILDERNESS

SHASTA–TRINITY
NATIONAL FOREST

Trinity River
Denny
Salver

d

299
Trinity Center

TO CARRVILLE
Burnt
Ranch
Del
Loma
Dedrick

e

Helena
Big Bar
Trinity
Lake

Junction City

f

Hyampom
Weaverville
Lewiston
Lake
Lewiston

Trinity River
299

g

Douglas City
299
French Gulch
Buckhorn Summit
3,213 feet

Hayfork
3
TO REDDING

Hayfork Summit
3,660 feet

h

TO MAD RIVER
Peanut

36

i

Forest
Glen
Wildwood
Ono

Ruth
Lake
A16
TO IGO

j

Ruth
Platina
Beegum

Mad River
SHASTA–TRINITY
NATIONAL FOREST
36

TO RED BLUFF

0   1   2   3   4   5   6   7   8   9

Chapter B1 features:

❶ Horse Ridge National Recreation Trail

13.0 mi. one way/2.0 days

Location: In Six Rivers National Forest on the western edge of the Trinity Alps Wilderness east of Hoopa; map B1, grid a1.

User groups: Hikers, dogs, and horses. No mountain bikes. No wheelchair facilities.

Permits: A wilderness permit is required for hikers planning on camping. Parking and access are free.

Directions: From Arcata, go east on Highway 299 to Willow Creek. Turn north on Highway 96 and drive about 10 miles into Hoopa Valley to Big Hill Lookout Road. Turn east on Big Hill Lookout Road and drive 11 miles to the Six Rivers National Forest border. (Big Hill Lookout Road becomes Forest Service Road 8N01.) Drive another four miles to the trailhead.

Maps: For a map of Six Rivers National Forest, send $4 to USDA-Forest Service, 630 Sansome Street, San Francisco, CA 94111. To obtain topographic maps of the area, ask for Tish Tang Point and Trinity Mountain from the USGS.

Contact: Six Rivers National Forest, Lower Trinity Ranger District, P.O. Box 68, Willow Creek, CA 95573; (916) 629-2118 or fax (916) 629-2102.

Trail notes: This is one of the lesser-known National Recreation Trails in the western U.S.,
but it has many excellent features, and alas, a few negative ones as well. While Horse Ridge can be hiked from one end to the other in a weekend, leaving a shuttle vehicle at both trailheads, our suggestion is to make the six-mile trip to Mill Creek Lakes, set in the least explored western sector of the Salmon Mountains/Trinity Alps. This is a good overnighter and will provide you with a feel for the area. From the trailhead at 4,800 feet, the grades are gradual with relatively easy elevation climbs and descents, and the trail is well wooded for the entire route. If you want to add to your trip, you can extend it southward on the Horse Ridge National Recreation Trail. It peaks out at Trinity Summit, at about 5,800 feet, where there's a historic cabin. Other hikers are rare in this area, and most of the time you'll feel as if you have the entire universe to yourself.

Special note: Water is scarce along the trail, but cattle are not; whatever water you find, don't drink it without first treating it with the best water filtration system you can afford.

❷ Trail Creek Trail

7.0 mi/2.0 days

Location: In the Russian Wilderness west of Callahan; map B1, grid a8.

User groups: Hikers, dogs, and horses. Mountain bikes are allowed only outside of the wilderness border. No wheelchair facilities.

Permits: A wilderness permit is required for hikers planning to camp. Parking and access are free.

Directions: From Redding, drive north on Interstate 5 for 70 miles. Just past Weed, take the Edgewood exit. At the stop sign, turn left and drive through the underpass to another stop sign. Turn right on old Highway 99 and drive about six miles to Gazelle. At Gazelle, turn left on Gazelle-Callahan Road and drive about 20 miles to Callahan. From Callahan on Highway 3, turn west on County Road 402 (Cecilville Road) and drive 17 miles to Trail Creek Campground. The trail heads north from a gravel road located across from the campground.

Maps: For a map of Klamath National Forest or the Trinity Alps Wilderness, send $4 to USDA-Forest Service, 630 Sansome Street, San Francisco, CA 94111. To obtain topographic maps of the area, ask for Deadman Peak and Eaton Peak from the USGS.

Contact: Klamath National Forest, Scott River Ranger District, 11263 North Highway 3, Fort Jones, CA 96032; (916) 468-5351 or fax (916) 468-5654.

Trail notes: The Russian Wilderness is a place so pristine, yet so small, that it just can't handle many visitors. Luckily, very few make the trip. If you go, walk softly and treat the area with fragile care. The Trail Creek Trail involves a steep climb and drop, then a short cross-country jaunt. The trailhead is located a short distance up a gravel road across from Trail Creek Campground, which is set on Cecilville-Callahan Road. For the first 1.5 miles, the trail heads steeply up on an old fire lane. A few mountain bikers like walking up this portion, then ripping back downhill to the campground. As you near the crest, you'll junction with the Pacific Crest Trail; turn left, then just five minutes later, turn again and follow the trail down to Syphon, Russian, Waterdog, and Lower Russian Lakes. The last quarter-mile to Russian Lake, the feature lake in the basin, is off-trail. Many years ago, our friend Paul Wertz filled some 10-gallon milk cans with water and juvenile golden trout, and with a donkey hauling those milk cans, tromped in all the way to this basin and stocked these lakes with those baby golden trout. If you catch one of their progeny, consider what Paul went through to get these

fish here, and you may feel special satisfaction by releasing the fish, rather than killing it.

❸ Long Gulch Lake Trail

4.5 mi/3.25 hrs

Location: In the Trinity Alps Wilderness west of Callahan; map B1, grid b8.

User groups: Hikers, dogs, and horses. No mountain bikes. No wheelchair facilities.

Permits: A wilderness permit is required for hikers planning to camp. Parking and access are free.

Directions: From Redding, drive north on Interstate 5 for 70 miles. Just past Weed, take the Edgewood exit. At the stop sign, turn left and drive through the underpass to another stop sign. Turn right on old Highway 99 and drive about six miles to Gazelle. At Gazelle, turn left on Gazelle-Callahan Road and drive about 20 miles to Callahan. From Callahan on Highway 3, turn west on County Road 402 (Cecilville Road) and drive 11 miles. Turn left on Forest Service Road 39N08 and drive 1.5 miles to the trailhead.

Maps: For a map of Klamath National Forest or the Trinity Alps Wilderness, send $4 to USDA-Forest Service, 630 Sansome Street, San Francisco, CA 94111. To obtain topographic maps of the area, ask for Deadman Peak and Billys Peak from the USGS.

Contact: Klamath National Forest, Scott River Ranger District, 11263 North Highway 3, Fort Jones, CA 96032; (916) 468-5351 or fax (916) 468-5654.

Trail notes: The Long Gulch Lake Trail rises along Long Gulch Creek, steeply at times, but in just 2.25 miles arrives at Long Gulch Lake. That makes it close enough to go in and out in a day, or better yet, you can make it a good weekend overnighter without tremendous strain. Set northeast of Deadman Peak (7,741 feet) in the Trinity Alps Wilderness, the round, pretty lake is stocked by airplane every year with small trout, a nice bonus. Another bonus is how simple it is to extend your trip either to other mountain lakes, or beyond deep into the Trinity Alps Wilderness. Trail Gulch Lake is just another three miles from Long Gulch Lake, a good side trip. If you choose to extend into the Trinity Alps instead, the trail is routed along North Fork Coffee Creek to Kickapoo Waterfall, about nine miles from Long Gulch Lake. This trip is crowded on summer weekends.

❹ New River Trailhead

18.0 mi/2.0 days

Location: In the Trinity Alps Wilderness east of Willow Creek; map B1, grid c2.

User groups: Hikers, dogs, and horses. No mountain bikes. No wheelchair facilities.

Permits: A wilderness permit is required for hikers planning to camp.

Directions: From Weaverville, drive west on Highway 299 about 32 miles. Turn north on County Road 402 (Denny Road) and drive about 21 miles, then turn left on Forest Service Road 7N15 and drive four miles north to the trailhead parking area.

Maps: For a map of Shasta-Trinity National Forest or the Trinity Alps Wilderness, send $4 to USDA-Forest Service, 630 Sansome Street, San Francisco, CA 94111. To obtain topographic maps of the area, ask for Jim Jam Ridge, Dees Peak, and Trinity Mountain from the USGS.

Contact: Shasta-Trinity National Forest, Big Bar Ranger District, Star Route 1, Box 10, Big Bar, CA 96010; (916) 623-6106 or fax (916) 623-6123.

Trail notes: Most backpackers in the Trinity Alps Wilderness like high mountain lakes, but here is a trail that features small streams. The highlights are the headwaters of the New River, a tributary to the Trinity River, and Mary Blaine Meadow. Because this is a river trail, not a lake trail, it gets far less use than other routes in the region. The trail starts right along the New River, then immediately begins climbing. In about a mile, you'll reach Megram Cabin, the first landmark along the trail. After another mile, bear right at the fork in the trail and hike along the well-wooded section of Slide Creek. After two miles, you'll arrive again at a fork, and again stay to the right. The trail passes Robbers Roost Mine, Emmons Cabin, and the Old Denny Cabin Site, all on the way to Mary Blaine Meadow, a distance of about nine miles from the trailhead. The meadow is set below Mary Blaine Mountain, and to the north, Dees Peak. The whole region is cut with small streams in crevices and canyons.

❺ East Fork Loop

20.0 mi/3.0 days

Location: In the Trinity Alps Wilderness east of Willow Creek; map B1, grid c3.

User groups: Hikers, dogs, and horses. No mountain bikes. No wheelchair facilities.

Permits: A wilderness permit is required for hikers planning to camp.

Directions: From Weaverville, turn west on Highway 299 and drive about 32 miles. Turn north on County Road 402 (Denny Road) and drive about 26 miles to the trailhead parking area.

Maps: For a map of Shasta-Trinity National Forest or the Trinity Alps Wilderness, send $4 to USDA-Forest Service, 630 Sansome Street, San Francisco, CA 94111. To obtain a topographic map of the area, ask for Jim Jam Ridge from the USGS.

Contact: Shasta-Trinity National Forest, Big Bar Ranger District, Star Route 1, Box 10, Big Bar, CA 96010; (916) 623-6106 or fax (916) 623-6123.

Trail notes: The East Fork Trailhead provides access to one of the more primitive, less-traveled regions of the Trinity Alps Wilderness. It's an area known for streams and forests in the lower reaches and bare limestone ridges in the higher reaches. The trip starts at the East Fork Trailhead, adjacent to the East Fork New River. It climbs along this pretty watershed, and after two miles turns before coming to Pony Creek. In the next six miles, which include sections that are quite steep, the trail climbs to Limestone Ridge near little Rattlesnake Lake. At Limestone Ridge, turn right on the New River Divide Trail and head south for six miles, passing Cabin Peak at 6,870 feet and arriving at White Creek Lake. To complete the loop, turn right on the trail at White Creek Lake and start the trip back, descending most of the way. The trail goes past Jakes Upper Camp and Jakes Lower Camp before linking up again with the East Fork Trail for the jog back to the parking area.

❻ Little South Fork Lake Trail

13.0 mi/2.0 days

Location: In the Trinity Alps Wilderness near Cecilville; map B1, grid c7.

User groups: Hikers only. No dogs, horses, or mountain bikes. No wheelchair facilities.

Permits: A wilderness permit is required for hikers planning to camp.

Directions: From Redding, drive north on Interstate 5 for 70 miles. Just past Weed, take the Edgewood exit. At the stop sign, turn left and drive through the underpass to another stop sign. Turn right on old Highway 99 and drive about six miles to Gazelle. Turn left on Gazelle-Callahan Road and drive about 27 miles to Callahan. From Callahan on Highway 3, turn west on Cecilville Road and drive about 28 miles. Turn left (south) on Caribou Road/South Fork Road (across from East Fork Campground) and drive about six miles to the Summerville Trailhead.

Maps: For a map of Klamath National Forest or the Trinity Alps Wilderness, send $4 to USDA-Forest Service, 630 Sansome Street, San Francisco, CA 94111. To obtain a topographic map of the area, ask for Thompson Peak from the USGS.

Contact: Klamath National Forest, Salmon River Ranger District, P.O. Box 280, Etna, CA 96027; (916) 467-5757 or fax (916) 468-5654.

Trail notes: You have to be a little bit crazy to try this trip, and that's why we signed up. There's just no easy way to reach Little South Fork Lake and its two idyllic campsites, excellent swimming, and large trout. This route is largely off-trail and requires skirting a big waterfall, but there's no better way in (see the special note below); we've tried them all. From the Summerville Trailhead, the trip starts out easy enough, with four miles of good trail, first along the Salmon River, then veering to the right along Little South Fork Creek. In the spring and early summer, high water can make this impassable. The trail dead-ends into Little South Fork Creek (a faint route on the other side that climbs through brush and up the canyon should be avoided). From here, you're on your own, heading upstream, with no trail available. We found the best strategy, though still steep and difficult, is to lateral across the slope on the right side of the stream, even though this is where Tom got chased and stung by a horde of bees on one trip. After leaving the trail, it's about 1.25 miles to a beautiful waterfall, divine and pristine; we named it Crystal Falls. To get around the

waterfall, loop to the right; if you go to the left, you'll add several dreadful hours to the trip. Guess how we know? Heh heh. It's another 1.25 miles to the lake, with very slow going all the way, scrambling up and across the wooded slope, seemingly going on forever at a snail's pace, before suddenly emerging from the forest onto granite plates. Ahead is the lake, beautifully set in a rock bowl, framed by a high back wall. There are excellent campgrounds at each end of the lake.

Special note: We hiked into this lake once from Caribou Lakes by climbing the Sawtooth Ridge, the entire route being off-trail, a slippery and dangerous proposition while carrying full packs. On another trip from Caribou Lakes, we dropped down into Little South Fork Canyon, losing thousands of feet in altitude and in the process getting caught in a brush field like bugs in a spider web. Neither route is recommended.

---

❼ Caribou Lakes Trail

18.0 mi/2.0 days

Location: In the Trinity Alps Wilderness northwest of Trinity Lake; map B1, grid c8.

User groups: Hikers, dogs, and horses. No mountain bikes. No wheelchair facilities.

Permits: A wilderness permit is required for hikers planning to camp.

Directions: From Weaverville, drive north on Highway 3 past Trinity Lake. At the Coffee Creek Ranger Station, turn west (left) on County Road 104 (Coffee Creek Road) and drive 17 miles to the trailhead at the end of the road.

Maps: For a map of Klamath National Forest or the Trinity Alps Wilderness, send $4 to USDA-Forest Service, 630 Sansome Street, San Francisco, CA 94111. To obtain a topographic map of the area, ask for Caribou Lakes from the USGS.

Contact: Klamath National Forest, Salmon River Ranger District, P.O. Box 280, Etna, CA 96027; (916) 467-5757 or fax (916) 468-5654.

Trail notes: The Caribou Lakes Basin provides the classic Trinity Alps scene: three high mountain lakes, beautiful and serene, with the back wall of the Sawtooth Ridge casting a monumental backdrop on one side, and on the other side, a drop-off and great views of a series of mountain peaks and ridgelines. Sunsets are absolutely remarkable when viewed from here. Because it's a nine-mile hike to the Caribou Lakes Basin, this makes an excellent first-day destination for backpackers exploring this section of the Trinity Alps Wilderness. The trail starts at the bottom of the Salmon River, however, and like all trails that start at the bottom of canyons, it means you begin the trip with a terrible climb that never seems to end. Plan on drinking a full canteen of water, then be certain not to miss the natural spring that's available near the crest, just off to the right. After reaching the crest, the trail travels counterclockwise around the mountain, then drops into the Caribou Lakes Basin. Ignore your urge to stop at the first lake, because the best campsites, swimming, and views are from Caribou Lake, the last and largest lake you'll reach in this circuit. Because this is a popular destination, fishing is often poor.

❽ Union Lake Trail

12.0 mi/2.0 days

Location: In the Trinity Alps Wilderness northwest of Trinity Lake; map B1, grid c8.

User groups: Hikers, dogs, and horses. No mountain bikes. No wheelchair facilities.

Permits: A wilderness permit is required for hikers planning to camp.

Directions: From Weaverville, drive north on Highway 3 past Trinity Lake. At the Coffee Creek Ranger Station, turn west (left) on County Road 104 (Coffee Creek Road) and drive about 10 miles to the trailhead on the left.

Maps: For a map of Shasta-Trinity National Forest or the Trinity Alps Wilderness, send $4 to USDA-Forest Service, 630 Sansome Street, San Francisco, CA 94111. To obtain a topographic map of the area, ask for Caribou Lakes from the USGS.

Contact: Shasta-Trinity National Forest, Weaverville Ranger District, P.O. Box 1190, Weaverville, CA 96093; (916) 623-2121 or fax (916) 623-6010.

Trail notes: Union Lake sits in a granite basin below Red Rock Mountain. The hike in and out is a good weekend affair, but most visitors are backpackers who are using the camp at the lake as a first-day destination for a multi-day trip. Of the trailheads on Coffee Creek Road, this one is often overlooked. The trail starts near an old sawmill along Coffee Creek, heads south (to the left), and in less than a mile, starts the climb adjacent to Union Creek (on your right). Like most hikes that start at a streambed, you pay for your pleasure, going up, not down. After about two miles, the trail crosses Union Creek and continues on for a few miles, now with the stream on your left. You'll pass a trail junction for Bullards Basin, and about half a mile later, turn right on the cutoff trail to Union Lake.

❾ Boulder Lake Trail

12.0 mi/2.0 days

Location: In the Trinity Alps Wilderness northwest of Trinity Lake; map B1, grid c9.

User groups: Hikers, dogs, and horses. No mountain bikes. No wheelchair facilities.

Permits: A wilderness permit is required for hikers planning to camp.

Directions: From Weaverville, drive north on Highway 3 past Trinity Lake. At the Coffee Creek Ranger Station, turn west (left) on County Road 104 (Coffee Creek Road) and drive about 6.5 miles to Goldfield Campground and the trailhead parking area.

Maps: For a map of Shasta-Trinity National Forest or the Trinity Alps Wilderness, send $4 to USDA-Forest Service, 630 Sansome Street, San Francisco, CA 94111. To obtain a topographic map of the area, ask for Ycatapom Peak from the USGS.

Contact: Shasta-Trinity National Forest, Weaverville Ranger District, P.O. Box 1190, Weaverville, CA 96093; (916) 623-2121 or fax (916) 623-6010.

Trail notes: The hike to Boulder Lake and back makes for a great weekend backpack trip. Two trails head out from the Goldfield Campground, each routed to Union Lake. Our choice is to take the trail that runs adjacent to Boulder Creek. The grade is long and steady, but the nearby cold flows of water have a way of keeping you mentally refreshed. As you near Sugar Pine Butte at 8,033 feet, the trail turns sharply to the left, loops in a clockwise direction around a butte, and then connects with the short cutoff trail that leads to Boulder Lake, a pretty lake set in a spectacular basin. This has become a very popular weekend hike and camping trip. If there are campers at the lake already, nearby Little Boulder Lake, about a 45-minute walk beyond, provides an option.

⑩ Burnt Ranch Falls

0.5 mi/0.5 hr

Location: In Shasta-Trinity National Forest on Highway 299 east of Willow Creek; map B1, grid d1.

User groups: Hikers and dogs. No horses or mountain bikes. No wheelchair facilities.

Permits: No permits are required.

Directions: From Weaverville, drive west on Highway 299 to Burnt Ranch. From Burnt Ranch, drive half a mile west on Highway 299 to the trailhead at Burnt Ranch Campground.

Maps: For a map of Shasta-Trinity National Forest, send $4 to USDA-Forest Service, 630 Sansome Street, San Francisco, CA 94111. To obtain a topographic map of the area, ask for Ironside Mountain from the USGS.

Contact: Shasta-Trinity National Forest, Big Bar Ranger District, Star Route 1, Box 10, Big Bar, CA 96010; (916) 623-6106 or fax (916) 623-6123.

Trail notes: Burnt Ranch Falls isn't a spectacular cascade of water like other more famous waterfalls, but it is the center of a very pretty, easy-to-reach scene on the Trinity River. It's a relatively small but wide waterfall, comprised of about 10 feet of rock that in low-water conditions creates a natural barrier for migrating salmon and steelhead. Thus, the highlight comes when river flows rise a bit in the fall, and you can watch the spectacular sight of salmon and steelhead jumping and sailing through the air to get over and past the falls.

The trail is a short but steep quarter-mile jaunt down from the Burnt Ranch Campground. When you arrive at the river, walk out a short way on the rocky spot to watch the fish jump. The setting in an area along Highway 299 has a magnificent natural landscape. Looking up from the river, the Trinity canyon walls look like they ascend into the sky. Unlike most waterfalls, Burnt Ranch Falls is a far less compelling scene at high water. During high, turbid flows, it becomes much more difficult to see fish jumping past the falls.

⑪ New River Divide Trail

30.0 mi/3.0 days

Location: In the Trinity Alps Wilderness north of Trinity River's Big Bar; map B1, grid d3.

User groups: Hikers, dogs, and horses. No mountain bikes. No wheelchair facilities.

Permits: A wilderness permit is required.

Directions: From Weaverville, drive west on Highway 299 about nine miles past Big Bar. Turn north on Forest Service Road 4 and follow the signs to the Green Mountain parking area.

Maps: For a map of Shasta-Trinity National Forest or the Trinity Alps Wilderness, send $4 to USDA-Forest Service, 630 Sansome Street, San Francisco, CA 94111. To obtain a topographic map of the area, ask for Del Loma from the USGS.

Contact: Shasta-Trinity National Forest, Big Bar Ranger District, Star Route 1, Box 10, Big Bar, CA 96010; (916) 623-6106 or fax (916) 623-6123.

Trail notes: The New River Divide Trail provides access to the Limestone Ridge of the Trinity Alps, taking a ridgeline route most of the way. This is an area known for lookouts from mountain rims, the headwaters of many small feeder streams, and few people. The trip starts at the Green Mountain Trailhead at an elevation of 5,052 feet, and in the first three miles, the route skirts around the southern flank of Brushy Mountain, past Panther Camp and Stove Camp, and along the eastern flank of Green Mountain. As the trail climbs up toward the Limestone Ridge, you'll find yourself perched on a "divide," where the streams on each side of you pour into different watersheds. Eventually, the trail rises all the way to Cabin Peak at 6,870 feet and beyond to little Rattlesnake Lake, a one-way distance of about 15 miles.

⑫ Grizzly Lake Trail

40.0 mi/5.0 days

Location: In the Trinity Alps Wilderness north of Junction City; map B1, grid d4.

User groups: Hikers, dogs, and horses. No mountain bikes. No wheelchair facilities.

Permits: A wilderness permit is required for hikers planning to camp.

Directions: From Weaverville, drive 13 miles west on Highway 299 to Helena. Turn north on East Fork Road (County Road 421) and drive 3.9 miles. Turn left on Hobo Gulch Road (Forest Service Road 34N07Y) and drive 12 miles to the Hobo Gulch Trailhead, located at Hobo Gulch Campground.

Maps: For a map of Shasta-Trinity National Forest or the Trinity Alps Wilderness, send $4 to USDA-Forest Service, 630 Sansome Street, San Francisco, CA 94111. To obtain a topographic map of the area, ask for Thurston Peaks from the USGS.

Contact: Shasta-Trinity National Forest, Big Bar Ranger District, Star Route 1, Box 10, Big Bar, CA 96010; (916) 623-6106 or fax (916) 623-6123.

Trail notes: The Hobo Gulch Campground is the site of an appealing trailhead, thanks to its setting quite deep in the national forest along Backbone Ridge. That means a lot of miles, 16 of them from Highway 299, are taken care of by car instead of on foot. However, the trailhead still doesn't provide short access to any lakes. Grizzly Lake, the nearest feature lake destination, is about 20 rough miles away. So instead of camping along lakes, hikers camp along pretty streams and flats.

The trail starts by heading straight north about five miles along the North Fork Trinity River to Rattlesnake Camp, then continues another three miles past the old Morrison Cabin and on to Pfeiffer Flat. Here the North Fork Trinity is joined by Grizzly Creek, an attractive backpacking destination. From Pfeiffer Flat, the trail follows Grizzly Creek, rising high toward the Trinity Sawtooth Ridge and requiring a long, tiring pull to beautiful Grizzly Meadows and then to Grizzly Lake, the final mile a scramble over bare rock. Grizzly Lake is a gorgeous high mountain lake, similar to many set in the glacial-carved bowls here. It's located below Thompson Peak at 8,663 feet, the most impressive peak in the Trinity Alps. Climbing the lake bowl in a clockwise direction makes for an exciting scramble to Thompson Peak and a perch just below the rock summit; to reach the tip-top of the mountain requires a technical climb. Grizzly Lake, which can be reached from other trailheads, has become very popular, and at times, even crowded by wilderness standards.

⓫ Granite Lake Trail

11.0 mi/2.0 days

Location: In the Trinity Alps Wilderness west of Trinity Center; map B1, grid d8.

User groups: Hikers, dogs, and horses. No mountain bikes. No wheelchair facilities.

Permits: A wilderness permit is required for hikers planning to camp.

Directions: From Weaverville, drive north on Highway 3 for 28 miles to Trinity Center. At Swift Creek Road, turn left and drive 6.8 miles to the parking area at the wilderness border.

Maps: For a map of Shasta-Trinity National Forest or the Trinity Alps Wilderness, send $4 to USDA-Forest Service, 630 Sansome Street, San Francisco, CA 94111. To obtain topographic maps of the area, ask for Covington Mill and Trinity Center from the USGS.

Contact: Shasta-Trinity National Forest, Weaverville Ranger District, P.O. Box 1190, Weaverville, CA 96093; (916) 623-2121 or fax (916) 623-6010.

Trail notes: When hikers scan wilderness maps, they often search for trails that are routed a short distance to a beautiful lake for a first night's camp. That's exactly what you get at Granite Lake, but though the trip in is only about five miles, it's anything but easy. From the trailhead, the hike starts simply enough, tracing along the right side of Swift Creek. Don't be fooled. Just beyond the confluence of Swift and Granite Creeks, you must cross the stream to the left and then pick up the Granite Lake Trail. This trail runs along the right side of Granite Creek for four miles, and includes a very steep section in the final mile that will have you wondering why you ever thought this was going to be such a short, easy trip. Finally you'll rise to Gibson Meadow, and just beyond, Granite Lake, a gorgeous sight below Gibson Peak. For a natural mountain water lake, it's a fair size, with good swimming during the day and trout fishing in the evening. This is a gorgeous spot, and also quite popular.

⓮ East Fork Trailhead

14.0 mi/2.0 days

Location: In the Trinity Alps Wilderness northwest of Trinity Lake; map B1, grid d8.

User groups: Hikers, dogs, and horses. No mountain bikes. No wheelchair facilities.

Permits: A wilderness permit is required for hikers planning to camp.

Directions: From Weaverville, drive north on Highway 3 to Covington Mill. Turn west on a signed Forest Service Road and drive for 2.5 miles to the trailhead.

Maps: For a map of Shasta-Trinity National Forest or the Trinity Alps Wilderness, send $4 to USDA-Forest Service, 630 Sansome Street, San Francisco, CA 94111. To obtain a topographic map of the area, ask for Covington Mill from the USGS.

Contact: Shasta-Trinity National Forest, Weaverville Ranger District, P.O. Box 1190, Weaverville, CA 96093; (916) 623-2121 or fax (916) 623-6010.

Trail notes: Your mission, should you choose to accept it, is the 6.5-mile largely uphill hike to the west side of Gibson Peak, where Deer Lake, Summit Lake, Luella Lake, Diamond Lake, and Siligo Peak can provide days of side-trip destinations. From the trailhead, the trip starts by tracing along the East Fork Stuart Fork, a feeder creek to Trinity Lake. After two miles, you'll arrive at a fork in the trail. Take the right fork (the left fork is routed to Bowerman Meadows and little Lake Anna), which climbs further along the stream, then traces past the southern flank of Gibson Peak. At times the trail is steep in this area, but finally you'll pass Gibson Peak, and Siligo Peak will come into view. The trail also junctions with a loop trail that circles Siligo Peak, and in the process, provides access to four high mountain lakes. Summit Lake is the favorite.

⓰ Stuart Fork Trailhead

25.0 mi/4.0 days

Location: In the Trinity Alps Wilderness northwest of Trinity Lake; map B1, grid e6.

User groups: Hikers, dogs, and horses. No mountain bikes. No wheelchair facilities.

Permits: A wilderness permit is required for hikers planning to camp.

Directions: From Weaverville on Highway 299, turn north on Highway 3 and drive 15 miles to Trinity Lake. Turn left on Trinity Alps Road and drive 2.5 miles to the trailhead at Bridge Camp.

Maps: For a map of Shasta-Trinity National Forest or the Trinity Alps Wilderness, send $4 to USDA-Forest Service, 630 Sansome Street, San Francisco, CA 94111. To obtain a topographic map of the area, ask for Covington Mill from the USGS.

Contact: Shasta-Trinity National Forest, Weaverville Ranger District, P.O. Box 1190, Weaverville, CA 96093; (916) 623-2121 or fax (916) 623-6010.

Trail notes: Don't say we didn't warn you; this trail doesn't have a difficulty rating of 5 for nothing. The hike requires an endless climb—very steep at times, particularly as you near the Sawtooth Ridge—spanning nearly 12 miles to Emerald Lake. But after arriving and resting up for a night, the ecstasy follows. Emerald Lake is one of three lakes set in line in a canyon below the Sawtooth Ridge, the others being Sapphire and Mirror. The surroundings are stark and prehistoric looking, and the lakes are gem-like, blue and clear, with big rainbow trout and water that is perfect for refreshing swims. The trail continues a mile past Emerald Lake to Sapphire Lake, and from there, it's an off-trail scramble, often across big boulders, as you climb another mile to reach Mirror Lake. The entire scene is surreal.

Special note: On the way in to Emerald Lake, you might notice a cutoff trail to the right, then see on your trail map that it crosses the Sawtooth Ridge and empties into the acclaimed Caribou Lakes Basin. On the map, it appears to be a short, easy trip, but in reality it involves a terrible climb with more than 100 switchbacks.

⓱ Canyon Creek Lakes Trailhead

15.0 mi/2.0 days

Location: In the Trinity Alps Wilderness north of Weaverville; map B1, grid e6.

User groups: Hikers, dogs, and horses. No mountain bikes. No wheelchair facilities.

Permits: A wilderness permit is required for hikers planning to camp.

Directions: From Weaverville, turn left on Highway 299 and drive eight miles to Junction City. Turn north on Canyon Creek Road and drive 13 miles to the trailhead at the end of the road.

Maps: For a map of Shasta-Trinity National Forest or the Trinity Alps Wilderness, send $4 to

USDA-Forest Service, 630 Sansome Street, San Francisco, CA 94111. To obtain a topographic map of the area, ask for Dedrick from the USGS.

Contact: Shasta-Trinity National Forest, Weaverville Ranger District, P.O. Box 1190, Weaverville, CA 96093; (916) 623-2121 or fax (916) 623-6010.

Trail notes: This is the kind of place where wilderness lovers can find religion. The destination is Canyon Creek Lakes, set high in a mountain canyon, framed by Sawtooth Mountain to the east and a series of high granite rims to the north. The route in is no mystery, heading straight upstream along Bear Creek for about a quarter of a mile, then crossing Bear Creek (a dry ford) before continuing along Canyon Creek. Four miles out, you'll reach the first of four waterfalls. The first is the smallest; then they get progressively taller, and all are gorgeous. After the last waterfall, walk for half a mile to reach Lower Canyon Creek Lake, seven miles out from the trailhead. From here, now largely above tree line, cross Stonehouse Gulch to reach the first of two lakes. The trail skirts past the left side of the first of the Canyon Creek Lakes, then in half a mile, arrives at the head of the larger of the two. They are like jewels set in the bottom of a gray, stark, high mountain canyon, and once you've seen them, you'll have their picture branded permanently in your mind. This has become a special weekend favorite for hikers from Eureka.

⑰ South Fork National Recreation Trail

20.0 mi/2.0 days

Location: In Shasta-Trinity National Forest east of Ruth Lake on Highway 36; map B1, grid i2.

User groups: Hikers and dogs. No horses or mountain bikes. No wheelchair facilities.

Permits: Campfire permits are required.

Directions: From Redding, drive west on Highway 299 for 43 miles to Douglas City. Turn left (south) on Highway 3 and drive about 25 miles to Hayfork. From Hayfork, drive southwest on Highway 3 for 10 miles to Highway 36. Turn west and drive 10 miles to the turnoff for Hell Gate Campground on the left. Drive on Forest Service Road 1S26 to the trailhead.

Maps: For a map of Shasta-Trinity National

Forest, send $4 to USDA-Forest Service, 630 Sansome Street, San Francisco, CA 94111. To obtain a topographic map of the area, ask for Forest Glen from the USGS.

Contact: Shasta-Trinity National Forest, Hayfork Ranger District, P.O. Box 159, Hayfork, CA 96041; (916) 628-5227 or fax (916) 628-5212.

Trail notes: This is an obscure trail for people who like walking along a stream in virtual oblivion. It's routed along the South Fork Trinity River, heading south toward the Yolla Bolly Wilderness. There are no lakes anywhere near the trail, and for the most part, the trail just meanders along, with that stream nearby providing a constant point of reference. Even the trailhead, a short drive out of the Hell Gate Campground, is remote and obscure. Immediately, the trail picks up the stream, and in less than an hour, you'll feel as if you've discovered your own private little universe. The temperatures can really smoke out here in the summer, and the stream is your savior. How far might you go? For many, an hour in and an hour out is plenty. You can keep going to Jacques Place, an unrenowned abandoned camp about 10 miles further one-way, or even beyond another five miles to the trail's end at Double Cabin Site, where you can leave a shuttle car and make this a one-way trip.

⑱ North Fork Beegum Trailhead

10.0 mi/2.0 days

Location: In Shasta-Trinity National Forest west of Red Bluff; map B1, grid j5.

User groups: Hikers, dogs, horses, and mountain bikes. No wheelchair facilities.

Permits: No permits are required.

Directions: From Interstate 5 at Red Bluff, turn west on Highway 36 and drive about 45 miles to the Yolla Bolly Ranger Station (west of Platina). Turn south on Stuart Gap Road and drive about eight miles to the trailhead at North Fork Beegum Campground.

Maps: For a map of Shasta-Trinity National Forest, send $4 to USDA-Forest Service, 630 Sansome Street, San Francisco, CA 94111. To obtain a topographic map of the area, ask for Pony Buck Peak from the USGS.

Contact: Shasta-Trinity National Forest, Yolla Bolla Ranger District, HC01, P.O. Box 450, Platina, CA 96076; (916) 352-4211 or fax (916) 352-4312.

Trail notes: You want to be by yourself? This region of California gets only a scant number of visitors. While it lacks high mountains, sweeping views, and lakeside campsites, there is another benefit here that has become far more difficult to find in California: absolute peace and quiet. The trail starts out of the North Fork Beegum Campground and is routed south along Beegum Creek for the first few miles. Much of this is quite rocky and difficult, but hey, you wanted to be alone, right? It then rises up to Pole Corral Gap, set at 4,360 feet and adjacent to Little Red Mountain. For most visitors, this is far enough. If you want to turn this into a one-way hike with a shuttle, the route continues down another seven miles to Pattymocus Butte, where there's an old Forest Service lookout station, accessible by vehicle.

Special note: A portion of the trail on this route runs across posted private property, the Seeliger Ranch. So stay on the trail. Got it?

⑲ Basin Gulch Trailhead

3.0 mi/2.0 hrs

Location: In Shasta-Trinity National Forest west of Red Bluff; map B1, grid j5.

User groups: Hikers, dogs, horses, and mountain bikes. No wheelchair facilities.

Permits: No permits are required.

Directions: From Interstate 5 at Red Bluff, turn west on Highway 36 and drive about 45 miles to the Yolla Bolly Ranger Station (west of Platina). Turn south on Stuart Gap Road and drive three miles to the trailhead at Basin Gulch Campground.

Maps: For a map of Shasta-Trinity National Forest, send $4 to USDA-Forest Service, 630 Sansome Street, San Francisco, CA 94111. To obtain a topographic map of the area, ask for Map File No. 01914/Pony Buck Peak from the USGS.

Contact: Shasta-Trinity National Forest, Yolla Bolla Ranger District, HC01, P.O. Box 450, Platina, CA 96076; (916) 352-4211 or fax (916) 352-4312.

Trail notes: Your destination on this hike is Noble Ridge. In a relatively short time, the trail

leaves any semblance of civilization far behind, the main attraction for many hikers. From the trailhead at Basin Gulch Campground, elevation 2,772 feet, the trail loops in a half circle, climbing as it goes, reaching the ridge at 3,200 feet in just 1.5 miles. Making the climb here is punishment enough, and after a picnic lunch, hikers often return back to the camp. But the determined few can go onward, hiking along Noble Ridge all the way for another four miles to a survey marker that marks the ridge top at 3,933 feet. The trail ends at a Forest Service road just three miles from Platina, allowing for a possible one-way hike with a shuttle.

Pacific Crest Trail (PCT) Section Overview

21.0 mi. one way/2–3 days

Trail sections in this area extend from Scott Mountain east of Callahan to the border of the Russian Wilderness.

This segment of the Pacific Crest Trail doesn't travel north to south, but rather is routed east to west. Because it only skirts the northern edge of the Trinity Alps Wilderness, it gets less use than many of the lake-destination trails in the wilderness to the south. Regardless, this route features many excellent, short side trips to small mountain lakes in both the Trinity Alps and the Russian Wilderness, making it attractive to both weekend hikers as well as those on longer expeditions. The following provide specific information about major trail sections in this zone.

PCT-44 Scott Mountain to Cecilville Road

18.0 mi. one way/2.0 days

Location: From Highway 3 at Scott Mountain Campground to Cecilville Road near the northern border of the Trinity Alps Wilderness; map B1, grid a9.

User groups: Hikers, dogs, and horses. No mountain bikes. No wheelchair facilities.

Permits: A wilderness permit is required for camping in the Trinity Alps Wilderness. Contact the Weaverville Ranger District at the address below for information.

Directions: From Callahan, drive south on Highway 3 about seven miles to the trailhead at Scott Mountain Campground.

Maps: To obtain topographic maps of the area, ask for Scott Mountain, Tangle Blue Lake, Billys Peak, and Deadman Peak from the USGS.

Contact: Shasta-Trinity National Forest, Weaverville Ranger District, P.O. Box 1190, Weaverville, CA 96093; (916) 623-2121 or fax (916) 623-6010.

Trail notes: Short hikes on spur trails to a number of wilderness lakes are the highlight of this section of the Pacific Crest Trail. From the camp at Scott Mountain, the trail is routed west for five miles, where the first of a series of lakes is situated within half a mile of the trail. They include Upper Boulder, East Boulder, Mid Boulder, and Telephone Lakes, all quite pretty and accessible from the main trail. After hiking past Eagle Peak, set at 7,789 feet, you'll pass additional short cutoffs that are routed to West Boulder, Mavis, and Fox Creek Lakes. Hikers often camp at one of these lakes, before dropping elevation to the South Fork Scott River, then crossing and heading north into the Russian Wilderness.

Trail notes: The long, steady climb up to the southern border of the Russian Wilderness starts from the bottom of the canyon at the North Fork Scott River. From the trailhead, a good side trip (to the south) is the short hike to Hidden Lake or South Fork Lakes. Those venturing onward on the PCT enter a complex habitat web that includes the headwaters of the Scott, Salmon, and Trinity Rivers, along with the beautiful scenery that such diversity creates. This section of the trail is rarely used, with less than 1,000 people a year estimated to hike here. Most of them use this as a jump-off spot, heading north into the Russian Wilderness.

Special note: For those driving to this trailhead, parking at Carter Meadows is recommended. While this will add about a quarter of a mile to your hike, water and a vault toilet are available there.

PCT Continuation: To continue hiking along the Pacific Crest Trail, see chapter A1.

PCT-45 Cecilville Road to Russian Wilderness

3.0 mi. one way/1.0 day

Location: From Cecilville Road west of Callahan to the southern border of the Russian Wilderness; map B1, grid a8.

User groups: Hikers, dogs, and horses. No mountain bikes. No wheelchair facilities.

Permits: No permits are required for this section. Parking and access are free.

Directions: From Callahan on Highway 3, turn west on Cecilville Road and drive 11.5 miles to the Cecilville Summit. Parking is limited here; a larger parking area is located just past Cecilville Summit at the Carter Meadows Trailhead.

Maps: To obtain topographic maps of the area, ask for Deadman Peak and Eaton Peak from the USGS.

Contact: Klamath National Forest, Scott River Ranger District, 11263 North Highway 3, Fort Jones, CA 96032; (916) 468-5351 or fax (916) 468-5654.

Map B2

Adjoining Maps: East: B3 ...... *page* 86   West: B1 54
North: A2 32   South: C2 124

Northern California Map .... *page 2*

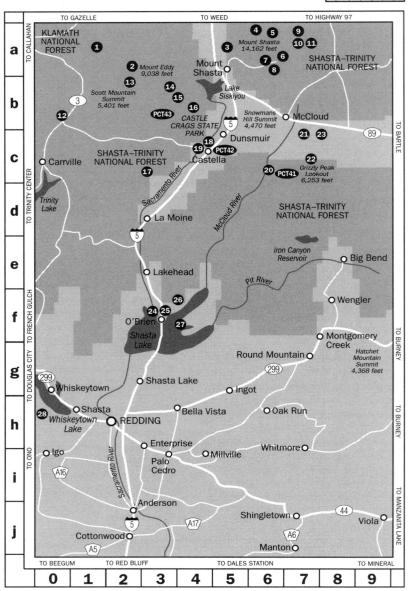

Chapter B2 features:

1 Kangaroo Lake Trailhead

3.0 mi/2.25 hrs

Location: In Klamath National Forest east of Callahan; map B2, grid a2.

User groups: Hikers, dogs, horses, and mountain bikes. The fishing is wheelchair accessible.

Permits: No permits are required. Parking and access are free.

Directions: From Interstate 5 north of Mount Shasta, take the Edgewood exit, then turn left and drive a short distance to old Highway 99. Turn right and drive approximately six miles to Gazelle. Turn left on Gazelle-Callahan Road and drive over the summit. Drive down the other side of the mountain about five miles, then turn left on Rail Creek Road and drive about five miles. The road dead-ends at the parking area for Kangaroo Lake. The trail starts to the right, down the road from the campground.

Maps: A trail guide can be obtained by contacting Klamath National Forest at the address below. For a map of Klamath National Forest, send $4 to USDA-Forest Service, 630 Sansome Street, San Francisco, CA 94111. To obtain a topographic map of the area, ask for Scott Mountain from the USGS.

Contact: Klamath National Forest, Scott River Ranger District, 11263 North Highway 3, Fort Jones, CA 96032; (916) 468-5351 or fax (916) 468-5654.

Trail notes: A remote paved road leads right to Kangaroo Lake, set at 6,050 feet, providing one of the most easily reached pristine mountain lakes with a campground, wheelchair-accessible fishing, and a great trailhead. From the campground, the trail rises up steeply and connects with the Pacific Crest Trail. From the Pacific Crest Trail you can make the scramble to Cory Peak at 7,737 feet for a 360-degree view. This is a great picnic site. All of Northern California's prominent mountain peaks are in view here, and immediately below you to the west is Kangaroo Lake, which looks like a large sapphire. The lake only covers 21 acres, but often produces large brook trout, most of them 12- to 14-inchers. Backpackers can extend this trip eastward four miles on the Pacific Crest Trail past Robbers Meadow to Bull Lake, a small lake in a relatively sparse setting.

❷ Deadfall Lakes Trail

5.0 mi/3.0 hrs

Location: In Shasta-Trinity National Forest west of Mount Shasta; map B2, grid a2.

User groups: Hikers, dogs, and horses. No mountain bikes. No wheelchair facilities.

Permits: No permits are required.

Directions: From Interstate 5 north of Weed, take the Edgewood exit and drive northwest on old Highway 99 for about half a mile. Turn left on Stewart Springs Road and drive to the road's end. Turn right on Forest Service Road 17 and drive 12 miles to the Deadfall Lakes parking area at the Trinity Divide. The Parks Creek Trailhead for the Pacific Crest Trail is on the left.

Maps: For a map of Shasta-Trinity National Forest, send $4 to USDA-Forest Service, 630 Sansome Street, San Francisco, CA 94111. To obtain a topographic map of the area, ask for Mount Eddy from the USGS.

Contact: Shasta-Trinity National Forest, Mount Shasta Ranger District, 204 West Alma, Mount Shasta, CA 96067; phone (916) 926-4511 or fax (916) 926-5120.

Trail notes: The sight of Middle Deadfall Lake is always a happy shock to newcomers. Here, secreted away on the west side of Mount Eddy, are three wilderness lakes, the prize being Middle Deadfall. At 25 acres, it's far larger than you might expect, and far prettier, too. Because the parking area and trailhead are at ridgeline, the hike in to this lake is much easier than to other wilderness lakes, making for an excellent day hike. The trail is routed through a mixed conifer forest, with views of the Trinity Alps off to the west, and it's a gentle rising grade most of the way. As you near the lake, you'll have to cross a stream (a no-wading, rock-hopping prospect) and a meadow, and then suddenly below you is Middle Deadfall Lake at 7,300 feet, one of the highlights along the Pacific Crest Trail. The best and most secluded campsite here is around the back side of the lake. There are two other lakes nearby, tiny and rarely visited Upper Deadfall at 7,800 feet, and Lower Deadfall at 7,150 feet, which covers five acres and is overlooked in the shadow of its nearby big brother. You should also note that a great side trip for campers at Middle Deadfall Lake is making the 3.5-mile hike to the top of Mount Eddy at 9,025 feet, a 1,700-foot climb. It's one of Northern California's greatest lookouts, with no better view anywhere of the western slopes of Mount Shasta.

❸ Black Butte Trail

5.0 mi/3.5 hrs

Location: In Shasta-Trinity National Forest between Interstate 5 and Mount Shasta; map B2, grid a5.

User groups: Hikers and dogs. No horses or mountain bikes. No wheelchair facilities.

Permits: No permits are required.

Directions: From Interstate 5 at Mount Shasta City, take the Central Mount Shasta exit and drive east on Lake Street. Bear left on Washington Drive. (Washington Drive becomes Everitt Memorial Highway.) Drive on Everitt Memorial Highway for about two miles to the first Penny Pines sign. Turn left on Forest Service Road 41N18 (Ash Flat). Drive about 200 yards and bear right, continuing on Forest Service Road 41N18 for 2.5 miles. After the road crosses under the overhead power line, turn left on Forest Service Road 41N18A (Black Butte Road) and drive to the trailhead. Parking is very limited; be sure to park off the road.

Maps: A trail information sheet is available by contacting the Mount Shasta Ranger District at the address below. For a map of Shasta-Trinity National Forest, send $4 to USDA-Forest Service, 630 Sansome Street, San Francisco, CA 94111. To obtain a topographic map of the area, ask for City of Mount Shasta from the USGS.

Contact: Shasta-Trinity National Forest, Mount Shasta Ranger District, 204 West Alma, Mount Shasta, CA 96067; (916) 926-4511 or fax (916) 926-5120.

Trail notes: Anybody who has cruised Interstate 5 north to Oregon and gawked in astonishment at Mount Shasta has inevitably seen Black Butte right alongside the highway. That's right, it's that conical-shaped, barren cindercone set between the highway and Mount Shasta, and it can pique a traveler's curiosity. The trail is routed right to the top and can answer all of your questions. But you may not like all the answers. Over the course of 2.5 miles, you'll climb 1,845 feet, much of it steep, most of it rocky, and in the summer, all of it hot and dry. Shade is nonexistent. There are only two rewards: one is claiming the summit, at 6,325 feet, where you'll find the foundation of an old Forest Service lookout and great 360-degree views; and the other is that the hike is an excellent warm-up for people who are planning to climb Mount Shasta. That is, providing you don't need a week to recover.

❹ Whitney Falls/Bolam Creek Trailhead

3.4 mi/2.5 hrs

Location: On the northwest slope of Mount Shasta; map B2, grid a6.

User groups: Hikers only. No dogs, horses, or mountain bikes. No wheelchair facilities.

Permits: You must obtain a wilderness permit for a fee from Shasta-Trinity National Forest.

Directions: From Interstate 5 at Weed, take the Highway 97 exit and drive through Weed. After about 11 miles, turn right on Bolam Road (Forest Service Road 43N21). Bolam Road is not signed. If you reach Siskiyou County Road A12, on the left, you have gone a quarter of a mile too far. Drive on Bolam Road toward the mountain (Mount Shasta), cross the railroad tracks, and continue to the trailhead at the end of the road. A high-clearance vehicle is required.

Maps: A trail map of the Mount Shasta Wilderness can be purchased for $7 from the Mount Shasta Ranger District at the address below. For a map of Shasta-Trinity National Forest, send $4 to USDA-Forest Service, 630 Sansome Street, San Francisco, CA 94111. To obtain a topographic map of the area, ask for Mount Shasta from the USGS.

Contact: Shasta-Trinity National Forest, Mount Shasta Ranger District, 204 West Alma, Mount Shasta, CA 96067; (916) 926-4511 or fax (916) 926-5120.

Trail notes: Mount Shasta, at 14,162 feet tall, is the most prominent landmark in Northern California, and it's well-known for its outstanding summit routes on its southern slopes. What is less known, however, is that there are four trailheads set on Shasta's northern and eastern

foothills that grant hikers choice day walks and mountaineers a starting point for difficult climbs over glaciers to the top. Those four forgotten trailheads are at Bolam Creek, North Gate, Brewer Creek, and Watkins Glacier. The Bolam Creek Trailhead is at about 5,600 feet, and from it, the trail heads uphill, for the most part tracing a gulch, which is the headwaters of a small stream. The trail traverses the creek a few times on the way, all easy crossings on a moderate-grade, surrounded primarily by old, gnarled Shasta red firs. The trail spans 1.6 miles to a fork at 6,400 feet, and for day hikers, the best bet is turning right, climbing partially up the treeless slope for a fantastic lookout and picnic site. Here you'll discover hidden Whitney Falls, a 250-foot waterfall, with its thin, silvery wisp tumbling through a narrow chute in a dramatic ashen gorge.

Special note: If you turn left at the fork instead, you'll venture through forest, then up through another barren stream drainage. The trail ends, and mountaineers will have to pass both Coquette Falls, and then near the peak at the Bolam Glacier, in order to make the summit. Safety gear and expert climbing skills are required.

❺ North Gate Trailhead

4.0 mi/2.75 hrs

Location: On the north slope of Mount Shasta; map B2, grid a6.

User groups: Hikers only. No dogs, horses, or mountain bikes. No wheelchair facilities.

Permits: You must obtain a wilderness permit for a fee from Shasta-Trinity National Forest.

Directions: From Interstate 5 at Weed, take the Highway 97 exit and drive through Weed. After about 13.5 miles, turn right on Forest Service Road 43N19 (Military Pass Road) and drive approximately five miles. Turn right on Forest Service Road 42N16 (Andesite Logging Road) and drive another three miles. Turn left on Forest Service Road 42N16A (Andesite Spur A) and drive to the parking area at the end of the road.

Maps: A trail map of the Mount Shasta Wilderness can be purchased for $7 from the Mount Shasta Ranger District at the address below. For a map of Shasta-Trinity National Forest, send $4 to USDA-Forest Service, 630 Sansome Street, San

Francisco, CA 94111. To obtain a topographic map of the area, ask for Mount Shasta from the USGS.

Contact: Shasta-Trinity National Forest, Mount Shasta Ranger District, 204 West Alma, Mount Shasta, CA 96067; (916) 926-4511 or fax (916) 926-5120.

Trail notes: The North Gate Trailhead, set at about 7,000 feet, is one of Mount Shasta's most obscure and least-used trails. It sits on the north flank of Shasta, just below a mountain mound called North Gate. The route skirts around this mound, following a small stream uphill for 1.6 miles; then further along, the trail deteriorates and disappears as you near tree line at 8,400 feet. From here, most day hikers will climb up another 400 feet to the source of the creek, a small spring, and have lunch and enjoy the view to the north.

Special note: Mountain climbers who use this route to climb to the Shasta Summit will discover the going is quite easy at first after leaving tree line. The trip then becomes very steep, difficult and dangerous, whether crossing Bolam or Hotlum Glacier. This route is for experienced mountain climbers only, who are aware of the extreme risks of crossing steep, sheer glaciers.

➏ Sand Flat Trailhead

3.4 mi/2.75 hrs

Location: On the southern slope of Mount Shasta; map B2, grid a6.

User groups: Hikers only. No dogs, horses, or mountain bikes. No wheelchair facilities.

Permits: You must obtain a wilderness permit for a fee from Shasta-Trinity National Forest.

Directions: From Interstate 5 at Mount Shasta City, take the Central Mount Shasta exit and drive east on Lake Street. Bear left on Washington Drive. (Washington Drive becomes Everitt Memorial Highway.) Drive about eight miles on Everitt Memorial Highway. Turn left on Forest Service Road 41N60 (Sand Flat Loop) and drive to the trailhead.

Maps: A trail map of the Mount Shasta Wilderness can be purchased for $7 from the Mount Shasta Ranger District at the address below. For a map of Shasta-Trinity National Forest, send $4 to USDA-Forest Service, 630 Sansome Street, San

Francisco, CA 94111. To obtain a topographic map of the area, ask for Mount Shasta from the USGS.

Contact: Shasta-Trinity National Forest, Mount Shasta Ranger District, 204 West Alma, Mount Shasta, CA 96067; (916) 926-4511 or fax (916) 926-5120.

Trail notes: The hike from Sand Flat to Horse Camp, a distance of 1.7 miles, will give you a good taste of the Mount Shasta experience, and you're likely to savor the flavors. Many who make this day hike are often compelled to return to climb all the way to the top. We were!

Sand Flat provides a good shaded parking area to start from at a 6,800-foot elevation. The trail immediately takes off uphill, gradually at first, and then becomes quite steep. At 7,360 feet, it intersects with the Bunny Flat Trail, and then continues rising through the forest. Along the way, there are amazing examples of how avalanches have knocked down entire sections of forest in this area. When you reach Horse Camp at 7,800 feet, nearing timber line, you'll find many rewards. The first is spring water flowing continuously out of a piped fountain near the Sierra Hut, perhaps the best tasting water in the world. The second is the foreboding view of Red Bank, which forms the mountain rim above Horse Camp. The third is the opportunity to hike up a short way above tree line for the sweeping views to the south of Castle Crags and Lake Siskiyou. After taking the first steps on the Summit Trail, you'll likely yearn to keep going all the way to the very top of this magic mountain. If you wish to hike the Summit Trail, see the following hike out of Bunny Flat Trailhead.

➐ Shasta Summit Trail

13.6 mi/1.5 days

Location: At Bunny Flat Trailhead on the southern slope of Mount Shasta; map B2, grid a6.

User groups: Hikers only. No dogs, horses, or mountain bikes. No wheelchair facilities.

Permits: You must obtain a wilderness permit for a fee from Shasta-Trinity National Forest. The Forest Service is also debating whether or not to establish a Shasta Summit permit, and possibly set a trailhead quota with a reservation system.

Call Shasta-Trinity National Forest prior to planning your trip.

Directions: From Interstate 5 at Mount Shasta City, take the Central Mount Shasta exit and drive east on Lake Street. Bear left on Washington Drive. (Washington Drive becomes Everitt Memorial Highway.) Drive about 10 miles on Everitt Memorial Highway to the trailhead at Bunny Flat.

Maps: A trail map of the Mount Shasta Wilderness can be purchased for $7 from the Mount Shasta Ranger District at the address below. For a map of Shasta-Trinity National Forest, send $4 to USDA-Forest Service, 630 Sansome Street, San Francisco, CA 94111. To obtain a topographic map of the area, ask for Mount Shasta from the USGS.

Contact: Shasta-Trinity National Forest, Mount Shasta Ranger District, 204 West Alma, Mount Shasta, CA 96067; (916) 926-4511 or fax (916) 926-5120. A 24-hour climbing report is available by phoning (916) 926-5555. Ice axes and crampons are available for rent at Fifth Season in Mount Shasta at (916) 926-3606. If you'd like to climb Mount Shasta with an experienced guide, call Michael Zanger of Shasta Mountain Guides at (916) 926-3117.

Trail notes: The hike to the top of Mount Shasta is a great challenge, an ascent of 7,000 feet over ice, snow, and rock while trying to suck what little oxygen you can out of the thin air. It may be the greatest adventure in the West that most people have an honest chance of achieving. While there are dangers, from tumbling boulders (see the special note below) to bad weather (which stops half the people who try the climb), hikers in good condition who start the trip very early and have the proper equipment can make it all the way to the top and back in a day. Early? You should depart from Bunny Flat by 3:30 A.M., or hike in a day early, set up a base camp at Horse Camp (tree line), and start no later than 4:30 A.M. Equipment? A daypack with warm clothes, a windbreaker, two canteens of water (refill wherever you find a rivulet of water, occasionally possible at Red Bank), food, and an ice ax and crampons are mandatory.

The trip starts out of Bunny Flat at 6,900 feet, leads through a forest of Shasta red firs, climbs up to where the trail intersects with the route out of Sand Flat, then turns right and rises to Horse Camp, at an elevation of 7,800 feet and a distance of 1.8 miles. After filling your canteens at the spring, start the Summit Trail, your first steps made across a series of large stones called "Olberman's Causeway." From here, the trail quickly rises above timber line, then after a short time becomes a faint path. Often, this is where the snow and ice start, and you must stop and strap your crampons on your boots. The walking is easy with crampons, the metal spikes poking holes into the ice surface. The trail climbs up Avalanche Gulch, and some people stop to make trail camps at a flat spot called Helen Lake at 10,440 feet. Hikers not acclimated to high altitudes may begin experiencing some dizziness, but there's no relief in sight. At this point, the hike gets steeper, about a 35-degree slope, and many give up before reaching Red Bank, a huge red volcanic outcrop at about 12,500 feet. At Red Bank, you'll need your ice ax, pulling your way through a narrow and steep rock/ice chute, where a slip is certain without crampons.

When you emerge atop Red Bank, you are nearly 13,000 feet high, at the foot of a glacier field and Misery Hill, named because it's a long, slow climb, and many mistake it for being the peak. Once atop Misery Hill, though, you'll see the true Shasta Summit, a massive pinnacle of lava which seems to jut straight up into the air. With a final push, follow the trail, grabbing rocks to help pull you up, sucking the thin air, and with a few last steps, you'll be on top. On clear days, you can see hundreds of miles in all directions, and at 14,162 feet, the sky is a deeper cobalt blue than you ever imagined. On top, you'll sign your name in a logbook in an old rusted metal box, then take in the grand wonders surrounding you. It's a remarkable trip, one we plan on making every year for as long as our bodies can take it.

Special note, part I: It's an absolute must to make an early start. In the hot summer months, towering cumulus clouds sometimes form on Mount Shasta during the afternoon, and by then you'll want to be making the trip down. If towering cumulus begin forming by noon, intense thunderstorms are possible by mid-afternoon.

Special note, part II: The biggest danger and largest number of injuries on Mount Shasta come not from falling, but from being hit by tumbling boulders. In fact, our research assistant, Robyn Schlueter, was struck in the foot by a boulder in her first attempt at climbing Shasta. She was hit so hard that it knocked her hiking boot off, breaking her foot and requiring an emergency helicopter airlift out for medical treatment. Always keep a good distance between your hiking partners, don't hike in a vertical line, and if a rock comes bouncing down, always shout, "Rock! Rock!" By the way, Robyn returned to Mount Shasta the following two years and made it to the top on both trips.

Special note, part III: The mountain is best hiked when it still has a good coating of snow and ice, which allows for excellent footing with crampons. When the snow and ice melt off in late fall, tromping through the small volcanic rocks is like slogging in mushy sand.

Special note, part IV: Drink lots of water. In high altitudes, dehydration is a common problem and can result in early exhaustion and extreme vulnerability to mountain sickness.

❽ Panther Meadows

2.8 mi/1.75 hrs

Location: On the southern slope of Mount Shasta; map B2, grid a6.

User groups: Hikers only. No dogs, horses, or mountain bikes. No wheelchair facilities.

Permits: You must obtain a wilderness permit for a fee from Shasta-Trinity National Forest.

Directions: From Interstate 5 at Mount Shasta, take the Central Mount Shasta exit and drive east on Lake Street. Bear left on Washington Drive. (Washington Drive becomes Everitt Memorial Highway.) Drive about 13 miles on Everitt Memorial Highway to the trailhead at Panther Meadows.

Maps: A trail map of the Mount Shasta Wilderness can be purchased for $7 from the Mount Shasta Ranger District at the address below. For a map of Shasta-Trinity National Forest, send $4 to USDA-Forest Service, 630 Sansome Street, San Francisco, CA 94111. To obtain a topographic map of the area, ask for Mount Shasta from the USGS.

Contact: Shasta-Trinity National Forest, Mount Shasta Ranger District, 204 West Alma, Mount

Shasta, CA 96067; (916) 926-4511 or fax (916) 926-5120.

Trail notes: Panther Meadows is considered a sacred Native American site, and even those who are unaware of it seem to intuitively realize this is a special place and find themselves walking softly and talking quietly when visiting. The trail is easy to reach, located just off to the right of the wide, paved, two-laner Everitt Memorial Highway. This hike is a short one, from Panther Meadows to Gray Butte and back.

From the parking area, the trail starts by heading east past meadow and forest, and after six-tenths of a mile, turns right and begins a steady climb for eight-tenths of a mile to the top of Gray Butte at 8,108 feet. It's a perfect lookout to the south, with Castle Crags, Mount Lassen, and the dropoff in the Sacramento Valley all prominent. If you continue on for half a mile, you'll discover a place called "The Gate," which some mountain visitors consider a sacred portal to the spiritual dimension.

❾ Brewer Creek Trailhead

4.2 mi/3.0 hrs

Location: On the northeast slope of Mount Shasta; map B2, grid a7.

User groups: Hikers only. No dogs, horses, or mountain bikes. No wheelchair facilities.

Permits: You must obtain a wilderness permit for a fee from Shasta-Trinity National Forest.

Directions: From Interstate 5 south of Mount Shasta City, take the McCloud-Reno exit and turn east on Highway 89. Drive 12 miles to McCloud, then eight miles further on Highway 89. Turn north on Military Pass Road (Forest Service Road 19). Drive about 12 miles, then turn left on Forest Service Road 42N02 (Gravel Creek Road) and drive about three miles. Turn right on Forest Service Road 42N10 (Brewer Creek Road) and drive to the parking area.

Maps: A trail map of the Mount Shasta Wilderness can be purchased for $7 from the Mount Shasta Ranger District at the address below. For a map of Shasta-Trinity National Forest, send $4 to USDA-Forest Service, 630 Sansome Street, San Francisco, CA 94111. To obtain a topographic map of the area, ask for Mount Shasta from the USGS.

Contact: Shasta-Trinity National Forest, Mount Shasta Ranger District, 204 West Alma, Mount Shasta, CA 96067; (916) 926-4511 or fax (916) 926-5120.

Trail notes: It's so quiet here that you can practically hear the wildflowers bloom. We've hiked the north slope of Shasta out of the Brewer Creek Trailhead several times and have never seen another person. The trip is a perfect day hike. The trailhead is set near Brewer Creek (7,200 feet), hence the name, and after a short walk through a section of forest that was selectively logged many years ago, you'll enter the Shasta Wilderness and be surrounded by old-growth firs, many quite scraggly from enduring harsh winters and the short growing season. Here the trail gets more steep, a steady climb up through forest, gradual switchbacks as it goes. When you near tree line at 7,700 feet, the trail turns to the left and begins to lateral across the mountain. It's 2.1 miles to timber line from the trailhead, and most people hike to this point, then turn back. However, you can add an easy mile or two by climbing a wide, volcanic slope with good footing all the way and rising to 9,500 feet. This is a great spot for a picnic, providing nice views to the north, and also perhaps inspiring dreams of the day when you'll next climb all the way to the top of Shasta.

Special note: Mountaineers who try to climb Shasta from this trailhead have only one good route from the point where the trail meets tree line, which is to head to the right up and over Hotlum Glacier. This route is extremely difficult, very steep, and dangerous.

⑩ Mud Creek Falls

3.0 mi/1.5 hrs

Location: On the southeast slope of Mount Shasta; map B2, grid a7.

User groups: Hikers only. No dogs, horses, or mountain bikes. No wheelchair facilities.

Permits: You must obtain a wilderness permit for a fee from Shasta-Trinity National Forest.

Directions: From Interstate 5 south of Mount Shasta City, take the McCloud-Reno exit and turn east on Highway 89. Drive 12 miles to McCloud, then another three miles to Pilgrim

Creek Road (Forest Service Road 13). Turn left and drive about five miles (paved) to Forest Service Road 41N15 (Widow Springs Road). Turn left and drive about five miles to Forest Service Road 31 (McKenzie Butte). Cross this road and drive on Forest Service Road 41N61 (Cold Creek Road), a dirt and gravel road, about one mile, then turn left on Forest Service Road 41N25Y (Clear Creek Road) and drive about three miles to the parking area. The road is well-signed but there are several spur roads enroute that can be confusing to newcomers.

Maps: A trail map of the Mount Shasta Wilderness can be purchased for $7 from the Mount Shasta Ranger District at the address below. For a map of Shasta-Trinity National Forest, send $4 to USDA-Forest Service, 630 Sansome Street, San Francisco, CA 94111. To obtain a topographic map of the area, ask for Mount Shasta from the USGS.

Contact: Shasta-Trinity National Forest, Mount Shasta Ranger District, 204 West Alma, Mount Shasta, CA 96067; (916) 926-4511 or fax (916) 926-5120.

Trail notes: A short walk on the remote southeast flank of Mount Shasta can provide entry into a land of enchantment that features deep canyons and views of glaciers and Mount Shasta's prettiest waterfall. The drive in is circuitous but well-signed, and it's a surprise to find other cars parked at the trailhead. The hike starts on an old overgrown jeep road, slowly emerging from a sparse forest of Shasta red fir, climbing to the eastern edge of the dramatic Mud Creek Canyon at about 7,000 feet elevation. From here, most climb on for another 15 minutes, arriving at a perfect view of the waterfall at the bottom of the canyon below. The waterfall, best viewed with binoculars, is perhaps 125 feet high, wide, and silver but distant. This area is rich in natural history, the canyon having been carved by a glacier and still fed with water from the towering, fractured Konwakiton Glacier above, running the color of volcanic silt.

⑪ Old Ski Bowl Trailhead

2.5 mi/2.0 hrs

Location: On the southern slope of Mount Shasta; map B2, grid a7.

User groups: Hikers only. No dogs, horses, or mountain bikes. No wheelchair facilities.

Permits: You must obtain a wilderness permit for a fee from Shasta-Trinity National Forest.

Directions: From Interstate 5 at Mount Shasta, take the Central Mount Shasta exit and drive east on Lake Street. Bear left on Washington Drive. (Washington Drive becomes Everitt Memorial Highway.) Drive about 14 miles on Everitt Memorial Highway to the trailhead in the upper parking area.

Maps: A trail map of the Mount Shasta Wilderness can be purchased for $7 from the Mount Shasta Ranger District at the address below. For a map of Shasta-Trinity National Forest, send $4 to USDA-Forest Service, 630 Sansome Street, San Francisco, CA 94111. To obtain a topographic map of the area, ask for Mount Shasta from the USGS.

Contact: Shasta-Trinity National Forest, Mount Shasta Ranger District, 204 West Alma, Mount Shasta, CA 96067; (916) 926-4511 or fax (916) 926-5120.

Trail notes: One of the great hikes on Mount Shasta is climbing from the Old Ski Bowl lodge site up to Green Butte. At 7,800 feet, it's the highest drive-to trailhead on Mount Shasta, set just above timber line. That means the entire route is across a volcanic slope, with great views every step of the way and a unique destination as well. Green Butte, a huge rock outcrop set at 9,193 feet, is a perfect perch.

At the parking area, there's an obvious trail (though it's unsigned) that leads up toward Green Butte, which is also clearly obvious just a mile away. But while the trip is short in distance, it's very steep, with a 1,300-foot elevation gain. Along the way, a great bonus is a natural spring set about halfway up the butte; be sure to find it and fill your canteen with this sweet tasting spring water. While Green Butte is the destination of most visitors here, the hiking route continues to 9,600 feet before disintegrating in the lava rubble and snow. The "Old Ski Bowl" is one of the legendary spots on Shasta. It was here that a developer desecrated Shasta wildlands by building a ski area above tree line. Well, nature gives and nature takes back. With no trees to hold snow in place, the old mountain wiped out the ski lifts with an avalanche, and again, Shasta is untouched, rising like a diamond in a field of coal.

⑫ Big Bear Lake Trail

8.0 mi/2.0 days

Location: In the Trinity Alps Wilderness south of Callahan; map B2, grid b1.

User groups: Hikers, dogs, and horses. No mountain bikes. No wheelchair facilities.

Permits: A wilderness permit is required for hikers planning to camp in the wilderness.

Directions: From Interstate 5 at Yreka, take the Highway 3/Fort Jones exit and drive about 40 miles to Callahan. Head south on Highway 3 for about 13 miles to the turnoff for the Bear Creek Parking Area. Turn right and drive to the trailhead.

Maps: For a map of Shasta-Trinity National Forest, send $4 to USDA-Forest Service, 630 Sansome Street, San Francisco, CA 94111. To obtain a topographic map of the area, ask for Tangle Blue Lake from the USGS.

Contact: Shasta-Trinity National Forest, Weaverville Ranger District, P.O. Box 1190, Weaverville, CA 96093; (916) 623-2121 or fax (916) 623-6010.

Trail notes: The four-mile hike up to Big Bear Lake, a large, beautiful lake by wilderness standards, can make for a perfect weekend backpack trip. If there's a negative to this trip, it's this: the trail ends at the lake, so if the lakeside campsites are already taken when you arrive, you're out of luck for a quality place to camp for the night. The trailhead is easy to reach, just off Highway 3 north of Trinity Lake. The route is simple but not easy. It follows Bear Creek for the entire route, with one stream crossing but climbing all the way. Once you reach the lake, a bonus is the side trip to Little Bear Lake, which takes about a mile of scrambling cross-country style to reach.

⑬ Toad Lake Trail

1.5 mi/2.0 days

Location: In Shasta-Trinity National Forest west of Mount Shasta; map B2, grid b2.

User groups: Hikers, dogs, horses, and mountain bikes. No wheelchair facilities.

Permits: No permits are required.

Directions: From Interstate 5 at Mount Shasta City, take the Central Mount Shasta exit and drive west on Lake Street/Hatchery Road to the intersection with Old Stage Road. Turn left on Old Stage Road and drive half a mile. Turn right on W.A. Barr Road. Go past Box Canyon Dam and the Lake Siskiyou Campground entrance where W.A. Barr Road becomes Forest Service Road 26 (South Fork Road). Just past the concrete bridge over the South Fork Sacramento River, turn right on Forest Service Road 40N53 (Toad Lake Road) and at the next junction, head left on Forest Service Road 40N53. Drive to the parking area below Toad Lake. Four-wheel-drive vehicles are recommended.

Maps: For a map of Shasta-Trinity National Forest, send $4 to USDA-Forest Service, 630 Sansome Street, San Francisco, CA 94111. To obtain a topographic map of the area, ask for Mount Eddy from the USGS.

Contact: Shasta-Trinity National Forest, Mount Shasta Ranger District, 204 West Alma, Mount Shasta, CA 96067; (916) 926-4511 or fax (916) 926-5120.

Trail notes: What? How is this possible? Are we suffering from some rare form of mental illness? While the latter might be true, that's not why a 1.5-mile round-trip hike, rating only a 1 in difficulty, is projected as a two-day trip. The reason is that the drive to the trailhead is endless, the road winding and twisting its way up the slopes of Mount Eddy, and no one should go up and back in a day. Keep your tongue in your mouth, because the ride is so jarring that you might bite the end of it when you hit a big pothole. But once parked, you'll immediately notice the perfect calm, and then with a 15-minute walk to the lake at a 6,950-foot elevation, you'll be furnished with a picture-perfect lakeside campsite.

The lake covers 23 acres, provides excellent swimming, fair fishing for small trout, and great side trips. The best is the one-mile hike from Toad Lake to Porcupine Lake, an idyllic spot for a picnic or a walk along the shore. To get there from Toad Lake, take the trail that's routed behind the lake up to the Pacific Crest Trail, then walk south for a quarter of a mile on the PCT to the Porcupine Lake cutoff on the right.

 Sisson-Callahan

17.0 mi/2.0 days

Location: In Shasta-Trinity National Forest near Lake Siskiyou west of Mount Shasta; map B2, grid b3.

User groups: Hikers, dogs, and horses. No mountain bikes. No wheelchair facilities.

Permits: No permits are required.

Directions: From Interstate 5 at Mount Shasta City, take the Central Mount Shasta exit and drive west on Lake Street/Hatchery Road to the intersection with Old Stage Road. Turn left on Old Stage Road and drive half a mile. Turn right on W.A. Barr Road and go a short distance to North Shore Road. Turn right on North Shore, which will become Forest Service Road 40N27 (Deer Creek Road). Drive across the wooden bridge on Deer Creek and at the next major junction, turn left on Forest Service Road 40N27C, and stop. Park along the edge of the road before the ford on the North Fork Sacramento. (The water here is sometimes deeper than it looks; don't be tempted to drive it.) The Sisson-Callahan Road starts on the other side of the ford, on an old logging skid road that goes to the right. Within half a mile it turns into the Sisson-Callahan Trail.

Maps: For a map of Shasta-Trinity National Forest, send $4 to USDA-Forest Service, 630 Sansome Street, San Francisco, CA 94111. To obtain topographic maps of the area, ask for City of Mount Shasta and Mount Eddy from the USGS.

Contact: Shasta-Trinity National Forest, Mount Shasta Ranger District, 204 West Alma, Mount Shasta, CA 96067; (916) 926-4511 or fax (916) 926-5120.

Trail notes: The Sisson-Callahan Trail is something of a legend in the Mount Shasta area, long ago being a well-known, well-traveled route up to Mount Eddy and Deadfall Lakes. But with a much easier route now available from the Deadfall Lakes Trailhead, this trail is often passed over. Why? The route is long, steep, and hot, climbing 5,000 feet to the top of Mount Eddy at 9,025 feet, then nine miles to Deadfall Lakes for the nearest first-class campground. In addition, the great scenic beauty doesn't start until you've climbed several thousand feet, and by then, you'll care more about how much water is left in your canteen than about the incredible sweeping view of Mount Shasta to the east. Alas, even worse are the killer switchbacks you'll have to traverse to reach the Eddy ridge. All in all, this is a genuine booger-country, butt-kicker of a trail.

⓯ Gumboot Lake Trailhead

1.5 mi/1.5 hrs

Location: In Shasta-Trinity National Forest west of Mount Shasta; map B2, grid b3.

User groups: Hikers only. No dogs, horses, or mountain bikes. No wheelchair facilities.

Permits: No permits are required.

Directions: From Mount Shasta City on Interstate 5, take the Central Mount Shasta exit and drive west on Lake Street/Hatchery Road to the intersection with Old Stage Road. Turn left on Old Stage Road and go half a mile. Make a right turn on W.A. Barr Road, driving past Box Canyon Dam and the Lake Siskiyou Campground entrance. W.A. Barr Road becomes Forest Service Road 26 (South Fork Road). Continue on Forest Service Road 26, turn left on Forest Service Road 40N37 (Gumboot Lake Road), and drive to the parking area at Gumboot Lake.

Maps: For a map of Shasta-Trinity National Forest, send $4 to USDA-Forest Service, 630 Sansome Street, San Francisco, CA 94111. To obtain a topographic map of the area, ask for Mumbo Basin from the USGS.

Contact: Shasta-Trinity National Forest, Mount Shasta Ranger District, 204 West Alma, Mount Shasta, CA 96067; (916) 926-4511 or fax (916) 926-5120.

Trail notes: If you must always have a trail to hike on, well, this trip is not for you. But if you don't mind a little cross-country scramble to a mountain rim, then a short cutoff to a peak for spectacular views of Gumboot Lake and beyond of Mount Shasta, then sign up for this hike. Starting at an elevation of 6,050 feet at Gumboot Lake, a pretty lake with good trout fishing, you circle the lake on the right side, where there's a good trail. At the back of the lake, break off the trail to the right and start climbing the slope, heading up towards the ridge that circles the

back of the lake. A little less than halfway to the top, you'll pass Little Gumboot Lake, then scramble your way to the ridge, where you'll intersect with the Pacific Crest Trail. Head to the left for a short distance, then again break off the trail, this time to the left, heading on the mountain spine toward the peak that towers over Gumboot Lake, with Mount Shasta the backdrop off to the east. This peak is your destination. The world may not be perfect, but from this lookout, it comes close.

⓰ Heart Lake Trail

3.0 mi/2.25 hrs

Location: At Castle Lake in Shasta-Trinity National Forest west of Mount Shasta; map B2, grid b4.

User groups: Hikers and dogs. Not suitable for horses or mountain bikes. No wheelchair facilities.

Permits: A wilderness permit is required to enter the Castle Crags Wilderness.

Directions: From Interstate 5 at Mount Shasta City, take the Central Mount Shasta exit and drive west on Lake Street/Hatchery Road to the intersection with Old Stage Road. Turn left on Old Stage Road and go half a mile, then turn right on W.A. Barr Road. Drive past Box Canyon Dam and turn left on Castle Lake Road. Contine on this road to the parking area at Castle Lake.

Maps: For a map of Shasta-Trinity National Forest, send $4 to USDA-Forest Service, 630 Sansome Street, San Francisco, CA 94111. A map of Castle Crags Wilderness can also be purchased for $7. To obtain a topographic map of the area, ask for City of Mount Shasta from the USGS.

Contact: Shasta-Trinity National Forest, Mount Shasta Ranger District, 204 West Alma, Mount Shasta, CA 96067; (916) 926-4511 or fax (916) 926-5120.

Trail notes: The tale of Castle Lake, set at an elevation of 5,450 feet, is that the water is like none other in the world, which has lead some people to jump into the lake for complete renewal. In reality, the water is so pure, containing few nutrients of any kind, that UC-Davis has a water sampling station here in an ongoing comparison study with Lake Tahoe.

The trailhead is on the left side of the lake, just across the outlet stream. From there, the trail rises up along the slope just left of the lake. Below is Castle Lake, a pretty sight set in a rock bowl with a high back wall. The trail rises up to a saddle at 5,900 feet. At the saddle, bear uphill to the right on the faint trail. It's an easy scramble, rising up over a lip at 6,050 feet, where little Heart Lake is secreted away. Because the lake is small, the water warms up by midsummer, making it great for swimming. In addition, if you scramble up the back wall of the little lake, you'll get a breathtaking view of Mount Shasta. Also note that the best drive-to spot anywhere for photographs of Mount Shasta is on Castle Lake Road at a turnout about half a mile downhill from the Castle Lake parking area.

Trail notes: This is sacred country for field-scout John Reginato, who at 78 knows the outback of Northern California better than any soul who has ever lived. It's Tamarack Lake that is his favorite spot, set high in the Trinity Divide at 5,900 feet. John plans on having his ashes scattered here. It's easy to see why—Tamarack is a beautiful alpine lake and a place of remarkable serenity. If you can pull yourself away from it, there's a rugged, cross-country route to the north that approaches the summit of Grey Rocks, a series of dark, craggy peaks. The route is steep and difficult, but the view of Castle Crags, Mount Shasta, the ridges of the Trinity Divide, and the Sacramento River Canyon will have you thanking a higher power for the privilege of breathing the air here.

⑰ Tamarack Lake Trailhead

5.0 mi/4.0 hrs

Location: In Shasta-Trinity National Forest southwest of Mount Shasta; map B2, grid c3.

User groups: Hikers and dogs. Not suitable for horses or mountain bikes. No wheelchair facilities.

Permits: No permits are required.

Directions: From Interstate 5 south of Dunsmuir, take the Castella/Castle Crags State Park exit and drive west on Castle Creek Road through the park for about 2.5 miles. Castle Creek Road will become Forest Service Road 25 (Whalen Road). Continue about 12.5 miles on Forest Service Road 25. Turn left on Forest Service Road 38N17 (Tamarack Road) and go about six miles to the trailhead. This road is extremely rough, with the last mile passable only to four-wheel-drive vehicles with large tires and high clearance. A primitive parking area is available on the right side for other vehicles to park prior to this bad section of road.

Maps: For a map of Shasta-Trinity National Forest, send $4 to USDA-Forest Service, 630 Sansome Street, San Francisco, CA 94111. To obtain a topographic map of the area, ask for Chicken Hawk Hill from the USGS.

Contact: Shasta-Trinity National Forest, Mount Shasta Ranger District, 204 West Alma, Mount Shasta, CA 96067; (916) 926-4511 or fax (916) 926-5120.

⑱ Root Creek Trail

2.5 mi/1.75 hrs

Location: In Castle Crags State Park south of Mount Shasta; map B2, grid c4.

User groups: Hikers only. No dogs, horses, or mountain bikes. No wheelchair facilities.

Permits: No permits are required. A $5 state park entrance fee is charged for each vehicle.

Directions: From Interstate 5 south of Mount Shasta, take the Castle Crags State Park exit. Turn west and follow the signs to the park entrance on the right. Just past the kiosk, bear right and follow the road to its end at the parking area for Vista Point.

Maps: A trail map can be obtained for a fee by contacting Castle Crags State Park at the address below. To obtain a topographic map of the area, ask for Dunsmuir from the USGS.

Contact: Castle Crags State Park, P.O. Box 80, Castella, CA 96017; (916) 235-2684 or fax (916) 235-2684.

Trail notes: Castle Crags State Park features a series of huge, ancient granite spires that tower over the Sacramento River Canyon, the kind of sight that can take your breath away the first time you see it from Interstate 5. That sight inspires a lot of people to take one of the hikes at the park, and while most don't have the time, energy, or body conditioning to complete the Crags Trail, the Root Creek Trail is a good second choice.

From the parking area, walk back down the road about 40 yards to reach the signed trailhead at 2,500 feet. Take the Kettlebelly Trail for a quarter of a mile, then turn right on Root Creek Trail. From here the trail is routed through a thick, cool forest, an easy walk that most visitors overlook. It continues to Root Creek, a pretty, babbling stream. Note that the park brochure mistakenly rates this hike as moderately strenuous (it's nearly flat), and the park map shows the trail breaking out above tree line (it doesn't).

⑲ Crags Trail

6.1 mi/4.0 hrs

Location: In Castle Crags State Park south of Mount Shasta; map B2, grid c4.

User groups: Hikers only. No dogs, horses, or mountain bikes. No wheelchair facilities.

Permits: No permits are required. A $5 state park entrance fee is charged for each vehicle.

Directions: From Interstate 5 south of Mount Shasta, take the Castle Crags State Park exit. Turn west and follow the signs to the park entrance. Just past the kiosk, bear right and follow the road to the parking area adjacent to Vista Point.

Maps: A trail map can be obtained for a fee by contacting Castle Crags State Park at the address below. To obtain a topographic map of the area, ask for Dunsmuir from the USGS.

Contact: Castle Crags State Park, P.O. Box 80, Castella, CA 96017; (916) 235-2684, (916) 538-2200, or fax (916) 235-2684.

Trail notes: From Vista Point in Castle Crags State Park, you can gaze up at the wondrous crags and spot Castle Dome, at 4,966 feet, the leading spire on the crags ridge. This is a high, rounded, missile-shaped piece of rock, and yes, this is your destination on the Crags Trail. If you're out of shape, this climb is a butt-kicker, gaining elevation all the way.

The well-signed trailhead is located about 40 yards down the road from the parking area at an elevation of 2,500 feet. Start by taking the Kettlebelly/Crags Trail for a quarter of a mile, then when you reach a three-trail junction, take off on the Crags Trail. Here the trail rises through a thick forest, climbing steeply at times before eventually turning to the right, emerging from the forest, and winding through the lower Crags. Once above tree line, the views get better with each rising step. In spring, snow and ice fields are common up this high. An excellent picnic spot is at Indian Springs at 3,600 feet, and many hikers get no further than this point. But the trail goes onward, always climbing, then getting quite steep before finally reaching a saddle at the foot of Castle Dome, where a few trees have somehow gained toeholds. When you set foot on this divine perch, gazing north at Mount Shasta, it will be a moment you'll prize forever.

⑳ McCloud Nature Trail

4.5 mi/2.5 hrs

Location: At Ah-Di-Na Campground on the McCloud River south of McCloud; map B2, grid c6.

User groups: Hikers only. No dogs, horses, or mountain bikes. No wheelchair facilities.

Permits: No permits are required.

Directions: From Interstate 5 south of Mount Shasta City, take the McCloud-Reno exit and turn east on Highway 89. Drive 12 miles to McCloud, turn right on Squaw Valley Road, and go about five miles south. (Squaw Valley Road becomes Forest Service Road 11/Hawkins Creek Road). Continue on Forest Service Road 11, past the McCloud boat ramp and going right to the sharp curve at the end of Battle Creek Cove. Turn right on Forest Service Road 38N53 (Ah-Di-Na Road) and drive about seven miles, past Ah-Di-Na Campground to the road's end at Wheelbarrow Creek. The Nature Conservancy boundary is half a mile down the trail.

Maps: For a map of Shasta-Trinity National Forest, send $4 to USDA-Forest Service, 630 Sansome Street, San Francisco, CA 94111. To obtain a topographic map of the area, ask for Lake McCloud from the USGS.

Contact: Shasta-Trinity National Forest, McCloud Ranger District, P.O. Box 1620, McCloud, CA 96057; (916) 964-2184 or fax (916) 964-2938.

Trail notes: Have you ever yearned for a place where old trees are left standing, deer and bobcat roam without fear, and where a crystal-perfect river flows free in an untouched canyon? The McCloud River Preserve is such a place, and because it's managed by The Nature Conservancy, it will always remain that way. While the lower McCloud River is best known for its flyfishing for trout, there's an excellent hiking trail that runs alongside the river, spanning more than two miles from the parking area on downstream. It's an easy yet beautiful walk among woods and water, requiring a bit of boulder hopping in a few spots. It's well worth it to hike out to the end, where the river plunges into a series of deep holes and gorges.

Though the McCloud is a well-known blue-ribbon trout stream, the trout can be a lot more difficult to catch than you might have heard. The best technique is to use weighted nymphs with a strike indicator, and being equipped with chest waders and a wading staff for the very slippery river bottom. Please remember that removing anything from this preserve, even a leaf or a stone, is not permitted.

㉑ Lower McCloud Falls

0.25 mi/0.5 hr

Location: In Shasta-Trinity National Forest east of McCloud; map B2, grid c7.

User groups: Hikers, wheelchairs, and dogs. Not suitable for horses or mountain bikes.

Permits: No permits are required.

Directions: From Interstate 5 south of Mount Shasta City, take the McCloud-Reno exit and turn east on Highway 89. Drive 12 miles to McCloud, then another five miles east on Highway 89. At the sign for Fowler's Camp, turn right on Forest Service Road 39N28 and follow the signs to Lower Falls.

Maps: For a map of Shasta-Trinity National Forest, send $4 to USDA-Forest Service, 630 Sansome Street, San Francisco, CA 94111. To obtain a topographic map of the area, ask for Lake McCloud from the USGS.

Contact: Shasta-Trinity National Forest, McCloud Ranger District, P.O. Box 1620, McCloud, CA 96057; (916) 964-2184 or fax (916) 964-2938.

Trail notes: The Lower McCloud Falls may not be the most majestic waterfall in California, but there may be none better for swimming. On hot summer days, youngsters jump off the granite rim, then fly through the air for about 15 feet

and land in the waterfall's pool like cannon balls. You can drive right to the Lower Falls. After parking, there are two routes upstream. The better of the two is to rock hop your way right along the river for 10 or 15 minutes, then pick a nice little spot to sit and watch the water go by. The more common trail is the paved walkway that is routed from Lower Falls to Fowler's Camp. Lower Falls is a chute-like waterfall, in which a chute of water pours into a large pool, surrounded by a granite rim. A ladder is available for swimmers and jumpers.

㉒ Middle Falls Trail

0.5 mi/0.5 hr

Location: At Fowler's Camp in Shasta-Trinity National Forest east of McCloud; map B2, grid c8.

User groups: Hikers and dogs. No horses or mountain bikes. No wheelchair facilities.

Permits: No permits are required.

Directions: From Interstate 5 south of Mount Shasta City, take the McCloud-Reno exit and turn east on Highway 89. Drive 12 miles to McCloud, then another five miles east on Highway 89. At the sign for Fowler's Camp, turn right on Forest Service Road 39N28 and head to the campground entrance. At the entrance station, park on the loop to the left and walk into the campground, taking the road to the left. The trail begins directly across from the rest rooms.

Maps: For a map of Shasta-Trinity National Forest, send $4 to USDA-Forest Service, 630 Sansome Street, San Francisco, CA 94111. To obtain a topographic map of the area, ask for McCloud from the USGS.

Contact: Shasta-Trinity National Forest, McCloud Ranger District, P.O. Box 1620, McCloud, CA 96057; (916) 964-2184 or fax (916) 964-2938.

Trail notes: One of the prettiest waterfalls in Northern California, the Middle Falls of the McCloud River is a wide and tall cascade of water that pours over a 75-foot cliff and then falls into a deep pool in a rock bowl. The easy hike is a 10- to 15-minute walk on a trail that skirts the left side of the McCloud River. You'll round a bend, probably hear the waterfall before you see it, and then suddenly, there it is, this wide sheet of falling water. It's something like a miniature

Niagara Falls. On summer weekends, teenagers climb to the rim above the falls, then plunge 100 feet into the pool like human missiles. It's a dangerous venture that we don't recommend. Because of the remarkable beauty of this waterfall, it has become extremely popular in the summer. Plans are in the works to make the trail wheelchair accessible. The one frustrating element is that some visitors litter at this pristine spot, or worse, discard their cigarette butts on the trail. We'd like to demonstrate the collective evil of small offenses by strapping the offenders into a chair, then grabbing their upper lips with a pair of pliers and stretching their lips right over the backs of their heads.

㉓ Grizzly Peak

0.25 mi/0.25 hr

Location: In Shasta-Trinity National Forest southeast of Mount Shasta; map B2, grid c7.

User groups: Hikers and dogs. Horses and mountain bikes are not advised. No wheelchair facilities.

Permits: No permits are required.

Directions: From Interstate 5 south of Mount Shasta City, take the McCloud-Reno exit and turn east on Highway 89. Drive 12 miles to McCloud, turn right on Squaw Valley Road, and drive about five miles. (Squaw Valley Road becomes Forest Service Road 11/Hawkins Creek Road.) Continue on Forest Service Road 11, keeping right past the McCloud boat ramp. About one mile past the Deer Creek Bridge, turn left at the signed intersection on Forest Service Road 39N06 (Stouts Meadow Road) and go 5.8 miles to Grizzly Peak. The road is long, bumpy, and steep in places, and four-wheel-drive vehicles with good clearance are recommended.

Maps: For a map of Shasta-Trinity National Forest, send $4 to USDA-Forest Service, 630 Sansome Street, San Francisco, CA 94111. To obtain a topographic map of the area, ask for Grizzly Peak from the USGS.

Contact: Shasta-Trinity National Forest, McCloud Ranger District, P.O. Box 1620, McCloud, CA 96057; (916) 964-2184 or fax (916) 964-2938.

Trail notes: At 6,252 feet, Grizzly Peak provides a sweeping view to the west of the McCloud Flats—a sea of conifers—and beyond to the eastern facing slopes of Mount Shasta at 14,162 feet. To get here requires a long, dusty, bumpy, and circuitous drive past Brushy Butte and Mica Gulch. Once at Grizzly Peak, you'll find a forest fire lookout station, which is a perfect spot to scan hundreds of thousands of acres of forest. The short walk is about a 15-minute traipse to the peak, the trail routed through low-lying brush. Lightning rods are set up here, and if you look below to the east, you'll spot a little-used segment of the Pacific Crest Trail. On our visit, Tom was just one step from the peak when he heard a strange buzzing sound, looked down, and saw that he was about to plant his size-13 boot right atop a five-foot rattlesnake. He somehow managed to hold up just in time, as if paralyzed. A moment later, while he was explaining the importance of staying calm in rattlesnake country, a small lizard scurried across the trail, and Tom nearly levitated from shock, as if he'd been poked with a cattle prod. Calm? Yeah, sure.

㉔ Waters Gulch Overlook

3.0 mi/1.5 hrs

Location: At Packers Bay on Shasta Lake north of Redding; map B2, grid f3.

User groups: Hikers and dogs. Not suitable for horses or mountain bikes. No wheelchair facilities.

Permits: No permits are required.

Directions: From Interstate 5 at Redding, drive north to Shasta Lake and take the Packers Bay exit. Drive southwest on Packers Bay Road to the trailhead, located a quarter of a mile before the boat ramp.

Maps: A detailed trail map can be obtained by contacting Earthwalk Press, 2239 Union Street, Eureka, CA 95501; (800) 828-MAPS. For a map of Shasta-Trinity National Forest, send $4 to USDA-Forest Service, 630 Sansome Street, San Francisco, CA 94111. To obtain a topographic map of the area, ask for O'Brien from the USGS.

Contact: Shasta-Trinity National Forest, Shasta Lake Ranger District, 14221 Holiday Road, Mountain Gate, CA 96003; (916) 275-1587 or fax (916) 275-1512.

Trail notes: Shasta Lake is so big—the biggest reservoir in California—that it can be difficult to know where to start in your mission to explore it. A good answer is right here on the Waters Gulch Loop. It connects to the Overlook Trail, an eight-tenths-of-a-mile cutoff that climbs atop a small mountain and furnishes a view of the main lake. The trailhead is at Packers Bay, easily accessible off Interstate 5. The trail heads west across a peninsula, then turns right at Waters Gulch, a cove on the main Sacramento River arm of the lake. While there are many drive-to areas where you can get lake views, here you can get a little seclusion as well.

㉕ Bailey Cove Loop Trail

2.8 mi/1.5 hrs

Location: On the McCloud arm of Shasta Lake north of Redding; map B2, grid f3.

User groups: Hikers, dogs, and mountain bikes. No horses. No wheelchair facilities.

Permits: No permits are required.

Directions: From Interstate 5 north of Redding, take the Shasta Caverns exit and follow the signs to Bailey Cove Boat Ramp and Picnic Area.

Maps: A detailed trail map can be obtained by contacting Earthwalk Press, 2239 Union Street, Eureka, CA 95501; (800) 828-MAPS. For a map of Shasta-Trinity National Forest, send $4 to USDA-Forest Service, 630 Sansome Street, San Francisco, CA 94111. To obtain a topographic map of the area, ask for O'Brien from the USGS.

Contact: Shasta-Trinity National Forest, Shasta Lake Ranger District, 14221 Holiday Road, Mountain Gate, CA 96003; (916) 275-1587 or fax (916) 275-1512.

Trail notes: Our favorite part of Shasta Lake is the McCloud arm, where the mountain canyon features limestone formations and the lake's clear emerald waters. This trail provides a great view of these phenomena, as well as a close-to-the-water loop hike on one of the lake's featured peninsulas. From the trailhead, start by hiking on the left fork, which takes you out along Bailey Cove. As you continue, the loop trail heads in a clockwise direction, first along the McCloud arm of the lake, then back to the parking area along John's Creek Inlet. When you reach the mouth of Bailey Cove, stop and enjoy the view. Directly

across the lake are the limestone formations, featuring North Gray Rocks at 3,114 feet, and topped by Horse Mountain at 4,025 feet. The famous Shasta Caverns are located just below North Gray Rocks.

㉖ Hirz Bay Trail

3.2 mi/1.75 hrs

Location: On the McCloud arm of Shasta Lake north of Redding; map B2, grid f4.

User groups: Hikers, dogs, and mountain bikes. No horses. No wheelchair facilities.

Permits: No permits are required.

Directions: From Interstate 5 north of Redding, take the Gilman Road exit and drive east on Gilman Road to Hirz Bay Campground.

Maps: A detailed trail map can be obtained by contacting Earthwalk Press, 2239 Union Street, Eureka, CA 95501; (800) 828-MAPS. For a map of Shasta-Trinity National Forest, send $4 to USDA-Forest Service, 630 Sansome Street, San Francisco, CA 94111. To obtain a topographic map of the area, ask for O'Brien from the USGS.

Contact: Shasta-Trinity National Forest, Shasta Lake Ranger District, 14221 Holiday Road, Mountain Gate, CA 96003; (916) 275-1587 or fax (916) 275-1512.

Trail notes: Most people discover this trail by accident, usually while camping either at Hirz Bay Group Camp or the tiny two-site Dekkas Rock Camp. That is because this trail links those two campsites, routed along the west side of the beautiful McCloud arm of Shasta Lake. The trail traces the shoreline of the lake, in and out along small coves and creek inlets. Straight across the lake are pretty views of the deep coves at Campbell Creek and Dekkas Creek, unique limestone outcrops, and Minnesota Mountain at 4,293 feet.

㉗ Greens Creek
Boat-In Trail

1.0-12.0 mi/0.5-7.0 hrs

Location: On the McCloud arm of Shasta Lake north of Redding; map B2, grid f4.

User groups: Hikers and dogs. No horses or mountain bikes. No wheelchair facilities.

Permits: No permits are required.

Directions: This trail can be accessed only by boat. Boat ramps are located to the north at Hirz Bay Campground (see the directions in the previous hike for the Hirz Bay Trail) or to the south at Lakeview Marina Resort (off Shasta Caverns Road). The trailhead is at Greens Creek Boat-In Camp on the east side of the McCloud River arm.

Maps: A detailed trail map can be obtained by contacting Earthwalk Press, 2239 Union Street, Eureka, CA 95501; (800) 828-MAPS. For a map of Shasta-Trinity National Forest, send $4 to USDA-Forest Service, 630 Sansome Street, San Francisco, CA 94111. To obtain a topographic map of the area, ask for O'Brien from the USGS.

Contact: Shasta-Trinity National Forest, Shasta Lake Ranger District, 14221 Holiday Road, Mountain Gate, CA 96003; (916) 275-1587 or fax (916) 275-1512.

Trail notes: Let's get a few things straight from the start: 1) Almost no one hikes this entire trail; 2) Almost no one hikes part of this trail; and 3) Almost no one even knows about this trail. Why? Because even with two million people estimated to visit Shasta Lake every year, the only way to access this trail is from an obscure boat-in campsite at Greens Creek on the east side of the McCloud arm of the lake. At the back of the cove at Greens Creek, you'll find a small Forest Service billboard, posted with recreation guide sheets, and behind it is the campground and trailhead. The trip is easily shortened, and usually is, because there are many fascinating side trips on the steep climb up toward a saddle between Town Mountain at 4,325 feet and Horse Mountain at 4,025 feet. The trail enters an oak/madrone forest that is interspersed with limestone formations. The latter are worth exploring, and if you spend enough time hiking and investigating, you may find some small caves, a highlight of the trip. Most people are inspired to hike just high enough to get a good clear view of the lake below, but not much farther.

㉘ Davis Gulch Trail

6.0 mi/3.5 hrs

Location: At Whiskeytown Lake National Recreation Area west of Redding; map B2, grid h0.

User groups: Hikers, dogs, and horses. No mountain bikes. No wheelchair facilities.

Permits: A free permit is required for hikers planning to camp in the backcountry. Parking and access are free.

Directions: From Interstate 5 at Redding, turn west on Highway 299 and drive seven miles. At the Whiskeytown Visitors Center, turn left on J.F. Kennedy Memorial Drive and follow the signs to Brandy Creek Picnic Area.

Maps: For a detailed trail map, contact Whiskeytown National Recreation Area at the address below. To obtain a topographic map of the area, ask for Igo from the USGS.

Contact: Whiskeytown National Recreation Area, P.O. Box 188, Whiskeytown, CA 96095; (916) 241-6584 or fax (916) 246-1225.

Trail notes: The Davis Gulch Trail is Whiskeytown Lake's best hike, an easy, meandering route along the southwest end of the lake. It starts out of the Brandy Creek Picnic Area at 1,300 feet and climbs up to 1,650 feet, making for a moderate climb on a wide, flat footpath. Most of the trees are oaks or madrones, and as you go, there are many good views of Whiskeytown Lake. The trail spans three miles and dead-ends at an information billboard along an access road. That means with two vehicles, it's possible to turn this into a one-way hike, and better yet, hike the whole route downhill—ending at the Brandy Creek Picnic Area instead of starting there.

Pacific Crest Trail (PCT) Section Overview

90.0 mi. one way/8-9 days

Trail sections extend from Ash Camp at the McCloud River south of McCloud Reservoir to Highway 3 at Scott Mountain.

This section of the Pacific Crest Trail traverses some of the most diverse and dynamic country in Northern California. It includes the lush and vibrant McCloud River and Sacramento River, where the trail drops as low as 2,000 feet, and it climbs to the Trinity Divide Ridge and its dozens of small, untouched lakes. A short side trip is available to the top of Mount Eddy, at an elevation of 9,025 feet. The trail also runs right beneath the series of sculpted granite spires of Castle Crags, a setting that can astonish newcomers. Following is more specific information on major trail sections in this zone.

PCT-41 Ash Camp to Castle Crags Wilderness

30.0 mi. one way/2.0 days

Location: From Ash Camp on the McCloud River west into Castle Crags State Park; map B2, grid c7.

User groups: Hikers, dogs, and horses. No mountain bikes. No wheelchair facilities.

Permits: Wilderness permits are required only in Castle Crags Wilderness.

Directions: From Interstate 5 south of Mount Shasta, take the McCloud-Reno exit and turn east on Highway 89. Drive 12 miles to McCloud, then turn right on Squaw Valley Road and go about 14 miles, past McCloud Reservoir, to the trailhead at Ash Camp.

Maps: To obtain topographic maps of the area, ask for Shoeinhorse Mountain, Yellowjacket Mountain, and Dunsmuir from the USGS.

Contact: Shasta-Trinity National Forest, McCloud Ranger District, P.O. Box 1620, McCloud, CA 96057; (916) 964-2184 or fax (916) 964-2938.

Trail notes: Of the hundreds of rivers along the Pacific Crest Trail, it's the McCloud River that often seems most vibrant with life. This segment of the PCT starts right alongside the McCloud River at Ash Camp, set at about 3,000 feet. The trail is then routed downstream along the McCloud for 2.5 miles, one of the most prized sections of trail in this region. At Ah-Di-Na Camp, the trail starts to rise, eventually turning up Squaw Valley Creek and climbing beyond to top Girard Ridge at 4,500 feet. When you top the ridge, Mount Shasta, Black Butte, and Castle Crags suddenly pop into view. After traversing the ridge for a few miles, the trail suddenly drops and cascades down to the Sacramento River Canyon. Your toes will be jamming into your boots as you head downhill. At the river, you might stop to soak your feet before picking up and heading west into Castle Crags State Park.

PCT-42 Castle Crags to Mumbo Basin

25.0 mi. one way/2.0 days

Location: From Castle Crags State Park west into Shasta-Trinity National Forest; map B2, grid c5.

User groups: Hikers and horses. No dogs are allowed on trails in Castle Crags State Park. No mountain bikes. No wheelchair facilities.

Permits: A permit is required to enter the Castle Crags Wilderness. A $5 parking fee is charged. There is no fee if you park outside and walk in.

Directions: From Interstate 5 south of Mount Shasta, take the Castle Crags State Park exit and drive west to the park entrance. Just past the kiosk is a special parking area for PCT hikers.

Maps: To obtain topographic maps of the area, ask for Dunsmuir, Seven Lakes Basin, and Mumbo Basin from the USGS.

Contact: Castle Crags State Park, P.O. Box 80, Castella, CA 96017; (916) 235-2684 or fax (916) 235-2684.

Trail notes: This is a key juncture for the PCT, where the trail climbs out of a river canyon and back to high ridgelines. It's in a classic region, the Trinity Divide, known for sculpted lakes in granite and sweeping views of Mount Shasta. From the Sacramento River at Castle Crags, at an elevation of 2,000 feet, the trail laterals up the north side of Castle Creek Canyon, rising just below the base of the awesome Crags, then finally hitting the rim at the back side of Castle Ridge. It follows the rim in a half-circle to the west, to the Seven Lakes Basin and beyond to the Mumbo Basin and the Gumboot Lake Trailhead. The final five miles of this segment pass by a dozen pristine mountain lakes. The biggest is Echo Lake at 5,900 feet, set just below Boulder Peak, and the highest is Helen Lake at 6,700 feet, requiring a half-mile side trip.

PCT-43 Mumbo Basin to Scott Mountain

35.0 mi. one way/4.0 days

Location: In Shasta-Trinity National Forest, from Gumboot Trailhead to Scott Mountain; map B2, grid b3.

User groups: Hikers, dogs, and horses. No mountain bikes. No wheelchair facilities.

Permits: No permits are required.

Directions: From Mount Shasta City on Interstate 5, take the Central Mount Shasta exit and drive to the stop sign. Turn left, cross the highway, and go to another stop sign at W. A. Barr Road. Turn west and drive a total of 18.5 miles on W.A. Barr Road (Forest Service Road 26) to the Gumboot Saddle/PCT parking area. The parking area is about 2.5 miles past the Gumboot Lake turnoff.

Maps: To obtain topographic maps of the area, ask for Mumbo Basin, South China Mountain, and Scott Mountain from the USGS.

Contact: Shasta-Trinity National Forest, McCloud Ranger District, P.O. Box 1620, McCloud, CA 96057; (916) 964-2184 or fax (916) 964-2938.

Trail notes: The PCT starts at a popular trailhead but quickly jumps northward into remote, beautiful country. The first highlight, only a mile up the trail, is the view below to the left of secluded Picayune Lake. The trail heads on, passing little Porcupine Lake, an idyllic setting which requires a quarter-mile side trip, and then over the rim and down to Deadfall Lakes, an excellent camping spot. From the ridge, an irresistible side trip is the one-mile trek to the top of Mount Eddy, 9,025 feet, with its incomparable view of Mount Shasta. From Deadfall Lakes, the trail continues down, rounds the headwaters of the Trinity River, then climbs back up Chilcoot Pass and Bull Lake. From here, it's a 10-mile pull to the Scott Mountain Summit Trailhead.

PCT Continuation: To continue hiking along the Pacific Crest Trail, see chapter B1.

Leave No Trace Tips

Properly Dispose of What You Can't Pack Out

If no refuse facility is available, deposit human waste in catholes dug six to eight inches deep at least 200 feet from water, camps, or trails. Cover and disguise the catholes when you're finished.

To wash yourself or your dishes, carry the water 200 feet from streams or lakes and use small amounts of biodegradable soap. Scatter the strained dishwater.

Map B3

Adjoining Maps: East: B4 .... *page* 100   West: B2 66
North: A3 36   South: C3 130

Northern California Map .... *page* 2

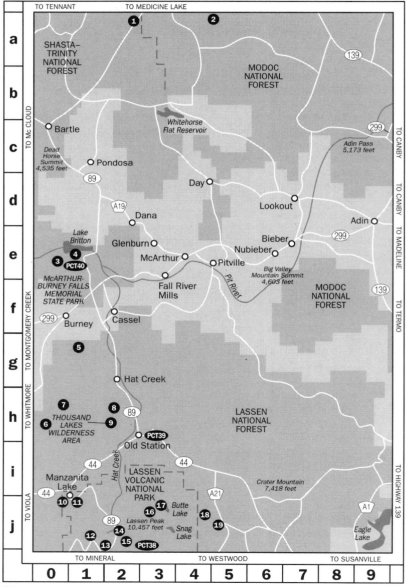

Chapter B3 features:

❶ Ice Caves Trail

0.25 mi/0.5 hr

Location: In Modoc National Forest south of Medicine Lake; map B3, grid a2.

User groups: Hikers and dogs. The terrain is not suitable for mountain bikes or horses. No wheelchair facilities.

Permits: No permits are required. Parking and access are free.

Directions: From Redding, drive north on Interstate 5 about 56 miles. Take the McCloud-Reno exit and go 29 miles east on Highway 89 through Bartle. Just past Bartle, turn northeast on Powder Hill Road (Forest Service Road 49) and drive about 21 miles to the ice caves, which are just off the road on the west side.

Maps: For a map of Modoc National Forest, send $4 to USDA-Forest Service, 630 Sansome Street, San Francisco, CA 94111. To obtain a topographic map of the area, ask for Medicine Lake from the USGS.

Contact: Modoc National Forest, Doublehead Ranger District, P.O. Box 818, Tulelake, CA 96134; (916) 667-2246 or fax (916) 667-4808.

Trail notes: If you're curious about the volcanic formations of the Medicine Lake area, but don't necessarily want to sign up for an expedition to explore them, the Ice Caves Trail is the perfect hike for you. The caves are located just off the road, requiring only a short walk to reach them. What you'll find here is a series of strange-looking caves, mostly shallow gouges in the volcanic rocks except for one that is deep and wide, a hollowed out grotto in a lava flow. Call it our imagination, but on our visit here we sensed the presence of old spirits, perhaps the ghosts of the Modoc Indians that used this area. Perhaps not. Regardless, it felt strange and uncomfortable and we left quickly.

❷ Burnt Lava Flow

2.5 mi/1.5 hrs

Location: In Modoc National Forest south of Medicine Lake; map B3, grid a5.

User groups: Hikers and dogs. The terrain is not suitable for mountain bikes or horses. No wheelchair facilities.

Permits: No permits are required. Parking and access are free.

Directions: From Redding, turn north on Interstate 5 and drive 56 miles. Take the McCloud-Reno exit and go 29 miles east on Highway 89 through Bartle. Just past Bartle, turn northeast on Powder Hill Road (Forest Service Road 49) and drive about 24 miles. Turn east on Forest Service Road 42N25 and head to the Burnt Lava Flow Geologic Area.

Maps: For a map of Modoc National Forest, send $4 to USDA-Forest Service, 630 Sansome Street, San Francisco, CA 94111. To obtain a topographic map of the area, ask for Porcupine Butte from the USGS.

Contact: Modoc National Forest, Doublehead Ranger District, P.O. Box 818, Tulelake, CA 96134; (916) 667-2246 or fax (916) 667-4808.

Trail notes: When you walk across the Burnt Lava Flow, a land of "rocks that float and mountains of glass," it may seem like you're exploring some prehistoric area that resembles the moon. But get this: the lava formation is only about 200 years old, the youngest flow in the Medicine Lake Highlands. It's located south of Glass Mountain, and covers some 8,760 acres, with little "islands" of forests amid the bare, jet-black lava flow. When we took an aerial survey of the area, the Burnt Lava Flow was one of the most fascinating portions of the entire region. On foot, it's even stranger. There is no trail, so you just pick your direction, with most visitors going from tree island to tree island. There are a few weird spots where the ground can be like quicksand when dry and wet concrete when wet. Just walk around those spots, staying on the hard, black lava flow.

❸ Burney Falls Trail

1.0 mi/0.5 hr

Location: In McArthur-Burney Falls State Park north of Burney; map B3, grid e1.

User groups: Hikers only. No dogs, horses, or mountain bikes. There is paved wheelchair access at the falls overlook point at the beginning of the trail.

Permits: No permits are required. A $5 state park day-use fee is charged for each vehicle.

Directions: From Interstate 5 at Redding, turn east on Highway 299 and drive 50 miles to Burney. Drive five miles east on Highway 299, then turn north on Highway 89 and go 5.8 miles to the state park entrance. Park at the main lot and follow the signs to the trailhead.

Maps: A trail guide can be obtained by contacting the state park at the address below. To obtain a topographic map of the area, ask for Burney Falls from the USGS.

Contact: McArthur-Burney Falls State Park, 24898 Highway 89, Burney, CA 96013; (916) 335-2777, (916) 538-2200, or fax (916) 335-5483.

Trail notes: Visitors from across the West are attracted to this state park to see Burney Falls. It is spectacular, 129 feet high, wide, and cascading. The waterfall plunges over a cliff in two pieces, split at the rim by a small bluff where two trees have managed toeholds, although the river flows over the top of them during high water from the spring snowmelt. Underground lava tubes also transport water to the site, where it seems to ooze and drip right from the surrounding moss. From the park entrance station, it's about a 50-foot walk to a rocky overlook, a perfect place for photographs of the waterfall. This spot also marks the start of the Burney Falls Trail, an easy one-mile loop around the waterfall and back. It's a self-guided nature trail, but rather than having to carry a brochure with you along the trail, you can just read the small signs that explain the feature sites. A great little side trip is to hike upstream of the falls, cross Burney Creek on the small bridge, then hike back downstream to a breathtaking overlook of the falls.

❹ Rim Trail

3.0 mi/1.75 hrs

Location: At Lake Britton in McArthur-Burney Falls State Park north of Burney; map B3, grid e1.

User groups: Hikers only. No dogs, horses, or mountain bikes. No wheelchair facilities.

Permits: No permits are required. A $5 state park day-use fee is charged for each vehicle.

Directions: From Interstate 5 at Redding, turn east on Highway 299 and drive 50 miles to Burney. Go five miles east on Highway 299, then turn north on Highway 89 and head 5.8 miles to the state park entrance. The trailhead is just opposite campground number 12.

Maps: A trail guide can be obtained by contacting the state park at the address below. To obtain a topographic map of the area, ask for Burney Falls from the USGS.

Contact: McArthur-Burney Falls State Park, 24898 Highway 89, Burney, CA 96013; (916) 335-2777, (916) 538-2200, or fax (916) 335-5483.

Trail notes: The Rim Trail provides an ideal hike for campers at Burney Falls State Park. The trail starts at the campground, then is routed to the rim of Lake Britton, a distance of 1.5 miles. It's an easy walk and pretty, too, heading first through forest, then emerging with a good lookout of the lake. An easy side trip is down to the beach. The lake is set in a gorge, and the water seems to have special qualities, sometimes shimmering with effervescence. The fishing is good, too, especially for crappie, but with bass, bluegill, and trout plentiful as well.

❺ Burney Mountain Summit

0.25 mi/0.25 hr

Location: In Lassen National Forest south of Burney; map B3, grid g1.

User groups: Hikers, dogs, horses, and mountain bikes. No wheelchair facilities.

Permits: No permits are required. Parking and access are free.

Directions: From Interstate 5 at Redding, turn east on Highway 299 and drive 50 miles to Burney. Go five more miles east, then turn south on Highway 89 and drive 10.5 miles. Turn west on Forest Service Road 34N19 and go 10 miles, then turn right on Forest Service Road 34N23 and head seven miles to the mountain summit. In the winter, the summit access road is blocked with a locked gate, where you can park and then hike to the top.

Maps: For a map of Lassen National Forest, send $4 to USDA-Forest Service, 630 Sansome Street, San Francisco, CA 94111. To obtain topographic maps of the area, ask for Burney Mountain West and Burney Mountain East from the USGS.

Contact: Lassen National Forest, Hat Creek Ranger District, P.O. Box 220, Falls River Mills, CA 96028; (916) 336-5521 or fax (916) 336-5758.

Trail notes: The view is just so good from the top of Burney Mountain (elevation 7,863 feet) that we had to include this trip in the book. The "hike" consists of just moseying around the summit, gazing off in all directions. However, if you show up in the winter when the access road is gated, it's a four-mile hike up the road to the top of the mountain. Almost nobody makes that trip. Burney Mountain often gets lost in the shadow of its big brothers, Mount Lassen and Mount Shasta, but of the three, the view just might be best from Burney. That's because sighting Lassen or Shasta makes for impressive panoramas in both directions—a view that just can't be duplicated.

❻ Magee Trailhead

10.0 mi/2.0 days

Location: On the southwest boundary of the Thousand Lakes Wilderness north of Lassen Volcanic National Park; map B3, grid h0.

User groups: Hikers, dogs, and horses. No mountain bikes. No wheelchair facilities.

Permits: No permits are required. Parking and access are free.

Directions: From Interstate 5 at Redding, turn east on Highway 299 and drive 50 miles to Burney. Go east five more miles, then turn south on Highway 89 and drive 31 miles. Turn right on Forest Service Road 16 and go 9.5 miles, then turn right on Forest Service Road 32N48 and head to the parking area at the end of the road.

Maps: For a map of Lassen National Forest, send $4 to USDA-Forest Service, 630 Sansome Street, San Francisco, CA 94111. To obtain topographic maps of the area, ask for Thousand Lakes Valley and Jacks Backbone from the USGS.

Contact: Lassen National Forest, Hat Creek Ranger District, P.O. Box 220, Falls River Mills, CA 96028; (916) 336-5521 or fax (916) 336-5758.

Trail notes: The Thousand Lakes Wilderness is a tiny, overlooked wilderness, but it's excellent for short hikes, either for a day or a weekend. The hike to Magee Lake and back is a great weekender. From the trailhead at 6,120 feet, you head east for 2.5 miles, then turn north toward Magee Peak, climbing all the way. The trail skirts the eastern slope of that mountain, and a possibility here is bushwhacking a quarter of a mile off the trail to the summit at 8,550 feet. After reaching the top of Magee Peak, you'll descend for about two miles to Magee Lake. For overnighters, a mandatory side trip is to Everett Lake, which is located less than a quarter of a mile to the northeast.

❼ Cypress Trailhead

6.0 mi/3.75 hrs

Location: On the north boundary of the Thousand Lakes Wilderness north of Lassen Volcanic National Park; map B3, grid h0.

User groups: Hikers, dogs, and horses. No mountain bikes. No wheelchair facilities.

Permits: No permits are required. Parking and access are free.

Directions: From Interstate 5 at Redding, turn east on Highway 299 and drive 50 miles to Burney. Go east five more miles, then turn south on Highway 89 and drive 10.5 miles. Turn west on Forest Service Road 34N19 and go 8.5 miles, then turn south on Forest Service Road 34N60 and head 2.5 miles to the parking area.

Maps: For a map of Lassen National Forest, send $4 to USDA-Forest Service, 630 Sansome Street, San Francisco, CA 94111. To obtain topographic maps of the area, ask for Thousand Lakes Valley and Jacks Backbone from the USGS.

Contact: Lassen National Forest, Hat Creek Ranger District, P.O. Box 220, Falls River Mills, CA 96028; (916) 336-5521 or fax (916) 336-5758.

Trail notes: You like lakes? You came to the right place. The Cypress Trailhead at 5,400 feet is the number one starting point for the Thousand Lakes Wilderness, with many small lakes sprinkled about in a radius of just two miles. After taking off down the trail, you'll hike for three miles before coming to Eiler Lake, the largest lake in this region, set just below Eiler Butte. Since the hike is only six miles round-trip, some locals do it in a day. But a network of trails here connects to other lakes, so an option is to keep on going for an overnighter. From the south side of Eiler Lake, the trail loops deeper into the wilderness in a clockwise arc. In the process, it passes near several other lakes, including Box and Barrett Lakes. Both of these provide good fishing for small trout.

⑧ Tamarack Trailhead

6.0 mi/3.5 hrs

Location: On the east boundary of the Thousand Lakes Wilderness north of Lassen Volcanic National Park; map B3, grid h1.

User groups: Hikers, dogs, and horses. No mountain bikes. No wheelchair facilities.

Permits: No permits are required. Parking and access are free.

Directions: From Interstate 5 at Redding, turn east on Highway 299 and drive 50 miles to Burney. Go east five more miles, then turn south on Highway 89 and drive about 14 miles. Turn west on Forest Service Road 33N25 and go five miles, then turn right on Forest Service Road 33N23Y and head to the parking area at the end of the road.

Maps: For a map of Lassen National Forest, send $4 to USDA-Forest Service, 630 Sansome Street, San Francisco, CA 94111. To obtain topographic maps of the area, ask for Thousand Lakes Valley and Jacks Backbone from the USGS.

Contact: Lassen National Forest, Hat Creek Ranger District, P.O. Box 220, Falls River Mills, CA 96028; (916) 336-5521 or fax (916) 336-5758.

Trail notes: From the Tamarack Trailhead, your first destination is Eiler Lake, a three-mile hike. A variety of activities are available from here. Have a picnic, swim or fish, and then return, or if you have backpacking gear, head onward to several other wilderness lakes. The trailhead elevation is 5,200 feet, and from this point, the trail is routed into the northwestern interior of the Thousand Lakes Wilderness. After two miles you'll reach a fork in the trail; turn left (south) to reach Barrett Lake in just another mile of hiking. Note that there is a complex trail network in this area with many junctions, creating a situation in which backpackers can invent their own multi-day route. From Barrett Lake, other attractive destinations include Durbin Lake, half a mile to the south, and Everett and Magee Lakes, another 2.7 miles away.

⑨ Bunchgrass Trailhead

8.0 mi/2.0 days

Location: On the south boundary of the Thousand Lakes Wilderness north of Lassen Volcanic National Park, map B3, grid h1.

User groups: Hikers, dogs, and horses. No mountain bikes. No wheelchair facilities.

Permits: No permits are required. Parking and access are free.

Directions: From Interstate 5 at Redding, turn east on Highway 299 and drive 50 miles to Burney. Go east five more miles, then turn south on Highway 89 and drive 31 miles. Turn right on Forest Service Road 16 and go seven miles, then turn right on Forest Service Road 32N45 and drive two miles. Turn left on Forest Service Road 32N42Y and head to the parking area at the end of the road.

Maps: For a map of Lassen National Forest, send $4 to USDA-Forest Service, 630 Sansome Street, San Francisco, CA 94111. To obtain topographic maps of the area, ask for Thousand Lakes Valley and Jacks Backbone from the USGS.

Contact: Lassen National Forest, Hat Creek Ranger District, P.O. Box 220, Falls River Mills, CA 96028; (916) 336-5521.

Trail notes: This trailhead is obscure and difficult to reach, and because of that, few visitors choose it as a jump-off spot for their treks. The destination is Durbin Lake, a four-mile hike one way, making for an easy weekend backpack trip. The trailhead elevation is 5,680 feet, and from there it's a fair walk in, a little up and down, and if you're not in shape, you'll know it well before you reach the lake. You'll come to Hall Butte at 7,187 feet and then Durbin Lake. A side-trip option is to hike out on the trail for three miles, skirting the western side of Hall Butte, then bushwhacking off-trail for half a mile to reach the top.

⑩ Manzanita Lake Trail

1.5 mi/1.5 hr

Location: At the western entrance to Lassen Volcanic National Park on Highway 44; map B3, grid j1.

User groups: Hikers only. No dogs, horses, or mountain bikes. No wheelchair facilities.

Permits: A wilderness permit is required for hikers planning to camp in the backcountry. A national park day-use fee is charged for each vehicle.

Directions: From Interstate 5 at Redding, turn east on Highway 44 and drive 46 miles to the park entrance. The trailhead is at Manzanita Lake just past the visitors center.

Maps: Trail maps are available for $7.24 (including tax and mailing). To order a map, contact Loomis Museum, c/o Lassen Volcanic National Park at the address below. For a map of Lassen National Forest, send $4 to USDA-Forest Service, 630 Sansome Street, San Francisco, CA 94111. To obtain a topographic map of the area, ask for Manzanita Lake from the USGS.

Contact: Lassen Volcanic National Park, P.O. Box 100, Mineral, CA 96063-0100; (916) 595-4444 or fax (916) 595-3262.

Trail notes: There's no prettier lake in Lassen Park that you can reach by car than Manzanita Lake. That is why the campground here is considered such a perfect destination for many. It's the largest camp in the park, with 179 sites, and it's easy to reach, located just beyond the entrance station at the western boundary of the park. The trail simply traces around the shoreline of this pretty lake at a 5,950-foot elevation, and is easily accessible from either the parking area just beyond the entrance station or from the campground. A good side trip is across the road to Reflection Lake, a small and also very pretty lake, which adds about half a mile to the trip.

⑪ Nobles Emigrant Trail

2–10 mi/1 hr–1 day

Location: From the Manzanita Lake Trailhead in Lassen Volcanic National Park east of Red Bluff; map B3, grid j1.

User groups: Hikers only. No dogs, horses, or mountain bikes. No wheelchair facilities.

Permits: A wilderness permit is required for hikers planning to camp in the backcountry. A national park day-use fee is charged for each vehicle.

Directions: From Interstate 5 at Redding, turn east on Highway 44 and drive 46 miles to the park entrance. The trailhead is across the road from Manzanita Lake, just past the visitors center.

Maps: Trail maps are available for $7.24 (including tax and mailing). To order a map, contact Loomis Museum, c/o Lassen Volcanic National Park at the address below. For a map of Lassen National Forest, send $4 to USDA-Forest Service, 630 Sansome Street, San Francisco, CA 94111. To obtain a topographic map of the area, ask for Manzanita Lake from the USGS.

Contact: Lassen Volcanic National Park, P.O. Box 100, Mineral, CA 96063-0100; (916) 595-4444 or fax (916) 595-3262.

Trail notes: The most difficult part of this hike is the first two steps. Why? Because the trailhead is set near the park entrance amid a number of small roads and a maintenance area, and despite a trail sign, many visitors can't find it and give up. It's worth the search, because it's a great day hike for campers staying at Manzanita Lake. The trail, with its easy, moderate grade, is routed first through an old forest, with towering firs, cedars, and Jeffrey pines. About 2.5 miles in, however, you'll arrive at Lassen's strange "Dwarf Forest." Not only are you surrounded by stunted trees, but you also get views of Chaos Crags, a jumble of pinkish rocks constituting what's left of an old broken-down volcano. Many visitors hike to this point, then turn around and return to the campground. The trail follows part of a historical route that was originally an east-west portion of the California Trail used by immigrants in the 1850s. There is no water available on the trail, so be sure to have at least one filled canteen per hiker. Because of the moderate slope, this trail makes for an ideal cross-country ski route in the winter months.

⑫ Lassen Summit Trail

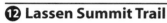

5.0 mi/4.0 hrs

Location: In Lassen Volcanic National Park east of Red Bluff; map B3, grid j1.

User groups: Hikers only. No dogs, horses, or mountain bikes. No wheelchair facilities.

Permits: A wilderness permit is required for hikers planning to camp in the backcountry. A national park day-use fee is charged for each vehicle.

Directions: From Interstate 5 at Red Bluff, turn east on Highway 36 and drive about 47 miles. Turn north on Highway 89 and go 4.5 miles to the park entrance. Drive 7.5 miles to the parking area and trailhead on the left.

Maps: Trail maps are available for $7.24 (including tax and mailing). To order a map, contact Loomis Museum, c/o Lassen Volcanic National Park at the address below. For a map of Lassen National Forest, send $4 to USDA-Forest Service, 630 Sansome Street, San Francisco, CA 94111. To obtain a topographic map of the area, ask for Lassen Peak from the USGS.

Contact: Lassen Volcanic National Park, P.O. Box 100, Mineral, CA 96063-0100; (916) 595-4444 or fax (916) 595-3262.

Trail notes: At 10,457, feet, the Mount Lassen Summit is a huge volcanic flume with hardened lava flows, craters, outcrops, and extraordinary views in all directions. Exploring Lassen Peak has become such a popular hike—perhaps the best introduction to mountain climbing a hiker could desire—that the National Park Service may enforce a trail quota in the future. The climb to the top is a 2.5-mile zigzag of a hike on a hard, flat trail, ascending just more than 2,000 feet in the process. The trailhead at 8,500 feet is adjacent to a large parking area set at the base of the summit along Highway 89, which means that many visitors can spontaneously decide to try the climb. Our suggestion is to plan it instead, starting early, at least by 7:30 A.M. (when the temperature is still cool). Bring a lunch and a canteen or two of water. In the morning, with the air still cool, it's about a two-hour walk to the top, a 15-percent grade most of the way. The views are superb, with Mount Shasta 100 miles north appearing close enough to reach out and grab. To the east are hundreds of miles of forests and lakes, and to the west, the land drops off to several small volcanic cones and the northern Sacramento Valley.

Special note: Winds are common at Lassen Summit, especially on summer afternoons. Hikers should stash a windbreaker in their daypacks. It's always a mistake to suddenly climb the summit without planning the trip. Stay at lower elevations if there's any chance of lightning activity.

⑬ Shadow Lake Trail

1.6 mi/1.0 hr

Location: In Lassen Volcanic National Park east of Red Bluff; map B3, grid j2.

User groups: Hikers. No dogs, horses, or mountain bikes. No wheelchair facilities.

Permits: A wilderness permit is required for hikers planning to camp in the backcountry. A national park day-use fee is charged for each vehicle.

Directions: From Interstate 5 at Red Bluff, turn east on Highway 36 and drive about 47 miles. Turn north on Highway 89 and go 4.5 miles to the park entrance. Continue 9.5 miles to the trailhead on the left.

Maps: Trail maps are available for $7.24 (including tax and mailing). To order a map, contact Loomis Museum, c/o Lassen Volcanic National Park at the address below. For a map of Lassen National Forest, send $4 to USDA-Forest Service, 630 Sansome Street, San Francisco, CA 94111. To obtain a topographic map of the area, ask for Reading Peak from the USGS.

Contact: Lassen Volcanic National Park, P.O. Box 100, Mineral, CA 96063-0100; (916) 595-4444 or fax (916) 595-3262.

Trail notes: A hike of less than a mile on this trail will bring you past little Terrace Lake, and then shortly after, to Shadow Lake. It's rare to reach such a pretty lake surrounded by wildlands in such a short distance. The trail involves a short, steep climb to Terrace Lake, and then a quarter of a mile juncture to skirt the southeast shoreline of Shadow Lake (at least five times the size of Terrace Lake). The lakes are set just north of Reading Peak, which reaches 8,701 feet. The trailhead is at 8,000 feet, and because of the altitude, some hikers may experience shortness of breath making the climb up to the lakes.

⑭ Summit Lake Loop

0.5 mi/0.5 hr

Location: In Lassen Volcanic National Park east of Red Bluff; map B3, grid j2.

User groups: Hikers and horses. No dogs or mountain bikes. No wheelchair facilities.

Permits: A wilderness permit is required for hikers planning to camp in the backcountry and for equestrians. A national park day-use fee is charged for each vehicle.

Directions: From Interstate 5 at Redding, turn east on Highway 44 and drive 46 miles to the park entrance at Highway 89. Head southeast on Highway 89 for 12 miles to the trailhead at Summit Lake.

Maps: Trail maps are available for $7.24 (including tax and mailing). To order a map, contact Loomis Museum, c/o Lassen Volcanic National Park at the address below. For a map of Lassen National Forest, send $4 to USDA-Forest Service, 630 Sansome Street, San Francisco, CA 94111. To obtain a topographic map of the area, ask for Reading Peak from the USGS.

Contact: Lassen Volcanic National Park, P.O. Box 100, Mineral, CA 96063-0100; (916) 595-4444 or fax (916) 595-3262.

Trail notes: At 7,000 feet, Summit Lake is a beautiful spot where deer visit almost every summer evening. Nearby campgrounds on both sides of the lake (north and south) are set in conifers, with a pretty meadow just south of the lake along Kings Creek. This hike is a simple walk around Summit Lake, best taken at dusk when the changing evening colors reflect a variety of tints across the lake surface. Though no lakes in Lassen Park are stocked with trout and the fishing is typically poor, you may still see a rising trout or two. The best place to see wildlife, especially deer, is in the meadow adjacent to Kings Creek, the lake's outlet stream.

⑮ Summit Lake Trailhead

8.0 mi/5.5 hrs

Location: In Lassen Volcanic National Park east of Red Bluff; map B3, grid j2.

User groups: Hikers only. Horses are allowed at the base, but are not permitted to climb the trail. No dogs or mountain bikes. No wheelchair facilities.

Permits: A wilderness permit is required for hikers planning to camp in the backcountry and for equestrians. A national park day-use fee is charged for each vehicle.

Directions: From Interstate 5 at Redding, turn east on Highway 44 and drive 46 miles to the park entrance at Highway 89. Go southeast on Highway 89 for 12 miles to the trailhead at Summit Lake.

Maps: Trail maps are available for $7.24 (including tax and mailing). To order a map, contact Loomis Museum, c/o Lassen Volcanic National Park at the address below. For a map of Lassen National Forest, send $4 to USDA-Forest Service, 630 Sansome Street, San Francisco, CA 94111. To obtain a topographic map of the area, ask for Reading Peak from the USGS.

Contact: Lassen Volcanic National Park, P.O. Box 100, Mineral, CA 96063; (916) 595-4444 or fax (916) 595-3262.

Trail notes: You get it all on this hike to Lower

Twin Lake: beautiful lakes, forest, meadows, and wildflowers, all of it a prime testimonial to the beauty of the Lassen Wilderness. It makes an outstanding day hike for campers staying at the Summit Lake Campground, or an easy overnighter for backpackers. The trail starts on the north side of Summit Lake, rising 500 feet in the first mile. If you can endure this climb, the rest of the hike will be a breeze. You'll arrive at Echo Lake in just another mile, and then at Upper Twin and Lower Twin in the next two miles, dropping 500 feet on your way. It's all very pretty, and a great bonus for Summit Lake campers.

Special note: No campfires are permitted in Lassen Park.

⑯ Cinder Cone Trail

4.0 mi/3.0 hrs

Location: From Butte Lake Trailhead in Lassen Volcanic National Park; map B3, grid j3.

User groups: Hikers only. Horses are allowed at the base, but are not permitted to climb the trail. No dogs or mountain bikes. No wheelchair facilities.

Permits: A wilderness permit is required for hikers planning to camp in the backcountry and for equestrians. A national park day-use fee is charged for each vehicle.

Directions: From Interstate 5 at Redding, turn east on Highway 44 and drive 60 miles. At the town of Old Station, go east on Highway 44 for 10.5 miles. Turn south on Butte Lake Road and drive seven miles to the trailhead at Butte Lake.

Maps: Trail maps are available for $7.24 (including tax and mailing). To order a map, contact Loomis Museum, c/o Lassen Volcanic National Park at the address below. For a map of Lassen National Forest, send $4 to USDA-Forest Service, 630 Sansome Street, San Francisco, CA 94111. To obtain a topographic map of the area, ask for Prospect Peak from the USGS.

Contact: Lassen Volcanic National Park, P.O. Box 100, Mineral, CA 96063-0100; (916) 595-4444 or fax (916) 595-3262.

Trail notes: Huge chunks of Lassen Park are overlooked by visitors simply because access is not off the park's main roadway, Highway 89.

Butte Lake and the Cinder Cone Trail, set in the northeastern corner of the park, are such areas. When you first arrive by car, you'll find large, attractive Butte Lake, quite a surprise for newcomers. The trailhead for the Nobles Emigrant Trail/Cinder Cone Trail (elevation 6,100 feet) is located at the northwest corner of the lake. The trail starts out easy, heading southwest through forest. But don't be fooled. After 1.5 miles, you'll reach the Cinder Cone cutoff, and there everything suddenly changes. The last half-mile rises to the top of the Cinder Cone, a short but very intense climb of 800 feet to the summit at 6,907 feet. The views are unforgettable, especially south to the Painted Dunes and Fantastic Lava Beds, a classic volcanic landscape.

⑰ Prospect Peak Trail

6.6 mi/4.5 hrs

Location: At Butte Lake in Lassen Volcanic National Park; map B3, grid j3.

User groups: Hikers only. Horses are allowed at the base, but are not permitted to climb the trail. No dogs or mountain bikes. No wheelchair facilities.

Permits: A wilderness permit is required for hikers planning to camp in the backcountry and for equestrians. A national park day-use fee is charged for each vehicle.

Directions: From Interstate 5 at Redding, turn east on Highway 44 and drive 60 miles. At the town of Old Station, go east on Highway 44 for 10.5 miles. Turn south on Butte Lake Road and drive seven miles to the Nobles Emigrant Trailhead at the lake. Hike about half a mile, then turn north toward Prospect Peak.

Maps: Trail maps are available for $7.24 (including tax and mailing). To order a map, contact Loomis Museum, c/o Lassen Volcanic National Park at the address below. For a map of Lassen National Forest, send $4 to USDA-Forest Service, 630 Sansome Street, San Francisco, CA 94111. To obtain a topographic map of the area, ask for Prospect Peak from the USGS.

Contact: Lassen Volcanic National Park, P.O. Box 100, Mineral, CA 96063-0100; (916) 595-4444 or fax (916) 595-3262.

Trail notes: Hiking to the top of most mountains requires a long, grinding climb, and, alas, gaining the summit of Prospect Peak is no different. Your reward is some of the best views in Lassen Park, and a trail that gets little use compared to the others in the park. The trailhead (Nobles Emigrant Trail), at elevation 6,100 feet, is adjacent to Butte Lake, and after less than half a mile, you'll turn right at the junction with the Prospect Peak Trail. The trail immediately starts to climb, and get used to it, because there's no respite for several hours. It climbs more than 2,200 feet over the course of just 3.3 miles, finally topping the summit at 8,338 feet. From here you can see most of the prominent peaks in the park, including Mount Lassen, Mount Hoffman, and Crater Butte, along with thousands and thousands of acres of national forest to the north. Since the snowmelt occurs earlier here than in the rest of the park, this trip makes a perfect hike in the early spring when the air is still cool. If you wait until summer, you'll find this a dry, forsaken place.

⑱ Cone Lake Trailhead

4.0 mi/2.5 hrs

Location: On the northern boundary of the Caribou Wilderness east of Lassen Volcanic National Park; map B3, grid j4.

User groups: Hikers only. No dogs, horses, or mountain bikes. No wheelchair facilities.

Permits: No permits are required. Parking and access are free.

Directions: From Interstate 5 at Redding, turn east on Highway 44 and drive 60 miles. At the town of Old Station, go east on Highway 44 for 30 miles. At the Bogard Work Station, turn right on Forest Service Road 10 and drive five miles, then turn right on Forest Service Road 32N09 and head 1.5 miles to the Cone Lake Trailhead.

Maps: For a map of Lassen National Forest, send $4 to USDA-Forest Service, 630 Sansome Street, San Francisco, CA 94111. To obtain a topographic map of the area, ask for Bogard Buttes from the USGS.

Contact: Lassen National Forest, Almanor Ranger District, P.O. Box 767, Chester, CA 96020; (916) 258-2141 or fax (916) 258-3491.

Trail notes: The prize destination on this excellent day hike is Triangle Lake, a pretty spot set in the northern Caribou Wilderness near Black Butte. The trailhead is located at tiny Cone Lake, just outside the wilderness. From here, you hike for nearly a mile before passing the wilderness boundary, which is clearly marked. At that point, you can sense the change in features as the land becomes wild and untouched, in striking contrast to the start of the hike. You head a mile south, arriving at Triangle Lake, which provides good fishing during the evening for pan-sized trout. If you want more, you can get more, heading onward from the lake. Here, the trail forks. The right fork is routed right into Lassen Volcanic National Park, a distance of only 1.5 miles, from which you can access Widow Lake (a Lassen wilderness permit is required). The left fork, on the other hand, leads to Twin Lakes over the course of just half a mile.

⑲ Caribou Lakes Trailhead

12.0 mi/2.0 days

Location: On the eastern boundary of the Caribou Wilderness east of Lassen Volcanic National Park; map B3, grid j5.

User groups: Hikers only. No dogs, horses, or mountain bikes. No wheelchair facilities.

Permits: No permits are required. Parking and access are free.

Directions: From Interstate 5 at Red Bluff, turn east on Highway 36 and drive 83 miles to the town of Westwood (located east of Lake Almanor). Turn north on County Road A21 and go 12.5 miles, then turn left on Silver Lake Road and head past Silver Lake to the trailhead parking area at Caribou Lake.

Maps: For a map of Lassen National Forest, send $4 to USDA-Forest Service, 630 Sansome Street, San Francisco, CA 94111. To obtain a topographic map of the area, ask for Red Cinder from the USGS.

Contact: Lassen National Forest, Almanor Ranger District, P.O. Box 767, Chester, CA 96020; (916) 258-2141 or fax (916) 258-3491.

Trail notes: The Caribou Lakes Trailhead provides a hiking trip that is a parade past mountain lakes. Rarely are this many wilderness lakes so close to a trailhead. This trip starts at Caribou

Lake, heading west, and in no time, you start passing all kinds of tiny lakes. The first one, Cowboy Lake, is only a quarter of a mile down the trail. In another 15 minutes, you'll come to Jewel Lake. This procession of lakes never seems to stop—Eleanor Lake is next, then after turning left at the fork (two miles in), you pass Black Lake, North and South Divide Lakes, and further on, Long Lake. This lake six miles from the trailhead should be your destination, since it makes for a great two-day backpack adventure. The Caribou Wilderness is quite small, just nine miles from top to bottom, and only five miles across, with elevations ranging from 5,000 to 7,000 feet. This trip will provide a visit to the best of it.

Pacific Crest Trail (PCT) Section Overview

114.0 mi. one way/9.0 days

Trail sections extend from Lassen Volcanic National Park north to Shasta-Trinity National Forest west of McArthur-Burney Falls State Park.

You get a little bit of bliss, a little bit of paradise, then a big load of bull pucky on the 114-mile segment of the Pacific Crest Trail that crosses through this chapter's map. The bliss is in Lassen Volcanic National Park, where the trail passes by high mountain lakes circled with conifers, then goes by a strange but compelling volcanic area. The paradise comes at Burney Falls, a 129-foot waterfall that is a portrait of serenity, along with nearby Lake Britton. Then it's off to no man's land, and here you'll be swearing your way up to Grizzly Peak in a place where water and breezes are rare, and where an endless climb through brushy terrain will have you wondering why you're doing this. It gets worse when you can scarcely follow the trail because of logging roads, brush, and zero trail maintenance. Following is more specific information on major trail sections in this zone.

PCT-38 Lassen Volcanic National Park to Highway 44

32.0 mi. one way/3.0 days

Location: From Warner Valley Campground in Lassen Volcanic National Park to Highway 44; map B3, grid j3.

User groups: Hikers only. No dogs, horses, or mountain bikes are allowed in the Lassen Volcanic National Park section of the hike. No wheelchair facilities.

Permits: A wilderness permit is required for hikers planning to camp in the Lassen Volcanic National Park backcountry and for equestrians. You may not camp with horses in the national park's backcountry. A corral is available by reservation for overnighters. A $5-per-vehicle or $3-per-hiker park entrance fee is charged.

Directions: From Interstate 5 at Red Bluff, turn east on Highway 36 and drive 70 miles to the town of Chester. Turn north on Warner Valley Road (improved dirt) and go 16 miles to the campground.

Maps: To obtain topographic maps of the route, ask for Reading Peak, West Prospect Peak, and Old Station from the USGS.

Contact: Lassen Volcanic National Park, P.O. Box 100, Mineral, CA 96063-0100; (916) 595-4444 or fax (916) 595-3262. Lassen National Forest, Hat Creek Ranger District, P.O. Box 220, Falls River Mills, CA 96028; (916) 336-5521.

Trail notes: Every step is a pleasure in Lassen Volcanic National Park, starting from the wooded Warner Valley (at 5,680 feet) at Springs Creek and then heading north into the park's most remote terrain. The trail is routed across Grassy Swale, past Swan Lake, and on to Lower Twin Lake (seven miles in), a pretty body of water circled by conifers.

From here, the trail heads north, skirting the western flank of Fairfield Peak (7,272 feet) and then onward, turning west past Soap Lake and Badger Flat, then continuing out past the park's boundary. As you hike toward Highway 44, you'll be lateraling across Badger Mountain (6,973 feet) to your right, with the Hat Creek drainage off to your immediate left. In this latter stretch of trail, you'll cross no major lakes or streams (plan your water well), but just forge on through the national forest, mostly second-growth, crossing a few roads along the way. In the spring, wildflowers are exceptional on the Hat Creek rim. A small, primitive Forest Service campground is located on the trail about 10 miles north of the border of Lassen Volcanic National Park.

PCT-39 Highway 44 to McArthur-Burney Falls State Park

40.0 mi. one way/3.0 days

Location: From the Highway 44 parking area north to McArthur-Burney Falls State Park; map B3, grid h3.

User groups: Hikers, dogs (except in the state park boundaries) and horses. No mountain bikes. No wheelchair facilities.

Permits: No permits are required. The park entrance fee is $5 per vehicle or $3 per hiker.

Directions: From Interstate 5 at Redding, turn east on Highway 44 and drive 60 miles. At the town of Old Station, go east on Highway 44 about a quarter of a mile beyond the Old Station Post Office. Turn right on Forest Service Road 32N20. The trail crosses the road about half a mile from the junction of Highway 44 and Forest Service Road 32N20.

Maps: To obtain topographic maps of the route, ask for Cassel, Dana, Old Station, Murken Bench, Hogback Ridge, and Burney Falls from the USGS.

Contact: Lassen National Forest, Hat Creek Ranger District, P.O. Box 220, Falls River Mills, CA 96028; (916) 336-5521 or fax (916) 336-5758.

Trail notes: The features of this segment of the Pacific Crest Trail are Hat Creek, Baum Lake, Crystal Lake, and the spectacular Burney Falls. From the trailhead at Highway 44, the stream is routed through the wooded watershed of Hat Creek, then to a long, shadeless section that will have you counting the drops of water in your canteen. After departing from Hat Creek, the PCT heads past Baum and Crystal Lakes, the latter 27 miles in from the trailhead. You cross Highway 299, and from there, it's an eight-mile romp to Burney Falls State Park and its breathtaking 129-foot waterfall.

PCT-40 McArthur-Burney Falls State Park to Ash Camp

52.0 mi. one way/4.0 days

Location: From McArthur-Burney Falls State Park west into Ash Camp in Shasta-Trinity National Forest; map B3, grid e1.

User groups: Hikers, dogs (except in the state park boundaries), and horses. No mountain bikes. No wheelchair facilities.

Permits: No permits are required. A $5-per-vehicle or $3-per-hiker park entrance fee is charged.

Directions: From Interstate 5 at Redding, turn east on Highway 299 and drive 50 miles to Burney. Continue five miles east on Highway 299, then turn north on Highway 89, and drive 5.8 miles to the state park entrance. Follow the signs to the trailhead.

Maps: To obtain topographic maps of the route, ask for Burney Falls, Skunk Ridge, and Grizzly Peak from the USGS.

Contact: McArthur-Burney Falls State Park, 24898 Highway 89, Burney, CA 96013; (916) 335-2777 or fax (916) 335-5483.

Trail notes: It may be difficult to leave the woods, waters, and aura of Burney Falls, but off you go, facing dry country and some of Northern California's least-used portions of the Pacific Crest Trail. It's called Hat Creek Rim, but with no water for nearly 30 miles, most call it hell. Virtually the only hikers who complete this section are the ones hiking the entire route, from Mexico to Canada; they're virtually forced to endure it, often at great hardship. This is the absolute worst section of the entire 2,700-mile PCT, where a single drop of water will be valued more than a $10,000 bill.

From Burney Falls, the PCT heads west, touching the Pit River Arm of Lake Britton, and then forward into Lassen Volcanic National Forest, crossing into Shasta-Trinity National Forest and up to Grizzly Peak. Much of this route is across dry, hot exposed slopes, where the trail has deteriorated in many spots due to the encroachment of brush and zero trail maintenance by the Forest Service. Knowing you're smack between the lush beauty of Burney Falls (behind you) and the McCloud River (ahead of you) can make dealing with the present brush-infested landscape a frustrating encounter. Always fill your canteens with water wherever you find it, and don't hesitate to make a camp if, late in the day, you find even a small flat spot with water nearby. Unfortunately, there just doesn't seem to be much water. In bad dry years, you can go 30 miles without finding water. After the hot, beastly climb near Grizzly Peak, most hikers will want to make a lightning-fast descent down to the eden of the McCloud River at Ash Camp. But hold your horses. As long as you've come this far, make the short side trip to Grizzly Peak, and while you're looking at the incredible view of Mount Shasta and the McCloud flats, congratulate yourself for completing such a terrible hike. Considering the PCT is the feature national recreation trail in America, this stretch is an embarrassment to the U.S. Forest Service and an abomination to hikers.

PCT Continuation: To continue hiking along the Pacific Crest Trail, see chapter B2.

Leave No Trace Tips

Keep the Wilderness Wild

Treat our natural heritage with respect. Leave plants,
rocks, and historical artifacts as you found them.

Good campsites are found, not made. Do not alter a campsite.

Let nature's sounds prevail; keep loud voices and noises to a minimum.

Do not build structures or furniture or dig trenches.

Map B4

Adjoining Maps: West: B3 ..... *page* 86
North: A4 42   South: C4 148

Northern California Map .... *page* 2

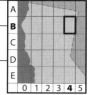

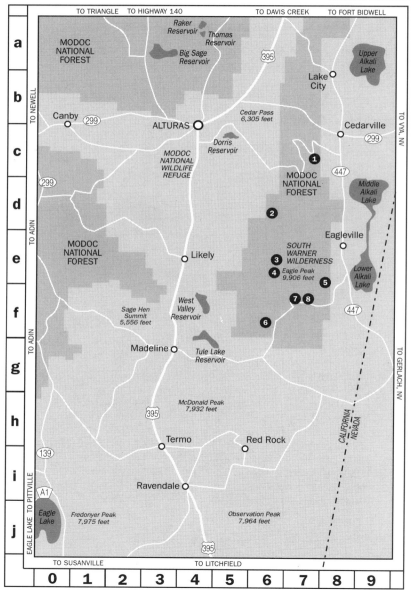

❶ Pepperdine Trailhead

12.0 mi/2.0 days

Location: On the northern boundary of the South Warner Wilderness east of Alturas; map B4, grid c7.

User groups: Hikers, dogs, and horses. No mountain bikes. No wheelchair facilities.

Permits: No permit is required. Parking and access are free.

Directions: From the south end of Alturas, turn east on County Road 56 and drive 13 miles to the Modoc National Forest boundary. Head west for six miles on Parker Creek Road, then turn south at the sign for Pepperdine Campground and drive to the trailhead.

Maps: For a map of the South Warner Wilderness, send $4 to USDA-Forest Service, 630 Sansome Street, San Francisco, CA 94111. To obtain a topographic map of the area, ask for Warren Peak from the USGS.

Contact: Modoc National Forest, Warner Mountain Ranger District, P.O. Box 220, Cedarville, CA 96104; (916) 279-6116 or phone or fax (916) 279-6118.

Trail notes: The six-mile trip on the Summit Trail to Patterson Lake is the most popular hike in the South Warner Wilderness. That still doesn't mean you'll run into other people or horses, because the Warners are a remote, lonely place rarely visited by hikers from the Bay Area, Sacramento, or Los Angeles. Patterson Lake is set in a rock basin at 9,000 feet, just below Warren Peak (9,718 feet), the highest lake in the wilderness and the highlight destination for most visitors. The Pepperdine Trailhead at 6,900 feet is located just beyond Porter Reservoir, where a primitive campground and a horse corral are available. The hike is a sustained climb, gaining 2,100 feet in elevation, passing to the right of Squaw Peak (8,646 feet) and then tiny Cotton-

wood Lake. From Squaw Peak looking east, it will seem as if you're looking across hundreds of miles of a stark, uninhabited landscape.

❷ Pine Creek Trailhead

4.0 mi/3.0 hrs

Location: On the northwestern boundary of the South Warner Wilderness east of Alturas; map B4, grid d6.

User groups: Hikers, dogs, and horses. No mountain bikes. No wheelchair facilities.

Permits: No permit is required. Parking and access are free.

Directions: From the south end of Alturas, turn east on County Road 56 and drive 13 miles to the Modoc National Forest boundary. Turn south on West Warner Road and go about 10 miles to the sign for the Pine Creek Trailhead. Turn east and head 1.75 miles to the parking area.

Maps: For a map of the South Warner Wilderness, send $4 to USDA-Forest Service, 630 Sansome Street, San Francisco, CA 94111. To obtain a topographic map of the area, ask for Eagle Peak from the USGS.

Contact: Modoc National Forest, Warner Mountain Ranger District, P.O. Box 220, Cedarville, CA 96104; (916) 279-6116 or phone or fax (916) 279-6118.

Trail notes: Modoc County is the least populated and least-known region of California, with only 15,000 residents sprinkled across a huge area. Yet there are many outstanding adventures available here, including one of the truly great short hikes available anywhere. And here it is, the Pine Creek Trail, which provides a magnificent yet short traipse into one of the most attractive areas of the South Warner Wilderness.

The trail starts along the South Fork of Pine Creek, about 6,800 feet in elevation, then heads straight east into the wilderness, climbing up the lush west-facing slopes. In the course of two miles, the trail rises up 1,000 feet to the Pine Creek Basin. Along the trail are several small lakes, the largest being the two set right along the trail as you enter the basin. Above you is a granite-faced rim, stark and with few trees, where the headwaters of eight small creeks start from springs, then pour down the mountain, join, and flow into Pine Creek Lake.

Some hikers use the Soup Spring Trail as a way of climbing up near the Warner Rim and intersecting with the Summit Trail, the feature hike in the South Warner Wilderness. That makes sense, with a free, primitive campground and corral at the trailhead, and then a four-mile romp uphill to the Summit Trail junction. It includes a 1,000-foot climb on the way, with the trail routed up the Slide Creek Canyon over the last two miles.

❸ Soup Spring Trailhead

3.0 mi/2.0 hrs

Location: On the western boundary of the South Warner Wilderness east of Alturas; map B4, grid e6.

User groups: Hikers, dogs, and horses. No mountain bikes. No wheelchair facilities.

Permits: No permit is required. Parking and access are free.

Directions: From the south end of Alturas, turn east on County Road 56 and drive 13 miles to the Modoc National Forest boundary. Turn south on West Warner Road and go about 13 miles to the sign for Soup Spring Campground. Turn east and drive 3.5 miles. Turn left on Soup Spring Campground Road and head about half a mile to the campground parking lot.

Maps: For a map of the South Warner Wilderness, send $4 to USDA-Forest Service, 630 Sansome Street, San Francisco, CA 94111. To obtain a topographic map of the area, ask for Eagle Peak from the USGS.

Contact: Modoc National Forest, Warner Mountain Ranger District, P.O. Box 220, Cedarville, CA 96104; (916) 279-6116 or phone or fax (916) 279-6118.

Trail notes: Mill Creek is a small, pristine trout stream that brings the lonely Warner Mountains to life. It's a short hike to get here, up a hill, over it, and then down heading into a valley. In this valley floor you'll find Mill Creek, only a 1.5-mile walk out of the Soup Spring Trailhead. Mill Creek is a great spot for a picnic lunch or a high-finesse fishing trip. The trout are extremely sensitive, so anything clumsy, like letting your shadow hit the water or clanking your boots on the shore, will spook them off the bite. The trout are small, dark, and chunky, unlike any seen elsewhere.

❹ Mill Creek Falls Trailhead

0.5 mi/0.5 hr

Location: On the southwestern boundary of the South Warner Wilderness east of Alturas; map B4, grid e6.

User groups: Hikers and dogs. Some wheelchair-accessible facilities are available at nearby campgrounds. No horses or mountain bikes.

Permits: No permit is required. Parking and access are free.

Directions: From Alturas, drive south on U.S. 395 about 18.5 miles to Likely. Turn east on Jess Valley Road and go nine miles. When the road forks, bear left and drive 2.5 miles, then turn right and head two miles to the trailhead.

Maps: For a map of the South Warner Wilderness, send $4 to USDA-Forest Service, 630 Sansome Street, San Francisco, CA 94111. To obtain a topographic map of the area, ask for Eagle Peak from the USGS.

Contact: Modoc National Forest, Warner Mountain Ranger District, P.O. Box 220, Cedarville, CA 96104; (916) 279-6116 or phone or fax (916) 279-6118.

Trail notes: The short, easy walk from the Mill Creek Falls Trailhead to Clear Lake will lead you to one of the prettiest spots in Modoc County. The trail skirts along the perimeter of the lake, a pretty high mountain water set at 6,000 feet. Of the lakes and streams in the Warners, it's Clear Lake that has the largest fish, with big brown and rainbow trout ranging to more than 10 pounds. There just aren't that many of them. Backpackers can head onward from Clear Lake on the Poison Flat Trail, but expect a very steep howler of a climb before intersecting with the Mill Creek Trail.

❺ Emerson Trailhead

7.0 mi/2.0 days

Location: On the eastern boundary of the South Warner Wilderness east of Alturas; map B4, grid e8.

User groups: Hikers, dogs, and horses. No mountain bikes. No wheelchair facilities.

Permits: No permit is required. Parking and access are free.

Directions: From Alturas, turn east on Highway 299 and drive 22 miles to Cedarville, then turn south on County Road 1 and go approximately 16 miles to Eagleville. Drive another 1.5 miles south on County Road 1, then turn right on Emerson Road and head three miles to the trailhead. Emerson Road is very steep and can be slippery when wet.

Maps: For a map of the South Warner Wilderness, send $4 to USDA-Forest Service, 630 Sansome Street, San Francisco, CA 94111. To obtain a topographic map of the area, ask for Emerson Peak from the USGS.

Contact: Modoc National Forest, Warner Mountain Ranger District, P.O. Box 220, Cedarville, CA 96104; (916) 279-6116 or phone or fax (916) 279-6118.

Trail notes: Don't be yelpin' about the dreadful climb up to North Emerson Lake, because we're warning you right here, loud and clear, that it qualifies as a first-class booger-country butt-kicker. If you choose to go anyway, well, you asked for it. The trail climbs 2,000 feet in 3.5 miles, but much of that is in a hellish half-mile stretch that'll have you howling for relief. Your reward is little North Emerson Lake, located in a wonderland-like setting at 7,800 feet in a rock bowl with a high sheer back wall.

The Emerson Trailhead, the most remote of those providing access to the Warners, is located on the east side of the mountain rim near stark, dry country. A primitive campground is available here at the trailhead. Out of camp, take the North Emerson Trail. And while you're at it, get yourself in the right frame of mind to cheerfully accept that you'll be getting your butt kicked. But rest assured that North Emerson Lake is worth every step.

❻ Blue Lake Loop

2.4 mi/1.25 hrs

Location: At Blue Lake in Modoc National Forest southeast of Alturas; map B4, grid f6.

User groups: Hikers and dogs. The fishing pier and rest room are wheelchair accessible. No horses or mountain bikes.

Permits: No permit is required. Parking and access are free.

Directions: From Alturas, drive south on U.S. 395 about 18.5 miles to Likely. Turn east on Jess Valley Road and go nine miles. When the road forks, bear right and head seven miles on Blue Lake Road. Turn right at the sign for Blue Lake and drive to the parking area.

Maps: For a map of Modoc National Forest, send $4 to USDA-Forest Service, 630 Sansome Street, San Francisco, CA 94111. To obtain a topographic map of the area, ask for Jess Valley from the USGS.

Contact: Modoc National Forest, Warner Mountain Ranger District, P.O. Box 220, Cedarville, CA 96104; (916) 279-6116 or phone or fax (916) 279-6118.

Trail notes: Blue Lake, shaped like an egg and rimmed with trees, is one of the prettiest lakes you can reach by driving. That makes the easy 2.4-mile loop hike around the lake on the Blue Lake Loop National Recreation Trail very special. With a campground at the lake, this trail makes a good side trip for overnight visitors. In addition, there is a fishing pier and wheelchair accessible rest room available. A bonus is that there are some huge trout in this lake—brown trout in the 10-pound class—and they provide quite a treasure hunt amid good numbers of foot-long rainbow trout.

❼ East Creek Loop

15.0 mi/2.0 days

Location: On the southern boundary of the South Warner Wilderness east of Alturas; map B4, grid f7.

User groups: Hikers, dogs, and horses. No mountain bikes. No wheelchair facilities.

Permits: No permit is required. Parking and access are free.

Directions: From Alturas, drive south on U.S. 395 about 18.5 miles to Likely. Turn east on Jess Valley Road and go until you reach South Warner Road. Turn south and drive southeast, heading toward Patterson Campground. Turn left at the East Creek Trailhead access road and continue a short distance to the parking area.

Maps: For a map of the South Warner Wilderness, send $4 to USDA-Forest Service, 630 Sansome Street, San Francisco, CA 94111. To obtain a topographic map of the area, ask for Emerson Peak from the USGS.

Contact: Modoc National Forest, Warner Mountain Ranger District, P.O. Box 220, Cedarville, CA 96104; (916) 279-6116 or phone or fax (916) 279-6118.

Trail notes: The East Creek Loop is our favorite loop hike in the Warner Mountains. It can be completed in a weekend, not including driving time, and provides a capsule look at the amazing contrasts of the Warners. The hike includes small, pristine streams as well as high barren mountain rims. The East Creek Trail, elevation 7,100 feet, is routed 5.5 miles north into the wilderness. Just before the junction with Poison Flat Trail, there is a spring located on the left side of the trail. Don't miss it—you'll need the water for the upcoming climb. Turn right at the junction with the Poison Flat Trail, then make the 800-foot climb above tree line, and turn right again on the Summit Trail.

The loop is completed by taking the Summit Trail back south, crossing high, stark country, most of it more than 8,000 feet in elevation. In the last two miles, the trail drops sharply, descending 1,000 feet on the way to Patterson Campground, which marks the end of the loop trail. Reaching the parking area at East Creek Trailhead requires a half-mile walk on the Forest Service Road.

❽ Summit Trail

45.0 mi/4.0 days

Location: On the southern boundary of the South Warner Wilderness east of Alturas; map B4, grid f7.

User groups: Hikers and horses. No dogs or mountain bikes. No wheelchair facilities.

Permits: No permit is required. Parking and access are free.

Directions: From Alturas, turn south on U.S. 395 and drive about 18.5 miles to Likely. Turn east on Jess Valley Road and drive until you reach South Warner Road. Turn south and drive southeast to Patterson Campground. The trailhead is at the camp.

Maps: For a map of the South Warner Wilderness, send $4 to USDA-Forest Service, 630 Sansome Street, San Francisco, CA 94111. To obtain a topographic map of the area, ask for Emerson Peak from the USGS.

Contact: Modoc National Forest, Warner Mountain Ranger District, P.O. Box 220, Cedarville, CA 96104; (916) 279-6116 or phone or fax (916) 279-6118.

Trail notes: The Warner Mountains have a mystique about them, a charm cultivated by the thoughts of hikers who dream of an area where the landscape is remote and untouched and the trails are empty. That is why the Summit Loop is the backpacking trek that most hikers yearn to take some day. However, only rarely do they get around to it. For most, the Warners are just too remote and too far away, and the trip requires too much time. If you are one of the lucky few to get here, you'll find this hike traverses both sides of the Warner ridge, providing an intimate look at a diverse place. The west side of the Warner Mountains is a habitat filled with small pine trees, meadows, and the headwaters of many small streams. The east side, however, is stark and rugged, with great long-distance lookouts to the east across high desert and miles of sagebrush and juniper.

Start the trip at the Patterson Camp Trailhead, elevation 7,200 feet, and from there, the trail climbs quickly, rising to 8,200 feet in two miles, accessing high, barren country. Great views abound from here as you head north. To reach the north end of the wilderness, take the turn at the Owl Creek Trail and hike to Linderman Lake, set at the foot of Devils Knob (8,776 feet), and beyond past Squaw Peak (8,646 feet). To return, make the hairpin left turn at the Summit Trail, and walk back on the mostly lush western slopes of the Warners. Highlights on the return loop include Patterson Lake (9,000 feet), the headwaters of Mill Creek and North Fork East Creek, and many beautiful and fragile meadows. The trail ends at the East Creek parking area, a half-mile walk from the Patterson Camp Trailhead. Savor every moment of this trip—it's one of the greatest little-known hikes anywhere in the United States.

Map CØ

Adjoining Maps: East: C1 ..... *page* 116
                    North: BØ 46   South: DØ 150

Northern California Map .... *page* 2

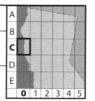

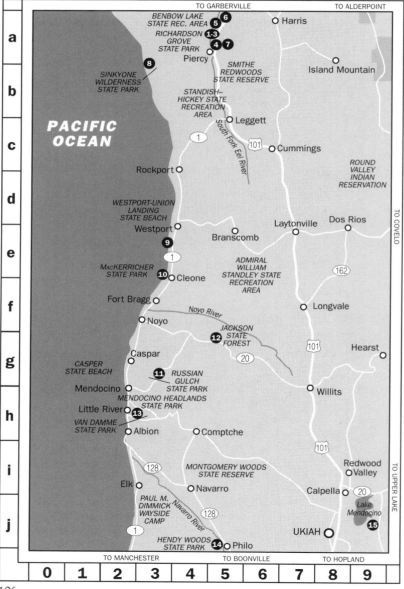

TO GARBERVILLE   TO ALDERPOINT

a

BENBOW LAKE
STATE REC. AREA **5** **6**   ○ Harris

RICHARDSON **1-3**
GROVE
STATE PARK **4** **7**
Piercy ○

SMITHE
REDWOODS
STATE RESERVE   Island Mountain ○

SINKYONE **8**
WILDERNESS
STATE PARK

STANDISH–
HICKEY STATE
RECREATION
AREA

b

**PACIFIC
OCEAN**

○ Leggett

Leggett

① ○ Cummings

c

South Fork Eel River

101

Rockport ○

ROUND
VALLEY
INDIAN
RESERVATION

d

WESTPORT-UNION
LANDING
STATE BEACH

Westport ○

Laytonville ○   Dos Rios ○

e

9

①

MacKERRICHER
STATE PARK **10** ○ Cleone

○ Branscomb

ADMIRAL
WILLIAM
STANDLEY STATE
RECREATION
AREA

162

TO COVELO

f

Fort Bragg ○

○ Noyo

Noyo River

JACKSON **12**
STATE
FOREST

Longvale ○

g

CASPER
STATE BEACH

Caspar ○

20

101

Hearst ○

11 RUSSIAN
GULCH
STATE PARK

Mendocino ○

MENDOCINO HEADLANDS
STATE PARK

Willits ○

h

Little River ○ **13**

VAN DAMME
STATE PARK ○ Albion

○ Comptche

101

i

128

MONTGOMERY WOODS
STATE RESERVE

Redwood
Valley ○

Elk ○

○ Navarro

Calpella ○   20

TO UPPER LAKE

j

PAUL M.
DIMMICK
WAYSIDE
CAMP

①

Navarro River

128

Lake
Mendocino

15

UKIAH ○

HENDY WOODS
STATE PARK **14** ○ Philo

TO MANCHESTER   TO BOONVILLE   TO HOPLAND

0   1   2   3   4   5   6   7   8   9

❶ Lookout Point Loop Trail

1.7 mi/1.0 hr

Location: In Richardson Grove State Park south of Garberville; map CØ, grid a5.

User groups: Hikers only. No dogs, horses, or mountain bikes. No wheelchair facilities.

Permits: No permits are required. A $5 state park entrance fee is charged for each vehicle.

Directions: From Santa Rosa, drive north on U.S. 101 to the junction with Highway 1 at Leggitt. Head north on Highway 1 about 17 miles to the park entrance on the west side of the highway. Follow the signs to the Redwood Day-Use Parking Area. Access to the trailhead is at the parking area and also out of Madrone Campground and Hartsook Inn.

Maps: For a trail guide and brochure, send $1.50 to Richardson Grove State Park at the address below. To obtain a topographic map of the area, ask for Garberville from the USGS.

Contact: Richardson Grove State Park, 1600 U.S. Highway 101, Suite 8, Garberville, CA 95542; (707) 247-3318, (707) 445-6547, or fax (707) 247-3300.

Trail notes: Big woods. Big water. That's what the Lookout Point Loop Trail supplies, with a tour through giant redwoods culminating at the canyon rim over the South Fork Eel River. Giant redwoods approaching 300 feet tall and an estimated 1,000 years in age are the highlight of Richardson Grove, while younger redwoods, fir, and tan oak fill out the forest. The trail passes through forest and rises to Lookout Point, where there's an excellent view of the South Fork. You can also see the Oak Flat Campground from here. As a free-flowing river, the South Fork Eel River can seem like a small trickle in late summer or a howling torrent during peak flows in winter. When looking down from Lookout Point during summer, it may seem hard to imagine how high the Eel has risen in high water years. In 1955, 1963, and 1986, the river actually flooded its banks and wiped out several campgrounds in the state park. This is an easy and popular hike, both for daytime park visitors, overnighters at Madrone Camp, or people staying at Hartsook Inn. From the latter, there's a half-mile spur trail that's connected to the Lookout Point Loop Trail.

❷ Durphy Creek Loop

4.5 mi/3.0 hrs

Location: In Richardson Grove State Park south of Garberville; map CØ, grid a5.

User groups: Hikers only. No dogs, horses, or mountain bikes. No wheelchair facilities.

Permits: No permits are required. A $5 state park entrance fee is charged for each vehicle.

Directions: From Santa Rosa, drive north on U.S. 101 to the junction with Highway 1 at Leggitt. Drive north on Highway 1 about 17 miles to the park entrance on the west side of the highway. Follow the signs to the Redwood Day-Use Parking Area. The trailhead is located in the parking area.

Maps: For a trail guide and brochure, send $1.50 to Richardson Grove State Park at the address below. To obtain a topographic map of the area, ask for Garberville from the USGS.

Contact: Richardson Grove State Park, 1600 U.S. Highway 101, Suite 8, Garberville, CA 95542; (707) 247-3318, (707) 445-6547, or fax (707) 247-3300.

Trail notes: Be ready for a good climb, have a full canteen of water, and note that no whiners are allowed. Why? Because this loop trail is the most challenging hike in Richardson Grove State Park. It starts easily enough, routed right along the left side of Durphy Creek at a tolerant grade. But when the trail turns left and starts to climb up the canyon, all tolerance is forgotten. The trail climbs 800 feet in less than half a mile, with a short cutoff to Tan Oak Springs, then onward to the ridge at 1,400 feet. On the way back down, the route descends through a dense forest of tan oaks and is quite steep in the last half mile, including some switchbacks. To complete the loop, turn left at the Lookout Point Trail and hike back toward the park office.

❸ Redwood Exhibit Trail

0.25 mi/0.25 hr

Location: In Richardson Grove State Park south of Garberville; map CØ, grid a5.

User groups: Hikers only. No dogs, horses, or mountain bikes. No wheelchair facilities.

Permits: No permits are required. A $5 state park entrance fee is charged for each vehicle.

Directions: From Santa Rosa, drive north on U.S. 101 to the junction with Highway 1 at Leggitt. Drive north on Highway 1 about 17 miles to the park entrance on the west side of the highway. Follow the signs to the Redwood Day-Use Parking Area. The trailhead is located in the parking area.

Maps: For a trail guide and brochure, send $1.50 to Richardson Grove State Park at the address below. To obtain a topographic map of the area, ask for Garberville from the USGS.

Contact: Richardson Grove State Park, 1600 U.S. Highway 101, #8, Garberville, CA 95542; (707) 247-3318, (707) 445-6547, or fax (707) 247-3300.

Trail notes: U.S. 101 cuts a swath right through the center of Richardson Grove State Park, and even the long-distance freeway burners slow down to 25 miles per hour to gawk at the giant redwoods. Some even park. If that includes you, the Redwood Exhibit Trail furnishes a short, easy stroll amid many of the park's largest and oldest trees. The actual exhibit trail is

only a quarter of a mile long, but it's possible to continue on, linking up with the Lookout Point Trail (hike number 1). After walking among those old giant redwoods, you may notice that you don't have the desire to drive quite so fast on the highway anymore.

❹ Settlers Loop Trail

0.7 mi/0.5 hr

Location: In Richardson Grove State Park south of Garberville; map CØ, grid a5.

User groups: Hikers only. No dogs, horses, or mountain bikes. No wheelchair facilities.

Permits: No permits are required. A $5 state park entrance fee is charged for each vehicle.

Directions: From Santa Rosa, drive north on U.S. 101 to the junction with Highway 1 at Leggitt. Drive north on Highway 1 about 17 miles to the park entrance on the west side of the highway. The trailhead is adjacent to the parking lot.

Maps: For a trail guide and brochure, send $1.50 to Richardson Grove State Park at the address below. To obtain a topographic map of the area, ask for Garberville from the USGS.

Contact: Richardson Grove State Park, 1600 U.S. Highway 101, Suite 8, Garberville, CA 95542; (707) 247-3318, (707) 445-6547, or fax (707) 247-3300.

Trail notes: The Settlers Loop Trail is the most popular hike for campers staying at the Oak Flat Campground, the largest camp in Richardson Grove State Park. The trail is short and simple, set on the east side of the South Fork Eel River, and features an easy walk through Settler's Meadow. If you want to extend the hike, the Settlers Loop Trail intersects with the southern end of the Toumey Trail (hike number 7). From this intersection, the Toumey Trail climbs 250 feet over the course of about half a mile to reach Panorama Point. From here, there's a sweeping view of Richardson Grove's giant redwoods, well worth the short climb.

❺ Woodland's Loop Trail

1.6 mi/1.0 hr

Location: In Richardson Grove State Park south of Garberville; map CØ, grid a5.

User groups: Hikers only. No dogs, horses, or mountain bikes. No wheelchair facilities.

Permits: No permits are required. A $5 state park entrance fee is charged for each vehicle.

Directions: From Santa Rosa, drive north on U.S. 101 to the junction with Highway 1 at Leggitt. Drive north on Highway 1 about 17 miles to the park entrance on the west side of the highway. The trailhead is accessible from the parking lot, just inside the entrance.

Maps: For a trail guide and brochure, send $1.50 to Richardson Grove State Park at the address below. To obtain a topographic map of the area, ask for Garberville from the USGS.

Contact: Richardson Grove State Park, 1600 U.S. Highway 101, Suite 8, Garberville, CA 95542; (707) 247-3318, (707) 445-6547, or fax (707) 247-3300.

Trail notes: You want easy? You get easy. You want forest? You get forest. You want a campground trailhead? You get a campground trailhead. The Woodland's Loop, an easy, pretty trail that starts at the Huckleberry Campground, does all that and more. The trail crosses North Creek, then is routed through both redwoods and tan oaks, which are dense at times. It also includes a gentle uphill portion, rising about 250 feet. The trail and camp are set on the west side of U.S. 101, and with the South Fork Eel River on the east side of the highway, there's no direct river access from this trail or the nearby campground.

➏ Pioneer Meadow Loop

3.5 mi/2.5 hrs

Location: In Benbow Lake State Recreation Area south of Garberville; map CØ, grid a5.

User groups: Hikers only. No dogs, horses, or mountain bikes. No wheelchair facilities.

Permits: No permits are required. A $5 state park entrance fee is charged for each vehicle.

Directions: From Santa Rosa, drive north on U.S. 101 to Leggitt, and continue for 22 miles to the Benbow exit. Take the Benbow exit, turn right, and head to the Benbow Lake State Recreation Area Campground. The trailhead is located at campsite number 73.

Maps: A map and brochure can be obtained by contacting Benbow Lake State Recreation Area at the address below. To obtain a topographic map of the area, ask for Garberville from the USGS.

Contact: Benbow Lake State Recreation Area, c/o Richardson Grove State Park, 1600 U.S. Highway 101, Suite 8, Garberville, CA 95542; (707) 923-3238, (707) 445-6547, or fax (707) 247-3300.

Trail notes: You can scan map after map and never find Benbow Lake. Not because it doesn't exist, but rather because it doesn't exist most of the year. You see, Benbow Lake is a seasonal lake, created each summer only by a temporary dam on the Eel River. When the Eel is dammed, Benbow Lake becomes a popular recreation site for sunbathing, swimming, nonpower boating, and camping. Hiking is also a viable alternative, especially on this loop trail.

Start on the Pratt Mill Trail near campground number 73 at an elevation of 400 feet; you can create a 3.5-mile loop by connecting to the Pioneer Trail. This route features some river frontage, a sprinkling of giant redwoods, a meadow, and a portion of trail along Benbow Lake. There's also the option of taking the Ridge Trail cutoff, a one-mile spur that climbs another 250 feet to an excellent 1,000-foot lookout, with views of the Eel River drainage.

➐ Toumey Grove Trail

3.8 mi/2.75 hrs

Location: In Richardson Grove State Park south of Garberville; map CØ, grid a5.

User groups: Hikers only. No dogs, horses, or mountain bikes. No wheelchair facilities.

Permits: No permits are required. A $5 state park entrance fee is charged for each vehicle.

Directions: From Santa Rosa, drive north on U.S. 101 to the junction with Highway 1 at Leggitt. Drive north on Highway 1 about 17 miles to the park entrance on the west side of the highway. Follow the signs to Oak Flat Campground, or to the parking area near the Summer Bridge. The trailheads are at both locations. This trail can only be accessed in the summer months.

Maps: For a trail guide and brochure, send $1.50 to Richardson Grove State Park at the address below. To obtain a topographic map of the area, ask for Garberville from the USGS.

Contact: Richardson Grove State Park, 1600 U.S. Highway 101, Suite 8, Garberville, CA 95542; (707) 247-3318, (707) 445-6547, or fax (707) 247-3300.

Trail notes: The Toumey Trail is one of Richardson Grove State Park's feature summer hikes. It includes walking over the South Fork Eel River on the "Summer Bridge" (a temporary bridge that crosses the river only in summer), through a majestic stand of old redwoods, up to Kauffman Springs, and beyond to the Panorama Point Lookout. The trail can be accessed at two spots, either at the north end near a parking area at Summer Bridge, or at the south end at Oak Flat Campground (see hike number 4, the Settlers Loop Trail). If you're not camping at Oak Flat, we suggest starting this hike at the parking area near the Summer Bridge. From here, the trail crosses the river and enters the redwoods; take your time and enjoy the surroundings. The trail climbs 300 feet, rising quickly with a few switchbacks, then arrives at Panorama Point, with excellent views of the Eel River Canyon and Richardson Grove Redwoods. Many hikers simply return from this point, but the trail can be extended another mile down to the Oak Flat Campground.

Special note: This trail can only be accessed in the summer months.

❽ Lost Coast Trail

16.7 mi. one way/2.0 days

Location: In Sinkyone Wilderness State Park south to Usal Campground on the Mendocino coast; map CØ, grid b3.

User groups: Hikers only. Horses are allowed only on the section of trail between Orchard Camp and Wheeler Camp. No dogs or mountain bikes. No wheelchair facilities.

Permits: No permits are required. Parking and access are free unless you plan to camp.

Directions: From U.S. Highway 101 north of Garberville, take the Redway exit and turn west on Briceland Road. Drive 36 miles to the park, past Needle Rock Barn to the visitors center, and

park at Orchard Camp. Be aware that the access road is unpaved, may close unexpectedly in the winter, and four-wheel-drive vehicles are often required in wet weather. There are no signs pointing the way to the park.

Maps: A trail map and brochure can be obtained by sending $1.50 to Sinkyone Wilderness State Park at the address below. To obtain a topographic map of the area, ask for Bear Harbor from the USGS.

Contact: Sinkyone Wilderness State Park, P.O. Box 245, Whitethorn, CA 95489; (707) 986-7711, (707) 445-6547, or fax (707) 441-5737.

Trail notes: The remote and rugged wilderness that once symbolized the Northern California coast is now protected forever in Sinkyone Wilderness State Park. Not many folks hike it, or even know how to get here. There are no directional signs along roads, no highways leading here, and the park is virtually never promoted. The few people that do visit will find a primitive, steep, and unforgiving terrain that provides a rare coastal wilderness experience. The best way to get it is on the Lost Coast Trail, best hiked north to south to keep the north winds out of your face.

From the northern trailhead at Orchard Camp, we advise you to split your trip in two by camping at Little Jackass Creek Camp. That will make your first day's hike 10.2 miles, the second 6.5 miles. Following is a more detailed breakdown.

Day 1: From the trailhead at Orchard Camp, the trail starts out flat and pleasant, arcing around Bear Harbor Cove. From here, the trail climbs 800 feet and then back down, in the process passing through a redwood grove and also breaking out for sweeping coastal views. Enjoy them, because the hike gets more difficult, including a steep climb up, over, and down a mountain, finally descending into Little Jackass Creek Camp, set beside a small stream. Day 2: The closeout of a two-day hike should always be as enjoyable as possible, and so it is here, with divine views in many spots along the 6.5-mile route. Alas, there's usually payment for views, and that payment comes in several rugged climbs in the park's most remote sections. After climbing to nearly 1,000 feet, the trail ends with an 800-foot downgrade over the last mile, descending to the Usal Campground parking area.

Special note: At the northern boundary of the Sinkyone Wilderness, this trail continues north into the King Range National Conservation Area, where it's routed for another 30 miles to the mouth of the Mattole River. See chapter BØ for more hikes in this area.

⑨ Bruhel Point Tide Pools

1.2 mi/1.0 hr

Location: On the Mendocino coast north of Fort Bragg; map CØ, grid e3.

User groups: Hikers and dogs. Not suitable for mountain bikes or horses. No wheelchair facilities.

Permits: No permits are required. Parking and access are free.

Directions: From Westport, drive south on Highway 1 about two miles to milepost marker 74.09. The tide pools are located a short walk from the Vista Point parking lot.

Maps: To obtain a topographic map of the area, ask for Inglenook from the USGS.

Contact: CalTrans, P.O. Box 3700, Eureka, CA 95502; (707) 445-6444 or fax (707) 445-6314.

Trail notes: Some of the best tide pools on the Pacific Coast can be found in Mendocino, and one of the best of the best is here, located just south of Bruhel Point. When you first arrive, you'll find a roadside vista point (no overnight parking), rest rooms, and a beach access trail. This is your calling. The trail is routed north toward Bruhel Point, much of it along the edge of ocean bluffs. We don't recommend freelancing a descent down the bluff, but rather urge you take only the cutoff trails, which lead to the best tide pool areas. Time your trip during a low tide, or better yet, a minus low tide. That is when the ocean pulls back, leaving a series of holes and cuts in a rock basin that remain filled with water, providing the perfect habitat and viewing areas for all kinds of tiny marine life.

⑩ Lake Cleone Trail

1.0 mi/0.5 hr

Location: In MacKerricher State Park on the Mendocino coast north of Fort Bragg; map CØ, grid e3.

User groups: Hikers and wheelchairs (the trail is partially wheelchair accessible). No dogs, horses, or mountain bikes. Horse trails are available elsewhere in the park.

Permits: No permits are required. Parking and access are free.

Directions: From Fort Bragg, drive north on U.S. Highway 1 for three miles to the park entrance. Turn left and drive to the parking area beside the lake. The trailhead is on the east side of the parking lot.

Maps: For a brochure and trail map, send $1 to MacKerricher State Park at the address below. To obtain a topographic map of the area, ask for Inglenook from the USGS.

Contact: MacKerricher State Park, P.O. Box 440, Mendocino, CA 95460; (707) 937-5804 or fax (707) 937-2953.

Trail notes: MacKerricher State Park is filled with enticing highlights, including free day-use access and the loop trail around Lake Cleone, which is not only easy, but is definitely something special. Mrs. MacKerricher aptly named the trail, which means gracious or beautiful in Greek. The route includes several sections on raised wooden walkways, which provide routes through marshy areas which are partially wheelchair accessible. In the winter months, the southern part of the trail (without the boardwalk) can be flooded. Be sure to wear your high boots.

The trail burrows through a variety of trees and lush vegetation, providing many glimpses of pretty Lake Cleone. It loops all the way around the lake, which is almost always full, with the beautiful Pacific Ocean just beyond to the west, a cypress grove to the south, and a marsh to the east. Historically, the lake is stocked with trout by the Department of Fish and Game three times prior to Memorial Day weekend.

Special note: From the parking lot adjacent to the lake, you can walk under the built-up foundation of an old railroad line, now a bicycle trail called the Old Haul Road, and connect to the Headlands Trail. This is a must-do, an easy and short walk, much of it on a raised walkway, that leads to the best seal and whale watching station on the coast, as well as a series of tide pools.

⑪ Falls Loop Trail

7.0 mi/4.0 hrs

Location: In Russian Gulch State Park on the Mendocino coast south of Fort Bragg; map CØ, grid g3.

User groups: Hikers only. No mountain bikes, dogs, or horses. However, a paved trail for bicycles and wheelchairs is routed 2.5 miles to the trailhead of the Falls Loop Trail (see special note).

Permits: No permits are required. A $5 state park entrance fee is charged for each vehicle.

Directions: From Fort Bragg, drive south on Highway 1 for six miles to the Russian Gulch State Park entrance. Turn left and follow the signs to the trailhead.

Maps: For a brochure and trail map, send $1 to Russian Gulch State Park at the address below. To obtain a topographic map of the area, ask for Mendocino from the USGS.

Contact: Russian Gulch State Park, P.O. Box 440, Mendocino, CA 95460; (707) 937-5804 or (707) 445-6547.

Trail notes: A 35-foot waterfall in deep forest makes this walk one of the prettiest on the Mendocino coast. Most of the year, this waterfall is a narrow silvery stream that pours atop and across a boulder. In winter, it can build into a more powerful chute and land in the rock basin with surging splashes.

The route is simple, taking the North Trail for 2.5 miles out to its junction with the Falls Loop Trail. At this junction, turn left and you'll hike less than a mile to reach the falls. Even in the summer months, this is a pretty, if narrow, silver cascade, streaming 20 feet across a granite boulder and down into a pool. The entire trip has very little elevation gain—it's an easy walk out to the Falls Loop Trail, then only a 200-foot gain to reach the waterfall. As you go, you'll delve deeper and deeper into dense forest, and although a lot of the old-growth was taken a long time ago, much is still divine.

Special note: A paved bicycle trail runs parallel to the North Trail and makes a great bike trip. But please note that bikes are not permitted on the dirt Falls Loop Trail. Bike racks are available at the intersection of these two trails,

meaning bikers can make the trip to the falls with only a one-mile hike. In other words, ride to the Falls Loop Trail junction, park your bike, and walk one mile from there. This bike trail is also wheelchair accessible.

⑫ Chamberlain Creek Waterfall Trail

0.5 mi/0.5 hr

Location: In Jackson State Forest east of Fort Bragg; map CØ, grid g5.

User groups: Hikers and dogs. No horses or mountain bikes. No wheelchair facilities.

Permits: No permits are required. Parking and access are free.

Directions: From Willits, drive west on Highway 20 for 17 miles. Turn right on County Road 200 and drive 1.2 miles, then bear left as the road forks. Drive about three more miles. Park on the side of the road and follow the hand railing down a steep slope to access the trail. Note that County Road 200 is sometimes closed due to weather; call ahead for the status.

Maps: For a free trail map, contact Jackson State Forest at the address below. To obtain a topographic map of the area, ask for Northspur from the USGS.

Contact: Jackson State Forest, 802 North Main Street, Fort Bragg, CA 95437; (707) 964-5674 or fax (707) 964-0941.

Trail notes: Hidden in Jackson State Forest is a 50-foot waterfall set in a canyon framed by redwoods, the kind of place where explorers can get religion. Set back off an old dirt logging road, the trail is short, yet steep, secluded, and beautiful. This access road, by the way, can get muddy in the winter and can be impassable for two-wheel drive vehicles. After parking, you'll find the trail routed down the canyon to the stream, starting with a short series of steps. The trail simply heads down the canyon directly to the base of the waterfall. A sprinkling of hike-in campgrounds are located amid giant redwoods about a quarter of a mile west of the waterfall. Despite the beauty of the area and the popularity of the Mendocino coast, Jackson State Forest is typically overlooked by most visitors, meaning you'll most likely have the place to yourself.

⓭ Fern Canyon Trail

8.1 mi/5.0 hrs

Location: In Van Damme State Park on the Mendocino coast south of Mendocino; map CØ, grid h2.

User groups: Hikers only. Wheelchairs and mountain bikes are allowed on the first 2.3 miles of the trail only.

Permits: No permits are required. A $5 state park entrance fee is charged for each vehicle.

Directions: From Mendocino, drive south on Highway 1 for 2.5 miles to the park entrance. Turn left and follow the signs to the trailhead. For campers, start near campsite number 26.

Maps: For a brochure and trail map, send $1 to Van Damme State Park at the address below. To obtain a topographic map of the area, ask for Mendocino from the USGS.

Contact: Van Damme State Park, P.O. Box 440, Mendocino, CA 95460; (707) 937-5804 or (707) 445-6547.

Trail notes: This beautiful streamside walk amid coastal redwoods is one of the most popular trails on the Mendocino coast. The trail starts at the bottom of a canyon along the Little River, then heads upstream, rising gently along the way, with a series of little bridges crisscrossing the water. The creek is pretty and often clear, the forest canopy is towering, and the understory of fern and sorrel is lush. Most people hike 2.3 miles (paved all the way) out to the junction of the Loop Trail, then turn around and head back. You can add on a three-mile loop, including a visit to the delightful Pygmy Forest, where an elevated wood walkway is routed amid this unusual setting. Note that heavy rains can flood out the trail and wash out the bridges.

Special note: Do not get this "Fern Canyon Trail" confused with the "Fern Canyon Trail" on the Humboldt County coast, which is detailed in chapter AØ.

⓮ Big Hendy Grove Trail

1.0 mi/0.5 hr

Location: In Hendy Woods State Park in Mendocino National Forest; map CØ, grid j5.

User groups: Hikers and wheelchairs (for a quarter of a mile). No dogs, horses, or mountain bikes.

Permits: No permits are required. A $5 state park entrance fee is charged for each vehicle.

Directions: From Mendocino, drive south on Highway 1 for about five miles to Highway 128. Go east on Highway 128 about 20 miles to the entrance of Hendy Woods State Park on the left. The trailhead begins just off the small parking lot.

Maps: For a brochure and trail map, send $1 to Hendy Woods State Park at the address below. To obtain a topographic map of the area, ask for Philo from the USGS.

Contact: Hendy Woods State Park, P.O. Box 440, Mendocino, CA 95460; (707) 895-3141, (707) 895-3537, or fax (707) 895-2012.

Trail notes: This easy and short walk through an ancient redwood forest can have visitors to Hendy Woods smiling for days. Hendy Woods is located in the redwood-filled canyon of the Navarro River, which flows to the sea on the Mendocino coast. While the park covers 845 acres, it's the two old-growth redwood groves that are most compelling. The groves are called Little Hendy (20 acres) and Big Hendy (80 acres).

When you first arrive, amid the foothill grassland country, you'll be stunned at the sudden interface with redwoods. At Big Hendy, start by taking the half-mile Discovery Trail, which leaves the grasslands and enters the grove on a dirt path. Suddenly you'll be walking among towering redwoods, moss-covered stumps, and a sprinkling of giant fallen trees, all set amid ferns and sorrel. A great side trip is to walk uphill on the cutoff trail to the old hermit's hut, where one of the last of the real hermits lived in a hollowed-out tree stump for years.

⓯ Glen Eden Trail

8.0 mi/5.0 hrs

Location: In Cow Mountain Recreation Area east of Ukiah; map CØ, grid j9.

User groups: Hikers, horses, and mountain bikes. No wheelchair facilities.

Permits: No permits are required. Parking and access are free.

Directions: From Ukiah on U.S. 101, drive east on Talmage Road to West Side Road. Turn right and go about a quarter of a mile on West Side Road. At the sign for Cow Mountain, turn left on Mill Creek Road and drive about three miles. You'll pass two ponds; at the upper end of the second pond, look for the small parking lot on the left side of the road. If you reach Mill Creek County Park, you've gone too far. The Mayacamas Trailhead (which leads to the Glen Eden Trail) is here.

Maps: For a free trail map of the Cow Mountain Recreation Area, contact the Bureau of Land Management at the address below. To obtain a topographic map of the area, ask for Cow Mountain from the USGS.

Contact: Bureau of Land Management, Ukiah District Office, 555 Leslie Street, Ukiah, CA 95482; (707) 468-4000.

Trail notes: This trail will have you sweating like Charles Manson's cellmate. The Glen Eden Trail is not only difficult to find (follow our directions precisely), but has several steep sections, and is typically quite hot. The chaparral-covered slopes are peppered with pine and oak, with many miles of trails and fire roads. But it's extremely rare to see other hikers, and no off-road vehicles are allowed (unlike the southern portion of the Cow Mountain Recreation Area). In addition, the views of Clear Lake and the Mayacamas Range are outstanding.

Start the trip by hiking up the Mayacamas Trail, which traces first Willow Creek and then Mill Creek. In little over a mile, you'll junction with the Glen Eden Trail. Turn right and climb out— the trail eventually crosses Mendo Rock Road (another trailhead possibility) and continues up to a series of great overlooks of Clear Lake. To return, retrace your route.

Leave No Trace Tips

Minimize Use and Impact of Fires

Campfires can have a lasting impact on the backcountry. Always carry a lightweight stove for cooking, and use a candle lantern instead of building a fire whenever possible.

Where fires are permitted, use established fire rings only.

Do not scar the natural setting by snapping the branches off live, dead, or downed trees.

Completely extinguish your campfire and make sure it is cold before departing. Remove all unburned trash from the fire ring and scatter the cold ashes over a large area well away from any camp.

Map C1

Adjoining Maps: East: C2 ..... *page* 124   West: CØ 106
North: B1 54   South: D1 156

Northern California Map .... *page* 2

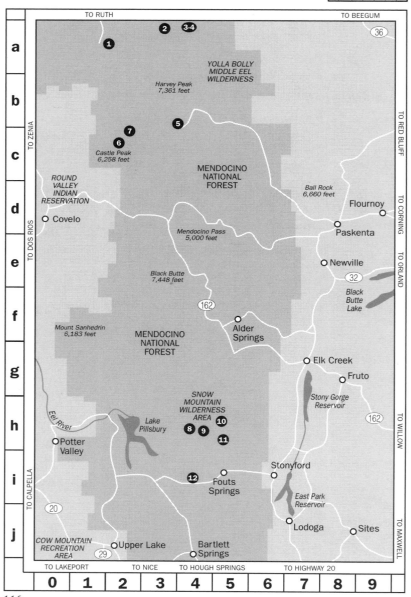

Chapter C1 features:

❶ Waterspout Loop

17.0 mi/2.0 days

Location: On the western boundary of the Yolla Bolly Wilderness west of Red Bluff; map C1, grid a2.

User groups: Hikers, dogs, and horses. No mountain bikes. No wheelchair facilities.

Permits: A campfire permit is required for hikers planning to camp. Parking and access are free.

Directions: From Interstate 5 at Red Bluff, drive west on Highway 36 about 50 miles to the Harrison Gulch Ranger Station. Go 8.5 miles east on Highway 36, then turn south on Forest Service Road 30 (Wildwood-Mad River Road). Drive approximately 24 miles, turn south on Forest Service Road 27N02, and continue to the Waterspout Trailhead on the left.

Maps: For a map of Mendocino National Forest, send $4 to USDA-Forest Service, 630 Sansome Street, San Francisco, CA 94111. To obtain a topographic map of the area, ask for Yolla Bolly from the USGS.

Contact: Mendocino National Forest, Corning Ranger District, P.O. Box 1019, Corning, CA 96021; (916) 824-5196 or fax (916) 824-6034.

Trail notes: The Yolla Bolly Wilderness is known for providing little-traveled routes to an intricate series of small streams, including the headwaters of different forks of the Eel and Trinity Rivers. That is the appeal of this loop trail, which traces the headwaters of the North Fork of the Middle Fork Eel, then loops back on Buck Ridge. There are no lakes along the route, but, then again, there are usually no people either. The trail starts at the remote Waterspout Trailhead, named for a spring located along the access road about a mile from the parking area.

Within a mile, the trail crosses the stream, then is routed along it southward for seven miles. The nearby Morrison Trail camp is a good spot for an overnighter. From there you can loop back by turning left at Wrights Valley, then turning left again a mile later, hiking Buck Ridge and the Yellowjacket Trail back to Waterspout.

❷ Black Rock Lake Trail

4.5 mi/3.0 hrs

Location: On the northern boundary of the Yolla Bolly Wilderness west of Red Bluff; map C1, grid a3.

User groups: Hikers, dogs, and horses. No mountain bikes. No wheelchair facilities.

Permits: A campfire permit is required for hikers planning to camp.

Directions: From Interstate 5 at Red Bluff, drive west on Highway 36 about 50 miles to the Harrison Gulch Ranger Station. Go 8.5 miles east on Highway 36, then turn south on Forest Service Road 30 (Wildwood-Mad River Road). Drive approximately nine miles, then turn east on Forest Service Road 35 and head to the Stuart Gap Trailhead.

Maps: For a map of Shasta-Trinity National Forest, send $4 to USDA-Forest Service, 630 Sansome Street, San Francisco, CA 94111. To obtain a topographic map of the area, ask for North Yolla Bolly from the USGS.

Contact: Shasta-Trinity National Forest, Yolla Bolla Ranger District, Platina, CA 96076; (916) 352-4211 or fax (916) 352-4312.

Trail notes: The 2.25-mile hike from the Stuart Gap Trailhead to Black Rock Lake is one of the best day hikes in the Yolla Bolly Wilderness. The trailhead is at the northern tip of the wilderness at 5,600 feet, where you hike about a mile along the northwestern flank of North Yolla Bolly Mountain (7,863 feet) toward Pettyjohn Basin. You then turn right and tromp another 1.25 miles to the lake, with the trail contouring through open stands of pine and fir and some small meadows. Small Black Rock Lake is set just below Black Rock Mountain (7,755 feet), and is ideal for swimming, but only rarely has it ever been stocked with trout. There are many other excellent day hikes from this trailhead, including to Yolla Bolly Lake (which has trout), Black Rock Mountain (great views), North Yolla Bolly Mountain (more sweeping vistas), and Cedar Basin (several creeks). Any of these make for classic days, remote and quiet. The trailhead can also be used as a jump-off spot for a hike straight south on the Pettyjohn Trail into the wilderness interior.

❸ Tomhead Saddle Loop

15.0 mi/2.0 days

Location: Near the eastern boundary of the Yolla Bolly Wilderness west of Red Bluff; map C1, grid a4.

User groups: Hikers, dogs, and horses. No mountain bikes. No wheelchair facilities.

Permits: A campfire permit is required for hikers planning to camp.

Directions: From Interstate 5 at Red Bluff, drive west on Highway 36 about 13 miles. Turn left (south) on Cannon Road and go approximately five miles to Pettyjohn Road. Turn west on Pettyjohn Road to Saddle Camp, then turn south on Forest Service Road 27N06 and drive three miles to the parking area at Tomhead Saddle Campground.

Maps: For a map of Shasta-Trinity National Forest, send $4 to USDA-Forest Service, 630 Sansome Street, San Francisco, CA 94111. To obtain a topographic map of the area, ask for North Yolla Bolly from the USGS.

Contact: Shasta-Trinity National Forest, Yolla Bolla Ranger District, Platina, CA 96076; (916) 352-4211 or fax (916) 352-4312.

Trail notes: Why is it that many backpacking trips with treacherous sections often start out easy, leading hikers into a misplaced sense of calm? While we don't know the answer, we do know this trail does exactly that. From the trailhead at Tomhead Saddle, elevation 5,500 feet, take the Humboldt Trail west toward East Low Gap. It seems an easy walk, with little elevation gain or loss. "What, me worry?" Well, you turn left on the Sanford Ridge Trail, eventually dropping down into Burnt Camp, an eight-mile first day. But get this: no water is available anywhere along the route. If your canteen is dry, Burnt Camp will seem like Eden, set along the South Fork of Cottonwood Creek. All seems right again. But it isn't, at least not if you don't like slippery stream crossings. The second day, hiking out from Burnt Camp, you'll take the Cottonwood Trail to Hawk Camp, then take the Syd Cabin Ridge Trail back to the parking area at Tomhead Saddle. This includes five stream crossings, some of them across slick bedrock. We were thinking of making a video of people crossing the river, then selling it as the "Yolla Bolly Guide to Ballet."

❹ Syd Cabin Ridge Trail

8.0 mi/2.0 days

Location: On the eastern boundary of the Yolla Bolly Wilderness west of Red Bluff; map C1, grid a4.

User groups: Hikers, dogs, and horses. No mountain bikes. No wheelchair facilities.

Permits: A campfire permit is required for hikers planning to camp.

Directions: From Interstate 5 at Red Bluff, drive west on Highway 36 about 13 miles. Turn left (south) on Cannon Road and go approximately five miles to Pettyjohn Road. Turn west on Pettyjohn Road and drive to Saddle Camp, then turn south on Forest Service Road 27N06 and continue three miles to the parking area at Tomhead Saddle Campground.

Maps: For a map of Shasta-Trinity National Forest, send $4 to USDA-Forest Service, 630 Sansome Street, San Francisco, CA 94111. To obtain a topographic map of the area, ask for North Yolla Bolly from the USGS.

Contact: Shasta-Trinity National Forest, Yolla Bolla Ranger District, Platina, CA 96076; (916) 352-4211 or fax (916) 352-4312.

Trail notes: Not many people hike into the Yolla Bolly Wilderness, set up a camp, then hike back out the next day. But here is a chance to do exactly that. The trailhead is at the Tomhead Saddle, located just west of Tomhead Mountain, elevation 6,757 feet. From here you hike past Tomhead Spring on the Syd Cabin Ridge Trail, then drop down into Hawk Camp. Expect a steady climb with no water between Tomhead Spring and Hawk Camp. Set just below the confluence of three feeder streams, Hawk Camp is an ideal spot to overnight. If you plan on extending your trip for several days into the wilderness, a network of trails intersects just beyond Hawk Camp, but note that a stream crossing is required.

❺ Ides Cove National Recreation Trail

10.5 mi/5.5 hrs

Location: On the southeastern boundary of the Yolla Bolly Wilderness west of Red Bluff; map C1, grid b4.

User groups: Hikers, dogs, and horses. No mountain bikes. No wheelchair facilities.

Permits: A campfire permit is required for hikers planning to camp.

Directions: From Corning on Interstate 5, take the Corning Road/Paskenta Road exit and drive west about 20 miles. In the town of Paskenta, Corning/Paskenta Road will split and become Round Valley Road on the left and, straight ahead, County Road M2/Toomes Creek Road. Continue straight on County Road M2/Toomes Creek Road to Cold Springs Ranger Station. Turn right on County Road M22 and go about 15 miles to the trailhead. For an alternate route from Red Bluff, turn west on County Road 356 (Forest Route 22) and drive about 41 miles. Then turn right on a signed access road and drive to the Ides Cove Trailhead.

Maps: For a map of Mendocino National Forest, send $4 to USDA-Forest Service, 630 Sansome Street, San Francisco, CA 94111. To obtain a topographic map of the area, ask for South Yolla Bolly from the USGS.

Contact: Mendocino National Forest, Corning Ranger District, P.O. Box 1019, Corning, CA 96021; (916) 824-5196 or fax (916) 824-6034.

Trail notes: At 8,092 feet, South Yolla Bolly Mountain is the highest point in this wilderness.

The Ides Cove National Recreation Trail skirts this mountain as part of one of the top one-day loop trails available in the Yolla Bollys, and a bonus is that a shorter loop hike (3.5 miles) is also convenient here. Another bonus is that a free campground with horse facilities is available at the trailhead. Despite that, the trail gets only light use. From the Ides Cove Trailhead, the trail drops down to the headwaters of Slide Creek, then is routed out to the foot of Harvey Peak at 7,361 feet, which is the halfway point and a good spot for lunch. The trail then turns sharply and is routed back along the flank of the South Yolla Bolly Mountains. On the way, it passes both Long and Square Lakes, both tiny water holes stocked with brook trout.

❻ Wrights Valley Trail

8.0 mi/4.5 hrs

Location: On the southern boundary of the Yolla Bolly Wilderness west of Red Bluff; map C1, grid c2.

User groups: Hikers, dogs, and horses. No mountain bikes. No wheelchair facilities.

Permits: A campfire permit is required for hikers planning to camp. Parking and access are free.

Directions: From Willits, drive north on U.S. 101 for 13 miles to Longvale. Turn east on Highway 162 and go to Covelo. Head east on Highway 162 for 13 miles to the Eel River Bridge. Turn left (north) at the bridge on Forest Service Road M1 and drive about 24 miles. Turn left on Forest Service Road 25N15C and continue to the Rock Cabin Trailhead.

Maps: For a map of Mendocino National Forest, send $4 to USDA-Forest Service, 630 Sansome Street, San Francisco, CA 94111. To obtain a topographic map of the area, ask for South Yolla Bolly from the USGS.

Contact: Mendocino National Forest, Covelo Ranger District, 78150 Covelo Road, Covelo, CA 95428; (707) 983-6118 or fax (707) 983-8004.

Trail notes: The Rock Cabin Trail extends north into the Yolla Bolly Wilderness, and up, over, then down a short ridge before pouring into Wrights Valley. It's about a four-mile trip one way. Here you'll find the headwaters of the Middle Fork of the Eel River, one of the prettiest streams in the wilderness. The trail is well marked and includes two creek crossings. While the Yolla Bollys provide few lakes, the Middle Fork awaits you, offering some of the best trout fishing in the region. Check with the Department of Fish and Game for updated fishing regulations.

Special note: Map-gazing hikers will likely notice a small lake, Henthorne Lake, complete with two wilderness cabins, set just 2.5 miles from the Rock Cabin Trailhead. Resist the urge to visit. This is maintained as private property, a nature reserve for some lucky soul. Hikers are often tempted to hike in via a very faint cowboy trail (with a river crossing) and camp here illegally. The Forest Service has purchased this property, but it's held as a "life estate" with all rights reserved to the former owners.

❼ Soldier Ridge Trail

8.0 mi/2.0 days

Location: On the southern boundary of the Yolla Bolly Wilderness west of Red Bluff; map C1, grid c3.

User groups: Hikers, dogs, and horses. No mountain bikes. No wheelchair facilities.

Permits: A campfire permit is required for hikers planning to camp. Parking and access are free.

Directions: From Willits, drive north on U.S. 101 for 13 miles to Longvale. Turn east on Highway 162 and head to Covelo. Continue driving east on Highway 162 for 13 miles to the Eel River Bridge. Turn left (north) at the bridge and go about 27 miles on Forest Service Road M1 to the trailhead at the end of the road.

Maps: For a map of Mendocino National Forest, send $4 to USDA-Forest Service, 630 Sansome Street, San Francisco, CA 94111. To obtain a topographic map of the area, ask for South Yolla Bolly from the USGS.

Contact: Mendocino National Forest, Covelo Ranger District, 78150 Covelo Road, Covelo, CA 95428; (707) 983-6118 or fax (707) 983-8004.

Trail notes: This is a mighty short walk as backpack trips go, just 3.5 miles to Kingsley Lake. But the rugged climb on the Soldier Ridge Trail to get there, along with the charm of this little lake, will compel you to stay overnight anyway. Actually, it's a long drive in the middle of nowhere just to

reach the trailhead, and then when you get there, you'll face a daunting 3.5-mile climb up the spine of Soldier Ridge toward the Yolla Bolly Crest. At the crest are three mountains lined in a row, Sugarloaf Mountain (elevation 7,367 feet), Solomon Peak (7,581 feet), and Hammerhorn Mountain (7,567 feet). The trail crosses through a saddle between Sugarloaf Mountain and Solomon Peak, then drops down to little Kingsley Lake, created from the headwaters of Thomas Creek. All is quiet and peaceful here.

❽ Waterfall Loop

13.0 mi/1.0 day

Location: On the northwestern boundary of the Snow Mountain Wilderness in Mendocino National Forest; map C1, grid h4.

User groups: Hikers, dogs, and horses. No mountain bikes. No wheelchair facilities.

Permits: A campfire permit is required for hikers planning to camp. Parking and access are free.

Directions: From Willows on Interstate 5, drive 21 miles west on Highway 162 to the town of Elk Creek. Turn west on Ivory Mill Road (Road 308) and go 15 miles to Forest Service Road M3. Turn south on Forest Service Road M3 and head 15.5 miles to the West Crockett Trailhead.

Maps: For a map of Mendocino National Forest, send $4 to USDA-Forest Service, 630 Sansome Street, San Francisco, CA 94111. To obtain topographic maps of the area, ask for Crockett Peak and St. John Mountain from the USGS.

Contact: Mendocino National Forest, Stonyford Ranger District, P.O. Box 160, Stonyford, CA 95979; (916) 963-3128 or fax (916) 963-3123.

Trail notes: Very few people know about the Snow Mountain Wilderness, and far fewer know about this excellent loop trail that traverses the region's most treasured areas. Double-peaked Snow Mountain itself is the big ridge located about midway between Interstate 5 at Willows and U.S. 101 at Willits. This trail starts at the northern boundary of the wilderness at the West Crockett Trailhead (just west of Crockett Peak), crosses the headwaters of Stony Creek (the last water for four miles), and then is routed along the Milk Ranch Trail toward Snow Mountain. A waterfall is located on a spur trail off the loop,

2.5 miles from the trailhead. The trail climbs much of the way, reaching a small loop set between East Snow Mountain (7,056 feet) and West Snow Mountain (7,038 feet). To return, take the North Ridge Trail, which drops down from Snow Mountain and traces along the Middle Fork of Stony Creek for a good portion of the route back to the parking area. Much of this area can be quite dry and hot in the peak of summer, especially on the North Ridge. Two notes: Rattlesnakes are common, and hikers should always be certain to carry a lot of water here—twice as much as usual.

❾ Upper Nye Trailhead

4.0 mi/2.5 hrs

Location: On the northern boundary of the Snow Mountain Wilderness in Mendocino National Forest; map C1, grid h4.

User groups: Hikers, dogs, and horses. No mountain bikes. No wheelchair facilities.

Permits: A campfire permit is required for hikers planning to camp. Parking and access are free.

Directions: From Willows on Interstate 5, drive west on Highway 162 about 21 miles to the town of Elk Creek. Turn west on Ivory Mill Road (Road 308) and go about 15 miles to Forest Service Road M3. Turn south on Forest Service Road M3 and head 14 miles to the trailhead.

Maps: For a map of Mendocino National Forest, send $4 to USDA-Forest Service, 630 Sansome Street, San Francisco, CA 94111. To obtain topographic maps of the area, ask for Crockett Peak and St. John Mountain from the USGS.

Contact: Mendocino National Forest, Stonyford Ranger District, P.O. Box 160, Stonyford, CA 95979; (916) 963-3128 or fax (916) 963-3123.

Trail notes: Much of Mendocino National Forest has been logged, with large patch cuts that in many cases have been slow to regrow. But the Snow Mountain Wilderness is like a little protected island amid the devastation, and this trail furnishes a short hike to one of its least visited, quiet streamside settings.

The trail has no head marker, is not maintained, and is hard to find. Start at the Upper Nye Trailhead (the primitive Waters Camp is a quarter of a mile away), then hike the eastern slopes of the

Snow Mountain Ridge down to Bear Wallow Creek. It's a two-mile hike, with one steep section. The small creek is a lovely spot to lean against a tree and relax for a while. Be forewarned that temperatures get quite warm in this region in the summer, particularly on hikes on the east-facing slopes, such as this one.

❿ Windy Point Trailhead

3.25 mi/1.75 hrs

Location: On the northern boundary of the Snow Mountain Wilderness in Mendocino National Forest; map C1, grid h5.

User groups: Hikers, dogs, and horses. No mountain bikes. No wheelchair facilities.

Permits: A campfire permit is required for hikers planning to camp. Parking and access are free.

Directions: From Willows on Interstate 5, drive west on Highway 162 about 21 miles to the town of Elk Creek. Turn west on Ivory Mill Road (Road 308) and head about 15 miles to Forest Service Road M3. Turn south on Forest Service Road M3 and go 13 miles to the trailhead.

Maps: For a map of Mendocino National Forest, send $4 to USDA-Forest Service, 630 Sansome Street, San Francisco, CA 94111. To obtain topographic maps of the area, ask for Crockett Peak and St. John Mountain from the USGS.

Contact: Mendocino National Forest, Stonyford Ranger District, P.O. Box 160, Stonyford, CA 95979; (916) 963-3128 or fax (916) 963-3123.

Trail notes: Every wilderness has secret spots, and so it is here in the Snow Mountain Wilderness. On a hot summer day, when every drop of water is counted as if it were liquid gold, you'll find a simple paradise on this short walk to the headwaters of a tiny fork of Bear Wallow Creek. The hike starts at Windy Point, the northernmost trailhead in the Snow Mountains. The trail heads straight east on the Bear Wallow Trail for a little more than a mile across very dry country. About 1.5 miles in, start looking for a spur trail on the right side, and when you see it, take it. This spur drops a short distance down to the source of the North Fork of Bear Wallow Creek, a truly secret little spot. If you think there are too many people in the world, just come here and look around.

⑪ Bear Wallow Trailhead

4.0 mi/2.5 hrs

Location: On the eastern boundary of the Snow Mountain Wilderness in Mendocino National Forest; map C1, grid h5.

User groups: Hikers, dogs, and horses. No mountain bikes. No wheelchair facilities.

Permits: A campfire permit is required for hikers planning to camp. Parking and access are free.

Directions: From Willows on Interstate 5, drive 21 miles west on Highway 162 to the town of Elk Creek. Turn south and head approximately 15 miles to Stonyford. Go west on Fouts Springs Road and drive about eight miles, then turn north on Forest Service Road 18N06 and drive to the parking area.

Maps: For a map of Mendocino National Forest, send $4 to USDA-Forest Service, 630 Sansome Street, San Francisco, CA 94111. To obtain a topographic map of the area, ask for Fouts Springs from the USGS.

Contact: Mendocino National Forest, Stonyford Ranger District, P.O. Box 160, Stonyford, CA 95979; (916) 963-3128 or fax (916) 963-3123.

Trail notes: Whoa, it can get hot out here. In summer, an early start for a hike is mandatory, particularly on the east-facing slopes of the Snow Mountain Wilderness. Your destination is a pretty section of Bear Wallow Creek, a small feeder stream to the Middle Fork of Stony Creek. The hike starts at the Bear Wallow Trailhead. From here, the Bear Wallow Trail is routed north for two miles; at that point, start looking for a trail junction on the left side. Be sure not to miss it. Turn left and take the quarter-mile traipse down to Bear Wallow Creek, a pretty spot and a decent destination for a day's walk. If you miss the turn, the Bear Wallow Trail continues all the way to Windy Point Trailhead, and, with no water available, you'll be saying, "Beam me up, Scotty."

⑫ Box Spring Loop

10.0 mi/1.0 day

Location: On the southwestern boundary of the Snow Mountain Wilderness in Mendocino National Forest; map C1, grid i4.

User groups: Hikers, dogs, and horses. No mountain bikes. No wheelchair facilities.

Permits: A campfire permit is required for hikers planning to camp. Parking and access are free.

Directions: From Willows on Interstate 5, drive 21 miles west on Highway 162 to the town of Elk Creek. Turn south and drive 15 miles to Stonyford. Turn west on Fouts Springs Road and drive about 32 miles, then go north on a signed access road and drive to the parking area at the end of the road at the Summit Spring Trailhead.

Maps: For a map of Mendocino National Forest, send $4 to USDA-Forest Service, 630 Sansome Street, San Francisco, CA 94111. To obtain a topographic map of the area, ask for Fouts Springs from the USGS.

Contact: Mendocino National Forest, Stonyford Ranger District, P.O. Box 160, Stonyford, CA 95979; (916) 963-3128 or fax (916) 963-3123.

Trail notes: This is not a trail for the indifferent. Do you yearn for the passion of the mountain experience? Do you crave the zest of life when you have a bad case of dry-mouth and discover a mountain spring? Is the price of a climb worth it for the mountaintop payoff? You need to answer yes, yes, and yes to be ready for this loop hike. It includes two killer climbs, a wonderful little spring along the trail, and the ascent of West Snow Mountain, 7,038 feet. Still interested? Then read on.

The trail starts at the Summit Spring Trailhead, and in the first mile, includes a no-fun clamber up to High Rock. At the trail junction here, turn right on the Box Spring Loop Trail and hike past the headwaters of Trout Creek to Box Spring, located just to the right of the trail near another trail junction. In hot weather, typically all summer, this spot is paradise. Turn left and make the three-mile climb up West Snow Mountain, sweating it out every step of the way. Enjoy this victory for a while before dropping back down for the final three miles back to the trailhead and parking area. This is an excellent loop hike, one that furnishes several rewards, but makes you earn every one of them.

Leave No Trace Tips

Plan Ahead and Prepare

Learn about the regulations and
special concerns of the area you are visiting.

Visit the backcountry in small groups.

Avoid popular areas during peak-use periods.

Choose equipment and clothing in subdued colors.

Pack food in reusable containers.

Map C2

Adjoining Maps: East: C3 ..... *page* 130   West: C1 116
North: B2 66   South: D2 162

Northern California Map .... *page* 2

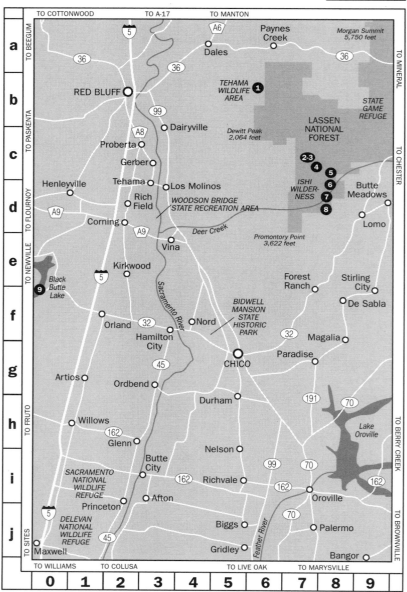

❶ McClure Trail

9.0 mi/1.0 day

Location: In the Tehama Wildlife Area east of Red Bluff; map C2, grid b6.

User groups: Hikers, dogs, and mountain bikes. No horses. No wheelchair facilities.

Permits: No permits are required. Parking and access are free.

Directions: From Interstate 5 at Red Bluff, turn east on Highway 36 and drive 20 miles to the town of Paynes Creek. Turn south on Plum Creek Road and go to Ishi Conservation Camp. Drive about 2.5 miles south to High Trestle Road and follow it to Hogsback Road. Park across from the intersection of High Trestle and Hogsback Roads and walk about a quarter of a mile on the dirt road to the trailhead. Access to the Tehama Wildlife Area is closed to the public from December 1 through the first Saturday in April. Access is also restricted for a short period during deer season in late September. There are no closures on U.S. Forest Service trails.

Maps: For a free map, contact the Tehama Wildlife Area at the address below. To obtain a topographic map of the area, ask for Dewitt Peak from the USGS.

Contact: Department of Fish and Game, Tehama Wildlife Area, P.O. Box 188, Paynes Creek, CA 96075; phone or fax (916) 597-2201.

Trail notes: At first glance the Tehama Wildlife Area might just appear to be nothing more than rolling oak woodlands. This is a habitat managed expressly for wildlife, and it includes a beautiful stream, abundant vegetation, and plenty of animals. This trail accesses the best of it, heading down a steep canyon to Antelope Creek, buffered by riparian vegetation. Wild pigs roam the canyons, deer are rampant in late fall (typically migrating in after the hunting season is over), and there are also lots of squirrels, hawks, and, alas, rattlesnakes. In late winter and spring, the canyons and hillsides come alive in green, and all wildlife seems to prosper. They'd better when they have the chance, because the heat here can seem unbearable in summer.

❷ Table Mountain Trail

3.2 mi/2.5 hrs

Location: In the Ishi Wilderness east of Red Bluff; map C2, grid c7.

User groups: Hikers, dogs, and horses. No mountain bikes. No wheelchair facilities.

Permits: A campfire permit is required for hikers planning to camp. Parking and access are free.

Directions: From Interstate 5 at Red Bluff, turn east on Highway 36 and drive to the town of Paynes Creek. Turn south on Little Giant Mill Road (Road 202) and go about seven miles until you reach an intersection. Turn south at Ponderosa Way and drive about 10 miles, then turn west on Forest Service Road 28N57 and follow the Peligreen Jeep Trail for six miles to the trailhead. The last five miles of road are suitable for four-wheel-drive vehicles only.

Maps: For a free trail map, contact the Almanor Ranger District at the address below. To obtain topographic maps of the area, ask for Panther Spring and Butte Meadows from the USGS.

Contact: Lassen National Forest, Almanor Ranger District, P.O. Box 767, Chester, CA 96020; (916) 258-2141 or fax (916) 258-3491.

Trail notes: This trail may be short, but it's anything but sweet. Except, that is, from the top of Table Mountain, elevation 2,380 feet, where you're supplied with a sweeping view of the Sacramento Valley and the surrounding land of Ishi. This is where Ishi, the last survivor of the Yahi Yana Indian tribe, escaped from a band of white settlers who exterminated the rest of the Yahis. Before being killed off, the Indians had lived here for 3,000 years; another stellar moment in the real history of the western frontier.

The trail starts from the northwest corner of the wilderness at the Table Mountain Trailhead, and then is routed 1.6 miles to the summit. It's very steep and challenging, and most hikers will be wheezing like worn-out donkeys before making the top. Because of the hot summers, it's absolutely critical to either start the trip very early in the morning or time it during cool weather, and to bring plenty of water for your built-in radiator.

Special Note: A trail map is strongly advised for those hiking in the Ishi Wilderness.

❸ Rancheria Trail

4.0 mi/2.75 hrs

Location: In the Ishi Wilderness east of Red Bluff; map C2, grid c7.

User groups: Hikers, dogs, and horses. No mountain bikes. No wheelchair facilities.

Permits: A campfire permit is required for hikers planning to camp. Parking and access are free.

Directions: From Interstate 5 at Red Bluff, turn east on Highway 36 and drive to the town of Paynes Creek. Turn south on Little Giant Mill Road (Road 202) and go about seven miles until you reach an intersection. Turn south at Ponderosa Way and drive about 10 miles, then turn west on Forest Service Road 28N57 and follow the Peligreen Jeep Trail for two miles to the Rancheria Trailhead. The last two miles of road are suitable for four-wheel-drive vehicles only.

Maps: For a free trail map, contact the Almanor Ranger District at the address below. To obtain topographic maps of the area, ask for Panther Spring and Butte Meadows from the USGS.

Contact: Lassen National Forest, Almanor Ranger District, P.O. Box 767, Chester, CA 96020; (916) 258-2141 or fax (916) 258-3491.

Trail notes: On a map, the Rancheria Trailhead looks like the closest and easiest trailhead to reach into the Ishi Wilderness from Red Bluff. And what the heck, the trail looks pretty short, too. But when you go there, a completely different picture comes into focus. First off, the

trailhead access road is quite rough, impassable for most cars, and that's just a prelude to what lies ahead. The trail starts by following an old jeep road, then leaves the road at a fence line off to the right. If it's hot, which is typical here most of the year, you'll already be reaching for your canteen. The trail then drops like a cannonball for a thousand feet into the Mill Creek Canyon, a surprising and awesome habitat, with some of the prettiest areas of the Ishi. Too bad you can't enjoy them more, because shadowing your every move is the knowledge that you have to climb back out of that canyon, most likely during the hottest part of the day. By the time you reach the car, your butt will be thoroughly kicked.

Special note: A trail map is strongly advised for those hiking in the Ishi Wilderness.

❹ Lower Mill Creek

13.0 mi/1.0 day

Location: In the Ishi Wilderness east of Red Bluff; map C2, grid c7.

User groups: Hikers, dogs, and horses. No mountain bikes. No wheelchair facilities.

Permits: A campfire permit is required for hikers planning to camp. Parking and access are free.

Directions: From Interstate 5 at Red Bluff, turn east on Highway 36 and drive to the town of Paynes Creek. Turn south on Little Giant Mill Road (Road 202) and go about seven miles until you reach an intersection. Turn south at Ponderosa Way and head about 17 miles to the Mill Creek Trailhead.

Maps: For a free trail map, contact the Almanor Ranger District at the address below. To obtain topographic maps of the area, ask for Panther Spring and Butte Meadows from the USGS.

Contact: Lassen National Forest, Almanor Ranger District, P.O. Box 767, Chester, CA 96020; (916) 258-2141 or fax (916) 258-3491.

Trail notes: If you only have time for one trail in the Ishi Wilderness, the Mill Creek Trail is the one to pick. That goes whether you want to invest just an hour or a full day, because any length of trip can be a joy here. The trail simply parallels the creek for 6.5 miles to its headwaters at Papes Place, with magnificent scenery and many good fishing and swimming holes along the way. This is a dramatic canyon, and as you stand along the stream, the walls can seem to ascend into heaven. It's a land shaped by thousands of years of wind and water.

Directly across from the trailhead on Ponderosa Way is another trailhead, this one for a route that follows Upper Mill Creek into Lassen National Forest. While not as spectacular as Lower Mill Creek, it provides a viable option for hiking, fishing, and swimming.

Special note: A trail map is strongly advised for those hiking in the Ishi Wilderness.

❺ Lassen Trail

12.6 mi/1.0 day

Location: In the Ishi Wilderness east of Red Bluff; map C2, grid c8.

User groups: Hikers, dogs, and horses. No mountain bikes. No wheelchair facilities.

Permits: A campfire permit is required for hikers planning to camp. Parking and access are free.

Directions: From Interstate 5 at Red Bluff, turn east on Highway 36 and drive to the town of Paynes Creek. Turn south on Little Giant Mill Road (Road 202) and go about seven miles until you reach an intersection. Turn south at Ponderosa Way and head about 24 miles to the Lassen Trailhead.

Maps: For a free trail map, contact the Almanor Ranger District at the address below. To obtain topographic maps of the area, ask for Panther Spring and Butte Meadows from the USGS.

Contact: Lassen National Forest, Almanor Ranger District, P.O. Box 767, Chester, CA 96020; (916) 258-2141 or fax (916) 258-3491.

Trail notes: In the gold rush days, the miners built this trail as part of a link between Deer Creek to the south and Mill Creek to the north. It's the only north/south trail in the Ishi Wilderness, crossing the volcanic tablelands to the gold fields. Be warned that the ridge is dry, often hot, and no water is available, so don't even dream of making this hike without a full canteen. What's worse is that the trip fools a lot of visitors, starting out very easy for the first 3.2 miles, heading along an old abandoned road.

Easy, eh? It then changes moods, and believe us, so will you. The trail descends to Boat Gunwale Creek, weaving through some nasty hillside brush. After crossing the creek, the trail deteriorates, virtually disappearing at times. The persistent and adept few will find the trail (or a resemblance of one) is routed all the way to Mill Creek Canyon, although it's easy to get confused on the way there. Most folks, however, won't have to worry about finding the trail to Mill Creek Canyon, since they will have turned around long before that juncture, heading straight back to their car. We almost didn't include this trip in the book, but for those who like self-inflicted torture, the book wouldn't be "The Complete Guide" without it.

Special note: A trail map is strongly advised for those hiking in the Ishi Wilderness.

❻ Moak Trail

14.0 mi/1.5 days

Location: In the Ishi Wilderness east of Red Bluff; map C2, grid d8.

User groups: Hikers, dogs, and horses. No mountain bikes. No wheelchair facilities.

Permits: A campfire permit is required for hikers planning to camp. Parking and access are free.

Directions: From Interstate 5 at Red Bluff, turn east on Highway 36 and drive to the town of Paynes Creek. Turn south on Little Giant Mill Road (Road 202) and go about seven miles until you reach an intersection. Turn south at Ponderosa Way and head about 26 miles to the Moak Trailhead.

Maps: For a free trail map, contact the Almanor Ranger District at the address below. To obtain topographic maps of the area, ask for Panther Spring and Butte Meadows from the USGS.

Contact: Lassen National Forest, Almanor Ranger District, P.O. Box 767, Chester, CA 96020; (916) 258-2141 or fax (916) 258-3491.

Trail notes: Hit it right in the spring, and the Moak Trail is likely the best overnight hike in California's foothill country. Hit it wrong in the summer and you'll wonder what you did to deserve such a terrible fate. In the spring, the foothill country is loaded with wildflowers and tall, fresh grass, and the views of the Sacramento Valley are spectacular. The trail includes a poke-and-probe section over a lava rock boulder field, and there are good trail camps at Deep Hole (2,800 feet) and Drennan. It's an excellent weekend trip, including a loop route by linking the Moak Trail with the Buena Vista Trail, most of it easy walking. Alas, try this trip in the summer or fall and you'll need to have your gray matter examined at Red Bluff General. No wildflowers, no shade, 100-degree temperatures, and as for water, yer dreamin'.

Special note: A trail map is strongly advised for those hiking in the Ishi Wilderness.

❼ Deer Creek Trail

14.0 mi/1.5 days

Location: In the Ishi Wilderness east of Red Bluff; map C2, grid d8.

User groups: Hikers, dogs, and horses. No mountain bikes. No wheelchair facilities.

Permits: A campfire permit is required for hikers planning to camp. Parking and access are free.

Directions: From Interstate 5 at Red Bluff, turn east on Highway 36 and drive to the town of Paynes Creek. Turn south on Little Giant Mill Road (Road 202) and go about seven miles until you reach an intersection. Turn south at Ponderosa Way and head about 32 miles to the Deer Creek Trailhead.

Maps: For a free trail map, contact the Almanor Ranger District at the address below. To obtain topographic maps of the area, ask for Panther Spring and Butte Meadows from the USGS.

Contact: Lassen National Forest, Almanor Ranger District, P.O. Box 767, Chester, CA 96020; (916) 258-2141 or fax (916) 258-3491.

Trail notes: It's no accident the Deer Creek Trail is the most popular hike in the Ishi Wilderness. Not only are you rewarded with striking surroundings, but the hike is a pleasurable romp even if you cut the trip short to just an hour or two. That's because the trail runs midway up naked slopes, offering spectacular views of Deer Creek Canyon's basaltic cliffs and spires, and of the stream below. The trailhead is at the southeast border of the wilderness, and right from the start, it's routed along the north shore of Deer Creek. Iron Mountain at 3,274 feet is located to the immediate north. The trail is directed along the stream into the wilderness interior, skirting past the northern edge of what is called the Graham Pinery—a dense island of ponderosa pine growing on a mountain terrace. A bonus is good trout fishing in Deer Creek, birdwatching for hawks, eagles, and falcons at the rock cliffs, and looking for a large variety of wildlife, including rattlesnakes (here's your warning), wild pigs, and lots of squirrels and quail.

Special note: A trail map is strongly advised for those hiking in the Ishi Wilderness.

❽ Devil's Den Trail

9.0 mi/1.0 day

Location: In the Ishi Wilderness east of Red Bluff; map C2, grid d8.

User groups: Hikers, dogs, and horses. No mountain bikes. No wheelchair facilities.

Permits: A campfire permit is required for hikers planning to camp. Parking and access are free.

Directions: From Interstate 5 at Red Bluff, turn east on Highway 36 and drive to the town of Paynes Creek. Turn south on Little Giant Mill Road (Road 202) and go about seven miles until you reach an intersection. Turn south at Ponderosa Way and head about 32.5 miles to the Devil's Den Trailhead, just south of the Deer Creek Trailhead.

Maps: For a free trail map, contact the Almanor Ranger District at the address below. To obtain topographic maps of the area, ask for Panther Spring and Butte Meadows from the USGS.

Contact: Lassen National Forest, Almanor Ranger District, P.O. Box 767, Chester, CA 96020; (916) 258-2141 or fax (916) 258-3491.

Trail notes: The Devil's Den Trailhead is less than half a mile from the Deer Creek Trailhead, but there the similarities between the two end. This trail includes a rough climb, beastly in summer, with no water available over the stretch where you'll need it most. The main attractions here are, one, nobody else is usually around, and two, the trail is routed through a series of habitat zones over the course of the first 3.5 miles, providing a number of striking contrasts. The trail starts easy, routed along Deer Creek for the first mile. Enjoy yourself because what follows is not exactly a picnic. The trail turns left, climbing up Little Pine Creek all the way to the ridge top, with the last mile on an old, hot, and chunky abandoned road. In the process, the vegetation changes from riparian along the creek, to woodland on the slopes, then chaparral on the ridge. In addition, an island of conifers, the Graham Pinery, is available for viewing with a quarter-of-a-mile side trip.

Special note: A trail map is strongly advised for those hiking in the Ishi Wilderness.

⑨ Big Oak Trail

1.0 mi/0.5 hr

Location: At the head of Black Butte Reservoir west of Chico; map C2, grid f0.

User groups: Hikers and dogs. No horses or mountain bikes. No wheelchair facilities.

Permits: No permits are required. Parking and access are free.

Directions: From Interstate 5 at Orland, take the Black Butte Lake exit. Drive 10 miles west on Newville Road (County Road 200), then turn left on County Road 206. Follow it to County Road 200A and drive to the trailhead.

Maps: A free brochure is available by contacting the U.S. Army Corps of Engineers at the address below. To obtain a topographic map of the area, ask for Julian Rocks from the USGS.

Contact: U.S. Army Corps of Engineers, Black Butte Lake, 19225 Newville Road, Orland, CA 95963; (916) 865-4781 or fax (916) 865-5283.

Trail notes: The Army Corps of Engineers has really screwed up some of California's once-great riverside habitat with massive rip-rap projects, but here they actually did something right: they protected Stony Creek by doing nothing but building a trail (of course, they had to build a dam here first). The route, an easy jaunt, follows the Stony Creek drainage above the head of Black Butte Reservoir. The riparian habitat here is in a protected state, providing an excellent area to see wildlife and birds in the sparse foothills of the Sacramento Valley. It has become part of California's Watchable Wildlife system. Alas, this hike is not without problems. First is the weather, which is close to intolerable in the summer—a real temperature tantrum—and very hot in spring and fall as well, and that's when most people have time to visit the area. Second is that during the prime times, spring and fall, it seems just about everybody camping at the lake gets around to walking this trail (hey, you can't blame them), so you can expect to run into folks. The best time for hiking is at dusk, when wildlife viewing is at its best.

Map C3

Adjoining Maps: East: C4 ..... *page* 148 West: C2 124
North: B3 .... 86 South: D3 166

Northern California Map .... *page* 2

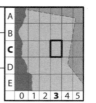

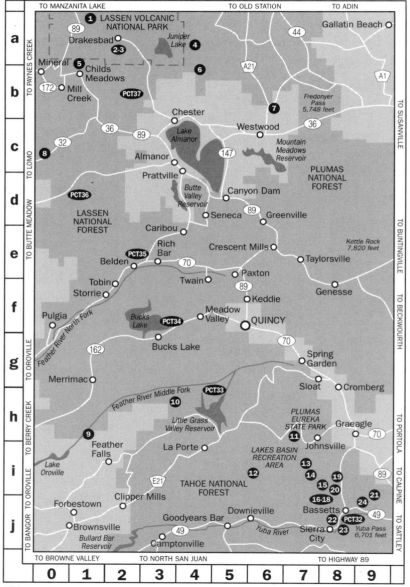

Chapter C3 features:

❶ Bumpass Hell Trail

6.0 mi/3.0 hrs

Location: In Lassen Volcanic National Park east of Red Bluff; map C3, grid a1.

User groups: Hikers only. No dogs, horses, or mountain bikes. No wheelchair facilities.

Permits: A free wilderness permit is required for hikers planning to camp in the backcountry. A national park day-use fee is charged for each vehicle.

Directions: From Interstate 5 at Red Bluff, drive east on Highway 36 for about 47 miles. Turn north on Highway 89 and go 4.5 miles to the park entrance, then 6.3 miles to the trailhead on the right.

Maps: Trail maps are available for $7.24 (including tax and mailing). To order a map, contact Loomis Museum, c/o Lassen Volcanic National Park, at the address below. To obtain a topographic map of the area, ask for Lassen Peak from the USGS.

Contact: Lassen Volcanic National Park, P.O.

Box 100, Mineral, CA 96063-0100; (916) 595-4444 or fax (916) 595-3262.

Trail notes: Bumpass Hell is like a walk into the land of perdition, complete with steam vents, boiling mud pots, and hot springs. It's all set amid volcanic rock and is prehistoric looking and a bit creepy, as if at any moment a dinosaur might come charging around the bend and start eating tourists. The trip to Bumpass Hell is the most popular hike in the park, and it makes sense because it's not only the park's largest thermal area, but an excellent morning walk.

The trail starts with a gradual 500-foot climb over the first mile, then descends 250 feet into the thermal area. It sits in a pocket just below Bumpass Mountain (8,753 feet), with a self-guiding leaflet available that explains the area. There are typically large numbers of tourists at Bumpass Hell, but you can get beyond them by extending your trip to Cold Boiling Lake, another 3.5 miles (one way), which includes two steep portions of trail.

Special note: For obvious reasons, it's important to stay on the trail or boardwalk near hydrothermal areas.

❷ Devil's Kitchen Trail

4.4 mi/2.5 hrs

Location: At Drakesbad in Lassen Volcanic National Park; map C3, grid a2.

User groups: Hikers only. No dogs, horses, or mountain bikes. No wheelchair facilities.

Permits: A free wilderness permit is required for hikers planning to camp in the backcountry. A national park day-use fee is charged for each vehicle.

Directions: From Chico, drive north on Highway 32 to the junction with Highway 89/36. Turn right (east) and take Highway 36 to Chester. Go left (north) on Warner Valley Road and drive 16.5 miles to the trailhead, located about half a mile past Warner Valley Campground.

Maps: Trail maps are available for $7.24 (including tax and mailing). To order a map, contact Loomis Museum, c/o Lassen Volcanic National Park, at the address below. To obtain a topographic map of the area, ask for Reading Peak from the USGS.

Contact: Lassen Volcanic National Park, P.O. Box 100, Mineral, CA 96063-0100; (916) 595-4444 or fax (916) 595-3262.

Trail notes: Drakesbad is the undiscovered Lassen—beautiful, wild, and remote. It gets missed by nearly everybody because access is obscure and circuitous out of Chester. In other words, there's no way to get here when entering from either of the main park entrances. But those who persevere will find a quiet paradise, along with this easy trip to Devil's Kitchen, a unique geologic thermal area. The trail is an easy hike, heading west above Hot Springs Creek. After two miles, it drops down into this barren pocket of steaming vents and boiling pots, where you'll immediately see why it was tagged Devil's Kitchen. A great side trip is available here, but few people know about it. From Devil's Kitchen, if you walk just a quarter of a mile upstream on Hot Springs Creek, you'll discover a delightful little waterfall. The trail is not marked and it's a good idea to talk to a ranger first.

❸ Drake Lake Trail

4.5 mi/2.75 hrs

Location: At Drakesbad in Lassen Volcanic National Park; map C3, grid a2.

User groups: Hikers only. No dogs, horses, or mountain bikes. No wheelchair facilities.

Permits: A free wilderness permit is required for hikers planning to camp in the backcountry. A national park day-use fee is charged for each vehicle.

Directions: From Chico, drive north on Highway 32 to the junction with Highway 89/36. Turn right (east) and take Highway 36 to Chester. Go left (north) on Warner Valley Road and drive 16.5 miles to the trailhead, located about half a mile past Warner Valley Campground.

Maps: Trail maps are available for $7.24 (including tax and mailing). To order a map, contact Loomis Museum, c/o Lassen Volcanic National Park, at the address below. To obtain a topographic map of the area, ask for Reading Peak from the USGS.

Contact: Lassen Volcanic National Park, P.O. Box 100, Mineral, CA 96063-0100; (916) 595-4444 or fax (916) 595-3262.

Trail notes: Drake is a beautiful alpine lake where deer are more plentiful than people. Set in a remote forested pocket, it's very secluded and pristine, and just difficult enough of a climb that many take a pass on the trip. From the trailhead at Drakesbad at about 5,700 feet, it's nearly an 800-foot climb over the course of two miles to Drake Lake (6,482 feet). Midway up the grade, the hike becomes quite steep and stays that way for nearly 45 minutes.

The lake is the payoff, emerald green and circled by firs. After you catch your breath, you may feel like jumping in and cooling off, particularly if it's a hot summer day. Well, we've got news for you. In early summer the water is still ice cold, and just when you realize that, a battalion of mosquitoes will show up and start feasting on all your bare, sumptuous flesh. Then what? Jump in and freeze your buns? Stand there and get devoured? Heck no, you'll have your clothes back on in record time.

❹ Juniper Lake Loop

12.0 mi/2.0 days

Location: In Lassen Volcanic National Park north of Lake Almanor; map C3, grid a4.

User groups: Hikers only. No dogs, horses, or mountain bikes. No wheelchair facilities.

Permits: A free wilderness permit is required for hikers planning to camp in the backcountry. A national park day-use fee is charged for each vehicle.

Directions: From Chico, drive north on Highway 32 to the junction with Highway 89/36. Turn right (east) and take Highway 36 to Chester. Go left (north) on Warner Valley Road and drive two miles. At the Y, bear right on Juniper Lake Road and go 11 miles to the trailhead near the ranger station. The access road is quite rough, so trailers and motor homes aren't recommended.

Maps: Trail maps are available for $7.24 (including tax and mailing). To order a map, contact Loomis Museum, c/o Lassen Volcanic National Park, at the address below. To obtain a topographic map of the area, ask for Mount Harkness from the USGS.

Contact: Lassen Volcanic National Park, P.O. Box 100, Mineral, CA 96063-0100; (916) 595-4444 or fax (916) 595-3262.

Trail notes: The Juniper Lake Loop explores Lassen Park's least known yet most beautiful backcountry, with nine lakes, many lookouts, and pretty trail camps along this 12-mile route. It starts at the trailhead adjacent to the Juniper Lake Ranger Station, which requires a long bumpy ride out of Chester just to reach. If you arrive late, a campground is available at the lake, elevation 6,792 feet. At the north end of Juniper Lake, the trail heads straight north, and though it has plenty of ups and downs, along with a fairly level stretch through Cameron Meadow, it's mostly down, descending 800 feet to Snag Lake, elevation 6,076 feet. Here the trail turns left and climbs 600 feet in less than a mile, topping a ridge and then pouring out to Rainbow Lake, a mile later to Lower Twin Lake (6,537 feet), and another mile further to Swan Lake (6,628 feet). Any of these can make for a good trail camp. On the second day, you'll loop back,

skirt the south flank of Crater Butte (7,267 feet), head past Horseshoe Lake and then to the starting point. Alas, this trip is not flawless. The fishing is poor, mosquitoes are rampant in the early summer, and nights are very cold in the fall. Note: From the north end of Juniper Lake, a great side trip is the half-mile, 400-foot climb to Inspiration Point, which provides a memorable view of Lassen Park's backcountry.

❺ Spencer Meadow Trail

10.0 mi/1.0 day

Location: In Lassen National Forest just south of Lassen Volcanic National Park; map C3, grid b0.

User groups: Hikers, dogs, horses, and mountain bikes. No wheelchair facilities.

Permits: No permits are required. Parking and access are free.

Directions: From Interstate 5 at Red Bluff, drive east on Highway 36 about 43 miles to Mineral. Continue east on Highway 36 for about seven miles to the trailhead parking area on the left.

Maps: For a map of Lassen National Forest, send $4 to USDA-Forest Service, 630 Sansome Street, San Francisco, CA 94111. To obtain a topographic map of the area, ask for Childs Meadows from the USGS.

Contact: Lassen National Forest, Almanor Ranger District, P.O. Box 767, Chester, CA 96020; (916) 258-2141 or fax (916)258-3491.

Trail notes: Spencer Meadow is a pretty, high mountain meadow on the southern flank of Lassen. Here explorers can discover an effervescent spring pouring forth, the source of Mill Creek and the creation of the headwaters of a Sacramento River tributary. Hiking access is easy, with the trailhead located at a parking area just off Highway 36. From here you hike straight north toward Lassen on the Spencer Meadow Trail. Over the course of five miles, the trail passes a small spring (about halfway in, look for the faint spur trail on the left), then tiny Patricia Lake (on the right, hidden), and finally Spencer Meadow and the Mill Creek Spring.

Special note: There is a trailhead closer to Spencer Meadow on Forest Service Road 29N40, but reaching it involves a long, rough drive.

❻ Indian Meadow Trail

6.0 mi/2.0 days

Location: On the southern boundary of the Caribou Wilderness north of Lake Almanor; map C3, grid b4.

User groups: Hikers, dogs, and horses. No mountain bikes. No wheelchair facilities.

Permits: No permits are required. Parking and access are free.

Directions: From Red Bluff, drive northeast on Highway 36 to Chester. From Chester, head five miles east on Highway 36 and turn north on Forest Service Road 10. Drive about 9.5 miles, then turn left on Forest Service Road 30N25 and go to the trailhead.

Maps: For a map of Lassen National Forest, send $4 to USDA-Forest Service, 630 Sansome Street, San Francisco, CA 94111. To obtain a topographic map of the area, ask for Childs Meadows from the USGS.

Contact: Lassen National Forest, Almanor Ranger District, P.O. Box 767, Chester, CA 96020; (916) 258-2141 or fax (916)258-3491.

Trail notes: Hidden between South Caribou Mountain and Black Cinder Rock is a little alpine pocket where dozens of small alpine lakes are sprinkled about the southern Caribou Wilderness. It's a slice of paradise that some hikers call the "Hiking Lakes." The trail out of Indian Meadow is a loop route that crosses right through these lakes, including the area's larger and most divine settings, Beauty Lake, Long Lake, Posey Lake, and Evelyn Lake. While the trip can be made in a day, you likely won't feel like leaving, and we recommend planning an easy overnight backpacking trip. Another bonus of an overnight trip is that you can take the side trip up to Hidden Lakes, a series of several small but pretty waters, set just below South Caribou Mountain.

After arriving at the trailhead at Indian Meadow, the trip starts easily enough, crossing Hay Meadow. In another mile, you'll reach Beauty Lake, the first of five major lakes on this loop hike. They are all good for swimming, although a bit cold, and Beauty and Posey have the best trout fishing. Note that although the Caribou Wilderness abuts Lassen Volcanic National Park, it's often overlooked in the big park's shadow. That's to your benefit, as long as you know about this trail.

❼ Bizz Johnson

25 mi. one way/3.0 days

Location: In Lassen National Forest west of Susanville; map C3, grid b6.

User groups: Hikers, dogs, horses, and mountain bikes. No wheelchair facilities.

Permits: No permits are required. Parking and access are free.

Directions: In Susanville on Highway 36, turn south on South Weatherton Street. Drive two blocks south (Weatherton becomes Richmond Road) and continue on Richmond Road for about a quarter of a mile to the Susanville Depot and the trailhead. For an alternate route, from Westwood on Highway 36, turn north on County Road A21 and drive four miles to the trailhead parking area.

Maps: For a free brochure, contact the Bureau of Land Management at the address below. For a map of Lassen National Forest, send $4 to USDA-Forest Service, 630 Sansome Street, San Francisco, CA 94111. To obtain topographic maps of the area, ask for Westwood East, Fredonyer Pass, and Susanville from the USGS.

Contact: Lassen National Forest, Eagle Lake Ranger District, 55 South Sacramento Street, Susanville, CA 96130; (916) 257-2151. Bureau of Land Management, Eagle Lake Resource Area, 2545 Riverside Drive, Susanville, CA 96130; (916) 257-5381 or fax (916) 257-4150.

Trail notes: In the 1960s, when Shasta legend John Reginato heard that Southern Pacific was going to abandon a rail line between Westwood and Susanville, he urged that it be converted to a hiking trail. The idea struck home, and the Bureau of Land Management worked with the U.S. Forest Service to develop and refine it. Now in the 1990s, this trail is one of the true multiple-use routes in Northern California, with plenty of room for hikers, mountain bikers, and horseback riders. In the winter, it makes a great trip on cross-country skis or on a snowmobile, with many trailheads providing different access points. The route traces the old Fernley and Lassen railroad line, following the Susan River Canyon for most of the way. It features beautiful views in many areas, and passes through two old railroad tunnels. Yet it's raw and primitive. You won't cross any developed areas. Guess they had it right when they built that first railroad line. The one negative: it's way too wide for a hiking trail.

❽ Deer Creek Trail

1–8 mi/1.0 day

Location: In Lassen National Forest along Highway 32 west of Lake Almanor; map C3, grid c0.

User groups: Hikers, dogs, and horses. Mountain bikes aren't advised. No wheelchair facilities.

Permits: No permits are required. Parking and access are free.

Directions: From Chico, drive north on Highway 32 for 40 miles. Just after crossing a small concrete bridge that crosses Deer Creek, park on the south side of the road where there's a dirt pullout. The trailhead is located on the north side of the road, just up from the bridge.

Maps: For a map of Lassen National Forest, send $4 to USDA-Forest Service, 630 Sansome Street, San Francisco, CA 94111. To obtain a topographic map of the area, ask for Onion Butte from the USGS.

Contact: Lassen National Forest, Almanor Ranger District, P.O. Box 767, Chester, CA 96020; (916) 258-2141 or fax (916)258-3491.

Trail notes: The Deer Creek Trail has all the ingredients to make it ideal for a trout angler, explorer, or somebody just looking for a dunk on a hot day. The gorgeous stream runs right alongside the trail, with good access throughout—and fish, often plenty of them in the summer months. From the parking area, the trail is routed downstream along the river for about 10 miles, but rarely does anybody ever walk all the way to the end. Instead they take their time, perhaps fishing along the way, maybe stopping a bit to enjoy a pretty waterfall 3.5 miles from the trailhead. In summer, Deer Creek is cold and clear, tumbling its way over rocks and into pools, seemingly with trout in

every one. There are a series of deep pools perfect for swimming, and while cold, the water is remarkably refreshing on hot summer days. A sidelight here is that the canyon rim is made up of a series of volcanic crags, like something out of Jurassic Park.

❾ Feather Falls National Recreation Trail

9.5 mi/4.0 hrs

Location: In Plumas National Forest east of Lake Oroville; map C3, grid h2.

User groups: Hikers, dogs, horses, and mountain bikes. No wheelchair facilities.

Permits: No permits are required. Parking and access are free.

Directions: From Oroville, drive east on Highway 162 about eight miles to Forbestown Road. Take Forbestown Road east six miles to Lumpkin Road. Turn left on Lumpkin Road and go ten miles to the sign for the Feather Falls Trail. Turn left and proceed 1.5 miles to the parking area at the end of the road. If you reach the town of Feather Falls, you've gone a mile too far.

Maps: For a map of Plumas National Forest, send $4 to USDA-Forest Service, 630 Sansome Street, San Francisco, CA 94111. To obtain a topographic map of the area, ask for Brush Creek from the USGS.

Contact: Plumas National Forest, Feather River Ranger District, 875 Mitchell Avenue, Oroville, CA 95965; (916) 534-6500.

Trail notes: Feather Falls is heaven to look at—a 640-foot silver band of water free-falling into a granite canyon, the kind of sight that can leave you feeling refreshed for weeks. In the spring, it's wide and powerful, and in years with big snowpacks in the Sierra, it stays that way well into July. But it runs all year and is beautiful even in the fall. The trail is pretty easy, climbing gently over the course of four miles, but so many people run out of water on the way that it becomes difficult for them. Some even end up feeling like a dry sponge by the time they get there, the result of hot temperatures and not enough drinking water.

From the trailhead, this hike descends for a mile

and then is flat for the most part, with a short climb near the end. The only real climb you'll face is on the return trip, just in the last mile. Even then, you can avoid that climb by taking the new loop trail that's now available. Right, there are actually two trails here, the older 7.6-mile route, or the new option that spans a total of 9.5 miles, which is longer but easier.

⑩ Hartman Bar National Recreation Trail

4.0 mi/3.0 hrs

Location: In Plumas National Forest east of Lake Oroville; map C3, grid h3.

User groups: Hikers, dogs, and horses. No mountain bikes. No wheelchair facilities.

Permits: No permits are required. Parking and access are free.

Directions: From Oroville, drive north on Highway 70/89 to Quincy. From Quincy, go south on Highway 70/89, then turn right on Quincy-La Porte Road. Drive 1.5 miles to Little Grass Valley Road, turn right (north), and drive to Black Rock Campground. Go left on Forest Service Road 94 and proceed to Forest Service Road 22N42Y. Turn right and head to the parking area at the end of the road.

Maps: For a map of Plumas National Forest, send $4 to USDA-Forest Service, 630 Sansome Street, San Francisco, CA 94111. To obtain topographic maps of the area, ask for Cascade and Haskins Valley from the USGS.

Contact: Plumas National Forest, Feather River Ranger District, 875 Mitchell Avenue, Oroville, CA 95965; (916) 534-6500.

Trail notes: Hikers often pay for their pleasure, and this hike involves two installments. The trail descends from the Hartman Ridge down the canyon to Hartman Bar Ridge on the Middle Fork Feather River. Going down will have your toes jamming into your boots, and the trip back can have your heart firing off like cannon shots. But awaiting is the Middle Fork Feather, one of the prettiest streams around, and with some of the best trout fishing as well. In fact, of the hundreds of trout streams in California, the Middle Fork Feather is clearly in the top five. If you don't like to fish, but would rather explore further, a foot-

bridge crosses the stream and climbs up the other side of the canyon, meeting Catrell Creek in half a mile. If you want to split the trip in two, the primitive Dan Beebe Camp is available along the river.

⑪ Eureka Peak Loop

3.0 mi/2.0 hrs

Location: In Plumas-Eureka State Park south of Quincy; map C3, grid h7.

User groups: Hikers only. No dogs, horses, or mountain bikes. No wheelchair facilities.

Permits: No permits are required. Parking and access are free.

Directions: From Sacramento, drive northeast on Interstate 80 to Truckee. In Truckee, take Highway 89 north and proceed past the town of Clio to County Road A14 (Graeagle-Johnsonville Road). Turn left (west) and drive to the park entrance. The trailhead is located at the north end of Eureka Lake.

Maps: For a trail map, send $6.50 and a self-addressed, stamped envelope to Plumas-Eureka State Park at the address below. To obtain a topographic map of the area, ask for Johnsville from the USGS.

Contact: Plumas-Eureka State Park, 310 Johnsville Road, Blairsden, CA 96103; (916) 836-2380 or fax (916) 525-0138. U.S. Forest Service, Mohawk Ranger Station, (916) 525-7232.

Trail notes: A panorama of the southern Sierra Nevada awaits from Eureka Peak, elevation 7,447 feet. The view includes all the peaks of the Gold Lakes Basin, with Mount Elwell (7,812 feet) most prominent to the south, and Plumas National Forest to the north and west, crowned by Blue Nose Mountain (7,290 feet), Stafford Mountain (7,019 feet), and Beartrap Mountain (7,232 feet). It's the vista that compels people to make the climb, a serious three-mile loop, with the first half a grunt to the top. The trailhead starts at Eureka Lake, elevation 6,300 feet. It then climbs 1,150 feet, a good, hard pull to the top. Many people start this trail by accident, after seeing the trailhead sign while visiting the lake. That's a mistake. The trip should be planned, bringing plenty of water and snacks with you to enjoy from the summit.

⑫ Chimney Rock Trail

2.0 mi/1.25 hrs

Location: North of Downieville in Tahoe National Forest; map C3, grid i6.

User groups: Hikers, dogs, and horses. Mountain bikes aren't advised. No wheelchair facilities.

Permits: No permits are required. Parking and access are free.

Directions: From Sacramento on Interstate 80, drive east to Auburn. In Auburn, take Highway 49 north to Nevada City. In Nevada City, continue on Highway 49 (it jogs to the left in Nevada City, then narrows) for about 40 miles to Saddleback Road (a few miles before the town of Downieville). Turn left on Saddleback Road, a dirt road. Drive eight miles north to a five-way intersection. Go straight through to Road 25-23-1 and continue for 2.6 miles, then bear right on Road 25-23-1-2 (look for the "Dead End" sign). Drive about half a mile to an intersection and head straight through. After about 100 yards, bear left on an obscure road (Poker Flat Trail) and drive for one mile to a turnout at the base of Bunker Hill. Park here and hike in six-tenths of a mile to the trailhead. The total mileage from Downieville is 13 miles. Note: Sections of the road are quite rough.

Maps: For a map of Tahoe National Forest, send $4 to USDA-Forest Service, 630 Sansome Street, San Francisco, CA 94111. To obtain a topographic map of the area, ask for Mount Fillmore from the USGS.

Contact: Tahoe National Forest, Downieville Ranger District, 15924 Highway 49, Camptonville, CA 95922; (916) 288-3231 or fax (916) 288-0727.

Trail notes: Chimney Rock is a huge volcanic cone that's 12 feet in diameter at its base, then rises nearly straight up for 25 feet. The great views from the top are well worth the trip. Yet because the route to the trailhead is so complicated, few either know of Chimney Rock or get around to making the hike. From the trailhead at 6,400 feet, it's a 400-foot climb over the course of a mile to reach it. While enjoying the perch atop Chimney Rock, you may choose to extend your trip or just make the easy descent back to the trailhead. The trip can be lengthened into an eight-mile loop. To do so, from Chimney Rock, take the trail eastward. It descends at first, then rises again around Needle Point and Rattlesnake Peak. For explorers, additional side trips into beautiful Empire Creek Canyon are possible when you intersect with the Empire Creek Trail.

⑬ Upper Jamison Trail

8.2 mi/2.0 days

Location: In Plumas-Eureka State Park on the northern boundary of Gold Lakes Basin, south of Quincy; map C3, grid i7.

User groups: Hikers only. No dogs, horses, or mountain bikes. No wheelchair facilities.

Permits: No permits are required. Parking and access are free.

Directions: From Sacramento, drive northeast on Interstate 80 to Truckee. In Truckee, take Highway 89 north and continue past the town of Clio to County Road A14 (Graeagle-Johnsonville Road); turn left (west) and drive 4.5 miles. Before reaching the Jamison Creek Bridge, look for a sign that reads, "Jamison Mine-Glass Lake Mine Complex." Turn left and drive on the dirt road about one mile to the Jamison Mine Complex. The trailhead starts at the far end of the parking lot.

Maps: For a trail map, send 50 cents and a self-addressed, stamped envelope to Plumas-Eureka State Park at the address below. To obtain a topographic map of the area, ask for Johnsville from the USGS.

Contact: Plumas-Eureka State Park, 310 Johnsville Road, Blairsden, CA 96103; (916) 836-2380, (916) 525-7232, or fax (916) 525-7232.

Trail notes: There's no reason to rush your way through this trail, which passes Grass, Jamison, and Rock Lakes, but rather take your time at it, stopping to enjoy the lakes along the way. Or take our suggestion and turn it into an overnight backpacking trip. The trail provides a glimpse of the beauty of the northern section of Lakes Basin Recreation Area, a country of beautiful alpine lakes and beveled granite mountains.

From the trailhead at the Jamison Mine building, start the trip by taking the Grass Lake Trail. It follows along Little Jamison Creek, rising two miles to Grass Lake, with the trail skirting along the east side of the lake. For many on a day hike, this is far enough. However, we urge you to forge onward. It's another two miles to Jamison Lake, with the trail climbing more steeply, then crossing the creek twice before arriving at the outlet of Jamison Lake. Another quarter of a mile will route you over to Rock Lake, a pretty sight below Mount Elwell, elevation 7,812 feet. Several good trail camps are available at Rock, Jamison, and Grass Lakes.

⑭ Mount Elwell Trail

6.0 mi/3.5 hrs

Location: At Smith Lake in Gold Lakes Basin south of Quincy; map C3, grid i7.

User groups: Hikers, dogs, and horses. No mountain bikes. No wheelchair facilities.

Permits: No permits are required. Parking and access are free.

Directions: From Sacramento, drive northeast on Interstate 80 to Truckee. In Truckee, take Highway 89 north to the town of Clio. Continue a short distance north on Highway 89 to Forest Service Road 24 (Gold Lake Highway). Turn left (west) on Gold Lake Highway and proceed to the sign for Gray Eagle Lodge. Turn right and drive to the Smith Lake Trailhead.

Maps: For a map of Plumas National Forest, send $4 to USDA-Forest Service, 630 Sansome Street, San Francisco, CA 94111. To obtain a topographic map of the area, ask for Gold Lake from the USGS.

Contact: Plumas National Forest, Beckwourth Ranger District, P.O. Box 7, Blairsden, CA 96103; (916) 836-2576 or fax (916) 836-0493.

Trail notes: From atop Mount Elwell, 7,812 feet, you're surrounded by the Gold Lakes Basin, a wildland filled with alpine lakes and granite mountains. You'll find yourself dreaming of the days when you might visit them. This trail is a good way to start. It begins at the Smith Lake Trailhead and passes near Smith Lake (6,700 feet) on the Smith Lake-Gray Eagle Lodge Trail, climbing all the way—1,100 feet over the course of three miles—to the top of Mount Elwell. It makes a great day trip for folks staying at the Gray Eagle Lodge at Smith Lake. Though few go onward from Mount Elwell, the trip can be extended simply enough. The trail continues

past Mount Elwell, descending three-quarters of a mile to the Long Lake Trail junction, then another three-quarters of a mile to a four-wheel-drive route. From this junction, you can also make a loop back to the Smith Lake Trailhead by descending to Long Lake and continuing north three miles on the Long Lake Trail. This is one of the true great hikes in the north Sierra.

⑮ Bear Lakes Loop

5.6 mi/3.0 hrs

Location: North of Sierra City; map C3, grid i7.

User groups: Hikers, dogs, and horses. No mountain bikes. No wheelchair facilities.

Permits: No permits are required. Parking and access are free.

Directions: From Sacramento, drive northeast on Interstate 80 to Truckee. In Truckee, take Highway 89 north to the town of Clio. Continue a short distance north on Highway 89 to Forest Service Road 24 (Gold Lake Highway). Turn left on Gold Lake Highway and proceed about six miles until you see the sign for the Long Lake Trailhead on the right (west) side of the ride.

Maps: For a map of Plumas National Forest, send $4 to USDA-Forest Service, 630 Sansome Street, San Francisco, CA 94111. To obtain a topographic map of the area, ask for Gold Lake from the USGS.

Contact: Plumas National Forest, Beckwourth Ranger District, P.O. Box 7, Blairsden, CA 96103; (916) 836-2575 or fax (916)836-0493.

Trail notes: Long Lake is one of the celestial settings in the heaven-like Gold Lakes Basin. It's the feature destination on this hike, and a good tromp that includes some steep rocky portions. The trailhead is at the Lakes Basin Campground, elevation 6,300 feet. From here, the trail is clear and well maintained, but requires a huff and a puff of a mile. Here you'll see the turnoff for a spur trail that's routed a quarter of a mile to Long Lake, one mile to little Silver Lake, three-quarters of a mile to Cub Lake, and another half a mile to Little Bear and Big Bear Lakes, and then three-quarters of a mile back to the trailhead. Long Lake is always a surprise to newcomers, since it's much larger than most high-country lakes and very pretty. The trail skirts along the southeast shoreline.

Special note: No camping is permitted at either Long or Silver Lakes.

⑯ Butcher Ranch Trail

8.0 mi/5.0 hrs

Location: West of Packer Lake in Tahoe National Forest; map C3, grid i7.

User groups: Hikers, dogs, horses, and mountain bikes. No wheelchair facilities.

Permits: No permits are required. Parking and access are free.

Directions: From Sacramento on Interstate 80, drive east to Auburn. In Auburn, take Highway 49 north to Nevada City. From Nevada City, go northwest on Highway 49/Gold Country Highway to Bassetts. Turn left (north) on Gold Lake Highway and proceed 1.4 miles, then turn left on Sardine Lake Road and drive a short distance. Cross the Salmon Creek Bridge, go three-tenths of a mile, and turn right on Packer Lake Road. Drive 2.5 miles to Packer Lake. The road forks here; take the left fork (Packer Saddle Road) and proceed 2.1 miles. Turn left at the sign for Sierra Buttes Lookout. Drive half a mile and bear right, then go another half a mile to a sign indicating Butcher Ranch. Take the right fork and drive seven-tenths of a mile to a sign directing you to the trailhead. Note: The road is quite steep and is recommended for high-clearance or four-wheel-drive vehicles only. Passenger cars can park at the sign for the trailhead and hike in half a mile to the trailhead.

Maps: For a map of Tahoe National Forest, send $4 to USDA-Forest Service, 630 Sansome Street, San Francisco, CA 94111. To obtain a topographic map of the area, ask for Sierra City from the USGS.

Contact: Tahoe National Forest, Downieville Ranger District, 15924 Highway 49, Camptonville, CA 95922; (916) 288-3231 or fax (916) 288-0727.

Trail notes: This is a hike for those who yearn for a mountain canyon paradise where wildflowers are abundant, fishing is good, and a side trip will take you to a pristine stream with gorgeous deep pools. The Butcher Ranch Trail furnishes all of that and more, and getting there isn't even too difficult. It's the getting back that will wear you out, but hey, we'll get to that. The trailhead is obscure and hard to reach, and that keeps many people away.

When you start hiking, you may wonder why we rated it a 4 for difficulty. After all, the trail follows the contour of Butcher Creek for 1.5 miles to the confluence of Pauley and Butcher Ranch Creeks. You then parallel Pauley Creek, with its deep and beautiful pools. On the way down, you'll drop nearly 2,000 feet in elevation over the course of four miles. Try not to laugh on your way down; what goes down must come up, and on the return, you'll be wondering why you ever talked yourself into this trip.

⑰ Pauley Creek Trail

12.0 mi/2.0 days

Location: West of Packer Lake in Tahoe National Forest; map C3, grid i7.

User groups: Hikers, dogs, horses, and mountain bikes. No wheelchair facilities.

Permits: No permits are required. Parking and access are free.

Directions: From Sacramento on Interstate 80, drive east to Auburn. In Auburn, take Highway 49 north to Nevada City, then drive northeast on Highway 49/Gold Country Highway to Bassetts. Turn left (north) on Gold Lake Highway at Bassetts, drive 1.4 miles, then turn left and cross the Salmon Creek Bridge. Proceed three-tenths of a mile and turn right on Packer Lake Road and drive for 2.5 miles to Packer Lake. The road forks here; take the left fork (Packer Saddle Road) and head 2.1 miles. Turn left at the sign for Sierra Buttes Lookout, drive half a mile, bear right, and go another half a mile to a sign indicating Butcher Ranch. Take the right fork and drive seven-tenths of a mile to a sign directing you to the trailhead. Note: The road is quite steep and only high-clearance or four-wheel-drive vehicles are advised. Passenger cars can park at the trailhead sign and hike in half a mile to the Butcher Creek Trailhead. To reach the Pauley Creek Trail, you must hike 1.5 miles west on the Butcher Creek Trail to its intersection with Pauley Creek.

Maps: For a map of Tahoe National Forest, send $4 to USDA-Forest Service, 630 Sansome Street,

San Francisco, CA 94111. To obtain topographic maps of the area, ask for Downieville, Sierra City, and Gold Lake from the USGS.

Contact: Tahoe National Forest, Downieville Ranger District, 15924 Highway 49, Camptonville, CA 95922; (916) 288-3231 or fax (916) 288-0727.

Trail notes: It's extremely rare when a side trip hike is awarded with its own separate mention, but the Pauley Creek Trail is one of those rare places that deserves a detailed listing. This is a side trip from the Butcher Ranch Trail (hike number 16). By extending that walk on the Pauley Creek Trail, you'll enter a land where there are streamside trail camps, spectacular wildflower blooms in early summer, and excellent trout fishing. Wildlife is also abundant in this watershed. The trailhead is difficult to reach and the return hike out of the canyon back to the trailhead involves a 2,000-foot climb. So much for the rough stuff. It's beautiful all along the stream and rare to see other people. Out here you can feel as if you've entered a time machine, exploring a wild land as if it were 200 years ago.

⑱ Deer Lake Trail

5.0 mi/3.5 hrs

Location: West of Packer Lake in Tahoe National Forest; map C3, grid i8.

User groups: Hikers, dogs, horses, and mountain bikes. No wheelchair facilities.

Permits: No permits are required. Parking and access are free.

Directions: From Sacramento on Interstate 80, drive east to Auburn. In Auburn, take Highway 49 north to Nevada City and proceed northeast on Highway 49/Gold Country Highway to Bassetts. Turn left (north) on Gold Lake Highway at Bassetts. Drive 1.4 miles, turn left, and cross the Salmon Creek Bridge. Go three-tenths of a mile, then turn right on Packer Lake Road. Drive two miles to the trailhead. Parking is available in the Packsaddle camping area just opposite the trailhead.

Maps: For a map of Tahoe National Forest, send $4 to USDA-Forest Service, 630 Sansome Street, San Francisco, CA 94111. To obtain a topographic map of the area, ask for Sierra City from the USGS.

Contact: Tahoe National Forest, Downieville Ranger District, 15924 Highway 49, Camptonville, CA 95922; (916) 288-3231 or fax (916) 288-0727.

Trail notes: Most lakes are green, but Deer Lake is the deepest azure blue you can imagine, and with the spectacular Sierra Buttes in the background, it's easy to understand why this trip is so popular. And popular it is, with the trail getting some of the heaviest use of any in this section of Tahoe National Forest. It's a 2.5-mile hike to the lake, in the process climbing 1,000 feet, topping out at 7,110 feet. From the trailhead, you'll climb up through a basin and receive a sweeping view of the massive Sierra Buttes and the surrounding forested slopes. As you head on, you'll cross a signed spur trail, a quarter-mile route to Grass Lake. It's well worth the short detour, but approach quietly because deer are common here. Then it's onward, over the ridge and down to Deer Lake. On warm evenings, the brook trout can leave countless circles while feeding on surface insects. This hike has it all, and, alas, that's why it often includes so many other people.

⑲ Frazier Falls Trail

1.0 mi/1.0 hr

Location: North of Sierra City; map C3, grid i8.

User groups: Hikers, dogs, and horses. No mountain bikes. No wheelchair facilities.

Permits: No permits are required. Parking and access are free.

Directions: From Sacramento, drive northeast on Interstate 80 to Truckee. In Truckee, take Highway 89 north to the town of Clio. Continue a short distance on Highway 89 north to Forest Service Road 24 (Gold Lake Highway). Turn left (west) on Forest Service Road 24 (Gold Lake Highway) and drive until you see the sign for Frazier Falls. Turn left and go to the end of the road.

Maps: For a map of Plumas National Forest, send $4 to USDA-Forest Service, 630 Sansome Street, San Francisco, CA 94111. To obtain a topographic map of the area, ask for Gold Lake from the USGS.

Contact: Plumas National Forest, Beckwourth Ranger District, P.O. Box 7, Blairsden, CA 96103; (916) 836-2575 or fax (916) 836-0493.

Trail notes: Frazier Falls is a 178-foot, silver-tasseled waterfall that tumbles out of a chute into a rocky basin where refracted light through the water droplets can make it all seem blessed. And maybe it is. The trail is a breeze, a half-mile romp on a gentle route that leads to the scenic overlook of the falls. The best time to visit is early summer, when snowmelt from the high country is peaking, filling Frazier Falls like a huge fountain. In addition, wildflower blooms along the trail in early summer add a splash of color, with violet lupine the most abundant. The road to the trailhead is paved all the way, the hike is easy, the falls are beautiful, and as you might expect, thousands of people make the trip every summer.

㉑ Round Lake Trailhead

1.4 mi/1.0 hr

Location: On the southern boundary of Gold Lakes Basin north of Sierra City; map C3, grid i8.

User groups: Hikers, dogs, and horses. No mountain bikes. No wheelchair facilities.

Permits: No permits are required. Parking and access are free.

Directions: From Sacramento, drive northeast on Interstate 80 to Truckee. In Truckee, take Highway 89 north to the town of Clio. Continue a short distance on Highway 89 north to Forest Service Road 24 (Gold Lake Highway). Turn left (west) on Forest Service Road 24 (Gold Lake Highway) and drive until you see the sign for Round Lake Trail. Turn right and continue to the parking area.

Maps: For a map of Plumas National Forest, send $4 to USDA-Forest Service, 630 Sansome Street, San Francisco, CA 94111. To obtain a topographic map of the area, ask for Gold Lake from the USGS.

Contact: Plumas National Forest, Beckwourth Ranger District, P.O. Box 7, Blairsden, CA 96103; (916) 836-2575 or fax (916) 836-0493.

Trail notes: The seven-tenths of a mile hike to Big Bear Lake is an easy, popular, and pretty walk, most commonly taken by visitors staying at Gold Lake Lodge. The trailhead is located alongside the parking lot next to the road to the lodge, and the trail itself is actually a closed road,

good for horseback riding. It's routed west to Big Bear Lake, the first in a series of beautiful alpine lakes in the Gold Lakes Basin. While most day users return after a picnic at Big Bear Lake, the trip can easily be extended, either west to Round Lake or north to Long Lake or Silver Lake. Most of this country is in the 6,000- to 7,000-foot elevation range, and is high granite country filled with alpine lakes.

㉑ Haskell Peak Trail

3.0 mi/2.0 hrs

Location: North of Highway 49 in Tahoe National Forest; map C3, grid i9.

User groups: Hikers, dogs, horses, and mountain bikes. No wheelchair facilities.

Permits: No permits are required. Parking and access are free.

Directions: From Sacramento on Interstate 80, drive east to Auburn. In Auburn, take Highway 49 north to Nevada City and proceed northeast on Highway 49/Gold Country Highway to Bassetts. Turn left (north) on Gold Lake Highway at Bassetts, drive 3.7 miles, then turn right on Forest Service Road 9 (Haskell Peak Road) and drive 8.4 miles. The trailhead is on the left; parking is available on either side of the road.

Maps: For a map of Tahoe National Forest, send $4 to USDA-Forest Service, 630 Sansome Street, San Francisco, CA 94111. To obtain a topographic map of the area, ask for Clio from the USGS.

Contact: Tahoe National Forest, Downieville Ranger District, 15924 Highway 49, Camptonville, CA 95922; (916) 288-3231 or fax (916) 288-0727.

Trail notes: Haskell Peak is one of the great, yet unknown, lookouts. On clear days you can see many mountains both nearby and distant, including Mount Shasta and Mount Lassen in Northern California, Mount Rose in Nevada, and the closer Sierra Buttes. To get this view requires a 1,100-foot climb over the course of 1.5 miles, topping out at the 8,107-foot summit. The trail climbs at a decent, steady grade through heavy forest for the first mile. It then flattens and reaches an open area where Haskell Peak comes into view. From here, it's only a quarter-mile but very steep climb to the top. You'll discover that Haskell Peak is the flume of an old volcano, and has many unusual volcanic rock formations. You'll also discover that just about nobody knows about this great hike.

㉒ Sierra Buttes Trail

5.0 mi/3.5 hrs

Location: Near Packer Lake in Tahoe National Forest; map C3, grid j8.

User groups: Hikers, dogs, and horses. No mountain bikes. No wheelchair access.

Permits: No permits are required. Parking and access are free.

Directions: From Sacramento on Interstate 80, drive east to Auburn. In Auburn, take Highway 49 north to Nevada City and proceed northeast on Highway 49/Gold Country Highway to Bassetts. Turn left (north) on Gold Lake Highway at Bassetts. Go 1.4 miles, turn left, and cross the Salmon Creek Bridge. Drive a short distance and turn right on Packer Lake Road. Proceed a quarter of a mile past the lake to the trailhead. The trail starts as a jeep road, located immediately behind the small parking area.

Maps: For a map of Tahoe National Forest, send $4 to USDA-Forest Service, 630 Sansome Street, San Francisco, CA 94111. To obtain a topographic map of the area, ask for Sierra City from the USGS.

Contact: Tahoe National Forest, Downieville Ranger District, 15924 Highway 49, Camptonville, CA 95922; (916) 288-3231 or fax (916) 288-0727.

Trail notes: The Sierra Buttes Lookout Station, 8,587 feet high and with a railed stairway to the top, provides a destination for one of California's best day hikes and greatest viewpoints. The trip starts near Packer Lake, at 6,000 feet in elevation. The trail climbs through a series of switchbacks to 6,700 feet. You loop around the mountain bowl that frames Sardine Lake in a counterclockwise direction, passing Tamarack Lakes, and then climbing some 1,500 feet to reach the top. The trail traces the rim to the lookout and is capped by a stairway with 176 steps that seem to project into wide open space. Climbing it is an astounding sensation, almost like climbing the cable at Half Dome. The lookout itself also juts out into space, and it can seem quite eery

as you scan miles and miles of Sierra mountain country, from Mount Lassen in the north all the way to the Tahoe Rim to the south. Stand here one time and you'll never forget it the rest of your life.

㉓ Haypress Creek Trail

6.0 mi/1.0 day

Location: East of Sierra City in Tahoe National Forest; map C3, grid j8.

User groups: Hikers, dogs, and horses. No mountain bikes. No wheelchair facilities.

Permits: No permits are required. Parking and access are free.

Directions: From Sacramento on Interstate 80, drive east to Auburn. In Auburn, take Highway 49 north to Nevada City and proceed northeast on Highway 49/Gold Country Highway to Sierra City. At the eastern end of Sierra City, turn off Highway 49 on Wild Plum Road at the sign for Wild Plum Campground. Drive one mile on this road to the Wild Plum Trailhead parking area. Walk through the campground and follow the trail to an intersection a quarter of a mile past a bridge over Haypress Creek. The trail is to the right.

Maps: For a map of Tahoe National Forest, send $4 to USDA-Forest Service, 630 Sansome Street, San Francisco, CA 94111. To obtain a topographic map of the area, ask for Haypress Valley from the USGS.

Contact: Tahoe National Forest, Downieville Ranger District, 15924 Highway 49, Camptonville, CA 95922; (916) 288-3231 or fax (916) 288-0727.

Trail notes: A canyon with a hidden stream and a waterfall that's surrounded by old-growth red fir make this a wonderful day hike for the properly inspired. Why properly inspired? Because the trail climbs from 4,400 feet up Haypress Creek to 5,840 feet, a 1,440-foot rise over just three miles. The trail starts out almost flat for the first half of a mile, then crosses over Haypress Creek on a footbridge. There's an excellent view of the Sierra Buttes in this area. Then you continue on the Haypress Creek Trail, rising past a rocky area and into forest, and, alas, passing some logging activity where the trail turns to road for a short spell. Don't despair. The trail soon enters an old-growth forest, contouring along Haypress Canyon, and passes by a lovely waterfall. This hike makes for a great day hike with a picnic lunch, and trail use is typically quite light.

㉔ Chapman Creek Trail

3.0 mi/2.0 hrs

Location: East of Sierra City in Tahoe National Forest; map C3, grid j9.

User groups: Hikers, dogs, horses, and mountain bikes. No wheelchair facilities.

Permits: No permits are required. Parking and access are free.

Directions: From Sacramento on Interstate 80, drive east to Auburn. In Auburn, take Highway 49 north to Nevada City and proceed northeast on Highway 49/Gold Country Highway to Sierra City. Take Highway 49 east and drive eight miles to Chapman Creek Campground. The trailhead and a parking area are located at the north end of the campground.

Maps: For a map of Tahoe National Forest, send $4 to USDA-Forest Service, 630 Sansome Street, San Francisco, CA 94111. To obtain a topographic map of the area, ask for Sierra City from the USGS.

Contact: Tahoe National Forest, Downieville Ranger District, 15924 Highway 49, Camptonville, CA 95922; (916) 288-3231 or fax (916) 288-0727.

Trail notes: Chapman Creek is a babbling brook where you can walk along, perhaps stopping to picnic, fish a little, or do absolutely nothing. That's right, nothing. It's that kind of place. The trailhead, elevation 5,840 feet, is set at a campground, providing easy access. Outside of campers, few others know of it. The trail winds easily along the contours of Chapman Creek under the canopy of a dense forest, rising gently along the way. It climbs to 6,400 feet, or 560 feet in a span of 1.5 miles. The river is the lifeblood for a variety of birds and wildlife, but few visitors make the trip for that reason. Rather they come to stroll and let their minds wander and be free.

Pacific Crest Trail (PCT) Section Overview

161.0 mi. one way/2.0 wks

Trail sections extend from the northern border of Tahoe National Forest (Yuba River) to Lassen Volcanic National Park.

If you plan on hiking only one section of the Pacific Crest Trail in this region, then make your selection with care. Highlights here include the Sierra Buttes, Gold Lakes Basin, Bucks Lake Wilderness, and Middle Fork Feather River, all world-class settings. But there are lowlights as well, including terrible chunks of trail through dry, hot country where there are too many rattlesnakes to take lightly. Much of the country ranges 5,000 to 7,000 feet in elevation, yet drops as low as 2,310 feet on the North Fork Feather River at Belden and 3,180 feet on the Middle Fork Feather. That means you'll face long, slow climbs and descents as you hike in and out of river canyons. Following is more specific information on major trail sections in this zone.

PCT-32 Yuba River to Fowler Creek

51.0 mi. one way/4.0 days

Location: In Tahoe National Forest, off Highway 49 east of Sierra City; map C3, grid j8.

User groups: Hikers, dogs, and horses. No mountain bikes. No wheelchair access.

Permits: No permits are required. Parking and access are free.

Directions: From Sacramento on Interstate 80, drive east to Auburn. In Auburn, take Highway 49 north to Nevada City. From Nevada City, go northeast on Highway 49/Gold Country Highway to Sierra City. Take Highway 49 northeast for two-tenths of a mile to the Pacific Crest Trail access point.

Maps: To obtain topographic maps of the area, ask for Haypress Valley, Sierra City, Mount Fillmore, and Onion Valley from the USGS.

Contact: Tahoe National Forest, Downieville Ranger District, 15924 Highway 49, Camptonville, CA 95922; (916) 288-3231 or fax (916) 288-0727.

Trail notes: Pristine alpine lakes and high mountain lookouts highlight this section of the Pacific Crest Trail. While just as beautiful as the section of trail south near Tahoe, this stretch gets far less use. It starts at the Yuba River, and in the first two miles, climbs an endless series of switchbacks up the back side of the Sierra Buttes—a terrible climb with a great reward. Note that the spur trail up to the Sierra Buttes Fire Lookout is an additional 1,400-foot climb, but furnishes one of the top lookouts in California. The trail then heads north, skirting past the western border of the Gold Lakes Basin, where a dozen high alpine lakes make for easy side trips and camps. With some terrible switchbacks, the PCT passes Mount Gibraltar (7,343 feet), Stafford Mountain (7,019 feet), and Mount Etna (7,163 feet), and flanks below Pilot Peak (7,457 feet). It then drops down the western slope, eventually descending to the Fowler Creek Trailhead.

PCT-33 Fowler Creek to Bucks Summit

26.0 mi. one way/3.0 days

Location: At Fowler Creek north of Little Grass Valley Reservoir in Plumas National Forest; map C3, grid h5.

User groups: Hikers, dogs, and horses. No mountain bikes. No wheelchair access.

Permits: No permits are required. Parking and access are free.

Directions: From Oroville, drive north on Highway 70/89 North to Quincy. From Quincy, drive south on Highway 70/89 South. Turn right on Quincy-La Porte Road and proceed 1.5 miles to Little Grass Valley Road. Turn north on Little Grass Valley Road and drive to Black Rock Campground. Bear left on Forest Service Road 94 and head to Forest Service Road 22N65Y. Turn right and drive to the parking area.

Maps: To obtain topographic maps of the area, ask for Onion Valley, Dogwood Peak, and Bucks Lake from the USGS.

Contact: Plumas National Forest, Feather River Ranger District, 875 Mitchell Ave., Oroville, CA 95965; (916) 534-6500 or fax (916) 532-1210.

Trail notes: Most PCT hikers will want to sprint through this section of trail. From Fowler Creek,

it passes through Plumas National Forest country until reaching the southern border of the Bucks Lake Wilderness. It starts quite nicely, dropping down to the Middle Fork Feather River (3,180 feet), a great trout stream, where an excellent footbridge gets you across a gorge. Enjoy it, because the rest of this route won't exactly have you writing postcards over the euphoria. It climbs out from the Middle Fork Feather to Lookout Rock, elevation 6,955 feet, and a long, dry pull, then drops down to Bucks Creek. Most of this region is dry rattlesnake country, so watch your step—and time your water stops.

PCT-34 Bucks Summit to Feather River

20.0 mi. one way/2.0 days

Location: At Bucks Summit Trailhead at the southern boundary of the Bucks Lake Wilderness west of Quincy; map C3, grid f3.

User groups: Hikers, dogs, and horses. No mountain bikes. No wheelchair access.

Permits: A fire permit is required in Bucks Lake Wilderness. Parking and access are free.

Directions: From Quincy, turn west on Bucks Lake Road and drive about 11 miles to the trailhead, located at Bucks Summit.

Maps: To obtain a topographic map of the area, ask for Bucks Lake from the USGS.

Contact: Plumas National Forest, Mount Hough Ranger District, 39696 Highway 70, Quincy, CA 95971; (916) 283-0555 or fax (916) 283-1821.

Trail notes: It's 20 miles from Bucks Summit to Belden, all of it on the Pacific Crest Trail through the Bucks Lake Wilderness. In the process, the trail passes across a granitic-based alpine area, where forest is interspersed with glacial-smoothed rock peaks. The trailhead is at Bucks Summit, elevation 5,531 feet, and from here the route generally follows the ridgeline for many miles, climbing to the southern flank of Mount Pleasant, 6,924 feet. Along the way, a short spur trail to little Rock Lake provides a good side trip. The trail heads past Three Lakes, where another spur trail provides another option, this one to Kellogg Lake. From here, the trail begins descending, then drops very sharply to the

North Fork Feather River at Belden, all the way down to 2,310 feet. Your big toes will be sore for days from jamming into the front of your boots.

PCT-35 Feather River to Humboldt Summit

26.0 mi. one way/2.0 days

Location: At the Belden Trailhead on Highway 70 in Plumas National Forest; map C3, grid e2.

User groups: Hikers, dogs, and horses. No mountain bikes. No wheelchair facilities.

Permits: No permits are required. Parking and access are free.

Directions: From Quincy, drive west on Highway 70 about 26 miles to the trailhead, located at the roadside rest area at Belden.

Maps: To obtain topographic maps of the area, ask for Belden and Humboldt Peak from the USGS.

Contact: Plumas National Forest, Feather River Ranger District, 875 Mitchell Ave., Oroville, CA 95965; (916) 534-6500 or fax (916) 532-1210.

Trail notes: The trail is not only rough from Belden to Humboldt Summit, but it's not particularly pretty, especially compared to the nearby wilderness. The climb is a mighty dry slice of life. From the North Fork Feather River at Belden, elevation 2,310 feet, the PCT climbs 4,777 feet over the course of this two-day thumper to Humboldt Summit at 7,087 feet. There are no lakes along this trail, only a few small waterholes requiring short side trips. Instead, the prettiest sections are along streams, the first being Chips Creek, which runs adjacent to the trail for eight miles, then later a short crossing over the headwaters of Willow Creek. Some might prefer to take three days instead of two to hike this section, but with Lassen Volcanic National Park looming ahead, you'll put in long days to get through this area.

PCT-36 Humboldt Summit to Domingo Springs

28.0 mi. one way/2.0 days

Location: At Humboldt Summit in Lassen National Forest southwest of Lake Almanor; map C3, grid d1.

User groups: Hikers, dogs, and horses. No mountain bikes. No wheelchair facilities.

Permits: No permits are required. Parking and access are free.

Directions: From Chico, drive north on Highway 32 to the junction with Highway 89/36. Turn right (east) and take Highway 36 toward Chester. Turn west on Highway 36 and drive two miles to the junction with Highway 89. Turn south on Highway 89 and proceed four miles, then turn right on County Road 308 (Humboldt Road) and drive 15 miles to the trailhead parking area.

Maps: To obtain topographic maps of the area, ask for Humboldt Peak and Stover Mountain from the USGS.

Contact: Lassen National Forest, Almanor Ranger District, P.O. Box 767, Chester, CA 96020; (916) 258-2141 or fax (916) 258-3491.

Trail notes: The idea of back-to-back 14-mile days to get through this chunk of trail may not appeal to many hikers, especially while carrying full-weight expedition packs. But that's standard for most hikers on this stretch of PCT, with little here to tarry for and with Lassen Volcanic National Park beckoning ahead. The trail starts just below Humboldt Peak at 7,087 feet and heads north along the ridge line, for the most part, past Butt Mountain (7,866 feet) and down to Soldier Meadows. A spring and stream make this a delightful stop before crossing Highway 36, forging onward another three miles to the Stove Springs Campground. The trail then skirts around the western flank of North Stove Mountain and drops down to Domingo Springs, where another campground is available.

PCT-37 Domingo Springs to Lassen Volcanic National Park

11.0 mi. one way/1.0 day

Location: At the Domingo Springs Trailhead in Lassen National Forest west of Lake Almanor; map C3, grid b2.

User groups: Hikers, dogs, and horses. No mountain bikes. No wheelchair facilities.

Permits: No permits are required. Parking and access are free.

Directions: From Chico, drive north on Highway 32 to the junction with Highway 89/36. Turn right (east) and take Highway 36 toward Chester. Turn north on Warner Valley Road (County Road 312) and drive about six miles. Turn left on Old Red Bluff Road (County Road 311) and go three miles to the parking area at Domingo Springs.

Maps: To obtain a topographic map of the area, ask for Stover Mountain from the USGS.

Contact: Lassen National Forest, Almanor Ranger District, P.O. Box 767, Chester, CA 96020; (916) 258-2141 or fax (916) 258-2141.

Trail notes: With each passing step, the scenery gets better and better. Finally you leave dry, hot forest country and enter Lassen Volcanic National Park at Warren Valley. All the suffering seems over and only paradise awaits. From Domingo Springs, the Pacific Crest Trail is routed straight north through Lassen National Forest. The Little North Fork of the North Fork Feather is located a quarter of a mile to the west and is a good side trip, both for swimming and fishing for large brown trout. As you enter Lassen Volcanic National Park, you'll pass Little Willow Lake, and two miles later arrive at Boiling Springs Lake and the Warner Valley Campground. This is a good layover spot, with the side trip to Devil's Kitchen recommended.

PCT Continuation: To continue hiking along the Pacific Crest Trail, see chapter B3.

Leave No Trace Tips

Travel and Camp with Care

On the trail:

Stay on designated trails. Walk single file in the middle of the path.

Do not take shortcuts on switchbacks.

When traveling cross-country where there are no trails, follow animal trails or spread out your group so no new routes are created. Walk along the most durable surfaces available, such as rock, gravel, dry grasses, or snow.

Use a map and compass to eliminate the need for rock cairns, tree scars, or ribbons.

If you encounter pack animals, step to the downhill side of the trail and speak softly to avoid startling them.

At camp:

Choose an established, legal site that will not be damaged by your stay.

Restrict activities to areas where vegetation is compacted or absent.

Keep pollutants out of the water by camping at least 200 feet (about 70 adult steps) from lakes and streams.

Control pets at all times, or leave them at home with a sitter. Remove dog feces.

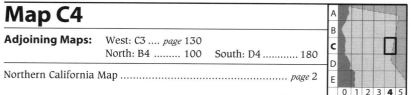

Map C4

Adjoining Maps: West: C3 .... *page* 130
North: B4 100   South: D4 180

Northern California Map .... *page* 2

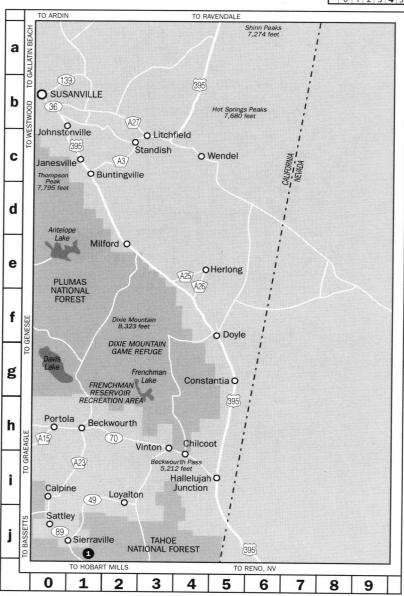

TO ARDIN   TO RAVENDALE

Shinn Peaks
7,274 feet

a

TO GALLATIN BEACH

139

b O SUSANVILLE
36

TO WESTWOOD

395
A27

Johnstonville   O Litchfield
395   Standish

Hot Springs Peaks
7,680 feet

c Janesville O   A3
O Buntingville   O Wendel

Thompson
Peak
7,795 feet

CALIFORNIA
NEVADA

d

Antelope
Lake

e Milford O

PLUMAS
NATIONAL
FOREST

A25 O Herlong
A26

TO GENESEE

f Dixie Mountain
8,323 feet

DIXIE MOUNTAIN
GAME REFUGE   O Doyle

Davis
Lake

g Frenchman
Lake

FRENCHMAN   Constantia O
RESERVOIR
RECREATION AREA

395

h Portola
O   O Beckwourth

TO GRAEAGLE

A15   70
Vinton O   O Chilcoot

i A23
Beckwourth Pass
5,212 feet

Calpine   Hallelujah O
O   49 Loyalton   Junction

j Sattley
O

TO BASSETTS

89
O Sierraville   TAHOE
❶   NATIONAL FOREST   395

TO HOBART MILLS   TO RENO, NV

| 0 | 1 | 2 | 3 | 4 | 5 | 6 | 7 | 8 | 9 |

Chapter C4 features:

❶ Cottonwood Creek Botanical Trail

1.0 mi/0.5 hr

Location: In Tahoe National Forest; map C4, grid j1.

User groups: Hikers, dogs, and horses, though horses aren't recommended. No mountain bikes. No wheelchair facilities.

Permits: No permits are required. Fees are required for parking in the campground parking lot and for camping; reservations are available.

Directions: From Truckee, drive north on Highway 89 about 20 miles to the Cottonwood Creek Campground entrance on the right. The trailhead is at the upper end of the campground. Just south of the campground entrance on the right is a large turnout providing free parking for day use. Alternate route from Sierraville is to drive four miles southeast on Highway 89 to Cottonwood Creek Campground on your left.

Maps: For a map of Tahoe National Forest, send $4 to USDA-Forest Service, 630 Sansome Street, San Francisco, CA 94111.

Contact: Tahoe National Forest, Sierraville Ranger District, P.O. Box 95, Sierraville, CA 96126; (916) 994-3401 or fax (916) 991-3143.

Trail notes: The Cottonwood Creek Botanical Trail is a half-mile nature trail that follows along little Cottonwood Creek. The trailhead is at the Cottonwood Creek Campground, set at 5,800 feet in the Sierra Nevada. The trail leads out of camp, with a brochure available at the trailhead. The brochure has listings that correspond to numbered posts along the trail, which explain a variety of plants and trees unique to the area. This is a short, easy trip along a refreshing stream with a little botany lesson along the way. A good side trip is to Campbell Hot Springs, located a very short drive west of Sierraville off Highway 49.

Map DØ

Adjoining Maps: East: D1 .... *page* 156
                      North: CØ 106

Northern California Map .... *page* 2

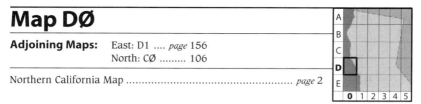

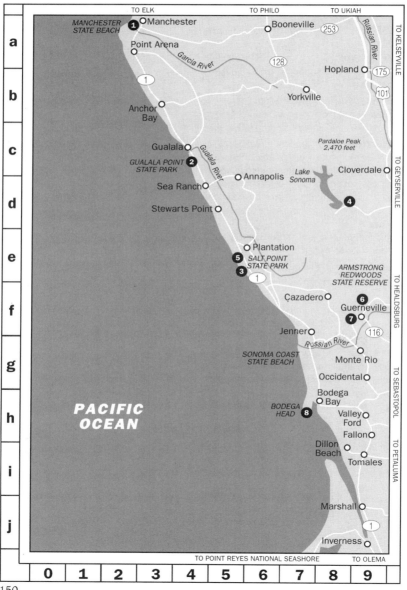

TO ELK
TO PHILO
TO UKIAH

MANCHESTER STATE BEACH

① ○Manchester

○ Booneville (253)

Point Arena ○

Garcia River

(128)

Russian River

TO KELSEYVILLE

Hopland ○ (175)

(1)

Yorkville ○ (101)

Anchor Bay ○

Gualala ○

GUALALA POINT STATE PARK ②

Gualala River

Pardaloe Peak 2,470 feet

Sea Ranch ○

○ Annapolis

Lake Sonoma

Cloverdale ○

TO GEYSERVILLE

Stewarts Point ○

④

○ Plantation

⑤ SALT POINT STATE PARK

③ (1)

ARMSTRONG REDWOODS STATE RESERVE

TO HEALDSBURG

Cazadero ○

⑥

Guerneville ○

⑦ (116)

Jenner ○

Russian River

○ Monte Rio

SONOMA COAST STATE BEACH

Occidental ○

PACIFIC OCEAN

BODEGA HEAD ⑧

Bodega ○ Bay

Valley ○ Ford

Fallon ○

TO SEBASTOPOL

Dillon Beach ○

○ Tomales

TO PETALUMA

Marshall ○

(1)

Inverness ○

TO POINT REYES NATIONAL SEASHORE
TO OLEMA

0 1 2 3 4 5 6 7 8 9

Chapter DØ features:

❶ Alder Creek Trail

4.0 mi/1.75 hrs

Location: In Manchester Beach State Park on the Mendocino coast north of Point Arena; map DØ, grid a2.

User groups: Hikers and horses. No dogs. The terrain isn't suitable for mountain bikes. No wheelchair facilities.

Permits: No permits are required. A $5 state park day-use fee is charged for each vehicle.

Directions: From Point Arena, drive north on Highway 1 to Kinney Lane. Turn left and go a short distance to the park entrance.

Maps: For a brochure and trail map, send $1 to Manchester Beach State Park at the address below. To obtain a topographic map of the area, ask for Point Arena from the USGS.

Contact: Manchester Beach State Park, P.O. Box 440, Mendocino, CA 95460; (707) 937-5804, (707) 865-2391, or fax (707) 937-2953.

Trail notes: Manchester State Beach has two moods, one sweet, one foul. In late winter and fall, radiant sunbeams set the Mendocino coast aglow, making for flawless beach walks. But in spring and early summer, with winds powering out of the north, it can feel like your head would blow off if it wasn't attached by the neck. The hike here starts adjacent to park headquarters and is routed past Lake Davis to the beach, continuing north along the beach to the mouth of Alder Creek. This is an attractive coastal lagoon, known for many species of birds, including whistling swans. It's also the area where the San Andreas Fault heads off from land into the sea. Time it right here and all can seem perfect.

❷ Headlands Loop

1.5 mi/0.75 hr

Location: In Gualala Point Regional Park on the Mendocino coast; map DØ, grid c4.

User groups: Hikers and dogs. No horses. One trail is suitable for wheelchairs and mountain bikes.

Permits: No permits are required. There is a $3 parking fee.

Directions: From Gualala, drive south on Highway 1 for a quarter of a mile (over the Gualala River) and turn west into the park entrance. Continue to the visitors center.

Maps: To obtain a topographic map of the area, ask for Gualala from the USGS.

Contact: Gualala Point Regional Park, P.O. Box 95, Gualala, CA 95445; (707) 785-2377 or (707) 527-2041.

Trail notes: The Headlands to Beach Loop is an easy, short walk that furnishes coastal views and a lookout over the Gualala River, not to mention a route amid giant coastal cypress trees. From the visitors center, the trail is routed along the Gualala River, then turns and loops to the left. Here you can take the short cutoff trail that leads to the beach. On the way back, the trail traces along the ocean bluffs for a short spell, and with it comes the coastal views. Then the trail turns inland and returns to the visitors center. Bonuses here include excellent whale watching during the winter and good wildflower blooms on the grassy hillsides in spring.

❸ Stockoff Creek Loop

1.25 mi/0.75 hr

Location: In Stillwater Cove Regional Park north of Jenner; map DØ, grid e5.

User groups: Hikers and dogs. No horses or mountain bikes. No wheelchair facilities.

Permits: No permits are required. A $3 day-use fee is charged for each vehicle.

Directions: From Santa Rosa on U.S. 101, take the Russian River exit. Turn left and follow River Road, past Monte Rio. Go right on Highway 116 and drive to Highway 1. Turn right and head north, past the town of Jenner for 16 miles to the park entrance on the right, at mile marker 37.01.

Maps: For a free brochure, contact Stillwater Cove Regional Park at the address below. To obtain a topographic map of the area, ask for Plantation from the USGS.

Contact: Stillwater Cove Regional Park, 2300 County Center Drive, Suite 120, Building A, Santa Rosa, CA 95403; (707) 847-3245 or (707) 785-2377. Regional Parks Department; (707) 527-2041 or fax (707) 785-3741.

Trail notes: Highway 1 is one of the top tourist drives in the U.S., which explains why the coastal state parks get such heavy use in the summer months. This little regional park, however, is sometimes overlooked by out-of-state traffic. The trailhead is located at the day-use parking lot, and after starting the walk, you'll almost immediately enter a surprising forest comprised of firs and redwoods. You then come to the Loop Trail junction, where you turn right. The trail is routed along the creek, crosses a few bridges, then eventually rises above the watershed and loops back through forest to the parking area. It's an easy, pretty, and secluded loop hike. A bonus is visiting Stillwater Cove, which requires crossing Highway 1 and then dropping down to the beach, which has a dramatic rock-strewn shore.

❹ South Lake Trailhead

5.0 mi/2.5 hrs

Location: At Lake Sonoma northwest of Healdsburg; map DØ, grid d8.

User groups: Hikers and dogs. No horses or mountain bikes. No wheelchair facilities.

Permits: No permits are required. Parking and access are free.

Directions: From Santa Rosa, drive 12 miles north on U.S. 101 to the town of Healdsburg. Turn left at the Dry Creek Road exit and drive about 11 miles, crossing Dry Creek River (Dry Creek Road becomes Skaggs Springs Road) and continuing to Skaggs Springs-Stewart Point Road. Turn left and go a quarter of a mile, then go right and drive to the base of the dam, the visitors center, and the trailhead.

Maps: For a free map, contact the U.S. Corps of Engineers at the address below. To obtain a topographic map of the area, ask for Warm Springs Dam from the USGS.

Contact: U.S. Arrmy Corps of Engineers, Lake Sonoma, 3333 Skaggs Springs Road, Geyserville, CA 95441; (707) 433-9483.

Trail notes: Lake Sonoma is one of the best examples in California of where the government folks have done something right. They not only built this lake, but added a superb boat ramp, marina, and campgrounds (some boat-in), and started a good bass fishery. They also cut 43 miles of trail, enough to spend days traipsing around the hills. The South Lake Trailhead is the best starting point, though the short trail at Vista Point has the best views (and the most wind in the spring and heat in the summer).

From the trailhead, the route traces along the lake, enters and exits a series of small groves, and extends along the lake's fingers. When you've had enough, just turn back. Many trails bisect the route and extend into more remote surrounding country, allowing ambitious hikers to create longer adventures. This area gets very hot in the summer. Most of the habitat is oak grasslands, and rarely you may see wild pigs, deer, or rattlesnakes.

❺ Stump Beach Trail

3.5 mi/1.5 hrs

Location: In Salt Point State Park north of Jenner; map DØ, grid e5.

User groups: Hikers only. Dogs, horses, and mountain bikes are only allowed on select trails. One trail (Gerstle Cove) is paved for wheelchairs.

Permits: No permits are required. A $5 state park day-use fee is charged per vehicle.

Directions: From San Francisco, drive north on U.S. 101 past Petaluma to Cotati and the junction with Highway 116. Turn northwest on Highway 116 and head to Highway 1. Go right on Highway 1 and drive about 20 miles (nine miles past Fort Ross) to the park entrance. Turn right and drive to the entrance kiosk. The trailhead is at the Salt Point parking area.

Maps: For a trail map, send 50 cents to Salt Point State Park at the address below. To obtain a topographic map of the area, ask for Plantation from the USGS.

Contact: Salt Point State Park, 25050 Coast Highway 1, Jenner, CA 95450; (707) 847-3221 or (707) 865-2391.

Trail notes: The dramatic, rocky shoreline of Salt Point State Park is memorable to anyone who has seen it. This trail provides the best look at it, including some simply awesome views from a 400-foot-high ocean bluff. The trailhead is at the parking area set near the tip of Salt Point, and from there, you hike north, over Warren Creek, a seasonal stream, and then across the bluffs. You can practically feel the crashing of ocean breakers below you, the spray rocketing skyward. The trail eventually winds around and down to Stump Beach Cove, a pretty, sandy beach where the calm waters are in sharp contrast to the nearby mauling ocean breakers. Salt Point State Park is known for excellent sport abalone diving in season, and also for providing one of the few marine reserves (Gerstle Cove) where no form of marine life may be taken or disturbed.

❻ Gilliam Creek Loop

8.9 mi/1.0 day

Location: In Austin Creek State Recreation Area north of Guerneville; map DØ, grid f9.

User groups: Hikers and horses. No dogs or mountain bikes. No wheelchair facilities.

Permits: No permits are required. A $5 state park day-use fee is charged for each vehicle.

Directions: From Santa Rosa, drive north on U.S. 101 to the Guerneville-Highway 116 exit. Turn west and drive to Guerneville, then go north on Armstrong Woods Road. Drive 2.5 miles to the Armstrong Redwoods State Reserve entrance. The trailhead is about 2.5 miles past the entrance.

Maps: For a trail map, send 50 cents to Armstrong Redwoods State Reserve at the address below. To obtain a topographic map of the area, ask for Guerneville from the USGS.

Contact: Armstrong Redwoods State Reserve, 17000 Armstrong Redwoods Road, Guerneville, CA 95446; (707) 869-2015 or (707) 865-2391.

Trail notes: The rolling hills, open forests, and streamside riparian habitat in Austin Creek State Recreation Area can seem a million miles away from the redwood forests of Armstrong Redwoods. Yet the two parks are actually coupled, forming 5,000 acres of contiguous parkland. While most tourists are walking around the redwoods at Armstrong, this trail offers a quieter and more ambitious alternative. From the trailhead at 1,100 feet, you contour across the slope, then drop down to the headwaters of Stonehouse Creek at 400 feet. The trail then follows along the stream, past the confluence with Gilliam Creek, extending 3.7 miles into the back country, all the way down to a 200-foot elevation. At the confluence of Austin Creek, you turn right and hike deeper into wild, hilly country along the stream, then return on the loop on the East Austin Creek Trail. The final two miles retrace your steps, climbing 700 feet in the process. At this point, you may ask, "Are we having fun yet?" Visitors who love Armstrong Redwoods tend not to speak of the adjoining Austin Creek Recreation Area with any terms of endearment.

❼ East Ridge Trail

6.8 mi/1.0 day

Location: In Armstrong Redwoods State Reserve north of Guerneville; map DØ, grid f9.

User groups: Hikers and horses. No dogs or mountain bikes. No wheelchair facilities.

Permits: No permits are required. A $5 state park day-use fee is charged for each vehicle.

Directions: From Santa Rosa on U.S. 101, take the Guerneville-Highway 116 exit. Turn west and drive to Guerneville, then go north on Armstrong Woods Road. Drive 2.5 miles to the Armstrong Redwoods State Reserve entrance. The trailhead is adjacent to the visitors center.

Maps: For a trail map, send 50 cents to Armstrong Redwoods State Reserve at the address below. To obtain a topographic map of the area, ask for Guerneville from the USGS.

Contact: Armstrong Redwoods State Reserve, 17000 Armstrong Redwoods Road, Guerneville, CA 95446; (707) 869-2015 or (707) 865-2391.

Trail notes: It's almost obligatory to hike either the Discovery Trail or Armstrong Nature Trail in Armstrong Redwoods, both very short and beautiful strolls through the park's grove of huge redwoods. But after that taste, your appetite will likely be whetted for something more inspiring. The East Ridge Trail provides it, rising 1,400 feet over the course of 3.4 miles, at times offering lookouts below into a sea of redwood tops. The trailhead is at a 200-foot elevation, adjacent to Fife Creek. The route climbs gradually at first, then in the first half-mile rises to cross the headwaters of Fife Creek, elevation 600 feet. Your climb has only just begun, and if you're already running out of gas, you'd best head back. The trail continues on, climbing all the way, contouring its way up towards McCray Mountain (1,940 feet), topping out at a service road at 1,600 feet.

❽ Bodega Head Loop

1.5 mi/1.0 hr

Location: On the Sonoma coast west of Bodega Bay; map DØ, grid h7.

User groups: Hikers only. No horses, dogs, or mountain bikes. No wheelchair facilities.

Permits: No permits are required. Parking and access are free.

Directions: From U.S. 101 at Petaluma, take the East Washington exit to East Washington Street and drive 26 miles to Bodega Bay (the road will turn into Highway 1). At the town of Bodega Bay, turn left on East Shore Road and drive less than half a mile. At the stop sign, turn west on Bay Flat Road and head around Bodega Bay (the road turns into West Side Road). Drive past Spud Point Marina to the Bodega Head parking area.

Maps: For a brochure, send 80 cents to SOS, P.O. Box 221, Duncan Mills, CA 95430.

Contact: For a free travel packet, write to the Bodega Bay Chamber of Commerce, P.O. Box 146, Bodega Bay, CA 94923, or call (707) 875-3422. You can also contact Sonoma Coast State Beach, P.O. Box 123, Duncan Mills, CA 95430; (707) 875-3483.

Trail notes: A short loop hike at Bodega Head will provide an introduction to one of California's great coastal areas. The trail starts at the east parking lot, and in just 1.5 miles, will take you

into a wonderland, with views of cliffs, untouched beaches, and southward to the sea and beyond. For a side trip, take a short tromp on a spur trail up to the tip-top of Bodega Head for 360-degree views. Rarely does the ocean seem so vast as it does from here. In spring and early summer, the wind can really howl. In late summer, fall, or early winter, Bodega Bay gets its warmest—and often wind-free—weather of the year.

Leave No Trace Tips

Pack It In and Pack It Out

Take everything you bring into the wild back out with you.

Protect wildlife and your food by storing rations securely.
Pick up all spilled foods.

Use toilet paper or wipes sparingly; pack them out.

Inspect your campsite for trash and any evidence of your stay.
Pack out all trash—even if it's not yours!

Map D1

Adjoining Maps: East: D2 .... *page* 162 West: DØ 150
North: C1 .... 116 South: E1 .... 216, 270

Northern California Map .... *page* 2

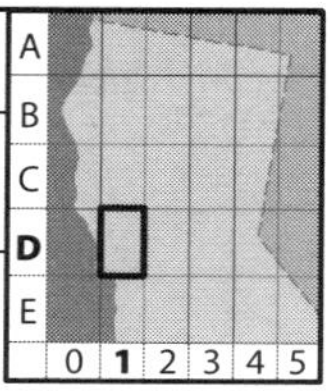

A
B
C
D
E
0 1 2 3 4 5

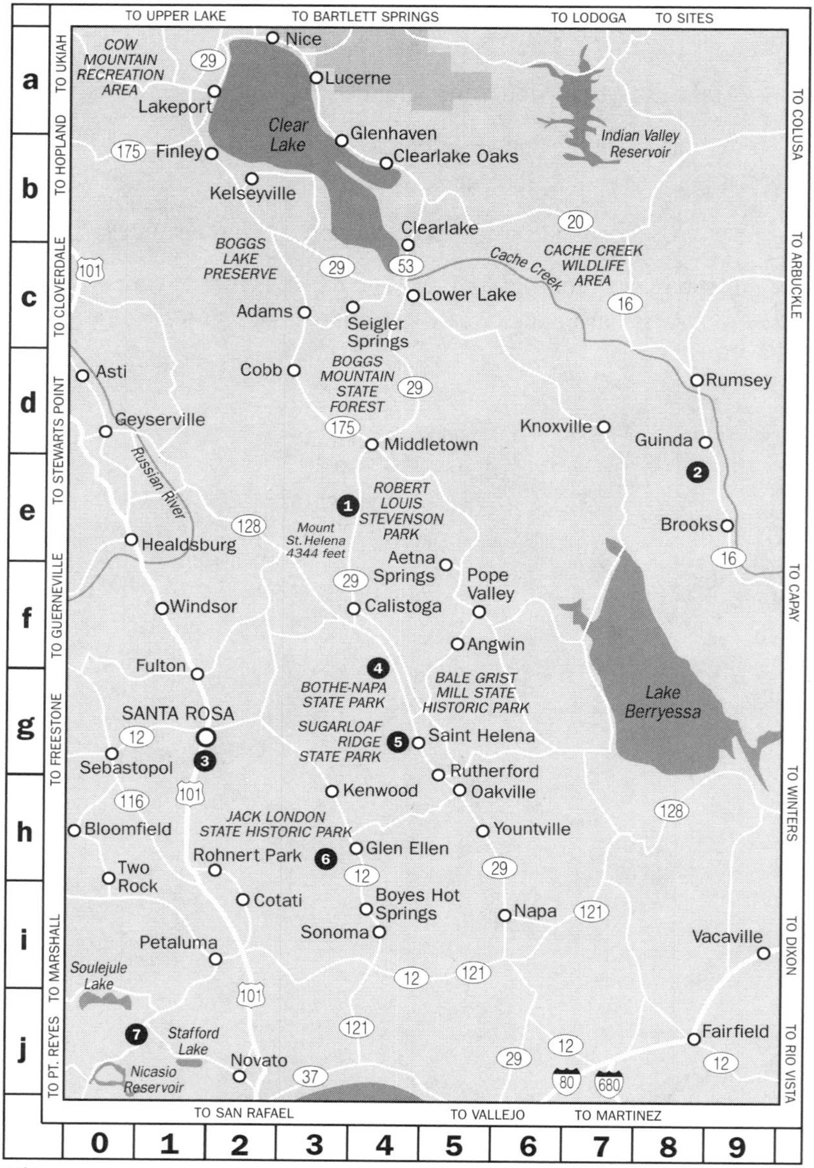

TO UPPER LAKE
TO BARTLETT SPRINGS
TO LODOGA
TO SITES
TO UKIAH
TO HOPLAND
TO CLOVERDALE
TO STEWARTS POINT
TO GUERNEVILLE
TO FREESTONE
TO MARSHALL
TO PT. REYES
TO COLUSA
TO ARBUCKLE
TO CAPAY
TO WINTERS
TO DIXON
TO RIO VISTA
TO SAN RAFAEL
TO VALLEJO
TO MARTINEZ
a
b
c
d
e
f
g
h
i
j
0
1
2
3
4
5
6
7
8
9
COW MOUNTAIN RECREATION AREA
Nice
Lucerne
Lakeport
Clear Lake
Glenhaven
Clearlake Oaks
Finley
Kelseyville
Indian Valley Reservoir
Clearlake
BOGGS LAKE PRESERVE
CACHE CREEK WILDLIFE AREA
Cache Creek
Lower Lake
Adams
Seigler Springs
Cobb
BOGGS MOUNTAIN STATE FOREST
Asti
Rumsey
Geyserville
Knoxville
Guinda
Middletown
Russian River
ROBERT LOUIS STEVENSON PARK
Mount St. Helena 4344 feet
Brooks
Healdsburg
Aetna Springs
Pope Valley
Windsor
Calistoga
Angwin
Fulton
BOTHE-NAPA STATE PARK
BALE GRIST MILL STATE HISTORIC PARK
Lake Berryessa
SANTA ROSA
SUGARLOAF RIDGE STATE PARK
Saint Helena
Sebastopol
Rutherford
Kenwood
Oakville
JACK LONDON STATE HISTORIC PARK
Bloomfield
Yountville
Rohnert Park
Glen Ellen
Two Rock
Cotati
Boyes Hot Springs
Napa
Sonoma
Vacaville
Petaluma
Soulejule Lake
Stafford Lake
Fairfield
Novato
Nicasio Reservoir
29
175
101
20
53
16
128
12
116
121
37
80
680
1
2
3
4
5
6
7

❶ Mount St. Helena Trail

10.0 mi/4.5 hrs

Location: In Robert Louis Stevenson State Park north of Calistoga; map D1, grid e3.

User groups: Hikers only. No dogs, horses, or mountain bikes. Mountain bikes are allowed on a nearby fire road, a quarter of a mile north on Highway 29. No wheelchair facilities.

Permits: No permits are required. Parking and access are free.

Directions: From Calistoga, drive about eight miles north on Highway 29 to the signed trailhead at the edge of the parking area on the west side of the highway at Robert Louis Stevenson State Park.

Maps: To obtain a topographic map of the area, ask for Mount St. Helena from the USGS.

Contact: Robert Louis Stevenson State Park, c/o Bothe-Napa Valley State Park, 3801 St. Helena Highway North, Calistoga, CA 94515; (707) 942-4575 or (707) 938-1519.

Trail notes: Mount St. Helena is Sonoma County's highest mountain, the peak that strikes such a memorable silhouette when viewed from the Bay Area. This trail climbs to the summit at 4,343 feet, requiring an ascent of 2,068 feet over the course of five miles. The route follows a moderate grade for the most part, then rises above the forest and includes two steep sections, one at the very end of your climb. In the summer, the hike can be pure hell, since much of the trail is actually an abandoned road with little shade, there's no water anywhere along the route, and the heat commonly blazes in the 90s and 100s out here. Most visitors make the trip when temperatures are more tolerable, of course, which makes the gradient feel pretty moderate. The mountain is most often visited in the winter, when the summit is commonly flecked with snow from passing storms, quite a treat for most folks in the area. In fact, when the snow level drops to 3,500 feet, the entire mountaintop can get a good pasting of a foot of snow. In spring, north winds clear the air. Visibility is best at this time, with remarkable views in all directions. No matter when you hike, be certain to bring plenty of water, a day pack with high-energy food, a windbreaker, and a change of shirts (so you won't be making the return downhill trip with a cold, wet shirt).

❷ Blue Ridge Trail

1–16 mi/1.0 day

Location: North of Lake Berryessa; map D1, grid e8.

User groups: Hikers and dogs. Horses and mountain bikes, while allowed, aren't recommended because of the steep, rocky terrain. No wheelchair facilities.

Permits: No permits are required. Parking and access are free.

Directions: From Interstate 5 at Woodland, drive west on Highway 16 for about 30 miles. At Lower Yolo County Park, turn left on a gravel road and look for a concrete bridge. After crossing the bridge, look for the trailhead on the left. Park in the unpaved area near Cache Creek. Walk down the dirt road through a meadow to the trailhead. In the winter, the dirt road is blocked by a locked gate; park instead at Lower Yolo County Park and walk down to the trailhead.

Maps: For a free primitive trail map, contact the Bureau of Land Management at the address below. To obtain a topographic map of the area, ask for Guinda from the USGS.

Contact: Bureau of Land Management, Clear Lake Resource Area, 2550 North State Street, Ukiah, CA 95482; (707) 468-4000.

Trail notes: There are relatively few trails on BLM property in Northern California, but all of them are special in one way or the other. Unfortunately, usually it's the other. The Blue Ridge Trail, for instance, includes a stretch with a 2,000-foot elevation gain in just three miles, and many pieces of trail that are very steep, rocky, and dry. The trail follows the ridge for eight miles (most folks don't last anywhere near that long), and you'd better be as fit as a Tibetan sherpa to try it. But hey, in spring this can be a sensational hike, with wildflowers ablaze and bushes and trees in full bloom. You'll see songbirds, swallows, falcons, and eagles flitting, hovering, and soaring. There are also a good share of lizards and rattlesnakes. The views are exceptional in all directions, with the Sutter Buttes and Snow Mountain most prominent, but with even Shasta and Lassen in view on clear days. In fact, the area has just about everything; everything that is, except water. You either bring at least two or three quarts per person, or you surrender, swearing never to hike here again.

❸ Spring Lake Trail

2.0 mi/1.0 hr

Location: In Spring Lake Regional Park in eastern Santa Rosa; map D1, grid g2.

User groups: Hikers and dogs. Horses are allowed only on designated trails. The park has 2.3 miles of trail that are paved for wheelchair and bicycle use.

Permits: No permits are required. There is a $3 parking fee.

Directions: From U.S. 101 in Santa Rosa, turn east on Highway 12 and continue east as it becomes Hoen Avenue. Turn left on Newanga Avenue and drive to the park entrance. The various trailheads are well marked and easily accessible from the parking area at the lake.

Maps: For a detailed trail map, send 25 cents to Spring Lake Regional Park at the address below. To obtain a topographic map of the area, ask for Santa Rosa from the USGS.

Contact: Spring Lake Regional Park, 5390 Montgomery Drive, Santa Rosa, CA 95409; (707) 539-8082.

Trail notes: Spring Lake is Santa Rosa's backyard fishing hole, a popular place for trout fishing, an evening picnic, or a short hike. For newcomers, we suggest the walk along the west shore of Spring Lake to the west dam, then turning left and heading into adjoining Howarth Park to Ralphine Lake. It's an easy, enjoyable stroll, though nothing serious. The lake is stocked with trout in winter and spring and provides a fair warm-water fishery in the summer. Nonpowered boating keeps things fun and quiet. For children, pony rides are quite popular. Robyn Schlueter, our research editor, remembers those pony rides fondly. "My grandmother used to take me here when I was little."

❹ Coyote Peak/Redwood Trail Loop

5.0 mi/3.0 hrs

Location: In Bothe-Napa Valley State Park south of Calistoga; map D1, grid g4.

User groups: Hikers only. No dogs. Horses and mountain bikes are allowed on fire roads only. No wheelchair facilities.

Permits: No permits are required. A $5 state park fee is charged per vehicle.

Directions: From the town of St. Helena, drive five miles north on Highway 128/29, past Bale Grist Mill State Park, to the park entrance on the left side of the road. Drive just past the Ritchey Creek Campground turnoff, near the picnic area where there's parking for about six cars near the trailhead.

Maps: For a brochure and trail map, send 75 cents to Bothe-Napa Valley State Park at the address below. To obtain a topographic map of the area, ask for Calistoga from the USGS.

Contact: Bothe-Napa Valley State Park, 3801 St. Helena Highway North, Calistoga, CA 94515; (707) 942-4575 or (707) 938-1519.

Trail notes: Who ever heard of redwoods in the Napa Valley? Who ever heard of a mountain peak there, too? Only those who also know of Bothe-Napa Valley State Park, which is like an island of wildlands in a sea of winery tourist traffic. Bothe-Napa has some of the most easterly stands of coastal redwoods, plus Douglas fir and an excellent lookout from Coyote Peak, all quite a surprise for newcomers. The best way to see it is on the Coyote Peak/Redwood Trail Loop, starting just past the Ritchey Creek Campground turnoff, near the picnic area. The first half-mile is on the Ritchey Trail, a very pretty stretch of trail along beautiful Ritchey Creek. Then veer left on the Redwood Trail, where you'll be surrounded by some of the park's highest stands of redwoods. The trail continues along Ritchey Creek for a quarter of a mile, then connects to the Coyote Peak Trail. Take the Coyote Peak Trail, which rises quickly, skirting the northern flank of Coyote Peak. (A short spur trail will take you all the way to the top, elevation 1,170 feet.) Then the trail drops down the other side of the hill and intersects with the South Fork Trail, which heads all the way back down to Ritchey Creek. Note that temperatures can be extremely hot in the summer— as high as 105 degrees in unshaded areas—but you'll find a cool paradise along Ritchey Creek.

⑤ Bald Mountain Loop

8.2 mi/1.0 day

Location: In Sugarloaf Ridge State Park north of Sonoma; map D1, grid g4.

User groups: Hikers, horses, and mountain bikes, though check for special trail restrictions on mountain bikes. No dogs. No wheelchair facilities.

Permits: No permits are required. A $5 state park day-use fee is charged for each vehicle.

Directions: From U.S.101 at Santa Rosa, turn east on Fourth Street/Highway 12 and drive through Kenwood to Adobe Canyon Road. Turn left and drive to the main entrance.

Maps: For a trail map and brochure, send 75 cents to Sugarloaf Ridge State Park at the address below. To obtain a topographic map of the area, ask for Kenwood from the USGS.

Contact: Sugarloaf Ridge State Park, 2605 Adobe Canyon Road, Kenwood, CA 95452; (707) 833-5712 or (707) 938-1519.

Trail notes: Bald Mountain, elevation 2,729 feet, overlooks the Napa Valley, with Mount St. Helena set to the north. On clear days from the summit, you can see portions of the San Francisco Bay Area, and then be thankful you're here instead of there. The old mountain is the cen-

terpiece of Sugarloaf Ridge State Park, a 2,700-acre park featuring redwoods in Sonoma Creek watershed, open meadows peppered with oaks on the hilltops, and some chaparral on ridges. The most ambitious hike in the park is the Bald Mountain Loop, an 8.2-mile trek that starts at the parking lot, then is routed in a loop by taking the Bald Mountain, Gray Meadow, Brushy Peaks, and Meadow Trails. Many less demanding hikes are available in the park, but this route will give you the greatest sense of the park's wildest lands. It's best hiked in the spring, when the air is still cool, the hills are green, and the wildflowers are in bloom. There's an extra bonus as well: when Sonoma Creek is flowing well, a beautiful 25-foot waterfall set in a wooded canyon tumbles downstream from the campground; a short trail is available from the park's entrance road.

⑥ Lake Trail

1.5 mi/0.75 hr

Location: In Jack London State Historic Park north of Sonoma; map D1, grid h3.

User groups: Hikers only. No dogs. Horses and mountain bikes are allowed on selected trails only. No wheelchair facilities.

Permits: No permits are required. A $5 state park day-use fee is charged for each vehicle.

Directions: From U.S. 101 at Santa Rosa, turn east on Highway 12 and drive to Kenwood. Turn right on Warm Springs Road and proceed to Arnold Drive. Turn right and drive a short distance, then turn right on London Ranch Road and go to the park entrance.

Maps: For a trail map and brochure, send $1 to Jack London State Historic Park at the address below. To obtain a topographic map of the area, ask for Glen Ellen from the USGS.

Contact: Jack London State Historic Park, 2400 London Ranch Road, Glen Ellen, CA 95442; (707) 938-5216 or (707) 938-1519.

Trail notes: You'll likely feel the shadow of the ghost of Jack London as you walk in his steps on the Lake Trail. It was here that London created his dreams as one of America's true great writers and philosophers. It was also here that those dreams were shattered, first from a fire that devoured his ranch home, then from an illness at age 40 from which he couldn't recover. Most visitors start the trip by touring London's cottage, winery ruins, barns, and distillery. Yearning for more, the Lake Trail easily provides it. The short walk leads to a small pond, which served as a favorite recreation area for London and his guests. The trail circles it, then returns back to the parking area.

However, this short trip alone doesn't do justice to the passion London had for the Sonoma Mountains. From the lake, you can extend your trip on the Mountain Trail, a steep, four-mile, 1,800-foot climb to the Sonoma Mountain summit at 2,363 feet. Note that the actual summit is outside park boundaries, and that you'll come to a gate on the fire road/trail when you cross into private property. Always check with park rangers for access status prior to making the summit climb.

❼ Soulejule Lake Trail

1.5 mi/0.75 hr

Location: In Sonoma County southwest of Petaluma; map D1, grid j0.

User groups: Hikers and dogs. Horses and mountain bikes, while allowed, aren't advised. No wheelchair facilities.

Permits: No permits are required. Parking and access are free.

Directions: From U.S. 101 at Novato, take the San Marin exit and drive west to Novato Boulevard. Turn right and proceed nine miles. Turn right again on Petaluma-Point Reyes Road and drive a quarter of a mile, then turn left on Wilson Hill Road. Drive three miles northwest, then turn left on Marshall-Petaluma Road, and go about five miles to the signed turnoff on the left. Park at the base of the dam.

Maps: To obtain a topographic map of the area, ask for Hicks Mountain from the USGS.

Contact: Marin Water District, 220 Mellen Avenue, Corte Madera, CA 94925; (415) 924-4600 or fax (415) 927-4953.

Trail notes: How do you pronounce Soulejule? Probably not the right way, but when you make this easy hike to this secluded lake, then start

catching the bass here, you won't care much. Soulejule is a little-known, hike-in lake in northern Marin. You can drive to the base of the dam, then make the short hike to the lake's edge. As you walk around the lake, stop now and then and make a cast, using either a white Crappie Killer or a one-inch floating Rapala. It's a great way to spend a spring evening, walking a little, fishing a little, maybe catching a little, with small bass and crappie cooperating during the winter-to-summer transition. By the way, how do you pronounce Soulejule? Like this: Soo-La-Hoo-Lee. Just like it looks.

Leave No Trace Tips

Properly Dispose of What You Can't Pack Out

If no refuse facility is available, deposit human waste in catholes dug six to eight inches deep at least 200 feet from water, camps, or trails. Cover and disguise the catholes when you're finished.

To wash yourself or your dishes, carry the water 200 feet from streams or lakes and use small amounts of biodegradable soap. Scatter the strained dishwater.

Map D2

Adjoining Maps: East: D3 .... *page* 166   West: D1 156
North: C2 124   South: E2 320

Northern California Map .... *page* 2

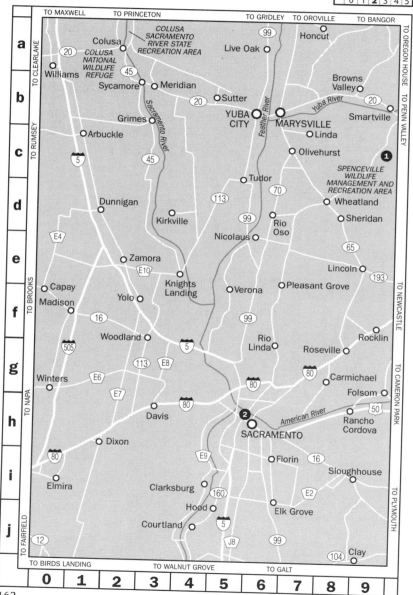

❶ Dry Creek Falls

5.0 mi/2.5 hrs

Location: In Spenceville Wildlife Area near Smartville; map D2, grid c9.

User groups: Hikers, dogs, horses, and mountain bikes. No wheelchair facilities.

Permits: No permits are necessary. Parking and access are free.

Directions: From Marysville, drive east on either Highway 20 or Hammonton-Smartville Road for about 15 miles to Smartville, then turn right (south) on Smartville Road. Drive 4.5 miles to Waldo Road and bear left onto the gravel road. Follow Waldo Road for 2.1 miles to Spenceville Road, then turn left and drive two miles to the end of the road at a blocked-off bridge. Park by the bridge and hike across.

Maps: Free maps of Spenceville Wildlife Area are available at information signposts in the refuge. To obtain a topographic map of the area, ask for Camp Far West from the USGS.

Contact: Spenceville Wildlife Area, c/o Oroville Wildlife Area, Department of Fish and Game, (916) 538-2236.

Trail notes: From the first autumn rain till midsummer, Dry Creek is anything but dry. Although it's located in Spenceville Wildlife Area, in the middle of arid oak-and-grassland country in the Central Valley, the stream supports a surprising variety of creekside vegetation, including various oaks, willows, and alders. Even more surprising, the stream produces a couple of sizable waterfalls, which are easily reached by a five-mile round-trip hike. Don't be put off by the worn-out bridge at the trailhead; just cross it carefully and start hiking to your right on the fire road on the other side. Dry Creek will be on your right, gurgling over rounded rocks. After walking nearly a mile, you'll bear right and hike south on another dirt road. At 2.5 miles from the trailhead, you'll come to the road's end at the larger of the two waterfalls. This one drops 60

feet into an immense pool, and its steep cliffs are walled off by a chain-link fence. If you follow use trails downstream along the creek, you'll find a smaller waterfall about 100 yards downstream. Both make fine spots for a springtime visit. Best time to hike the trail? December through April, preferably soon after a rain.

❷ American River Parkway/Jedediah Smith Trail

23.0 mi. one way/1.0 day

Location: Along the American River from Sacramento to Folsom; map D2, grid h6.

User groups: Hikers, dogs, horses, and mountain bikes. Note the restrictions for mountain bikes and hikers in the trail notes below. Wheelchairs are not allowed on the actual trail, but wheelchair-accessible rest rooms, fishing areas, and picnic grounds are available along the way.

Permits: No permits are required. Each county park charges a $4 fee per vehicle.

Directions: The trail begins at Discovery Park in Sacramento on the north side of the American River. From Interstate 5, take the Richards Boulevard exit and drive west to Jiboom Street. Turn north and follow the road into the park. Note: The trail's prettiest access point is Goethe Park in Rancho Cordova. To get to Goethe Park, on the south side of the Sacramento River, drive east on U.S. 50 and take the Bradshaw North exit. Follow Bradshaw Road to Folsom and turn east. Continue to Rod Braudy Drive and turn north. Follow the road into the park.

Maps: For a free trail map, contact the County Parks Department at the address below. To obtain topographic maps of the area, ask for Sacramento East, Carmichael, Citrus Heights, and Folsom from the USGS.

Contact: County of Sacramento, Parks and Recreation Division, Park Ranger Section 4040, Bradshaw Road, Sacramento, CA 95827; (916) 875-6961 or fax (916) 875-6632.

Trail notes: The idea for the American River Parkway sounded good in concept, and it works even better in practice. The plan was to create a route along the American River, linking Sacramento all the way upstream past Rancho Cordova and Fair Oaks. The result was this multiple-use trail that runs 23 miles from Discovery Park in Sacramento up to Folsom. There are actually two separate, parallel trails, one paved for bicyclists only and a dirt trail for horses. Walkers and joggers should stay off the paved portion and instead use the shoulder of either trail. Virtually no one hikes the entire length, of course; most people simply enjoy short sections, usually on evening walks, jogs, or rides.

Spring and fall are when the American River is prettiest. In spring, the trees and grass are green, the water is rolling fresh, and by May, schools of shad are swimming upstream. Come autumn, the leaves of the adjacent trees turn bright colors, lighting up the river. In the intervening summer months, 100-degree temperatures keep trail use low during the day, but when evening shade emerges, so do joggers and walkers.

Leave No Trace Tips

Keep the Wilderness Wild

Treat our natural heritage with respect. Leave plants, rocks, and historical artifacts as you found them.

Good campsites are found, not made. Do not alter a campsite.

Let nature's sounds prevail; keep loud voices and noises to a minimum.

Do not build structures or furniture or dig trenches.

Map D3

Adjoining Maps: East: D4 .... *page* 180   West: D2 162
North: C3 130   South: E3 324

Northern California Map .... *page* 2

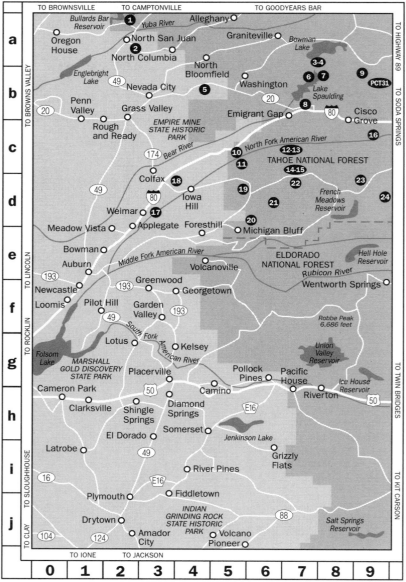

TO BROWNSVILLE   TO CAMPTONVILLE   TO GOODYEARS BAR

a

Bullards Bar
Reservoir
1 Yuba River   Alleghany○
Oregon
House   ○North San Juan   Graniteville○   Bowman
Lake
2
North Columbia   ○   North
Bloomfield   **3-4**
○

TO BROWNS VALLEY

b

Englebright
Lake   49   ○Nevada City   Washington   **6 7**   Lake
Spaulding   **9**
5   20   PCT31
Penn
Valley   Grass Valley   **8**
○   Rough   EMPIRE MINE   Emigrant Gap○   80   Cisco
Grove
and Ready   STATE HISTORIC   ○
20   PARK

TO SODA SPRINGS

c

174   Bear River   North Fork American River   **16**
Colfax   **10**   **12-13**
18   **11**   TAHOE NATIONAL FOREST
14-15

d

49   80   **19**   **22**   **23**
○Iowa
Hill   French
Meadows
Reservoir   **24**
Weimar○ **17**   **21**
Meadow Vista○   ○Applegate   Foresthill   **20**
○Michigan Bluff

e

Bowman○   Middle Fork American River   ELDORADO   Hell Hole
Reservoir
Auburn○   Volcanoville   NATIONAL FOREST
193   ○   Rubicon River
Newcastle○   Greenwood   Wentworth Springs○
Loomis○   193   ○Georgetown

TO LINCOLN

f

Pilot Hill   Garden
49   Valley   193
○   Robbe Peak
6,686 feet

TO ROCKLIN

g

Lotus○   South Fork   Union
Valley
Reservoir
○Kelsey   American River
Folsom
Lake   MARSHALL
GOLD DISCOVERY
STATE PARK   Placerville○   Pollock
Pines○   Pacific
House   Ice House
Reservoir

h

Cameron Park○   50   Camino   Riverton○   50
Clarksville○   Shingle   Diamond
Springs   Springs   E16
Somerset○
El Dorado○   Jenkinson Lake

i

Latrobe○   49   Grizzly
Flats
16   ○River Pines

TO SLOUGHHOUSE

j

E16
Plymouth○   ○Fiddletown
Drytown○   INDIAN
GRINDING ROCK   88   Salt Springs
Reservoir
104   124   STATE HISTORIC
○Amador   PARK
City   ○Volcano
Pioneer○

TO CLAY

TO IONE   TO JACKSON

0   1   2   3   4   5   6   7   8   9

TO HIGHWAY 89

TO TWIN BRIDGES

TO KIT CARSON

❶ Bullards Bar Trail

1–7 mi/1.0 day

Location: On Bullards Bar Reservoir in Tahoe National Forest; map D3, grid a1.

User groups: Hikers, dogs, horses, and mountain bikes. No wheelchair facilities.

Permits: No permits are required. Parking and access are free.

Directions: From Nevada City, drive north on Highway 49 to Marysville Road (south of Camptonville). Turn left and follow the signs to the Dark Day Picnic Area/Boat Ramp turnoff. Turn right and drive half a mile. Take the left fork to the picnic area and the trailhead.

Maps: For a map of Tahoe National Forest, send $4 to USDA-Forest Service, 630 Sansome Street, San Francisco, CA 94111. To obtain topographic maps of the area, ask for Camptonville and Challenge from the USGS.

Contact: Tahoe National Forest, Downieville Ranger District, 15924 Highway 49, Camptonville, CA 95922; (916) 288-3231 or fax (916) 288-0727.

Trail notes: Don't be spooked by the seven-mile length of this trail (12 if you include the two loops). Most folks just saunter along for a few miles, maybe take a dunk in the water or cast out a fishing line and sit a spell, then turn back.

From the trailhead at the Dark Day Picnic Area, the trail leads west and east along the shore of Bullards Bar Reservoir to Vista Point, overlooking the dam. The path is nearly flat, ranging between 2,243 and 2,250 feet in elevation. Along the way there are many good fishing and swimming spots and a sprinkling of huge ponderosa pines and Douglas firs. A heck of a lot of folks go for walks on this trail, one of the most heavily used in the county.

❷ South Yuba Independence Trail

4.0 mi/2.0 hrs

Location: Near Nevada City; map D3, grid a2.

User groups: Hikers, dogs, and wheelchairs. No horses or mountain bikes.

Permits: No permits are necessary. Parking and access are free.

Directions: From Interstate 80 at Auburn, drive north on Highway 49 for 27 miles to Nevada City. Continue on Highway 49 for eight miles past Nevada City to the trailhead parking area along the highway (just before the South Yuba River bridge). Park at the large paved pullout—it's well signed but comes up fast.

Maps: Trail maps/brochures are available at the trailhead or from the Bridgeport Ranger Station.

To obtain a topographic map of the area, ask for Nevada City from the USGS.

Contact: South Yuba River Project, Bridgeport Ranger Station; (916) 432-2546 or Sequoya Challenge, P.O. Box 3166, Grass Valley, CA 95945; (916) 272-3823.

Trail notes: The South Yuba Independence Trail is the first identified wheelchair wilderness trail in the United States, and it solves the biggest complaint that wheelchair users have about wheelchair-accessible trails: It's not paved. Without pavement, the outdoors really feels natural, like it should, which gives wheelchair users a higher-quality experience. The trail is a stroke of genius, built on a combination of hard-packed dirt and refurbished wooden flumes. It travels for six miles through beautiful forested terrain along the Yuba River Canyon, and it's equally loved (and used) by wheelchair hikers and two-legged hikers. The path was originally a canal route, built in 1859 to carry water from the Yuba to a hydraulic mining site in Smartville. The canal followed a nearly level contour along the steep hillsides above the river, and wooden flumes allowed the canal passage over creeks. Since 1970, the old canal trail has been undergoing a transformation, as more and more sections are being rehabilitated for all-access hiking. In many places, two trails run side by side, one for wheelchairs and one for hiking legs. Wheelchair-accessible outhouses, and picnicking and fishing platforms, have also been put in place.

From the trailhead, you have a choice of hiking east or west. First-timers should hike to the west (go right) to visit Rush Creek Falls and spectacular Flume 28, one mile from the trailhead. Flume 28 makes an impressive horseshoe-shaped turn around Rush Creek's canyon, with the waterfall dropping above and below the flume. From there, you can hike another mile to Jones Bar Road, then turn around and reverse your steps for a four-mile round-trip.

③ Lindsey Lakes Trail

7.0 mi/3.75 hrs

Location: In Tahoe National Forest north of Emigrant Gap; map D3, grid a7.

User groups: Hikers, dogs, and horses. Mountain bikes are not advised. No wheelchair facilities.

Permits: No permits are required. Parking and access are free.

Directions: From Auburn, drive east on Interstate 80 to four miles past Emigrant Gap. Take the Highway 20 exit and head west, driving about five miles to Bowman Lake Road (Forest Service Road 18). Turn right and drive north until you see a sign that says "Lindsey Lake, Feely Lake, Carr Lake." Turn right and follow the signs to the parking area for Lindsey Lake. The road can be extremely rough; four-wheel-drive vehicles are advised.

Maps: For a map of Tahoe National Forest, send $4 to USDA-Forest Service, 630 Sansome Street, San Francisco, CA 94111. To obtain topographic maps of the area, ask for English Mountain and Graniteville from the USGS.

Contact: Tahoe National Forest, Nevada City Ranger District, P.O. Box 6003, Nevada City, CA 95959; (916) 265-4531, (916) 478-6187, or fax (916) 478-6109.

Trail notes: The featured hike of the Grouse Lakes area—a classic Sierra basin in the 6,000-foot range—is the Lindsey Lakes Trail. This 3.5-mile trail dead-ends after climbing past the three Lindsey Lakes and offers a great optional side trip. From the trailhead at Lower Lindsey Lake, elevation 6,160 feet, you hike up to the other lakes on a short trail that's quite steep in several places, before topping out at 6,400 feet. The route gets medium use and accesses good swimming holes with cold water, though the fishing is poor. The best fishing in this basin is at nearby Culbertson Lake, where you can make a wonderful side trip by hiking out to Rock Lakes and up to Bullpen Lake. The latter is one of the few lakes anywhere that has been stocked with Arctic grayling. Another side trip from the Lindsey Lakes Trail is the Crooked Lakes Trail (hike number 4).

④ Crooked Lakes Trail

6.0 mi/3.5 hrs

Location: In Tahoe National Forest north of Emigrant Gap; map D3, grid a7.

User groups: Hikers, dogs, and horses. Mountain bikes are not recommended. No wheelchair facilities.

Permits: No permits are required. Parking and access are free.

Directions: From Auburn, drive east on Interstate 80 to four miles past Emigrant Gap. Take the Highway 20 exit and head west, driving about five miles to Bowman Lake Road (Forest Service Road 18). Turn right and drive north until you see a sign that says "Lindsey Lake, Feely Lake, Carr Lake." Turn right and follow the signs to the parking area. Take the Lindsey Lake Trail to the junction with the Crooked Lakes Trail. The road can be extremely rough; four-wheel-drive vehicles are advised.

Maps: For a map of Tahoe National Forest, send $4 to USDA-Forest Service, 630 Sansome Street, San Francisco, CA 94111. To obtain a topographic map of the area, ask for English Mountain from the USGS.

Contact: Tahoe National Forest, Nevada City Ranger District, P.O. Box 6003, Nevada City, CA 95959; (916) 265-4531, (916) 478-6187, or fax (916) 478-6109.

Trail notes: You start this hike by walking on the Lindsey Lakes Trail, then taking the turnoff for the Crooked Lakes Trail. In the course of 2.25 miles, the route climbs up to the most scenic lakes in the Grouse Lakes area. Your destination is Upper Rock Lake, a small pool in a high Sierra setting. From the trailhead you'll climb 700 feet before topping out at 6,880 feet. To extend the trip, head south from Upper Rock Lake, past Penner, Crooked, and Island Lakes.

❺ Pioneer Trail

24.0 mi/2.0 days

Location: East of Nevada City, off of Highway 20 in Tahoe National Forest; map D3, grid b4.

User groups: Hikers, dogs, and horses. No mountain bikes. No wheelchair facilities.

Permits: No permits are required. Parking and access are free.

Directions: From Nevada City, drive about seven miles east on Highway 20 to the trailhead, across from Lone Grave. If the parking lot there is full, additional parking and trail access are available at Skillman Flat, Upper Burlington

Ridge, and the Omega Rest Area, all located to the east of Highway 20.

Maps: For a map of Tahoe National Forest, send $4 to USDA-Forest Service, 630 Sansome Street, San Francisco, CA 94111. To obtain a topographic map of the area, ask for Washington from the USGS.

Contact: Tahoe National Forest, Nevada City Ranger District, P.O. Box 6003, Nevada City, CA 95959; (916) 265-4531, (916) 478-6187, or fax (916) 478-6109.

Trail notes: Hiking the Pioneer Trail is like taking a history lesson, as you trace the route of the first wagon road opened by emigrants and gold seekers in 1850. Along the way there are three campgrounds for backpackers, but the trail is better suited for mountain biking. From the trailhead at Lone Grave, elevation 3,500 feet, the trail heads east for 12 miles to Bear Valley, gaining 2,000 feet. You will pass Central House (once a stagecoach stop), White Cloud (where the largest mill on the West Coast once operated), Skillman Flat (site of a burned-down mill), and the Omega Overlook (site of a huge hydraulic gold mining operation). From the Omega Overlook, you will get dramatic views of the Yuba River and the surrounding granite cliffs. The amount of traffic on this trail is increasing, particularly with all the mountain bikers making the one-way trip downhill from Bear Valley to Lone Grave. If you encounter others, demonstrate the utmost courtesy: bikers should always dismount and walk when passing hikers.

❻ Round Lake Trail

4.5 mi/3.0 hrs

Location: At Carr Lake in Tahoe National Forest north of Emigrant Gap; map D3, grid b7.

User groups: Hikers, dogs, and horses. Mountain bikes are not recommended. No wheelchair facilities.

Permits: No permits are required. Parking and access are free.

Directions: From Auburn, drive east on Interstate 80 to four miles past Emigrant Gap. Take the Highway 20 exit and head west, driving about five miles to Bowman Lake Road (Forest Service Road 18). Turn right and drive north until you see a sign that says "Lindsey Lake, Feely Lake, Carr Lake." Turn right and follow the signs to the parking area at Carr Lake, then continue on foot to the trailhead at Feely Lake. The road can be extremely rough; four-wheel-drive vehicles are advised.

Maps: For a map of Tahoe National Forest, send $4 to USDA-Forest Service, 630 Sansome Street, San Francisco, CA 94111. To obtain topographic maps of the area, ask for English Mountain and Graniteville from the USGS.

Contact: Tahoe National Forest, Nevada City Ranger District, P.O. Box 6003, Nevada City, CA 95959; (916) 265-4531 or fax (916) 478-6187.

Trail notes: The Round Lake Trail accesses a series of Sierra lakes, including Island Lake, Long Lake, Round Lake, and Milk Lake. Because of this it's very popular, despite being demanding and, in places, steep. From the trailhead at Feely Lake, elevation 6,720 feet, the route heads east, climbing first to Island Lake. This lake, which is named for the little rocky islands sprinkled about, has several good campgrounds. Forging on, the trail passes Long Lake and then Round Lake before arriving at Milk Lake. The latter is a deep cobalt blue, as blue as Lake Tahoe, and has campsites near the east and west ends. If these sites are full, a short, steep hike just south of the lake will bring you to another camp on Grouse Ridge.

❼ Grouse Ridge Trail

6.0–16.2 mi/1–2 days

Location: In Tahoe National Forest north of Emigrant Gap; map D3, grid b8.

User groups: Hikers, dogs, horses, and mountain bikes. No wheelchair facilities.

Permits: No permits are required. Parking and access are free.

Directions: From Auburn, drive east on Interstate 80 to four miles past Emigrant Gap. Take the Highway 20 exit and head west, driving about five miles to Bowman Lake Road (Forest Service Road 18). Turn right and drive north to Granite-ville Road, then turn right again and continue for three miles. Turn right on Faucherie Lake Road and drive for a quarter mile to the Sawmill Lake Trailhead. The road can be extremely rough; four-wheel-drive vehicles are advised.

Maps: For a map of Tahoe National Forest, send $4 to USDA-Forest Service, 630 Sansome Street, San Francisco, CA 94111. To obtain topographic maps of the area, ask for Cisco Grove and English Mountain from the USGS.

Contact: Tahoe National Forest, Nevada City Ranger District, P.O. Box 6003, Nevada City, CA 95959; (916) 265-4531, (916) 478-6187, or fax (916) 478-6109.

Trail notes: A truly gorgeous hike, the Grouse Ridge Trail weaves up and down from a mountain crest, connecting Sawmill Lake to the north with the Eagle Lakes for a one-way distance of 8.25 miles. The beauty of this hike is that along the way there are a number of short side trips you can take to make quick hits at a half dozen lakes. In fact, many people use the Grouse Ridge Trail as a jump-off point to take short and spectacular day hikes. The elevation varies from 6,160 to 6,400 feet, with the ups and downs coming in short yet serious spurts. From Sawmill Lake, you climb up a timbered slope to a ridge and a turnoff for Rock Lake, itself worth a visit. You then pass Shotgun Lake (actually a wet meadow) and continue onward to Middle Lake, Crooked Lakes, and Milk Lake. The views are divine much of the way.

Special note: At Sawmill Lake, the trail crosses the spillway of the dam, which may be impassable in spring and early summer when high water spills into Canyon Creek.

❽ Sierra Discovery Trail

1.0 mi/0.5 hr

Location: Off Highway 20 near Lake Spaulding; map D3, grid b6.

User groups: Hikers, dogs, and wheelchairs. No horses or mountain bikes.

Permits: No permits are necessary. Parking and access are free.

Directions: From Auburn, drive east on Interstate 80 for 40 miles to the Highway 20 exit. Drive northwest on Highway 20 for 4.3 miles to Bowman Lake Road. Turn right and drive six-tenths of a mile to the Sierra Discovery Trail parking lot on the left side of the road.

Maps: To obtain a topographic map of the area, ask for Blue Canyon from the USGS.

Contact: PG&E Sierra Discovery Trail, P.O. Box 277444, Sacramento, CA 95827; (916) 386-5164.

Trail notes: The Pacific Gas and Electric Company has done a good deed in the form of the PG&E Sierra Discovery Trail at Bear Valley, where everyone, regardless of hiking ability, can take a pleasant loop trip along the Bear River. The trail surface is pavement and gravel with some boardwalk sections, all of which are suitable for wheelchairs and baby strollers. The one-mile loop packs in a lot of information about Bear Valley's ecosystems, wildlife, geology, and cultural history, as it winds through a forest of pines and incense cedars. Highlights along the trail include a boardwalk section over a lush meadow, green with corn lilies in the spring, and a small waterfall on the Bear River. If you get lucky, you may see a water ouzel flitting in and out of the falls' streaming water. The ouzel is the only American songbird that can swim below the surface of the water.

❾ Beyers Lakes Trail

12.5 mi/2.0 days

Location: In Tahoe National Forest northwest of Donner; map D3, grid b8.

User groups: Hikers, dogs, and horses. Mountain bikes are not advised. No wheelchair facilities.

Permits: No permits are required. Parking and access are free.

Directions: From Auburn, drive east on Interstate 80 to four miles past Emigrant Gap. Take the Highway 20 exit and head west, driving about five miles to Bowman Lake Road (Forest Service Road 18). Turn right and drive 19 miles, then turn right again on Meadow Lake Road and drive about six miles to the trailhead at Meadow Lake. The road can be extremely rough; four-wheel-drive vehicles are advised.

Maps: For a map of Tahoe National Forest, send $4 to USDA-Forest Service, 630 Sansome Street, San Francisco, CA 94111. To obtain topographic maps of the area, ask for Cisco Grove and English Mountain from the USGS.

Contact: Tahoe National Forest, Nevada City Ranger District, P.O. Box 6003, Nevada City, CA

95959; (916) 265-4531, (916) 478-6187, or fax (916) 478-6109.

Trail notes: Beautiful Baltimore Lake and the Beyers Lakes are the prime destinations of this trail, which offers excellent opportunities for camping, fishing, and swimming (that is, if you don't mind freezing your buns off) and is an excellent choice for a two-day backpacking trip. The trailhead is at Meadow Lake, elevation 5,500 feet, set below Hartley Butte (7,457 feet). From there the trail heads southwest on a rough, old four-wheel-drive route to Baltimore Lake, set in a timbered basin. The evening trout bite here is often good, and there are lakeside campsites. Continuing on from Baltimore Lake, the trail climbs over a mountain saddle at 7,140 feet, then descends into the Beyers Lakes Basin. The panorama before you is pristine, with four lakes nestled in granite and bordered by a sprinkling of fir trees.

❿ Euchre Bar Trail

6.0 mi/3.5 hrs

Location: On the North Fork American River near Baxter in Tahoe National Forest; map D3, grid c5.

User groups: Hikers, dogs, and horses. Mountain bikes are not advised. No wheelchair facilities.

Permits: No permits are required. Parking and access are free.

Directions: From Interstate 80 east of Auburn, take the Alta exit. Turn right on Morton, then left on Casa Loma. Follow Casa Loma until you see the sign for the Rawhide Mine, then turn right. Follow the road three-quarters of a mile past the second railroad crossing to a parking area. The trailhead is 0.1 miles beyond the parking area.

Maps: For a map of Tahoe National Forest, send $4 to USDA-Forest Service, 630 Sansome Street, San Francisco, CA 94111. To obtain topographic maps of the area, ask for Dutch Flat and Westville from the USGS.

Contact: Tahoe National Forest, Foresthill Ranger District, 22830 Foresthill Road, Foresthill, CA 95631; (916) 367-2224 or fax (916) 367-2992.

Trail notes: A river runs through almost every Sierra gulch and canyon, and so it is with this portion of the North Fork American River. From the trailhead, the route winds steeply down to the river and Euchre Bar, where a suspension footbridge crosses the water. The trail then leads upriver for 2.4 miles, along an excellent stretch of water for fishing, camping, panning for gold, and swimming (it is cold). If you want a lesson in pain, continue hiking another five miles. You'll climb the old Dorer Ranch Road, passing mining ruins and abandoned equipment from the Gold Rush era, gaining 2,000 feet in elevation through this dry, dusty country.

⑪ Italian Bar Trail

4.5 mi/3.5 hrs

Location: Near the North Fork American River in Tahoe National Forest; map D3, grid c5.

User groups: Hikers, dogs, and horses. Mountain bikes are not advised. No wheelchair facilities.

Permits: No permits are required. Parking and access are free.

Directions: From Interstate 80 at Auburn, turn east on Foresthill Road and drive 16 miles to the town of Foresthill. Drive another 13 miles northeast on Foresthill Road to Humbug Ridge Road (Forest Service Road 66), then turn left and drive three miles north to the trailhead.

Maps: For a map of Tahoe National Forest, send $4 to USDA-Forest Service, 630 Sansome Street, San Francisco, CA 94111. To obtain a topographic map of the area, ask for Westville from the USGS.

Contact: Tahoe National Forest, Foresthill Ranger District, 22830 Foresthill Road, Foresthill, CA 95631; (916) 367-2224 or fax (916) 367-2992.

Trail notes: Miners in the 1850s were like mountain goats, and they knew the most direct route between two points was a straight line. As a result, this route that miners once used to reach the North Fork American River is almost straight down going in and straight up coming out, gaining 3,000 feet in elevation over the course of 2.25 miles. It's about as fun as searching for a tiny gold nugget on the beach. As you head down from the trailhead, which is at 5,400

feet, you get little help from switchbacks. The trail ends at the river, and from there you must scramble and hop from rock to rock along the riverbanks. Eventually you end up at a secluded spot where all seems perfect—until you start the hike back. When you face the 3,000-foot climb out, you will wonder how you ever talked yourself into doing this hike.

⑫ Mumford Bar Trail

6.5 mi/1.0 day

Location: Near the North Fork American River in Tahoe National Forest; map D3, grid c6.

User groups: Hikers, dogs, and horses. Mountain bikes are not advised. No wheelchair facilities.

Permits: No permits are required. Parking and access are free.

Directions: From Interstate 80 at Auburn, turn east on Foresthill Road and drive 16 miles to the town of Foresthill. Drive another 15 miles northeast on Foresthill Road to the Mumford Trailhead on the left side of the road.

Maps: For a map of Tahoe National Forest, send $4 to USDA-Forest Service, 630 Sansome Street, San Francisco, CA 94111. To obtain topographic maps of the area, ask for Duncan Peak and Westville from the USGS.

Contact: Tahoe National Forest, Foresthill Ranger District, 22830 Foresthill Road, Foresthill, CA 95631; (916) 367-2224 or fax (916) 367-2992.

Trail notes: You'd have to be part mountain goat and part idiot to want to try this hike. Guess how we know? The trail leads almost straight down to the North Fork American River for more than 3.25 miles, and you know what that means. Right, it's almost straight up coming back.

From the trailhead at 5,360 feet, the first mile of trail follows an old four-wheel-drive route that deteriorates and then drops down to the river canyon at 2,640 feet. This stretch of river is designated as Wild and Scenic and is quite pretty, with good canyon views and fishing spots. We recommend that you extend your walk by taking the American River Trail (hike number 13) and staying overnight. Otherwise you will have to climb back out of the canyon on the same day, something even most mountain goats would not choose to do.

⑬ American River Trail

21.4 mi/2.0 days

Location: On the North Fork American River east of Foresthill in Tahoe National Forest; map D3, grid c6.

User groups: Hikers, dogs, and horses. Mountain bikes are not advised. No wheelchair facilities.

Permits: No permits are required. Parking and access are free.

Directions: From Interstate 80 at Auburn, turn east on Foresthill Road and drive 16 miles to the town of Foresthill. Drive another 15 miles northeast on Foresthill Road to the Mumford Trailhead on the left side of the road.

Maps: For a map of Tahoe National Forest, send $4 to USDA-Forest Service, 630 Sansome Street, San Francisco, CA 94111. To obtain a topographic map of the area, ask for Duncan Peak from the USGS.

Contact: Tahoe National Forest, Foresthill Ranger District, 22830 Foresthill Road, Foresthill, CA 95631; (916) 367-2224 or fax (916) 367-2992.

Trail notes: A 90-minute hike from the Mumford Trailhead (see hike number 12) gets you down into a steep canyon and alongside the beautiful and remote North Fork American River. There you turn right and start hiking upstream on the American River Trail. This is what you came for, the chance to walk along a pristine stretch of river on a steady, easy grade. You will pass old mining sites and abandoned cabins, alternating between dense vegetation and pretty river views. This trail makes for a great getaway, and hikers can enjoy exploring and trout fishing. Alas, nothing is perfect, and this hike does have some foibles: It crosses two creeks, Tadpole and New York, which are difficult, even dangerous to ford when running high during the snowmelt period in spring and early summer. A mile upriver of Tadpole Creek, and then again at New York Creek, the trail runs adjacent to private property—check your map and stay on the trail in these places. Plus, the hike back out of the canyon to your car is a terrible grunt, going from 2,640 feet along

the river up to 5,360 feet—a gain of 2,720 feet in just 3.25 miles.

Special note: The Mumford Trailhead is also accessible from the Sailor Flat Trail (see hike number 15).

⑭ Beacroft Trail

4.5 mi/1.0 day

Location: Near the North Fork American River in Tahoe National Forest; map D3, grid c7.

User groups: Hikers, dogs, and horses. Mountain bikes are not advised. No wheelchair facilities.

Permits: No permits are required. Parking and access are free.

Directions: From Interstate 80 at Auburn, turn east on Foresthill Road and drive 16 miles to the town of Foresthill. Drive another 19 miles northeast on Foresthill Road to the trailhead on the left side of the road, one mile past Secret House Campground.

Maps: For a map of Tahoe National Forest, send $4 to USDA-Forest Service, 630 Sansome Street, San Francisco, CA 94111. To obtain a topographic map of the area, ask for Duncan Peak from the USGS.

Contact: Tahoe National Forest, Foresthill Ranger District, 22830 Foresthill Road, Foresthill, CA 95631; (916) 367-2224 or fax (916) 367-2992.

Trail notes: The Beacroft Trail is the "no-option" option to hiking down to the North Fork American River. The trailhead is located four miles beyond the Mumford Trailhead, and after having reviewed the steep descent and climb required for that hike, you might want to look elsewhere for an easier route down. That's where the Beacroft Trail comes in. Still, it isn't a much better option, requiring an even more hellacious effort, as it drops 3,240 feet in only 2.25 miles. The trip back will have you howling. How can such a short trail be so steep? Ask the people who built the darn thing; those gold miners apparently had neither an abundance of useful gray matter between their ears nor much gold to carry on the return trip. When you reach the river, you can turn left on the American River Trail, which traces some of the most beautiful, accessible portions of this stream. Alas, even here you face an obstacle.

Within the first mile, you must cross New York Creek, a difficult (and sometimes dangerous) ford when full of snowmelt in early summer.

⑮ Sailor Flat Trail

6.5 mi/1.0 day

Location: Near the North Fork American River in Tahoe National Forest; map D3, grid c7.

User groups: Hikers, dogs, and horses. Mountain bikes are not advised. No wheelchair facilities.

Permits: No permits are required. Parking and access are free.

Directions: From Interstate 80 at Auburn, turn east on Foresthill Road and drive 16 miles to the town of Foresthill. Drive 25 more miles northeast on Foresthill Road to Sailor Flat Road. Turn left and drive one mile north to the trailhead.

Maps: For a map of Tahoe National Forest, send $4 to USDA-Forest Service, 630 Sansome Street, San Francisco, CA 94111. To obtain topographic maps of the area, ask for Royal Gorge and Duncan Peak from the USGS.

Contact: Tahoe National Forest, Foresthill Ranger District, 22830 Foresthill Road, Foresthill, CA 95631; (916) 367-2224 or fax (916) 367-2992.

Trail notes: Of the series of trailheads on Foresthill Road that provide access to the North Fork American River, this is the most distant, most remote, and, yes, most difficult. The Sailor Flat Trailhead lies at the end of the road, out in the middle of nowhere at an elevation of 6,400 feet, yet the remains of a long-abandoned gold stamp mill still stand nearby. The hike starts out easily enough, with the first 1.5 miles following an old mining road on which hikers will confront nothing serious. Don't be fooled though. The trail grows much steeper, with switchback after switchback leading down into the canyon. When you reach the river, at 3,360 feet, you will have dropped 3,040 feet in only 3.25 miles. You can explore further by turning left on the American River Trail (hike number 13), which traces the most beautiful sections of this river, heading downstream past meadows, canyon views, and good spots to fish and pan for gold.

Special note: With a shuttle vehicle and a partner, you can create an excellent one-way hike covering 15.6 miles. From the Sailor Flat Trailhead, hike down to the American River Trail, turn left, hike along the river to Mumford Bar, make a left turn and hike out to Foresthill Road (see hike numbers 12 and 13).

⑯ Loch Leven Lakes

7.0 mi/1.0 day

Location: South of Cisco Grove in Tahoe National Forest; map D3, grid c9.

User groups: Hikers, dogs, and horses. Mountain bikes are not advised. No wheelchair facilities.

Permits: No permits are required. Parking and access are free.

Directions: From Sacramento, follow Interstate 80 east and take the Big Bend exit, or follow Interstate 80 west and take the Rainbow Road exit. Follow the signs to the Big Bend Visitor Center, located adjacent to the highway. The parking area and trailhead are about a quarter mile east of the visitor center.

Maps: For a map of Tahoe National Forest, send $4 to USDA-Forest Service, 630 Sansome Street, San Francisco, CA 94111. To obtain a topographic map of the area, ask for Cisco Grove from the USGS.

Contact: Tahoe National Forest, Nevada City Ranger District, P.O. Box 6003, Nevada City, CA 95959; (916) 478-6187 or fax (916) 478-6109.

Trail notes: Most people would like to know what heaven is like, but they aren't very willing to sign up for the trip. The 3.5-mile hike to Loch Leven Lakes furnishes some answers, because, after all, heaven should look something like this. You get sweeping vistas of ridges and valleys, gorgeous high alpine meadows, and glaciated mountain terrain with a series of pristine lakes. Because the trailhead is so easily accessible from Interstate 80, this hike has become very popular.

The trail starts at 5,680 feet, then works its way upward on a moderate grade to the southwest. Granite outcrops are numerous, and huge boulders (deposited by receding glaciers) lie sprinkled among Jeffrey pine and lodgepole pine. The trail crosses a creek and railroad tracks, climbs through a cool forest, then tops the summit and winds down to Lower Loch Leven Lake. Many people stop here, content just taking in the surroundings. But you can forge on for another mile, circling Middle Loch Leven Lake, then heading east up to High Loch Leven Lake at 6,800 feet.

At Middle Loch Leven Lake, you'll find the recently rebuilt Cherry Point Trail. Adventurous hikers can take that trail to the Big Granite Trail, also rebuilt, and from there continue to the North Fork American River, for a distance of about six miles. Fishing is fair during the evening bite, and there are backcountry campgrounds at each lake.

⑰ Codfish Creek Trail

3.0 mi/1.5 hrs

Location: In Auburn State Recreation Area; map D3, grid d3.

User groups: Hikers, dogs, horses, and mountain bikes. No wheelchair facilities.

Permits: No permits are necessary. Parking and access are free.

Directions: From Sacramento, drive east on Interstate 80 for 40 miles to Weimar. Take the Weimar/Cross Road exit, then turn south on Ponderosa Way. In three miles, Ponderosa Way turns to dirt. In 2.5 additional miles, you reach a bridge over the American River (total 5.5 miles on Ponderosa Way). Don't cross the bridge, but park along the road near it. Begin hiking on the trail on the north side of the bridge, heading west (downstream).

Maps: For a map of Tahoe National Forest, which includes Auburn State Recreation Area lands, send $4 to USDA-Forest Service, 630 Sansome Street, San Francisco, CA 94111. To obtain a topographic map of the area, ask for Colfax from the USGS.

Contact: Auburn State Recreation Area, P.O. Box 3266, Auburn, CA 95604; (916) 885-4527.

Trail notes: The Codfish Creek Trail is a little-known but well-loved route along the North Fork American River which follows an old mining route downstream along its edge, then cuts up the canyon of Codfish Creek. Compared to most other hiking trails along the American River, this one is surprisingly well maintained,

and it's cared for by a great group of people called PARC, for Protect the American River Canyon. The trail begins at the north side of the bridge on Ponderosa Way, and heads downstream on sunny and exposed slopes. At 1.2 miles, the trail turns right and leads upstream along Codfish Creek, heading away from the river. This section of trail is shaded by big manzanitas and deciduous trees, a pleasant contrast to the grassy slopes along the river. The path brings you to a series of cascades on Codfish Creek, where Indian rhubarb grows in profusion along the water's edge. If you can, plan your trip for February, March, or April, when you get the double bonus of a full-flowing waterfall and lots of blooming wildflowers.

⑱ Stevens Trail

9.0 mi/5.0 hrs

Location: Near Colfax; map D3, grid d3.

User groups: Hikers, dogs, horses, and mountain bikes. No wheelchair facilities.

Permits: No permits are necessary. Parking and access are free.

Directions: From Sacramento, drive east on Interstate 80 for 45 miles to Colfax. Take the Colfax/Grass Valley exit, turn left at the stop sign, and drive east on the frontage road (North Canyon Way) for seven-tenths of a mile to the trailhead parking area.

Maps: To obtain a topographic map of the area, ask for Colfax from the USGS.

Contact: Bureau of Land Management, Folsom Resource Area, 63 Natoma Street, Folsom, CA 95630; (916) 985-4474.

Trail notes: The Stevens Trail is a surprisingly lush and peaceful trail that leaves noisy Interstate 80 in Colfax and drops down into the shady canyon of the North Fork of the American River. Along the way, it passes a huge variety of wildflowers and blooming buckeye trees in springtime, and tunnels through a mixed forest of oak, pine, fir, and dogwood. There are a few junctions to watch for, but the trail is well signed all the way. After a long stint in the forest, the trail opens out to lovely views of the American River canyon. To your left and above you, you can see the railroad line, which was built by Chinese laborers dangling from rope-strung baskets from the cliffs above. Since the path to the river is all downhill, you must remember to save some water and energy for the climb back up, which has a 1,200-foot elevation gain. Luckily, 1.5 miles from the trailhead is a seasonal waterfall on Stevens Creek. On your uphill return, you'll be grateful for its little upstream pools, where you can cool off your feet, and maybe some other body parts, too.

⑲ Green Valley Trail

4.5 mi/1.0 day

Location: On the North Fork American River near Sugar Pine Reservoir; map D3, grid d5.

User groups: Hikers, dogs, and horses. Mountain bikes are not advised. No wheelchair facilities.

Permits: No permits are required. Parking and access are free.

Directions: From Interstate 80 at Auburn, turn east on Foresthill Road and drive about 16 miles to the town of Foresthill. Head northeast on Foresthill Road for about seven miles, then turn left on Forest Service Road 10 and follow it for five miles until you cross the Sugar Pine Dam. Drive one mile past the dam, then turn north on Elliot Ranch Road and drive three miles to the trailhead.

Maps: For a map of Tahoe National Forest, send $4 to USDA-Forest Service, 630 Sansome Street, San Francisco, CA 94111. To obtain a topographic map of the area, ask for Dutch Flat from the USGS.

Contact: Tahoe National Forest, Foresthill Ranger District, 22830 Foresthill Road, Foresthill, CA 95631; (916) 367-2224 or fax (916) 367-2992.

Trail notes: It's amazing what people will go through to create a space that feels like their own. Hikers can do just that on the Green Valley Trail by finding an idyllic spot along the North Fork American River and soaking up the serenity. But the price is steep, and the return trip will put you through more punishment than is typically handed out at Folsom Prison.

The trip starts at a little-known trailhead near Sugar Pine Reservoir, at elevation 4,080 feet.

From there, the Green Valley Trail is steep and often rocky, dropping 2,240 feet in 2.25 miles before reaching the river. We do not advise extending your trip from here. It is possible to continue downriver a short way, or cross the river (good luck) and hike upstream into Green Valley. However, these sections of the trail are in very poor condition, and the upstream route crosses private property owned by people who don't take kindly to visitors.

⑳ Western States Trail/ Michigan Bluff

4.0 mi/2.5 hrs

Location: In Tahoe National Forest east of Foresthill; map D3, grid d5.

User groups: Hikers, dogs, horses, and mountain bikes. No wheelchair facilities.

Permits: No permits are required. Parking and access are free.

Directions: From Interstate 80 at Auburn, turn east on Foresthill Road and drive about 16 miles to the town of Foresthill. Continue northeast on Foresthill Road and follow the signs to Michigan Bluff. The trailhead is located about a quarter-mile east of Michigan Bluff.

Maps: For a map of Tahoe National Forest, send $4 to USDA-Forest Service, 630 Sansome Street, San Francisco, CA 94111. To obtain a topographic map of the area, ask for Michigan Bluff from the USGS.

Contact: Tahoe National Forest, Foresthill Ranger District, 22830 Foresthill Road, Foresthill, CA 95631; (916) 367-2224 or fax (916) 367-2992.

Trail notes: If only the Forest Service would ban motorcycles, or "dirt bikes" as they're called, from this trail, this hike would be just about perfect. While it is rare to run into dirt bikes here, they are legal and it's only a matter of time until word circulates among the bikers. The attraction is beautiful Eldorado Canyon, where you can fish for trout and camp along Eldorado Creek. From the trailhead at 3,520 feet, the trail quickly drops about two miles into the canyon, with switchbacks leading to a footbridge over Eldorado Creek. Extend the trip by crossing the bridge, then hiking up the other side of the canyon to scenic views of the rugged topography.

Special note: The Michigan Bluff Trail is a section of the Western States Trail, which spans from Squaw Valley to Auburn.

㉑ Grouse Falls

1.0 mi/0.5 hr

Location: In Tahoe National Forest near Foresthill; map D3, grid d6.

User groups: Hikers, dogs, horses, and mountain bikes. No wheelchair facilities.

Permits: No permits are necessary. Parking and access are free.

Directions: From Interstate 80 at Auburn, take the Foresthill/Auburn Ravine Road exit, then drive 16 miles east to Foresthill. In Foresthill, turn right (east) on Mosquito Ridge Road, across from the Foresthill post office. Drive 19 miles to Peavine Road (Road 33). Turn left on Peavine Road and drive 5.5 miles to the Grouse Falls turnoff on the left. Turn left and drive a half mile to the trailhead.

Maps: For a map of Tahoe National Forest, send $4 to USDA-Forest Service, 630 Sansome Street, San Francisco, CA 94111. To obtain a topographic map of the area, ask for Michigan Bluff from the USGS.

Contact: Tahoe National Forest, Foresthill Ranger District, 22830 Foresthill Road, Foresthill, CA 95631; (916) 367-2224.

Trail notes: Some waterfalls are simply mind-boggling in their beauty, and Grouse Falls is one of those. Sure, it's a long drive to get there, but it's a scenic route through a rugged, tree-filled canyon—the kind of place that makes you feel like you're really getting away from it all. When at last you reach the trailhead, the walk to the waterfall overlook is surprisingly short. It only takes about 15 minutes from the time you park your car, and the trail is slightly downhill all the way, through a dense and beautiful old-growth conifer forest.

You don't see or hear immense Grouse Falls until just before you come out to the overlook, and when you do, it's a shock to your system. Although the waterfall is about a half mile away across the canyon, it is huge, as in several hundred feet tall. When running full, it's a waterfall of Yosemite quality. The overlook is a wooden platform with benches, where you can sit and admire the beauty for as long as you please. In addition to viewing Grouse Falls, you're also looking out over a deep, wide, forested canyon, with absolutely no sign of human development. Hallelujah.

㉒ Forest View Trail

1.5 mi/0.75 hr

Location: In Tahoe National Forest east of Foresthill; map D3, grid d7.

User groups: Hikers and dogs. No horses or mountain bikes. No wheelchair facilities.

Permits: No permits are required. Parking and access are free.

Directions: From Interstate 80 at Auburn, turn east on Foresthill Road and drive about 16 miles to the town of Foresthill. Turn east on Mosquito Ridge Road and drive 23 miles to the trailhead.

Maps: Free interpretive brochures are available at the trailhead. For a map of Tahoe National Forest, send $4 to USDA-Forest Service, 630 Sansome Street, San Francisco, CA 94111. To obtain a topographic map of the area, ask for Greek Store from the USGS.

Contact: Tahoe National Forest, Foresthill Ranger District, 22830 Foresthill Road, Foresthill, CA 95631; (916) 367-2224 or fax (916) 367-2992.

Trail notes: Giant Sequoias, the world's largest trees, attract many visitors to this easy, well-maintained interpretive trail that leads through California's northernmost grove of Sequoia redwoods. It is set at 5,200 feet on Mosquito Ridge Road, which provides generous views of the wild and superb landscape. The trail meanders through virgin old-growth forest, home to half a dozen truly monster-sized trees. Along the half-mile Big Trees Interpretive Trail, there are 16 stops marked with numbers that coincide with numbered listings in a brochure available at the trailhead, allowing visitors to take an interesting and informative self-guided tour of the fascinating history of these massive trees. Linked with the Forest View Trail, the entire loop extends 1.5 miles. Despite the long drive to the trailhead on Mosquito Ridge, the trail gets quite a bit of use.

⑳ Western States Trail/ McGuire

7.8 mi/4.0 hrs

Location: At French Meadows Reservoir in Tahoe National Forest; map D3, grid d8.

User groups: Hikers, dogs, horses, and mountain bikes. No wheelchair facilities.

Permits: No permits are required. Parking and access are free.

Directions: From Interstate 80 at Auburn, turn east on Foresthill Road and drive about 16 miles to the town of Foresthill. Turn east on Mosquito Ridge Road and drive 36 miles to the French Meadows Reservoir Dam. Cross the dam and continue east, skirting the south side of the lake. At the northeast end of the lake, turn left and follow the signs to McGuire Boat Ramp.

Maps: For a map of Tahoe National Forest, send $4 to USDA-Forest Service, 630 Sansome Street, San Francisco, CA 94111. To obtain a topographic map of the area, ask for Bunker Hill from the USGS.

Contact: Tahoe National Forest, Foresthill Ranger District, 22830 Foresthill Road, Foresthill, CA 95631; (916) 367-2224 or fax (916) 367-2992.

Trail notes: The McGuire Trail has become a favorite side trip for families visiting or camping at French Meadows Reservoir (elevation 5,290 feet). The trail traces the north shore of the lake, poking in and out of timber, then follows an easy grade to the top of Red Star Ridge (5,600 feet), which offers good views of the reservoir below. French Meadows is a good-sized lake, covering nearly 2,000 acres when full, and is stocked each year with more than 30,000 trout, joining a healthy population of resident brown trout and holdovers from stocks of rainbow trout from previous years. Water drawdowns are a common problem in late summer, as this exposes many stumps and boulders, creating a navigational hazard for boaters.

㉔ Hell Hole Trail

13.0 mi. one way/2.0 days

Location: In the Granite Chief Wilderness, east of Hell Hole Reservoir in Tahoe National Forest; map D3, grid d9.

User groups: Hikers, dogs, and horses. No mountain bikes. No wheelchair facilities.

Permits: A campfire permit is required. Parking and access are free.

Directions: From Interstate 80 in Truckee, turn south on Highway 89 and drive to Tahoe City. Continue four miles south on Highway 89 to the Caspian Picnic Area. Turn west (right) on Blackwood Canyon Road and drive 2.3 miles, then cross the creek and continue for another 4.8 miles to Barker Pass.

Note: Blackwood Canyon Road is subject to closure. When closed, follow these alternate directions: From Interstate 80 in Truckee, turn south on Highway 89 and drive past Tahoe City. Turn west (right) on McKinney Creek Road (a high-clearance, four-wheel-drive vehicle is required) and drive about 15 miles to Barker Pass, where the pavement ends. Go another 2.3 miles to the Powderhorn Trailhead and then park. Walk four miles on the Powderhorn Trail to Diamond Crossing, where the trail intersects the Hell Hole Trail.

Maps: For a map of Tahoe National Forest, send $4 to USDA-Forest Service, 630 Sansome Street, San Francisco, CA 94111. To obtain a topographic map of the area, ask for Wentworth Springs from the USGS.

Contact: Tahoe National Forest, Truckee Ranger District, 10342 Highway 89 North, Truckee, CA 96161; (916) 587-3558 or fax (916) 587-6914.

Trail notes: Do you yearn for a challenging trek in a very remote high-mountain wilderness setting? This is it. Way out in booger country, the Hell Hole Trail requires hikers to have wilderness skills and, worst of all, be prepared for a difficult stream crossing and traversing a landslide. Sound fun? Who said anything about fun?

Start at the remote Powderhorn Trailhead, set at 6,400 feet on the boundary of the Granite Chief Wilderness. From there you hike four miles down to Diamond Crossing (fording Powderhorn Creek), where you will meet the Hell Hole Trail. Shortly after turning left, you will have to cross Five Lakes Creek, a difficult and sometimes dangerous endeavor, especially during snowmelt. If you make it, you will then descend to Little Buckskin Creeks (two more fords, both a lot easier than the first one) and into Steamboat

Canyon. Approximately one-half mile from Steamboat Canyon, hikers face a slippery landslide that demands extreme caution. The trail then drops toward the Rubicon River and Hell Hole Reservoir. Few hikers attempt this trail, and those that do must not be too concerned about living long, healthy lives.

Special note I: The stream crossings required on this hike can be life-threatening during periods of high snowmelt and runoff.

Special note II: For an excellent day hike or a weekend camping trip, start the trail at the Hell Hole Dam and walk three miles to a hike-in camp set at the head of the lake.

PCT-31 Donner Pass to the Yuba River

38.0 mi. one way/3.0 days

Location: From Highway 80 to Highway 49 in Tahoe National Forest; map D3, grid b9.

User groups: Hikers, dogs, and horses. No mountain bikes. No wheelchair facilities.

Permits: Wilderness permits are not required for this section of the Pacific Crest Trail, but campfire permits are. Parking and access are free.

Directions: From Auburn, drive east on Interstate 80 to Boreal/Donner Summit. Take the exit for the Pacific Crest Trailhead parking area. There is no parking in the Donner Summit rest area.

Maps: For a map of Tahoe National Forest, send $4 to USDA-Forest Service, 630 Sansome Street, San Francisco, CA 94111. To obtain topographic maps of the area, ask for Norden, Soda Springs, Webber, Haypress Valley, Independence Lake, and English Mountain from the USGS.

Contact: Tahoe National Forest, Truckee Ranger District, 10342 Highway 89, North Truckee, CA 96161; (916) 587-3558 or fax (916) 587-6914. Tahoe National Forest, Sierraville Ranger District, P.O. Box 95, Highway 89, Sierraville, CA 96126; (916) 994-3401 or fax (916) 994-3143.

Trail notes: Though not one of the more glamorous sections of the Pacific Crest Trail, this stretch is hardly a stinker. For the most part, it follows a crest connecting a series of small mountaintops before dropping down to Jackson Meadow Reservoir and Highway 49. Some good views are to be had on the first leg of the trail, so many that some PCT hikers begin to take them for granted after awhile. Here the trail is routed past Castle Peak (elevation 9,103 feet), Basin Peak (9,015 feet), and Lacey Mountain (8,214 feet). Covering this much terrain makes for an ambitious first day, perhaps with stops at Paradise Lake or White Rock Lake. As the trail drops to Jackson Meadow Reservoir, the views end, but in time you'll catch sight of the lake; surrounded by fir trees, it is quite pretty. The PCT then skirts the east side of the reservoir, passes several drive-to campgrounds, heads through Bear Valley (not *the* Bear Valley), and drops steeply to Milton Creek and four miles beyond that to Loves Falls at Highway 49.

PCT Continuation: To continue hiking along the Pacific Crest Trail, see chapter C3.

Map D4

Adjoining Maps: West: D3 ... *page* 166
North: C4 148   South: E4 326

Northern California Map .... *page* 2

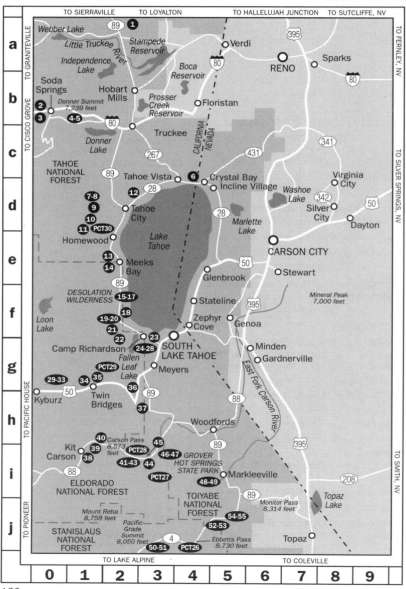

Chapter D4 features:

❶ Cottonwood Creek

0.75 mi/0.5 hr

Location: In Tahoe National Forest north of Truckee; map D4, grid a2.

User groups: Hikers and dogs. No horses or mountain bikes. No wheelchair facilities.

Permits: No permits are required. Parking and access are free.

Directions: From Truckee, drive north on Highway 89 for 18 miles to the campground entrance road on the right, a half mile past Cold Creek Camp. Turn right and drive a quarter mile to the campground and trailhead.

Maps: For a map of Tahoe National Forest, send $4 to USDA-Forest Service, 630 Sansome Street, San Francisco, CA 94111. To obtain a topographic map of the area, ask for Hobart Mills from the USGS.

Contact: Tahoe National Forest, Sierraville Ranger District, P.O. Box 95, Highway 89, Sierraville, CA 96126; (916) 994-3401 or fax (916) 994-3143.

Trail notes: This ain't nothin' but a little ol' interpretive trail, but we like it just the same. The Cottonwood Creek Botanical Trail is so good, it's too bad it only gets visited by campers at Cottonwood Creek Campground. Along its short length, you get to learn how to identify white fir, alders, manzanita, cottonwoods, incense cedars, quaking aspen, junipers . . . you get the idea. The best tip we learned on the trail? On warm days, smell the bark on the sunny side of a Jeffrey pine. Try it; you'll see why. The trail is a half-mile loop, but you can add on a quarter-mile spur trail to an overlook of the Sierra Valley. It's a great place to watch the sun set before crawling into your sleeping bag.

❷ Lower Lola Montez Lake

6.0 mi/3.0 hrs

Location: In Tahoe National Forest near Soda Springs; map D4, grid b0.

User groups: Hikers, dogs, horses, and mountain bikes. No wheelchair facilities.

Permits: No permits are required. Parking and access are free.

Directions: From Auburn, drive east on Interstate 80 for 55 miles to Soda Springs. Take the Soda Springs/Norden exit and cross over the overpass to the north side of the freeway. Follow the paved road east, past the fire station for three-tenths of a mile to the trailhead parking area.

Maps: For a map of Tahoe National Forest, send $4 to USDA-Forest Service, 630 Sansome Street, San Francisco, CA 94111. To obtain topographic maps of the area, ask for Soda Springs and Norden from the USGS.

Contact: Tahoe National Forest, Truckee Ranger District, 10342 Highway 89 North, Truckee, CA 96161; (916) 587-3558 or fax (916) 587-6914.

Trail notes: Partly because it's so easy, partly because it's right off the highway, and partly because the trail is favored by mountain bikers, the hike to Lower Lola Montez Lake is a bad choice for a July or August weekend afternoon. For hikers who enjoy peace and quiet, this is definitely an off-season trail, best left for the days of autumn when the vacationers have abandoned Lake Tahoe. The path cuts through Toll Mountain Estates, a private community, and is a mix of wide dirt roads and single-track trails. The first quarter mile is on single-track, then you reach a dirt road and turn right, cross Castle Creek and continue until the road becomes single-track again. And so it goes. Luckily, the route is marked all the way, and with all the people who visit here, it's unlikely you'll get lost and not be able to get found. The good news is that the Lower Lola Montez Lake is not popular without reason; it's a beautiful alpine lake set at 7,200 feet that is shallow enough to warm up for swimming. Fishing is half-decent, but best early in the year.

❸ Palisade Creek Trail to Heath Falls

10.0 mi/6.0 hrs

Location: In Tahoe National Forest near Soda Springs; map D4, grid b0.

User groups: Hikers, dogs, and horses. No mountain bikes. No wheelchair facilities.

Permits: No permits are required. Parking and access are free.

Directions: From Auburn, drive east on Inter-

User groups: Hikers, dogs, horses, and mountain bikes. No wheelchair facilities.

Permits: No permits are required. Parking and access are free.

Directions: From Tahoe City, drive north on Highway 89 for five miles and turn west on Squaw Valley Road. Drive 2.2 miles to the Squaw Valley Fire Station, where the trail begins on its east side. You must leave your car in the large parking lot by the ski lift buildings, not by the fire station. Walk back across the bridge to the trailhead.

Maps: For a map of Tahoe National Forest, send $4 to USDA-Forest Service, 630 Sansome Street, San Francisco, CA 94111. To obtain topographic maps of the area, ask for Tahoe City and Granite Chief from the USGS.

Contact: Tahoe National Forest, Truckee Ranger District, 10342 Highway 89 North, Truckee, CA 96161; (916) 587-3558 or fax (916) 587-6914.

Trail notes: Tinker Knob is not an easy summit to attain, but those who reach it always remember it. From the Squaw Valley fire station, it's a demanding 3.5-mile hike to the intersection of the Granite Chief Trail and the Pacific Crest Trail. The total gain is 2,000 feet; most of the climb is forested but there are occasional openings with views of Lake Tahoe and surrounding peaks. When at last you gain the PCT at 8,200 feet in elevation, turn right (north) toward Tinker Knob. Now it's another 3.5 miles, most of it on an easier, winding grade along the top of a ridge, passing an intersection with the Painted Rock Trail on the left. The last section of trail is a series of switchbacks up to the Tinker Knob Saddle, then a brief quarter-mile climb to the summit of Tinker Knob at 8,950 feet. You like views? How about this one—a head-swiveling vista of Anderson Peak, Painted Rock, Silver Peak, the American River Canyon, Donner Lake, and Lake Tahoe. To cut some mileage off your trip, you can hike this trail as a shuttle trip, leaving one car at the Coldstream Trailhead near Donner Memorial State Park. (It's at the horseshoe bend in the railroad tracks at the end of Coldstream Creek access road.) The Coldstream Trail meets the PCT just below the summit of Tinker Knob, so after gaining the summit via the route described above, you can follow Cold-stream Trail four miles down to its trailhead. This makes an 11-mile one-way hike with a shuttle.

---

⑧ Granite Chief Trail to Emigrant Pass

12.0 mi/7.0 hrs

Location: In Tahoe National Forest near Squaw Valley; map D4, grid d1.

User groups: Hikers, dogs, horses, and mountain bikes. No wheelchair facilities.

Permits: No permits are required. Parking and access are free.

Directions: From Tahoe City, drive north on Highway 89 for five miles and turn west on Squaw Valley Road. Drive 2.2 miles to the Squaw Valley Fire Station, where the trail begins on its east side. You must leave your car in the large parking lot by the ski lift buildings, not by the fire station. Walk back across the bridge to the trailhead.

Maps: For a map of Tahoe National Forest, send $4 to USDA-Forest Service, 630 Sansome Street, San Francisco, CA 94111. To obtain topographic maps of the area, ask for Tahoe City and Granite Chief from the USGS.

Contact: Tahoe National Forest, Truckee Ranger District, 10342 Highway 89 North, Truckee, CA 96161; (916) 587-3558 or fax (916) 587-6914.

Trail notes: The Granite Chief Trail begins at the Squaw Valley fire station at 6,200 feet and climbs, climbs, and climbs some more till it reaches the Pacific Crest Trail, 3.5 miles later. This is why many hikers choose to ride the tram at Squaw Valley to reach the PCT, then start hiking around from there. But not you; you like a challenge. Okay, here it is.

Climb 2,000 feet over those 3.5 miles, roughly paralleling Squaw Creek and mostly in the woods, then when you reach the PCT, turn left (south) toward Twin Peaks. What's that big blue spot down there? It's Lake Tahoe for sure. Hike for one mile on the PCT, still climbing, to the eastern flank of Granite Chief Peak, elevation 9,086. Finally you begin to descend, and in one more mile, reach an intersection with the Western States Trail. Turn left and take a half-mile walk to visit the Watson Monument, a stone marker at Emigrant Pass. You probably won't stay long; although the views are lovely, the wind howls.

❾ Five Lakes

4.2 mi/2.0 hrs

Location: In the Granite Chief Wilderness near Alpine Meadows; map D4, grid d1.

User groups: Hikers, dogs, and horses. No mountain bikes. No wheelchair facilities.

Permits: No permits are required for day hiking. Parking and access are free.

Directions: From Tahoe City, drive north on Highway 89 for 3.5 miles to Alpine Meadows Road. Turn west on Alpine Meadows Road and drive two miles to the trailhead on the right. Park alongside the road.

Maps: For a map of Tahoe National Forest, send $4 to USDA-Forest Service, 630 Sansome Street, San Francisco, CA 94111. To obtain topographic maps of the area, ask for Tahoe City and Granite Chief from the USGS.

Contact: Tahoe National Forest, Truckee Ranger District, 10342 Highway 89 North, Truckee, CA 96161; (916) 587-3558 or fax (916) 587-6914.

Trail notes: There are those who say that this trek into the Granite Chief Wilderness is too easy, and they may be right. Although the trail has a steep grade, it's mercifully short, which makes it incredibly popular with hikers, especially on weekends. Make your trip in the off-season or during the week, and definitely make this a day trip instead of an overnight, to minimize impact at the five granite-bound lakes. Do you promise? Okay. With that said, prepare for a gorgeous trip, with spectacular alpine scenery all the way.

The first half mile is the steepest grade, and the next three-quarters of a mile continue the ascent to the top of a ridge. There are switchbacks galore, and almost no shade along the manzanita-lined trail as you climb 1,000 feet. At 1.8 miles, you reach the Granite Chief Wilderness boundary and enter a land of red fir, white fir, and rocks. A signed junction a quarter mile further points you toward the lakes, with your trail heading directly downhill to the largest of them. From there, you can follow numerous side trails to the four other lakes, all east of the big one. Remember: Minimize your impact. The Five Lakes are set at 7,400 feet.

❿ Ward Creek

6.0 mi/3.0 hrs

Location: In Tahoe National Forest near Tahoe City; map D4, grid d1.

User groups: Hikers, dogs, horses, and mountain bikes. No wheelchair facilities.

Permits: No permits are required. Parking and access are free.

Directions: From Tahoe City, drive two miles south on Highway 89 to Pineland Drive, just north of Kilner Park. Turn right on Pineland Drive for a half mile to Twin Peaks Drive. Turn left and drive 1.7 miles. (Twin Peaks Drive becomes Ward Creek Boulevard.) At 1.7 miles, park in the pull-out on the left side of the highway, and begin hiking at the gated dirt road, Forest Service Road 15N62. If the gate is open, you can drive inside and park along the dirt road.

Maps: For a map of Lake Tahoe Basin Management Unit, send $4 to USDA-Forest Service, 630 Sansome Street, San Francisco, CA 94111. To obtain a topographic map of the area, ask for Tahoe City from the USGS.

Contact: Lake Tahoe Basin Management Unit, 870 Emerald Bay Road, South Lake Tahoe, CA 96150; (916) 573-2600 or fax (916) 573-2693.

Trail notes: Compared to some of the more famous hikes at Lake Tahoe, the Ward Creek Trail is rather tame: No stellar waterfall, no drop-dead gorgeous lake views, no towering granite monoliths. But then again, there are no crowds either. For many, the trade-off is a good one. The route passes through fields of mule's ears and forests of sugar pines, with enough open sections to provide wide-open views of the surrounding mountain ridges.

The trail begins as an old dirt road, paralleling Ward Creek for 1.5 miles to a washed-out bridge and a "Road Closed" sign. You cross the creek on logs and continue hiking, now on single-track. The trail climbs a little higher above Ward Creek, then enters a dense, lovely pine forest. You can go as far as you like (the trail continues to Twin Peaks, 5.3 miles from the trailhead), but for the mileage suggested above, turn around when you are about a half mile into the trees, then take an easy stroll home.

⑪ Ellis Peak

5.0 mi/2.5 hrs

Location: In Tahoe National Forest near Tahoe City; map D4, grid d1.

User groups: Hikers, dogs, horses, and mountain bikes. No wheelchair facilities.

Permits: No permits are required. Parking and access are free.

Directions: From Tahoe City, drive four miles south on Highway 89 to Forest Service Road 03 (Barker Pass Road). Turn right (west) and drive seven miles to the summit of Barker Pass, where the pavement ends. The trailhead is on the left (south) side of the road.

Maps: For a map of Lake Tahoe Basin Management Unit, send $4 to USDA-Forest Service, 630 Sansome Street, San Francisco, CA 94111. To obtain a topographic map of the area, ask for Homewood from the USGS.

Contact: Lake Tahoe Basin Management Unit, 870 Emerald Bay Road, South Lake Tahoe, CA 96150; (916) 573-2600 or fax (916) 573-2693.

Trail notes: This short but steep trek leads to the top of Ellis Peak and fabulous views of Lake Tahoe, Granite Chief and Desolation Wildernesses, and Hell Hole Reservoir. There is a 900-foot elevation gain from the trailhead to the peak at 8,740 feet, but the route is beautiful all the way, with close-up wildflowers rivaling the far-off views. Plenty of switchbacks and abundant shade make the initial climb easy, then the route follows a ridgeline for 1.5 miles with wide-open vistas. Hey, is that Lake Tahoe down there? Yessiree Bob.

When you meet up with a wide dirt road, bear left to begin the trek to Ellis Peak. In a quarter mile, you'll see a short left spur to tiny Ellis Lake, a worthy side trip. Continue 100 yards further past the spur trail, then turn east (left) on another dirt road. In a quarter mile you reach Knee Ridge, from which the summit of Ellis Peak is plainly visible. Go for it. Note that the only downer along this route is that much of it is accessible to off-road vehicles and mountain bikes, although we saw none of the former on our trip. Still, plenty of people hike the trail the old-fashioned way—on foot.

⑫ Burton Creek Loop

5.0 mi/2.5 hrs

Location: Off Highway 28 near Tahoe City; map D4, grid d2.

User groups: Hikers, dogs, horses, and mountain bikes. No wheelchair facilities.

Permits: No permits are required. Parking and access are free.

Directions: From Tahoe City, drive northeast on Highway 28 for 2.3 miles to Old Mill Road. Turn left and drive four-tenths of a mile, then turn left on Polaris Road and drive a half mile to North Tahoe High School and the dirt road by the school parking lot. Park alongside the dirt road, being careful not to block the gate.

Maps: Currently, there is no Burton Creek State Park map available. To obtain a topographic map of the area, ask for Tahoe City from the USGS.

Contact: Tahoe State Recreation Area, (916) 525-7232, (916) 583-3074, or (916) 525-7982. Or fax (916) 525-0138.

Trail notes: Burton Creek State Park is Lake Tahoe's second largest state park at more than 2,000 acres, so you might wonder why few people have ever heard of it. It's because the park has no visitor center, no campground, no entrance kiosk, and, unfortunately, no trail signs. What really matters is that it has no crowds, a major bonus at Lake Tahoe. A five-mile loop trip is possible in the park, starting near North Tahoe High School and wandering through a mix of fir and pine forest, open meadows, and creekside riparian habitat. Although the trail is not signed at present, there are numbers painted at most intersections, which help you stay on track. (The route is frequently used for 10K races in the summer.) A quarter mile from the trailhead is the start of the loop; you can hike it in either direction. Just make sure you remember what the spur trail looks like that leads from the loop back to the trailhead; otherwise you'll walk right past it on your return trip, like we did. Some advice: If you're visiting this park in summer, stop in at the campground at Tahoe State Recreation Area (it's across Highway 28 from the turnoff to Burton Creek State Park). Check with the kiosk to see if they have a map or updated trail information on Burton Creek.

⑱ General Creek to Lily Pond

7.0 mi/3.5 hrs

Location: In Sugar Pine Point State Park near Lake Tahoe; map D4, grid e1.

User groups: Hikers and mountain bikes. No dogs or horses. No wheelchair facilities.

Permits: No permits are required. A $5 day-use fee is charged per vehicle.

Directions: From Tahoe City, drive eight miles south on Highway 89 to the General Creek Campground entrance on the right. Park in one of the day-use areas by the entrance kiosk, then walk into the campground to site #149 and the start of the trail. (You can walk into the camp on the park road, or take the single-track trail that leads from the parking lot.)

Maps: A map of Sugar Pine Point State Park is available for $1 at the entrance station. To obtain a topographic map of the area, ask for Homewood from the USGS.

Contact: Sugar Pine Point State Park, P.O. Box 266, Tahoma, CA 96142; (916) 525-7982 or (916) 525-7232. Or fax (916) 525-0138.

Trail notes: This trail in Sugar Pine Point State Park follows a flat, open stretch of General Creek and then leads gently uphill through the forest to marshy Lily Pond, a pretty, serene spot. Most of the trail is part of a popular cross-country skiing loop in the winter, which means it's on a wide logging road. There are a couple key factors to enjoying this walk: If you're not staying in the General Creek Campground, the day-use parking area is more than a half mile from campsite #149, where the trail begins. To make this walk to the trailhead more pleasant, be sure to take the single-track trail from the parking lot, instead of walking along the paved camp road. The trail is somewhat hidden from view, so if you don't see it, ask the attendant in the entrance kiosk where it is. Next, when you finally meet up with the loop, be sure to take the north side of it, which is prettier than the south side, with lots of big sugar pines interspersed with Jeffreys and lodgepoles. (The south side is mostly open meadows. If you're a history buff, it was the site of the 1960 Olympics biathlon.) At 2.5 miles from the campground, at the far end of the loop, you'll see the single-track turnoff signed for Lily Pond and Lost Lake. It's a one-mile hike through a rocky, dense forest to the pond, which is indeed covered with lilies. On your return, you can always take the south side of the loop for variety, then turn left on the bridge over General Creek to return to the start of the loop.

⑲ Meeks Creek Trail to Rubicon Lake

15.0 mi/1–2 days

Location: In the Desolation Wilderness; map D4, grid e1.

User groups: Hikers, dogs, and horses. No mountain bikes. No wheelchair facilities.

Permits: Day hikers must fill out a self-serve day-use permit at the wilderness trailhead. A wilderness permit is required for overnight stays; they are available from the South Lake Tahoe Ranger Station or the Lake Tahoe Visitor Center. Quotas are in effect from June 15 to Labor Day; permits are available in advance by mail for this period for a fee.

Directions: From Tahoe City, drive south on Highway 89 for 10 miles to Meeks Bay Resort. Look for a small dirt parking lot on the west side of the highway, directly across from the resort, and park there. The trailhead is well marked.

Maps: For a map of Lake Tahoe Basin Management Unit or Desolation Wilderness, send $4 to USDA-Forest Service, 630 Sansome Street, San Francisco, CA 94111. A Desolation Wilderness map is also available for a fee from Tom Harrison Cartography at (415) 456-7940. To obtain topographic maps of the area, ask for Homewood and Rockbound Valley from the USGS.

Contact: Lake Tahoe Basin Management Unit, 870 Emerald Bay Road, South Lake Tahoe, CA 96150; (916) 573-2600 or fax (916) 573-2693.

Trail notes: If you don't mind sharing the trail with lots of other folks, this trek into the Desolation Wilderness is a moderate backpacking trip that's loaded with alpine lakes and classic Tahoe scenery. A closed dirt road (Road 14N42) leads from the Desolation Wilderness sign near Meeks Bay for 1.3 level miles to a trail sign for Phipps Pass and Tahoe-Yosemite Trail. (This is a popular cross-country skiing route in winter.) Bear right here and begin the gradual climb to a chain of alpine lakes, beginning with Lake Genevieve at 4.5 miles and culminating with Rubicon Lake at 7.5 miles. Parallel Meeks Creek on a gently climbing trail, and pass the wilderness boundary at 2.5 miles. You're in forest most of the time, so don't expect a lot of panoramic views, but, then again, don't expect any brutal, sunny, exposed ascents. Cross Meeks Creek and continue straight to Lake Genevieve, a shallow, swimmable body of water. The trail then climbs up to larger Crag Lake, then continues to climb further to small, lily-covered Shadow Lake. (A right fork beyond Crag Lake leads to small Hidden Lake, less than a quarter mile off the main trail, a good side trip.) From Shadow Lake, it's a mile further to Stony Ridge Lake, the largest of this series of lakes, and then yet another mile to Rubicon Lake, 7.5 miles from the trailhead and with a total elevation gain of only 2,000 feet. The main steep stretch is right at the end, between Stony Ridge Lake and Rubicon Lake. Campsites can be found at most all of the lakes, but Rubicon Lake is the preferred site, since it's the most scenic of the group.

⑮ Rubicon and Lighthouse Loop

2.0 mi/1.0 hr

Location: In D.L. Bliss State Park on the west shore of Lake Tahoe; map D4, grid f2.

User groups: Hikers only. No dogs, horses, or mountain bikes. No wheelchair facilities.

Permits: No permits are required. A $5 day-use fee is charged per vehicle.

Directions: From Tahoe City, drive south on Highway 89 for 15 miles and turn left at the sign for D.L. Bliss State Park. Drive a half mile to the entrance station, then continue for seven-tenths of a mile to a fork. Turn right and drive another seven-tenths of a mile to Calawee Cove Beach and parking lot. The Rubicon Trail begins on the far side of the lot. (If this lot is full, you will have to use one of the other day-use parking lots in the park.)

Maps: A map of D.L. Bliss State Park is available for $1 at the entrance station. To obtain a topographic map of the area, ask for Emerald Bay from the USGS.

Contact: D.L. Bliss State Park, P.O. Box 266, Tahoma, CA 96142; (916) 525-7277 or (916) 525-7232. Or fax (916) 525-0138.

Trail notes: Not everybody is up for hiking the entire length of the Rubicon Trail (see trail notes for hike number 16). But if you're visiting Lake Tahoe, you should not leave the area without sampling at least a piece of this magnificent pathway, which edges along the steep cliffs on the west side of the lake. An excellent short trip on the Rubicon is this loop, which starts from Calawee Cove Beach at D.L. Bliss State Park. Although the hike has very little elevation gain, it's not for those who are afraid of heights, because there are 100-foot dropoffs along the trail's edge, leading straight down to Lake Tahoe. Cables are in place in some sections to keep people from falling off the trail. You hike a quarter mile to a spur trail to the old lighthouse (don't bother with the spur; there's nothing to see), then continue beyond it for another half mile. The lake and mountain views are mind-boggling every step of the way. Bear right at the trail junction and walk to a parking lot, where you can pick up the Lighthouse Trail and loop back to Calawee Cove Beach. On the other hand, if you want to see those lake vistas one more time, forget about the loop and just head back the way you came.

⑯ Rubicon Trail

9.0 mi/5.0 hrs

Location: In D.L. Bliss State Park on the west shore of Lake Tahoe; map D4, grid f2.

User groups: Hikers only. No dogs, horses, or mountain bikes. No wheelchair facilities.

Permits: No permits are required. A $5 day-use fee is charged per vehicle.

Directions: From Tahoe City, drive south on Highway 89 for 15 miles and turn left at the sign for D.L. Bliss State Park. Drive a half mile to the entrance station, then continue for seven-tenths of a mile to a fork. Turn right and drive another seven-tenths of a mile to Calawee Cove Beach and parking lot. The Rubicon Trail begins on the far side of the lot. (If this lot is full, you will have to use one of the other day-use parking lots in the park.)

Maps: A map of D.L. Bliss State Park is available for $1 at the entrance station. To obtain a topographic map of the area, ask for Emerald Bay from the USGS.

Contact: D.L. Bliss State Park, P.O. Box 266, Tahoma, CA 96142; (916) 525-7277 or (916) 525-7232. Or fax (916) 525-0138.

Trail notes: The Rubicon Trail is the premier Lake Tahoe day hike. Accept no substitutes; if you want the best scenery that Lake Tahoe offers, this is the trail to hike. The only problem? Right; it's you and about a zillion other hikers. If you possibly can, walk this trail in the off-season (late September is great) and do it on a weekday. Then get ready for eye-popping, film-burning scenery, as you gaze out across the surface and deep into the depths of sparkling clear, 12-mile-wide Lake Tahoe, and gawk at the rim of mountains that surround it. The trail stays close to the lake edge and has very little elevation change, just some mild ups and downs, holding steady near 6,300 feet. Highlights include Rubicon Point, Emerald Point, Fannette Island, and Vikingsholm Castle (see hike number 18). If you prefer, you can start and end your Rubicon hike at Vikingsholm Castle; just leave your car in the Emerald Bay Overlook parking lot. But you'll add on nearly two miles round-trip getting from the parking lot to Vikingsholm, with a 600-foot elevation change.

⓱ Balancing Rock

1.0 mi/0.5 hr

Location: In D.L. Bliss State Park on the west shore of Lake Tahoe; map D4, grid f2.

User groups: Hikers only. No dogs, horses, or mountain bikes. No wheelchair facilities.

Permits: No permits are required. A $5 day-use fee is charged per vehicle.

Directions: From Tahoe City, drive south on Highway 89 for 15 miles and turn left at the sign for D.L. Bliss State Park. Drive a half mile to the entrance station, then continue for seven-tenths of a mile to a fork. Turn left and drive a quarter mile to the Balancing Rock parking lot on the left.

Maps: A map of D.L. Bliss State Park is avail-

able for $1 at the entrance station. To obtain a topographic map of the area, ask for Emerald Bay from the USGS.

Contact: D.L. Bliss State Park, P.O. Box 266, Tahoma, CA 96142; (916) 525-7277 or (916) 525-7232. Or fax (916) 525-0138.

Trail notes: It sounds kind of dumb, but it's quite popular and more interesting than you might expect. The Balancing Rock is a big hunk of granite that has been a curiosity at Lake Tahoe for eons. It's a 130-ton rock that sits balanced on a small rock pedestal, like a giant golf ball on an itty-bitty golf tee. The trail's interpretive brochure explains that eventually erosion will wear away the pedestal and cause the Balancing Rock to lose its balance, but Tahoe-lovers have been awaiting this event forever and it still hasn't happened. In addition to Balancing Rock, the trail shows off many of the plants and trees of the Tahoe area. It's a good learning experience for both kids and adults.

⓲ Vikingsholm

2.0 mi/1.0 hr

Location: In Emerald Bay State Park on the west shore of Lake Tahoe; map D4, grid f2.

User groups: Hikers only. No dogs, horses, or mountain bikes. No wheelchair facilities.

Permits: No permits are required. Parking and access are free, but there is a fee to tour the inside of the castle.

Directions: From South Lake Tahoe, drive northwest on Highway 89 for nine miles to the Emerald Bay Overlook parking lot on the east side of Highway 89. The trail begins from the lake side of the parking lot.

Maps: A map of Emerald Bay and D.L. Bliss State Parks is available for $1 at the visitor center by Vikingsholm. To obtain a topographic map of the area, ask for Emerald Bay from the USGS.

Contact: Emerald Bay State Park, P.O. Box 266, Tahoma, CA 96142; (916) 525-7277 or (916) 525-7232. Or fax (916) 525-0138.

Trail notes: If you can take this walk very early in the morning, and preferably during a weekday, you'll get to experience the incredible beauty that has made Lake Tahoe the revered vacation destination that it is. If you take this walk at almost any other time . . . well, let's just say we hope you like a lot of company. Although the destination of this one-mile trail (really a dirt road) is Vikingsholm, a fancy replica of a Viking castle that belonged to an heiress in the 1930s, the beauty lies in the scenery spread out before you as you hike downhill. You see spectacular Fannette Island and the deep blue waters of Emerald Bay, and travel through an old-growth cedar and pine forest. You even gain access to some of Lake Tahoe's coveted sandy shoreline. Although you have to pay a fee to tour the inside of the castle, you can hike to it for free and add on a side trip to the base of 150-foot Eagle Falls, a quarter mile from Vikingsholm. For many people, the surprise on this trail is that the return hike has a 500-foot elevation gain. What, you mean we have to breathe hard?

Special note: Be sure to arrive early. By midmorning on weekends, visitors are forced to park up to two miles away.

⑲ Eagle Falls and Eagle Lake

2.0 mi/1.0 hr

Location: Off Highway 89 near South Lake Tahoe; map D4, grid f2.

User groups: Hikers and dogs. No horses or mountain bikes. No wheelchair facilities.

Permits: Day hikers must fill out a self-serve permit at the wilderness trailhead. A $3 day-use fee is charged per vehicle.

Directions: From South Lake Tahoe, drive northwest on Highway 89 for 8.5 miles to the Eagle Falls Picnic Area and Trailhead. Turn left into the parking area, or park in the roadside pullout just north of the picnic area on the west side of Highway 89.

Maps: For a map of Lake Tahoe Basin Management Unit, send $4 to USDA-Forest Service, 630 Sansome Street, San Francisco, CA 94111. To obtain a topographic map of the area, ask for Emerald Bay from the USGS.

Contact: Lake Tahoe Basin Management Unit, 870 Emerald Bay Road, South Lake Tahoe, CA 96150; (916) 573-2600 or fax (916) 573-2693.

Trail notes: Next to the trail to Vikingsholm (see hike number 18), this may be the most-

walked trail around Lake Tahoe. From the Eagle Falls Picnic Area, a sign by the rest room points you to the Eagle Falls Trail. Unfortunately, this is something of a "designer" path, with natural granite cut into flagstone-like stairsteps and an elaborate wooden bridge that escorts you over the top of the falls. Still, it's a beautiful walk, best taken early in the morning and during the week, when the masses aren't around. The waterfall pours right under the hikers' bridge. (If you want to see the "other" Eagle Falls, the one that drops right along Highway 89, see the trail notes for the Vikingsholm Trail.) Immediately following the bridge, the "designer" aspect of the trail ends, as you enter the Desolation Wilderness and climb 400 feet in less than a mile to reach rocky Eagle Lake, surrounded by granite cliffs. People fish and picnic here; some even try to swim in the icy water.

⑳ Velma Lakes

10.0 mi/5.0 hrs

Location: In the Desolation Wilderness; map D4, grid f2.

User groups: Hikers, dogs, and horses. No mountain bikes. No wheelchair facilities.

Permits: Day hikers must fill out a self-serve day-use permit at the wilderness trailhead. A wilderness permit is required for overnight stays; they are available from the South Lake Tahoe Ranger Station or the Lake Tahoe Visitor Center. Quotas are in effect from June 15 to Labor Day; permits are available in advance by mail for this period for a fee.

Directions: From South Lake Tahoe, drive northwest on Highway 89 for 8.5 miles to the Eagle Falls Picnic Area and Trailhead. Turn left into the parking area, or park in the roadside pullout just north of the picnic area on the west side of Highway 89.

Maps: For a map of Lake Tahoe Basin Management Unit or Desolation Wilderness, send $4 to USDA-Forest Service, 630 Sansome Street, San Francisco, CA 94111. A Desolation Wilderness map is also available for a fee from Tom Harrison Cartography at (415) 456-7940. To obtain topographic maps of the area, ask for Emerald Bay and Rockbound Valley from the USGS.

Contact: Lake Tahoe Basin Management Unit, 870 Emerald Bay Road, South Lake Tahoe, CA 96150; (916) 573-2600 or fax (916) 573-2693.

Trail notes: Remember to bring your sunscreen, because the trail to the Velma Lakes is rocky, exposed, and open. The route follows the trail to Eagle Falls and Eagle Lake for the first mile (see trail notes for hike number 19), then climbs seriously through a rugged, glaciated landscape, with only occasional hardy lodgepole pines and twisted junipers providing meager shade. The lack of trees and the abundance of rock means wide-open views and plenty of granite drama; welcome to the Sierra high country. At three miles you intersect the trail to Dicks Lake heading southwest (left), and you should head northwest (right) for Velma Lakes. Your trail heads directly to Middle Velma Lake in one mile, the most popular of the lakes. It has several granite islands and is favored for swimming. You can take a left cutoff just before Middle Velma Lake and head south to Upper Velma Lake in a half mile, or follow a use trail north along a creek to Lower Velma Lake (on your right, also a half mile away). Note that you can also begin the Velma Lakes hike from the trailhead at Bayview Campground, but then you miss out on seeing Eagle Lake, and a world-class view of Tahoe.

㉑ Cascade Falls

2.0 mi/1.0 hr

Location: Off Highway 89 near South Lake Tahoe; map D4, grid f2.

User groups: Hikers and dogs. No horses or mountain bikes. No wheelchair facilities.

Permits: No permits are required. Parking and access are free.

Directions: From South Lake Tahoe, drive northwest on Highway 89 for 7.5 miles to the Bayview Campground. Turn left and drive to the far end of the campground to the trailhead parking area. If it's full, park on the shoulder of Highway 89 by the campground entrance.

Maps: For a map of Lake Tahoe Basin Management Unit, send $4 to USDA-Forest Service, 630 Sansome Street, San Francisco, CA 94111. To obtain a topographic map of the area, ask for Emerald Bay from the USGS.

Contact: Lake Tahoe Basin Management Unit, 870 Emerald Bay Road, South Lake Tahoe, CA 96150; (916) 573-2600 or fax (916) 573-2693.

Trail notes: We rate this trail as far and away the best easy hike at Lake Tahoe. It's short and flat enough for almost anybody to make the trip, including young children, but still feels like wilderness. The one-mile trail leads to a stunning 200-foot cascade that drops into the southwest end of Cascade Lake. Make sure you visit in spring or early summer when the fall is flowing full and wide, because by August, it loses its drama. From the trailhead at Bayview Campground, take the left fork signed for Cascade Falls. In five minutes you get tremendous views of Cascade Lake, elevation 6,464 feet, then you start to hear and see the falls. The trail disintegrates as it nears the waterfall's edge, and hikers with children shouldn't get too close. But no matter; the best views are actually further back on the trail. Upstream of the falls are some lovely pools surrounded by wide shelves of granite.

㉒ Mount Tallac from Tallac Trailhead

9.0 mi/6.0 hrs

Location: In the Desolation Wilderness near Fallen Leaf Lake; map D4, grid f2.

User groups: Hikers and dogs. No horses or mountain bikes. No wheelchair facilities.

Permits: Day hikers must fill out a self-serve day-use permit at the wilderness trailhead. A wilderness permit is required for overnight stays; they are available from the South Lake Tahoe Ranger Station or the Lake Tahoe Visitor Center. Quotas are in effect from June 15 to Labor Day; permits are available in advance by mail for this period for a fee.

Directions: From South Lake Tahoe, drive northwest on Highway 89 for 3.8 miles to the signed turnoff for Mount Tallac and Camp Concord on the left, across the highway from the sign for Baldwin Beach. Drive four-tenths of a mile, then turn left and drive six-tenths of a mile to the trailhead.

Maps: For a map of Lake Tahoe Basin Management Unit or Desolation Wilderness, send $4 to USDA-Forest Service, 630 Sansome Street, San

Francisco, CA 94111. A Desolation Wilderness map is also available for a fee from Tom Harrison Cartography at (415) 456-7940. To obtain a topographic map of the area, ask for Emerald Bay from the USGS.

Contact: Lake Tahoe Basin Management Unit, 870 Emerald Bay Road, South Lake Tahoe, CA 96150; (916) 573-2600 or fax (916) 573-2693.

Trail notes: Hikers short on time and long on energy like hiking to 9,735-foot Mount Tallac from the Mount Tallac Trailhead rather than from the Glen Alpine Trailhead (see hike number 26). The payment this trail extracts from you is a 2,600-foot climb over the final three miles (plus another 900 feet in the first mile and a half), but in exchange you get a gorgeous route that passes by Floating Island Lake and Cathedral Lake on its way to Tallac's spectacular summit. It's 1.5 miles from the trailhead to Floating Island Lake, with excellent views along the way of Fallen Leaf Lake and Lake Tahoe. Then it's another six-tenths of a mile to a trail junction just before Cathedral Lake, where a trail from Fallen Leaf Lake joins this trail. Cathedral Lake is a good rest spot before making the final ascent to the top of Mount Tallac, a 2.4-mile butt-kicker of a climb on a rocky trail. It's made easier by a constant and ever-changing parade of vistas, including long looks at Gilmore Lake, Susie Lake, and Lake Aloha. The trail ends a quarter mile before the summit, where it meets the other Mount Tallac trail coming from Gilmore Lake, and you turn right and boulder-hop your way to the top. Not surprisingly, the views are wide-reaching—of the Desolation Wilderness, Fallen Leaf Lake, Lake Tahoe, and even Mount Rose, far off to the east. Hope the sun is shining and the skies are clear.

㉓ Rainbow and Lake of the Sky Trails

0.5 mi/0.5 hr

Location: In Tahoe National Forest near South Lake Tahoe; map D4, grid f2.

User groups: Hikers and wheelchairs. No dogs, horses, or mountain bikes.

Permits: No permits are required. Parking and access are free.

Directions: From South Lake Tahoe, drive northwest on Highway 89 for three miles to the Lake Tahoe Visitor Center turnoff on the right. Turn right and drive to the visitor center parking lot, where the trails begin.

Maps: For a map of Lake Tahoe Basin Management Unit, send $4 to USDA-Forest Service, 630 Sansome Street, San Francisco, CA 94111. To obtain a topographic map of the area, ask for Emerald Bay from the USGS.

Contact: Lake Tahoe Basin Management Unit, 870 Emerald Bay Road, South Lake Tahoe, CA 96150; (916) 573-2600 or fax (916) 573-2693.

Trail notes: Several short interpretive walks begin at the Lake Tahoe Visitor Center, the best of which are the Rainbow Trail and Lake of the Sky Trail. You can hike them both from the same starting point at the visitor center, and combine an interesting nature lesson with a walk along Lake Tahoe's shoreline for exceptional scenery and views. Start with the Rainbow Trail, which leads from the visitor center's west side and takes you to Taylor Creek and its Stream Profile Chamber. The creek is where thousands of kokanee salmon come to spawn in the fall, and you can view them through the glass walls of the profile chamber. (You can also just see them the ordinary way, just peering into the creek as you walk.) Then loop back to the visitor center and pick up the Lake of the Sky Trail. You'll pass by Taylor Creek Marsh on your way to Tallac Point and Tahoe's shoreline. In summer, people go swimming at this sandy stretch of beach.

㉔ Susie and Heather Lakes

10.0 mi/5.0 hrs

Location: In the Desolation Wilderness near Fallen Leaf Lake; map D4, grid g3.

User groups: Hikers, dogs, and horses. No mountain bikes. No wheelchair facilities.

Permits: Day hikers must fill out a self-serve day-use permit at the wilderness trailhead. A wilderness permit is required for overnight stays; they are available from the South Lake Tahoe Ranger Station or the Lake Tahoe Visitor Center. Quotas are in effect from June 15 to Labor Day; permits are available in advance by mail for this period for a fee.

Directions: From South Lake Tahoe, drive northwest on Highway 89 for 2.9 miles to Fallen Leaf Lake Road. Turn left and drive 4.8 miles on an increasingly narrow road. Take the left fork on Road 1216, signed for Lily Lake and the Desolation Wilderness. Drive seven-tenths of a mile to the trailhead.

Maps: For a map of Lake Tahoe Basin Management Unit or Desolation Wilderness, send $4 to USDA-Forest Service, 630 Sansome Street, San Francisco, CA 94111. A Desolation Wilderness map is also available for a fee from Tom Harrison Cartography at (415) 456-7940. To obtain a topographic map of the area, ask for Emerald Bay from the USGS.

Contact: Lake Tahoe Basin Management Unit, 870 Emerald Bay Road, South Lake Tahoe, CA 96150; (916) 573-2600 or fax (916) 573-2693.

Trail notes: Since the beautiful Desolation Wilderness is being loved to death by hordes of summer backpackers, do the area a favor and take a day hike to Susie and Heather Lakes instead. You'll minimize your impact on the land and still have a terrific outdoor experience in this area of rugged alpine beauty.

The trail to Susie and Heather Lakes begins as a rocky road and passes some summer cabins and a waterfall on Glen Alpine Creek. At 1.2 miles, the road ends near an old resort and you'll see a sign for Gilmore, Susie, and Grass Lakes. Start to climb, and shortly you'll enter the Desolation Wilderness boundary. You can take the short left cutoff to little Grass Lake (adding one mile each way to your trip) or continue straight, signed for Susie, Heather, and Aloha Lakes. At four miles, you'll reach the eastern shore of Susie Lake, then hike alongside it and around the lake's southern edge to continue another mile to Heather Lake. The granite-lined lake is deep and wide, and set in a landscape of classic high Sierra scenery.

㉕ Fallen Leaf Lake Trail

2.0 mi/1.0 hr

Location: In Tahoe National Forest near South Lake Tahoe; map D4, grid g3.

User groups: Hikers, dogs, horses, and mountain bikes. No wheelchair facilities.

Permits: No permits are required. Parking and access are free.

Directions: From South Lake Tahoe, drive northwest on Highway 89 for 2.9 miles to Fallen Leaf Lake Road. Turn left and drive eight-tenths of a mile to the Fallen Leaf Lake Trailhead.

Maps: For a map of Lake Tahoe Basin Management Unit, send $4 to USDA-Forest Service, 630 Sansome Street, San Francisco, CA 94111. To obtain a topographic map of the area, ask for Emerald Bay from the USGS.

Contact: Lake Tahoe Basin Management Unit, 870 Emerald Bay Road, South Lake Tahoe, CA 96150; (916) 573-2600 or fax (916) 573-2693.

Trail notes: Fallen Leaf Lake at 6,400 feet in elevation is the second largest lake in the Tahoe Basin, and some say it's the prettiest. Too bad most of it is privately owned, but luckily this path allows you access to the part that is public. The short, mostly flat trail leads from the trailhead to the lake and then along its northern edge to the dam, which you can walk across. Much of the trail hugs the lake's shoreline, so you can look out across the blue water and feel that sense of peace that comes from the sight of deep, sapphire waters. You get excellent views of Glen Alpine Canyon and Mount Tallac. In the fall, the shoreline of Fallen Leaf Lake is one of the best spots near Tahoe to admire the quaking aspens turning gold. Campers staying at Fallen Leaf Lake Campground can access this trail from their tents.

㉖ Mount Tallac Loop (Glen Alpine Trailhead)

11.6 mi/7.5 hrs

Location: In the Desolation Wilderness near Fallen Leaf Lake; map D4, grid g3.

User groups: Hikers and dogs. No horses or mountain bikes. No wheelchair facilities.

Permits: Day hikers must fill out a self-serve day-use permit at the wilderness trailhead. A wilderness permit is required for overnight stays; they are available from the South Lake Tahoe Ranger Station or the Lake Tahoe Visitor Center. Quotas are in effect from June 15 to Labor Day; permits are available in advance by mail for this period for a fee.

Directions: From South Lake Tahoe, drive northwest on Highway 89 for 2.9 miles to Fallen Leaf Lake Road. Turn left and drive 4.8 miles on an increasingly narrow road. Take the left fork on Road 1216, signed for Lily Lake and the Desolation Wilderness. Drive seven-tenths of a mile to the trailhead.

Maps: For a map of Lake Tahoe Basin Management Unit or Desolation Wilderness, send $4 to USDA-Forest Service, 630 Sansome Street, San Francisco, CA 94111. A Desolation Wilderness map is also available for a fee from Tom Harrison Cartography at (415) 456-7940. To obtain a topographic map of the area, ask for Echo Lake from the USGS.

Contact: Lake Tahoe Basin Management Unit, 870 Emerald Bay Road, South Lake Tahoe, CA 96150; (916) 573-2600 or fax (916) 573-2693.

Trail notes: You can hike to the top of 9,735-foot Mount Tallac from either of two trailheads. This trip, from Glen Alpine, is considered the more gradual route, but it's only more gradual if you hike it out and back. (See the trail notes for hike number 22.) Most people hike this trail as a loop, which means the ascent from Glen Alpine up the back side of Mount Tallac is fairly gradual, but the descent down the front face is knee-jarring and intense. Hikers who need to be kind to their joints should consider an out-and-back trip from Glen Alpine; everyone else can follow this trail as a loop if they please.

Start at the Glen Alpine Trailhead, elevation 6,560 feet, and follow the main trail to the Grass Lake and Gilmore Lake junction, 1.5 miles in. Bear right and get ready for an intense series of switchbacks out of Glen Alpine Canyon, with some, but not nearly enough, shade to keep you refreshed. The first good rest stop is at Gilmore Lake, 3.5 miles in, where you can stretch your hamstrings and eat a Power Bar. From there it's just under two miles to the top of Mount Tallac, climbing up its smooth back side. The official trail ends just below the summit; you must scramble over and around boulders for the last quarter mile to reach the top. After enjoying thoroughly tremendous views of the Desolation Wilderness, Fallen Leaf Lake, Lake Tahoe, and Mount Rose, climb back down to the trail's terminus and look for another trail heading east,

toward Fallen Leaf Lake. Hikers with strong knees can take this route for a steep and fast downhill return on a loop; everyone else should retrace their steps back to Glen Alpine. When loop hikers reach tiny Cathedral Lake, 2.3 miles from the summit, they should watch for a right fork shortly beyond it, which leads to Stanford Camp and then to the road to Glen Alpine Trailhead.

㉗ Gilmore Lake

7.6 mi/4.0 hrs

Location: In the Desolation Wilderness near Fallen Leaf Lake; map D4, grid g3.

User groups: Hikers and dogs. No horses or mountain bikes. No wheelchair facilities.

Permits: Day hikers must fill out a self-serve day-use permit at the wilderness trailhead. A wilderness permit is required for overnight stays; they are available from the South Lake Tahoe Ranger Station or the Lake Tahoe Visitor Center. Quotas are in effect from June 15 to Labor Day; permits are available in advance by mail for this period for a fee.

Directions: From South Lake Tahoe, drive northwest on Highway 89 for 2.9 miles to Fallen Leaf Lake Road. Turn left and drive 4.8 miles on an increasingly narrow road. Take the left fork on Road 1216, signed for Lily Lake and the Desolation Wilderness. Drive seven-tenths of a mile to the trailhead.

Maps: For a map of Lake Tahoe Basin Management Unit or Desolation Wilderness, send $4 to USDA-Forest Service, 630 Sansome Street, San Francisco, CA 94111. A Desolation Wilderness map is also available for a fee from Tom Harrison Cartography at (415) 456-7940. To obtain a topographic map of the area, ask for Emerald Bay from the USGS.

Contact: Lake Tahoe Basin Management Unit, 870 Emerald Bay Road, South Lake Tahoe, CA 96150; (916) 573-2600 or fax (916) 573-2693.

Trail notes: If we only had time to day hike to one destination near South Lake Tahoe, Gilmore Lake would be our choice. Everything about it is a classic Lake Tahoe and Desolation Wilderness trip, a roundup of the best the area has to offer. You get to visit a scenic alpine lake, and along the way you are treated to fields of wild-flowers, mountain vistas, beautiful conifer forests, and more. Of course, we're not the only ones who like this trail, so all the usual disclaimers apply about timing your trip for the off-season or during the week.

With that said, take off from the Glen Alpine Trailhead and hike down the road past all the private cabins. The rocky road eventually becomes a rocky trail. Bear right at the junction with the Grass Lake Trail, 1.5 miles in. Get ready to do the majority of this trail's climbing, heading for more trail junctions that await around three miles in, where paths lead off to the left to Susie and Heather Lakes. Bear right instead for Gilmore Lake, the largest lake in this area between Fallen Leaf Lake and Lake Aloha. You'll reach it at 3.5 miles, with a 1,700-foot elevation gain, so you'll be exercised but not completely worn out when you arrive. Despite the fact that hundreds of people cruise by Gilmore Lake each day on their way to climb Mount Tallac, few take the time to hang out for long by the lake's sapphire blue waters. The lake manages to stay secluded and pristine, and is ringed by grassy, flower-filled meadows.

㉘ Angora Lakes Trail

1.0 mi/0.5 hr

Location: In Tahoe National Forest near Fallen Leaf Lake; map D4, grid g3.

User groups: Hikers, dogs, horses, and mountain bikes. No wheelchair facilities.

Permits: No permits are required. Parking and access are free.

Directions: From South Lake Tahoe, drive northwest on Highway 89 for 2.9 miles to Fallen Leaf Lake Road. Turn left and drive eight-tenths of a mile to a fork. Go left and drive a half mile, then turn right on Forest Service Road 12N14. Drive 2.3 miles, past the Angora Fire Lookout, to the road's end and the trailhead.

Maps: For a map of Lake Tahoe Basin Management Unit, send $4 to USDA-Forest Service, 630 Sansome Street, San Francisco, CA 94111. To obtain a topographic map of the area, ask for Echo Lake from the USGS.

Contact: Lake Tahoe Basin Management Unit,

870 Emerald Bay Road, South Lake Tahoe, CA 96150; (916) 573-2600 or fax (916) 573-2693.

Trail notes: First, a warning: It's unwise to hike the Angora Lakes Trail unless you are accompanied by a person under the age of seven. The Angora Lakes are extremely popular with children's day camps and groups, and all summer long the little ones outnumber us old folks. Still, it's a pretty hike, and the Upper Angora Lake is a sight to behold. Head uphill from the parking lot on the signed dirt road, and in 15 minutes you'll be looking at Lower Angora Lake, which has a few cabins on its far side. Continue beyond its edge another quarter mile and, voilá, you reach the upper lake and Angora Lakes Resort, built in 1917. Although the resort cabins are always rented out way in advance, day users can buy a lemonade and sit at a picnic table to watch the action at the small, picturesque lake. Action? What action? Anglers fish from shore or rent rowboats for a few bucks per hour, toddlers wade around at the shallow beach area, and plenty of folks just plunk themselves down along the shoreline to stare at the bowl-shaped, glacial cirque lake. It has a high granite wall on its far side, where in early summer a waterfall of snowmelt flows down to the lake.

㉙ Lyons Creek Trail

9.0 mi/4.5 hrs

Location: In the Desolation Wilderness; map D4, grid g0.

User groups: Hikers, dogs, and horses. No mountain bikes. No wheelchair facilities.

Permits: Wilderness permits are required for both day hikers and backpackers; they are available for a fee from the Eldorado National Forest office (address below) or from Wrights Lake. Quotas are in effect from June 15 to Labor Day.

Directions: From Placerville, drive east on Highway 50 for 45 miles to the signed turnoff for Wrights Lake on the north side of the highway. (It's about 15 miles west of South Lake Tahoe and five miles east of Kyburz.) Drive north on Wrights Lake Road for four miles, then turn right at the sign for Lyons Creek Trail.

Maps: For a map of Eldorado National Forest or Desolation Wilderness, send $4 to USDA-

Forest Service, 630 Sansome Street, San Francisco, CA 94111. A Desolation Wilderness map is also available for a fee from Tom Harrison Cartography at (415) 456-7940. To obtain a topographic map of the area, ask for Pyramid Peak from the USGS.

Contact: Eldorado National Forest, 3070 Camino Heights Drive, Camino, CA 95709; (916) 644-6048 or fax (916) 644-3034.

Trail notes: If you're fond of walking along coursing waterways, following the gurgle and babble of a creek as you hike, this trip along Lyons Creek to Lake Sylvia will suit you just fine. Wildflowers proliferate near the water, and views of Pyramid Peak (just shy of 10,000 feet in elevation) will inspire you as you gently ascend. Keep to the south side of the creek for four solid miles, then cross it and reach a junction a tenth of a mile further. Lyons Lake is to the left and steeply uphill; Lake Sylvia is a half mile to the right. Bear right and wander the final distance to the lake, which is shadowed by Pyramid Peak. Campsites can be found on its shores. The ambitious can take the side trip to Lyons Lake, a half mile from the junction but with a nasty 450-foot climb.

⏱️ Grouse Lake

4.0 mi/2.0 hrs

Location: In the Desolation Wilderness; map D4, grid g0.

User groups: Hikers, dogs, and horses. No mountain bikes. No wheelchair facilities.

Permits: Day hikers must fill out a self-serve day-use permit at the wilderness trailhead. A wilderness permit is required for overnight stays; they are available for a fee from the Eldorado National Forest office (address below). Quotas are in effect from June 15 to Labor Day.

Directions: From Placerville, drive east on Highway 50 for 45 miles to the signed turnoff for Wrights Lake on the north side of the highway. (It's about 15 miles west of South Lake Tahoe and five miles east of Kyburz.) Drive north on Wrights Lake Road for eight miles to the Wrights Lake Campground, then continue beyond it for 1.3 miles (take the right fork) to the end of the road and the Twin Lakes and

Grouse Lakes Trailhead. If you are backpacking, you must park before the campground in the backpackers' parking lot.

Maps: For a map of Eldorado National Forest or Desolation Wilderness, send $4 to USDA-Forest Service, 630 Sansome Street, San Francisco, CA 94111. A Desolation Wilderness map is also available for a fee from Tom Harrison Cartography at (415) 456-7940. To obtain a topographic map of the area, ask for Pyramid Peak from the USGS.

Contact: Eldorado National Forest, 3070 Camino Heights Drive, Camino, CA 95709; (916) 644-6048 or fax (916) 644-3034.

Trail notes: The Crystal Basin area is a magical place on the western edge of Desolation Wilderness, where the nearly 10,000-foot peaks of the Crystal Range overlook the basin and its multitude of lakes. Several excellent day hikes and backpacking trips are possible in this area, most of which begin from the Wrights Lake Campground. Of those, this trip to Grouse Lake is the shortest, and a good trail for first-timers wanting to sample the area. From the day-use parking area, the Twin Lakes Trail winds past a meadow (sometimes filled with cud-chewing bovines) and then enters a pine and fir forest interspersed with stretches of hard granite. You reach a trail junction 1.2 miles out, and head right at the sign for Smith Lake. Grouse Lake is less than a mile away, and although some backpackers camp here, most head for Hemlock or Smith Lakes further on, and leave Grouse Lake for the day users. That means you can spread out a picnic or strip down to your bathing suit, then lounge around on the rocky shoreline and soak up some sun. If you want to walk further, Hemlock Lake is another half mile away, but getting there involves a steep climb.

⏱️ Twin and Island Lakes

6.4 mi/4.0 hrs

Location: In the Desolation Wilderness; map D4, grid g0.

User groups: Hikers, dogs, and horses. No mountain bikes. No wheelchair facilities.

Permits: Day hikers must fill out a self-serve day-use permit at the wilderness trailhead. A wilderness permit is required for overnight stays; they are available for a fee from the Eldorado National Forest office (address below). Quotas are in effect from June 15 to Labor Day.

Directions: From Placerville, drive east on Highway 50 for 45 miles to the signed turnoff for Wrights Lake on the north side of the highway. (It's about 15 miles west of South Lake Tahoe and five miles east of Kyburz.) Drive north on Wrights Lake Road for eight miles to the Wrights Lake Campground, then continue beyond it for 1.3 miles (take the right fork) to the end of the road and the Twin Lakes and Grouse Lakes Trailhead. If you are backpacking, you must park before the campground in the backpackers' parking lot.

Maps: For a map of Eldorado National Forest or Desolation Wilderness, send $4 to USDA-Forest Service, 630 Sansome Street, San Francisco, CA 94111. A Desolation Wilderness map is also available for a fee from Tom Harrison Cartography at (415) 456-7940. To obtain a topographic map of the area, ask for Pyramid Peak from the USGS.

Contact: Eldorado National Forest, 3070 Camino Heights Drive, Camino, CA 95709; (916) 644-6048 or fax (916) 644-3034.

Trail notes: The only downer on the trip to Twin and Island Lakes is the sheer number of people who make this journey every day during the summer months. Of course, when you see the lakes, you'll know why they are so darn popular. Of all the hiking possibilities in the Wrights Lake area, this trip is hands-down the most scenic, with possibly the best views in the entire Desolation Wilderness, and miles of solid granite under your feet as you walk. The first 1.2 miles from the day-use trailhead have only a gentle climb to the intersection with the trail to Grouse, Hemlock, and Smith Lakes. Bear left and climb up over granite, until three-quarters of a mile later you crest a ridge and start to descend. The vistas of jagged mountains to the northeast make an awesome backdrop. At 2.5 miles you'll reach the dam at Lower Twin Lake, then cross it and continue hiking along the lake's northwest shore to a couple tiny lakes at 3.0 miles. Another quarter mile brings you to the south end of Island Lake, where vistas of the Crystal Range are the best of the trip, and most hikers burn a heck of a lot of film.

❷ Gertrude and Tyler Lakes

8.0 mi/4.0 hrs

Location: In the Desolation Wilderness; map D4, grid g0.

User groups: Hikers, dogs, and horses. No mountain bikes. No wheelchair facilities.

Permits: Day hikers must fill out a self-serve day-use permit at the wilderness trailhead. A wilderness permit is required for overnight stays; they are available for a fee from the Eldorado National Forest office (address below). Quotas are in effect from June 15 to Labor Day.

Directions: From Placerville, drive east on Highway 50 for 45 miles to the signed turnoff for Wrights Lake on the north side of the highway. (It's about 15 miles west of South Lake Tahoe and five miles east of Kyburz.) Drive north on Wrights Lake Road for eight miles to the Wrights Lake Campground, then continue beyond it for 1.3 miles (take the right fork) to the end of the road and the Twin Lakes and Grouse Lakes Trailhead. If you are backpacking, you must park before the campground in the backpackers' parking lot.

Maps: For a map of Eldorado National Forest or Desolation Wilderness, send $4 to USDA-Forest Service, 630 Sansome Street, San Francisco, CA 94111. A Desolation Wilderness map is also available for a fee from Tom Harrison Cartography at (415) 456-7940. To obtain topographic maps of the area, ask for Pyramid Peak and Rockbound Valley from the USGS.

Contact: Eldorado National Forest, 3070 Camino Heights Drive, Camino, CA 95709; (916) 644-6048 or fax (916) 644-3034.

Trail notes: There's a ton of hiking to be accomplished in the Wrights Lake area, and among all the possibilities, this trip to Gertrude and Tyler Lakes stands out. It's the perfect length for a day trip, with an easy to moderate elevation gain. Begin by crossing the creek and taking the trail signed for Maud Lake and Rockbound Pass from the trailhead parking lot (not the Twin Lakes Trail). Follow the signs at several junctions, staying straight on the route to Rockbound Pass until you see a sign for the Tyler Lake Trail at 1.7

miles, where the Rockbound Pass Trail forks to the left. Bear right and start to climb harder. Your ascent is interspersed with a few short drops and level stretches, with Crystal Range peaks now coming into view. At 3.5 miles you'll reach a short left spur trail (100 yards long) to the grave of William Tyler, marked with a white stone, who died here in a blizzard in the 1920s. A half mile beyond this spur are Gertrude and Tyler Lakes at 8,000 feet in elevation; Gertrude is accessible via the left fork (really straight) and Tyler is via the right fork. Gertrude is shallow and good for swimming, but Tyler is more beautiful, set in a granite basin with a few sparse pines on its shores. Both lakes can be easily visited in one trip, although Tyler Lake requires a bit more of a climb. Campsites are found at both lakes.

③ Rockbound Pass and Lake Doris

12.0 mi/6.0 hrs or 2.0 days

Location: In the Desolation Wilderness; map D4, grid g0.

User groups: Hikers, dogs, and horses. No mountain bikes. No wheelchair facilities.

Permits: Day hikers must fill out a self-serve day-use permit at the wilderness trailhead. A wilderness permit is required for overnight stays; they are available for a fee from the Eldorado National Forest office (address below). Quotas are in effect from June 15 to Labor Day.

Directions: From Placerville, drive east on Highway 50 for 45 miles to the signed turnoff for Wrights Lake on the north side of the highway. (It's about 15 miles west of South Lake Tahoe and five miles east of Kyburz.) Drive north on Wrights Lake Road for eight miles to the Wrights Lake Campground, then continue beyond it for 1.3 miles (take the right fork) to the end of the road and the Twin Lakes and Grouse Lakes Trailhead. If you are backpacking, you must park before the campground in the backpackers' parking lot.

Maps: For a map of Eldorado National Forest or Desolation Wilderness, send $4 to USDA-Forest Service, 630 Sansome Street, San Francisco, CA 94111. A Desolation Wilderness map is also available for a fee from Tom Harrison Cartography at (415) 456-7940. To obtain topographic maps of the area, ask for Pyramid Peak and Rockbound Valley from the USGS.

Contact: Eldorado National Forest, 3070 Camino Heights Drive, Camino, CA 95709; (916) 644-6048 or fax (916) 644-3034.

Trail notes: To make the epic trip to 8,650-foot Rockbound Pass, follow the trail notes for hike number 32, the route to Gertrude and Tyler Lakes, for the first 1.7 miles. (You can also start your trip from the trailhead at Dark Lake, on the west side of Wrights Lake, but it's a half mile longer than from this trailhead.) At the junction at 1.7 miles, bear left to stay on the Rockbound Pass Trail, and hike through mixed conifers to get your first glimpse of Rockbound Pass at 2.5 miles—a distant notch in the mountains to the north. To get to it, you must descend a bit and cross the Jones Fork of Silver Creek, then parallel the stream on its course from Maud Lake. You're traveling in very rocky terrain now; the trail is sometimes blasted out of granite. Reach the western shores of Maud Lake at 4.2 miles, where some people make camp while others continue the ascent to the pass. It's not much further; after a steady climb you gain its summit at 5.6 miles. The views of Desolation Wilderness open wide, but the howling wind often prevents you from staying too long. If that's the case, descend a half mile to Lake Doris, just to the left of the trail, where you can make camp, or if you're day hiking, just hang out and rest. The total elevation gain on this trip is 1,700 feet, plus a short descent to Lake Doris.

③ Horsetail Falls Vista

2.0 mi/1.0 hrs

Location: In Eldorado National Forest near South Lake Tahoe; map D4, grid g1.

User groups: Hikers and dogs. No horses or mountain bikes. No wheelchair facilities.

Permits: No permits are required (if you stay out of the wilderness boundary.) Parking and access are free.

Directions: From South Lake Tahoe, drive south on Highway 89 for five miles to Highway 50. Drive west on Highway 50 for about 15 miles to Twin Bridges, where there is a huge pullout on the north side of the highway just before the bridge. (The pullout is a half mile west of the turnoff for Camp Sacramento.) Park in the pullout, then walk across the highway bridge about 500 feet to the well-marked trailhead.

Maps: For a map of Eldorado National Forest, send $4 to USDA-Forest Service, 630 Sansome Street, San Francisco, CA 94111. To obtain a topographic map of the area, ask for Echo Lake from the USGS.

Contact: Eldorado National Forest, 3070 Camino Heights Drive, Camino, CA 95709; (916) 644-6048 or fax (916) 644-3034.

Trail notes: Horsetail Falls is that plainly visible waterfall that takes your breath away as you're driving west along U.S. 50. Approximately 15,000 people each summer see the falls and pull over at the giant parking area by the trailhead, then hike part of the way to reach it. The trail has been a source of controversy for many years, because the waterfall is located within the boundary of the Desolation Wilderness on a rough but serviceable route, but the first mile of trail is outside the wilderness boundary and extremely accessible. That means that plenty of inexperienced people try to hike to the falls, and then get lost, injured, or worse when they enter the wilderness boundary and lose the trail, or slip and fall in the dangerous waters near Horsetail Falls. The Forest Service is carrying out the wilderness mandate by not making man-made alterations to the trail, like building bridges or blasting an obvious trail into the granite, but some hikers feel that because the route is so popular, it should be more developed. We think the best way to solve the dilemma is to hike only the first mile of the route, to the edge of the wilderness boundary. It's a perfect easy hike for families or anybody wanting to get off the highway and stretch their legs, and although it doesn't go all the way to Horsetail Falls, it provides many excellent views of it, as well as of Pyramid Creek's glacier-carved canyon. Just turn around when you reach the wilderness boundary sign. One tragic note: In September 1995, some ingrate vandalized this trail by spray-painting 90 green arrows on the pristine granite along the trail. The Forest Service is working to remove the graffiti, but for now, it's there.

35 Ralston Peak

8.0 mi/5.0 hrs

Location: In the Desolation Wilderness near South Lake Tahoe; map D4, grid g1.

User groups: Hikers and dogs. No horses or mountain bikes. No wheelchair facilities.

Permits: Wilderness permits are required for both day hikers and backpackers; they are available for a fee from the Eldorado National Forest office (address below). Quotas are in effect from June 15 to Labor Day.

Directions: From South Lake Tahoe, drive south on Highway 89 for five miles to Highway 50. Drive west on Highway 50 for about 14 miles to the turnoff for Camp Sacramento. (If you reach Twin Bridges, you've gone 1.5 miles too far west.) There is a parking area off the north side of Highway 50, and a sign for the Ralston Trail to Lake of the Woods.

Maps: For a map of Eldorado National Forest or Desolation Wilderness, send $4 to USDA-Forest Service, 630 Sansome Street, San Francisco, CA 94111. A Desolation Wilderness map is also available for a fee from Tom Harrison Cartography at (415) 456-7940. To obtain a topographic map of the area, ask for Echo Lake from the USGS.

Contact: Eldorado National Forest, 3070 Camino Heights Drive, Camino, CA 95709; (916) 644-6048 or fax (916) 644-3034.

Trail notes: The route to Ralston Peak has a little of everything—dense forest, open manzanita-covered slopes, meadows, and granite ridges. And a lot of one thing—elevation gain. From trailhead to summit, you ascend from 6,400 feet to 9,240 feet over the course of four miles. Begin by walking northward up the paved road from the east side of the parking area for 200 yards; look for the trail leading off on the left. Climb upward through nonstop trees (and nonstop switchbacks) for a mile, then enter a more open area as you pass the wilderness boundary sign at 1.5 miles. The views start to widen. Your lungs request a lunch break, but they don't get one until 2.5 miles up, when you finally gain the ridge. A half mile later, the break is over, and you climb again, this time to another ridge at 3.5 miles, covered in meadow grasses and wildflowers. Part ways with the main trail and look for a trail leading to your right to the top of Ralston Peak, a half mile away. Scramble up over jumbled rock to gain the 9,235-foot summit, and take in the view of Lake Tahoe, Fallen Leaf Lake, Carson Pass, Echo Lakes, and below you (to the north), Ralston Lake. Wow, what a view. Wow, what a climb. Is your butt kicked?

③⑥ Boat Taxi to Lake Aloha

12.0 mi/6.0 hrs

Location: In the Desolation Wilderness; map D4, grid g2.

User groups: Hikers only. No dogs, horses, or mountain bikes. No wheelchair facilities.

Permits: Day hikers must fill out a self-serve day-use permit at the wilderness trailhead. A wilderness permit is required for overnight stays; they are available for a fee from the South Lake Tahoe Ranger Station or the Lake Tahoe Visitor Center. Quotas are in effect from June 15 to Labor Day.

Directions: From South Lake Tahoe, drive south on Highway 89 for five miles to Highway 50. Drive west on Highway 50 for 5.5 miles to the signed turnoff for Echo Lakes on the right. (It's one mile west of Echo Summit.) Turn right and drive a half mile, then turn left. Drive one mile to Echo Lake and park in the hikers' parking lot.

Maps: For a map of Lake Tahoe Basin Management Unit or Desolation Wilderness, send $4 to USDA-Forest Service, 630 Sansome Street, San Francisco, CA 94111. A Desolation Wilderness map is also available for a fee from Tom Harrison Cartography at (415) 456-7940. To obtain a topographic map of the area, ask for Echo Lake from the USGS.

Contact: Lake Tahoe Basin Management Unit, 870 Emerald Bay Road, South Lake Tahoe, CA 96150; (916) 573-2600 or fax (916) 573-2693.

Trail notes: Some people just like to take boat rides, and if you're one of them, you can have a great all-day adventure by taking the boat taxi at Echo Lakes, a private resort, and then hiking to Lake Aloha. If you think it's wimpy to ride the boat instead of walking all the way, you're wrong. Those who ride will still end up tired at the end of the day, having completed a 10- to 14-mile hike (depending on how many side trips you take to other lakes) with a decent amount of ups and downs. Those who take the boat will also end up a little poorer, because the ride costs about eight bucks. From the parking lot, walk a quarter mile downhill to the lake and the boat launch area to reach the boat taxi, which leaves at regularly scheduled intervals (in summer only). The boat carries you two miles to the far end of Upper and Lower Echo Lakes, and from there you hike uphill to gain the main trail and head to your left. It's three miles to the eastern edge of Lake Aloha, passing about a million trail junctions along the way, all of which lead to various lakes in very short distances. (Maybe not quite a million.) Most people don't stop when they reach Lake Aloha's shore; instead they hike along its beautiful north side for another one or two miles, and admire the rocky coves of the giant lake. Its elevation is 8,116 feet. On the way back, you can take one of the signed trail junctions and hike to Lake of the Woods, Lake Lucille, Lake Margery, Tamarack Lake, or Ralston Lake, all less than one mile off the Lake Aloha Trail.

③⑦ Dardanelles Lake

7.6 mi/4.5 hrs

Location: Near Carson Pass; map D4, grid h3.

User groups: Hikers, dogs, horses, and mountain bikes. No wheelchair facilities.

Permits: No permits are required. Parking and access are free.

Directions: From South Lake Tahoe, drive south on Highway 89 for approximately 10 miles to the Big Meadow Trailhead parking area, which is 5.5 miles south of the junction of U.S. 50 and Highway 89. The trail to Dardanelles begins on the south side of the road.

Maps: For a map of Lake Tahoe Basin Management Unit, send $4 to USDA-Forest Service, 630 Sansome Street, San Francisco, CA 94111. To obtain a topographic map of the area, ask for Echo Lake from the USGS.

Contact: Lake Tahoe Basin Management Unit, 870 Emerald Bay Road, South Lake Tahoe, CA 96150; (916) 573-2600 or fax (916) 573-2693.

Trail notes: The route to Dardanelles Lake along the Tahoe Rim Trail starts out steep but gets easier as it goes. It enters Meiss Country, that large and wonderful roadless area south of Lake Tahoe, where the forces that shaped the land were ice (glaciers) and fire (volcanic action). Both have made their presence clearly visible. The trail heads south from the freeway, climbs through fir and pine forest to Big Meadow, then continues to a trail junction at two miles. There, you turn sharply right (on the Meiss Meadow Trail toward Christmas Valley) and walk less than a quarter mile, then turn left and cross a creek for the final 1.2 miles to Dardanelles Lake. The trail surface is smooth, not rocky, which makes the 1,400-foot climb pretty easy. The lake is perfect for swimming, fishing, and picnicking. If you can time your trip for autumn, you'll be treated to a marvelous color display from the aspens and alders that grow along this trail's many streams.

⑱ Minkalo Trail

7.0 mi/3.5 hrs

Location: Near Silver Lake; map D4, grid i1.

User groups: Hikers, dogs, horses, and mountain bikes. No wheelchair facilities.

Permits: No permits are required. Parking and access are free.

Directions: From Meyers at the junction of Highway 50 and Highway 89, drive south on Highway 89 for 11 miles to Highway 88. Turn west on Highway 88 and drive 15.5 miles to the Kit Carson Lodge turnoff on the north side of the road. (It's 10.8 miles west of Carson Pass Summit, at Silver Lake.) Turn north and drive past Kit Carson Lodge, go left at the first fork, go right at the second fork, and wind up at the parking for the Minkalo Trail. (It's a total 1.4 miles from Highway 88.) Walk back down the road for about 40 yards to find the start of the trail.

Maps: For a map of Eldorado National Forest, send $4 to USDA-Forest Service, 630 Sansome Street, San Francisco, CA 94111. To obtain a topographic map of the area, ask for Caples Lake from the USGS.

Contact: Eldorado National Forest, 3070 Camino Heights Drive, Camino, CA 95709; (916) 644-6048 or fax (916) 644-3034. Or Amador Ranger District, 26820 Silver Drive, Pioneer, CA 95666; (209) 295-4251, or fax (209) 295-5998.

Trail notes: Since Silver Lake has a fair number of private homes on its shore, it appears less "wild" than nearby Caples Lake. Still, the big blue lake at 7,300 feet in elevation is beautiful, and if you want to hike near it, the Minkalo Trail is your best bet. The trail leads to Granite Lake in one mile, and Plasse's Resort (on the south side of the lake) in three miles. We say, why not hike to both, then buy a pizza or a Power Bar at Plasse's Resort Trading Post to fuel up for the hike back to the Minkalo Trailhead. The trail starts out rocky and stays that way for the first quarter mile. You cross a bridge over Squaw Creek and shortly see the right fork that leads to Plasse's Resort. Take the left fork first, heading to Granite Lake, which you'll reach in about 20 minutes after a moderate climb. It's a pretty lake and good for swimming. After you've visited, return to the trail junction and hike southward, soon coming close to the edge of Silver Lake and staying in its proximity. You'll have many pretty lake views from here on out, including long looks at Treasure Island, Silver Lake's large island. It takes about an hour to reach the campground at Plasse's, an excellent place for horse-lovers (and pizza-lovers).

⑲ Emigrant Lake

8.0 mi/4.0 hrs

Location: In the Mokelumne Wilderness near Caples Lake; map D4, grid i1.

User groups: Hikers, dogs, and horses. No mountain bikes. No wheelchair facilities.

Permits: No day-hiking permits are required. A free wilderness permit is required for overnight stays between April 1 and November 30; they are available from the Amador Ranger Station, the Carson Pass Information Station, or the Eldorado Information Center.

Directions: From Meyers at the junction of Highway 50 and Highway 89, drive south on Highway 89 for 11 miles to Highway 88. Turn west on Highway 88 and drive 14 miles to the west side of Caples Lake and the trailhead parking area. (It's five miles west of Carson Pass Summit.)

Maps: For a map of Eldorado National Forest, send $4 to USDA-Forest Service, 630 Sansome Street, San Francisco, CA 94111. To obtain a topographic map of the area, ask for Caples Lake from the USGS.

Contact: Eldorado National Forest, 3070 Camino Heights Drive, Camino, CA 95709; (916) 644-6048 or fax (916) 644-3034. Or Amador Ranger District, 26820 Silver Drive, Pioneer, CA 95666; (209) 295-4251, or fax (209) 295-5998.

Trail notes: The trailhead at Caples Lake is always jam-packed with backpackers, so do yourself a favor—visit here in the off-season and make your trip a day hike instead of an overnight. Still, crowds or no crowds, the scenery is tremendous and the path is excellent every step of the way. The trail leads from the spillway at Caples Lake up and along the lake's south side, following an old emigrant route. The first two miles are right along the lake's edge, climbing gently above the shoreline, always in the shade of big conifers. More climbing alongside Emigrant Creek leads you to a stream crossing at 3.5 miles, followed by another crossing. A few switchbacks carry you up to Emigrant Lake, a beautiful cirque lake set at 8,600 feet, with many fine sunbathing rocks. Just before the lake is a small, pristine meadow, almost as pretty as the lake itself, with some serious wildflowers in season. Covered Wagon Peak and Thimble Peak at 9,500 feet rise above the scene. The total elevation gain is less than 1,000 feet, making this a surprisingly easy day hike even with its eight-mile distance.

⑩ Lake Margaret

4.6 mi/3.0 hrs

Location: Near Carson Pass and Kirkwood Lake; map D4, grid i1.

User groups: Hikers, dogs, horses, and mountain bikes. No wheelchair facilities.

Permits: No permits are required. Parking and access are free.

Directions: From Meyers at the junction of Highway 50 and Highway 89, drive south on Highway 89 for 11 miles to Highway 88. Turn west on Highway 88 and drive 14.5 miles to the Lake Margaret sign on the north side of the road. (It's 5.5 miles west of Carson Pass Summit, and 5.5 miles east of Silver Lake.) Turn north and park at the trailhead parking area.

Maps: For a map of Eldorado National Forest, send $4 to USDA-Forest Service, 630 Sansome Street, San Francisco, CA 94111. To obtain a topographic map of the area, ask for Caples Lake from the USGS.

Contact: Eldorado National Forest, 3070 Camino Heights Drive, Camino, CA 95709; (916) 644-6048 or fax (916) 644-3034. Or Amador Ranger District, 26820 Silver Drive, Pioneer, CA 95666; (209) 295-4251, or fax (209) 295-5998.

Trail notes: A hike to an alpine lake with a less-than-1,000-foot elevation gain? If it seems too good to be true, you need an easy trail fix, and Lake Margaret should do the trick. This is one of the few hikes along Highway 88 that leads from the north side of the highway, which means you can say farewell to most of the crowds at Caples and Silver Lakes' campgrounds and trailheads on the south side of the highway.

The trail undulates gently up and down, never gaining or losing more than a couple hundred feet, with the pleasant sound of Caples Creek keeping you company along the way. You'll cross the creek on a wide bridge a half mile in. The path passes by a couple of minuscule lakes, really more like ponds if you visit in late summer or fall, and climbs a bit over duck-marked granite. A lovely grove of aspens grows along Caples Creek, near where you cross it again at two miles. At 2.3 miles, you reach the granite shoreline of Lake Margaret, after about an hour of walking and only a minor expenditure of energy. Note that although most of the trails in this area are good for wildflower-lovers, the proximity of Caples Creek makes the bloom especially showy here.

④ Winnemucca Lake from Woods Lake

3.0 mi/1.5 hrs

Location: In the Mokelumne Wilderness near Carson Pass; map D4, grid i2.

User groups: Hikers, dogs, and horses. No mountain bikes. No wheelchair facilities.

Permits: No day-hiking permits are required. A free wilderness permit is required for overnight stays between April 1 and November 30; they are available from the Amador Ranger Station, the Carson Pass Information Station, or the Eldorado Information Center.

Directions: From Meyers at the junction of Highway 50 and Highway 89, drive south on Highway 89 for 11 miles to Highway 88. Turn west on Highway 88 and drive 12 miles to the Woods Lake Campground turnoff on the south side of the road. (It's 1.5 miles west of Carson Pass Summit.) Turn left and drive 1.5 miles to the trailhead parking area at Woods Lake, by the picnic area. (Backpackers must park in a special overnight section of the campground.)

Maps: For a map of Eldorado National Forest, send $4 to USDA-Forest Service, 630 Sansome Street, San Francisco, CA 94111. To obtain topographic maps of the area, ask for Caples Lake and Carson Pass from the USGS.

Contact: Eldorado National Forest, 3070 Camino Heights Drive, Camino, CA 95709; (916) 644-6048 or fax (916) 644-3034. Or Amador Ranger District, 26820 Silver Drive, Pioneer, CA 95666; (209) 295-4251 or fax (209) 295-5998.

Trail notes: Woods Lake is a little magical spot where you can drive right up, walk a few feet to the water's edge, and plunk in your fishing line. It's also the trailhead for numerous great hikes into the Mokelumne Wilderness, including this easy trip to deep blue Winnemucca Lake, set at the base of fantastic-looking Mount Round Top, elevation 10,381 feet. The land here has been formed by volcanic action, so as you walk, you have to constantly remind yourself that you aren't at Mount Lassen or Mount Shasta, you're just south of Tahoe in Carson Pass.

After crossing the footbridge at the trailhead and setting off down the trail, you pass by the remains of an arrastra, a device used for crushing gold or silver ore—evidence of this area's mining past. Continue walking through big conifers until you come out to a glacial moraine, where your views open wide of Mount Round Top, a huge old volcanic vent. It is best seen when it has a light dusting of snow on it. In 1.5 miles you reach the edge of Winnemucca Lake, right at the foot of the mountain, where many people like to set up camp for the night. It's a gorgeous spot. If you hike to your left along the lake's edge, you get a great view over your left shoulder of Caples Lake.

㊷ Winnemucca Lake Loop

5.0 mi/3.0 hrs

Location: In the Mokelumne Wilderness near Carson Pass; map D4, grid i2.

User groups: Hikers, dogs, and horses. No mountain bikes. No wheelchair facilities.

Permits: No day-hiking permits are required. A free wilderness permit is required for overnight stays between April 1 and November 30; they are available from the Amador Ranger Station, the Carson Pass Information Station, or the Eldorado Information Center.

Directions: From Meyers at the junction of Highway 50 and Highway 89, drive south on Highway 89 for 11 miles to Highway 88. Turn west on Highway 88 and drive 12 miles to the Woods Lake Campground turnoff on the south side of the road. (It's 1.5 miles west of Carson Pass Summit.) Turn left and drive 1.5 miles to the trailhead parking area at Woods Lake, by the picnic area. (Backpackers must park in a special overnight section of the campground.)

Maps: For a map of Eldorado National Forest, send $4 to USDA-Forest Service, 630 Sansome Street, San Francisco, CA 94111. To obtain topographic maps of the area, ask for Caples Lake and Carson Pass from the USGS.

Contact: Eldorado National Forest, 3070 Camino Heights Drive, Camino, CA 95709; (916) 644-6048 or fax (916) 644-3034. Or Amador Ranger District, 26820 Silver Drive, Pioneer, CA 95666; (209) 295-4251 or fax (209) 295-5998.

Trail notes: If you want all the scenic beauty of the Winnemucca Lake Trail described in hike number 41, but a longer walk and a little more solitude, try this loop trip instead. The trail is the same route as the Winnemucca Lake Trail for the first 1.5 miles to Winnemucca's edge, but then you bear right and cross the stream on the west side of the lake. From there it's one mile uphill to Round Top Lake, steep enough to get you puffing, but the gorgeous scenery makes it all worthwhile. Round Top Lake is set below The Sisters, two peaks that are both at 10,000 feet-plus, but you also have views of Mount Round Top and Fourth of July Peak. It's incredibly dramatic. It's also windy, so you might not stay long. From there, follow the lake's outlet creek on the

Lost Cabin Mine Trail for two miles back to Woods Lake Campground, then wind your way through the camp back to the Woods Lake Picnic Area, where you left your car if you're day hiking.

⓭ Fourth of July Lake

8.8 mi/4.5 hrs

Location: In the Mokelumne Wilderness near Caples Lake; map D4, grid i2.

User groups: Hikers, dogs, and horses. No mountain bikes. No wheelchair facilities.

Permits: No day-hiking permits are required. A free wilderness permit is required for overnight stays between April 1 and November 30; they are available from the Amador Ranger Station, the Carson Pass Information Station, or the Eldorado Information Center.

Directions: From Meyers at the junction of Highway 50 and Highway 89, drive south on Highway 89 for 11 miles to Highway 88. Turn west on Highway 88 and drive 12 miles to the Woods Lake Campground turnoff on the south side of the road. (It's 1.5 miles west of Carson Pass Summit.) Turn left and drive one mile to the campground. Park in the backpackers' parking lot and walk to site #13, where a sign reads "Lost Cabin Mine Trail—Follow this road to trailhead."

Maps: For a map of Eldorado National Forest, send $4 to USDA-Forest Service, 630 Sansome Street, San Francisco, CA 94111. To obtain a topographic map of the area, ask for Caples Lake from the USGS.

Contact: Eldorado National Forest, 3070 Camino Heights Drive, Camino, CA 95709; (916) 644-6048 or fax (916) 644-3034. Or Amador Ranger District, 26820 Silver Drive, Pioneer, CA 95666; (209) 295-4251 or fax (209) 295-5998.

Trail notes: The biggest problem in planning a trip to Fourth of July Lake is deciding which way to go. There are so many ways, from so many trailheads, including ones at Carson Pass and Upper Blue Lake. The shortest and most direct route is from Woods Lake Campground near campsite 13, and it includes a nice stopover at Round Top Lake, two miles in. Follow the dirt road from the campground for a half mile to the start of the Lost Cabin Mine Trail. Pass the eastern flank of 9,000-foot Black Butte, an old volcanic vent that is similar in appearance to Mount Round Top, a few miles to the east. In less than an hour you arrive at Round Top Lake, a worthy destination in itself and a good spot for a snack break, beneath the sturdy shoulders of the two peaks of The Sisters. It's only two more miles to Fourth of July Lake, but they are steep and downhill, which means you have to climb back out on the way home. In addition to the tough grade, the route is usually dusty. If you make it to the lake, fishing is good for brook trout, and many campsites are found in the lake's basin. Remember the rules, though: No campfires are allowed, and your camp must be 100 feet from the water. Late in the summer, a sandy beach gets exposed, perfect for swimmers.

⓮ Frog Lake

1.8 mi/1.0 hr

Location: In the Mokelumne Wilderness near Carson Pass; map D4, grid i3.

User groups: Hikers, dogs, and horses. No mountain bikes. No wheelchair facilities.

Permits: No day-hiking permits are required. A free wilderness permit is required for overnight stays between April 1 and November 30; they are available from the Amador Ranger Station, the Carson Pass Information Station, or the Eldorado Information Center.

Directions: From Meyers at the junction of Highway 50 and Highway 89, drive south on Highway 89 for 11 miles to Highway 88. Turn west on Highway 88 and drive 10 miles to Carson Pass Summit. The parking area and trailhead is on the left, by the Carson Pass Information Station.

Maps: For a map of Eldorado National Forest, send $4 to USDA-Forest Service, 630 Sansome Street, San Francisco, CA 94111. To obtain a topographic map of the area, ask for Carson Pass from the USGS.

Contact: Eldorado National Forest, 3070 Camino Heights Drive, Camino, CA 95709; (916) 644-6048 or fax (916) 644-3034. Or Amador Ranger District, 26820 Silver Drive, Pioneer, CA 95666; (209) 295-4251 or fax (209) 295-5998.

Trail notes: Any hiking trip from the Carson Pass Trailhead is going to be packed with people, but we say take this walk anyway just because it's so interesting and educational. At the trailhead, you can learn about Kit Carson, the great explorer for whom this pass was named, and you can learn about the geologic forces that shaped this region, which is called the Round Top Geologic Area. Evidence of both glaciers and volcanoes can be seen with every step you take. The short walk to Frog Lake is suitable even for small children, and if you're more ambitious, you can continue another 1.5 miles to beautiful Winnemucca Lake. At Frog Lake, you are provided with a fascinating vista of Elephant Back, elevation 9,585 feet, which looks exactly like its name. It's a lava dome, a round mass of solid lava. The lake is a beautiful turquoise color, perfect for picnicking alongside, although because the area is rather open and exposed, the wind sometimes blows with ferocity.

㊺ Showers Lake

10.0 mi/6.0 hrs

Location: Near Caples Lake; map D4, grid i3.

User groups: Hikers, dogs, and horses. No mountain bikes. No wheelchair facilities.

Permits: No permits are required. Parking and access are free.

Directions: From Meyers at the junction of Highway 50 and Highway 89, drive south on Highway 89 for 11 miles to Highway 88. Turn west on Highway 88 and drive 10 miles to Carson Pass Summit. The parking area and trailhead is on the right (north), across the highway from (and slightly west of) the Carson Pass Information Station.

Maps: For a map of Eldorado National Forest, send $4 to USDA-Forest Service, 630 Sansome Street, San Francisco, CA 94111. To obtain topographic maps of the area, ask for Caples Lake and Carson Pass from the USGS.

Contact: Eldorado National Forest, 3070 Camino Heights Drive, Camino, CA 95709; (916) 644-6048 or fax (916) 644-3034. Or Amador Ranger District, 26820 Silver Drive, Pioneer, CA 95666; (209) 295-4251 or fax (209) 295-5998.

Trail notes: Here's a short trip on the Pacific Crest Trail into the land of Meiss Country, headwaters for the Upper Truckee River and home of the endangered Lahontan cutthroat trout.

Although Meiss Country is not designated wilderness, it might as well be, because there are no roads cutting into it and all is peaceful and serene. The Pacific Crest Trail and a completed stretch of the Tahoe Rim Trail are the main routes through Meiss Country. For the trip to Showers Lake, head uphill from the trailhead on the PCT, climbing through Meiss Pass and then dropping into a huge valley basin. Views along the way include Mount Round Top, Elephant's Back, and Red Lake Peak, expanding to include far-off Lake Tahoe to the north. It's 2.9 miles to a fork with the Tahoe Rim Trail, just beyond a crossing of the Upper Truckee River, which is little more than a stream here. The right fork leads 2.2 miles to Round Lake, Meiss Country's largest lake and a popular destination, but stay left on the PCT and TRT, and cross the river again on your way to Showers Lake, 2.1 miles further. The last half mile of trail is a 350-foot descent to Showers Lake, with 9,590-foot Little Round Top poking up above it to the west. The trail leads along the east side of the lake, where campsites can be found. The lake is set at 8,790 feet, and is the highest lake in the Upper Truckee River Basin.

㊻ Raymond Lake

11.0 mi/1–2 days

Location: In the Mokelumne Wilderness near Blue Lakes; map D4, grid i3.

User groups: Hikers, dogs, and horses. No mountain bikes. No wheelchair facilities.

Permits: No day-hiking permits are required. A free wilderness permit is required for overnight stays between April 1 and November 30; they are available from the ranger station in Markleeville or at the Carson Pass Information Station.

Directions: From Meyers at the junction of Highway 50 and Highway 89, drive south on Highway 89 for 11 miles to Highway 88. Turn west on Highway 88 and drive 2.5 miles to the Blue Lakes turnoff on the south side of the road. Turn south and drive 11 miles to the left turnoff for Tamarack Lake and Wet Meadows. Bear left and drive three miles to the left turnoff for Lower Sunset Lake. Turn left and drive a short distance to the trailhead.

Maps: For a map of Toiyabe National Forest–Carson District, send $4 to USDA-Forest Service, 630 Sansome Street, San Francisco, CA 94111. To obtain topographic maps of the area, ask for Pacific Valley and Ebbetts Pass from the USGS.

Contact: Toiyabe National Forest, Carson Ranger District, 1536 South Carson Street, Carson City, NV 89701; (702) 882-2766 or fax (702) 884-8199.

Trail notes: Considering how difficult it is, we're not sure why this trip to Raymond Lake is so popular, except if you figure in the gorgeous alpine scenery. The trip has become something of a right of passage for hikers in the Carson Pass area, and the trail is busy almost as soon as it is snow free, with even not-too-fit hikers making the 3,000-foot climb to the rocky alpine lake. The trail starts near Lower Sunset Lake, and heads east from the access road on the Pacific Crest Trail. Keep following the PCT trail markers for 4.5 miles, then turn right on the Raymond Lake Trail. (Most of those 4.5 miles are a moderate ascent.) The final stretch is only a mile but a butt-kicker, mostly because you're already getting tired when you begin it. The lake is about 10 acres in size and set at 9,000 feet. It's popular with people who want to catch themselves a golden trout. The best thing about the lake has nothing to do with fishing, but everything to do with the fact that it is set below 10,000-foot Raymond Peak, a ruggedly beautiful mountain.

㊼ Granite Lake

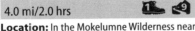

4.0 mi/2.0 hrs

Location: In the Mokelumne Wilderness near Blue Lakes; map D4, grid i3.

User groups: Hikers, dogs, and horses. No mountain bikes. No wheelchair facilities.

Permits: No day-hiking permits are required. A free wilderness permit is required for overnight stays between April 1 and November 30; they are available from the Amador Ranger Station, the Carson Pass Information Station, or the Eldorado Information Center.

Directions: From Meyers at the junction of Highway 50 and Highway 89, drive south on Highway 89 for 11 miles to Highway 88. Turn west on Highway 88 and drive 2.5 miles to the

Blue Lakes turnoff on the south side of the road. Turn south and drive 12 miles to the fork at Lower Blue Lake. Turn right and drive 1.5 miles to the dam by Upper Blue Lake, shortly beyond Middle Creek Campground; turn into the parking area. The Granite Lake and Grouse Lake Trail leads from the west side of the parking area.

Maps: For a map of Eldorado National Forest, send $4 to USDA-Forest Service, 630 Sansome Street, San Francisco, CA 94111. To obtain a topographic map of the area, ask for Pacific Valley from the USGS.

Contact: Eldorado National Forest, 3070 Camino Heights Drive, Camino, CA 95709; (916) 644-6048 or fax (916) 644-3034. Or Amador Ranger District, 26820 Silver Drive, Pioneer, CA 95666; (209) 295-4251 or fax (209) 295-5998.

Trail notes: Campers at Middle Creek Campground can just set out from their tents on this trail to Granite Lake, but everyone else must begin by the dam at Upper Blue Lake and follow a well-signed but meandering route to enter the Mokelumne Wilderness, one mile in. It's only one more mile from the wilderness boundary to Granite Lake, with a total 550-foot climb over well-graded trail. You'll notice you're climbing, but not enough to make anybody start whining. A quarter mile past the boundary sign you'll see a large pond, but don't mistake that for Granite Lake, which is another 20 minutes further on the trail. The granite basin it's set in, and the granite that lines its shores, is a dead giveaway that you've made it to the proper destination. Hope you brought your swimsuit for the deep, chilly waters.

㊽ Hot Springs Creek Waterfall

3.0 mi/1.5 hr

Location: In Grover Hot Springs State Park near Markleeville; map D4, grid i4.

User groups: Hikers only. No dogs, horses, or mountain bikes. No wheelchair facilities.

Permits: No permits are required. A $5 day-use fee is charged per vehicle.

Directions: From Meyers at the junction of Highway 50 and Highway 89, drive south on Highway 89 for 24 miles to Markleeville. At

Markleeville, turn right (west) on Hot Springs Road and drive 3.5 miles to the state park entrance. The signed trailhead is a quarter mile beyond the entrance station and campground turnoffs at a gated dirt road.

Maps: A map of Grover Hot Springs State Park is available for $1 at the entrance station. To obtain a topographic map of the area, ask for Markleeville from the USGS.

Contact: Grover Hot Springs State Park, P.O. Box 188, Markleeville, CA 96120; (916) 694-2248 or (916) 525-7232. Or fax (916) 694-2502.

Trail notes: Even without a waterfall, this would be a great trail to walk, because it leads through the giant sugar pines of Hot Springs Valley, enclosed by rocky cliffs and 10,000-foot peaks. The route leaves from just beyond the campgrounds in Grover Hot Springs State Park and follows the Burnside Lake and Charity Valley Trails for a half mile, then branches off on a left fork. The trail is well signed for the waterfall, so you'll have no chance of getting lost. (There's only one questionable part, where the trail reaches a jumbled pile of boulders, but the correct answer is simply to go up and over them.) Hot Springs Canyon gradually narrows on its way to the falls, and when you near the creek's edge, you'll see many small trout swimming in its pools. The waterfall is about 50 feet high and best seen from April to July. Technically, it is outside of state park land and in Toiyabe National Forest, so you'll see backpackers' campfire rings on the cliff above the falls.

49 Burnside Lake

8.4 mi/5.0 hrs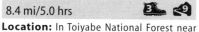

Location: In Toiyabe National Forest near Markleeville; map D4, grid i4.

User groups: Hikers, dogs, horses, and mountain bikes. No wheelchair facilities.

Permits: No permits are required. A $5 day-use fee is charged per vehicle. Parking and access are free if you begin at the trailhead outside of the state park.

Directions: From Meyers at the junction of Highway 50 and Highway 89, drive south on Highway 89 for 24 miles to Markleeville. At Markleeville, turn right (west) on Hot Springs

Road and drive 3.5 miles to the state park entrance. The signed trailhead is a quarter mile beyond the entrance station and campground turnoffs at a gated dirt road. (Another trailhead is located outside of the state park, on Hot Springs Road three-quarters of a mile before the state park entrance, signed for Charity Valley.)

Maps: For a map of Toiyabe National Forest–Carson District, send $4 to USDA-Forest Service, 630 Sansome Street, San Francisco, CA 94111. A map of Grover Hot Springs State Park is available for $1 at the entrance station. To obtain a topographic map of the area, ask for Markleeville from the USGS.

Contact: Grover Hot Springs State Park, P.O. Box 188, Markleeville, CA 96120; (916) 694-2248 or (916) 525-7232. Or Toiyabe National Forest, Carson Ranger District, 1536 South Carson Street, Carson City, NV 89701; (702) 882-2766 or fax (702) 884-8199.

Trail notes: The Burnside Lake Trail leaves Grover Hot Springs State Park at 5,900 feet in elevation and climbs west to Burnside Lake at 8,160 feet. The climb is spaced out over four miles, so it's a steady workout to the lake but not grueling. Along the way you pass tall and majestic sugar pines and rocky outcrops, with 10,023-foot Hawkins Peak and 9,417-foot Markleeville Peak towering over the scene. The lake is about 10 surface acres, and popular for fishing. Although you can start hiking on the trail from Hot Springs Road shortly before the state park entrance, we recommend you start from the park's trailhead. Not only does it shave two miles off your trip, but also when you return from your hike, you can take a dip in the 102-degree hot springs and soothe those aching muscles. (Note: Although you may encounter some mountain bikers on the trail at first, they will soon branch off on their way to Charity Valley.)

50 Heiser Lake

4.8 mi/2.5 hrs

Location: In the Carson-Iceberg Wilderness near Ebbetts Pass; map D4, grid j3.

User groups: Hikers, dogs, and horses. No mountain bikes. No wheelchair facilities.

Permits: No day-hiking permits are required. Parking and access are free.

Directions: From Angels Camp at the intersection of Highways 4 and 49, go east on Highway 4 for 40 miles to Bear Valley. Set your odometer at Bear Valley and drive 10 miles further east on Highway 4 to the Mosquito Lakes Trailhead and the Heiser Lake Trail. Park on the right (south) side of the road, across from the campground; there is only enough space for a few cars.

Maps: For a map of Stanislaus National Forest, send $4 to USDA-Forest Service, 630 Sansome Street, San Francisco, CA 94111. A map of the Carson-Iceberg Wilderness is also available from the Forest Service for $4. To obtain topographic maps of the area, ask for Pacific Valley and Spicer Meadow Reservoir from the USGS.

Contact: Stanislaus National Forest, Calaveras Ranger District, P.O. Box 500, Hathaway Pines, CA 95323; (209) 795-1381 or fax (209) 795-6849.

Trail notes: When a trailhead is located at a spot as pretty as the Mosquito Lakes on Highway 4, you just know you're in for a good trip. The tiny little lakes are popular with fishermen from the nearby campgrounds, but this trail is popular with nature lovers, who set out on the short, moderate day hike to Heiser Lake for a few hours of peace in the Carson-Iceberg Wilderness. The trail climbs and descends, then climbs and descends some more, mostly heading in a straight-line course due south to the lake. It's one of those trails where you've got to work equally hard traveling in both directions. At a junction with the trail from Bull Run Lake two miles in, bear left and finish out the last half mile to Heiser Lake, set at 8,000 feet in elevation. The lake is granite bound, with a couple of tiny islands sticking out of its shallow waters.

(51) Bull Run Lake

7.0 mi/4.0 hrs

Location: In the Carson-Iceberg Wilderness near Ebbetts Pass; map D4, grid j3.

User groups: Hikers, dogs, and horses. No mountain bikes. No wheelchair facilities.

Permits: No day-hiking permits are required. Parking and access are free.

Directions: From Angels Camp at the intersection of Highways 4 and 49, drive east on Highway 4 for 40 miles to Bear Valley. Set your odometer at Bear Valley and drive 8.5 miles further east on Highway 4 to the Stanislaus Meadow turnoff on the right (Road 8N13). Turn right and drive a short distance to the trailhead parking area.

Maps: For a map of Stanislaus National Forest, send $4 to USDA-Forest Service, 630 Sansome Street, San Francisco, CA 94111. A map of the Carson-Iceberg Wilderness is also available from the Forest Service for $4. To obtain topographic maps of the area, ask for Pacific Valley and Spicer Meadow Reservoir from the USGS.

Contact: Stanislaus National Forest, Calaveras Ranger District, P.O. Box 500, Hathaway Pines, CA 95323; (209) 795-1381 or fax (209) 795-6849.

Trail notes: You might have to share the trail to Bull Run Lake with some horses (their owners like the big parking lot at the trailhead, large enough for horse trailers), but as long as you remember to pack along a few extra apples or carrots, things should turn out okay. Although longer than the nearby trail to Heiser Lake, this trip to Bull Run Lake is actually easier, because the trail is well graded and the only really steep section is in the last half mile. The first 1.3 miles are almost level, traveling slightly downhill through a grassy meadow, which is filled with wildflowers in the early summer and turns golden by September. After that you start to climb, mostly through pine forest and over duck-lined stretches of granite. Watch for a trail junction at 2.2 miles, where you should turn right for Bull Run Lake (straight ahead is Heiser Lake). After a brief flat stretch, prepare for a final mile of climbing, with the last part being the most challenging. The lake is a fine reward for your panting effort, set in a steep-walled granite bowl and with many smooth rock slabs to lay on. (Note that the ambitious can add on a trip to Heiser Lake, which is two miles away from the junction but with a steep up and down. It's better saved for backpackers, or day hikers who have gotten a very early start.)

(52) Noble Lake

9.0 mi/4.5 hrs

Location: In Toiyabe National Forest near Ebbetts Pass; map D4, grid j5.

User groups: Hikers, dogs, horses, and mountain bikes. No wheelchair facilities.

Permits: No day-hiking permits are required. Parking and access are free.

Directions: From Angels Camp at the intersection of Highways 4 and 49, go east on Highway 4 for 40 miles to Bear Valley. Set your odometer at Bear Valley and drive 15 miles further east on Highway 4 to Ebbetts Pass and the trailhead parking area. The trail is on the south side of the road. (If you are coming from Markleeville, drive south on Highway 89/Highway 4 for 15 miles to Ebbetts Pass.)

Maps: For a map of Toiyabe National Forest–Carson District, send $4 to USDA-Forest Service, 630 Sansome Street, San Francisco, CA 94111. To obtain a topographic map of the area, ask for Ebbetts Pass from the USGS.

Contact: Toiyabe National Forest, Carson Ranger District, 1536 South Carson Street, Carson City, NV 89701; (702) 882-2766 or fax (702) 884-8199.

Trail notes: Noble Lake lies just outside of the Carson-Iceberg Wilderness, and is reachable by a long, butt-kicking hike on the Noble Canyon Trail out of Silver Creek Campground, or a shorter, gentler route from Ebbetts Pass. Guess which one we like better? Right. From Ebbetts Pass, elevation 8,700 feet, there's a mere 1,200-foot climb to the lake at 9,440 feet (which includes some descent as well). The lake is a fine spot for camping or just spending an afternoon. The scenery is classic high Sierra—big conifers, snow-capped peaks, hard granite, and lush meadows. The hiking season is brief at this elevation, usually only about three months from July to September, but that just makes being here seem all the more special.

The lake route follows the access trail to the Pacific Crest Trail from the trailhead parking area. In a quarter mile of climbing, you will join the PCT proper and head south, first climbing and then making a long descent into Noble Canyon. The trail from Silver Creek Campground joins your trail here, and some switchbacks follow. At three miles you will cross Noble Creek, then climb again to a high meadow. Soon you can see Noble Lake; the main lake is to the right of the trail, but a smaller unnamed lake is off to the left, an eighth mile off the trail. Both have decent campsites and many good rocks to sit on and relax. In springtime, fishing is reportedly good at Noble Lake.

(53) Kinney Lakes

5.0 mi/2.5 hrs

Location: In Toiyabe National Forest near Ebbetts Pass; map D4, grid j5.

User groups: Hikers, dogs, horses, and mountain bikes. No wheelchair facilities.

Permits: No day-hiking permits are required. Parking and access are free.

Directions: From Angels Camp at the intersection of Highways 4 and 49, drive east on Highway 4 for about 40 miles to Bear Valley. Set your odometer at Bear Valley and drive 15 miles further east on Highway 4 to Ebbetts Pass and the trailhead parking area. The trail is on the north side of the road. (If you are coming from Markleeville, drive south on Highway 89/Highway 4 for 15 miles to Ebbetts Pass.)

Maps: For a map of Toiyabe National Forest–Carson District, send $4 to USDA-Forest Service, 630 Sansome Street, San Francisco, CA 94111. To obtain a topographic map of the area, ask for Ebbetts Pass from the USGS.

Contact: Toiyabe National Forest, Carson Ranger District, 1536 South Carson Street, Carson City, NV 89701; (702) 882-2766 or fax (702) 884-8199.

Trail notes: The route to Kinney Lakes follows the Pacific Crest Trail in the opposite direction of the hike to Noble Lake (see hike number 52), heading north past minuscule Sherrold Lake on the way to large Upper Kinney Lake. You start hiking at 8,700 feet at the pass, so even though this trail has an easy to moderate grade, your lungs feel like they're getting a workout. The trail leads through a landscape of big conifers with little undergrowth, typical of the high country. When the trees disperse, your views open wide. Raymond Peak and Reynold Peak rule the skyline. At 1.6 miles you reach a signed junction for Upper and Lower Kinney Lakes, and you can take your pick as to which one to visit first. The Pacific Crest Trail leads directly to the upper lake, while the lower lake must be visited by following an

Map Section D4—page 180

eastward fork from the PCT. The upper lake, though smaller, is the prettiest of the two.

54 Wolf Creek Trail

6.0 mi/3.0 hrs

Location: In the Carson-Iceberg Wilderness near Markleeville; map D4, grid j5.

User groups: Hikers, dogs, and horses. No mountain bikes. No wheelchair facilities.

Permits: No day-hiking permits are required. A free wilderness permit is required for overnight stays; they are available at the trailhead. Parking and access are free.

Directions: From Meyers at the junction of Highway 50 and Highway 89, drive south on Highway 89 for 24 miles to Markleeville. At Markleeville, continue south on Highway 89/Highway 4 for 7.5 miles to the signed turnoff for Wolf Creek on the left. Turn left (east) and drive 5.5 miles to the end of the road at Wolf Creek Meadows. The trail begins at the south end of the meadow, near the campground.

Maps: For a map of Toiyabe National Forest–Carson District, send $4 to USDA-Forest Service, 630 Sansome Street, San Francisco, CA 94111. A map of the Carson-Iceberg Wilderness is also available from the Forest Service for $4. To obtain a topographic map of the area, ask for Wolf Creek from the USGS.

Contact: Toiyabe National Forest, Carson Ranger District, 1536 South Carson Street, Carson City, NV 89701; (702) 882-2766 or fax (702) 884-8199.

Trail notes: When the temperature heats up around Markleeville, you've got two choices: Head for the mineral springs at Grover Hot Springs State Park (the cool pool, not the hot pool), or take a hike on the Wolf Creek Trail. We know, it's a tough choice. But if you pick the latter, you're in for a fine time on this easy trail along Wolf Creek, starting at 6,480 feet in elevation. The trail is wide enough to hold hands with your hiking partner (it's an old jeep road), and it meanders upstream and slightly uphill for a total of nine miles one way. A perfect day hike is just to stroll along the creek for an hour or two, find a good spot along the stream to hang out for a while, then turn around and stroll back.

Energetic types can hike four miles out to a right fork for the steep trail to Bull Lake, then continue a half mile beyond the fork to Wolf Creek Falls. The waterfall is quite impressive early in the summer, thundering over a cliff of volcanic rock.

55 East Carson River Trail

4.0 mi/2.0 hrs

Location: In the Carson-Iceberg Wilderness near Markleeville; map D4, grid j5.

User groups: Hikers, dogs, and horses. No mountain bikes. No wheelchair facilities.

Permits: No day-hiking permits are required. A free wilderness permit is required for overnight stays; they are available at the trailhead. Parking and access are free.

Directions: From Meyers at the junction of Highway 50 and Highway 89, drive south on Highway 89 for 24 miles to Markleeville. At Markleeville, continue south on Highway 89/Highway 4 for 7.5 miles to the signed turnoff for Wolf Creek on the left. Turn left (east) and drive 3.5 miles to the left turnoff signed for the East Carson River Trail. Turn left and drive one mile to the trailhead.

Maps: For a map of Toiyabe National Forest–Carson District, send $4 to USDA-Forest Service, 630 Sansome Street, San Francisco, CA 94111. A map of the Carson-Iceberg Wilderness is also available from the Forest Service for $4. To obtain a topographic map of the area, ask for Wolf Creek from the USGS.

Contact: Toiyabe National Forest, Carson Ranger District, 1536 South Carson Street Carson City, NV 89701; (702) 882-2766 or fax (702) 884-8199.

Trail notes: If it's springtime and you're itching to go hiking but there's still too much snow around Ebbetts Pass, the East Carson River Trail can be your salvation. Trailhead elevation is only 6,240 feet at the north side of Wolf Creek Meadows, which means it's snow free before other nearby areas. Bear left at the trail junction just uphill from the trailhead. An interesting journey is 1.5 miles in to Wolf Creek Lake (sometimes dry) and Railroad Canyon, the site of 19th-century logging operations. Although this trail continues onward and eventually meets up with the High Trail out of Wolf Creek Meadows, it's nearly impossible to make a loop trip out of the two trails, especially in early season. The High Trail reaches an elevation of nearly 8,000 feet and is often covered in snow. So just hike as far as you like, then head back the way you came.

Pacific Crest Trail (PCT) Section Overview

98.6 mi. one way/10.0 days

Trail elevations within this section—which extends from Highway 4 near Ebbetts Pass to the trailhead parking area near Donner Pass—range from 7,000 feet to over 10,000 feet. Although the lower reaches of the PCT are open from mid-June to mid-October, several high passes within the region may remain snow covered until mid-July, making hiking difficult. Snow-covered passes are impossible to navigate with pack stock and horses. For this reason, the highest usage period for the most heavily traveled section of the California PCT occurs during the month of August.

PCT-26 Ebbetts Pass to Blue Lakes Road

12.0 mi. one way/1.0 day

Location: From Highway 4 near Ebbetts Pass north to Blue Lakes Road just south of Carson Pass and Highway 88; map D4, grid j4.

User groups: Hikers, dogs, and horses. No mountain bikes. No wheelchair facilities.

Permits: A backcountry permit is required for traveling through various wilderness and special-use areas the trail traverses. In addition, a campfire permit is required for the use of portable camp stoves or the building of campfires (where permitted). To make it simple, you can contact the national forest, BLM, or national park office at your point of entry for a combined permit that is good for traveling through multiple-permit areas during your dates of travel.

Directions: To reach the Ebbetts Pass Trailhead, from Angels Camp, head east on Highway 4 to Ebbetts Pass. For the Blue Lakes Road Trailhead, from the Highway 88/89 interchange at Hope Valley, head west on Highway 88 to Blue

Lakes Road and turn left. Stay on Blue Lakes Road to the trailhead parking area, just before reaching Blue Lakes.

Maps: For an overall view of the trail route in this section, send $4 for each map ordered to the USDA-Forest Service, 630 Sansome Street, San Francisco, CA 94111, and ask for Lake Tahoe Basin Management Unit, Tahoe National Forest, Eldorado National Forest, and Stanislaus National Forest maps. For topographic maps of the route, request Ebbetts Pass, Pacific Valley, and Carson Pass from the USGS.

Contact: Eldorado National Forest, Information Center, 3070 Camino Heights Drive, Camino, CA 95709; (916) 644-6048.

Trail notes: As you depart Ebbetts Pass, you'll cross a series of fantastic volcanic formations in the Mokelumne Wilderness. The country here may look stark from a distance, but it is loaded with tiny wildflowers. The trail is quite good—a lot of hikers make great time in this area—but the lack of available water can become a concern. We suggest tanking up when you get the chance, such as at Eagle Creek below Reynold Peak (9,690 feet). The Mokelumne Wilderness is a relative breeze, and you'll find yourself approaching civilization at a series of small lakes in Tahoe National Forest. The trail rises up a stark, wind-blown, sandy ridge, with excellent views of the Blue Lakes, but again, no water for several miles until you drop down near Lost Lake. You'll actually cross several roads on this stretch of trail, and maybe even see a car—a moment of irony for long-distance PCT hikers.

PCT-27 Blue Lakes Road to Carson Pass

12.0 mi. one way/1.0 day

Location: From Blue Lakes Road north to Carson Pass and Highway 88; map D4, grid i3.

User groups: Hikers, dogs, and horses. No mountain bikes. No wheelchair access.

Permits: A backcountry permit is required for traveling through various wilderness and special-use areas that the trail traverses. In addition, a campfire permit is required for the use of portable camp stoves or the building of campfires (where permitted). To make it simple, you can contact the national forest, BLM, or national park office at your point of entry for a combined permit that is good for traveling through multiple-permit areas during your dates of travel.

Directions: To reach the Blue Lakes Road Trailhead, from the Highway 88/89 junction at Hope Valley, go west on Highway 88 to Blue Lakes Road and turn left. Stay on Blue Lakes Road for 11 miles to the trailhead parking, just before reaching Blue Lakes. For the Carson Pass Trailhead, from the Highway 88/89 junction at Hope Valley, go west on Highway 88 to Carson Pass.

Maps: For an overall view of the trail route in this section, send $4 for each map ordered to the USDA-Forest Service, 630 Sansome Street, San Francisco, CA 94111, and ask for Lake Tahoe Basin Management Unit, Tahoe National Forest, Eldorado National Forest, and Stanislaus National Forest maps. For topographic maps of the route, request Pacific Valley and Carson Pass from the USGS.

Contact: Eldorado National Forest, Information Center, 3070 Camino Heights Drive, Camino, CA 95709; (916) 644-6048.

Trail notes: Many hikers underestimate the climb over Elephant Back to reach Carson Pass. After all, on a map it doesn't look like much, and from a distance, as you size it up, it looks easy enough. Wrong! It's a long, grueling pull. The trip out of Blue Lakes starts easily, with a dirt road often in view and adding a bit of early angst to the affair. As you go, you keep wondering when the climb will start. Well, eventually it does, and, alas, it takes a couple of hours, enough to kick the butt of anybody who's not in shape. Guess how we know? After topping the Elephant Back, the route drops down to Carson Pass at a rest stop, where you'll likely meet humanity, but believe it or not, no water. Conserve yours if you plan to go onward, because it takes another hour of hiking before you'll reach the next trickle.

Carson Pass to Echo Lake Resort

15.8 mi. one way/1–2 days

Location: From Carson Pass at Highway 88 north to Echo Lake near Highway 50, just south of Lake Tahoe; map D4, grid i3.

User groups: Hikers, dogs, and horses. No mountain bikes. No wheelchair facilities.

Permits: A backcountry permit is required for traveling through various wilderness and special-use areas that the trail traverses. In addition, a campfire permit is required for the use of portable camp stoves or the building of campfires (where permitted). To make it simple, you can contact the national forest, BLM or national park office at your point of entry for a combined permit that is good for traveling through multiple-permit areas during your dates of travel.

Directions: To reach the Carson Pass Trailhead, from the Highway 88/89 interchange at Hope Valley, head west on Highway 88 to Carson Pass. For the Echo Lake Resort Trailhead, take Highway 50 west from Lake Tahoe to Echo Lake and Echo Summit.

Maps: For an overall view of the trail route in this section, send $4 for each map ordered to the USDA-Forest Service, 630 Sansome Street, San Francisco, CA 94111, and ask for Lake Tahoe Basin Management Unit, Tahoe National Forest, Eldorado National Forest, and Stanislaus National Forest maps. For topographic maps of the route, ask for Carson Pass, Caples Lake, and Echo Lake from the USGS.

Contact: Eldorado National Forest, Information Center, 3070 Camino Heights Drive, Camino, CA 95709; (916) 644-6048. Lake Tahoe Basin Management Unit, 870 Emerald Bay Road, Suite 1, South Lake Tahoe, CA 96150; (916) 573-2600.

Trail notes: When you've hiked on the Pacific Crest Trail for weeks, the first glimpse of Lake Tahoe in the distance can seem like a privileged view into heaven. From Ebbetts Pass, the view is just a few miles distant. You start by hiking over a short mountain rim (nice view to the west of Caples Lake), then dropping into the headwaters of the Truckee River. After making the rim, as you gaze northward, Lake Tahoe suddenly comes into view. It's like having a divine vision. In addition, finally there is water available, with several small creeks from which you can pump liquid as you walk into the Truckee headwaters. At the same time, you will be greeted by a beautiful high meadow surrounded by a light forest. All seems right with the world again. With Echo Lake Resort within one day's hiking time, you will be amazed at how inspired you can get on this section of trail. It's very pretty, weaving in and out of lush canyons, along creeks, and eventually to beautiful and tiny Showers Lake. Here the trail seems to drop off to Never-Never Land, descending very quickly and steeply in the march toward Tahoe. Contentment reigns. When you reach Little Norway, however, reality sets in. Cars are everywhere. The trail suddenly grinds down amid cabins and vacation property. There's one last hill to climb, then the PCT drops quickly to the parking lot for Echo Lake.

Almost nobody hiking the PCT immediately heads north into the Desolation Wilderness from here. Virtually everyone stops for at least a day to get cleaned up, resupplied, and fed by something other than a Power Bar. But after a day, the trail calls again. If you hear it, well, you just have to answer it.

PCT-29 Echo Lake Resort to Barker Pass

32.3 mi. one way/3.0 days

Location: From Echo Lake near U.S. 50 south of Lake Tahoe to Forest Route 3 near Barker Pass northwest of Emerald Bay; map D4, grid g2.

User groups: Hikers, dogs, and horses. No mountain bikes. No wheelchair facilities.

Permits: A backcountry permit is required for traveling through various wilderness and special-use areas the trail traverses. In addition, a campfire permit is required for the use of portable camp stoves or the building of campfires (where permitted). To make it simple, you can contact the national forest, BLM, or national park office at your point of entry for a combined permit that is good for traveling through multiple-permit areas during your dates of travel.

Directions: To reach the Echo Lake Resort Trailhead, take Highway 50 south from Lake Tahoe to Echo Lake and Echo Summit. For the Barker Pass Trailhead, from Tahoe Pines on Highway 89, head north for half a mile to the Kaspian Picnic Grounds and then bear left (west) for seven miles on Forest Service Road 15N03.

Maps: For topographic maps of the route, request Echo Lake, Emerald Bay, and Rockbound Valley from the USGS.

Contact: Lake Tahoe Basin Management Unit, 870 Emerald Bay Road, Suite 1, South Lake Tahoe, CA 96150; (916) 573-2600 or fax (916) 573-2693.

Trail notes: Before hiking this area, we first flew over it in a small airplane and understood why so many hikers are captivated with it. The Desolation Wilderness (and the neighboring Granite Chief Wilderness) are filled with sculpted granite domes and hundreds of gemlike lakes. All is pristine, yet access is also quite easy, making this the most heavily used section of the PCT all summer long. The trip starts at Echo Lake, elevation 7,400 feet, climbs up through pines, past Upper Echo Lake, and then continues up and north toward Triangle Lake, one of dozens of lakes you pass on your northward route. They come and go—Lake Margery, Lake Aloha, and then Heather, Susie, Gilmore, and finally Dicks Lake (9,380 feet); so many, in fact, that you can plan on a perfect campsite near a lake every night, providing you don't mind the company of other hikers who are drawn by classic beauty. The views are dramatic as well, across miles and miles of the glacial-carved granite, all of it pristine high Sierra landscape. As you continue, you'll discover Upper and Middle Velma Lakes, both very pretty, with good fishing. The trail skirts the ridgeline, keeping the higher knobs to the east as it gradually descends toward Richardson Lake, just beyond the Desolation Wilderness boundary—ready now to enter the Granite Chief Wilderness.

PCT-30 Barker Pass to Donner Pass

31.4 mi. one way/3.0 days

Location: From Forest Route 3 near Barker Pass northwest of Emerald Bay north to the trailhead parking area near Interstate 80 and old Highway 40 at Donner Pass; map D4, grid e1.

User groups: Hikers, dogs, and horses. No mountain bikes. No wheelchair facilities.

Permits: A backcountry permit is required for traveling through various wilderness and special-use areas the trail traverses. In addition, a campfire permit is required for the use of portable camp stoves or the building of campfires (where permitted). To make it simple, you can contact the national forest, BLM, or national park office at your point of entry for a combined permit that is good for traveling through multiple-permit areas during your dates of travel.

Directions: To reach the Barker Pass Trailhead, from Tahoe Pines on Highway 89, head north for half a mile to the Kaspian Picnic Grounds and then bear left (west) for seven miles on Forest Service Road 15N03. For the Donner Pass Trailhead, drive west on Interstate 80 from Truckee and exit at Castle Peak Area Boreal Ridge, just west of the Donner Summit roadside rest area. The sign for the Pacific Crest Trailhead is what you're looking for, and it's located on the south side of the highway.

Maps: For topographic maps of the route, request Emerald Bay, Rockbound Valley, Homewood, Tahoe City, Granite Chief, and Norden from the USGS.

Contact: Tahoe National Forest, Truckee Ranger District, 10342 Highway 89, North Truckee, CA 96161; (916) 587-3558 or fax (916) 587-6914. Lake Tahoe Basin Management Unit, 870 Emerald Bay Road, Suite 1, South Lake Tahoe, CA 96150; (916) 573-2600 or (916) 573-2693.

Trail notes: The trailhead at Barker Pass, 7,650 feet, is one of the best anywhere, with direct access to the Granite Chief Wilderness to the north (or the Desolation Wilderness to the south). Heading north on the PCT, the trip starts with a climb of 800 feet to enter Granite Chief, and once on the ridge, you're rewarded with 360-degree views of this high-mountain landscape, a mix of volcanic rock and granite ridges, much of it above tree line. Though hikers don't face the long, sustained climbs so common in the southern Sierra, it's enough of a roller-coaster ride to require hikers to be in excellent shape. The trail cuts the flank of Ward Peak at 8,470 feet, then switchbacks steeply down to Five Lakes and Five Lakes Creek (where there's good camping), and then continues up and down canyons all the way to Donner Pass. You can expect to see lots of other hikers. One reason is that along the way you'll pass near two ski resorts, Alpine Meadows and Squaw Valley, where hikers can use the ski lifts in the summer to gain easy elevation to the ridgeline, rather than having to grind out long, all-day climbs. Before making the final push to Donner Pass, a descent of more than 1,000 feet, hikers can enjoy breathtaking views of Donner Lake and miles of surrounding high country.

PCT Continuation: To continue hiking along the Pacific Crest Trail, see chapter D3.

Map E1–Marin

Adjoining Maps: East: E1 ..... *page* 270
North: D1 .... 156 South: E1 250

Note: Section E1 is divided into four chapters. For other E1 sections see pages 250 (San Francisco), 270 (East Bay), and 294 (South Bay).

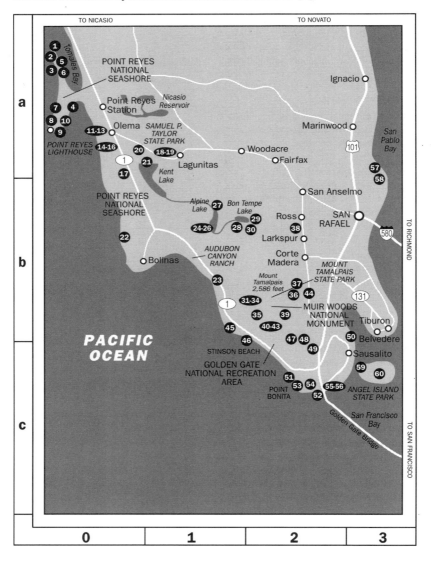

Chapter E1–Marin features:

1 Tomales Point Trail

6.0 mi/3.5 hrs

Location: In Point Reyes National Seashore in northwest Marin County; map E1–Marin, grid a0.

User groups: Hikers and horses. (Note: It is a violation of federal law to herd, chase, or otherwise harass elk.) Pierce Ranch is accessible by wheelchairs; the Tomales Point Trail is not. No dogs or mountain bikes.

Permits: No permits are required. Parking and access are free.

Directions: From U.S. 101 in Marin, take the Sir Francis Drake Boulevard exit and drive about 20 miles west on Sir Francis Drake Boulevard to the town of Olema. Turn right on Highway 1 and drive two miles. Turn left at Sir Francis Drake Highway and drive north for 6.4 miles to Pierce Ranch Road. Turn right and drive 9.5 miles to the Pierce Ranch parking area and the trailhead.

Maps: For a free map of Point Reyes National Seashore, write to them at the address below. To obtain a topographic map of the area, ask for Tomales from the USGS.

Contact: Superintendent, Point Reyes National Seashore, Point Reyes, CA 94956. Bear Valley Visitor Center, (415) 663-1092 or fax (415) 663-8132.

Trail notes: Imagine meeting up with an elk that stands five feet at the shoulders and has antlers that practically poke holes in the clouds. That just might happen on this trail, the best choice in California for those who want to see wildlife. Elk often wander quite close to the parking area, and in the evening the herd will usually congregate near a watering area set in a valley about three miles from the trailhead. We have seen as many as 75 elk in a single trip; on another, we counted 13 elk, six deer, three rabbits, and a fox —all within a two-hour span.

The trail, which has a flat walking surface and easy grades, is flanked to the west by the Pacific Ocean and to the east by Tomales Bay—both beautiful sights. By following elk paths through the low brush, you can take numerous off-trail side trips. For a bonus, continue hiking the extra mile all the way to Tomales Point. The only negative to this trip is that wind and fog occasionally envelop the area, creating poor conditions for hiking.

❷ McClures Beach Trail

1.0 mi/0.5 hr

Location: In Point Reyes National Seashore in northwest Marin County; map E1–Marin, grid a0.

User groups: Hikers only. No dogs, horses, or mountain bikes. No wheelchair facilities.

Permits: No permits are required. Parking and access are free.

Directions: From U.S. 101 in Marin, take the Sir Francis Drake Boulevard exit and drive about 20 miles west on Sir Francis Drake Boulevard to the town of Olema. Turn right on Highway 1 and drive two miles. Turn left at Sir Francis Drake Highway and drive north for 6.4 miles to Pierce Ranch Road. Turn right and drive 9.5 miles to Pierce Ranch, then turn left and drive a half mile to the parking area and the trailhead.

Maps: For a free map of Point Reyes National Seashore, write to them at the address below. To obtain a topographic map of the area, ask for Tomales from the USGS.

Contact: Superintendent, Point Reyes National Seashore, Point Reyes, CA 94956. Bear Valley Visitor Center, (415) 663-1092 or fax (415) 663-8132.

Trail notes: In the divine panorama of Point Reyes, McClures Beach is one easy-to-reach spot that is often overlooked. It sits in the shadow of nearby Pierce Ranch, with its 200-strong elk herd, and most visitors never drive the quarter mile to the road's end, except perhaps to use the rest rooms and telephone there. But an easy, half-mile walk will lead you to McClures Beach, where you'll find tide pools to the south and beachfront to the north. The best time to visit is during minus low tides, so you can survey the tide pools and watch all manner of tiny marine creatures playing their war games. Beachcombing along McClures Beach and Driftwood Beach (to the immediate north) during these low tides also can unveil unusual finds. One other thing: The sunsets here can be spectacular, especially during fall and early winter, when the skies often look like a scene from *The Ten Commandments*.

Special note: Tide pooling at this beach can be dangerous, as incoming tides can cut you off, leaving no way to escape. Consult a tide table and never, ever turn your back on the waves.

❸ Abbotts Lagoon Trail

3.2 mi/1.5 hrs

Location: In Point Reyes National Seashore in northwest Marin County; map E1–Marin, grid a0.

User groups: Hikers and mountain bikes (bikers on the first mile only; do not cross the bridge). Wheelchair accessible with assistance. No dogs or horses.

Permits: No permits are required. Parking and access are free.

Directions: From U.S. 101 in Marin, take the Sir Francis Drake Boulevard exit and drive about 20 miles west on Sir Francis Drake Boulevard to the town of Olema. Turn right on Highway 1 and drive two miles, then turn left at Sir Francis Drake Highway and drive north for 6.4 miles to

Pierce Point Road. Turn right and drive 3.3 miles to a small parking area with rest rooms. The trailhead is on the left side of the road.

Maps: For a free map of Point Reyes National Seashore, write to them at the address below. To obtain a topographic map of the area, ask for Drake's Bay from the USGS.

Contact: Superintendent, Point Reyes National Seashore, Point Reyes, CA 94956. Bear Valley Visitor Center, (415) 663-1092 or fax (415) 663-8132.

Trail notes: A short ridge shields Abbotts Lagoon from the sight of park visitors driving on Pierce Point Road. That is what keeps this trail secluded, despite being an easy walk to an excellent destination. The trail is surfaced with what is known as "soil cement" and is wheelchair accessible about halfway to the ocean bluff. From the trailhead (look for the rest rooms), the trail climbs the low ridge. Just like that, below you lies Abbotts Lagoon, and beyond that, the Pacific Ocean. The lagoon is an ideal place for novice canoeists and kayakers, providing you don't mind the one-mile portage. Bird-watching is often good here, thanks to a rare mix of waterfowl that require freshwater and seabirds migrating along the coast. If you walk past the lagoon (for a distance of 1.6 miles from the trailhead), you'll arrive at Point Reyes Beach, where there are miles and miles of sand dunes and untouched waterfront stretching to the north and south.

❹ Estero Trail

8.8 mi/4.0 hrs

Location: In Point Reyes National Seashore in northwest Marin County; map E1–Marin, grid a0.

User groups: Hikers, horses, and mountain bikes (restricted at Drake's Head). The first two miles are wheelchair accessible, with assistance. No dogs.

Permits: No permits are required. Parking and access are free.

Directions: From U.S. 101 in Marin, take the Sir Francis Drake Boulevard exit and drive about 20 miles west on Sir Francis Drake Boulevard to the town of Olema. Turn right on Highway 1 and drive two miles, then turn left at Sir Francis Drake Highway and drive north for 8.2 miles.

Turn left and drive one mile to the parking area for the Estero Trailhead.

Maps: For a free map of Point Reyes National Seashore, write to them at the address below. To obtain a topographic map of the area, ask for Drake's Bay from the USGS.

Contact: Superintendent, Point Reyes National Seashore, Point Reyes, CA 94956. Bear Valley Visitor Center, (415) 663-1092 or fax (415) 663-8132.

Trail notes: The Estero Trail crosses a valley, parallels a bay, ascends a ridge, then leads down to the waterfront, where a perfect, quiet picnic spot awaits. It's an ideal hike for newcomers to Point Reyes National Seashore, providing glimpses of a variety of settings. In addition, the round-trip is long enough for a workout yet is quite pleasant, with no gut-wrenching climbs. From the parking area, you walk 2.4 miles, then turn left at the signed junction. The compensation for climbing Drake's Head is a view of Drake's Estero, an outstanding kayaking location; the walk from the turnoff to the ridge is just 0.6 miles. From there, you turn right and walk 1.4 miles to the waterfront bordering Estero de Limantour. This is a beautiful spot, and we suggest you get an early start so you can enjoy it fully without having to rush to beat darkness on the 4.4-mile return trip.

❺ Marshall Beach Trail

2.4 mi/1.25 hrs

Location: In Point Reyes National Seashore in northwest Marin County; map E1–Marin, grid a0.

User groups: Hikers, horses, and mountain bikes. No dogs. No wheelchair facilities.

Permits: No permits are required. Parking and access are free.

Directions: From U.S. 101 in Marin, take the Sir Francis Drake Boulevard exit and drive about 20 miles west on Sir Francis Drake Boulevard to the town of Olema. Turn right on Highway 1 and drive two miles, then turn left at Sir Francis Drake Highway and drive 6.4 miles to Pierce Ranch Road. Turn right and drive 1.3 miles to just beyond the access road to Tomales Bay State Park. Turn right on Duck Cove/Marshall Beach Road and drive 2.6 miles to the parking area for the Marshall Beach Trail.

Maps: For a free map of Point Reyes National Seashore, write to them at the address below. To obtain a topographic map of the area, ask for Tomales from the USGS.

Contact: Superintendent, Point Reyes National Seashore, Point Reyes, CA 94956. Bear Valley Visitor Center, (415) 663-1092 or fax (415) 663-8132.

Trail notes: What's the most secluded beach in Marin County? Marshall Beach might just qualify. This pretty spot is set on the demure waters of Tomales Bay, sheltered from north winds by Inverness Ridge. The trailhead tends to be overlooked because there are no signs directing hikers to it until you reach the trailhead itself. In addition, the beach is overshadowed by Tomales Bay State Park, which you must drive past in order to get here—and many people don't continue driving. The hike is 1.2 miles one way, taking an elliptical route down into a gulch to a protected cove that helps shelter the beach. It's the kind of place where you can just sit and watch the water lap gently at the shore. Somehow, that is plenty.

❻ Johnstone Trail

8.0 mi/4.0 hrs

Location: In Tomales Bay State Park in northwest Marin County; map E1–Marin, grid a0.

User groups: Hikers only. The park headquarters is wheelchair accessible, but the trail is not. No dogs, horses, or mountain bikes.

Permits: A state park day-use fee is charged at the entrance station.

Directions: From U.S. 101 in Marin, take the Sir Francis Drake Boulevard exit and drive about 20 miles west on Sir Francis Drake Boulevard to the town of Olema. Turn right on Highway 1 and drive two miles, then turn left at Sir Francis Drake Highway and drive north for 6.4 miles to Pierce Ranch Road. Turn right and drive 1.2 miles, then turn right again on the access road for Tomales Bay State Park and drive 1.5 miles to the parking area and the trailhead.

Maps: A small map/brochure is available for a fee at the entrance station to Tomales Bay State Park. To obtain a topographic map of the area, ask for Tomales from the USGS.

Contact: Tomales Bay State Park, Star Route,

Inverness, CA 94937; (415) 669-1140, (415) 893-1580, or fax (415) 669-1701.

Trail notes: The centerpiece hike of Tomales Bay State Park is the Johnstone Trail, ranging from Hearts Desire Beach to Shell Beach for a one-way trip of four miles. In the process, you will pass through a procession of different habitats, including beaches, forests, meadows, and fields. The highlight is the gentle waterfront of Tomales Bay, protected from north winds by Inverness Ridge at Point Reyes. When viewed from the ridge, the bay appears cobalt blue, beautiful, and soft, unlike most saltwater bays, which look green and harsh. Up close, its docile nature makes it perfect for wading, waterplay, hand-launching small boats, or, during low tides, clamming (you must obtain a fishing license). For a good side trip, take the Jepson Trail cutoff to gain quick access to a dramatic grove of craggy, virgin Bishop pine. In the spring, wildflower blooms can be spectacular.

❼ South Beach Trail

0.1 mi/0.25 hr

Location: In Point Reyes National Seashore in northwest Marin County; map E1–Marin, grid a0.

User groups: Hikers, dogs, and horses. No mountain bikes. No wheelchair facilities.

Permits: No permits are required. Parking and access are free.

Directions: From U.S. 101 in Marin, take the Sir Francis Drake Boulevard exit and drive about 20 miles west on Sir Francis Drake Boulevard to the town of Olema. Turn right on Highway 1 and drive two miles, then turn left at Sir Francis Drake Highway and drive north for 13.6 miles. Turn right and drive to the parking lot for South Beach.

Maps: For a free map of Point Reyes National Seashore, write to them at the address below. To obtain a topographic map of the area, ask for Drake's Bay from the USGS.

Contact: Superintendent, Point Reyes National Seashore, Point Reyes, CA 94956. Bear Valley Visitor Center, (415) 663-1092 or fax (415) 663-8132.

Trail notes: If you desire miles of untouched beachfront, you've come to the right place. The Point Reyes beach extends for nearly 10 miles, all of it pristine with surf that rolls on endlessly. This short trail leads to South Beach, about three miles north of the Point Reyes Lighthouse. The beach makes a good picnic site where you can usually walk your dog on the sand (leashed, of course), and is one of the few places at Point Reyes where dogs are permitted. (Dogs may not be allowed at certain times of the year in order to protect marine mammals.) For the best stroll, walk south for about a mile to an expanse of sand dunes. It is wise to call ahead for weather conditions, as low fog is common, especially during the summer. A word of warning: Do not swim or bodysurf here. This stretch of coast is known for its treacherous undertow, the kind that can trap even the strongest swimmers, pulling people under and pushing them out to sea, despite their attempts to swim back to the beach.

8 Point Reyes Lighthouse

0.8 mi/0.5 hr

Location: In Point Reyes National Seashore in northwest Marin County; map E1–Marin, grid a0.

User groups: Hikers and mountain bikes (bikes are restricted from the stairs). Partially accessible to wheelchairs. No dogs or horses.

Permits: No permits are required. Parking and access are free. A national park day-use fee may be charged.

Directions: From U.S. 101 in Marin, take the Sir Francis Drake Boulevard exit and drive about 20 miles west on Sir Francis Drake Boulevard to the town of Olema. Turn right on Highway 1 and drive two miles, then turn left at Sir Francis Drake Highway and drive north for 18.4 miles. The road dead-ends at the parking area for the Point Reyes Lighthouse.

Maps: For a free map of Point Reyes National Seashore, write to them at the address below. To obtain a topographic map of the area, ask for Drake's Bay from the USGS.

Contact: Superintendent, Point Reyes National Seashore, Point Reyes, CA 94956. Bear Valley Visitor Center, (415) 663-1092 or fax (415) 663-8132.

Trail notes: There may be no better place on land from which to watch migrating whales. From Point Reyes, you scan the ocean, searching for what looks like a little puff of smoke on the water's surface: a whale spout. When you find one, you zoom in closer, perhaps using binoculars. If you are lucky, you might even get a tail salute. The chances are good, as 21,000 gray whales migrate past here every winter on the great whale highway just offshore of Point Reyes. The trail to the lookout is short and paved, and includes a dramatic descent on a railed stairway. On the way back, of course, you face a modest climb, steep for some, so stop to pant a bit at the three rest stops. On clear weekends, particularly in winter, the place can be crowded. A fence on the edge of the cliff keeps visitors from falling overboard and provides one of the most dramatic coastal lookouts anywhere. Sunsets are unforgettable.

9 Chimney Rock Trail

2.8 mi/1.25 hrs

Location: In Point Reyes National Seashore in northwest Marin County; map E1–Marin, grid a0.

User groups: Hikers and mountain bikes. The first quarter mile of the trail is wheelchair accessible. No dogs or horses.

Permits: No permits are required. Parking and access are free.

Directions: From U.S. 101 in Marin, take the Sir Francis Drake Boulevard exit and drive about 20 miles west on Sir Francis Drake Boulevard to the town of Olema. Turn right on Highway 1 and drive two miles, then turn left at Sir Francis Drake Highway and drive north for 17.3 miles. Turn left and drive 0.9 miles to the parking lot for the Chimney Rock Trail.

Maps: For a free map of Point Reyes National Seashore, write to them at the address below. To obtain a topographic map of the area, ask for Drake's Bay from the USGS.

Contact: Superintendent, Point Reyes National Seashore, Point Reyes, CA 94956. Bear Valley Visitor Center, (415) 663-1092 or fax (415) 663-8132.

Trail notes: A lot of visitors miss out on Chimney Rock because of its proximity to the Point Reyes Lighthouse, the feature destination of the national seashore. But the Chimney Rock lookout is easy to reach (it's about a half-hour hike), and the trail accesses a cutoff to a vista that is nearly the equal of that from the lighthouse.

From the parking area, the trail is routed 1.4 miles to land's end. Chimney Rock, or at least what is supposed to be Chimney Rock, sits right offshore. Just beyond the halfway point to land's end, hikers can take a short cutoff trail that provides great views of the Pacific Ocean. During the winter, especially between late December and March, this is a great spot to watch for the spouts of migrating whales. Another bonus is that on the way back, you can complete the last 0.8 miles on a loop trail, so you don't have to walk the same route you followed on the way in. One note: At the end of the trail, where a wooden guardrail keeps people from falling over the edge, you will look down at an assortment of coastal rocks and ask, "So, which one of those suckers is Chimney Rock?" Good question. Like most visitors, we never figured it out.

⑩ Sir Francis Drake Trail

1.9 mi/1.0 hr

Location: In Point Reyes National Seashore in northwest Marin County; map E1–Marin, grid a0.

User groups: Hikers and mountain bikes. No dogs or horses. No wheelchair facilities.

Permits: No permits are required. Parking and access are free.

Directions: From U.S. 101 in Marin, take the Sir Francis Drake Boulevard exit and drive about 20 miles west on Sir Francis Drake Boulevard to the town of Olema. Turn right on Highway 1 and drive two miles, then turn left at Sir Francis Drake Highway and drive north for 13.1 miles. Turn left and drive 1.2 miles to the parking lot at the Kenneth Patrick Visitor Center and the trailhead.

Maps: For a free map of Point Reyes National Seashore, write to them at the address below. To obtain a topographic map of the area, ask for Drake's Bay from the USGS.

Contact: Superintendent, Point Reyes National Seashore, Point Reyes, CA 94956. Bear Valley Visitor Center, (415) 663-1092 or fax (415) 663-8132.

Trail notes: Hey, this spot is not exactly a secret. In fact, you might as well stand on the Golden Gate Bridge with a megaphone and announce its existence to the world. At the trailhead, for instance, you will discover a large parking lot and visitor center, complete with exhibits, maps, and books (maybe even this one). The trail traces the back of the arcing beaches along Drake's Bay, providing scenic lookouts onto the bay's protected waters. The trail continues to the mouth of Drake's Estero, then returns via an inland loop that includes a short climb up, then down, a waterfront bluff. This is one of the more popular hikes at Point Reyes National Seashore, and why not? It is an easy walk, provides great scenic beauty, and traces three habitats: beach frontage, the mouth of a lagoon, and hillside bluffs. Just don't expect solitude.

⑪ Muddy Hollow Loop

7.1 mi/3.25 hrs

Location: In Point Reyes National Seashore at Limantour Beach in northwest Marin County; map E1–Marin, grid a0.

User groups: Hikers and horses. Muddy Hollow Road is accessible to wheelchair users who have assistance. No dogs or mountain bikes.

Permits: No permits are required. Parking and access are free.

Directions: From U.S. 101 in Marin, take the Sir Francis Drake Boulevard exit and drive about 20 miles west on Sir Francis Drake Boulevard to the town of Olema. Turn right on Highway 1 and drive 100 yards. Turn left on Bear Valley Road and drive north for two miles to Limantour Road. Turn left and drive about 7.6 miles to Limantour Beach and the trailhead.

Maps: For a free map of Point Reyes National Seashore, write to them at the address below. To obtain a topographic map of the area, ask for Drake's Bay from the USGS.

Contact: Superintendent, Point Reyes National Seashore, Point Reyes, CA 94956. Bear Valley Visitor Center, (415) 663-1092 or fax (415) 663-8132.

Trail notes: This is one of the greatest coastal loop hikes anywhere. The Muddy Hollow Loop is routed through various settings and terrain, but starts and ends right on the beach. The most striking element of the hike is witnessing the regenerative powers of the land, as these coastal foothills—ravaged by the wildfire of October 1995—are now blooming and revegetating. From the trailhead at Limantour Beach, you hike north up Muddy Hollow, a shallow valley that drains rainfall into the Estero de Limantour. After 1.4 miles, turn left on Muddy Hollow "Road" and hike 2.1 miles. Here the trail crosses the coastal hills, climbing to about 300 feet then dropping into another valley and crossing Glenbrook Creek. Seeing the remnants of fire damage being overcome by budding plant life can provide a profound and lasting impact. Turn left at the Glenbrook/Estero Trail, which leads back to the parking area over the course of 3.9 miles. The latter sector traces the shore of the Estero, a serene setting on calm, blue-sky days. From the Limantour parking area, this is also an excellent jump-off spot for canoeing and kayaking. The Estero de Limantour is protected by the narrow Limantour sand spit.

⑫ Coast Trail

15.0 mi. one way/2.5 days

Location: In Point Reyes National Seashore in northwest Marin County; map E1–Marin, grid a0.

User groups: Hikers and horses. Mountain bikes are permitted only from the Laguna Trailhead to the Coast Campground and are otherwise prohibited. Partially accessible to wheelchair users who have assistance. No dogs.

Permits: No permits are required. Parking and access are free.

Directions: From U.S. 101 in Marin, take the Sir Francis Drake Boulevard exit and drive about 20 miles west on Sir Francis Drake Boulevard to the town of Olema. Turn right on Highway 1 and drive about 100 yards. Turn left at Bear Valley Road and drive north for two miles to Limantour Road. Turn left and drive six miles. Turn left on the access road for the Point Reyes Hostel. The trailhead is just before the hostel, on the right.

Maps: For a free map of Point Reyes National Seashore, write to them at the address below. To obtain topographic maps of the area, ask for Inverness and Double Point from the USGS.

Contact: Superintendent, Point Reyes National Seashore, Point Reyes, CA 94956. Bear Valley Visitor Center, (415) 663-1092 or fax (415) 663-8132.

Trail notes: Of the handful of overnight hiking trips available in the Bay Area, the Coast Trail provides the most extended tour into a land of charm. Located north of Bolinas on the remote Marin Coast, the trail offers camps at ocean bluffs, great ridge lookouts, coastal lakes, a beach with sculptured rocks and tide pools, and a rare coastal waterfall. The continuous backcountry route is 15 miles long, enough to allow lingering hikers to spend a weekend at it (Friday evening through Sunday) and short enough for the ambitious to tackle in a single day. There are only a few catches: You need a hiking partner who will double as a shuttle driver, so you can leave a car at each end of the trail. While camping is free, you must make a reservation through the headquarters of Point Reyes National Seashore. You'll need to come prepared to cook your food using a small backpack stove, not a campfire. And tents are recommended, because the coastal weather is the most unpredictable in the Bay Area—clear, calm, and warm one day, then suddenly foggy, windy, and clammy the next.

The best trailhead for the Coast Trail is at the Point Reyes Hostel, from where you will hike north to south, keeping the wind at your back and out of your face. The first camp, Coast Camp, is an easy 2.8-miler, ideal for those heading out on a Friday evening after work. As you hike in, you'll have a panoramic view of the reborn coastal foothills, which were burned in the wildfire of October 1995, though luckily the campground and trail were untouched. The sound of ocean waves will waft you to sleep. The next day, you will hike south, getting glimpses along the way of Sculptured Beach, with its magnificent rock stacks and tunnels. A 0.2-mile cutoff drops down to the beach, allowing you to explore the unique geologic formations and tide pools there. Continuing on, the Coast Trail eventually turns inland, then drops down a canyon and to Wildcat Camp, set on a bluff overlooking the ocean. This ends a 6.6-mile day, seven miles if you take the cutoff to Sculptured Beach.

On day three, figure on a 5.6-mile closeout, with plenty of sideshows. You will hike past a series of coastal lakes, nearby Wildcat Lake, and little Ocean Lake, and have the opportunity to see Alamere Falls, a pretty waterfall that tumbles to the beach. After climbing to a short ridge, you will skirt above Pelican Lake and along the northern shore of Bass Lake. The trail then heads up a coastal hill, topping out at 563 feet, before lateraling down a canyon and back to ocean bluffs. Following the trail, you turn left and in a mile arrive at the Palomarin Trailhead. You will be ready to reach your shuttle car and head for the barn. If you have a shuttle partner, this is one of the Bay Area's greatest hikes.

⑬ Laguna Loop Trail

5.5 mi/2.5 hrs

Location: In Point Reyes National Seashore in northwest Marin County; map E1–Marin, grid a0.

User groups: Hikers and horses. Mountain bikes are permitted only from the Laguna Trailhead to the Coast Campground and are otherwise prohibited. No dogs. No wheelchair facilities.

Permits: No permits are required. Parking and access are free.

Directions: From U.S. 101 in Marin, take the Sir Francis Drake Boulevard exit and drive about 20 miles west on Sir Francis Drake Boulevard to the town of Olema. Turn right on Highway 1 and drive about 100 yards. Turn left at Bear Valley Road and drive north for two miles to Limantour Road. Turn left and drive six miles. Turn left on the access road for the Point Reyes Hostel and drive 0.2 miles past the hostel to the trailhead on the right side of the road.

Maps: For a free map of Point Reyes National Seashore, write to them at the address below. To obtain a topographic map of the area, ask for Inverness from the USGS.

Contact: Superintendent, Point Reyes National Seashore, Point Reyes, CA 94956. Bear Valley Visitor Center, (415) 663-1092 or fax (415) 663-8132.

Trail notes: The Laguna Loop Trail allows hikers to witness an amazing process known as the genesis effect, in which land devoured by fire is now being reborn. The trailhead is just 0.2 miles down the road from the Point Reyes Hostel, adjacent to the park's Environmental Education Center. From there, the trail continues 1.8 miles up to Inverness Ridge, with great views of Drake's Bay on the way. At the ridge, you turn right and hike 0.7 miles toward Mount Wittenberg, at 1,407 feet the highest point at Point

Reyes National Seashore. On the north flank of Mount Wittenberg, hikers should turn right on the Fire Lane Trail, which loops back around for three miles to the Laguna Trailhead. This excellent loop hike entails a bit of a climb and offers Pacific lookouts, yet is short enough to complete in a few hours. Camping overnight is an option: When you reach the Mount Wittenberg trail junction, continue south on the Sky Trail (instead of turning right on the loop trail). In just half a mile you will reach Sky Camp, the most easily accessible of the Point Reyes environmental campsites.

⑭ Mount Wittenberg Loop

8.6 mi/5.0 hrs

Location: In Point Reyes National Seashore near Olema in northwest Marin County; map E1–Marin, grid a0.

User groups: Hikers and horses. No dogs or mountain bikes. No wheelchair facilities.

Permits: No permits are required. Parking and access are free.

Directions: From U.S. 101 in Marin, take the Sir Francis Drake Boulevard exit and drive about 20 miles west on Sir Francis Drake Boulevard to the town of Olema. Turn right on Highway 1 and drive about 100 yards. Turn left at Bear Valley Road and drive north for 0.7 miles. Turn left at the Seashore Information sign and drive to the parking lot for the Bear Valley Visitor Center.

Maps: For a free map of Point Reyes National Seashore, write to them at the address below. To obtain a topographic map of the area, ask for Inverness from the USGS.

Contact: Superintendent, Point Reyes National Seashore, Point Reyes, CA 94956. Bear Valley Visitor Center, (415) 663-1092 or fax (415) 663-8132.

Trail notes: The Sky Trail/Mount Wittenberg Trail is the least used of the hikes that start at Point Reyes park headquarters. Why? Simple, because this sucker is the most direct route (1.7 miles) from park headquarters at elevation 105 feet to Mount Wittenberg at 1,407 feet. That means there are fewer people here than on the other trails, and that alone is plenty reason to inspire a few wise, well-conditioned hikers. At Mount Wittenberg, the trail turns left and traces

Inverness Ridge southward, breaking out of trees as it nears the coast for ocean views. You'll also have a panoramic shot of the coastal foothills, which are recovering from the wildfire of October 1995. Along the way, you will have the option of turning left and looping back on other trails if you desire to cut the trip short. We suggest you continue to the Baldy cutoff (another three miles), then complete the loop by returning to park headquarters via the Bear Valley Trail, though it can be rather crowded. This way you have the option of making the 1.5-mile trip down to Kelham Beach from the Sky Trail/Baldy Trail junction. However, this is only for the ambitious, as it requires a 1,000-foot climb out on the way back. But hey, you wanted to be alone, right? At the least, the climb up Wittenberg and back down—a 3.4-mile round-trip, just a quick huff and a puff—is worth tightening your boots for.

⑮ Bear Valley Trail

8.2 mi/4.0 hrs

Location: In Point Reyes National Seashore near Olema in northwest Marin County; map E1–Marin, grid a0.

User groups: Hikers, horses (weekdays only), and mountain bikes (first three miles only). The 1.5-mile trail to Divide Meadow is wheelchair accessible with a lot of assistance. No dogs.

Permits: No permits are required. Parking and access is free.

Directions: From U.S. 101 in Marin, take the Sir Francis Drake Boulevard exit and drive about 20 miles west on Sir Francis Drake Boulevard to the town of Olema. Turn right on Highway 1 and drive about 100 yards. Turn left at Bear Valley Road and drive north for 0.7 miles. Turn left at the Seashore Information sign and drive to the parking lot for the Bear Valley Visitor Center.

Maps: For a free map of Point Reyes National Seashore, write to them at the address below. To obtain a topographic map of the area, ask for Inverness from the USGS.

Contact: Superintendent, Point Reyes National Seashore, Point Reyes, CA 94956. Bear Valley Visitor Center, (415) 663-1092 or fax (415) 663-8132.

Trail notes: The Bear Valley Trail has all the ingredients needed to earn a "10" rating. Starting with a pretty route through forests, it leads past Divide Meadow to Bear Valley then down along Coast Creek to the beach, Arch Rock, and the Sea Tunnel, where the views are marvelous. So, you ask, why is it rated only a "6"? The answer is because the trail is actually a park service road made of compressed rock, and it gets a ton of traffic, including bicycles. This is the most heavily used trail in Point Reyes National Seashore. The best element is that it is wheelchair accessible and is in fact one of the prettiest wheelchair routes in California. Just put it in power drive, for there's a modest 215-foot climb from park headquarters to Divide Meadow. Wheelchairs and bikes are permitted to the Glen Camp Trail, 3.2 miles from park headquarters. After that, you hike down the Coast Creek drainage on a 0.7-mile trek to the beach.

⑯ Rift Zone Trail

5.2 mi. one way/2.25 hrs

Location: In Point Reyes National Seashore near Olema in northwest Marin County; map E1–Marin, grid a0.

User groups: Hikers and horses. No dogs or mountain bikes. No wheelchair facilities.

Permits: No permits are required. Parking and access are free.

Directions: From U.S. 101 in Marin, take the Sir Francis Drake Boulevard exit and drive about 20 miles west on Sir Francis Drake Boulevard to the town of Olema. Turn right on Highway 1 and drive about 100 yards. Turn left at Bear Valley Road and drive north for 0.7 miles. Turn left at the Seashore Information sign and drive to the parking lot for the Bear Valley Visitor Center.

Maps: For a free map of Point Reyes National Seashore, write to them at the address below. To obtain a topographic map of the area, ask for Inverness from the USGS.

Contact: Superintendent, Point Reyes National Seashore, Point Reyes, CA 94956. Bear Valley Visitor Center, (415) 663-1092 or fax (415) 663-8132.

Trail notes: Some of the best advice we ever got was this: Don't let school interfere with your education. Well, the Rift Zone Trail provides a lesson from the University of Nature, with one of the world's classic examples of an earthquake fault line: the San Andreas Fault. From park headquarters, it's a 5.2-mile one-way hike to the Five Brooks Trailhead, best completed with a shuttle car. Along the way, the trail traces along Olema Creek, where horizontal movement of 21 feet was recorded during the 1906 earthquake. Much evidence of earthquake activity is visible on this trail, including parallel ridges, but the most obvious sign is the clear difference in vegetation types on each side of the fault. The trail gets heavy use, has no difficult grades, and requires only a few short ups and downs near its southern junction with the Five Brooks Trailhead.

⑰ Olema Valley

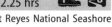

Location: In Point Reyes National Seashore south of Olema in northwest Marin County; map E1–Marin, grid a0.

User groups: Hikers, horses, and mountain bikes. No dogs. No wheelchair facilities.

Permits: No permits are required. Parking and access are free.

Directions: From U.S. 101 in Marin, take the Sir Francis Drake Boulevard exit and drive about 20 miles west on Sir Francis Drake Boulevard to the town of Olema. Turn left on Highway 1 and drive 3.6 miles to the Five Brooks Trailhead, located on the west side of the road.

Maps: For a free map of Point Reyes National Seashore, write to them at the address below. To obtain a topographic map of the area, ask for Bolinas from the USGS.

Contact: Superintendent, Point Reyes National Seashore, Point Reyes, CA 94956. Bear Valley Visitor Center, (415) 663-1092 or fax (415) 663-8132.

Trail notes: The phenomenon of two parallel creeks running in opposite directions is the featured attraction of the Olema Valley Trail, which starts at the Five Brooks Trailhead (elevation 180 feet) and runs adjacent to the San Andreas Fault rift zone. Two earth plates moving in opposite directions created the fault line, resulting in the strange marvel of Olema Creek and Pine Gulch Creek. From the trailhead, it's 1.3 miles to the headwaters of Pine Gulch Creek. From there, you can hike southward for four miles along the pretty creek, before the trail ends at Highway 1.

Most hikers turn back long before that, but with a partner and a shuttle car, it makes a great one-way hike, 5.3 miles in all.

⑱ Barnabe Trail

5.0 mi/3.5 hrs

Location: In Samuel P. Taylor State Park west of San Rafael; map E1–Marin, grid a1.

User groups: Hikers, dogs, and mountain bikes (bikes are not permitted on spur trails). The park headquarters is wheelchair accessible, but the trail is not. No horses.

Permits: A $5 state park day-use fee is charged at the entrance station.

Directions: From U.S. 101 in Marin, take the Sir Francis Drake Boulevard exit. Turn west on this road and drive 14.5 miles to the park entrance on the left.

Maps: A small map/brochure is available for a fee at the entrance station to Samuel P. Taylor State Park. To obtain a topographic map of the area, ask for San Geronimo from the USGS.

Contact: Samuel P. Taylor State Park, P.O. Box 251, Lagunitas, CA 94938; (415) 488-9897 or fax (415) 488-4315. Marin District Headquarters, (415) 893-1580.

Trail notes: Samuel P. Taylor State Park is a beautiful redwood retreat set along the primary access road to Point Reyes. The Barnabe Trail, a steep fire road through the park, climbs 2.5 miles up to Barnabe Peak (1,466 feet in elevation). It's a love/hate deal for hikers because the trail is steep and not all that intimate, yet the summit is a scenic viewpoint, with Inverness Ridge, Point Reyes, and the Pacific Ocean off to the west. From the peak it is also common on warm days to see hawks and vultures floating aloft on rising thermals with nary a wingbeat.

The landscape of the park changes dramatically over the course of this hike. The canyon bottoms and north-facing slopes are cool and shaded, marked with coastal redwoods. As you climb out of the canyon on the 1,300-foot ascent to the summit, you will rise to open grasslands that are always lush and green by spring. Since the trail is a dirt service road, leashed dogs and bicycles are permitted and all users are urged to share the route, using the utmost courtesy.

⑲ Pioneer Tree Trail

2.0 mi/1.0 hrs

Location: In Samuel P. Taylor State Park west of San Rafael; map E1–Marin, grid a1.

User groups: Hikers only. The park headquarters is wheelchair accessible, but the trail is not. No dogs, horses, or mountain bikes.

Permits: A $5 state park day-use fee is charged at the entrance station.

Directions: From U.S. 101 in Marin, take the Sir Francis Drake Boulevard exit. Turn west on this road and drive 14.5 miles to the park entrance on the left.

Maps: A small map/brochure is available for a fee at the entrance station to Samuel P. Taylor State Park. To obtain a topographic map of the area, ask for San Geronimo from the USGS.

Contact: Samuel P. Taylor State Park, P.O. Box 251, Lagunitas, CA 94938; (415) 488-9897 or fax (415) 488-4315. Marin District Headquarters, (415) 893-1580.

Trail notes: If you like big trees and a simple, quiet walk, the Pioneer Tree Trail in Samuel P. Taylor State Park will provide it. This loop circles through the park's prize grove of coastal redwoods, the species that produces the tallest trees in the world. The trailhead is at the south side of Lagunitas Creek at the Redwood Grove Picnic Area, about a quarter mile from park headquarters. From there, you hike up Wildcat Canyon, then traverse across to the Irving Creek drainage and follow that creek down near its confluence with Lagunitas Creek. The last half mile traces the southern edge of the creek back to the picnic area. It's a pleasant hike on a soft dirt trail, surrounded by the scent of redwoods, and includes a 400-foot climb and drop. Bicycles are prohibited on this route from all but the half-mile service road along Lagunitas Creek.

⑳ Bolinas Ridge

10.2 mi. one way/4.5 hrs

Location: In northwest Marin County west of San Rafael; map E1–Marin, grid a1.

User groups: Hikers, dogs, horses, and mountain bikes. No wheelchair facilities.

Permits: No permits are required. Parking and access are free.

Directions: From U.S. 101 in Marin, take the Sir Francis Drake Boulevard exit. Turn west on this road and drive 18 miles (or 3.4 miles past the entrance station to Samuel P. Taylor State Park). The trailhead is on the left side of the road. Park along the road.

Maps: This trail is included on a free map of Point Reyes National Seashore; write to Superintendent, Point Reyes National Seashore, Point Reyes, CA 94956. To obtain topographic maps of the area, ask for Inverness, San Geronimo, and Bolinas from the USGS.

Contact: Golden Gate National Recreation Area (GGNRA), Fort Mason, Building 201, San Francisco, CA 94123; (415) 663-1092, (415) 556-0560, or fax (415) 331-1428.

Trail notes: Spectacular lookouts across miles of foothills as well as an excellent mountain bike route make this a premier trip. It is a perfect one-way hike, if you arrange to have a shuttle car waiting for you at trail's end. The surrounding landscape offers a heavily wooded slope and Kent Lake to the east, Olema Valley and Inverness Ridge to the west, and Bolinas Lagoon and the Pacific Ocean to the south. The trail crosses atop Bolinas Ridge, through some of the most remote land in the GGNRA. The trailhead near Olema starts with a 700-foot climb in the first 2.5 miles. Many hikers call it quits here, stopping to enjoy the view, then turning around and heading home. Continue, though, and the trail keeps climbing, all the way to 1,329 feet in the first four miles. From that point on, the hike becomes much easier, with only moderate drops and ascents over the last 6.2 miles to the trail's end on Bolinas-Fairfax Road. Mountain biking is permitted, but hikers need not fear: the trail is not only wide enough for everyone, but has very few hidden turns. Note: Some people (especially bicyclists) prefer to complete this trail in the opposite direction in order to avoid the climb.

㉑ Kent Dam Trail

1.8 mi/1.0 hr

Location: In northwest Marin County west of San Rafael; map E1–Marin, grid a1.

User groups: Hikers, dogs, and mountain bikes. No horses. No wheelchair facilities.

Permits: No permits are required. Groups are limited to 19 people. Parking and access are free.

Directions: From U.S. 101 in Marin, take the Sir Francis Drake Boulevard exit. Turn west on this road and drive about 12 miles, just past Shafter Bridge, which spans Paper Mill Creek. Park here and look for the locked gate at the entrance to the trailhead on the left.

Maps: This trail is included on a free map of Point Reyes National Seashore; write to Superintendent, Point Reyes National Seashore, Point Reyes, CA 94956. To obtain topographic maps of the area, ask for San Geronimo and Bolinas from the USGS.

Contact: Marin Water District, (415) 924-4600 or fax (415) 927-4953. North Marin Water District, (415) 897-4133. Western Boat in San Rafael, (415) 454-4177.

Trail notes: Most people are astounded the first time they see Kent Lake, for they have no idea such a huge lake is secreted away in a Marin canyon. But here it is, nearly four miles from north to south, with an additional large arm extending east into Big Carson Creek. One reason the lake remains little known to outsiders is that the parking at the trailhead is quite poor, just a few spaces along Sir Francis Drake Boulevard. From there you hike on a ranch road along Lagunitas Creek for about a mile, arriving at the east side of Peters Dam. By damming the canyon on Lagunitas Creek, the Marin Water District created this massive lake and at the same time annihilated the runs of steelhead and silver salmon by dewatering the stream and blocking the migratory path to spawning areas. No water contact is permitted, but quite a few people go swimming here anyway in the summer. Some get caught and cited when water district officials make the occasional patrol. Fishing is only fair for bass, and the Department of Fish and Game never makes stocks.

㉒ Alamere Falls Trail

8.4 mi/4.0 hrs

Location: In Point Reyes National Seashore northwest of Bolinas; map E1–Marin, grid b0.

User groups: Hikers and horses. No dogs or mountain bikes. No wheelchair facilities.

Permits: No permits are required. Parking and access are free.

Directions: From U.S. 101 in Marin, take the Sir Francis Drake Boulevard exit and drive about 20 miles west on Sir Francis Drake Boulevard to the town of Olema. Turn left on Highway 1 and drive 8.9 miles south to Olema-Bolinas Road. Turn right and drive 2.1 miles to Mesa Road. Turn right and drive 5.8 miles to the Palomarin Trailhead.

Maps: For a free map of Point Reyes National Seashore, write to them at the address below. To obtain topographic maps of the area, ask for Bolinas and Double Point from the USGS.

Contact: Superintendent, Point Reyes National Seashore, Point Reyes, CA 94956. Bear Valley Visitor Center, (415) 663-1092 or fax (415) 663-8132.

Trail notes: The water from Alamere Falls tumbles down Alamere Creek and over an ocean bluff, cascading 40 feet to the beach below and into the Pacific Ocean. It is one of the few ocean bluff waterfalls anywhere, and after winter rains it is amazing how full, big, and beautiful it can become. The best starting point is the Palomarin Trailhead, from which you'll hike the southern end of the Coast Trail. The trail is routed along the ocean for about a mile, then heads up in the coastal hills to an elevation of about 500 feet and back down westward for two miles to the falls. In the process, you will skirt the northern end of Bass Lake, and a mile later, along the ridge overlooking larger Pelican Lake. When you near the ocean, an option is to take the 0.4-mile cutoff trail to Double Point, which provides a great ocean lookout and a close-up view of Stormy Stack, a huge sea rock.

㉓ Audubon Canyon Ranch Trail

0.4 mi/0.25 hr

Location: On the Marin coast near Bolinas Lagoon; map E1–Marin, grid b1.

User groups: Hikers only. No dogs, horses, or mountain bikes. No wheelchair facilities.

Permits: Entrance to the ranch is free, but donations are requested. The ranch is only open on weekends and holidays from spring through midsummer.

Directions: From U.S. 101 in Marin, take the Sir Francis Drake Boulevard exit and drive about 20 miles west on Sir Francis Drake Boulevard to the town of Olema. Turn left on Highway 1 and drive south for 10.5 miles, then turn left into Audubon Canyon Ranch.

Maps: A small trail map/brochure is available at ranch headquarters. To obtain a topographic map of the area, ask for Bolinas from the USGS.

Contact: Audubon Canyon Ranch, 4900 Highway 1, Stinson Beach, CA 94970; (415) 868-9244.

Trail notes: Here is a little slice of paradise, the premier place on the Pacific Coast to view herons and egrets, those large, graceful sea-birds, as they court, mate, nest, and rear their young. From ranch headquarters, the hike is short but steep, requiring about 20 minutes to reach the canyon overlook. Benches are provided for rest stops. Spotting scopes installed at the top can be used to peer across the valley and zero in on the giant nests in the redwoods. Bird-watchers might want to repeat this great trip again and again, tracking the mating process of the great birds. May and June are usually the best times to come. In May the eggs start hatching, and by June there can be as many as 200 hatchlings in the different nests. They eagerly await breakfast, lunch, and dinner, provided when their huge parents return from Bolinas Lagoon and vomit the goodies all over the nest. Hey, what's for dessert?

Special note: It is important to remember that Audubon Canyon Ranch is open only on weekends and holidays, 10 A.M. to 4 P.M., spring through midsummer. It is closed the rest of the year.

㉔ Alpine/Kent Lake Pump Trail

6.0 mi/3.0 hrs

Location: On the northwest slopes of Mount Tamalpais at Alpine Lake Dam; map E1—Marin, grid b1.

User groups: Hikers, dogs, horses, and mountain bikes. No wheelchair facilities.

Permits: No permits are required. Groups are limited to 19 people. Parking and access are free.

Directions: From U.S. 101 in Marin, take the Sir Francis Drake Boulevard exit and drive six miles west to the town of Fairfax. Turn left at the first gas station in Fairfax on Pacheco Road and then make an immediate right onto Broadway Avenue. In one block, turn left on Bolinas Road and drive west about five miles, continuing along Alpine Lake. Park on the right side of the road near the hairpin turn and look for the gated service road/trailhead.

Alternate route: From U.S. 101 in Marin, take the Sir Francis Drake Boulevard exit and head west into San Anselmo. Turn left at Center Boulevard and drive to the town of Fairfax, where Center Boulevard becomes Broadway Avenue. In Fairfax, turn left on Bolinas Road and drive west about five miles, continuing along Alpine Lake. Park on the right side of the road near the hairpin turn and look for the gated service road/trailhead.

Maps: For a hiking/biking map, write to the Marin Water District at the address below. A detailed hiking map of the area is available for a fee from Olmsted Brothers Map Company, P.O. Box 5351, Berkeley, CA 94705. To obtain a topographic map of the area, ask for Bolinas from the USGS.

Contact: Marin Water District, 220 Nellen Avenue, Corte Madera, CA 94925; (415) 924-4600 or fax (415) 927-4953. North Marin Water District, (415) 897-4133.

Trail notes: Hiking this trail can make you feel like you're exploring a slice of Tennessee wilderness, not a location just five miles from the Marin suburbs. Tracing the ins and outs of Lagunitas Creek amid oak and madrone woodlands, the trail is quite pretty. It is actually a service road for the pump station between Alpine Dam and the headwaters of Kent Lake, following Lagunitas Creek as it pours northward. The trailhead is located at the north side of Alpine Dam; from there, the route follows a gentle grade down along the stream. It's about 1.5 miles to the headwaters of Kent Lake; another half mile after that you will begin seeing the main lake. Throughout this area, you can take a short departure from the trail at any point to find an ideal setting for a picnic. Many trails require hikers to make a great physical investment in return for peace and solitude. Not this one.

㉕ Cataract Falls

2.5 mi/1.5 hrs

Location: On the northwest slopes of Mount Tamalpais at Alpine Lake Dam; map E1–Marin, grid b1.

User groups: Hikers and dogs. No horses or mountain bikes. No wheelchair facilities.

Permits: No permits are required. Groups are limited to 19 people. Parking and access are free.

Directions: From U.S. 101 in Marin, take the Sir Francis Drake Boulevard exit and drive six miles west to the town of Fairfax. Turn left at the first gas station in Fairfax on Pacheco Road and then make an immediate right onto Broadway Avenue. In one block, turn left on Bolinas Road. Drive about five miles, continuing along Alpine Lake. Cross the dam and park on the side of the road at the hairpin turn on Bolinas Road.

Alternate route: From U.S. 101 in Marin, take the Sir Francis Drake Boulevard exit and head west into San Anselmo. Turn left at Center Boulevard and drive to the town of Fairfax, where Center Boulevard becomes Broadway Avenue. In Fairfax, turn left on Bolinas Road and drive about five miles, continuing along Alpine Lake. Cross the dam and park on the side of the road at the hairpin turn on Bolinas Road.

Maps: A map/brochure of Mount Tamalpais State Park is available for a small fee at the visitor center or by writing to the state park at the address below. A detailed hiking map of the area is available for a fee from Olmsted Brothers Map Company, P.O. Box 5351, Berkeley, CA 94705. To obtain a topographic map of the area, ask for Bolinas from the USGS.

Contact: Mount Tamalpais State Park, 801 Panoramic Highway, Mill Valley, CA 94941; (415) 388-2070 or fax (415) 388-2968. Marin District Headquarters, (415) 893-1580. Marin Water District, (415) 924-4600 or fax (415) 927-4953.

Trail notes: Cataract Falls is not a single waterfall, but a series of cascades that rush down a beautifully wooded canyon set in the northwest slopes of Mount Tamalpais. And you pay for this one. The hike is quite challenging, er, make that steep, um, make that a real heart-thumper. From the trailhead at the south end of Alpine Lake at elevation 644 feet, you face a 750-foot climb over the span of just a mile to reach the falls at 1,400 feet. That is why many hikers take the easier route from the Laurel Dell Trailhead, a 240-foot drop over 0.4 miles.

In late winter, especially when the skies have just cleared after heavy rains, the cascades in this canyon can look like something found in Hawaii. That is particularly true when rays of sunlight catch the droplets of springwater just right, making them sparkle. From top to bottom, there's one cascade after another, bottomed out by a silvery chute pouring into a plunge pool. This is the best-known fall in the region (so popular that finding a parking spot at the trailhead can be difficult on weekends). After getting your fill of this sight, return the way you came.

㉖ Lily Gulch Trail

0.6 mi/0.45 hr

Location: On the northwest slopes of Mount Tamalpais at Alpine Lake Dam; map E1–Marin, grid b1.

User groups: Hikers, dogs, horses, and mountain bikes. No wheelchair facilities.

Permits: No permits are required. Groups are limited to 19 people. Parking and access are free.

Directions: From U.S. 101 in Marin, take the Sir Francis Drake Boulevard exit and drive six miles west to the town of Fairfax. Turn left at the first gas station in Fairfax on Pacheco Road and then make an immediate right onto Broadway Avenue. In one block, turn left on Bolinas Road. Drive about five miles, continuing along Alpine Lake. Park along the road at Alpine Lake's second major cove, Lily Gulch.

Alternate route: From U.S. 101 in Marin, take the Sir Francis Drake Boulevard exit and head west into San Anselmo. Turn left at Center Boulevard and drive to Fairfax, where Center Boulevard becomes Broadway Avenue. In Fairfax, turn left on Bolinas Road and head west about five miles, continuing along Alpine Lake. Park along the road at Alpine Lake's second major cove, Lily Gulch.

Maps: For a hiking/biking map, write to the Marin Water District at the address below. A detailed hiking map of the area is available for a fee from Olmsted Brothers Map Company, P.O. Box 5351, Berkeley, CA 94705. To obtain a topographic map of the area, ask for Bolinas from the USGS.

Contact: Marin Water District, 220 Nellen Avenue, Corte Madera, CA 94925; (415) 924-4600 or fax (415) 927-4953.

Trail notes: If you don't have much time, but want to make an aerobic climb to a Marin landmark, the Lily Gulch Trail to Dutchman's Rock provides that opportunity. The trailhead is very easy to reach; you'll find it at a pullout on the right side of Bolinas-Fairfax Road where the road bends and rises steeply around one of Alpine Lake's arms. From there, the trail is routed up Lily Gulch, which displays a winsome creek in the winter, but after just 0.2 miles, you turn right on the Dutchman's Rock cutoff trail and start ascending. In little more than a tenth of a mile, you will reach ol' Dutchman, set at 1,217 feet, one of the highest points—along with Liberty Peak at 1,410 feet to the immediate north— near the north shore of Alpine Lake. In all, you'll climb more than 500 feet over the course of 0.3 miles. Some trails on Mount Tam can get crowded, but this one never does. Why? Most people don't like hiking up.

㉗ Pine Mountain/ Carson Falls

3.0 mi/1.5 hrs

Location: On the northwest slopes of Mount Tamalpais west of Fairfax; map E1–Marin, grid b1.

User groups: Hikers, dogs, horses, and mountain bikes. No wheelchair facilities. Note that mountain bikes are allowed on Pine Mountain and Oat Hill Roads, but not on the hiking trail down to Carson Falls.

Permits: No permits are required. Groups are limited to 19 people. Parking and access are free.

Directions: From U.S. 101 in Marin, take the Sir Francis Drake Boulevard exit and drive six miles west to the town of Fairfax. Turn left at the first gas station in Fairfax on Pacheco Road and then make an immediate right onto Broadway Avenue. In one block, turn left on Bolinas Road. Drive about five miles, continuing along Alpine Lake. The parking area is located at the first

hairpin turn at Alpine Lake, along the left side of the road. Park and walk across the road to the trailhead.

Alternate route: From U.S. 101 in Marin, take the Sir Francis Drake Boulevard exit and head west into San Anselmo. Turn left at Center Boulevard and drive to the town of Fairfax, where Center Boulevard becomes Broadway Avenue. In Fairfax, turn left on Bolinas Road and head west about five miles, continuing along Alpine Lake. The parking area is located at the first hairpin turn at Alpine Lake, along the left side of the road. Park and walk across the road to the trailhead.

Maps: For a hiking/biking map, write to the Marin Water District at the address below. A detailed hiking map of the area is available for a fee from Olmsted Brothers Map Company, P.O. Box 5351, Berkeley, CA 94705. To obtain a topographic map of the area, ask for Bolinas from the USGS.

Contact: Marin Water District, 220 Nellen Avenue, Corte Madera, CA 94925; (415) 924-4600 or fax (415) 927-4953.

Trail notes: Your destination is Carson Falls, a set of small waterfalls that tumble into granite pools. The walk to this quiet, divine spot hidden on the north slopes of Mount Tamalpais is an easy stroll across hilly grasslands, often accompanied by a hawk or two floating about overhead, followed by a short jog down a canyon into the Carson Creek drainage.

The trailhead (1,078 feet) is adjacent to one of the better parking areas provided on lands administered by the Marin Water District. After parking, you cross Bolinas-Fairfax Road to reach the trailhead, Pine Mountain Road (a water district service road). The road climbs 400 feet over the course of a mile, reaching a junction with Oat Hill Road on the crest of a hill flanked on both sides by foothill grasslands. Turn left here, hike 0.3 miles, then turn right on the hiking trail that is routed 0.2 miles down to Carson Creek and the series of waterfalls. The lowest of the falls is a stunning, high silver stream that flows over a notch in a boulder and freefalls 30 feet into a beautiful pool. Of course, the cascades are best seen after a good rain, but there is usually at least a trickle of water into early summer.

㉘ Three Lakes Trail

5.5 mi/2.5 hrs

Location: On the northwest slopes of Mount Tamalpais at Lagunitas Lake near San Anselmo; map E1–Marin, grid b1.

User groups: Hikers only. No dogs, horses, or mountain bikes. No wheelchair facilities.

Permits: A $3 day-use fee is charged at the entrance station. Groups are limited to 19 people.

Directions: From U.S. 101 in Marin, take the Sir Francis Drake Boulevard exit and drive six miles west to the town of Fairfax. Turn left at the first gas station in Fairfax on Pacheco Road and then make an immediate right onto Broadway Avenue. In one block, turn left on Bolinas Road and head west about 1.5 miles. Turn left at Sky Oaks Road, drive to the park entrance, then continue past the entrance station to Lagunitas Lake.

Alternate route: From U.S. 101 in Marin, take the Sir Francis Drake Boulevard exit and head west into San Anselmo. Bear left onto Center Boulevard and drive to the town of Fairfax, where Center Boulevard becomes Broadway Avenue. In Fairfax, turn left on Bolinas Road and head west about 1.5 miles. Turn left at Sky Oaks Road, drive to the park entrance, and continue past the entrance station to Lagunitas Lake.

Maps: A map/brochure is available for a fee at the park entrance station or by contacting the Sky Oaks Ranger Station at the address below. A detailed hiking map of the area is available for a fee from Olmsted Brothers Map Company, P.O. Box 5351, Berkeley, CA 94705. To obtain a topographic map of the area, ask for San Rafael from the USGS.

Contact: Sky Oaks Ranger Station, P.O. Box 865, Fairfax, CA 94978; (415) 459-5267. Marin Water District, (415) 924-4600 or fax (415) 927-4953.

Trail notes: There is no officially designated Three Lakes Trail, so don't look for a sign. Instead, this loop hike—one of the Bay Area's best—is made up of a series of trails that lead past a trio of lakes, the focus of this adventure. No other hike in the Bay Area connects in such intimate fashion with some of the prettiest lakes around. The trailhead lies at elevation 740 feet at the Lagunitas Picnic Area, adjacent to Lagunitas

Lake, the smallest of Marin County's eight lakes. Walk west along the Bon Tempe Shadyside Trail, tracing the western shore of Bon Tempe Lake. Beyond that, connect to the Kent Trail, which follows the pristine southern edge of Alpine Lake for two miles. To loop back to Lagunitas Lake, turn left on the Kent Trail (elevation 760 feet) and climb 400 feet up Mount Tamalpais. At the junction with the Stocking Trail, turn left and loop back down (making a short jog right on Rocky Ridge Road) to the lake. A map will be very helpful, of course, so pick one up at the Sky Oaks Ranger Station.

㉙ Deer Park Trail

2.0 mi/1.25 hrs

Location: On the northwest slopes of Mount Tamalpais near San Anselmo; map E1–Marin, grid b2.

User groups: Hikers only. No dogs, horses, or mountain bikes. No wheelchair facilities.

Permits: No permits are required. Groups are limited to 19 people. Parking and access are free.

Directions: From U.S. 101 in Marin, take the Sir Francis Drake Boulevard exit and drive six miles west to the town of Fairfax. Turn left at the first gas station in Fairfax on Pacheco Road and then make an immediate right onto Broadway Avenue. In one block, turn left on Bolinas Road. Drive one-half mile, turn left on Porteous Avenue, and proceed to Deer County Park.

Alternate route: From U.S. 101 in Marin, take the Sir Francis Drake Boulevard exit and head west into San Anselmo. Turn left onto Center Boulevard and drive to the town of Fairfax, where Center Boulevard becomes Broadway Avenue. In Fairfax, turn left on Bolinas Road. Drive one-half mile, turn left on Porteous Avenue, and proceed to Deer County Park.

Maps: For a hiking/biking map, write to the Marin Water District at the address below. A detailed hiking map of the area is available for a fee from Olmsted Brothers Map Company, P.O. Box 5351, Berkeley, CA 94705. To obtain a topographic map of the area, ask for San Rafael from the USGS.

Contact: Marin Water District, 220 Nellen Avenue, Corte Madera, CA 94925; (415) 924-4600 or fax (415) 927-4953.

Trail notes: The trailhead at Deer Park is quite popular, but by taking the Deer Park Trail rather than one of the other options, you can find peace in addition to having quite a workout. You get both of these things because the trail climbs about 350 feet in less than a mile. That's steep, and this is one of those situations where you must pay for your pleasure. But pleasure you will get. As the trail rises up the slopes of Bald Hill, views open up around you, and not just of the surrounding countryside; it is common to see deer in this area, and wildflower blooms are quite good in the spring. If you want even more, you'll have an opportunity to link up with a spiderweb network of other trails in the area.

③⓪ Phoenix Lake Trail

2.7 mi/1.5 hrs

Location: On the north slope of Mount Tamalpais near Ross; map E1–Marin, grid b2.

User groups: Hikers, leashed dogs, horses, and mountain bikes (restricted from the lake's southern shoreline). No wheelchair facilities.

Permits: No permits are required. Groups are limited to 19 people. Parking and access are free.

Directions: From U.S. 101 in Marin, take the Sir Francis Drake Boulevard exit and head west for 2.5 miles. Turn left on Lagunitas Road and drive 1.1 miles into Natalie Coffin Greene Park. The lake is a quarter mile from the parking area. Parking is extremely limited.

Maps: For a hiking/biking map, write to the Marin Water District at the address below. A detailed hiking map of the area is available for a fee from Olmsted Brothers Map Company, P.O. Box 5351, Berkeley, CA 94705. To obtain a topographic map of the area, ask for San Rafael from the USGS.

Contact: Marin Water District, 220 Nellen Avenue, Corte Madera, CA 94925; (415) 924-4600 or fax (415) 927-4953.

Trail notes: Of the eight lakes in Marin County, Phoenix is the least accessible. Not only is the parking situation poor, but newcomers can have trouble finding the lake, an intolerable situation considering how beloved it is. And the little 25-acre jewel set in a pocket just west of the town of Ross is indeed well loved. From Natalie Coffin Greene Park, it's an easy 0.2-mile walk to the lake. Stairs on one side of the small dam take visitors down to a trail at the water's edge. The distance around the entire lake is 2.3 miles. In the winter, the lake is stocked with trout twice a month, and in the spring, bass fishing can be decent. As at all Marin lakes, no one is permitted to make contact with the water.

③① Laurel Dell Loop

2.5 mi/1.5 hrs

Location: In Mount Tamalpais State Park; map E1–Marin, grid b2.

User groups: Hikers and dogs. No horses or mountain bikes. No wheelchair facilities.

Permits: No permits are required. Parking and access are free.

Directions: From U.S. 101 in Marin, take the Stinson Beach/Highway 1 exit. Drive west to the stoplight at the T intersection. Turn left and drive about 2.5 miles uphill to Panoramic Highway. Turn right on Panoramic Highway and continue up the hill for 5.5 miles (past the turnoff to Muir Woods). Turn right on Pantoll Road and drive about 1.5 miles to the T intersection. Turn left on Ridgecrest Road and drive 1.4 miles to the parking area for the Laura Dell Trailhead.

Maps: A map/brochure of Mount Tamalpais State Park is available for a small fee at the visitor center or by writing to the address below. A detailed hiking map of the area is available for a fee from Olmsted Brothers Map Company, P.O. Box 5351, Berkeley, CA 94705. To obtain topographic maps of the area, ask for Bolinas and San Rafael from the USGS.

Contact: Mount Tamalpais State Park, 801 Panoramic Highway, Mill Valley, CA 94941; (415) 388-2070 or fax (415) 388-2968. Marin District Headquarters, (415) 893-1580. Marin Water District, (415) 924-4600 or fax (415) 927-4953.

Trail notes: Cataract Falls is the most adored waterfall on Mount Tamalpais, and the Laura Dell Trailhead provides the easiest route there. Instead of the gut-wrenching climb from Alpine Lake (see hike number 25), here you start high and glide down to the falls, then return via a gentle loop. The trailhead is at 1,640 feet, and from there you hike 0.4 miles on the Laurel Dell

Trail to the Laurel Dell Picnic Area. At the edge of the picnic area, get on the Cataract Falls Trail and continue to the waterfall at 1,400 feet. When running at full strength, this cascade is a truly precious sight, especially when you realize it's so close to an urban setting. At the falls, turn right on the High Marsh Trail, hike onward, then right at any of the next three trail intersections to return to the Laurel Dell Trailhead. Of the three choices, the second makes the best return loop, as the short cutoff will put you within a few hundred yards of the trailhead.

㉜ Rock Springs Trail

0.6 mi/0.5 hr

Location: In Mount Tamalpais State Park; map E1–Marin, grid b2.

User groups: Hikers only. No dogs, horses, or mountain bikes. No wheelchair facilities.

Permits: No permits are required. Parking and access are free.

Directions: From U.S. 101 in Marin, take the Stinson Beach/Highway 1 exit. Drive west to the stoplight at the T intersection. Turn left and drive about 2.5 miles uphill to Panoramic Highway. Turn right on Panoramic Highway and continue up the hill for 5.5 miles (past the turnoff to Muir Woods). Turn right on Pantoll Road and drive 1.5 miles to a parking area across from a T intersection. This is the Rock Springs Trailhead.

Maps: A map/brochure of Mount Tamalpais State Park is available for a small fee at the visitor center or by writing to the address below. A detailed hiking map of the area is available for a fee from Olmsted Brothers Map Company, P.O. Box 5351, Berkeley, CA 94705. To obtain a topographic map of the area, ask for San Rafael from the USGS.

Contact: Mount Tamalpais State Park, 801 Panoramic Highway, Mill Valley, CA 94941; (415) 388-2070 or fax (415) 388-2968. Marin District Headquarters, (415) 893-1580. Marin Water District, (415) 924-4600 or fax (415) 927-4953.

Trail notes: Five trails start at Rock Springs, but our favorite is the shorty to O'Rourke's Bench, where you can have a picnic while enjoying an awesome view to the west. On one trip, the coast was socked in with low stratus clouds, appearing from this lookout as if it were a sea of fog dotted with protruding mountaintops that resembled islands. On another day, we caught an extraordinary sunset there. O'Rourke's Bench is quite easy to reach. After parking at Rock Springs, cross Ridgecrest Boulevard and take the O'Rourke's Bench Trail for 0.3 miles. After some 10 or 15 minutes, you will come upon this little bench set on a knoll at 2,071 feet. A plaque next to the bench reads: "Give me these hills and the friends I love. I ask no other heaven. To our dad O'Rourke, in joyous celebration of his 76th birthday, Feb. 25th, 1927. From the friends to whom he showed this heaven."

㉝ Barth's Retreat

2.0 mi/1.0 hr

Location: In Mount Tamalpais State Park; map E1–Marin, grid b2.

User groups: Hikers only. No dogs, horses, or mountain bikes. No wheelchair facilities.

Permits: No permits are required. Parking and access are free.

Directions: From U.S. 101 in Marin, take the Stinson Beach/Highway 1 exit. Drive west to the stoplight at the T intersection. Turn left and drive about 2.5 miles uphill to Panoramic Highway. Turn right on Panoramic Highway and continue up the hill for 5.5 miles (past the turnoff to Muir Woods). Turn right on Pantoll Road and drive 1.5 miles to a parking area across from a T intersection. This is the Rock Springs Trailhead, but there is a sign indicating Barth's Retreat.

Maps: A map/brochure of Mount Tamalpais State Park is available for a small fee at the visitor center or by writing to the address below. A detailed hiking map of the area is available for a fee from Olmsted Brothers Map Company, P.O. Box 5351, Berkeley, CA 94705. To obtain a topographic map of the area, ask for San Rafael from the USGS.

Contact: Mount Tamalpais State Park, 801 Panoramic Highway, Mill Valley, CA 94941; (415) 388-2070 or fax (415) 388-2968. Marin District Headquarters, (415) 893-1580. Marin Water District, (415) 924-4600 or fax (415) 927-4953.

Trail notes: Rarely can the features of the land change more quickly than on the hike to Barth's

Retreat on Mount Tamalpais. In just a mile, you cross a serpentine swale, pass a small creek with riparian habitat, go through a forest, and then arrive at an open area called Barth's Retreat. Barth, by the way, was one Emil Barth, a prolific musician/hiker/trail builder who constructed a camp here in the early 1900s. This hike provides a quick glimpse of the diversity Mount Tam offers. When you link it with the short hike to O'Rourke's Bench (see hike number 32), which also starts from Rock Springs, you can feel like you've seen the world in a two-hour time span.

㉞ Mountain Theater

3.0 mi/1.5 hrs

Location: In Mount Tamalpais State Park; map E1–Marin, grid b2.

User groups: Hikers only. No dogs, horses, or mountain bikes. No wheelchair facilities.

Permits: No permits are required. Parking and access are free.

Directions: From U.S. 101 in Marin, take the Stinson Beach/Highway 1 exit. Drive west to the stoplight at the T intersection. Turn left and drive about 2.5 miles uphill to Panoramic Highway. Turn right on Panoramic Highway and continue up the hill for 5.5 miles (past the turnoff to Muir Woods). Turn right on Pantoll Road and drive 1.5 miles to the T intersection. Turn right, drive a quarter mile to the parking area on the right side of the road, then walk the short distance to the Mountain Theater Trailhead.

Maps: A map/brochure of Mount Tamalpais State Park is available for a small fee at the visitor center or by writing to the address below. A detailed hiking map of the area is available for a fee from Olmsted Brothers Map Company, P.O. Box 5351, Berkeley, CA 94705. To obtain a topographic map of the area, ask for San Rafael from the USGS.

Contact: Mount Tamalpais State Park, 801 Panoramic Highway, Mill Valley, CA 94941; (415) 388-2070 or fax (415) 388-2968. Marin District Headquarters, (415) 893-1580. Marin Water District, (415) 924-4600 or fax (415) 927-4953.

Trail notes: The round-trip from the Mountain Theater to West Point Inn is a classic Mount Tamalpais walk—pretty, easy, and with a landmark on each end. The theater, Mount Tam's masterpiece outdoor amphitheater, is actually a very short distance from the parking area; you cross right behind it on the Rock Springs Trail en route to West Point Inn. The trail is quiet and tranquil—especially since it's off-limits to bikes—and weaves in and out of a hardwood forest, descending easily for most of the way. Over the course of 1.5 miles, you drop 295 feet, from a trailhead elevation of 2,080 feet to the trail's end at 1,785 feet. West Point Inn offers great views and a perfect spot for a picnic lunch, and lemonade is often available inside. Here's a secret: small cabins without electricity can be rented for overnight stays; for years, we have sworn not to tell anybody about them. Until now, heh, heh, we've kept that promise.

Special note: Much of this trail is on Marin Water District land; contact this agency for a detailed map.

㉟ Bootjack Loop

6.2 mi/3.0 hrs

Location: In Mount Tamalpais State Park; map E1–Marin, grid b2.

User groups: Hikers only. No dogs, horses, or mountain bikes. No wheelchair facilities.

Permits: No permits are required. A $5 parking fee is charged.

Directions: From U.S. 101 in Marin, take the Stinson Beach/Highway 1 exit. Drive west to the stoplight at the T intersection. Turn left and drive about 2.5 miles uphill to Panoramic Highway. Turn right on Panoramic Highway and continue up the hill for 5.5 miles (past the turnoff to Muir Woods) to Pantoll Road. Turn left at the parking area, where you'll find the Pantoll Ranger Station and Trailhead.

Maps: A map/brochure of Mount Tamalpais State Park is available for a small fee at the visitor center or by writing to the address below. A detailed hiking map of the area is available for a fee from Olmsted Brothers Map Company, P.O. Box 5351, Berkeley, CA 94705. To obtain a topographic map of the area, ask for San Rafael from the USGS.

Contact: Mount Tamalpais State Park, 801 Panoramic Highway, Mill Valley, CA 94941; (415)

388-2070 or fax (415) 388-2968. Marin District Headquarters, (415) 893-1580. Marin Water District, (415) 924-4600 or fax (415) 927-4953.

Trail notes: Few hikes provide glimpses of such a dynamic, diverse, and delightful habitat as the Bootjack Loop. The trail crosses a meadow, oak woodlands, and some hilly grasslands, then submerges deep into a redwood forest and climbs back out, all in the space of 6.2 miles. It entails a steady downgrade, so you face a huff-puffer climb on the return trip, but the redwoods make it worth the grunt.

Starting at the Pantoll Ranger Station and Trailhead, elevation 1,500 feet, in Mount Tamalpais State Park, you hike north for 0.4 miles on the Alpine Trail to Van Wyck Meadow, descending 450 feet in the process. From there, you turn right on the Bootjack Trail, heading downhill along a small stream. This leg leads 1.3 miles into Muir Woods National Monument, where you turn right on the Ben Johnson Trail and begin the steep return trip. Over the next mile, the trail climbs 500 feet, flanked the entire way by one of the Bay Area's richest redwood groves, home to many gigantic trees. To complete the loop, continue up, up, and up on the Ben Johnson Trail (to the Stapelveldt Trail) for the final 0.9 miles to the Pantoll Trailhead, a total elevation gain of 1,080 feet.

㊱ East Peak Mount Tamalpais

0.2 mi/0.25 hrs

Location: In Mount Tamalpais State Park; map E1–Marin, grid b2.

User groups: Hikers only. Dogs are permitted on the paved trail, but not on the mountaintop overlook. No horses or mountain bikes. No wheelchair access on the trail, but good views are available from the wheelchair-accessible parking lot.

Permits: No permits are required. A $5 parking fee is charged.

Directions: From U.S. 101 in Marin, take the Stinson Beach/Highway 1 exit. Drive west to the stoplight at the T intersection. Turn left and drive about 2.5 miles uphill to Panoramic Highway.

Turn right on Panoramic Highway and continue up the hill for 5.5 miles (past the turnoff to Muir Woods). Turn right on Pantoll Road and drive about 1.5 miles to the T intersection. Turn right on Ridgecrest Road and drive two miles to the East Peak. The road dead-ends at the parking area at the base of the summit.

Maps: A map/brochure of Mount Tamalpais State Park is available for a small fee at the visitor center, located adjacent to the parking area, or by writing to the address below. A detailed hiking map of the area is available for a fee from Olmsted Brothers Map Company, P.O. Box 5351, Berkeley, CA 94705. To obtain a topographic map of the area, ask for San Rafael from the USGS.

Contact: Mount Tamalpais State Park, 801 Panoramic Highway, Mill Valley, CA 94941; (415) 388-2070 or fax (415) 388-2968. Marin District Headquarters, (415) 893-1580. Marin Water District, (415) 924-4600 or fax (415) 927-4953.

Trail notes: There is simply no better place in the Bay Area to watch the sun set than atop Mount Tamalpais's East Peak, for the feelings this experience inspires will stay with you for many weeks. Mount Tam is one of those rare spots that project a feeling of power, and while standing on its highest point, you can sense that power flowing right through you. The hike is very short—after all, a parking lot is set right at the foot of the summit trail—but quite steep, rising about 330 feet to the top at an elevation of 2,571 feet. An old lookout station is positioned at the summit, and hikers usually try to find a perch as close as possible to the top.

Looking off to the east, the bay resembles the Mediterranean Sea, an azure pool sprinkled with islands. And at nighttime, the lights of the bridges and the surrounding cities can give the Bay Area an almost surreal look. But the true magic happens at sunset, particularly on foggy days. The peak stands well above the fogline, and when the fiery sun dips into that low stratus to the west, orange light is refracted for hundreds of miles around. Witness this stunning sight even one time and you will gain a new perspective about what might be possible in this world. Perhaps you'll even set some new horizons for yourself.

㊲ Inspiration Point

2.6 mi/1.0 hrs

Location: In Mount Tamalpais State Park; map E1–Marin, grid b2.

User groups: Hikers, dogs, and mountain bikes. No horses. No wheelchair access on the trail, but good views are available from the wheelchair-accessible parking lot.

Permits: No permits are required. A $5 parking fee is charged.

Directions: From U.S. 101 in Marin, take the Stinson Beach/Highway 1 exit. Drive west to the stoplight at the T intersection. Turn left and drive about 2.5 miles uphill to Panoramic Highway. Turn right on Panoramic Highway and continue up the hill for 5.5 miles (past the turnoff to Muir Woods). Turn right on Pantoll Road and drive 1.5 miles to the T intersection. Turn right on Ridgecrest Road and drive two miles to the East Peak. The road dead-ends at the parking area at the base of the summit.

Maps: A map/brochure of Mount Tamalpais State Park is available for a small fee at the visitor center, located adjacent to the parking area, or by writing to the address below. A detailed hiking map of the area is available for a fee from Olmsted Brothers Map Company, P.O. Box 5351, Berkeley, CA 94705. To obtain a topographic map of the area, ask for San Rafael from the USGS.

Contact: Mount Tamalpais State Park, 801 Panoramic Highway, Mill Valley, CA 94941; (415) 388-2070 or fax (415) 388-2968. Marin District Headquarters, (415) 893-1580. Marin Water District, (415) 924-4600 or fax (415) 927-4953.

Trail notes: Inspiration Point provides a nearby alternative to the East Peak, ideal if you want the same kind of magic found at that popular summit (see hike number 36), yet without all the people. To get there, instead of heading up to the East Peak after parking, go the opposite direction and turn right on the fire road, Eldridge Grade. The trail wraps around the northern flank of the East Peak, then makes a hairpin turn to the left around North Knee, set at 2,000 feet. At this point, the bay comes into view to the east and you start to understand the attraction. But keep on, because Inspiration Peak awaits just down the road. At the hairpin

right turn, take the short but steep cutoff trail on the left and you will quickly reach the top at 2,040 feet, your vantage point for miles and miles of charmed views. All seems enchanted.

Special note: Much of this trail is on Marin Water District land, where leashed dogs are permitted.

㊳ Dawn Falls

1.4 mi/0.75 hr

Location: On the eastern slopes of Mount Tamalpais near Larkspur; map E1–Marin, grid b2.

User groups: Hikers, dogs, horses (on the adjacent fire road), and mountain bikes. No wheelchair facilities.

Permits: No permits are required. Groups are limited to 19 people. Parking and access are free.

Directions: From U.S. 101 in Marin, take the Tamalpais Drive exit, then head west on Tamalpais Drive to Corte Madera Avenue. Turn right and drive about a half mile, then turn left on Madrone Avenue and drive to Valley Way. The trailhead is at the road's end.

Maps: For a trail map, write to the Marin Water District at the address below. A detailed hiking map of the area is available for a fee from Olmsted Brothers Map Company, P.O. Box 5351, Berkeley, CA 94705. To obtain a topographic map of the area, ask for San Rafael from the USGS.

Contact: Marin Water District, 220 Nellen Avenue, Corte Madera, CA 94925; (415) 924-4600 or fax (415) 927-4953.

Trail notes: The Bay Area has many hidden waterfalls, but this one is both easy to reach and, in winter and spring, a beautiful and energizing sight. Dawn Falls, a 25-foot fountain of water, is best seen in the early morning, when rays of sunlight penetrate the atmosphere. Note, however, that in summer and fall, day after day of dry weather reduces the cascade to a trickle, and in drought years, it can go completely dry. At the trailhead, don't get confused and take the Baltimore Canyon Fire Road; that route is far less intimate than the Dawn Falls Trail, which probes a dense woodland, with model riparian habitat on each side of Larkspur Creek near the falls. This walk starts out easy and stays that way, even with the moderate 300-foot rise to the waterfall.

③ Mountain Home Trail

2.4 mi/1.0 hr

Location: In Mount Tamalpais State Park; map E1–Marin, grid b2.

User groups: Hikers only. No dogs, horses, or mountain bikes. No wheelchair facilities.

Permits: No permits are required. Parking and access are free.

Directions: From U.S. 101 in Marin, take the Stinson Beach/Highway 1 exit. Drive west to the stoplight at the T intersection. Turn left and drive about 2.5 miles uphill to Panoramic Highway. Turn right on Panoramic Highway and continue up the hill for 5.5 miles (past the turnoff to Muir Woods). Turn right on Pantoll Road and continue to the Mountain Home Inn parking area. The trailhead (Panoramic Trail) is on the west side of the road.

Maps: A map/brochure of Mount Tamalpais State Park is available for a small fee at the visitor center or by writing to the address below. A detailed hiking map of the area is available for a fee from Olmsted Brothers Map Company, P.O. Box 5351, Berkeley, CA 94705. To obtain a topographic map of the area, ask for San Rafael from the USGS.

Contact: Tourist Club, (415) 388-9987. Mount Tamalpais State Park, 801 Panoramic Highway, Mill Valley, CA 94941; (415) 388-2070 or fax (415) 388-2968. Marin District Headquarters, (415) 893-1580. Marin Water District, (415) 924-4600 or fax (415) 927-4953.

Trail notes: Want unique? You got unique: a 1.2-mile hike at Mount Tamalpais that ends at a great little inn called the Tourist Club, where you can slake your thirst with your favorite elixir. This walk is short and has only one small steep portion. To reach the Tourist Club, park at the lot at Mountain Home along Panoramic Highway. From there, take the Panoramic Trail for 0.4 miles (it parallels Panoramic Highway) to its junction with the Redwood Trail, which you then follow for three-quarters of a mile. The route laterals across the mountain slope before dropping into a pocket where the Tourist Club is perched on a slope. On weekends at this wood-framed building, not only can you get liquid refreshments, you can often drink while listening to German

music. There is no other hiking destination like it in California.

④ Matt Davis Trail

3.2 mi. one way/1.5 hr

Location: On the western slopes of Mount Tamalpais; map E1–Marin, grid b2.

User groups: Hikers only. No dogs, horses, or mountain bikes. No wheelchair facilities.

Permits: No permits are required. A $5 parking fee is charged.

Directions: From U.S. 101 in Marin, take the Stinson Beach/Highway 1 exit. Drive west to the stoplight at the T intersection. Turn left and drive about 2.5 miles uphill to Panoramic Highway. Turn right on Panoramic Highway and drive up the hill for 5.5 miles (past the turnoff to Muir Woods) to Pantoll Road. Turn left at the parking area, where you'll find the Pantoll Ranger Station and Trailhead.

Maps: A map/brochure of Mount Tamalpais State Park is available for a small fee at the visitor center or by writing to the address below. A detailed hiking map of the area is available for a fee from Olmsted Brothers Map Company, P.O. Box 5351, Berkeley, CA 94705. To obtain a topographic map of the area, ask for San Rafael from the USGS.

Contact: Mount Tamalpais State Park, 801 Panoramic Highway, Mill Valley, CA 94941; (415) 388-2070 or fax (415) 388-2968. Marin District Headquarters, (415) 893-1580. Marin Water District, (415) 924-4600 or fax (415) 927-4953.

Trail notes: The 3.2-mile section of the Matt Davis Trail from the Pantoll Trailhead down to Stinson Beach offers dramatic views of the Pacific Ocean. There are many places where you can stop, spread your arms wide, and feel as if the entire world were within your grasp. It is a great one-way hike—just make sure you go with a partner and have a shuttle car waiting at the trail's end at the Stinson Beach Firehouse. After parking at Pantoll, elevation 1,500 feet, cross the road and look for the sign marking the Matt Davis/Coastal Trail. Soon enough, you will start descending toward the beach, but not before first entering a lush grove of fir trees. Here the trail is level for nearly a mile. When you emerge, the trail begins its steep descent across open grasslands down to Stinson Beach. Only thick fog can ruin the day. Note that the entire Matt Davis Trail is technically nearly double our suggested route, with the trailhead at Mountain Home.

⑪ Steep Ravine Trail

4.0 mi/1.5 hrs

Location: On the western slopes of Mount Tamalpais; map E1–Marin, grid b2.

User groups: Hikers only. No dogs, horses, or mountain bikes. No wheelchair facilities.

Permits: No permits are required. A $5 parking fee is charged.

Directions: From U.S. 101 in Marin, take the Stinson Beach/Highway 1 exit. Drive west to the stoplight at the T intersection. Turn left on Shoreline Highway/Highway 1 and drive about 2.5 miles uphill to Panoramic Highway. Turn right on Panoramic Highway and continue up the hill for 5.5 miles (past the turnoff to Muir Woods) to Pantoll Road. Turn left at the parking area, where you'll find the Pantoll Ranger Station and Trailhead.

Maps: A map/brochure of Mount Tamalpais State Park is available for a small fee at the visitor center or by writing to the address below. A detailed hiking map of the area is available for a fee from Olmsted Brothers Map Company, P.O. Box 5351, Berkeley, CA 94705. To obtain a topographic map of the area, ask for San Rafael from the USGS.

Contact: Mount Tamalpais State Park, 801 Panoramic Highway, Mill Valley, CA 94941; (415) 388-2070 or fax (415) 388-2968. Marin District Headquarters, (415) 893-1580. Marin Water District, (415) 924-4600 or fax (415) 927-4953.

Trail notes: Hiking the Steep Ravine Trail is like being baptized by the divine spirit of nature, and those who set foot on it will find a place where they can get their own brand of religion. The trail passes through remarkably beautiful terrain, including cathedral-like redwoods, lush undergrowth, and a pretty stream. Believe it or not, this is one of the few hikes that is best done during a rainstorm. In the canyon, the forest canopy protects you from a direct assault by the raindrops. Everything becomes vibrant with life

as it drips with water. From the trailhead at Pantoll, the route descends 1,100 feet over the course of two miles, ending at Highway 1 near Rocky Point. After departing and heading downhill, it doesn't take long before the redwoods surround you. The trail follows along Webb Creek, crossing the stream eight times in all. The junction with the Dipsea Trail is a trail landmark; from this point, it's half a mile to the end.

⑫ Main Trail

2.0 mi/1.0 hr

Location: In Muir Woods National Monument near Mill Valley; map E1–Marin, grid b2.

User groups: Hikers only. No dogs (except for seeing-eye dogs), horses, or mountain bikes. The first section of the trail is wheelchair accessible.

Permits: No permits are required. Parking and access are free. Donations for printed materials are requested.

Directions: From U.S. 101 in Marin, take the Stinson Beach/Highway 1 exit. Drive west to the stoplight at the T intersection. Turn left on Shoreline Highway/Highway 1 and drive 2.5 miles uphill to Panoramic Highway. Turn right and drive 0.7 miles to the Muir Woods junction. Turn left and drive 0.8 miles to the Muir Woods parking area.

Maps: A map/brochure is available for a fee at the visitor center or by contacting Muir Woods National Monument at the address below. To obtain a topographic map of the area, ask for San Rafael from the USGS.

Contact: Muir Woods National Monument, Mill Valley, CA 94941; (415) 388-2596.

Trail notes: This just might be the most heavily used trail in the Bay Area, yet not necessarily by Bay Area residents. You see, tourists from all over the world visiting San Francisco tend to follow the same routine: After taking the obligatory picture of the Golden Gate Bridge from Vista Point, they drive to Muir Woods to see a real redwood tree. Soon enough, they find themselves on the Main Trail, a paved route set along Redwood Creek and completely encompassed by the giant trees. The trail is both very pretty and easy to walk, but more often than not it resembles a parade route. After about a mile, the trail starts to climb to the left; just like that, most of the tourists head back to the parking lot. An option is to turn this into a loop hike by taking the Hillside Trail up the west side of the canyon and looping back to the Muir Woods headquarters. The loop trail is three miles long and includes a pleasant climb.

㊸ Ocean View Trail (Panoramic Highway Trail)

3.0 mi/1.75 hrs

Location: In Muir Woods National Monument near Mill Valley; map E1–Marin, grid b2.

User groups: Hikers only. No dogs (except for seeing-eye dogs), horses, or mountain bikes. The first section of the trail is wheelchair accessible.

Permits: No permits are required. Parking and access are free. Donations for printed materials are requested.

Directions: From U.S. 101 in Marin, take the Stinson Beach/Highway 1 exit. Drive west to the stoplight at the T intersection. Turn left on Shoreline Highway/Highway 1 and drive 2.5 miles uphill to Panoramic Highway. Turn right and drive 0.7 miles to the Muir Woods junction. Turn left and drive 0.8 miles to the Muir Woods parking area.

Maps: A map/brochure is available for a fee at the visitor center or by contacting Muir Woods National Monument at the address below. To obtain a topographic map of the area, ask for San Rafael from the USGS.

Contact: Muir Woods National Monument, Mill Valley, CA 94941; (415) 388-2596.

Trail notes: When you arrive at Muir Woods and see tour buses shooting out people like popcorn from a popping machine, you'll be glad you read this, because the Ocean View Trail provides the best chance of getting away from the crowds. After passing the information stand and starting down the paved path on the valley floor, turn right on the Ocean View Trail. In under a minute, you will enter a different world, a world of solitude, beautiful redwoods, and, alas, a steep ascent.

From the valley floor, the trail heads up the east side of the canyon on a steady grade, steep enough to get you puffing. It climbs 570 feet in 1.2 miles, rising above the valley to where you can look down into a sea of redwoods. To complete the loop, turn left on the Lost Trail, elevation 750 feet, which descends quite steeply over just 0.4 miles back to the valley floor at 300 feet. There you turn left and return to headquarters on the Fern Creek Trail. A great escape.

Special note: While this trail is listed as the Ocean View Trail, most people call it the Panoramic Highway Trail. It is listed both ways on various maps and signs. Ironically, there is no ocean view.

㊹ Dipsea Trail

6.6 mi. one way/3.5 hrs

Location: On Mount Tamalpais from Mill Valley to Stinson Beach; map E1–Marin, grids b1 and b2.

User groups: Hikers only. No dogs, horses, or mountain bikes. No wheelchair facilities.

Permits: No permits required. A $5 parking fee is charged.

Directions: From U.S. 101 in Marin, take the East Blithedale/Tiburon Boulevard exit. Head west on East Blithedale (it becomes Throckmorton Street) into Mill Valley, then follow Throckmorton to Old Mill Park. The trailhead is at Old Mill Creek and the bridge, which leads to the stepped staircase.

Maps: The Dipsea Trail crosses several jurisdictions. A map/brochure of Mount Tamalpais State Park is available for a small fee at the visitor center or by contacting Mount Tamalpais State Park at the address below. A detailed hiking map of the area is available for a fee from Olmsted Brothers Map Company, P.O. Box 5351, Berkeley, CA 94705. To obtain topographic maps of the area, ask for San Rafael and Bolinas from the USGS.

Contact: Mount Tamalpais State Park, 801 Panoramic Highway, Mill Valley, CA 94941; (415) 388-2070 or fax (415) 388-2968. Marin District Headquarters, (415) 893-1580. Marin Water District, (415) 924-4600. Muir Woods National Monument, Mill Valley, CA 94941; (415) 388-2596.

Trail notes: For Marin hikers, completing the Dipsea Trail is a rite of passage, an experience that offers a glimpse into both heaven and hell in a single morning. The annual Dipsea Race has turned the trail into something of a legend, and many people have developed a classic love-hate relationship with the hike. They love it because it's the perfect east-to-west crossing of Mount Tamalpais, from Mill Valley to Stinson Beach, passing through Muir Woods in the process and making a beautiful descent to the coast. Yet they hate it because it starts at an infamous set of seemingly unending staircase steps, crosses paved roads, and, just when hikers start to get tired, throws in a killer climb up Cardiac Hill. Of course, if you haven't figured it out by now, this is a one-way-only hike, shuttle partner required.

The trail starts in Mill Valley on Cascade Way at those hated steps, 671 in all. According to park rangers, the steps spawned the legend that Marin hikers never die, they just reach the 672nd step. When the trail tops the stairs and reaches pavement, look for the faint arrows painted on the street to mark the way. They will route you along Sequoia Road, Walsh Drive, then Bay View, where you cross Panoramic Highway and finally get off the pavement and start descending into Muir Woods. From there, the trail is well signed. Noted spots include Cardiac Hill, where you are handed a 480-foot climb in 0.4 miles. In return, you are also presented with phenomenal views of the Pacific Ocean and San Francisco, as well as the knowledge that most of the rest of the trail is downhill. Over the final 2.3 miles, you descend across the Marin hills, dip into lush Steep Ravine Canyon, and push across coastal bluffs to the parking area at Stinson Beach. Like we said, it's a rite of passage.

⑮ Rocky Point Trail

0.2 mi/0.25 hr

Location: On the Marin coast south of Stinson Beach; map E1–Marin, grid b1.

User groups: Hikers only. No dogs, horses, or mountain bikes. No wheelchair facilities.

Permits: Day-use parking and access are free. For overnight stays, a reservation is required at Steep Ravine Cabins/Environmental Campsites (phone 10 days in advance, 800/444-7275).

Directions: From U.S. 101 in Marin, take the Stinson Beach/Highway 1 exit and drive to the coast at the Muir Beach Overlook. Drive about four miles north on Highway 1 to the Rocky Point access road (gated) on the left side of the highway. Directions for how to get through the access road are included in the reservation confirmation information for the Steep Ravine Environmental Cabins.

Maps: A map/brochure of Mount Tamalpais State Park is available for a small fee at the visitor center or by contacting Mount Tamalpais State Park at the address below. A detailed hiking map of the area is available for a fee from Olmsted Brothers Map Company, P.O. Box 5351, Berkeley, CA 94705. To obtain topographic maps of the area, ask for Bolinas and Point Bonita from the USGS.

Contact: Mount Tamalpais State Park, 801 Panoramic Highway, Mill Valley, CA 94941; (415) 388-2070 or fax (415) 388-2968. Marin District Headquarters, (415) 893-1580.

Trail notes: One of the hidden secrets of the great outdoors is here at Rocky Point, where primitive cabins set on an ocean bluff are available for overnight rentals. It is one of the most dramatic camp settings on the Pacific coast, with views of passing whales, pelicans and murres, freighters and fishing boats. Sunsets can be exceptional. The cabins cost $30 per night, plus a $6.75 reservation fee, and include a wood stove, picnic table, and flat wood surface for sleeping. You bring everything else, which should include good walking shoes to make the short hike down to the beach. From the cabins, you head back to the Rocky Point access road, turn right, then take the trail down to the cove, a descent of about 80 feet. Another beach trail on the north side of Rocky Point leads down to the southern end of Redrock Beach.

⑯ Owl Trail

3.5 mi/1.5 hr

Location: On the Marin coast south of Stinson Beach; map E1–Marin, grid c1.

User groups: Hikers only. No dogs, horses, or mountain bikes. The Muir Beach Overlook is wheelchair accessible, but the Owl Trail is not.

Permits: No permits are required. Parking and access are free.

Directions: From U.S. 101 in Marin, take the Stinson Beach/Highway 1 exit and drive to the coast. Turn left at the Muir Beach Overlook and drive a short distance to the parking area.

Maps: A map/brochure is available at the Marin Headlands Visitor Center or by contacting the Golden Gate National Recreation Area, Marin Headlands, at the address below. A detailed hiking map of the area is available for a fee from Olmsted Brothers Map Company, P.O. Box 5351, Berkeley, CA 94705. To obtain a topographic map of the area, ask for Point Bonita from the USGS.

Contact: Muir Woods National Monument, Mill Valley, CA 94941; (415) 388-2596 or fax (415) 389-2596. Golden Gate National Recreation Area (GGNRA), Marin Headlands, Building 1056, Fort Cronkite, Sausalito, CA 94965. Marin Headlands Visitor Center, (415) 331-1540. GGNRA headquarters, (415) 556-0560.

Trail notes: A delightful walk, this trail laterals down the coastal hillside to a secluded, rocky beach, with several sideshows along the way. The trailhead is near the Muir Beach Overlook, which alone is worth the trip for the great views of the southern Marin coast. Don't stop there like so many visitors do, but instead hike northward on the Owl Trail. From the unsigned trailhead on the north side of the parking area, the trail is routed through low-lying brush, which makes wearing shorts a sticky proposition. Starting at 440 feet, the trail descends 240 feet in 0.9 miles on its northward course to Slide Ranch. Slide Ranch consists of a hamlet of wood huts and a small farm with goats, sheep, chickens, and even some ducks, all favorites of youngsters. Two-foot-tall great horned owls sometimes roost in the giant cypress trees at Slide Ranch, but they can be difficult to see in their natural camouflage. From here the trip down to the beach adds another 15 minutes to your walk; the descent is slippery, and a rope has been affixed to aid hikers through the worst spot. Once down, you can explore numerous secret spots amid rocks of all sizes, stacks, and tide pools. On one visit, we saw what must have been hundreds of tiny rock crabs sparring in the shallows.

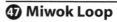 Miwok Loop

3.5 mi/2.0 hrs

Location: In the Marin Headlands near Sausalito; map E1–Marin, grid c2.

User groups: Hikers, dogs, horses, and mountain bikes (partial access). No wheelchair facilities.

Permits: No permits are required. Parking and access are free.

Directions: From U.S. 101 in Marin, take the Stinson Beach/Highway 1 exit. Drive 0.6 miles and turn left on Tennessee Valley Road. Drive two miles until the road dead-ends at the trailhead.

Maps: A map/brochure is available at the Marin Headlands Visitor Center or by contacting the Golden Gate National Recreation Area, Marin Headlands, at the address below. A detailed hiking map of the area is available for a fee from Olmsted Brothers Map Company, P.O. Box 5351, Berkeley, CA 94705. To obtain a topographic map of the area, ask for Point Bonita from the USGS.

Contact: Golden Gate National Recreation Area (GGNRA), Marin Headlands, Building 1056, Fort Cronkite, Sausalito, CA 94965. Marin Headlands Visitor Center, (415) 331-1540. GGNRA headquarters, (415) 556-0560.

Trail notes: The Miwok Loop is a near circular hike that traverses the pretty grasslands of the Marin Headlands, connecting a number of trails to provide a decent physical workout. Good views are found throughout, including those from a great 880-foot lookout to the west at the junction of Ridge Road and the Fox Trail. The hike starts at the Miwok Stables, elevation 200 feet, where you head north on the Miwok Trail, rising into higher country. The trail turns left, then heads west for 0.6 miles, still climbing to the junction of the Miwok Trail and Coyote Ridge Road. At this point, to make the loop hike, turn left on Ridge Road, where the trail tops out at 1,000 feet. The next mile offers spectacular views of the ocean, and every step can be special. To return to the Miwok Stables, turn left at the Fox Trail and hike 1.1 miles, go left again on the paved Tennessee Valley Trail, and hike out the last 0.4 miles to the stables. Trail use is typically high on weekends, and that includes mountain bike traffic on Coyote Ridge Road.

⓭ Tennessee Valley

4.2 mi/2.0 hrs

Location: In the Marin Headlands near Sausalito; map E1–Marin, grid c2.

User groups: Hikers, horses, and mountain bikes.(Horses and mountain bikes must take the forked fire road.) No dogs. No wheelchair facilities.

Permits: No permits are required. Parking and access are free.

Directions: From U.S. 101 in Marin, take the Stinson Beach/Highway 1 exit.Drive 0.6 miles and turn left on Tennessee Valley Road. Drive two miles until the road dead-ends at the trailhead.

Maps: A map/brochure is available at the Marin Headlands Visitor Center or by contacting the Golden Gate National Recreation Area, Marin Headlands, at the address below. A detailed hiking map of the area is available for a fee from Olmsted Brothers Map Company, P.O. Box 5351, Berkeley, CA 94705. To obtain a topographic map of the area, ask for Point Bonita from the USGS.

Contact: Golden Gate National Recreation Area (GGNRA), Marin Headlands, Building 1056, Fort Cronkite, Sausalito, CA 94965. Marin Headlands Visitor Center, (415) 331-1540. GGNRA headquarters, (415) 556-0560.

Trail notes: This very popular, scenic trail in the Marin Headlands traces Tennessee Valley out to Tennessee Cove and the Pacific Ocean. While the area is not wooded, the views of the Pacific Ocean can be gorgeous and the sunsets memorable.The best trailhead is at the Miwok Stables, elevation 200 feet. From there, the first 0.8 miles is paved and attracts many mountain bikers.The route turns to gravel for the final 1.1 miles, tracing alongside a pretty lagoon before dropping the final 0.2 miles to Tennessee Cove. With the easy, meandering grade, hard surface, and ocean views, the trail has become a favorite of family hikers.

⓮ Morning Sun Trail

0.2 mi/0.5 hr

Location: In the Marin Headlands near Sausalito; map E1–Marin, grid c2.

User groups: Hikers only. No dogs, horses, or mountain bikes. No wheelchair facilities.

Permits: No permits are required. Parking and access are free.

Directions: From San Francisco, take U.S. 101 north into Marin.After passing through the tunnel and driving down the grade, take the Spencer Road exit. Drive a half mile on Spencer Road (on the west side of U.S.101) to the parking area and the trailhead.

Maps: A map/brochure is available at the Marin Headlands Visitor Center or by contacting the Golden Gate National Recreation Area, Marin Headlands, at the address below. A detailed hiking map of the area is available for a fee from Olmsted Brothers Map Company, P.O. Box 5351, Berkeley, CA 94705. To obtain a topographic map of the area, ask for San Francisco North from the USGS.

Contact: Golden Gate National Recreation Area (GGNRA), Marin Headlands, Building 1056, Fort Cronkite, Sausalito, CA 94965. Marin Headlands Visitor Center, (415) 331-1540. GGNRA headquarters, (415) 556-0560.

Trail notes: This trail didn't get its name by accident. After the short but steep climb to the junction with the Alta Trail, you will discover this is a magnificent location to watch the sun rise, casting varying hues of yellow and orange across San Francisco Bay. In fact, it is one of the best places in the Bay Area to catch a sunrise. There is a good parking area at the trailhead,and from there you climb about 400 feet, peaking out at 800 feet at the Alta Trail junction. From Alta, you can easily extend your trip in either direction,or create a pretty 5.2-mile loop by linking the Rodeo Valley Trail and the Bobcat Trail.

⓯ Bicentennial Bike Path

4.5 mi/2.0 hrs

Location: On the San Francisco Bay shoreline from Sausalito to Corte Madera; map E1–Marin, grid c3.

User groups: Hikers, dogs, mountain bikes, and wheelchairs. No horses.

Permits: No permits are required. Parking and access are free.

Directions: From San Francisco, drive north on U.S. 101 over the Golden Gate Bridge. In Marin, take the Sausalito exit. Follow Second Street/Bridgeway through Sausalito to Harbor Drive, then park. The trail starts there.

Maps: A detailed hiking map of the area is available for a fee from Olmsted Brothers Map Company, P.O. Box 5351, Berkeley, CA 94705. To obtain a topographic map of the area, ask for San Francisco North from the USGS.

Contact: Richardson Bay Audubon Center, (415) 388-2524.

Trail notes: Can folks out for an easy stroll mix well with joggers and bikers? The Bicentennial Bike Path proves this is possible, primarily because it was designed just for that purpose. This paved byway starts in Sausalito and heads north, tracing the shoreline of Richardson Bay into Corte Madera. It is a great nature walk, easy and pleasant. From Sausalito, the route passes beneath the U.S. 101 overpass, then pushes toward Bothin Marsh along the edge of Richardson Bay, crossing two exceptional little bridges that provide passage over tidelands. At low tide, hundreds of tiny sandpipers frequently poke around in the mud; in the nearby sloughs bordered by pickleweed, you can often spot egrets, night herons, and maybe even a pelican. Drop into the Richardson Bay Audubon Center for a good side trip. Bikers can continue all the way to Ross but will have to make a few connections on city streets to do so.

51 Coastal Trail/ Fort Cronkite

5.2 mi/2.5 hrs

Location: In the Marin Headlands at the mouth of San Francisco Bay; map E1–Marin, grid c2.

User groups: Hikers, dogs, horses, and mountain bikes. Fort Cronkite and the picnic area are partially wheelchair accessible.

Permits: No permits are required. Parking and access are free.

Directions: From San Francisco, drive north on U.S. 101 over the Golden Gate Bridge. In Marin, take the Alexander Avenue exit and turn left underneath the highway. Take the wide paved road to the right (Conzelman Road, but there is

no sign), then look for the Marin Headlands sign. Drive for one mile, make a right on McCullough Road (the downhill fork), and soon after turn left on Bunker Road. Drive about 2.5 miles to where the road dead-ends at the Fort Cronkite/Rodeo Beach parking lot.

Maps: A map/brochure is available at the Marin Headlands Visitor Center or by contacting the Golden Gate National Recreation Area, Marin Headlands, at the address below. A detailed hiking map of the area is available for a fee from Olmsted Brothers Map Company, P.O. Box 5351, Berkeley, CA 94705. To obtain a topographic map of the area, ask for Point Bonita from the USGS.

Contact: Golden Gate National Recreation Area (GGNRA), Marin Headlands, Building 1056, Fort Cronkite, Sausalito, CA 94965. Marin Headlands Visitor Center, (415) 331-1540. GGNRA headquarters, (415) 556-0560.

Trail notes: Fort Cronkite, perched on an ocean bluff above Rodeo Beach, was the "support community" for the Headlands military fortifications in the 1930s and 1940s. From here, a paved pathway extends north up to Wolf Ridge, climbing to a 960-foot summit at what is known as "Hill 88." The land consists primarily of coastal grasslands, so from the summit you get outstanding views of the Pacific Ocean. The entire route is paved, and you may encounter bikers who careen downhill hell-bent for leather, sending hikers scattering for the bushes. Enforcement of the speed limit has helped, as has peer pressure from more ethical riders. While the round-trip distance is 5.2 miles, you'll surely make the 2.6-mile return hike at least twice as fast as the journey up.

52 Upper Fisherman's Trail

0.6 mi/0.5 hr

Location: In the Marin Headlands at the mouth of San Francisco Bay; map E1–Marin, grid c2.

User groups: Hikers only. No dogs, horses, or mountain bikes. No wheelchair facilities.

Permits: No permits are required. Parking and access are free.

Directions: From San Francisco, drive north on U.S. 101 over the Golden Gate Bridge. In Marin, take the Alexander Avenue exit and turn left underneath the highway. Take the wide paved road to the right (Conzelman, but there is no sign), then look for the Marin Headlands sign. Drive one mile, make a right on McCullough Road (the downhill fork), and soon after turn left on Bunker Road. Drive a short distance and take the first left to the Upper Fisherman's parking area and the trailhead.

Maps: A map/brochure is available at the Marin Headlands Visitor Center or by contacting the Golden Gate National Recreation Area, Marin Headlands, at the address below. A detailed hiking map of the area is available for a fee from Olmsted Brothers Map Company, P.O. Box 5351, Berkeley, CA 94705. To obtain a topographic map of the area, ask for Point Bonita from the USGS.

Contact: Golden Gate National Recreation Area (GGNRA), Marin Headlands, Building 1056, Fort Cronkite, Sausalito, CA 94965. Marin Headlands Visitor Center, (415) 331-1540. GGNRA headquarters, (415) 556-0560.

Trail notes: A delightful beach and a sea-level view of the entrance to the bay await at Bonita Cove. If only the weather was better. . . . Instead, summer days are typically cold and foggy here. From the parking area, the trail embarks on about a half-mile walk with an elevation change of some 300 feet—you'll know it when you make the return trip up—before emerging onto a beach sheltered by nearby Point Bonita and Point Diablo. The trail was named for the anglers who have used it over the years in the summer months to fish for striped bass and halibut. The cove is a good fishing spot because it's protected by Point Diablo, where baitfish often congregate during tidal transitions. Those baitfish, typically schools of anchovies, in turn attract the larger fish.

Special note: The rocky cliffs here can be dangerous; use extreme caution.

53 Coastal Trail/Fort Barry

1.4 mi/0.75 hr

Location: In the Marin Headlands near Rodeo Lagoon; map E1–Marin, grid c2.

User groups: Hikers, dogs, and horses. No mountain bikes. No wheelchair facilities.

Permits: No permits are required. Parking and access are free.

Directions: From San Francisco, drive north on U.S. 101 over the Golden Gate Bridge. In Marin, take the Alexander Avenue exit and turn left underneath the highway. Take the wide paved road to the right (Conzelman, but there is no sign), then look for the Marin Headlands sign. Drive one mile, make a right on McCullough Road (the downhill fork), and soon after turn left on Bunker Road. Proceed a short distance to Fort Barry. After parking, walk from the visitor center across the street and up the hill to the trailhead.

Maps: A map/brochure is available at the Marin Headlands Visitor Center or by contacting the Golden Gate National Recreation Area, Marin Headlands, at the address below. A detailed hiking map of the area is available for a fee from Olmsted Brothers Map Company, P.O. Box 5351, Berkeley, CA 94705. To obtain a topographic map of the area, ask for Point Bonita from the USGS.

Contact: Golden Gate National Recreation Area (GGNRA), Marin Headlands, Building 1056, Fort Cronkite, Sausalito, CA 94965. Marin Headlands Visitor Center, (415) 331-1540. GGNRA headquarters, (415) 556-0560.

Trail notes: Fort Barry was a nerve center for military operations in an era long past. Today it's a place that can calm the nerves of frazzled hikers. After parking and exploring at Fort Barry a bit, take the unpaved road/trail that heads west from the fort. Covering just 0.7 miles, the trail is routed along the south side of Rodeo Lagoon and out to the bluffs overlooking the ocean. This is a great, easy walk, with good views all around on clear days. The fort, set at the foot of Rodeo Valley, offers a living history lesson.

54 Hawk Hill

0.1 mi/0.25 hr

Location: In the Marin Headlands near Rodeo Lagoon; map E1–Marin, grid c2.

User groups: Hikers only. There are some wheelchair-accessible facilities, but the trail is steep and assistance may be needed. No dogs, horses, or mountain bikes.

Permits: No permits are required. Parking and access are free.

Directions: From San Francisco, drive north on U.S. 101 over the Golden Gate Bridge. In Marin, take the Alexander Avenue exit and turn left underneath the highway. Take the wide paved road to the right (Conzelman, but there is no sign), then look for the Marin Headlands sign. Continue on Conzelman (veering left at the fork with McCullough Road) and drive a short distance. Just before Conzelman becomes a one-way road, park on the shoulder. Note: The Conzelman access road is closed each day at sunset.

Maps: A map/brochure is available at the Marin Headlands Visitor Center or by contacting the Golden Gate National Recreation Area, Marin Headlands, at the address below. A detailed hiking map of the area is available for a fee from Olmsted Brothers Map Company, P.O. Box 5351, Berkeley, CA 94705. To obtain a topographic map of the area, ask for San Francisco North from the USGS.

Contact: Golden Gate National Recreation Area (GGNRA), Marin Headlands, Building 1056, Fort Cronkite, Sausalito, CA 94965. Marin Headlands Visitor Center, (415) 331-1540. GGNRA headquarters, (415) 556-0560.

Trail notes: Awesome views make this a choice trip. Each year more than 10,000 hawks fly over the Marin Headlands during their five-month migration season, peaking in September and October, and the raptors are best viewed from this lookout. In addition, there may be no better spot to see the Golden Gate Bridge, with the San Francisco skyline providing a backdrop. The hike is easy and fun, especially for youngsters. You can drive nearly to the top of Hawk Hill; after parking, hike a short distance, equivalent to a few blocks, to reach the lookout summit. As many as 2,800 hawks have been counted on a single day from this spot. The most commonly seen raptors are the red-tailed hawk, Cooper's hawk, turkey vulture, American kestrel, and northern harrier. All you need is a clear October day.

55 Vista Point/East Fort Baker

2.5 mi/1.5 hrs

Location: In the Marin Headlands at the northern foot of the Golden Gate Bridge; map E1–Marin, grid c2.

User groups: Hikers, dogs, and mountain bikes. Vista Point is wheelchair accessible, but the trail is not. No horses.

Permits: No permits are required. Parking and access are free.

Directions: From San Francisco, drive north on U.S. 101 over the Golden Gate Bridge, get in the right lane, and take the Vista Point exit.

Maps: A map/brochure is available at the East Fort Baker Visitor Center or by contacting the Golden Gate National Recreation Area, Marin Headlands, at the address below. A detailed hiking map of the area is available for a fee from Olmsted Brothers Map Company, P.O. Box 5351, Berkeley, CA 94705. To obtain a topographic map of the area, ask for San Francisco North from the USGS.

Contact: Golden Gate National Recreation Area (GGNRA), Marin Headlands, Building 1056, Fort Cronkite, Sausalito, CA 94965. Marin Headlands Visitor Center, (415) 331-1540. GGNRA headquarters, (415) 556-0560.

Trail notes: Vista Point, the famous lookout at the northern end of the Golden Gate Bridge, is like a mini United Nations, as travelers from around the world stop there to take photos. Little do they know that with a short walk, they can get even better views. From the parking area, a paved trail loops under the north foot of the bridge, then works its way back and forth, descending to East Fort Baker. There you will find a bay cove; as you look up from the shoreline, the Golden Gate Bridge is even more inspiring. You can stroll along the shore and out to a fishing pier or check out the children's Bay Area Discovery Museum. A nearby large grassy area makes an excellent picnic site, and picnic tables are available near Lime Point, set below the north end of the bridge. You can also extend the trip out to Yellow Bluff (see hike number 56), for more spectacular views and picnic sites.

56 Yellow Bluff Trail

1.5 mi/1.0 hr

Location: In the Marin Headlands at the northern foot of the Golden Gate Bridge; map E1–Marin, grid c2.

User groups: Hikers, dogs, and mountain

bikes. Fort Baker is wheelchair accessible, but the trail is not. No horses.

Permits: No permits are required. Parking and access are free.

Directions: From San Francisco, drive north on U.S. 101 over the Golden Gate Bridge. In Marin, take the Alexander Avenue exit and stay to the right at the split. Drive a very short distance, then turn left and drive a few hundred yards to a stop sign. Turn right and drive a half mile to the parking area for Fort Baker.

Maps: A map/brochure is available at the East Fort Baker Visitor Center or by contacting the Golden Gate National Recreation Area, Marin Headlands, at the address below. A detailed hiking map of the area is available for a fee from Olmsted Brothers Map Company, P.O. Box 5351, Berkeley, CA 94705. To obtain a topographic map of the area, ask for San Francisco North from the USGS.

Contact: Golden Gate National Recreation Area (GGNRA), Marin Headlands, Building 1056, Fort Cronkite, Sausalito, CA 94965. Marin Headlands Visitor Center, (415) 331-1540. GGNRA headquarters, (415) 556-0560.

Trail notes: From your vantage point on Yellow Bluff, San Francisco looks like the land of Oz, the Golden Gate Bridge like a link to Valhalla. This is a little piece of heaven. Yellow Bluff, the first major land point along the Marin shore east of the Golden Gate, provides a stunning lookout across San Francisco Bay and the surrounding landmarks. The trail is flat, short, and, best of all, unpublicized, and there are a few picnic tables nearby. From East Fort Baker, walk on the trail that heads east near the shoreline of the bay. You can turn the trip into a triangular loop hike by continuing along the shore, heading toward Sausalito, then turning left at the trail junction and hiking back to Fort Baker. One of the great features of this area is that it is often sunny, even when the Marin Headlands to the west lie buried in fog.

57 Shoreline Trail

5.0 mi/2.0 hrs

Location: In China Camp State Park east of San Rafael; map E1–Marin, grid b3.

User groups: Hikers, horses, and mountain bikes. No dogs. No wheelchair facilities.

Permits: No permits are required. A $5 state park day-use fee is charged at the entrance station.

Directions: From U.S. 101 in San Rafael, take the North San Pedro exit and drive east for four miles to the park entrance.

Maps: A small map/brochure is available for a fee at park headquarters or by contacting the State Parks district office at the address below. To obtain a topographic map of the area, ask for San Quentin from the USGS.

Contact: China Camp State Park, (415) 456-0766. State Parks, Marin District Headquarters, 7665 Redwood Boulevard, Suite 150, Novato, CA 94945; (415) 893-1580.

Trail notes: The Shoreline Trail is the best introduction to China Camp State Park a hiker could ask for. From the well-signed trailhead at the parking area, the trail meanders along the shore of San Pablo Bay, bordered by undisturbed hills on one side and waterfront on the other. The first mile provides good lookouts across the bay; the last half crosses a meadow, then runs adjacent to tidal areas, marshes, and wetlands, home to many species of waterfowl. Because the hike does not involve serious elevation gains or losses, you won't face any surprise climbs on the way back. An option on the return trip is to take the Miwok Fire Trail, which loops back to headquarters with a 300-foot climb and drop.

58 Bay View Trail

11.5 mi/4.5 hrs

Location: In China Camp State Park east of San Rafael; map E1–Marin, grid b3.

User groups: Hikers, horses, and mountain bikes. No dogs. No wheelchair facilities.

Permits: No permits are required. A $3 day-use and parking fee is charged at China Camp Village.

Directions: From U.S. 101 in San Rafael, take the North San Pedro exit and drive east for five miles to China Camp Village.

Maps: A small map/brochure is available for a fee at park headquarters or by contacting the State Parks district office at the address below.

To obtain a topographic map of the area, ask for San Quentin from the USGS.

Contact: China Camp State Park, (415) 456-0766. State Parks, Marin District Headquarters, 7665 Redwood Boulevard, Suite 150, Novato, CA 94945; (415) 893-1580.

Trail notes: The Bay View Trail is the most ambitious hike anywhere along the shore of San Pablo Bay. From China Camp Village, start hiking out on the Shoreline Trail (hike number 57), then link the Peacock Gap Trail to the Bay View Trail to access the park's most remote reaches. The Bay View Trail climbs to about 600 feet, traversing much of China Camp in the process. To visit the highest point in the park, take the Back Ranch Fire Trail to the Ridge Fire Trail, for panoramic vistas of San Pablo Bay, San Francisco Bay, Mount St. Helena, Mount Diablo, Angel Island, and San Francisco. We recommend that you return to the trailhead by dropping down to the Back Ranch Meadows Campground and walking back on the Shoreline Trail. On our visit, a nearly tame deer bedded down in the meadow adjacent to the parking lot and stared at us for an hour and a half; nothing we could do would satisfy its curiosity.

59 Perimeter Road

5.0 mi/2.5 hrs

Location: In Angel Island State Park in San Francisco Bay; map E1–Marin, grid c3.

User groups: Hikers and mountain bikes (helmets are required for bikers aged 17 and under). The Perimeter Road is accessible to wheelchairs, but many portions are too steep. No dogs (except for seeing-eye dogs) or horses.

Permits: No permits are required. Ferry boat ticket fees, which include day-use fees, vary according to departure point and season; the average round-trip price per person is $6 from Tiburon, $10 from San Francisco, $10 from Vallejo, and $12 from Oakland/Alameda; add $1 per bicycle.

Directions: Ferry service to Angel Island is available from Tiburon, San Francisco, Vallejo, and Oakland/Alameda. *To reach the Tiburon Ferry:* Take U.S. 101 in Marin to Tiburon Boulevard. Head east on Tiburon Boulevard, curving along the bay's shoreline. Park at one of the pay lots in Tiburon, then walk a short distance to the Tiburon Ferry, which is well signed. *To reach the San Francisco Ferry:* Take U.S. 101 to the Marina Boulevard exit near the southern foot of the Golden Gate Bridge. Follow Marina Boulevard toward Fisherman's Wharf. The ferry departs from Pier 43 1/2. *To reach the Vallejo Ferry:* Take Interstate 80 to U.S. 780. Drive to Curtola Parkway (which becomes Mare Island Way), and continue to 495 Mare Island Way, where free parking is available. The docking area is directly across from the parking lot. *To reach the Oakland/Alameda Ferry:* In Oakland, drive south on Highway 980, take the Webster exit, and drive west to the ferry dock and parking lot at Jack London Square.

Maps: You can purchase a topographic map/brochure for $1 at the park or by sending $2 to the Angel Island Association, Box 866, Tiburon, CA 94920. To obtain a topographic map of the area, ask for San Francisco North from the USGS.

Contact: Angel Island State Park, (415) 435-1915. Marin State Park District Headquarters, (415) 893-1580. Tiburon Ferry, (415) 435-2131. San Francisco's Red and White Fleet, (800) 229-2784. (Note: At press time, the fleet was being purchased by the Blue and Gold Fleet; if no answer, call 705-5444.) Vallejo Blue and Gold Fleet, (707) 64-FERRY. Oakland/Alameda Ferry, (510) 522-3300.

Trail notes: A hike around Angel Island on the Perimeter Trail provides great views of the bay and a historical tour amid remnants of the island's military past. Plus, it's long enough to provide a decent workout to boot. The trail winds past old barracks and abandoned military buildings, climbs through lush eucalyptus forests and across high bluffs, and looks out over San Francisco Bay and its world-class landmarks. Heavy logging of non-native eucalyptus has dramatically changed the character of this island and the trail. When linked with the North Ridge/Sunset Trail (hike number 60), this is the most scenic hike in the entire Bay Area. The only downer is that the trail is actually a road, yet somehow it still manages to inspire. From each lookout you see San Francisco Bay from a completely new angle.

⑥⓪ North Ridge/Sunset Trail

6.0 mi/3.0 hrs

Location: In Angel Island State Park in San Francisco Bay; map E1–Marin, grid c3.

User groups: Hikers only. No dogs (except for seeing-eye dogs), horses, or mountain bikes (they may not even be walked on this trail). No wheelchair facilities.

Permits: No permits are required. Ferry boat ticket fees, which include day-use fees, vary according to departure point and season; the average round-trip price per person is $6 from Tiburon, $10 from San Francisco, $10 from Vallejo, and $12 from Oakland/Alameda; add $1 per bicycle.

Directions: Ferry service to Angel Island is available from Tiburon, San Francisco, Vallejo, and Oakland/Alameda. *To reach the Tiburon Ferry:* Take U.S. 101 in Marin to Tiburon Boulevard. Head east on Tiburon Boulevard, curving along the bay's shoreline. Park at one of the pay lots in Tiburon, then walk a short distance to the Tiburon Ferry, which is well signed. *To reach the San Francisco Ferry:* Take U.S. 101 to the Marina Boulevard exit near the southern foot of the Golden Gate Bridge. Follow Marina Boulevard toward Fisherman's Wharf. The ferry departs from Pier 43 1/2. *To reach the Vallejo Ferry:* Take Interstate 80 to U.S. 780. Drive to Curtola Parkway (which becomes Mare Island Way), and continue to 495 Mare Island Way, where free parking is available. The docking area is directly across from the parking lot. *To reach the Oakland/Alameda Ferry:* In Oakland, drive south on Highway 980, take the Webster exit, and drive west to the ferry dock at Jack London Square.

Maps: You can purchase a topographic map/brochure for $1 at the park or by sending $2 to the Angel Island Association, Box 866, Tiburon, CA 94920. To obtain a topographic map of the area, ask for San Francisco North from the USGS.

Contact: Angel Island State Park, (415) 435-1915. Marin State Park District Headquarters, (415) 893-1580. Tiburon Ferry, (415) 435-2131. San Francisco's Red and White Fleet, (800) 229-2784. (Note: At press time, the fleet was being purchased by the Blue and Gold Fleet; if no answer, call 705-5444.) Vallejo Blue and Gold Fleet, (707) 64-FERRY. Oakland/Alameda Ferry, (510) 522-3300.

Trail notes: When standing atop Mount Livermore, you will be surrounded by dramatic scenery in every direction. That is because at 781 feet, this is the highest point on Angel Island, the virtual center of San Francisco Bay. The views are superb even at night, when the Golden Gate Bridge and the city are charmingly lit. The trail is steep, with a 550-foot climb in just a half mile, which will have even the best-conditioned hikers puffing like locomotives by the time they reach the top. The Summit Trail is actually a cut-off from the Perimeter Trail (hike number 59); for the ambitious, it's the highlight of a six-mile loop hike on Angel Island.

Map E1–S.F. Peninsula

Adjoining Maps: East: E1 ..... *page* 270
North: E1 216   South: E1 294

Note: Section E1 is divided into four chapters. For other E1 sections see pages 216 (Marin), 270 (East Bay), and 294 (South Bay).

Northern California Map .... *page* 2

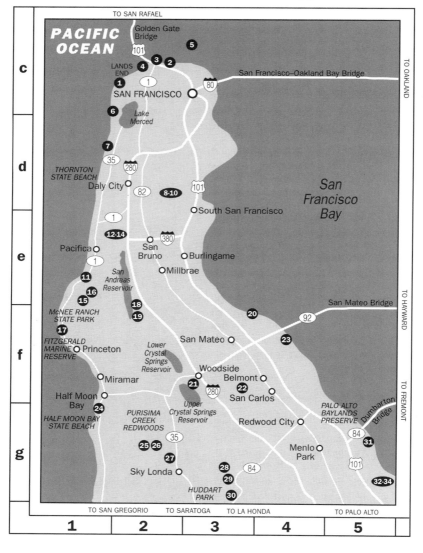

Chapter E1–San Francisco Peninsula features:

❶ Lands End Trail

2.5 mi/1.0 hr

Location: On the San Francisco headlands at the entrance to San Francisco Bay; map E1–San Francisco Peninsula, grid c1.

User groups: Hikers, wheelchairs, dogs, and mountain bikes (mountain bikes must be walked through narrow sections of the trail). No horses.

Permits: No permits are required. Parking and access are free.

Directions: From the Peninsula, take Interstate 280 to Highway 1 in San Bruno. Turn west and drive one mile to Highway 35 (Skyline Boulevard). Turn right on Highway 35 and drive past Lake Merced in San Francisco, jogging left at the lake, and continue to the Cliff House Restaurant. Or, from San Francisco, take Geary Boulevard west until it dead-ends at the ocean and the Cliff House Restaurant. Parking is available along Geary Boulevard, Skyline Boulevard, and in a lot across from Louis' Restaurant.

Maps: For a free map, contact the Golden Gate National Recreation Area at the address below.

To obtain a topographic map of the area, ask for San Francisco North from the USGS.

Contact: Golden Gate National Recreation Area, Fort Mason, Building 201, San Francisco, CA 94123; (415) 561-4323, (415) 556-0560, or fax (415) 556-0693. Cliff House Visitor Center, (415) 556-8642.

Trail notes: From Lands End, one glance can take in the mouth of San Francisco Bay and the crashing breakers, with the Golden Gate Bridge and Marin Headlands in the foreground and the Pacific Ocean, Farallon Islands, and Point Reyes in the background. By now you've probably figured out that this is one of San Francisco's greatest lookouts. From the trailhead near the Cliff House Restaurant, you meander eastward on a dirt trail set near bluffs topped with cypress trees. The scenic, nearly flat path traces the Coastal Trail between Lands End and China Beach on a 2.5-mile round-trip course from the parking area. It is especially popular on Sunday mornings, when hikers will take a brisk walk, enjoying the sea breeze on their faces, followed by brunch at one of two nearby restaurants, the Cliff House or Louis'.

❷ Golden Gate Promenade

3.0 mi/1.25 hrs

Location: On the shore of San Francisco Bay in San Francisco; map E1–San Francisco Peninsula, grid c2.

User groups: Hikers, wheelchairs, dogs, and mountain bikes. No horses.

Permits: No permits are required. Parking and access are free.

Directions: From U.S. 101 at the southern end of the Golden Gate Bridge in San Francisco, take the Marina Boulevard exit. Head southeast toward Fisherman's Wharf. Parking lots are available off Marina Boulevard at Fort Mason, Marina Green, Crissy Field, and near the St. Francis Yacht Club.

Maps: For a free map, contact the Golden Gate National Recreation Area at the address below. To obtain a topographic map of the area, ask for San Francisco North from the USGS.

Contact: Golden Gate National Recreation Area, Fort Mason, Building 201, San Francisco, CA 94123; (415) 561-4323, (415) 556-0560, or fax (415) 556-0693.

Trail notes: This paved trail leads along the shoreline of San Francisco Bay from Marina Green to Fort Point. It is virtually flat and the views are magnificent, with a scenic backdrop of the Golden Gate Bridge, Alcatraz, Tiburon, Sausalito, and the bay itself. From the parking area at Marina Green, simply follow the paved pathway through Crissy Field, along the Presidio and out to Fort Point, then to the southern foot of the Golden Gate Bridge. The entire trail is popular with joggers and walkers, especially in the morning. In the afternoon, it can get quite windy. People looking for a workout will find one of the Bay Area's most popular par courses at Marina Green. Side trips include the old Muni Pier, the Presidio, which borders much of the route, and Fort Point.

❸ Golden Gate Bridge

3.0 mi/1.25 hrs

Location: From San Francisco to Marin; map E1–San Francisco Peninsula, grid c2.

User groups: Hikers, wheelchairs, dogs, and mountain bikes (on the west side of the bridge only). No horses.

Permits: No permits are required. Parking and access are free.

Directions: From U.S. 101 at the southern end of the Golden Gate Bridge, take the toll plaza parking area exit. Limited parking is available directly east of the toll plaza. There is additional unpaved parking 50 yards west of the toll plaza; from there you must walk through a short tunnel to reach the foot of the bridge.

Maps: For a free map, contact the Golden Gate National Recreation Area at the address below. To obtain a topographic map of the area, ask for San Francisco North from the USGS.

Contact: Golden Gate National Recreation Area, Fort Mason, Building 201, San Francisco, CA 94123; (415) 561-4323, (415) 556-0560, or fax (415) 556-0693. Fort Funston Visitor Center, (415) 239-2366.

Trail notes: Relatively few Bay Area residents ever get around to taking the number one tourist walk in the world: the Golden Gate Bridge. From the center of the bridge, the view is incomparable. Looking eastward, you can see Alcatraz, Angel Island, and the bay framed by the San Francisco waterfront and the East Bay hills. Parking is available at the north end of the bridge at Vista Point, and at the south end, on each side of the toll station. If you park on the west side, you walk through a short tunnel that runs under Highway 101 and loops up to the pathway entrance. The path on the east side of the bridge is reserved for pedestrians, while the west side is for bicyclists only on weekends and evenings. From one end to the other, the bridge is 1.22 miles long (and 220 feet above the water), but most folks walk only halfway out then return to their cars, for a round-trip of 1.5 miles.

❹ Coastal Trail

2.5 mi/1.0 hr

Location: In the Presidio on the San Francisco headlands; map E1–San Francisco Peninsula, grid c2.

User groups: Hikers and wheelchairs. Dogs are not advised. No horses or mountain bikes.

Permits: No permits are required. Parking and access are free.

Directions: From U.S. 101 at the southern end of the Golden Gate Bridge, take the toll plaza parking area exit. Limited parking is available directly east of the toll plaza. After parking, you must walk through a short tunnel to reach the trailhead. There is additional unpaved parking 50 yards west of the toll plaza near the trailhead.

Maps: For a free map, contact the Golden Gate National Recreation Area at the address below. To obtain a topographic map of the area, ask for San Francisco North from the USGS.

Contact: Golden Gate National Recreation Area, Fort Mason, Building 201, San Francisco, CA 94123; (415) 561-4323, (415) 556-0560, or fax (415) 556-0693.

Trail notes: While Vista Point at the northern foot of the Golden Gate Bridge may be the most popular place from which to take snapshots of the bridge, a lookout on the Coastal Trail provides a more scenic view. This spot is just north of Baker Beach, where San Francisco Bay, the bridge, and the Marin coast all fit easily into a 35 mm frame, a postcardlike scene.

After parking, hike southwest on the Coastal Trail, passing the Fort Scott Overlook, Battery Crosby, and Battery Chamberlin en route to the south end of Baker Beach. The best strategy for would-be photographers is to make the 30-minute walk in, scanning for photo opportunities along the way, and then capture any ideas on film on the return trip. The soft dirt pathway is set in cypress, but don't forget that this is the big, bad city: hikers should travel in pairs or go very early in the morning. For more postcard views of the bridge, take a side trip down to mile-long Baker Beach.

❺ Agave Trail

1.5 mi/1.5 hrs

Location: On Alcatraz Island; map E1–San Francisco Peninsula, grid c3.

User groups: Hikers only. No dogs, horses, or mountain bikes. No wheelchair facilities.

Permits: No permits are required. The following fees include ferry boat ride to the island, park day-use fee, and audio cassette tour: $10 for

adults, $8.25 for seniors, and $4.75 for children. (Without the audio cassette tour, it's a few dollars less.) Ferries depart from Pier 41 in San Francisco at 9:45 A.M., 10:15 A.M., and every half hour thereafter until 2:15 P.M. or 4:15 P.M., depending upon the season and the day of the week. Schedules are subject to change on short notice; call for current information.

Directions: From U.S. 101 heading south into San Francisco, take the Marina Boulevard exit near the southern foot of the Golden Gate Bridge. Follow Marina Boulevard toward Fisherman's Wharf. Park in a pay lot, walk to Pier 41 at Fisherman's Wharf, and look for the prominent sign for the Red and White Fleet.

Maps: For a free map/brochure, contact the Golden Gate National Recreation Area at the address below. To obtain a topographic map of the area, ask for San Francisco North from the USGS.

Contact: Golden Gate National Recreation Area, Fort Mason, Building 201, San Francisco, CA 94123; (415) 561-4323, (415) 556-0560, or fax (415) 556-0693. The Red and White Fleet, (415) 546-2700. Advance tickets can be purchased by phone using a credit card (with a reservation fee).

Note: At press time, the fleet was being purchased by the Blue and Gold Fleet; if you can't reach the above number, call (415) 705-5444 for information.

Trail notes: The Agave Trail at Alcatraz Island, opened in the winter of 1994–95, is bound to become one of the more popular hikes in California. Not only has it made accessible one-third of the island that was previously closed to visitors, it also provides some of the most breathtaking views found on any of the 15,000 miles of hiking trails in the Bay Area. The trail—named after the agave plant, which is common here—starts at the ferry landing on the east side of Alcatraz and traces the rim of the island to its southern tip. It is quite wide, with a few benches and cement picnic tables situated for sweeping views of both the East Bay and San Francisco.

From its southern end, the trail is routed back to the historic parade ground atop the island, where you'll find some masterpieces of sculpture, which includes 110 stone steps. The parade ground is a haven for nesting birds, and this area is closed to the public in the spring each year so the birds will not be disturbed. If you visit during a low tide, you can discover some relatively little known tide pools at the island's southwest corner. This part of the island also has abundant bird life, including a population of night herons; for pure cuteness, they're right up there with chipmunks and baby ducks. The old cell block is located at the center of the island, with other buildings sprinkled along the eastern shore and on the northern tip. Ranger-led tours of the park are available, and visitors can rent audio tapes for a self-guided cellhouse tour. The ghost of Al Capone is said to roam here, trying to figure out a way to pay his taxes.

❻ Ocean Beach Esplanade

6.0 mi/2.25 hrs

Location: On the San Francisco coast; map E1– San Francisco Peninsula, grid d1.

User groups: Hikers, dogs, and horses. Partially wheelchair accessible. No mountain bikes.

Permits: No permits are required. Parking and access are free.

Directions: From the Peninsula, take Interstate 280 to Highway 1 in San Bruno. Turn west and drive one mile to Highway 35 (Skyline Boulevard). Turn right on Highway 35 and drive five miles, jogging left to pass Lake Merced. Park on the left along the beach. Or, from San Francisco, take Geary Boulevard west until it dead-ends at the ocean and the Cliff House Restaurant. Turn left on the Great Highway and drive one mile to the parking area on the right.

Maps: For a free map, contact the Golden Gate National Recreation Area at the address below. To obtain a topographic map of the area, ask for San Francisco South from the USGS.

Contact: Golden Gate National Recreation Area, Fort Mason, Building 201, San Francisco, CA 94123; (415) 561-4323, (415) 556-0560, or fax (415) 556-0693.

Trail notes: At Ocean Beach, located along San Francisco's coastal Great Highway, you will discover a long expanse of sand, a paved jogging trail, and miniature parks at Fort Funston and Thornton Beach. The nature of both the trail and the adjacent beach allows visitors to create trips

of any length. The beach spans four miles from Seal Rock near the Cliff House south to Fort Funston; from there, if desired, you can continue to explore south all the way past Center Hole to Mussel Rock at the north end of Pacifica. The huge swath of sand at Ocean Beach is popular with joggers, especially during low tides when the hard-packed sand is uncovered. A paved jogging trail is located just east of the Great Highway.

❼ Fort Funston Sunset Trail

1.5 mi/0.5 hr

Location: On the San Francisco coast; map E1– San Francisco Peninsula, grid d1.

User groups: Hikers, dogs, and horses. Partially wheelchair accessible. No mountain bikes.

Permits: No permits are required. Parking and access are free.

Directions: From the Peninsula, take Interstate 280 to Highway 1 in San Bruno. Turn west and drive one mile to Highway 35 (Skyline Boulevard). Turn right on Highway 35 and drive five miles, jogging left to pass Lake Merced. Park on the left along the beach. Or, from San Francisco, take Geary Boulevard west until it dead-ends at the ocean and the Cliff House Restaurant. Turn left on the Great Highway and drive four miles to the parking area on the right.

Maps: For a free map, contact the Golden Gate National Recreation Area at the address below. To obtain a topographic map of the area, ask for San Francisco South from the USGS.

Contact: Golden Gate National Recreation Area, Fort Mason, Building 201, San Francisco, CA 94123; (415) 561-4323, (415) 556-0560, or fax (415) 556-0693. Fort Funston Visitor Center, (415) 239-2366.

Trail notes: Fort Funston is perched on San Francisco's coastal bluffs, with the ocean on one side and Lake Merced on the other. The park is one of the most popular places around to take dogs. It is also the top hang gliding spot in the Bay Area, and watching those daredevils soar is the main attraction. A viewing deck is provided adjacent to the parking area, where the Sunset Trail begins. From there, the trail is routed north through coastal bluffs and above sand dunes for three-quarters of a mile to the park's border. The only problem here is the weather. If the wind doesn't get you, the fog likely will, especially in the summer months. But don't write the place off, because in the fall and winter, the fog clears and each evening the kind of sunsets that can make your spine tingle put on quite a show. Those hang gliders are worth gawking at, too, especially in the spring when the north winds come up every afternoon. We'll even tell you a little secret: A lot of sand dollars seem to turn up on the beach walk that leads south from Fort Funston less than a mile to Thornton Beach. Remember that collecting them is a violation of park rules.

❽ Summit Loop Trail

3.1 mi/1.5 hrs

Location: In San Bruno Mountain State and County Park near South San Francisco; map E1– San Francisco Peninsula, grid d2.

User groups: Hikers and horses. No dogs or mountain bikes. No wheelchair facilities.

Permits: No permits are required. There is a $3 entrance fee.

Directions: From U.S. 101 north of South San Francisco, take the Cow Palace exit and drive to Guadalupe Canyon Parkway. Turn left and follow Guadalupe Canyon Parkway for about two miles to the park entrance on the right.

Maps: For a free trail map, contact San Bruno Mountain State and County Park at the address below. To obtain a topographic map of the area, ask for San Francisco South from the USGS.

Contact: San Bruno Mountain State and County Park, 555 Guadalupe Canyon Parkway, Brisbane, CA 94005; (415) 587-7511 or fax (415) 992-6770.

Trail notes: San Bruno Mountain is a unique island of open space in an urban setting. This Bay Area landmark, best known to Peninsula residents as that "big ol' hill" west of Highway 101 near Candlestick Park, has elevations ranging to 1,314 feet. The summit is private and inaccessible to the public; the highest accessible point is the top parking lot at 1,225 feet. Wind and fog can be big-time downers here. For the inspired, the Summit Loop Trail is the most demanding and rewarding hike in the park. It starts at the parking area on the south side of Guadalupe Canyon Parkway. If you are inspired, you can connect to the Ridge Trail and add up to five miles to your hike by walking out and back on the East Ridge, which provides beautiful vistas. On the return trip, we suggest you veer right at the Dairy Ravine Trail, taking the switchback down the canyon, then heading right again at the Eucalyptus Trail (named for trees that have since been removed), which will bring you to the parking area.

❾ Saddle Trail

2.5 mi/1.25 hrs

Location: In San Bruno Mountain State and County Park; map E1–San Francisco Peninsula, grid d2.

User groups: Hikers and horses. No dogs or mountain bikes. No wheelchair facilities.

Permits: No permits are required. There is a $3 entrance fee.

Directions: From U.S. 101 north of South San Francisco, take the Cow Palace exit and drive to Guadalupe Canyon Parkway. Turn left and follow Guadalupe Canyon Parkway for about two miles to the park entrance on the right.

Maps: For a free trail map, contact San Bruno Mountain State and County Park at the address below. To obtain a topographic map of the area, ask for San Francisco South from the USGS.

Contact: San Bruno Mountain State and County Park, 555 Guadalupe Canyon Parkway, Brisbane, CA 94005; (415) 587-7511 or fax (415) 992-6770.

Trail notes: Guadalupe Canyon Parkway splits San Bruno Mountain State and County Park in two, leaving hikers to decide which section to visit on a given day. The north half provides a pair of good loop hikes: the Saddle Trail, the featured hike from the parking area/trailhead on the north side, and the Bog Trail (hike number 10). Both are easier than the Summit Loop/ Ridge Trail in the park's southern half. For this hike, from the north parking area, start walking on the Old Guadalupe Trail, which junctions with the Saddle Trail after about 20 minutes. From there, take the Saddle Trail and loop around the northern boundaries of the park, climbing about 150 feet in the process. The wind can absolutely howl through this area at times, so pick your hiking days with care. Most of the surrounding terrain is open hillside grasslands, so the views of the South Bay are unblocked and, on clear days, just spectacular.

⑩ Bog Trail

0.8 mi/0.5 hr

Location: In San Bruno Mountain State and County Park; map E1–San Francisco Peninsula, grid d2.

User groups: Hikers only. The upper part of the trail is wheelchair accessible. No dogs, horses, or mountain bikes.

Permits: No permits are required. There is a $3 entrance fee.

Directions: From U.S. 101 north of South San Francisco, take the Cow Palace exit and drive to Guadalupe Canyon Parkway. Turn left and follow Guadalupe Canyon Parkway for about two miles to the park entrance on the right.

Maps: For a free trail map, contact San Bruno Mountain State and County Park at the address below. To obtain a topographic map of the area, ask for San Francisco South from the USGS.

Contact: San Bruno Mountain State and County Park, 555 Guadalupe Canyon Parkway, Brisbane, CA 94005; (415) 587-7511 or fax (415) 992-6770.

Trail notes: The Bog Trail provides a good introduction to San Bruno Mountain State and County Park, although you'll need to hike other trails here if you desire a more passionate experience. The trail starts at the trailhead on the north side of Guadalupe Canyon Parkway and is routed along the north flank of the mountain, changing only 30 feet in elevation. By turning right at the junction with the Old Guadalupe Trail, you can make this a short loop hike. Open hillsides surround the trail and are quite pretty on clear days in the spring when the grasslands turn green and are sprinkled with an explosion of wildflowers. Hikers who make this easy trip quickly get a sense of the importance of the open space buffer the park provides for the congested North Peninsula.

⑪ Rockaway Point Trail

2.5 mi/1.5 hrs

Location: On the Pacifica shoreline near Pacifica State Beach; map E1–San Francisco Peninsula, grid e1.

User groups: Hikers and dogs. No horses or mountain bikes. No wheelchair facilities.

Permits: No permits are required. Parking and access are free.

Directions: From San Francisco, head south on Interstate 280 to Daly City. Turn south on Highway 1 and drive about five miles into Pacifica. Drive to the southern end of Pacifica and turn right at the parking lot for Pacifica State Beach (Linda Mar). The trail starts at the north end of the beach.

Maps: To obtain a topographic map of the area, ask for Montara Mountain from the USGS.

Contact: City of Pacifica, Planning Division, 170 Santa Maria Avenue, Pacifica, CA 94044; (415) 738-7335 or fax (415) 359-5807.

Trail notes: Sure, you could probably hike this route to the end and back in a flash. But sometimes, as you will discover here, taking the time to go slow sure beats rushing through as quickly as possible. You just plain won't want to miss anything after you park at the Pacifica State Beach parking lot and start hiking north on the beach. The northern end of this stretch of sand is a great place to throw sticks to a dog (but be aware that the sand dune area provides habitat for the endangered snowy plover) and to fish for striped bass in the summertime.

At the end of the beach, climb up on the dirt trail that traces around Rockaway Point. Here you will find beautiful views of San Pedro Point, Montara Mountain, and of course the Pacific Ocean. Just meander along, listen to the waves, and let the beauty flow through you. Then, when you feel like it, turn around and follow the same route back to your car. When you first drive up, don't get spooked if the parking lot seems crowded. Why? Because many people often prefer to spend time philosophizing about life while looking down into the mouth of a beer bottle, rather than taking this walk and experiencing the full fabric of the place.

⑫ Milagra Ridge

2.0 mi/0.75 hr

Location: In Pacifica near Skyline College; map E1–San Francisco Peninsula, grid e2.

User groups: Hikers and mountain bikes (allowed on only one mile of paved trail). Wheelchair accessible with assistance. No dogs or horses.

Permits: No permits are required. Parking and access are free.

Directions: From Interstate 280 in San Bruno, take the Westborough exit, then drive west up the hill and across Highway 35 (Skyline Boulevard). Drive to College Avenue and turn right. Continue a very short distance to the end of the road and the trailhead. Limited parking is available.

Maps: For a free map, contact the Golden Gate National Recreation Area at the address below. To obtain a topographic map of the area, ask for San Francisco South from the USGS.

Contact: Golden Gate National Recreation Area, Fort Mason, Building 201, San Francisco, CA 94123; (415) 561-4323, (415) 556-0560, or fax (415) 556-0693.

Trail notes: A mile-long paved road/trail is routed to the top of Milagra Ridge, one of the best places imaginable to fly a kite. Those coastal breezes can almost put a strong kite in orbit; some people even use saltwater fishing rods and reels filled with line to fly theirs, "playing" the kite as if it were a big fish. Kite flying is allowed only inside the gate on the hill to the left. Hikers must stay on the trail to protect the endangered mission blue butterfly.

The parking area that hikers use to gain access to Milagra Ridge is small and obscure—nobody winds up here by accident. Once you park your car, the hike up to the top of the ridge is an easy mile and is suitable for wheelchair users who have some assistance. The summit was flattened in the 1950s to accommodate a missile site, long since abandoned. Looking westward, visitors will be surprised at the sheer dropoff from the ridge down into Pacifica. Alas, in the summer months this can be one of the foggiest places in the world.

⑬ Sweeney Ridge

4.4 mi/2.5 hrs

Location: On the Peninsula ridgeline in San Bruno; map E1–San Francisco Peninsula, grid e2.

User groups: Hikers, dogs, horses, and mountain bikes. No wheelchair facilities.

Permits: No permits are required. Parking and access are free.

Directions: From Interstate 280 in San Bruno, take the Westborough exit and drive west up the hill to Highway 35 (Skyline Boulevard). Turn left on Highway 35 and drive a short distance to College Drive, then turn right and drive to the Skyline College campus. At the stop sign turn left and drive to lot number 2. The trailhead is located at the back of the parking lot. Bikes can also access the trail from Sneath Lane in San Bruno.

Maps: For a free map, contact the Golden Gate National Recreation Area at the address below. To obtain a topographic map of the area, ask for San Francisco South from the USGS.

Contact: Golden Gate National Recreation Area, Fort Mason, Building 201, San Francisco, CA 94123; (415) 561-4323, (415) 556-0560, or fax (415) 556-0693. Fort Funston Visitor Center, (415) 239-2366.

Trail notes: Hikers usually have to pay dearly to get a 360-degree mountaintop view, but at Sweeney Ridge, payment is made via a 2.2-mile hike from the trailhead at Skyline College. This is the Bay Discovery Site, where Captain Portola became the first of the New World explorers to get a glimpse of what is now San Francisco Bay. You can make the same discovery on the steady grade up to the ridge; it takes about an hour for most people, more for some. The route traces through coastal scrub and grassland, topping out at 1,200 feet. On clear days, several of the Bay Area's most impressive mountains stand in clear view: Mount Tamalpais, Mount Diablo, and nearby Montara Mountain. In 15 minutes of hiking, the views of the South Bay on one side and the Pacific Ocean on the other offer another extraordinary perspective. In the spring, when all is green, look closely and you will find surprising numbers of wildflowers with their tiny blooms.

⑭ Montara Mountain/ Brooks Creek Trail

7.0 mi/2.5 hrs

Location: In San Pedro Valley County Park in Pacifica; map E1–San Francisco Peninsula, grid e2.

User groups: Hikers and horses (on designated trails only). Some trails and facilities are wheelchair accessible. No dogs or mountain bikes.

Permits: No permits are required. There is a $3 entrance fee.

Directions: From San Francisco, take Highway 1 south into Pacifica. Turn east on Linda Mar Boulevard and drive until it dead-ends at Oddstad Boulevard. Turn right and drive to the park entrance, located about 50 yards on the left. The trailhead is on the southwest side of the parking lot.

Maps: For a free trail map, contact San Pedro Valley County Park at the address below. To obtain a topographic map of the area, ask for Montara Mountain from the USGS.

Contact: San Pedro Valley County Park, 600 Oddstad Boulevard, Pacifica, CA 94044; (415) 355-8289 or fax (415) 363-4020.

Trail notes: Just 20 minutes south of San Francisco is this secluded trail in San Pedro Valley County Park, where visitors are few, the coastal beauty divine, and hikers can carve out their own personal slice of heaven. The Montara Mountain/Brooks Creek Trail is the prize of the park, featuring the best viewing area for Brooks Falls (read on) and great lookouts to the Pacific Coast. After parking, walk about 50 yards along the Montara Mountain/Brooks Creek Trail. The trail then splits, with the Brooks Creek Trail on the left and the Montara Mountain Trail on the right; the two merge again about one mile up Brooks Creek and continue as a common route to the peak. Turn right on the well-signed Montara Mountain Trail. From here, the next mile climbs several hundred feet, and suddenly, the waterfall appears in a surprising freefall down a canyon.

The falls are connected in three narrow, silver-tasseled tiers, falling 175 feet in all. And though they are viewed from some distance across the canyon, they are still among the most impressive falls in the Bay Area. One reason they are so little known is that they don't flow year-round. As a tributary to San Pedro Creek, Brooks Creek runs only in late winter and spring, best of course after several days of rain. Note that a great coastal lookout is available another 10 minutes up the trail on a dramatic rock outcrop. The hike continues all the way to the North Peak of Montara Mountain at 1,898 feet, 3.5 miles one way, including a final 1.1-mile push on a fire road to reach the summit. On a clear spring day, the views are absolutely stunning in all directions, highlighted by the Pacific Ocean and the Farallon Islands.

Special note: This route is the first link in one of the few great one-way hikes (using a shuttle) in the Bay Area. From the top of Montara Mountain, you enter McNee Ranch State Park and hike 3.8 miles to Montara State Beach, descending all the way, with glorious views for the entire route. (See hike number 16, Montara Mountain/ McNee Ranch.) So, with cars parked at each end of the trail, you can hike 7.3 miles one way from San Pedro Valley County Park, up Montara Mountain, and down to Montara State Beach.

⑮ San Pedro Mountain

6.0 mi/2.5 hrs

Location: In McNee Ranch State Park in Montara; map E1–San Francisco Peninsula, grid e1.

User groups: Hikers and dogs. No horses or mountain bikes. No wheelchair facilities.

Permits: No permits are required. Parking and access are free.

Directions: From San Francisco, drive about 17 miles south on Highway 1. Continue through Pacifica, then through Devil's Slide, and down to the base of the hill. Look for a small pullout area on the left. The access point is at a yellow gate with a state park property sign. There is room enough to accommodate only three cars, so if the pullout is full, go south on Highway 1 a short distance and park at the lot on the west side of the highway at Montara State Beach.

Maps: To obtain a topographic map of the area, ask for Montara Mountain from the USGS.

Contact: California State Parks, Bay Area District, 95 Kelly Avenue, Half Moon Bay, CA 94019; (415) 726-8800.

Trail notes: For people who like dramatic coastal views, this is the ideal trail, tracing the top of coastal bluffs. Many spots along the way provide perches for flawless vistas. To get to them, take note at the entrance gate and look for the trail that is routed off to the left and up through the hilly grasslands. With those first few steps, it doesn't look like much of a trail. But as you continue, rising atop the first crest, you will see how it tracks up the spine of the coastal ridgeline, eventually providing a lookout above Gray Whale Cove. From this viewpoint, you may feel an odd sense of irony: Below you is Highway 1, typically filled with a stream of slow-moving cars driven by people who want to get somewhere else; meanwhile, you are in a place of peace and serenity, happy right where you are. The hike includes a few short climbs across grasslands and can be converted to a loop hike by turning right at the junction with the Montara Mountain Trail.

⑯ Montara Mountain/ McNee Ranch

7.6 mi/3.75 hrs

Location: In McNee Ranch State Park in Montara; map E1–San Francisco Peninsula, grid e1.

User groups: Hikers, dogs, and mountain bikes. No horses. No wheelchair facilities.

Permits: No permits are required. Parking and access are free.

Directions: From San Francisco, drive about 17 miles south on Highway 1. Continue through Pacifica, then through Devil's Slide, and down to the base of the hill. Look for a small pullout area on the left. The access point is at a yellow gate with a state park property sign. There is room enough to accommodate only three cars, so if the pullout is full, go south on Highway 1 a short distance and park at the lot on the west side of the highway at Montara State Beach.

Maps: To obtain a topographic map of the area, ask for Montara Mountain from the USGS.

Contact: California State Parks, Bay Area District, 95 Kelly Avenue, Half Moon Bay, CA 94019; (415) 726-8800.

Trail notes: On a clear day from the top of Montara Mountain, the Farallon Islands to the northwest appear so close you may think you could reach out and pluck them from the ocean. To the east, it looks like you could take a giant leap across the bay and land atop Mount Diablo. Some 10 miles to the north and south there's nothing but mountain wilderness connecting Sweeney Ridge to an off-limits state game preserve. By now, you should be properly inspired for the climb, which for many is a genuine gut-wrencher. From the main access gate to the top it's 3.8 miles, a rise of nearly 2,000 feet that includes three killer "ups." From the gate, follow the ranch road up the ridgeline of San Pedro Mountain to the Montara Coastal Range; at the fork, stay to the right on the dirt road as it climbs and turns. After a 20-minute wheezer of an ascent, look for a garbage can at a flat spot on the left side of the trail—30 yards down a cutoff from here you'll find a perch for a dazzling view of the Pacific Coast. After catching your breath, continue on, heading up, up, and up, eventually topping out at the summit. Only the radio transmitter there mars an otherwise pristine setting. All you need for this hike is a clear day, some water, and plenty of inspiration.

⑰ Fitzgerald Marine Reserve

1.0 mi/1.0 hr

Location: In Moss Beach; map E1–San Francisco Peninsula, grid f1.

User groups: Hikers only. No dogs, horses, or mountain bikes. No wheelchair facilities.

Permits: No permits are required. Parking and access are free.

Directions: From San Francisco, take Interstate 280 to Highway 1 in Daly City and drive through Pacifica, over Devil's Slide, and into Moss Beach. Turn right at the signed turnoff at California Street and continue one mile to the parking area.

Alternate route: From the Peninsula, take Highway 92 into Half Moon Bay, then head north on Highway 1 for seven miles to Moss Beach. Turn left at the signed turnoff at California Street and drive one mile to the parking area.

Maps: To obtain a topographic map of the area, ask for Montara Mountain from the USGS.

Contact: Fitzgerald Marine Reserve, P.O. Box 451, Moss Beach, CA 94038; (415) 728-3584 or fax (415) 728-3621.

Trail notes: The closer you look, the better it gets. When you go tide-pool hopping, there is nothing more fascinating than discovering a variety of tiny sea creatures. That is what makes the Fitzgerald Marine Reserve—a shallow 30-acre reef that exposes hundreds and hundreds of tidal pockets every time a minus low tide rolls back the ocean—so attractive. After parking, it's a short walk down to the tide pools; from there, you walk on exposed rock, watching the wonders of the tidal waters. Be sure to wear boots that grip well, and take care not to crush any fragile sea plants as you walk. In the tide pools you will discover hermit crabs, rock crabs, sea anemones, sculpins, starfish, sea snails, and many plants and animals in various colors. An option is to continue walking south on the beach to the Moss Beach Distillery, a popular watering hole. A few notes: No dogs, no beachcombing, no shell gathering. In other words, OK looky, but no touchy. After all, this is a preserve.

⑱ San Andreas Trail

6.0 mi/2.5 hrs

Location: In the San Mateo County foothills southwest of San Bruno; map E1–San Francisco Peninsula, grid f2.

User groups: Hikers, horses, and mountain bikes. Note that the northern section is paved, but the southern section is not. There are some wheelchair-accessible facilities. No dogs.

Permits: No permits are required. Parking and access are free.

Directions: To access the north gate: From Interstate 280 in San Bruno, take the Westborough exit and drive west up the hill to the intersection with Highway 35 (Skyline Boulevard). Turn left on Highway 35 and drive about 2.5 miles to the trailhead entrance on the right side of the road. To access the south gate: From the south, take Highway 280 to the Millbrae Avenue exit. Head north on what appears to be a frontage road (Skyline Boulevard) and drive to the parking area on the left.

Maps: For a free trail map, contact San Mateo

County Parks at the address below. To obtain a topographic map of the area, ask for Montara Mountain from the USGS.

Contact: San Mateo County Parks, 590 Hamilton Street, Redwood City, CA 94063; (415) 363-4020 or fax (415) 599-1721.

Trail notes: Winding its way through wooded foothills, the San Andreas Trail overlooks Upper San Andreas Lake. The only downer is that much of the route runs adjacent to Highway 35 (Skyline Boulevard). Regardless, it is worth the trip, because to the west you can see the untouched slopes of Montara Mountain, a game preserve, and that sparkling lake, all off-limits to the public. The trail starts near the northern end of the lake; a signed trailhead marker is posted on Skyline Boulevard. It goes about three miles until the next access point at Hillcrest Boulevard, and from there connects to the Sawyer Camp Trail (hike number 19). The view of Montara Mountain to the west is particularly enchanting during the summer when rolling fog banks crest the ridgeline. It's quite a spectacle.

⑲ Sawyer Camp Trail

12.0 mi/5.0 hrs

Location: In the San Mateo County foothills south of San Bruno; map E1–San Francisco Peninsula, grid f2.

User groups: Hikers, horses, and mountain bikes. There are some wheelchair-accessible facilities at the south end. No dogs.

Permits: No permits are required. Parking and access are free.

Directions: From Interstate 280 in San Bruno, take the Westborough exit and drive west up the hill to the intersection with Highway 35 (Skyline Boulevard). Turn left on Highway 35 and drive about six miles to the trailhead entrance on the right.

Maps: For a free trail map, contact San Mateo County Parks at the address below. To obtain a topographic map of the area, ask for Montara Mountain from the USGS.

Contact: San Mateo County Parks, 590 Hamilton Street, Redwood City, CA 94063; (415) 363-4020 or fax (415) 599-1721.

Trail notes: With the Sawyer Camp Trail you get everything that there is on the connecting link to the north, the San Andreas Trail (hike number 18), and more. The trail is set away from the road, so you get more peace. It is routed along a lake and through a forest, so you get more nature. But, since this route is paved and hardly a secret, you also get more people. In fact, ever since the biking speed limit was raised to 15 miles per hour, there's been a real problem with hikers being used as flags in a slalom course. While the listed one-way distance is six miles, at any point you can just turn around and go back, cutting the trip as short as you wish. Or better yet, bring two vehicles, leave one at each of the two trailheads along Highway 35 (Skyline Boulevard), and make it a one-way walk. From north to south, the hike includes a drop of 400 feet, so if you plan on a return trip, there will be a little huff-and-puff on the way back. Park benches are provided at viewpoints along the lake, where you can often see trout rising and feeding on summer evenings.

⑳ Coyote Point Trail

0.4 mi/0.5 hr

Location: In Coyote Point County Park in San Mateo; map E1–San Francisco Peninsula, grid f3.

User groups: Hikers, wheelchairs, and mountain bikes. No dogs or horses.

Permits: No permits are required. There is a $4 parking fee.

Directions: In San Mateo on U.S. 101, take the Poplar Avenue exit and drive half a block to Humboldt Street. Turn right and drive a few blocks to Peninsula Street. Turn right and drive over, then under, U.S. 101, bearing left on the frontage road. Follow the frontage road a short distance to the Coyote Point County Park entrance.

Alternate route: In San Mateo on U.S. 101, take the Dore exit, then make an immediate left turn on the frontage road and drive a short distance to the Coyote Point County Park entrance.

Maps: For a free trail map, contact Coyote Point County Park at the address below. To obtain a topographic map of the area, ask for San Mateo from the USGS.

Contact: Coyote Point County Park, 1701 Coyote Point Drive, San Mateo, CA 94401; (415) 573-2592.

Trail notes: The trail is so short and flat, some hikers may question why they should bother. But give it a try and you'll see. From the lookout over the pretty South Bay on a clear day, it looks as if you could get a running start, jump, and glide across the water to the land's edge. To hike the trail, park adjacent to the boat ramp and walk out to land's end at Coyote Point. This is a good fishing area, by the way, for jacksmelt in the spring. From this point, you can scan miles of open water, spotting Mount Diablo to the east, the San Mateo Bridge to the south, and on especially clear days, the Bay Bridge to the north. Many are surprised at just how big the South Bay is. An optional side trip is to hike north along the bay's shore.

㉑ Crystal Springs Trail

6.4 mi/3.0 hrs

Location: Along Crystal Springs Reservoir in the Woodside foothills; map E1–San Francisco Peninsula, grid f3.

User groups: Hikers and mountain bikes. No dogs or horses. No wheelchair facilities.

Permits: No permits are required. Parking and access are free.

Directions: From Interstate 280 in San Mateo, take the Highway 92 exit and drive west to Cañada Road/Highway 95. Turn south on Cañada Road and drive 0.2 miles to the parking area on the right.

Maps: For a free trail map, contact San Mateo County Parks at the address below. To obtain a topographic map of the area, ask for San Mateo from the USGS.

Contact: San Mateo County Parks, 590 Hamilton Street, Redwood City, CA 94063; (415) 363-4020 or fax (415) 599-1721.

Trail notes: Crystal Springs is the forbidden paradise of the Bay Area, and this trail is as close as the bureaucrats will let you get. Enjoy the view, but don't touch and don't dare trespass or fish; they'll slam you in the pokey before you know what hit you. From the parking area, the trail runs along the border of San Francisco watershed land, adjacent to Cañada Road. Beautiful Crystal Springs Reservoir is off to the west, occasionally disappearing from view behind a hill as you walk south. Deer are commonly seen in this area, a nice bonus. Your destination is 3.2 miles away, the Pulgas Water Temple (closed to the public), where waters from Hetch Hetchy in Yosemite arrive via canal and thunder into this giant bathtub-like structure surrounded by Roman pillars and a canopy. At the Pulgas Water Temple, you have the option of continuing for another 4.2 miles to Huddart Park. With a shuttle car, that makes a great one-way hike.

㉒ Waterdog Lake Trail

4.0 mi/1.75 hrs

Location: In the Belmont foothills; map E1– San Francisco Peninsula, grid f3.

User groups: Hikers and mountain bikes. No dogs or horses. No wheelchair facilities.

Permits: No permits are required. Parking and access are free.

Directions: From Highway 92 in San Mateo, take the Ralston Avenue exit and turn south on Lyall Way. Drive to the corner of Lyall Way and Lake Road to find the parking entrance. Parking is available along the street.

Maps: For a trail map, contact the City of Belmont Parks at the address below. To obtain a topographic map of the area, ask for San Mateo from the USGS.

Contact: City of Belmont Parks, 1225 Ralston Avenue, Belmont, CA 94002; (415) 595-7441 or fax (415) 595-7419.

Trail notes: The lack of public access to a half-dozen lakes on the Peninsula makes little Waterdog Lake all the more special. Out of the way and often forgotten, the lake was created by damming Belmont Creek in Diablo Canyon. While not exactly a jewel, it still makes for a unique recreation site, but it gets overlooked because the parking access is so obscure. It takes only 15 minutes to reach the lake, with the trail skirting the northern edge of the shore. Many people stop here, but if you forge on, you will be well compensated. The trail, which is more of a dirt road, rises above the lake and enters John Brooks Memorial Open Space. At the crest

of the hill, reached after a climb of about 300 feet, there are pretty views of Crystal Springs Reservoir. An option is to extend your trip on the Sheep Camp Trail, a dirt road that is linked to a gravel road set adjacent to the San Francisco Fish and Game Refuge.

㉓ San Mateo Pier

5.0 mi/2.0 hrs

Location: In South San Francisco Bay in Foster City; map E1–San Francisco Peninsula, grid f4.

User groups: Hikers, wheelchairs, and mountain bikes. No dogs or horses.

Permits: No permits are required. The parking fee is $4 per vehicle.

Directions: From U.S. 101 in San Mateo, take the Hillsdale exit east and drive approximately three miles until the road dead-ends at the pier's parking lot.

Maps: To obtain a topographic map of the area, ask for Redwood Point from the USGS.

Contact: San Mateo County Parks, 590 Hamilton Street, Redwood City, CA 94063; (415) 363-4020 or fax (415) 599-1721. For detailed information or fishing updates, phone Sun Valley Bait and Tackle, (415) 343-6837.

Trail notes: When does a fishing pier make for an excellent hike? When you visit the San Mateo Pier, which provides an unusual adventure, great views, and for people who live nearby, a fresh look at familiar surroundings. The pier was once the old San Mateo Bridge; when its replacement was built, they let the old bridge stand at the western footing in Foster City. It extends 2.5 miles into the main channel of the South Bay and is accessible for free to everyone. Most of the visitors are people out fishing for sharks, rays, perch, kingfish, and even the occasional sturgeon.

Since the pier extends past a mile of tidal flats, there is an abundance of bird life, with dozens of species of seabirds and waterfowl. During minus low tides, the South Bay is a weird sight, as it becomes miles of mudflats with a narrow band of water in the center. By the way, some people call it the San Mateo Pier, some the Foster City Pier, others the Werder Pier. By any name, it's an unusual place to hike.

㉔ Pillar Point

2.5 mi/1.5 hrs

Location: In Princeton at Half Moon Bay; map E1–San Francisco Peninsula, grid g1.

User groups: Hikers, dogs, and horses (not advised). No mountain bikes. No wheelchair facilities.

Permits: No permits are required. Parking and access are free.

Directions: From the Peninsula, take Interstate 280 to San Mateo and Highway 92. Turn west on Highway 92 and drive to Half Moon Bay. Turn right on Highway 1 and drive five miles to Princeton. Turn left at the traffic signal, drive about a half mile through Princeton Village, and turn left again, going one mile toward a radar station. There is limited parking on the left side of the road. Follow the trail on the west side of the harbor.

Maps: To obtain a topographic map of the area, ask for Half Moon Bay from the USGS.

Contact: There is no managing agency. For general information, phone Huck Finn Sportfishing, (415) 726-7133.

Trail notes: One of the truly great coastal walks, this place is nevertheless overlooked by many visitors and locals alike. It includes a secluded beach with inshore kelp beds and sea lions playing peek-a-boo, and during low tide, you can walk "around the corner" at Pillar Point and boulder-hop in wondrous seclusion. Watch your tide book, because the Pillar Point tidal area is under water most of the time.

To start, park at the western side of Princeton Harbor, just below the radar station, then walk out along the west side of the harbor. The trail here is on hard-packed dirt above two quiet beaches where grebes, cormorants, and pelicans often cavort. During the evening, the harbor lights are quite pretty here. When you reach the Princeton jetty, turn right and walk along the beach toward Pillar Point; this is where the sea lions frequently play "Now-you-see-me, now-you-don't." At low tides, continue around Pillar Point and enjoy the rugged beauty, solitude, and ocean views, taking your time as you hop along from rock to rock.

㉕ Harkins Ridge Trail

3.2 mi. one way/1.5 hrs

Location: In Purisima Creek Redwoods Open Space Preserve, on Skyline Ridge near San Mateo; map E1–San Francisco Peninsula, grid g2.

User groups: Hikers, horses, and mountain bikes. No dogs. No wheelchair facilities.

Permits: No permits are required. Parking and access are free.

Directions: From San Francisco, drive south on Interstate 280 for about 15 miles to the Highway 92 cutoff. Turn west on Highway 92 and drive to Highway 35 (Skyline Boulevard). Turn south (left) on Highway 35 and drive 4.5 miles to the Whittemore Gulch Trailhead on the right. If you are planning a shuttle trip, drive a second car to the Higgins Purisima Road parking area (see hike number 26).

Maps: For a free map, contact the Midpeninsula Regional Open Space District at the address below or pick one up at the trailhead. To obtain a topographic map of the area, ask for Woodside from the USGS.

Contact: Midpeninsula Regional Open Space District, 330 Distel Circle, Los Altos, CA 94022; (415) 691-1200 or fax (415) 691-0485.

Trail notes: Purisima Creek Redwoods is a magnificent 2,633-acre redwood preserve set on the western slopes of the Santa Cruz Mountains from Skyline Boulevard down to Half Moon Bay. One of the best ways to explore the area is on the Harkins Ridge Trail. We recommend making it a one-way trip by having a shuttle car waiting at the trail's end at the Higgins Purisima parking access.

The trail starts at the Whittemore Gulch access on Skyline Boulevard, elevation 2,000 feet, and descends over 3.2 miles to 400 feet; the last portion of the trail drops quite steeply in a series of switchbacks. (To turn this into a loop hike, return via the Whittemore Gulch Trail, hike number 26. However, that involves a steep, exposed ascent, and rangers have had to provide emergency assistance to unprepared hikers suffering from exhaustion.) In the process, you are routed through redwoods that many people don't even realize exist. For those who want a pristine experience, a good option is to take the Soda Gulch Trail; about a mile down the Harkins Ridge Trail, turn left at the junction. No mountain bikes are allowed on this portion of the trail, which heads past giant trees, redwood sorrel, and fern-lined creek banks.

㉖ Whittemore Gulch

4.3 mi/3.25 hrs

Location: In Purisima Creek Redwoods Open Space Preserve, near Half Moon Bay; map E1–San Francisco Peninsula, grid g2.

User groups: Hikers only. Horses and mountain bikes are sometimes restricted due to wet weather, so check with a ranger beforehand. No dogs. No wheelchair facilities.

Permits: No permits are required. Parking and access are free.

Directions: From San Francisco, drive south on Interstate 280 for about 15 miles to the Highway 92 cutoff. Turn west on Highway 92 and drive to Half Moon Bay. At the stoplight, turn left on Main Street and drive south through town to Higgins Purisima Road. Turn left and drive on the winding road for four miles to the trailhead parking area on the left.

Maps: For a free map, contact the Midpeninsula Regional Open Space District at the address below or pick one up at the trailhead. To obtain a topographic map of the area, ask for Woodside from the USGS.

Contact: Midpeninsula Regional Open Space District, 330 Distel Circle, Los Altos, CA 94022; (415) 691-1200 or fax (415) 691-0485.

Trail notes: Most folks come to this popular trailhead to take a short stroll along Purisima Creek and then turn back. The Whittemore Gulch Trail, however, offers more of a challenge, especially near the end. It also forms the return route for a loop hike starting at Skyline Boulevard (see hike number 25).

The trail begins innocently enough from the Higgins Purisima parking area, routed right up Whittemore Gulch for a gentle climb over the first mile. This stretch is even suitable for wheelchairs and strollers. All seems well with the world as you pass through a grove of shaded redwoods and by a small stream. Then the bubble pops: In a series of switchbacks, the trail climbs 600 feet in just over a quarter mile, at about a 10 percent grade. After the switchbacks, the trail climbs another 400 feet in a more gracious fashion to reach the Whittemore Gulch parking access on Skyline Boulevard, which, at 2,000 feet, features a great lookout of Half Moon Bay and Pillar Point Harbor. The trailhead elevation is 400 feet, so that means it's a 1,600-foot climb to Skyline Boulevard, taking any of three different trails to get there.

㉗ Redwood Trail

0.5 mi/0.5 hr

Location: In Purisima Creek Redwoods Open Space Preserve, on Skyline Ridge near Woodside; map E1–San Francisco Peninsula, grid g2.

User groups: Hikers and wheelchairs. No dogs, horses, or mountain bikes.

Permits: No permits are required. Parking and access are free.

Directions: From San Francisco, drive south on Interstate 280 for approximately 15 miles to the Highway 92 cutoff. Turn west on Highway 92 and continue driving to Highway 35 (Skyline Boulevard). Turn west on Highway 35 and drive to the Purisima Creek parking area, located at mile marker 16.65.

Maps: For a free map, contact the Midpeninsula Regional Open Space District at the address below or pick one up at the trailhead. To obtain a topographic map of the area, ask for Woodside from the USGS.

Contact: Midpeninsula Regional Open Space District, 330 Distel Circle, Los Altos, CA 94022; (415) 691-1200 or fax (415) 691-0485.

Trail notes: The quarter-mile-long Redwood Trail allows just about anybody to experience the grandeur of a redwood forest. Anybody? People with baby strollers, wheelchairs, or walkers, and those recovering from poor health will be able to do this trail. It starts at 2,000 feet on Skyline Boulevard and is routed north under a canopy of giant redwoods. At the end are picnic tables and rest rooms. And the return trip is just as easy. Most people don't really hike the trail, they just kind of mosey along, seeing how it feels to wander freely among ancient trees.

㉘ Huddart Park Loop

5.0 mi/3.25 hrs

Location: In the Woodside foothills; map E1– San Francisco Peninsula, grid g3.

User groups: Hikers and horses. Mountain bikes are permitted on paved roads only. Limited wheelchair facilities. No dogs.

Permits: No permits are required. A $4 park entrance fee is charged when the kiosk is attended.

Directions: From Interstate 280 in Woodside, take the Woodside Road/Highway 84 exit and drive about nine miles west to King's Mountain Road. Turn right and drive 2.2 miles to the park entrance.

Maps: For a trail map, contact Huddart Park at the address below. To obtain a topographic map of the area, ask for Woodside from the USGS.

Contact: Huddart Park, 1100 King's Mountain Road, Woodside, CA 94062; (415) 851-1210, (415) 851-0326, or fax (415) 851-9558. San Mateo County Parks, 590 Hamilton Street, Redwood City, CA 94063; (415) 363-4020 or fax (415) 691-0485.

Trail notes: A Peninsula treasure, Huddart Park covers 1,000 acres from the foothills near Woodside on up to Skyline Boulevard. Redwoods grow on much of the land, a creek runs right through the park, and when you hike high on the east slope, there are occasional views of the South Bay. While several short loop trips are available here, including the half-mile Redwood Trail, we recommend creating a loop hike and circling the park. A map is a necessity, of course. At the Werder Picnic Area, start on the Dean Trail. To make a complete loop and return to the trailhead, connect to the Richard Road's Trail, Summit Springs Trail, and Archery Fire Trail. In the process you will get a good overview of the entire area and discover why this is one of the best hiking parks on the Peninsula. A unique option is taking the Skyline Ridge Trail (see hike number 29), which connects Huddart Park with Wunderlich Park.

Special note: The Chickadee Trail at Huddart Park is wheelchair accessible. Also, horses are allowed on many other park trails.

㉙ Skyline Trail

8.0 mi. one way/4.5 hrs

Location: From Huddart Park to Skylonda, near the Skyline Ridge and Woodside; map E1– San Francisco Peninsula, grid g3.

User groups: Hikers and horses. No dogs or mountain bikes. No wheelchair facilities.

Permits: No permits are required. A $4 park entrance fee is charged when the kiosk is attended.

Directions: From San Francisco, drive south on Interstate 280 for about 15 miles to the Highway 92 cutoff. Turn west on Highway 92 and drive to Highway 35 (Skyline Boulevard). Turn south (left) on Highway 35 and drive 6.5 miles to the trailhead on the east side of the road. Look for the blue sign marking the Bay Ridge Trail.

Maps: For a trail map, contact Huddart Park at the address below. To obtain a topographic map of the area, ask for Woodside from the USGS.

Contact: Huddart Park, 1100 King's Mountain Road, Woodside, CA 94062; (415) 851-1210, (415) 851-0326, or fax (415) 851-9558. San Mateo County Parks, 590 Hamilton Street, Redwood City, CA 94063; (415) 363-4020 or fax (415) 691-0485.

Trail notes: Great ridgeline views of the South Bay, giant stumps and trees, and a good, long walk are the highlights of the Skyline Trail. This route connects Huddart Park to Wunderlich Park, for an excellent one-way-only walk with a shuttle partner. The trip includes a climb of about 700 feet followed by a descent of some 1,000 feet. For the most part, though, it traces through redwoods along the Skyline Ridge, which provides wonderful views. From Huddart Park heading south, the trail emerges from the park and crosses King's Mountain Road, then climbs gradually (it has been reconstructed to avoid a steep grade) to the Skyline Ridge before turning south again. Skyline Boulevard/Highway 35 may be nearby, but there are few reminders, as the trail is routed to trace ridges and laterals above canyons. Some of the old tree stumps in the area are huge; when you start spotting them, look closely for the Methuselah Tree. The centerpiece of the forest, this colossal survivor spans 15 feet in diameter. When you enter Wunderlich Park, the trail descends sharply in a series of switchbacks, then turns tightly for the last half mile to Skylonda.

⑳ Meadows Loop Trail

5.5 mi/3.0 hrs

Location: In Wunderlich Park in the Woodside foothills; map E1–San Francisco Peninsula, grid g3.

User groups: Hikers and horses. No dogs or mountain bikes. No wheelchair facilities.

Permits: No permits are required. Parking and access are free.

Directions: From Interstate 280 on the Peninsula in Woodside, take the Woodside/Highway 84 exit. Drive west for 2.5 miles to the park on the right.

Maps: For a free map, contact San Mateo County Parks at the address below. To obtain a topographic map of the area, ask for Woodside from the USGS.

Contact: Wunderlich Park, (415) 851-1210, (415) 851-7570, or fax (415) 851-9558. San Mateo County Parks, 590 Hamilton Street, Redwood City, CA 94063; (415) 363-4020 or fax (415) 691-0485.

Trail notes: Wunderlich Park is one of the best spots on the Peninsula for clearing out the brain cobwebs. The network of trails here provides a variety of adventures, from short strolls to all-day treks. Take your pick. Ours is the Meadows Loop, which circles much of the park, crossing first through oak woodlands, rising to open grasslands, then passing a redwood forest on the way back. This hike includes an elevation gain of nearly 1,000 feet, so come prepared for a workout. Make sure you have a trail map, then take this route: Near the park office, look for the signed trailhead for the Alambique Trail and hike about a half mile. At the junction with the Meadows Trail, turn right, hike a short distance, then turn left on the Meadows Trail and climb up to The Meadows. This is a perfect picnic site, with rolling hills, grasslands, and great views. To complete the loop, forge onward, then turn right at the Bear Gulch Trail and take it all the way back, including switchbacks, to the park entrance.

㉛ Ravenswood Open Space Preserve

2.0 mi/0.75 hr

Location: On the shore of South San Francisco Bay at Ravenswood; map E1–San Francisco Peninsula, grid g5.

User groups: Hikers, wheelchairs, and mountain bikes. No dogs or horses.

Permits: No permits are required. Parking and access are free.

Directions: From U.S. 101 in Palo Alto, take the University Avenue exit and drive east to Bay Road. Turn right on Bay Road and drive to the end of the road. The preserve entrance is adjacent to Cooley Landing.

Maps: For a free map, contact the Midpeninsula Regional Open Space District at the address below. To obtain a topographic map of the area, ask for Mountain View from the USGS.

Contact: Midpeninsula Regional Open Space District, 330 Distel Circle, Los Altos, CA 94022; (415) 691-1200 or fax (415) 691-0485.

Trail notes: This 370-acre parcel of land is rich in marshland habitat and home to many types of birds. The first trails became accessible in 1992, along with two excellent observation decks. From the parking area at the end of Bay Road, backtrack by walking across a bridged slough to the trailhead on the north side of the road. You will immediately come to a fork in the road. You can turn right and walk 200 feet to an observation deck with great views of the South Bay. Go left instead and you will find a hard-surface path that heads north and hooks out toward the bay to another wood observation deck. This is the primary destination for most visitors.

㉜ Baylands Catwalk

0.25 mi/0.5 hr

Location: On the shore of South San Francisco Bay in Palo Alto; map E1–San Francisco Peninsula, grid g5.

User groups: Hikers only. No dogs, horses, or mountain bikes. No wheelchair facilities.

Permits: No permits are required. Parking and access are free.

Directions: From U.S. 101 in Palo Alto, take the Embarcadero exit east. Drive toward the bay, jogging left past the airport. Drive past the yacht harbor until you reach a sharp right turn. Park at the lot on the right. The nature preserve is on the left.

Maps: To obtain a topographic map of the area, ask for Mountain View from the USGS.

Contact: Palo Alto Baylands Interpretive Center, 1451 Middlefield Road, Palo Alto, CA 94301; (415) 329-2261, (415) 329-2506, or fax (415) 691-0485.

Trail notes: What the heck is the Baylands Catwalk, you ask? As you will discover, it is an old wooden walkway placed across tidal marshland and routed under giant electrical towers and out to the shoreline of South San Francisco Bay. In recent years, the Catwalk has been improved, with a new observation deck set on the edge of the bay waters. You start at the Baylands Interpretive Center, which houses exhibits explaining the marshland habitat. From there, you can make the short walk straight east out to the observation deck, about a 10-minute trip. The marsh supports an abundant population of bird life, especially egrets, coots, and ducks.

Special note: The Catwalk extends north and south across the marsh for a mile. This was once a great, easy walk, but access is now forbidden in order to protect an endangered mouse and passage is blocked by a barbed-wire-edged gate.

㉝ Baylands Trail

4.0 mi/1.5 hrs

Location: On the shore of South San Francisco Bay in Palo Alto; map E1–San Francisco Peninsula, grid g5.

User groups: Hikers, wheelchairs, and mountain bikes. No dogs or horses.

Permits: No permits are required. Parking and access are free.

Directions: From U.S. 101 in Palo Alto, take the Embarcadero East exit. At the second light, across from Ming's Restaurant, turn left on Geng Street and drive to the end of the road. The trailhead is right behind the Baylands Baseball Park grandstand.

Maps: To obtain a topographic map of the area, ask for Mountain View from the USGS.

Contact: Palo Alto Baylands Interpretive Center, 1451 Middlefield Road, Palo Alto, CA 94301; (415) 329-2261, (415) 329-2506, or fax (415) 691-0485.

Trail notes: The farther you go on this trail, the better it gets. The Baylands Trail starts without much fanfare, a simple hard-gravel road with an ugly slough on your left and the Palo Alto golf course on your right. If you keep looking ahead, you will often see ground squirrels scurrying about, along with an occasional jackrabbit. The trail then reaches a fork. Bikers should turn left, taking the outstanding Baylands bike trail; it extends all the way to Dumbarton Bridge, which has a bike lane, and across the bay to Fremont. Hikers are better off turning right. Here the trail softens and the slough melds into the tidal waters of San Francisquito Creek. The pathway continues along past the golf course, then crosses the departure runway for the Palo Alto Airport and leads out to land's end, where the creek pours into the bay. This is a classic salt marsh habitat, with lots of birds and wildlife. The views are pretty, the walk is as flat as it gets, and hikers are always sighting squirrels, rabbits, egrets, coots, and ducks.

㉞ South Bay Nature Trail

2.0 mi/1.0 hr

Location: In San Francisco Bay National Wildlife Refuge near Alviso; map E1–San Francisco Peninsula, grid g5.

User groups: Hikers and mountain bikes. No dogs or horses. No wheelchair facilities.

Permits: No permits are required. Parking and access are free.

Directions: From U.S. 101 near Sunnyvale, take Highway 237 east to Zanker Street. Turn left on Zanker Street and drive to the parking area at the Environmental Education Center.

Maps: To obtain a topographic map of the area, ask for Mountain View from the USGS.

Contact: San Francisco Bay National Wildlife Refuge, P.O. Box 524, Newark, CA 94560; (510)

792-4275 or (510) 792-0222. Environmental Education Center, (408) 262-2867.

Trail notes: Everybody knows about the San Francisco Bay National Wildlife Refuge, right? That's the big nature center located at the eastern foot of the Dumbarton Bridge, right? Very popular, right? Wrong, wrong, and wrong. A little-known portion of the wildlife refuge is set deep in the South Bay marsh near Alviso, where it receives scant attention compared to its big brother to the north. Headquarters are at the Environmental Education Center; from there, you walk on a dirt path along a wild tidal marshland. As you stroll northward, you will delve into wilder and wilder habitat, and in the process have a chance at seeing a dozen species of birds in a matter of minutes. The endangered harvest salt mouse lives in this habitat. Guided nature walks are held regularly on weekend mornings, and they are well worth attending.

Leave No Trace Tips

Minimize Use and Impact of Fires

Campfires can have a lasting impact on the backcountry. Always carry a lightweight stove for cooking, and use a candle lantern instead of building a fire whenever possible.

Where fires are permitted, use established fire rings only.

Do not scar the natural setting by snapping the branches off live, dead, or downed trees.

Completely extinguish your campfire and make sure it is cold before departing. Remove all unburned trash from the fire ring and scatter the cold ashes over a large area well away from any camp.

Map E1–East Bay

Adjoining Maps: East: E2 ..... *page* 320   West: E1 ..... 216, 250
North: D1 156   South: E1 294

Note: Section E1 is divided into four chapters. For other E1 sections
see pages 216 (Marin), 250 (San Francisco), and 294 (South Bay).

Northern California Map .... *page* 2

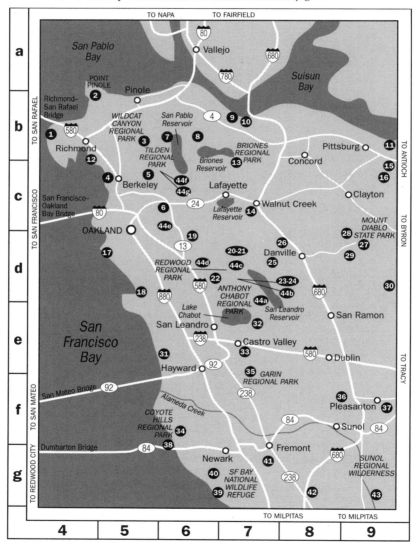

❶ False Gun Vista Point

1.0 mi/0.75 hr

Location: In Miller-Knox Regional Shoreline west of Richmond on the shore of San Francisco Bay; map E1–East Bay, grid b4.

User groups: Hikers and dogs. No horses or mountain bikes. No wheelchair facilities.

Permits: No permits are required. Parking and access are free.

Directions: In Richmond, drive south on Interstate 80, exit west at Cutting Boulevard, and drive to Garrard Boulevard. Turn left and drive through the tunnel. The road becomes Dornan Drive; follow Dornan Drive for a half mile to the parking area on the right. From Berkeley, drive north on Interstate 80 and bear left on Interstate 580 west. Turn left at the Cutting Boulevard exit and proceed as above.

Maps: For a free trail map, contact the East Bay Regional Parks District at the address below and ask for the Miller-Knox Regional Shoreline brochure. To obtain a topographic map of the area, ask for San Quentin from the USGS.

Contact: East Bay Regional Parks District, 2950 Peralta Oaks Court, P.O. Box 5381, Oakland, CA 94605; (510) 635-0135, extension 2200, or fax (510) 569-1417.

Trail notes: A little-known lookout over San Francisco Bay is the highlight of Miller-Knox Regional Shoreline, and getting to it requires only a short hike and climb. This parkland covers 260 acres of hill and shoreline property at Point Richmond, where strong afternoon winds in the summer create excellent conditions for kite flying. While most people make the short stroll along Keller Beach, we prefer this hike. From the parking area, it leads about half a mile up Old Country

Road and the Marine View Trail, making a right turn on the Crest Trail to reach the False Gun Vista Point. In the process the trail climbs 300 feet to the lookout at 322 feet. On clear days, you get picture-perfect views of San Francisco Bay and its many surrounding landmarks.

❷ Bay View Loop

3.0 mi/1.5 hrs

Location: In Point Pinole Regional Shoreline; map E1–East Bay, grid b5.

User groups: Hikers, dogs, horses, and mountain bikes. The trail is partially wheelchair accessible.

Permits: No permits are required. A $3 parking fee is charged when the kiosk is attended. The shuttle bus costs $1 for ages 12 through 61 and 50 cents for seniors and youngsters 6 through 11. Children under six and disabled people ride free.

Directions: From Interstate 80 in San Pablo, take the Hilltop exit. Drive west on Hilltop to the intersection with San Pablo Avenue. Turn right on San Pablo Avenue and drive north for a short distance, then turn left on Richmond Parkway. Drive a few miles to Giant Highway. Turn right and drive a short distance to the well-signed park entrance on the left. Take the shuttle bus to the bay.

Maps: For a free trail map, contact the East Bay Regional Parks District at the address below and ask for the Point Pinole Regional Shoreline brochure. To obtain a topographic map of the area, ask for Richmond from the USGS.

Contact: East Bay Regional Parks District, 2950 Peralta Oaks Court, P.O. Box 5381, Oakland, CA 94605; (510) 635-0135, extension 2200, or fax (510) 569-1417. Point Pinole Regional Shoreline, (510) 237-6896.

Trail notes: On the Bay View Loop, you can walk several miles along the shore of San Pablo Bay and see nothing but water, passing ships, and birds. That's because visitors to Point Pinole must park at the entrance station and catch a shuttle bus to the shoreline. There you will find a long, pretty cobbled beach and beautiful views of San Pablo Bay, Marin, and Mount Tamalpais. An excellent fishing pier is also available. The park covers 2,147 acres, and this loop trail is a great way to explore it. From the parking area, it is routed along the shore to Point Pinole, then swings back on the Woods Trail, which runs through a large grove of eucalyptus.

❸ San Pablo Ridge Loop

6.2 mi/3.0 hrs

Location: In Wildcat Canyon Regional Park in the Richmond foothills; map E1–East Bay, grid b5.

User groups: Hikers, dogs, horses, and mountain bikes. No wheelchair facilities.

Permits: No permits are required. Parking and access are free.

Directions: In Richmond, head north on Interstate 80 to the Amador/Solano exit, turn east, and drive three blocks on Amador. Turn right on McBryde Avenue and head east. After passing Arlington Boulevard, drive straight (the road is now Park Avenue) and bear left through a piped gate to the parking area.

Maps: For a free trail map, contact the East Bay Regional Parks District at the address below and ask for the Wildcat Canyon Regional Park brochure. To obtain a topographic map of the area, ask for Richmond from the USGS.

Contact: East Bay Regional Parks District, 2950 Peralta Oaks Court, P.O. Box 5381, Oakland, CA 94605; (510) 635-0135, extension 2200, or fax (510) 569-1417. Tilden Nature Area, (510) 525-2233.

Trail notes: Newcomers to Wildcat Canyon Regional Park may find it hard to believe how quickly they can get to a remote land with great views. But it is true. Just east of Richmond, San Pablo Ridge rises about a thousand feet high; it takes a short grunt of a hike to get to the top, but you'll find it well worth the grunting. That's because you get great views of San Pablo Reservoir and Briones Reservoir off one side of the ridge, and of San Francisco Bay on the other. Of all the views of San Francisco, this is certainly one of the best. Start at the parking area and hike up the Belgum Trail, turning right at San Pablo Ridge and climbing about 700 feet over the course of 2.5 miles. Once on top, slow down and enjoy the cruise. To loop around, turn right on the Mezue Trail then right again on the Wildcat Creek Trail and walk back to the parking area.

❹ Berkeley Pier

1.2 mi/0.75 hr

Location: Near Berkeley on the shore of San Francisco Bay; map E1–East Bay, grid b5.

User groups: Hikers and wheelchairs. No dogs, horses, or mountain bikes.

Permits: No permits are required. Parking and access are free.

Directions: From Interstate 80 in Berkeley, take the University Avenue exit and follow the signs to the Berkeley Marina. The pier is at the foot of University Avenue, just past the bait shop and marina.

Maps: To obtain a topographic map of the area, ask for Oakland West from the USGS.

Contact: Berkeley Marina, 201 University Avenue, Berkeley, CA 94701; (510) 644-6376.

Trail notes: This historic structure extends 3,000 feet into San Francisco Bay amidst landmarks that people come from around the world to see. The walk is easy—straight, flat, and long—and while most people can get to the end of the pier in 20 minutes, there is no reason to hurry. The Golden Gate Bridge is a classic sight from your vantage point at the end of the pier, especially during sunsets, when you will discover how the Golden Gate earned its name. Things look different out here, especially if you bring a loaf of French bread to nibble on and maybe your favorite elixir to wash it down. Fishing success varies, but the best time is in the early summer, when halibut school on the Berkeley Flats.

❺ Nimitz Way

10.0 mi/4.25 hrs

Location: In Tilden Regional Park at Inspiration Point in the Berkeley hills; map E1–East Bay, grid c5.

User groups: Hikers, dogs, horses, and mountain bikes. The trail is partially wheelchair accessible.

Permits: No permits are required. Parking and access are free.

Directions: From Highway 24 in the East Bay, drive to just east of the Caldecott Tunnel and take the Fish Ranch Road exit west to Grizzly Peak Boulevard. Turn right, drive up the hill, and turn right again on South Park Drive. Drive one mile to Wildcat Canyon Road, bear right, and drive to the parking area at Inspiration Point on the left. South Park Drive is closed each year from November through March to protect migrating newts. To avoid South Park Drive, from Highway 24 drive through the Caldecott Tunnel and exit at Orinda. Turn left on Camino Pablo. Drive north for about two miles, turn left on Wildcat Canyon Road, and follow it to Inspiration Point on the right.

Maps: For a free trail map, contact the East Bay Regional Parks District at the address below and ask for the Tilden Regional Park brochure. To obtain a topographic map of the area, ask for Briones Valley from the USGS.

Contact: East Bay Regional Parks District, 2950 Peralta Oaks Court, P.O. Box 5381, Oakland, CA 94605; (510) 635-0135, extension 2200, or fax (510) 569-1417. Tilden Nature Area, (510) 525-2233.

Trail notes: When you start down this trail, you might wonder why we rated it so high. The views? Sure, the sweeping vistas of the East Bay foothills are great, but hey, the paved trail seems more appropriate for bikes, wheelchairs, and joggers than hikers. And so it is for the first four miles, until suddenly you enter a different universe. After passing a gate, the trail turns to dirt and, just like that, there's no one else around as you climb San Pablo Ridge. The views are stunning in all directions, particularly of Briones and San Pablo Reservoirs to the east, and San Francisco Bay and the city's skyline to the west. Your goal should be to climb at least to Wildcat Peak, elevation 1,250 feet, and two miles out before turning around and heading for home. This is one of the best sections of the 31-mile East Bay Skyline National Trail.

❻ Round Top Loop Trail

1.7 mi/1.0 hr

Location: In the Robert Sibley Volcanic Regional Preserve in the Berkeley hills; map E1–East Bay, grid c6.

User groups: Hikers and dogs. The trail is partially accessible to wheelchairs, horses, and mountain bikes.

Permits: No permits are required. Parking and access are free.

Directions: From Highway 24 in the East Bay, drive to just east of the Caldecott Tunnel and take the Fish Ranch Road exit west to Grizzly Peak Boulevard. Turn left and drive to Skyline Boulevard, then drive straight ahead for another quarter mile to the park entrance and parking area on the left.

Alternate route: From Montclair Village, east of Highway 13 in Oakland, take Snake Road uphill to Skyline Boulevard. Turn left on Skyline Boulevard and drive to the park entrance.

Maps: For a free trail map, contact the East Bay Regional Parks District at the address below and ask for the Sibley Volcanic Regional Preserve brochure. To obtain a topographic map of the area, ask for Briones Valley from the USGS.

Contact: East Bay Regional Parks District, 2950 Peralta Oaks Court, P.O. Box 5381, Oakland, CA 94605; (510) 635-0135, extension 2200, or fax (510) 569-1417.

Trail notes: The remains of the Bay Area's long-extinct volcano, Mount Round Top, can be explored at Sibley Preserve. As you walk along the exposed volcanic rock, you can take a self-guided tour using a pamphlet available at the trailhead. After the volcano blasted out its lava contents about nine million years ago, the interior of the mountain collapsed into the void left by the outburst and blocks of volcanic stone lay scattered everywhere around the flanks of the mountain. A gated road leads to the top at elevation 1,763 feet, but the best way to see the mountain is on the Round Top Loop Trail. Hike in a clockwise direction so the numbered posts (1 through 9) on the self-guided tour correspond in order with the most interesting volcanic outcrops.

❼ Laurel Loop Trail

0.7 mi/0.5 hr

Location: In the Kennedy Grove Regional Recreation Area near the San Pablo Reservoir in El Sobrante; map E1–East Bay, grid b6.

User groups: Hikers, dogs, horses, and mountain bikes. No wheelchair facilities.

Permits: No permits are required. There is a $3-per-vehicle parking fee when the kiosk is attended.

Directions: From Interstate 80 in Richmond, take the San Pablo Dam Road exit. Turn east and drive through El Sobrante for 3.5 miles to the park entrance on the left. From the entrance, follow the pavement to the northwestern parking lot. From Orinda, turn left on Camino Pablo and drive north along San Pablo Reservoir to the park entrance on the right.

Maps: For a free trail map, contact the East Bay Regional Parks District at the address below and ask for the Kennedy Grove Regional Recreation Area brochure. To obtain a topographic map of the area, ask for Richmond from the USGS.

Contact: East Bay Regional Parks District, 2950 Peralta Oaks Court, P.O. Box 5381, Oakland, CA 94605; (510) 635-0135, extension 2200, or fax (510) 569-1417. Kennedy Grove Regional Recreation Area, (510) 223-7840.

Trail notes: Kennedy Grove is set at the base of San Pablo Dam, where visitors will discover a rich grove of eucalyptus located adjacent to a large lawn/meadow. This loop hike takes hikers through the eucalyptus and then back, skirting the lawn areas. It is best hiked in a clockwise direction, departing from the trailhead at the gate at the northeast corner of the parking area. This is the kind of park where people toss Frisbees, pass a football, or play a low-key game of softball.

Special note: A new hiking and equestrian trail is located off the Laurel Loop Trail. The one-mile Seafoam Trail can be accessed from the other side of the grove. It ascends a hill through a woodland of bay and oak trees and provides spectacular views of San Pablo Ridge and the North Bay.

❽ Sobrante Ridge Trail

1.6 mi/1.0 hr

Location: In the Sobrante Ridge Regional Preserve near El Sobrante; map E1–East Bay, grid b6.

User groups: Hikers, dogs, horses, and mountain bikes. No wheelchair facilities.

Permits: No permits are required. Parking and access are free.

Directions: From Interstate 80 in Richmond, take the San Pablo Dam Road exit. Drive east for three miles and turn left on Castro Ranch Road. Drive about two miles to Conestoga Way, then turn left and proceed to Carriage Drive. Turn left again and drive two blocks to Coach Way. Turn right and proceed to the park entrance and parking area at the end of the road.

Maps: For a free trail map, contact the East Bay Regional Parks District at the address below and ask for the Sobrante Ridge Regional Preserve brochure. To obtain a topographic map of the area, ask for Briones Valley from the USGS.

Contact: East Bay Regional Parks District, 2950 Peralta Oaks Court, P.O. Box 5381, Oakland, CA 94605; (510) 635-0135, extension 2200, or fax (510) 569-1417. Sobrante Ridge Regional Preserve, (510) 223-7840.

Trail notes: Sobrante Ridge Park was the missing link in an East Bay corridor of open space until finally being acquired in the mid-1980s. The wild and scenic land is now protected, and should remain that way forever. The park covers 277 acres of rolling hills, open ridgeline, and wooded ravines, and this hike accesses the best of it. From the trailhead at Coach Drive, take the Sobrante Ridge Trail, which rises in an elliptical half-loop to the left. After 0.7 miles, you will come to the junction with the Broken Oaks Trail. Turn left here and make the short loop (less than a quarter-mile long), then retrace your steps on the Sobrante Ridge Trail. This walk provides an easy yet intimate look at one of the Bay Area's newest parklands.

⑨ Franklin Ridge Loop Trail

3.1 mi/1.75 hrs

Location: At Carquinez Strait Regional Shoreline near Martinez; map E1–East Bay, grid b7.

User groups: Hikers, dogs, horses, and mountain bikes. No wheelchair facilities.

Permits: No permits are required. Parking and access are free.

Directions: From Highway 4 in Martinez, take the Alhambra Avenue exit and drive north for

two miles toward the Carquinez Strait. Turn left on Escobar Street, drive three blocks, and turn right on Talbart Street, which becomes Carquinez Scenic Drive. Follow that road for about a half mile to the parking area on the left.

Maps: For a free trail map, contact the East Bay Regional Parks District at the address below and ask for the Carquinez Strait Regional Shoreline brochure. To obtain a topographic map of the area, ask for Benicia from the USGS.

Contact: East Bay Regional Parks District, 2950 Peralta Oaks Court, P.O. Box 5381, Oakland, CA 94605; (510) 635-0135, extension 2200, or fax (510) 569-1417.

Trail notes: Set on the hillsides overlooking Martinez, this land is the gateway to the San Joaquin Delta. The Franklin Ridge Loop Trail is the best way to explore the park, rising to 750 feet. From the ridge, there are spectacular views of Carquinez Strait, Mount Diablo, and Mount Tamalpais. From the parking area at the Carquinez Strait East Staging Area, the hike heads south on the California Riding and Hiking Trail toward Franklin Ridge, climbing as it goes, at times quite steeply, then connects to the Franklin Ridge Loop. When you reach the loop, note that this trail is best hiked in a clockwise direction. Most of the park consists of open, rolling grasslands, but there are some groves of eucalyptus and a few wooded ravines.

⑩ Martinez Shoreline

2.2 mi/1.0 hr

Location: At Martinez Regional Shoreline near Martinez; map E1–East Bay, grid b7.

User groups: Hikers, dogs, horses, and mountain bikes. The rest rooms are wheelchair accessible, but the trail is not.

Permits: No permits are required. Parking and access are free.

Directions: From Highway 4 in Martinez, take the Alhambra Avenue exit. Drive north on Alhambra Avenue for two miles and turn right on Escobar Street. Continue for three blocks to Ferry Street and turn left. Drive across the railroad tracks and bear right onto Joe DiMaggio Drive. Turn left on North Coast Street and drive to the parking area next to the fishing pier.

Maps: For a free trail map, contact the East Bay Regional Parks District at the address below and ask for the Martinez Regional Shoreline brochure. To obtain a topographic map of the area, ask for Benicia from the USGS.

Contact: East Bay Regional Parks District, 2950 Peralta Oaks Court, P.O. Box 5381, Oakland, CA 94605; (510) 635-0135, extension 2200, or fax (510) 569-1417.

Trail notes: The Shoreline Trail is the most attractive walk at Martinez Waterfront Park, a 343-acre parcel that includes marshlands and bay frontage. Start hiking from the parking area located at the foot of the Martinez Fishing Pier and walk back on North Court Street to the trailhead at Sand Beach. The hike skirts a pond, crosses Arch Bridge over Alhambra Creek, and runs along the waterfront, past an old schooner hull, to the park's western boundary. The trail is easy and flat, with the bay on one side, marshlands on the other. It is popular for bicycling, jogging, and bird-watching. An option is to walk a short distance from the parking lot to the Martinez Pier, one of the few piers in the Bay Area where steelhead are caught in the winter.

⑪ Antioch Pier

0.5 mi/0.5 hr

Location: At Antioch Regional Shoreline near Antioch; map E1–East Bay, grid b9.

User groups: Hikers, wheelchairs, dogs, and mountain bikes. No horses.

Permits: No permits are required. Parking and access are free. To fish from the shore or the pier, people 16 and over must obtain a fishing license.

Directions: From Highway 4 in Antioch, take the Wilbur Avenue exit and turn right on Wilbur Avenue. Make an immediate left on Bridgehead Road; the parking area is at the end of the road.

Maps: For a free trail map, contact the East Bay Regional Parks District at the address below and ask for the Antioch Regional Shoreline brochure. To obtain a topographic map of the area, ask for Antioch North from the USGS.

Contact: East Bay Regional Parks District, 2950 Peralta Oaks Court, P.O. Box 5381, Oakland, CA 94605; (510) 635-0135, extension 2200, or fax (510) 569-1417.

Trail notes: This is a short but scenic walk along a marshland and out to the end of a 550-foot pier, one of the best fishing piers in the Bay Area. The parkland encompasses only 7.5 acres, but it is set along the lower San Joaquin River just upstream from the Antioch Bridge. From the parking lot, the trail leads 0.14 miles to the foot of the pier, with a gated, wheelchair-accessible road on your right and wetlands on your left. The pier extends into the San Joaquin River, right into the pathway of migrating striped bass, sturgeon, and at other times, catfish and even salmon. If you don't catch any fish, you can still go to the end of the pier and catch views of the Antioch Bridge and the San Joaquin River at its widest point.

⑫ Point Isabel Shoreline

1.0 mi/0.75 hr

Location: At Point Isabel Regional Shoreline near Berkeley; map E1–East Bay, grid c4.

User groups: Hikers and dogs. No horses or mountain bikes. The rest rooms are wheelchair accessible, but the trail is not.

Permits: No permits are required. Parking and access are free.

Directions: From Interstate 80 in south Richmond, take the Central Avenue exit and drive west to Isabel Street. Turn right and drive to the parking area at the end of the road.

Maps: For a free trail map, contact the East Bay Regional Parks District at the address below and ask for the Point Isabel Regional Shoreline brochure. To obtain a topographic map of the area, ask for Richmond from the USGS.

Contact: East Bay Regional Parks District, 2950 Peralta Oaks Court, P.O. Box 5381, Oakland, CA 94605; (510) 635-0135, extension 2200, or fax (510) 569-1417.

Trail notes: Beautiful bayfront views of San Francisco and the Golden Gate, plus the fact that it's a popular place to walk dogs, attract visitors to the Point Isabel Regional Shoreline. The point extends into San Francisco Bay just north of Golden Gate Fields Racetrack, and the 21-acre park provides an easy shoreline walk, rich bird-watching opportunities, and those great views. From the parking area, the trail extends northward along the shore of the bay, then east along Hoffman Channel, and ends with a short loop trail around the edge of Hoffman Marsh. The best time to see birds here is in the fall, when year-round residents are joined by migratory species.

⑬ Briones Crest Loop

5.6 mi/3.25 hrs

Location: In Briones Regional Park north of Lafayette; map E1–East Bay, grid c7.

User groups: Hikers, dogs, and horses. Mountain bikes are allowed on all but the last mile of the loop. No wheelchair facilities.

Permits: No permits are required. There is a $3-per-vehicle parking fee when the kiosk is attended.

Directions: From Interstate 680 north of Pleasant Hill, take Highway 4 west for three miles to the Alhambra Avenue exit. Turn south on Alhambra Avenue, drive for a half mile, and bear right onto Alhambra Valley Road. Drive another mile to Reliez Valley Road. Turn left and follow Reliez Valley Road a half mile to the parking area on the right. Look for the trailhead indicating the Alhambra Creek Trail.

Maps: For a free trail map, contact the East Bay Regional Parks District at the address below and ask for the Briones Regional Park brochure. To obtain a topographic map of the area, ask for Briones Valley from the USGS.

Contact: East Bay Regional Parks District, 2950 Peralta Oaks Court, P.O. Box 5381, Oakland, CA 94605; (510) 635-0135, extension 2200, or fax (510) 569-1417.

Trail notes: Briones Regional Park is a 5,700-acre sanctuary of peace set amid several fast-growing communities. It is one of the best parks for hiking in the East Bay, with an intricate network of trails, and this is the best of the lot. There are many trail junctions on the loop, and a map will help you from making a wrong turn. From the trailhead, take the Alhambra Creek Trail and the Spengler Trail (turn right) to the Briones Crest Trail and turn left. This stretch rises to Briones Peak at 1,483 feet in just 2.5 miles. It is the highest point in the park and grants a panoramic view of the East Bay's rolling hillsides,

quiet and tranquil. The view includes Mount Diablo, the west Delta, Suisun Bay, and the mothball fleet. To complete the loop, turn left on the Spengler Trail, then right on the Diablo View Trail. The latter closes out the hike in 1.1 miles, offering great views of the slopes of Mount Diablo.

⑭ Lafayette-Moraga Trail

7.75 mi. one way/4.0 hrs

Location: North of the San Leandro Reservoir; map E1–East Bay, grid c7.

User groups: Hikers, wheelchairs, dogs, horses, and mountain bikes.

Permits: No permits are required. Parking and access are free.

Directions: From Highway 24 near Lafayette, take the Pleasant Hill exit south. Turn right on Olympic Boulevard and park at the Olympic Staging Area.

Maps: For a free trail map, contact the East Bay Regional Parks District at the address below and ask for the Lafayette-Moraga Regional Trail brochure. To obtain topographic maps of the area, ask for Walnut Creek and Las Trampas Ridge from the USGS.

Contact: East Bay Regional Parks District, 2950 Peralta Oaks Court, P.O. Box 5381, Oakland, CA 94605; (510) 635-0135, extension 2200, or fax (510) 569-1417.

Trail notes: The Lafayette-Moraga Trail is a 7.75-mile linear park. In other words, the trail is a park that forms a line from Lafayette to Moraga. Much of it is paved, while the rest is either dirt or compacted soil, making most of the route more popular with bikers and joggers than hikers. The hike starts at the Olympic Staging Area in Lafayette and curls to the left for the first 3.5 miles, eventually heading south along Las Trampas Creek to Bollinger Canyon. It then passes through downtown Moraga to the Valle Vista Staging Area on Canyon Road. For most, this is the end of the trip, as bicycles, dogs, and horses are not allowed to continue. Hikers, however, may keep walking west on land managed by the East Bay Municipal Utility District. Permits are required on East Bay MUD lands; phone (510) 287-0469.

⑮ Prospect Tunnel Loop

4.5 mi/2.5 hrs

Location: In the Black Diamond Mines Regional Preserve in the Mount Diablo foothills near Antioch; map E1–East Bay, grid c9.

User groups: Hikers, dogs, horses, and mountain bikes. A short portion of the trail is accessible to hikers only. No wheelchair facilities.

Permits: No permits are required. The parking fee is $3 per vehicle from November through February and $4 from March through October; there's a $1 dog fee year-round.

Directions: From Highway 4 at Antioch, take the Lone Tree Way exit and drive south to Blue Rock Drive. Turn right, drive to Frederickson Lane, bear right, and drive to the gate. There is limited parking on the left. Note: The signs along the way say "Contra Loma Regional Park," not "Black Diamond Mines." Once past the gate, you will be in Black Diamond Mines Regional Preserve.

Maps: For a free trail map, contact the East Bay Regional Parks District at the address below and ask for the Black Diamond Mines Regional Preserve brochure. To obtain a topographic map of the area, ask for Antioch South from the USGS.

Contact: East Bay Regional Parks District, 2950 Peralta Oaks Court, P.O. Box 5381, Oakland, CA 94605; (510) 635-0135, extension 2200, or fax (510) 569-1417.

Trail notes: Bring a flashlight with fresh batteries so you can explore 200 feet of mountain tunnel, the featured attraction of Black Diamond Mines Regional Preserve. The Prospect Tunnel, driven in the 1860s by miners in search of coal, probes 400 feet into the side of Mount Diablo, and half of that length is now accessible to the public. To reach the tunnel, it's about a 1.5-mile hike from the trailhead, taking the Stewartville Trail off Frederickson Lane. Most of the surrounding area is grasslands and foothill country. After exploring the Prospect Tunnel, you can tack a loop onto your hike. Turn left on the Star Mine Trail, which loops for 1.6 miles and passes by a barred tunnel, one of the last active coal mines in the area. The Prospect Tunnel and the Star Mine are two of the most unusual spots in the preserve's 3,700 acres.

⑯ Contra Loma Loop

1.6 mi/1.0 hr

Location: In Contra Loma Regional Park near Antioch; map E1–East Bay, grid c9.

User groups: Hikers, wheelchairs, dogs, horses, and mountain bikes.

Permits: No permits are required. The parking fee is $3 per vehicle from November through February and $4 from March through October; there's a $1 dog fee year-round.

Directions: From Highway 4 at Antioch, take the Lone Tree Way exit and drive south to Blue Rock Drive. Turn right, drive to Frederickson Lane, bear right, and drive to the gate. There is limited parking on the left side of the road. Take a right turn, pass the kiosk, and bear left. Drive to the parking lot by the beach.

Maps: For a free trail map, contact the East Bay Regional Parks District at the address below and ask for the Contra Loma Regional Park brochure. To obtain a topographic map of the area, ask for Antioch South from the USGS.

Contact: East Bay Regional Parks District, 2950 Peralta Oaks Court, P.O. Box 5381, Oakland, CA 94605; (510) 635-0135, extension 2200, or fax (510) 569-1417.

Trail notes: Most people go to Contra Loma Regional Park to fish at Contra Loma Lake, swim and sunbathe, or picnic. This short loop trail provides an alternative to those activities, tracing along the northwest shore of the lake, then climbing up and over a short hill and looping back to the starting point. From the parking area, head out on the trail to the Cattail Cove Picnic Area. Just after that, the trail turns right and follows the shore of the lake, passes a fishing pier, and then starts a 10-minute climb up a small hill. To close out the loop, glide down the hill. The trail turns left and a mile later returns to the Cattail Cove Picnic Area.

⑰ Shoreline Trail

5.0 mi/2.25 hrs

Location: At Crown Memorial State Beach on the shore of San Francisco Bay in Alameda; map E1–East Bay, grid d5.

User groups: Hikers, wheelchairs, dogs (on the paved trail only, not the beach), and mountain bikes. No horses.

Permits: No permits are required. There is a $3 parking fee when the entrance kiosk is attended.

Directions: From Interstate 580, take Interstate 980 west into Oakland. Take the 12th Street/Alameda exit. Follow the road under Interstate 880 and turn left onto Fifth Street. Drive to the Oakland/Alameda Tube. At the end of the tube, you will be on Webster Street, which deadends at Central. Turn left on Central, then right on Eighth Street and drive a quarter mile to Crown Beach.

Maps: For a free trail map, contact the East Bay Regional Parks District at the address below and ask for the Crown Memorial State Beach brochure. To obtain a topographic map of the area, ask for Oakland West from the USGS.

Contact: East Bay Regional Parks District, 2950 Peralta Oaks Court, P.O. Box 5381, Oakland, CA 94605; (510) 635-0135, extension 2200, or fax (510) 569-1417.

Trail notes: The tide book is your bible at Crown Memorial State Beach, which is set along the shore of San Francisco Bay just south of Crab Cove. High tide is the best time to observe seabirds such as loons, grebes, and ducks. Low tide, however, is the best time to watch shorebirds such as sandpipers poking around the exposed mudflats. The trail is a paved bicycle path that follows the bay's shoreline, running 2.5 miles south to an overlook of the Elsie Roemer Bird Sanctuary. The bay views are also quite good. When the wind is down, this is one of the best swimming areas in the bay; when the wind is up, it's excellent for windsurfing.

⓲ Arrowhead Marsh

2.0 mi/1.0 hr

Location: At Martin Luther King Regional Shoreline on San Leandro Bay near Oakland; map E1–East Bay, grid d5.

User groups: Hikers, wheelchairs, and mountain bikes. No dogs or horses.

Permits: No permits are required. Parking and access are free.

Directions: From Interstate 880 in Oakland, take the Hegenberger Road exit and follow it toward the airport and Doolittle Drive. Turn right on Doolittle Drive and proceed to Swan Way. Turn right again and drive a short distance to the park entrance. Turn left and drive to the parking area at the end of the road.

Alternate route: From Interstate 880 in Oakland, take the Hegenberger Road exit and drive a short distance to Pardee Drive. Turn right and drive a few blocks to Swan Way. Turn left and drive one block to Gravel Access Road. Turn right on Gravel Access Road and drive a short distance to the marsh area.

Maps: For a free trail map, contact the East Bay Regional Parks District at the address below and ask for the Martin Luther King Regional Shoreline brochure. To obtain a topographic map of the area, ask for San Leandro from the USGS.

Contact: East Bay Regional Parks District, 2950 Peralta Oaks Court, P.O. Box 5381, Oakland, CA 94605; (510) 635-0135, extension 2200, or fax (510) 569-1417.

Trail notes: Arrowhead Marsh is one of the best bird-watching areas in the East Bay, with 30 species commonly sighted, including several pairs of blue-winged teal. At high tide, this is also a top spot to see rails, typically elusive birds that are more often heard than seen. The paved trail skirts the edge of the marsh, which is set along San Leandro Bay. From the parking area, the trail is routed one mile out along the Airport Channel, with the marsh on your left. If you want, you can extend your walk across a bridge at San Leandro Creek, then continue along the shore to Garretson Point, adding 1.4 miles round-trip. This parkland covers 1,220 acres, including some of the bay's most valuable wetland habitat.

⓳ Huckleberry Loop Path

1.7 mi/1.25 hrs

Location: In the Huckleberry Botanic Regional Preserve in the Oakland hills; map E1–East Bay, grid d6.

User groups: Hikers only. No dogs, horses, or mountain bikes. No wheelchair facilities.

Permits: No permits are required. Parking and access are free.

Directions: From Highway 24 in the East Bay, drive to just east of the Caldecott Tunnel and take the Fish Ranch Road exit west to Grizzly Peak Boulevard. Bear left onto Skyline Boulevard. Drive a short distance past Sibley Volcanic Preserve to the park entrance and parking lot on the left.

Maps: For a free trail map, contact the East Bay Regional Parks District at the address below and ask for the Huckleberry Botanic Regional Preserve brochure. To obtain a topographic map of the area, ask for Oakland East from the USGS.

Contact: East Bay Regional Parks District, 2950 Peralta Oaks Court, P.O. Box 5381, Oakland, CA 94605; (510) 635-0135, extension 2200, or fax (510) 569-1417.

Trail notes: If you know what you're looking for, this is a trip into an ecological wonderland. If you don't, well, it's still a rewarding, tranquil venture. The only reason people come to Huckleberry is to hike, not to play games or fish. That is because the Huckleberry Loop is routed through a remarkable variety of rare and beautiful plants. From the parking area, follow the path to the left fork, where you then descend steeply through a mature bay forest for a mile. The trail returns by turning right and climbing 0.7 miles out of the canyon. This last section is particularly rich in diverse plant life.

comes Redwood Road, and continue as above to the parking area.

Maps: For a free trail map, contact the East Bay Regional Parks District at the address below and ask for the Redwood Regional Park brochure. To obtain a topographic map of the area, ask for Oakland East from the USGS.

Contact: East Bay Regional Parks District, 2950 Peralta Oaks Court, P.O. Box 5381, Oakland, CA 94605; (510) 635-0135, extension 2200, or fax (510) 569-1417.

Trail notes: Newcomers to Redwood Regional Park are often amazed at the beauty of this trail. After all, who ever heard of redwood forests and trout streams in Oakland? But visitors to this park know you get both of these things here. For the best loop route, hike up the Stream Trail for a quarter mile, then turn left on the French Trail. You will climb along the western slopes of the redwood canyon, rising to 1,000 feet. With the puffing behind you (always hike up when you're fresh), you will turn right on the Fern Trail and soon junction with the Stream Trail. The rest of the route back to the park entrance is easy and downhill, tracing along pretty Redwood Creek through the center of the redwood forest. In late winter and spring, trout swim upstream from San Leandro Reservoir to spawn in these waters (fishing is not permitted).

⑳ Stream Trail Loop

3.5 mi/2.0 hrs

Location: In Redwood Regional Park in the Oakland hills; map E1–East Bay, grid d7.

User groups: Hikers, wheelchairs, dogs, and horses. No mountain bikes.

Permits: No permits are required. There is a $3-per-vehicle parking fee when the kiosk is attended.

Directions: From Highway 24 in Oakland, turn south on Highway 13 and drive to Redwood Road. Turn left on Redwood Road and drive two miles past Skyline Boulevard to the park entrance. Park at the Canyon Meadow Staging Area at the end of the road.

Alternate route: From the Oakland side of the Bay Bridge, take Highway 580 to the 35th Avenue exit. Drive east on 35th Avenue, which be-

㉑ East Ridge Loop

4.0 mi/2.5 hrs

Location: In Redwood Regional Park in the Oakland hills; map E1–East Bay, grid d7.

User groups: Hikers, dogs, and horses. Mountain bikes and wheelchairs are permitted on the paved part of the trail.

Permits: No permits are required. There is a $3-per-vehicle parking fee when the kiosk is attended.

Directions: From Highway 24 in Oakland, turn south on Highway 13 and drive to Redwood Road. Turn left on Redwood Road and drive two miles past Skyline Boulevard to the park entrance. Park at the Canyon Meadow Staging Area at the end of the road.

Maps: For a free trail map, contact the East Bay Regional Parks District at the address below and ask for the Redwood Regional Park brochure. To obtain a topographic map of the area, ask for Oakland East from the USGS.

Contact: East Bay Regional Parks District, 2950 Peralta Oaks Court, P.O. Box 5381, Oakland, CA 94605; (510) 635-0135, extension 2200, or fax (510) 569-1417.

Trail notes: From atop the East Ridge at 1,100 feet, you can look down into a canyon that appears to be a sea of redwoods. The view is quite a treat after climbing nearly 900 feet from the trailhead. The payback comes when you turn left and loop down into that canyon, where Redwood Creek awaits under the cool canopy of a lush forest. This trip is an option to the Stream Trail Loop (hike number 20) for ambitious hikers and mountain bikers; unlike that trail, bikes are allowed on the East Ridge. From the parking area, turn right on the Canyon Trail, climbing up to the East Ridge in half a mile. Turn left and make the loop by hiking out on the ridge, climbing much of the way, then turn left again on Prince Road and return on the Stream Trail.

㉒ Graham Trail Loop

0.75 mi/0.5 hr

Location: In the Roberts Regional Recreation Area in the Oakland hills; map E1–East Bay, grid d7.

User groups: Hikers and dogs. No horses or mountain bikes. The rest room is wheelchair accessible, but the trail is not.

Permits: No permits are required. There is a $3-per-vehicle parking fee.

Directions: From Highway 24 in the East Bay, drive to Highway 13 in Oakland. Turn south on Highway 13 (follow the signs carefully) and drive three miles to Joaquin Miller Road. Head east on Joaquin Miller Road to Skyline Boulevard. Turn left on Skyline Boulevard and drive about one mile to the park entrance on the right.

Maps: For a free trail map, contact the East Bay Regional Parks District at the address below and ask for the Roberts Regional Recreation Area and Redwood Regional Park brochures. To obtain a topographic map of the area, ask for Oakland East from the USGS.

Contact: East Bay Regional Parks District, 2950 Peralta Oaks Court, P.O. Box 5381, Oakland, CA 94605; (510) 635-0135, extension 2200, or fax (510) 569-1417.

Trail notes: Because the entrance to Roberts Regional Recreation Area lies amid redwood trees, it has proven to be a popular stop for visitors who want to see *Sequoia sempervirens* with a minimum effort. If you want to enter a redwood forest in the East Bay without having to walk far, this is the best bet. From the entrance of the parking area, near the swimming pool, take the short trail that is linked to the Graham Trail. Turn right and you will be routed in a short circle past a rest room to Diablo Vista, then turn right and head back to the parking area. The walk is short and sweet, just right for those who do not wish for a more challenging encounter.

㉓ Grass Valley Loop

2.8 mi/1.5 hrs

Location: In Anthony Chabot Regional Park in the Oakland hills; map E1–East Bay, grid d7.

User groups: Hikers, dogs, horses, and mountain bikes. No wheelchair facilities.

Permits: No permits are required. Parking and access are free.

Directions: From Interstate 580 in Oakland, take the 35th Avenue exit and drive east (35th Avenue becomes Redwood Road). Follow Redwood Road past Skyline Boulevard and drive three more miles to the Bort Meadow Staging Area on the right.

Maps: For a free trail map, contact the East Bay Regional Parks District at the address below and ask for the Anthony Chabot Regional Park brochure. To obtain a topographic map of the area, ask for Las Trampas Ridge from the USGS.

Contact: East Bay Regional Parks District, 2950 Peralta Oaks Court, P.O. Box 5381, Oakland, CA 94605; (510) 635-0135, extension 2200, or fax (510) 569-1417.

Trail notes: Grass Valley lies hidden in the East Bay hills, providing a simple paradise. This meadow lines more than a mile of a valley floor, framed on each side by the rims of miniature mountains. In the spring, the land glows with the various hues of green from wild grasses, along with wild radish, blue-eyed grass, and golden poppies. The scene is quiet and beautiful, and the Grass Valley Trail is one of the quickest routes into tranquillity. Starting at the Bort Meadow Staging Area, at a trailhead for the East Bay Skyline National Trail, hike downhill to the Bort Meadow picnic area, turn left, head south through Grass Valley and on to Stone Bridge, for a distance of 1.5 miles. To get back from Stonebridge, walk north on the Brandon Trail, which is routed along the west side of Grass Valley. To crown a perfect day, end the hike with lunch at Bort Meadow.

24 Bort Meadow

5.4 mi/3.25 hrs

Location: In Anthony Chabot Regional Park north of Castro Valley; map E1–East Bay, grid d7.

User groups: Hikers, dogs, horses, and mountain bikes. No wheelchair facilities.

Permits: No permits are required. Parking and access are free.

Directions: From Interstate 580 in Oakland, take the 35th Avenue exit and drive east (35th Avenue becomes Redwood Road). Follow Redwood Road past Skyline Boulevard and drive three more miles to the Bort Meadow Staging Area on the right.

Maps: For a free trail map, contact the East Bay Regional Parks District at the address below and ask for the Anthony Chabot Regional Park brochure. To obtain a topographic map of the area, ask for Las Trampas Ridge from the USGS.

Contact: East Bay Regional Parks District, 2950 Peralta Oaks Court, P.O. Box 5381, Oakland, CA 94605; (510) 635-0135, extension 2200, or fax (510) 569-1417.

Trail notes: This trail has good views of a beautiful valley and, in the spring, a diverse array of pretty wildflowers. You start at the Bort Meadow Staging Area, a trailhead for the East Bay Skyline National Trail. Head out north (to the right) where the trail meanders along an old ranch road, climbing only slightly above Bort Meadow and Grass Valley. At the ridge, turn and look south for a great view of Grass Valley, a divine sight in the springtime. From the ridge, the trail proceeds north, with valley and hilltop views along the way; watch closely for the hidden bench on the right side of the trail, so you can sit and look out over the remote foothill country. After enjoying the views, return the way you came.

25 Rocky Ridge Loop

4.4 mi/2.5 hrs

Location: In Las Trampas Regional Wilderness south of Moraga; map E1–East Bay, grid d7.

User groups: Hikers, dogs, and horses. No mountain bikes. No wheelchair facilities.

Permits: No permits are required. Parking and access are free.

Directions: From Interstate 680 in San Ramon, take the Crow Canyon Road exit and head west to Bollinger Canyon Road. Turn north on Bollinger Canyon Road and follow it for five miles to the parking area.

Maps: For a free trail map, contact the East Bay Regional Parks District at the address below and ask for the Las Trampas Regional Wilderness brochure. To obtain a topographic map of the area, ask for Las Trampas Ridge from the USGS.

Contact: East Bay Regional Parks District, 2950 Peralta Oaks Court, P.O. Box 5381, Oakland, CA 94605; (510) 635-0135, extension 2200, or fax (510) 569-1417.

Trail notes: Rocky Ridge is the prime destination for hikers visiting the 3,800-acre Las Trampas Regional Wilderness. The grassy rolling ridge with sandstone outcrops provides spectacular views to the east and the west. The outcrops have been beautifully sculpted by the wind and are colored by various lichen species. You can spend an entire day, if you so desire, just poking around the ridge. To reach Rocky Ridge, begin at the staging area at the end of Bollinger Road. Take the Rocky Ridge Trail, which starts out with a steep climb, rising about 800 feet over the course of 1.5 miles. Have faith, because once that climb is behind you, you'll be atop Rocky Ridge and the trail eases up. Head south down the ridge (take the Upper Trail) for a mile, enjoying the views on the way. To hike out the loop, turn left on the Elderberry Trail and walk two miles downhill to the staging area.

Special note: For an added adventure, explore the Wind Caves. To reach these hollowed openings in the sandstone outcrops from the Upper Trail, turn right on the Sycamore Trail and hike a steep 0.3 miles down to the caves.

㉖ Iron Horse Regional Trail

15.0 mi. one way/1.0 day

Location: In the San Ramon Valley from San Ramon to Walnut Creek; map E1–East Bay, grid d8.

User groups: Hikers, wheelchairs, dogs, horses, and mountain bikes.

Permits: No permits are required. Parking and access are free.

Directions: From Interstate 680 in Danville, take the Rudgear Road exit and park at either the Park and Ride lot (on the east side of the freeway) or the Staging Area (south side).

Maps: For a free trail map, contact the East Bay Regional Parks District at the address below and ask for the Iron Horse Regional Trail brochure. To obtain a topographic map of the area, ask for Las Trampas Ridge from the USGS.

Contact: East Bay Regional Parks District, 2950 Peralta Oaks Court, P.O. Box 5381, Oakland, CA 94605; (510) 635-0135, extension 2200, or fax (510) 569-1417.

Trail notes: The Iron Horse Regional Trail is a focal point of the national "Rails to Trails" program, which converts abandoned rail lines into hiking trails. When complete, the Iron Horse Trail will span northward from Shadow Cliffs Lake in Pleasanton all the way to Suisun Bay near Martinez. The rail route that it follows was established in 1890 and abandoned officially in 1976. It took only two years to remove all the tracks, but the trail conversion is requiring quite a bit more time.

The completed portion starts at Pine Valley Intermediate School in San Ramon and heads about 15 miles north to Walnut Creek. It is often hot and dry out here, with little shade (the trail is 75 feet wide in places) and no water available, but the trail deserves mention anyway. When shade trees are planted, piped water is made available, and the route is lengthened, Iron Horse will become a prominent long-distance trail for jogging, biking, and even walking.

㉗ Mount Diablo Summit Loop

0.7 mi/0.5 hr

Location: In Mount Diablo State Park near Danville; map E1–East Bay, grid d9.

User groups: Hikers and horses. No dogs or mountain bikes. The first half of the trail is designed for wheelchair use.

Permits: No permits are required. A $5-per-vehicle state park entrance fee is charged.

Directions: From Interstate 680 in Danville, take the Diablo Road exit and drive east for three miles. Turn left on Mount Diablo Scenic Boulevard, which will take you right into the park. Drive to the summit, stopping just before the road becomes a one-way road. The trailhead is just above the lower parking area.

Maps: For a trail map, send $5 (brochure is $1) to Mount Diablo State Park at the address below. To obtain a topographic map of the area, ask for Diablo from the USGS.

Contact: Mount Diablo State Park, P.O. Box 250, Diablo, CA 94528; (510) 837-2525 or (415) 726-8800.

Trail notes: One of the best lookouts in the world is at the top of Mount Diablo. No matter how fouled up things get, you can't foul up that view. This loop—called both the Fire Interpretive Trail and the Diablo Summit Loop—allows hikers to take a short, easy walk around the top of this East Bay landmark. Since you can drive nearly to the top of the mountain at 3,849 feet, it is the easiest hike in the park, yet also provides the best views.

Looking west, you can see across the bay to the Golden Gate Bridge, the Pacific Ocean, and, 25 miles out to sea, the Farallon Islands. To the north, you can see up the Central Valley. To the east, the frosted Sierra crest is often in view; using binoculars on a perfect day, it is even possible to see a piece of Half Dome sticking out from Yosemite Valley (135 miles). The view from the top of Mount Diablo is said to be second only to that of Mount Kilimanjaro in terms of the amount of visible earth surface. We once encountered a surprise patch of ladybugs and they were suddenly everywhere, thousands of them. Many decided to use our arms, shoulders, and heads as landing platforms.

28 Giant Loop

8.6 mi/4.75 hrs

Location: In Mount Diablo State Park near Danville; map E1–East Bay, grid d9.

User groups: Hikers and horses. No dogs or mountain bikes. No wheelchair facilities.

Permits: No permits are required. A $5-per-vehicle state park entrance fee is charged.

Directions: From Interstate 680 in Danville, take the Ygnacio Valley Road exit and drive 7.5 miles on Ygnacio Valley Road. Turn right on Clayton Road and drive one mile to Mitchell Canyon Road. Turn right and drive to the trailhead at the end of the road.

Maps: For a trail map, send $5 (brochure is $1) to Mount Diablo State Park at the address below. To obtain a topographic map of the area, ask for Diablo from the USGS.

Contact: Mount Diablo State Park, P.O. Box 250, Diablo, CA 94528; (510) 837-2525 or (415) 726-8800.

Trail notes: You face an endurance test on this hike, but it allows you to get a real feel for Mount Diablo with the least chance of meeting up with other park visitors. The Giant Loop Trail, set on the north side of Mount Diablo, involves an 1,800-foot climb to Deer Flat, then a steep descent into Donner Canyon. On the way, you will pass flower-strewn grasslands (spectacular in the spring) and take in seemingly endless views of Northern California. Deer Flat is a good spot for lookouts. In addition, the Giant Loop offers the chance to take a great side trip to Eagle Peak, elevation 2,369 feet, another of the mountain's best lookouts. This hike can be hot, dry, and difficult, so set aside most of a day and enjoy it slowly.

29 China Wall Loop

3.3 mi/2.0 hrs

Location: In Diablo Foothills Regional Park on the northwest slopes of Mount Diablo near Danville; map E1–East Bay, grid d9.

User groups: Hikers, dogs, horses, and mountain bikes. No wheelchair facilities.

Permits: No permits are required. Parking and access are free.

Directions: From Interstate 680 in Walnut Creek, take the Ygnacio Valley Road exit. Turn right, drive several miles to Walnut Avenue, then turn right. Drive to Oak Grove Road, turn right, then turn right again on Castle Rock Road and drive to Borges Ranch Road. The parking area is at the end of Borges Ranch Road.

Alternate route: From Interstate 680, drive south to the North Main Street exit. Drive south on North Main Street to Ygnacio Valley Road. Turn left and proceed as above.

Maps: For a free trail map, contact the East Bay Regional Parks District at the address below and ask for the Diablo Foothills Regional Park brochure. To obtain a topographic map of the area, ask for Diablo from the USGS.

Contact: East Bay Regional Parks District, 2950 Peralta Oaks Court, P.O. Box 5381, Oakland, CA 94605; (510) 635-0135, extension 2200, or fax (510) 569-1417.

Trail notes: First of all, there is no sign for the China Wall Loop at the trailhead. After taking this hike, we came up with that name. The China Wall rock formation sits on the slopes of Mount Diablo. What you see on this hike is a line of rocks that looks like the Great Wall of China in miniature (well, kind of)—they are prehistoric-looking sandstone formations. In addition, on the hike out, you will get glimpses to the east of Castle Rocks and other prominent sandstone outcrops located just outside the park's boundary. Look closer and you might also see golden eagles, hawks, and falcons, all of which nest here. To reach China Wall requires only a 1.5-mile hike from the Borges Ranch Trailhead, heading off on the Briones-to-Mount Diablo Trail. Turn right at the junction with the Alamo Trail, which runs a half mile along the base of China Wall. To complete the loop, turn right again on the Hanging Valley Trail and hike back to the trailhead.

30 Volvon Loop Trail

5.7 mi/3.0 hrs

Location: In the Morgan Territory Regional Preserve north of Livermore; map E1–East Bay, grid d9.

User groups: The first half of the loop is accessible to hikers, dogs, horses, and mountain bikes. The second half is for hikers and dogs only. No wheelchair facilities.

Permits: No permits are required. Parking and access are free.

Directions: From Interstate 580 in Livermore, take the North Livermore Avenue exit. Drive north to Highland Road and turn left, then drive a short distance and turn right on Morgan Territory Road. Follow Morgan Territory Road to the parking area just past the ridge summit.

Maps: For a free trail map, contact the East Bay Regional Parks District at the address below and ask for the Morgan Territory Regional Preserve brochure. To obtain a topographic map of the area, ask for Tassajara from the USGS.

Contact: East Bay Regional Parks District, 2950 Peralta Oaks Court, P.O. Box 5381, Oakland, CA 94605; (510) 635-0135, extension 2200, or fax (510) 569-1417.

Trail notes: Morgan Territory is located within the traditional homeland of the Volvon, one of five historical Indian nations in the Mount Diablo area. This trail, named after the first people to live here, is the park's featured hike. The trip is excellent, tracing along a ridge as it rises along sandstone hills to a ridgeline with terrific views. From the trailhead at 2,000 feet, take the Volvon Trail, which is routed northward up along the highest point in the park at 1,977 feet. The trail loops around this peak, then returns via the Coyote Trail (hikers only) back down the grade to the starting point. This parkland is most beautiful in the spring, and not just because the hills are greened up; one of the best wildflower displays in the Bay Area occurs here at that time.

㉛ Cogswell Marsh Loop

2.8 mi/1.5 hrs

Location: At Hayward Regional Shoreline on South San Francisco Bay in Hayward; map E1–East Bay, grid e6.

User groups: Hikers and mountain bikes. No dogs or horses. No wheelchair facilities.

Permits: No permits are required. Parking and access are free.

Directions: From Interstate 880 in Hayward, take the West Winton Avenue exit and follow the road west toward the bay to the entrance and parking area.

Maps: For a free trail map, contact the East Bay Regional Parks District at the address below and ask for the Hayward Regional Shoreline brochure. To obtain a topographic map of the area, ask for San Leandro from the USGS.

Contact: East Bay Regional Parks District, 2950 Peralta Oaks Court, P.O. Box 5381, Oakland, CA 94605; (510) 635-0135, extension 2200, or fax (510) 569-1417.

Trail notes: Cogswell Marsh is the heart of an 800-acre marshy wetlands, a great place to take short nature hikes and try to identify many rare birds. It's always a good choice for viewing shorebirds; as a bonus, peregrine falcons are typically seen either hovering over the marsh or perched on power pylons. As many as 200 white pelicans have been seen here, along with the occasional merlin. From the parking area, the trail starts with a .37-mile hike across landfill, then enters the marshlands, where a loop trail circles the most vital habitat. To keep feet from getting wet, two short sections are bridged. The loop is best hiked clockwise, so you face the Bay Bridge and the San Francisco skyline, an outstanding view, as you walk along the water's edge of the South Bay. Guided weekend nature walks are available.

㉜ Shoreline Loop Trail

1.75 mi/1.0 hr

Location: In the Cull Canyon Regional Recreation Area in the Castro Valley foothills; map E1–East Bay, grid e7.

User groups: Hikers and dogs. No horses or mountain bikes. No wheelchair facilities.

Permits: No permits are required. There is a $1.50 to $2.50 swim fee to enter the lagoon area (closed in winter).

Directions: From Interstate 580 East in Castro Valley, take the Center Street exit and drive north to Heyer Avenue. Turn right on Heyer and proceed to Cull Canyon Road, then make a left and drive to the park entrance. From Interstate 580 West, take the Castro Valley exit and turn left onto Castro Valley Boulevard. Drive to Crow Canyon Road, turn right, and drive a half mile. Turn left on Cull Canyon Road and drive to the park entrance.

Maps: For a free trail map, contact the East Bay Regional Parks District at the address below and ask for the Cull Canyon Regional Recreation Area brochure. To obtain a topographic map of the area, ask for Hayward from the USGS.

Contact: East Bay Regional Parks District, 2950 Peralta Oaks Court, P.O. Box 5381, Oakland, CA 94605; (510) 635-0135, extension 2200, or fax (510) 569-1417.

Trail notes: Little Cull Canyon Reservoir, covering just 18 acres, is the backdrop for a picnic lunch in a canyon, and this short hike along the lake is popular with park visitors. From the parking area, walk over to the picnic areas, then turn left along the Shoreline Trail. It skirts the western bank of the narrow lake, then loops back along a lagoon. Most of the year, this is a pleasant walk. However, just plain forget it on summer afternoons, when the hot sun brands everything in sight. That is why this park is most famous for its swimming complex, complete with bathhouse and snack bar, not for the hiking and, heaven knows, not for the fishing.

㉝ Don Castro Lake Loop

1.7 mi/1.0 hr

Location: In the Don Castro Regional Recreation Area in the Castro Valley foothills; map E1–East Bay, grid e7.

User groups: Hikers and dogs. Portions of the trail are paved for bicycle and wheelchair use. No horses.

Permits: No permits are required. A $1.50 to $2.50 entrance fee, which includes swimming, is charged when the kiosk is attended.

Directions: From Interstate 580 East in Castro Valley, take the Center Street exit and turn right. Drive to Kelly Street and turn left. Drive a short distance, turn left onto Woodroe, and drive to the park entrance. From Interstate 580 West, take the Castro Valley exit and drive west on East Castro Valley Boulevard to Grove Way. Turn left and drive to Center Street. Drive a short distance, turn left, and drive to Kelly Street. Make another

left onto Kelly Street and drive to Woodroe. Turn left once again and drive to the park entrance.

Maps: For a free trail map, contact the East Bay Regional Parks District at the address below and ask for the Don Castro Regional Recreation Area brochure. To obtain a topographic map of the area, ask for Hayward from the USGS.

Contact: East Bay Regional Parks District, 2950 Peralta Oaks Court, P.O. Box 5381, Oakland, CA 94605; (510) 635-0135, extension 2200, or fax (510) 569-1417.

Trail notes: Don Castro is a small (23 acres) but pretty lake that attracts swimmers to its lagoon and clear, warm, blue waters. Hiking is typically an afterthought for visitors, who come primarily to picnic or fish. The trail, actually a road, is routed completely around the lake for an easy walk or jog in a nice setting. From the parking area, walk a short distance along the West Lawn to the dam and start your hike there, circling the water in a clockwise direction. In the first quarter mile, with the lake on your right, you will pass a fishing pier and the swimming lagoon (on your left). The route continues to the headwaters of the lake at San Lorenzo Creek, crosses the creek, then hems the southern shoreline all the way to the lake's spillway. After climbing a short staircase, you will be on top and can hike over the dam and back to the parking area. It's an easy circle.

㉞ Bayview Trail

3.0 mi/1.5 hrs

Location: In Coyote Hills Regional Park on the shore of the South Bay near Fremont; map E1–East Bay, grid f6.

User groups: Hikers, dogs, horses, and mountain bikes. The trail is paved and technically wheelchair accessible, but is quite steep in some sections.

Permits: No permits are required. There is a $3-per-vehicle parking fee when the kiosk is attended.

Directions: From Fremont, drive west on Highway 84 to the Paseo Padre Parkway exit. Turn right on Paseo Padre Parkway and drive to Patterson Ranch Road. Turn left and drive to the parking area. Or, from Highway 880 in Fremont, take the Highway 84/Decoto Road exit, turn right on Ardenwood Boulevard, and continue to Commerce Drive. Turn left on Commerce (which becomes Patterson Ranch Road) and drive to the park entrance.

From the Peninsula, turn east on Highway 84, cross the Dumbarton Bridge, and take the Thornton Avenue exit. Turn left (the road becomes Paseo Padre Parkway) and drive north to Patterson Ranch Road. Turn left on Patterson Ranch Road and drive to the parking area.

Maps: For a free trail map, contact the East Bay Regional Parks District at the address below and ask for the Coyote Hills Regional Park brochure. To obtain a topographic map of the area, ask for Newark from the USGS.

Contact: East Bay Regional Parks District, 2950 Peralta Oaks Court, P.O. Box 5381, Oakland, CA 94605; (510) 635-0135, extension 2200, or fax (510) 569-1417. Coyote Hills Regional Park, (510) 795-9385.

Trail notes: Evidence of Coyote Hills Regional Park's rich history is visible throughout its 966 acres: four Indian shell mounds, heaps of accumulated debris from ancient living areas, can be seen. The Shoreline Trail is the favorite hike in the park, offering excellent views of the South Bay. This walk circles the park, including a 1.5-mile stretch that borders the bay and a shorter piece that runs adjacent to a marsh. The park is a wildlife sanctuary, with grassy hills and marshes that provide significant habitat for numerous migrating waterfowl. The best way to hike this loop is in a counterclockwise direction from the main parking area. For a short but enjoyable side trip from the main parking area, by the way, take the wooden boardwalk out through the North Marsh.

㉟ High Ridge Loop

3.3 mi/2.0 hrs

Location: In Garin Regional Park in the Hayward foothills; map E1–East Bay, grid f7.

User groups: Hikers, dogs, horses, and mountain bikes. No wheelchair facilities.

Permits: No permits are required. There is a $3-per-vehicle parking fee when the kiosk is attended.

Directions: From Fremont, take Highway 238 (Mission Boulevard) north through Union City to Garin Avenue. Turn right onto Garin Avenue and drive one mile to the park entrance.

Maps: For a free trail map, contact the East Bay Regional Parks District at the address below and ask for the Garin and Dry Creek Pioneer Regional Parks brochure. To obtain a topographic map of the area, ask for Hayward from the USGS.

Contact: East Bay Regional Parks District, 2950 Peralta Oaks Court, P.O. Box 5381, Oakland, CA 94605; (510) 635-0135, extension 2200, or fax (510) 569-1417.

Trail notes: The hilltops in Garin Regional Park render sweeping views of the East Bay foothills westward to South San Francisco Bay, the number one attraction at this 3,000-acre parkland. The hills span for miles, and in the fall, there are times late in the day when sunbeams will pour through openings between cumulus clouds, creating a divine scene. Of the 20 miles of trails in the park, the Ridge Loop Trail is the best way to see the surrounding wildlands, primarily oak grasslands amid rolling foothills. From the parking area (at 380 feet), walk a quarter mile past the picnic areas to Arroyo Flats, then turn left on the High Ridge Trail. In another quarter mile, it links up with the Vista Peak Loop, best hiked in a clockwise direction. You will start climbing, rising 550 feet in a mile, topping out at Vista Peak (934 feet) and shortly after, Garin Peak (948 feet). Take your time and enjoy the views.

㊱ Ridgeline Trail

7.0 mi/4.0 hrs

Location: In Pleasanton Ridge Regional Park west of Pleasanton; map E1–East Bay, grid f9.

User groups: Hikers, dogs, horses, and mountain bikes. No wheelchair facilities.

Permits: No permits are required. Parking and access are free.

Directions: From Interstate 680 in Pleasanton, take the Bernal Road exit west and drive to Foothill Road. Turn left and drive three miles to the parking area and information center.

Maps: For a free trail map, contact the East Bay Regional Parks District at the address below and ask for the Pleasanton Ridge Regional Park brochure. To obtain a topographic map of the area, ask for Dublin from the USGS.

Contact: East Bay Regional Parks District, 2950 Peralta Oaks Court, P.O. Box 5381, Oakland, CA 94605; (510) 635-0135, extension 2200, or fax (510) 569-1417.

Trail notes: People often overlook Pleasanton Ridge Regional Park, not knowing it offers a quiet, natural setting with excellent views from the Ridgeline Trail. Development in and around the park has purposely been limited so the surroundings could retain as natural a feel as possible. The plan has succeeded, and the best way to experience it is on this hike. The Ridgeline Trail climbs to elevations of 1,600 feet, with the northern sections giving way to sweeping views featuring miles of rolling foothills and valleys at the threshold of Mount Diablo. From the parking area, elevation 300 feet, start hiking on the Oak Tree Trail, which is routed 1.4 miles up to the Ridgeline Trail, climbing 750 feet. Turn right and hike two miles along the ridge. You can return on a loop route by turning left on the Thermalito Trail, which we recommend.

㊲ North Arroyo Trail

1.3 mi/0.75 hr

Location: In the Shadow Cliffs Regional Recreation Area in Pleasanton; map E1–East Bay, grid f9.

User groups: Hikers and dogs. Portions of the trail are accessible to horses and mountain bikes. No wheelchair facilities.

Permits: No permits are required. The parking fee is $4 from March through October, $3 from November through February; there's a $1 dog fee year-round.

Directions: From Interstate 580 in Pleasanton, take Santa Rita Road south. Drive two miles, turn left on Valley Avenue, and drive to Stanley Boulevard. Turn left and drive to the park entrance.

Maps: For a free trail map, contact the East Bay Regional Parks District at the address below and ask for the Shadow Cliffs Regional Recreation Area brochure. To obtain a topographic map of the area, ask for Livermore from the USGS.

Contact: East Bay Regional Parks District, 2950 Peralta Oaks Court, P.O. Box 5381, Oakland, CA 94605; (510) 635-0135, extension 2200, or fax (510) 569-1417.

Trail notes: Though you can't walk all the way around Shadow Cliffs Lake, you can explore a series of smaller ponds in the Arroyo area. There's no place else like it in the East Bay. From the back of the first parking area, you take a trail over the top of a levee and down to the shore of the first pond. Then, just follow the North Arroyo Trail along the shores of several ponds for about half a mile. For a view of the ponds, make the short climb up the adjacent levee. These ponds are water holes left over from a gravel quarry. Shadow Cliffs Lake, the biggest pond, covering some 80 acres, has been stocked with trout and is one of the better fishing spots in the East Bay. It is also a good place to swim, as the water is often quite clear.

㊳ Dumbarton Bridge

4.5 mi/2.5 hrs

Location: On the Dumbarton Bridge from Fremont to East Palo Alto; map E1–East Bay, grid g6.

User groups: Hikers, wheelchairs, and mountain bikes. No dogs or horses.

Permits: No permits are required. Parking and access are free.

Directions: From Redwood City, head east on Highway 84 and cross the Dumbarton Bridge. Take the first exit after the toll plaza, Thornton Avenue. Turn right and drive a quarter mile to Marshland Road. Turn right and drive four miles to the parking area at the fishing pier.

Maps: To obtain a topographic map of the area, ask for Newark from the USGS.

Contact: San Francisco Bay National Wildlife Refuge, P.O. Box 524, Newark, CA 94560; (510) 792-4275, (510) 792-0222, or fax (510) 792-5828.

Trail notes: Let this be a lesson for future bridge designers. When the Dumbarton Bridge was constructed, a biking and hiking path was added along the south side of the roadway, separated from traffic by a cement cordon. That means you can safely hike to the top of the center span for a unique view of the South Bay. This hike is best started from the Fremont side of the bridge, because it is unsafe to leave cars unat-

Map Section E1–East Bay—page 270

tended at the western foot of the bridge in East Palo Alto.

Special note: The bridge is a link in an outstanding bicycle trip. Start at the Alameda Creek Regional Trail in Niles, head over the Dumbarton Bridge, turn left on the Baylands Trail and ride through Palo Alto, then go farther south at Charleston Slough on the Baylands Trail to Mountain View Baylands.

㊴ Dumbarton Pier

1.0 mi/1.0 hr

Location: In South San Francisco Bay in the San Francisco Bay National Wildlife Refuge in Fremont; map E1–East Bay, grid g6.

User groups: Hikers, wheelchairs, and mountain bikes. No dogs or horses.

Permits: No permits are required. Parking and access are free.

Directions: From San Francisco, drive south on U.S. 101 to the Willow Road–Dumbarton exit. Drive east across the Dumbarton Bridge and take the first exit (Thornton Avenue) after the toll plaza. Turn right and drive to Marshlands Road. Turn right again and drive past the San Francisco Bay National Wildlife Refuge entrance and visitor center for about three miles, following the signs to Dumbarton Pier (and the entrance to a leg of the Bay bicycle trail).

Maps: For a free brochure, contact the refuge at the address below. To obtain a topographic map of the area, ask for Newark from the USGS.

Contact: San Francisco Bay National Wildlife Refuge, P.O. Box 524, Newark, CA 94560; (510) 792-4275, (510) 792-0222, or fax (510) 792-5828.

Trail notes: Here is an example of how the government did something right. This pier was once the old Dumbarton Bridge, but when the new high-rise span was built in the 1980s, the roadway extending from Fremont was converted to a fishing pier and made part of the San Francisco Bay National Wildlife Refuge. The pier reaches all the way to the channel of the South Bay, a natural migratory pathway for sharks (in the summer), bat rays (winter), sturgeon (winter), perch (late fall), and jacksmelt (spring). Many seabirds and waterfowl live in this area

year-round. The easy walk out to the end of the pier also renders pretty sea views of the South Bay's shoreline; looking north on a clear day, you can see the city of San Francisco as well as the San Mateo and Bay Bridges.

㊵ Tidelands Trail

2.5 mi/1.5 hrs

Location: In the San Francisco Bay National Wildlife Refuge at the eastern foot of the Dumbarton Bridge; map E1–East Bay, grid g7.

User groups: Hikers, dogs, and mountain bikes. There are no wheelchair facilities, but the trail can be navigated by most wheelchair users. No horses.

Permits: No permits are required. Parking and access are free.

Directions: From San Francisco, drive south on U.S. 101 to the Willow Road–Dumbarton exit. Drive east across the Dumbarton Bridge and take the first exit (Thornton Avenue) after the toll plaza. Turn right and drive a quarter mile to Marshland Road. Turn right and drive a short distance to the visitor center.

Maps: For a free brochure, contact the refuge at the address below. To obtain a topographic map of the area, ask for Newark from the USGS.

Contact: San Francisco Bay National Wildlife Refuge, P.O. Box 524, Newark, CA 94560; (510) 792-4275, (510) 792-0222, or fax (510) 792-5828.

Trail notes: Bird-watchers won't soon forget the diversity of bird life at the San Francisco Bay National Wildlife Refuge, with more than 250 species in a given year using this habitat for food, resting space, and nesting sites. In just 15 or 20 minutes, it is not unusual to see a half-dozen species of ducks, an egret, sandpiper, willet, and herons. The refuge is big, covering 23,000 acres in all, and the Tidelands Trail pours right through it. This is actually a wide dirt pathway on a levee routed amid salt marsh and bay tidewaters. Group nature tours on this trail are offered regularly on weekends. The views of the South Bay and, on clear days, the surrounding foothills make for a panoramic urban backdrop. Don't forget to stop by refuge headquarters before your hike to see the exhibits and pamphlets that will make your walk more enjoyable.

ⓐ Alameda Creek Regional Trail

11.0 mi. one way/4.5 hrs

Location: On Alameda Creek from Niles to the South Bay; map E1–East Bay, grid g7.

User groups: South Trail: Hikers, dogs, and mountain bikes. North Trail: Hikers, dogs, and horses. No wheelchair facilities.

Permits: No permits are required. Parking and access are free.

Directions: From Interstate 680 in Fremont, take the Mission Boulevard exit and drive west to Highway 84/Niles Canyon Road. Turn right and make another immediate right on Old Canyon Road. The staging area is on the left.

Maps: For a free trail map, contact the East Bay Regional Parks District at the address below and ask for the Alameda Creek Regional Trail brochure. To obtain a topographic map of the area, ask for Niles from the USGS.

Contact: East Bay Regional Parks District, 2950 Peralta Oaks Court, P.O. Box 5381, Oakland, CA 94605; (510) 635-0135, extension 2200, or fax (510) 569-1417.

Trail notes: An unusual solution to the biker vs. hiker conflict has been implemented here with the construction of a double trail. There are two trails, one on each side of Alameda Creek, routed from Niles Community Park to the shoreline of the South Bay. The trail on the north bank is designed for horseback riders and hikers. The one on the south bank is paved, perfect for bicyclists and joggers. Markers set at quarter-mile intervals help joggers keep track of their exact distances. From Niles, the trail routes past Shinn Pond, Alameda Creek Quarries, and Coyote Hills Regional Park. For access to Coyote Hills Regional Park and the San Francisco Bay National Wildlife Refuge, take the trail on the south side of the creek; there is no direct access to either of those areas on the north-side trail.

User groups: Hikers, dogs, and horses. No mountain bikes. No wheelchair facilities.

Permits: No permits are required. A parking fee is charged at the Ohlone College lot.

Directions: From Fremont, take Highway 238 (Mission Boulevard) to the Ohlone College campus. Turn left and park at Lot D or H. Go through the gate at the back of the campus to access the trail.

Maps: For a free trail map, contact the East Bay Regional Parks District at the address below and ask for the Mission Peak Regional Preserve brochure. To obtain a topographic map of the area, ask for Niles from the USGS.

Contact: East Bay Regional Parks District, 2950 Peralta Oaks Court, P.O. Box 5381, Oakland, CA 94605; (510) 635-0135, extension 2200, or fax (510) 569-1417.

Trail notes: In one of the most intense climbs in the Bay Area, this trail takes you from elevation 400 feet at the trailhead to the summit of Mission Peak at 2,517 feet in a span of just 3.5 miles. That is why many people stay away, far away. But in the spring, it is one of the best hikes around, when the grasslands are such a bright green that the hills seem to glow, wildflowers are blooming everywhere, and there are sweeping views of San Francisco, the Santa Cruz Mountains, and on crystal clear days, the Sierra crest to the east. Two trails lead up, but the best choice is to start at the parking lot at Ohlone College, for a route that's less steep than from the other trailhead at the end of Stanford Avenue in Fremont. After parking at Ohlone College, take the Spring Valley Trail, which intersects with the Peak Trail and continues along the northern flank of the mountain up to the summit. It's a good idea to bring a spare shirt for this hike, especially in the colder months. That's because you will likely sweat through whatever you are wearing on the way up, then when you stop to enjoy the views, get cold and clammy. An extra shirt solves that problem.

ⓑ Peak Trail

7.0 mi/5.0 hrs

Location: In the Mission Peak Regional Preserve near Fremont; map E1–East Bay, grid g8.

ⓒ Sunol Loop

4.75 mi/3.5 hrs

Location: In the Sunol Regional Wilderness near Sunol; map E1–East Bay, grid g9.

User groups: Hikers, dogs, horses, and mountain bikes. The Indian Joe Creek section of the loop is limited to hikers. No wheelchair facilities.

Permits: No permits are required. Parking and access are free.

Directions: From Interstate 680 in the East Bay, take the Calaveras Road exit in Sunol. Turn south on Calaveras Road to Geary Road. Turn left on Geary Road and continue into the park.

Maps: For a free trail map, contact the East Bay Regional Parks District at the address below and ask for the Sunol-Ohlone Regional Wilderness brochure. To obtain a topographic map of the area, ask for La Costa Valley from the USGS.

Contact: East Bay Regional Parks District, 2950 Peralta Oaks Court, P.O. Box 5381, Oakland, CA 94605; (510) 635-0135, extension 2200, or fax (510) 569-1417. Sunol Regional Wilderness, (510) 862-2244.

Trail notes: There are hidden places around the Bay Area that make you feel as if only you know about them. This is one such place. Sunol Preserve is a 6,400-acre wilderness, and this loop trail leads past many of the most striking spots: Little Yosemite, a miniature canyon with a pretty stream; Cerro Este, at 1,720 feet, one of the higher points in the park; Cave Rocks, a series of natural, gouged-out rock forms; and Indian Joe Creek, a little brook that runs along the start of the trail. From the parking area, begin your loop hike by heading north on the Indian Joe Creek Trail, then climbing one mile to Cave Rocks. Turn right on Rocks Road/Cerro Este Trail and climb up over the summit, then down the other side, all the way to the Canyon View Trail. Turn right and return to the parking area. A great option on the Canyon View Trail is to take the short gated cutoff trail that drops down to the floor of Little Yosemite. In the winter, the creek at the bottom of the valley has many tiny pool-and-drop waterfalls.

44 East Bay Skyline National Trail

31.0 mi. one way/3.0 days

Location: In the East Bay Regional Parks District, from Chabot Regional Park near Castro Valley to Wildcat Canyon Regional Park in the Richmond hills; map E1–East Bay, grids c5, c6, d6, d7.

User groups: Hikers, dogs, horses, and mountain bikes. Horses and mountain bikes are restricted in some sections.

Permits: No permits are required. A parking fee may be charged at some trailheads.

Directions: See individual trailhead listings below for specific directions.

Maps: For a brochure and map of the East Bay Skyline National Trail or individual maps on each regional park, contact the East Bay Regional Parks District at the address below.

Contact: East Bay Regional Parks District, 2950 Peralta Oaks Court, P.O. Box 5381, Oakland, CA 94605; (510) 635-0135, extension 2200, or fax (510) 569-1417.

Trail notes: A 31-mile trail along the East Bay's skyline offers a unique opportunity for a long-distance hike that can be chopped into many short segments over the course of days or even weeks. The trail spans from the Castro Valley foothills northward to the ridgeline behind Richmond, crossing six regional parks for a view into the area's prettiest and wildest lands. Called the East Bay Skyline National Trail, it is the Bay Area's longest single continuous trail. We hiked the route from south to north in two days, but the trail can be divided into seven sections from the different access points available at parking areas. Bicycles and horses are permitted on the 65 percent of the trail that is wide enough to accommodate them.

It is a great trip, whether you do it all in one weekend or cover a bit at a time over several weeks. No permits are needed, leashed dogs are permitted, and access is free. The only drawbacks are the lack of campgrounds along the way, which makes backpacking and overnights impossible, and the absence of piped drinking water. Water is available at only four points over the 31 miles, at Lomas Cantadas, Sibley Preserve, Skyline Gate, and Bort Meadow. So come prepared with a full canteen or two of water per person, along with a hat and sunscreen. Following is a detailed description of the trail from south to north:

44a. Proctor Gate to Bort Meadow, Chabot Regional Park

Directions: From Interstate 580 in Oakland, take the 35th Avenue exit and drive east (35th

Avenue becomes Redwood Road). Drive on Redwood Road to the Proctor Gate Staging Area, located on the east border of the park, next to a golf course.

Trail notes: The trail starts adjacent to a golf course, is routed up a ridge, then meanders on a ranch road in Chabot Regional Park. At Stonebridge (don't turn left at the trail junction!), the trail leads into Grass Valley and on to Bort Meadow. Distance: 6.5 miles; climbs 600 feet, then drops 320 feet.

44b. Bort Meadow to MacDonald Gate, Chabot Regional Park

Directions: From Interstate 580 in Oakland, take the 35th Avenue exit and drive east (35th Avenue becomes Redwood Road). Drive on Redwood Road, three miles past Skyline Boulevard to the Bort Meadow Staging Area on the right.

Trail notes: Here the trail climbs steeply out of Bort Meadow. At the ridge, turn and look south for the great view of Grass Valley. Hikers are completely exposed on the ascent; it's hot and dry in the afternoon, so it's best to go early in the morning. From the ridge, the trail proceeds through a hardwood forest with some chaparral in the mix, drops into a canyon, crosses Redwood Road, and puts you at the entrance to Redwood Regional Park. Distance: 2.7 miles; climbs 300 feet, then drops 500 feet.

44c. MacDonald Gate to Skyline Gate, Redwood Regional Park

Directions: From Interstate 580 to the west or Interstate 680 to the east, drive to Highway 24, then to Highway 13 and go south. Drive to Redwood Road and turn left. Drive to the park entrance, then turn south and park at the MacDonald Gate Staging Area.

Trail notes: Hikers have two options here, and our preference is to split off at the French Trail to hike up the canyon bottom on the Stream Trail, enveloped by redwoods. Note that bikes are banned from this section. The alternative, a must for bikers, is to take the West Ridge Trail for a steep climb to the canyon rim, then drop to the junction at Skyline Gate. Distance: 5 miles; the French Trail drops 200 feet, then climbs 400 feet; the West Ridge Trail climbs 900 feet, then drops 200 feet.

44d. Skyline Gate through Huckleberry Preserve to Sibley Preserve

Directions: From Highway 24 in Oakland, drive east to Highway 13. Go south and drive to Joaquin Miller Road, then head east until you hit Skyline Boulevard. Turn left on Skyline Boulevard and drive to the Skyline Gate Staging Area.

Trail notes: This section of trail is a choice hike for nature lovers, who will see an abundance of bird life and other animals, especially in the early morning and late evening. The trail passes through a deciduous woodland habitat, with a short but quite steep climb after entering Huckleberry Preserve. Distance: 3 miles; drops 200 feet, then climbs 480 feet.

44e. Sibley Preserve to Lomas Cantadas, Tilden Regional Park

Directions: From Interstate 580 to the west or Interstate 680 to the east, drive to Highway 24. Continue to just east of the Caldecott Tunnel and take the Fish Ranch Road exit west to Grizzly Peak Boulevard. Turn left and drive to Skyline Boulevard. The park entrance and parking area are on the left.

Trail notes: A unique section of trail, this part crosses over the Caldecott Tunnel in a relatively unpeopled area. Many hawks are seen here, a nice bonus. Sibley is best known for its volcanic past, and hikers can take a side trip to Mount Round Top, a one-time volcano that blew its top off. No bicycles are permitted. Distance: 3.4 miles; drops 300 feet, then climbs 600 feet.

44f. Lomas Cantadas to Inspiration Point, Tilden Regional Park

Directions: From Interstate 580 to the west or Interstate 680 to the east, drive to Highway 24. Drive to just east of the Caldecott Tunnel and take the Fish Ranch Road exit to Grizzly Peak Boulevard. At the stop sign, turn right and drive on Grizzly Peak Boulevard to Lomas Cantadas Road. Turn right, then immediately turn left, following the signs for the Steam Train to the parking area.

Trail notes: This section of trail starts at a major access area off Grizzly Peak Boulevard, with an adjacent side trip available to Vollmer

Peak, the highest point on the East Bay Skyline National Trail. The trail is then routed north to Inspiration Point at Wildcat Canyon Road, another well-known access point, losing elevation most of the way. Many sweeping views of the East Bay's untouched foothills are found on this hike. Distance: 3 miles; drops 860 feet.

44g. Inspiration Point (Tilden) to Wildcat Canyon Regional Park

Directions: From Interstate 580 to the west or Interstate 680 to the east, drive to Highway 24. Continue to just east of the Caldecott Tunnel and take the Fish Ranch Road exit west to Grizzly Peak Boulevard. Turn right, drive up the hill, and turn right on South Park Drive. Drive one mile to Wildcat Canyon Road, bear right, and drive to the parking area at Inspiration Point on the left.

Alternate Route: To avoid South Park Drive, which is sometimes closed in the winter due to newt migrations, from Highway 24, go through the Caldecott Tunnel and exit at Orinda. Turn left on Camino Pablo. Drive north for about two miles, then turn left on Wildcat Canyon Road. Follow the road to Inspiration Point on the right.

Trail notes: The last stretch starts at the most heavily used section of the entire route, then crosses its most dramatic and unpeopled terrain. From Inspiration Point, the trail is actually paved for four miles, ideal for bicycles and wheelchairs. Beyond that, the trail turns to dirt and traces San Pablo Ridge, with inspiring views in all directions, before dropping steeply into Wildcat Canyon Regional Park in the Richmond foothills. Distance: 7.2 miles; drops 800 feet.

Map E1–South Bay

Adjoining Maps: East: E2 ..... *page* 320
North: E1 .. 250, 270   South: F1 384

Note: Section E1 is divided into four chapters. For other E1 sections
see pages 216 (Marin), 250 (San Francisco), and 270 (East Bay).

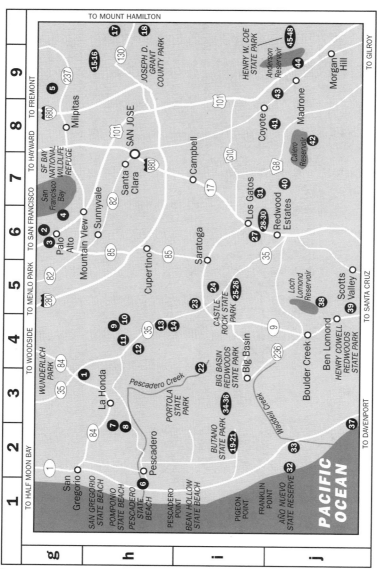

Chapter E1–South Bay features:

❶ Windy Hill Loop

8.2 mi/4.5 hrs

Location: In the Windy Hill Open Space Preserve in the Portola Valley foothills; map E1–South Bay, grid g3.

User groups: Hikers, dogs, and horses. No mountain bikes (except on the preserve's Spring Ridge Trail). There are wheelchair facilities in the picnic area adjacent to the parking area.

Permits: No permits are required. Parking and access are free.

Directions: From Interstate 280 or U.S. 101 on the Peninsula, take Highway 84 west to Highway 35 (Skyline Boulevard). Turn left on Highway 35 and drive 2.3 miles to the parking area.

Maps: For a free trail map and brochure, contact the Midpeninsula Regional Open Space District at the address below. To obtain a topographic map of the area, ask for Mindego Hill from the USGS.

Contact: Midpeninsula Regional Open Space District, 330 Distel Circle, Los Altos, CA 94022; (415) 691-1200 or fax (415) 691-0485.

Trail notes: Windy Hill may be known for the north winds that blow through on spring afternoons, but it is even better known for offering remarkable views on clear days in any season. From the 1,900-foot summit, a grass-covered hilltop west of Portola Valley, hikers can see San Francisco Bay on one side and the Pacific Ocean on the other. If views are all you want, the 0.7-mile Anniversary Trail, which is routed from the parking area to the summit, provides them. If you want more, you can get more by taking an excellent loop hike that drops down into forests then climbs back out to grasslands. To do this, take the Hamms Gulch Trail, dropping 1,000 feet in elevation through a remote, pristine, wooded environment. Loop back on the Razorback Ridge Trail, hiking an extended series of switchbacks to make the return climb. The trail emerges from the woodlands, then turns right on the Lost Trail. The last 2.1 miles to the parking area offer great views and a refreshing end to the hike.

❷ Charleston Slough

4.0 mi/1.5 hrs

Location: In a South Bay marshland in Palo Alto; map E1–South Bay, grid g6.

User groups: Hikers and mountain bikes. No dogs or horses. No wheelchair facilities.

Permits: No permits are required. Parking and access are free.

Directions: From U.S. 101 in south Palo Alto, take the San Antonio exit and turn east toward the bay. After a short distance, turn left on Bayshore Frontage Road and drive about a mile to Charleston Slough. The parking area is on the right side of the road.

Maps: To obtain a topographic map of the area, ask for Mountain View from the USGS.

Contact: Palo Alto Baylands Interpretive Center, 1451 Middlefield Road, Palo Alto, CA 94301; (415) 329-2506.

Trail notes: This trail is actually an old levee road that borders Charleston Slough, providing access to an expanse of wetlands and marsh habitat. It connects to a similar levee road that connects to Shoreline Regional Park in Mountain View—a great bike route and also good for hikes. From this trailhead, the best option is to head straight out the levee along the slough. Within 10 or 15 minutes, with each step you will gain access to marshland that has been preserved completely in its native state. From afar the surroundings may appear to be nothing more than pickleweed and mud, but look closer and you will begin to see the huge diversity of birds and wildlife that thrive in this very rich ecosystem. Way back in the 1950s, striped bass used to enter the mouth of Charleston Slough here and provide some excellent fishing. While the stripers are long gone, the serene atmosphere

and the variety of birds remain, making this a favorite destination for many people. The trail/road extends out near the shore of the South Bay, near the mouth of San Francisquito Creek. An added bonus is a large pit with mounds of dirt that are great for mountain bike jumping, known by locals as "The Moguls."

❸ Shoreline Regional Park

2.0 mi/1.0 hr

Location: Along South San Francisco Bay in Mountain View; map E1–South Bay, grid g6.

User groups: Hikers, wheelchairs, and mountain bikes. No dogs or horses.

Permits: No permits are required. Parking and access are free.

Directions: From U.S. 101 in Mountain View, take Shoreline Boulevard east and drive past the Shoreline Amphitheater to the park entrance station.

Maps: To obtain a topographic map of the area, ask for Mountain View from the USGS.

Contact: Shoreline Regional Park, City of Mountain View, 3070 North Shoreline Boulevard, Mountain View, CA 94043; (415) 903-6392 or fax (415) 903-6099.

Trail notes: An ideal family destination, Shoreline Regional Park offers a wide variety of activities, including pleasant walks and bike rides on wide, crushed-gravel byways. There's also a small lake that makes an excellent spot for windsurfing, and many good kite-flying areas on tiny hills. The best trail at the park is routed along the east side of the lake and then northward on a levee through marshlands. It is quite popular with bird-watchers, who can spot everything from egrets to LBJs (Little Brown Jobs). A concession stand near the lake gets a lot of use from the corn dog-and-Coke crowd, which kind of puts everything in perspective.

❹ Sunnyvale Baylands

2.0 mi/1.0 hr

Location: On South San Francisco Bay in Sunnyvale; map E1–South Bay, grid g7.

User groups: Hikers only. No dogs, horses, or mountain bikes. No wheelchair facilities.

Permits: No permits are required. A $3 parking fee is charged.

Directions: From Highway 237 in Sunnyvale, take the Lawrence Expressway exit north to Caribbean Drive and follow the signs to the park.

Maps: For a free map, write to Sunnyvale Baylands County Park at the address below. To obtain a topographic map of the area, ask for Mountain View from the USGS.

Contact: Sunnyvale Baylands County Park, P.O. Box 3707, Sunnyvale, CA 94088; (408) 730-7709 or fax (408) 745-7116.

Trail notes: Sunnyvale Baylands County Park really isn't much of a park at all, but rather a wildlife preserve surrounded by a levee that makes a good trail for hiking and jogging. It covers 220 acres of South Bay marshland, home to blue herons, great egrets, avocets, black-necked stilts, mallards, pintails, and burrowing owls. On nearly every trip you will also see a jackrabbit or two. In fact, these rabbits have a way of scaring the bejesus out of hikers. They hide in the weeds, it seems, until you get close, then suddenly pop up and take off at warp speed, shocking you every time.

From the parking area adjacent to Highway 237, hike along the levee, turning left as it parallels Calabazas Creek. To your left is a seasonal wetland preserve. The trail continues along the creek, then turns left again and runs alongside Guadalupe Slough. An open water bird preserve lies to the left.

---

❺ Monument Peak Trail

7.5 mi/4.0 hrs

Location: In Ed R. Levin County Park in the Milpitas foothills; map E1–South Bay, grid g9.

User groups: Hikers and horses. No dogs or mountain bikes. No wheelchair facilities.

Permits: No permits are required. A $3 day-use fee is charged.

Directions: From San Jose, take Interstate 680 north to Milpitas. Take the Calaveras Road East exit and follow Calaveras Road to the park. The trail starts near the northwest end of Sandy Wool Lake.

Maps: For a free trail map, contact Ed R. Levin County Park at the address below. To obtain

topographic maps of the area, ask for Milpitas and Calaveras Reservoir from the USGS.

Contact: Ed R. Levin County Park, 3100 Calaveras Road, Milpitas, CA 95035; (408) 262-6980 or fax (408) 946-7610.

Trail notes: At 2,594 feet, Monument Peak offers views that nearly rival those on Mount Hamilton, with far-ranging vistas over the Santa Clara Valley. Yet the peak gets bypassed by many people, including regular visitors to Ed R. Levin County Park. Of the 13 trails in the park, the summit hike is clearly the longest, steepest, and most difficult. And most park visitors do not come for a challenge, but rather to play golf at Spring Valley, go fishing at Sandy Wool Lake, or just enjoy a picnic. Those who do want a challenge will find one on this climb. There are two routes to the top: The Monument Peak Trail is actually a road, and you may run head-on into mountain bikers ripping downhill on it. We suggest you take the Tularcitos/Agua Caliente Trail for a more gentle climb without having to contend with bikes. It junctions with the Monument Peak Road near the top, where you turn left for the final push to the summit. With the trailhead at 300 feet at Sandy Wool Lake, figure on a 2,300-foot climb over the course of about 3.75 miles.

---

❻ Pescadero Marsh

3.0 mi/1.5 hrs

Location: In Pescadero Marsh south of Pescadero; map E1–South Bay, grid h1.

User groups: Hikers only. No dogs, horses, or mountain bikes. No wheelchair facilities.

Permits: No permits are required. A $5 parking/access fee is charged.

Directions: From the Peninsula in San Mateo, take Highway 92 west to Half Moon Bay. Turn south on Highway 1 and drive 18 miles to Pescadero Marsh. Cross the Pescadero Bridge and park at the dirt area on the left side of the highway at Pescadero Road. The trailhead is at the northeastern end of the bridge.

Maps: To obtain a topographic map of the area, ask for San Gregorio from the USGS.

Contact: California State Parks, 95 Kelly Avenue, Half Moon Bay, CA 94019; (415) 726-8820 or (415) 879-2170.

Trail notes: Here is one of the few remaining natural marshlands on the entire central California coast, a 600-acre parcel that is home to more than 250 species of birds. The most spectacular is the blue heron, which often grows nearly four feet tall and can have a wingspan of seven feet. A classic experience at any wetland is watching these huge birds lift off with labored wingbeats. The trail is nearly flat, so this is an easy walk for almost anyone. It starts just northeast of the Pescadero Bridge on Highway 1, where a dirt path is routed amid pampas grass and bogs along the edge of wetland habitat. For the best route, take the North Pond Trail to Audubon Marsh, then turn and head east and trace the southern edge of the marsh on the Sequoia Trail along Pescadero Creek. The marsh is bordered by the Pacific Ocean on one side and Pescadero Creek on the other, creating a unique setting that attracts birds who live in both saltwater and freshwater environments. Guided nature walks are conducted on most weekends by volunteers from the Half Moon Bay State Parks Department.

❼ McDonald Loop

3.1 mi/1.5 hrs

Location: In Sam McDonald County Park near La Honda; map E1–South Bay, grid h2.

User groups: Hikers only. No dogs, horses, or mountain bikes. No wheelchair facilities.

Permits: No permits are required. Parking and access are free.

Directions: From Interstate 280 on the Peninsula, take the Woodside/Highway 84 exit. Drive up the hill past Skyline Boulevard and continue another 10 miles to La Honda. Turn left on La Honda/Pescadero Road, bear left at the Y, and drive 1.5 miles to Sam McDonald County Park.

Maps: For a free trail map, contact Sam McDonald County Park at the address below. To obtain a topographic map of the area, ask for La Honda from the USGS.

Contact: Sam McDonald County Park, San Mateo County Parks and Recreation Department, 590 Hamilton Street, Redwood City, CA 94063; (415) 879-0238 or (415) 363-4020.

Trail notes: Though not a long trail, for many people the McDonald Loop is long enough, with a few surprise "ups" providing a challenge. The 1,000-acre park is best known for its redwoods, complete with the classic fern/sorrel understory, and is kept in a primitive state. Its trail network is linked by fire trail to Memorial County Park and Portola Redwood State Park. (The fire trails, by the way, are among the best mountain bike routes on the Peninsula.) This loop trail provides a fine introduction to the area and makes an excellent hike year-round; in the winter, especially during the week, you'll rarely encounter other hikers. For a great side trip, visit the adjacent Heritage Grove, which is accessible on Alpine Road about one mile east of the park. Several ancient redwoods grow there, and you can view them on a short, pleasant walk.

❽ Pescadero Creek Trail

6.0 mi/2.5 hrs

Location: In Memorial County Park near La Honda; map E1–South Bay, grid h2.

User groups: Hikers only. No dogs, horses, or mountain bikes. No wheelchair facilities.

Permits: No permits are required. A $4 day-use fee is charged.

Directions: From Interstate 280 on the San Mateo Peninsula, take the Woodside/Highway 84 exit. Drive up the hill past Skyline Boulevard and continue another 10 miles to La Honda. Turn left on La Honda/Pescadero Road, bear right at the Y, and drive six miles to Memorial County Park.

Maps: For a free trail map, contact Memorial County Park at the address below. To obtain a topographic map of the area, ask for La Honda from the USGS.

Contact: Memorial County Park, San Mateo Parks and Recreation Department, 590 Hamilton Street, Redwood City, CA 94063; (415) 879-0238 or (415) 363-4020.

Trail notes: Memorial County Park lies tucked in a pocket of redwoods between the tiny towns of La Honda and Loma Mar. Fifty miles of trails lead throughout the area, and one of our favorites is the Iverson Trail, routed along the very pretty Pescadero Creek. In the winter, when the water is clear enough, hikers can sometimes see steelhead preparing to spawn. In the summer, those "little trout" you see are actually steelhead smolts, trying to grow bigger before swimming out to sea, and no fishing is permitted. The area has many fire roads that are excellent for mountain biking, a bonus for visitors.

⑨ San Andreas Fault Trail

0.6 mi/0.5 hr

Location: In Los Trancos Open Space Preserve in the Palo Alto foothills; map E1—South Bay, grid h4.

User groups: Hikers only. The trail is not wheelchair accessible, but the parking lot is and offers a nice view. No dogs, horses, or mountain bikes.

Permits: No permits are required. Parking and access are free.

Directions: From Interstate 280 in Palo Alto, turn west on Page Mill Road and drive seven twisty miles to the signed parking area on the right. The Monte Bello Open Space Preserve is directly across the street.

Maps: For a free trail map, contact the Midpeninsula Regional Open Space District at the address below. A map and trail guide are also available at the parking area. To obtain a topographic map of the area, ask for Mindego Hill from the USGS.

Contact: Midpeninsula Regional Open Space District, 330 Distel Circle, Los Altos, CA 94022; (415) 691-1200 or fax (415) 691-0485.

Trail notes: The air at Los Trancos Open Space Preserve is always fresh, scented with bay leaves and damp woods. There are only seven miles of trails at the preserve, but one of the Peninsula's prize hikes is found here: the San Andreas Fault Trail. This is a self-guided tour of an "earthquake trail" and includes several examples of fault movement. The 13 numbered signposts along the way correspond with numbered explanations in the park brochure. If you don't want a geology lesson, you may be content with the good views of the Peninsula from the 2,000-foot ridgeline. Most hikers connect the San Andreas Fault Trail to the Lost Creek Loop Trail, a pleasant and easy bonus leg that is routed into secluded spots along a pretty creek. With the Monte Bello Open Space Preserve just on the other side of Page Mill Road, there are nearly 3,000 contiguous acres of public open space here.

⑩ Stevens Creek Nature Trail

3.5 mi/2.0 hrs

Location: In the Monte Bello Open Space Preserve in the Palo Alto foothills; map E1—South Bay, grid h4.

User groups: Hikers, horses, and mountain bikes (restricted from some trails). This trail is not open to wheelchairs, but the parking lot and a short side trail are wheelchair accessible and offer a good view. No dogs.

Permits: No permits are required unless you plan to use the preserve's backpack camp; phone (415) 691-1200 for information.

Directions: From Interstate 280 in Palo Alto, turn west on Page Mill Road and drive seven twisty miles to the signed parking area on the left. Los Trancos Open Space Preserve is directly across the street.

Maps: For a free trail map, contact the Midpeninsula Regional Open Space District at the address below. A map and trail guide are also available at the trailhead. To obtain a topographic map of the area, ask for Mindego Hill from the USGS.

Contact: Midpeninsula Regional Open Space District, 330 Distel Court, Los Altos, CA 94022; (415) 691-1200 or fax (415) 691-0485.

Trail notes: The Monte Bello Open Space Preserve encompasses more than 2,700 acres of the most natural and scenic lands on the Peninsula. It includes 2,800-foot Black Mountain, the headwaters of Stevens Creek, and this pretty nature trail. The hike starts by lateraling across a grasslands bluff, then drops 450 feet into the creek's wooded headwaters. As you descend through the forest, you will smell spicy bay leaves, feel the cool dampness on your skin, and see moss growing on so many trees. The trail emerges from the forest and is routed back along the San Andreas Fault, evidenced by two starkly contrasting images: dense woodlands stand to the west, while grasslands and chaparral lie off to the east. The two habitats are the product of the differences in soil composition created by fault movement. The nature trail has signed points of interest, with explanations for each in the brochure. Longer hikes are available in the park, the most ambitious being the 7.6-mile (one-way) Canyon Trail to Saratoga Gap.

⑪ Coal Creek Open Space

4.0 mi/2.0 hrs

Location: In the Coal Creek Open Space Preserve on the Peninsula's Skyline Ridge; map E1–South Bay, grid h4.

User groups: Hikers, dogs, horses, and mountain bikes. No wheelchair facilities.

Permits: No permits are required. Parking and access are free.

Directions: From Highway 280 in Palo Alto, take the Page Mill Road exit and drive west on a winding two-lane road up the mountain to Skyline Boulevard. Turn right on Skyline Boulevard and drive one mile to the parking area, located on the right at the CalTrans Vista Point.

Maps: For a free trail map, contact the Midpeninsula Regional Open Space District at the address below. To obtain a topographic map of the area, ask for Mindego Hill from the USGS.

Contact: Midpeninsula Regional Open Space District, 330 Distel Circle, Los Altos, CA 94022; (415) 691-1200 or fax (415) 691-0485.

Trail notes: Most residents of the Peninsula have never heard of the Coal Creek Open Space Preserve. That makes sense, as this is one of the lesser-developed parklands in the Bay Area. Yet it is worth making a trip to the 490-acre parcel of land set just east of Skyline Ridge, with its rolling meadows, open grasslands, and the forested headwaters of two creeks. The park's trails—actually old ranch roads—cover only four miles as they traverse the grasslands past a classic-looking barn and down along a small creek. Plan on enjoying nothing more than a short walk and a picnic. A bonus is that the parking area is adjacent to the CalTrans Vista Point, one of the best lookouts on the Peninsula.

⑫ Borel Hill Trail

1.4 mi/1.0 hr

Location: In the Russian Ridge Open Space Preserve on the Peninsula's Skyline Ridge; map E1–South Bay, grid h4.

User groups: Hikers, horses, and mountain bikes. A wheelchair-accessible trail starting at the parking area leads to Alpine Pond in the Skyline Ridge Open Space Preserve. No dogs.

Permits: No permits are required. Parking and access are free.

Directions: From Interstate 280 in Palo Alto, take the Page Mill Road exit and drive west on a winding two-lane road up the mountain to Skyline Boulevard. Cross Skyline Boulevard and turn right into the parking lot at the northwest corner of the intersection.

Maps: For a free trail map, contact the Midpeninsula Regional Open Space District at the address below. Maps are usually available at the trailhead. To obtain a topographic map of the area, ask for Mindego Hill from the USGS.

Contact: Midpeninsula Regional Open Space District, 330 Distel Circle, Los Altos, CA 94022; (415) 691-1200 or fax (415) 691-0485.

Trail notes: Borel Hill is one of the great lookouts on the San Francisco Peninsula, topping out at 2,572 feet and surrounded by grasslands so hikers get unobstructed, 360-degree views. Yet the hill is not well known, and remains a favorite destination of only a few hikers who visit the Russian Ridge Open Space Preserve. Russian Ridge is that big grassy ridge near the intersection of Alpine Road and Skyline Boulevard above Palo Alto, hike southeast on the Ridge Trail, climbing about 250 feet over the course of 0.7 miles to Borel Hill. You'll see it just southwest of the trail: the hill is the highest spot around, bordered by grasslands and no trees. From the summit, with just a sweeping turn of the head, you can see Monterey Bay one moment, then Mount Diablo and the South Bay the next. There are several other trails at the preserve, the best being the 2.6-mile (one-way) hike out to the Mindego Ridge Trail, which is routed through an oak woodland forest. A return loop trail was completed in 1995.

⑬ Skyline Ridge Trail

3.0 mi/1.5 hrs

Location: In the Skyline Ridge Open Space Preserve on the Peninsula's Skyline Ridge; map E1–South Bay, grid h4.

User groups: Hikers, horses, and mountain bikes. A wheelchair-accessible trail leads to Horseshoe Lake. No dogs.

Permits: No permits are required. Parking and access are free.

Directions: From Highway 280 in Palo Alto, take the Page Mill Road exit and drive west on a winding two-lane road up the mountain to Skyline Boulevard. Turn left on Skyline Boulevard and drive 0.8 miles to the main entrance and parking area on the right.

Maps: For a free trail map, contact the Midpeninsula Regional Open Space District at the address below. To obtain a topographic map of the area, ask for Mindego Hill from the USGS.

Contact: Midpeninsula Regional Open Space District, 330 Distel Circle, Los Altos, CA 94022; (415) 691-1200 or fax (415) 691-0485.

Trail notes: Most people discover this park by accident in December, when they come up Skyline Boulevard (Highway 35) to the choose-and-cut Christmas tree farm owned by the Open Space District. They see the parking area and maybe a trailhead, and become a little curious. At some point, many return to satisfy their curiosity with a hike, and most leave feeling well compensated for the effort. From the parking area on the west side of Skyline Boulevard, the Skyline Ridge Trail is routed around Horseshoe Lake, a pretty little farm pond. From there, the trail pushes into the interior of the parkland, skirting the flank of the highest mountain in park boundaries (2,493 feet), and loops back to Skyline Boulevard. You play peek-a-boo here, heading in and out of woodlands and gaining occasional views of plunging canyons to the west. You can create a loop hike, but that requires going back on a fire road; most people return to the parking area via the same route they walked in on the way in.

⑭ Long Ridge Loop

4.6 mi/2.0 hrs

Location: In the Long Ridge Open Space Preserve in the Santa Cruz Mountains; map E1–South Bay, grid h4.

User groups: Hikers, horses, and mountain bikes. No dogs. No wheelchair facilities.

Permits: No permits are required. Parking and access are free.

Directions: From Highway 280 in Palo Alto, take the Page Mill Road exit and drive west on a winding two-lane road up the mountain to Skyline Boulevard. Turn left on Skyline Boulevard and drive three miles to a dirt parking area along the shoulder on the right side of the road.

Maps: For a free trail map, contact the Midpeninsula Regional Open Space District at the address below. Maps are usually available at the trailhead. To obtain a topographic map of the area, ask for Mindego Hill from the USGS.

Contact: Midpeninsula Regional Open Space District, 330 Distel Circle, Los Altos, CA 94022; (415) 691-1200 or fax (415) 691-0485.

Trail notes: When you walk the ridgeline here, you are rewarded with gorgeous views of the western slopes of the Santa Cruz Mountains, highlighted by Big Basin Redwoods and Butano State Parks. From the southern part of the park on a clear day, the Pacific Coast comes into view as well. The Long Ridge Open Space Preserve covers more than 1,000 acres and offers a scenic loop hike that peaks out at 2,400 feet, climbing the ridge and ducking down into pretty, wooded canyons in the process. After departing from the trailhead, you cross a small creek, then turn right to start the looping hike up Long Ridge. The trail climbs up to Long Ridge Road, turns, and is routed south across the grassy hilltops. From here, the views of the coastal foothills and the ocean beyond can be wondrous. At the four-corners trail junction, turn left for the steep, switchback route down the canyon. At the end of the switchbacks, the trail passes the beautiful Jikoji Retreat, a private Zen center set along a surprising little pond, then turns left and loops back to the parking area. You wind up near a pretty oak woodland, with an apple orchard in one area.

⑮ Eagle Rock Loop

2.2 mi/1.0 hr

Location: In Alum Rock City Park in the San Jose foothills; map E1–South Bay, grid h9.

User groups: Hikers and mountain bikes. No dogs or horses. No wheelchair facilities.

Permits: No permits are required. A $3 parking fee is charged.

Directions: From Interstate 680 in San Jose, take Alum Rock Avenue east for 3.5 miles to the park entrance.

Maps: For a free trail map, contact Alum Rock City Park at the address below. To obtain a topographic map of the area, ask for Calaveras Reservoir from the USGS.

Contact: Alum Rock City Park, 16240 Alum Rock Avenue, San Jose, CA 95127; (408) 277-4539 or (408) 259-5477.

Trail notes: Eagle Rock is pretty short as far as mountains go, only 795 feet. But at Alum Rock City Park, it's the best perch around for a picnic site and a view of the Santa Clara Valley. In the winter, after rain has cleared the air, it becomes a choice spot. For this hike, park at the lot at the road's end at the eastern end of the park, where you'll find a major trailhead for several routes. Take the one on the left, the North Rim Trail, to reach Eagle Rock. The hike climbs 300 feet to a canyon rim overlooking the valley cut by Penitencia Creek, before a short, signed cutoff trail takes you to Eagle Rock. To complete the loop, return to the North Rim Trail and continue on, working your way back down the valley floor. Turn left on the Creek Trail (more like a road), which is routed along Penitencia Creek to the parking area. Thirteen miles of trails provide access to the park's 700 acres, but this hike is our favorite.

⓰ Penitencia Creek

4.0 mi/1.75 hrs

Location: In Penitencia Creek County Park in east San Jose; map E1–South Bay, grid h9.

User groups: Hikers and mountain bikes. No dogs or horses. No wheelchair facilities.

Permits: No permits are required. A $3 parking fee is charged.

Directions: From Interstate 680 in San Jose, take the Berryessa Road exit east. Turn right on Capitol Avenue and drive to Penitencia Creek Road. Turn left and drive to the Alum Rock City Park entrance. The trailhead is at the western end of that park.

Maps: For a free trail map, contact Penitencia Creek County Park at the address below. To obtain a topographic map of the area, ask for Calaveras Reservoir from the USGS.

Contact: Penitencia Creek County Park, c/o Ed R. Levin County Park, 3100 Calaveras Road, Milpitas, CA 95035; (408) 262-6980 or fax (408) 946-7610.

Trail notes: To be honest, this isn't much of a hiking trail and is really more of a bike path. But with the stream running alongside, it makes a pleasant route for a leisurely stroll, jog, or bicycle ride. Two more bonuses make it worth a trip: The park's eastern boundary abuts Alum Rock City Park, providing access to an additional 13 miles of trails. And near Piedmont Road, behind the fire station, you'll find an additional 40 acres called Creek Park, which is linked to this trail, providing an optional loop hike. The Penitencia Creek Trail traces the stream for four miles, adjacent to Penitencia Creek Road, so joggers making the round-trip can have an easy eight-miler. Most hikers do about half that or extend their walks into Creek Park or Alum Rock City Park.

⓱ Halls Valley Loop

5.5 mi/3.0 hrs

Location: In Joseph D. Grant County Park in the Mount Hamilton foothills east of San Jose; map E1–South Bay, grid h9.

User groups: Hikers, horses, and mountain bikes. No dogs. No wheelchair facilities.

Permits: No permits are required. A $3 entrance fee is charged daily from April to September and on weekends and holidays the rest of the year. A small, slotted register is posted at the parking area, so you pay the do-it-yourself way.

Directions: From U.S. 101 in San Jose, go south on Interstate 680. Drive to the Alum Rock Avenue East exit, turn right on Mount Hamilton Road, and drive eight miles east to the parking area on the left.

Maps: For a free trail map, contact Joseph D. Grant County Park at the address below. To obtain a topographic map of the area, ask for Lick Observatory from the USGS.

Contact: Joseph D. Grant County Park, 18405

Mount Hamilton Road, San Jose, CA 95140; (408) 274-6121.

Trail notes: Grant Ranch is the Bay Area's great undiscovered playland. The wild area covers 9,000 acres in the foothills of Mount Hamilton, yet gets relatively little use, despite being the perfect setting for hiking and mountain biking. There is plenty of room for both endeavors, with nearly 40 miles of hiking trails (horses permitted) and 20 miles of abandoned ranch roads for both mountain biking and hiking. The Halls Valley Loop provides the best introduction to Grant Ranch. From the parking area along Mount Hamilton Road, take the main trail/road out past Grant Lake and bear left at the junction on the Halls Valley Trail. This route skirts Halls Valley to the left, an open landscape of foothills and grasslands sprinkled with oaks, a quiet and pretty scene. The trail heads out 2.5 miles, climbing east toward Mount Hamilton until it meets the Cañada de Pala Trail. Turn right, hike up 0.4 miles, and turn right again on the Los Huecos Trail to complete the loop. From here, it's a 1.8-mile trip back to the parking area, descending steeply most of the way.

Special note: There are many great side trips on this route. After a rain, one of the best is searching out the little creek at the bottom of Halls Valley, then following it upstream to discover a procession of little waterfalls. For the ambitious, another is climbing 2.2 miles and 500 feet up the ridge on the Pala Seca Trail above Halls Valley to the park's highest point; from Antler Point at 2,995 feet, you can look out over the Santa Clara Valley.

⑱ Hotel Trail

7.0 mi/3.25 hrs

Location: In Joseph D. Grant County Park in the Mount Hamilton foothills east of San Jose; map E1—South Bay, grid h9.

User groups: Hikers, horses, and mountain bikes. No dogs. No wheelchair facilities.

Permits: No permits are required. A $3 entrance fee is charged daily from April to September and on weekends and holidays the rest of the year. A small, slotted register is posted at the parking area, so you pay the do-it-yourself way.

Directions: From U.S. 101 in San Jose, go south on Interstate 680. Drive to the Alum Rock Avenue East exit, turn right on Mount Hamilton Road, and drive eight miles east to the parking area on the left. The Hotel Trail starts on the other side of the road, opposite the parking area.

Maps: For a free trail map, contact Joseph D. Grant County Park at the address below. To obtain a topographic map of the area, ask for Lick Observatory from the USGS.

Contact: Joseph D. Grant County Park, 18405 Mount Hamilton Road, San Jose, CA 95140; (408) 274-6121.

Trail notes: People? What people? The remote landscape around Eagle Lake in Grant County Park provides visitors with precious tranquillity as well as good chances of seeing wildlife. Eagle Lake, set in the southernmost reaches of the park's 9,000 acres, is the prime destination of the Hotel Trail. After parking at the lot along Mount Hamilton Road, cross the road and look for the trailhead on the south side. Start hiking southeast on the ranch road (the Hotel Trail), scanning your surroundings for the wild turkeys that are commonly seen in this area. As you head deeper into the interior, you will be hiking through foothill country; bovines are the most frequently encountered animal (keep your distance from the bulls, of course), but you might see a herd of wild pigs, too. These pigs tend to sprint off when they see or hear people, so don't worry about playing out the stereotypical fearless-hiker-meets-ferocious-boar scene. The route to Eagle Lake is a direct shot of 3.5 miles, climbing a couple of hundred feet in the process. There are several options for side trips along the way: the best is to turn right on the Cañada de Pala Trail and drop down about a half mile to San Felipe Creek, the prettiest stream in the park.

⑲ Año Nuevo Lookout

2.75 mi/1.5 hrs

Location: In Butano State Park near Pescadero; map E1—South Bay, grid i2.

User groups: Hikers only. No dogs, horses, or mountain bikes. No wheelchair facilities.

Permits: No permits are required. A $5-per-vehicle state park entrance fee is charged.

Directions: From Interstate 280 in San Mateo, go west on Highway 92 and drive to Half Moon Bay. Turn south on Highway 1 and drive about 18 miles to the Pescadero turnoff. Turn east on Pescadero Road and drive past the town of Pescadero. Turn right (south) on Cloverdale Road and drive to the signed park entrance on the left. Park at the entrance station.

Maps: For a free trail map, contact Butano State Park at the address below. To obtain a topographic map of the area, ask for Franklin Point from the USGS.

Contact: Butano State Park, P.O. Box 3, Pescadero, CA 94060; (415) 879-2040 or (415) 330-6300.

Trail notes: Just pick a clear day, tighten your boots, and this trail will reward you with a fairly steep climb and a great view. Park at the entrance station, then start down the trailhead directly to the right. The trail climbs 730 feet in less than a mile to the lookout. From the lookout point, Año Nuevo Island to the south and the Pacific Ocean seem framed perfectly by conifers. We advise continuing on the Año Nuevo Trail, then returning on the Goat Hill Trail to complete the loop. Although short, this loop hike provides a good climb, a great lookout, and a chance to walk through redwoods on the return descent. Note: The name is pronounced "BUTE-uh-no" and not, we repeat, *not* "Bew-TAH-no."

㉗ Mill Ox Loop

5.0 mi/2.75 hrs

Location: In Butano State Park near Pescadero; map E1–South Bay, grid i2.

User groups: Hikers only. No dogs, horses, or mountain bikes. No wheelchair facilities.

Permits: No permits are required. A $5-per-vehicle state park entrance fee is charged.

Directions: From Interstate 280 in San Mateo, go west on Highway 92 and drive to Half Moon Bay. Turn south on Highway 1 and drive about 18 miles to the Pescadero turnoff. Turn east on Pescadero Road and drive past the town of Pescadero. Turn right (south) on Cloverdale Road and continue to the signed park entrance. The trailhead is a short distance past the entrance station on the left.

Maps: For a free trail map, contact Butano State Park at the address below. To obtain a topographic map of the area, ask for Franklin Point from the USGS.

Contact: Butano State Park, P.O. Box 3, Pescadero, CA 94060; (415) 879-2040 or (415) 330-6300.

Trail notes: If you love redwoods and ferns but are also partial to sun and warm afternoons, the Mill Ox Loop at Butano State Park may be the ideal hike for you. Why? Because you get all these things in good doses. The trail starts by crossing a small creek in a dense redwood forest, then heads up a very steep grade on switchbacks, emerging at the top of the canyon on the Butano Fire Road. Here you turn right and climb more gradually as you head toward the park's interior. The fire road gets plenty of sun, and plenty of shirts come off en route to 1,138 feet. Excellent views of the Pacific Ocean are to be had along the way if you turn and look back to the west. When you reach a junction with the Jackson Flats Trail, turn right; the trail descends quite steeply over a bare rock facing for a quarter mile, then drops into Butano Canyon and the surrounding redwood forest. The rest of the hike is beautiful and pleasant, a meandering walk past ferns, trillium, redwoods, and rarely in the spring, blooming wild orchids. This is one of our favorites.

㉘ Butano Loop

11.0 mi/2.0 days

Location: In Butano State Park near Pescadero; map E1–South Bay, grid i2.

User groups: Hikers only. No dogs, horses, or mountain bikes. No wheelchair facilities.

Permits: No permits are required. A $5-per-vehicle state park entrance fee is charged.

Directions: From Interstate 280 in San Mateo, go west on Highway 92 and drive to Half Moon Bay. Turn south on Highway 1 and drive about 18 miles to the Pescadero turnoff. Turn east on Pescadero Road and drive past the town of Pescadero. Turn right (south) on Cloverdale Road and continue to the signed park entrance. The trailhead is a short distance past the entrance station on the left.

Maps: For a free trail map, contact Butano State

Park at the address below. To obtain a topographic map of the area, ask for Franklin Point from the USGS.

Contact: Butano State Park, P.O. Box 3, Pescadero, CA 94060; (415) 879-2040 or (415) 330-6300.

Trail notes: A trail camp makes this one of the few loop hikes in the Bay Area that can be turned into an overnight backpack trip. Note that water for drinking and cooking is usually not available at the camp, so campers must pack in their own. In addition, most of the route is on fire roads, and with the boom in mountain bike use, fewer and fewer people are making the trip on foot. Regardless, you can still arrange it so that almost half of the trip follows trails, not roads, and enjoy a mix of redwood-filled canyons and sunny lookouts from ridgelines. By following our suggested route, the first day of your hike will be spent primarily in the sun, and you'll walk through redwoods for most of the second day.

Start at the Mill Ox Trailhead (see hike number 20) at elevation 200 feet, then hike up the steep grade, turning right on the Butano Fire Road (700 feet). From here, you trace the rim of Butano Canyon, enjoying views of the redwood-filled valley below and the Pacific Ocean off to the west. The trail climbs steadily before reaching 1,713 feet, crosses an old abandoned airstrip on the ridgeline, then drops down to the Butano Trail Camp at 1,550 feet, for a first-day total of 5.5 miles. Reservations are required, and since this is an environmental camp, only lightweight camp stoves are permitted for cooking. On day two, you return by turning right on the Olmo Fire Trail, then taking the Doe Ridge/Goat Hill Trails back to the starting point. Much of this route laterals and descends into the south side of Butano Canyon on a soft dirt trail amid redwoods. During the winter, when the Sierra Nevada is entombed in snow and ice, this loop is the perfect answer for those looking for an overnight backpack trip.

㉒ Sequoia Trail

1.0 mi/0.5 hr

Location: In Portola Redwood State Park in the Santa Cruz Mountains; map E1–South Bay, grid i4.

User groups: Hikers only. No dogs, horses, or mountain bikes. No wheelchair facilities.

Permits: No permits are required. A $6-per-vehicle state park entrance fee is charged; pay at the visitor station, one mile into the park.

Directions: From Interstate 280 in Palo Alto, take the Page Mill Road exit. Turn west and drive about 10 miles to Highway 35 (Skyline Boulevard). Cross Highway 35 and continue on Alpine Road for three miles. Turn left at Portola State Park Road and drive three miles to the park. The trailhead is just south of park headquarters.

Maps: For a trail map, send a legal-sized stamped envelope and 75 cents to Portola Redwood State Park at the address below. To obtain a topographic map of the area, ask for Mindego Hill from the USGS.

Contact: Portola Redwood State Park, P.O. Box F, Route 2, La Honda, CA 94020; (415) 948-9098.

Trail notes: The Shell Tree is one of the most unusual forest specimens on the Peninsula. This giant redwood is a strange-looking creature that has been ravaged by fire yet still lives, and now measures some 17 feet in diameter. We suggest you hike the Sequoia Trail, a short, easy loop, just to see this tree. Even on such a short hike, the surrounding forest, much of it redwood and Douglas fir, can provide a sense of remoteness. If you want more of a workout, the Sequoia Trail is linked to the Summit Trail (across from the group camping area), which ventures into remote lands on the eastern border of the park. Portola Redwood State Park covers about 1,000 acres, primarily second-growth redwoods, though a few ancient monsters remain. The park has only 14 miles of trails, but the Iverson Trail connects to Memorial County Park and an additional trail network.

㉓ Saratoga Gap Loop

9.0 mi/5.0 hrs

Location: In the Saratoga Gap Open Space Preserve on Skyline Ridge in the Santa Cruz Mountains; map E1–South Bay, grid i5.

User groups: Hikers, horses, and mountain bikes. No dogs. No wheelchair facilities.

Permits: No permits are required. Parking and access are free.

Directions: From Interstate 280 near Santa Clara, turn west on Saratoga Avenue and drive to Highway 9. Drive west on Highway 9 to the junction with Highway 35 (Skyline Boulevard). Look for the CalTrans parking area on the left. The preserve is on the north side of Highway 9, across the road from the parking lot.

Maps: For a free trail map, contact the Midpeninsula Regional Open Space District at the address below. Maps are usually available at the trailhead. To obtain topographic maps of the area, ask for Mindego Hill and Cupertino from the USGS.

Contact: Midpeninsula Regional Open Space District, 330 Distel Circle, Los Altos, CA 94022; (415) 691-1200 or fax (415) 691-0485.

Trail notes: Saratoga Gap serves as a trailhead center for hikers exploring the Peninsula's Skyline Ridge. Trails from here lead to five other parklands, making it possible for hikers to create trips of any length. The best is the nine-mile Saratoga Gap Loop. After parking, the trail starts off northward, adjacent to Highway 35 on the Skyline Ridge. After one mile, turn right on Charcoal Road, which is routed down the slope (bikes are permitted on the uphill here!) and into Upper Stevens Creek County Park. The trail descends to the headwaters of Stevens Creek, a quiet, wooded spot. Cross the creek and soon you will reach a trail junction, where you turn left (west) on the Canyon Trail; after crossing a small creek, turn left on the Grizzly Flat Trail. That trail climbs back to Skyline Boulevard, where you cross the road, enter the Long Ridge Open Space Preserve, and hike south to where the trail crosses Skyline Boulevard once again. Return on the Saratoga Gap Trail to the parking area. The hills here are grassy knobs sprinkled with oaks and madrones, while the canyons are heavily wooded, most prominently with Douglas firs.

㉔ Summit Rock Loop

2.0 mi/1.0 hr

Location: In Sanborn-Skyline County Park on Skyline Ridge in the Santa Cruz Mountains; map E1–South Bay, grid i5.

User groups: Hikers and horses. No dogs or mountain bikes. No wheelchair facilities.

Permits: No permits are required. A $3-per-vehicle day-use fee is charged.

Directions: From Interstate 280 near Santa Clara, turn west on Saratoga Avenue and drive to Highway 9. Drive west on Highway 9 to the junction with Highway 35 (Skyline Boulevard). Turn south and drive 2.5 miles to Sanborn-Skyline County Park. The trailhead is located across from Castle Rock State Park on Skyline Boulevard.

Maps: For a free trail map, contact Sanborn-Skyline County Park at the address below. To obtain a topographic map of the area, ask for Castle Rock Ridge from the USGS.

Contact: Sanborn-Skyline County Park, 16055 Sanborn Road, Saratoga, CA 95070; (408) 867-9959.

Trail notes: The Santa Clara Valley never looks prettier than it does from Summit Rock, set just east of the Skyline Ridge. This is the ideal perch for a lookout to the valley below, and getting there is not difficult when you take the featured hike at Sanborn-Skyline County Park. The park is so named because it connects Sanborn Creek with the Skyline Ridge, covering some 2,850 acres of mountain terrain in between. From the trailhead, across Highway 35 from Castle Rock State Park, hikers start on the Skyline Trail and head north, adjacent to the road. The Skyline Trail leads right into the Summit Rock Loop, providing easy access to this great lookout. For people who like their views to come even easier, a popular option at the Skyline Trailhead is the quarter-mile hike that leads to Indian Rock. Note that park headquarters are not located at this trailhead, but rather off Sanborn Road, where full facilities and other trails are available.

㉕ Trail Camp Loop

5.5 mi/3.0 hrs

Location: In Castle Rock State Park on Skyline Ridge in the Santa Cruz Mountains; map E1–South Bay, grid i5.

User groups: Hikers and horses. No dogs or mountain bikes. No wheelchair facilities.

Permits: No permits are required, but you must self-register at the park entrance. A $3 day-use fee is charged.

Directions: From Interstate 280 near Santa Clara, turn west on Saratoga Avenue and drive to Highway 9. Drive west on Highway 9 to the junction with Highway 35 (Skyline Boulevard). Turn south and drive 2.5 miles to the entrance to Castle Rock State Park on the right.

Maps: For a free brochure, contact Castle Rock State Park at the address below. To obtain a topographic map of the area, ask for Castle Rock Ridge from the USGS.

Contact: Castle Rock State Park, 15000 Skyline Boulevard, Los Gatos, CA 95030; (408) 867-2952 or (408) 429-2851.

Trail notes: Castle Rock State Park is well known to rock climbers, who practice their art here on Castle Rock and Goat Rock, two honeycombed sandstone formations. But hikers, too, are attracted to the park, a 3,600-acre semi-wilderness with 32 miles of hiking trails. The park is located on the west side of Skyline Ridge at an elevation of 3,000 feet, high enough to be above the smog, receive light snowfall in the winter, and provide scenic views to the west of Big Basin and Monterey Bay. The Trail Camp Loop offers the best introduction to the park. From the parking lot, take the Saratoga Gap Trail to Trail Camp for a 2.8-mile trip that passes a gorgeous waterfall then crosses a rock face, with excellent views. To return from Trail Camp, reverse your direction and follow the Ridge Trail, passing Goat Rock (a great lookout) and mixed forest in 2.7 miles en route to the parking area. Because the sandstone you see is filled with tiny holes, we call this park "Swiss Cheese State Park."

㉖ Skyline-to-Sea Trail

31.6 mi. one way/3.0 days

Location: From Castle Rock State Park via Big Basin to Waddell Creek on the Pacific coast; map E1–South Bay, grid i5.

User groups: Hikers and horses. No dogs or mountain bikes. No wheelchair facilities.

Permits: Unless you are camping, no permits are required, but everyone must self-register at the park entrance. A $4 state park day-use fee is charged. If you plan to camp, the fee is $10, which includes parking.

Directions: From Interstate 280 near Santa Clara, turn west on Saratoga Avenue and drive to Highway 9. Drive west on Highway 9 to the junction with Highway 35 (Skyline Boulevard). Turn south and drive 2.5 miles to the entrance to Castle Rock State Park on the right. For a one-way shuttle trip, leave a car at Waddell Creek (see hike number 33).

Maps: For a free brochure, contact Castle Rock State Park at the address below. To obtain topographic maps of the area, ask for Castle Rock Ridge and Big Basin from the USGS.

Contact: Castle Rock State Park, 15000 Skyline Boulevard, Los Gatos, CA 95030; (408) 867-2952. Big Basin Redwoods State Park, 21600 Big Basin Way, Boulder Creek, CA 95006; (408) 338-8860, (408) 429-2851, or fax (408) 429-2876.

Trail notes: What began as a good idea has been transformed into one of the most worshiped trails in the Bay Area. Years ago someone had a vision to create a trail that connected Castle Rock State Park on Skyline Ridge to Big Basin and out by way of Waddell Creek to the coast. The result, much of it built by volunteers, is this 38-mile backpack route, complete with primitive trail camps. It is ideal in many ways, including the fact that the hike is generally downhill, starting at 3,000 feet at Castle Rock and dropping all the way down to sea level. Fantastic views, redwood forests, waterfalls, and the camps are among the rewards. Only in extremely rare conditions will you come across a discarded cigarette butt or a piece of litter; after all, most people won't trash a piece of heaven. The trail is best hiked in four days, but most do it in three. Of course, it is a must that you have a shuttle car waiting at the end of the trail at Waddell Creek on Highway 1.

From the trailhead at Castle Rock State Park, head out to the Waterman Gap trail camp (water is available) for a first-day hike of 9.6 miles. This portion includes crossing an open rock facing with fantastic views of Big Basin and the Pacific Coast to the west, which will help you envision the upcoming route. The logical plan for the second day is to hike 9.5 miles to Jay Camp at Big Basin headquarters. This is not exactly a back-country experience, as the camp has rest rooms and drinking water. On the last day you face a real grunt, hiking 12.5 miles out, up, and over the Big

Basin rim then down a wooded canyon, passing beautiful 70-foot Berry Creek Falls, crossing Waddell Creek, and finishing up at the coast. If you want to split the last day in two, an excellent option is to take a bonus day by turning right at Berry Creek Falls, then hiking up past Cascade Falls to the Sunset Camp (no piped water), the most remote camp in Big Basin.

㉗ Ridge Trail

6.0 mi/2.75 hrs

Location: In El Sereno Open Space Preserve in the Saratoga foothills; map E1–South Bay, grid i6.

User groups: Hikers, horses, and mountain bikes. No dogs. No wheelchair facilities.

Permits: No permits are required. Parking and access are free.

Directions: From the intersection of Interstate 280 and Highway 17 in San Jose, turn south on Highway 17 and drive about eight miles to Los Gatos. Continue south for about three miles to Montevina Road. Turn right and park at the roadside turnout at the end of the road. There is space for only a few cars.

Maps: For a free trail map, contact the Midpeninsula Regional Open Space District at the address below. To obtain a topographic map of the area, ask for Castle Rock Ridge from the USGS.

Contact: Midpeninsula Regional Open Space District, 330 Distel Circle, Los Altos, CA 94022; (415) 691-1200 or fax (415) 691-0485.

Trail notes: El Sereno Open Space is one of the lesser-used parklands in the Bay Area. Why? Not only is it remote, but there's room at the trailhead for only two vehicles to park. The preserve covers 1,112 acres and is named for Mount El Sereno, a prominent peak on the adjacent ridge. From the trailhead at the pullout on Montevina Road, hike on the jeep trail, which traces a ridgeline. Though the trail bobs and weaves, you will generally head east, topping out on a rim and then descending toward Los Gatos, for a distance of three miles to the end of the trail. This is where you'll find panoramic views of Lyndon Canyon, Lexington Reservoir, and the South Bay. After taking time to enjoy the vistas, return via the same route.

㉘ St. Joseph's Hill Trail

2.7 mi/1.75 hrs

Location: In the St. Joseph's Hill Open Space Preserve near Lexington Reservoir; map E1–South Bay, grid i6.

User groups: Hikers, dogs, and mountain bikes. No horses. No wheelchair facilities.

Permits: No permits are required. Parking and access are free.

Directions: From Los Gatos, drive about four miles south on Highway 17 to the Alma Bridge Road exit at Lexington Reservoir. Turn east and drive 1.5 miles across the dam. Parking is available just east of the dam in Lexington Reservoir County Park. The trail starts opposite the boat launching area beyond the dam.

Maps: For a free trail map, contact the Midpeninsula Regional Open Space District at the address below. To obtain a topographic map of the area, ask for Los Gatos from the USGS.

Contact: Midpeninsula Regional Open Space District, 330 Distel Circle, Los Altos, CA 94022; (415) 691-1200 or fax (415) 691-0485.

Trail notes: For most people to be willing to hike up, there had better be considerable compensation waiting at the trail's end. And so there is on this hike, which climbs 600 feet in the space of about 1.5 miles to a perch on top of St. Joseph's Hill, with views of Lexington Reservoir, the Santa Clara Valley, and the adjacent Sierra Azul Range. From the parking area, just east of the dam at elevation 645 feet, you hike north adjacent to Los Gatos Creek for about a half mile. At the trail junction, turn right and begin the climb up St. Joseph's Hill; a loop route is available near the top. Lexington Reservoir never looked so good.

㉙ Lexington Dam Trail

1.0 mi/0.5 hr

Location: In Lexington Reservoir County Park in the Saratoga foothills; map E1–South Bay, grid i6.

User groups: Hikers and limited mountain bikes. No dogs or horses. No wheelchair facilities.

Permits: No permits are required. A $3 day-use fee is charged.

Directions: From Los Gatos, drive about four miles south on Highway 17 to the Alma Bridge Road exit at Lexington Reservoir. Turn east and drive 1.5 miles across the dam. Parking is available just east of the dam.

Maps: For a free trail map, contact Lexington Reservoir County Park at the address below. To obtain a topographic map of the area, ask for Los Gatos from the USGS.

Contact: Lexington Reservoir County Park, c/o Vasona Lake County Park, 298 Garden Hill Drive, Los Gatos, CA 95030; (408) 356-2729.

Trail notes: Lexington Reservoir can be one of the prettiest places in Santa Clara County, as well as one of the ugliest. The lake might be full of water one year, then drained down to nothing the next. And after a hot summer it can resemble a dust bowl. Park at the lot just east of the dam, then walk across the dam and turn right on the "Pedway." That's as far as many people get, as most come for the view of the lake from the dam. Keep walking, though, and you will be surprised, as the trail drops down along Los Gatos Creek. After 1.5 miles, it links up with the Los Gatos Creek Trail, which you can follow all the way into town; it's a popular bike route. Note: Alma Bridge Road circles the reservoir, and for more ambitious walks, there are several parklands nearby.

⓷ Sierra Azul Loop

6.1 mi/4.5 hrs

Location: In the Sierra Azul Open Space Preserve near Lexington Reservoir; map E1–South Bay, grid i6.

User groups: Hikers, horses, and mountain bikes. No dogs. No wheelchair facilities.

Permits: No permits are required. Parking and access are free.

Directions: From Los Gatos, drive about four miles south on Highway 17 to the Alma Bridge Road exit at Lexington Reservoir. Turn east and drive 1.5 miles across the dam to the parking area.

Maps: For a free trail map, contact the Midpeninsula Regional Open Space District at the address below. To obtain a topographic map of the area, ask for Santa Teresa Hills from the USGS.

Contact: Midpeninsula Regional Open Space District, 330 Distel Circle, Los Altos, CA 94022; (415) 691-1200 or fax (415) 691-0485.

Trail notes: This is Santa Clara Valley's backyard wilderness. Many people find it difficult to believe these wildlands could exist so close to so many homes. But they do, and you can explore them on the Sierra Azul Loop, a strenuous hike that climbs, climbs, and climbs as it probes the Sierra Azul Range.

At the entrance to the Sierra Azul Open Space Preserve, the trail rises in the first mile to 1,762 feet at Priest Rock. There it nearly levels out for about a mile, until you reach the loop junction. Veer to the left; the trail starts climbing again, and in the next 1.5 miles climbs another thousand feet or so to reach the ridgeline at 2,628 feet. Turn right at the ridge and enjoy finally being on top, cruising over the 1.6-mile stretch on the mountain rim. Turn right at the next ridge junction and take the trail back (three miles to the loop junction), relaxing on the downhill cruise.

⓷ Bald Mountain Trail

1.0 mi/1.0 hr

Location: In the Sierra Azul Range south of Los Gatos; map E1–South Bay, grid i7.

User groups: Hikers, horses, and mountain bikes. No dogs. No wheelchair facilities.

Permits: No permits are required. Parking and access are free.

Directions: From San Jose, drive south on the Almaden Expressway. Turn west on Camden Avenue and drive to the intersection with Hicks Road. Go south, drive to Mount Umunhum Road, then turn west and continue to the two-car parking area at district pipe gate SA-7. There is limited roadside parking only, not a designated parking area.

Maps: For a free trail map, contact the Midpeninsula Regional Open Space District at the address below. To obtain a topographic map of the area, ask for Santa Teresa Hills from the USGS.

Contact: Midpeninsula Regional Open Space District, 330 Distel Court, Los Altos, CA 94022; (415) 691-1200 or fax (415) 691-0485.

Trail notes: It's hard to beat standing atop a mountain, especially when you're near Mount Umunhum, at 3,486 feet, the highest point in the Sierra Azul Range. From anywhere in the Santa Clara Valley, Mount Umunhum is the most prominent landmark on the western horizon—it's that mountain with the big abandoned radar station on top. Alas, the public is not permitted to hike to the summit of Umunhum due to toxic contaminates and restrictions related to private property. But the trip to adjacent Bald Mountain is the next best thing. The trail here is a half-mile route on Mount Umunhum Road to Bald Mountain, a hilltop knoll with views of the Almaden Valley and across San Jose to Mount Hamilton, then south to San Benito County. As we said, public access to Mount Umunhum is prohibited, and the Midpeninsula Regional Open Space District requests that you call them prior to visiting Bald Mountain. By the way, guess what "Umunhum" means in the Ohlone Indian language: 1. Eagle? 2. Bear? 3. Hummingbird? The answer: hummingbird.

㉜ Año Nuevo Trail

2.5 mi/2.0 hrs

Location: In Año Nuevo State Reserve on the San Mateo County coast south of Pescadero; map E1–South Bay, grid j2.

User groups: Hikers only. No dogs, horses, or mountain bikes. No wheelchair facilities.

Permits: From April through November, you must obtain a permit to hike in the park's Wildlife Protection Area. Permits are available at the park on a first-come, first-served basis. From December through March, access to the park is available only by accompanying a ranger on a scheduled walk. To make a reservation, phone Destinet at (800) 444-7275. A $5 parking fee is charged. Seal walk tickets are $4 per person.

Directions: From Interstate 280 in San Mateo, turn west on Highway 92 and drive to Half Moon Bay. Turn left (south) on Highway 1 and drive about 30 miles to the park entrance on the right.

Maps: For a map and brochure, send 75 cents to Año Nuevo State Reserve at the address below. To obtain a topographic map of the area, ask for Año Nuevo from the USGS.

Contact: Año Nuevo State Reserve, New Year's Creek Road, Pescadero, CA 94060; (415) 879-2025 or (415) 726-8800.

Trail notes: One of the more curious adventures in the Bay Area has become one of the most popular: touring Año Nuevo State Reserve to see the elephant seals. Yep, this is the place where these giant creatures arrive every winter to fight, mate, give birth, sunbathe, and make funny noises. So many people now want to watch them that you must make reservations and join a tour group, typically from December through March. Elephant seals look like giant slugs, often weighing 2,000 to 3,000 pounds—even the newborns weigh 75 pounds. The old boars reach nearly 20 feet in length and weigh as much as 5,000 pounds. As part of a tour group, you'll walk along roped-off trails, winding your way amid the animals. They will appear to have no interest in you, and if you keep your distance, that is just how it should be. With a 200 mm camera lens, you can get excellent pictures. The best times to visit are in mid-December, when the males battle for harems, and in late January, when hundreds of pups are born. The rest of the year, this is a nice place to enjoy a quiet beach walk. It's hard to believe then that such a phenomenon takes place here in the winter.

㉝ Waddell Creek Trail

9.0 mi/4.0 hrs

Location: In Big Basin Redwoods State Park on the Santa Cruz County coast south of Año Nuevo; map E1–South Bay, grid j2.

User groups: Hikers, horses (not permitted past the Henry Trail), and mountain bikes (not permitted past Waddell Creek Bridge). No dogs. No wheelchair facilities.

Permits: No permits are required. A $6-per-vehicle state park entrance fee is charged.

Directions: From Interstate 280 in San Mateo, turn west on Highway 92 and drive to Half Moon Bay. Turn left (south) on Highway 1 and drive about 30 miles, past Año Nuevo State Reserve. Drive south for about three miles and look for the signs indicating Big Basin Redwoods State Park/Rancho del Oso, just past the Santa Cruz

County line. Park along the right (west) side of Highway 1 at the entrance to Rancho del Oso.

Maps: Contact Big Basin Redwoods State Park for the availability and prices of trail maps. To obtain a topographic map of the area, ask for Franklin Point from the USGS.

Contact: Big Basin Redwoods State Park, 21600 Big Basin Way, Boulder Creek, CA 95006; (408) 338-8860, (408) 429-2851, or fax (408) 429-2876.

Trail notes: If the only wildlife you ever see is on the back of a quarter, this trail can change that, particularly during the last two hours of light on a weekday evening. Deer seem to sprout out of nowhere at a huge meadow on the north side of the trail; rabbits, squirrels, and quail are often seen hip-hopping around; baby steelhead swim in Waddell Creek; and ducks and herons make year-round homes in the marsh near the coast. The trailhead is located on Highway 1 just south of the Santa Cruz County line at the Rancho del Oso outpost. The trail, actually a ranch road, starts by skirting a marsh, then runs adjacent to Waddell Creek. You can turn around at any point, of course, but we suggest walking all the way out to the bridge over Berry Creek. The trail is nearly flat and has become very popular on weekends with mountain bikers, who typically go too fast and spook the wildlife. That's why you should hike during the week, if you can, when trail users are few and tranquility abounds. It's the perfect setting for an evening wildlife walk.

㉞ Redwood Loop

0.6 mi/0.5 hr

Location: In Big Basin Redwoods State Park in the Santa Cruz Mountains near Boulder Creek; map E1–South Bay, grid i3.

User groups: Hikers only. Partially wheelchair accessible. No dogs, horses, or mountain bikes.

Permits: No permits are required. A $6-per-vehicle state park entrance fee is charged.

Directions: From the San Francisco Peninsula, take Interstate 280 to Sunnyvale/Saratoga Road. Turn south and drive five miles to Saratoga. Turn right at Highway 9 and drive up the hill for about seven miles to Skyline Ridge. Continue over the

other side of Highway 9 about seven more miles to Highway 236. Turn right and drive about 10 miles to Big Basin Redwoods State Park. Note: Highway 236 is extremely twisty and not recommended for motor homes or trailers.

Alternate route: From San Francisco, take Highway 1 south to Santa Cruz. Go north on Highway 9 and drive about 12 miles. At the traffic light in Boulder Creek, turn left on Highway 236. Drive about 10 miles to park headquarters.

Maps: Contact Big Basin Redwoods State Park for availability and prices of trail maps. To obtain a topographic map of the area, ask for Franklin Point from the USGS.

Contact: Big Basin Redwoods State Park, 21600 Big Basin Way, Boulder Creek, CA 95006; (408) 338-8860, (408) 429-2851, or fax (408) 429-2876.

Trail notes: Most people come to Big Basin Redwoods State Park to see giant redwoods, and the Redwood Loop is a short, easy, scenic path that wanders amid many of the park's largest trees. This trail gets a lot of use, which is why we knocked the rating down a few notches. By using the numbered posts along the way and a trail brochure, you can take a self-guided nature walk. The sights include pretty Opal Creek, the Chimney Tree (which has survived many fires), and several other ancient redwoods. The Santa Clara Tree, located across Opal Creek at signpost 3, is 17 feet in diameter; the Father-of-the-Forest is about 2,000 years old and stands at signpost 8; and the Mother-of-the-Forest, the tallest tree in the park at 329 feet, is at signpost 9. Many people take as much as an hour to complete the loop. There is no reason to rush.

㉟ Berry Creek Falls

12.0 mi/5.5 hrs

Location: In Big Basin Redwoods State Park in the Santa Cruz Mountains near Boulder Creek; map E1–South Bay, grid i3.

User groups: Hikers only. No dogs, horses, or mountain bikes. No wheelchair facilities.

Permits: No permits are required. A $6-per-vehicle state park entrance fee is charged.

Directions: From the San Francisco Peninsula, take Interstate 280 to Sunnyvale/Saratoga Road.

Turn south and drive five miles to Saratoga. Turn right at Highway 9 and drive up the hill for about seven miles to Skyline Ridge. Continue over the other side of Highway 9 about seven more miles to Highway 236. Turn right and drive about 10 miles to Big Basin Redwoods State Park. Note: Highway 236 is extremely twisty and not recommended for motor homes or trailers.

Alternate route: From San Francisco, take Highway 1 south to Santa Cruz. Go north on Highway 9 and drive about 12 miles. At the traffic light in Boulder Creek, turn left on Highway 236. Drive about 10 miles to park headquarters.

Maps: Contact Big Basin Redwoods State Park for availability and prices of trail maps. To obtain a topographic map of the area, ask for Franklin Point from the USGS.

Contact: Big Basin Redwoods State Park, 21600 Big Basin Way, Boulder Creek, CA 95006; (408) 338-8860, (408) 429-2851, or fax (408) 429-2876.

Trail notes: The prettiest sight in the Bay Area just might be Berry Creek Falls, a 70-foot waterfall framed by a canyon, complete with ferns, redwoods, and the sound of rushing water. We think it's the number one hike in the Bay Area, one that we repeat over and over again. Getting an early start really helps you have a carefree trip, with no pressure to complete the loop by a certain time. You start at park headquarters, taking the Skyline-to-Sea Trail (hike number 26) amid the giant redwoods up to the Big Basin rim, then head down the other side, hiking west toward to the coast. After topping the rim (at 1,200 feet), the hike descends 600 feet over the course of about four miles to Berry Creek Falls (4.7 miles from the trailhead). You round a bend and suddenly, there it is, this divine waterfall. A small bench is perfectly situated for viewing the scene while eating a picnic lunch.

To return, we recommend going the long way, up the staircase and past the Cascade Falls—both Silver Falls and Golden Falls—then returning on the Sunset Trail. At Silver Falls, it is possible to dunk your head into the streaming water without getting the rest of your body wet, a real thrill. The Sunset Trail takes you to the most remote sections of the park, loops back into redwoods, then leads back to park headquarters. However, you can trim the hiking time down to about 4.5

hours if you double back on the same trail you came in on. But in such a beautiful place, why cut the experience short?

36 Meteor Trail

5.2 mi/2.5 hrs

Location: In Big Basin Redwoods State Park in the Santa Cruz Mountains near Boulder Creek; map E1–South Bay, grid i3.

User groups: Hikers only. No dogs, horses, or mountain bikes. No wheelchair facilities.

Permits: No permits are required. A $6-per-vehicle state park entrance fee is charged.

Directions: From the San Francisco Peninsula, take Interstate 280 to Sunnyvale/Saratoga Road. Turn south and drive five miles to Saratoga. Turn right at Highway 9 and drive up the hill for about seven miles to Skyline Ridge. Continue over the other side of Highway 9 about seven more miles to Highway 236. Turn right and drive about 10 miles to Big Basin Redwoods State Park. Note: Highway 236 is extremely twisty and not recommended for motor homes or trailers.

Alternate route: From San Francisco, take Highway 1 south to Santa Cruz. Go north on Highway 9 and drive about 12 miles. At the traffic light in Boulder Creek, turn left on Highway 236. Drive about 10 miles to park headquarters.

Maps: Contact Big Basin Redwoods State Park for the availability and prices of trail maps. To obtain a topographic map of the area, ask for Franklin Point from the USGS.

Contact: Big Basin Redwoods State Park, 21600 Big Basin Way, Boulder Creek, CA 95006; (408) 338-8860, (408) 429-2851, or fax (408) 429-2876.

Trail notes: Under the heavy redwood canopy of Big Basin, most hikers don't worry about whether or not it's foggy on the coast. But on this hike there's a unique reason to worry, as the park's best coastal lookout is at the trail's end. The Meteor Trail starts at park headquarters on the Skyline-to-Sea Trail (hike number 26) and heads northeast. (If you see a sign for Berry Creek Falls, you're going in the wrong direction.)

For much of the route you hike along Opal Creek, a pretty stream in the spring, surrounded by redwoods. Two miles out, you will arrive at the intersection with the Meteor Trail, where you turn left and climb 400 feet over the space of a mile to the Middle Ridge Fire Road. From here, the Ocean View Summit (1,600 feet) is only a couple hundred yards off, featuring a great glimpse to the west of the Waddell Creek watershed and the Pacific Coast—though the view is largely eclipsed now by trees. Return by doubling back the way you came. If you visit Big Basin and don't have time for the Berry Creek Falls hike, this is the next best option.

㊲ Davenport Beach

1.0 mi/1.0 hr

Location: On the Santa Cruz County coast north of Santa Cruz; map E1–South Bay, grid j3.

User groups: Hikers, dogs, and horses. No mountain bikes. No wheelchair facilities.

Permits: No permits are required. Parking and access are free.

Directions: From the San Francisco Peninsula, take Interstate 280 to Highway 92, turn west, and drive to Half Moon Bay. Turn south on Highway 1. Drive past Año Nuevo State Reserve and continue driving another nine miles to Davenport. Park on the right side of the highway at the spacious beach area, one mile north of the high ocean bluff.

Maps: To obtain a topographic map of the area, ask for Davenport from the USGS.

Contact: There is no managing agency for this location.

Trail notes: If you have a passion for wide-open ocean frontage, the beach at Davenport will certainly satisfy. It is made up of pristine, open sand dunes that are often deserted. Except, that is, for the daredevil hang gliders who use the coastal thermals to float off a cliff at the southern end of the beach and then glide through the sky in apparent comfort. Well, it is a heck of a lot more comforting to take a stroll along the vast beach, a haven of tranquillity. During the winter venture off on a side trip up along the bluffs, one of the best land-based spots to the see the spouts of passing gray whales. Just look for the little "puff of smoke" out at sea. This is also one of the top windsurfing spots in California.

㊳ Loch Lomond Loop

5.0 mi/3.25 hrs

Location: In Loch Lomond Park in the Santa Cruz foothills near Ben Lomond; map E1–South Bay, grid j5.

User groups: Hikers only. No dogs, horses, or mountain bikes. No wheelchair facilities.

Permits: No permits are required. A $3 day-use fee is charged. The Loch Lomond Recreation Area is open only from March 1 through September 15. Rangers are on duty during the winter and will cite trespassers.

Directions: From San Jose, go south on Highway 17, drive to Scotts Valley, and take the Mount Hermon Road exit. Drive three miles west on Mount Hermon Road to Graham Hill Road. Turn left and drive about 0.8 miles, then turn left on Zayante Road and continue five miles to Lompico Road. Turn left and drive another five miles to West Drive. Turn left again and go to Sequoia Road. Turn right and continue into the park.

Maps: For a free trail map, contact Loch Lomond Park at the address below. To obtain a topographic map of the area, ask for Felton from the USGS.

Contact: Loch Lomond Park, 100 Loch Lomond Way, Felton, CA 95018; (408) 335-7424.

Trail notes: There is no prettier lake in the greater Bay Area than Loch Lomond Reservoir, a jewel set in the Santa Cruz Mountains, complete with an island and circled by conifers. Newcomers are always surprised by its beauty, and by the nearby hiking opportunities as well. Of the 12 miles of trails here, the best hike is the Loch Lomond Loop. You start east on the Loch Trail, a level path that extends along the lakeshore for 1.5 miles out to Deer Flat. There you turn uphill on the Highland Trail, climbing and looping to the right up the ridge on a moderate ascent. It peaks out at a remote weather station where you get a great view of the lake below. Bring your camera. To complete the loop, continue on the trail, which is routed down to the upper picnic area; or you can take the paved road back to the starting point. A bonus at Loch Lomond is good trout fishing, especially in April. Great lake, great views, great hike.

㊴ Eagle Creek Trail

3.0 mi/1.5 hrs

Location: In Henry Cowell Redwoods State Park near Santa Cruz; map E1–South Bay, grid j5.

User groups: Hikers and horses. No dogs or mountain bikes. No wheelchair facilities.

Permits: No permits are required. A $5-per-vehicle state park entrance fee is charged.

Directions: From San Jose, turn south on Highway 17, drive to Scotts Valley, and take the Mount Hermon Road exit. Drive three miles west on Mount Hermon Road, then turn left on Graham Hill Road and continue driving south to the park entrance. The trailhead is adjacent to the campground.

Maps: For a trail map, send $1.50 to Mountain Parks Foundation, 525 North Big Trees Park Road, Felton, CA 95018; (408) 335-3174. To obtain a topographic map of the area, ask for Felton from the USGS.

Contact: Henry Cowell Redwoods State Park, 101 North Big Trees Road, Felton, CA 95018; (408) 335-4598 or (408) 429-2851.

Trail notes: There are two places you just plain shouldn't miss on a visit to Henry Cowell Redwoods State Park. The first one is the Eagle Creek Trail, the most direct hiking route to the River Trail and the San Lorenzo River. The other is the park's observation deck, offering first-class views (we'll get to that).

The Eagle Creek Trail starts between campsites 82 and 84, crosses Eagle Creek, then continues adjacent to the stream as it heads out toward the San Lorenzo River. As you hike this portion of the trail you are surrounded by redwoods. The trail then crosses Pipeline Road and junctions with the River Trail. Many people turn around and head back at this point. However, a great way to extend your hike is to head north on the River Trail along the river, adding an extra three miles to the trip. Another bonus is the observation deck, the highest point in the park, with great sweeping views of Santa Cruz and Monterey Bay. It's only a 0.3-mile hike from the campground via the Pine Trail, which starts near campsite 49.

㊵ Mine Hill Loop

14.5 mi/7.0 hrs

Location: In Almaden Quicksilver County Park in the San Jose foothills; map E1–South Bay, grid j7.

User groups: Hikers and horses. No dogs or mountain bikes. No wheelchair facilities.

Permits: No permits are required. Park entrance is free.

Directions: From San Jose, take Highway 85 south to the Almaden Expressway. Continue driving south on the Almaden Expressway to Almaden Road. Take Almaden Road through the historic town of New Almaden to the park entrance on the right.

Maps: For a free trail map, contact Almaden Quicksilver County Park at the address below. A trail map is also available at the trailhead. To obtain a topographic map of the area, ask for Santa Teresa Hills from the USGS.

Contact: Almaden Quicksilver County Park, c/o Calero Reservoir County Park, 23205 McKean Road, San Jose, CA 95120; (408) 268-3883.

Trail notes: You want pleasure? You want pain? You want love? You want hate? This hike provides all of these. Of the dozen trails at Almaden Quicksilver County Park, this is the most challenging, one of the longest single-day hikes at a Bay Area park. Almaden covers 3,600 acres, and with two lakes (Almaden and Guadalupe) and evidence of historical mining operations, it's also one of the most fascinating.

The Mine Hill Trail leads past remnants of old burnt ore dumps. The trail starts at the park entrance about a mile north of Almaden Reservoir, then is routed far into the backcountry, eventually skirting above and past Guadalupe Reservoir to a trail junction, for a trip of 8.5 miles one way. To return, turn left on the Guadalupe Trail, which explores even more remote country on the way back, passes the shore of Guadalupe Reservoir, then connects again with the Mine Hill Trail for the last three-quarters of a mile to the trailhead. Note that some areas adjacent to the Mine Hill Trail are closed to public access because of hazardous residual materials from the mercury mines.

⓪ Coyote Peak Loop

3.4 mi/2.0 hrs

Location: In Santa Teresa County Park south of San Jose; map E1–South Bay, grid j8.

User groups: Hikers, leashed dogs, and horses. No mountain bikes, except on the Ohlone Trail. No wheelchair facilities.

Permits: No permits are required. Park entrance is free.

Directions: From U.S. 101 between San Jose and Morgan Hill, take Bernal Road east and drive to the day-use parking area. Park in the main day-use lot.

Maps: For a free trail map, contact Santa Teresa County Park at the address below. To obtain a topographic map of the area, ask for Santa Teresa Hills from the USGS.

Contact: Santa Teresa County Park, 985 Heller Avenue, San Jose, CA 95111; (408) 225-0225. Parks Administration, (408) 358-3741.

Trail notes: Golfers know Santa Teresa County Park best, but hikers are discovering that the park has something for them as well. Most notable is the walk up to Coyote Peak, the feature destination of a good loop hike that provides a surprise lookout to the southern Santa Clara Valley. This park covers 1,688 acres, but the main attractions are the golf course, driving range, bar, and restaurant. You can quickly leave development behind, however, by hiking south from the Hidden Springs Trailhead off Bernal Road. After one mile, the trail junctions with the Coyote Peak Trail, which climbs up Coyote Peak, with a short loop cutoff getting you to the summit. To complete the loop, continue on the Coyote Peak Trail, then take the Ohlone Trail one mile back to the parking area. Compared to the manicured greens of the golf course, this trail provides an insight into the park's most primitive and rugged areas, and gives you a good view for your efforts.

⓬ Juan Crespi Loop

4.8 mi/2.0 hrs

Location: In Calero Reservoir County Park southeast of San Jose; map E1–South Bay, grid j8.

User groups: Hikers and horses. No dogs or mountain bikes. No wheelchair facilities.

Permits: No permits are required. Park entrance is free.

Directions: From San Jose, drive south on U.S. 101 for five miles to Coyote. Take the Bernal Road exit west and drive a short distance to the Monterey Highway exit. Head south a short way to Bailey Avenue and turn right. Turn left on McKean Road and drive to the sign for the horse stables. Park adjacent to the ranger office.

Maps: For a free map, contact Calero Reservoir County Park at the number below. To obtain a topographic map of the area, ask for Santa Teresa Hills from the USGS.

Contact: Calero Reservoir County Park, (408) 268-3883. Parks Administration, (408) 358-3741.

Trail notes: You'd better know the difference between horse droppings and Shinola if you plan to do this hike. Why? Because this is a very popular horseback trail, if you don't watch where you're going, well, you won't be stepping in shoe polish. And many people have trouble watching their step because of the nice views of Calero Reservoir to the north. Start near the entrance gate and follow the Juan Crespi Trail, turning right toward Calero Reservoir. The trail runs along the southern shoreline of the lake for more than a mile before making a nearly 180-degree looping left turn. There it becomes the Los Cerritos Trail and climbs the ridgeline bordering the southern end of the lake. When it tops the ridge, it connects to the Pena Trail. To complete the loop, turn left on the Pena Trail, making a descent. A great way to go is to descend the Pena Trail, turn right on the Vallecitos Trail and then left on the Figueroa Trail. It adds two miles to the trip, but is well worth it.

⓭ Del Coyote Nature Trail

1.2 mi/0.5 hr

Location: In Coyote-Hellyer County Park downstream of Anderson Dam, south of San Jose; map E1–South Bay, grid j9.

User groups: Hikers only. No dogs, horses, or mountain bikes. No wheelchair facilities.

Permits: No permits are required. A $3 day-use fee is charged from May through September.

Directions: From San Jose, drive south on U.S. 101 and take the Hellyer Avenue exit. Drive about 300 yards to the park entrance on the left.

Maps: For a free map, contact Coyote-Hellyer County Park at the address below. To obtain a topographic map of the area, ask for Morgan Hill from the USGS.

Contact: Coyote-Hellyer County Park, 985 Hellyer Avenue, San Jose, CA 95111; (408) 225-0225. Parks Administration, (408) 358-3741.

Trail notes: Thousands and thousands of people roar up and down U.S. 101 south of San Jose with nary a clue about the peaceful little park that sits so nearby. Yet just east of the highway is Coyote-Hellyer County Park with its small, shaded stream that is stocked with rainbow trout in the late spring and early summer. The hike starts at a picnic area, meandering along the stream from there. The flowing waters come from nearby Anderson Dam, and steady releases are made well into summer. That is what makes this park so attractive to local residents, who know this is a nice spot for a respite.

㊹ Serpentine Trail

0.8 mi/0.5 hr

Location: In Anderson Lake County Park near Morgan Hill; map E1–South Bay, grid j9.

User groups: Hikers only. No dogs, horses, or mountain bikes. No wheelchair facilities.

Permits: No permits are required. A $3 day-use fee is charged from May through September.

Directions: From San Jose, drive south on U.S. 101 to the Cochran Road exit. Take Cochran Road east to the park entrance.

Maps: For a free trail map, contact Anderson Lake County Park at the address below. To obtain topographic maps of the area, ask for Mount Sizer and Morgan Hill from the USGS.

Contact: Anderson Lake County Park, 1105 Burnett Avenue, Morgan Hill, CA 95037; (408) 779-3634. Parks Administration, (408) 358-3741.

Trail notes: The size of Anderson Lake, nearly 1,000 acres, always shocks first-time visitors to this water-filled canyon set among the oak woodlands and foothills of the Gavilan Mountains. One of the best viewpoints at the park is the dam overlook, reached by taking a short walk on the Serpentine Trail. It starts between the Live Oak and Toyon group areas and is simply routed to the northwest corner of the dam. One major problem at Anderson Lake is the fluctuating water levels. This lake needs a lot of water to stay full, and it seems as though the water managers like to almost empty the thing every four or five years. When they do that, you might as well arrange a trip to the Grand Canyon.

㊺ Middle Ridge Loop

4.5 mi/3.0 hrs

Location: In Henry W. Coe State Park in the Diablo Range east of Morgan Hill; map E1–South Bay, grid j9.

User groups: Hikers, horses, and mountain bikes. No dogs. No wheelchair facilities.

Permits: No permits are required unless you plan to camp in the backcountry. A $5 state park day-use fee is charged.

Directions: From U.S. 101 in Morgan Hill, take the East Dunne Avenue exit and drive east for 13 slow and twisty miles to the park entrance. From park headquarters, take the Northern Heights Route Trailhead.

Maps: For a trail map, send $2 and a postpaid envelope to Henry W. Coe State Park at the address below. To obtain topographic maps of the area, ask for Mississippi Creek, Gilroy Hot Springs, Mount Stakes, Mustang Peak, Pacheco Peak, Wilcox Ridge, and Mount Sizer from the USGS.

Contact: Henry W. Coe State Park, P.O. Box 846, Morgan Hill, CA 95038; (408) 779-2728 or (209) 826-1196.

Trail notes: A good pair of hiking boots and a reality check are your tickets to the 80,000 acres of wildlands that comprise Henry W. Coe State Park, a place for anyone who wants solitude (and quality fishing) and isn't averse to rugged hiking. The Middle Ridge Loop is a short day hike that provides a glimpse of the park's primitive charms, along with some serious ups and downs. From park headquarters, you start by taking the Northern Heights Route over the top of Pine Ridge (elevation 3,000 feet) and then dropping 600 feet down to Little Coyote Creek, then going back up past Frog Lake and to the

Middle Ridge Trail (2,800 feet). This first leg is about two miles, and most visitors will stop along the creek for a reality check and to reassess what awaits in the wilderness. Turn right on the Middle Ridge Trail, hike two miles to the junction with the Fish Trail, then turn right again and follow the trail down across Little Coyote Creek. This is one of the prettier sections of the little stream, and really puts a nice capper on the walk. To finish the loop, you have to climb back out of the canyon, over Pine Ridge, and back to the headquarters. This hike gives you just enough to whet your appetite for more challenging routes into the park's interior.

46 Coit Lake Trail

26.0 mi/2.0 days

Location: In Henry W. Coe State Park in the Diablo Range east of Morgan Hill; map E1–South Bay, grid j9.

User groups: Hikers, horses, and mountain bikes. No dogs. No wheelchair facilities.

Permits: No permits are required unless you plan to camp in the backcountry. A $5 state park day-use fee is charged.

Directions: From U.S. 101 in Morgan Hill, take the East Dunne Avenue exit and drive east over Morgan Hill and Anderson Lake for 13 miles on the twisty road to park headquarters. From there, take the Coit Route Trailhead.

To reach the Coyote Creek entrance: From U.S. 101 in Gilroy, take the Leavesley Road exit and drive east on Leavesley Road for less than two miles. Turn left on New Avenue, then right on Roop Road. Drive up into the hills to the Coyote Lake County Park turnoff. Drive straight across the cattle guard to Gilroy Hot Springs Road and continue five miles to the end of the road.

Maps: For a trail map, send $2 and a postpaid envelope to Henry W. Coe State Park at the address below. To obtain topographic maps of the area, ask for Mississippi Creek and Mount Sizer from the USGS.

Contact: Henry W. Coe State Park, P.O. Box 846, Morgan Hill, CA 95038; (408) 779-2728 or (209) 826-1196.

Trail notes: On some spring days at Coit Lake you can catch nearly a bass per cast just by flipping out a one-inch floating Rapala lure. It is often the best pond-style fishing in the greater Bay Area. Unfortunately, that fact inspires many excited people to start hiking off to the lake without first taking a litmus test of the quest they are about to undertake. This is a long hike with difficult climbs both ways, particularly if the weather is hot and dry, as it commonly is out here. Many get busted by the heat before reaching the lake and return frustrated without making a cast.

Heading out on the Coit Route, it's a little less than 12 miles to the lake. Right off, there's a 1,150-foot drop into China Hole, then a 1,200-foot climb over five miles, much of it through Mahoney Meadow, followed by two easier up-and-downs. Coit Lake is best fished during the last two hours of the evening, but the nearest trail camp is the Pacheco Horse Camp, a mile from the lake, making the first day a 13-miler. The return trip is even tougher because near the end, when you are nearly worn out, you will have to make that 1,150-foot climb out of China Hole back to park headquarters—over the span of only two miles. Add in a hot afternoon and you'll be ready to surrender when you reach your car.

Special note: This section of the park is more easily reached from the Coyote Creek access gate. Unattended cars have been vandalized there, but park officials hope to have a parking attendant working on weekends in the spring. Hikers who choose to enter by the Coyote Creek access point must have a trail map; overnight users are still required to obtain a permit from headquarters.

47 Mississippi Lake Trail

22.0 mi/2.0 days

Location: In Henry W. Coe State Park in the Diablo Range east of Morgan Hill; map E1–South Bay, grid j9.

User groups: Hikers, horses, and mountain bikes. No dogs. No wheelchair facilities.

Permits: No permits are required unless you plan to camp in the backcountry. A $5 state park day-use fee is charged.

Directions: From U.S. 101 in Morgan Hill, take the East Dunne Avenue exit and drive east over Morgan Hill and Anderson Lake for 13 miles on the twisty road to park headquarters. From there, take the Pacheco Route Trailhead.

To reach the Bell Station access point: From U.S. 101 in Gilroy, exit east on Highway 152 East/Pacheco Pass and drive about 10 miles to the junction with Highway 156. Drive six miles northeast on Pacheco Pass Highway and exit north at the sign for the Bell Station Café. Park a quarter mile from the highway, near the parked trailer (above the hill, behind the café). From here, hike six miles past two locked gates to reach the main body of the park.

Maps: For a trail map, send $2 and a postpaid envelope to Henry W. Coe State Park at the address below. To obtain topographic maps of the area, ask for Mississippi Creek and Mount Sizer from the USGS.

Contact: Henry W. Coe State Park, P.O. Box 846, Morgan Hill, CA 95038; (408) 779-2728 or (209) 826-1196.

Trail notes: Even though Henry W. Coe State Park was just opened to the public in 1981, a few legends have already developed, and the most mysterious involves Mississippi Lake. Set virtually in the center of the park's 125 square miles, it's the biggest and prettiest lake here. The mystery has nothing to do with scenic beauty, but rather its strange ability to create huge trout: scientists have documented 26-inch wild trout that were only 18 months old. They are all but gone now, as low water in the feeder creek prevented spawning during the 1988–92 drought; any trout you catch should be released immediately. (Bass were planted in 1991 and have taken over the lake, providing good fishing.) Still, the legendary huge trout of Mississippi Lake have inspired many to make the trip out. Provided you get a very early start, you can have an excellent weekend trip.

From park headquarters, you hike eight miles out on the Pacheco Route, and that includes a long drop followed by a killer climb, gaining 1,400 feet over 2.6 miles, from East Fork Coyote Creek over Willow Crest and to the junction with the Interior Route. Turn left on the Interior Route and the trail becomes a lot easier. In 3.5 miles, you will be skirting the southern shore of the lake. The nearest trail camp, Mississippi Creek Horse Camp, is about a half mile south of the lake. This

is a long, grueling hike from headquarters, and many unprepared hikers have suffered from dehydration and had to be rescued by park staff.

Special note: This section of the park is more easily reached from the Bell Station access gate. But visitors trespassing on private land there may cause this access point to be closed to the public. Hikers who choose to enter by the Bell Station access point must have a trail map; overnight users are still required to obtain a permit from headquarters.

48 Rooster Comb Loop

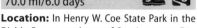

70.0 mi/6.0 days

Location: In Henry W. Coe State Park in the Diablo Range southeast of San Jose; map E1–South Bay, grid j9.

User groups: Hikers, horses, and mountain bikes. No dogs. No wheelchair facilities.

Permits: No permits are required unless you plan to camp in the backcountry. A $5 state park day-use fee is charged.

Directions: From U.S. 101 in Morgan Hill, take the East Dunne Avenue exit and drive east over Morgan Hill and Anderson Lake for 13 miles on the twisty road to park headquarters. From there, take the Pacheco Route Trailhead.

Maps: For a trail map, send $2 and a postpaid envelope to Henry W. Coe State Park at the address below. To obtain topographic maps of the area, ask for Mississippi Creek and Mount Sizer from the USGS.

Contact: Henry W. Coe State Park, P.O. Box 846, Morgan Hill, CA 95038; (408) 779-2728 or (209) 826-1196.

Trail notes: "I've always been crazy," Waylon Jennings once said, "because it's kept me from going insane." Well, you have to be something of a deranged soul to try this hike, and that's why we signed up! Not only is it just plain long, but it includes seven climbs that'll have you cussing and explores the park's most remote and arid wildlands, where anything over 10 inches of rain a year is considered a flood. So why do it? Because no trail on public land in the Bay Area leads to a more isolated spot, because Paradise Lake will seem like a mirage after you've walked

33 miles, and hey, you're a little deranged anyway, right? Highlights on the trek in include Kelly Lake (about 10.5 miles in), Coit Lake (12 miles), and in the remote Orestimba Drainage, Paradise Lake and Robinson Falls. A spectacular spot is the loop's namesake, the Rooster Comb, a perch overlooking the Orestimba Valley.

The only thing simple is the route: You take the Pacheco Trail (16.7 miles) out to the park's southern boundary, then turn left on the Gill Trail (10.5 miles), then hike the loop on the Rooster Comb Trail (10.1 miles), reconnect with the Gill Trail (5 miles), and then head back the way you came. We suggest taking a week to do it, arriving and camping at park headquarters the first night so you can go through your gear and make an early getaway the next morning, then average 11.6 miles per day for six days. Several trail camps are situated along the way, and camping is permitted throughout the wilderness area. If the weather turns hot, physically unprepared hikers can find themselves in real danger. Regardless of your physical condition, when you return to your car at park headquarters, you won't feel so crazy anymore.

Map E2

Adjoining Maps: East: E3 ..... *page* 324   West: E1 ..... 270, 294
North: D2 162   South: F2 402

Northern California Map .... *page* 2

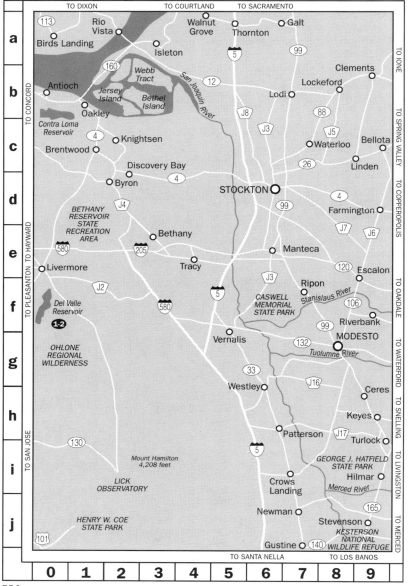

❶ Ohlone Wilderness Trail

28.0 mi. one way/3.0 days

Location: In the Sunol-Ohlone Regional Wilderness, from Del Valle Regional Park south of Livermore to Mission Peak in Fremont; map E2, grid f1.

User groups: Hikers, dogs (daytime only), and horses. No mountain bikes. No wheelchair facilities.

Permits: A trail permit/map for the Ohlone Wilderness Trail is required. You can obtain one for $2 at the park office or $2.50 by mail. To receive your permit by mail, contact the East Bay Regional Parks District at the address below. The park entrance fee is $3.

Directions to the east trailhead: From Interstate 580 East at Livermore, take the North Livermore Avenue exit. Turn south and follow North/South Livermore Road (which becomes Tesla Road) to Mines Road. Turn right on Mines Road and drive about three miles south to Del Valle Road. Turn right and continue for three miles to the entrance to Del Valle Regional Park. Park at the south end of Del Valle Reservoir, which is close to the trailhead.

Directions to the west trailhead: From Highway 680 near Fremont, take the Mission Boulevard exit. Turn east on Stanford Avenue and drive to the parking lot and trailhead at the end of the road.

Maps: You will receive a trail map when you purchase your permit. To obtain a topographic map of the area, ask for Mendenhall Springs from the USGS.

Contact: East Bay Regional Parks District, 2950 Peralta Oaks Court, P.O. Box 5381, Oakland, CA 94605. For information, contact Sunol-Ohlone Regional Wilderness, (510) 862-2244 or fax (510) 862-0810; Regional Park Headquarters, (510) 635-0135, extension 2200; or Del Valle Regional Park, (510) 373-0332.

Trail notes: Hikers can traverse the East Bay's most unspoiled backcountry via the spectacular 28-mile Ohlone Wilderness Trail, which lies entirely on wildlands. Starting south of Livermore at Del Valle Regional Park and cutting west to Fremont, the trail rises through fields of wildflowers, grasslands, and oaks and climbs three major summits: Rocky Ridge, Rose Peak (elevation 3,817 feet), and Mission Peak (2,517 feet). It makes an ideal three-day backpacking venture, as hikers can set up trail camps at Sunol and Ohlone Regional Parks. Backpackers will cover about 12 miles the first day, followed by two days at about eight miles each. Some people close out the final 16 miles in one day. And it's not unusual for cross-country runners, feeling somewhat deranged, to run the entire route in a single day; an organized race is even held here.

Hiking the trail east to west is the only way to fly. That way you'll face the steepest ascent right at the beginning, when you are still fresh. Starting at Del Valle Regional Park, the route first tackles Rocky Ridge, for an elevation gain of 1,600 feet in just 1.5 miles. (A side trip from here, by the way, is to Murietta Falls; see hike number 2). As you crest the final ridge, Mission Peak, you'll face a moment of truth: you can actually see your car waiting at the parking lot, yet it is still so far away. This last stretch drops 2,100 feet in 3.5 miles, a terrible toe-jammer that will have your knees and thighs screaming for mercy. Weeks later, though, when you replay this adventure in your memory banks, the hike will suddenly seem like "fun."

❷ Murietta Falls Trail

11.0 mi/1.0 day

Location: In the Sunol-Ohlone Regional Wilderness, from Del Valle Regional Park south of Livermore to Mission Peak in Fremont; map E2, grid f1.

User groups: Hikers, dogs (daytime only), and horses. No mountain bikes. No wheelchair facilities.

Permits: A trail permit/map for the Ohlone Wilderness Trail is required. You can obtain one for $2 at the park office or $2.50 by mail. To receive your permit by mail, contact the East Bay Regional Parks District at the address below. The park entrance fee is $3.

Directions: From Interstate 580 East at Livermore, take the North Livermore Avenue exit. Turn south and follow North/South Livermore Road (which becomes Tesla Road) to Mines Road. Turn right on Mines Road and drive about three miles south to Del Valle Road. Turn right and drive three miles to the entrance to Del Valle Regional Park. Park at the south end of Del Valle Reservoir, which is close to the trailhead.

Maps: You will receive a trail map when you purchase your permit. To obtain a topographic map of the area, ask for Mendenhall Springs from the USGS.

Contact: East Bay Regional Parks District, 2950 Peralta Oaks Court, P.O. Box 5381, Oakland, CA 94605; (510) 635-0135, extension 2200. Del Valle Regional Park, (510) 373-0332.

Trail notes: Little known and only rarely seen, the Bay Area's highest waterfall lies hidden away in the southern Alameda County wilderness, where few venture. Murietta Falls, named after a legendary outlaw of the 1800s, Joaquin Murietta, is set in the Sunol-Ohlone Regional Wilderness, where a free-flowing creek runs through a rocky gorge, then plunges 100 feet over a cliff onto the rocks below. Upstream, more small pools and cascades await, and along with Murietta Falls, they make this a destination like nowhere else in the East Bay.

Why do so few people know about this place? Getting there requires a butt-kicker of a hike: It's 5.5 miles one way, most of which climbs a terribly steep ridge. You'll first ascend 1,600 feet in just 1.5 miles, the worst stretch of the Ohlone Wilderness Trail (hike number 1). The route tops out at Rocky Ridge, drops into Williams Gulch, then climbs again even higher toward Wauhab Ridge. You will gain as much as 3,300 feet in elevation before turning right on the Springboard Trail (signpost 35, not 36). From there, it's one mile to the waterfall. Walk along a ridge about a quarter mile, then turn left on the Greenside Trail, which descends into a valley and to the falls. Unfortunately, you can't get a clear view of Murietta Falls from the Greenside Trail. Once at the creek on the valley bottom, leave the trail and work your way carefully downstream for a few hundred yards to the top of the falls. An option is to take an unsigned side road/trail off the Greenside Trail, located past the stream. Turn right on this road/trail, which drops in a looping turn down to the floor, providing a better view of the cascade.

When Murietta Falls first comes into view, it stands in contrast to the East Bay hills, a grassland/oak habitat where one does not expect to find steep cliffs and waterfalls. But there it is, all 100 feet. In the springtime the rapidly greening hills frame the falls, providing a refuge of tranquillity only a few miles from suburbia, concrete, and traffic jams. But given the difficulty of the hike, many are disappointed by how little water there can be here. It can be like a bad joke. Even in big rain years, though, the creek is reduced to a trickle by summer, and sometimes even goes dry. In addition, it gets hot out here in the summer, really smokin', like 100 degrees. By July, the hills are brown, the waterfall has disappeared, and only the ghost of Murietta remains to laugh as you struggle on that 1,600-foot climb.

Special note: If you want to stay overnight in the wilderness, a trail camp (Stewart's Camp) is available about half a mile from Murietta Falls; reservations are required.

Leave No Trace Tips

Travel and Camp with Care

On the trail:

Stay on designated trails. Walk single file in the middle of the path.

Do not take shortcuts on switchbacks.

When traveling cross-country where there are no trails,
follow animal trails or spread out your group so no new routes are
created. Walk along the most durable surfaces available,
such as rock, gravel, dry grasses, or snow.

Use a map and compass to eliminate
the need for rock cairns, tree scars, or ribbons.

If you encounter pack animals, step to the downhill side
of the trail and speak softly to avoid startling them.

At camp:

Choose an established, legal site that will not be damaged by your stay.

Restrict activities to areas where vegetation is compacted or absent.

Keep pollutants out of the water by camping at least 200 feet
(about 70 adult steps) from lakes and streams.

Control pets at all times, or leave them at home
with a sitter. Remove dog feces.

Map E3

Adjoining Maps: East: E4 ..... *page* 326   West: E2 320
North: D3 166   South: F3 408

Northern California Map .... *page* 2

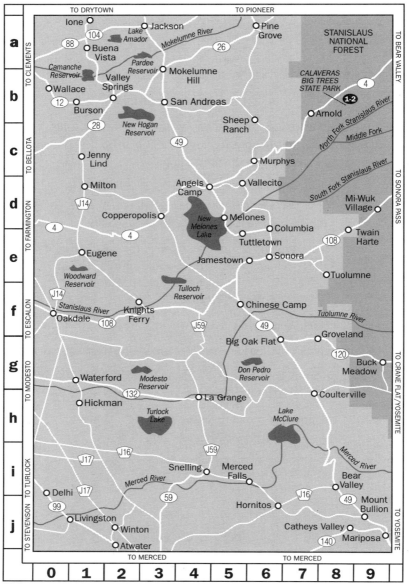

❶ North Grove Loop

1.0 mi/0.5 hr

Location: Northeast of Arnold on Highway 4; map E3, grid b8.

User groups: Hikers and wheelchairs. No dogs, horses, or mountain bikes.

Permits: No permits are required. There is a $5 state park entrance fee for each vehicle.

Directions: From Highway 99 at Stockton, turn east on Highway 4 and drive to the junction of Highways 4 and 49 at Angels Camp. Drive east on Highway 4 for 26 miles to the park, located four miles east of Arnold. The trailhead is adjacent to the park entrance.

Maps: For a brochure and complete trail map, send $1 to Calaveras Big Trees State Park at the address below. Interpretive brochures are also available at the trailhead for 25 cents. To obtain a topographic map of the area, ask for Dorrington from the USGS.

Contact: Calaveras Big Trees State Park, P.O. Box 120, Arnold, CA 95223; (209) 795-2334 or fax (209) 795-7306.

Trail notes: Even though there are 150 giant sequoias at Calaveras Big Trees State Park, the highlight is actually the one known as "The Big Stump." Lore has it that the gent who first found this place wanted to prove how big the trees were, so naturally he cut one down, leaving behind the giant stump. Makes perfect sense, right? Just like you'd shoot Bigfoot. . . . Well, the state park gets a lot of visitors, and this is the most popular walk here, so you can expect other people—lots of 'em. The easy trail is routed among the giant sequoias, and the sweet fragrance of the massive trees fills the air. You will never forget that scent. These trees, of course, are known not for their height but for their tremendous diameter: it can take a few dozen people, linking hands, to encircle one.

❷ South Grove Loop

5.0 mi/3.0 hrs

Location: Northeast of Arnold on Highway 4; map E3, grid b8.

User groups: Hikers only. No dogs, horses, or mountain bikes. No wheelchair facilities.

Permits: No permits are required. There is a $5 state park entrance fee for each vehicle.

Directions: From Highway 99 at Stockton, turn east on Highway 4 and drive to the junction of Highways 4 and 49 at Angels Camp. Drive east on Highway 4 for 26 miles to the park, located four miles east of Arnold. From the park entrance, head down the parkway for nine miles to the trailhead. Note: The road is closed in winter.

Maps: For a brochure and complete trail map, send $1 to Calaveras Big Trees State Park at the address below. To obtain a topographic map of the area, ask for Boards Crossing from the USGS.

Contact: Calaveras Big Trees State Park, P.O. Box 120, Arnold, CA 95223; (209) 795-2334 or fax (209) 795-7306.

Trail notes: The two largest giant sequoias in Calaveras Big Trees State Park are found on a spur trail of this hike, and that makes it a must-do for visitors. But so many tourists are content to just walk the little trail at the North Grove, look at the giant stump, then hit the road. Why rush? As long as you're at the park, take the South Grove Loop. The loop itself is 3.5 miles long, but the highlight is a spur trail that branches off for three-quarters of a mile to the Agassiz Tree and the Palace Hotel Tree, two monster-sized specimens. For a great photograph, have someone take a picture of you standing at the base of one of these trees; you will look like a Lilliputian from *Gulliver's Travels*.

Map E4

Adjoining Maps: East: E5 ..... *page* 370   West: E3 324
                 North: D4 180   South: F4 410

Northern California Map .... *page* 2

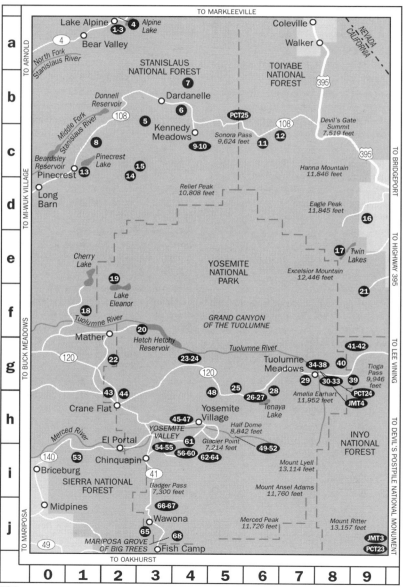

Chapter E4 Features:

❶ Osborne Hill

2.6 mi/1.5 hrs

Location: On Highway 4 near Lake Alpine; map E4, grid a2.

User groups: Hikers, dogs, horses, and mountain bikes. No wheelchair facilities.

Permits: No permits are required. Parking and access are free.

Directions: From Angels Camp at the intersection of highways 4 and 49, drive east on Highway 4 for 40 miles to Bear Valley. Set your odometer at Bear Valley and drive three miles further east on Highway 4 to the Osborne Ridge Trailhead, just east of Silvertip Campground. Take the trail that leads from the south side of the road.

Maps: For a map of Stanislaus National Forest, send $4 to USDA-Forest Service, 630 Sansome Street, San Francisco, CA 94111. To obtain a topographic map of the area, ask for Tamarack from the USGS.

Contact: Stanislaus National Forest, Calaveras Ranger District, P.O. Box 500, Hathaway Pines, CA 95323; (209) 795-1381, or fax (209) 795-6849.

Trail notes: We like the way Lake Alpine looks from close-up on the Lakeshore Trail, but then again we like the way Lake Alpine looks from far up on Osborne Hill, also known as Osborne Point. A short, healthy climb brings you to the point, from which you can look down at the lake and beyond into the Carson-Iceberg Wilderness. The trail ends there, but connects to the Emigrant West Trail if you wish to hike further. If you're itching for winter to be over so you can go hiking, you'll be happy to know that Highway 4 is always open as far east as Silvertip Campground, but not always further. That means that if the snow is dwindling, you'll have

access to this trailhead often long before you can access the others near Lake Alpine.

❷ Lakeshore Trail and Inspiration Point

4.0 mi/2.0 hrs

Location: On Highway 4 near Lake Alpine; map E4, grid a2.

User groups: Hikers, dogs, and horses. No mountain bikes. No wheelchair facilities.

Permits: No permits are required. Parking and access are free.

Directions: From Angels Camp at the intersection of highways 4 and 49, drive east on Highway 4 for 40 miles to Bear Valley. Set your odometer at Bear Valley and drive 4.3 miles further east on Highway 4 to the Lake Alpine East Shore Trailhead turnoff on the right. Turn right, drive a quarter mile, then turn right again and drive one-tenth of a mile past Pine Marten Campground to the signed parking area and the trailhead.

Maps: For a map of Stanislaus National Forest, send $4 to USDA-Forest Service, 630 Sansome Street, San Francisco, CA 94111. To obtain a topographic map of the area, ask for Spicer Meadow Reservoir from the USGS.

Contact: Stanislaus National Forest, Calaveras Ranger District, P.O. Box 500, Hathaway Pines, CA 95323; (209) 795-1381, or fax (209) 794-6849.

Trail notes: It's hard to say which trail is better, the Lakeshore Trail or the trail to Inspiration Point. To solve the dilemma, hike both of them together. The trip starts with a short walk down a dirt road, then you turn right onto single-track. In a mere 10 minutes of hiking through thick lodgepole pine forest littered with tiny pine cones, you're at the edge of Lake Alpine, elevation 7,350 feet. Follow the trail to your left, and in another 10 minutes, reach a left fork for Inspiration Point (the Lakeshore Trail continues straight). You'll want to head out and back on both trails; it makes no difference which one you take first.

The Lakeshore Trail is flat and stays within 100 feet of the water's edge, offering many pretty lake vistas. Eventually the trail meets up with Slick Rock four-wheel-drive road, but there's no need to go that far. Just walk a mile or so to the dam, then turn around and head back. The Inspiration Point Trail is more of a workout, a steep one-mile climb to the summit at Inspiration Point, from which you can see for miles. Pick a clear day and you'll be pointing out Lake Alpine, Elephant Rock, the Dardanelles, and Spicer Meadow Reservoir.

❸ Duck Lake

3.0 mi/1.5 hrs

Location: In the Carson-Iceberg Wilderness off Highway 4 near Lake Alpine; map E4, grid a2.

User groups: Hikers, dogs, and horses. No mountain bikes. No wheelchair facilities.

Permits: No day-use permits are required. Parking and access are free.

Directions: From Angels Camp at the intersection of highways 4 and 49, drive east on Highway 4 for 40 miles to Bear Valley. Set your odometer at Bear Valley and drive 4.3 miles further east on Highway 4 to the Lake Alpine East Shore Trailhead turnoff on the right. Turn right and continue straight to Silver Valley Camp and the Silver Valley Trailhead.

Maps: For a map of Stanislaus National Forest, send $4 to USDA-Forest Service, 630 Sansome Street, San Francisco, CA 94111. A map of the Carson-Iceberg Wilderness is also available from the Forest Service for $4. To obtain a topographic map of the area, ask for Spicer Meadow Reservoir from the USGS.

Contact: Stanislaus National Forest, Calaveras Ranger District, P.O. Box 500, Hathaway Pines, CA 95323; (209) 795-1381, or fax (209) 794-6849.

Trail notes: The trailhead at Silver Valley Campground is the start of the route to Duck Lake, and

it's also one of the busiest trailheads into the Carson-Iceberg Wilderness. The trip to Duck Lake is a perfect easy hike for families or people just in the mood for a stroll, and the more ambitious can continue past the lake on an eight-mile round-trip to Rock Lake. It's only one mile to reach Duck Lake, but once you're there you'll want to walk the loop trail around its perimeter, adding another mile to your trip. The area is the site of a historic cow camp where animals have grazed since the late 1800s. You can examine the remains of a couple early 20th-century pioneer cabins.

❹ Woodchuck Basin to Wheeler Lake

6.4 mi/3.5 hrs

Location: In the Mokelumne Wilderness off Highway 4 near Lake Alpine; map E4, grid a2.

User groups: Hikers, dogs, and horses. No mountain bikes. No wheelchair facilities.

Permits: No day-use permits are required. Parking and access are free.

Directions: From Angels Camp at the intersection of highways 4 and 49, drive east on Highway 4 for 40 miles to Bear Valley. Set your odometer at Bear Valley and drive 5.5 miles further east on Highway 4 to the Woodchuck Basin Trailhead on the left. Turn left and drive a quarter mile to the parking area.

Maps: For a map of Stanislaus National Forest, send $4 to USDA-Forest Service, 630 Sansome Street, San Francisco, CA 94111. To obtain a topographic map of the area, ask for Spicer Meadow Reservoir from the USGS.

Contact: Stanislaus National Forest, Calaveras Ranger District, P.O. Box 500, Hathaway Pines, CA 95323; (209) 795-1381, or fax (209) 794-6849.

Trail notes: Located only a mile from the campgrounds at Lake Alpine, the Woodchuck Basin Trailhead at elevation 7,800 feet should have a parking lot full of cars, but it rarely does. The trail leads into the Mokelumne Wilderness, and after climbing uphill on it for 1.7 forested miles, you reach a junction where you can go left for Underwood Valley or right for tiny Wheeler Lake. Bearing right, you pass a Mokelumne Wilderness sign, and in moments you are heading for a 1.5-mile steep descent to Wheeler Lake. Think it over before you go, because you'll need to gain those 1,000 feet back on the way home. But if you're willing to take the plunge, you're treated to a picturesque, tree- and granite-lined lake, where you can pass the afternoon with little fear that you'll be bugged by a busload of other hikers.

❺ Eagle Meadow to Dardanelle

4.0 mi one way/2.0 hrs

Location: Near Dardanelle; map E4, grid b3.

User groups: Hikers, dogs, horses, and mountain bikes. No wheelchair facilities.

Permits: No permits are required. Parking and access are free.

Directions: From Sonora, drive east on Highway 108 for 41 miles to the turnoff for Niagara Creek Campground, on the right side of the highway. (The turnoff is approximately 12 miles east of Strawberry.) Turn right, then in a quarter mile, turn right again on Road 5N01. Follow Road 5N01 for seven miles to Eagle Meadow. This is the start of the one-way shuttle hike; the finish is at Dardanelle Resort on Highway 108, eight miles east of the Niagara Creek turnoff.

Maps: For a map of Stanislaus National Forest, send $4 to USDA-Forest Service, 630 Sansome Street, San Francisco, CA 94111. To obtain topographic maps of the area, ask for Donnell Lake and Dardanelle from the USGS.

Contact: Stanislaus National Forest, Summit Ranger District, #1 Pinecrest Lake Road, Pinecrest, CA 95364; (209) 965-3434, or fax (209) 965-3372.

Trail notes: If you can convince someone to drop you off at Eagle Meadow and pick you up at Dardanelle Resort, or if you have two cars for a shuttle hike, you can take a scenic downhill stroll paralleling Eagle Creek. It's a trip for lovers of subalpine meadows, especially in the first mile. After it leaves the meadow, the trail enters a thick and lovely conifer forest, so you get a bit of shade along the path. The route gets a bit steep in sections, so make sure your knees are in good enough shape for four miles of downhill before you make the trip.

❻ Columns of the Giants

0.5 mi/0.5 hr

Location: Near Dardanelle; map E4, grid b3.

User groups: Hikers and dogs. No horses or mountain bikes. No wheelchair facilities.

Permits: No permits are required. Parking and access are free.

Directions: From Sonora, drive east on Highway 108 for 50 miles to Pigeon Flat Campground, two miles east of Dardanelle and on the south side of the highway. (If you're traveling west on Highway 108, the campground is 15 miles west of Sonora Pass.) Park in the day-use parking lot just outside the camp.

Maps: For a map of Stanislaus National Forest, send $4 to USDA-Forest Service, 630 Sansome Street, San Francisco, CA 94111. To obtain a topographic map of the area, ask for Dardanelle from the USGS.

Contact: Stanislaus National Forest, Summit Ranger District, #1 Pinecrest Lake Road, Pinecrest, CA 95364; (209) 965-3434, or fax (209) 965-3372.

Trail notes: This is Highway 108's answer to Devils Postpile National Monument, and, take it from us, it's no cheap imitation. The rock formations at the end of the Columns of the Giants geological trail were formed 150,000 years ago when a series of volcanic eruptions occurred. The lava flow cooled rapidly, probably during cold weather, and cracked into narrow, hexagonal, basalt columns.

Some of the remaining columns are 30 to 40 feet in height and three to four feet in diameter. While many are still standing tall, or at least at an angle, others have shattered into thousands of pieces and created a giant pile of rubble. An interpretive trail sign explains that underneath this rock pile is evidence of the last small ice age in the Sierra—frozen remnants of ice fields that are replenished each year by winter snow and cold. All this historical information gives you plenty to think about during your very short walk. Make sure you bring your camera—it's lots of fun taking pictures of your hiking partner standing right next to the jumbled heap of rocks.

❼ Clark Fork and Boulder Lake

8.0 mi/4.0 hrs

Location: In the Carson-Iceberg Wilderness, on Clark Fork Stanislaus River; map E4, grid b3.

User groups: Hikers, dogs, and horses. No mountain bikes. No wheelchair facilities.

Permits: A free wilderness permit is required for overnight stays; they are available from the Summit Ranger Station. Parking and access are free.

Directions: From Sonora, drive east on Highway 108 for 46 miles to the left turnoff for Clark Fork Road. (The turnoff is approximately 17 miles east of Strawberry.) Turn left and follow Clark Fork Road for about seven miles to its end at the Clark Fork Trailhead at Iceberg Meadow.

Maps: For a map of Stanislaus National Forest, send $4 to USDA-Forest Service, 630 Sansome Street, San Francisco, CA 94111. A map of the Carson-Iceberg Wilderness is also available from the Forest Service for $4. To obtain a topographic map of the area, ask for Donnell Lake from the USGS.

Contact: Stanislaus National Forest, Summit Ranger District, #1 Pinecrest Lake Road, Pinecrest, CA 95364; (209) 965-3434, or fax (209) 965-3372.

Trail notes: From this trailhead at Iceberg Meadow, you immediately enter the Carson-Iceberg Wilderness, at the base of imposing Iceberg Peak. Hiking upstream on the northern edge of the Clark Fork Stanislaus River, you'll enjoy good wildflowers and a lovely mixed forest of white firs and Jeffrey pines. At the water's edge, the trees are more leafy, including cottonwoods and aspens. The river pools are cold, but useful for cooling off on a hot day. At 2.5 miles, you have a choice: Bear right (really straight) and continue along the Clark Fork, or turn left and hike steeply uphill along Boulder Creek. We suggest the left fork, following Boulder Creek for 1.5 miles uphill to tiny Boulder Lake. It's a good workout to a pretty destination. But hey, if you get tired, just cut the trip short, turning around when you reach Boulder Creek. Plenty of fishing holes and picnic spots can be found along the Clark Fork.

❽ Trail of the Gargoyles

3.0 mi/1.5 hrs

Location: Near Strawberry and Pinecrest Lake; map E4, grid c1.

User groups: Hikers and dogs. No horses or mountain bikes. No wheelchair facilities.

Permits: No permits are required. Parking and access are free.

Directions: From Sonora, drive east on Highway 108 for 34 miles to Herring Creek Road (Road 4N12), 2.4 miles east of Strawberry. Turn right on Herring Creek Road, then continue for 6.7 miles to an often unsigned left turnoff. Turn left and drive two-tenths of a mile to the trailhead.

Maps: For a map of Stanislaus National Forest, send $4 to USDA-Forest Service, 630 Sansome Street, San Francisco, CA 94111. To obtain a topographic map of the area, ask for Pinecrest from the USGS.

Contact: Stanislaus National Forest, Summit Ranger District, #1 Pinecrest Lake Road, Pinecrest, CA 95364; (209) 965-3434, or fax (209) 965-3372.

Trail notes: When you park your car at the nondescript trailhead, it's hard to guess what's in store on the Trail of the Gargoyles. Sure, the odd rock formations that line the trail are fascinating to look at, but what's more significant is that they (and you) are perched at the edge of a cliff at 7,400 feet in elevation. You walk just inches away from what appears to be the edge of the world, with only thin air between you and the densely forested basin several hundred feet below. It's an easy and nearly flat trail, but if you have kids with you, keep a hand-hold on them at all times. By the way, the rock formations don't look much like gargoyles, except for the fact that they are hanging off the edge of this abrupt abyss. The trailhead is in the middle of this 1.5-mile trail, which means you'll want to walk out and back in both directions. The trail on the north rim is slightly steeper.

❾ Relief Reservoir

6.0 mi/3.0 hrs

Location: On the edge of the Emigrant Wilderness near Dardanelle; map E4, grid c4.

User groups: Hikers, dogs, and horses. No mountain bikes. No wheelchair facilities.

Permits: No day-use permits are required. Parking and access are free.

Directions: From Sonora, go east on Highway 108 for 55 miles to the Kennedy Meadows turn-off, six miles east of Dardanelle on the south side of the highway. Turn right and follow the road one mile to the well-signed parking area. Day hikers can park a half mile further down the road, near Kennedy Meadows Resort. (If you're traveling west on Highway 108, the Kennedy Meadows turnoff is 9.6 miles west of Sonora Pass.)

Maps: For a map of Stanislaus National Forest, send $4 to USDA-Forest Service, 630 Sansome Street, San Francisco, CA 94111. A map of the Emigrant Wilderness is also available from the Forest Service for $7. To obtain a topographic map of the area, ask for Sonora Pass from the USGS.

Contact: Stanislaus National Forest, Summit Ranger District, #1 Pinecrest Lake Road, Pinecrest, CA 95364; (209) 965-3434, or fax (209) 965-3372.

Trail notes: From the mammoth trailhead and parking lot at Kennedy Meadows, you can hike to Relief Reservoir (elevation 7,200 feet), do a little fishing, then hike back out. The only downers are that pack animals have roughed up the trail, and the route is seriously overused. On weekends, it seems you must constantly pull off the path to let horses (and other hikers) go by. The route, called the Huckleberry Trail, leads along the Stanislaus River, enters the Emigrant Wilderness at one mile, then skirts its edge. Quickly you understand why this trip is so popular—the river canyon gets more and more beautiful as you head deeper into it. The trail had to be blasted into the steep and rocky hillside. Pass the left turnoff for roaring Kennedy Creek and Kennedy Lake at 2.6 miles, then proceed straight for another half mile to an overlook of the reservoir. It's a steep drop down to the water's edge in the last quarter mile, which must be regained on the return trip.

⑩ Kennedy Lake

14.8 mi/2.0 days

Location: In the Emigrant Wilderness near Dardanelle; map E4, grid c4.

User groups: Hikers, dogs, and horses. No mountain bikes. No wheelchair facilities.

Permits: A free wilderness permit is required for overnight stays; they are available from the Summit Ranger Station. Parking and access are free.

Directions: From Sonora, drive east on Highway 108 for 55 miles to the turnoff for Kennedy Meadows, six miles east of Dardanelle and on the south side of the highway. Turn right and follow the road for one mile to the large parking area. (If you're traveling west on Highway 108, the Kennedy Meadows turnoff is 9.6 miles west of Sonora Pass.)

Maps: For a map of Stanislaus National Forest, send $4 to USDA-Forest Service, 630 Sansome Street, San Francisco, CA 94111. A map of the Emigrant Wilderness is also available from the Forest Service for $7. To obtain a topographic map of the area, ask for Sonora Pass from the USGS.

Contact: Stanislaus National Forest, Summit Ranger District, #1 Pinecrest Lake Road, Pinecrest, CA 95364; (209) 965-3434, or fax (209) 965-3372.

Trail notes: If the number of cars in the Kennedy Meadows parking lot is scaring you, take heart. Many of them belong to people day hiking to fish at Relief Reservoir. If you have the time and inclination for a longer trip to Kennedy Lake, you will leave a lot of your fellow hikers behind. Even so, don't expect solitude. You'll likely share the lake with other backpackers, horse packers, and grazing cows. Follow the trail notes in hike number 9 to Relief Reservoir, but at 2.6 miles take the left fork for Kennedy Lake. The trail climbs for another 1.6 miles, then goes flat for the final 3.2 miles to the lake. It's an easy two-day backpack trip, with low mileage and only a 1,200-foot elevation gain. Note that all the campsites are downstream of the lake, rather than along its shoreline.

⑪ Sardine Falls

2.0 mi/1.0 hr

Location: Near Sonora Pass; map E4, grid c6.

User groups: Hikers and dogs. No horses or mountain bikes. No wheelchair facilities.

Permits: No permits are required. Parking and access are free.

Directions: From the junction of U.S. 395 and Highway 108, drive 12.5 miles west on Highway 108. (You will be 2.5 miles east of Sonora Pass Summit.) Park along the road in the gravel pullouts, near the overgrown jeep roads on the northwest side of the meadow.

Maps: For a map of Toiyabe National Forest (Bridgeport District), send $4 to USDA-Forest Service, 630 Sansome Street, San Francisco, CA 94111. To obtain a topographic map of the area, ask for Pickel Meadow from the USGS.

Contact: Toiyabe National Forest, Bridgeport Ranger District, P.O. Box 595, Bridgeport, CA 93517; (760) 932-7070, or fax (760) 932-1299.

Trail notes: An easy hike through a high alpine meadow, culminating at a pretty waterfall, is our idea of a fine way to spend an afternoon. The trip to Sardine Falls requires a little route-finding because there is no formal trail, but since you can see the falls from the road and there are several overgrown jeep routes to follow, the going is easy. From where you've left your car, head across the northwest side of the meadow. (Look for a route that is signed "Route Closed" to motorized vehicles; it's the most direct path.) Cross Sardine Creek, which parallels Highway 108, then walk up the right side of larger McKay Creek. After climbing uphill over a rise, you'll hear and then see Sardine Falls, gracefully framed by a few sparse lodgepole pines.

⑫ Secret and Poore Lakes

6.5 mi/3.5 hrs

Location: Near Sonora Pass; map E4, grid c7.

User groups: Hikers, dogs, horses, and mountain bikes. No wheelchair facilities.

Permits: No permits are required. Parking and access are free.

Directions: From the junction of U.S. 395 and Highway 108, drive seven miles west on Highway 108 to Leavitt Meadows Campground on the south side of the road. (If you are coming from the west, the camp is eight miles east of Sonora Pass.) Day hikers may park inside the campground; backpackers must park a quarter mile west of the camp on Highway 108.

Maps: For a map of Toiyabe National Forest (Bridgeport District), send $4 to USDA-Forest

Service, 630 Sansome Street, San Francisco, CA 94111. To obtain a topographic map of the area, ask for Pickel Meadow from the USGS.

Contact: Toiyabe National Forest, Bridgeport Ranger District, P.O. Box 595, Bridgeport, CA 93517; (760) 932-7070, or fax (760) 932-1299.

Trail notes: This 6.5-mile loop trip begins at a footbridge over the West Walker River at Leavitt Meadows Campground. In a quarter mile, take the left fork for Secret Lake (you won't be alone, most likely). Climb for nearly two miles through sage and Jeffrey pines, then descend for a half mile to Secret Lake. Much larger Poore Lake is visible over your left shoulder. Take a break at Secret Lake, then continue around the right side of the lake, hiking through sparse junipers and pines for a half mile to the left turnoff for Poore Lake. Take the more rough, three-quarter mile route to the large lake. Keep your fingers crossed that there are no loud off-road-vehicles racing around it. If it's quiet, you can swim or fish for a few hours, then retrace your steps to the junction. From there, loop back to the campground on a lower trail that follows closer to the West Walker River, through Leavitt Meadow. (If Poore Lake turns out to be less than perfect, you can always hike further, beyond the return loop junction, to little Roosevelt Lake.) One caveat: As you depart the trailhead at Leavitt Meadows Camp, don't be shocked if you hear a lot of shouting and see people running through the woods across the West Walker River. It's just the U.S. Marines in training at the nearby Mountain Warfare Training Center. They scared the heck out of us.

⑬ Pinecrest Lake National Recreation Trail

4.0 mi/2.0 hrs

Location: On Pinecrest Lake near Strawberry; map E4, grid d1.

User groups: Hikers and dogs. No horses or mountain bikes. No wheelchair facilities except at the fishing ramp and day-use area.

Permits: No permits are required. Parking and access are free.

Directions: From Sonora, drive east on Highway 108 for 31 miles to the Pinecrest turnoff.

Turn right on Pinecrest Lake Road, then continue for one mile to the day-use parking area on the south side of the lake. Park as close to the end of the road as possible.

Maps: For a map of Stanislaus National Forest, send $4 to USDA-Forest Service, 630 Sansome Street, San Francisco, CA 94111. To obtain a topographic map of the area, ask for Pinecrest from the USGS.

Contact: Stanislaus National Forest, Summit Ranger District, #1 Pinecrest Lake Road, Pinecrest, CA 95364; (209) 965-3434, or fax (209) 965-3372.

Trail notes: Pinecrest Lake is a tremendously popular family vacation resort just off Highway 108, the kind of place that people go year after year for a week of boating, camping, and fishing. The trail that circles its banks is a lot like the lake itself—it's pretty, it's popular, and it's no place to go if you like solitude. However, the four-mile loop makes a good early morning walk or run, if you're up and at it before the crowds get out of bed. In the afternoons, you can hike to the east side of the lake, then take a spur trail along the South Fork Stanislaus River to some excellent swimming holes, called "Cleo's Bath." The main downer: The south side of the loop is littered with vacation homes. The weird part: There are pay telephones positioned right along the trail.

⑭ Camp and Bear Lakes

8.0 mi/4.0 hrs

Location: In the Emigrant Wilderness near Pinecrest Lake; map E4, grid d2.

User groups: Hikers, dogs, and horses. No mountain bikes. No wheelchair facilities.

Permits: A free wilderness permit is required for overnight stays; they are available from the Summit Ranger Station. Parking and access are free.

Directions: From Sonora, drive east on Highway 108 for 31 miles to the Pinecrest turnoff. Turn right on Pinecrest Lake Road, then continue for a half mile to the right fork for Dodge Ridge Ski Area. Bear right and drive 2.9 miles, then turn right at the sign for Aspen Meadow and Gianelli Trailhead. Drive a half mile, then turn left and drive four miles to the right turnoff for Crabtree Trailhead. Turn right and drive a quarter mile to the Crabtree Trailhead. The route is well signed.

Maps: For a map of Stanislaus National Forest, send $4 to USDA-Forest Service, 630 Sansome Street, San Francisco, CA 94111. A map of the Emigrant Wilderness is also available from the Forest Service for $7. To obtain a topographic map of the area, ask for Pinecrest from the USGS.

Contact: Stanislaus National Forest, Summit Ranger District, #1 Pinecrest Lake Road, Pinecrest, CA 95364; (209) 965-3434, or fax (209) 965-3372.

Trail notes: The Crabtree Trailhead at elevation 7,180 feet is the trailhead of choice for most hikers and backpackers entering the Emigrant Wilderness. It's easy to reach, and allows access to many excellent destinations with a relatively short walk. From Crabtree, it's a moderate 2.5-mile hike to Camp Lake, just inside the wilderness boundary. Campsites can be found on the ridge on the south side of the lake. If there are too many people there, you can go an extra 1.5 miles to Bear Lake, accessible via a one-mile-long left spur trail off the Crabtree Trail. Both lakes offer stellar granite-country scenery, good campsites, and the chance of seeing plenty of wildflowers along the route in summer. We were wowed by the wandering daisies, big blue lupine, and yellow daisies.

⑮ Burst Rock/Powell Lake

4.0 mi/2.5 hrs

Location: In the Emigrant Wilderness near Pinecrest Lake; map E4, grid d2.

User groups: Hikers, dogs, and horses. No mountain bikes. No wheelchair facilities.

Permits: A free wilderness permit is required for overnight stays; permits are available from the Summit Ranger Station. Parking and access are free.

Directions: From Sonora, drive east on Highway 108 for 31 miles to the Pinecrest turnoff. Turn right on Pinecrest Lake Road, then continue for a half mile to the right fork for Dodge Ridge Ski Area. Bear right and drive 2.9 miles, then turn right at the sign for Aspen Meadow and Gianelli Trailhead. Drive a half mile, then turn left and drive 8.3 miles to the trailhead parking area. The route is well signed.

Maps: For a map of Stanislaus National Forest, send $4 to USDA-Forest Service, 630 Sansome

Street, San Francisco, CA 94111. A map of the Emigrant Wilderness is also available from the Forest Service for $7. To obtain a topographic map of the area, ask for Pinecrest from the USGS.

Contact: Stanislaus National Forest, Summit Ranger District, #1 Pinecrest Lake Road, Pinecrest, CA 95364; (209) 965-3434, or fax (209) 965-3372.

Trail notes: Both Burst Rock and Powell Lake are supreme day hike destinations, but they come with a surprise for first-time visitors: Neither one is located right along the trail, and since this is wilderness land, neither one is signed. This results in a lot of people wandering around asking, "Which rock is Burst Rock?" The short answer is: It doesn't matter. After hiking gently but steadily uphill for one mile, you'll reach an interpretive sign which details the difficulties of pioneers who tried to use this route (called the West Walker-Sonora Emigrant Trail) to cross the Sierras in the 1850s.

From the wilderness boundary sign, cut off to your left for about 50 yards and you'll witness an incredible vista and drop-off to the valley below, and who knows, you might even be standing on Burst Rock. After feeling suitably humbled, retrace your steps and continue another mile on the trail, until you reach an unsigned fork which leads to the left for less than a quarter mile to Powell Lake, a favorite spot of young anglers. (If you miss the fork, shortly you'll catch sight of the lake off to your left, and you'll know to go back and find it.) If you're lucky and smart enough to be the first visitors here in the morning, you can make a wish, take off all your clothes, and dive in to the lake from the peninsula of rocks in its center. The experience can feel downright religious.

⑯ Buckeye Creek Trail

5.0 mi/2.5 hrs

Location: In Toiyabe National Forest west of Bridgeport and Highway 395; map E4, grid d8.

User groups: Hikers, dogs, and horses. No mountain bikes. No wheelchair facilities.

Permits: No day-use permits are required. Parking and access are free for day hikers; backpackers must pay a $5 parking fee.

Directions: From Bridgeport on U.S. 395, drive west on Twin Lakes Road for seven miles to the Buckeye Road turnoff. Turn right on Buckeye Road (dirt) and drive about 3.5 miles to the Buckeye Campground and trailhead.

Maps: For a map of Toiyabe National Forest (Bridgeport District), send $4 to USDA-Forest Service, 630 Sansome Street, San Francisco, CA 94111. To obtain a topographic map of the area, ask for Twin Lakes from the USGS.

Contact: Toiyabe National Forest, Bridgeport Ranger District, P.O. Box 595, Bridgeport, CA 93517; (760) 932-7070, or fax (760) 932-1299.

Trail notes: You can hike up to eight miles one-way along Buckeye Creek, most of it pretty flat, although few people go that far. Most hikers just take off from Buckeye Campground (7,000 feet), maybe pack along their fishing rods, and walk a couple of miles each way up and down the stream. Brook trout are planted here all summer, close to the campground. It's rare to be able to hike in the eastern Sierra without having to climb, but that's what you get here on the bottom of Buckeye Canyon. If you don't like to fish, there's plenty of other stuff to do, like admire the wildflowers in the meadows or gape at the impressive walls of glacial summits and ridges that surround you.

⑰ Robinson Creek Trail

7.8 mi/5.0 hrs

Location: In the Hoover Wilderness west of Bridgeport; map E4, grid e8.

User groups: Hikers, dogs, and horses. No mountain bikes. No wheelchair facilities.

Permits: No day-use permits are required. Parking and access are free for day hikers; backpackers must pay a $5 parking fee.

Directions: From Bridgeport on U.S. 395, drive west on Twin Lakes Road for 13.2 miles to the signed parking area on the west end of the lakes, near Mono Village Campground.

Maps: For a map of Toiyabe National Forest (Bridgeport District) or the Hoover Wilderness, send $4 to USDA-Forest Service, 630 Sansome Street, San Francisco, CA 94111. To obtain a topographic map of the area, ask for Twin Lakes from the USGS.

Contact: Toiyabe National Forest, Bridgeport Ranger District, P.O. Box 595, Bridgeport, CA 93517; (760) 932-7070, or fax (760) 932-1299.

Trail notes: Some call it the Barney Lake Trail, others the Robinson Creek Trail, but whatever you call it, you need to know that this is the busiest trail into the Hoover Wilderness. Why? It's one of the few that's not a butt-kicker, as it gains only 1,200 feet along its four-mile length. The remedy for the crowds? Start hiking very early in the day, before the hundreds of campers in the Twin Lakes area have arisen from their sleeping bags. You must park outside Mono Village Campground and then walk straight through it to reach the trailhead, which is signed for Barney Lake. The trail parallels Robinson Creek the whole way, with off-and-on views of the mammoth, jagged Sawtooth Ridge. It enters the Hoover Wilderness at 2.6 miles, then climbs a bit more steeply, and reaches the lake at 3.9 miles. If you get there before everyone else does, you can congratulate yourself and call the lake your own.

⑱ Preston Flat Trail

6.0 mi/3.0 hrs

Location: In Stanislaus National Forest, on Tuolumne River near Cherry Lake; map E4, grid f1.

User groups: Hikers, dogs, and horses. No mountain bikes. No wheelchair facilities.

Permits: No permits are required. Parking and access are free.

Directions: From Groveland, drive east on Highway 120 for 13 miles to the Cherry Lake Road turnoff on the left (Road 1N03). Turn left and drive three miles to the left turnoff for Early Intake Powerhouse and the trailhead parking area. Turn left and drive to the trailhead.

Maps: For a map of Stanislaus National Forest, send $4 to USDA-Forest Service, 630 Sansome Street, San Francisco, CA 94111. To obtain a topographic map of the area, ask for Cherry Lake South from the USGS.

Contact: Stanislaus National Forest, Groveland Ranger District, 24545 Highway 120, Groveland, CA 95321; (209) 962-7825, or fax (209) 962-7412.

Trail notes: If the crowds in Yosemite are getting you down, step outside the park borders and take a hike on the Preston Flat Trail in Stanislaus National Forest. The elevation is low here—2,200 feet—so plan your trip for spring, when the air is cool and the fishing is good. The trail leads along the north side of the Wild and Scenic Tuolumne River, tracing its path for 4.5 miles almost to the edge of the national park. Few people hike that far, though. Most just head out for two or three miles upstream, carrying a fishing rod or a camera to photograph the beautiful wildflowers.

⑲ Lake Eleanor

3.0 mi/1.5 hrs

Location: In northwest Yosemite National Park; map E4, grid f2.

User groups: Hikers and horses. No dogs or mountain bikes. No wheelchair facilities.

Permits: No day-hiking permits are required. Parking and access are free.

Directions: From Groveland, drive east on Highway 120 for 13 miles, toward Yosemite National Park. Turn left on Cherry Lake Road (Road 1N03), signed for Cherry Lake and Sweetwater Camp. Follow Cherry Lake Road to near the edge of Cherry Lake, then turn left on a dirt road that is signed for Lake Eleanor. Follow the dirt road to its end, a quarter mile south of the lake.

Maps: Free park maps are available at park entrance stations or by contacting Yosemite National Park at the address below. A more detailed map is available for a fee from Tom Harrison Cartography, (415) 456-7940. To obtain a topographic map of the area, ask for Lake Eleanor from the USGS.

Contact: Yosemite National Park Public Information Office, P.O. Box 577, Yosemite National Park, CA 93589; (209) 372-0200, or fax (209) 372-0371.

Trail notes: Up here in the Hetch Hetchy region of Yosemite, elevations are low and temperatures can heat up. While that may not be good news in July and August, it's great news early in the year, when the rest of Yosemite is still buried in snow. You can fish all year at Lake Eleanor, elevation 4,657 feet, as long as the road is open and you can get in, and you can also hike the easy trail around the lake's edge. Swimming and canoeing are popular in summer. The access road to Lake Eleanor ends a quarter mile before the lake, so you start your hike there, then cruise around the lake to find your campsite or drop a line in the water.

Special note: Check your calendar before you go. The gate at Cherry Lake is closed every year one week before deer season, which is usually sometime in September. If you choose to go to Lake Eleanor anyway, you must add 4.5 miles to your hike (one way).

20 Hetch Hetchy Reservoir

13.0 mi/1–2 days

Location: In northwest Yosemite National Park; map E4, grid f3.

User groups: Hikers and horses. No dogs or mountain bikes. No wheelchair facilities.

Permits: There is a $20 entrance fee at Yosemite National Park, good for seven days. A free wilderness permit is required for overnight stays. They are available on a first-come, first-served basis up to one day in advance at the Yosemite Wilderness kiosk near your chosen trailhead, or further in advance by mail or phone for a $3 reservation fee; call (209) 372-0740.

Directions: From Groveland, drive east on Highway 120 for 22.5 miles to the Evergreen Road turnoff signed for Hetch Hetchy Reservoir (one mile west of the Big Oak Flat entrance to Yosemite). Follow Evergreen Road north to Camp Mather, then bear right and continue on Hetch Hetchy Road for a total of 16 miles to the dam and trailhead.

Maps: Free park maps are available at park entrance stations or by contacting Yosemite National Park at the address below. A more detailed map is available for a fee from Tom Harrison Cartography, (415) 456-7940. To obtain a topographic map of the area, ask for Hetch Hetchy Reservoir from the USGS.

Contact: Yosemite National Park Public Information Office, P.O. Box 577, Yosemite National Park, CA 93589; (209) 372-0200, or fax (209) 372-0371.

Trail notes: You're hungering for a Yosemite backpacking trip, but Tuolumne Meadows is knee-deep in melting snow. There's no better time than spring to hike the northern edge of Hetch Hetchy Reservoir, elevation 3,796 feet, admiring three stunning waterfalls along the way: Tueeulala, Wapama, and Rancheria. It's a long round-trip day hike or an easy overnight backpacking trip to the eastern edge of the reservoir and Rancheria Falls, where the bears are some of the boldest in all of Yosemite. (Bring a bear-proof food canister or hang your food high.) While Rancheria Falls is a series of cascades, Wapama Falls on Tiltill Creek is a Bridalveil-like plume of whitewater, plunging daringly into the reservoir. In spring, Wapama Falls sometimes flows so furiously that they have to close the trail. In contrast, Tueeulala Falls is a delicate wisp of whitewater, and it dries up by early summer. The trail is mostly flat, with a total elevation gain of only 1,000 feet, and manageable for beginning backpackers. Fishing in the reservoir is good in spring and fall, but remember: No swimming allowed. The trail starts by crossing the giant O'Shaughnessy Dam. This gives you pause to think about the San Francisco politicians who in 1908 believed that flooding Hetch Hetchy's valley, a nearly exact twin to stunning Yosemite Valley, was a good idea. It just goes to show—the good old days were not always so good.

21 Green, East, and West Lakes

8.0 mi/5.0 hrs

Location: In the Hoover Wilderness west of Bridgeport; map E4, grid f9.

User groups: Hikers, dogs, and horses. No mountain bikes. No wheelchair facilities.

Permits: No day-use permits are required. Parking and access are free.

Directions: From Bridgeport, drive south on U.S. 395 for five miles to Green Lake Road (dirt). Turn west and drive 8.5 miles to the signed trailhead parking area, shortly before Green Creek Campground.

Maps: For a map of Toiyabe National Forest (Bridgeport District) or the Hoover Wilderness, send $4 to USDA-Forest Service, 630 Sansome

Street, San Francisco, CA 94111. To obtain a topographic map of the area, ask for Twin Lakes from the USGS.

Contact: Toiyabe National Forest, Bridgeport Ranger District, P.O. Box 595, Bridgeport, CA 93517; (760) 932-7070, or fax (760) 932-1299.

Trail notes: All three lakes—Green, East, and West—are situated at over 9,000 feet in elevation, offer decent trout fishing, and are accessible via the Green Creek Trail. It's only five miles round-trip to Green Lake, but you can go two miles further for a nine-mile round-trip that includes East Lake as well, or take a 1.5-mile spur off the main trail for a jaunt to West Lake. Options; you've got options. Some people make a short backpacking trip out of it and see all three lakes. The trail climbs, of course, but not so much that you'll be worn out when you reach the lakes, just enough to give you stellar valley views most of the way. Wildflowers are excellent along the trail, as it closely parallels the West Fork of Green Creek. The turnoff for West Lake is on the right at 2.4 miles, and the main trail reaches Green Lake at 2.6 miles, then East Lake at 4.6 miles.

㉒ Carlon Falls

4.5 mi/2.5 hrs

Location: On the border of Stanislaus National Forest and northwest Yosemite National Park; map E4, grid g2.

User groups: Hikers only. No dogs, horses, or mountain bikes. No wheelchair facilities.

Permits: No permits are required. Parking and access are free.

Directions: From Groveland, drive east on Highway 120 for 22.5 miles to the Evergreen Road turnoff signed for Hetch Hetchy Reservoir (one mile west of the Big Oak Flat entrance to Yosemite). Follow Evergreen Road north for one mile to the far side of the bridge, just past Carlon Day-Use Area. Park on the right at the closed-off road on the north side of the bridge. (There is room for about five cars.) Begin hiking on the closed road, heading upstream. The road turns to single-track after about 100 yards.

Maps: For a map of Stanislaus National Forest, send $4 to USDA-Forest Service, 630 Sansome Street, San Francisco, CA 94111. To obtain a topo-

graphic map of the area, ask for Ackerson Mountain from the USGS.

Contact: Stanislaus National Forest, Groveland Ranger District, 24545 Highway 120, Groveland, CA 95321; (209) 962-7825, or fax (209) 962-7412.

Trail notes: Carlon Falls is a pretty cascade on the South Fork Tuolumne River in the far western region of Yosemite. It's so far west that the trailhead is actually in Stanislaus National Forest, outside the park border. You hike into Yosemite National Park. That means no $20 entrance fee, no waiting in line at the entrance kiosk, and no crowds. The trailhead is just outside of Carlon Day-Use Area, a popular picnicking spot on the Tuolumne River. Hike along the northern bank of the river to reach the falls in just over two miles; the trail is smooth, flat, and easy to follow. The waterfall drops in two tiers over wide granite ledges, and the riverbanks surrounding it are covered in tall hardwoods and dense foliage. A bonus is that unlike most Yosemite waterfalls, Carlon Falls runs year-round, and it's great to visit in the autumn when the deciduous trees in the area show their brilliant colors.

㉓ Lukens Lake

1.5 mi/1.0 hr

Location: Off Tioga Road in Yosemite National Park; map E4, grid g4.

User groups: Hikers only. No dogs, horses, or mountain bikes. No wheelchair facilities.

Permits: No permits are required. There is a $20 entrance fee at Yosemite National Park, good for seven days.

Directions: From Merced, drive 70 miles northeast on Highway 140 to Yosemite National Park. Follow the signs to Yosemite Valley, entering through the Arch Rock entrance station. Continue 4.5 miles to the left turnoff for Tioga Road/Highway 120, looping back out of the valley on Big Oak Flat Road. In 9.3 miles, turn right on Tioga Road and drive 16.2 miles to the Lukens Lake Trailhead parking area on the south side of the road. The trail begins on the north side of the road.

Maps: Free park maps are available at park entrance stations or by contacting Yosemite National Park at the address below. A more detailed map is available for a fee from Tom Harrison Cartography, (415) 456-7940. To obtain a topographic map of the area, ask for Tamarack Flat from the USGS.

Contact: Yosemite National Park Public Information Office, P.O. Box 577, Yosemite National Park, CA 93589; (209) 372-0200, or fax (209) 372-0371.

Trail notes: The Lukens Lake Trail is the perfect introductory lake hike for families in Yosemite National Park. It has all the best features of a long backpacking trip to a remote alpine area, without the long miles, steep climbs, and heavy weight to carry. A six-year-old could make the trip easily. A bonus is that the trailhead is on the western end of Tioga Road, so it's quickly reached from points in Yosemite Valley. The trail is three-quarters of a mile long, leading from Tioga Road up to a saddle, then dropping down to the lake. It winds through a red fir forest, then cuts across a corn lily-filled meadow to the edge of the shallow lake. Don't forget your picnic.

㉔ Ten Lakes/Grant Lakes

12.6 mi/1–2 days

Location: Off Tioga Road in Yosemite National Park; map E4, grid g4.

User groups: Hikers only. No dogs, horses, or mountain bikes. No wheelchair facilities.

Permits: There is a $20 entrance fee at Yosemite National Park, good for seven days. A free wilderness permit is required for overnight stays. They are available on a first-come, first-served basis up to one day in advance at the Yosemite Wilderness kiosk near your chosen trailhead, or further in advance by mail or phone for a $3 reservation fee; call (209) 372-0740.

Directions: From Merced, drive 70 miles northeast on Highway 140 to Yosemite National Park. Follow the signs toward Yosemite Valley, entering through the Arch Rock entrance station. Continue 4.5 miles to the left turnoff for Tioga Road/Highway 120, looping back out of the valley on Big Oak Flat Road. In 9.3 miles, turn right on Tioga Road and drive 19.4 miles to the Yosemite Creek and Ten Lakes Trailhead parking area which is on the south side of the road. The trail begins on the north side of the road.

Maps: Free park maps are available at park entrance stations or by contacting Yosemite National Park at the address below. A more detailed map is available for a fee from Tom Harrison Cartography, (415) 456-7940. To obtain topographic maps of the area, ask for Yosemite Falls and Ten Lakes from the USGS.

Contact: Yosemite National Park Public Information Office, P.O. Box 577, Yosemite National Park, CA 93589; (209) 372-0200, or fax (209) 372-0371.

Trail notes: Those who enjoy serious punishment would hike to Ten Lakes and Grant Lakes from Yosemite Valley, traveling almost the entire length of Yosemite Creek. The rest of us start at the Tioga Road Trailhead (elevation 7,500 feet) and enter the Ten Lakes Basin via a much shorter route, so we still have plenty of time and energy left to relax and enjoy ourselves. The Ten Lakes area is incredibly popular, so get your wilderness permit early and choose your camping spot based on where you can get the most solitude. If you can't get a permit, get an early-morning start and make this trip as a long day hike; just be prepared for some serious climbing at a high elevation. From the same trail, you can hike to either the Grant Lakes (take the right cutoff five miles out, and hike one mile further) or Ten Lakes (continue straight to the trail's end, 6.3 miles from the trailhead). The Grant Lakes offer a little more solitude (good for day hikers), but the two larger of the Ten Lakes have the best campsites, with many trees along their shorelines offering protection from the wind. All of the lakes are sparkling, rockbound beauties.

㉕ May Lake

2.4 mi/2.0 hrs

Location: Off Tioga Road in Yosemite National Park; map E4, grid g5.

User groups: Hikers and horses. No dogs or mountain bikes. No wheelchair facilities.

Permits: No permits are required. There is a $20 entrance fee at Yosemite National Park, good for seven days.

Directions: From Merced, drive 70 miles northeast on Highway 140 to Yosemite National Park. Follow the signs toward Yosemite Valley, entering through the Arch Rock entrance station. Continue 4.5 miles to the left turnoff for Tioga Road/Highway 120, looping back out of the valley on Big Oak Flat Road. In 9.3 miles, turn right on Tioga Road and drive 26.6 miles to the May Lake Road turnoff on the left (near road marker T-21). Drive two miles to the trailhead parking lot.

Maps: Free park maps are available at park entrance stations or by contacting Yosemite National Park at the address below. A more detailed map is available for a fee from Tom Harrison Cartography, (415) 456-7940. To obtain a topographic map of the area, ask for Tenaya Lake from the USGS.

Contact: Yosemite National Park Public Information Office, P.O. Box 577, Yosemite National Park, CA 93589; (209) 372-0200, or fax (209) 372-0371.

Trail notes: Here's a hike that you can take the kids on. It's an easy 1.25 miles to May Lake, tucked in below 10,850-foot Mount Hoffman. The trail's total elevation gain is only 400 feet, and, better yet, it's downhill all the way home. They say May Lake is the exact geographical center of Yosemite National Park, but what matters more to most people is that it's a round, blue lake set at 9,329 feet, with a spectacular mountain backdrop. The trail begins at the Snow Flat Trailhead two miles off Tioga Road, then passes through a lodgepole pine forest and climbs up to granite country, then drops down to the lake's southern shore. A High Sierra Camp is located along the shore, but this trip is so easy that it's best suited for a day hike.

㉖ Clouds Rest

14.0 mi/8.0 hrs

Location: Off Tioga Road in Yosemite National Park; map E4, grid g5.

User groups: Hikers only. No dogs, horses, or mountain bikes. No wheelchair facilities.

Permits: No permits are required. There is a $20 entrance fee at Yosemite National Park, good for seven days.

Directions: From Merced, drive 70 miles northeast on Highway 140 to Yosemite National Park.

Follow the signs toward Yosemite Valley, entering through the Arch Rock entrance station. Continue 4.5 miles to the left turnoff for Tioga Road/Highway 120, looping back out of the valley on Big Oak Flat Road. In 9.3 miles, turn right on Tioga Road and drive 30.3 miles to the Sunrise Lakes Trailhead on the south side of Tioga Road, just west of Tenaya Lake.

Maps: Free park maps are available at park entrance stations or by contacting Yosemite National Park at the address below. A more detailed map is available for a fee from Tom Harrison Cartography, (415) 456-7940. To obtain a topographic map of the area, ask for Tenaya Lake from the USGS.

Contact: Yosemite National Park Public Information Office, P.O. Box 577, Yosemite National Park, CA 93589; (209) 372-0200, or fax (209) 372-0371.

Trail notes: Hiking to Clouds Rest is a trip that's as epic as climbing Half Dome, and with less people elbowing you along the way. But with a 2,300-foot climb and 14 miles to cover, it's not for those who are out of shape.

The trail ascends steadily for the first four miles, then descends steeply for a half mile, then climbs again, with only a short breather in the middle where the trail goes flat (too briefly). The final summit ascent is a little dicey because of the terrifying dropoffs, but as with other Yosemite peaks, watch your footing on the granite slabs and you'll be fine. Overall, the route is far safer than climbing Half Dome, although the summit is actually higher. The view from the top of Clouds Rest—of Yosemite Valley, Half Dome, Tenaya Lake, and various peaks and ridges—will knock your socks off. Hope you brought along an extra pair.

㉗ Sunrise Lakes

7.5 mi/4.5 hrs or 2.0 days

Location: Off Tioga Road in Yosemite National Park; map E4, grid g5.

User groups: Hikers only. No dogs, horses, or mountain bikes. No wheelchair facilities.

Permits: There is a $20 entrance fee at Yosemite National Park, good for seven days. A free wilderness permit is required for overnight stays. They are available on a first-come, first-served basis up to one day in advance at the Yosemite Wilderness kiosk near your chosen trailhead, or further in advance by mail or phone for a $3 reservation fee; call (209) 372-0740.

Directions: From Merced, drive 70 miles northeast on Highway 140 to Yosemite National Park. Follow the signs toward Yosemite Valley, entering through the Arch Rock entrance station. Continue 4.5 miles to the left turnoff for Tioga Road/Highway 120, looping back out of the valley on Big Oak Flat Road. In 9.3 miles, turn right on Tioga Road and drive 30.3 miles to the Sunrise Lakes trailhead on the south side of Tioga Road, just west of Tenaya Lake.

Maps: Free park maps are available at park entrance stations or by contacting Yosemite National Park at the address below. A more detailed map is available for a fee from Tom Harrison Cartography, (415) 456-7940. To obtain a topographic map of the area, ask for Tenaya Lake from the USGS.

Contact: Yosemite National Park Public Information Office, P.O. Box 577, Yosemite National Park, CA 93589; (209) 372-0200, or fax (209) 372-0371.

Trail notes: With all the people hiking to Clouds Rest, combined with all the people hiking to the Sunrise Lakes, the Sunrise Trailhead can look like a mall parking lot on a Saturday. But don't be scared off; the hike to Sunrise Lakes is a great day hike or easy backpacking trip, especially during the week or off-season, with only a 1,000-foot elevation gain and a ton of stellar scenery, including great views of Clouds Rest.

You follow the trail as it climbs above the edge of Tenaya Canyon, then at 2.5 miles, turn left at the sign for the Sunrise High Sierra Camp, leaving the hordes of Clouds Rest hikers behind. Before you know it, Lower Sunrise Lake shows up on the right, and the other lakes appear shortly after it on the left. The upper lake is the largest and by far the most popular; lots of folks like to swim and picnic there on warm summer days. Backpackers can pick a site here or continue onward for two more miles to the backpackers' camp or the High Sierra Camp, depending on where they've made their plans.

28 Tenaya Lake

2.0 mi/1.0 hr

Location: Off Tioga Road in Yosemite National Park; map E4, grid g6.

User groups: Hikers only. No dogs, horses, or mountain bikes. No wheelchair facilities.

Permits: No permits are required. There is a $20 entrance fee at Yosemite National Park, good for seven days.

Directions: From Merced, drive 70 miles northeast on Highway 140 to Yosemite National Park. Follow the signs toward Yosemite Valley, entering through the Arch Rock entrance station. Continue 4.5 miles to the left turnoff for Tioga Road/Highway 120, looping back out of the valley on Big Oak Flat Road. In 9.3 miles, turn right on Tioga Road and drive 31.7 miles to the eastern Tenaya Lake picnic area (there is another Tenaya Lake picnic area one-half mile west of this one). The trail leads from the parking lot.

Maps: Free park maps are available at park entrance stations or by contacting Yosemite National Park at the address below. A more detailed map is available for a fee from Tom Harrison Cartography, (415) 456-7940. To obtain a topographic map of the area, ask for Tenaya Lake from the USGS.

Contact: Yosemite National Park Public Information Office, P.O. Box 577, Yosemite National Park, CA 93589; (209) 372-0200, or fax (209) 372-0371.

Trail notes: Lots of people drive east down Tioga Road in a big rush to get to Tuolumne Meadows, but when they see giant Tenaya Lake right along the road, it stops them in their tire tracks. Luckily the 150-acre, sapphire-blue lake has a parking lot and picnic area at its east end, where you can leave your car and take a stroll down to the lake's edge. While most people stop at the white-sand beach and picnic tables to watch the rockclimbers on nearby Polly Dome, you can leave the crowds behind and stroll to the south side of the beach. Pick up the trail there that leads along the back side of Tenaya Lake, far from the road on the north side. When you get to the west end of the lake, where the trail continues but the water views end, just turn around and walk back. It's a perfect, easy hike, at the edge of one of the most beautiful lakes in Yosemite.

㉙ Cathedral Lakes

7.4 mi/4.0 hrs or 2.0 days

Location: Near Tuolumne Meadows in Yosemite National Park; map E4, grid g7.

User groups: Hikers and horses. No dogs or mountain bikes. No wheelchair facilities.

Permits: There is a $20 entrance fee at Yosemite National Park, good for seven days. A free wilderness permit is required for overnight stays. They are available on a first-come, first-served basis up to one day in advance at the Yosemite Wilderness kiosk near your chosen trailhead, or further in advance by mail or phone for a $3 reservation fee; call (209) 372-0740.

Directions: From Merced, drive 70 miles northeast on Highway 140 to Yosemite National Park. Follow the signs toward Yosemite Valley, entering through the Arch Rock entrance station. Continue 4.5 miles to the left turnoff for Tioga Road/Highway 120, looping back out of the valley on Big Oak Flat Road. In 9.3 miles, turn right on Tioga Road and drive 37.4 miles to the Cathedral Lakes Trailhead parking on the right.

Maps: Free park maps are available at park entrance stations or by contacting Yosemite National Park at the address below. A more detailed map is available for a fee for Tom Harrison Cartography, (415) 456-7940. To obtain a topographic map of the area, ask for Tenaya Lake from the USGS.

Contact: Yosemite National Park Public Information Office, P.O. Box 577, Yosemite National Park, CA 93589; (209) 372-0200, or fax (209) 372-0371.

Trail notes: The Cathedral Lakes are a tremendously popular easy backpacking destination in Yosemite, but it's such a short hike to reach them that it also makes a great day trip. Located on a half mile spur off the John Muir Trail, the lakes are within a classic glacial cirque, tucked in below 10,940-foot Cathedral Peak. It's as scenic a spot as you'll find anywhere. Campsites are found close to the lakes, but you will need to secure your wilderness permit way in advance

in order to spend the night there. From the trail's start at Tioga Road, it's a 3.2-mile walk on the John Muir Trail, then a right turn on the Cathedral Lake spur. The total climb is only 1,000 feet, and much of the trail is shaded by lodgepole pines. When the path breaks out of the trees, views of surrounding peaks (especially distinctive Cathedral Peak) keep you oohing and ahhing the whole way. The last half mile is a flat stroll through a meadow, following the lake's inlet stream to the water's edge.

㉚ Vogelsang Loop

19.0 mi/3–4 days

Location: Near Tuolumne Meadows in Yosemite National Park; map E4, grid g7.

User groups: Hikers and horses. No dogs or mountain bikes. No wheelchair facilities.

Permits: There is a $20 entrance fee at Yosemite National Park, good for seven days. A free wilderness permit is required for overnight stays. They are available on a first-come, first-served basis up to one day in advance at the Yosemite Wilderness kiosk near your chosen trailhead, or further in advance by mail or phone for a $3 reservation fee; call (209) 372-0740.

Directions: From Merced, drive 70 miles northeast on Highway 140 to Yosemite National Park. Follow the signs toward Yosemite Valley, entering through the Arch Rock entrance station. Continue 4.5 miles to the left turnoff for Tioga Road/Highway 120, looping back out of the valley on Big Oak Flat Road. In 9.3 miles, turn right on Tioga Road and drive 39.5 miles to the PCT/John Muir Trail Trailhead and the Wilderness Permit Station.

Maps: Free park maps are available at park entrance stations or by contacting Yosemite National Park at the address below. A more detailed map is available for a fee from Tom Harrison Cartography, (415) 456-7940. To obtain a topographic map of the area, ask for Vogelsang Peak from the USGS.

Contact: Yosemite National Park Public Information Office, P.O. Box 577, Yosemite National Park, CA 93589; (209) 372-0200, or fax (209) 372-0371.

Trail notes: Although this loop is popular with backpackers using the Vogelsang High Sierra

Camp, hikers who plan early can get a wilderness permit for their own self-designed backpacking trip. Then they can take the loop at their leisure and spend a few peaceful days in the Yosemite backcountry. The traditional route is to head out on the western side of the loop along Rafferty Creek, then take a short spur off the loop and spend the night at Vogelsang Lake, which is without question the most visually dramatic spot to be seen on this trip. It's flanked by Fletcher Peak, a steep and rugged wall of glacially-carved granite. Only a few trees dare grow in this sparse high alpine environment. The next day you rejoin the loop and continue eastward to Evelyn Lake, another favorite camping spot. When it's time to return, you hike down to Lyell Fork, a 2,000-foot descent that takes a few hours, then meet up with the John Muir Trail and follow it north, through lush green and gorgeous Lyell Canyon, back to the trailhead at Tuolumne Meadows. The trailhead is at 8,600 feet, plenty high to start, and, for the most part, the trail undulates along, never gaining or losing more than 2,000 feet.

㉛ Lower Gaylor Lake

8.0 mi/4.0 hrs

Location: Near Tioga Pass in Yosemite National Park; map E4, grid g7.

User groups: Hikers only. No dogs, horses, or mountain bikes. No wheelchair facilities.

Permits: No permits are required. There is a $20 entrance fee at Yosemite National Park, good for seven days.

Directions: From Merced, drive 70 miles northeast on Highway 140 to Yosemite National Park. Follow the signs toward Yosemite Valley, entering through the Arch Rock entrance station. Continue 4.5 miles to the left turnoff for Tioga Road/Highway 120, looping back out of the valley on Big Oak Flat Road. In 9.3 miles, turn right on Tioga Road and drive 39.5 miles to the trailhead for the PCT/John Muir Trail near Tuolumne Lodge and the Wilderness Permit Station, on the south side of Tioga Road.

Maps: Free park maps are available at park entrance stations or by contacting Yosemite National Park at the address below. A more detailed map is available for a fee from Tom Harrison Cartography, (415) 456-7940. To obtain topographic maps of the area, ask for Vogelsang Peak and Tioga Pass from the USGS.

Contact: Yosemite National Park Public Information Office, P.O. Box 577, Yosemite National Park, CA 93589; (209) 372-0200, or fax (209) 372-0371.

Trail notes: A variation on the Middle and Upper Gaylor Lakes hike (see trail number 40), this trail starts at Tuolumne Lodge and meanders along the Dana Fork Tuolumne River, then crosses Tioga Road and heads to Lower Gaylor Lake. Note that if you want to get to the Upper and Middle Gaylor Lakes from the lower lake, you have to go cross-country; the shorter way to reach them is to drive to the Tioga Pass Trailhead and follow the trail notes in hike number 40. This hike, however, draws fewer crowds, which is why we prefer it. Elevation at this trailhead is 9,250 feet; the total gain is about 800 feet to Lower Gaylor Lake, a gentle climb the whole way. The lake is a deep turquoise color and hemmed in by granite, and from its edge you get wide vistas of the peaks in the Tuolumne Meadows area. Occasional hearty whitebark pines try to eke out a living in Lower Gaylor Lake's basin.

㉜ Elizabeth Lake

4.5 mi/2.5 hrs

Location: Near Tuolumne Meadows in Yosemite National Park; map E4, grid g7.

User groups: Hikers only. No dogs, horses, or mountain bikes. No wheelchair facilities.

Permits: No permits are required. There is a $20 entrance fee at Yosemite National Park, good for seven days.

Directions: From Merced, drive 70 miles northeast on Highway 140 to Yosemite National Park. Follow the signs toward Yosemite Valley, entering through the Arch Rock entrance station. Continue 4.5 miles to the left turnoff for Tioga Road/Highway 120, looping back out of the valley on Big Oak Flat Road. In 9.3 miles, turn right on Tioga Road and drive 39 miles to the Tuolumne Meadows Campground on the right. The trail begins across from the group camp rest rooms.

Maps: Free park maps are available at park entrance stations or by contacting Yosemite National Park at the address below. A more detailed map is available for a fee from Tom Harrison Cartography, (415) 456-7940. To obtain a topographic map of the area, ask for Vogelsang Peak from the USGS.

Contact: Yosemite National Park Public Information Office, P.O. Box 577, Yosemite National Park, CA 93589; (209) 372-0200, or fax (209) 372-0371.

Trail notes: Starting at the trailhead elevation of 8,600 feet, you have a mere 900-foot elevation gain over 2.25 miles to get to pretty Elizabeth Lake, a day hike that is attainable for almost everybody. The only problem is that almost nobody can find the trailhead, tucked into the back of Tuolumne Meadows Campground, across from the group camp rest rooms. Once you locate it, be prepared to climb steeply for the first mile, then breathe easier when the trail levels out. Luckily the route is mostly shaded by lodgepole pines. Your reward is a gorgeous little lake at the base of Unicorn Peak, the kind of place to spread out a picnic, or for the brave to take a swim. Some folks try to climb Unicorn Peak (10,880 feet) from the lake, but most are happy to sit around and admire the views of it and its neighboring peaks in the Cathedral Range.

㉝ Lyell Canyon

6.0 mi/3.0 hrs

Location: Near Tuolumne Meadows in Yosemite National Park; map E4, grid g7.

User groups: Hikers and horses. No dogs or mountain bikes. No wheelchair facilities.

Permits: No permits are required. There is a $20 entrance fee at Yosemite National Park, good for seven days.

Directions: From Merced, drive 70 miles northeast on Highway 140 to Yosemite National Park. Follow the signs toward Yosemite Valley, entering through the Arch Rock entrance station. Continue 4.5 miles to the left turnoff for Tioga Road/Highway 120, looping back out of the valley on Big Oak Flat Road. In 9.3 miles, turn right on Tioga Road and drive 39.5 miles to the Tuolumne Lodge and Wilderness Permit Station parking lot on the

right. Look for the trail sign for the John Muir Trail/Pacific Crest Trail.

Maps: Free park maps are available at park entrance stations or by contacting Yosemite National Park at the address below. A more detailed map is available for a fee from Tom Harrison Cartography, (415) 456-7940. To obtain a topographic map of the area, ask for Vogelsang Peak from the USGS.

Contact: Yosemite National Park Public Information Office, P.O. Box 577, Yosemite National Park, CA 93589; (209) 372-0200, or fax (209) 372-0371.

Trail notes: This hike is one of the easiest in the Yosemite high country, and since it is virtually flat, and also starts out beautiful and stays that way all along, you can hike it as long or as short as you like. The total trail length is eight miles one way, paralleling the Lyell Fork of the Tuolumne River on the Pacific Crest Trail/John Muir Trail, but most people just head out for two or three miles, often carrying a fishing rod, then turn back. To reach the Lyell Fork, you must first cross the Dana Fork on a footbridge near the wilderness permit station and parking lot. Then in a quarter mile you cross the Lyell Fork on a second footbridge, and walk upstream along the river's southwest side. If you like looking at gorgeous meadows and a meandering river, this is your hike. A bonus is that there are backpacking sites three to four miles out on the trail, so if you get a wilderness permit, you can linger for a few days in paradise.

㉞ Young Lakes Loop

12.5 mi/1–2 days

Location: Near Tuolumne Meadows in Yosemite National Park; map E4, grid g7.

User groups: Hikers and horses. No dogs or mountain bikes. No wheelchair facilities.

Permits: There is a $20 entrance fee at Yosemite National Park, good for seven days. A free wilderness permit is required for overnight stays. They are available on a first-come, first-served basis up to one day in advance at the Yosemite Wilderness kiosk near your chosen trailhead, or further in advance by mail or phone for a $3 reservation fee; call (209) 372-0740.

Directions: From Merced, drive 70 miles northeast on Highway 140 to Yosemite National Park.

Follow the signs toward Yosemite Valley, entering through the Arch Rock entrance station. Continue 4.5 miles to the left turnoff for Tioga Road/Highway 120, looping back out of the valley on Big Oak Flat Road. In 9.3 miles, turn right on Tioga Road and drive 39 miles to the Lembert Dome/Soda Springs/Dog Lake/Glen Aulin Trailhead parking on the left. Begin hiking on the western edge of the parking lot, where there is a gated dirt road signed "Soda Springs, 0.5 mile."

Maps: Free park maps are available at park entrance stations or by contacting Yosemite National Park at the address below. A more detailed map is available for a fee from Tom Harrison Cartography, (415) 456-7940. To obtain topographic maps of the area, ask for Tioga Pass and Falls Ridge from the USGS.

Contact: Yosemite National Park Public Information Office, P.O. Box 577, Yosemite National Park, CA 93589; (209) 372-0200, or fax (209) 372-0371.

Trail notes: Starting from the Lembert Dome parking lot, the Young Lakes Loop is a classic Yosemite trip that works equally well as a short backpacking trip or a long day hike. The destination is a series of lakes that are set in a deep and wide glacial cirque—the kind of awesome scenery that sticks in your mind months later when you're sitting at a desk somewhere staring at your computer screen.

The trip starts with a walk down the wide dirt road that leads to Soda Spring, on the west side of the Lembert Dome parking lot. Pick up the trail near Parson's Lodge that leads to Glen Aulin and follow it through lodgepole pines for 1.8 miles until you see the right turnoff for Young Lakes. Follow the Young Lakes Trail for three more miles, climbing steadily. At five miles out from the trailhead you'll see the return leg of your loop leading off to the right, but you'll continue straight for another 1.5 miles to Lower Young Lake and a stunning view of Mount Conness and White Mountain. Two more lakes are accessible within a half mile to the east. When you're ready to head home, retrace your steps to the junction and take the eastern (left) fork, returning via Dog Lake and Lembert Dome. A nice bonus is that the return leg of the loop is shorter—from the junction, it's only 3.5 miles back to your car.

㉟ Waterwheel Falls

16.0 mi/1–2 days

Location: Near Tuolumne Meadows in Yosemite National Park; map E4, grid g7.

User groups: Hikers and horses. No dogs or mountain bikes. No wheelchair facilities.

Permits: There is a $20 entrance fee at Yosemite National Park, good for seven days. A free wilderness permit is required for overnight stays. They are available on a first-come, first-served basis up to one day in advance at the Yosemite Wilderness kiosk near your chosen trailhead, or further in advance by mail or phone for a $3 reservation fee; call (209) 372-0740.

Directions: From Merced, drive 70 miles northeast on Highway 140 to Yosemite National Park. Follow the signs toward Yosemite Valley, entering through the Arch Rock entrance station. Continue 4.5 miles to the left turnoff for Tioga Road/Highway 120, looping back out of the valley on Big Oak Flat Road. In 9.3 miles, turn right on Tioga Road and drive 39 miles to the Lembert Dome/Soda Springs/Dog Lake/Glen Aulin Trailhead parking on the left. Begin hiking on the western edge of the parking lot, where there is a gated dirt road signed "Soda Springs, 0.5 mile."

Maps: Free park maps are available at park entrance stations or by contacting Yosemite National Park at the address below. A more detailed map is available for a fee from Tom Harrison Cartography, (415) 456-7940. To obtain topographic maps of the area, ask for Tioga Pass and Falls Ridge from the USGS.

Contact: Yosemite National Park Public Information Office, P.O. Box 577, Yosemite National Park, CA 93589; (209) 372-0200, or fax (209) 372-0371.

Trail notes: This hike is the Epic Waterfall Trip. If you hike the entire route, you'll see so many waterfalls and so much water along the way that you'll have enough memories to get you through a 10-year drought. The best way to do it is to arrange for a wilderness permit in advance, or reserve a stay at the Glen Aulin High Sierra Camp, so that you can divide the 16 miles of trail over two or more days. If you're in good enough shape, you can do the trip in one day, because the trail is nearly flat for the first four miles (a 400-foot elevation loss), then descends some more over the next four miles (a 1,500-foot elevation loss). Unfortunately, all the climbing must be done on the way home, so you must reserve your energy, and have plenty of food and water. Follow the trail notes in hike number 36 for Glen Aulin and Tuolumne Falls for the first four miles of trail, then continue downstream past Glen Aulin Camp, alternating between stretches of stunning flower- and aspen-lined meadows and stark granite slabs. Waterwheel Falls is only three miles from the camp, and two other major cascades, California and LeConte, are along the way. To see all three falls, make sure you take every spur trail you see that leads to the left off the main trail; none of the waterfalls are apparent from the main trail. (People will stop you on the trail to ask if you know where the waterfalls are.) While all three falls are long whitewater cascades, Waterwheel is considered Yosemite's most unusual-looking waterfall, because it has sections of churning water that dip into deep holes in the granite, then shoot out with such velocity that they seem to double back on themselves. When the river level is high, they actually appear to circle around like waterwheels.

㊱ Glen Aulin and Tuolumne Falls

9.0 mi/5.0 hrs

Location: Near Tuolumne Meadows in Yosemite National Park; map E4, grid g7.

User groups: Hikers and horses. No dogs or mountain bikes. No wheelchair facilities.

Permits: No permits are required. There is a $20 entrance fee at Yosemite National Park, good for seven days.

Directions: From Merced, drive 70 miles northeast on Highway 140 to Yosemite National Park. Follow the signs toward Yosemite Valley, entering through the Arch Rock entrance station. Continue 4.5 miles to the left turnoff for Tioga Road/ Highway 120, looping back out of the valley on Big Oak Flat Road. In 9.3 miles, turn right on Tioga Road and drive 39 miles to the Lembert Dome/ Soda Springs/Dog Lake/Glen Aulin Trailhead parking on the left. Begin hiking on the western edge of the parking lot, where there is a gated dirt road signed "Soda Springs, 0.5 mile."

Maps: Free park maps are available at park entrance stations or by contacting Yosemite National Park at the address below. A more detailed map is available for a fee from Tom Harrison Cartography, (415) 456-7940. To obtain topographic maps of the area, ask for Tioga Pass and Falls Ridge from the USGS.

Contact: Yosemite National Park Public Information Office, P.O. Box 577, Yosemite National Park, CA 93589; (209) 372-0200, or fax (209) 372-0371.

Trail notes: Those who aren't up for the Epic Waterfall Trip to Waterwheel Falls described in hike number 35 can take this trip instead, and maybe even sneak in a good meal at the Glen Aulin High Sierra Camp. (To stay in the camp, you must reserve a space a year in advance, but you can often purchase a hot meal just by showing up.) Tuolumne Falls drops right by the High Sierra Camp, and reaching it requires only a 4.5-mile one-way walk with a 400-foot elevation loss. The return climb is easy, with most of the ascent being in the first mile as you head up and over the various cascades of Tuolumne Falls on granite stairsteps. Follow the dirt road from the Lembert Dome parking lot toward Soda Spring, then when you near Parson's Lodge, veer right on the signed trail to Glen Aulin. You'll walk through forest, then move closer to the Tuolumne River and get incredible views of Cathedral and Unicorn peaks and Fairview Dome. After three miles, you'll cross the Tuolumne on a footbridge and in a quarter mile, reach the first stunning drop of Tuolumne Falls, a 100-foot churning freefall. Keep descending past more cascades to the base of the falls, where another footbridge leads back across the river and to Glen Aulin. Pick a spot downstream beside a river pool or near the bridge at the base of the waterfall, have a seat, and ponder how beautiful the world is.

㊲ Lembert Dome

2.8 mi/1.5 hrs

Location: Near Tuolumne Meadows in Yosemite National Park; map E4, grid g7.

User groups: Hikers only. No dogs, horses, or mountain bikes. No wheelchair facilities.

Permits: No permits are required. There is a

$20 entrance fee at Yosemite National Park, good for seven days.

Directions: From Merced, drive 70 miles northeast on Highway 140 to Yosemite National Park. Follow the signs toward Yosemite Valley, entering through the Arch Rock entrance station. Continue 4.5 miles to the left turnoff for Tioga Road/Highway 120, looping back out of the valley on Big Oak Flat Road. In 9.3 miles, turn right on Tioga Road and drive 39 miles to the Lembert Dome/Soda Springs/Dog Lake/Glen Aulin Trailhead parking on the left. Begin hiking on the trail near the rest rooms.

Maps: Free park maps are available at park entrance stations or by contacting Yosemite National Park at the address below. A more detailed map is available for a fee from Tom Harrison Cartography, (415) 456-7940. To obtain a topographic map of the area, ask for Tioga Pass from the USGS.

Contact: Yosemite National Park Public Information Office, P.O. Box 577, Yosemite National Park, CA 93589; (209) 372-0200, or fax (209) 372-0371.

Trail notes: Lembert Dome is a *roche moutonnée,* which is a French geologic term that means it looks something like a sheep. Well, we never saw the resemblance, but we did feel like a couple of mountain goats when we climbed Lembert Dome, elevation 9,450 feet. From the parking area at Lembert Dome's base, you can see rock climbers practicing their stuff on the steep side of the dome, but luckily the hiker's trail leads you around to the more sloped back side, where you can walk right up the granite—no ropes necessary. The Dog Lake and Lembert Dome Trail winds its way steeply around to the dome's north side (see the trail notes for Dog Lake, hike number 38); from there you pick any route along the granite that looks manageable. When you reach the top of the dome, you know you've accomplished something. The view from its highest point—of Tuolumne Meadows and surrounding peaks and domes—is more than worth the effort.

38 Dog Lake

3.4 mi/2.0 hrs

Location: Near Tuolumne Meadows in Yosemite National Park; map E4, grid g7.

User groups: Hikers and horses. No dogs or mountain bikes. No wheelchair facilities.

Permits: No permits are required. There is a $20 entrance fee at Yosemite National Park, good for seven days.

Directions: From Merced, drive 70 miles northeast on Highway 140 to Yosemite National Park. Follow the signs toward Yosemite Valley, entering through the Arch Rock entrance station. Continue 4.5 miles to the left turnoff for Tioga Road/Highway 120, looping back out of the valley on Big Oak Flat Road. In 9.3 miles, turn right on Tioga Road and drive 39 miles to the Lembert Dome/Soda Springs/Dog Lake/Glen Aulin Trailhead parking on the left. Begin hiking on the trail near the rest rooms.

Maps: Free park maps are available at park entrance stations or by contacting Yosemite National Park at the address below. A more detailed map is available for a fee from Tom Harrison Cartography, (415) 456-7940. To obtain a topographic map of the area, ask for Tioga Pass from the USGS.

Contact: Yosemite National Park Public Information Office, P.O. Box 577, Yosemite National Park, CA 93589; (209) 372-0200, or fax (209) 372-0371.

Trail notes: Dog Lake is an easy-to-reach destination from Tuolumne Meadows, a perfect place for a family to spend an afternoon in the high country. The hike begins near the base of Lembert Dome, then heads through a gorgeous meadow which offers views of snowy Cathedral and Unicorn Peaks. The trail traverses a granite slab, then splits off from the path to Lembert Dome and starts to climb steeply through a lodgepole pine and fir forest. When you reach an intersection with the Young Lakes Trail, you're only a quarter mile from Dog Lake. The lake is a delight to see when you finally arrive—it's set at 9,170 feet in elevation, and it's wide, shallow, and deeply blue. You can hike around its perimeter if you please, try a swim in late summer, or just sit by its peaceful shore and relax.

39 Mono Pass

8.0 mi/4.0 hrs

Location: Near Tioga Pass in Yosemite National Park; map E4, grid g8.

User groups: Hikers and horses. No dogs or mountain bikes. No wheelchair facilities.

Permits: No permits are required. There is a $20 entrance fee at Yosemite National Park, good for seven days.

Directions: From Merced, drive 70 miles northeast on Highway 140 to Yosemite National Park. Follow the signs toward Yosemite Valley, entering through the Arch Rock entrance station. Continue 4.5 miles to the left turnoff for Tioga Road/Highway 120, looping back out of the valley on Big Oak Flat Road. In 9.3 miles, turn right on Tioga Road and drive 44.5 miles to the Mono Pass Trailhead parking on the south side of the road (near road marker T-37, 1.5 miles west of Tioga Pass).

Maps: Free park maps are available at park entrance stations or by contacting Yosemite National Park at the address below. A more detailed map is available for a fee from Tom Harrison Cartography, (415) 456-7940. To obtain a topographic map of the area, ask for Tioga Pass from the USGS.

Contact: Yosemite National Park Public Information Office, P.O. Box 577, Yosemite National Park, CA 93589; (209) 372-0200, or fax (209) 372-0371.

Trail notes: With an elevation gain of only 900 feet spread out over four miles, you'll hardly even notice you're climbing on the route to Mono Pass. That's if you're acclimated, of course, because you're starting out at 9,700 feet, where the air is mighty thin. The trail passes through barren, high-elevation lodgepole pine forests and meadows, and crosses the Dana Fork of the Tuolumne River (an easy boulder-hop). Besides Mono Pass itself, the big attractions on the trail are the old mining cabins from the 19th century, some which have been restored. Take the right spur trail at 3.7 miles to see the best group of them. The hike to the pass offers great views of Mount Gibbs, Mount Dana, and the Kuna Crest. If you have the energy, continue past the pass for another half mile for even more expansive views.

㊵ Middle and Upper Gaylor Lakes

4.0 mi/2.5 hrs 3 9

Location: Near Tioga Pass in Yosemite National Park; map E4, grid g8.

User groups: Hikers only. No dogs, horses, or mountain bikes. No wheelchair facilities.

Permits: No permits are required. There is a $20 entrance fee at Yosemite National Park, good for seven days.

Directions: From Merced, drive 70 miles northeast on Highway 140 to Yosemite National Park. Follow the signs toward Yosemite Valley, entering through the Arch Rock entrance station. Continue 4.5 miles to the left turnoff for Tioga Road/Highway 120, looping back out of the valley on Big Oak Flat Road. In 9.3 miles, turn right on Tioga Road and drive 46 miles to the parking lot just west of the Tioga Pass Entrance Station, on the north side of Tioga Road.

Maps: Free park maps are available at park entrance stations or by contacting Yosemite National Park at the address below. A more detailed map is available for a fee from Tom Harrison Cartography, (415) 456-7940. To obtain a topographic map of the area, ask for Tioga Pass from the USGS.

Contact: Yosemite National Park Public Information Office, P.O. Box 577, Yosemite National Park, CA 93589; (209) 372-0200, or fax (209) 372-0371.

Trail notes: The trail to Middle and Upper Gaylor Lakes is incredibly popular, which is another way of saying that it offers world-class scenery that completely wows visitors. Starting near Tioga Pass at nearly 10,000 feet, the trail climbs a ridge and then drops down to Middle Gaylor Lake. Though it's only a mile of hiking, you'll be panting when you arrive. From there, you can follow the creek to reach smaller Upper Gaylor Lake in another mile. Just north of it by a few hundred yards is the site of the Great Sierra Mine and the remains of an old cabin. The Great Sierra Mine turned out not to be so great—no silver ore was ever refined and the mine was eventually abandoned. The hauntingly beautiful glacial scenery is what remains. Total elevation gain on the hike to Upper Gaylor Lake is about 1,000 feet.

㊶ Gardisky Lake

2.0 mi/2.0 hrs 4 8

Location: In Inyo National Forest just east of Tioga Pass; map E4, grid g9.

User groups: Hikers and dogs. No horses or mountain bikes. No wheelchair facilities.

Permits: No permits are required. Parking and access are free.

Directions: From Merced, drive 70 miles northeast on Highway 140 to Yosemite National Park. Follow the signs toward Yosemite Valley, entering through the Arch Rock entrance station. Continue 4.5 miles to the left turnoff for Tioga Road/Highway 120, looping back out of the valley on Big Oak Flat Road. In 9.3 miles, turn right on Tioga Road and drive 48 miles to the Saddlebag Lake turnoff on the left, two miles east of Tioga Pass. Turn left and go 1.3 miles to the trailhead parking area on the west side of the road (before your reach Saddlebag Lake). The trail begins on the east side of the road.

Maps: For a map of Inyo National Forest, send $4 to USDA-Forest Service, 630 Sansome Street, San Francisco, CA 94111. To obtain a topographic map of the area, ask for Tioga Pass from the USGS.

Contact: Inyo National Forest, Mono Lake Ranger District, P.O. Box 429, Lee Vining, CA 93541; (760) 647-3044, or fax (760) 647-3046.

Trail notes: How can a two-mile round-trip hike be rated a 4 for difficulty? It can because it goes straight up, gaining 1,000 feet in just one mile with not nearly enough switchbacks. Although the trail distance is short, the trailhead is set at 10,000 feet, which means you don't have much oxygen for that kind of intense climbing. Hope you're acclimated. The trip offers many rewards, though, such as fewer people than nearby Saddlebag Lake, and a stellar high alpine setting. That 11,500-foot mountain you're looking at (ahead and to your right as you climb) is Tioga Peak.

㉜ Saddlebag Lake Loop

3.6 mi/2.0 hrs

Location: In Inyo National Forest just east of Tioga Pass; map E4, grid g9.

User groups: Hikers and dogs. No horses or mountain bikes. No wheelchair facilities.

Permits: No day-use permits are required. Parking and access are free.

Directions: From Merced, drive 70 miles northeast on Highway 140 to Yosemite National Park. Follow the signs toward Yosemite Valley, entering through the Arch Rock entrance station. Continue 4.5 miles to the left turnoff for Tioga Road/Highway 120, looping back out of the valley on Big Oak Flat Road. In 9.3 miles, turn right on Tioga Road and drive 48 miles to the Saddlebag Lake turnoff on the left, two miles east of Tioga Pass. Turn left and drive another 2.5 miles to the trailhead parking area.

Maps: For a map of Inyo National Forest, send $4 to USDA-Forest Service, 630 Sansome Street, San Francisco, CA 94111. To obtain a topographic map of the area, ask for Tioga Pass from the USGS.

Contact: Inyo National Forest, Mono Lake Ranger District, P.O. Box 429, Lee Vining, CA 93541; (760) 647-3044, or fax (760) 647-3046.

Trail notes: Located just east of Tioga Pass and in the heart of the 20 Lakes Basin, Saddlebag Lake at 10,087 feet is a slice of paradise that's just outside the border of Yosemite National Park. The high alpine setting is as good as anything in the park, and, unfortunately, on summer weekends the crowds are just as apparent. A fun aspect of hiking here is that you can make a shuttle trip by hiking one way along the length of Saddlebag Lake, then take the boat taxi back (for a fee). It cuts 1.5 miles off your total mileage, and it increases the number of places you can access if you wish to go further than this loop around the lake. (You can also take the shuttle both ways and cut three miles off your trip.) The only downer to the boat taxi is that because of it, hikers sometimes have to contend with yahoos who bring coolers of food and drink with them, then leave their litter behind. Hopefully with increased education and awareness, this ludicrous behavior will stop; spread the word to offenders about "leaving no trace."

To hike along Saddlebag Lake, you can take either of two trails, on the lake's east or west side. The trail on the west side is closest to the hiker parking area and campground, and it leads 1.5 miles to little Greenstone Lake. Look to your right and you'll see the trail coming from Saddlebag Lake's east side. To make a short 3.6-

mile loop, turn right here and head back. If you continue onward instead, you'll start to climb in earnest, but your reward is the chance to visit several more lakes in the Hoover Wilderness, including Wasco, Steelhead, Shamrock, and Helen. No matter how far you go, you'll be awed by the incredibly stark scenery—just granite, water, and the occasional hearty whitebark pine.

⓭ Merced Grove

4.0 mi/2.5 hrs

Location: In western Yosemite National Park; map E4, grid h2.

User groups: Hikers only. No dogs, horses, or mountain bikes. No wheelchair facilities.

Permits: No permits are required. There is a $20 entrance fee at Yosemite National Park, good for seven days.

Directions: From Merced, drive 70 miles northeast on Highway 140 to Yosemite National Park. Follow the signs toward Yosemite Valley, entering through the Arch Rock entrance station. Continue 4.5 miles to the left turnoff for Tioga Road/Highway 120, looping back out of the valley on Big Oak Flat Road. Continue straight on Big Oak Flat Road for 15 miles (past the Tioga Road turnoff) to the Merced Grove parking area on the left. (If you enter Yosemite from the Big Oak Flat entrance station on Highway 120, you'll drive south on Big Oak Flat Road for five miles to reach the grove on your right.)

Maps: Free park maps are available at park entrance stations or by contacting Yosemite National Park at the address below. A more detailed map is available for a fee from Tom Harrison Cartography, (415) 456-7940. To obtain a topographic map of the area, ask for Ackerson Mountain from the USGS.

Contact: Yosemite National Park Public Information Office, P.O. Box 577, Yosemite National Park, CA 93589; (209) 372-0200, or fax (209) 372-0371.

Trail notes: There are three giant Sequoia groves in Yosemite National Park—Merced, Tuolumne, and Mariposa. Although all are popular, the Merced Grove is usually the quietest of the lot, which in our opinion, makes it the best. Generally it only gets visited by people who enter Yosemite from the Big Oak Flat entrance in the north, who must drive by it on their way to Yosemite Valley. The hiking is on closed-off dirt roads (which make good cross-country skiing trails in winter), but you can leave the roads and just take your time wandering among the big Sequoias, which are mixed in with white firs, incense cedars, ponderosa pines, and sugar pines. In addition to their immense size, the cinnamon color of the Sequoias' bark always gives away their identity.

⓮ Tuolumne Grove

5.0 mi/2.5 hrs

Location: In western Yosemite National Park; map E4, grid h2.

User groups: Hikers and mountain bikes. No dogs or horses. No wheelchair facilities.

Permits: No permits are required. There is a $20 entrance fee at Yosemite National Park, good for seven days.

Directions: From Merced, drive 70 miles northeast on Highway 140 to Yosemite National Park. Follow the signs toward Yosemite Valley, entering through the Arch Rock entrance station. Continue 4.5 miles to the left turnoff for Tioga Road/Highway 120, looping back out of the valley on Big Oak Flat Road. In 9.3 miles, turn right on Tioga Road, then drive one-third mile to the Tuolumne Grove parking lot on the left, near Crane Flat.

Maps: Free park maps are available at park entrance stations or by contacting Yosemite National Park at the address below. A more detailed map is available for a fee from Tom Harrison Cartography, (415) 456-7940. To obtain a topographic map of the area, ask for Ackerson Mountain from the USGS.

Contact: Yosemite National Park Public Information Office, P.O. Box 577, Yosemite National Park, CA 93589; (209) 372-0200, or fax (209) 372-0371.

Trail notes: What's nice about the Tuolumne Grove of giant Sequoias in Yosemite National Park is that you have to walk a mile and a half to access it. The grove is located on the "old" Big Oak Flat Road, which is a six-mile historic road/trail that is open to bikes and hikers but closed to cars. Leave your car at the parking lot near Crane Flat, then hike into the big trees. The Tuolumne Grove's big claim to fame is that it has one of the two remaining walk-through trees in Yosemite; this one is called the Dead Giant. It's a stump that was tunneled in 1878. Go ahead, walk through it—everybody does. The grove is especially beautiful in early spring, when you can take a snowshoe walk or cross-country ski trek through the Sequoias. Of all the sights to be seen in Yosemite, there's nothing quite like the vision of those giant trees crowned with snow.

㊺ Upper Yosemite Fall

7.2 mi/6.0 hrs

Location: In Yosemite Valley; map E4, grid h4.

User groups: Hikers only. No dogs, horses, or mountain bikes. No wheelchair facilities.

Permits: No permits are required. There is a $20 entrance fee at Yosemite National Park, good for seven days.

Directions: From Merced, drive 70 miles northeast on Highway 140 to Yosemite National Park. Follow the signs toward Yosemite Valley, entering through the Arch Rock entrance station. Continue on Highway 140/El Portal Road, which becomes Southside Drive, for 10.5 miles. Just beyond the Yosemite Chapel, bear left at the fork and head toward the village and visitor center, then turn left and drive west on Northside Drive for three-quarters of a mile to the Yosemite Lodge parking lot. Turn left and park in the lot, then walk to the Upper Fall Trailhead, which is across the road and a quarter mile to the west, between the parking lot for Sunnyside Walk-In Campground and the camp itself. You may not park in the Sunnyside lot unless you are camping there. (If you are riding the free Yosemite Valley shuttle bus, take stop number 8 and walk to the trailhead.)

Maps: Free park maps are available at park entrance stations or by contacting Yosemite National Park at the address below. A more detailed map is available for a fee from Tom Harrison Cartography, (415) 456-7940. To obtain a topographic map of the area, ask for Yosemite Falls from the USGS.

Contact: Yosemite National Park Public Information Office, P.O. Box 577, Yosemite National Park, CA 93589; (209) 372-0200, or fax (209) 372-0371.

Trail notes: If you tucker out on this demanding climb to Upper Yosemite Fall, just remember that you always have a fallback position: You can hike only 1.2 miles one way to the Columbia Point viewpoint (also called Columbia Rock), a total gain of 1,200 feet in elevation, and call it a day. The view of Yosemite Valley from Columbia Point is a stunner, and plenty of people who planned on hiking to Upper Yosemite Fall turn around here and still leave satisfied.

Those who push on are also rewarded: After a flat section of trail and then a short descent, the trail switchbacks up and up and up until, at 3.7 miles and after gaining a total of 2,700 feet, you reach the brink of Upper Yosemite Fall. You get an incredible perspective on the fall's drop and the valley floor far below. (Make sure you take the cutoff trail on your right for the best overlook point; the main trail continues on a bridge over the top of the fall.) It's a great feeling to stand at the overlook and realize that you're standing on top of the tallest waterfall in North America. Still haven't had enough? You can continue another three-quarters of a mile, crossing the bridge above the falls, to Yosemite Point (6,936 feet), where you get a stunning view of the south rim of the canyon, plus Half Dome and North Dome, and a look at the top of Lost Arrow Spire, a single shaft of granite jutting into the sky. Believe it or not, it's a popular rock climbing route.

㊻ Eagle Peak

13.5 mi/1–2 days

Location: In Yosemite Valley; map E4, grid h4.

User groups: Hikers only. No dogs, horses, or mountain bikes. No wheelchair facilities.

Permits: There is a $20 entrance fee at Yosemite National Park, good for seven days. A free wilderness permit is required for overnight stays. They are available on a first-come, first-served basis up to one day in advance at the Yosemite Wilderness kiosk near your chosen trailhead, or further in advance by mail or phone for a $3 reservation fee; call (209) 372-0740.

Directions: From Merced, drive 70 miles northeast on Highway 140 to Yosemite National Park. Follow the signs toward Yosemite Valley, and enter through the Arch Rock entrance station. Continue on Highway 140/El Portal Road, which becomes Southside Drive, for 10.5 miles. Just beyond the Yosemite Chapel, bear left at the fork and head toward the village and visitor center, then turn left and drive west on Northside Drive for three-quarters of a mile to the Yosemite Lodge parking lot. Turn left and park in the lot, then walk to the Upper Yosemite Fall Trailhead, which is across the road and a quarter mile to the west, between the parking lot for Sunnyside Walk-In Campground and the camp itself. You may not park in the Sunnyside lot unless you are camping there. (If you are riding the free Yosemite Valley shuttle bus, take stop number 8 and walk to the trailhead.)

Maps: Free park maps are available at park entrance stations or by contacting Yosemite National Park at the address below. A more detailed map is available for a fee from Tom Harrison Cartography, (415) 456-7940. To obtain a topographic map of the area, ask for Yosemite Falls from the USGS.

Contact: Yosemite National Park Public Information Office, P.O. Box 577, Yosemite National Park, CA 93589; (209) 372-0200, or fax (209) 372-0371.

Trail notes: If you seek more of a challenge than the day hike to Upper Yosemite Fall, the trail to Eagle Peak gives you all of the stunning destinations of the shorter trip—Columbia Point, Lower Yosemite Fall, Upper Yosemite Fall—plus an additional three miles one way to a lookout atop of the highest rock of the Three Brothers formation. From here, you can see not just the whole of Yosemite, but also all the way to the mountains and foothills of the Coast Range. Just make sure you pick a clear day.

Follow the trail notes for hike number 45 to Upper Yosemite Fall, then after taking the spur trail to the fall's brink, backtrack a quarter mile to the trail junction for the Eagle Peak Trail. Take the Eagle Peak Trail northwest for 1.5 miles, then hike south for one mile through Eagle Peak Meadows. At a trail junction with the El Capitan Trail, bear left for the final half-mile ascent to your final destination—the summit of Eagle Peak, elevation 7,779 feet. After completing this trip, you'll never view the Three Brothers the same way again.

47 Lower Yosemite Fall

0.5 mi/0.5 hr

Location: In Yosemite Valley; map E4, grid h4.

User groups: Hikers and wheelchairs. No dogs, horses, or mountain bikes.

Permits: No permits are required. There is a $20 entrance fee at Yosemite National Park, good for seven days.

Directions: From Merced, drive 70 miles northeast on Highway 140 to Yosemite National Park. Follow the signs to Yosemite Valley, entering through the Arch Rock entrance station. Continue on Highway 140/El Portal Road, which becomes Southside Drive, for 10.5 miles. Just beyond the Yosemite Chapel, bear left at the fork and head toward the village and visitor center, then turn left and drive west on Northside Drive for three-quarters of a mile to the Lower Yosemite Fall parking lot on your right. (If you are riding the free Yosemite Valley shuttle bus, take stop number 7.)

Maps: Free park maps are available at park entrance stations or by contacting Yosemite National Park at the address below. To obtain a topographic map of the area, ask for Half Dome from the USGS.

Contact: Yosemite National Park Public Information Office, P.O. Box 577, Yosemite National Park, CA 93589; (209) 372-0200, or fax (209) 372-0371.

Trail notes: It's so short you can hardly call it a hike, and the route is paved and crawling with people, but, nonetheless, Lower Yosemite Fall is an absolute must-do walk for visitors to Yosemite Valley. One thing is for sure: You won't need a map for this trip. From the Lower Yosemite Fall parking lot, head up the pavement to the footbridge below the falls, where in the spring you can get soaking wet from the incredible mist and spray. It's a terrific cheap thrill. The only downer to Lower Yosemite Fall is that by late summer, it and its big brother, Upper Yosemite Fall, often dry up completely. If you like water, plan your trip for sometime between April and July. The best time of day to make the trip? Check out full moon nights in the spring, when you can sometimes see "moonbows" in the lower fall. And by the way, if you want to visit Upper Yosemite Fall as well, be informed that you can't hike there from here, even though you can see the upper fall from the parking lot and on the first part of this walk. The only way to hike to the upper fall is from the trailhead near Sunnyside Campground (see hike number 45).

48 North Dome

9.0 mi/5.0 hrs

Location: Off Tioga Road in Yosemite National Park; map E4, grid h4.

User groups: Hikers only. No dogs, horses, or mountain bikes. No wheelchair facilities.

Permits: There is a $20 entrance fee at Yosemite National Park, good for seven days. A free wilderness permit is required for overnight stays. They are available on a first-come, first-served basis up to one day in advance at the Yosemite Wilderness kiosk near your chosen trailhead, or further in advance by mail or phone for a $3 reservation fee; call (209) 372-0740.

Directions: From Merced, drive 70 miles northeast on Highway 140 to Yosemite National Park. Follow the signs toward Yosemite Valley, entering through the Arch Rock entrance station. Continue 4.5 miles to the left turnoff for Tioga Road/Highway 120, looping back out of the valley on Big Oak Flat Road. In 9.3 miles, turn right on Tioga Road and drive 24.5 miles to the Porcupine Creek Trailhead parking area on the right, a mile past Porcupine Flat Campground.

Maps: Free park maps are available at park entrance stations or by contacting Yosemite National Park at the address below. A more detailed map is available for a fee from Tom Harrison Cartography, (415) 456-7940. To obtain a topographic map of the area, ask for Yosemite Falls from the USGS.

Contact: Yosemite National Park Public Information Office, P.O. Box 577, Yosemite National Park, CA 93589; (209) 372-0200, or fax (209) 372-0371.

Trail notes: There are those who say that climbing Half Dome is a disappointment, and not just because of the crowds. When you reach the top and check out the commanding view, the panorama is not quite as awesome as you might expect, and that's because you can't see Half Dome; you're standing on it. If Half Dome is an absolute necessity in your view of Yosemite,

climb North Dome instead, which offers a heart-stopping view of that big piece of granite. The route is not for the faint of heart, but when you are way up high looking down at Tenaya Canyon and across at Half Dome and Clouds Rest, well, you'll know why you came. There are two main routes to North Dome—the first is via Yosemite Valley and the Yosemite Falls Trail, but it's a long, butt-kicking trip. The better route begins at the Porcupine Creek Trailhead near Porcupine Flat Campground on Tioga Road. The dirt access road shortly brings you to a proper trail signed as Porcupine Creek. Continue straight at two possible junctions near the 2.5-mile mark, heading due south for North Dome. After the third mile your views begin to open up, providing fine vistas of North Dome and Half Dome and increasing your anticipation. At a trail junction at four miles, take the left spur for the ascent to North Dome's summit. Hope you brought plenty of film with you.

49 Mist Trail to Top of Vernal Fall

3.0 mi/2.0 hrs

Location: In Yosemite Valley; map E4, grid h5.

User groups: Hikers only. No dogs, horses, or mountain bikes. No wheelchair facilities.

Permits: No permits are required. There is a $20 entrance fee at Yosemite National Park, good for seven days.

Directions: From Merced, drive 70 miles northeast on Highway 140 to Yosemite National Park. Follow the signs toward Yosemite Valley, entering through the Arch Rock entrance station. Continue on Highway 140/El Portal Road, which becomes Southside Drive, for 11.6 miles to the day-use parking lot at Curry Village. Then, ride the free Yosemite Valley shuttle bus to Happy Isles, stop number 16. In winter, when the shuttle does not run, you must hike from the day-use parking lot in Curry Village, adding two miles to your round-trip. (Trails may be closed in winter; call to check on weather conditions.)

Maps: Free park maps are available at park entrance stations or by contacting Yosemite National Park at the address below. A more detailed map is available for a fee from Tom

Harrison Cartography, (415) 456-7940. To obtain a topographic map of the area, ask for Half Dome from the USGS.

Contact: Yosemite National Park Public Information Office, P.O. Box 577, Yosemite National Park, CA 93589; (209) 372-0200, or fax (209) 372-0371.

Trail notes: To hike to the top of Vernal Fall, you have to take the free Yosemite shuttle bus to Happy Isles to start your trip (or add an extra mile each way, hiking from the day-use parking area in Curry Village to Happy Isles). But once that's accomplished, prepare yourself for a stellar, world-class walk to one of the most photographed waterfalls in the world. The only minus is the hordes of people, so make your trip more enjoyable by starting early in the morning, before they're out in full force.

While many people hike only to the Vernal Fall footbridge, eight-tenths of a mile from Happy Isles, it's definitely worth the extra effort to push on another half mile to reach the top of Vernal Fall. To do so means ascending the Mist Trail's famous granite stairway that curves around the side of Vernal Fall, so close to it that you feel like you are practically a part of the waterfall. Actually, you are—hikers are inevitably drenched in spray and mist, particularly in springtime. Be sure to bring a rain poncho if you don't like getting wet. The route is an easy climb to the Vernal Falls bridge, then a steep tromp up the seemingly endless stairs to the top of the falls. Total elevation gain is 1,050 feet. It's a trip you have to do at least once in your life.

㊿ Mist and John Muir Loop to Nevada Fall

6.5 mi/4.0 hrs

Location: In Yosemite Valley; map E4, grid h5.

User groups: Hikers only. No dogs or mountain bikes. Horses are allowed only on the John Muir Trail. No wheelchair facilities.

Permits: No permits are required. There is a $20 entrance fee at Yosemite National Park, good for seven days.

Directions: From Merced, drive 70 miles northeast on Highway 140 to Yosemite National Park. Follow the signs toward Yosemite Valley, entering through the Arch Rock entrance sta-

tion. Continue on Highway 140/El Portal Road, which becomes Southside Drive, for 11.6 miles to the day-use parking lot at Curry Village. Then ride the free Yosemite Valley shuttle bus to Happy Isles, stop number 16. In winter, when the shuttle does not run, you must hike from the day-use parking lot in Curry Village, adding two miles to your round-trip. (Trails may be closed in winter; call to check on weather conditions.)

Maps: Free park maps are available at park entrance stations or by contacting Yosemite National Park at the address below. A more detailed map is available for a fee from Tom Harrison Cartography, (415) 456-7940. To obtain a topographic map of the area, ask for Half Dome from the USGS.

Contact: Yosemite National Park Public Information Office, P.O. Box 577, Yosemite National Park, CA 93589; (209) 372-0200, or fax (209) 372-0371.

Trail notes: You can hike either the John Muir Trail or the Mist Trail to reach Yosemite's classic Nevada Fall, and since both trails are stunning scenery all the way, the choice is really about how you like your steep parts—on the way up or the way down? Many people prefer to hike up on the Mist Trail, even though it's much steeper, because you can look around at the scenery while you're climbing up on the Mist Trail's treacherous granite staircase, but you have to look down at your feet while descending. Others want the easiest ascent, which makes the John Muir Trail the preferred choice for the way up. Both trails join at two different points, above and below Nevada Fall, so take your pick.

For either route, start at Happy Isles and walk to the footbridge over the Merced River. Shortly after the bridge, the two trails diverge, then merge again just above Nevada Fall. (You can also transfer from one trail to the other via a quarter-mile connector trail at Clark Point, just above Vernal Fall.) Our vote is to stay on the Mist Trail for the first 1.2 miles to the top of Vernal Fall, then take your pick for the route between Vernal and Nevada Falls, and take your pick again for the return trip. Total elevation gain to the top of 594-foot-tall Nevada Fall is 2,600 feet, a healthy climb. But when you get to walk this close to two world-class waterfalls, who's complaining?

(51) Mirror Lake/Tenaya Canyon Loop

4.5 mi/2.0 hrs 1 8

Location: In Yosemite Valley; map E4, grid h5.

User groups: Hikers only. No dogs, horses, or mountain bikes. No wheelchair facilities.

Permits: No permits are required. There is a $20 entrance fee at Yosemite National Park, good for seven days.

Directions: From Merced, drive 70 miles northeast on Highway 140 to Yosemite National Park. Follow the signs toward Yosemite Valley, entering through the Arch Rock entrance station. Continue on Highway 140/El Portal Road, which becomes Southside Drive, for 11.6 miles to the day-use parking lot at Curry Village. Then ride the free Yosemite Valley shuttle bus to Mirror Lake Junction, stop number 17.

Maps: Free park maps are available at park entrance stations or by contacting Yosemite National Park at the address below. A more detailed map is available for a fee from Tom Harrison Cartography, (415) 456-7940. To obtain a topographic map of the area, ask for Half Dome from the USGS.

Contact: Yosemite National Park Public Information Office, P.O. Box 577, Yosemite National Park, CA 93589; (209) 372-0200, or fax (209) 372-0371.

Trail notes: If you start your trip from Mirror Lake Junction (you can take the shuttle bus to stop number 17 or add on an extra 1.5 miles round-trip from the Curry Village parking area), you can get away from a good chunk of the valley traffic on this easy, mostly flat loop trip into Tenaya Canyon. Walk a half mile on pavement to Mirror Lake, then follow the foot trail beyond it up Tenaya Creek for 1.5 miles, then circle back. Check out the great views of Half Dome and Basket Dome. If you want to see Mirror Lake looking more like a lake and less like a meadow, make this trip in springtime. The lake is slowly undergoing the process of sedimentation—it's filling with sand and gravel from Tenaya Creek—and even in spring is quite shallow. The loop trail is nearly flat the whole way, and once you get past Mirror Lake and into Tenaya Canyon, you may even find a little privacy.

Special note: As of early 1997, this trail is undergoing a transformation, as the park begins to remove the asphalt from sections of Yosemite Valley. As a result, the shuttle bus stop may be moved to a new location, and parts of the route may no longer be paved.

(52) Half Dome

17.0 mi/1–2 days 5 9

Location: In Yosemite Valley; map E4, grid h5.

User groups: Hikers only. No dogs, horses, or mountain bikes. No wheelchair facilities.

Permits: A free wilderness permit is required for overnight stays. They are available on a first-come, first-served basis up to one day in advance at the Yosemite Wilderness kiosk near your chosen trailhead, or further in advance by mail or phone for a $3 reservation fee; call (209) 372-0740. There is a $20 entrance fee at Yosemite National Park, good for seven days.

Directions: From Merced, drive 70 miles northeast on Highway 140 to Yosemite National Park. Follow the signs toward Yosemite Valley, entering through the Arch Rock entrance station. Continue on Highway 140/El Portal Road, which becomes Southside Drive, for 11.6 miles to the day-use parking lot at Curry Village. Then, ride the free Yosemite Valley shuttle bus to Happy Isles, stop number 16.

Maps: Free park maps are available at park entrance stations or by contacting Yosemite National Park at the address below. A more detailed map is available for a fee from Tom Harrison Cartography, (415) 456-7940. To obtain a topographic map of the area, ask for Half Dome from the USGS.

Contact: Yosemite National Park Public Information Office, P.O. Box 577, Yosemite National Park, CA 93589; (209) 372-0200, or fax (209) 372-0371.

Trail notes: No argument about it, Half Dome is one of those once-in-your-life-you-gotta-do-it hikes. Just be sure you know what you're in for before you set out on this epic trail: You're looking at 17 miles round-trip, a 4,800-foot elevation gain, and an incredible amount of company. Plenty of people make the journey as a day hike, and if you do so, make sure to bring a load of water and food with you. You'll be handing it out to others who are not so well prepared, as well as gulping it down yourself. Follow either the John Muir Trail or the Mist Trail from Happy Isles to the top of Nevada Fall (see hike number 50), then go left and enter Little Yosemite Valley, where backpackers can make camp. At 6.2 miles, the John Muir Trail splits off from the Half Dome Trail, and you head left for Half Dome. Everything usually goes smoothly until you reach the steel cables that run 200 yards up the back of the dome, at which point you'll start praying a lot and wishing there weren't so many other hikers on the cables with you. Do some soul-searching before you begin the cable ascent—turning around is not an option once you're halfway up. When you reach the top, the views are so incredible that you forget all about your tired arms and feet. During the summer, about 500 people a day make this trip. To make it easier, camp at Little Yosemite Valley (4.7 miles in, wilderness permit required) and save the final ascent for the next day.

(53) Hites Cove

9.0 mi/5.0 hrs 2 10

Location: On the South Fork of the Merced River; map E4, grid i1.

User groups: Hikers, dogs, horses, and mountain bikes. No wheelchair facilities.

Permits: All hikers must register at Savage's Trading Post. Parking and access are free.

Directions: From Mariposa, drive 22 miles east on Highway 140 to Savage's Trading Post. The parking area is on the north side of the road, but the trail actually begins on the south side, near Savage's Trading Post.

Maps: For a map of Sierra National Forest, send $4 to USDA-Forest Service, 630 Sansome Street, San Francisco, CA 94111. To obtain a topographic map of the area, ask for El Portal from the USGS.

Contact: Sierra National Forest, Mariposa Ranger District, 41969 Highway 41, Oakhurst, CA 93644; (209) 683-4665 or fax (209) 683-7258.

Trail notes: The best part of the 22-mile South Fork of the Merced River Trail is the Hites Cove portion that begins at Savage's Trading Post on Highway 140. It runs 4.5 miles one way to Hites Cove four-wheel-drive road. Considered by many to be the premier Sierra spring wildflower trail, the Hites Cove Trail offers hikers a look at 60 flower varieties, including goldfields, lupine, poppies, brodaiea, monkeyflower, shooting stars, fiesta flowers, fairy lanterns, baby blue eyes, and Indian pinks. To see them, visit from March to May, before the show is over. (Often this is the only time during the year when the trail is open.) The only downers along the route are the hordes of people who flock here during that brief period, and the fact that the first three-quarters of a mile of trail are on private property. (You start hiking on a paved driveway.)

Hikers wishing to turn this into an overnight can camp at Hites Cove, the sight of the 1879 Hites Cove Hotel, then continue hiking to Devil's Gulch, 2.5 miles further. To do so, however, requires crossing the South Fork Merced River at Hites Cove, a difficult feat early in the year.

Special note: Call the Mariposa Ranger District to make sure this trail is open before planning your trip. Usually the trail is only open for two or three months in the spring.

(54) Inspiration and Stanford Points

7.6 mi/4.0 hrs 3 9

Location: In Yosemite Valley near the Wawona Tunnel; map E4, grid i3.

User groups: Hikers only. No dogs, horses, or mountain bikes. No wheelchair facilities.

Permits: No permits are required. There is a $20 entrance fee at Yosemite National Park, good for seven days.

Directions: From Merced, drive 70 miles northeast on Highway 140 to Yosemite National Park. Follow the signs to Yosemite Valley, entering through the Arch Rock entrance station. Continue on Highway 140/El Portal Road, which becomes Southside Drive, for 6.3 miles, then turn right at the fork for Highway 41/Wawona/Fresno. Continue 1.5 miles to the parking lots on either side of the road just before you enter the Wawona Tunnel. The trailhead is at the parking lot on the left (south) side of the road.

Maps: Free park maps are available at park

entrance stations or by contacting Yosemite National Park at the address below. A more detailed map is available for a fee from Tom Harrison Cartography, (415) 456-7940. To obtain a topographic map of the area, ask for El Capitan from the USGS.

Contact: Yosemite National Park Public Information Office, P.O. Box 577, Yosemite National Park, CA 93589; (209) 372-0200, or fax (209) 372-0371.

Trail notes: You need a little inspiration? You came to the right place. The view from the Wawona Tunnel Trailhead should be enough to inspire you (check out the panorama of Yosemite Valley, El Capitan, Half Dome, and Bridalveil Fall), but if it's not, just do a little climbing on the Pohono Trail to Inspiration Point and Stanford Point. The trail is uphill but well graded, and just long enough to give you a good workout. The first mile of trail is mostly forested, exhibiting no sign of the vistas to come, and the trail climbs 1,000 feet over this stretch. At 1.3 miles the route reaches Inspiration Point, where the view is somewhat obscured by trees, but keep heading upward for another 1,000-foot climb and eventually you'll cross Meadow Brook and reach the left cutoff trail for Stanford Point. You're 3.8 miles from the trailhead and you've climbed 2,200 feet, but your reward is an eagle's-eye view of the valley floor 3,000 feet below.

55 Bridalveil Fall

0.5 mi/0.5 hr

Location: In Yosemite Valley; map E4, grid i3.

User groups: Hikers and wheelchairs. No dogs, horses, or mountain bikes.

Permits: No permits are required. There is a $20 entrance fee at Yosemite National Park, good for seven days.

Directions: From Merced, drive 70 miles northeast on Highway 140 to Yosemite National Park. Follow the signs toward Yosemite Valley, entering through the Arch Rock entrance station. Continue on Highway 140/El Portal Road, which becomes Southside Drive, for 6.3 miles, then turn right at the fork for Highway 41/Wawona/Fresno. Turn left almost immediately into the Bridalveil Fall parking lot. The trail begins at the end of the parking lot. (If you are driving into the park from

the southern entrance near Wawona, watch for the Bridalveil Fall turnoff on your right as you drive into the valley on Highway 41.)

Maps: Free park maps are available at park entrance stations or by contacting Yosemite National Park at the address below. To obtain a topographic map of the area, ask for El Capitan from the USGS.

Contact: Yosemite National Park Public Information Office, P.O. Box 577, Yosemite National Park, CA 93589; (209) 372-0200, or fax (209) 372-0371.

Trail notes: Bridalveil Fall is right up there with Lower Yosemite Fall as a must-do walk for visitors to Yosemite Valley. Like that other famous waterfall walk, the path to Bridalveil Fall is paved and crowded with people. Still, it's awesome. The best thing about this waterfall is that unlike the other falls in Yosemite Valley, Bridalveil runs year-round; it never dries up and disappoints visitors. The walk to its overlook is short and nearly level, and the small viewing area is about 70 yards from the fall. You can look straight up and see Bridalveil Creek plunging 620 feet off the edge of the south canyon wall. In high wind, the fall billows and sways, and if you are lucky, you might see rainbows dancing in its mist. Another bonus is that in spring, your position at the Bridalveil overlook is such that if you turn around, you get an excellent view of Ribbon Fall flowing off the northern Yosemite Valley rim. Ribbon Fall is the highest single drop in the park at 1,612 feet.

56 McGurk Meadow

2.0 mi/1.0 hr

Location: Off Glacier Point Road in Yosemite National Park; map E4, grid i4.

User groups: Hikers only. No dogs, horses, or mountain bikes. No wheelchair facilities.

Permits: No permits are required. There is a $20 entrance fee at Yosemite National Park, good for seven days.

Directions: From Merced, drive 70 miles northeast on Highway 140 to Yosemite National Park. Follow the signs toward Yosemite Valley, entering through the Arch Rock entrance station. Continue on Highway 140/El Portal Road, which becomes Southside Drive, for 6.3 miles, then turn right at the fork for Highway 41/ Wawona/Fresno. Continue for 9.2 miles, then turn left on Glacier Point Road and drive 7.5 miles to the McGurk Meadow Trailhead on the left. Park in the pullout about 75 yards further up the road.

Maps: Free park maps are available at park entrance stations or by contacting Yosemite National Park at the address below. A more detailed map is available for a fee from Tom Harrison Cartography, (415) 456-7940. To obtain a topographic map of the area, ask for Half Dome from the USGS.

Contact: Yosemite National Park Public Information Office, P.O. Box 577, Yosemite National Park, CA 93589; (209) 372-0200, or fax (209) 372-0371.

Trail notes: Some hikes make you feel overjoyed to be alive, and the McGurk Meadow Trail is one of those. The trailhead is the first one you reach as you wind along Glacier Point Road to spectacular Glacier Point, and it's definitely worth stopping to take the short walk through a fir and pine forest to pristine McGurk Meadow. A quarter mile before you reach the meadow, you pass an old pioneer cabin on your left, still standing in half-decent repair. Then you come out to the mile-long meadow, and a footbridge carries you across a tiny stream that makes lazy S-turns through the grasses. You can follow the trail along the north edge of McGurk Meadow as far as you please (the route connects to the Pohono Trail, which traverses Yosemite's south rim), or do what we did: Just stand there on the footbridge and be touched by the beauty.

🔟 Bridalveil Creek

3.4 mi/1.5 hrs

Location: Off Glacier Point Road in Yosemite National Park; map E4, grid i4.

User groups: Hikers only. No dogs, horses, or mountain bikes. No wheelchair facilities.

Permits: No permits are required. There is a $20 entrance fee at Yosemite National Park, good for seven days.

Directions: From Merced, drive 70 miles northeast on Highway 140 to Yosemite National Park. Follow the signs toward Yosemite Valley, entering through the Arch Rock entrance station. Con-

tinue on Highway 140/El Portal Road, which becomes Southside Drive, for 6.3 miles, then turn right at the fork for Highway 41/Wawona/Fresno. Continue for 9.2 miles, then turn left on Glacier Point Road and drive another 8.9 miles to the Ostrander Lake Trailhead on the right.

Maps: Free park maps are available at park entrance stations or by contacting Yosemite National Park at the address below. A more detailed map is available for a fee from Tom Harrison Cartography, (415) 456-7940. To obtain a topographic map of the area, ask for Half Dome from the USGS.

Contact: Yosemite National Park Public Information Office, P.O. Box 577, Yosemite National Park, CA 93589; (209) 372-0200, or fax (209) 372-0371.

Trail notes: Maybe the best time to hike to Bridalveil Creek from Glacier Point Road is to do it immediately after visiting Bridalveil Fall. After a short walk through a fire-scarred area, you wind up at the edge of Bridalveil Creek, a babbling brook that seems far too tame to be able to produce the giant waterfall downstream. It's a great lesson for children, as is the abundance of new growth in the burned areas of the forest.

To make the trip, follow the Ostrander Lake Trail from Glacier Point Road for 1.4 miles, then when the trail splits, take the right fork toward Bridalveil Creek. You reach it in less than a quarter mile. The stream is so tame here that there is no bridge to cross it—it's just an easy rock-hop by midsummer. Pick a spot along its banks, and spend some time counting the wildflowers.

🔟 Ostrander Lake

12.5 mi/1–2 days

Location: Off Glacier Point Road in Yosemite National Park; map E4, grid i4.

User groups: Hikers only. No dogs, horses, or mountain bikes. No wheelchair facilities.

Permits: There is a $20 entrance fee at Yosemite National Park, good for seven days. A free wilderness permit is required for overnight stays. They are available on a first-come, first-served basis up to one day in advance at the Yosemite Wilderness kiosk near your chosen trailhead, or further in advance by mail or phone for a $3 reservation fee; call (209) 372-0740.

Directions: From Merced, drive 70 miles northeast on Highway 140 to Yosemite National Park. Follow the signs toward Yosemite Valley, entering through the Arch Rock entrance station. Continue on Highway 140/El Portal Road, which becomes Southside Drive, for 6.3 miles, then turn right at the fork for Highway 41/Wawona/Fresno. Continue for 9.2 miles, then turn left on Glacier Point Road and drive 8.9 miles to the Ostrander Lake Trailhead on the right.

Maps: Free park maps are available at park entrance stations or by contacting Yosemite National Park at the address below. A more detailed map is available for a fee from Tom Harrison Cartography, (415) 456-7940. To obtain topographic maps of the area, ask for Half Dome and Mariposa Grove from the USGS.

Contact: Yosemite National Park Public Information Office, P.O. Box 577, Yosemite National Park, CA 93589; (209) 372-0200, or fax (209) 372-0371.

Trail notes: While many people take short day hikes from Glacier Point Road, a longer 12.5-mile trip to Ostrander Lake may better suit your desires. You can hike out and back in a day, or get a wilderness permit and camp near the lake's shores. The wide blue lake, set at 8,580 feet, is a popular destination of cross-country skiers in the winter, as is evidenced by the stone Ostrander Ski Hut. Although the trail (really an old road) begins in a burned area, it then traverses through a typical high country landscape of firs, pines, and as you ascend, granite. You have to gain 1,600 feet along the way, most of it in the final three miles to the lake, but you are continually spurred on by excellent views of Half Dome, North Dome, and Liberty Cap. Now that's incentive.

⑤⑨ Sentinel Dome

2.0 mi/1.0 hr

Location: Off Glacier Point Road in Yosemite National Park; map E4, grid i4.

User groups: Hikers only. No dogs, horses, or mountain bikes. No wheelchair facilities.

Permits: No permits are required. There is a $20 entrance fee at Yosemite National Park, good for seven days.

Directions: From Merced, drive 70 miles north-

east on Highway 140 to Yosemite National Park. Follow the signs to Yosemite Valley, entering through the Arch Rock entrance station. Continue on Highway 140/El Portal Road, which becomes Southside Drive, for 6.3 miles, then turn right at the fork for Highway 41/Wawona/Fresno. Continue for 9.2 miles, then turn left on Glacier Point Road and drive 13.2 miles to the Taft Point/Sentinel Dome Trailhead parking lot, on the left side of the road.

Maps: Free park maps are available at park entrance stations or by contacting Yosemite National Park at the address below. A more detailed map is available for a fee from Tom Harrison Cartography, (415) 456-7940. To obtain a topographic map of the area, ask for Half Dome from the USGS.

Contact: Yosemite National Park Public Information Office, P.O. Box 577, Yosemite National Park, CA 93589; (209) 372-0200, or fax (209) 372-0371.

Trail notes: It's hard to believe you can get so much for so little, but on the Sentinel Dome Trail, you can. The granite dome is located about a mile before Glacier Point on Glacier Point Road, and its elevation is 1,000 feet higher than the point's. That means stellar views are yours for the asking. A nearly flat one-mile walk leads you to the base of the dome, and a 50-yard scramble up its smooth granite back side brings you to its summit. There you are greeted by stunning vistas in all directions, including an unusual perspective on Upper and Lower Yosemite Falls. Sentinel Dome is a great family hike, and to make a longer day of it, you can easily combine it with hike number 60 to Taft Point and The Fissures, which starts from the same trailhead but heads in the opposite direction.

⑥⓪ Taft Point and The Fissures

2.0 mi/1.0 hr

Location: Off Glacier Point Road in Yosemite National Park; map E4, grid i4.

User groups: Hikers only. No dogs, horses, or mountain bikes. No wheelchair facilities.

Permits: No permits are required. There is a $20 entrance fee at Yosemite National Park, good for seven days.

Directions: From Merced, drive 70 miles northeast on Highway 140 to Yosemite National Park. Follow the signs to Yosemite Valley, entering through the Arch Rock entrance station. Continue on Highway 140/El Portal Road, which becomes Southside Drive, for 6.3 miles, then turn right at the fork for Highway 41/Wawona/Fresno. Continue for 9.2 miles, then turn left on Glacier Point Road and drive 13.2 miles to the Taft Point/Sentinel Dome Trailhead parking lot, on the left side of the road.

Maps: Free park maps are available at park entrance stations or by contacting Yosemite National Park at the address below. A more detailed map is available for a fee from Tom Harrison Cartography, (415) 456-7940. To obtain a topographic map of the area, ask for Half Dome from the USGS.

Contact: Yosemite National Park Public Information Office, P.O. Box 577, Yosemite National Park, CA 93589; (209) 372-0200, or fax (209) 372-0371.

Trail notes: It's not so much the sweeping vista from Taft Point that you remember; although certainly you could say that the views of Yosemite's north rim and the valley floor are stunning. What you remember is the incredible sense of awe that you feel, perhaps mixed with a little fear and a lot of respect, as you peek down into The Fissures in Taft Point's granite—huge cracks in the rock that plunge hundreds of feet down toward the valley. One of the fissures has a couple of large boulders captured in its jaws; they're stuck there waiting for the next big earthquake or Ice Age to set them free. Be sure to walk to the piped railing along the edge of the cliff, where you can hold on tight and peer down at the valley far, far below. If you have kids with you, or anyone who is afraid of heights, be sure to keep a tight hand-hold on them.

Directions: From Merced, drive 70 miles northeast on Highway 140 to Yosemite National Park. Follow the signs to Yosemite Valley, entering through the Arch Rock entrance station. Continue on Highway 140/El Portal Road, which becomes Southside Drive, for 9.5 miles. The trailhead is located next to mile marker V18, on the right side of Southside Drive. Park in the pullouts along the road.

Maps: Free park maps are available at park entrance stations or by contacting Yosemite National Park at the address below. A more detailed map is available for a fee from Tom Harrison Cartography, (415) 456-7940. To obtain a topographic map of the area, ask for Half Dome from the USGS.

Contact: Yosemite National Park Public Information Office, P.O. Box 577, Yosemite National Park, CA 93589; (209) 372-0200, or fax (209) 372-0371.

Trail notes: Many years ago, one of us hiked this trail on our first-ever visit to Yosemite, and was shocked when we got to the top and found a giant parking lot and refreshment stand located there. What, you mean we could have driven to the high point on this trail? It's true, but your arrival at dramatic Glacier Point is somehow made all the more meaningful if you get there the hard way, which means hiking the Four-Mile Trail all the way up from the valley floor, gaining 3,220 feet in 4.8 miles (not four miles, as the name implies). The trail is partially shaded, and makes for a terrific day hike with an early morning start, then you can have a leisurely brunch or lunch from your bird's-eye perch on Glacier Point. From the point, you get unobstructed views of just about everything, most notably Half Dome, Basket Dome, Yosemite Falls, Vernal and Nevada Falls, and the valley floor, far, far below you.

61 Four-Mile Trail

9.6 mi/6.0 hrs

Location: In Yosemite Valley; map E4, grid i4.

User groups: Hikers only. No dogs, horses, or mountain bikes. No wheelchair facilities.

Permits: No permits are required. There is a $20 entrance fee at Yosemite National Park, good for seven days.

62 Pohono Trail

13.0 mi. one way/7.0 hrs

Location: Off Glacier Point Road in Yosemite National Park; map E4, grid i5.

User groups: Hikers only. No dogs, horses, or mountain bikes. No wheelchair facilities.

Permits: There is a $20 entrance fee at Yosemite National Park, good for seven days. A free wilderness permit is required for overnight stays. They are available on a first-come, first-served basis up to one day in advance at the Yosemite Wilderness kiosk near your chosen trailhead, or further in advance by mail or phone for a $3 reservation fee; call (209) 372-0740.

Directions: From Merced, drive 70 miles northeast on Highway 140 to Yosemite National Park. Follow the signs to Yosemite Valley, entering through the Arch Rock entrance station. Continue on Highway 140/El Portal Road, which becomes Southside Drive, for 6.3 miles, then turn right at the fork for Highway 41/Wawona/Fresno. Continue for 9.2 miles, then turn left on Glacier Point Road and drive 15.7 miles to Glacier Point. The Pohono Trail heads west from the point and crosses over Glacier Point Road two times (near the parking lot).

Maps: Free park maps are available at park entrance stations or by contacting Yosemite National Park at the address below. A more detailed map is available for a fee from Tom Harrison Cartography, (415) 456-7940. To obtain topographic maps of the area, ask for Half Dome and El Capitan from the USGS.

Contact: Yosemite National Park Public Information Office, P.O. Box 577, Yosemite National Park, CA 93589; (209) 372-0200, or fax (209) 372-0371.

Trail notes: If you can arrange a shuttle trip, the Pohono Trail from Glacier Point downhill to its end at Wawona Tunnel has some incredible offerings. The two ends of the trail have the best drive-to viewpoints in all of Yosemite, and in between you are treated to dozens of other scenic spots, including Sentinel Dome at 1.5 miles, Taft Point at 3.8 miles, as well as four bird's-eye lookouts over the valley floor: Inspiration, Stanford, Dewey, and Crocker Points.

Starting at Glacier Point and ending at Wawona Tunnel, you'll cover a 2,800-foot descent, but there are some ups along the way, too, like at the very beginning from Glacier Point to Sentinel Dome. Remember to bring along a good map, because many of the best offerings are just off the trail, and if you don't take the spur routes to reach them, you'll miss out on some spectacular scenery. Note: The view of Yosemite Falls from the Pohono Trail in front of Sentinel Dome is the best in all of Yosemite.

(63) Panorama Trail

8.5 mi. one way/5.0 hrs

Location: Off Glacier Point Road in Yosemite National Park; map E4, grid i5.

User groups: Hikers only. No dogs, horses, or mountain bikes. No wheelchair facilities.

Permits: No permits are required. There is a $20 entrance fee at Yosemite National Park, good for seven days.

Directions: From Merced, drive 70 miles northeast on Highway 140 to Yosemite National Park. Follow the signs to Yosemite Valley, entering through the Arch Rock entrance station. Continue on Highway 140/El Portal Road, which becomes Southside Drive, for 6.3 miles, then turn right at the fork for Highway 41/Wawona/Fresno. Continue for 9.2 miles, then turn left on Glacier Point Road and drive 15.7 miles to Glacier Point. The Panorama Trail heads east from the point.

Maps: Free park maps are available at park entrance stations or by contacting Yosemite National Park at the address below. A more detailed map is available for a fee from Tom Harrison Cartography, (415) 456-7940. To obtain a topographic map of the area, ask for Half Dome from the USGS.

Contact: Yosemite National Park Public Information Office, P.O. Box 577, Yosemite National Park, CA 93589; (209) 372-0200, or fax (209) 372-0371.

Trail notes: It's an incredibly spectacular route to walk from Glacier Point to Yosemite Valley, downhill most of the way, passing more mind-boggling scenery than you can shake a stick at, but you've got to have a shuttle car waiting at the end, or it's a heck of a long climb back up. A great option is to take the Glacier Point Hiker's Bus for one leg of the trip (phone 209/372-1240 for rates and pickup times). The well-named Panorama Trail begins at Glacier Point, elevation 7,214 feet, the trailhead with what is probably the grandest view in the West. You switchback down from the point, accompanied by ever-changing perspectives on Half Dome, Basket Dome, North Dome, Liberty Cap, and far-off Vernal and Nevada Falls. You will gape a lot. After passing Illilouette Fall and climbing a bit for the first time on the trip, continue eastward to the

Panorama Trail's end near the top of Nevada Fall. Take the short spur to the top of the fall, then continue downhill (and now westward) on either the John Muir Trail or the Mist Trail, passing Vernal Fall along the way. (If you take the John Muir Trail, make sure you take the spur trail off it that leads to Vernal Fall. The Mist Trail goes directly by Vernal Fall.) The hike ends at Happy Isles, where you can take the free valley shuttle bus to the pickup point for the Glacier Point Hiker's Bus, or to your shuttle car parked somewhere in the valley. Note that the entire route has a 3,200-foot elevation loss over its course, but there is also a 760-foot climb to make after you cross Illilouette Creek. Also be forewarned that while the starting miles of the trip are very peaceful, the final two miles by Vernal Fall can be a parade of people.

⑥④ Illilouette Fall

4.0 mi/2.5 hrs

Location: Off Glacier Point Road in Yosemite National Park; map E4, grid i5.

User groups: Hikers only. No dogs, horses, or mountain bikes. No wheelchair facilities.

Permits: No permits are required. There is a $20 entrance fee at Yosemite National Park, good for seven days.

Directions: From Merced, drive 70 miles northeast on Highway 140 to Yosemite National Park. Follow the signs to Yosemite Valley, entering through the Arch Rock entrance station. Continue on Highway 140/El Portal Road, which becomes Southside Drive, for 6.3 miles, then turn right at the fork for Highway 41/Wawona/Fresno. Continue for 9.2 miles, then turn left on Glacier Point Road and drive 15.7 miles to Glacier Point. The trail begins on the right side of the point.

Maps: Free park maps are available at park entrance stations or by contacting Yosemite National Park at the address below. A more detailed map is available for a fee from Tom Harrison Cartography, (415) 456-7940. To obtain a topographic map of the area, ask for Half Dome from the USGS.

Contact: Yosemite National Park Public Information Office, P.O. Box 577, Yosemite National Park, CA 93589; (209) 372-0200, or fax (209) 372-0371.

Trail notes: Those who can't afford the time or make the car shuttle arrangements necessary to hike the entire Panorama Trail should at least take this incredible out-and-back trip on the top portion of the route. Glacier Point is your starting point and the bridge above Illilouette Fall becomes your destination, but what happens in between is sheer magic. Some say that hiking the Panorama Trail is like staring at a life-size Yosemite postcard, but we say it's more like being in the postcard. As you walk, you feel like you've become one with the magnificent panorama of Half Dome, Basket Dome, North Dome, Liberty Cap, and far-off Vernal and Nevada Falls. The trail is downhill all the way to Illilouette Fall in two miles, which means you have a 1,200-foot elevation gain on the return trip. The path is extremely well graded, though, so even children can make the climb. After viewing the waterfall from a trailside overlook, walk another quarter mile and stand on the bridge that is perched just above the 370-foot drop. Don't think about swimming here, for obvious reasons.

⑥⑤ Wawona Meadow Loop

3.2 mi/1.25 hrs

Location: Off Highway 41 near Wawona, in Yosemite National Park; map E4, grid j3.

User groups: Hikers, dogs, and mountain bikes. No horses. No wheelchair facilities.

Permits: No permits are required. There is a $20 entrance fee at Yosemite National Park, good for seven days.

Directions: From Merced, drive 70 miles northeast on Highway 140 to Yosemite National Park. Follow the signs toward Yosemite Valley, entering through the Arch Rock entrance station. Continue on Highway 140/El Portal Road, which becomes Southside Drive, for 6.3 miles, then turn right at the fork for Highway 41/Wawona/Fresno. Drive 27 miles to the trailhead, which is just south of the golf course and across the road from the Wawona Hotel.

Maps: Free park maps are available at park entrance stations or by contacting Yosemite National Park at the address below. A more detailed map is available for a fee from Tom Harrison Cartography, (415) 456-7940. To obtain a topographic map of the area, ask for Wawona from the USGS.

Contact: Yosemite National Park Public Information Office, P.O. Box 577, Yosemite National Park, CA 93589; (209) 372-0200, or fax (209) 372-0371.

Trail notes: Hey, sometimes you just want to take a stroll in the park, and the Wawona Meadow Loop is just that. On one trip to Yosemite, we ignored this trail because of its proximity to the Wawona Golf Course, the presence of which insulted our hiking sensibilities. But on another trip we gave the Wawona Meadow Loop a try, and wound up liking it. On the easy, flat trail, you see and smell terrific wildflowers in late spring and summer, enjoy the good company of butterflies, and generally have a terrific lazy stroll around a pretty meadow. From the signed trailhead across the road from the Wawona Hotel, hike to your left on the dirt road, following the split rail fence, then loop around the meadow. You can even bring your dog or ride your bike, a rarity in Yosemite. If you're staying at the Wawona Hotel, you can hike from there, crossing the Wawona Road on your way out and back.

---

66 Chilnualna Falls

8.2 mi/5.0 hrs

Location: Off Highway 41 near Wawona, in Yosemite National Park; map E4, grid j3.

User groups: Hikers and horses. No dogs or mountain bikes. No wheelchair facilities.

Permits: There is a $20 entrance fee at Yosemite National Park, good for seven days. A free wilderness permit is required for overnight stays. They are available on a first-come, first-served basis up to one day in advance at the Yosemite Wilderness kiosk near your chosen trailhead, or further in advance by mail or phone for a $3 reservation fee; call (209) 372-0740.

Directions: From Merced, drive 55 miles northeast on Highway 140 to Yosemite National Park. Follow the signs to Yosemite Valley, entering through the Arch Rock entrance station. Continue on Highway 140/El Portal Road, which becomes Southside Drive, for 6.3 miles, then turn right at the fork for Highway 41/Wawona/Fresno. Drive south on the Wawona Road (Highway 41) for 25

miles to Wawona, then turn left on Chilnualna Falls Road. Drive 1.7 miles east and park in the lot on the right side of the road. Walk back to Chilnualna Falls Road and pick up the single-track trail across the pavement.

Maps: Free park maps are available at park entrance stations or by contacting Yosemite National Park at the address below. A more detailed map is available for a fee from Tom Harrison Cartography, (415) 456-7940. To obtain topographic maps of the area, ask for Wawona and Mariposa Grove from the USGS.

Contact: Yosemite National Park Public Information Office, P.O. Box 577, Yosemite National Park, CA 93589; (209) 372-0200, or fax (209) 372-0371.

Trail notes: Are you ready to climb? Pick a nice, cool day, since you're here in the lower-elevation part of Yosemite, and prepare for a steady four-mile uphill, gaining 2,400 feet to reach Chilnualna Falls. Your nose will be continually assaulted with the intoxicating smell of bear clover, which together with manzanita and oaks makes up the majority of the vegetation along the route. Halfway up you get a great view of Wawona Dome (elevation 6,897 feet) from a granite overlook. This is a great place to take a break and stretch your hamstrings. Shortly thereafter you begin to glimpse a section of Chilnualna Falls, high up on a cliff wall, still far ahead of you. When you get closer, you see that the lower drop of the waterfall is a plunging freefall. The trail leads you on top of the freefall (unfortunately not in front of it, so you never get to see it head-on) to a series of cascades. Keep walking until you reach the top cascade, consisting of five pool-and-drop tiers, which is just 100 yards to the right of the granite-lined trail. It's a great spot for a picnic before you begin the long descent back downhill.

---

67 Alder Creek Falls

8.2 mi/5.0 hrs

Location: Off Highway 41 near Wawona, in Yosemite National Park; map E4, grid j3.

User groups: Hikers and horses. No dogs or mountain bikes. No wheelchair facilities.

Permits: There is a $20 entrance fee at Yosemite National Park, good for seven days. A free wilderness permit is required for overnight stays. They are available on a first-come, first-served basis up to one day in advance at the Yosemite Wilderness kiosk near your chosen trailhead, or further in advance by mail or phone for a $3 reservation fee; call (209) 372-0740.

Directions: The easiest way to find this unmarked trailhead is to travel north from Wawona. Follow the directions for Chilnualna Falls, hike number 66, but from the turnoff for Chilnualna Falls Road, drive north on the Wawona Road (Highway 41) for 4.2 miles. (You can also set your odometer at Wawona Campground; the trailhead is 3.4 miles north of the camp.) The trailhead is at a hairpin turn on the east side of the Wawona Road. There is no marker except for a Yosemite Wilderness sign, which you cannot see from your car. Park in the large dirt pullout on the west side of the road.

Maps: Free park maps are available at park entrance stations or by contacting Yosemite National Park at the address below. A more detailed map is available for a fee from Tom Harrison Cartography, (415) 456-7940. To obtain a topographic map of the area, ask for Wawona from the USGS.

Contact: Yosemite National Park Public Information Office, P.O. Box 577, Yosemite National Park, CA 93589; (209) 372-0200, or fax (209) 372-0371.

Trail notes: Maybe the best thing about Alder Creek Falls is that with all the world-famous waterfalls in Yosemite, this one just plain gets overlooked. Or maybe the best thing is the fun hike to reach it, starting with the challenge of locating the trailhead along Highway 41. After you accomplish this, you begin with a one-mile beeline hike straight uphill through the forest, which is sure to get your heart pumping. At the top of the ridge and a trail junction, turn left and lateral through the trees for two more miles, still heading uphill, but now more gently. Three miles from the trailhead, the route suddenly goes flat as it joins an old railroad grade, and then it's a one-mile easy stroll to the spot where Alder Creek takes the plunge off a granite lip. The waterfall is about 250 feet tall, and the best view of it is from the trail, as you stand about 100 yards in front of it. If you choose to keep hiking beyond the falls, you'll find many picnic spots amongst meadows and wildflowers.

 **68 Mariposa Grove**

2.0 mi/1.0 hrs

Location: Off Highway 41 near Wawona, in Yosemite National Park; map E4, grid j4.

User groups: Hikers only. No dogs, horses, or mountain bikes. No wheelchair facilities.

Permits: No permits are required. There is a $20 entrance fee at Yosemite National Park, good for seven days.

Directions: From Merced, drive 70 miles northeast on Highway 140 to Yosemite National Park. Follow the signs toward Yosemite Valley, entering through the Arch Rock entrance station. Continue on Highway 140/El Portal Road, which becomes Southside Drive, for 6.3 miles, then turn right at the fork for Highway 41/Wawona/Fresno. Drive 32 miles to the well-signed Mariposa Grove access road, by Yosemite's south entrance. Turn east and drive two miles to the parking lot. Note that this two-mile stretch of road may be closed in winter. (If you enter the park on Highway 41 from the south, the Mariposa Grove is on the right, just after you drive through the park entrance station.)

Maps: Free park maps are available at park entrance stations or by contacting Yosemite National Park at the address below. A more detailed map is available for a fee from Tom Harrison Cartography, (415) 456-7940. A map of the Mariposa Grove is available at the trailhead for 50 cents. To obtain a topographic map of the area, ask for Mariposa Grove from the USGS.

Contact: Yosemite National Park Public Information Office, P.O. Box 577, Yosemite National Park, CA 93589; (209) 372-0200, or fax (209) 372-0371.

Trail notes: The Mariposa Grove is the largest of the three groves of giant Sequoias in Yosemite National Park. That's why on summer weekends, the parking lot fills up and people wait in line in their cars to see the 250 or so big trees here. We hate to spill the beans, but the truth is that there are far better (and more peaceful) groves of Sequoias just a few miles south in Sierra National Forest, such as the Nelder Grove described in Chapter F4. Still, if you're in Yosemite and you want to see the Sequoias, this is the place. The star tree in the Mariposa Grove is the Grizzly

Giant, with a circumference of more than 100 feet. It's one of the oldest known giant Sequoias, at approximately 2,700 years old, which gives you some perspective on your short time on Earth. If you want to see only the most famous trees in the grove—the Grizzly Giant, California Tunnel Tree, and the Bachelor and Three Graces—take the well-signed two-mile hike through the lower grove, and turn around when you see the signs pointing to the upper grove. If you hike the entire lower and upper grove, you will cover about 6.5 miles.

Pacific Crest Trail (PCT) Section Overview

135.8 mi. one way/14.0 days

Trail elevations within this section, extending from the Agnew Meadows Trailhead north to Ebbetts Pass, range from 7,000 feet to over 10,000 feet. Although the lower reaches of the PCT are open from mid-June to mid-October, several high passes within the region may remain covered with snow until mid-July, making hiking difficult. Snow-covered passes are impossible to navigate with pack stock and horses.

PCT-23 Agnew Meadows to JMT-3 Tuolumne Meadows

28.0 mi. one way/3.0 days

Location: From the Agnew Meadows Trailhead north to the trailhead parking area at Tuolumne Meadows on Highway 120; map E4, grid j9.

User groups: Hikers and horses. No dogs or mountain bikes. No wheelchair facilities.

Permits: A wilderness permit is required for traveling through various wilderness and special-use areas the trail traverses. Contact either the Inyo National Forest at (760) 647-3000 or Wilderness Office of the National Park Service at (209) 372-0200 for a permit that is good for the length of your trip.

Directions: From Lee Vining, drive 26 miles south on Highway 395 to Mammoth Junction. Turn west on Highway 203 (Minaret Summit Road) to the town of Mammoth Lakes and drive 14 miles to the Agnew Meadows Campground and the trailhead parking area.

Maps: For an overall view of the trail route in this section, send $4 for each map ordered to the USDA-Forest Service, 630 Sansome Street, San Francisco, CA 94111, and ask for the maps of Inyo National Forest and the Sierra National Forest. For topographic maps of the route, request Vogelsang Peak, Mount Ritter, Koip Peak, and Mammoth Mountain from the USGS.

Contact: Public Information Office, National Park Service, P.O. Box 577, Yosemite National Park, CA 95389; (209) 372-0200 or fax (209) 372-0371. Inyo National Forest, Mono Lake Ranger District, P.O. Box 429, Lee Vining, CA 93541; (760) 647-3000 or fax (760) 647-3027.

Trail notes: This section of trail features breathtaking views of the Minarets, many glacial-cut lakes, and the wondrous descent into Yosemite. The PCT starts here by leaving Reds Meadows, an excellent place to arrange a food drop (and a chance to eat your first cheeseburger in weeks). The trail heads out into the most beautiful section of Inyo National Forest and the Ansel Adams Wilderness. All in a row, the PCT passes Rosalie Lake, Shadow Lake, Garnet Lake, and Thousand Island Lake. If they look like Ansel Adams' pictures in real life, it's because they are. The background setting of Banner and Ritter Peaks is among the most spectacular anywhere.

From Thousand Island Lake, the PCT makes a fair climb over Island Pass (10,200 feet), then drops down into the headwaters of Rush Creek, where emerald-green flows swirl over boulders, pouring like a wilderness fountain. From here, it's a decent, steady ascent back above treeline to Donohue Pass (11,056 feet), the southern wilderness border of Yosemite National Park. It was here, while munching a trail lunch, that we saw a huge landslide on the westward canyon wall. A massive amount of rock material fell in just a few seconds—an unforgettable showing of natural forces.

The trail becomes quite blocky at Donohue Pass, and you rock-hop your way down to the headwaters of Lyell Fork, a pretzel-like stream that meanders through the meadows. It pours all the way to Tuolumne Meadows, and following it, the trail is nearly flat for more than four miles. At Tuolumne Meadows, you can resupply—and get yourself another cheeseburger.

Special note: To continue on the Pacific Crest Trail, see PCT-24 (following John Muir Trail-4).

JMT-4 Tuolumne Meadows to Yosemite Valley

22 mi. one way /2.0 days

Location: From Tuolumne Meadows Campground in Yosemite, map E4, grid g7, to Happy Isles in Yosemite Valley, map E4, grid h5.

User groups: Hikers and horses. No dogs or mountain bikes. No wheelchair facilities.

Permits: A wilderness permit is required for traveling through various wilderness and special-use areas that the trail traverses. Contact the Wilderness Office of the National Park Service at (209) 372-0200 for a permit that is good for the length of your trip.

Directions: From Groveland in the Central Valley foothills, drive east on Highway 120 into Yosemite National Park and continue toward Yosemite Valley. At Crane Flat, turn left on Highway 120 (Tioga Pass Road) and continue for about an hour, driving past Tenaya Lake to the Tuolumne Meadows Campground. There is a signed trailhead parking area for the John Muir Trail here.

Maps: For topographic maps of the route, request Vogelsang Peak, Half Dome, Yosemite Falls, and Tenaya Peak from the USGS. For other maps of Yosemite, see hike number 19.

Contact: Public Information Office, National Park Service, P.O. Box 577, Yosemite National Park, CA 95389; (209) 372-0200 or fax (209) 372-0371.

Trail notes: The first glimpses of Yosemite Valley will seem like a privileged view into heaven after having hiked the entire John Muir Trail from Mount Whitney. For hikers only making this 22-mile section, the rewards can seem just as profound. The trip starts at Tuolumne Meadows, where backpackers can buy a good, cheap breakfast, obtain wilderness permits, and camp in a special area set aside for JMT hikers. When you take your first steps away from Tuolumne Meadows, resist the urge to rush to the finish line in order to close out a historic expedition. Instead relax and enjoy the downhill glide, always remembering that you are in sacred land.

Compared to the rest of the JMT, this leg will come with far less strain, starting with a 3.1-mile tromp past Cathedral Lakes (requiring a half-mile walk on a signed cutoff trail). If you can time it right, this can make for a great layover camp, with deep, emerald-green water, and Cathedral Peak in the background. At dawn, when there isn't a breath of wind, it can seem like a mountain church. Beyond Cathedral Lakes, the trail makes a relatively short 500-foot climb over Cathedral Pass, skirts Tresidder Peak, then descends down and through pristine Long Meadow. After passing Sunrise Trail Camp, a decent layover, the trail picks up little Sunrise Creek and follows it all the way down to Little Yosemite Valley, a popular trail camp. From Cathedral Lakes, it's 14.5 miles to the junction of the Half Dome Trail, and another 2.2 miles to Little Yosemite.

For JMT hikers, making the climb to the top of Half Dome is a must, even though it often means putting up with a parade of people, and even delays waiting for the line to move at the climbing cable. The Half Dome climb starts with a steep hike for the first mile, followed by steep switchbacks across granite on good trail to the foot of Half Dome's back wall. Here you'll find climbing cables to aid your final 300-foot ascent, and as you go, you'll discover breathtaking views of Tenaya Canyon. This is considered one of the world's glamour hikes, and while it turns hiking into an act of faith, we have seen eight-year-olds and 70-year-olds make the cable climb. By the way, if you take on Half Dome, be certain to have two canteens of water per person. Adding the Half Dome side trip to the rest of the JMT leg will add a round-trip of 5.2 miles to your hike. Because of its proximity to Half Dome, the Little Yosemite Valley Trail Camp is often crowded. From here, though, it's an easy five-mile hike downhill to Yosemite Valley. Again, try not to speed through to the end, even though it's an easy tromp downhill all the way. The magic is in the moment.

From Little Yosemite, the JMT is routed along the Merced River. In a mile, you'll reach Liberty Cap, and shortly later, Nevada Falls. Then down, down you go, with the trail often turning to giant granite steps, down past Emerald Pool and then to Vernal Falls, another spectacular waterfall.

Since Vernal Falls is just 1.7 miles from the end of the trail, you'll start meeting lots of day hikers coming from the other direction, many gasping for breath as they make the uphill climb out of Yosemite Valley. Many will ask how far you've hiked, some may even want to take your photograph. It may feel a bit inane, but, hey, enjoy it. After all, you just finished the John Muir Trail, the greatest hiking trail in the world.

PCT-24 Tuolumne Meadows to Sonora Pass

77.0 mi. one way/8.0 days

Location: From the trailhead parking at Tuolumne Meadows on Highway 120 north to the Sonora Pass Trailhead; map E4, grid g8.

User groups: Hikers and horses. No dogs or mountain bikes. No wheelchair facilities.

Permits: A wilderness permit is required for traveling through various wilderness and special-use areas the trail traverses. Contact either the Wilderness Office of the National Park Service at (209) 372-0200 or the Stanislaus National Forest at (209) 795-1381 for a permit that is good for the length of your trip.

Directions: From Lee Vining, drive west on Highway 120/Tioga Pass Road to Tuolumne Meadows and the signed trailhead parking area for the John Muir Trail/PCT and Lyell Fork.

Maps: For an overall view of the trail route in this section, send $4 for each map ordered to the USDA-Forest Service, 630 Sansome Street, San Francisco, CA 94111, and ask for the Stanislaus National Forest, Toiyabe National Forest, and the Inyo National Forest maps. For topographic maps of the route, request Pickel Meadow, Tower Peak, Piute Mountain, Matterhorn Peak, Dunderberg Peak, Vogelsang Peak, Tioga Pass, Falls Ridge, Buckeye Ridge, and Sonora Pass from the USGS.

Contact: Public Information Office, National Park Service, P.O. Box 577, Yosemite National Park, CA 95389; (209) 372-0200 or fax (209) 372-0371. Stanislaus National Forest, Calaveras Ranger Station, P.O. Box 500, Hathaway Pines, CA 95233; (209) 795-1381 or fax (209) 795-6849.

Trail notes: Yosemite National Park is well known for its crowded conditions in the valley,

but you can go for days and see almost no one on this section of trail. The beauty of the deep canyons, glacial-cut peaks, untouched meadows, and abundant wildlife make it a surreal paradise.

But it's real enough. From Tuolumne Meadows, the trail starts out deceptively easily as it follows the Tuolumne River towards the Grand Canyon of the Tuolumne River. It stays easy to Glen Aulin, where you get a great view of Tuolumne Falls, an excellent day trip from the Tuolumne Meadows drive-in camp. When you cross the bridge here and head up-canyon, you'll be leaving most people behind. In the next three days, you'll go up one canyon and down the next, one after another, with breathtaking views and long, demanding climbs. Highlights include Matterhorn Canyon (many deer, trout, and views), Benson Lake (the largest white sand beach in the Sierra Nevada), Dorothy Lake (panoramic views to the north), and many beautiful meadows, each like a wilderness church. The one serious negative is the incredible clouds of mosquitoes at the Wilmer Lake area during late spring and early summer.

When you leave Yosemite and enter Toiyabe National Forest, the landscape changes quickly from glacial-cut granite to volcanic rock, with the trail dropping past several pretty lakes and into a river drainage. Here the trail can be difficult to follow in parts, and in others, your chance of meeting grazing cows is high, particularly by the midsummer months. It will inspire you to head out to make the long climb up toward Leavitt Pass, set just below 10,800-foot Leavitt Peak, much of it a long, slow, uphill pull, almost all above treeline in gray, stark country. At Leavitt Pass, the wind whistles by at high speed almost year-round, a product of the "venturi effect," in which valley winds are continually forced through the narrow saddle at the pass, and must speed up to make it through.

The final drop down to Sonora Pass is a one-hour descent that seems to wind all over the mountain, and can be extremely dangerous and slippery when snow covered. When you reach Highway 108, cross the road and walk about 100 yards west to a large day-use parking area. The trail picks up again there.

PCT-25 Sonora Pass to Ebbetts Pass

30.8 mi. one way/3.0 days 🥾 🔟

Location: From Highway 108 at Sonora Pass north to Highway 4 near Ebbetts Pass; map E4, grid b5.

User groups: Hikers, dogs, and horses. No mountain bikes. No wheelchair facilities.

Permits: A wilderness permit is required for traveling through various wilderness and special-use areas the trail traverses. Contact the Stanislaus National Forest at (209) 532-3671 to obtain a permit that is good for the length of your trip.

Directions: From Sonora, head east on Highway 108 to the trailhead and parking area at Sonora Pass.

Maps: For topographic maps of the route, request Pickel Meadow, Disaster Peak, Dardanelles Cone, and Ebbetts Pass from the USGS.

Contact: Stanislaus National Forest, Supervisor's Office, 19777 Greenley Road, Sonora, CA 95370; (209) 532-3671 or fax (209) 533-1890.

Trail notes: While this section of the Pacific Crest Trail may not have the glamorous reputation of the stretch of trail in the southern Sierra, it's just as compelling for those who know it. From Sonora Pass, you're forced to climb out for a good hour or two, then rise over Wolf Creek Gap (10,300 feet) and make the easy drop down the Carson Canyon. This is the start of the Carson-Iceberg Wilderness, a giant swath of land that is a rare, unpeopled paradise. The Sierra riparian zones here are lined with flowers, seemingly all kinds and all colors, often in luxuriant beds of greenness.

The PCT climbs out of Carson Canyon, around Boulder Peak, then down and up two more canyons. All the while you keep crossing these little creeks filled with natural gardens. You wind your way across and through these areas, and eventually climb up a ridge, then head down, steeply at times, to Ebbetts Pass. Alas, there's no water here. No problem. A short, half-hour climb and you can be pumping water, and maybe setting up camp, too, at little Sherrold Lake, not far from the edge of the Mokelumne Wilderness.

PCT Continuation: To continue hiking along the Pacific Crest Trail, see chapter D4.

Leave No Trace Tips

Pack It In and Pack It Out

Take everything you bring into the wild back out with you.

Protect wildlife and your food by storing rations securely.
Pick up all spilled foods.

Use toilet paper or wipes sparingly; pack them out.

Inspect your campsite for trash and any evidence of your stay.
Pack out all trash—even if it's not yours!

Map E5

Adjoining Maps: West: E4 .... *page* 326
                      South: F5 422

Northern California Map .... *page* 2

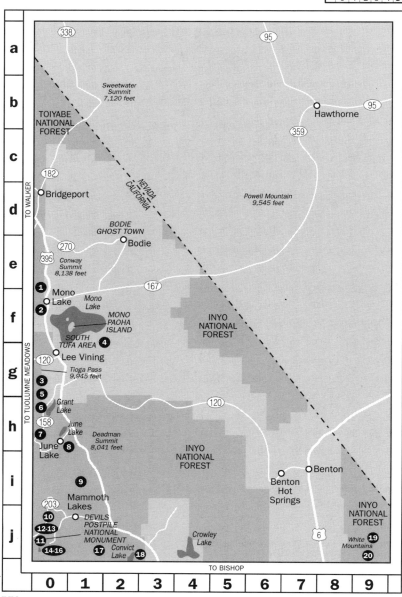

TO WALKER

TO TUOLUMNE MEADOWS

A
B
C
D
E
0 1 2 3 4 **5**

(338)

(95)

Sweetwater Summit 7,120 feet

Hawthorne

(95)

TOIYABE NATIONAL FOREST

(359)

NEVADA CALIFORNIA

(182)

Bridgeport

Powell Mountain 9,545 feet

BODIE GHOST TOWN

(270)

Bodie

(395) *Conway Summit 8,138 feet*

(167)

1

Mono Lake

Mono Lake

2

MONO PAOHA ISLAND

INYO NATIONAL FOREST

SOUTH TUFA AREA **4**

(120) Lee Vining

Tioga Pass 9,945 feet

3

5

6 *Grant Lake*

(120)

(158) *June Lake*

7

June Lake **8**

Deadman Summit 8,041 feet

INYO NATIONAL FOREST

9

Benton

Mammoth Lakes

Benton Hot Springs

INYO NATIONAL FOREST

(203)

10

DEVILS POSTPILE NATIONAL MONUMENT

12-13

11

Crowley Lake

(6)

White Mountains **19**

14-16

17 *Convict Lake* **18**

20

TO BISHOP

0   1   2   3   4   5   6   7   8   9

① Virginia Lakes Trail

7.0 mi/2.0 days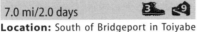

Location: South of Bridgeport in Toiyabe National Forest; map E5, grid f0.

User groups: Hikers, dogs, and horses. No mountain bikes. No wheelchair facilities.

Permits: Hikers planning to camp must obtain a wilderness permit. Parking and access are free. Campfires are prohibited at Summit and Cooney Lakes.

Directions: From Bridgeport, drive 13.5 miles south on U.S. 395. Turn west on Virginia Lakes Road and drive seven miles to the trailhead at the Big Virginia Day-Use Area.

Maps: For a map of Toiyabe National Forest, send $4 to USDA-Forest Service, 630 Sansome Street, San Francisco, CA 94111. To obtain a topographic map of the area, ask for Dunderberg Peak from the USGS.

Contact: Toiyabe National Forest, Bridgeport Ranger District, P.O. Box 595, Bridgeport, CA 93517; (619) 932-7070 or fax (619) 932-1299.

Trail notes: Virginia Lakes form the gateway to a beautiful high-mountain basin that contains eight small alpine lakes within a two-mile radius. The trailhead is at the Big Virginia Day-Use Area, set at 9,600 feet between mountain peaks that jut 12,000 feet into the sky. From here, you hike west past Blue Lake to Cooney Lake and on to Frog Lakes (one mile), then start climbing seriously, continuing two more miles to Summit Lake. This lake is set just below the Sierra ridge, between Camiaca Peak (11,739 feet) to the

north and Excelsior Mountain (12,446 feet) to the south. The lake makes a good first-night camp, but it can be cold and windy here. If you want to take a longer trip into even wilder country, you can do so from this point. The trail skirts the north end of Summit Lake, then enters one of the most remote sections in Yosemite National Park, dropping down into Virginia Canyon along Return Creek.

② Lundy Lake Trailhead

6.5 mi/4.0 hrs

Location: South of Bridgeport in the Hoover Wilderness, within Inyo National Forest; map E5, grid f0.

User groups: Hikers, dogs, horses, and mountain bikes (up to the wilderness border). No wheelchair facilities.

Permits: Hikers planning to camp must obtain a wilderness permit.

Directions: From the junction of Highway 167 and U.S. 395 at Mono Lake, turn west on Lundy Lake Road and drive five miles to Lundy Lake. Drive two miles west past Lundy Lake to the trailhead at the end of the road.

Maps: For a map of Inyo National Forest, send $4 to USDA-Forest Service, 630 Sansome Street, San Francisco, CA 94111. To obtain topographic maps of the area, ask for Lundy and Dunderberg Peak from the USGS.

Contact: Inyo National Forest, Mono Lake Ranger District, P.O. Box 429, Lee Vining, CA 93541; (619) 647-3044 or fax (619) 647-3046.

Trail notes: When you use the Lundy Lake Trailhead as a jump-off point for a backpack trip, you get a passport into the sculpted-granite high country, complete with half a dozen gemlike lakes. The trailhead lies about two miles past Lundy Lake, a long, narrow pool set at 7,800 feet. From there, the trail rises along Mill Creek into the Hoover Wilderness, passes several small waterfalls, and after three miles arrives at Lake Helen. The next mile brings you to Odell Lake and little Twin Lake, take your pick. This region has Yosemite-style high-country beauty, yet it's located just to the east of the park boundary. You can extend your trip quite easily, creating a great one-way hike with a shuttle. To do so, cross over the top of Lundy Pass, then drop down past Hummingbird Lake to Saddlebag Lake, which at 10,087 feet is the highest drive-to lake in California. That makes it a one-way hike of seven miles.

❸ Gibbs Lake Trail

5.4 mi/3.75 hrs

Location: West of Lee Vining on the northern boundary of the Ansel Adams Wilderness; map E5, grid g0.

User groups: Hikers, dogs, horses, and mountain bikes (up to the wilderness border). No wheelchair facilities.

Permits: Hikers planning to camp must obtain a wilderness permit.

Directions: From Lee Vining, drive about one mile south on U.S. 395, then turn west (right) on Forest Service Road 1N16 (look for the sign indicating Upper Horse Meadow). Drive about three miles to the trailhead at the end of the road. Note: Forest Service Road 1N16 requires a four-wheel-drive vehicle.

Maps: For a map of Inyo National Forest, send $4 to USDA-Forest Service, 630 Sansome Street, San Francisco, CA 94111. To obtain topographic maps of the area, ask for Lee Vining and Mount Dana from the USGS.

Contact: Inyo National Forest, Mono Lake Ranger District, P.O. Box 429, Lee Vining, CA 93541; (619) 647-3044 or fax (619) 647-3046.

Trail notes: The 2.7-mile hike from Upper Horse Meadow to Gibbs Lake truly is one of the greatest day hikes in California. Since the trail-

head isn't located at a lake or other attractive setting, nobody gets here by accident. The trail starts at Upper Horse Meadow, elevation 8,000 feet, and climbs up Gibbs Canyon to Gibbs Lake, at 9,530 feet. That's about a 1,500-foot climb, and except for a half mile of switchbacks at the beginning, most of the route is on a steady grade along Gibbs Creek. It is a pretty spot, backed by bare granite and fronted by conifers. The trail ends at Gibbs Lake, so you will not have to compete for trail space or a lakeside picnic site with backpackers arriving from other trails.

❹ South Tufa Trail

1.0 mi/0.5 hr

Location: East of Lee Vining in the Mono Lake Tufa State Reserve, at the southern end of Mono Lake; map E5, grid g1.

User groups: Hikers, wheelchairs, and dogs. No horses or mountain bikes.

Permits: No permits are required. Parking and access are free.

Directions: From Lee Vining, drive five miles south on U.S. 395, then take Highway 120 east for five miles. Turn left at the sign for South Tufa and follow the dirt road to the parking area.

Maps: For a free map of the lake, contact the Mono Lake Tufa State Reserve at the address below. To obtain topographic maps of the area, ask for Lee Vining and Mono Mills from the USGS.

Contact: Mono Lake Tufa State Reserve, P.O. Box 99, Lee Vining, CA 93541; (619) 647-6331. Mono Basin National Forest Scenic Area, P.O. Box 429, Lee Vining, CA 93541; (619) 525-7232 or fax (619) 647-6331.

Trail notes: The strange and remarkable tufa towers, spires, and knobs at Mono Lake embellish one of the most extraordinary landscapes in California. The terrain resembles a moonscape and has even been called "a landing pad for spaceships," but by anybody's definition is a peculiar place that lures thousands of people every summer who come to take a short walk. Mono Lake itself is vast—covering 60 square miles—and is estimated to be more than 700,000 years old, making it one of the oldest lakes in North America. The lake's basin has become one of the world's most prolific stopover points for gulls, grebes, plovers, and phalaropes during their annual southbound flights. That's because the alkaline properties of the water create prime habitat for brine shrimp (an ideal food for these birds), and the lake's islands provide isolation from predators. The actual loop trail is only one mile long, but there are several spurs that can add extra miles to your hike. You will stroll along the southern shore of the lake, near the South Tufa Area. This is where the strange and gigantic tufa spires sit like old, untouched earth castles.

❺ Walker Lake Trailhead

8.2 mi/5.0 hrs

Location: Southwest of Lee Vining at the northeastern boundary of the Ansel Adams Wilderness; map E5, grid h0.

User groups: Hikers, dogs, horses, and mountain bikes (up to the wilderness border). No wheelchair facilities.

Permits: Hikers planning to camp must obtain a wilderness permit.

Directions: From Lee Vining, drive about four miles south on U.S. 395 to Walker Lake Road. Turn west and continue to the trailhead at the east end of the lake.

Maps: For a map of Inyo National Forest, send $4 to USDA-Forest Service, 630 Sansome Street, San Francisco, CA 94111. To obtain topographic maps of the area, ask for Mount Dana and Koip Peak from the USGS.

Contact: Inyo National Forest, Mono Lake Ranger District, P.O. Box 429, Lee Vining, CA 93541; (619) 647-3044 or fax (619) 647-3046.

Trail notes: Lower Sardine Lake is a jewel cradled in a high glacial bowl at 9,888 feet, the kind of lake that made the Ansel Adams Wilderness one of the most treasured places in the world. The hike in is tough and steep, with only one short, flat section to provide much of a break. At first, the route is easy and beautiful, skirting the northern edge of Walker Lake to its headwaters, Walker Creek. From here, you head up Bloody Canyon, climbing nearly 2,000 feet in less than two miles. The hike parallels Walker Creek, requiring two stream crossings on the way up to Lower Sardine Lake. For anyone who is either out of

shape or not acclimated to the altitude, the climb can be rough going, a real wheezer. The trail usually opens by mid-June, though this varies each year depending on the snowpack. Backpackers can opt to continue hiking up and over Mono Pass and into some of Yosemite National Park's most remote backcountry.

❻ Parker Lake Trail

4.4 mi/2.5 hrs

Location: South of Lee Vining in the Ansel Adams Wilderness, west of Grant Lake; map E5, grid h0.

User groups: Hikers, dogs, and horses. No mountain bikes. No wheelchair facilities.

Permits: Hikers planning to camp must obtain a wilderness permit.

Directions: From Lee Vining, drive about four miles south on U.S. 395 to Highway 158 (June Lake Loop). Turn south and drive 1.5 miles, then turn right on Parker Lake Road and drive two miles. Turn left on Forest Service Road 1S26 and drive one mile until the road dead-ends at the trailhead at Parker Creek.

Maps: For a map of Inyo National Forest, send $4 to USDA-Forest Service, 630 Sansome Street, San Francisco, CA 94111. To obtain topographic maps of the area, ask for Mount Dana and Koip Peak from the USGS.

Contact: Inyo National Forest, Mono Lake Ranger District, P.O. Box 429, Lee Vining, CA 93541; (619) 647-3044 or fax (619) 647-3046.

Trail notes: The high Sierra is known for the long killer grades hikers must take to reach pristine high mountain lakes, but the Parker Lake Trail provides an easy alternative. Not only is the walk to the lake just 2.2 miles long, but it entails an elevation gain of a mere 300 feet. Yes, there is a God! Though the nearby June Lake Loop gets a lot of vacation traffic, this trailhead is obscure enough that most visitors pass it by. Beginning at an elevation of 8,000 feet along Parker Creek, the trail follows the creek upstream—an easy romp for most—before arriving at Parker Lake at 8,318 feet. The lake is surrounded by granite walls, which are impassable. No trails lead out of the basin, save for the one easy route along Parker Creek. This hike makes an excellent day trip.

❼ Silver Lake Trail

19.2 mi/3.0 days

Location: On the eastern boundary of the Ansel Adams Wilderness, west of June Lake; map E5, grid h0.

User groups: Hikers, dogs, and horses. No mountain bikes. No wheelchair facilities.

Permits: Hikers planning to camp must obtain a wilderness permit.

Directions: From Lee Vining, drive about 11 miles south on U.S. 395 to June Lake Junction. Make a right turn on Highway 158 (June Lake Road) and drive six miles to the trailhead at Silver Lake Campground.

Maps: For a map of Inyo National Forest, send $4 to USDA-Forest Service, 630 Sansome Street, San Francisco, CA 94111. To obtain topographic maps of the area, ask for June Lake and Koip Peak from the USGS.

Contact: Inyo National Forest, Mono Lake Ranger District, P.O. Box 429, Lee Vining, CA 93541; (619) 647-3044 or fax (619) 647-3046.

Trail notes: Some places will never change, and people are drawn to them because they provide a sense of permanence that can't be found anywhere else. That is how it is at the headwaters of Rush Creek. Created from drops of melting snow near the Sierra crest at 10,500 feet, this stream runs downhill for miles, rolling into the forest like a swirling emerald green fountain. Even a short visit requires a long drive to the trailhead followed by a demanding backpacking trek. In the process hikers contend with a 10-mile climb out, ice-cold stream crossings, and the possibility of afternoon thunderstorms in which lightning bolts and thunderclaps rattle off the canyon rims.

The trailhead lies at Silver Lake, elevation 7,200 feet. After departing Silver Lake, hikers follow the trail adjacent to Lower Rush Creek upstream toward the Ansel Adams Wilderness. After three miles, you arrive at beautiful Gem Lake (8,052 feet), then, at the seven-mile point, at Waugh Lake (9,424 feet). Many visitors never venture farther than these lakes, simply stopping to camp, swim, or fish. But upstream of Waugh Lake is where you will find the headwaters of Rush Creek, along with the flawless symmetry of the untouched high country. Getting there requires a climb of 3,300 feet over the course of 9.6 miles, but it is one of the prettiest streams anywhere, and well worth the effort.

❽ Yost Lake Trail

9.5 mi/1.0 day

Location: On the eastern boundary of the Ansel Adams Wilderness, at June Lake; map E5, grid i0.

User groups: Hikers, dogs, and horses. No mountain bikes. No wheelchair facilities.

Permits: Hikers planning to camp must obtain a wilderness permit.

Directions: From Lee Vining, drive about 11 miles south on U.S. 395 to June Lake Junction. Go right on Highway 158 (June Lake Road) and drive two miles to the town of June Lake. The trailhead is opposite the June Lake boat ramp.

Maps: For a map of Inyo National Forest, send $4 to USDA-Forest Service, 630 Sansome Street, San Francisco, CA 94111. To obtain topographic maps of the area, ask for June Lake and Mammoth Mountain from the USGS.

Contact: Inyo National Forest, Mono Lake Ranger District, P.O. Box 429, Lee Vining, CA 93541; (619) 647-3044 or fax (619) 647-3046.

Trail notes: Yost Lake is a small glacial lake hidden at 9,000 feet on the slopes of June Mountain. Many people visit the June Lakes area for years without even knowing Yost exists. But it is up there, tucked away and accessible only to those willing to hike. From the trailhead (7,800 feet) at June Lake, the trail rises very steeply in the first half mile, climbing nearly 1,000 feet. That discourages many from going farther; after all, it is 4.75 miles to the lake. Ah, but after that first grunt of a climb, the trail gets much easier, contouring across the slopes of the mountain. It rises gradually to the headwaters of Yost Creek, then drops into the small basin that guards the lake.

❾ Inyo Craters

0.75 mi/1.5 hrs

Location: In Inyo National Forest north of Mammoth; map E5, grid i1.

User groups: Hikers and dogs. No horses or mountain bikes. No wheelchair facilities.

Permits: No permits are required.

Directions: From Lee Vining, drive about 20 miles south on U.S. 395 to the Mammoth Lakes Scenic Loop (Forest Service Road 3S23). Turn right and drive about three miles, then turn right again on Forest Service Road 3S30. Follow this road to Forest Service Road 3S29, then turn right and drive to the parking area for the Inyo Craters Picnic Area.

Maps: For a map of Inyo National Forest, send $4 to USDA-Forest Service, 630 Sansome Street, San Francisco, CA 94111. To obtain a topographic map of the area, ask for Mammoth Mountain from the USGS.

Contact: Inyo National Forest, Mammoth Ranger District, P.O. Box 148, Mammoth Lakes, CA 93546; (619) 934-2505, (619) 924-5500, or fax (619) 924-5537.

Trail notes: A geologic phenomenon, the Inyo Craters make a great destination for an easy day hike in the Mammoth Lakes area. The craters are phreatic tips, meaning that they were created by an explosion of steam. Long ago when the mountain was a smoldering volcano, melted snow poured into it, and when the cold water hit hot magma—kaboom! The hike is easy and short, less than a half mile through open forest sprinkled with red fir and Jeffrey pine. In each of the two craters there's a tiny pond that's filled with the collected drops of melting snow each spring.

⑩ Upper Soda Springs Trailhead

2.75 mi/2.0 hrs

Location: In the Ansel Adams Wilderness, west of Mammoth; map E5, grid j0.

User groups: Hikers, dogs, and horses. No mountain bikes. No wheelchair facilities.

Permits: Hikers planning to camp in the wilderness must obtain a wilderness permit.

Directions: From Lee Vining, drive 25 miles south on U.S. 395 to Highway 203. Turn west and follow the road to the town of Mammoth Lakes. Drive about 17 miles west on Minaret Summit Road into Devils Postpile National Monument. Look for the signs for Upper Soda Springs Campground and follow them to the camping area. The trailhead is just west of there. During the summer months, from 7:30 A.M. to 5:30 P.M., visitors are required to take the shuttle bus from the Mammoth Ski Area; the fee is $7 per adult and $4 per child.

Maps: For a map of Inyo National Forest, send $4 to USDA-Forest Service, 630 Sansome Street, San Francisco, CA 94111. To obtain a topographic map of the area, ask for Mammoth Mountain from the USGS.

Contact: Inyo National Forest, Mammoth Ranger District, P.O. Box 148, Mammoth Lakes, CA 93546; (619) 934-2505, (619) 924-5500, or fax (619) 924-5537.

Trail notes: The Upper San Joaquin River is an angler's paradise, a beautiful stream that tumbles over rocks and into pools. There have been days in late June and July when we've caught and released 50 to 60 trout. Most of them are little guys, rarely more than 10 inches long, but they include brook, rainbow, and brown trout, and even the occasional golden trout. Things are much different just a mile or two downriver near Devils Postpile, where a small stretch of water that is easily accessible from campgrounds gets hammered day after day all summer long.

For the best fishing, hike from the Soda Springs Campground on the River Trail upstream along the San Joaquin River, heading out at least a mile before wetting a line. Along the way, enjoy the canyon views and lush streamside vegetation. The best technique is to fly-fish using a floating line, a nine-foot leader, nymphs, and a strike indicator (many of the strikes are very soft).

If you want to hike, not fish, it is a 6.9-mile trek from the trailhead to Thousand Island Lake (9,833 feet), a divine spot where huge boulders dot the surface waters, creating the appearance of miniature islands. The views of Banner and Ritter Peaks, along with the rest of the Minarets, are unsurpassed from this vantage point. It is the favorite hike of Scott Greenstein, a Forest Service volunteer who told us that a new variety of wildflower blooms every week in the springtime.

⓫ Rainbow Falls Trail

1.5 mi/1.5 hrs

Location: In Devils Postpile National Monument west of Mammoth; map E5, grid j0.

User groups: Hikers, dogs, and horses. No mountain bikes. No wheelchair facilities.

Permits: No permits are required.

Directions: From Lee Vining, drive 25 miles south on U.S. 395 to Highway 203. Turn west and follow the road to the town of Mammoth Lakes. Drive about 17 miles west on Minaret Summit Road into Devils Postpile National Monument. Look for the signs for Upper Soda Springs Campground and follow them to the camping area. The trailhead is just west of there. During the summer, from 7:30 A.M. to 5:30 P.M., visitors are required to take the shuttle bus from the Mammoth Ski Area; the fee is $7 per adult and $4 per child. Take the shuttle to Reds Meadows Resort at the end of the road in Devils Postpile National Monument.

Maps: For a map of Inyo National Forest, send $4 to USDA-Forest Service, 630 Sansome Street, San Francisco, CA 94111. To obtain a topographic map of the area, ask for Mammoth Mountain from the USGS.

Contact: Devils Postpile National Monument, (619) 934-2289. Inyo National Forest, Mammoth Ranger District, P.O. Box 148, Mammoth Lakes, CA 93546; (619) 934-2505, (619) 924-5500, or fax (619) 924-5537.

Trail notes: The first time you lay eyes on Rainbow Falls, this tall, wide, and often forceful waterfall comes as an awesome surprise. The cascade inspires as much as it astonishes, yet it is often overlooked for nearby Devils Postpile (the world's best example of columnar rock), the adjacent Ansel Adams Wilderness, and of course Mammoth Lakes and the dozens of nearby recreation destinations. But this is still one of the best short hikes in California. The trail starts at the Reds Meadows Resort, which is actually more of a headquarters for horseback riders, then is routed south down into the canyon of the Middle Fork San Joaquin River. A short cutoff trail allows hikers to loop down to the base of the falls for a classic vantage point. You also can hike another half mile downstream to find a smaller waterfall. For such a short walk, the Rainbow Falls Trail is a classic.

⓬ Minaret Lake Trail

14.8 mi/2.0 days

Location: In the Ansel Adams Wilderness, west of Mammoth; map E5, grid j0.

User groups: Hikers, dogs, and horses. No mountain bikes. No wheelchair facilities.

Permits: Hikers planning to camp in the wilderness must obtain a wilderness permit.

Directions: From Lee Vining, drive 25 miles south on U.S. 395 to Highway 203. Turn west and follow the road to the town of Mammoth Lakes. Drive west for 17 miles on Minaret Summit Road into Devils Postpile National Monument. Look for the signs for Upper Soda Springs Campground and follow them to the camping area. The trailhead is just west of there. You must hike 1.5 miles on the John Muir Trail to reach the Minaret Lake Trailhead. During the summer, from 7:30 A.M. to 5:30 P.M., visitors are required to take the shuttle bus from the Mammoth Ski Area; the fee is $7 per adult and $4 per child.

Maps: For a map of Inyo National Forest, send $4 to USDA-Forest Service, 630 Sansome Street, San Francisco, CA 94111. To obtain topographic maps of the area, ask for Mammoth Mountain and Mount Ritter from the USGS.

Contact: Inyo National Forest, Mammoth Ranger District, P.O. Box 148, Mammoth Lakes, CA 93546; (619) 934-2505, (619) 924-5500, or fax (619) 924-5537.

Trail notes: With an early start and a fresh head of steam, you can make the 7.4-mile, 1,800-foot climb from Devils Postpile to Minaret Lake in a good morning's effort. There's perhaps no better place to have a picnic lunch. It is enchanting, and Minaret Lake is a real prize, set just below the awesome glacial-carved Minaret Range at 9,793 feet. From the trailhead, you hike north on the John Muir Trail to just beyond Johnston Lake, then take the left fork along Minaret Creek. The trail rises with the creek, and in the last mile climbs steeply above tree line before skirting the outlet of Minaret Lake. A high, impassable back wall frames the lake, and the trail circles around the northern shore. You've made it to the kind of place where John Muir got religion.

⑬ Fern Lake Loop

13.0 mi/2.0 days

Location: In the Ansel Adams Wilderness, west of Mammoth; map E5, grid j0.

User groups: Hikers, dogs, and horses. No mountain bikes. No wheelchair facilities.

Permits: Hikers planning to camp in the wilderness must obtain a wilderness permit.

Directions: From Lee Vining, drive 25 miles south on U.S. 395 to Highway 203. Turn west and follow the road to the town of Mammoth Lakes. Drive about 17 miles west on Minaret Summit Road into Devils Postpile National Monument. Look for the signs for Upper Soda Springs Campground and follow them to the camping area. The trailhead is just west of there. During the summer, from 7:30 A.M. to 5:30 P.M., visitors are required to take the shuttle bus from the Mammoth Ski Area; the fee is $7 per adult and $4 per child.

Maps: For a map of Inyo National Forest, send $4 to USDA-Forest Service, 630 Sansome Street, San Francisco, CA 94111. To obtain topographic maps of the area, ask for Crystal Crag and Cattle Mountain from the USGS.

Contact: Inyo National Forest, Mammoth Ranger District, P.O. Box 148, Mammoth Lakes, CA 93546; (619) 934-2505, (619) 924-5500, or fax (619) 924-5537.

Trail notes: Fern Lake can be the focal point of an ambitious day hike into and back out of Devils Postpile, or better, the start of a great 13-mile loop trip. Either way you go, this is an excellent hike, and one that has become very popular—the only drawback.

Starting at Devils Postpile, you hike five miles to Fern Lake, climbing most of the way. This small lake is set in a rock bowl at tree line, below Iron Mountain in the Minarets. From there, the trail contours north across the mountain, poking in and out of sparse forest and bare granite, to Beck Cabin (a 1.1-mile side trip will take you to Beck Lakes, 9,803 feet). The route back

drops 4.8 miles down to the John Muir Trail, including a very steep half mile on switchbacks. To complete the loop, turn right and hike the final 1.4 miles to Devils Postpile. We strongly advise taking the side trip to Beck Lakes, set in a glacial-formed pocket just below the Minarets ridge amid celestial mountain scenery.

⑭ Red Cone Loop

6.7 mi/4.0 hrs

Location: At Horseshoe Lake in Mammoth Lakes; map E5, grid j0.

User groups: Hikers, dogs, and horses. No mountain bikes are allowed past the wilderness border. No wheelchair facilities.

Permits: Hikers planning to camp must obtain a wilderness permit.

Directions: From Lee Vining, drive south on U.S. 395 for 25 miles to Highway 203. Turn west and follow the road to the town of Mammoth Lakes. Turn south on Lake Mary Road and drive to the road's end. The trailhead is on the west side of Horseshoe Lake.

Maps: For a map of Inyo National Forest, send $4 to USDA-Forest Service, 630 Sansome Street, San Francisco, CA 94111. To obtain a topographic map of the area, ask for Crystal Crag from the USGS.

Contact: Inyo National Forest, Mammoth Ranger District, P.O. Box 148, Mammoth Lakes, CA 93546; (619) 934-2505, (619) 924-5500, or fax (619) 924-5537.

Trail notes: Horseshoe Lake, elevation 8,900 feet, lies at the end of the road to the Mammoth Lakes, an excellent trailhead that makes for a great day hike. The loop trail tops out near Crater Meadow, a beautiful little spot set just below Red Cones, about a five-minute walk off the main trail. This is your destination, a spot where you can have a picnic lunch in virtual peace before enjoying the walk back down. The contrast is striking: Just a short distance below there are typically many people at Twin Lakes, Lake Mary, Lake Mamie, and Lake George, yet you are separated from them by Mammoth Pass. You will be surprised at how relatively few people take this loop hike and happy that you made the choice to do so.

⓯ Lake George Trailhead

1.0 mi/0.5 hr

Location: At Lake George in Mammoth Lakes; map E5, grid j0.

User groups: Hikers and dogs. Mountain bikes are not advised. No horses. No wheelchair facilities.

Permits: No permits are required.

Directions: From Lee Vining, drive south on U.S. 395 for 25 miles to Highway 203. Turn west and follow the road to the town of Mammoth Lakes. Turn south on Lake Mary Road and follow it to Lake Mary. Turn south at Lake Mary and follow the signs to Lake George. The trailhead is at the campground near the northeast shore of the lake.

Maps: For a map of Inyo National Forest, send $4 to USDA-Forest Service, 630 Sansome Street, San Francisco, CA 94111. To obtain a topographic map of the area, ask for Crystal Crag from the USGS.

Contact: Inyo National Forest, Mammoth Ranger District, P.O. Box 148, Mammoth Lakes, CA 93546; (619) 934-2505, (619) 924-5500, or fax (619) 924-5537.

Trail notes: Campers at Lake George will be pleased to find that this easy, short trail provides access to hidden TJ Lake. It's a revelation to many that a pretty alpine lake within easy reach can also be very secluded. The trail starts at the campground at Lake George, then leads up the inlet stream to TJ Lake. It's only about half a mile, and an easy grade to boot. Crystal Crag (10,377 feet) towers above the lake, adding great natural beauty to the scene. The trail skirts along the eastern shoreline of the lake before deadending at the small inlet stream.

⓰ Blue Crag Loop

3.4 mi/1.75 hrs

Location: At Lake Mary in Mammoth Lakes; map E5, grid j0.

User groups: Hikers, dogs, and horses. No mountain bikes are allowed past the wilderness boundary. No wheelchair facilities.

Permits: Hikers planning to camp must obtain a wilderness permit.

Directions: From Lee Vining, drive south on U.S. 395 for 25 miles to Highway 203. Turn west and follow the road to the town of Mammoth Lakes. Turn south on Lake Mary Road and follow it to Lake Mary. The trailhead is south of Lake Mary, just beyond the Coldwater Campground.

Maps: For a map of Inyo National Forest, send $4 to USDA-Forest Service, 630 Sansome Street, San Francisco, CA 94111. To obtain a topographic map of the area, ask for Crystal Crag from the USGS.

Contact: Inyo National Forest, Mammoth Ranger District, P.O. Box 148, Mammoth Lakes, CA 93546; (619) 934-2505, (619) 924-5500, or fax (619) 924-5537.

Trail notes: Nature's artwork is just about perfect here. The scenic Blue Crag Loop offers hikers access to three small, jewel-like lakes, a pretty meadow, and a close-up view of towering Blue Crag. The trail starts just south of Lake Mary, at the end of the road beyond the Coldwater Campground. The hike starts by climbing up to Arrowhead Lake (a short spur trail provides shoreline access), then heads up to the base of Blue Crag, overlooking Skelton Lake. To complete the loop, turn right at Blue Crag, pass Gentian Meadow and little Emerald Lake, and head back down along Coldwater Creek to the trailhead. This short, scenic loop provides a glimpse of classic high Sierra country, most of it ranging between 9,000 and 9,700 feet in elevation.

⓱ Valentine Lake Trailhead

11.2 mi/1.0 day

Location: In Inyo National Forest south of Mammoth Lakes; map E5, grid j1.

User groups: Hikers, dogs, and horses. No mountain bikes are allowed past the wilderness boundary. No wheelchair facilities.

Permits: Hikers planning to camp must obtain a wilderness permit.

Directions: From Lee Vining, drive south on U.S. 395 for about 27 miles to Sherwin Creek Road (about two miles south of the Mammoth Lakes turnoff). Turn west and drive approximately 2.5 miles. About one mile before you reach Sherwin Creek Campground, turn left on a spur road and drive a short distance to the trailhead.

Maps: For a map of Inyo National Forest, send $4 to USDA-Forest Service, 630 Sansome Street, San Francisco, CA 94111. To obtain a topographic map of the area, ask for Crystal Crag from the USGS.

Contact: Inyo National Forest, Mammoth Ranger District, P.O. Box 148, Mammoth Lakes, CA 93546; (619) 934-2505, (619) 924-5500, or fax (619) 924-5537.

Trail notes: The Mammoth Lakes area is one of the star attractions of the eastern Sierra, yet nearby Valentine Lake, though not quite lost, is largely forgotten. Perhaps the little lake is overlooked because the trailhead (7,600 feet) is not found at one of the lakes in the Mammoth Lakes Basin or at nearby Devils Postpile. Or perhaps it's because the climb required to get there is so steep. Regardless of the reason, a morning's hike—rising some 2,100 feet over 5.6 miles—will get you to the lake, which sits at 9,698 feet.

Some say the lake is shaped like a teardrop, hence the name, but when we visited, we thought it looked more like a drop of sweat. The hike starts out with a very steep climb, including a half mile of switchbacks, until you reach 8,500 feet. After that, the trail laterals along Sherwin Creek, including two more sets of switchbacks, before finally taking you to the lake's outlet. Valentine Lake is surrounded by high mountain walls on three sides, making it impossible to go much farther.

⑱ Convict Lake Trailhead

15.4 mi/2.0 days

Location: On the eastern boundary of the John Muir Wilderness, south of Mammoth; map E5, grid j3.

User groups: Hikers, dogs, and mountain bikes. No horses. No wheelchair facilities.

Permits: No permits are required.

Directions: From Lee Vining, drive south on U.S. 395 for about 31 miles to Convict Lake Road. Turn right and drive to the lake at the end of the road. The trailhead is off a short spur road to the right as you near the lake.

Maps: For a map of Inyo National Forest, send $4 to USDA-Forest Service, 630 Sansome Street, San Francisco, CA 94111. To obtain a topo-

graphic map of the area, ask for Bloody Mountain from the USGS.

Contact: Inyo National Forest, Mammoth Ranger District, P.O. Box 148, Mammoth Lakes, CA 93546; (619) 934-2505, (619) 924-5500, or fax (619) 924-5537.

Trail notes: Framed by a back wall of bare granite peaks, Convict Lake is a mountain shrine, and the trail that leads from here into the backcountry wilderness makes hikers feel as if they're ascending into heaven. But this is no easy trip. Not only is there a long, grueling climb—gaining 3,000 feet in 7.7 miles—but a tricky and sometimes dangerous stream crossing is involved. The trail starts near Convict Lake (the trailhead is well signed) at 7,621 feet, skirts along the north shore of the lake, then leads up through a canyon alongside Convict Creek. About three miles in, you have to ford Convict Creek, which usually requires getting wet and can be dangerous in the early summer because of high snowmelt. (Many attempts to bridge this crossing have failed, as the bridge always gets washed out by high flows in early summer.) If you get past that crossing, the trail is routed up to a series of large, untouched lakes: Mildred Lake, Dorothy Lake (10,275 feet), Lake Genevieve (10,000 feet), Bighorn Lake, Edith Lake, and Cloverleaf Lake. Take your pick. You can spend days exploring this high-mountain paradise.

⑲ White Mountain Peak Trail

7.5 mi/6.0 hrs

Location: In Inyo National Forest northeast of Bishop; map E5, grid j9.

User groups: Hikers only. Due to extremely high altitudes, dogs, horses, and mountain bikes are strongly not advised. No wheelchair facilities.

Permits: No permits are required.

Directions: From U.S. 395 at Big Pine, take Highway 168 northeast toward Nevada. Drive about 15 miles, then turn left on White Mountain Road. Drive north for 22 miles past Ancient Bristlecone Pine Forest to the locked gate at the road's end. This is the trailhead. Park to the side, making sure you aren't blocking the road.

Maps: For a map of Inyo National Forest, send

$4 to USDA-Forest Service, 630 Sansome Street, San Francisco, CA 94111. To obtain a topographic map of the area, ask for White Mountain Peak from the USGS.

Contact: Inyo National Forest, White Mountain Ranger District, 798 North Main Street, Bishop, CA 93514; (619) 873-2500, (619) 873-2400, or fax (619) 973-2458.

Trail notes: White Mountain Peak is the third tallest peak in California, only 249 feet lower than the highest, Mount Whitney (Mount Williamson is second in line), yet it is little known to hikers outside of the area. It's so tall that the 14,246-foot summit is the site of a University of California high-altitude research lab. This hike is a butt-kicker, following an old Navy-built road as it climbs 2,600 feet in 7.5 miles at high altitude. The trail starts at a locked gate, then leads past Mount Barcroft (13,040 feet) on a long grind. The summit constitutes an impressive granite massif with grand views. To the east, you can see a hundred miles into Nevada, and to the west, the Owens Valley and Volcanic Tableland. As you hike you'll feel like you're entering a different world. When you reach the top, you'll realize that you are.

Contact: Inyo National Forest, White Mountain Ranger District, 798 North Main Street, Bishop, CA 93514; (619) 873-2500, (619) 873-2400, or fax (619) 973-2458.

Trail notes: The Methuselah Tree is the prize of the Ancient Bristlecone Pine Forest. Here for more than 4,000 years, it's the oldest living tree documented in the world. But forest rangers won't tell you which one it is, out of fear that some dimwit will cut it down. So you'll have to be satisfied just knowing you have walked among the ancients, rather than actually seeing the grandfather of the forest. The trail starts at the Schulman Grove Picnic Area, where little birds will sometimes eat right out of your hand. Schulman Grove, elevation 10,100 feet, is where you'll find the oldest trees in Bristlecone, and they look their age. Centuries of fire, sand, ice, and wind have sculpted them, giving them the appearance of living driftwood. The trail loops among these trees, with a few short climbs along the way. You will never forget this short, unusual hike.

㉒ Methuselah Trail

3.0 mi/1.75 hrs

Location: In Inyo National Forest northeast of Bishop; map E5, grid j9.

User groups: Hikers and dogs. No horses or mountain bikes. No wheelchair facilities.

Permits: No permits are required.

Directions: From U.S. 395 at Big Pine, take Highway 168 northeast toward Nevada. Drive about 15 miles, then turn left on White Mountain Road. Drive north for eight miles past the entrance to the Ancient Bristlecone Pine Forest to the Schulman Grove Picnic Area. Turn right and drive a short distance to the parking area and the trailhead.

Maps: For a map of Inyo National Forest, send $4 to USDA-Forest Service, 630 Sansome Street, San Francisco, CA 94111. To obtain a topographic map of the area, ask for Westgard Pass from the USGS.

Central California

Featured Areas .... *pages* 382–383

Overall Rating									
1	2	3	4	5	6	7	8	9	10

Poor .... Fair .... Great

Difficulty				
1	2	3	4	5

A stroll .... Moderate ...... A real butt-kicker!

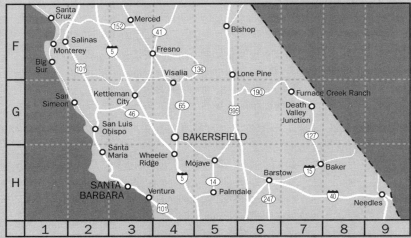

Featured Areas in Central California

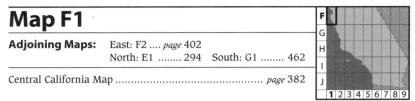

Map F1

Adjoining Maps: East: F2 .... *page* 402
North: E1 294   South: G1 462

Central California Map .... *page 382*

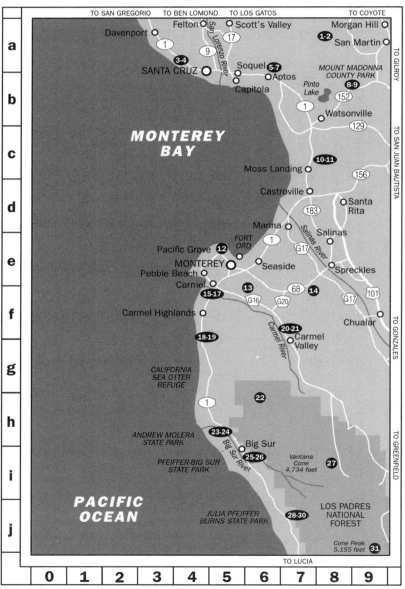

TO SAN GREGORIO   TO BEN LOMOND   TO LOS GATOS   TO COYOTE

a

Davenport
Felton
Scott's Valley
Morgan Hill
1-2
San Martin
3-4
1
9
17
SANTA CRUZ
Soquel **5-7**
Aptos
MOUNT MADONNA
COUNTY PARK

b

Capitola
Pinto Lake
8-9
152
1
Watsonville
129

MONTEREY
BAY

c

Moss Landing
10-11
156

d

Castroville
183
Santa Rita

e

Marina
Salinas
FORT ORD
1
Pacific Grove **12**
G17
MONTEREY
Pebble Beach
Seaside
Spreckles
Carmel
13
68
14
G17
101

f

15-17
G16
G20
Carmel Highlands
20-21
Carmel Valley
Chualar

g

18-19
CALIFORNIA
SEA OTTER
REFUGE
Carmel River
22

h

1
ANDREW MOLERA
STATE PARK
23-24
Big Sur
25-26
PFEIFFER-BIG SUR
STATE PARK
Big Sur River
Ventana
Cone
4,734 feet
27

i

j

PACIFIC
OCEAN
JULIA PFEIFFER
BURNS STATE PARK
28-30
LOS PADRES
NATIONAL
FOREST
Cone Peak
5,155 feet
31
TO LUCIA

TO GILROY   TO SAN JUAN BAUTISTA   TO GONZALES   TO GREENFIELD

0   1   2   3   4   5   6   7   8   9

❶ Uvas Park Waterfall Loop

1.0 mi/0.5 hr

Location: In Uvas Canyon County Park near Morgan Hill; map F1, grid a7.

User groups: Hikers and dogs. No horses or mountain bikes. No wheelchair facilities.

Permits: No permits are required. Parking and access are free.

Directions: From San Jose, take U.S. 101 south and exit at Bernal Road. At the stoplight, turn right, then right again, to reach Monterey Highway. Turn left (south) on Monterey Highway. Turn right on Bailey Avenue and drive 2.8 miles to McKean Road. Turn left on McKean Road and drive six miles (McKean Road becomes Uvas Road). Turn right on Croy Road and drive 4.5 miles to the park (continue past Svaedal, a private camp and resort). Park near the park visitor center or further up the hill in one of the picnic area parking lots. The trailhead is the gated dirt road at Black Oak Picnic Area.

Maps: A free map of Uvas Canyon County Park is available at the visitor center. To obtain a topographic map of the area, ask for Loma Prieta from the USGS.

Contact: Uvas Canyon County Park, 8515 Croy Road, Morgan Hill, CA 95037; (408) 779-9232 or fax (408) 779-3315.

Trail notes: Uvas Canyon County Park is a little slice of waterfall heaven on the east side of the Santa Cruz Mountains. Although the park has only a small length of hiking trails, it's living proof that good things come in small packages. What's the one key element to a perfect trip? Visit during the rainy season, preferably just after a good downpour. Although the park's creeks flow year-round, only immediately following a good rain can you witness the full watery spectacle. The one-mile Waterfall Loop Trail parades around Swanson Creek's canyon, crossing wooden footbridges and passing 30-foot Black Rock Falls and several smaller falls. Be sure to walk a tenth of a mile past the far end of the loop to see Basin Falls and Upper Falls (both pretty cascades 15 to 25 feet high). The entire canyon comes alive with the sound of rushing water, and a myriad of ferns and foliage grow on every inch of ground. It's a happy place, where you can hike around in your rain gear and be smiling the whole time.

❷ Alec Canyon and Contour Loop

4.5 mi/2.5 hrs

Location: In Uvas Canyon County Park near Morgan Hill; map F1, grid a7.

User groups: Hikers and dogs. No horses or mountain bikes. No wheelchair facilities.

Permits: No permits are required. Parking and access are free.

Directions: From San Jose, take U.S. 101 south and exit at Bernal Road. At the stoplight, turn right, then right again, to reach Monterey Highway. Turn left (south) on Monterey Highway. Turn right on Bailey Avenue and drive 2.8 miles to McKean Road. Turn left on McKean Road and drive six miles (McKean Road becomes Uvas Road). Turn right on Croy Road and drive 4.5 miles to the park (continue past Sveadal, a private camp and resort). Park near the park visitor center or further up the hill in one of the picnic area parking lots. The trailhead is the gated dirt road at Black Oak Picnic Area.

Maps: A free map of Uvas Canyon County Park is available at the visitor center. To obtain a topographic map of the area, ask for Loma Prieta from the USGS.

Contact: Uvas Canyon County Park, 8515 Croy Road, Morgan Hill, CA 95037; (408) 779-9232 or fax (408) 779-3315.

Trail notes: For hikers looking for more of a workout than what the Waterfall Loop in Uvas Park provides, this hike up Alec Canyon Trail will get your heart pumping. It's a good trip for a clear winter day, when the views from the trail's overlook at Manzanita Point are at their best. Start hiking on the gated road at Black Oak Picnic Area, then bear left, heading up and away from the canyon and the Waterfall Loop Trail. (You'll get to hike that trail on your way back downhill.) A steep climb up the wide road brings you to Manzanita Point, where you can see far

off to the north and east. Wow, there's a whole huge valley way out there. Continue a quarter mile beyond the point and take the right cutoff to cascading Triple Falls, the most secluded of all the waterfalls in Uvas Park. Then retrace your steps on Alec Canyon Trail, this time bearing left on the Contour Trail less than a half mile past Manzanita Point. Contour Trail is pure fun, winding like a snake along the hillsides, with minimal elevation change but many curves and twists. Finally it drops back down to Swanson Creek, where you can walk back to the trailhead via the Waterfall Loop (see trail description in hike number 1).

❸ Old Landing Cove Trail

2.5 mi/1.5 hrs

Location: In Wilder Ranch State Park north of Santa Cruz; map F1, grid b3.

User groups: Hikers and mountain bikes. No horses or dogs. No wheelchair facilities.

Permits: No permits are required. A $6 day-use fee is charged per vehicle.

Directions: From Santa Cruz, drive north on Highway 1 for four miles. Turn left into the entrance for Wilder Ranch State Park, then follow the park road to its end at the main parking area. Take the trail signed as "Nature Trail" from the southwest side of the parking lot.

Maps: A free map of Wilder Ranch State Park is available at the entrance station. To obtain a topographic map of the area, ask for Santa Cruz from the USGS.

Contact: Wilder Ranch State Park, 1401 Old Coast Road, Santa Cruz, CA 95060; (408) 423-9703 or fax (408) 423-3763.

Trail notes: When you visit Wilder Ranch, you may notice that on some maps and park signs this trail is called "Old Cove Landing," while on others, it's called "Old Landing Cove." Take your pick. The Old Landing Cove Trail is a gem of a coastal hike that offers a look at a seal rookery, some spectacular pocket beaches, and a hidden fern cave. Although the trail is open to both hikers and mountain bikers, everybody seems to mind their manners and get along fine, probably because there's enough spectacular scenery to go around. The trail leads past brussels sprouts fields to the coast. An odd but interesting fact is that 12 percent of our nation's brussels sprouts production happens right here in this park. Once you're beyond the farming fields, turn right and walk along the tops of coastal bluffs. In an eighth of a mile you reach the trail's namesake, Old Landing Cove, where small schooners loaded lumber in the late 1800s. A little more walking brings you to the seal rookery, where you look down on huge flat rocks covered in wall-to-wall seals. Finally, near post number 8, a spur trail leads down to a small beach. If you take the spur, you find a shallow cave on the inland side of the beach filled with ferns from floor to ceiling. A quarter mile past the fern cave beach is another excellent pocket beach, perfect for picnicking or lying around.

④ Wilder Ridge and Zane Grey Trails

6.0 mi/3.0 hrs

Location: In Wilder Ranch State Park north of Santa Cruz; map F1, grid b3.

User groups: Hikers, horses, and mountain bikes. No dogs. No wheelchair facilities.

Permits: No permits are required. A $6 day-use fee is charged per vehicle.

Directions: From Santa Cruz, drive north on Highway 1 for four miles. Turn left into the entrance for Wilder Ranch State Park, then follow the park road to its end at the main parking area. Take the trail signed as "Nature Trail" from the southwest side of the parking lot. Walk down the park road to the Wilder Ranch and Cultural Preserve, then walk through the cultural preserve to the picnic area and chicken coops to reach the tunnel that leads underneath Highway 1.

Maps: A free map of Wilder Ranch State Park is available at the entrance station. To obtain a topographic map of the area, ask for Santa Cruz from the USGS.

Contact: Wilder Ranch State Park, 1401 Old Coast Road, Santa Cruz, CA 95060; (408) 423-9703 or fax (408) 423-3763.

Trail notes: Once you find your way to the hiker/biker tunnel underneath Highway 1 near the farm buildings at Wilder Ranch, you're on your way to a great six-mile day hike with just

enough of a climb to give you a workout, and a spectacular vista of Monterey Bay. Keep in mind that this side of the park is the domain of mountain bikers—hundreds of them on the weekends—but the trails are wide and there's plenty of room for everybody to have a good experience. The Wilder Ridge Trail has a 500-foot climb to a gorgeous overlook, and you reach it by exiting the tunnel and heading straight and then uphill on Wilder Ridge, then bearing right on the right side of the Wilder Ridge Loop. At about 2.5 miles out, shortly after the Twin Oaks Trail forks right, you come out to an obvious grassy overlook at the top of the ridge, only about 40 feet off the main trail. Enjoy the wide-reaching vista for as long as you please, then continue along the ridgetop on Wilder Ridge Loop. For an interesting loop, take the Zane Grey cutoff on the left (it's single-track), then go left again on the other side of the Wilder Ridge Loop. Altogether, it's a great trip, especially in springtime when the hillside grasses are green and the summer fog is not yet visiting.

⑤ Maple Falls

7–9 mi/4.5 hrs

Location: Near Aptos, south of Santa Cruz; map F1, grid b6.

User groups: Hikers only. No dogs or horses. Mountain bikes are allowed only on fire roads. No wheelchair facilities.

Permits: No permits are required. A $3 day-use fee is charged per vehicle.

Directions: From Santa Cruz, drive south on Highway 1 for six miles to the Aptos exit. Bear left at the exit, then turn right on Soquel Drive and drive a half mile. Turn left on Aptos Creek Road. Stop at the entrance kiosk, then continue up the park road and park at Porter Picnic Area. In the winter months, you must park at George's Picnic Area, a mile before Porter Picnic Area, because the park road is gated off at that point.

Maps: A free map of The Forest of Nisene Marks State Park is available at the entrance kiosk. To obtain topographic maps of the area, ask for Laurel, Soquel, and Loma Prieta from the USGS.

Contact: The Forest of Nisene Marks State

Park, c/o Sunset State Beach, 201 Sunset Beach Road, Watsonville, CA 95076; (408) 763-7063 or (408) 429-2850, or fax (408) 763-7124.

Trail notes: It's either a seven-mile or a nine-mile round-trip to Maple Falls, and it all depends on whether or not they've gated off the park road to Porter Picnic Area, the main trailhead. In winter and spring, the road is usually closed off, which means you need to walk an extra mile in each direction in order to see the falls. Of course, winter and spring are the best seasons to go, because that's when Maple Falls is flowing at its fullest. The trip starts out with an easy walk on Aptos Creek Fire Road, which you'll share with mountain bikers. Follow it to a quarter mile past Porter Picnic Area, where you cut off on the Loma Prieta Grade Trail on the left. The second-growth redwood and Douglas fir forest just keeps getting thicker, greener, and better, and the trail is now sweet single-track. Where Loma Prieta Grade splits, stay to the right, heading toward Bridge Creek Historic Site, for the shortest route to the falls. (You can take the other side of the Loma Prieta Grade loop on your way back if you still have the energy.) When you reach Bridge Creek Historic Site, the site of a former logging camp, the maintained trail ends and you begin a fun, half-mile stream scramble to Maple Falls, following the course of Bridge Creek. The canyon narrows as you travel through a dense green world of ferns, moss, foliage, and water, and at last you reach the back of the canyon, where 40-foot Maple Falls spills over the back wall. Wow, what a great hike.

❻ Loma Prieta Epicenter

4.0 mi/2.0 hrs

Location: Near Aptos, south of Santa Cruz; map F1, grid b6.

User groups: Hikers and mountain bikes. No dogs or horses. No wheelchair facilities.

Permits: No permits are required. A $3 day-use fee is charged per vehicle.

Directions: From Santa Cruz, drive south on Highway 1 for six miles to the Aptos exit. Bear left at the exit, then turn right on Soquel Drive and drive a half mile. Turn left on Aptos Creek Road. Stop at the entrance kiosk, then continue

up the park road and park at Porter Picnic Area. In the winter months, you must park at George's Picnic Area, a mile before Porter Picnic Area, because the park road is gated off at that point.

Maps: A free map of The Forest of Nisene Marks State Park is available at the entrance kiosk. To obtain topographic maps of the area, ask for Laurel, Soquel, and Loma Prieta from the USGS.

Contact: The Forest of Nisene Marks State Park, c/o Sunset State Beach, 201 Sunset Beach Road, Watsonville, CA 95076; (408) 763-7063 or (408) 429-2850, or fax (408) 763-7124.

Trail notes: The destination on this trail is the epicenter of the 1989 Loma Prieta earthquake, but the pleasure of the trip has little to do with its interesting geological focus. Instead, the joy is in the scenery, which is a lush second-growth redwood forest that has regenerated after a clear-cut operation at the turn of the century. The walk follows the Aptos Creek Fire Road, which you share with mountain bikers as it leads gently uphill. At 1.5 miles from the Porter Picnic Area, cross a footbridge and descend a bit on the trail until you come to the spot where a large sign once stood, proclaiming the proximity of the earthquake epicenter (the sign was stolen). There's a small bike rack there. Cross the creek and continue up the single-track trail for a half mile to the actual epicenter, where you will see surprisingly little evidence of anything earth-shaking, but rather a lovely and peaceful redwood forest. Turn around here for a four-mile round-trip (or six miles if you had to start from George's Picnic Area instead of Porter Picnic Area).

❼ West Ridge and Aptos Creek Loop

12.5 mi/7.0 hrs or 2.0 days

Location: Near Aptos, south of Santa Cruz; map F1, grid b6.

User groups: Hikers and mountain bikes. No dogs or horses. No wheelchair facilities.

Permits: No permits are required. A $3 day-use fee is charged per vehicle. An advance reservation is necessary to stay overnight at West Ridge Trail Camp; phone the park for reservations.

Directions: From Santa Cruz, drive south on Highway 1 for six miles to the Aptos exit. Bear left at the exit, then turn right on Soquel Drive and drive a half mile. Turn left on Aptos Creek Road. Stop at the entrance kiosk, then continue up the park road and park at George's Picnic Area.

Maps: A free map of The Forest of Nisene Marks State Park is available at the entrance kiosk. To obtain a topographic map of the area, ask for Laurel, Soquel, and Loma Prieta from the USGS.

Contact: The Forest of Nisene Marks State Park, c/o Sunset State Beach, 201 Sunset Beach Road, Watsonville, CA 95076; (408) 763-7063 or (408) 429-2850, or fax (408) 763-7124.

Trail notes: The West Ridge and Aptos Creek Loop is the grand tour of The Forest of Nisene Marks State Park, suitable only for hikers in good condition and with a lot of time on their hands. An option is to get advance reservations for West Ridge Trail Camp and turn this into an overnight trip; the camp is situated conveniently near spectacular Sand Point Overlook—great for sunsets. (Backpacking stoves are necessary; no campfires are allowed.) From George's Picnic Area, walk up Aptos Creek Road for a quarter mile to the left cutoff for West Ridge Trail, then start climbing uphill along the West Ridge of Aptos Canyon. (You can also take the Loma Prieta Grade Trail, if you prefer, then follow the left side of its loop and take the connector trail to meet up with West Ridge Trail.) Finally you ascend all the way to Hinckley Ridge at 1,300 feet, then meet up with the fire road that leads to West Ridge Trail Camp and Sand Point Overlook. From the overlook at 1,500 feet, you can see down into the densely forested Bridge Creek drainage, and far off across sky-blue Monterey Bay. Finish out the loop with a long downhill walk on Aptos Creek Fire Road, a wide path through dense redwoods and Douglas firs.

❽ White Deer Trail

0.5 mi/0.25 hr

Location: In Mount Madonna County Park in the Santa Cruz Mountains west of Gilroy; map F1, grid b8.

User groups: Hikers and wheelchairs. No dogs, horses, or mountain bikes.

Permits: No permits are required. A $3 day-use fee is charged.

Directions: From San Jose, take U.S. 101 south to Gilroy. Turn west on Highway 152 and drive 10 miles, then turn right on Poleline Road and drive to the parking area.

Maps: For a free trail map, contact Mount Madonna County Park at the address below. To obtain a topographic map of the area, ask for Mount Madonna from the USGS.

Contact: Mount Madonna County Park, 7850 Poleline Road, Watsonville, CA 95076; (408) 842-2341.

Trail notes: The remainders of a rare herd of white deer are the star attraction at Mount Madonna County Park. These animals are similar to black-tailed deer, the most common deer in California, except they are larger and completely white. In late summer, the bucks develop a huge set of antlers, quite a sight. They are kept in a pen that stands about 30 feet from the parking lot next to headquarters to protect them, because in the early 1990s, a group of poachers with rifles was killing them off at night, one at a time. Justice was served when one of the gunmen shot himself by accident and was left behind by his fellow culprits. Karma. Only three deer survived the poaching incidents, but two fawns were born in 1994, giving some cause for hope. Today the herd is rebuilding itself, and you can typically see five to 10 of these rare animals here. The "white deer" are actually white fallow deer, descendants of a pair donated in 1932 by William Randolph Hearst.

❾ Bayview Loop

2.5 mi/1.75 hrs

Location: In Mount Madonna County Park in the Santa Cruz Mountains west of Gilroy; map F1, grid b8.

User groups: Hikers and horses. No dogs or mountain bikes. No wheelchair facilities.

Permits: No permits are required. A $3 day-use fee is charged.

Directions: From San Jose, take U.S. 101 south to Gilroy. Turn west on Highway 152 and drive

10 miles, then turn right on Poleline Road and drive to the entrance station. The trailhead is on the left.

Maps: For a free trail map, contact Mount Madonna County Park at the address below. To obtain a topographic map of the area, ask for Mount Madonna from the USGS.

Contact: Mount Madonna County Park, 7850 Poleline Road, Watsonville, CA 95076; (408) 842-2341.

Trail notes: Mount Madonna County Park provides great scenic beauty, good hiking, camping, and horseback riding. The park is set around the highest peak in the southern range of the Santa Cruz Mountains, and with 18 miles of hiking trails, the best routes are combinations of different trails. So it is with this triangular loop, starting at the park entrance station at Hecker Pass, elevation 1,270 feet. Take the Bayview Trail and hike north for 1.1 miles, scanning west to Monterey Bay along the way. Turn right on the Redwood Trail (it will cross Poleline Road) and you will walk from those coastal lookouts into forest, getting the best of both worlds. To complete the loop, take the Redwood/Rock Springs/Blackhawk/Bayview Trails as they junction in sequence. Confused? This park is filled with a spiderweb of short hikes. By linking them you can customize your adventure. Our suggested loop provides a look at some of the park's prettiest settings.

⑩ Elkhorn Slough South Marsh Loop

2.8 mi/1.5 hrs

Location: Near Moss Landing; map F1, grid c7.

User groups: Hikers only. No dogs, horses, or mountain bikes. Some facilities are wheelchair accessible.

Permits: No permits are required. A $2.50 entrance fee is charged per person. (Children under 16 enter free, and anyone in possession of a California fishing or hunting license can enter free.)

Directions: From Highway 1 at Moss Landing, turn east on Dolan Road (by the Pacific Gas and Electric Company power station). Drive three miles to Elkhorn Road, then turn left (north) and

drive two miles to the reserve entrance. The trail begins by the visitor center.

Maps: A free map of Elkhorn Slough is available at the parking lot or the visitor center. To obtain a topographic map of the area, ask for Moss Landing from the USGS.

Contact: Elkhorn Slough National Estuarine Reserve, 1700 Elkhorn Road, Moss Landing, CA; (408) 728-2822, or fax (408) 649-2894.

Trail notes: Elkhorn Slough is 2,500 acres of marsh and tidal flats, the precious borderline between sea and land that is home to thousands of species of birds, fish, and invertebrates. It's the second largest salt marsh in California, and in the peak of the migration season, over 20,000 birds per day congregate here. Hikers with binoculars (and sometimes with just their own eyes) frequently spot golden eagles and peregrine falcons here. Endangered clapper rails and least terns are also among the sanctuary's inhabitants. The South Marsh Loop Trail is a three-mile tour of this salty, marshy, bird-filled land, crossing footbridges over the slough and staying close to the water's edge and mudflats. Make sure you take all the short spurs off the loop. A highlight in the spring is walking through the heron rookery, where you may be able to spot tiny great blue heron babies. (If you want to walk more, two other loop trails are available.)

Special note: The reserve is open Wednesdays through Sundays only.

⑪ Moss Landing Wildlife Area Marsh Trail

3.0 mi/1.5 hrs

Location: In Moss Landing; map F1, grid c7.

User groups: Hikers only. No dogs, horses, or mountain bikes. No wheelchair facilities.

Permits: No permits are required. Parking and access are free.

Directions: From Moss Landing, drive north on Highway 1 for one mile to a dirt road on the right that is signed for Moss Landing Wildlife Area. (It's north of Struve Road.) Turn right (east) and drive a short distance to the trailhead. (If you are coming from the south, you can use the south entrance to the wildlife area. Cross the Elkhorn Slough bridge.)

Maps: A free map/brochure of Moss Landing Wildlife Area is available at the north entrance to Moss Landing Wildlife Area. To obtain a topographic map of the area, ask for Moss Landing from the USGS.

Contact: Department of Fish and Game, (408) 649-2870. Or contact the neighboring Elkhorn Slough Reserve, (408) 728-2822.

Trail notes: Located on the north bank of giant Elkhorn Slough, the Moss Landing Wildlife Area gets a little less human traffic than the more developed Elkhorn Slough Reserve, but no less bird traffic. Unlike the neighboring reserve, there's no day-use fee to visit here, and it's open seven days a week. From the trailhead, you leave the lettuce fields and wander into the salt marsh with your camera, binoculars, and bird book (or maybe just your lunch and a friend). The trail winds along the marsh for five-plus miles, but you can just go as far as you like, paying a visit to brown pelicans, egrets, herons, terns, gulls, and all their buddies. Brown pelicans summer here in large numbers. The terrain varies somewhat as you walk, moving into occasional groves of eucalyptus and oak woodlands, with a side-trip possible to some old salt harvesting ponds. Most people just walk 1.5 miles out, to a picnic area situated on a bluff above the slough.

⑫ Asilomar Coast Trail

2.4 mi/1.5 hrs

Location: In Pacific Grove; map F1, grid e5.

User groups: Hikers and dogs. No horses or mountain bikes. Portions of the trail are wheelchair accessible.

Permits: No permits are required. Parking and access are free.

Directions: From Salinas on U.S. 101, take the Highway 68/Monterey exit and continue into Monterey and then Pacific Grove, where Highway 68 becomes Sunset Drive. Continue to Asilomar State Beach. Park alongside Sunset Drive; the trail begins opposite the conference center.

Maps: To obtain a topographic map of the area, ask for Monterey from the USGS.

Contact: Asilomar State Beach, 804 Crocker Avenue, Pacific Grove, CA 93950; (408) 372-4076, or fax (408) 372-3759.

Trail notes: Even if you aren't lucky enough to attend a conference at the historic Asilomar Conference Center, you can still walk its adjoining Asilomar Coast Trail, a spectacular 1.2-mile trail along coastal bluffs above rugged, windswept Asilomar Beach. There's plenty to look at, and many side trails to explore. You'll see waves crashing against jagged rocks, plentiful tide pools, tiny pocket beaches, wide sandy stretches with big white dunes, and much sea life. Be sure to take the separate boardwalk trail (on the west side of the conference center) that leads across the dunes. Kite flying is also popular along some stretches of Asilomar Beach.

⑬ Skyline and Jacks Peak Trails

1.2 mi/0.5 hr

Location: In Jacks Peak County Park near Monterey; map F1, grid e5.

User groups: Hikers and dogs. No horses or mountain bikes. No wheelchair facilities.

Permits: No permits are required. A $2 entrance fee is charged per vehicle Monday through Thursday; $3 on Fridays, weekends, and holidays.

Directions: From Monterey, take Highway 68 east from Highway 1 for 1.7 miles to Olmsted Road. Turn right on Olmsted Road and drive 1.5 miles to Jacks Peak Drive, then follow Jacks Peak Drive to the park entrance. After passing through the entrance kiosk, turn right and drive to the parking area for Jacks Peak.

Maps: A free map of Jacks Peak County Park is available at the entrance station. To obtain a topographic map of the area, ask for Seaside from the USGS.

Contact: Jacks Peak County Park, 25020 Jacks Peak Road, Monterey, CA 93940; (408) 372-8551.

Trail notes: They've got a whole park centered around Jacks Peak, the highest point on the Monterey Peninsula at 1,068 feet. Hey, it's not the Sierra, but it's high and pretty. The park and the peak are named after David Jacks, the guy who got his name on Monterey Jack Cheese. The Skyline Nature Trail is an easy loop walk around the summit of Jacks Peak, set amid Monterey pines. The Jacks Peak Trail is a smaller loop inside the Skyline Nature Trail loop, and you can easily branch off the latter to join the former for a half-hour walk that provides unparalleled views of Carmel Valley, the Monterey Peninsula, Point Lobos, the Santa Lucia Mountains, and the Pacific Ocean. Even though the view is about the same on both trail loops, make sure you walk a leg of the Jacks Peak Trail to the top of Jacks Peak, where you can sit on a bench and pull out a picnic of Jack cheese sandwiches. Don't plan on watching the sun set from here, though; unfortunately, the park closes before then.

⑭ Ollason Peak

7.5 mi/3.5 hrs

Location: In Toro County Park near Monterey; map F1, grid e7.

User groups: Hikers, dogs, and horses. No mountain bikes. No wheelchair facilities.

Permits: No permits are required. A $3 entrance fee is charged per vehicle Monday through Thursday; $5 on Fridays, weekends, and holidays.

Directions: From Monterey, take Highway 68 east from Highway 1 for 13 miles to the park entrance, on the right (south) side of the road. Drive to the parking area by Quail Meadow Group Campground.

Maps: A free map of Toro County Park is available at the entrance station. To obtain a topographic map of the area, ask for Spreckels from the USGS.

Contact: Toro County Park, 501 Monterey Highway, Salinas, CA 93908; (408) 484-1108.

Trail notes: Pick a cool day in spring to take this inspiring jaunt to the top of Ollason Peak, elevation 1,800 feet, far from the madding crowds of popular Toro County Park. Even with a cool breeze, the Ollason Trail can be a butt-kicker, with many steep sections over a less-than-smooth route. It leads from the Quail Meadow Group Camp, and climbs through wide grasslands and occasional oak groves, most of the time on wide double-track. Increasingly wide

views, and an excellent variety of grassland wildflowers, are your reward for the work. After a long stint heading southwest, the trail suddenly veers east, then resumes its southern course for the final climb to Ollason Peak, four miles from the trailhead. You get lovely views toward Monterey Bay and the Central Valley from Ollason's summit. Retrace your steps from there, or continue a little further to Coyote Spring Trail, bearing left for a 7.5-mile loop. If you're making the loop, be sure to watch for the left turnoff on Cougar Ridge from Coyote Spring, which returns you to a connector trail back to Quail Meadow Camp.

⑮ Sea Lion Point Trail

0.6 mi/0.5 hr

Location: In Point Lobos State Reserve near Carmel; map F1, grid f4.

User groups: Hikers and wheelchairs. No dogs, horses, or mountain bikes. Part of the trail is wheelchair accessible.

Permits: No permits are required. A $6 day-use fee is charged per vehicle.

Directions: From Carmel at Rio Road, drive south on Highway 1 for three miles to the entrance to Point Lobos State Reserve on the right. Turn right and drive through the entrance kiosk, then continue straight to the information station and Sea Lion Point parking area.

Maps: A map of Point Lobos State Reserve is available for 50 cents at the entrance station. To obtain a topographic map of the area, ask for Monterey from the USGS.

Contact: Point Lobos State Reserve, Route 1, Box 62, Carmel, CA 93923; (408) 624-4909, or fax (408) 624-8413.

Trail notes: On summer weekends, the cars are parked in a long line along the road outside Point Lobos State Reserve, Carmel's crown jewel of parks. Even on weekdays, the parking lots are surprisingly full here, but the park's stunning coastal beauty and plentiful wildlife explains why. By far the biggest attraction at the park is the Sea Lion Point Trail, a round-trip loop of just over a half mile, part of which is suitable for wheelchairs. Along the way, you can look for cute little sea otters floating on their backs in the kelp, and chubby harbor seals hauling out on the rocks. When the trail reaches a rocky staircase, wheelchair users will have to turn back, but other visitors can continue down to a lower trail. Rock outcrops jut out of the breakers just offshore; these are named Sea Lion Rocks, for obvious reasons. Test your hiking partner's knowledge of American literature with this fact: Robert Louis Stevenson used Point Lobos as the inspiration for his novel *Treasure Island*.

16 Whaler's Knoll and Cypress Grove

4.0 mi/2.0 hrs

Location: In Point Lobos State Reserve near Carmel; map F1, grid f4.

User groups: Hikers only. No dogs, horses, or mountain bikes. No wheelchair facilities.

Permits: No permits are required. A $6 day-use fee is charged per vehicle.

Directions: From Carmel at Rio Road, drive south on Highway 1 for three miles to the entrance to Point Lobos State Reserve on the right. Turn right and drive through the entrance kiosk, then continue straight to the information station and Sea Lion Point parking area.

Maps: A map of Point Lobos State Reserve is available for 50 cents at the entrance station. To obtain a topographic map of the area, ask for Monterey from the USGS.

Contact: Point Lobos State Reserve, Route 1, Box 62, Carmel, CA 93923; (408) 624-4909, or fax (408) 624-8413.

Trail notes: Two excellent trails lead from the north side of the Sea Lion Point parking area (near the information station) at Point Lobos, and you can connect them to make a stellar four-mile round-trip. Start by hiking on the Cypress Grove Trail, which shows off the park's feature Monterey cypress trees. The grove is one of only two remaining natural cypress groves on earth. In addition to getting a look at the marvelous windswept trees, you walk through coastal scrub to rocky cliffs with picture-perfect ocean views. The trail loops around and heads back toward the parking area, but just before you reach it, you can turn left on the North Shore Trail and climb a bit to the right turnoff for the Whaler's Knoll Trail. Whaler's Knoll Trail makes

loose switchbacks uphill to the top of Whaler's Knoll, where you get the best view in the whole park. Luckily there's a bench there so you can sit down, catch your breath, and enjoy it. The knoll was where turn-of-the-century whalers would watch for whales, then hang a signal flag when they spotted them. You can continue hiking from there, heading downhill and making a loop back along the coast on the North Shore Trail.

17 Point Lobos Perimeter

6.0 mi/3.0 hrs

Location: In Point Lobos State Reserve near Carmel; map F1, grid f4.

User groups: Hikers only. No dogs, horses, or mountain bikes. No wheelchair facilities.

Permits: No permits are required. A $6 day-use fee is charged per vehicle.

Directions: From Carmel at Rio Road, drive south on Highway 1 for three miles to the entrance to Point Lobos State Reserve on the right. Turn right and drive through the entrance kiosk, then continue straight to the information station and Sea Lion Point parking area.

Maps: A map of Point Lobos State Reserve is available for 50 cents at the entrance station. To obtain a topographic map of the area, ask for Monterey from the USGS.

Contact: Point Lobos State Reserve, Route 1, Box 62, Carmel, CA 93923; (408) 624-4909, or fax (408) 624-8413.

Trail notes: The perimeter hike at Point Lobos connects a number of trails to view the best highlights of the park. Make sure you get a park map at the entrance station before hiking it, so you can scope out the many side-trip options that are possible (and the many shortcuts, if you're getting tired). Starting from the Sea Lion Point parking area, make your first destination Sea Lion Point (see trail notes for hike number 15), then bear left on Sand Hill Trail and connect to South Shore Trail. The latter leads along the quieter south part of the park, past numerous spectacular beaches and coves, to Bird Island Trail. Make sure you take the short side path to Bird Island Overlook, then maybe walk the stairs down to the sandy beaches at China Cove and Gibson Beach. (China Cove is one of the most beautiful spots on earth, in our opinion.) From the Bird Island Trail you connect with the South Plateau Trail, follow it northward and cross the park road to follow Carmelo Meadow Trail, then bear right for a side trip to Granite Point. Don't miss this; it's a rocky outcrop on a short loop trail with great views toward Carmel to the north. Then retrace your steps along the Granite Point Trail and finish out your loop by hiking along the park's northern shoreline, following Granite Point Trail to Cabin Trail to North Shore Trail. Possible side trips are to the Whaler's Cabin Museum, or a spur trail to a lookout of Guillemot Island and its millions of birds, or the Whaler's Knoll and Cypress Grove (see hike number 16 for details on these). If you take all of the possible side trips along the route, this hike will take you almost all day, and what a fine day it will be.

⑱ Rocky Ridge and Soberanes Canyon Loop

6.0 mi/3.0 hrs

Location: In Garrapata State Park south of Carmel; map F1, grid f4.

User groups: Hikers only. No dogs, horses, or mountain bikes. No wheelchair facilities.

Permits: No permits are required. Parking and access are free.

Directions: From Carmel at Rio Road, drive south on Highway 1 for seven miles to marker 13 and the dirt pullouts along the highway at Garrapata State Park. (It's four miles south of Point Lobos State Park and easy to miss; go slow and watch for cars parked alongside the road.) The Soberanes Canyon Trail begins on the inland side of the road.

Maps: To obtain a topographic map of the area, ask for Soberanes Point from the USGS.

Contact: Garrapata State Park, c/o Pfeiffer Big Sur State Park, Big Sur, CA 93920; (408) 667-2315, (408) 649-2836, or (408) 624-7195.

Trail notes: It sounds impossible. A state park that's free on the Monterey Coast? But it's true—it won't cost you a dime to park alongside Highway 1 and hike around all day on the excellent trails of Garrapata State Park. The park is situated on both sides of Highway 1, with some trails leading to the ocean and others leading

up inland canyons and hillsides. Hikers looking for a long leg-stretching walk will enjoy this loop trip on the inland side of the park, which travels through a remarkable variety of terrain. You want diversity, you get diversity. Begin hiking on the Soberanes Canyon Trail. What starts out as a ranch road through chaparral-covered hillsides quickly becomes single-track through an increasingly narrow and wet canyon. The big surprise is a gorgeous stand of redwoods along Soberanes Creek, a complete contrast to the chaparral, cactus, and dry-country wildflowers at the start of the trail. The grove is a good turnaround spot for those looking for a shorter trip. If you continue on, the trail makes a substantial climb and heads north to a spur to the Peak Trail (also signed as North Ridge Trail) and an intersection with the Rocky Ridge Trail. Forget the spur and finish out your loop on Rocky Ridge Trail, where on a clear day you can look out over the ocean for miles. The trail then winds back down the hillsides and deposits you back at your car on Highway 1.

⑲ Soberanes Point Trail

2.0 mi/1.0 hrs

Location: In Garrapata State Park south of Carmel; map F1, grid f4.

User groups: Hikers only. No dogs, horses, or mountain bikes. No wheelchair facilities.

Permits: No permits are required. Parking and access are free.

Directions: From Carmel at Rio Road, drive south on Highway 1 for seven miles to marker 13 and the dirt pullouts along the highway at Garrapata State Park. (It's four miles south of Point Lobos State Park and easy to miss; go slow and watch for cars parked alongside the road.) The Soberanes Point Trail begins on the inland side of the road.

Maps: To obtain a topographic map of the area, ask for Soberanes Point from the USGS.

Contact: Garrapata State Park, c/o Pfeiffer Big Sur State Park, Big Sur, CA 93920; (408) 667-2315, (408) 649-2836, or (408) 624-7195.

Trail notes: You can access the Soberanes Point Trail from three different gates along Highway 1, so if you miss marker 13 you can always stop at markers 15 or 16. Wherever you begin from, you'll end up on a spectacular and easy set of trails that join in a series of loops around Soberanes Point, all basically centering around Whale Peak. If you time your trip properly, you'll have access to some excellent tide pools at low tide, and even if not, you get views of rocky shoreline bluffs and plenty of animal and bird life. Many anglers try their luck rock fishing here at the point, and it's also a popular spot for whale watching from November to January. Note that if you start from marker 13, you can hike a short loop to your right and then a much larger loop to your left. If you start from marker 15, you're at the middle of the larger loop, so you can start hiking either right or left. Just wander as you please; the coastline and the perimeter of the point makes it impossible to get lost.

⓴ Lupine, Waterfall, and Mesa Loop

3.0 mi/1.5 hrs

Location: In Garland Ranch Regional Park near Carmel; map F1, grid f6.

User groups: Hikers, dogs, and horses. No mountain bikes. No wheelchair facilities.

Permits: No permits are required. Parking and access are free.

Directions: From Highway 1 at Carmel, turn east on Carmel Valley Road. Drive 8.6 miles on Carmel Valley Road to the Garland Ranch parking area on the right side of the road. Walk across the river bridge to get to the visitor center and trailheads.

Maps: A free map of Garland Ranch Regional Park is available at the visitor center. To obtain topographic maps of the area, ask for Mount Carmel and Carmel Valley from the USGS.

Contact: Garland Ranch Regional Park, P.O. Box 395, Carmel Valley, CA 93924; (408) 659-6063 or (408) 659-4488.

Trail notes: Garland Ranch's excellent visitor center is the perfect place to begin your trip to the park. Take a look inside, get a trail map, and learn a few things about the area's animals, trees, and wildflowers. The center is also the trailhead for this combined loop on the Lupine, Waterfall, and Mesa Trails. Although the park's

waterfall only flows during the rainy season, the trails are good to walk year-round, and they're well maintained and well signed to boot. Begin by heading to the left (northwest) from the visitor center on the Lupine Loop, which travels along the open, flat floodplains of the Carmel River. In a half mile, leave the loop and continue straight on the Waterfall Trail, then climb through a more shady area to the rocky cliff where the waterfall sometimes falls. Beyond it, you'll ascend more seriously, following a few switchbacks to the mesa, a large high meadow with views of Carmel Valley and beyond. Follow the Mesa Trail back downhill to the other side of the Lupine Loop, and take the Lupine Loop back to the visitor center. Expect an excellent wildflower show in the grasslands in springtime.

㉑ Snivley's Ridge Trail

5.6 mi/3.0 hrs

Location: In Garland Ranch Regional Park near Carmel; map F1, grid f6.

User groups: Hikers, dogs, and horses. No mountain bikes. No wheelchair facilities.

Permits: No permits are required. Parking and access are free.

Directions: From Highway 1 at Carmel, turn east on Carmel Valley Road. Drive 8.6 miles on Carmel Valley Road to the Garland Ranch parking area on the right side of the road. Walk across the river bridge to get to the visitor center and trailheads.

Maps: A free map of Garland Ranch Regional Park is available at the visitor center. To obtain topographic maps of the area, ask for Mount Carmel and Carmel Valley from the USGS.

Contact: Garland Ranch Regional Park, P.O. Box 395, Carmel Valley, CA 93924; (408) 659-6063 or (408) 659-4488.

Trail notes: If it's winter or spring, a trip to the top of Snivley's Ridge could be just what you need to keep your hiking legs in shape. It's a healthy 1,600-foot climb up to the ridge, plus a 250-foot climb to get to the ridge's highest point, so be prepared to pant a little. Much of the walk is exposed; be sure to bring water and pick a cool day to hike the trail. From the park visitor center, set out on either side of the Lupine

Loop (heading left is a little shorter), then continue uphill on the Mesa Trail to its junction with Fern Trail. This stretch is moist and shady, so enjoy it while you're in it. Follow Fern Trail, then turn left and quickly right on Sky Trail, and begin the serious portion of the climb. Well-graded switchbacks make it easier. Many people stop where Sky Trail meets Snivley's Ridge Trail, at a bench with a panoramic view of Carmel Valley, the forested Santa Lucia Mountains, and the ocean. But those determined to go as high as possible should turn right on Snivley's Ridge, walk another half mile, then turn left on a spur trail that leads to the park's highest point, at 2,038 feet.

㉒ Skinner Ridge Viewpoint

4.4 mi/2.5 hrs

Location: In the Ventana Wilderness near Carmel Valley; map F1, grid g6.

User groups: Hikers, dogs, and horses. No mountain bikes. No wheelchair facilities.

Permits: No permits are required. A national forest recreation pass is required for each vehicle; fees are $5 for one day or $30 for a year.

Directions: From Carmel, drive south on Highway 1 for 12 miles, past Garrapata State Park, to the left (east) turnoff for Palo Colorado Road (it's just south of Rocky Point Restaurant). Turn left and drive eight miles to Bottcher's Gap Campground. The Skinner Ridge Trail is signed at the edge of the parking lot.

Maps: For a map of Los Padres National Forest or the Ventana Wilderness, send $4 to USDA-Forest Service, 630 Sansome Street, San Francisco, CA 94111. To obtain topographic maps of the area, ask for Mount Carmel and Big Sur from the USGS.

Contact: Los Padres National Forest, Monterey Ranger District, 406 South Mildred Avenue, King City, CA 93930; (408) 385-5434.

Trail notes: What's the best thing about this trip? The vistas from Skinner Ridge Viewpoint? The white marble of giant Pico Blanco to the southwest? The ocean views in the first mile of the climb? The colors of the oak leaves in autumn? Or the many possible side trips from Skin-

ner Ridge? It's hard to decide; you'd better go see for yourself. The trailhead is at 2,000 feet, and the initial climb is through chaparral, with wide-open views. Then the trail enters the trees (madrones and oaks), and winds and twists its way around before making a short but steep ascent to the top of Skinner Ridge, elevation 3,450 feet. Most people stop here, 2.2 miles out, feeling fully oxygenated and exercised, and glad to be alive in a place where the views are this spectacular. The good news is that on the way back downhill, you get to see even more. Those who have extra energy to burn can continue three-quarters of a mile further to a trail junction and turn left to descend to Turner Creek (Apple Tree Camp is one mile away, a good place for an overnight). Or proceed straight ahead for the climb to Devil's Peak (elevation 4,158 feet, and one mile further).

㉓ Molera Point Trail

2.5 mi/1.5 hrs

Location: In Andrew Molera State Park north of Big Sur; map F1, grid h5.

User groups: Hikers, dogs, horses, and mountain bikes. No wheelchair facilities.

Permits: No permits are required. A $4 day-use fee is charged per vehicle.

Directions: From Carmel, drive 22 miles south on Highway 1 to Andrew Molera State Park's main entrance, on the west side of the highway. Trails begin at the parking lot. (The park is two miles north of Big Sur.)

Maps: A map of Andrew Molera State Park is available for 50 cents at this park's entrance station or at the entrance to Pfeiffer Big Sur State Park. To obtain a topographic map of the area, ask for Big Sur from the USGS.

Contact: Andrew Molera State Park, c/o Pfeiffer Big Sur State Park, Big Sur, CA 93920; (408) 667-2315 or (408) 624-7195, or fax (408) 667-2886.

Trail notes: Andrew Molera is a low-key state park, without all the development and fanfare that often comes with state park status. That means it's good for hikers—people who just want a good trail to walk on and not much else. An easy trail leads from the park's main parking lot to Molera Point, where you can look down on spectacular Molera Beach and count the sea lions lying on the rocks. To reach the point, take the trail from the right side of the parking lot, which stays on the north side of the Big Sur River. The trail is really a dirt road, and follows the river as it winds past the park's walk-in camp and historic Cooper Cabin, which was built in 1861 and is the oldest structure on the Big Sur coast. At the river's mouth, a bridge leads to the beach (the bridge is in place only in summer), and a spur trail leads to the right, out to Molera Point. Take the spur trail and check out the view, then if the tide is low and the bridge is in place, go play on the beach for a while before heading back.

㉔ Molera State Park Loop

7.8 mi/4.0 hrs

Location: In Andrew Molera State Park north of Big Sur; map F1, grid h5.

User groups: Hikers, dogs, horses, and mountain bikes. No wheelchair facilities.

Permits: No permits are required. A $4 day-use fee is charged per vehicle.

Directions: From Carmel, drive 22 miles south on Highway 1 to Andrew Molera State Park's main entrance, on the west side of the highway. Trails begin at the parking lot. (The park is two miles north of Big Sur.)

Maps: A map of Andrew Molera State Park is available for 50 cents at this park's entrance station or at the entrance to Pfeiffer Big Sur State Park. To obtain a topographic map of the area, ask for Big Sur from the USGS.

Contact: Andrew Molera State Park, c/o Pfeiffer Big Sur State Park, Big Sur, CA 93920; (408) 667-2315 or (408) 624-7195, or fax (408) 667-2886.

Trail notes: This big loop around the western side of Andrew Molera State Park is possible only in summertime, when the footbridge is in place over the Big Sur River. If the bridge is there, don't miss out on this trail, which offers six miles of lovely vistas. Start by taking the path from the ocean side of the parking lot and immediately crossing the footbridge. Follow either of the trails that skirt the edges of Creamery Meadow, then turn left on Ridge Trail and hike southward, paralleling the ocean. It's views, views, views all

the way. See any whales waving at you? Three miles out, you meet up with Panorama Trail and turn right. Descend to the Bluffs Trail, and follow it for three miles back to the Creamery Meadow trails. (Halfway along the Bluffs Trail, a side trip is possible on the Spring Trail, which leads a short distance down to the beach.) The Bluffs Trail offers long and beautiful looks at Molera Point and beach and Point Sur Light Station.

㉕ Pfeiffer Falls and Valley View Loop

1.6 mi/1.0 hrs

Location: In Pfeiffer Big Sur State Park near Big Sur; map F1, grid i6.

User groups: Hikers only. No dogs, horses, or mountain bikes. No wheelchair facilities.

Permits: No permits are required. A $6 day-use fee is charged per vehicle.

Directions: From Carmel, drive 26 miles south on Highway 1 to Pfeiffer Big Sur State Park, on the east side of the highway. (It's two miles south of Big Sur.) Drive through the entrance kiosk, turn left at the lodge, then turn right, following the signs to Pfeiffer Falls Trailhead and Nature Center. Park just beyond the nature center. The trail is on the left side of the lot, signed as Oak Grove Trail, Valley View Trail, and Pfeiffer Falls Trail. (If the small parking lot is full, you may have to park by the lodge and walk to the trailhead.)

Maps: A map of Pfeiffer Big Sur State Park is available for $1 at the entrance station. To obtain a topographic map of the area, ask for Big Sur from the USGS.

Contact: Pfeiffer Big Sur State Park, Big Sur, CA 93920; (408) 667-2315 or (408) 649-2836, or fax (408) 667-2886.

Trail notes: A loop hike to a 60-foot waterfall and an overlook of the Big Sur Valley? Sounds great; let's go. And don't forget, there's a gorgeous redwood forest along the way. You get all of this when you set out on the Pfeiffer Falls Trail from the nature center at Pfeiffer Big Sur State Park, then return on the Valley View Trail. After a slightly uphill walk on the Pfeiffer Falls Trail along Pfeiffer Redwood Creek (ignore all the trail junctions and stay along the creek, crossing it a couple of times on bridges), you'll wind up at the foot of tall and narrow Pfeiffer Falls, which streams down a vertical, dark rock face. You can sit for a while at the waterfall's viewing platform, then backtrack along the trail a tenth of a mile to its junction with the Valley View Trail. Follow Valley View Trail as it climbs up and out of the canyon. You'll leave the redwoods almost immediately and hike in an oak forest for a half mile, until the trail reaches a wide overlook of the Big Sur Valley and Point Sur. From there, head back down Valley View Trail and take the right fork (a quarter mile from the viewpoint) to finish out your loop hike near the trailhead.

㉖ Buzzards Roost Trail

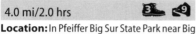

4.0 mi/2.0 hrs

Location: In Pfeiffer Big Sur State Park near Big Sur; map F1, grid i6.

User groups: Hikers only. No dogs, horses, or mountain bikes. No wheelchair facilities.

Permits: No permits are required. A $6 day-use fee is charged per vehicle.

Directions: From Carmel, drive 26 miles south on Highway 1 to Pfeiffer Big Sur State Park, on the east side of the highway. (It's two miles south of Big Sur.) Drive through the entrance kiosk, continue past the lodge and turn right to cross the bridge over the Big Sur River. A parking area is on the left side of the road. At the parking area, the Buzzards Roost Trail is signed. (You can also park at the Big Sur Lodge and walk from there.)

Maps: A map of Pfeiffer Big Sur State Park is available for $1 at the entrance station. To obtain topographic maps of the area, ask for Big Sur and Pfeiffer Point from the USGS.

Contact: Pfeiffer Big Sur State Park, Big Sur, CA 93920; (408) 667-2315 or (408) 649-2836, or fax (408) 667-2886.

Trail notes: Hikers looking for a bit of a challenge in Pfeiffer Big Sur State Park will want to try out this trail to the Buzzards Roost Overlook. Compared to the Pfeiffer Falls Trail, this trail gets surprisingly little traffic, except if there are large groups camping at the nearby group campground. The trail leads along the Big Sur River through a forest of many splendid redwoods,

then switchbacks uphill onto slopes filled with oaks and bays, and finally climbs into chaparral country. You get to walk in some of every kind of Big Sur terrain. High up on Pfeiffer Ridge, there's a 360-degree view of the Pacific Ocean, the Big Sur River gorge, and the Santa Lucia Mountains, providing a fine reward for your effort in climbing up here. The trailhead is at 200 feet in elevation and the overlook is at nearly 1,000 feet.

㉗ Pine Valley

10.6 mi/6.0 hrs or 2.0 days

Location: In the Ventana Wilderness near Carmel Valley; map F1, grid i8.

User groups: Hikers, dogs, and horses. No mountain bikes. No wheelchair facilities.

Permits: A free campfire permit is required for overnight stays from May through December; they are available from the Monterey Ranger District or the Big Sur Station. A national forest recreation pass is required for each vehicle; fees are $5 for one day or $30 for a year.

Directions: From Greenfield on U.S. 101, take the G-16/Monterey County Road exit and drive west for 29 miles. Turn south on Tassajara Road and drive 1.3 miles to Cachagua Road. Turn left and drive nine miles to the trailhead, located just past the turnoff for China Campground. (High-clearance vehicles are recommended. The county sometimes closes the road during bad weather; phone the Monterey Ranger District before traveling.)

Maps: For a map of Los Padres National Forest or the Ventana Wilderness, send $4 to USDA-Forest Service, 630 Sansome Street, San Francisco, CA 94111. To obtain a topographic map of the area, ask for Chews Ridge from the USGS.

Contact: Los Padres National Forest, Monterey Ranger District, 406 South Mildred Avenue, King City, CA 93930; (408) 385-5434.

Trail notes: The Pine Valley hike is a great one-night backpacking trip or long day hike into the Ventana Wilderness, and can easily be extended into a 13-mile loop. The hike begins on the northern end of the Pine Ridge Trail at China Campground, following an up-and-down course that soon becomes more down than up. At 3.5

miles, you turn right on the Carmel River Trail and descend some more to the headwaters of the Carmel River and the beginning of fir and ponderosa pine forest. Pine Valley Camp is 5.3 miles from the trailhead, set in lush Pine Valley, a spacious high meadow lined with ferns, ponderosa pines, and rocky sandstone formations. A short side trip to Pine Falls is possible from the camp; follow a well-worn route downstream along the river for a half mile to the waterfall. From there, you can retrace your steps back to the trailhead for a 10.6-mile round-trip, or make camp at Pine Valley, or take the trail from the upper end of camp, which meets up with the Pine Ridge Trail. Turn left on Pine Ridge Trail and hike back to the trailhead to complete a 13-mile loop.

28 McWay Falls Overlook

0.5 mi/0.5 hr

Location: In Julia Pfeiffer Burns State Park south of Big Sur; map F1, grid j7.

User groups: Hikers only. No dogs, horses, or mountain bikes. The McWay Falls Overlook Trail is wheelchair accessible via a special bridge that bypasses the stairs from the parking lot.

Permits: No permits are required. A $6 day-use fee is charged per vehicle.

Directions: From Carmel, drive 37 miles south on Highway 1 to Julia Pfeiffer Burns State Park, on the east side of the highway. (It's 13 miles south of Big Sur.) Drive through the entrance kiosk, then park near the rest rooms. The Overlook Trail starts across the pavement from the rest rooms, on a series of wooden stairs.

Maps: A map of Julia Pfeiffer Burns State Park is available for 50 cents at this park's entrance kiosk, or at the entrance kiosk for Pfeiffer Big Sur State Park. To obtain a topographic map of the area, ask for Partington Ridge from the USGS.

Contact: Julia Pfeiffer Burns State Park, c/o Pfeiffer Big Sur State Park, Big Sur, CA 93920; (408) 667-2315 or (408) 649-2836, or fax (408) 667-2886.

Trail notes: Next to Yosemite Falls and Bridalveil Fall, McWay Falls is probably the waterfall that appears most often on family snapshots of California vacations. Although few know its name, its image is unforgettable: An 80-foot waterfall leaping off a rugged ocean bluff and pouring gracefully into the Pacific. The walk to the waterfall's overlook is on a paved trail that leads through a tunnel underneath Highway 1, then comes out to a spectacular overlook of McWay Cove. A bench is placed along the trail, where you can sit and admire the action (and maybe even catch sight of a passing gray whale). You can also continue a few hundred feet beyond the bench, where the trail ends at the ruins of "Waterfall House," the home of Lathrop and Helen Hooper Brown in the 1940s. There's not much left of it now, but at one time, it was obviously quite a place.

29 Ewoldsen Loop Trail

4.3 mi/2.0 hr

Location: In Julia Pfeiffer Burns State Park south of Big Sur; map F1, grid j7.

User groups: Hikers only. No dogs, horses, or mountain bikes. No wheelchair facilities.

Permits: No permits are required. A $6 day-use fee is charged per vehicle.

Directions: From Carmel, drive 37 miles south on Highway 1 to Julia Pfeiffer Burns State Park, on the east side of the highway. (It's 13 miles south of Big Sur.) Drive through the entrance kiosk, then park near the rest rooms. The Ewoldsen Trail starts on the inland side of the parking area, near the picnic areas.

Maps: A map of Julia Pfeiffer Burns State Park is available for 50 cents at this park's entrance kiosk, or at the entrance kiosk for Pfeiffer Big Sur State Park. To obtain a topographic map of the area, ask for Partington Ridge from the USGS.

Contact: Julia Pfeiffer Burns State Park, c/o Pfeiffer Big Sur State Park, Big Sur, CA 93920; (408) 667-2315 or (408) 649-2836, or fax (408) 667-2886.

Trail notes: Some say that the Ewoldsen Trail is the best hiking trail in all of Big Sur, and they get no argument from us. The trail begins with an easy saunter along McWay Creek and its spectacular redwood forest, then the trail splits with Canyon Trail to the left and Ewoldsen Trail switchbacking uphill. Take the short Canyon Trail spur to its end, a quarter mile away, and visit McWay Canyon's sweet little waterfall. (It's not the big one in the park, which falls into the ocean and is described in hike number 28, but it's pretty to look at.) Then retrace your steps back to the junction and head uphill on the Ewoldsen Trail, which climbs steadily above the tops of the tall redwood trees below. The next fork, about 1.5 miles in, is the beginning of the loop, and most people hike the right side first. You alternate between dense redwood forest and more sparse oak woodland, till at 2.5 miles the trail reaches a ridgetop with good views out over McWay Canyon. There the loop begins its downhill return, affording many fine views of the ocean and then dropping back into redwood forest. Total elevation gain along the trail is 1,600 feet.

⑳ Partington Point and Tan Bark Trails

4.0 mi/2.0 hrs

Location: In Julia Pfeiffer Burns State Park south of Big Sur; map F1, grid j7.

User groups: Hikers only. No dogs, horses, or mountain bikes. No wheelchair facilities.

Permits: No permits are required. A $6 day-use fee is charged per vehicle in the main part of the park, but you can park for free alongside Highway 1 at the trailheads for Partington Point and the Tan Bark Trails.

Directions: From Carmel, drive 34 miles south on Highway 1 to a dirt pullout along the highway and the trailheads for the Partington Point and Tan Bark Trails. The trailheads are 10.5 miles south of Big Sur and 2.2 miles north of the main entrance to Julia Pfeiffer Burns State Park. (Partington Point Trail is on the west side of the highway, Tan Bark Trail is on the east side.)

Maps: A map of Julia Pfeiffer Burns State Park is available for 50 cents at this park's entrance kiosk, or at the entrance kiosk for Pfeiffer Big Sur State Park. To obtain a topographic map of the area, ask for Partington Ridge from the USGS.

Contact: Julia Pfeiffer Burns State Park, c/o Pfeiffer Big Sur State Park, Big Sur, CA 93920; (408) 667-2315 or (408) 649-2836, or fax (408) 667-2886.

Trail notes: If you want to hike at Julia Pfeiffer Burns State Park without the crowds or the day-use fees, a combined out-and-back trip on the Partington Point and Tan Bark Trails could be just your cup of tea. The two trails are about as different as any trails could be, except that they both start from the same point along Highway 1. You park your car in one spot and then hike a short ways on both sides of the highway. The Partington Point Trail is a dirt road that leads westward and downhill to Partington Point, home of the park's underwater playground of caves and natural bridges. Unless you're a scuba diver, you won't be able to see them, but you will be able to have a seat along the rocky cove and pretend you're a sea otter or a sea lion, or maybe a pelican. Keep your eyes peeled for spouting whales. Then hike back uphill and cross the highway to the start of the Tan Bark Trail, a thickly forested route that leads along Partington Creek, heading inland. You can hike a short half-mile loop on the trail (a bridge carries you across Partington Creek and then back down the other side), or you can continue further on the route, climbing steeply uphill for a mile or so until you gain some lovely views out to the coast.

㉛ Cone Peak Lookout Trail

4.0 mi/2.5 hrs

Location: In the Ventana Wilderness north of Lucia; map F1, grid j9.

User groups: Hikers, dogs, and horses. No mountain bikes. No wheelchair facilities.

Permits: No permits are required. A national forest recreation pass is required for each vehicle; fees are $5 for one day or $30 for a year.

Directions: From Carmel, drive 55 miles south on Highway 1 to Kirk Creek Campground, on the west side of the highway. Continue one mile further south on Highway 1 to the left turnoff for Nacimiento-Ferguson Road. Turn left and drive seven miles, then turn left on Cone Peak Road. Drive 5.4 miles to the trailhead on the left (do not follow the road to its end).

Maps: For a map of Los Padres National Forest or the Ventana Wilderness, send $4 to USDA-Forest Service, 630 Sansome Street, San Francisco, CA 94111. To obtain a topographic map of the area, ask for Cone Peak from the USGS.

Contact: Los Padres National Forest, Monterey

Ranger District, 406 South Mildred Avenue, King City, CA 93930; (408) 385-5434.

Trail notes: The two-mile climb to Cone Peak is a classic Ventana Wilderness adventure, and the fun begins with the drive to the trailhead. After leaving Highway 1, you get almost non-stop dramatic coastal views as your car chugs its way uphill. But that's nothing compared to the views you get at the fire lookout on Cone Peak, at 5,155 feet above sea level. The hike is a relentless climb, and the last mile sometimes seems to go straight up, but the total elevation gain is surprisingly only 1,500 feet. Make sure you have plenty of water with you. After switchbacking upward through a mix of low brush, hardwoods, and then conifers (mostly Coulter pines), you reach a trail junction at 1.8 miles. Go east (right) and walk the final quarter mile to the fire lookout. If it's staffed, say hello to the lookout person. Most likely, they'll be more than happy to name all the peaks and valleys in the 360-degree panorama that surrounds you.

Map F2

Adjoining Maps: East: F3 .... *page* 408   West: F1 384

North: E2 320   South: G2 466

Central California Map .... *page* 382

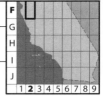

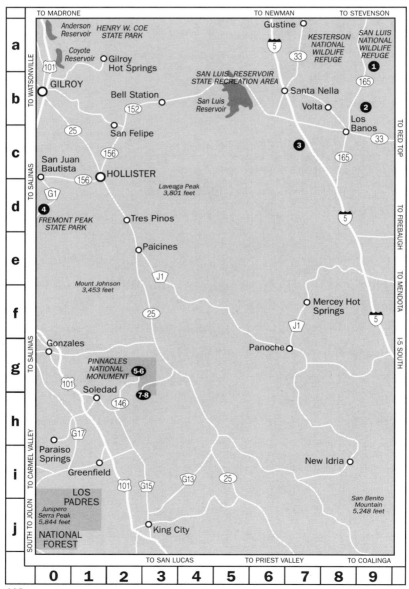

❶ Chester and Winton Marsh Trails

1.8 mi/1.0 hr

Location: In the San Luis National Wildlife Refuge north of Los Banos; map F2, grid a9.

User groups: Hikers and dogs. No horses or mountain bikes. No wheelchair facilities.

Permits: No permits are required. Parking and access are free.

Directions: From Los Banos on Highway 152/33, drive north on Highway 165 (Mercey Springs Road) for 6.4 miles to Wolfsen Road. Bear right and follow Wolfsen Road for 2.5 miles into the National Wildlife Refuge. Follow the signs for the Waterfowl Tour Route. The Chester Marsh Trail parking area will be on the left side of the road. Continue around the Waterfowl Tour Route loop to reach the Winton Marsh Trail parking area, also on the left side of the road.

Maps: A free map of the wildlife refuge is available by contacting the refuge headquarters at the address below. To obtain a topographic map of the area, ask for Los Banos from the USGS.

Contact: San Luis National Wildlife Refuge, P.O. Box 2176, Los Banos, CA 93635; (209) 826-3508, or fax (209) 826-1445.

Trail notes: While most people are taking the driving tour in San Luis National Wildlife Refuge, hoping to spot a big tule elk or a flock of birds from the windows of their cars, you can take two flat and short walks through bird-filled marshes, starting from two different trailheads along the Waterfowl Tour Route. As you drive the auto route, the first trailhead you reach is for the Chester Marsh Trail, on the north edge of the Waterfowl Tour Route. It's open for hiking only from February to September, because the birds get the run of the place in the fall and early winter. It's a one-mile interpretive loop, and you can

pick up an explanatory brochure at the trailhead. After your walk, get back in your car and continue driving along the Waterfowl Tour Route until you reach the trailhead for the Winton Marsh Trail. This trail is open year-round, is slightly shorter than the one at Chester Marsh, and has a wooden observation platform and several benches situated slightly above the marsh, so you can pull out your binoculars and peer at the feathered fowl below. What will you see? The usual cabal: Ducks, geese, moorhens, coots, pheasants, snipe, hawks, owls, egrets, herons, and even some rare types like the endangered tri-colored blackbird (it's black, white, and red). Even while just driving around, we saw a coyote and about a zillion bunnies, in addition to numerous Swainson's hawks.

❷ Los Banos Wildlife Area

2.0 mi/1.0 hr

Location: North of Los Banos; map F2, grid b8.

User groups: Hikers and dogs. No horses or mountain bikes. No wheelchair facilities.

Permits: Visitors must self-register at the entrance kiosk. A $2 entrance fee is charged per vehicle. If you are in possession of a valid California fishing or hunting license, entrance is free.

Directions: From Los Banos on Highway 152/33, drive north on Highway 165 (Mercey Springs Road) for three miles to Henry Miller Avenue. Turn right on Henry Miller Avenue, then left into the Los Banos Wildlife Area entrance. After registering, continue down the gravel road to the parking area by Little and Big Buttonwillow Lakes.

Maps: To obtain a topographic map of the area, ask for Los Banos from the USGS.

Contact: Los Banos Wildlife Area, 18110 West Henry Miller Avenue, Los Banos, CA 93635; (209) 826-0463 or (209) 826-5188.

Trail notes: Los Banos Wildlife Area is like the little brother of neighboring San Luis National Wildlife Refuge, but is run by the California Department of Fish and Game instead of the feds, but the birds don't care about the distinction. On our first trip here, we had barely driven past the registration kiosk when a giant sandhill crane lifted off 20 feet from our car. This was in June, which is not the sandhill crane's normal season for visiting. The two-mile loop trail near Little Buttonwillow Lake offers the best formal hiking in the preserve, although there are numerous other parking areas where you can just pull off the road and wander as you please. On the loop trail, you get to visit the sandhill crane viewing area, where you're almost guaranteed to see the huge, prehistoric-looking birds. Their large size, the distinctive crook in their necks, and the way they lay their feet back as they fly makes them easy to identify even if you've never seen them before. In autumn, when the waterfowl migration is in full swing, up to 50,000 birds show up here—hundreds of different species. The only downer? Unlike the federal wildlife refuge, this refuge doesn't have a separate area for hunters and hikers, so hikers are discouraged from visiting during the autumn hunting season, which is also the best bird-watching season.

❸ Path of the Padres

5.0 mi/3.0 hrs

Location: On Los Banos Creek, south of San Luis Reservoir; map F2, grid c6.

User groups: Hikers only. No dogs, horses, or mountain bikes. No wheelchair facilities.

Permits: Advance reservations are required; call to reserve a space during the first week of February. A $5 fee is charged per person for the reservation and guided tour. In addition, a $5 day-use fee is charged per vehicle.

Directions: From Interstate 5 at the junction with Highway 152 (south of Santa Nella), turn east on Highway 152 and drive 2.5 miles, then turn right (south) on Volta Road and drive one mile. Turn left (east) on Pioneer Road and drive eight-tenths of a mile, then turn right on Canyon Road. Drive south on Canyon Road for five miles to Los Banos Creek Reservoir. (You will

cross back to the west side of Interstate 5.) Park near the boat ramp.

Maps: To obtain a topographic map of the area, ask for Los Banos Valley from the USGS.

Contact: San Luis Reservoir State Recreation Area, Four Rivers District, 31426 West Highway 152, Gustine, CA 95322; (209) 826-1196.

Trail notes: You've got to plan way in advance to take this unusual hike at Los Banos Creek Reservoir. That's because the only way to go is by boat and with a guide, and guided trips are only offered on weekends in March and April. The trip has become so popular that it usually sells out as soon as reservations are available, which is the first week of February each year. That means don't procrastinate on making your call for reservations. If you've reserved a spot, your trip begins with a boat ride down the long and narrow reservoir, which is set in a steep-walled canyon and is popular for windsurfing and canoeing. At the reservoir's far end, everyone gets off the boat and starts hiking up the narrow canyon of Los Banos Creek, where old-growth sycamore groves and a cornucopia of spring wildflowers can be seen. The guide will teach you how to spot and identify various animal tracks along the canyon floor, and birders may thrill to see a peregrine falcon or other cliff-dwelling species. The hike ends with a climb to the top of a knoll, which offers wide views of the Los Banos valley. So why is this trail called the Path of the Padres? Because the fathers at Mission San Juan Bautista came here in the early 1800s to recruit the Yokut Indians to work for them. On the trip, you'll see bedrock mortars and other evidence of the Native Americans who once lived in this canyon.

❹ Fremont Peak Trail

0.6 mi/0.5 hr

Location: In Fremont Peak State Park near San Juan Bautista; map F2, grid d0.

User groups: Hikers only. No dogs, horses, or mountain bikes. No wheelchair facilities.

Permits: No permits are required. A $3 day-use fee is charged per vehicle.

Directions: From Gilroy, drive south on U.S. 101 for 10 miles to the Highway 156 East/San

Juan Bautista exit. Turn east on Highway 156 and drive three miles to San Juan Bautista, then turn right (south) on San Juan Canyon Road. (It's signed for the state park.) Follow it for 11 miles to its end in Fremont Peak State Park.

Maps: A free map of Fremont Peak State Park is available at the self-registration area. To obtain a topographic map of the area, ask for San Juan Bautista from the USGS.

Contact: Fremont Peak State Park, P.O. Box 787, San Juan Bautista, CA 95045; (408) 623-4255.

Trail notes: Fremont Peak State Park—it's a little tiny park with a great big view. There isn't much of a choice of hiking trails here, just a short six-tenths of a mile trail to the summit of Fremont Peak, elevation 3,169 feet. But that one little trip packs one heck of a punch. Pick a clear day in winter or spring (summer gets brutally hot and the visibility worsens), make the pretty drive from San Juan Bautista, and prepare for a panorama of Monterey Bay, Santa Cruz, Salinas, Watsonville, Hollister, and the Santa Lucia Mountains. (They say that on the clearest of days you can see the Sierra, but we've never seen it.) From the parking area, walk up the gated, paved service road for a few hundred yards, then cut off on the right on the signed Peak Trail, which winds its way up the mountain. The last tenth of a mile is very rocky, and the final summit climb is a bit of a scramble. Ignore the close-by transmitters and check out the far-off views. Note: Another popular activity at the park is stargazing—Fremont Peak Observatory is open to the public on certain weekends (call for a schedule) and rangers hold astronomy programs here.

❺ Balconies Caves

 2.4 mi/1.5 hrs

Location: In Pinnacles National Monument near Soledad; map F2, grid g2.

User groups: Hikers only. No dogs, horses, or mountain bikes. No wheelchair facilities.

Permits: No permits are required. There is a $4 entrance fee at Pinnacles National Monument, good for seven days.

Directions: From Salinas, drive south on U.S. 101 for 22 miles to Soledad and take the Soledad/Highway 146 exit. Drive east on High-

way 146 for 12 miles. (The road is signed for West Pinnacles.) Highway 146 dead-ends at the Chaparral Ranger Station and trailhead parking lot.

Maps: A free map of Pinnacles National Monument is available at the ranger station. To obtain topographic maps of the area, ask for Bickmore Canyon and North Chalone Peak from the USGS.

Contact: Pinnacles National Monument, 5000 Highway 146, Paicines, CA 95043; (408) 389-4485, or fax (408) 389-4489.

Trail notes: If you're coming from U.S. 101 and the western edge of California, the west side of Pinnacles National Monument is a heck of a lot easier to get to than the east side. But if you're disappointed to learn that the Pinnacles' famous Bear Gulch Caves can only be accessed from the east side of the park, don't despair. The west side has its own caves, and like the east side's Bear Gulch Caves, these are a barrel of fun. Got your flashlights? Okay; then set off on the Balconies Trail, hike past the campground and follow the often dry West Fork of Chalone Creek. A mere six-tenths of a mile brings you to some huge, colorful, lichen-covered volcanic rocks, a preview of the caves to come. The sound of the wind in the gray pines and the scurrying of squirrels keeps you company. At the left fork for Balconies Cliffs, take the right fork to enter the caves, and turn on your flashlights for some good clean fun and adventure, squeezing through clefts in the rock, ducking your head under ledges, and climbing down rocky staircases. When you exit the caves, you can turn left and loop back on the Balconies Cliffs Trail, gaining many lovely views as you climb over the top of the caves.

❻ Pinnacles High Peaks Loop

8.8 mi/5.0 hrs

Location: In Pinnacles National Monument near Soledad; map F2, grid g2.

User groups: Hikers only. No dogs, horses, or mountain bikes. No wheelchair facilities.

Permits: No permits are required. There is a $4 entrance fee at Pinnacles National Monument, good for seven days.

Directions: From Salinas, drive south on U.S.

101 for 22 miles to Soledad and take the Soledad/Highway 146 exit. Drive east on Highway 146 for 12 miles. (The road is signed for West Pinnacles.) Highway 146 dead-ends at the Chaparral Ranger Station and trailhead parking lot.

Maps: A free map of Pinnacles National Monument is available at the ranger station. To obtain topographic maps of the area, ask for Bickmore Canyon and North Chalone Peak from the USGS.

Contact: Pinnacles National Monument, 5000 Highway 146, Paicines, CA 95043; (408) 389-4485, or fax (408) 389-4489.

Trail notes: Pinnacles National Monument is a hiker's park. The first clue you get is that no roads connect the east and west sides of the park, so the only way to get from one side to the other is to walk. We think that's just fine, especially since the park's first-rate trail system makes it possible to string together a loop tour around the park on the Juniper Canyon Trail, High Peaks Trail, Old Pinnacles Trail, and Balconies Trail. If you follow the trails in this order, you get almost all your climbing done in the first half of the trip, and then have a fairly easy and flat home stretch. Begin hiking from the right side of the large parking lot near the Chaparral Ranger Station, following the Juniper Canyon Trail from grasslands into the rocky hills. The trail gets steeper as you go. Bear left on the Tunnel Trail, which in a half mile connects you to the High Peaks Trail, then continue on the latter for 2.5 miles further, all the way to the Chalone Creek picnic area. There you can fill up your water bottles, take a rest, and then head north on the Old Pinnacles Trail, a pleasant route that meanders along the West Fork of Chalone Creek. (In winter, the creek even has water in it.) In 2.3 miles, you'll reach a fork for the Balconies Trail, and if you've never been to Balconies Caves, you should take the left fork which leads you through them. (The right fork climbs above the caves for some excellent views.) After ducking your head and bending your knees a lot as you wander through the caves, you'll come out to an easy and flat section of the Balconies Trail, which brings you right back to the Chaparral parking lot. If you pick a cool day and carry plenty of water, this is a stellar long day hike in

Pinnacles. (Note that if you want more adventure, you should follow the Juniper Canyon Trail past the Tunnel Trail cutoff to the High Peaks Trail, then bear left and follow this rugged stretch of the High Peaks Trail, rather than taking the Tunnel Trail cutoff.)

❼ Condor Gulch and High Peaks Loop

5.0 mi/2.5 hr

Location: In Pinnacles National Monument near Soledad; map F2, grid g2.

User groups: Hikers only. No dogs, horses, or mountain bikes. No wheelchair facilities.

Permits: No permits are required. There is a $4 entrance fee at Pinnacles National Monument, good for seven days.

Directions: From King City on U.S. 101, take the First Street exit and head east. First Street turns into Highway G13/Bitterwater Road. Follow it for 15 miles to Highway 25, where you turn left (north). Follow Highway 25 for 14 miles to Highway 146. Turn left on Highway 146, and follow it for 4.8 miles to the park entrance and Bear Gulch visitor center. The trailhead for the Condor Gulch Trail is across the road from the visitor center.

Maps: A free map of Pinnacles National Monument is available at the ranger station. To obtain topographic maps of the area, ask for Bickmore Canyon and North Chalone Peak from the USGS.

Contact: Pinnacles National Monument, 5000 Highway 146, Paicines, CA 95043; (408) 389-4485, or fax (408) 389-4489.

Trail notes: The Condor Gulch Trail begins across the road from the Bear Gulch Ranger Station, and it's a good 30-minute climb up the hill on a smooth, switchbacked trail to an overlook of the High Peaks. The scent of wild sage and rosemary is enticingly aromatic along the route, and your eyes are continually drawn to the colorful lichen growing on equally colorful rocks. The overlook is just a piped railing on a ledge above a huge boulder, but it's a good spot to get your bearings and look out over the trail you just climbed. It's also a good turnaround spot if you don't want to go further. If you do, continue uphill to a junction with the High Peaks Trail at 1.7 miles and turn left. In just over a half mile, you'll reach a junction with the Tunnel Trail, where there are benches to rest your weary legs and enjoy the fine view to the west. Continue on the High Peaks Trail through narrow passageways and over and under steep rock formations. In many places the trail has been blasted into the rock, and the steep dropoffs can be dizzying. Make sure you use the hand-holds and guard rails. After seven-tenths of a mile, you'll reach an intersection with the Juniper Canyon Trail, where you should turn left and head back to Bear Gulch. You'll have to walk up the Bear Gulch Trail or the park road a short distance to get back to your car.

❽ Bear Gulch Caves

2.0 mi/1.0 hr

Location: In Pinnacles National Monument near Soledad; map F2, grid g2.

User groups: Hikers only. No dogs, horses, or mountain bikes. No wheelchair facilities.

Permits: No permits are required. There is a $4 entrance fee at Pinnacles National Monument, good for seven days.

Directions: From King City on U.S. 101, take the First Street exit and head east. First Street turns into Highway G13/Bitterwater Road. Follow it for 15 miles to Highway 25, where you turn left (north). Follow Highway 25 for 14 miles to Highway 146. Go left on Highway 146, and follow it for 4.8 miles to the park entrance and visitor center, then continue beyond it to the parking lot by Bear Gulch Picnic Area and the Bear Gulch Caves Trailhead.

Maps: A free map of Pinnacles National Monument is available at the ranger station. To obtain topographic maps of the area, ask for Bickmore Canyon and North Chalone Peak from the USGS.

Contact: Pinnacles National Monument, 5000 Highway 146, Paicines, CA 95043; (408) 389-4485, or fax (408) 389-4489.

Trail notes: Bear Gulch Caves is by far the most popular destination in Pinnacles National Monument, and it's easy and fun for all ages to enjoy. Make sure you've packed along a flashlight (preferably one for each person), then set off

from the Bear Gulch picnic area on the Bear Gulch Trail. A quarter mile down the trail you meet up with the Moses Spring Trail, where you bear left, pass through a rock tunnel, then reach another fork where you can either head into the caves directly or take the Moses Spring Trail up and over them. Which way you go makes no difference, because you can always go the other way on your return trip; however, most people have so much fun inside Bear Gulch Caves that they take the cave path in both directions. What kind of fun? How about this: Walk into water-sculpted volcanic caverns where only occasional beams of sunlight flash through the ceiling. Enter a circular cavern where water streams down the walls, the only sound being the constant drip of water. Climb up to rocky lookouts and down rocky staircases; duck through narrow passageways; stoop, twist, and turn your body, following the beam of your flashlight. It's a great adventure, with no real threat of danger. Kids have a ball in the caves, but then again, so do adults.

Special note: If you are planning to visit Pinnacles National Monument in the rainy season, call ahead to make sure that this trail is open. During wet periods, the park sometimes has to gate off the caves.

Map F3

Adjoining Maps: East: F4 .... *page* 410   West: F2 402
North: E3 324   South: G3 474

Central California Map .... *page* 382

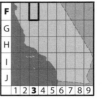

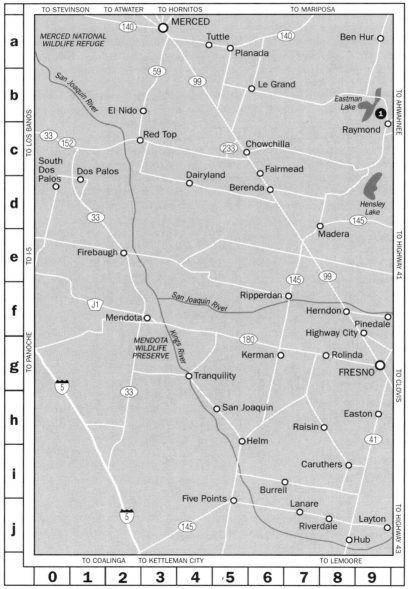

TO STEVINSON   TO ATWATER   TO HORNITOS   TO MARIPOSA

a

MERCED NATIONAL
WILDLIFE REFUGE

(140) **MERCED**

Tuttle (140)   Ben Hur

Planada

b

San Joaquin River

(59)

(99)

Le Grand

El Nido

Eastman
Lake

①

TO AHWAHNEE

Raymond

c

TO LOS BANOS

(33)

(152)

Red Top

(233) Chowchilla

d

South
Dos
Palos

Dos Palos

Dairyland

Fairmead

Berenda

Hensley
Lake

(33)

(145)

Madera

TO HIGHWAY 41

e

TO I-5

Firebaugh

f

(J1)

Mendota

San Joaquin River

(145) (99)

Ripperdan

Herndon

Highway City

Pinedale

g

TO PANOCHE

MENDOTA
WILDLIFE
PRESERVE

Kings River

(180)

Kerman

Rolinda

Tranquility

FRESNO

TO CLOVIS

⑤

(33)

h

San Joaquin

Easton

Raisin

Helm

(41)

i

Caruthers

Burrell

j

⑤

Five Points

(145)

Lanare

Riverdale

Layton

Hub

TO HIGHWAY 43

TO COALINGA   TO KETTLEMAN CITY   TO LEMOORE

| 0 | 1 | 2 | 3 | 4 | 5 | 6 | 7 | 8 | 9 |

❶ Lakeview Trail

2.0 mi/1.0 hr

Location: On the southeast shore of Eastman Lake, east of Chowchilla; map F3, grid b9.

User groups: Hikers, dogs, horses, and mountain bikes. No wheelchair facilities.

Permits: No permits are required. Parking and access are free.

Directions: From Merced, drive south on Highway 99 for 20 miles to Chowchilla. Take the Avenue 26 exit and head east for 17 miles. Turn north on County Road 29 and drive eight miles to the lake. Turn right and park in the lot by the spillway, just beyond the visitor center and park headquarters.

Maps: A free map of Eastman Lake is available at the visitor center. To obtain a topographic map of the area, ask for Raymond from the USGS.

Contact: U.S. Army Corps of Engineers, Eastman Lake, P.O. Box 67, Raymond, CA 93653; (209) 689-3255.

Trail notes: Let's get one thing straight: You don't want to hike here at midday in July. Got it? Good. But if it's March and the wildflowers are in bloom, you'd be wise to head out here to Eastman Lake, then hike the Lakeview Trail that leads along its south and east side. Sure, a reservoir is a reservoir, but when the water level is high, the grasslands are green, and the flowers are blooming, this reservoir can seem like a little slice of paradise in the Central Valley. The trail leads a total of four miles one way, but unfortunately much of the route is closed from December 1 to July 15, which includes the best hiking season. But if you start hiking from the spillway, you can hike along the south side of the lake for a mile to the group campground area, then continue from there along the east side of the lake for another mile before you reach the trail closure. The best part of the trail is this latter section, so if you're looking for a shorter trip, park in the trailhead parking lot at Codorniz Group Campground and hike north on the Lakeview Trail from there; that makes a two-mile round-trip.

Map F4

Adjoining Maps: East: F5 .... *page* 422   West: F3 408
North: E4 326   South: G4 476

Central California Map .... *page* 382

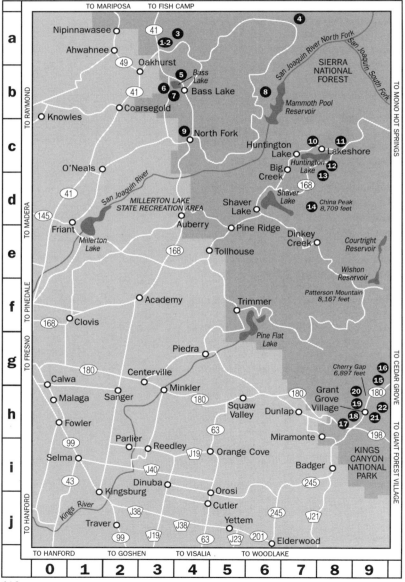

❶ Lewis Creek

4.0 mi/2.0 hrs

Location: Off Highway 41 north of Oakhurst; map F4, grid a3.

User groups: Hikers and dogs. No horses or mountain bikes. No wheelchair facilities.

Permits: No permits are required. Parking and access are free.

Directions: From Oakhurst, drive north on Highway 41 for eight miles to the signed trailhead for the Lewis Creek Trail, on the east side of the highway. (The trailhead is four miles south of Westfall Picnic Area.)

Maps: For a map of Sierra National Forest, send $4 to USDA-Forest Service, 630 Sansome Street, San Francisco, CA 94111. To obtain a topographic map of the area, ask for Ahwahnee from the USGS.

Contact: Sierra National Forest, Mariposa Ranger District, 43060 Highway 41, Oakhurst, CA 93644; (209) 683-4665, or fax (209) 683-7258.

Trail notes: There are three trailheads that access the Lewis Creek Trail, but unless you want to hike its entire 3.5-mile one-way distance, the best place to start is at the trail's midpoint just off Highway 41. From this roadside trailhead, you can take a 10-minute walk south to Corlieu Falls, then walk 1.8 miles north to see Red Rock Falls. Neither waterfall is a show-stopper, although both are pretty. Instead, the highlight of the trip is the hike itself, a gorgeous walk along flower-lined Lewis Creek that follows the route of the historic Madera Sugar Pine lumber flume. You'll pass many anglers along the way, as Lewis Creek is stocked with catchable trout. In addition, the white western azaleas along the streambanks bloom in profusion, shaded by a thick canopy of oaks, ponderosa pines, and incense cedars.

❷ Shadow of the Giants

1.2 mi/0.5 hr

Location: Off Highway 41 south of Yosemite National Park and north of Oakhurst; map F4, grid a3.

User groups: Hikers and dogs. No horses or mountain bikes. No wheelchair facilities.

Permits: No permits are required. Parking and access are free.

Directions: From Oakhurst, drive north on Highway 41 for five miles to Sky Ranch Road (Road 632). Turn east on Sky Ranch Road and drive six miles to the turnoff for Nelder Grove. Turn left, drive 1.5 miles, then take the left fork, signed for Shadow of the Giants. Drive a half mile to the trailhead.

Maps: For a map of Sierra National Forest, send $4 to USDA-Forest Service, 630 Sansome Street, San Francisco, CA 94111. To obtain a topographic map of the area, ask for Bass Lake from the USGS.

Contact: Sierra National Forest, Mariposa Ranger District, 43060 Highway 41, Oakhurst, CA 93644; (209) 683-4665, or fax (209) 683-7258.

Trail notes: Shadow of the Giants is a National Recreation Trail that is located within the Nelder Grove of giant Sequoias. For sheer numbers of Sequoias and blissful peace and quiet, it beats the heck out of the Sequoia groves a few miles north in Yosemite National Park. On a Saturday afternoon in June, we walked the one-mile interpretive trail all by ourselves. The self-guided signs along the trail are interesting and informative, and the babble of Nelder Creek is a perfect accompaniment to the huge, majestic trees. In addition to the Sequoias, the forest is filled with western azaleas, dogwoods, incense cedars, wild rose, sugar pines, and white firs. (What's the best thing we learned on the trail? The bark of mature Sequoias is so soft that squirrels use it to line their nests.) The trail makes an easy loop, and is set at 5,000 feet in elevation. The best redwoods are at the far end of the loop, so make sure you walk all the way.

❸ Fresno Dome

2.0 mi/1.0 hr

Location: Off Highway 41 south of Yosemite National Park and north of Oakhurst; map F4, grid a3.

User groups: Hikers, dogs, and mountain bikes. No horses. No wheelchair facilities.

Permits: No permits are required. Parking and access are free.

Directions: From Oakhurst, drive north on Highway 41 for five miles to Sky Ranch Road (Road 632). Turn east on Sky Ranch Road, drive approximately 12 miles, then turn left at the sign for Fresno Dome Campground and drive 4.8 miles to the trailhead (two miles past the camp).

Maps: For a map of Sierra National Forest, send $4 to USDA-Forest Service, 630 Sansome Street, San Francisco, CA 94111. To obtain a topographic map of the area, ask for Bass Lake from the USGS.

Contact: Sierra National Forest, Mariposa Ranger District, 43060 Highway 41, Oakhurst, CA 93644; (209) 683-4665, or fax (209) 683-7258.

Trail notes: We recommend one hour of time for this trip, but you might want to plan for more, because once you reach the top of Fresno Dome, you won't want to leave. The trailhead elevation is 8,000 feet, and the trail is beautiful right from the start, where it traverses a verdant meadow filled with corn lilies, quaking aspens, and lavender shooting stars. The first mile is completely flat; in the second mile you climb up the sloped back side of Fresno Dome. After a moderate ascent, manageable by almost anybody, you're rewarded with 360-degree views, mostly of conifer-filled valleys. You can just make out a corner of Bass Lake, the town of Oakhurst, and the far-off snowy peaks of the John Muir Wilderness. From up on top of Fresno Dome, it all looks like heaven.

❹ The Niche and Cora Lakes

11.0 mi/6.0 hrs or 2.0 days

Location: In the Ansel Adams Wilderness, southeast of Yosemite National Park; map F4, grid a6.

User groups: Hikers, dogs, and horses. No mountain bikes. No wheelchair facilities.

Permits: A free wilderness permit is required for overnight stays; they are available from the Minarets Ranger Station. Quotas are in effect from June to September; reservations are available in advance by mail for this period for a $3 fee. Parking and access are free.

Directions: From the town of North Fork (south of Bass Lake), drive southeast on Road 225 to Minarets Road. Turn left (north) on Minarets Road (Road 81) and follow it for approximately 50 winding miles to the Clover Meadow Ranger Station/Granite Creek turnoff on the right. Drive 4.5 miles to the Isberg trailhead just beyond Granite Creek Campground.

Maps: For a map of Sierra National Forest, send $4 to USDA-Forest Service, 630 Sansome Street, San Francisco, CA 94111. To obtain a topographic map of the area, ask for Timber Knob from the USGS.

Contact: Sierra National Forest, Minarets Ranger District, P.O. Box 10, North Fork, CA 93643; (209) 877-2218, or fax (209) 877-3173.

Trail notes: Reaching the trailhead for The Niche and Cora Lakes requires a long drive on the Sierra Vista National Scenic Byway, the showpiece road of the North Fork area, and if you have the time for it, it's a great trip. The best way to make the adventure work well is to drive out and spend the night at Granite Creek Campground or nearby Clover Meadow Campground, then start hiking the next day. The trip starts with a 1.5-mile ascent to the Niche at 8,000 feet, where you enter the Ansel Adams Wilderness boundary. Follow the well-marked signs to Cora Lake at 4.0 miles. The total ascent is only about 1,200 feet. If you still have energy left, retrace your steps to the Niche, then head northeast along the ridge toward Hemlock Crossing. Go as far as you please, but at least go for a mile or two, enjoying stellar views of Mount Ritter, Mount Banner, and the Minarets.

❺ Willow Creek

4.8 mi/2.5 hrs

Location: On the northeast end of Bass Lake near Oakhurst; map F4, grid b3.

User groups: Hikers and dogs. No horses or mountain bikes. No wheelchair facilities.

Permits: No permits are required. Parking and access are free.

Directions: From Oakhurst, drive north on Highway 41 for four miles, then turn right on Road 222. Drive four miles and bear left on Road 274. Drive one mile to the trailhead parking area on the left side of the road, on the west side of the highway bridge over Willow Creek. Alternatively, you can park near Falls Beach Picnic Area on Road 222 by Bass Lake's dam, then access the trail via a connector route alongside Willow Creek.

Maps: For a map of Sierra National Forest, send $4 to USDA-Forest Service, 630 Sansome Street, San Francisco, CA 94111. To obtain a topographic map of the area, ask for Bass Lake from the USGS.

Contact: Sierra National Forest, Mariposa Ranger District, 43060 Highway 41, Oakhurst, CA 93644; (209) 683-4665, or fax (209) 683-7258.

Trail notes: Most people hike the Willow Creek Trail with one of two things in mind: fishing or swimming. You can't blame them, since the trail runs alongside Willow Creek, and offers a myriad of quiet pools and fast, granite-lined cascades. The Forest Service requests that people don't swim upstream of Angel Falls, a wide cascade that looks like angel wings, because the creek is used as a domestic water supply. (Downstream swimming is okay, but be wary of slippery granite all along the creek.) At 2.4 miles from the trailhead, be sure to take the left spur for Devil's Slide, at a junction where the main trail continues to its end at McLeod Flat Road. Devil's Slide is a remarkable granite water slide, with large rounded indentations in the rock. A chain-link fence keeps hikers off the dangerously slick granite. From Devil's Slide, head back to the main trail and retrace your steps downhill. Expect to see some great views of bright blue Bass Lake on the return trip.

❻ Way of the Mono

0.5 mi/0.5 hr

Location: On the northwest end of Bass Lake near Oakhurst; map F4, grid b3.

User groups: Hikers and dogs. No horses or mountain bikes. No wheelchair facilities.

Permits: No permits are required. Parking and access are free.

Directions: From Oakhurst, drive north on Highway 41 for four miles, then turn right on Road 222. Drive four miles and bear right to stay on Road 222. The signed trailhead parking area is across from Little Denver Church Picnic Area, between the Forks Resort and the California Land Management Office.

Maps: For a map of Sierra National Forest, send $4 to USDA-Forest Service, 630 Sansome Street, San Francisco, CA 94111. To obtain a topographic map of the area, ask for Bass Lake from the USGS.

Contact: Sierra National Forest, Mariposa Ranger District, 43060 Highway 41, Oakhurst, CA 93644; (209) 683-4665, or fax (209) 683-7258.

Trail notes: Pick up an interpretive brochure at the Bass Lake Recreation Office before you set off on this half-mile loop trail. (Brochures are supposed to be available at the trailhead, but they weren't on our trip.) The Way of the Mono is an educational trail that teaches about the Western Mono Indians who once inhabited the Bass Lake area. You visit a grain grinding place, and learn about how the Monos survived through the changes of the seasons. In addition to a cultural history lesson, the trail also offers beautiful vistas of Bass Lake and its surroundings. Check out the view from the large granite outcrop.

❼ Goat Mountain Lookout

8.5 mi/5.0 hrs

Location: On the south end of Bass Lake near Oakhurst; map F4, grid b3.

User groups: Hikers and dogs. No horses or mountain bikes. No wheelchair facilities.

Permits: No permits are required. Parking and access are free.

Directions: From Oakhurst, drive north on Highway 41 for four miles, then turn right on Road 222. Drive four miles and bear right to stay on Road 222. Continue along the western shore of Bass Lake for about five miles to Spring Cove Campground. The Spring Cove Trail begins on the left side of the campground entrance. If there is no parking there, you can park at Rocky Point Picnic Area. (You can also hike to Goat Mountain Fire Lookout from Forks Campground, three miles north on Road 222.)

Maps: For a map of Sierra National Forest, send $4 to USDA-Forest Service, 630 Sansome Street, San Francisco, CA 94111. To obtain a topographic map of the area, ask for Bass Lake from the USGS.

Contact: Sierra National Forest, Mariposa Ranger District, 43060 Highway 41, Oakhurst, CA 93644; (209) 683-4665, or fax (209) 683-7258.

Trail notes: The 4.2-mile route to Goat Mountain Fire Lookout can be hiked from trailheads at either Forks Campground or Spring Cove Campground. Both are equally good, and of similar length, so take your pick. Both trails climb two miles on a moderate grade, then join and form one path for another half mile, before meeting up with a dirt road leading to Goat Mountain Fire Lookout. As you climb up the trail, you have nearly non-stop views of Bass Lake and the forested valleys surrounding it. You'll also be breathing hard. Heading south on the fire road, you'll reach the fire lookout, at elevation 4,675 feet, in 1.7 miles. Stop in and say hello to the lookout person. If you can talk someone into driving a second car to the other trailhead and campground, you can turn this into a pleasant semi-loop trip by hiking up one trail and down the other.

❽ French Trail at Mammoth Pool

4.0 mi/2.0 hrs

Location: At the Mammoth Pool Reservoir on the North Fork San Joaquin River; map F4, grid b6.

User groups: Hikers, dogs, horses, and mountain bikes. (No mountain bikes are allowed on the portion of the French Trail that enters the Ansel Adams Wilderness.) No wheelchair facilities.

Permits: No permits are required. Parking and access are free.

Directions: From the town of North Fork (south of Bass Lake), drive southeast on Road 225 to Minarets Road. Turn left (north) on Minarets Road (Road 81) and follow it for approximately 35 winding miles to the Mammoth Pool Road (Road 25) turnoff on the right. Turn right and drive past Wagner's Resort to the trailhead at Logan Meadow.

Maps: For a map of Sierra National Forest, send $4 to USDA-Forest Service, 630 Sansome Street, San Francisco, CA 94111. To obtain a topographic map of the area, ask for Mammoth Pool Dam from the USGS.

Contact: Sierra National Forest, Minarets Ranger District, P.O. Box 10, North Fork, CA 93643; (209) 877-2218, or fax (209) 877-3173.

Trail notes: The French Trail is a 75-mile trail that follows the route of the San Joaquin River from Redinger Lake near North Fork to south of Devils Postpile National Monument. It was surveyed in 1880 and was intended to become a wagon road, although there was never enough money or interest to make it happen. One section of the French Trail runs along the west side of Mammoth Pool Reservoir. Along this stretch, you hike through a pine and cedar forest and open chaparral hillsides with continual views of the big lake, which is a long, narrow reservoir with steep, high walls. Just remember this: If it's summertime, confine your activities at Mammoth Pool to swimming, boating, and fishing. It's too hot to hike at this 3,300-foot elevation except in spring and fall. Spring is best, because that's when the lake is full and pretty.

⑨ Cedars Interpretive

0.5 mi/0.5 hr

Location: In North Fork; map F4, grid c4.

User groups: Hikers, wheelchairs, and dogs. No horses or mountain bikes.

Permits: No permits are required. Parking and access are free.

Directions: From Oakhurst, drive north on Highway 41 for four miles, then turn right on Road 222. Drive four miles and bear left on Road 274, following it approximately 10 miles to its end in North Fork. At the four-way intersection, turn right and drive a quarter mile to the Minarets Ranger Station.

Maps: For a map of Sierra National Forest, send $4 to USDA-Forest Service, 630 Sansome Street, San Francisco, CA 94111. To obtain a topographic map of the area, ask for North Fork from the USGS.

Contact: Sierra National Forest, Minarets Ranger District, P.O. Box 10, North Fork, CA 93643; (209) 877-2218, or fax (209) 877-3173.

Trail notes: When people stop in at the North Fork Ranger Station to figure out how to spend their time in these parts, they'd be wise to take the half-mile Cedars Interpretive Walk that begins next to the station. That way they can learn about the local flora and fauna of the area, and about the people who lived on these lands long before us—the Mono Indians. A bonus is that the trail is surfaced, so wheelchair users can make the trip. Trailhead elevation is 2,600 feet.

⑩ Kaiser Peak

10.6 mi/6.0 hrs or 2.0 days

Location: In the Kaiser Wilderness north of Huntington Lake near Lakeshore; map E4, grid c7.

User groups: Hikers, dogs, and horses. No mountain bikes. No wheelchair facilities.

Permits: A free wilderness permit is required for overnight stays; they are available from the Pineridge Ranger Station. Quotas are in effect from June to September; permits are available in advance by mail for this period for a $3 fee. Parking and access are free.

Directions: From Fresno, drive northeast on

Highway 168 through Clovis for 70 miles to Huntington Lake, then turn left on Huntington Lake Road and drive one mile. Look for the large sign for the horse stables and pack station, and turn right. Follow the pack station road (Deer Creek Road) for a half mile to the hikers' parking area. The trailhead is signed "Kaiser Loop Trail."

Maps: For a map of Sierra National Forest or Kaiser Wilderness, send $4 to USDA-Forest Service, 630 Sansome Street, San Francisco, CA 94111. To obtain a topographic map of the area, ask for Kaiser Peak from the USGS.

Contact: Sierra National Forest, Pineridge Ranger District, P.O. Box 559, Prather, CA 93651; (209) 855-5360, or fax (209) 855-5375.

Trail notes: While many visitors to Huntington Lake take the short strolls to Rancheria Falls or the Indian Pools on Big Creek, far fewer attempt the ascent of Kaiser Peak. Why? Because it's a butt-kicking 5.3-mile climb to the top, gaining 3,000 feet of elevation on the way to the 10,320-foot peak. Luckily, you get many excellent views of Huntington Lake on the way up, and at the halfway point you can scramble up for a view and a rest on huge College Rock. Then it's up, up, and up some more, for what seems like an eternity. Finally you gain the rocky summit, and at last you know why you came. You're wowed by incredible 360-degree views, which take in Mammoth Pool Reservoir, Huntington Lake, Shaver Lake, Mount Ritter, and Mount Goddard. Wow. Backpackers looking for more mileage can turn the hike into a 14-mile loop trip.

⑪ George Lake

9.8 mi/6.0 hrs or 2.0 days

Location: In the Kaiser Wilderness north of Huntington Lake near Lakeshore; map E4, grid c8.

User groups: Hikers, dogs, and horses. No mountain bikes. No wheelchair facilities.

Permits: A free wilderness permit is required for overnight stays; they are available from the Pineridge Ranger Station. Quotas are in effect from June to September; permits are available in advance by mail for this period for a $3 fee. Parking and access are free.

Directions: From Fresno, drive northeast on Highway 168 through Clovis for 70 miles to Huntington Lake, then turn right on Kaiser Pass Road and drive 4.8 miles. Look for a trail sign for Trail 24E03, Twin Lakes and Potter Pass. Park on the south side of the road; the trail begins across on the north side of the road.

Maps: For a map of Sierra National Forest or Kaiser Wilderness, send $4 to USDA-Forest Service, 630 Sansome Street, San Francisco, CA 94111. To obtain a topographic map of the area, ask for Kaiser Peak from the USGS.

Contact: Sierra National Forest, Pineridge Ranger District, P.O. Box 559, Prather, CA 93651; (209) 855-5360, or fax (209) 855-5375.

Trail notes: Trails into the Kaiser Wilderness always seem to come with a climb, and the route to George Lake is no exception. But if you're willing to work your heart and lungs, your reward is a spectacular day hike or backpacking trip to scenic Twin Lakes and George Lake. Along the way, you must ascend to Kaiser Ridge, cross over it through Potter Pass, then leave most of your fellow hikers behind at Upper and Lower Twin Lakes as you press on to George Lake. You're witness to alpine meadows and conifer forests, and a classic Sierra view from Potter Pass. Then it's downhill from the pass to the granite-lined Twin Lakes, then uphill again to George Lake, 1.3 miles from Upper Twin Lake. The final push is definitely worth it. Trailhead elevation is 8,200 feet. (Another good route to these lakes is from the trailhead near Sample Meadow Campground, further north on Kaiser Pass Road. If you're willing to drive further, this route is not as crowded as the Potter Pass route, and has less of a climb.)

⑫ Rancheria Falls

2.0 mi/1.0 hr

Location: Off Highway 168 near Huntington Lake; map F4, grid c8.

User groups: Hikers, dogs, horses, and mountain bikes. No wheelchair facilities.

Permits: No permits are required. Parking and access are free.

Directions: From Fresno, drive northeast on Highway 168 through Clovis for 70 miles, past Shaver Lake. A half mile before reaching Huntington Lake, take the right turnoff signed for

Rancheria Falls (Road 8S31). Follow the dirt road for 1.3 miles to the signed trailhead at a sharp curve in the road. Park off the road.

Maps: For a map of Sierra National Forest, send $4 to USDA-Forest Service, 630 Sansome Street, San Francisco, CA 94111. To obtain a topographic map of the area, ask for Huntington Lake from the USGS.

Contact: Sierra National Forest, Pineridge Ranger District, P.O. Box 559, Prather, CA 93651; (209) 855-5360, or fax (209) 855-5375.

Trail notes: At 7,760 feet in elevation in Sierra National Forest, the air is clean and fresh, butterflies flutter amid the wildflowers, and a 150-foot waterfall sparkles in the sunlight. Wanna go? It's an easy trip, with the trailhead located close by popular Huntington Lake. The hike to Rancheria Falls is a well-graded one mile on a National Recreation Trail, suitable for hikers of all abilities. The route leads through a fir forest with an understory of wildflowers and gooseberry, and delivers you at Rancheria Falls' base, where you watch the creek tumble over a 50-foot-wide rock ledge. On weekends, the destination can be a little crowded, but you can pick a boulder downstream of the falls and call it your own. Then have a seat and watch the watery spectacle unfold.

⑬ Indian Pools

1.5 mi/1.0 hr

Location: Off Highway 168 near Huntington Lake; map F4, grid c8.

User groups: Hikers and dogs. No horses or mountain bikes. No wheelchair facilities.

Permits: No permits are required. Parking and access are free.

Directions: From Fresno, drive northeast on Highway 168 through Clovis for 70 miles, past Shaver Lake. One mile before reaching Huntington Lake, turn right at the signed Sierra Summit ski area. Drive a half mile to the end of the ski area parking lot and look for the signed trailhead for Indian Pools. (Occasionally they close the Sierra Summit parking lot and you must park on Highway 168 and walk the short distance into the ski area.)

Maps: For a map of Sierra National Forest, send

$4 to USDA-Forest Service, 630 Sansome Street, San Francisco, CA 94111. To obtain a topographic map of the area, ask for Huntington Lake from the USGS.

Contact: Sierra National Forest, Pineridge Ranger District, P.O. Box 559, Prather, CA 93651; (209) 855-5360, or fax (209) 855-5375.

Trail notes: When campers at Huntington Lake's many campgrounds are looking for a place to cool off in the afternoon, Indian Pools is where they go. The hike is really a walk, suitable for all ages and abilities, and you can stop almost anywhere you like along Big Creek, pick a pool, and wade in. The trail starts out on a private road but quickly changes to single-track. Flowers bloom in profusion along the streambanks. The official trail ends seven-tenths of a mile east of the trailhead, at a huge, clear pool, which usually you must share with other hikers and bathers. But a use trail continues further upstream, and if you take it, you can reach quieter, more private pools.

⑭ Dinkey Lakes

7.0 mi/4.0 hrs or 2.0 days

Location: Off Highway 168 near Shaver Lake; map F4, grid d7.

User groups: Hikers, dogs, and horses. No mountain bikes. No wheelchair facilities.

Permits: A free wilderness permit, available from the Pineridge Ranger Station, is required for overnight stays. Parking and access are free.

Directions: From Fresno, drive northeast on Highway 168 through Clovis for 50 miles to the town of Shaver Lake. Turn right on Dinkey Creek Road and drive nine miles. Turn left on Rock Creek Road (9S09) and drive six miles, then turn right on 9S10 and drive 4.7 miles. Turn right at the sign for Dinkey Lakes on Road 9S62 and drive 2.2 miles to the trailhead. These last two miles are very rough road. (Stay left at the fork to bypass the four-wheel-drive area and go straight to the trailhead.)

Maps: For a map of Sierra National Forest, send $4 to USDA-Forest Service, 630 Sansome Street, San Francisco, CA 94111. To obtain topographic maps of the area, ask for Huntington Lake and Dogtooth Peak from the USGS.

Contact: Sierra National Forest, Pineridge Ranger District, P.O. Box 559, Prather, CA 93651; (209) 855-5360, or fax (209) 855-5375.

Trail notes: We've never met anybody who doesn't love the Dinkey Lakes. What's not to love? There are dozens of lakes clustered into a small wilderness area, and most are so easily accessible that you can see them in a day hike, rather than packing along all your gear for an overnight stay. The trip begins with a stream crossing over Dinkey Creek, where immediately you'll be awed by the incredible array of colors in the rock streambed. Walk on flat trail through a flower-filled forest, then recross the creek and start to climb. At 1.3 miles, you reach the junction for the start of the loop. Go right and meet Mystery Lake at 1.6 miles, Swede Lake at 2.3 miles, South Lake at 3.2 miles, and finally First Dinkey Lake at 3.8 miles. First Dinkey Lake is the most beautiful of them all. After taking in the scenery, continue on the loop, now heading westward back to the parking lot. One caveat: Don't expect much solitude. The ease of the hiking makes this area extremely popular. Note that the loop we describe works as either a day hike or backpacking trip, but if you choose to backpack, you can explore much further, taking the spurs off the end of the main loop (between South Lake and First Dinkey Lake) to Second Dinkey Lake, Island Lake, Rock Lake, and so on.

⑮ Chicago Stump Trail

0.5 mi/0.5 hr

Location: In Sequoia National Forest, north of Grant Grove area of Kings Canyon National Park, map F4; grid g9.

User groups: Hikers and horses. No dogs or mountain bikes. No wheelchair facilities.

Permits: No permits are required. There is a $10 entrance fee at Sequoia and Kings Canyon National Parks, good for seven days.

Directions: From Fresno, drive east on Highway 180 for 55 miles to the Big Stump Entrance Station at Kings Canyon National Park. Continue 1.5 miles and turn left for Grant Grove. Drive approximately 4.5 miles, passing Grant Grove Village, then turn left at the sign for Forest Service Road 13S03. Drive two miles, then turn right on Road 13S65 and continue one-tenth of a mile to the Chicago Stump Trailhead.

Maps: Park maps are available for free at park entrance stations or by contacting Sequoia and Kings Canyon National Parks at the address below. A more detailed map is available for a fee from Tom Harrison Cartography at (415) 456-7940 or Trails Illustrated at (800) 962-1643. To obtain a topographic map of the area, ask for Hume from the USGS.

Contact: Sequoia and Kings Canyon National Parks, Three Rivers, CA 93271-9700; (209) 565-3134 or (209) 335-2856. Or contact Sequoia National Forest, Hume Lake Ranger District, 35860 East Kings Canyon Road, Dunlap, CA 93621; (209) 338-2251, or fax (209) 338-2131.

Trail notes: The Converse Basin was once the largest and finest grove of giant Sequoias in the world, before a couple of lumber companies got the bright idea to chop all the trees down. Now, where the giants once stood, second-growth Sequoias have taken hold. This short and easy stroll takes you through a regenerated mixed forest to the Chicago Stump, a massive stump that belonged to one of the largest trees in the world. It was cut down in 1892 so that a cross-section of the tree could be exhibited at the Chicago World's Fair. The stump is worth seeing, if only to remind yourself that these kinds of tragedies must never be repeated.

⓰ Boole Tree

2.0 mi/1.0 hr

Location: In Sequoia National Forest, north of the Grant Grove area of Kings Canyon National Park, map F4; grid g9.

User groups: Hikers and horses. No dogs or mountain bikes. No wheelchair facilities.

Permits: No permits are required. There is a $10 entrance fee at Sequoia and Kings Canyon National Parks, good for seven days.

Directions: From Fresno, drive east on Highway 180 for 55 miles to the Big Stump Entrance Station at Kings Canyon National Park. Continue 1.5 miles and turn left for Grant Grove. Drive approximately six miles, passing Grant Grove Village, then turn left at the sign for Forest Service Road 13S55, Boole Tree, Converse Basin, and

Stump Meadow. Drive 2.6 miles and park in the wide parking pullout.

Maps: Park maps are available for free at park entrance stations or by contacting Sequoia and Kings Canyon National Parks at the address below. A more detailed map is available for a fee from Tom Harrison Cartography at (415) 456-7940 or Trails Illustrated at (800) 962-1643. To obtain a topographic map of the area, ask for Hume from the USGS.

Contact: Sequoia and Kings Canyon National Parks, Three Rivers, CA 93271-9700; (209) 565-3134 or (209) 335-2856. Or contact Sequoia National Forest, Hume Lake Ranger District, 35860 East Kings Canyon Road, Dunlap, CA 93621; (209) 338-2251, or fax (209) 338-2131.

Trail notes: You have to drive through the entrance to Kings Canyon National Park to reach this trail in Sequoia National Forest, which means that most people who stop here are on their way to Cedar Grove or points eastward in the national park. The Boole Tree Trail gets surprisingly few visitors, especially when compared to the General Grant Grove of giant Sequoias, just a few miles away. Why? The Boole Tree is the only giant left standing in the Converse Basin grove, as the rest were clear-cut at the turn of the century. You climb 500 feet to the top of a ridge, then descend down the other side, to reach the Boole Tree in one mile. At 269 feet tall and with a diameter of 35 feet, it's the largest tree in any of the national forests, and it's one of the largest trees in the world.

⓱ Big Stump Trail

1.0 mi/0.5 hr

Location: In the Grant Grove area of Kings Canyon National Park, map F4; grid h8.

User groups: Hikers only. No dogs, horses, or mountain bikes. No wheelchair facilities.

Permits: No permits are required. There is a $10 entrance fee at Sequoia and Kings Canyon National Parks, good for seven days.

Directions: From Fresno, drive east on Highway 180 for 55 miles to the Big Stump Entrance Station at Kings Canyon National Park. The trail begins a half mile past the entrance station, at the Big Stump Picnic Area.

Maps: Park maps are available for free at park entrance stations or by contacting Sequoia and Kings Canyon National Parks at the address below. A more detailed map is available for a fee from Tom Harrison Cartography at (415) 456-7940 or Trails Illustrated at (800) 962-1643. To obtain a topographic map of the area, ask for Hume from the USGS.

Contact: Sequoia and Kings Canyon National Parks, Three Rivers, CA 93271-9700; (209) 565-3134 or (209) 335-2856.

Trail notes: Normally it would be hard for us to get excited about a trail called the "Big Stump Trail." In fact, this sort of thing is usually quite depressing. But the Big Stump Trail at the entrance to Kings Canyon National Park is a show-stopper, especially since it's the first thing you see as you enter the park from the Central Valley. The size of the mammoth trees, oops, make that stumps, just blows you away. All the trees here were cut for timber in the 1880s, and you can see the remains of logging activities. The loop trail crosses the park road in two places, which is why many people just hike the west side of the loop by the picnic area, where the Burnt Monarch and Mark Twain Stumps are found. The Mark Twain Stump belonged to a 26-foot-wide tree that took two men 13 days to cut down. You can pick up a trail brochure for this hike at the Grant Grove Visitor Center.

---

⑱ Sunset Trail

5.0 mi/2.5 hrs

Location: In the Grant Grove area of Kings Canyon National Park, map F4; grid h8.

User groups: Hikers only. No dogs, horses, or mountain bikes. No wheelchair facilities.

Permits: No permits are required. There is a $10 entrance fee at Sequoia and Kings Canyon National Parks, good for seven days.

Directions: From Fresno, drive east on Highway 180 for 55 miles to the Big Stump Entrance Station at Kings Canyon National Park. Continue 1.5 miles and turn left for Grant Grove. Drive 1.5 miles to Grant Grove Village and park in the large parking lot near the visitor center. Cross the road and walk on the paved trail toward Sunset Campground's amphitheater. Continue heading

left through the camp to site #179, where the trail begins.

Maps: Park maps are available for free at park entrance stations or by contacting Sequoia and Kings Canyon National Parks at the address below. A more detailed map is available for a fee from Tom Harrison Cartography at (415) 456-7940 or Trails Illustrated at (800) 962-1643. To obtain topographic maps of the area, ask for Hume and General Grant Grove from the USGS.

Contact: Sequoia and Kings Canyon National Parks, Three Rivers, CA 93271-9700; (209) 565-3134 or (209) 335-2856.

Trail notes: The Sunset Trail leaves Sunset Campground at elevation 6,590 feet and heads gently downhill for 2.25 miles to Ella Falls, a pretty 40-foot cascade on Sequoia Creek. At 1.5 miles down the trail, you reach a junction with the South Boundary Trail, and can take a short side trip to the left to Viola Falls, which isn't much of a waterfall but is a memorably scenic spot on granite-sculpted Sequoia Creek. Most people just mosey down the trail a ways, enjoying the big pines and firs and flowering western azaleas, and maybe stealing a kiss on one of the wooden footbridges. If you like, you can follow the trail for its entire 2.5-mile length to Sequoia Lake. Although the lake is privately owned, hikers are allowed to walk along its edge, as long as they stay out of the camp area. While you're having fun, don't forget that the return trip is all uphill with a 1,300-foot elevation gain, so save some water and energy.

---

⑲ North Grove Loop

1.5 mi/1.0 hr

Location: In the Grant Grove area of Kings Canyon National Park, map F4; grid h9.

User groups: Hikers only. No dogs, horses, or mountain bikes. No wheelchair facilities.

Permits: No permits are required. There is a $10 entrance fee at Sequoia and Kings Canyon National Parks, good for seven days.

Directions: From Fresno, drive east on Highway 180 for 55 miles to the Big Stump Entrance Station at Kings Canyon National Park. Continue 1.5 miles and turn left for Grant Grove. Drive two miles, passing Grant Grove Village, to the left turnoff for General Grant Tree. Turn left and follow the access road for one mile to the parking lot. The North Grove Loop starts from the far end of the lower parking lot.

Maps: Park maps are available for free at park entrance stations or by contacting Sequoia and Kings Canyon National Parks at the address below. A more detailed map is available for a fee from Tom Harrison Cartography at (415) 456-7940 or Trails Illustrated at (800) 962-1643. To obtain topographic maps of the area, ask for Hume and General Grant Grove from the USGS.

Contact: Sequoia and Kings Canyon National Parks, Three Rivers, CA 93271-9700; (209) 565-3134 or (209) 335-2856.

Trail notes: For people who want a little more hiking than the General Grant Tree Trail provides (see hike number 20), the North Grove Loop is the answer. The walk is along an old dirt road, which leads downhill through a grove of Sequoia, sugar pine, white fir, and dogwood. (Stay to the right at the first junction to make the loop.) At the far end of the loop, you'll pass a junction with another dirt road, which was once an old wagon road that was used to take the logged Sequoias to the mill. For a 1.5-mile loop, stay to the left and hike back uphill, gaining 400 feet, to reach the paved road that leads back to the parking area.

⑳ General Grant Tree

0.6 mi/0.5 hrs

Location: In the Grant Grove area of Kings Canyon National Park, map F4; grid h9.

User groups: Hikers and wheelchairs. No dogs, horses, or mountain bikes.

Permits: No permits are required. There is a $10 entrance fee at Sequoia and Kings Canyon National Parks, good for seven days.

Directions: From Fresno, drive east on Highway 180 for 55 miles to the Big Stump Entrance Station at Kings Canyon National Park. Continue 1.5 miles and turn left for Grant Grove. Drive two miles, passing Grant Grove Village, to the left turnoff for General Grant Tree. Turn left and follow the access road for one mile to the parking lot.

Maps: Park maps are available for free at park entrance stations or by contacting Sequoia and

Kings Canyon National Parks at the address below. A more detailed map is available for a fee from Tom Harrison Cartography at (415) 456-7940 or Trails Illustrated at (800) 962-1643. To obtain topographic maps of the area, ask for Hume and General Grant Grove from the USGS.

Contact: Sequoia and Kings Canyon National Parks, Three Rivers, CA 93271-9700; (209) 565-3134 or (209) 335-2856.

Trail notes: This paved loop through a giant Sequoia grove allows both wheelchair users and hikers to have a look at the General Grant Tree. Estimated at 1,800 to 2,000 years old, the General Grant is 267 feet tall and 107 feet in circumference at its base, making it the third largest tree in the world. Every year since 1926, the park has held a Christmas celebration around its base, and so the tree is dubbed "the nation's Christmas tree." Its neighbors include the Fallen Monarch (a hollow downed tree that is so wide, it was once used as a park employee camp) and a group of big Sequoias named after various U.S. states. It may seem a little campy, but there are many excellent photo opportunities in the grove.

㉑ Manzanita and Azalea Loop

3.3 mi/2.0 hrs

Location: In the Grant Grove area of Kings Canyon National Park, map F4; grid h9.

User groups: Hikers only. No dogs, horses, or mountain bikes. No wheelchair facilities.

Permits: No permits are required. There is a $10 entrance fee at Sequoia and Kings Canyon National Parks, good for seven days.

Directions: From Fresno, drive east on Highway 180 for 55 miles to the Big Stump Entrance Station at Kings Canyon National Park. Continue 1.5 miles and turn left for Grant Grove. Drive 1.5 miles to Grant Grove Village and park in the large parking lot near the visitor center. Walk on the service road behind the lodge buildings (and near the tent cabins) to reach the start of the Manzanita Trail.

Maps: Park maps are available for free at park entrance stations or by contacting Sequoia and Kings Canyon National Parks at the address below. A more detailed map is available for a fee from Tom Harrison Cartography at (415) 456-7940 or Trails Illustrated at (800) 962-1643. To obtain a topographic map of the area, ask for Hume from the USGS.

Contact: Sequoia and Kings Canyon National Parks, Three Rivers, CA 93271-9700; (209) 565-3134 or (209) 335-2856.

Trail notes: This hike is a good exercise route for vacationers staying in the cabins at Grant Grove Village or in the nearby campgrounds. It climbs 800 feet, which gives your heart and lungs a workout, and it's pretty every step of the way. From the end of the dirt road, the trail climbs a dry slope uphill to Park Ridge. Near the top, you'll parallel the dirt road that leads to the Park Ridge Fire Lookout. Then the Manzanita Trail meets up with the Azalea Trail, and you'll descend on a much shadier, moister slope. The azaleas bloom bright white in June and July. To complete the loop, the trail crosses the park road and then ends just across the road from the visitor center.

㉒ Panoramic Point and Park Ridge

4.7 mi/3.0 hrs

Location: In the Grant Grove area of Kings Canyon National Park, map F4; grid h9.

User groups: Hikers only. No dogs, horses, or mountain bikes. No wheelchair facilities.

Permits: No permits are required. There is a $10 entrance fee at Sequoia and Kings Canyon National Parks, good for seven days.

Directions: From Fresno, drive east on Highway 180 for 55 miles to the Big Stump Entrance Station at Kings Canyon National Park. Continue 1.5 miles and turn left for Grant Grove. Drive 1.5 miles to Grant Grove Village and turn right by the visitor center and store. Follow the road past some cabins, and take the right fork for Panoramic Point. It's 2.3 miles from the visitor center to Panoramic Point.

Maps: Park maps are available for free at park entrance stations or by contacting Sequoia and Kings Canyon National Parks at the address below. A more detailed map is available for a fee from Tom Harrison Cartography at (415) 456-

7940 or Trails Illustrated at (800) 962-1643. To obtain a topographic map of the area, ask for Hume from the USGS.

Contact: Sequoia and Kings Canyon National Parks, Three Rivers, CA 93271-9700; (209) 565-3134 or (209) 335-2856.

Trail notes: Start your trip by taking the 300-yard paved walk from the parking area to Panoramic Point, which delivers what its name implies. An interpretive display names the many peaks and valleys you can see, including the big pointy one—Mount Goddard at 13,560 feet. From Panoramic Point, take the dirt trail that leads to the right along the ridge. This trail intersects with a dirt road, which you follow all the way to the Park Ridge Fire Lookout. Check out the nifty outdoor shower at its base, and if there is someone in the tower and they give you permission to come up, do so and sign the visitor register. (The lookout person never gets any visitors on cloudy days, but he or she gets many when it's sunny and you can see for miles around.) This lookout is actually in Sequoia National Forest, not the national parks, which is why you'll see some logged areas along the road to it. The lookout is only operated during the fire season, which is usually May to October. For your return trip, you can walk down the trail back to Panoramic Point, or take the dirt road which also leads back to the parking lot.

Map F5

Adjoining Maps: East: F6 .... *page* 458   West: F4 410
North: E5 370   South: G5 478

Central California Map .... *page 382*

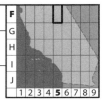

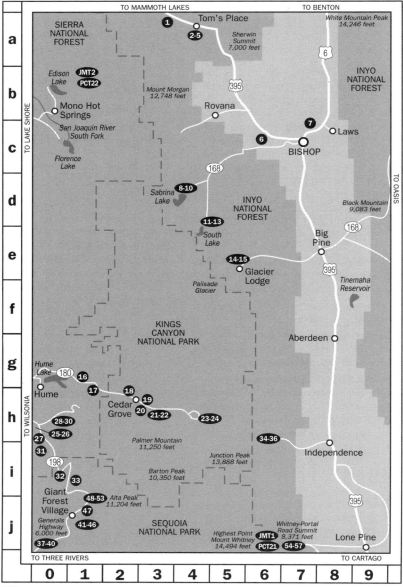

TO MAMMOTH LAKES   TO BENTON

SIERRA NATIONAL FOREST

Tom's Place

White Mountain Peak 14,246 feet

1

2-5

Sherwin Summit 7,000 feet

6

Edison Lake

JMT2

PCT22

INYO NATIONAL FOREST

Mount Morgan 12,748 feet

395

Mono Hot Springs

Rovana

San Joaquin River South Fork

7

Laws

6

BISHOP

Florence Lake

168

Sabrina Lake

8-10

INYO NATIONAL FOREST

11-13

South Lake

Big Pine

168

Black Mountain 9,083 feet

14-15

Glacier Lodge

395

Tinemaha Reservoir

Palisade Glacier

KINGS CANYON NATIONAL PARK

Aberdeen

Hume Lake

180

16

Hume

17

18

Cedar Grove

19

20

21-22

23-24

34-36

28-30

25-26

27

Palmer Mountain 11,250 feet

Junction Peak 13,888 feet

Independence

31

198

32

33

Barton Peak 10,350 feet

Giant Forest Village

48-53

Alta Peak 11,204 feet

47

Generals Highway 6,000 feet

41-46

SEQUOIA NATIONAL PARK

395

37-40

Highest Point Mount Whitney 14,494 feet

JMT1

PCT21

54-57

Whitney-Portal Road Summit 8,371 feet

Lone Pine

TO THREE RIVERS   TO CARTAGO

TO LAKE SHORE

TO WILSONIA

TO OASIS

| 0 | 1 | 2 | 3 | 4 | 5 | 6 | 7 | 8 | 9 |

Chapter F5 features:

① McGee Creek to Steelhead Lake

10.6 mi/6.0 hrs

Location: In the John Muir Wilderness; map F5, grid a3.

User groups: Hikers, dogs, and horses. No mountain bikes. No wheelchair facilities.

Permits: A free wilderness permit is required for overnight stays; they are available from the Bishop Ranger Station. Quotas are in effect from the last Friday in June to September 15; permits are available in advance by mail, phone, or fax for this period for a $3 fee. Mail permit requests to Wilderness Reservations, P.O. Box 430, Big Pine, CA 93513. Phone (888) 374-3773 or fax (760) 938-1137.

Directions: From U.S. 395 in Lee Vining, drive approximately 33 miles south to the McGee Creek Road turnoff on the right. (It's eight miles south of the Mammoth Lakes turnoff and 30 miles north of Bishop.) Drive three miles southwest on McGee Creek Road (past the pack station) to the trailhead.

Maps: For a map of Inyo National Forest, send $4 to USDA-Forest Service, 630 Sansome Street, San Francisco, CA 94111. To obtain a topographic map of the area, ask for Convict Lake from the USGS.

Contact: Inyo National Forest, White Mountain Ranger District, 798 North Main Street, Bishop, CA 93514; (760) 873-2500 or fax (760) 873-2563.

Trail notes: Unlike many trails leading into the John Muir Wilderness, the McGee Creek Trail has the benefit of starting out with a relatively flat stretch, giving your legs and lungs the opportunity for a warm-up before you start to climb. In the first two miles you pass through plains of sage and rabbit brush, heading toward a colorful and dramatic mountain backdrop: Mount Baldwin on the right, Mount Crocker on the left, and Red and White Mountain straight ahead—all 12,000-plus-foot peaks. To your left, along McGee Creek, grows a lush garden of aspens, birches, and cottonwoods. Pass Horsetail Falls on the right at two miles out, then carefully cross and recross McGee Creek. Soon the trail enters a lodgepole pine forest and the climb steepens, and at 4.2 miles you reach a junction with the Steelhead Lake Trail heading left (east). Switchbacks carry you to a short spur to tiny Grass Lake, then to much larger Steelhead Lake (10,350 feet). The total climb over 5.3 miles is 2,300 feet.

❷ Mono Pass

7.4 mi/4.0 hrs

Location: In the John Muir Wilderness; map F5, grid a4.

User groups: Hikers, dogs, and horses. No mountain bikes. No wheelchair facilities.

Permits: No day-hiking permits are required. Parking and access are free.

Directions: From U.S. 395 in Lee Vining, drive approximately 40 miles south to Tom's Place and the Rock Creek Road turnoff on the right. (It's 15 miles south of the Mammoth Lakes turnoff and 24 miles north of Bishop.) Follow Rock Creek Road southwest for 10.5 miles to its end, at the Mosquito Flat parking area.

Maps: For a map of Inyo National Forest, send $4 to USDA-Forest Service, 630 Sansome Street, San Francisco, CA 94111. To obtain topographic maps of the area, ask for Mount Morgan and Mount Abbot from the USGS.

Contact: Inyo National Forest, White Mountain Ranger District, 798 North Main Street, Bishop, CA 93514; (760) 873-2500 or fax (760) 873-2563.

Trail notes: Since wilderness permits are hard to come by for this trail, your best bet is a day hike up to scenic, austere Mono Pass, where William Brewer and his party crossed the Sierra in 1864. Trailhead elevation is 10,300 feet, and the pass is at 12,400 feet, so get ready to climb in thin air (gasp). Also, expect it to be cold and windy at the pass, no matter how warm it is at the trailhead. Start your trip by following the trail alongside Rock Creek, with a wall of mammoth mountain peaks surrounding you. A half mile in, bear right for Mono Pass, switchbacking uphill. As you climb, you get a view of Little Lakes Valley (see hike number 3), as well as continual eyefuls of classic Sierra scenery—clear blue sky, jagged mountain backdrops, and plenty of rock. When at last you gain the summit, you get a full 360-degree panoramic view, probably little different than when Brewer saw it more than a century ago.

❸ Little Lakes Valley

3–9 mi/2–5 hrs

Location: In the John Muir Wilderness; map F5, grid a4.

User groups: Hikers, dogs, and horses. No mountain bikes. No wheelchair facilities.

Permits: No day-hiking permits are required. A free wilderness permit is required for overnight stays; they are available from the Bishop Ranger Station. Quotas are in effect from the last

Friday in June to September 15; permits are available in advance by mail, phone, or fax for this period for a $3 fee. Mail permit requests to Wilderness Reservations, P.O. Box 430, Big Pine, CA 93513. Phone (888) 374-3773 or fax (760) 938-1137.

Directions: From U.S. 395 in Lee Vining, drive approximately 40 miles south to Tom's Place and the Rock Creek Road turnoff on the right. (It's 15 miles south of the Mammoth Lakes turnoff and 24 miles north of Bishop.) Follow Rock Creek Road southwest for 10.5 miles to its end, at the Mosquito Flat parking area.

Maps: For a map of Inyo National Forest, send $4 to USDA-Forest Service, 630 Sansome Street, San Francisco, CA 94111. To obtain topographic maps of the area, ask for Mount Morgan and Mount Abbot from the USGS.

Contact: Inyo National Forest, White Mountain Ranger District, 798 North Main Street, Bishop, CA 93514; (760) 873-2500 or fax (760) 873-2563.

Trail notes: If the mileage shown above reflects some indecision, that's because the Little Lakes Valley makes it hard to decide. Which lake to visit? How far to hike? It's best to decide as you go, depending on how many other people are at the lakes and how your energy is holding up. The Little Lakes Valley is a spectacularly beautiful, glacially carved area that is littered with lakes, both large and small, and surrounded by 13,000-foot peaks. What makes it even more special is that its trailhead is at 10,300 feet, so your car does most of the climbing. For this reason, the trail is extremely popular, especially with beginning backpackers, day hikers, and trout anglers.

The trail leads past Mack Lake and shallow Marsh Lake to Heart Lake, 1.5 miles in. A quarter mile further is larger Box Lake, then another quarter mile further is still larger Long Lake, both popular destinations right along the trail. Those with more stamina can continue to Chickenfoot Lake at three miles out, or the Gem Lakes at 3.5 miles. Those who are willing and able continue upward through 11,100-foot Morgan Pass, then descend a couple hundred feet to Upper and Lower Morgan Lake, at 4.0 and 4.5 miles out respectively. There are enough hiking options along this one trail to keep most lake-lovers busy for a week.

4 Tamarack Lakes

9.4 mi/6.0 hrs

Location: In the John Muir Wilderness; map F5, grid a4.

User groups: Hikers, dogs, and horses. No mountain bikes. No wheelchair facilities.

Permits: No day-hiking permits are required. A free wilderness permit is required for overnight stays; they are available from the Bishop Ranger Station. Quotas are in effect from the last Friday in June to September 15; permits are available in advance by mail, phone, or fax for this period for a $3 fee. Mail permit requests to Wilderness Reservations, P.O. Box 430, Big Pine, CA 93513. Phone (888) 374-3773 or fax (760) 938-1137.

Directions: From U.S. 395 in Lee Vining, drive approximately 40 miles south to Tom's Place and the Rock Creek Road turnoff on the right. (It's 15 miles south of the Mammoth Lakes turnoff and 24 miles north of Bishop.) Follow Rock Creek Road southwest for 8.5 miles to the east shore of Rock Creek Lake and the trailhead parking for Tamarack Lakes, on the left.

Maps: For a map of Inyo National Forest, send $4 to USDA-Forest Service, 630 Sansome Street, San Francisco, CA 94111. To obtain a topographic map of the area, ask for Mount Morgan from the USGS.

Contact: Inyo National Forest, White Mountain Ranger District, 798 North Main Street, Bishop, CA 93514; (760) 873-2500 or fax (760) 873-2563.

Trail notes: The trailhead elevation at Rock Creek Lake is nearly 10,000 feet, so the first two miles of this trail can be rather breathtaking (huff, puff) as you climb steeply to the turnoff for the Francis Lake Trail on the right and shortly thereafter, Kenneth Lake on the left. After the initial ascent, many people decide to head for one of these two lakes instead of continuing for two more miles to the Tamarack Lakes. Another left spur trail leads to Dorothy Lake at 2.5 miles. Those who continue onward will be rewarded (after more heavy breathing) with first the smaller Tamarack Lake and then the larger one, set in a steeply sloped rocky bowl. Despite the barren look of the cliffs on the lake's edges, the larger Tamarack Lake has good fishing for golden trout. If you stop at Dorothy Lake instead, you have a chance at catching brook trout or Lahontan cutthroat trout.

❺ Ruby Lake

4.5 mi/2.5 hrs

Location: In the John Muir Wilderness; map F5, grid a4.

User groups: Hikers, dogs, and horses. No mountain bikes. No wheelchair facilities.

Permits: No day-hiking permits are required. Parking and access are free.

Directions: From U.S. 395 in Lee Vining, drive approximately 40 miles south to Tom's Place and the Rock Creek Road turnoff on the right. (It's 15 miles south of the Mammoth Lakes turnoff and 24 miles north of Bishop.) Follow Rock Creek Road southwest for 10.5 miles to its end, at the Mosquito Flat parking area.

Maps: For a map of Inyo National Forest, send $4 to USDA-Forest Service, 630 Sansome Street, San Francisco, CA 94111. To obtain topographic maps of the area, ask for Mount Abbot and Mount Morgan from the USGS.

Contact: Inyo National Forest, White Mountain Ranger District, 798 North Main Street, Bishop, CA 93514; (760) 873-2500 or fax (760) 873-2563.

Trail notes: For both day hikers and backpackers, the Little Lakes Valley is the premier destination from the Rock Creek Canyon Trailhead. The only problem is the crowds, especially on the weekends, which can turn a supposedly peaceful wilderness experience into a large group encounter. A visit to Ruby Lake is a possible solution, because it's off the main trail that leads into the Little Lakes Valley, situated instead on the right fork that leads to Mono Pass. Since most hikers on this fork are heading to Mono Pass and the Pioneer Basin beyond, few take the time to stop at Ruby Lake, a quarter mile off the main trail. From the trailhead, hike a half mile and bear right at the junction for Mono Pass. Grunt it out through the switchbacks, enjoy a vista over the Little Lakes Valley, and reach the spur trail to Ruby Lake at two miles. A quarter mile of walking brings you to the cliff-bound lake, nearly as large in size as Rock Creek Lake by the trailhead, and set at 11,120 feet. The fishing is reportedly not great, but the picnicking is highly recommended.

❻ Honeymoon Lake

12.2 mi/7.0 hrs or 2.0 days

Location: In the John Muir Wilderness; map F5, grid c6.

User groups: Hikers, dogs, and horses. No mountain bikes. No wheelchair facilities.

Permits: A free wilderness permit is required for overnight stays; they are available from the Bishop Ranger Station. Quotas are in effect from the last Friday in June to September 15; permits are available in advance by mail, phone, or fax for this period for a $3 fee. Mail permit requests to Wilderness Reservations, P.O. Box 430, Big Pine, CA 93513. Phone (888) 374-3773 or fax (760) 938-1137.

Directions: From Bishop, drive north on U.S. 395 for seven miles and turn left (west) on Pine Creek Road. Drive 9.5 miles to the trailhead parking area, near the pack station on the left side of the road.

Maps: For a map of Inyo National Forest, send $4 to USDA-Forest Service, 630 Sansome Street, San Francisco, CA 94111. To obtain topographic maps of the area, ask for Bishop and Tungsten Hills from the USGS.

Contact: Inyo National Forest, White Mountain Ranger District, 798 North Main Street, Bishop, CA 93514; (760) 873-2500 or fax (760) 873-2563.

Trail notes: Since the trailhead elevation in Pine Creek Canyon is only 7,400 feet, the best destinations must be gained with a climb. That includes Honeymoon Lake, 6.1 miles and a 3,000-foot ascent away. Luckily you pass Upper and Lower Pine Lake along the route, and there's enough spectacular scenery to keep you motivated as you huff and puff. The route begins in the trees along Pine Creek, then joins a mining road which leads to the Brownstone Mine. As you climb out of the trees, you get views of the Owens River Valley and the desert-like White Mountains. You also get sweaty and overheated, switchbacking out in the open with no shade. Above the mine, the trail becomes extremely rocky, and ascends more switchbacks to meet first lower and then upper Pine Lake at 4.7 and 5.7 miles. This section of trail is blessed with some trees and the close proximity of Pine Creek. A quarter mile beyond the upper lake, reach a trail junction and take the right fork toward Italy Pass, heading west to Honeymoon Lake in a tenth of a mile. Many campsites are found near the granite-bound lake.

❼ Fish Slough

2.0 mi/1.0 hr

Location: In the Fish Slough Area of Critical Environmental Concern, north of Bishop; map F5, grid c7.

User groups: Hikers and dogs. No horses or mountain bikes (except on roads). No wheelchair facilities.

Permits: No permits are required. Parking and access are free.

Directions: From Bishop, drive north on U.S. 395 to Highway 6. Drive north on Highway 6 for 2.5 miles, then turn left (west) on Five Bridges Road. Drive 2.5 miles (past a gravel pit) to Fish Slough Road and turn right. Park anywhere along Fish Slough Road and begin hiking; there is no designated trail.

Maps: A free map/brochure is available from the Bureau of Land Management at the address below. To obtain a topographic map of the area, ask for Fish Slough from the USGS.

Contact: Bureau of Land Management Bishop Resource Area, 785 North Main Street, Suite E, Bishop, CA 93514; (760) 872-4881.

Trail notes: It's hard to believe you can see a great blue heron in the eastern Sierra, but here you can. The marshland in Fish Slough is watered by natural springs from the Owens Valley, making this area a rich riparian wetland in the middle of a giant desert and volcanic tableland. You walk in an oasis that teems with fish and wildlife, while gazing out over arid desert plains and mountains. Although the area gets less than six inches of rainfall per year, the water is stored in the underlying porous volcanic rock, creating a continuous reservoir for Fish Slough. When you look into the slough's clear pools, you can see bubbles coming up from the springs below. Because of the abundance of water, the wetlands are excellent for wildlife-watching (mostly birds and bunnies) and are home to rare and endangered species of fish, like the Owens pupfish. In addition to bird-watching, you can see Native American cultural artifacts at Fish Slough, including some prehistoric petroglyphs drawn on the rocks. Remember: Look but don't touch; they're protected by law.

❽ Blue Lake

6.0 mi/3.0 hrs

Location: In the John Muir Wilderness; map F5, grid d3.

User groups: Hikers, dogs, and horses. No mountain bikes. No wheelchair facilities.

Permits: No day-hiking permits are required. A free wilderness permit is required for overnight stays; they are available from the Bishop Ranger Station. Quotas are in effect from the last Friday in June to September 15; permits are available in advance by mail, phone, or fax for this period for a $3 fee. Mail permit requests to Wilderness Reservations, P.O. Box 430, Big Pine, CA 93513. Phone (888) 374-3773 or fax (760) 938-1137.

Directions: From Bishop on U.S. 395, turn west on Line Street (Highway 168) and drive 18.5 miles to Lake Sabrina. Day-use parking is at the end of the road. Backpackers' parking is located at a turnout near the road to North Lake, a half mile before the end of the road.

Maps: For a map of Inyo National Forest, send $4 to USDA-Forest Service, 630 Sansome Street, San Francisco, CA 94111. To obtain topographic maps of the area, ask for Mount Thompson and Mount Darwin from the USGS.

Contact: Inyo National Forest, White Mountain Ranger District, 798 North Main Street, Bishop, CA 93514; (760) 873-2500 or fax (760) 873-2563.

Trail notes: The Sabrina Basin Trail leads to a series of alpine lakes set below lofty, 13,000-foot granite peaks. Of these, one of the easiest to reach is scenic Blue Lake, a popular spot for photographers, trout anglers, and cold-water swimmers. If you catch the light just right, you can take pictures of Blue Lake with towering Mount Thompson and the Thompson Ridge mirrored on its surface. It's a 1,250-foot climb to the lake, spread out gradually over three miles. Start by hiking along the shore of Lake Sabrina, then switchback your way uphill to the lake. If you get inspired to see more, you can bear left from Blue Lake to Donkey Lake and the Baboon Lakes

(1.5 miles further), or bear right and hike eastward to the Emerald Lakes and Dingleberry Lake (1.8 miles further). Any of these are likely to have less visitors than Blue Lake.

⑨ Lamarck Lake

8.0 mi/4.0 hrs

Location: In the John Muir Wilderness; map F5, grid d3.

User groups: Hikers, dogs, and horses. No mountain bikes. No wheelchair facilities.

Permits: No day-hiking permits are required. A free wilderness permit is required for overnight stays; they are available from the Bishop Ranger Station. Quotas are in effect from the last Friday in June to September 15; permits are available in advance by mail, phone, or fax for this period for a $3 fee. Mail permit requests to Wilderness Reservations, P.O. Box 430, Big Pine, CA 93513. Phone (888) 374-3773 or fax (760) 938-1137.

Directions: From Bishop on U.S. 395, turn west on Line Street (Highway 168) and drive 18 miles toward Lake Sabrina. Just before reaching the lake, turn right at the turnoff for North Lake. Drive 1.5 miles and turn right to park in the hiker parking lot by North Lake, near the pack station. Then walk down the road to the trailhead at the far end of North Lake Campground.

Maps: For a map of Inyo National Forest, send $4 to USDA-Forest Service, 630 Sansome Street, San Francisco, CA 94111. To obtain topographic maps of the area, ask for Mount Thompson and Mount Darwin from the USGS.

Contact: Inyo National Forest, White Mountain Ranger District, 798 North Main Street, Bishop, CA 93514; (760) 873-2500 or fax (760) 873-2563.

Trail notes: The only downer on the Lamarck Lakes Trail is that from the trailhead parking area, you have to walk three-quarters of a mile down the road to get to the actual trailhead, which is located on the far side of North Lake Campground. With that dull stint out of the way, head through the aspens, cross Bishop Creek on a footbridge, and climb 1.7 miles to the left fork for Grass Lake, a small lake that is popular with campground anglers. Stay right and continue climbing for what seems like forever but is actually only three-quarters of a mile further, to

the short right spur to Lower Lamarck Lake, set in a rock-lined granite basin. (Although you gain only 1,500 feet in elevation on this trail, most of it is between the Grass Lake junction and Lower Lamarck Lake.) Cross the lake's outlet creek and climb to the Upper Lamarck Lake, a half mile further and nearly double in size. Look for Mount Emerson, Mount Lamarck, and the red-colored Piute Crags in the background.

⑩ Loch Leven Lake

4.6 mi/3.0 hrs

Location: In the John Muir Wilderness; map F5, grid d3.

User groups: Hikers, dogs, and horses. No mountain bikes. No wheelchair facilities.

Permits: No day-hiking permits are required. Parking and access are free.

Directions: From Bishop on U.S. 395, turn west on Line Street (Highway 168) and drive 18 miles toward Lake Sabrina. Just before reaching the lake, turn right at the turnoff for North Lake. Drive 1.5 miles and turn right to park in the hiker parking lot by North Lake, near the pack station. Then walk down the road to the trailhead at the far end of North Lake Campground.

Maps: For a map of Inyo National Forest, send $4 to USDA-Forest Service, 630 Sansome Street, San Francisco, CA 94111. To obtain topographic maps of the area, ask for Mount Thompson and Mount Darwin from the USGS.

Contact: Inyo National Forest, White Mountain Ranger District, 798 North Main Street, Bishop, CA 93514; (760) 873-2500 or fax (760) 873-2563.

Trail notes: If you're in the mood for a shorter hike in the Bishop Creek and North Lake area, Loch Leven Lake might just fit the bill. Take the trail marked for Piute Pass from the far end of North Lake Campground. A moderate but continual climb through the quaking aspens and lodgepole pines in the North Fork Bishop Creek Canyon brings you to the high ridge where Loch Leven Lake is nestled at 10,740 feet. A beautiful wildflower display accompanies you along the stream in summer, and in autumn, the quaking aspens can take your breath away. Mount Emerson and the reddish-colored Piute Crags are in full view at Loch Leven Lake, which is set in a rocky glacial bowl. Although there are campsites by the lake, most people just spend an hour or two there, whiling away their time by fishing, picnicking, or gazing at the beauty.

⑪ Tyee Lakes

7.0 mi/4.0 hrs

Location: In the John Muir Wilderness; map F5, grid d4.

User groups: Hikers, dogs, and horses. No mountain bikes. No wheelchair facilities.

Permits: No day-hiking permits are required. A free wilderness permit is required for overnight stays; they are available from the Bishop Ranger Station. Quotas are in effect from the last Friday in June to September 15; permits are available in advance by mail, phone, or fax for this period for a $3 fee. Mail permit requests to Wilderness Reservations, P.O. Box 430, Big Pine, CA 93513. Phone (888) 374-3773 or fax (760) 938-1137.

Directions: From Bishop on U.S. 395, turn west on Line Street (Highway 168) and drive 15 miles to the junction for South Lake. Go left and drive 4.5 miles on South Lake Road to the footbridge that crosses Bishop Creek and the Tyee Lakes and George Lake Trailhead on the right. Park alongside the road.

Maps: For a map of Inyo National Forest, send $4 to USDA-Forest Service, 630 Sansome Street, San Francisco, CA 94111. To obtain a topographic map of the area, ask for Mount Thompson from the USGS.

Contact: Inyo National Forest, White Mountain Ranger District, 798 North Main Street, Bishop, CA 93514; (760) 873-2500 or fax (760) 873-2563.

Trail notes: There's so much excellent hiking in the South Fork Bishop Creek Canyon, it's hard to choose where to go. Since so many backpackers opt for the Bishop Pass Trail and its many lakes (see hike number 13), day hikers might do well to choose this trail to the Tyee Lakes instead. Named for a brand of salmon eggs, the Tyee Lakes offer good trout fishing (what, you were expecting salmon fishing?) and plenty of classic high Sierra scenery. From the bridge over Bishop Creek, you climb through sagebrush and aspens through a few dozen switchbacks and into a lodgepole pine forest. After two miles of climbing, the trail grade eases up, and you reach one of the smaller, lower Tyee Lakes at 2.3 miles. A half mile more climbing brings you to the next small lake (called Tyee Lake number 2); then another half mile brings you to one of the larger ones (Tyee Lake number 3). A total of four Tyee Lakes are reachable by following the trail for 3.5 miles, with a total elevation gain of 2,000 feet. Anglers seek out rainbow and brown trout at the two largest lakes.

⑫ Green and Brown Lakes

6.0 mi/3.0 hrs

Location: In the John Muir Wilderness; map F5, grid d4.

User groups: Hikers, dogs, and horses. No mountain bikes. No wheelchair facilities.

Permits: No day-hiking permits are required. Parking and access are free.

Directions: From Bishop on U.S. 395, turn west on Line Street (Highway 168) and drive 15 miles to the junction for South Lake. Go left and drive six miles on South Lake Road to Parcher's Lodge and pack station on the left side of the road, just beyond Willow Campground.

Maps: For a map of Inyo National Forest, send $4 to USDA-Forest Service, 630 Sansome Street, San Francisco, CA 94111. To obtain a topographic map of the area, ask for Mount Thompson from the USGS.

Contact: Inyo National Forest, White Mountain Ranger District, 798 North Main Street, Bishop, CA 93514; (760) 873-2500 or fax (760) 873-2563.

Trail notes: Brown Lake and Green Lake are two excellent day-hiking destinations from the South Lake Trailhead in Bishop Creek's South Fork Canyon. With only a 1,500-foot climb, you can visit both lakes, maybe do a little fishing for rainbow trout, and be home in time for supper. Access the trail from the pack station trailhead, and follow a stock trail as it climbs along Bishop Creek through a conifer forest, and joins the main Green Lake Trail at one mile. Bear left and level out to an alpine meadow at two miles, then meet Brown Lake's outlet stream and the little lake itself at 2.5 miles. If you like fishing, this is your spot, but if you like scenery, continue another half mile to much larger Green Lake, surrounded by wildflowers and whitebark pines.

⑬ Ruwau and Chocolate Lakes Loop

6.0 mi/3.0 hrs

Location: In the John Muir Wilderness; map F5, grid d4.

User groups: Hikers, dogs, and horses. No mountain bikes. No wheelchair facilities.

Permits: No day-hiking permits are required. A free wilderness permit is required for overnight stays; they are available from the Bishop Ranger Station. Quotas are in effect from the last Friday in June to September 15; permits are available in advance by mail, phone, or fax for this period for a $3 fee. Mail permit requests to Wilderness Reservations, P.O. Box 430, Big Pine, CA 93513. Phone (888) 374-3773 or fax (760) 938-1137.

Directions: From Bishop on U.S. 395, turn west on Line Street (Highway 168) and drive 15 miles to the junction for South Lake. Go left and drive 7.5 miles on South Lake Road to the end of the road and the trailhead parking area.

Maps: For a map of Inyo National Forest, send $4 to USDA-Forest Service, 630 Sansome Street, San Francisco, CA 94111. To obtain a topographic map of the area, ask for Mount Thompson from the USGS.

Contact: Inyo National Forest, White Mountain Ranger District, 798 North Main Street, Bishop, CA 93514; (760) 873-2500 or fax (760) 873-2563.

Trail notes: Lakes, lakes, lakes everywhere. That's how it is on the Bishop Pass Trail, where in the space of only five miles you can access Long Lake, Spearhead Lake, Saddlerock Lake, Bishop Lake, and so on. But if you prefer a loop trip to an out-and-back hike, the Bishop Pass Trail provides another lake-filled option, which is a two-mile hike to Long Lake, then a circular route to Ruwau Lake, the Chocolate Lakes, and Bull Lake. It's the kind of trip that fills your mind with precious memories of blue-sky Sierra scenery and gemlike, rock-lined lakes. The trail begins on the south side of the parking lot, and you head uphill along the eastern shore of South Lake. The views begin almost immediately, particularly of Mount Thompson and Mount Goode. Take the left fork at three-quarters of a mile, heading for Long Lake and Bishop Pass. Continue straight, ignoring all turnoffs, as you hike up around the spectacular western shore of Long Lake, popular with anglers and backpackers. At 2.5 miles near the lake's far end, instead of continuing straight to Saddlerock Lake and Bishop Pass, take the left fork for Ruwau Lake, a half mile away. Then it's another half mile to the two Chocolate Lakes, set below Chocolate Peak, and still another half mile to Bull Lake. Note that the trail is rather indistinct in places, and it's often more like a route than a real trail, especially between Ruwau Lake and the Chocolate Lakes. Make sure you have a good map with you. From Bull Lake, you keep on hiking and quickly rejoin the Bishop Pass Trail. Turn right and walk just under two miles back to the parking lot. Wow, what a day.

⑭ First and Second Falls

3.0 mi/1.5 hrs

Location: In the John Muir Wilderness; map F5, grid e5.

User groups: Hikers, dogs, and horses. No mountain bikes. No wheelchair facilities.

Permits: No day-hiking permits are required. Parking and access are free.

Directions: From Bishop, drive 15 miles south on U.S. 395 to Big Pine. Turn right (west) on Crocker Street, which becomes Glacier Lodge Road, and drive 10.5 miles to Glacier Lodge and the Big Pine Canyon Trailhead, at the end of the road. Day hikers may park in the day-use area near the lodge, but backpackers must park a half mile east on Glacier Lodge Road in the backpackers' parking lot.

Maps: For a map of Inyo National Forest, send $4 to USDA-Forest Service, 630 Sansome Street, San Francisco, CA 94111. To obtain a topographic map of the area, ask for Coyote Flat from the USGS.

Contact: Inyo National Forest, White Mountain Ranger District, 798 North Main Street, Bishop, CA 93514; (760) 873-2500 or fax (760) 873-2563.

Trail notes: If you're camping or fishing in Big Pine Canyon, or maybe just wandering around exploring the area, there's a great walk to be taken starting from the end of the road near Glacier Lodge. Since it's just a day hike, you can park in the parking area right by the lodge, and save yourself the long walk from the backpackers' parking lot.

Head west from the trailhead on the wide road, passing some private cabins, and in seconds you cross a bridge over First Falls, a noisy, 200-foot-long whitewater cascade. Then bear right onto a narrower trail and start switchbacking uphill paralleling the cascade. As you climb, you get awesome views into Big Pine Canyon's South Fork. At the top of the falls, cross another bridge over the creek, then take a hard left onto a dirt road, staying along the creek. Now it's a flat stroll into the North Fork of Big Pine Canyon. Your goal is Second Falls, a larger, more impressive cascade than First Falls, less than one mile away and clearly visible from the trail. Since the route is set along the canyon bottom, you get many interesting vistas along the way, from the tall surrounding canyon walls to occasional lodgepole pines and many mountain wildflowers. When the trail starts to climb back out of the canyon, take the left spur cutoff to head closer to the waterfall, or just pick a big rock to sit on and admire the scenery.

⓯ First and Second Lakes

9.6 mi/6.0 hrs or 2.0 days

Location: In the John Muir Wilderness; map F5, grid e5.

User groups: Hikers, dogs, and horses. No mountain bikes. No wheelchair facilities.

Permits: A free wilderness permit is required for overnight stays; they are available from the Bishop Ranger Station. Quotas are in effect from the last Friday in June to September 15; permits are available in advance by mail, phone, or fax for this period for a $3 fee. Mail permit requests to Wilderness Reservations, P.O. Box 430, Big Pine, CA 93513. Phone (888) 374-3773 or fax (760) 938-1137.

Directions: From Bishop, drive 15 miles south on U.S. 395 to Big Pine. Turn right (west) on Crocker Street, which becomes Glacier Lodge Road, and drive 10.5 miles to Glacier Lodge and the Big Pine Canyon Trailhead, at the end of the road. Day hikers may park in the day-use area

near the lodge, but backpackers must park a half mile east on Glacier Lodge Road in the backpackers' parking lot.

Maps: For a map of Inyo National Forest, send $4 to USDA-Forest Service, 630 Sansome Street, San Francisco, CA 94111. To obtain topographic maps of the area, ask for Coyote Flat and Split Mountain from the USGS.

Contact: Inyo National Forest, White Mountain Ranger District, 798 North Main Street, Bishop, CA 93514; (760) 873-2500 or fax (760) 873-2563.

Trail notes: The trail to First and Second Lakes in Big Pine Canyon follows the same route as the trail to First and Second Falls (see hike number 14), but then continues onward, climbing up and over Second Falls on the well-graded trail to Cienaga Mirth at three miles out. Here you'll see a stone cabin built by movie star Lon Chaney, now a backcountry ranger residence. Wildflowers are excellent at the swampy, spring-fed mirth. You reach First Lake at 4.5 miles, then bear left and reach Second Lake at 4.8 miles. By Second Lake, you've climbed to over 10,000 feet and the lake water is a stunning glacial blue-green color. You'll see hardy hikers with climbing equipment continuing beyond Second Lake; they're hiking a full nine miles one way to the edge of Palisade Glacier, the southernmost glacier in the Sierra. With a 5,000-foot elevation gain, the route to the glacier is not for everybody.

⓰ Yucca Point

4.0 mi/2.25 hrs

Location: In Sequoia National Forest, west of the Cedar Grove area of Kings Canyon National Park; map F5, grid g1.

User groups: Hikers only. No dogs, horses, or mountain bikes. No wheelchair facilities.

Permits: No permits are required. Parking and access are free, but you will have to pay the $10 entrance fee to pass through the Big Stump entrance station at Kings Canyon National Park.

Directions: From Fresno, drive east on Highway 180 for 55 miles to the Big Stump entrance station at Kings Canyon National Park. Continue 1.5 miles and turn left for Grant Grove and Cedar Grove. Continue 16 miles on Highway 180, past Kings Canyon Lodge, to the Yucca Point

Trailhead on the left. Park in the pullouts alongside Highway 180.

Maps: For a map of Sequoia National Forest, send $4 to USDA-Forest Service, 630 Sansome Street, San Francisco, CA 94111. A detailed map is available for a fee from Tom Harrison Cartography at (415) 456-7940 or Trails Illustrated at (800) 962-1643. To obtain a topographic map of the area, ask for Wren Peak from the USGS.

Contact: Sequoia National Forest, Hume Lake Ranger District, 35860 East Kings Canyon Road, Dunlap, CA 93621; (209) 338-2251 or fax (209) 338-2131.

Trail notes: The Yucca Point Trail is an upside-down hike, the kind where you go down on the way in (so easy) and up on the way back (not so easy). The path descends from Highway 180 to the Kings River, dropping 1,200 feet along the way. We looked at it from the top and assumed it would be brutal on the way back, but as long as you don't climb uphill at high noon, it's not as bad as it looks. The trail is well graded; the only hardship is that the terrain is all chaparral so there's almost no shade, just the occasional tall yucca plant. The path is mostly used by anglers heading down to the wild trout section of the Kings River, but hikers like the excellent views it provides and the access to the river's cool, emerald-green pools.

⑰ Windy Cliffs

3.0 mi/1.5 hrs

Location: In Sequoia National Forest, west of the Cedar Grove area of Kings Canyon National Park; map F5, grid h1.

User groups: Hikers only. No dogs, horses, or mountain bikes. No wheelchair facilities.

Permits: No permits are required. Parking and access are free, but you will have to pay the $10 entrance fee to pass through the Big Stump entrance station at Kings Canyon National Park.

Directions: From Fresno, drive east on Highway 180 for 55 miles to the Big Stump entrance station at Kings Canyon National Park. Continue 1.5 miles and turn left for Grant Grove and Cedar Grove. Continue 22 miles on Highway 180 to the parking area for Boyden Cave, on the right side of the road.

Maps: For a map of Sequoia National Forest, send $4 to USDA-Forest Service, 630 Sansome Street, San Francisco, CA 94111. A detailed map is available for a fee from Tom Harrison Cartography at (415) 456-7940 or Trails Illustrated at (800) 962-1643. To obtain a topographic map of the area, ask for Wren Peak from the USGS.

Contact: Sequoia National Forest, Hume Lake Ranger District, 35860 East Kings Canyon Road, Dunlap, CA 93621; (209) 338-2251 or fax (209) 338-2131.

Trail notes: The Forest Service concessionaire charges a fee for tours of Boyden Cave, one of many limestone caverns in the vicinity of Kings Canyon and Sequoia National Park, and the parking lot is always busy with carloads and busloads full of people waiting to take the tour. But if you're low on cash, you can take this stellar hike instead, and get million-dollar views of Kings Canyon for free. From the cave gift shop, walk up the paved path and take the left fork near the entrance to the cave. The trail is signed as "unmaintained," but never fear, it's fairly well used. (It does have some steep dropoffs, however.) In no time you'll climb a little higher and see a sweeping panorama of the fast-flowing Kings River and Highway 180 below. In one mile, you'll see Boulder Creek cascading down the hillside. The path ends when it reaches creekside at 1.5 miles, and you turn around and head back.

⑱ Lewis Creek Trail

11.0 mi/6.0 hrs or 2.0 days

Location: Off Highway 180 in the Cedar Grove area of Kings Canyon National Park; map F5, grid h2.

User groups: Hikers and horses. No dogs or mountain bikes. No wheelchair facilities.

Permits: There is a $10 entrance fee at Sequoia and Kings Canyon National Parks, good for seven days. A free wilderness permit is required for overnight stays. They are available on a first-come, first-served basis at the wilderness kiosk near your chosen trailhead, or in advance by mail or fax after March 1; for more information phone (209) 565-3708.

Directions: From Fresno, drive east on Highway 180 for 55 miles to the Big Stump entrance station at Kings Canyon National Park. Continue 1.5 miles and turn left for Grant Grove and Cedar Grove. Continue 31 miles on Highway 180 to the Lewis Creek Trail parking area on the north side of the road (before you reach Cedar Grove Village).

Maps: Free park maps are available at park entrance stations or by contacting Sequoia and Kings Canyon National Parks at the address below. A more detailed map is available for a fee from Tom Harrison Cartography at (415) 456-7940 or Trails Illustrated at (800) 962-1643. To obtain a topographic map of the area, ask for Cedar Grove from the USGS.

Contact: Sequoia and Kings Canyon National Parks, Three Rivers, CA 93271-9700; (209) 565-3134 or (209) 335-2856.

Trail notes: Up, up, and up. If you're willing to climb 3,200 feet over the course of 5.5 miles, your reward is pristine Frypan Meadow at 7,800 feet in elevation. In summer, the meadow is green and littered with wildflowers, a glorious sight after climbing through hot, dusty chaparral. But there's no way to see it without first putting in some effort on the Lewis Creek Trail. The good news is that if the first mile or so proves to be too demanding (or too hot if you don't start first thing in the morning), you can always take the right fork at 1.3 miles and head back downhill on the Hotel Creek Trail, making an eight-mile loop out of the trip. If you grunt it out on the Lewis Creek Trail, most of the climbing is over in the first four miles. After you cross Lewis Creek, the last mile and a half is a piece of cake (relatively). If you've got your wilderness permit, campsites can be found by Frypan Meadow.

---

⑲ Hotel Creek Overlook

5.0 mi/2.5 hrs

Location: Off Highway 180 in the Cedar Grove area of Kings Canyon National Park; map F5, grid h3.

User groups: Hikers and horses. No dogs or mountain bikes. No wheelchair facilities.

Permits: No permits are required. There is a $10 entrance fee at Sequoia and Kings Canyon National Parks, good for seven days.

Directions: From Fresno, drive east on High-

way 180 for 55 miles to the Big Stump entrance station at Kings Canyon National Park. Continue 1.5 miles and turn left for Grant Grove and Cedar Grove. Continue 31.5 miles on Highway 180 and take the left fork for Cedar Grove Village. The Hotel Creek Trailhead is a quarter mile north of the Cedar Grove Lodge; drive north from the lodge for a quarter mile, heading for the stables. The parking area is on the left.

Maps: Free park maps are available at park entrance stations or by contacting Sequoia and Kings Canyon National Parks at the address below. A more detailed map is available for a fee from Tom Harrison Cartography at (415) 456-7940 or Trails Illustrated at (800) 962-1643. To obtain a topographic map of the area, ask for Cedar Grove from the USGS.

Contact: Sequoia and Kings Canyon National Parks, Three Rivers, CA 93271-9700; (209) 565-3134 or (209) 335-2856.

Trail notes: The destination on this trip is a stunning overlook of Kings Canyon, the deepest canyon in the continental United States. Actually, the canyon vistas are continual for most of the hike, so if you don't make it to the overlook, you'll still get an eyeful. The trail consists of dozens of switchbacks over open, sunny slopes, climbing 1,200 feet over two miles to a trail junction with the Lewis Creek Trail. Turn left to head to the overlook, which peers down on Cedar Grove and the length of Kings Canyon. Hope you came with picnic supplies. For a five-mile round-trip, retrace your steps back to Cedar Grove. But if you want to walk further, you can continue from the overlook turnoff for another 1.5 miles, then turn left and hike downhill on the Lewis Creek Trail, making an eight-mile loop out of the trip.

---

⑳ Lookout Peak

13.0 mi/7.0 hrs

Location: Off Highway 180 in the Cedar Grove area of Kings Canyon National Park; map F5, grid h3.

User groups: Hikers and horses. No dogs or mountain bikes. No wheelchair facilities.

Permits: No permits are required. There is a $10 entrance fee at Sequoia and Kings Canyon National Parks, good for seven days.

Directions: From Fresno, drive east on Highway 180 for 55 miles to the Big Stump entrance station at Kings Canyon National Park. Continue 1.5 miles and turn left for Grant Grove and Cedar Grove. Continue 31.5 miles on Highway 180 and take the right fork. The Don Cecil Trailhead is on the right side of the road, just beyond the turnoff for Cedar Grove Village and the visitor center. (If you reach Canyon View and Moraine campgrounds, you've gone too far.)

Maps: Free park maps are available at park entrance stations or by contacting Sequoia and Kings Canyon National Parks at the address below. A more detailed map is available for a fee from Tom Harrison Cartography at (415) 456-7940 or Trails Illustrated at (800) 962-1643. To obtain a topographic map of the area, ask for Cedar Grove from the USGS.

Contact: Sequoia and Kings Canyon National Parks, Three Rivers, CA 93271-9700; (209) 565-3134 or (209) 335-2856.

Trail notes: Lookout Peak at 8,531 feet in elevation is a summit worth ascending, even though it's an all-day trip with a 3,900-foot elevation gain. From the top, you get an unforgettable Sierra view, with Cedar Grove far below you and peaks and ridges all around. In addition, just a few hundred yards from the summit is Summit Meadow, filled with summer wildflowers. The key is to carry plenty of water and plan on an early-morning start to beat the heat. (You can filter water from Sheep Creek, one mile in.) Luckily, there's a decent amount of shade in the first few miles. Even though this trailhead is located right by the Cedar Grove Campgrounds, few people hike all the way to the peak, so you have a chance at peace and quiet while you gaze out from your mountaintop perch. If you're thinking about making the trip easier by splitting into two days, forget it—there's no overnight camping allowed.

㉑ Roaring River Falls

0.4 mi/0.25 hr

Location: Off Highway 180 in the Cedar Grove area of Kings Canyon National Park; map F5, grid h3.

User groups: Hikers and wheelchairs. No dogs, horses, or mountain bikes.

Permits: No permits are required. There is a $10 entrance fee at Sequoia and Kings Canyon National Parks, good for seven days.

Directions: From Fresno, drive east on Highway 180 for 55 miles to the Big Stump entrance station at Kings Canyon National Park. Continue 1.5 miles and turn left for Grant Grove and Cedar Grove. Continue 35 miles on Highway 180 to the sign for Roaring River Falls and the River Trail, three miles past Cedar Grove Village. The trailhead is on the right side of the road.

Maps: Free park maps are available at park entrance stations or by contacting Sequoia and Kings Canyon National Parks at the address below. A more detailed map is available for a fee from Tom Harrison Cartography at (415) 456-7940 or Trails Illustrated at (800) 962-1643. To obtain a topographic map of the area, ask for The Sphinx from the USGS.

Contact: Sequoia and Kings Canyon National Parks, Three Rivers, CA 93271-9700; (209) 565-3134 or (209) 335-2856.

Trail notes: It's really just an easy stroll to see Roaring River Falls, which drops through a narrow gorge into the South Fork Kings River. It's the only waterfall in Sequoia and Kings Canyon National Parks that is accessible via wheelchair. If hikers using two legs want a longer walk, they can continue downstream on the River Trail to Zumwalt Meadow in 1.6 miles or Road's End in 2.7 miles. What's extraordinary about the waterfall is not the cascade itself, but the giant rocky pool into which it falls, which is at least 50 feet wide. From where the paved trail ends at the edge of the pool, the waterfall is perfectly framed by two big conifers. About a zillion photos have been snapped here.

㉒ Zumwalt Meadow Loop

1.5 mi/1.0 hr

Location: Off Highway 180 in the Cedar Grove area of Kings Canyon National Park; map F5, grid h3.

User groups: Hikers only. No dogs, horses, or mountain bikes. No wheelchair facilities.

Permits: No permits are required. There is a $10 entrance fee at Sequoia and Kings Canyon National Parks, good for seven days.

Directions: From Fresno, drive east on Highway 180 for 55 miles to the Big Stump entrance station at Kings Canyon National Park. Continue 1.5 miles and turn left for Grant Grove and Cedar Grove. Continue 36 miles on Highway 180 to the parking area for Zumwalt Meadow, on the right side of the road.

Maps: Free park maps are available at park entrance stations or by contacting Sequoia and Kings Canyon National Parks at the address below. A more detailed map is available for a fee from Tom Harrison Cartography at (415) 456-7940 or Trails Illustrated at (800) 962-1643. To obtain a topographic map of the area, ask for Cedar Grove from the USGS.

Contact: Sequoia and Kings Canyon National Parks, Three Rivers, CA 93271-9700; (209) 565-3134 or (209) 335-2856.

Trail notes: What's the prettiest easy hike in Kings Canyon National Park? The Zumwalt Meadow Loop Trail wins hands down. A scenic 1.5-mile walk along the South Fork Kings River, the Zumwalt Meadow Loop is a delight for hikers of all abilities. Many people bring their fishing rods along to try their luck in the river, but for most, the hiking is better than the fishing. From the parking area, walk downstream along the river to an old suspension footbridge, then cross it and walk back upstream. The loop begins at an obvious fork, and you can hike it in either direction. The south side traverses a boulder field of jumbled rocks which have tumbled down from the Grand Sentinel, elevation 8,504 feet. The north side cuts through a thick, waist-high fern forest and follows a wooden walkway over a marsh. We were surprised by a deer who was up to his neck in the ferns. Views of 8,717-foot North Dome are awe inspiring. Trees, meadow, rock, stream, river, canyon walls—the Zumwalt Meadow Trail has it all.

㉓ Mist Falls

9.2 mi/5.0 hrs

Location: Off Highway 180 in the Cedar Grove area of Kings Canyon National Park; map F5, grid h4.

User groups: Hikers only. No dogs, horses, or mountain bikes. No wheelchair facilities.

Permits: No permits are required. There is a $10 entrance fee at Sequoia and Kings Canyon National Parks, good for seven days.

Directions: From Fresno, drive east on Highway 180 for 55 miles to the Big Stump entrance station at Kings Canyon National Park. Continue 1.5 miles and turn left for Grant Grove and Cedar Grove. Continue 38 miles on Highway 180 to Road's End, six miles past Cedar Grove Village. The trailhead is at the east end of the parking lot, near the wilderness ranger station.

Maps: Free park maps are available at park entrance stations or by contacting Sequoia and Kings Canyon National Parks at the address below. A more detailed map is available for a fee from Tom Harrison Cartography at (415) 456-7940 or Trails Illustrated at (800) 962-1643. To obtain a topographic map of the area, ask for The Sphinx from the USGS.

Contact: Sequoia and Kings Canyon National Parks, Three Rivers, CA 93271-9700; (209) 565-3134 or (209) 335-2856.

Trail notes: The Mist Falls Trail is probably the most well-used pathway in Kings Canyon National Park, with good reason. It's a stellar 4.6-mile walk to an impressive cascade on the South Fork Kings River, with only 650 feet in elevation gain along the way. Many backpackers use this trail to access Paradise Valley and points beyond, while most day hikers turn around at Mist Falls. The first two miles are flat, walking up the Kings River Valley with canyon walls towering above you on both sides. You spend a lot of time craning your neck, looking up at the high canyon rims, where springtime waterfalls cascade down. You're in open forest much of the time. At two miles, reach a trail junction and bear left, then start to climb over granite. The further you go, the more expansive the views become; make sure you keep turning around so you can take in the whole panorama. A highlight is the huge stone face of The Sphinx—you'll know it when you see it. At four miles, the river starts to get more waterfall-like, with crashing pools and rocky granite slides getting increasingly vertical. A half mile later you reach Mist Falls, which fans out over a 45-foot wide granite ledge and crashes into a boulder-lined pool. It creates a tremendous spray and mist in early summer, and mellows out as the season goes on. Now listen carefully: There are two ways to beat the crowds on this path—First, start early in the morning. Second, hike part of the route on an alternate trail on the south side of the river, which runs from the Road's End parking lot to the Bailey Bridge at the trail intersection mentioned above. If you get an early start, save this alternate route for the return trip. By then, the day hikers will be out in full force.

㉔ Copper Creek Trail

21.0 mi/3–4 days

Location: Off Highway 180 in the Cedar Grove area of Kings Canyon National Park; map F5, grid h4.

User groups: Hikers and horses. No dogs or mountain bikes. No wheelchair facilities.

Permits: There is a $10 entrance fee at Sequoia and Kings Canyon National Parks, good for seven days. A free wilderness permit is required for overnight stays. They are available on a first-come, first-served basis at the wilderness kiosk near the trailhead, or by mail or fax after March 1; for more information phone (209) 565-3708.

Directions: From Fresno, drive east on Highway 180 for 55 miles to the Big Stump entrance station at Kings Canyon National Park. Continue 1.5 miles and turn left for Grant Grove and Cedar Grove. Continue 38 miles on Highway 180 to Road's End, six miles past Cedar Grove Village. The trail begins at the long-term parking area.

Maps: Free park maps are available at park entrance stations or by contacting Sequoia and Kings Canyon National Parks at the address below. A more detailed map is available for a fee from Tom Harrison Cartography at (415) 456-7940 or Trails Illustrated at (800) 962-1643. To obtain a topographic map of the area, ask for The Sphinx from the USGS.

Contact: Sequoia and Kings Canyon National Parks, Three Rivers, CA 93271-9700; (209) 565-3134 or (209) 335-2856.

Trail notes: The Copper Creek Trailhead is at 5,000 feet, and Granite Lake is at 9,972 feet, so it's not hard to do the math. If you're up for a backpacking trip with a 5,000-foot elevation gain over 10 miles, the Granite Lake Basin is

your ticket to happiness. But keep in mind that the route can be hot and dry as it switchbacks up manzanita-covered slopes; this trail is considered one of the most strenuous in the Cedar Grove area. Your first night's camp is at Lower Tent Meadow, four miles in and at 7,800 feet. After that, things start to get really good. With Mount Hutchings looming over your left shoulder, the second day's six miles will go easier, bringing you to rocky, jewel-like Granite Lake in only a few hours. You must have a backpacking stove for camping by the lake, or anywhere above 10,000 feet.

㉕ Redwood Canyon

4.0 mi/2.0 hrs

Location: Southeast of the Grant Grove area of Kings Canyon National Park; map F5, grid h0.

User groups: Hikers only. No dogs, horses, or mountain bikes. No wheelchair facilities.

Permits: No permits are required. There is a $10 entrance fee at Sequoia and Kings Canyon National Parks, good for seven days.

Directions: From Fresno, drive east on Highway 180 for 55 miles to the Big Stump entrance station at Kings Canyon National Park. Continue 1.5 miles and turn right on the Generals Highway, heading for Sequoia National Park. Drive approximately three miles on the Generals Highway to Quail Flat (signed for Hume Lake to the left) and turn right on the dirt road to Redwood Saddle. Drive 1.5 miles and park in the parking lot. Take the trail signed for the Hart Tree and Redwood Canyon.

Maps: Free park maps are available at park entrance stations or by contacting Sequoia and Kings Canyon National Parks at the address below. A more detailed map is available for a fee from Tom Harrison Cartography at (415) 456-7940 or Trails Illustrated at (800) 962-1643. To obtain a topographic map of the area, ask for General Grant Grove from the USGS.

Contact: Sequoia and Kings Canyon National Parks, Three Rivers, CA 93271-9700; (209) 565-3134 or (209) 335-2856.

Trail notes: Several loop trips are possible in the Redwood Mountain area of Kings Canyon National Park, but one of the prettiest and simplest trips is just an out-and-back walk on the Redwood Canyon Trail, paralleling Redwood Creek. The beauty begins before you even start walking; on the last mile of the drive to the trailhead, the road winds through giant Sequoias that are so close, you can reach out your car window and touch them. The trail leads downhill from the parking area, and in a third of a mile you reach a junction and follow the Redwood Creek Trail to the right. You'll find that this Sequoia grove is far more lush with foliage than many; because it is situated by Redwood Creek, the Sequoias grow amid a dense background of dogwoods, firs, ceanothus, and mountain misery. The area seems much more like the damp, lush coastal redwood forests of northwestern California. While the standing Sequoias are impressive, some of the fallen ones along the trail are really amazing, because you get a close-up look at their immense size. Make sure you hike the full two miles to the stream crossing of Redwood Creek—some of the best tree specimens are down there, and also near the junction with the Sugar Bowl Loop Trail. The return trip is all uphill, but easier than you'd expect.

㉖ Redwood Mountain Loop

10.0 mi/5.0 hrs

Location: Southeast of the Grant Grove area of Kings Canyon National Park; map F5, grid h0.

User groups: Hikers only. No dogs, horses, or mountain bikes. No wheelchair facilities.

Permits: No permits are required. There is a $10 entrance fee at Sequoia and Kings Canyon National Parks, good for seven days.

Directions: From Fresno, drive east on Highway 180 for 55 miles to the Big Stump entrance station at Kings Canyon National Park. Continue 1.5 miles and turn right on the Generals Highway, heading for Sequoia National Park. Drive approximately three miles on the Generals Highway to Quail Flat (signed for Hume Lake to the left) and turn right on the dirt road to Redwood Saddle. Drive 1.5 miles and park in the parking lot. Take the trail signed as Burnt Grove/Sugar Bowl Loop.

Maps: Free park maps are available at park

entrance stations or by contacting Sequoia and Kings Canyon National Parks at the address below. A more detailed map is available for a fee from Tom Harrison Cartography at (415) 456-7940 or Trails Illustrated at (800) 962-1643. To obtain a topographic map of the area, ask for General Grant Grove from the USGS.

Contact: Sequoia and Kings Canyon National Parks, Three Rivers, CA 93271-9700; (209) 565-3134 or (209) 335-2856.

Trail notes: If you've got a whole day to hike in the Redwood Mountain area of Kings Canyon National Park, you're in luck. The Redwood Mountain Loop combines all the best highlights of the area into one long trail, on which you'll wander in near solitude among the giant Sequoias. If the paved trails to the General Grant Tree and the General Sherman Tree turn you off, this trail will turn you on. Start by hiking on the signed Burnt Grove/Sugar Bowl Loop Trail, which leads uphill from the parking lot. It's one mile to Burnt Grove and 2.5 miles to Sugar Bowl Grove, both very dense stands of Sequoias. Two miles east of there, you intersect with the Redwood Canyon Trail, head downhill and cross Redwood Creek, then proceed to the Fallen Goliath, a mammoth fallen tree. One mile further you see the Hart Tree, the largest tree in this area, and pass by beautiful Hart Meadow. Then simply continue for three miles back to the parking area. (In the final two miles, you get to walk through the Tunnel Log, a hollowed Sequoia.) Note that if you tire out halfway through this loop, you can always follow the Redwood Canyon Trail uphill back to the start.

㉗ Buena Vista Peak

2.0 mi/1.0 hr

Location: Southeast of the Grant Grove area of Kings Canyon National Park; map F5, grid h0.

User groups: Hikers only. No dogs, horses, or mountain bikes. No wheelchair facilities.

Permits: No permits are required. There is a $10 entrance fee at Sequoia and Kings Canyon National Parks, good for seven days.

Directions: From Fresno, drive east on Highway 180 for 55 miles to the Big Stump entrance station at Kings Canyon National Park. Continue 1.5

miles and turn right on the Generals Highway, heading for Sequoia National Park. Drive approximately five miles on the Generals Highway to the Buena Vista Trailhead on the right, just across the road and slightly beyond the large pullout for the Kings Canyon Overlook on the left.

Maps: Free park maps are available at park entrance stations or by contacting Sequoia and Kings Canyon National Parks at the address below. A more detailed map is available for a fee from Tom Harrison Cartography at (415) 456-7940 or Trails Illustrated at (800) 962-1643. To obtain a topographic map of the area, ask for General Grant Grove from the USGS.

Contact: Sequoia and Kings Canyon National Parks, Three Rivers, CA 93271-9700; (209) 565-3134 or (209) 335-2856.

Trail notes: Forget stopping at the drive-to Kings Canyon Overlook, because just across the road is a trailhead and an easy walk with all the same views, and more, plus a chance at a private picnic spot. Buena Vista Peak is really a rocky dome, peaking at 7,603 feet, one of the highest points west of Generals Highway. It offers 360-degree views: You can see a million conifers at your feet and the hazy foothills to the southwest, but the best vistas are to the east, looking out at the snow-capped peaks of the John Muir and Monarch Wildernesses. It's an easy half-hour walk up the back side of the dome, passing through pine and fir forest, manzanita and sage, and walking by some interesting rock formations (check out the giant boulder sculpture in the first quarter mile of trail). Then you can wander all around the top of the dome, taking in many different perspectives on the vistas, before heading back to the parking lot. It's downhill all the way.

㉘ Weaver Lake

4.2 mi/2.0 hrs or 2.0 days

Location: In the Jennie Lakes Wilderness; map F5, grid h0.

User groups: Hikers, dogs, and horses. No mountain bikes. No wheelchair facilities.

Permits: A free wilderness permit is required for overnight stays; they are available from the Hume Lake Ranger Station. Parking and access are free, but you will have to pay the $10 entrance fee to

pass through the Big Stump entrance station at Kings Canyon National Park.

Directions: From Fresno, drive east on Highway 180 for 55 miles to the Big Stump entrance station at Kings Canyon National Park. Continue 1.5 miles and turn right on the Generals Highway, heading for Sequoia National Park. Drive seven miles and turn left on Forest Service Road 14S11, at the sign for Big Meadow and Horse Corral. Drive four miles to the Big Meadow Campground, then continue past it, turn right and follow the signs for four miles to Fox Meadow and the Weaver Lake Trailhead.

Maps: For a map of Sequoia National Forest, send $4 to USDA-Forest Service, 630 Sansome Street, San Francisco, CA 94111. A detailed map is available for a fee from Tom Harrison Cartography at (415) 456-7940 or Trails Illustrated at (800) 962-1643. To obtain a topographic map of the area, ask for Muir Grove from the USGS.

Contact: Sequoia National Forest, Hume Lake Ranger District, 35860 East Kings Canyon Road, Dunlap, CA 93621; (209) 338-2251 or fax (209) 338-2131.

Trail notes: Tucked into a corner just outside the border of Kings Canyon and Sequoia National Parks, the Jennie Lakes Wilderness is a 10,500-acre wilderness area that is often overlooked by park visitors. It offers much of the same scenery as the parks—beautiful lakes, meadows, forests, and streams—but without all the fanfare. Weaver Lake is the easiest-to-reach destination in the wilderness, and it makes a perfect family backpacking trip, or an equally nice day hike. The trail is well signed and passes through a mix of fir forest and meadows. At seven-tenths of a mile, take the left fork for Weaver Lake, climbing up into granite country. At just over two miles out, you'll reach the shallow but pretty lake at 8,700 feet in elevation, where you can try your luck fishing or just find a lakeside seat and gaze out on the beauty. On warm days, the brave go swimming.

㉙ Jennie Lake

10.0 mi/6.0 hrs or 2.0 days

Location: In the Jennie Lakes Wilderness; map F5, grid h0.

User groups: Hikers, dogs, and horses. No mountain bikes. No wheelchair facilities.

Permits: A free wilderness permit is required for overnight stays; they are available from the Hume Lake Ranger Station. Parking and access are free, but you will have to pay the $10 entrance fee to pass through the Big Stump entrance station at Kings Canyon National Park.

Directions: From Fresno, drive east on Highway 180 for 55 miles to the Big Stump entrance station at Kings Canyon National Park. Continue 1.5 miles and turn right on the Generals Highway, heading for Sequoia National Park. Drive seven miles and turn left on Forest Service Road 14S11, at the sign for Big Meadow and Horse Corral. Drive four miles to the Big Meadow Campground, then continue past it, turn right and follow the signs for four miles to Fox Meadow and the Weaver Lake Trailhead.

Maps: For a map of Sequoia National Forest, send $4 to USDA-Forest Service, 630 Sansome Street, San Francisco, CA 94111. A detailed map is available for a fee from Tom Harrison Cartography at (415) 456-7940 or Trails Illustrated at (800) 962-1643. To obtain a topographic map of the area, ask for Muir Grove from the USGS.

Contact: Sequoia National Forest, Hume Lake Ranger District, 35860 East Kings Canyon Road, Dunlap, CA 93621; (209) 338-2251 or fax (209) 338-2131.

Trail notes: This trail into the Jennie Lakes Wilderness offers more of a challenge than the route to Weaver Lake (see hike number 28), climbing 1,500 feet over five miles with some short, steep pitches. The trail is the same as the Weaver Lake Trail for seven-tenths of a mile, but at the fork you bear right for Jennie Lake. The trail climbs and dips through fir and pine forest and manzanita, then crosses Poop Out Pass at 3.7 miles, the highest point on this trail. At five miles you reach the outlet stream for Jennie Lake, and shortly you come to the lake itself, set at 9,000 feet. With a white granite backdrop and some sparse trees, the shoreline looks austere and barren, but beautiful just the same. Campsites are found around the lake, and catching fish for dinner is a fair possibility. But if you only came for the day, make sure to find a comfortable spot to sit and enjoy the scenery before you head back.

㉚ Mitchell Peak

6.0 mi/3.0 hrs

Location: In the Jennie Lakes Wilderness; map F5, grid h0.

User groups: Hikers, dogs, and horses. No mountain bikes. No wheelchair facilities.

Permits: A free wilderness permit is required for overnight stays; they are available from the Hume Lake Ranger Station. Parking and access are free, but you will have to pay the $10 entrance fee to pass through the Big Stump entrance station at Kings Canyon National Park.

Directions: From Fresno, drive east on Highway 180 for 55 miles to the Big Stump entrance station at Kings Canyon National Park. Continue 1.5 miles and turn right on the Generals Highway, heading for Sequoia National Park. Drive seven miles and turn left on Forest Service Road 14S11, at the sign for Big Meadow and Horse Corral. Drive four miles to the Big Meadow Campground, then continue six more miles to Horse Corral Meadow. Turn right on Forest Service Road 13S12 and drive 2.8 miles to the Marvin Pass Trailhead.

Maps: For a map of Sequoia National Forest, send $4 to USDA-Forest Service, 630 Sansome Street, San Francisco, CA 94111. A detailed map is available for a fee from Tom Harrison Cartography at (415) 456-7940 or Trails Illustrated at (800) 962-1643. To obtain a topographic map of the area, ask for Muir Grove from the USGS.

Contact: Sequoia National Forest, Hume Lake Ranger District, 35860 East Kings Canyon Road, Dunlap, CA 93621; (209) 338-2251 or fax (209) 338-2131.

Trail notes: If you've got the legs for a 2,000-foot climb over 2.75 miles, you can stand atop the summit of Mitchell Peak, the highest point in the Jennie Lakes Wilderness, at 10,365 feet in elevation. It's a one-mile climb from the trailhead to Marvin Pass and the boundary of the Jennie Lakes Wilderness. Bear left (east), and climb some more. At 1.75 miles you reach the next junction, this one signed for Mitchell Peak. Head left (north) and in one more mile, you'll make the brief climb to Mitchell's summit, which straddles the border of Kings Canyon National Park. From your rocky perch, you can look out on the Great Western Divide and the Silliman Crest. It's not a bad spot to catch your breath.

③ Big Baldy

4.6 mi/2.5 hrs

Location: In Sequoia National Forest, southeast of the Grant Grove area of Kings Canyon National Park; map F5, grid i0.

User groups: Hikers only. No dogs, horses, or mountain bikes. No wheelchair facilities.

Permits: No permits are required. There is a $10 entrance fee at Sequoia and Kings Canyon National Parks, good for seven days.

Directions: From Fresno, drive east on Highway 180 for 55 miles to the Big Stump entrance station at Kings Canyon National Park. Continue 1.5 miles and turn right on the Generals Highway, heading for Sequoia National Park. Drive approximately 6.5 miles on the Generals Highway to the Big Baldy Trailhead on the right, shortly before the turnoff for Big Meadows on the left.

Maps: Free park maps are available at park entrance stations or by contacting Sequoia and Kings Canyon National Parks at the address below. A more detailed map is available for a fee from Tom Harrison Cartography at (415) 456-7940 or Trails Illustrated at (800) 962-1643. To obtain a topographic map of the area, ask for Muir Grove from the USGS.

Contact: Sequoia and Kings Canyon National Parks, Three Rivers, CA 93271-9700; (209) 565-3134 or (209) 335-2856.

Trail notes: The trip to Big Baldy comes with a million views and a little workout besides. Views? We're talking Redwood Canyon, Redwood Mountain, Buena Vista Peak, Little Baldy, the Silliman Crest, and the Great Western Divide. A workout? You've got to climb 1,000 feet, but it's nicely spread out over two miles, and the only noticeable ascent is in the last third of a mile to the top of Baldy's rocky knob. The trail begins in the trees but quickly opens up to wide views. They just keep changing and getting more interesting all the way to Big Baldy's 8,209-foot summit, where your panorama opens up to 360 degrees. This trail is so fun and rewarding, with so little suffering involved, you may feel like you're getting away with something.

③ Muir Grove

4.0 mi/2.0 hrs

Location: Northwest of the Lodgepole area of Sequoia National Park; map F5, grid i0.

User groups: Hikers only. No dogs, horses, or mountain bikes. No wheelchair facilities.

Permits: No permits are required. There is a $10 entrance fee at Sequoia and Kings Canyon National Parks, good for seven days.

Directions: From Fresno, drive east on Highway 180 for 55 miles to the Big Stump entrance station at Kings Canyon National Park. Continue 1.5 miles and turn right on the Generals Highway, heading for Sequoia National Park. Drive approximately 17 miles on the Generals Highway to the right turnoff for Dorst Campground. Turn right and park in the amphitheater parking lot in the campground.

Maps: Free park maps are available at park entrance stations or by contacting Sequoia and Kings Canyon National Parks at the address below. A more detailed map is available for a fee from Tom Harrison Cartography at (415) 456-7940 or Trails Illustrated at (800) 962-1643. To obtain a topographic map of the area, ask for Muir Grove from the USGS.

Contact: Sequoia and Kings Canyon National Parks, Three Rivers, CA 93271-9700; (209) 565-3134 or fax (209) 565-3730.

Trail notes: Nobody finds this trail unless they happen to be staying at Dorst Campground, so you have a lot better chance of seeing big Sequoias in solitude in the Muir Grove than at most places in the park. After crossing a wooden footbridge, the trail enters a mixed forest of red fir, white fir, sugar pines, and incense cedars. Take the left fork for 1.9 miles to reach the Muir Grove, a pristine grove of huge trees. For some reason, their cinnamon-colored bark really stands out here. So do the cinnamon-colored coats of black bears, who are often seen in this grove on their way to raid the dumpsters at Dorst Campground.

③ Little Baldy

3.5 mi/2.0 hrs

Location: Northwest of the Lodgepole area of Sequoia National Park; map F5, grid i0.

User groups: Hikers only. No dogs, horses, or mountain bikes. No wheelchair facilities.

Permits: No permits are required. There is a $10 entrance fee at Sequoia and Kings Canyon National Parks, good for seven days.

Directions: From Fresno, drive east on Highway 180 for 55 miles to the Big Stump entrance station at Kings Canyon National Park. Continue 1.5 miles and turn right on the Generals Highway, heading for Sequoia National Park. Drive approximately 18 miles on the Generals Highway to the Little Baldy Trailhead on the left, a mile beyond the turnoff for Dorst Campground.

Maps: Free park maps are available at park entrance stations or by contacting Sequoia and Kings Canyon National Parks at the address below. A more detailed map is available for a fee from Tom Harrison Cartography at (415) 456-7940 or Trails Illustrated at (800) 962-1643. To obtain a topographic map of the area, ask for Muir Grove and Giant Forest from the USGS.

Contact: Sequoia and Kings Canyon National Parks, Three Rivers, CA 93271-9700; (209) 565-3134 or fax (209) 565-3730.

Trail notes: Little Baldy, Big Baldy, Buena Vista Peak. . . . Along this stretch of the Generals Highway, there are so many big rocks you can hike up that provide far-reaching views, it's hard to know where to start. Start here, on the Little Baldy Trail. It's a little more challenging than the Buena Vista Peak Trail, but less so than the Big Baldy Trail, and offers similar mind-boggling views. Some claim that Little Baldy's view of the Silliman Crest, the Great Western Divide, Castle Rocks, Moro Rock, the Kaweah River Canyon, and the San Joaquin foothills is the best panorama in the park. An added bonus is that you can also view Big Baldy from this trail, an interesting perspective that you don't get from anywhere else, as well as well-named Chimney Rock. This path also rates high for best lupine displays. The bushes bloom dark purple right along the trail.

㉞ Kearsage Pass

10.0 mi/6.0 hrs or 2.0 days

Location: In the John Muir Wilderness in Inyo National Forest; map F5, grid i6.

User groups: Hikers, dogs, and horses. (Dogs are allowed to Kearsage Pass, but not beyond it.) No mountain bikes. No wheelchair facilities.

Permits: No day-hiking permits are required. A free wilderness permit is required for overnight stays; they are available from the Lone Pine Ranger Station. Quotas are in effect from the last Friday in June to September 15; permits are available in advance by mail, phone, or fax for this period for a $3 fee. Mail permit requests to Wilderness Reservations, P.O. Box 430, Big Pine, CA 93513. Phone (888) 374-3773 or fax (760) 938-1137.

Directions: From Lone Pine, drive 15 miles north on U.S. 395 to Independence. Turn west on Market Street, which becomes Onion Valley Road. Drive 14 miles to the end of the road and the trailhead at the hiker parking area.

Maps: For a map of Inyo National Forest, send $4 to USDA-Forest Service, 630 Sansome Street, San Francisco, CA 94111. To obtain a topographic map of the area, ask for Kearsage Peak from the USGS.

Contact: Inyo National Forest, Mount Whitney Ranger District, P.O. Box 8, Lone Pine, CA 93545; (760) 876-6200 or fax (760) 876-6202.

Trail notes: The trailhead elevation for the Kearsage Pass Trail is 9,200 feet, and the elevation at Kearsage Pass is 11,823 feet. There are five miles and a good amount of climbing in between, but the route is well graded and the scenery is spectacular. The trail, which was once an Indian trading route, leads to the backcountry of Kings Canyon National Park, but most day hikers just make the trip to the pass. Along the way, you pass several sparkling lakes and whitewater cascades, and a wealth of high-country wildflowers. Remember to bring sunglasses, sunscreen, and a jacket for the summit, which is windy and exposed. The trail climbs gradually from the trailhead, frequently nearing Independence Creek, then veering away through a multitude of switchbacks. You pass Little Pothole Lake at 1.5 miles, Gilbert Lake at 2.2 miles, and Flower Lake at 2.6 miles. Continue climbing high above treeline to Kearsage Pass. You'll get a long-distance view of Heart Lake, and pass the left spur trail leading to Big Pothole Lake along the way. Finally, just when you think you can climb no further, you reach the pass at 5.0 miles. A wooden sign announces your arrival in Kings Canyon Park, and extraordinary Sierra views surround you from every direction. Note that if you decide to turn this into an overnight trip, food storage regulations are in effect. The bears have smartened up to the old hang-the-food-in-the-tree routine, so bear-resistant canisters are required for all backpackers. Also, you must have a backpacking stove, because campfires are *ixnay*.

㉟ Flower and Matlock Lakes

6.4 mi/3.5 hrs

Location: In the John Muir Wilderness in Inyo National Forest; map F5, grid i6.

User groups: Hikers, dogs, and horses. No mountain bikes. No wheelchair facilities.

Permits: No day-hiking permits are required. Parking and access are free.

Directions: From Lone Pine, drive 15 miles north on U.S. 395 to Independence. Turn west on Market Street, which becomes Onion Valley Road. Drive 14 miles to the end of the road and the trailhead at the hiker parking area.

Maps: For a map of Inyo National Forest, send $4 to USDA-Forest Service, 630 Sansome Street, San Francisco, CA 94111. To obtain a topographic map of the area, ask for Kearsage Peak from the USGS.

Contact: Inyo National Forest, Mount Whitney Ranger District, P.O. Box 8, Lone Pine, CA 93545; (760) 876-6200 or fax (760) 876-6202.

Trail notes: If you don't have the time or the energy for the Kearsage Pass Trail, the route to Flower Lake and Matlock Lake is a close second choice. While it doesn't offer the astounding views that the pass has, it is still a stellar trip into dramatic granite country, where little grows in the harsh, exposed conditions above treeline. The beauty here can pull at your heartstrings, with both lakes being deep blue waterways that draw in all the color of the Sierra sky. The trail climbs gradually from the trailhead, switchbacking along Independence Creek. You pass Little Pothole Lake at 1.5 miles, Gilbert Lake at 2.2 miles, and reach a junction for Matlock Lake

at 2.5 miles. Continue straight for a tenth of a mile to Flower Lake, then retrace your steps to the junction and head south for seven-tenths of a mile to larger Matlock Lake. Pull out your camera and a picnic, and while away some time before returning to the trailhead.

㊱ Robinson Lake

3.0 mi/2.0 hrs

Location: In the John Muir Wilderness in Inyo National Forest; map F5, grid i6.

User groups: Hikers, dogs, and horses. No mountain bikes. No wheelchair facilities.

Permits: No day-hiking permits are required. A free wilderness permit is required for overnight stays; they are available from the Lone Pine Ranger Station. Quotas are in effect from the last Friday in June to September 15; permits are available in advance by mail, phone, or fax for this period for a $3 fee. Mail permit requests to Wilderness Reservations, P.O. Box 430, Big Pine, CA 93513. Phone (888) 374-3773 or fax (760) 938-1137.

Directions: From Lone Pine, drive 15 miles north on U.S. 395 to Independence. Turn west on Market Street, which becomes Onion Valley Road. Drive 14 miles to the end of the road and the hiker parking area. Walk into Onion Valley Campground to find the trailhead.

Maps: For a map of Inyo National Forest, send $4 to USDA-Forest Service, 630 Sansome Street, San Francisco, CA 94111. To obtain a topographic map of the area, ask for Kearsage Peak from the USGS.

Contact: Inyo National Forest, Mount Whitney Ranger District, P.O. Box 8, Lone Pine, CA 93545; (760) 876-6200 or fax (760) 876-6202.

Trail notes: The Robinson Lake Trail is best described as relentlessly steep but mercifully short. The hike is challenging in places due to the grade and relative obscurity of the trail, but the destination is superlative. In addition to beautiful Robinson Lake at 10,500 feet, you get a close and personal view of 11,744-foot Independence Peak, and an excellent wildflower display along Robinson Creek. Start by hiking up the stream just beyond car campsite number 8 in Onion Valley Campground. Watch out for overgrown vegetation which can sometimes hide the trail. Just climb, catch your breath, and climb some more. You'll reach the shallow lake in less than an hour. Campsites and picnicking sites are found in the sand on the lake's east side or in the pine forest on the northwest side. Plan your trip for July to September; the trail is usually free of snow to the lake by midsummer.

37 Marble Falls

7.0 mi/4.0 hrs

Location: Off Highway 198 in the Foothills region of Sequoia National Park; map F5, grid j0.

User groups: Hikers only. No dogs, horses, or mountain bikes. No wheelchair facilities.

Permits: No permits are required. There is a $10 entrance fee at Sequoia and Kings Canyon National Parks, good for seven days.

Directions: From Visalia, drive east on Highway 198 for 44 miles to the turnoff on the left for Potwisha Campground, 3.8 miles east of the Ash Mountain entrance station to Sequoia National Park. The trail begins next to site number 16 in Potwisha Campground; park in the day-use parking area in the camp.

Maps: Free park maps are available at park entrance stations or by contacting Sequoia and Kings Canyon National Parks at the address below. A more detailed map is available for a fee from Tom Harrison Cartography at (415) 456-7940 or Trails Illustrated at (800) 962-1643. To obtain a topographic map of the area, ask for Giant Forest from the USGS.

Contact: Sequoia and Kings Canyon National Parks, Three Rivers, CA 93271-9700; (209) 565-3134 or fax (209) 565-3730.

Trail notes: This is the waterfall to see in Sequoia and Kings Canyon in winter and spring, when there's no access to snowed-in Tokopah Falls or Mist Falls. March and April are particularly good months to visit, because of high flows in the Marble Fork Kaweah River and excellent spring wildflowers in the grasslands and chaparral that line the trail. From its rather pedantic start as a dirt road, this trail just keeps getting better as it contours along the Marble Fork. There are no trail junctions to worry about; at 3.5 miles, the path simply dead-ends near the lower cascades of Marble Falls. Although much of the falls are hidden in the narrow, rocky river gorge, tucked out of sight, what is visible is an impressive billowing cascade of fast whitewater. Be very careful on the slippery granite near the river's edges; the current and cold water are even more dangerous than they look. Aside from the waterfall and the wildflowers, the other highlights on this trail are the colorful outcroppings of marble, particularly in the last mile as you near the falls. Remember, though, that in summertime this area of the park can bake like an oven. If you make the trip to the falls from May to September, get an early morning start.

38 Potwisha to Hospital Rock

5.0 mi/2.5 hrs

Location: Off Highway 198 in the Foothills region of Sequoia National Park; map F5, grid j0.

User groups: Hikers only. No dogs, horses, or mountain bikes. No wheelchair facilities.

Permits: No permits are required. There is a $10 entrance fee at Sequoia and Kings Canyon National Parks, good for seven days.

Directions: From Visalia, drive east on Highway 198 for 44 miles to the turnoff on the left for Potwisha Campground, 3.8 miles east of the Ash Mountain entrance station to Sequoia National Park. Don't turn left into Potwisha campground; instead turn right on the paved road opposite the campground. Drive past the RV dumping station to the signed trailhead and parking area.

Maps: Free park maps are available at park entrance stations or by contacting Sequoia and Kings Canyon National Parks at the address below. A more detailed map is available for a fee from Tom Harrison Cartography at (415) 456-7940 or Trails Illustrated at (800) 962-1643. To obtain a topographic map of the area, ask for Giant Forest from the USGS.

Contact: Sequoia and Kings Canyon National Parks, Three Rivers, CA 93271-9700; (209) 565-3134 or fax (209) 565-3730.

Trail notes: First, some advice: Don't hike this trail on a hot day. If it's summertime and you want to the see the Monache Indian historical sites at Potwisha and Hospital Rock, drive to each of them and see them both separately. In winter or spring, however, it's far more fun to take this five-mile hike through chaparral and oak woodlands, especially in March when the wildflowers bloom. In the first 100 yards from the trailhead, you'll see Indian grinding holes and pictographs, which look roughly like people and animals. You'll also pass many tempting pools in the Middle Fork Kaweah, which see a lot of swimmers in the summertime. The trail climbs gradually 2.5 miles from Potwisha to Hospital Rock, crossing the highway after the first mile. When you reach Hospital Rock, which is just a few feet off the road to Buckeye Flat Campground, you see a huge display of pictographs on its side. Across the campground road are more grinding holes in the boulders, and near them, a short paved path leads to deep pools and sandy beaches on the Middle Fork. Another path leads from the camp road to the underside of Hospital Rock, where there's a large, cavelike shelter. This is where a Native American medicine man healed the sick and injured, resulting in a white man naming this place Hospital Rock.

🄴 Middle Fork Trail to Panther Creek

6.0 mi/3.0 hrs

Location: Off Highway 198 in the Foothills region of Sequoia National Park; map F5, grid j0.

User groups: Hikers only. No dogs, horses, or mountain bikes. No wheelchair facilities.

Permits: No permits are required. There is a $10 entrance fee at Sequoia and Kings Canyon National Parks, good for seven days.

Directions: From Visalia, drive east on Highway 198 for 47 miles to the turnoff on the right for Buckeye Flat Campground, across from Hospital Rock. Turn right and drive a half mile to a left fork just before the campground. Bear left on the dirt road and drive 1.3 miles to the trailhead and parking area. In the winter, you must park at Hospital Rock and walk in to the trailhead, adding 3.6 miles to your round-trip.

Maps: Free park maps are available at park entrance stations or by contacting Sequoia and

Kings Canyon National Parks at the address below. A more detailed map is available for a fee from Tom Harrison Cartography at (415) 456-7940 or Trails Illustrated at (800) 962-1643. To obtain a topographic map of the area, ask for Giant Forest from the USGS.

Contact: Sequoia and Kings Canyon National Parks, Three Rivers, CA 93271-9700; (209) 565-3134 or fax (209) 565-3730.

Trail notes: You want to be alone? You don't want to see anybody else on the trail? Okay, just sign up for this trip any time between June and September, when the foothills have warmed up to their summer extremes. Don't be fooled by this path's name: The Middle Fork Trail is no streamside meander. Rather, it's a shadeless, exposed trail that leads high along the canyon of the Middle Fork Kaweah River—always at least 250 feet above it. In summer, it's hot as Hades. Of course, that's what makes this trail perfect in winter and spring. While most other trails in Sequoia and Kings Canyon are still snowed under, you can take an early season day hike or backpacking trip along the Middle Fork Trail. The main destination is Panther Creek at three miles, where the trail leads right across the brink of Panther Creek's 100-foot dive into the Kaweah River. But you can hike further, if you wish. Although the Middle Fork Trail is set in grasslands and chaparral, it offers some stunning views of the area's geology, including Moro Rock, Castle Rocks, and the Great Western Divide. We hiked this trail in August, and despite the fact that we were wilting from the heat, the wide views kept our spirits up.

🄵 Paradise Creek Trail

1.2 mi/0.75 hr

Location: Off Highway 198 in the Foothills region of Sequoia National Park; map F5, grid j0.

User groups: Hikers only. No dogs, horses, or mountain bikes. No wheelchair facilities.

Permits: No permits are required. There is a $10 entrance fee at Sequoia and Kings Canyon National Parks, good for seven days.

Directions: From Visalia, drive east on Highway 198 for 47 miles to the turnoff on the right for Buckeye Flat Campground, across from Hospital

Rock. Turn right and drive six-tenths of a mile to the campground. Park in any of the dirt pullouts outside of the camp entrance; no day-use parking is allowed in the camp. (You can also park at Hospital Rock and walk to the campground.) The trailhead is near campsite number 28.

Maps: Free park maps are available at park entrance stations or by contacting Sequoia and Kings Canyon National Parks at the address below. A more detailed map is available for a fee from Tom Harrison Cartography at (415) 456-7940 or Trails Illustrated at (800) 962-1643. To obtain a topographic map of the area, ask for Giant Forest from the USGS.

Contact: Sequoia and Kings Canyon National Parks, Three Rivers, CA 93271-9700; (209) 565-3134 or fax (209) 565-3730.

Trail notes: From Buckeye Flat Campground, the Paradise Creek Trail meanders through oaks and buckeyes and crosses a long, picturesque footbridge over the Middle Fork Kaweah River. An inviting, Olympic-sized pool is on the right side of the bridge, where campers often go swimming on summer afternoons. Save the pool for after your hike; for now, take the signed Paradise Creek Trail at the far side of the bridge. You'll briefly visit the creek and then leave it, climbing into oak and grassland terrain. There are some high views of Moro Rock and Hanging Rock, but most of the beauty is right at your feet, in the springtime flowers that grow in the grasses and the leafy blue oaks that shade them. The maintained trail ends when it reaches Paradise Creek again, although a faint route continues along its banks.

🅸 Sunset Rock

2.0 mi/1.0 hr

Location: Off the Generals Highway in the Giant Forest area of Sequoia National Park; map F5, grid j1.

User groups: Hikers only. No dogs, horses, or mountain bikes. No wheelchair facilities.

Permits: No permits are required. There is a $10 entrance fee at Sequoia and Kings Canyon National Parks, good for seven days.

Directions: From Fresno, drive east on Highway 180 for 55 miles to the Big Stump entrance station at Kings Canyon National Park. Continue

1.5 miles and turn right on the Generals Highway, heading for Sequoia National Park. Drive approximately 30 miles on the Generals Highway, past Lodgepole and Wolverton, to the Giant Forest area of Sequoia National Park. Park near the village store.

Maps: Free park maps are available at park entrance stations or by contacting Sequoia and Kings Canyon National Parks at the address below. A more detailed map is available for a fee from Tom Harrison Cartography at (415) 456-7940 or Trails Illustrated at (800) 962-1643. To obtain a topographic map of the area, ask for Giant Forest from the USGS.

Contact: Sequoia and Kings Canyon National Parks, Three Rivers, CA 93271-9700; (209) 565-3134 or fax (209) 565-3730.

Trail notes: The trail to Sunset Rock is a first-rate easy hike, perfect at sunset or any time, that gets much less traffic than you might expect, considering its proximity to Giant Forest Village. To hike to the rock, first you must find a place to leave your car in the busy village, then use the crosswalk on the north side of the village to cross the road and pick up the signed trail. The path is lined with worn pavement, and is almost completely flat. It leads through a mixed forest (with a handful of giant Sequoias) and crosses Little Deer Creek on its way to Sunset Rock. The rock is a huge, flat piece of granite, about the size of a football field, set at 6,412 feet in elevation. Standing on it, you get a terrific overlook of Little Baldy to your right, and a sea of conifers below in the Marble Fork Kaweah River Canyon. A side note is that Giant Forest Village will soon be a thing of the past; the park is building a new visitor services center a few miles away, and they plan to remove all the buildings from Giant Forest by the year 2000. That way, the giant Sequoias can get a little more peace.

🅲 Moro Rock

0.6 mi/0.5 hr

Location: Off the Generals Highway in the Giant Forest area of Sequoia National Park; map F5, grid j1.

User groups: Hikers only. No dogs, horses, or mountain bikes. No wheelchair facilities.

Permits: No permits are required. There is a $10 entrance fee at Sequoia and Kings Canyon National Parks, good for seven days.

Directions: From Fresno, drive east on Highway 180 for 55 miles to the Big Stump entrance station at Kings Canyon National Park. Continue 1.5 miles and turn right on the Generals Highway, heading for Sequoia National Park. Drive approximately 30 miles on the Generals Highway, past Lodgepole and Wolverton, to the Giant Forest area of Sequoia National Park. Just beyond the village store, turn left on Crescent Meadow Road, drive 1.5 miles, and take the right fork to the Moro Rock parking area.

Maps: Free park maps are available at park entrance stations or by contacting Sequoia and Kings Canyon National Parks at the address below. A more detailed map is available for a fee from Tom Harrison Cartography at (415) 456-7940 or Trails Illustrated at (800) 962-1643. To obtain a topographic map of the area, ask for Giant Forest from the USGS.

Contact: Sequoia and Kings Canyon National Parks, Three Rivers, CA 93271-9700; (209) 565-3134 or fax (209) 565-3730.

Trail notes: Everybody has heard of Moro Rock, the prominent, pointy granite dome with the top-of-the-world sunset vistas, and if you're visiting the Giant Forest area of Sequoia National Park, well, you just have to hike to the top of it. When you climb those 380 stairs to the dome's summit and check out the view, you realize that unlike many famous attractions, Moro Rock is not overrated. It's as great as everybody says, maybe even better. If you start your trip from the Moro Rock parking area, it's only three-tenths of a mile to the top, climbing switchbacks, ramps, and granite stairs the whole way. (If you want to hike more, you can start your walk from Giant Forest Village on the Moro Rock, Bear Hill, or Soldiers Trails, adding about three miles to your round-trip.) Railings line the rock-blasted trail, to keep you from dropping off the 6,725-foot granite dome. What's the view like? Well, on a clear day, you can see all the way to the Coast Range, 100 miles away. In closer focus is the Middle Fork of the Kaweah River, the Great Western Divide, Castle Rocks at 9,180 feet, Triple Divide Peak at 12,634 feet, Mount Stewart at

12,205 feet . . . and on and on. In a word, it's awesome. And even better, you don't get this view just from the top of Moro Rock—you get it all the way up, at every turn in the trail.

⓭ Crescent Meadow and Tharp's Log

1.6 mi/1.0 hr

Location: Off the Generals Highway in the Giant Forest area of Sequoia National Park; map F5, grid j1.

User groups: Hikers and wheelchairs (with assistance). No dogs, horses, or mountain bikes.

Permits: No permits are required. There is a $10 entrance fee at Sequoia and Kings Canyon National Parks, good for seven days.

Directions: From Fresno, drive east on Highway 180 for 55 miles to the Big Stump entrance station at Kings Canyon National Park. Continue 1.5 miles and turn right on the Generals Highway, heading for Sequoia National Park. Drive approximately 30 miles on the Generals Highway, past Lodgepole and Wolverton, to the Giant Forest area of Sequoia National Park. Just beyond the village store, turn left on Crescent Meadow Road and drive 3.5 miles to the Crescent Meadow parking area.

Maps: Free park maps are available at park entrance stations or by contacting Sequoia and Kings Canyon National Parks at the address below. A more detailed map is available for a fee from Tom Harrison Cartography at (415) 456-7940 or Trails Illustrated at (800) 962-1643. To obtain topographic maps of the area, ask for Lodgepole and Giant Forest from the USGS.

Contact: Sequoia and Kings Canyon National Parks, Three Rivers, CA 93271-9700; (209) 565-3134 or fax (209) 565-3730.

Trail notes: Crescent Meadow is more than 1.5 miles long and surrounded by giant Sequoias. John Muir called it "the gem of the Sierras." We don't know how Muir would feel about the pavement that lines the trail around this precious meadow, but we hope he'd like this loop hike anyhow. Follow the pavement for 200 yards from eastern side of the parking lot, and just like that you're at the southern edge of beautiful Crescent Meadow. Take the right fork and head for Log

Meadow and Tharp's Log. Log Meadow is as large and beautiful as Crescent Meadow, and Tharp's Log was the homestead of Hale Tharp, the first white man to enter this forest. He grazed cattle and horses here, and built a modest home inside a fallen, fire-hollowed Sequoia. You can look inside Tharp's Log and see his bed, fireplace, dining room table, and the door and windows he fashioned into the log. (Children find this incredibly thrilling.) From Tharp's Log, continue your loop back to Crescent Meadow and around its west side, where you return to the north edge of the parking lot.

㊹ High Sierra Trail and Eagle View

1.5 mi/1.0 hr

Location: Off the Generals Highway in the Giant Forest area of Sequoia National Park; map F5, grid j1.

User groups: Hikers only. No dogs, horses, or mountain bikes. No wheelchair facilities.

Permits: No permits are required. There is a $10 entrance fee at Sequoia and Kings Canyon National Parks, good for seven days.

Directions: From Fresno, drive east on Highway 180 for 55 miles to the Big Stump entrance station at Kings Canyon National Park. Continue 1.5 miles and turn right on the Generals Highway, heading for Sequoia National Park. Drive approximately 30 miles on the Generals Highway, past Lodgepole and Wolverton, to the Giant Forest area of Sequoia National Park. Just beyond the village store, turn left on Crescent Meadow Road and drive 3.5 miles to the Crescent Meadow parking area.

Maps: Free park maps are available at park entrance stations or by contacting Sequoia and Kings Canyon National Parks at the address below. A more detailed map is available for a fee from Tom Harrison Cartography at (415) 456-7940 or Trails Illustrated at (800) 962-1643. To obtain topographic maps of the area, ask for Giant Forest and Lodgepole from the USGS.

Contact: Sequoia and Kings Canyon National Parks, Three Rivers, CA 93271-9700; (209) 565-3134 or fax (209) 565-3730.

Trail notes: Are you ready to be wowed? From the lower parking lot at Crescent Meadow, follow the trail that leads to the southern edge of Crescent Meadow, then at one-tenth of a mile, take the right fork that leads up the ridge on the High Sierra Trail, toward Eagle View. The High Sierra Trail is a popular trans-Sierra route that eventually leads to Mount Whitney, the highest peak in the contiguous United States. On this trip, you won't go quite that far, but you will get a taste of the visual delights of this extraordinary trail. In less than a half mile, you'll gain the ridge and start getting wondrous, edge-of-the-world views. Numerous wildflowers line the path, which contours along the edge of this high ridge. At seven-tenths of a mile, you'll reach Eagle View, an unsigned but obvious lookout from which you get a fascinating look at Moro Rock to your right, Castle Rocks straight ahead, and dozens of peaks and ridges of the Western Divide far across the canyon. The vistas are so fine, and the trail is so good, that you might just want to keep walking all the way to Mount Whitney.

㊺ High Sierra Trail to Hamilton Lake

30.0 mi/3.0 days

Location: Off the Generals Highway in the Giant Forest area of Sequoia National Park; map F5, grid j1.

User groups: Hikers only. No dogs, horses, or mountain bikes. No wheelchair facilities.

Permits: There is a $10 entrance fee at Sequoia and Kings Canyon National Parks, good for seven days. A free wilderness permit is required for overnight stays. They are available on a first-come, first-served basis at the wilderness kiosk near your chosen trailhead, or in advance by mail or fax after March 1; for more information phone (209) 565-3708.

Directions: From Fresno, drive east on Highway 180 for 55 miles to the Big Stump entrance station at Kings Canyon National Park. Continue 1.5 miles and turn right on the Generals Highway, heading for Sequoia National Park. Drive approximately 30 miles on the Generals Highway, past Lodgepole and Wolverton, to the Giant Forest area of Sequoia National Park. Just beyond the village store, turn left on Crescent Meadow Road and drive 3.5 miles to the Crescent Meadow parking area.

Maps: Free park maps are available at park entrance stations or by contacting Sequoia and Kings Canyon National Parks at the address below. A more detailed map is available for a fee from Tom Harrison Cartography at (415) 456-7940 or Trails Illustrated at (800) 962-1643. To obtain topographic maps of the area, ask for Giant Forest and Lodgepole from the USGS.

Contact: Sequoia and Kings Canyon National Parks, Three Rivers, CA 93271-9700; (209) 565-3134 or fax (209) 565-3730.

Trail notes: This is a classic easy-to-moderate three-day backpacking trip in the High Sierra, with a two-night stay at Bearpaw Meadow Camp, a shady campground that clings to the edge of a granite gorge. The route follows the High Sierra Trail from Crescent Meadow to Eagle View (see trail notes for hike number 44), then continues for 10 nearly level miles along the north rim of the Middle Fork Kaweah River Canyon. It's views, views, views all the way.

After a good night's sleep at Bearpaw Meadow, elevation 7,700 feet (advance reservations for a wilderness permit are definitely necessary in the summer months), you start out on an eight-mile round-trip day hike to Upper and Lower Hamilton Lake, at 8,300 feet, set in a glacially carved basin at the base of the peaks of the Great Western Divide. On the final day you hike 11 miles back to Crescent Meadow, once again witnessing 180-degree views from the sunny High Sierra Trail. By the time it's all over and you're back home, your mind is completely blown by all the high country beauty, and you've shot off about a million pictures, none of which can compare to the experience of actually being there.

㊻ Hazelwood and Huckleberry Loop

4.5 mi/2.0 hrs

Location: Off the Generals Highway in the Giant Forest area of Sequoia National Park; map F5, grid j1.

User groups: Hikers only. No dogs, horses, or mountain bikes. No wheelchair facilities.

Permits: No permits are required. There is a

$10 entrance fee at Sequoia and Kings Canyon National Parks, good for seven days.

Directions: From Fresno, drive east on Highway 180 for 55 miles to the Big Stump entrance station at Kings Canyon National Park. Continue 1.5 miles and turn right on the Generals Highway, heading for Sequoia National Park. Drive approximately 30 miles on the Generals Highway, past Lodgepole and Wolverton, to the Giant Forest area of Sequoia National Park. The Hazelwood Trailhead is on the south side of the highway, a quarter mile before you reach Giant Forest Village, near Giant Forest Lodge.

Maps: Free park maps are available at park entrance stations or by contacting Sequoia and Kings Canyon National Parks at the address below. A more detailed map is available for a fee from Tom Harrison Cartography at (415) 456-7940 or Trails Illustrated at (800) 962-1643. To obtain a topographic map of the area, ask for Giant Forest from the USGS.

Contact: Sequoia and Kings Canyon National Parks, Three Rivers, CA 93271-9700; (209) 565-3134 or fax (209) 565-3730.

Trail notes: This hike combines two loop trails in the Giant Forest area for an easy but excellent day hike, passing by many giant Sequoias and peaceful grassy meadows. A bonus: These trails are generally less crowded than the other day hikes in the Giant Forest area.

From the Generals Highway, pick up the Hazelwood Nature Trail and take the right side of the loop to join up with the Alta Trail and the Huckleberry Meadow Trail Loop. Take the Alta Trail for a quarter mile, then bear right on the Huckleberry Meadow Trail, following it for one mile to the site of Squatter's Cabin, one of the oldest structures in Sequoia National Park, dating back to the 1880s. The trail then skirts the edge of Huckleberry Meadow and heads north to Circle Meadow and the giant Sequoia trees that line the meadow's edges. A half mile further is a short spur trail on the left heading to the Washington Tree, the second largest tree in the world (after General Sherman), at 30 feet in diameter and 246.1 feet tall. Finally, the loop finishes out on the Alta Trail, where you return to the Hazelwood Nature Trail and walk the opposite side of the loop, back to the Generals Highway.

㊼ Congress Trail Loop

2.1 mi/1.0 hr

Location: Off the Generals Highway in the Giant Forest area of Sequoia National Park; map F5, grid j1.

User groups: Hikers only. No dogs, horses, or mountain bikes. No wheelchair facilities.

Permits: No permits are required. There is a $10 entrance fee at Sequoia and Kings Canyon National Parks, good for seven days.

Directions: From Fresno, drive east on Highway 180 for 55 miles to the Big Stump entrance station at Kings Canyon National Park. Continue 1.5 miles and turn right on the Generals Highway, heading for Sequoia National Park. Drive approximately 28 miles on the Generals Highway, past Lodgepole and Wolverton, to the signed turnoff on the left for the General Sherman Tree.

Maps: Free park maps are available at park entrance stations or by contacting Sequoia and Kings Canyon National Parks at the address below. A more detailed map is available for a fee from Tom Harrison Cartography at (415) 456-7940 or Trails Illustrated at (800) 962-1643. To obtain a topographic map of the area, ask for Giant Forest from the USGS.

Contact: Sequoia and Kings Canyon National Parks, Three Rivers, CA 93271-9700; (209) 565-3134 or fax (209) 565-3730.

Trail notes: The Congress Trail, a two-mile loop that starts (or ends) at the General Sherman Tree, is a much-traveled route through the Giant Forest's prize grove of giant Sequoias. The General Sherman gets the most visitors, of course, because it is recognized as the largest living thing in the world (not by height, but by volume). After you leave its side, the crowds lessen somewhat. You'll pass by many huge trees with very patriotic names, like the House and Senate clusters, the General McKinley Tree, the Lincoln Tree, and . . . you get the idea. If you can overlook all the plaques and signs and the rather silly tree-naming, the big Sequoias are truly impressive. Make sure you pick up an interpretive brochure at the trailhead or at the Lodgepole Visitor Center.

㊽ The Lakes Trail

13.0 mi/2–3 days

Location: Off the Generals Highway in the Wolverton area of Sequoia National Park; map F5, grid j1.

User groups: Hikers only. No dogs, horses, or mountain bikes. No wheelchair facilities.

Permits: There is a $10 entrance fee at Sequoia and Kings Canyon National Parks, good for seven days. A free wilderness permit is required for overnight stays. They are available on a first-come, first-served basis at the wilderness kiosk near your chosen trailhead, or in advance by mail or fax after March 1; for more information phone (209) 565-3708.

Directions: From Fresno, drive east on Highway 180 for 55 miles to the Big Stump entrance station at Kings Canyon National Park. Continue 1.5 miles and turn right on the Generals Highway, heading for Sequoia National Park. Drive approximately 27 miles on the Generals Highway, past the Lodgepole Village turnoff, to the Wolverton turnoff on the left (east) side of the road. Turn left and drive to the parking area and trailhead.

Maps: Free park maps are available at park entrance stations or by contacting Sequoia and Kings Canyon National Parks at the address below. A more detailed map is available for a fee from Tom Harrison Cartography at (415) 456-7940 or Trails Illustrated at (800) 962-1643. To obtain a topographic map of the area, ask for Lodgepole from the USGS.

Contact: Sequoia and Kings Canyon National Parks, Three Rivers, CA 93271-9700; (209) 565-3134 or fax (209) 565-3730.

Trail notes: The Wolverton trailhead is at 7,200 feet, which gives you a boost at the start for this trip into the high country. The Lakes Trail is the most popular backpacking trip in Sequoia National Park, and it's easy to see why. Wide-open views and dramatic granite walls are standard fare as you hike. Part of the route is on a loop, with one side of the loop traveling to the Watchtower, a 1,600-foot-tall granite cliff that offers incredible vistas of Tokopah Valley and beyond (see the trail notes for hike number 49). The trailside scenery begins in red fir forest, then enters polished granite country, and culminates in a rocky basin with three gemlike lakes—Heather, Emerald, and Pear—as well as many sparkling creeks. The total climb to Pear Lake is a mere 2,300 feet, spread out over 6.5 miles. Backpackers note: You may camp only at Emerald and Pear Lakes, and no campfires are allowed.

Special note: The Watchtower Trail isn't usually open until summer. When it is closed, you must take the alternate Hump Trail, which is not as scenic. If you're planning a trip for early in the year, check with the park to be sure the Watchtower Trail is open.

㊾ Heather Lake and the Watchtower

9.0 mi/5.0 hrs

Location: Off the Generals Highway in the Wolverton area of Sequoia National Park; map F5, grid j1.

User groups: Hikers only. No dogs, horses, or mountain bikes. No wheelchair facilities.

Permits: No permits are required. There is a $10 entrance fee at Sequoia and Kings Canyon National Parks, good for seven days.

Directions: From Fresno, drive east on Highway 180 for 55 miles to the Big Stump entrance station at Kings Canyon National Park. Continue 1.5 miles and turn right on the Generals Highway, heading for Sequoia National Park. Drive approximately 27 miles on the Generals Highway, past the Lodgepole Village turnoff, to the Wolverton turnoff on the left (east) side of the road. Turn left and drive to the parking area and trailhead.

Maps: Free park maps are available at park entrance stations or by contacting Sequoia and Kings Canyon National Parks at the address below. A more detailed map is available for a fee from Tom Harrison Cartography at (415) 456-7940 or Trails Illustrated at (800) 962-1643. To obtain a topographic map of the area, ask for Lodgepole from the USGS.

Contact: Sequoia and Kings Canyon National Parks, Three Rivers, CA 93271-9700; (209) 565-3134 or fax (209) 565-3730.

Trail notes: There's no reason that day hikers should be denied the incredible joys of hiking the Lakes Trail from the Wolverton area of

Sequoia National Park. You don't have to carry a backpack, get a wilderness permit, or have two or more free days to hike the first part of the Lakes Trail, making the mind-blowing ascent to the top of the 1,600-foot Watchtower and then continuing to rocky Heather Lake. If you're hiking in spring or early summer, call the park first to make sure the Watchtower Trail is open. Otherwise, you'll have to take the alternate Hump Trail, which is steeper and nowhere near as thrilling. The route to the Watchtower is a ledge trail, blasted into hard granite, which creeps along the high rim of Tokopah Valley. Your view is straight down, 1,500 feet below. You can even seen little tiny people walking on the path to Tokopah Falls. It's incredible (although not a good idea for people who are afraid of heights). Walking up to the Watchtower is plenty exciting, but it's even more so when you reach the other side, where you can look back and see what you were walking on. Three-quarters of a mile further you're at Heather Lake, which is designated for day-use only, so it has no campsites. It has a steep granite backdrop and a few rocky ledges to sit on. After a rest, you get to head back and hike the Watchtower route all over again.

㊿ Alta Peak

13.0 mi/1–2 days

Location: Off the Generals Highway in the Wolverton area of Sequoia National Park; map F5, grid j1.

User groups: Hikers only. No dogs, horses, or mountain bikes. No wheelchair facilities.

Permits: There is a $10 entrance fee at Sequoia and Kings Canyon National Parks, good for seven days. A free wilderness permit is required for overnight stays. They are available on a first-come, first-served basis at the wilderness kiosk near your chosen trailhead, or in advance by mail or fax after March 1; for more information phone (209) 565-3708.

Directions: From Fresno, drive east on Highway 180 for 55 miles to the Big Stump entrance station at Kings Canyon National Park. Continue 1.5 miles and turn right on the Generals Highway, heading for Sequoia National Park. Drive approximately 27 miles on the Generals Highway, past the Lodgepole Village turnoff, to the Wolverton turnoff on the left (east) side of the road. Turn left and drive to the parking area and trailhead.

Maps: Free park maps are available at park entrance stations or by contacting Sequoia and Kings Canyon National Parks at the address below. A more detailed map is available for a fee from Tom Harrison Cartography at (415) 456-7940 or Trails Illustrated at (800) 962-1643. To obtain a topographic map of the area, ask for Lodgepole from the USGS.

Contact: Sequoia and Kings Canyon National Parks, Three Rivers, CA 93271-9700; (209) 565-3134 or fax (209) 565-3730.

Trail notes: You say you like heights? You like vistas? Here's your trail, a 4,000-foot climb to the top of Alta Peak, an 11,204-foot summit in the Alta Country. Alta Peak and Mount Whitney are the only summits in Sequoia National Park that have established trails, but both of them are still butt-kickers to reach. The trail to Alta Peak and Alta Meadow starts out the same as the Lakes Trail from the Wolverton parking area, then heads south (right) to Panther Gap at 1.7 miles. After climbing through the forest to Panther Gap at 8,450 feet, you get your first set of eye-popping views—of the Middle Fork Kaweah River and the Great Western Divide. Continue to Mehrten Meadow at 3.5 miles, a popular camping spot, then reach a junction where you can go left for Alta Peak or right to Alta Meadow. You'll want to take both spurs if you have the time and energy. If you're exhausted, just walk to Alta Meadow, with its flower-filled grasses and mountain views, a flat one mile away. Alta Peak is two miles away via the left fork, with a 2,000-foot climb. These two miles are considered one of the toughest stretches of trail in Sequoia National Park, mostly because of the 10,000-plus foot elevation here above treeline. The summit is at 11,204 feet, and, of course, it offers a complete panorama of vistas. Even Mount Whitney and the Coast Range are visible on a clear day.

User groups: Hikers and horses. No dogs or mountain bikes. No wheelchair facilities.

Permits: No permits are required. There is a $10 entrance fee at Sequoia and Kings Canyon National Parks, good for seven days.

Directions: From Fresno, drive east on Highway 180 for 55 miles to the Big Stump entrance station at Kings Canyon National Park. Continue 1.5 miles and turn right on the Generals Highway, heading for Sequoia National Park. Drive approximately 27 miles on the Generals Highway, past the Lodgepole Village turnoff, to the Wolverton turnoff on the left (east) side of the road. Turn left and drive to the parking area and trailhead.

Maps: Free park maps are available at park entrance stations or by contacting Sequoia and Kings Canyon National Parks at the address below. A more detailed map is available for a fee from Tom Harrison Cartography at (415) 456-7940 or Trails Illustrated at (800) 962-1643. To obtain a topographic map of the area, ask for Lodgepole from the USGS.

Contact: Sequoia and Kings Canyon National Parks, Three Rivers, CA 93271-9700; (209) 565-3134 or fax (209) 565-3730.

Trail notes: If you're not up for the marathon trip to Alta Peak (see hike number 50), you can still get a taste of the high country on this loop from the Wolverton Trailhead. Start hiking on the Lakes Trail from the east end of the Wolverton parking lot, and at 1.7 miles bear right on the Alta Trail to parallel Wolverton Creek, following it to Panther Gap. Here, at 8,450 feet, you get an inspiring vista of the Middle Fork Kaweah River and the Great Western Divide. Check out 9,081-foot Castle Rocks, an obvious landmark. From the gap, turn right (west) and follow the Alta Trail to Panther Peak and Panther Meadow, then on to Red Fir Meadow. Finally, at 2.7 miles, bear right and complete the loop by descending to Long Meadow and then edging along its east side to return to the parking lot.

51 Alta Trail Loop

5.0 mi/2.5 hrs

Location: Off the Generals Highway in the Wolverton area of Sequoia National Park; map F5, grid j1.

52 Tokopah Falls

3.6 mi/2.0 hrs

Location: Off the Generals Highway in the Lodgepole area of Sequoia National Park; map F5, grid j1.

User groups: Hikers and horses. No dogs or mountain bikes. No wheelchair facilities.

Permits: No permits are required. There is a $10 entrance fee at Sequoia and Kings Canyon National Parks, good for seven days.

Directions: From Fresno, drive east on Highway 180 for 55 miles to the Big Stump entrance station at Kings Canyon National Park. Continue 1.5 miles and turn right on the Generals Highway, heading for Sequoia National Park. Drive approximately 25 miles on the Generals Highway to the Lodgepole Campground turnoff, then drive three-quarters of a mile to the Log Bridge area of Lodgepole Camp. Park in the large lot just before the bridge over the Marble Fork Kaweah River, and walk 150 yards to the trailhead, which is just after you cross the bridge.

Maps: Free park maps are available at park entrance stations or by contacting Sequoia and Kings Canyon National Parks at the address below. A more detailed map is available for a fee from Tom Harrison Cartography at (415) 456-7940 or Trails Illustrated at (800) 962-1643. To obtain a topographic map of the area, ask for Lodgepole from the USGS.

Contact: Sequoia and Kings Canyon National Parks, Three Rivers, CA 93271-9700; (209) 565-3134 or fax (209) 565-3730.

Trail notes: This is unquestionably the best waterfall day hike in Sequoia and Kings Canyon National Parks, leading to 1,200-foot-high Tokopah Falls. It's also a perfect family hike, easy on the feet and even easier on the eyes. The scenery is spectacular the whole way, from the up-close looks at wildflowers and granite boulders to the more distant views of the Watchtower, a 1,600-foot glacially carved cliff on the south side of Tokopah Valley. Then there's the valley itself, with Tokopah Falls pouring down the smooth back curve of its U-shape. Because the trail begins by the three huge Lodgepole Campgrounds, it sees a lot of foot traffic. Your best bet is to start early in the morning. Another unusual feature of the trail? Hikers see more yellow-bellied marmots on the Tokopah Falls route than anywhere else in the two parks. We saw at least 40 of the cute little blonde guys, sunning themselves on rocks. If you're lucky, one of them will whistle at you as you walk by.

53 Twin Lakes

13.6 mi/1–2 days

Location: Off the Generals Highway in the Lodgepole area of Sequoia National Park; map F5, grid j1.

User groups: Hikers and horses. No dogs or mountain bikes. No wheelchair facilities.

Permits: There is a $10 entrance fee at Sequoia and Kings Canyon National Parks, good for seven days. A free wilderness permit is required for overnight stays. They are available on a first-come, first-served basis at the wilderness kiosk near your chosen trailhead, or in advance by mail or fax after March 1; for more information phone (209) 565-3708.

Directions: From Fresno, drive east on Highway 180 for 55 miles to the Big Stump entrance station at Kings Canyon National Park. Continue 1.5 miles and turn right on the Generals Highway, heading for Sequoia National Park. Drive approximately 25 miles on the Generals Highway to the Lodgepole Campground turnoff, then drive three-quarters of a mile to the Log Bridge area of Lodgepole Camp. The Twin Lakes Trailhead is just beyond the Tokopah Falls Trailhead and the bridge over the Marble Fork Kaweah River.

Maps: Free park maps are available at park entrance stations or by contacting Sequoia and Kings Canyon National Parks at the address below. A more detailed map is available for a fee from Tom Harrison Cartography at (415) 456-7940 or Trails Illustrated at (800) 962-1643. To obtain a topographic map of the area, ask for Lodgepole from the USGS.

Contact: Sequoia and Kings Canyon National Parks, Three Rivers, CA 93271-9700; (209) 565-3134 or fax (209) 565-3730.

Trail notes: From the Lodgepole Campground Trailhead at 6,740 feet, the Twin Lakes are a mere 2,800-foot elevation gain and 6.8 miles away, making this a moderate backpacking trip or a long, strenuous day hike. It's a classic Sequoia National Forest trip, and one that is heavily traveled each summer. The terrain is dense conifer forests, glacial moraine, and open meadows along the way. From the trailhead, you climb past Wolverton's Rock to Cahoon Meadow at three miles, a half mile beyond a crossing of

Silliman Creek. You then continue to Cahoon Gap at 4.2 miles, cross over Clover Creek at five miles (campsites are found along the creek), bear right at the J.O. Pass Trail junction at 5.5 miles, and reach the Twin Lakes at 6.8 miles. The trail leads you directly to the larger Twin Lake; the smaller one you reach by following a spur. Both are shallow and have forested banks; some hikers try their luck fishing in the larger lake. Backpackers spending the night at Twin Lakes can hike further the next day, over rocky Silliman Pass at 10,100 feet to the less-visited Ranger Lakes, three miles further. Note that campfires are not allowed at Twin Lakes.

54 Whitney Portal National Recreation Trail

4.0 mi. one way/2.0 hrs

Location: In Inyo National Forest near Whitney Portal; map F5, grid J7.

User groups: Hikers, dogs, and horses. No mountain bikes. No wheelchair facilities.

Permits: No day-hiking permits are required. Parking and access are free.

Directions: From Lone Pine on U.S. 395, drive west on Whitney Portal Road for 13 miles to the end of the road and the trailhead, located across from the fishing pond. You will need to leave a shuttle car or arrange a pickup at Lone Pine Campground, four miles below off of Whitney Portal Road.

Maps: For a map of Inyo National Forest, send $4 to USDA-Forest Service, 630 Sansome Street, San Francisco, CA 94111. To obtain a topographic map of the area, ask for Mount Langley from the USGS.

Contact: Inyo National Forest, Mount Whitney Ranger District, P.O. Box 8, Lone Pine, CA 93545; (760) 876-6200 or fax (760) 876-6202.

Trail notes: Don't confuse this trail with the Mount Whitney Trail, because except for their nearby trailheads, they have zero in common. Although if you try to hike the Whitney Portal National Recreation Trail in both directions, instead of as a one-way downhill hike, you may find it feels darn near as demanding as the Mount Whitney Trail, which climbs nearly 6,000 feet to the top of Mount Whitney. (Okay, maybe

not quite that demanding.) The recreation trail begins at Whitney Portal, elevation 8,360 feet, and heads downhill through conifers and granite to Lone Pine Campground, elevation 5,640. The best thing about the route is that no matter how crowded it is at Whitney Portal, this trail gets surprisingly few hikers, especially after the first half mile, which skirts Whitney Portal Campground. You get to leave the multitudes behind as you walk downhill along Lone Pine Creek, among the good company of granite formations and big pines. Vistas are excellent along the way, including Mount Whitney to the west, and the Alabama Hills and White Mountains to the east.

55 Mount Whitney Trail

22.0 mi/15.0 hrs or 2–3 days

Location: In the John Muir Wilderness; map F5, grid J7.

User groups: Hikers only. No dogs, horses, or mountain bikes. (Dogs are allowed on the first 8.5 miles of trail, but not beyond.) No wheelchair facilities.

Permits: A wilderness permit is required for both day hikers and backpackers; they are available from the Lone Pine Ranger Station. Quotas are in effect for Mount Whitney from May 22 to October 15 for both day hikers and backpackers; permits are available in advance by phoning (888) 374-3773 or faxing (760) 938-1137, or by writing to Wilderness Reservations, P.O. Box 430, Big Pine, CA 93513. There is a $4 fee for overnight permit reservations, and a $2 fee for day hike permit reservations.

Directions: From Lone Pine on U.S. 395, drive west on Whitney Portal Road for 13 miles to the end of the road and the trailhead.

Maps: For a map of Inyo National Forest, send $4 to USDA-Forest Service, 630 Sansome Street, San Francisco, CA 94111. To obtain topographic maps of the area, ask for Mount Whitney and Mount Langley from the USGS.

Contact: Inyo National Forest, Mount Whitney Ranger District, P.O. Box 8, Lone Pine, CA 93545; (760) 876-6200 or fax (760) 876-6202.

Trail notes: Mount Whitney at 14,496 feet in elevation is the highest peak in the contiguous

United States, and also probably the most frequently climbed peak. It has become such a popular route that not only are quotas enforced for backpackers, but even day hikers must obtain a wilderness permit to hike the trail. And, yes, many people do hike the entire 22-mile trail in one day, ascending and descending more than a vertical mile along the way (6,131 feet in all), but it means a pre-dawn start and a grueling march. Many people who try this suffer from altitude sickness and never make it to the top; others make it but realize they would have had a lot more fun if they had divided the trip into two or even three days. So here's the smart way to hike Mount Whitney: Get your wilderness permit way in advance, and plan your trip for a weekday, not a weekend. If possible, wait to make the climb until September or early October, when the crowds have thinned considerably. (August is the month with the highest trail usage.) Spend a day or two hiking around at high elevation before you set out on the Whitney Trail, and come prepared with sunglasses, sunscreen, good boots, and warm clothes for the summit. And here's our Good Samaritan tip: Bring extra food and water so you can give it out to less fortunate hikers you meet along the trail. For more information on this spectacular but demanding trail, see the Pacific Crest Trail information at the end of this chapter on page 455.

56 Lone Pine Lake

5.8 mi/3.0 hrs

Location: In the John Muir Wilderness near Whitney Portal; map F5, grid j7.

User groups: Hikers and dogs. No horses or mountain bikes. No wheelchair facilities.

Permits: No day-hiking permits are required. Parking and access are free.

Directions: From Lone Pine on U.S. 395, drive west on Whitney Portal Road for 13 miles to the end of the road and the Mount Whitney Trailhead.

Maps: For a map of Inyo National Forest, send $4 to USDA-Forest Service, 630 Sansome Street, San Francisco, CA 94111. To obtain topographic maps of the area, ask for Mount Langley and Mount Whitney from the USGS.

Contact: Inyo National Forest, Mount Whitney Ranger District, P.O. Box 8, Lone Pine, CA 93545; (760) 876-6200 or fax (760) 876-6202.

Trail notes: The route to the top of Mount Whitney is so popular and so overcrowded that it has permits and quotas and regulations up the wazoo, but guess what? Sweet little Lone Pine Lake is just outside of the regulated Mount Whitney Zone, so you can hike to it any time without dealing with any bureaucracy first. It's a fun trip for people who have always dreamed of climbing Mount Whitney, because it follows the first three miles of the summit trail. While other people are trudging along carrying heavy backpacks, you're stepping lightly with only a sandwich and a bottle of water in your daypack. The trail leads through Jeffrey pines and manzanita to the John Muir Wilderness border at one mile, then switchbacks uphill and opens up to views of the Alabama Hills far below. You'll cross Lone Pine Creek at 2.8 miles, then bear left at a junction to leave the main Mount Whitney Trail and head a few hundred yards to Lone Pine Lake. It's a sweet spot, and although privacy is rare, you have a greater chance of it after Labor Day and on a weekday. Who knows, you might just get so inspired that next time you'll come back and hike all the way to the summit.

57 Meysan Lake

9.4 mi/6.0 hrs or 2.0 days

Location: In the John Muir Wilderness near Mount Whitney; map F5, grid j8.

User groups: Hikers and dogs. No horses or mountain bikes. No wheelchair facilities.

Permits: A free wilderness permit is required for overnight stays; they are available from the Lone Pine Ranger Station. Quotas are in effect from the last Friday in June to September 15; permits are available in advance by mail, phone, or fax for this period for a $3 fee. Mail permit requests to Wilderness Reservations, P.O. Box 430, Big Pine, CA 93513. Phone (888) 374-3773 or fax (760) 938-1137.

Directions: From Lone Pine on U.S. 395, drive west on Whitney Portal Road for 12 miles to Whitney Portal Campground and the Meysan Lake Trailhead. Park on the side of Whitney

Portal Road by the camp, then walk through the camp to reach the trailhead.

Maps: For a map of Inyo National Forest, send $4 to USDA-Forest Service, 630 Sansome Street, San Francisco, CA 94111. To obtain topographic maps of the area, ask for Mount Whitney and Mount Langley from the USGS.

Contact: Inyo National Forest, Mount Whitney Ranger District, P.O. Box 8, Lone Pine, CA 93545; (760) 876-6200 or fax (760) 876-6202.

Trail notes: The Meysan Lake Trail is less popular than the neighboring trail to the top of Mount Whitney, but still you should get your wilderness permit in advance or plan on day hiking. Better yet, plan your trip for late September and during the week. The trail to Meysan Lake is long, steep, and dry—let's just say it's grueling—but it leads to a beautiful alpine lake basin and provides spectacular views of granite walls. It also gives climbers access to climbing routes on Mount Mallory and Lone Pine Peak. The trail leads along Meysan Creek and is not well maintained, which makes it even more demanding. You pass tiny Grass Lake at 2.5 miles, where the first water is available, and then Camp Lake at 3.5 miles. The trail from Camp Lake to Meysan Lake is rather sketchy and on a steep and rocky slope. Meysan Lake is often still frozen as late as June, even though the trail can be as hot as an oven. Trailhead elevation is 7,900 feet; Meysan Lake is at 11,460 feet. No fires are allowed at Meysan Lake, so make sure you've got your stove packed.

Pacific Crest Trail (PCT) Section Overview

150.0 mi. one way/14.0 days

Welcome to the High Sierra, as this section, extending from the trailhead parking area at Whitney Portal north to Agnew Meadows, takes you into the heart of it. Bear precautions are at a premium now—no food in the tent and always hang your supplies. Streams may be swollen from the snowmelt and difficult to cross. Snow may still linger in the high passes as late as July. Do not attempt to cross any high angle snowpack or icepack unless you're skilled at handling the situation with an ice ax and crampons. The trail ranges from 7,000 to over 13,000 feet along this portion of the trail.

PCT-21 JMT-1 Whitney Portal to Lake Thomas Edison

112.0 mi. one way/11.0 days

Location: From the trailhead parking area at Whitney Portal north to the trailhead parking area at Lake Thomas Edison; map F5, grid j6.

User groups: Hikers and horses. No dogs or mountain bikes. No wheelchair facilities.

Permits: A wilderness permit is required for traveling through various wilderness and special-use areas the trail traverses. Contact the Inyo National Forest District Office at (619) 876-6200.

Directions: To reach the Mount Whitney Trailhead, from Lone Pine and Highway 395, head west on Whitney Portal Road for approximately 13 miles to Whitney Portal and the trailhead for the Mount Whitney Trail. To reach the Lake Thomas Edison Trailhead, from the town of Shaver Lake, drive north on Highway 168 for approximately 21 miles to the town of Lakeshore. Turn northeast onto Kaiser Pass Road (Forest Service 4S01). Kaiser Pass Road becomes Edison Lake Road at Mono Hot Springs. Drive another five miles north past town to the Vermillion Campground and parking area for backcountry hikers. The PCT begins near the east end of the lake.

Maps: For an overall view of the trail route in this section, send $4 for each map ordered to the USDA-Forest Service, 630 Sansome Street, San Francisco, CA 94111, and ask for the Sierra National Forest, Inyo National Forest, and Sequoia National Forest maps. For topographic maps of the route, request Mount Whitney, Mount Williamson, Kearsarge Peak, Mount Clarence King, Mount Pinchot, North Palisade, Mount Goddard, Mount Darwin, Mount Henry, Ward Mountain, Florence Lake, and Graveyard Peak from the USGS.

Contact: Inyo National Forest, Mount Whitney Ranger District, P.O. Box 8, Lone Pine, CA 93545; (619) 876-6200 or fax (619) 876-6202. Sierra National Forest, Pineridge Ranger District, P.O. Box 559, Prather, CA 93651; (209) 855-5360 or fax (209) 855-5375. Sequoia National Forest,

Cannell Meadow Ranger District, P.O. Box 6, Kernville, CA 93238; (619) 376-3781 or fax (619) 376-3795.

Trail notes: You can have a foothold in the sky with every step on the John Muir Trail (and with this section of the PCT). The trail starts at practically the tip-top of North America, Mount Whitney, and takes you northward across a land of 12,000-foot passes and Ansel Adams-style panoramic vistas.

From the trailhead at Whitney Portal, the hike climbs more than 6,100 feet over the course of 10 miles to reach the Whitney summit at 14,494 feet. That includes an ascent over 100 switchbacks (often snow covered) to top Wotan's Throne and reach Trail Crest (13,560 feet). Here you turn right and take the Summit Trail. In the final stretch to the top, the ridge is cut by huge notch windows in the rock; you look through and the bottom drops out more than 10,000 feet to the little town of Lone Pine below, at an elevation of 3,800 feet. Finally you make it to the top, and notice how the surrounding giant blocks of rock look as if they were sculpted with a giant hammer and chisel. From here, the entire Western Divide is visible, and to the north rows of mountain peaks are lined up for miles to the horizon. Be sure to sign your name in the register (kept in a lightning-proof metal box). You may feel a bit dizzy from the altitude, but know you're someplace very special.

The journey farther north is just as captivating. The route drops into Sequoia National Park, then climbs above treeline for almost a day's worth of hiking as it nears Forester Pass, 13,180 feet. It's not only the highest point on the PCT, but the most dangerous section of trail on the entire route as well. The trail is narrow and steep, cut into a high vertical slab of rock, and is typically icy, with an iced-over snowfield near the top that's particularly treacherous. An ice ax is an absolute must—slip here and you could fall thousands of feet.

Once through Forester, the trail heads onward into the John Muir Wilderness along Bubbs Creek, with great wildflowers at nearby Vidette Meadow. Then it's up and over Kearsage Pass (10,710 feet), and after a short drop, you're back climbing again, this time over Glen Pass (11,978

feet), a spectacular, boulder-strewn ridge with great views to the north looking into Kings Canyon National Park. Just two miles from Glen Pass is Rae Lakes, a fantasy spot for camping (one-night limit), with pristine meadows, shoreline campsites, and lots of eager brook trout.

The JMT/PCT then heads through Kings Canyon National Park by following pristine streams much of the way, finally climbing up and over Pinchot Pass (12,130 feet), then back down along the upper Kings River for a long, steady ascent over Mather Pass (12,100 feet). The wonders continue as you hike along Palisade Lakes, then down into LeConte Canyon, followed by an endless climb up to Muir Pass (11,965 feet). In early summer, snowfields are common here, and this can be the most difficult and trying section of the entire PCT, especially if your boots keep postholing through the snow. The country near Muir Pass is extremely stark—nothing but sculpted granite, ice, and a few small turquoise lakes—crowned by the stone-made Muir Hut at the pass, where hikers can duck in and hide for safety from sudden afternoon thunderstorms and lightning bolts.

The views astound many visitors as the trail drops into Evolution Valley. It's like a trip back to the beginning of time, where all is pure and primary, yet incredibly lush and beautiful. You finally leave Kings Canyon National Park, following the headwaters of the San Joaquin River into the Sierra National Forest. After bottoming out at 7,890 feet, the trail rises steeply in switchback after switchback as it enters the John Muir Wilderness. Finally you top Selden Pass (10,900 feet), take in an incredible view where the rows of surrounding mountaintops look like the Great Pyramids, then make the easy one-mile descent to Marie Lakes, a pretty campsite with excellent trout fishing near the lake's outlet.

The final push on this section of the PCT is climbing up Bear Mountain, then down a terrible, toe-jamming stretch to Mono Creek. Here you make a left turn and continue for two more miles until you come to Edison Lake, an excellent place to have a food stash waiting.

Special note: Crossing Mono Creek at the north fork can be dangerous in high runoff conditions.

PCT-22 JMT-2 Lake Thomas Edison to Agnew Meadows

38.0 mi. one way/3.0 days

Location: From Lake Thomas Edison north to Agnew Meadows; map F5, grid b1.

User groups: Hikers, dogs, and horses. No mountain bikes. No wheelchair facilities.

Permits: A wilderness permit is required for traveling through various wilderness and special-use areas the trail traverses. Contact the Inyo National Forest at (619) 934-2505 or the Sierra National Forest at (209) 841-3311.

Directions: From Fresno, drive northeast on Highway 168 for about 68 miles to the Lakeshore Resort Area at Huntington Lake. Turn northeast onto Kaiser Pass Road (Forest Service 4S01). Kaiser Pass Road becomes Edison Lake Road at Mono Hot Springs. Drive another five miles north past the Vermillion Resort and Campground and beyond to the parking area for backcountry hikers. The trail begins near the west end of the lake.

Maps: For an overall view of the trail route in this section, send $4 to USDA-Forest Service, 630 Sansome Street, San Francisco, CA 94111, and ask for the Inyo National Forest map. To obtain topographic maps of the route, request Mammoth Mountain, Crystal Crag, Bloody Mountain, Graveyard Peak, Mount Ritter, and Coip Peak from the USGS.

Contact: Inyo National Forest, Mammoth Ranger District, P.O. Box 148, Mammoth Lakes, CA 93546; (619) 934-2505 or fax (619) 924-5537. Sierra National Forest, Pineridge Ranger District, P.O. Box 559, Prather, CA 93651; (209) 855-5360 or fax (209) 855-5375.

Trail notes: The world is not perfect, but the scene from Silver Pass comes close. At 10,900 feet, you scan a bare, high-granite landscape sprinkled with alpine lakes. Just north of the pass are five small lakes: Chief, Papoose, Warrior, Squaw, and Lake of the Lone Indian. This is the highlight on this 38-mile section of the Pacific Crest Trail. The trip starts at Mono Creek, with a good resupply point at Edison Lake (7,650 feet), just two miles away. From the Mono Creek junction, you head north toward Silver Pass, climbing along Silver Pass Creek much of the way. Before you get to Silver Pass, there's a stream crossing that can be dangerous in high runoff conditions. Top Silver Pass at 10,900 feet, and enjoy a five-mile descent and then a quick up to Tully Hole (9,250 feet). Climbing north, you pass Deer Creek, Purple Lake, and Lake Virginia. You head up to Red Cones and then make a steady descent toward Devils Postpile National Monument. A good resupply point is at nearby Red's Meadow Pack Station.

Special note: For food drop information, call the Vermillion Valley Resort at (209) 855-6558. They are open only in summer and fall.

PCT Continuation: To continue hiking along the Pacific Crest Trail or the John Muir Trail, see chapter E4.

Map F6

Adjoining Maps: West: F5 ... *page* 422
                      South: G6 508

Central California Map .... *page* 382

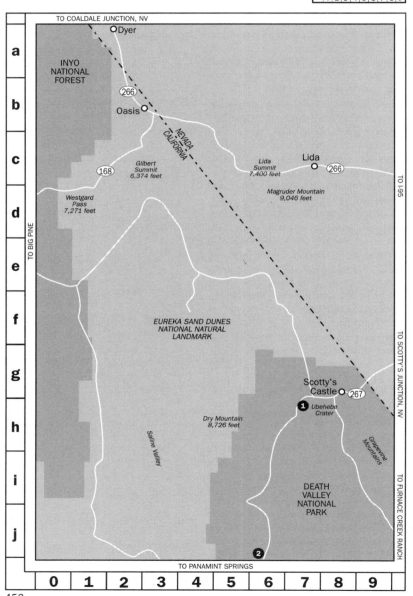

❶ Little Hebe Crater Trail

1.0 mi/0.5 hr

Location: In Death Valley National Park near Scotty's Castle; map F6, grid h7.

User groups: Hikers only. No dogs, horses, or mountain bikes. No wheelchair facilities.

Permits: No permits are required. There is a $10 entrance fee at Death Valley National Park, good for seven days.

Directions: From the Furnace Creek Visitor Center in Death Valley National Park, drive north on Highway 190 toward Scotty's Castle. In 48 miles, you will pass the Grapevine entrance station, then continue north for three miles (keep left; don't bear right for Scotty's Castle) to the turnoff for the Ubehebe Crater parking area. Bear left and drive to the parking area on the left.

Maps: Free park maps are available at park entrance stations or by contacting Death Valley National Park at the address below. A more detailed map is available for a fee from Tom Harrison Cartography at (415) 456-7940. To obtain a topographic map of the area, ask for Ubehebe Crater from the USGS.

Contact: Death Valley National Park, Death Valley, CA 92328; (760) 786-2331 or fax (760) 786-3283.

Trail notes: A walk along the rim of a not-so-ancient volcano is what you get on the Little Hebe Crater Trail. The trail leads along Ubehebe Crater's southwest rim to Little Hebe and several older craters. Ubehebe Crater is 500 feet deep and a half mile across, and was formed by volcanic activity that occurred between 1,000 and 2,000 years ago. Little Hebe and the other craters are smaller in size, but similar in appearance—mostly black and ash colored, but with eroded walls that reveal a colorful blend of orange and rust from the minerals in the rock. A half mile from the trailhead, you reach a junction where you can continue straight ahead to Little Hebe Crater, or just loop all the way around Ubehebe's rim. Take your pick—from the high rim of Ubehebe, it's easy to see where you're going, as well as down into the valley below and far off to the Last Chance Range. Note that the trail surface is a mix of gravel and cinders, and it's somewhat loose in places, so hiking boots or high-top shoes are a good idea.

❷ Ubehebe Peak

4.0 mi/3.0 hrs

Location: In Death Valley National Park; map F6, grid j6.

User groups: Hikers only. No dogs, horses, or mountain bikes. No wheelchair facilities.

Permits: No permits are required. There is a $10 entrance fee at Death Valley National Park, good for seven days.

Directions: From the Furnace Creek Visitor Center in Death Valley National Park, drive north on Highway 190 toward Scotty's Castle. In 48 miles, you will pass the Grapevine entrance station, then continue north for three miles (keep left; don't bear right for Scotty's Castle) to the turnoff for the Ubehebe Crater parking area. Bear left and continue past the Ubehebe Crater parking area on the dirt road signed for Racetrack. Turn onto Racetrack Road and drive 20 miles, then bear right at Teakettle Junction. Drive 5.8 miles to a pullout on the right side of the road, signed as the Grandstand parking area. (High-clearance vehicles are necessary on Racetrack Road.)

Maps: Free park maps are available at park entrance stations or by contacting Death Valley National Park at the address below. A more detailed map is available for a fee from Tom Harrison Cartography at (415) 456-7940. To obtain a topographic map of the area, ask for Ubehebe Peak from the USGS.

Contact: Death Valley National Park, Death Valley, CA 92328; (760) 786-2331 or fax (760) 786-3283.

Trail notes: The climb to Ubehebe Peak would be strenuous enough if you just accounted for the steep grade, but add in the fact that this is Death Valley and the hike becomes a butt-kicker. The peak offers tremendous views of both the snowy Sierra Nevada and the desert-like Last Chance Range, as well as Racetrack and Saline Valleys. The trail is a narrow miners' route that switchbacks up and up and up, and you can be darn sure that you won't come across any shade on the way. There is no real trail for the final half mile to the summit; most hikers content themselves with the view from the trail's end at a saddle 1.5 miles up. (If you stop here, you won't be missing out. The view is incredible.) Experienced climbers can make the final summit scramble. Total elevation gain is 1,900 feet; the summit is at 5,678 feet in elevation. Note: Before or after your trip, be sure to explore around the Racetrack area by the trailhead, where you can see the tracks of rocks that have slid along the surface of the mudflats, pushed by strong winds. Many a fine photograph has been shot of these fascinating rock tracks.

Leave No Trace Tips

Plan Ahead and Prepare

Learn about the regulations and special concerns of the area you are visiting.

Visit the backcountry in small groups.

Avoid popular areas during peak-use periods.

Choose equipment and clothing in subdued colors.

Pack food in reusable containers.

Map G1

Adjoining Maps: East: G2 ... *page* 466
North: F1 384

Central California Map .... *page* 382

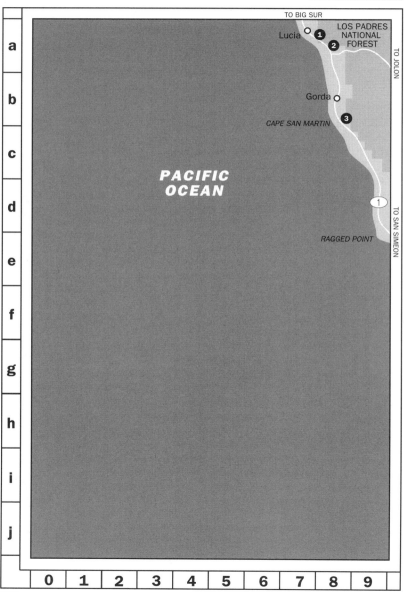

Chapter G1 features:

❶ Limekiln Trail

1.8 mi/1.0 hrs

Location: In Limekiln State Park south of Big Sur; map G1, grid a7.

User groups: Hikers only. No dogs, horses, or mountain bikes. No wheelchair facilities.

Permits: No permits are required. A $6 day-use fee is charged per vehicle.

Directions: From Carmel, drive 52 miles south on Highway 1 to Limekiln State Park, on the east side of the highway. (It's 2.5 miles south of Lucia, and 14.8 miles south of Julia Pfeiffer Burns State Park.) The trailhead is at the far side of the inland campground.

Maps: A map of Limekiln State Park is available for 50 cents at the entrance kiosk. To obtain a topographic map of the area, ask for Lopez Point from the USGS.

Contact: Limekiln State Park, c/o Pfeiffer Big Sur State Park, Big Sur, CA 93920; (408) 667-2315, (408) 649-2836, or (408) 667-2403.

Trail notes: What's Big Sur's best-kept secret? That's easy—the hiking trail at Limekiln State Park. The state park is so new, and so small, that it hasn't been inundated by visitors like Pfeiffer Big Sur or Julia Pfeiffer Burns State Parks. The Limekiln Trail leads from the inland campground into a gorgeous redwood forest. It follows Limekiln Creek for a half mile to the park's namesake limekilns, which were used to make limestone bricks and cement in the 1880s. The four kilns look like giant smokestacks with mossy, brick bottoms; they're interesting to see and photograph, but they're not the highlight of this trail. What is? A spur trail off the main route leads to Limekiln Falls, a spectacular 100-foot waterfall that drops over a limestone face. The spur is not marked, but it comes up immediately after you cross the second bridge on your way to the limekilns. (The first bridge is right by the campground.) Getting to the waterfall requires some

boulder-hopping, and in spring you may end up with wet feet, but it's good fun.

❷ Kirk Creek/Vicente Flat Trail

10.0 mi/6.0 hrs or 2.0 days

Location: In the Ventana Wilderness south of Lucia; map G1, grid a7.

User groups: Hikers, dogs, and horses. No mountain bikes. No wheelchair facilities.

Permits: A free campfire permit is required for overnight stays from May through December; they are available from the Monterey Ranger District or the Big Sur Station. A national forest recreation pass is required for each vehicle; fees are $5 for one day or $30 for a year.

Directions: From Carmel, drive 55 miles south on Highway 1 to Kirk Creek Campground, on the west side of the highway. (It's four miles south of Lucia, and six miles north of Gorda.) The trailhead is on the east side of the highway; you must park alongside Highway 1 in the pullout and not in the campground.

Maps: For a map of Los Padres National Forest or Ventana Wilderness, send $4 to USDA-Forest Service, 630 Sansome Street, San Francisco, CA 94111. To obtain topographic maps of the area, ask for Lopez Point and Cone Peak from the USGS.

Contact: Los Padres National Forest, Monterey Ranger District, 406 South Mildred Avenue, King City, CA 93930; (408) 385-5434.

Trail notes: What you see at the trailhead is not exactly what you get on this popular back-packing trail. You see chaparral and no shade, but you get chaparral and no shade only part of the time; the rest of the time you're hiking in shady redwood groves or along lush ravines. The Kirk Creek Trail (also called the Vicente Flat Trail) is full of surprises. The lack of trees in some sections is actually a positive, because it allows for wide-reaching views over the big blue Pacific. Your destination is Vicente Flat Camp in five miles, with a 1,700-foot elevation gain, mostly on well-graded trail. The trail leads steadily northeast, passing occasional odd-looking rocks and meandering in and out of the trees. Pass small Espinoza Camp at 3.2 miles, which is seldom used because of the superiority of Vicente Flat Camp, a larger camp with a nearby stream and a beautiful setting. The final half mile of trail is a descent to the Stone Ridge Trail junction, where you bear left for Vicente Flat Camp. You have a choice of sites in the shade or the sun; Hare Creek provides a water source.

❸ Salmon Creek Trail

4.2 mi/2.0 hrs or 2.0 days

Location: In the Silver Peak Wilderness south of Gorda; map G1, grid b8.

User groups: Hikers, dogs, and horses. No mountain bikes. No wheelchair facilities.

Permits: A free campfire permit is required for overnight stays from May through December; they are available from the Monterey Ranger District or the Big Sur Station. A national forest recreation pass is required for each vehicle; fees are $5 for one day or $30 for a year.

Directions: From Big Sur, drive 33 miles south on Highway 1 to Gorda, then continue 7.6 miles south of Gorda to the trailhead for the Salmon Creek Trail on the east side of the highway, at a hairpin turn. Park in the large parking pullout along the road. The Salmon Creek Trail leads from the south end of the guardrail.

Maps: For a map of Los Padres National Forest, send $4 to USDA-Forest Service, 630 Sansome Street, San Francisco, CA 94111. To obtain a topographic map of the area, ask for Villa Creek from the USGS.

Contact: Los Padres National Forest, Monterey Ranger District, 406 South Mildred Avenue, King City, CA 93930; (408) 385-5434.

Trail notes: While heading for a day hike or short backpacking trip on the Salmon Creek Trail, many people walk right by and miss seeing spectacular Salmon Creek Falls, which is just off the Salmon Creek Trail and a quarter-mile walk from Highway 1. Don't be one of them; start your trip at the signed Salmon Creek Trail but after walking a few hundred feet, cut off on any of the spur trails to your left and pay a visit to the impressive 100-foot waterfall, surrounded by cabin-sized boulders. Then return

to the Salmon Creek Trail, say good-bye to the creekside shade and dampness, and start a healthy climb to the ridge, where you can look back down at the highway and marvel at how far you've gone, and fast. From there, it's still more climbing, gaining a total of 800 feet, until you start to see Douglas firs, a sure sign that you're nearing misnamed Spruce Camp at 1,325 feet. At the Spruce Creek Trail fork, stay straight (left). The final tenth of a mile is downhill along Spruce Creek, a beautiful stream with a myriad of pools and cascades. The camp here is in gorgeous shade from Douglas firs, and there are many good spots to stick your feet (or other body parts) into the stream. If you want to spend the night but somebody already has this spot, you can continue another 1.5 miles to Estrella Camp.

Leave No Trace Tips

Travel and Camp with Care

On the trail:

Stay on designated trails. Walk single file in the middle of the path.

Do not take shortcuts on switchbacks.

When traveling cross-country where there are no trails,
follow animal trails or spread out your group so no new routes are
created. Walk along the most durable surfaces available,
such as rock, gravel, dry grasses, or snow.

Use a map and compass to eliminate
the need for rock cairns, tree scars, or ribbons.

If you encounter pack animals, step to the downhill side
of the trail and speak softly to avoid startling them.

At camp:

Choose an established, legal site that will not be damaged by your stay.

Restrict activities to areas where vegetation is compacted or absent.

Keep pollutants out of the water by camping at least 200 feet
(about 70 adult steps) from lakes and streams.

Control pets at all times, or leave them at home
with a sitter. Remove dog feces.

Map G2

Adjoining Maps: East: G3 ... *page* 474   West: G1 462
                     North: F2 402   South: H2 518

Central California Map .... *page* 382

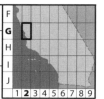

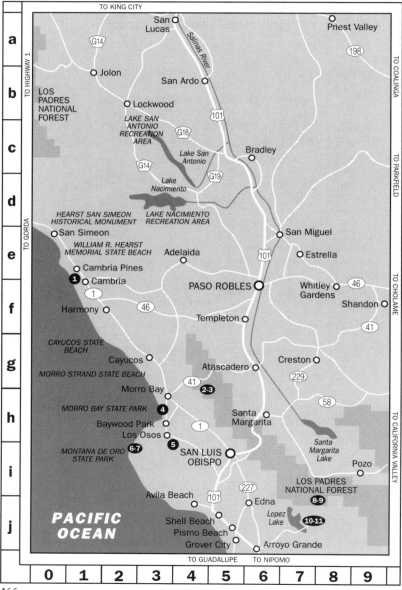

Chapter G2 features:

❶ Leffingwell Landing/ Moonstone Beach

4.0 mi/2.0 hrs

Location: Near Cambria; map G2, grid e1.

User groups: Hikers and dogs. No horses or mountain bikes. No wheelchair facilities.

Permits: No permits are required. Parking and access are free.

Directions: From north of Templeton on U.S. 101, take the Highway 46 West/Cambria/Hearst Castle exit. Drive west on Highway 46 for 22 miles to Highway 1, then continue three miles north on Highway 1, past Cambria, to Moonstone Beach Drive. Turn left on Moonstone Beach Drive and park at Leffingwell Landing.

Maps: To obtain a topographic map of the area, ask for Cambria from the USGS.

Contact: San Simeon State Beach, San Simeon District, 750 Hearst Castle Road, San Simeon, CA 93452; (805) 927-2020 or (805) 927-2068.

Trail notes: What's the best time to make the trip to Cambria? That's easy—in the spring, when the rolling hills along Highway 46 on the drive to the coast are lush and green. Of course, any time of year is a good time to walk the trail from Leffingwell Landing that leads along the bluffs above Moonstone Beach. Even though the trail parallels Moonstone Beach Drive all the way, the road isn't much of a bother, because the vistas out to sea hold all of your attention. The parking lot at Leffingwell Landing is in the middle of this trail, which means you can walk out and back in both directions. To the south, you may have a wet creek crossing at Leffingwell Creek, but you can go around it via the golf course. The bluff trail's southern terminus is at the intersection of Moonstone Beach Drive and

Weymouth Street, but you can descend to the beach there and keep walking. If you head in the other direction, about a quarter mile north of Leffingwell Landing the trail again descends on a wooden staircase to the beach, and you continue your walk there. In addition to the coastal vistas from the bluffs, there are many colorful patches of ice plant, cypress trees, and several benches and overlooks (accessible via short spurs off the main trail)—places where you can find a spot to call your own. We watched a winter squall come in from one of these overlooks; it was sudden, dramatic, and beautiful. Right below Leffingwell Landing there are fine tide pools to be explored. In winter, keep on the lookout for passing whales.

❷ Cerro Alto Summit

4.0 mi/2.0 hrs

Location: Off Highway 41, east of Morro Bay; map G2, grid g4.

User groups: Hikers, dogs, horses, and mountain bikes. No wheelchair facilities.

Permits: No permits are required. A national forest recreation pass is required for each vehicle; fees are $5 for one day or $30 for a year.

Directions: From Atascadero on U.S. 101, take the Highway 41 West/Morro Bay exit. Drive eight miles west on Highway 41 to Cerro Alto Campground on the left, midway between Atascadero and Morro Bay. Park in the signed hikers' parking lot near the camp host's residence, at the far end of the campground. Walk back down the camp road to the trailhead by the footbridge.

Maps: For a map of Los Padres National Forest, send $4 to USDA-Forest Service, 630 Sansome Street, San Francisco, CA 94111. To obtain a topographic map of the area, ask for Atascadero from the USGS.

Contact: Los Padres National Forest, Santa Lucia Ranger District, 1616 North Carlotti Drive, Santa Maria, CA 93454; (805) 925-9538 or fax (805) 349-0888.

Trail notes: We hope you like to climb, because that's what you do on the Cerro Alto Trail to the summit of Cerro Alto, elevation 2,620 feet. The 1,600-foot climb is divided over two miles of steep terrain, much of which burned in a 1994 arson fire, but the reward for your exertion is one of the finest views of the Central Coast—a panoramic vista of the Pacific Ocean, Whale Rock Reservoir, Morro Bay, Piedras Blancas Lighthouse, and the Santa Lucia Mountains. From the trailhead along the camp road (south of the parking area), you cross Morro Creek on a bridge, enter a bay and live oak forest, then leave it and head for chaparral country. In three-quarters of a mile, bear left, then shortly thereafter, bear right. After a series of switchbacks and some rocky sections of trail, you reach the road to the peak at 1.7 miles. Turn left and circle the peak as you climb another quarter mile to the summit.

❸ Cerro Alto Loop

2.5 mi/1.0 hr

Location: Off Highway 41, east of Morro Bay; map G2, grid g4.

User groups: Hikers, dogs, horses, and mountain bikes. No wheelchair facilities.

Permits: No permits are required. A national forest recreation pass is required for each vehicle; fees are $5 for one day or $30 for a year.

Directions: From Atascadero on U.S. 101, take the Highway 41 West/Morro Bay exit. Drive eight miles west on Highway 41 to Cerro Alto Campground on the left, midway between Atascadero and Morro Bay. Park in the signed hikers' parking lot near the camp host's residence, at the far end of the campground. Start hiking on the signed Cerro Alto Trail from there.

Maps: For a map of Los Padres National Forest, send $4 to USDA-Forest Service, 630 Sansome Street, San Francisco, CA 94111. To obtain a topographic map of the area, ask for Atascadero from the USGS.

Contact: Los Padres National Forest, Santa Lucia Ranger District, 1616 North Carlotti Drive, Santa Maria, CA 93454; (805) 925-9538 or fax (805) 349-0888.

Trail notes: Not everybody is up for the dry, steep hike to the top of Cerro Alto Peak, and if you're in that camp, you can take another hike from Cerro Alto Campground that offers many of its own rewards. Since some of this area burned in a 1994 fire, you'll see much evidence of regrowth (especially spring wildflowers) as well as many still standing, blackened trees. Take the trail from the far end of Cerro Alto Campground; you'll return on the trail by the bridge at the lower end of the camp. It's an up-and-down kind of deal, with not too much up or too much down. The first half mile is in a forest of oaks, bays, and madrones, with many ferns growing at your feet. As the trail climbs, the terrain changes to chaparral, and at one mile, you reach an old road junction. Turn right and in less than a mile, the path meets up with the Cerro Alto Trail to the summit. Keep following the old road and switchback to the west, then make a one-mile descent back to the camp.

❹ Cabrillo Peak

3.0 mi/1.5 hrs

Location: In Morro Bay State Park near Morro Bay; map G2, grid h3.

User groups: Hikers, horses, and mountain bikes. No dogs. No wheelchair facilities.

Permits: No permits are required. Parking and access are free.

Directions: From San Luis Obispo, take Highway 1 northwest for 11 miles to Morro Bay. Take the Morro Bay State Park exit and continue on South Bay Boulevard. In three-quarters of a mile, take the left fork (do not head for the main part of the park) and drive another half mile to the Cabrillo Peak dirt parking lot on the left side of the road. The first parking lot is for the Quarry Trail; another parking lot shortly following it is for the Park Ridge Trail. (Park at either—the two trails join.)

Maps: To obtain a topographic map of the area, ask for Morro Bay South from the USGS.

Contact: Morro Bay State Park, State Park Road,

Morro Bay, CA 93442; (805) 772-7434. Or San Luis Obispo Coast State Parks at (805) 549-3312.

Trail notes: You hardly realize you're in a state park when you reach the trailhead for Cabrillo Peak, which is just a small dirt parking lot alongside a busy road. Where's the entrance kiosk? What about the state park entrance fee? Where are all the campgrounds and rest rooms? None of that applies here at Morro Bay State Park's Cabrillo Peak, which is a quiet refuge from the hustle and bustle of Morro Bay tourism. Cabrillo Peak is one of nine "morros" or small volcanic peaks that lay in a loose chain along the central coast. (Morro Rock is another of these, and the most famous of the group.) Although no trail goes to the top of Cabrillo Peak, you can hike on the peak's lower reaches on the Quarry Trail and Park Ridge Trail. Both are accessible from two small parking areas off South Bay Boulevard; if you miss the first one, just take the second one. The Park Ridge Trail goes straight up, then veers left and joins the Quarry Trail. The Cabrillo Peak area contains a variety of native plants and grasslands, including these spring bloomers: bird's eye gilia, brodiea, and mariposa lilies. On the sunniest slopes, coastal sage scrub grows, including black sage and bush monkeyflower. Translation? No shade. That makes the views of Morro Bay and Morro Rock first class, but it also means you'd better carry water.

❺ Los Osos Oaks Reserve

2.0 mi/1.0 hr

Location: West of San Luis Obispo in Los Osos; map G2, grid h3.

User groups: Hikers only. No dogs, horses, or mountain bikes. No wheelchair facilities.

Permits: No permits are required. Parking and access are free.

Directions: From U.S. 101 in San Luis Obispo, take the Los Osos exit and head west on Los Osos Valley Road. Drive 8.5 miles on Los Osos Valley Road to the Los Osos Oaks Reserve on the left side of the road, which is marked by a small sign. (The reserve is located exactly one mile east of 10th Street in Los Osos, and just west of the bear statue on the road.) There is a small parking area by the trailhead, just off Los Osos Valley Road.

Maps: To obtain a topographic map of the area, ask for Morro Bay South from the USGS.

Contact: Los Osos Oaks Reserve, c/o Morro Bay State Park, State Park Road, Morro Bay, CA 93442; (805) 772-7434. Or San Luis Obispo Coast State Parks at (805) 549-3312.

Trail notes: It's hard to believe that a bunch of old oak trees right alongside a busy road could make for such great walking, but they do. The hike is an odd mix of elements, since you hear road noise much of the time, but the forest still seems peaceful. The venerable old oaks in Los Osos Oaks Reserve are as old as 800 years, and they can be visited by wandering on any of three short, flat trails. It's easy to walk a brief stretch on all of them. The Chumash Loop, Oak View Trail, and Los Osos Creek Trail all lead from the parking lot, then split off from each other. Oak View is just a short out-and-back trip through the trees and provides the best look at the reserve's highlights; Chumash Loop is a little longer and loops around the reserve. The Los Osos Creek Trail is the least impressive of the three, showing off the fewest fine tree specimens, and following a marshy stretch of creek. The oak forest is a mix of very large, old trees, with moss hanging down from their branches, and tiny, dwarfed ones. Some of the oaks' trunks and branches are so twisted, gnarled, and wrinkled that they look like a tangled web of elephants' trunks. If you're into photography, this is the kind of place that is best captured in black and white. And if the coast is fogged in, this hike is an ideal choice, because all the beauty of the forest is close enough to touch.

❻ Montana de Oro Bluffs Trail

3.0 mi/1.5 hrs

Location: In Montana de Oro State Park west of San Luis Obispo; map G2, grid i2.

User groups: Hikers and mountain bikes. No dogs or horses. No wheelchair facilities.

Permits: No permits are required. Parking and access are free.

Directions: From U.S. 101 in San Luis Obispo, take the Los Osos exit and head west on Los Osos Valley Road. Drive 12 miles on Los Osos Valley

Road to the Montana de Oro entrance, then continue 2.5 miles to the small parking area on the right side of the road, which is 100 yards beyond the left turnoff for the visitor center. The signed Bluffs Trail begins there.

Maps: A map of Montana de Oro State Park is available for $1 at the visitor center, or at Morro Bay State Park. To obtain a topographic map of the area, ask for Morro Bay South from the USGS.

Contact: Montana de Oro State Park, Los Osos, CA 93402; (805) 528-0513 or Morro Bay State Park at (805) 772-7434. Or San Luis Obispo Coast State Parks at (805) 549-3312.

Trail notes: How can a state park this good be free of charge? We can't figure it out, but we're glad it is. The Bluffs Trail at Montana de Oro State Park is one of the finest coast walks in Central and Southern California, blissfully free of the blight of human development and loaded with classic oceanside beauty. The flat trail contours along the top of Montana de Oro's shale and sediment bluffs, with nonstop views of rocky offshore outcrops, colorful rock cliffs and arches, and the big blue Pacific. Wooden railings keep hikers from leaning too far over the edge of the constantly eroding bluffs. In addition to all the coastal vistas, the grasses alongside the trail explode in a display of orange poppies and other wildflowers in February, March, and April. The trail ends at a barbed wire fence and Pacific Gas and Electric Company property (it's lined with huge cactus to keep people out). Just follow the tiny loop and then retrace your steps on the trail. A good side trip is to explore the beach that's right across from the visitor center turnoff, near where you left your car.

➐ Valencia and Oats Peaks

7.0 mi/3.5 hrs

Location: In Montana de Oro State Park west of San Luis Obispo; map G2, grid i2.

User groups: Hikers and horses. No dogs or mountain bikes. No wheelchair facilities.

Permits: No permits are required. Parking and access are free.

Directions: From U.S. 101 in San Luis Obispo, take the Los Osos exit and head west on Los Osos Valley Road. Drive 12 miles on Los Osos Valley

Road to the Montana de Oro entrance, then continue 2.5 miles to the small parking area on the right side of the road, which is 100 yards beyond the left turnoff for the visitor center. The Valencia Peak Tail begins on the left side of the road.

Maps: A map of Montana de Oro State Park is available for $1 at the visitor center, or at Morro Bay State Park. To obtain a topographic map of the area, ask for Morro Bay South from the USGS.

Contact: Montana de Oro State Park, Los Osos, CA 93402; (805) 528-0513 or Morro Bay State Park at (805) 772-7434. Or San Luis Obispo Coast State Parks at (805) 549-3312.

Trail notes: With a cool ocean breeze keeping you comfortable, this seven-mile round-trip hike to two coastal peaks is a spectacular day trip. If you forget to carry water and/or hike in the heat of high noon, it can be a nightmare. So get prepared, then head for the Valencia Peak Trailhead in Montana de Oro State Park. The wide route heads briefly south and then turns inland for a gradual ascent through grasslands and wildflowers, chaparral and scrub. There are several junctions; all are well marked.

In two miles and with an 1,100-foot elevation gain, you arrive at the top of Valencia Peak, elevation 1,347 feet. On a clear day you can see all the way from Point Sal in the south to Piedras Blancas in the north. From there you must descend for a mile (losing nearly 500 feet) to join a road that connects to the Oats Peak Trail, then hike upward once again on the Oats Peak Trail. (Sorry, but there's no other way to do it from the top of Valencia Peak.)

Oats Peak is more easily gained in 1.2 miles, and a survey marker tells you when you reach its summit at 1,373 feet. From there, you can walk along the ridgetop for a while to enjoy more of the spectacular views of the ocean, Morro Rock, and the inland mountains, or head back downhill. Keep to the Oats Peak Trail for your descent. If you take Oats Peak Trail all the way back down, you'll have a 10-minute walk on the park road to get back to your car. One more thing to think about: If you can possibly visit from February to April, you get a good chance at crystal-clear vistas and the best chance of seeing Montana de Oro's signature wildflower display. The park's hills are gorgeous in season.

❽ Big Falls

3.0 mi/1.5 hrs

Location: In the Santa Lucia Wilderness near Arroyo Grande; map G2, grid i8.

User groups: Hikers, dogs, and horses. No mountain bikes. No wheelchair facilities.

Permits: No day-use permits are required. A national forest recreation pass is required for each vehicle; fees are $5 for one day or $30 for a year.

Directions: From San Luis Obispo, drive 15 miles south on U.S. 101 to Arroyo Grande and the Highway 227/Lopez Lake exit. Head east on Highway 227, then turn right on Lopez Drive, following the signs toward Lopez Lake for 10.3 miles. Turn right on Hi Mountain Road (before Lopez Lake's entrance station). Drive eight-tenths of a mile, then turn left on Upper Lopez Canyon Road. Drive 6.3 miles, passing a Boy Scout Camp, then turn right. In one-tenth mile, the pavement ends. Continue for 3.5 miles on the dirt road, crossing Lopez Creek numerous times in the wet season, to the Big Falls Trailhead. The trailhead is not usually marked, so set your odometer and look for a small waterfall on the left side of the road. The trail leads from the right side of the road. (Note: Four-wheel-drive vehicles are recommended.)

Maps: For a map of Los Padres National Forest, send $4 to USDA-Forest Service, 630 Sansome Street, San Francisco, CA 94111. To obtain a topographic map of the area, ask for Tar Spring Ridge from the USGS.

Contact: Los Padres National Forest, Santa Lucia Ranger District, 1616 North Carlotti Drive, Santa Maria, CA 93454; (805) 925-9538 or fax (805) 349-0888.

Trail notes: The journey to Big Falls in the Santa Lucia Wilderness is a wacky, water-filled adventure. Even as late as June, the drive to the trailhead can require dozens of crossings of Lopez Creek. In places, the stream simply becomes the road. In comparison to the drive, the hike is surprisingly easy and fast. You walk through a fern- and flower-filled sycamore and oak forest to the first waterfall, only a half mile in. This is not actually Big Falls, it's a smaller waterfall, although plenty of people mistake it for Big Falls. This waterfall is only about 30 feet high, with many small trout swimming in its lower pool, and a much deeper pool just above its lip. People sunbathe by the rocky pools upstream. You can continue hiking beyond this cataract to the real Big Falls, another mile further. Wildflowers are excellent all along the route, and at their best in spring. The terrain gets drier and rockier as you climb up out of the canyon to Big Falls, and you'll find different types of flowers and foliage on this upper part of the trail. Big Falls is about 80 feet tall, but it's only impressive early in the year. By June, it has much less flow than the smaller waterfall downstream. (Note that if you want to hike more, the trail continues beyond Big Falls for another mile, making an exposed and steep ascent to Hi Mountain Road.)

❾ Little Falls

1.0 mi/0.5 hr

Location: In the Santa Lucia Wilderness near Arroyo Grande; map G2, grid i8.

User groups: Hikers, dogs, and horses. No mountain bikes. No wheelchair facilities.

Permits: No day-use permits are required. A national forest recreation pass is required for each vehicle; fees are $5 for one day or $30 for a year.

Directions: From San Luis Obispo, drive 15 miles south on U.S. 101 to Arroyo Grande and the Highway 227/Lopez Lake exit. Head east on Highway 227, then turn right on Lopez Drive, following the signs toward Lopez Lake for 10.3 miles. Turn right on Hi Mountain Road (before Lopez Lake's entrance station). Drive eight-tenths of a mile, then turn left on Upper Lopez Canyon Road. Drive 6.3 miles, passing a Boy Scout Camp, then turn right. In one-tenth mile, the pavement ends. Continue for 1.6 miles on the dirt road, crossing Lopez Creek numerous times in the wet season, to the Little Falls Trailhead. The trail leads from the right side of the road. (Note: Four-wheel-drive vehicles are recommended.)

Maps: For a map of Los Padres National Forest, send $4 to USDA-Forest Service, 630 Sansome Street, San Francisco, CA 94111. To obtain a topographic map of the area, ask for Tar Spring Ridge from the USGS.

Contact: Los Padres National Forest, Santa Lucia Ranger District, 1616 North Carlotti Drive, Santa Maria, CA 93454; (805) 925-9538 or fax (805) 349-0888.

Trail notes: Little Falls is just as pretty as its neighbor Big Falls in the Santa Lucia Wilderness, and getting to it requires the same wet and rugged drive, but less of it. If your car isn't up to the 3.5 miles of rocky road and stream crossings that it takes to get to Big Falls, maybe you can convince it to go only 1.6 miles to Little Falls. If even that's too much, you can always park where the pavement ends and walk to Little Falls, adding 3.2 miles round-trip to the mileage shown above. It's still a pretty easy hike, and with plenty of lovely scenery. From the trailhead, you hike along Little Falls Creek, a cool, shady stream that is teeming with small trout and lined with oaks, sycamores, bays, and maples. Maidenhair and giant woodwardia ferns line its rocky pools. After only 15 minutes of hiking (less than a half mile), you'll see a spur trail heading off to the left, which you can follow upstream for a few hundred feet to Little Falls, a 50-foot limestone waterfall. The main trail continues beyond this spur to many fine, water-carved pools, perfect for wading into. The trail eventually climbs out of the canyon to Hi Mountain Road.

⑩ Duna Vista and Two Waters Trails

2.2–6.6 mi/1–3 hrs

Location: At Lopez Lake east of Arroyo Grande; map G2, grid j7.

User groups: Hikers, horses, and mountain bikes. No dogs. No wheelchair facilities.

Permits: No permits are required. A $5 day-use fee is charged per vehicle.

Directions: From San Luis Obispo, drive 15 miles south on U.S. 101 to Arroyo Grande and the Highway 227/Lopez Lake exit. Head east on Highway 227, then turn right on Lopez Drive, following the signs to Lopez Lake for 10.4 miles. To reach the Two Waters Trailhead, you can take a boat ride up the Wittenberg or Lopez arms of the lake, or add four miles to your trip by hiking from the Wittenberg Trailhead. To reach the latter, drive 1.5 miles past the park entrance

station to the parking area near where the park road is gated off.

Maps: To obtain a topographic map of the area, ask for Tar Spring Ridge from the USGS.

Contact: Lopez Lake Recreation Area, 5800 Lopez Drive, Arroyo Grande, CA 93420; (805) 489-1122 or fax (805) 473-7181.

Trail notes: Most people on the Central Coast know that Lopez Lake is completely set up for water recreation—Jet skiing, waterskiing, windsurfing, fishing, you name it—but not everyone knows that the park is also great for hiking, especially in springtime. The best path in the park, Duna Vista Trail, is accessible via either a long hike or a short hike and a boat ride. The latter option works out great for people who want to go hiking while their loved ones go fishing; they can be dropped off and picked up later. (Guided trips are also frequently available; check with the park for dates and times.) If you're going by boat, there are two trailheads (docks) for the Two Waters Trail, one on the Lopez arm of the lake and one on the Wittenberg arm. You can start from either trailhead, or arrange a shuttle pickup with a friend so you can start at one end and finish at the other. From either trailhead, the Two Waters Trail runs for six-tenths of a mile to the Duna Vista Trail, which you then follow uphill for a half mile. California fuschias bloom along the trail, mixed in among the sage and chaparral. After a 600-foot climb, you're rewarded with views of the Santa Lucia Wilderness, the Pacific Ocean, and Pismo Dunes. (Oh yeah, Duna Vista—now we get it.) If you can't arrange a boat ride, you can hike to the start of the Two Waters Trail. Start walking from the end of the park road on the Wittenberg Trail, then meet up with the Tuouski Trail by Camp French (a Boy Scout Camp), and follow Tuouski Trail to its junction with the east end of the Two Waters Trail. Keep in mind that this changes a 2.2-mile round-trip into a 6.6-mile round-trip.

⑪ Blackberry Springs and High Ridge

3.0 mi/1.5 hrs

Location: At Lopez Lake east of Arroyo Grande; map G2, grid j7.

User groups: Hikers, horses, and mountain bikes. No dogs. No wheelchair facilities.

Permits: No permits are required. A $5 day-use fee is charged per vehicle.

Directions: From San Luis Obispo, drive 15 miles south on U.S. 101 to Arroyo Grande and the Highway 227/Lopez Lake exit. Head east on Highway 227, then turn right on Lopez Drive, following the signs to Lopez Lake for 10.4 miles. Continue past the entrance station to Squirrel Campground and the trailhead for the Blackberry Springs Trail.

Maps: To obtain a topographic map of the area, ask for Tar Spring Ridge from the USGS.

Contact: Lopez Lake Recreation Area, 5800 Lopez Drive, Arroyo Grande, CA 93420; (805) 489-1122 or fax (805) 473-7181.

Trail notes: Great views of the grassy hills and blue water of Lopez Lake are yours for the taking on the High Ridge Trail. Start from the Blackberry Springs Trailhead at Squirrel Campground, where you can pick up an interpretive brochure. Learn all about the Chumash Indians who once lived here as you follow the trail uphill through a foliage-rich creek canyon, which includes some blackberry bushes. Many of the other plants along the trail are also edible and were used by the Chumash. The trail steepens as it climbs to connect with High Ridge Trail at three-quarters of a mile, where you turn left and wander along a firebreak on Turkey Ridge, which has wide-open views. It's hot and sunny up here, so that may dictate how far you wander, but the trail leads for 1.5 miles before it drops down to the Wittenberg arm of the lake. Might as well just head out for a half mile or so, enjoy the views of the Santa Lucia Wilderness and the coast, then turn around and head back. Another option is to turn right instead of left on the High Ridge Trail, walk a half mile, then connect with the Turkey Ridge Trail. Take the Turkey Ridge Trail back to the parking lot by Squirrel Campground for a nice three-mile loop trip.

Map G3

Adjoining Maps: East: G4 ... *page* 476   West: G2 466
North: F3 408   South: H3 522

Central California Map .... *page* 382

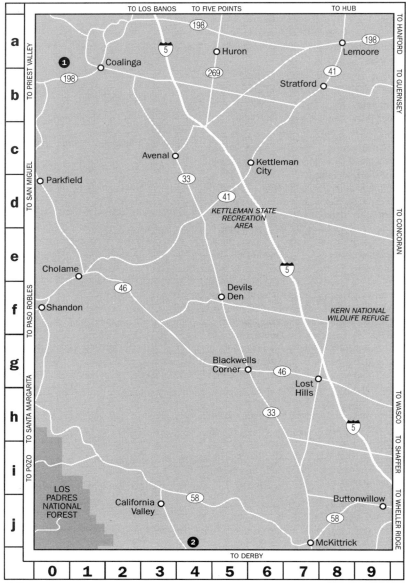

❶ Kreyenhagen Peak

4.0 mi/2.5 hrs

Location: Northwest of Coalinga; map G3, grid a1.

User groups: Hikers, dogs, horses, and mountain bikes. No wheelchair facilities.

Permits: No permits are required. A $3 day-use fee is charged per vehicle.

Directions: From Coalinga, drive 20 miles west on Highway 198 to Coalinga Mineral Springs Road. Turn right (north) and drive four miles to Coalinga Mineral Springs County Park.

Maps: To obtain a topographic map of the area, ask for Curry Mountain from the USGS.

Contact: Bureau of Land Management, Hollister Resource Area, 20 Hamilton Court, Hollister, CA 95023; (408) 637-8183.

Trail notes: Most people don't realize that there's a National Recreation Trail out here near Coalinga, the town that was made famous by an earthquake. But it's true, and in winter and spring, this is a first-class hike to the summit of Kreyenhagen Peak, elevation 3,558 feet, climbing through chaparral-covered hillsides. The trail begins at the far end of the picnic area and crosses a dry streambed, then begins to ascend. It's well graded all the way, with the second mile being slightly steeper than the first. The vista from the peak includes the Diablo Range, the San Joaquin Valley, and miles of surrounding Bureau of Land Management land. That's a pretty wide scope considering how little effort is required to obtain the view.

❷ Carrizo Plains and Painted Rock

1.0 mi/0.5 hr

Location: In eastern San Luis Obispo County, south of California Valley; map G3, grid j4.

User groups: Hikers only. No dogs, horses, or mountain bikes. No wheelchair facilities.

Permits: No permits are required. Parking and access are free.

Directions: From San Luis Obispo on U.S. 101, drive north for eight miles and take the Santa Margarita/Highway 58 exit. Drive east on Highway 58 for 52 miles to the Soda Lake Road turn-off on the right. Turn right (south) and drive 13.5 miles to the Painted Rock Trail and visitor center on the right side of the road.

Maps: A brochure on the Carrizo Plains is available from the BLM at the address below. To obtain a topographic map of the area, ask for Painted Rock from the USGS.

Contact: Bureau of Land Management, Caliente Resource Area, 3801 Pegasus Drive, Bakersfield, CA 93308; (805) 391-6000. Or the Goodwin Education Center at Carrizo Plains, open Thurdays through Sundays from October through May, at (805) 475-2131.

Trail notes: Carrizo Plains is considered to be California's largest nature preserve, and the big draw is the large number of sandhill cranes who hang around here from November to February. While thousands of migrating and resident birds can be seen in this area, it's the cranes that bring the hordes of bird-lovers and photographers to alkali Soda Lake and the surrounding plains. Since the birds don't stay in one place, most people spot them while driving around the Carrizo Plains area, or while stopping at the overlook platform near Soda Lake. (The birds are unmistakable—drab gray in color but with seven-foot wing spans and three-foot-long legs.) After checking out the big birds, head for the Painted Rock Interpretive Trail, where you can walk the short path that leads to 55-foot-tall Painted Rock. The interior of the rounded sandstone amphitheater has some of the best Native American pictographs in the country. Spring wildflowers are beautiful all across the plains.

Special note: Check your calendar before you go. The area is closed from March 1 to July 15 to protect nesting falcons. The best time to visit is November to February to see the sandhill cranes.

Map G4

Adjoining Maps: East: G5 ... *page* 478   West: G3 474
North: F4 410   South: H4 532

Central California Map .... *page* 382

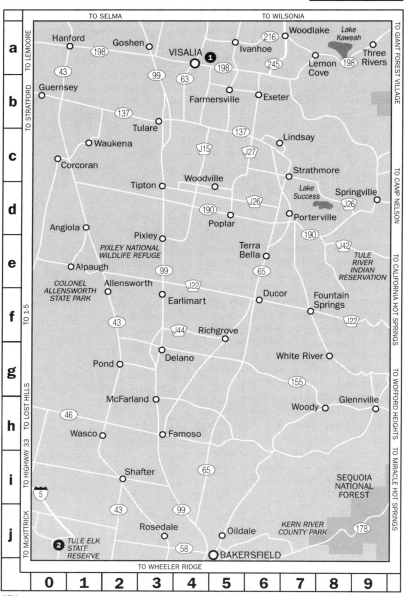

❶ Kaweah Oaks Preserve

2.0 mi/1.0 hr

Location: East of Visalia; map G4, grid a4.

User groups: Hikers, dogs, horses, and mountain bikes. No wheelchair facilities.

Permits: No permits are required. Parking and access are free.

Directions: From Tulare on Highway 99, drive north for 10 miles and turn east on Highway 198. Drive 13 miles on Highway 198, passing Visalia, to the left turnoff for Road 182. Turn left on Road 182 and drive four-tenths of a mile to the trailhead parking area on the left.

Maps: To obtain a topographic map of the area, ask for Visalia from the USGS.

Contact: Kaweah Oaks Preserve, c/o Four Creeks Land Trust, (209) 738-0211.

Trail notes: The Kaweah Oaks Preserve is Tulare County's premier nature preserve, the slim remains of the massive oak forest that once shaded Visalia and its environs. Some big oaks still stand, as well as wild grapes growing as high as 30 feet. From the parking area, go through the cattle gate, and walk down the old ranch road to the interpretive area and picnic tables on the left (about a third of a mile). Then cross the weir on the far side of the picnic area and walk the nature trail loop. You can also continue straight on the ranch road, but this is a cattle grazing area, so be sure to close all the gates behind you. As you walk, look for herons, hawks, and owls, as well as the preserve's four species of woodpeckers. In addition to the big old oaks and grapevines, you'll see some California sycamore, cottonwoods, and willows growing near the streams. This is a good walk for winter or spring, or early morning or evening in summer, when the valley is at its coolest.

❷ Tule Elk State Reserve

1.0 mi/0.5 hr

Location: Off Interstate 5 west of Bakersfield; map G4, grid j0.

User groups: Hikers only. No dogs, horses, or mountain bikes. Some facilities are wheelchair accessible.

Permits: No permits are required. A $3 day-use fee is charged per vehicle.

Directions: From the junction of Interstate 5 and Highway 99 north of the Grapevine, drive north on Interstate 5 for 33 miles to the Stockdale Highway exit. Drive west for 1.2 miles, then turn left (south) on Morris Road. Drive 1.5 miles on Morris Road, then turn right (west) on Station Road. Drive a quarter mile to the Tule Elk State Reserve. The route is well signed.

Maps: To obtain a topographic map of the area, ask for Tupman from the USGS.

Contact: Tule Elk State Reserve, 8653 Station Road, Buttonwillow, CA 93206; (805) 765-5004.

Trail notes: Most people just plain don't know that there's a huge herd of magnificent tule elk wandering around a few miles from I-5. If you're one of them, better pull off the highway and get yourself to the Tule Elk State Reserve, out here by the bustling metropolis of Tupman. There aren't a lot of trails to choose from, but if you've been driving on Interstate 5 long enough, just getting out of the car is a big deal. A dirt road runs along the east boundary of the reserve, popular with walkers and hopeful elk-seekers. The animals are most active in the autumn, when their rutting season begins. (Bring binoculars for your best chance at a good view.) Make sure you stop in at the visitor center and check out their interesting displays on the elk and the history of the Central Valley.

Map G5

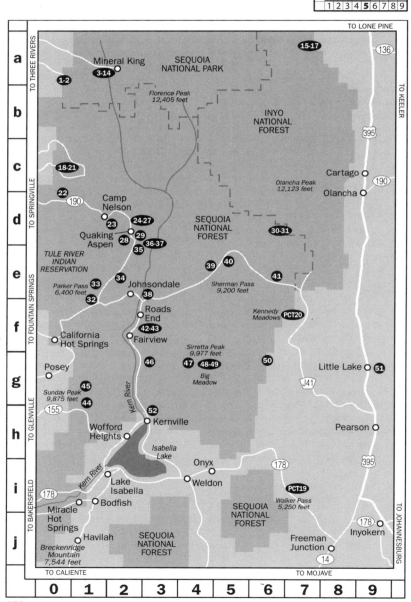

TO LONE PINE

TO THREE RIVERS

SEQUOIA NATIONAL PARK

15-17

136

a

Mineral King
3-14

1-2

Florence Peak
12,405 feet

INYO NATIONAL FOREST

b

TO KEELER

395

c

18-21

TO SPRINGVILLE

Cartago

190

Olancha Peak
12,123 feet

Olancha

190

22

190

Camp Nelson

d

24-27

23

SEQUOIA NATIONAL FOREST

30-31

Quaking Aspen

28   29

35   36-37

TULE RIVER INDIAN RESERVATION

e

Parker Pass
6,400 feet

33   34

32

39   40

Johnsondale

38

41

Sherman Pass
9,200 feet

TO FOUNTAIN SPRINGS

Roads End

f

42-43

Fairview

Kennedy Meadows   PCT20

California Hot Springs

Sirretta Peak
9,977 feet

46

47   48-49

50

g

Posey

45

44

Big Meadow

Little Lake   51

Sunday Peak
9,875 feet

155

J41

TO GLENVILLE

Kern River

h

Wofford Heights

52

Kernville

Pearson

Isabella Lake

i

Onyx

178

395

Kern River

178

Lake Isabella

Weldon

PCT19

TO BAKERSFIELD

Miracle Hot Springs

Bodfish

SEQUOIA NATIONAL FOREST

Walker Pass
5,250 feet

Inyokern

178

TO JOHANNESBURG

j

Havilah

SEQUOIA NATIONAL FOREST

Freeman Junction

Breckenridge Mountain
7,544 feet

14

TO CALIENTE

TO MOJAVE

0   1   2   3   4   5   6   7   8   9

❶ Ladybug Trail

3.8 mi/2.0 hrs

Location: Off Highway 198 in the South Fork region of Sequoia National Park; map G5, grid a1.

User groups: Hikers and horses. No dogs or mountain bikes. No wheelchair facilities.

Permits: No permits are required. There is a $10 entrance fee at Sequoia and Kings Canyon National Parks, good for seven days.

Directions: From Visalia, drive east on Highway 198 for 35 miles to one mile west of Three Rivers. Turn right on South Fork Drive and drive 12.8 miles to South Fork Campground. (At nine miles, the road turns to dirt.) Day-use parking is available just inside the camp entrance. The trailhead is at the far end of the campground loop.

Maps: Free park maps are available at park entrance stations or by contacting Sequoia and Kings Canyon National Parks at the address below. A more detailed map is available for a fee from Tom Harrison Cartography at (415) 456-7940 or Trails Illustrated at (800) 962-1643. To obtain a topographic map of the area, ask for Dennison Peak from the USGS.

Contact: Sequoia and Kings Canyon National Parks, Three Rivers, CA 93271-9700; (209) 565-3134 or fax (209) 565-3730.

Trail notes: The South Fork area is the forgotten region of Sequoia National Park. Accessible only by a 13-mile dead-end road out of Three Rivers, South Fork is the place to go when you just want to get away from it all. Solitude in a national park? You can find it here. The elevation is low—only 3,600 feet—so the area is accessible year-round, and there may be no finer winter walk than a hike on the Ladybug Trail out of South Fork. The trail leaves the far end of South Fork Campground and heads through an oak and bay forest along the South Fork Kaweah River. At 1.7 miles you reach Ladybug Camp, a primitive camping area along the river's edge, in the shade of pines and firs. A short scramble downstream of the camp gives you a look at Ladybug Falls, a 25-foot waterfall set in a rocky grotto. If you continue upstream, the trail leads another few hundred yards and then switchbacks uphill, heading for Whiskey Log Camp. But a use trail leaves the main trail and continues a short distance upriver, where there are many beautiful rocky pools. And in case you haven't guessed, the trail, camp, and falls are named for the millions of ladybugs that winter near the river, then alight in the spring to head back to the Central Valley to feed.

❷ Garfield-Hockett Trail

5.8 mi/3.0 hrs

Location: Off Highway 198 in the South Fork region of Sequoia National Park; map G5, grid a1.

User groups: Hikers and horses. No dogs or mountain bikes. No wheelchair facilities.

Permits: No permits are required. There is a $10 entrance fee at Sequoia and Kings Canyon National Parks, good for seven days.

Directions: From Visalia, drive east on Highway 198 for 35 miles to one mile west of Three Rivers. Turn right on South Fork Drive and drive 12.8 miles to South Fork Campground. (At nine miles,

the road turns to dirt.) Day-use parking is available just inside the camp entrance. The trailhead is at the far end of the campground loop.

Maps: Free park maps are available at park entrance stations or by contacting Sequoia and Kings Canyon National Parks at the address below. A more detailed map is available for a fee from Tom Harrison Cartography at (415) 456-7940 or Trails Illustrated at (800) 962-1643. To obtain a topographic map of the area, ask for Dennison Peak from the USGS.

Contact: Sequoia and Kings Canyon National Parks, Three Rivers, CA 93271-9700; (209) 565-3134 or fax (209) 565-3730.

Trail notes: The trip to the magnificent Garfield Grove is only 2.9 miles from South Fork Campground, and if you don't mind a steep climb and possibly sharing the trail with horse packers, you should be sure to take this hike. The trail climbs immediately and keeps climbing, but fortunately is shaded by oaks most of the way. The ascent rewards you with a continual view of distant Homer's Nose, a granite landmark that, although prominent, looks little like anybody's nose. In just under three miles of nonstop climbing, you reach the first of many Sequoias in the Garfield Grove. This grove is reported to be one of the largest groves in the national parks. By the time you reach it, you've gained 2,000 feet in elevation, so pick a big tree to lean against, pull out a snack, and take a breather.

❸ Paradise Ridge

5.0 mi/2.5 hrs

Location: Off Highway 198 in the Mineral King region of Sequoia National Park; map G5, grid a2.

User groups: Hikers and horses. No dogs or mountain bikes. No wheelchair facilities.

Permits: No permits are required. There is a $10 entrance fee at Sequoia and Kings Canyon National Parks, good for seven days.

Directions: From Visalia, drive east on Highway 198 for 38 miles to Mineral King Road, 2.5 miles east of Three Rivers. (If you reach the Ash Mountain entrance station, you've gone too far.) Turn right on Mineral King Road and drive 20 miles to the Hockett Trail parking area on the right, a quarter mile past Atwell Mill Camp. Park there and walk back west on Mineral King Road for a third of a mile to the trailhead for Paradise Ridge, on the north side of the road.

Maps: Free park maps are available at park entrance stations or by contacting Sequoia and Kings Canyon National Parks at the address below. A more detailed map is available for a fee from Tom Harrison Cartography at (415) 456-7940 or Trails Illustrated at (800) 962-1643. To obtain a topographic map of the area, ask for Silver City from the USGS.

Contact: Sequoia and Kings Canyon National Parks, Three Rivers, CA 93271-9700; (209) 565-3134 or fax (209) 565-3730.

Trail notes: Okay, you've just driven the 20 twisting miles in to Mineral King from Three Rivers. You're tired and dusty and itching to get out of the car and move your legs. What's the first trail you can reach in Mineral King? The Paradise Ridge Trail, and it climbs right away, enough to get you huffing and puffing and your lungs cleaned out of road dust. After the initial steepness of the trail, the grade becomes easier as it moves into switchbacks ascending the hill. The path is loaded with giant Sequoia trees, some in clusters as large as 10 or more. At your feet are tons of ferns. As you climb, the views just keep improving, of the East Fork Kaweah River Canyon below you and far off, the Great Western Divide. You can hike all the way to the top of the ridge at three miles, if you like, but the views aren't any better there than they are on the way up. Most people just cruise uphill a ways, then turn around when they've had enough. Besides the big trees and the big views, our favorite thing about this trail was that on our trip, we saw more bears than people.

❹ Hockett Trail to East Fork Bridge

4.0 mi/2.0 hrs

Location: Off Highway 198 in the Mineral King region of Sequoia National Park; map G5, grid a2.

User groups: Hikers and horses. No dogs or mountain bikes. No wheelchair facilities.

Permits: No permits are required. There is a $10 entrance fee at Sequoia and Kings Canyon National Parks, good for seven days.

Directions: From Visalia, drive east on Highway 198 for 38 miles to Mineral King Road, 2.5 miles east of Three Rivers. (If you reach the Ash Mountain entrance station, you've gone too far.) Turn right on Mineral King Road and drive 20 miles to the Hockett Trail parking area on the right, a quarter mile past Atwell Mill Camp. Park there and walk into the campground to site 16, where the trail begins.

Maps: Free park maps are available at park entrance stations or by contacting Sequoia and Kings Canyon National Parks at the address below. A more detailed map is available for a fee from Tom Harrison Cartography at (415) 456-7940 or Trails Illustrated at (800) 962-1643. To obtain a topographic map of the area, ask for Mineral King from the USGS.

Contact: Sequoia and Kings Canyon National Parks, Three Rivers, CA 93271-9700; (209) 565-3134 or fax (209) 335-2856.

Trail notes: The Hockett Trail makes a fine day-hiking path in Mineral King, suitable for all kinds of hikers. Families with small children can just walk a mile downhill to the footbridge over the East Fork Kaweah River, where there is a small waterfall and many sculptured granite pools, then turn around and head back. People looking for a longer trip can continue another mile to the East Fork Grove of Sequoias and Deer Creek. Both groups get to hike through a beautiful forest of big conifers—pines, cedars, and firs—and fields of mountain misery. The trail starts in an area of Sequoia stumps, near where the Atwell Mill cut lumber in the 1880s. Live Sequoias still flourish further down the path, near the river's edge; apparently they were spared because of their distance from the mill. The trail is well graded, and even the uphill return is only a moderate climb.

❺ Cold Springs Nature Trail

2.0 mi/1.0 hr

Location: Off Highway 198 in the Mineral King region of Sequoia National Park; map G5, grid a2.

User groups: Hikers and horses. No dogs or mountain bikes. No wheelchair facilities.

Permits: No permits are required. There is a

$10 entrance fee at Sequoia and Kings Canyon National Parks, good for seven days.

Directions: From Visalia, drive east on Highway 198 for 38 miles to Mineral King Road, 2.5 miles east of Three Rivers. (If you reach the Ash Mountain entrance station, you've gone too far.) Turn right on Mineral King Road and drive 23.5 miles to Cold Springs Campground on the right. The trail begins near site 6. If you aren't staying in the camp, you can park by the Mineral King Ranger Station and walk into the campground.

Maps: Free park maps are available at park entrance stations or by contacting Sequoia and Kings Canyon National Parks at the address below. A more detailed map is available for a fee from Tom Harrison Cartography at (415) 456-7940 or Trails Illustrated at (800) 962-1643. To obtain a topographic map of the area, ask for Mineral King from the USGS.

Contact: Sequoia and Kings Canyon National Parks, Three Rivers, CA 93271-9700; (209) 565-3134 or fax (209) 565-3730.

Trail notes: You may not expect much from a campground nature trail, but the Cold Springs Nature Trail is guaranteed to exceed your expectations. Not only is it lined with wildflowers along the East Fork Kaweah River and informative signposts that teach you to identify junipers, red and white firs, cottonwoods, and aspens, but the views of the Sawtooth Ridge are glorious. The loop is less than a half mile, but from the far end of it, the trail continues along the East Fork Kaweah River, heading another mile into Mineral King Valley. Walk to the loop's far end and then continue at least another quarter mile along the trail. It just gets prettier as it goes. Here's the best Mineral King tip we know: Take this walk right before sunset, when the valley's surrounding mountain peaks turn every imaginable shade of pink, orange, and coral, reflecting the sun setting in the west. The vistas are so beautiful, they can practically make you weep.

❻ Farewell Gap Trail to Aspen Flat

2.0 mi/1.0 hr

Location: Off Highway 198 in the Mineral King region of Sequoia National Park; map G5, grid a2.

User groups: Hikers and horses. No dogs or mountain bikes. No wheelchair facilities.

Permits: No permits are required. There is a $10 entrance fee at Sequoia and Kings Canyon National Parks, good for seven days.

Directions: From Visalia, drive east on Highway 198 for 38 miles to Mineral King Road, 2.5 miles east of Three Rivers. (If you reach the Ash Mountain entrance station, you've gone too far.) Turn right on Mineral King Road and drive 25 miles to the end of the road and the Eagle/Mosquito Trailhead. (Take the right fork at the end of the road to reach the parking area.) Walk back out of the parking lot and follow the road to the pack station; the Farewell Gap Trail begins just beyond it.

Maps: Free park maps are available at park entrance stations or by contacting Sequoia and Kings Canyon National Parks at the address below. A more detailed map is available for a fee from Tom Harrison Cartography at (415) 456-7940 or Trails Illustrated at (800) 962-1643. To obtain a topographic map of the area, ask for Mineral King from the USGS.

Contact: Sequoia and Kings Canyon National Parks, Three Rivers, CA 93271-9700; (209) 565-3134 or fax (209) 565-3730.

Trail notes: If ever there were a perfect family hike, this would have to be it. Actually, if ever there were a perfect hike for every two-legged person on the planet, this would have to be it. The glacial-cut Mineral King Valley, a peaceful paradise of meadows, streams, and 100-year-old cabins, has to be one of the most scenic places in the West, possibly in the world. An easy stroll along the canyon floor leads you past waterfalls and along the headwaters of the East Fork Kaweah River, in the awesome shelter of thousand-foot cliffs. After walking to the trailhead near the pack station, you follow the Farewell Gap Trail (an old dirt road) for a mile, then cross Crystal Creek and take the right fork off the main trail. This brings you closer to the river, where you follow a narrow use trail to Aspen Flat, a lovely grove of trees, or to Soda Springs, situated right along the river's edge. There you can see mineral springs bubbling up from the ground, turning the earth around them a bright orange color. Bring a fishing rod on this trail if you like, but be absolutely certain to bring your camera.

➐ Mosquito Lake

7.2 mi/4.0 hrs or 2.0 days

Location: Off Highway 198 in the Mineral King region of Sequoia National Park; map G5, grid a2.

User groups: Hikers and horses. No dogs or mountain bikes. No wheelchair facilities.

Permits: There is a $10 entrance fee at Sequoia and Kings Canyon National Parks, good for seven days. A free wilderness permit is required for overnight stays. They are available on a first-come, first-served basis at the ranger station near your chosen trailhead, or in advance by mail or fax after March 1; for more information phone (209) 565-3708.

Directions: From Visalia, drive east on Highway 198 for 38 miles to Mineral King Road, 2.5 miles east of Three Rivers. (If you reach the Ash Mountain entrance station, you've gone too far.) Turn right on Mineral King Road and drive 25 miles to the end of the road and the Eagle/Mosquito Trailhead. (Take the right fork at the end of the road to reach the parking area.) The trail begins at the far end of the parking lot.

Maps: Free park maps are available at park entrance stations or by contacting Sequoia and Kings Canyon National Parks at the address below. A more detailed map is available for a fee from Tom Harrison Cartography at (415) 456-7940 or Trails Illustrated at (800) 962-1643. To obtain a topographic map of the area, ask for Mineral King from the USGS.

Contact: Sequoia and Kings Canyon National Parks, Three Rivers, CA 93271-9700; (209) 565-3134 or fax (209) 565-3730.

Trail notes: Ah, paradise. You know you're in it as soon as you park your car at the end of Mineral King Road. The Eagle/Mosquito Trailhead is at 7,830 feet, and you set out from the parking lot near one of Mineral King's adorable cabins, left from early in the 20th century and privately owned. Feel jealous? Keep walking; you'll get over it. In minutes you cross a footbridge over Spring Creek's waterfall, called Tufa Falls because of the calcium carbonate in Spring Creek's water. The falls are well heard but not well seen from this trail. At one mile, reach the junction for Eagle Lake, the Mosquito Lakes, and White Chief, and take the right fork, climbing steadily all the way. At two miles, you reach the Mosquito Lakes junction and go right, leaving the Eagle Lake Trail for another day. Climb up and then down the other side of Miner's Ridge at 9,360 feet, and reach Mosquito Lake number 1 at 9,040 feet and 3.6 miles. This is the first of several Mosquito Lakes, all of which are linked by Mosquito Creek. Mosquito Lake number 1 is considered to be the easiest lake to reach in Mineral King (with only a 1,200-foot gain), but hikers with excess energy can follow the stream uphill to four more lakes. The climb from Lake number 1 to Lake number 2 is steep, but there is little elevation gain from Lake number 2 through Lake number 5. The first camp-sites are at Mosquito Lake number 2. Mosquito Lake number 5 is a total of five miles from the Eagle/Mosquito Trailhead. There is no maintained trail to the upper lakes, but the use trail along the creek is fairly easy to follow. The trout fishing improves at the upper lakes.

➑ Eagle Lake Trail

6.8 mi/4.0 hrs or 2.0 days

Location: Off Highway 198 in the Mineral King region of Sequoia National Park; map G5, grid a2.

User groups: Hikers and horses. No dogs or mountain bikes. No wheelchair facilities.

Permits: There is a $10 entrance fee at Sequoia and Kings Canyon National Parks, good for seven days. A free wilderness permit is required for overnight stays. They are available on a first-come, first-served basis at the ranger station near your chosen trailhead, or in advance by mail or fax after March 1; for more information phone (209) 565-3708.

Directions: From Visalia, drive east on Highway 198 for 38 miles to Mineral King Road, 2.5 miles east of Three Rivers. (If you reach the Ash Mountain entrance station, you've gone too far.) Turn right on Mineral King Road and drive 25 miles to the end of the road and the Eagle/Mosquito Trailhead. (Take the right fork at the end of the road to reach the parking area.) The trail begins at the far end of the parking lot.

Maps: Free park maps are available at park entrance stations or by contacting Sequoia and Kings Canyon National Parks at the address below. A more detailed map is available for a fee from Tom Harrison Cartography at (415) 456-7940 or Trails Illustrated at (800) 962-1643. To obtain a topographic map of the area, ask for Mineral King from the USGS.

Contact: Sequoia and Kings Canyon National Parks, Three Rivers, CA 93271-9700; (209) 565-3134 or fax (209) 565-3730.

Trail notes: Eagle Lake is the glamour destination in Mineral King, the trail to hike if you can only hike one trail in the area. Why? The blue-green lake is drop-dead gorgeous, that's why, and easy to reach for day hikers. The total elevation gain is only 2,200 feet. In addition, if you can stop staring at the scenery for a minute, you might even catch a fish or two. The Eagle Lake Trail is exactly the same route as the Mosquito Lake Trail (see trip notes for hike number 7) up until the two-mile point near the Eagle Sink Holes. These are noticeable holes in the ground where Eagle Creek suddenly goes underground. A trail junction follows the sink holes, and you go left (instead of bearing right for Mosquito Lake). You've got 1,000 feet to gain over 1.4 miles, and much of it is in an exposed, rocky area. Luckily there are plenty of well-graded switchbacks, and you arrive before you know it at Eagle Lake's dam. The big lake is surrounded by glacially carved rock, and the trail continues along the east side of it to many good picnicking spots and photo opportunities. Campsites are found near the lake.

❾ Franklin Lakes

10.8 mi/6.0 hrs or 2.0 days

Location: Off Highway 198 in the Mineral King region of Sequoia National Park; map G5, grid a2.

User groups: Hikers and horses. No dogs or mountain bikes. No wheelchair facilities.

Permits: There is a $10 entrance fee at Sequoia and Kings Canyon National Parks, good for seven days. A free wilderness permit is required for overnight stays. They are available on a first-come, first-served basis at the ranger station near your chosen trailhead, or in advance by mail or fax after March 1; for more information phone (209) 565-3708.

Directions: From Visalia, drive east on Highway 198 for 38 miles to Mineral King Road, 2.5 miles east of Three Rivers. (If you reach the Ash Mountain entrance station, you've gone too far.) Turn right on Mineral King Road and drive 25 miles to the end of the road and the Eagle/Mosquito Trailhead. (Take the right fork at the end of the road to reach the parking area.) Walk back out of the parking lot and follow the road to the pack station; the Farewell Gap Trail begins just beyond it.

Maps: Free park maps are available at park entrance stations or by contacting Sequoia and Kings Canyon National Parks at the address below. A more detailed map is available for a fee from Tom Harrison Cartography at (415) 456-7940 or Trails Illustrated at (800) 962-1643. To obtain a topographic map of the area, ask for Mineral King from the USGS.

Contact: Sequoia and Kings Canyon National Parks, Three Rivers, CA 93271-9700; (209) 565-3134 or fax (209) 565-3730.

Trail notes: Maybe the best thing about hiking to Franklin Lakes is the waterfalls you get to pass along the way, especially our favorite on Franklin Creek. Other than that, this trail is not much different from all the other trails in Mineral King Valley, which is the same as saying that it's incredibly awesome and spectacular and you'll want to visit again and again. The trail has only a 2,500-foot elevation gain over 5.4 miles. The first two miles are nearly flat, as the route winds along the bottom of Mineral King's canyon, following the Farewell Gap Trail alongside the East Fork Kaweah River. Pass Tufa Falls across the canyon at a quarter mile, then Crystal Creek Falls at one mile. The trail then leaves the valley floor and starts to climb moderately, till you reach Franklin Creek Falls at 1.7 miles. One switchbacked mile beyond the falls, the Franklin Lakes Trail forks left off the Farewell Gap Trail and starts climbing in earnest up the Franklin Creek Valley. At nearly 10,000 feet, the trail crosses Franklin Creek again (campsites are found here), then parallels the creek for another mile to the largest Franklin Lake. The lake is dammed and surrounded by steep slopes and a few pines and junipers. Rainbow Mountain is on its northeast side; Tulare Peak is to the south.

⑩ White Chief Mine Trail

5.8 mi/3.0 hrs

Location: Off Highway 198 in the Mineral King region of Sequoia National Park; map G5, grid a2.

User groups: Hikers and horses. No dogs or mountain bikes. No wheelchair facilities.

Permits: No permits are required. There is a $10 entrance fee at Sequoia and Kings Canyon National Parks, good for seven days.

Directions: From Visalia, drive east on Highway 198 for 38 miles to Mineral King Road, 2.5 miles east of Three Rivers. (If you reach the Ash Mountain entrance station, you've gone too far.) Turn right on Mineral King Road and drive 25 miles to the end of the road and the Eagle/Mosquito Trailhead. (Take the right fork at the end of the road to reach the parking area.) The trail begins from the far end of the parking lot.

Maps: Free park maps are available at park entrance stations or by contacting Sequoia and Kings Canyon National Parks at the address below. A more detailed map is available for a fee from Tom Harrison Cartography at (415) 456-7940 or Trails Illustrated at (800) 962-1643. To obtain a topographic map of the area, ask for Mineral King from the USGS.

Contact: Sequoia and Kings Canyon National Parks, Three Rivers, CA 93271-9700; (209) 565-3134 or fax (209) 565-3730.

Trail notes: If you're one of those liberated hikers who doesn't need to have an alpine lake in your itinerary to be happy, the trail to White Chief Bowl is a scenic route with much to offer. Since most hikers in Mineral King are heading for lakeside destinations, you can avoid some of the weekend crowds by hiking the White Chief Trail. The first mile of trail is the same as the route to Eagle and Mosquito Lakes, but you'll leave most everyone behind when you continue straight at the one-mile junction, while they bear right for the lakes (see trails number 7 and 8). The White Chief Trail continues on a steady grade to the ruins of Crabtree Cabin, where you can catch your breath as you examine what is reportedly the oldest remaining structure in Mineral King. The cabin belonged to the discoverer of the White Chief Mine in the 1870s. Next comes White Chief Meadows, filled with summer wildflowers in the wet areas around White Chief Creek. Cross the creek and continue gently upward along White Chief Bowl to White Chief Mine at 9,200 feet, which to this day is still private property within the national park. Although the route continues beyond the mine, it gets increasingly faint and climbs steeply over a rocky path, so turn around wherever you please and head back down the canyon.

⑪ Timber Gap Trail

4.0 mi/2.0 hrs

Location: Off Highway 198 in the Mineral King region of Sequoia National Park; map G5, grid a2.

User groups: Hikers and horses. No dogs or mountain bikes. No wheelchair facilities.

Permits: No permits are required. There is a $10 entrance fee at Sequoia and Kings Canyon National Parks, good for seven days.

Directions: From Visalia, drive east on Highway 198 for 38 miles to Mineral King Road, 2.5 miles east of Three Rivers. (If you reach the Ash Mountain entrance station, you've gone too far.) Turn right on Mineral King Road and drive 24.5 miles to the Sawtooth parking area, a half mile before the end of the road.

Maps: Free park maps are available at park entrance stations or by contacting Sequoia and Kings Canyon National Parks at the address below. A more detailed map is available for a fee from Tom Harrison Cartography at (415) 456-7940 or Trails Illustrated at (800) 962-1643. To obtain a topographic map of the area, ask for Mineral King from the USGS.

Contact: Sequoia and Kings Canyon National Parks, Three Rivers, CA 93271-9700; (209) 565-3134 or fax (209) 565-3730.

Trail notes: The first thing you need to know: If you don't like horses, you'd better find another trail to hike in Mineral King, because the Timber Gap Trail is popular with the folks at the pack station. If you don't mind some hooved companions, this is an excellent and interesting route, on which you can witness the mining history of Mineral King. The trail climbs steeply from the Sawtooth Trailhead on an old mining path along Monarch Creek, and forks in a quarter mile. Take the left fork for Timber Gap, which climbs through a dense fir forest and then opens out to switchbacks in a wide and treeless slope—the result of continual winter avalanches. The exposed slope is home to many mountain wildflowers. At two miles, the climb ends at Timber Gap, elevation 9,450 feet, a forested pass. The stumps you see among the red firs remain from early miners who cut down the trees to fuel their fires and support their mining tunnels. In addition to horses, expect to see many mule deer on this trail; the Mineral King Valley is full of them and they love to eat the young foliage along the hillsides.

⓬ Monarch Lakes

8.4 mi/5.0 hrs or 2.0 days

Location: Off Highway 198 in the Mineral King region of Sequoia National Park; map G5, grid a2.

User groups: Hikers and horses. No dogs or mountain bikes. No wheelchair facilities.

Permits: There is a $10 entrance fee at Sequoia and Kings Canyon National Parks, good for seven days. A free wilderness permit is required for overnight stays. They are available on a first-come, first-served basis at the ranger station near your chosen trailhead, or in advance by mail or fax after March 1; for more information phone (209) 565-3708.

Directions: From Visalia, drive east on Highway 198 for 38 miles to Mineral King Road, 2.5 miles east of Three Rivers. (If you reach the Ash Mountain entrance station, you've gone too far.) Turn right on Mineral King Road and drive 24.5 miles to the Sawtooth parking area, a half mile before the end of the road.

Maps: Free park maps are available at park entrance stations or by contacting Sequoia and Kings Canyon National Parks at the address below. A more detailed map is available for a fee from Tom Harrison Cartography at (415) 456-7940 or Trails Illustrated at (800) 962-1643. To obtain a topographic map of the area, ask for Mineral King from the USGS.

Contact: Sequoia and Kings Canyon National Parks, Three Rivers, CA 93271-9700; (209) 565-3134 or fax (209) 565-3730.

Trail notes: The Monarch Lakes Trail leads from the Sawtooth Trailhead at 8,000 feet in elevation and climbs 2,500 feet to the rocky, gemlike Monarch Lakes. Walk a quarter mile from the trailhead and take the right fork for Monarch and Crystal Lakes. After one steep mile, you'll reach Groundhog Meadow, named for the adorable yellow-bellied marmots that inhabit the area. (We like their blonde coats and shrill whistles.) Beyond the meadow, the trail starts switchbacking seriously in and out of red fir forest, then reaches barren Chihuahua Bowl at 3.2 miles (named for the Chihuahua Mine, not those little dogs) where the trail forks sharply right for Crystal Lake. Stay left for one more mile—a relatively smooth mile with the easiest grade of the whole route—to Lower Monarch Lake. Snow can often be found here even in late summer, and the vista is dramatic, with Sawtooth Peak dominating the skyline. If you have a wilderness permit and a backpacking stove, you can find a campsite near the lake. While the main trail continues north to Sawtooth Pass, a use trail leads south from the lower lake for a half mile to Upper Monarch Lake. The big surprise is that the upper lake has been dammed, like most of the lakes in Mineral King, and is operated by Southern California Edison. Still, it is wide, deep blue, and dramatic. Note: If you're backpacking and want to take a first-rate side trip, the trail to Sawtooth Pass is a 1.3-mile, 1,200-foot climb that's not easy, but Sawtooth Pass offers one of the best views in the Southern Sierra.

⓭ Crystal Lake Trail

9.8 mi/6.0 hrs or 2.0 days

Location: Off Highway 198 in the Mineral King region of Sequoia National Park; map G5, grid a2.

User groups: Hikers and horses. No dogs or mountain bikes. No wheelchair facilities.

Permits: There is a $10 entrance fee at Sequoia and Kings Canyon National Parks, good for seven days. A free wilderness permit is required for overnight stays. They are available on a first-come, first-served basis at the ranger station near your chosen trailhead, or in advance by mail or fax after March 1; for more information phone (209) 565-3708.

Directions: From Visalia, drive east on Highway 198 for 38 miles to Mineral King Road, 2.5 miles east of Three Rivers. (If you reach the Ash Mountain entrance station, you've gone too far.) Turn right on Mineral King Road and drive 24.5 miles to the Sawtooth parking area, a half mile before the end of the road.

Maps: Free park maps are available at park entrance stations or by contacting Sequoia and Kings Canyon National Parks at the address below. A more detailed map is available for a fee from Tom Harrison Cartography at (415) 456-7940 or Trails Illustrated at (800) 962-1643. To obtain a topographic map of the area, ask for Mineral King from the USGS.

Contact: Sequoia and Kings Canyon National Parks, Three Rivers, CA 93271-9700; (209) 565-3134 or fax (209) 565-3730.

Trail notes: The long and arduous path to Crystal Lake follows the same route as the trail to Monarch Lakes for the first 3.2 miles (see the trail notes for hike 12). There, in Chihuahua Bowl, a sharp right-hand turn puts you on the trail to Crystal Lake. In a half mile the trail leads past the ruins of the Chihuahua Mine on the right, one of Mineral King's last hopes for silver riches. Like the other mines in the area, it never produced ore to equal the miners' dreams. The trail climbs abruptly over a rocky slope to a ridge of reddish foxtail pines, where your vista opens wide. Far off you can see the Farewell Gap peaks, and down below you see the Cobalt Lakes and Crystal Creek, pouring down to the Mineral King Valley and the East Fork Kaweah River. The trail continues, following more switchbacks, to upper Crystal Creek and Crystal Lake, which has been dammed. Off to the left (north), Mineral Peak stands out at 11,500 feet, and to the right (south), Rainbow Mountain shows off its colorful rock. Views are spectacular in every direction. If you scramble a quarter mile off-trail toward Mineral Peak, you will reach Little Crystal Lake, where you have a near-guarantee of solitude and a vista you won't forget.

⑭ Black Wolf Falls

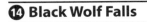 0.5 mi/0.5 hr

Location: Off Highway 198 in the Mineral King region of Sequoia National Park; map G5, grid a2.

User groups: Hikers only. No dogs, horses, or mountain bikes. No wheelchair facilities.

Permits: No permits are required. There is a $10 entrance fee at Sequoia and Kings Canyon National Parks, good for seven days.

Directions: From Visalia, drive east on Highway 198 for 38 miles to Mineral King Road, 2.5 miles east of Three Rivers. (If you reach the Ash Mountain entrance station, you've gone too far.) Turn right on Mineral King Road and drive 24.5 miles to the Sawtooth parking area, a half mile before the end of the road. Walk up the road toward Black Wolf Falls, then look for a use trail across the road from the "No Parking Any Time" sign, just beyond where Monarch Creek flows under the road.

Maps: Free park maps are available at park entrance stations or by contacting Sequoia and Kings Canyon National Parks at the address below. A more detailed map is available for a fee from Tom Harrison Cartography at (415) 456-7940 or Trails Illustrated at (800) 962-1643. To obtain a topographic map of the area, ask for Mineral King from the USGS.

Contact: Sequoia and Kings Canyon National Parks, Three Rivers, CA 93271-9700; (209) 565-3134 or fax (209) 565-3730.

Trail notes: This hike is really just a stroll, and the destination is readily apparent from the Sawtooth Trailhead: Black Wolf Falls, tumbling down the canyon wall in Mineral King Valley. But aside from the chance to get close to a pretty waterfall, the hike is interesting because of its historical significance. Black Wolf's name is actually an alteration of its original moniker, which was Black Wall Falls, named for the Black Wall copper mine that was located at the waterfall's base. Back in the 1870s, when miners believed that Mineral King was rich in more than just scenery, they mined the base of Monarch Creek with a modicum of success. Today you can walk right up to the falls and see the mine tunnel on its right side (it looks like a cave, but don't go inside; it's unstable). In summer, rangers lead group hikes to the waterfall and talk about Mineral King's mining history. Although the route to Black Wolf Falls isn't an official trail, the path is well used and clearly visible. If you can find its beginning across the road from the "No Parking Any Time" sign, the rest of the hike is easy.

⑮ Cottonwood Lakes

10.0 mi/6.0 hrs or 2.0 days

Location: In the John Muir Wilderness south of Mount Whitney; map G5, grid a7.

User groups: Hikers, dogs, and horses. No mountain bikes. No wheelchair facilities.

Permits: No day-hiking permits are required. A free wilderness permit is required for overnight stays; they are available from the Lone Pine Ranger Station. Quotas are in effect from the last Friday in June to September 15; permits are available in advance by mail, phone, or fax for this period for a $3 fee. Mail permit requests to Wilderness Reservations, P.O. Box 430, Big Pine, CA 93513. Phone (888) 374-3773 or fax (760) 938-1137.

Directions: From Lone Pine on U.S. 395, drive west on Whitney Portal Road for 3.3 miles and turn left (south) on Horseshoe Meadow Road. Continue 19.5 miles and bear right for the Cottonwood Lakes Trailhead parking area, near the end of Horseshoe Meadow Road.

Maps: For a map of Inyo National Forest, send $4 to USDA-Forest Service, 630 Sansome Street, San Francisco, CA 94111. To obtain a topographic map of the area, ask for Cirque Peak from the USGS.

Contact: Inyo National Forest, Mount Whitney Ranger District, P.O. Box 8, Lone Pine, CA 93545; (760) 876-6200 or fax (760) 876-6202.

Trail notes: Trailhead elevation is just over 10,000 feet here at Horseshoe Meadow, which makes this a wildly popular trailhead for climbing deeper into the backcountry of the John Muir Wilderness. With the trailhead situated so high, you get a jump on the ascent—your four wheels do the work instead of your two feet. An unusual feature of this hike is that it passes through two wilderness areas—first the Golden Trout Wilderness and then the John Muir Wilderness. Cottonwood Creek accompanies you for much of this trip, and the trail is a straightforward climb until 3.5 miles, where you reach a trail junction. Take your pick as to which way to go—the trail forms a loop around Cotton-

wood Lakes numbers 1, 2, and 3. If you just want to see the closest lake and then head back without making the loop, go left for Cottonwood Lake number 1, 1.5 miles from the junction. That will make your round-trip an even 10 miles. If you complete the whole loop, passing all three beautiful lakes, you'll travel 11.5 miles. (Lakes numbers 4 and 5 are located a half mile beyond the far end of the loop, if you want to see even more.) Total elevation gain is only 1,000 feet. Once at the lakes, there are a few things to remember: 1) Special fishing regulations are in effect, so get updated on the latest rules. 2) No wood fires are allowed, so bring your backpacking stove. 3) The wildflowers are spectacular, but the mosquitoes are voracious. Come prepared.

⑯ Cottonwood Pass

8.0 mi/5.0 hrs

Location: In the Golden Trout Wilderness; map G5, grid a7.

User groups: Hikers, dogs, and horses. No mountain bikes. No wheelchair facilities.

Permits: No day-hiking permits are required. A free wilderness permit is required for overnight stays; they are available from the Lone Pine Ranger Station. Quotas are in effect from the last Friday in June to September 15; permits are available in advance by mail, phone, or fax for this period for a $3 fee. Mail permit requests to Wilderness Reservations, P.O. Box 430, Big Pine, CA 93513. Phone (888) 374-3773 or fax (760) 938-1137.

Directions: From Lone Pine on U.S. 395, drive west on Whitney Portal Road for 3.3 miles and turn left (south) on Horseshoe Meadow Road. Continue 19.5 miles to the Horseshoe Meadow Trailhead on the left, at the end of Horseshoe Meadow Road.

Maps: For a map of Inyo National Forest or Golden Trout Wilderness, send $4 to USDA-Forest Service, 630 Sansome Street, San Francisco, CA 94111. To obtain a topographic map of the area, ask for Cirque Peak from the USGS.

Contact: Inyo National Forest, Mount Whitney Ranger District, P.O. Box 8, Lone Pine, CA 93545; (760) 876-6200 or fax (760) 876-6202.

Trail notes: The Cottonwood Pass Trail provides access to the Pacific Crest Trail and the Kern Plateau, a land of stark, subalpine meadows. You're entering the Golden Trout Wilderness, home of California's state fish, located at the very south end of the Sierra Nevada. This is where the steep, nearly perpendicular mountains start to mellow out into more gentle terrain, mostly in the form of rolling high-country hills and meadows. Start from wide Horseshoe Meadow and climb gently through forest for the first two miles of trail. After that, the switchbacks begin, and the views open up. After an 1,100-foot climb, you reach the pass at four miles, where you can gaze out at the Great Western Divide, Big Whitney Meadows, and the Inyo Mountains. Bring a jacket with you for the windy, 11,200-foot summit. Ambitious hikers can continue beyond the pass and take the right fork for Chicken Spring Lake, a half mile away on the Pacific Crest Trail (no campfires allowed).

⑰ Trail Pass

5.0 mi/3.0 hrs

Location: In Inyo National Forest; map G5, grid a7.

User groups: Hikers, dogs, and horses. No mountain bikes. No wheelchair facilities.

Permits: No day-hiking permits are required. A free wilderness permit is required for overnight stays; they are available from the Lone Pine Ranger Station. Quotas are in effect from the last Friday in June to September 15; permits are available in advance by mail, phone, or fax for this period for a $3 fee. Mail permit requests to Wilderness Reservations, P.O. Box 430, Big Pine, CA 93513. Phone (888) 374-3773 or fax (760) 938-1137.

Directions: From Lone Pine on U.S. 395, drive west on Whitney Portal Road for 3.3 miles and turn left (south) on Horseshoe Meadow Road. Continue 19.5 miles to the Horseshoe Meadow Trailhead on the right, at the end of Horseshoe Meadow Road.

Maps: For a map of Inyo National Forest, send $4 to USDA-Forest Service, 630 Sansome Street, San Francisco, CA 94111. To obtain a topographic map of the area, ask for Cirque Peak from the USGS.

Contact: Inyo National Forest, Mount Whitney Ranger District, P.O. Box 8, Lone Pine, CA 93545; (760) 876-6200 or fax (760) 876-6202.

Trail notes: Trail Pass may not be as spectacular as the other trails at Horseshoe Meadow, but it's got two things going for it—far less people and an easier grade. It's only five miles round-trip from the trailhead to the pass, with a mere 500-foot elevation gain, unheard of in these parts. The main folks using the trail are backpackers accessing the Pacific Crest Trail and Golden Trout Wilderness, so a lot of the time you can have this gently rolling, high-country terrain all to yourself. Follow the trail from the parking area to a junction a quarter mile in, then bear left. In another half mile the trail forks, and you bear right for Trail Pass. Pass by Horseshoe Meadow and Round Valley, where you'll have the company of many pack horses, who enjoy subalpine meadows as much as people do. Views are good of Mount Langley and Cirque Peak. The pass is situated at 10,500 feet, just below Trail Peak at 11,600 feet.

⑱ Balch Park Nature Trail

1.0 mi/0.5 hr

Location: In Mountain Home Demonstration State Forest, off Highway 190 near Springville; map G5, grid c0.

User groups: Hikers, dogs, and horses. No mountain bikes. No wheelchair facilities.

Permits: No permits are required. Parking and access are free.

Directions: From Porterville, drive east on Highway 190 for 18 miles to Springville. At Springville, turn left (north) on Balch Park Road/Road 239 and drive 3.5 miles, then turn right on Bear Creek Road/Road 220. Drive 14 miles to Mountain Home Demonstration State Forest Headquarters, pick up a free park map, then continue 1.5 miles further to the entrance to Balch Park and the nature trail.

Maps: A free map/brochure of Mountain Home Demonstration State Forest is available from park headquarters. To obtain a topographic map of the area, ask for Camp Wishon from the USGS.

Contact: Tulare County Parks and Recreation Department at (209) 733-6612, or Mountain

Home Demonstration State Forest, P.O. Box 517, Springville, CA 93265; (209) 539-2321 (summer) or (209) 539-2855 (winter).

Trail notes: Balch Park is the small county-run park within the borders of Mountain Home Demonstration State Park, and its easy, one-mile nature trail is a great place to take your kids for the afternoon. The trail begins next to the main entrance to Balch Park Camp, across from the museum, and your first stop is a visit to the Hollow Log, which was used as a dwelling by various pioneers, Indians, and prospectors. You also get to see the Lady Alice Tree, which was incorrectly billed in the early 1900s as the largest tree in the world. Nonetheless, it's no slacker in the size department. Continuing along the route, you'll see and learn all about dogwoods, bracken ferns, manzanita, and gooseberry. When you're finished hiking the nature trail, you can cross the road and throw a line into one of Balch Park's two small fishing ponds, which are stocked weekly.

⑲ Adam and Eve Loop Trail

2.0 mi/1.0 hr

Location: In Mountain Home Demonstration State Forest, off Highway 190 near Springville; map G5, grid c0.

User groups: Hikers, dogs, and horses. No mountain bikes. No wheelchair facilities.

Permits: No permits are required. Parking and access are free.

Directions: From Porterville, drive east on Highway 190 for 18 miles to Springville. At Springville, turn left (north) on Balch Park Road/Road 239 and drive 3.5 miles, then turn right on Bear Creek Road/Road 220. Drive 14 miles to Mountain Home Demonstration State Forest Headquarters, pick up a free park map, then continue one mile further and turn right at the sign for Hidden Falls Recreation Area. Drive three miles, to just past the pack station and before Shake Camp Campground, to the trailhead for the Adam and Eve Loop Trail on the left.

Maps: A free map/brochure of Mountain Home Demonstration State Forest is available from park headquarters. To obtain a topographic map of the area, ask for Camp Wishon from the USGS.

Contact: Mountain Home Demonstration State Forest, P.O. Box 517, Springville, CA 93265; (209) 539-2321 (summer) or (209) 539-2855 (winter).

Trail notes: On the Adam and Eve Loop Trail, you can see the Adam Tree standing tall and proud, but its companion the Eve Tree is no longer thriving. It (she?) was axed during the infamous Sequoia logging years, and it's strangely touching to see the gaping slash in her side. Begin your trip by taking the left side of the loop, heading uphill to the Adam Tree, the second largest tree in this state forest at 240 feet tall and 27 feet in diameter. The Eve Tree is shortly after. The big draw on the trail is visiting the "Indian bathtubs" at Tub Flat halfway around the loop—basins formed in solid granite that were probably used by Native Americans. No one is sure if they are man-made or geology-made. The basins are much larger than the traditional Indian grinding holes that are found elsewhere in the Sierra; they are truly large enough to take a bath in.

⑳ Redwood Crossing

4.0 mi/2.0 hrs

Location: In Mountain Home Demonstration State Forest, off Highway 190 near Springville; map G5, grid c0.

User groups: Hikers, dogs, and horses. No mountain bikes. No wheelchair facilities.

Permits: No permits are required. Parking and access are free.

Directions: From Porterville, drive east on Highway 190 for 18 miles to Springville. At Springville, turn left (north) on Balch Park Road/Road 239 and drive 3.5 miles, then turn right on Bear Creek Road/Road 220. Drive 14 miles to Mountain Home Demonstration State Forest Headquarters, pick up a free park map, then continue one mile further and turn right at the sign for Hidden Falls Recreation Area. Drive 3.5 miles to Shake Camp Campground. The Long Meadow Trailhead is located by the public corral.

Maps: A free map/brochure of Mountain Home Demonstration State Forest is available from park headquarters. To obtain a topographic map of the area, ask for Camp Wishon from the USGS.

Contact: Mountain Home Demonstration State Forest, P.O. Box 517, Springville, CA 93265; (209) 539-2321 (summer) or (209) 539-2855 (winter).

Trail notes: An excellent easy hike for campers and day visitors at Mountain Home Demonstration State Forest is the Long Meadow Trail from Shake Camp Campground to Redwood Crossing on the Tule River. The trail starts by the public corral at elevation 6,800 feet, and leads through logged Sequoia stumps to a thick mixed forest on the slopes high above the Wishon Fork Tule River. When the trail reaches clearings in the trees, views are excellent of the Great Western Divide. At two miles out, you reach Redwood Crossing, a boulder-lined stretch of the river. Those willing to ford can cross to the other side and head into the Golden Trout Wilderness, but day hikers should pull out a picnic at the river's edge and make an afternoon of it. (Overnighters heading for the wilderness need to secure a wilderness permit from the Tule River Ranger District office.)

㉑ Moses Gulch Trail

4.0 mi/2.0 hrs

Location: In Mountain Home Demonstration State Forest, off Highway 190 near Springville; map G5, grid c0.

User groups: Hikers, dogs, and horses. No mountain bikes. No wheelchair facilities.

Permits: No permits are required. Parking and access are free.

Directions: From Porterville, drive east on Highway 190 for 18 miles to Springville. At Springville, turn left (north) on Balch Park Road/Road 239 and drive 3.5 miles, then turn right on Bear Creek Road/Road 220. Drive 14 miles to Mountain Home Demonstration State Forest Headquarters, pick up a free park map, then continue one mile further and turn right at the sign for Hidden Falls Recreation Area. Drive 3.5 miles to Shake Camp Campground. The Moses Gulch Trailhead is located by the public corral.

Maps: A free map/brochure of Mountain Home Demonstration State Forest is available from park headquarters. To obtain a topographic map of the area, ask for Camp Wishon from the USGS.

Contact: Mountain Home Demonstration State Forest, P.O. Box 517, Springville, CA 93265; (209) 539-2321 (summer) or (209) 539-2855 (winter).

Trail notes: For a less-crowded alternate to the popular Redwood Crossing Trail, you can take the "other" trail from the public corral at Shake Flat Campground and wind your way through stands of beautiful virgin Sequoias to the Wishon Fork Tule River at Moses Gulch Campground. The Moses Gulch Trail crosses park roads twice—the only downer—but it's an easy walk for families, and peaceful besides. Once you reach the river at two miles, you have the option of hiking alongside it to the north or south, adding some distance to your trip. The northern stretch leads to Hidden Falls Campground, home of many small falls and pools, and the southern stretch crosses pretty Galena and Silver Creeks and leads past a mining cabin and an old copper mine.

㉒ Doyle Trail

6.0 mi/3.0 hrs

Location: In Sequoia National Forest near Springville; map G5, grid d0.

User groups: Hikers, dogs, horses, and mountain bikes. No wheelchair facilities.

Permits: No permits are required. Parking and access are free.

Directions: From Porterville, drive east on Highway 190 for 18 miles to Springville. From Springville, continue east on Highway 190 for 7.5 miles to Wishon Drive (Road 208), a left fork. Turn left and drive four miles on Wishon Drive, then take the left fork which is signed for day-use parking (above the campground). Drive a quarter mile and park off the road, near the gate.

Maps: For a map of Sequoia National Forest, send $4 to USDA-Forest Service, 630 Sansome Street, San Francisco, CA 94111. To obtain a topographic map of the area, ask for Camp Wishon from the USGS.

Contact: Sequoia National Forest, Tule River Ranger District, 32588 Highway 190, Springville, CA 93265; (209) 539-2607 or fax (209) 539-2067.

Trail notes: The Doyle Trail is a great alternative to the heat of the Springville and Porterville Valleys. It's in the transition zone between foothills and conifers, with plenty of shade from tall manzanita, oaks, madrones, and pines. Squirrels and lizards are your primary companions on the trail, which laterals along the slopes above the Wishon Fork of the Tule River. From the gated trailhead, hike up the paved road, then bear left to bypass Doyle Springs, a community of private cabins. Follow the trail that is signed as "Trail to Upstream Fishing." The route climbs gently through the forest for 2.5 miles, then suddenly descends to the same level as the river, where there are some primitive campsites available. Then the trail rises again, climbing for another half mile to a clearing on the right, where there is an outcrop of jagged green rock alongside the river. Leave the trail and cross over the rock, where you'll find a few picture-perfect swimming holes and small waterfalls.

㉓ Amos Alonzo Stagg Tree

0.5 mi/0.5 hr

Location: In Sequoia National Forest near Camp Nelson; map G5, grid d2.

User groups: Hikers, dogs, horses, and mountain bikes. No wheelchair facilities.

Permits: No permits are required. Parking and access are free.

Directions: From Porterville, drive 36 miles east on Highway 190 to 2.5 miles past Camp Nelson, and turn left on Redwood Drive. Follow Redwood Drive for about five miles as it turns into Alder Drive (dirt). Follow Alder Drive to the signed parking area for the Stagg Tree. Then hike down the dirt road.

Maps: For a map of Sequoia National Forest, send $4 to USDA-Forest Service, 630 Sansome Street, San Francisco, CA 94111. To obtain a topographic map of the area, ask for Camp Nelson from the USGS.

Contact: Sequoia National Forest, Tule River Ranger District, 32588 Highway 190, Springville, CA 93265; (209) 539-2607 or fax (209) 539-2067.

Trail notes: Can you name the six largest giant Sequoias in the world, and their general locations? Number one is the General Sherman Tree in Sequoia National Park. Number two is the Washington Tree in Sequoia National Park. Number three is the General Grant Tree in Kings Canyon National Park. Number four is the President Tree in Sequoia National Park. Number five is the Lincoln Tree in Sequoia National Park. And number six is the Stagg Tree in Sequoia National Forest, the largest tree outside of Sequoia and Kings

Canyon National Parks, and the largest Sequoia in the world that is under private ownership. The owner is a nice person and lets people come see his tree, via an easy half-mile hike. The Stagg Tree is 243 feet tall and 29 feet in diameter at its base, which is only about four-fifths the size of the number one tree, the General Sherman. Here's something to ponder: The Stagg Tree weighs about 2.5 million pounds.

㉔ Jordan Peak Lookout

1.8 mi/1.0 hr

Location: In Sequoia National Forest near Quaking Aspen; map G5, grid d2.

User groups: Hikers, dogs, horses, and mountain bikes. No wheelchair facilities.

Permits: No permits are required. Parking and access are free.

Directions: From Porterville, drive 45 miles east on Highway 190 to Forest Service Road 21S50 near Quaking Aspen Campground. Turn left on Road 21S50 and drive five miles, then bear left and continue on Road 21S50 for 2.8 miles, then bear left on Road 20S71, signed for Jordan Peak Lookout, and follow it one mile to its end at the trailhead.

Maps: For a map of Sequoia National Forest, send $4 to USDA-Forest Service, 630 Sansome Street, San Francisco, CA 94111. To obtain a topographic map of the area, ask for Sentinel Peak from the USGS.

Contact: Sequoia National Forest, Tule River Ranger District, 32588 Highway 190, Springville, CA 93265; (209) 539-2607 or fax (209) 539-2067.

Trail notes: You'll see some logging activity out here by Jordan Peak, but if you can put up with it, you can climb a mere 600 feet over less than a mile to reach the summit of this 9,100-foot mountain. Few summits are so easily attained (it's a well-graded and well-maintained trail), and this one is not lacking in dramatic vistas. You can see the Wishon Fork Canyon of the Tule River, Camp Nelson, the Sequoia Crest, and Slate Mountain, Maggie Mountain, and Moses Mountain close up, and the Tehachapis and the Coast Range far, far away. The peak is covered with microwave equipment, but it doesn't mar the stupendous view. Head west from the trailhead on the Jordan Lookout Trail, switchbacking up until you reach the catwalked stairs to the lookout, which was built in 1934.

㉕ Clicks Creek Trail

14.0 mi/2.0 days

Location: In the Golden Trout Wilderness near Quaking Aspen; map G5, grid d2.

User groups: Hikers, dogs, and horses. No mountain bikes. No wheelchair facilities.

Permits: A free wilderness permit is required for overnight stays; they are available from the Springville or Kernville ranger stations. Parking and access are free.

Directions: From Porterville, drive 45 miles east on Highway 190 to Forest Service Road 21S50 near Quaking Aspen Campground. Turn left on Road 21S50 and drive five miles, then bear left and continue on Road 21S50 for 1.5 miles to the Clicks Creek Trailhead at Log Cabin Meadow.

Maps: For a map of Sequoia National Forest or Golden Trout Wilderness, send $4 to USDA-Forest Service, 630 Sansome Street, San Francisco, CA 94111. To obtain a topographic map of the area, ask for Sentinel Peak from the USGS.

Contact: Sequoia National Forest, Tule River Ranger District, 32588 Highway 190, Springville, CA 93265; (209) 539-2607 or fax (209) 539-2067.

Trail notes: If you like peace and quiet on your backpacking trips, the Clicks Creek Trail in the Golden Trout Wilderness may suit you just fine. The trail leads northeast from Log Cabin Meadow (elevation 7,800 feet), heading steadily downhill along Clicks Creek to the Little Kern River. The route crosses the creek several times. Shade lovers will thrill at the conifer forests that line the route, interspersed by large and grassy meadows, and anglers can bring along their gear to try their luck with the golden trout in the river. There are many possible campsites along the Little Kern, where the elevation is 6,200 feet.

㉖ John Jordan/Hossack Meadow Trail

5.0 mi/2.5 hrs

Location: In Sequoia National Forest near Quaking Aspen; map G5, grid d2.

User groups: Hikers, dogs, horses, and mountain bikes. No wheelchair facilities.

Permits: No permits are required. Parking and access are free.

Directions: From Porterville, drive 45 miles east on Highway 190 to Forest Service Road 21S50 near Quaking Aspen Campground. Turn left on Road 21S50 and drive 6.6 miles, then bear left on Road 20S81. Follow Road 20S81 for 1.4 miles to the signed trailhead.

Maps: For a map of Sequoia National Forest, send $4 to USDA-Forest Service, 630 Sansome Street, San Francisco, CA 94111. To obtain a topographic map of the area, ask for Sentinel Peak from the USGS.

Contact: Sequoia National Forest, Tule River Ranger District, 32588 Highway 190, Springville, CA 93265; (209) 539-2607 or fax (209) 539-2067.

Trail notes: Your route on the John Jordan Trail begins with a crossing of McIntyre Creek, then traverses a level mile to an old fence and gate and McIntyre Rock, a huge pile of granite boulders with an excellent view. Climb on top of the rock's well-graded cracking granite back side and peer over its startlingly steep front side. Surprise—it's straight down about 600 feet. The trail then heads downhill through a red fir forest to Nelson Creek, the site of some logging work. Although you can walk another half mile to the trail's end at Hossack Meadow, most people turn around at the sight of logged trees, making for a five-mile round-trip with a 1,000-foot elevation gain on the return. So who was John Jordan, anyway? He was a trailblazer in the 1870s, who unfortunately was most famous for drowning in the Kern River on his way back to the Central Valley to tell everybody he had completed this trail, a proposed toll road.

㉗ Freeman Creek Trail

4.0 mi/2.0 hrs

Location: In Sequoia National Forest near Quaking Aspen; map G5, grid d2.

User groups: Hikers, dogs, horses, and mountain bikes. No wheelchair facilities.

Permits: No permits are required. Parking and access are free.

Directions: From Porterville, drive 45 miles

east on Highway 190 to Forest Service Road 21S50 near Quaking Aspen Campground. Turn left on Road 21S50 and drive a half mile, then turn right at the sign for the Freeman Creek Grove.

Maps: For a map of Sequoia National Forest, send $4 to USDA-Forest Service, 630 Sansome Street, San Francisco, CA 94111. To obtain a topographic map of the area, ask for Sentinel Peak from the USGS.

Contact: Sequoia National Forest, Tule River Ranger District, 32588 Highway 190, Springville, CA 93265; (209) 539-2607 or fax (209) 539-2067.

Trail notes: The easternmost grove of Sequoias in the world is your destination on the Freeman Creek Trail. Compared to most Sequoia groves in the Sierra, the trees of the 1,700-acre Freeman Creek Grove are mere adolescents—probably not more than 1,000 years old. Among them is a tree named for former President George Bush, who visited the grove in 1992. The trail is a pleasant downhill stroll along Freeman Creek, reaching the first Sequoias in about one mile, after crossing the creek. In between the big trees are large meadow areas, many of which bloom with spring and summer wildflowers, and forests of red firs. Many campsites are found along the creek. The path finally ends at Lloyd Meadows, three miles from the trailhead, but most people don't travel that far, since it requires too much climbing on the way back. Two miles out and back is just about perfect.

㉘ Summit Trail to Slate Mountain

8.0 mi/4.0 hrs

Location: In Sequoia National Forest near Quaking Aspen; map G5, grid d2.

User groups: Hikers, dogs, horses, and mountain bikes. No wheelchair facilities.

Permits: No permits are required. Parking and access are free.

Directions: From Porterville, drive 46 miles east on Highway 190 to Forest Service Road 21S78, which is a half mile south of Quaking Aspen Campground. Turn right on Road 21S78 and drive a half mile to the Summit Trailhead.

Maps: For a map of Sequoia National Forest, send $4 to USDA-Forest Service, 630 Sansome

Street, San Francisco, CA 94111. To obtain a topographic map of the area, ask for Sentinel Peak from the USGS.

Contact: Sequoia National Forest, Tule River Ranger District, 32588 Highway 190, Springville, CA 93265; (209) 539-2607 or fax (209) 539-2067.

Trail notes: If you're staying at Quaking Aspen Campground, you can set out on the Summit National Recreation Trail from outside your tent door, but if you're not, drive to the trailhead just south of the camp off Road 21S78. Few people hike all 12 miles of the trail, but many take this four-mile jaunt to the summit of 9,302-foot Slate Mountain, the highest peak in the area. The first two miles of trail are easy, climbing gently through meadows and forest (some logging activity can be seen), then the route climbs more steeply, ascending first the east side and then the north side of Slate Mountain. Views of the granite spires of the Needles and Olancha Peak can be seen. At 3.8 miles, you reach a junction with the Bear Creek Trail, and from there it's a short scramble to your left to the top of Slate Mountain, which is a big pile of rocks with a tremendous 360-degree view. There's no trail, but a couple well-worn routes are visible.

㉙ Needles Lookout

5.0 mi/2.5 hrs

Location: In Sequoia National Forest near Quaking Aspen; map G5, grid d2.

User groups: Hikers, dogs, horses, and mountain bikes. No wheelchair facilities.

Permits: No permits are required. Parking and access are free.

Directions: From Porterville, drive 46 miles east on Highway 190 to Forest Service Road 21S05, which is a half mile south of Quaking Aspen Campground. Turn left (east) on Road 21S05 and drive 2.8 miles to the trailhead.

Maps: For a map of Sequoia National Forest, send $4 to USDA-Forest Service, 630 Sansome Street, San Francisco, CA 94111. To obtain topographic maps of the area, ask for Sentinel Peak and Durrwood Creek from the USGS.

Contact: Sequoia National Forest, Tule River Ranger District, 32588 Highway 190, Springville, CA 93265; (209) 539-2607 or fax (209) 539-2067.

Trail notes: Here it is, the most perfect easy day hike in Sequoia National Forest. It's just long enough and with enough up and down to be challenging but not too physically demanding for beginning and intermediate hikers, and full of visual rewards. The trail starts with a placard bearing a great old black-and-white photo, which shows what the fire lookout on top of the Needles looked like earlier in this century. Five minutes down the trail you leave the forest and come out to two wooden benches, good places to stare out at the magnificent view of the Kern River Basin before you. If you look ahead, you get a glimpse of the fire lookout, perched in what looks like a precarious fashion on top of the Needles' tall granite spires. As you continue along the trail, you lose your view of it. The trail goes up, then down, then up again, undulating through firs, ponderosa and sugar pines, granite, and sand. The only steep section is the final set of switchbacks up the Needles, which lead to a series of stairs and catwalks that ascend to the lookout tower. When you reach the first catwalk, the rest is a cakewalk. A sign tells you if the tower is open and you may come up and visit. If it's closed, just climb up on any boulder to admire the view—it's just as fine from the base of the tower as it is from above. You look out over Lloyd Meadow and the western half of the Golden Trout Wilderness. This is a perfect place to take someone who needs to get inspired.

⑳ Casa Vieja Meadow

4.0 mi/2.0 hrs

Location: In the Golden Trout Wilderness; map G5, grid d6.

User groups: Hikers, dogs, and horses. No mountain bikes. No wheelchair facilities.

Permits: No permits are required for day hiking. Parking and access are free.

Directions: From Kernville on the north end of Lake Isabella, drive north on Sierra Way/Road 99 for 22 miles to the right turnoff for Sherman Pass Road (22S05). Turn right and drive approximately 35 miles on Sherman Pass Road to the Blackrock Information Station, then continue straight on Road 21S03, Blackrock Road. Follow Road 21S03 north for eight miles to the end of the road and the Blackrock Mountain Trailhead.

Maps: For a map of Sequoia National Forest, Inyo National Forest, or Golden Trout Wilderness, send $4 to USDA-Forest Service, 630 Sansome Street, San Francisco, CA 94111. To obtain a topographic map of the area, ask for Casa Vieja Meadows from the USGS.

Contact: Sequoia National Forest, Cannell Meadow Ranger District, P.O. Box 6, Kernville, CA 93238; (760) 376-3781 or fax (760) 376-3795. Or Inyo National Forest, Mount Whitney Ranger District, P.O. Box 8, Lone Pine, CA 93545; (760) 876-6200.

Trail notes: The Blackrock Mountain Trailhead at elevation 8,800 feet is the jump-off point for a variety of backpacking trips into the Golden Trout Wilderness. But day hikers can also sample the delights of this large, waterway-filled land, the home of California's state fish, the golden trout. From the end of Blackrock Road, walk for less than a quarter mile to the wilderness boundary, then head gently downhill through a red fir forest to the western edge of Casa Vieja Meadow. There, you'll find a snow survey cabin and a wide expanse of grass and wildflowers. Hope your daypack is full of picnic supplies. At the far end of the meadow, you must ford Ninemile Creek to continue hiking further, so make this your turnaround point. (Some people try their luck fishing here.) You'll have a gradual 800-foot elevation gain on your return trip.

㉛ Jordan Hot Springs

12.0 mi/7.0 hrs or 2.0 days

Location: In the Golden Trout Wilderness; map G5, grid d6.

User groups: Hikers, dogs, and horses. No mountain bikes. No wheelchair facilities.

Permits: A free wilderness permit is required for overnight stays; they are available from the Cannell Meadow or Lone Pine Ranger Stations. Parking and access are free.

Directions: From Kernville on the north end of Lake Isabella, drive north on Sierra Way/Road 99 for 22 miles to the right turnoff for Sherman Pass Road (22S05). Turn right and drive approximately 35 miles on Sherman Pass Road to the Blackrock Information Station, then continue straight on Road 21S03, Blackrock Road. Follow

Road 21S03 north for eight miles to the end of the road and the Blackrock Mountain Trailhead.

Maps: For a map of Sequoia National Forest, Inyo National Forest, or Golden Trout Wilderness, send $4 to USDA-Forest Service, 630 Sansome Street, San Francisco, CA 94111. To obtain a topographic map of the area, ask for Casa Vieja Meadows from the USGS.

Contact: Sequoia National Forest, Cannell Meadow Ranger District, P.O. Box 6, Kernville, CA 93238; (760) 376-3781 or fax (760) 376-3795. Or Inyo National Forest, Mount Whitney Ranger District, P.O. Box 8, Lone Pine, CA 93545; (760) 876-6200.

Trail notes: You can do it in a day, if you're ambitious, or you can take a more leisurely two-day trip to Jordan Hot Springs, but however you do it, it's critical to remember that almost all the work is on the way home. The trail is a descent (sometimes knee-jarring) to the grounds of an old hot springs resort, which was closed when this area became part of the Golden Trout Wilderness. The original buildings still stand, and the hot springs are still hot, which is the reason that this is one of the most popular trips in the wilderness. From the trailhead, take the Blackrock Trail for two miles to Casa Vieja Meadow (see trail notes for hike number 30), then cross Ninemile Creek and turn left (west) on the Jordan Hot Springs Trail. Hike another three miles downhill along Ninemile Creek, crossing it a few times more. Once you reach the old resort, have a good soak and pull your energy together, because you've got a 2,600-foot gain on the return trip.

way. Drive 2.4 miles to the trailhead parking area on the right, just before Redwood Meadow Campground. Cross the road to begin the trail.

Maps: For a map of Sequoia National Forest, send $4 to USDA-Forest Service, 630 Sansome Street, San Francisco, CA 94111. To obtain a topographic map of the area, ask for Johnsondale from the USGS.

Contact: Sequoia National Forest, Hot Springs Ranger District, Route 4, Box 548, California Hot Springs, CA 93207; (805) 548-6503 or fax (805) 548-6236.

Trail notes: The Trail of 100 Giants is as good as, and maybe better than, most of the giant Sequoia trails in Sequoia and Kings Canyon National Parks. Trailhead elevation is 6,400 feet, and the trail is an easy and nearly flat loop that is suitable for wheelchairs, baby strollers, and marathon runners alike. The giant Sequoias are dense here, situated amid a mixed forest of cedars and pines. As you walk in from the parking lot across the road, the first Sequoia tree on your right is a doozy—probably the best one on the loop. Of all the Sequoia groves we've seen and admired, the Trail of 100 Giants grove stands out because it has an unusual amount of twins—two Sequoias that are growing tightly side by side in order to share resources. In fact, this grove even has one twin that rangers call a "sequedar," a Sequoia and a cedar that have grown together. If you're staying at Redwood Meadow Campground, you have your own entrance to this loop, so you don't have to drive down the road to the main trailhead and parking lot.

㉜ Trail of 100 Giants

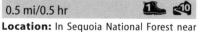
0.5 mi/0.5 hr

Location: In Sequoia National Forest near Johnsondale; map G5, grid e1.

User groups: Hikers, wheelchairs (with assistance), dogs, and horses. No mountain bikes.

Permits: No permits are required. Parking and access are free.

Directions: From Kernville on the north end of Lake Isabella, drive north on Sierra Way/Road 99 for 27 miles to Johnsondale R-Ranch. Continue west (the road becomes Road 50), then in 5.5 miles, turn right on the Western Divide High-

㉝ Mule Peak Lookout

1.2 mi/1.0 hr

Location: In Sequoia National Forest near Johnsondale; map G5, grid e1.

User groups: Hikers, dogs, horses, and mountain bikes. No wheelchair facilities.

Permits: No permits are required. Parking and access are free.

Directions: From Kernville on the north end of Lake Isabella, drive north on Sierra Way/Road 99 for 27 miles to Johnsondale R-Ranch. Continue west (the road becomes Road 50), then in 5.5 miles, turn right on the Western Divide Highway. Drive five miles to the left turnoff signed for Mule Peak, Road 22S03. Turn left and follow Road 22S03 for five miles to the Mule Peak Trailhead.

Maps: For a map of Sequoia National Forest, send $4 to USDA-Forest Service, 630 Sansome Street, San Francisco, CA 94111. To obtain a topographic map of the area, ask for Sentinel Peak from the USGS.

Contact: Sequoia National Forest, Hot Springs Ranger District, Route 4, Box 548, California Hot Springs, CA 93207; (805) 548-6503 or fax (805) 548-6236.

Trail notes: While rock climbers come to Mule Peak to do their daring work, hikers can take a not-so-daring walk up the back side of Mule Peak. The area around the peak has been logged, unfortunately, but growth is coming back with moderate success. The trail follows a series of easy switchbacks up the hillside, gaining 600 feet to the summit of Mule Peak, elevation 8,142 feet. A lookout tower is positioned there, still in operation by Sequoia National Forest, and views are excellent of Onion Meadow Peak, Table Mountain, and the Tule River Valley. We have friends who took their four-year-old on this hike; it's attainable for all ages and levels of hikers.

🕙 Nobe Young Falls

1.0 mi/1.0 hr

Location: In Sequoia National Forest near Johnsondale; map G5, grid e2.

User groups: Hikers, dogs, horses, and mountain bikes. No wheelchair facilities.

Permits: No permits are required. Parking and access are free.

Directions: From Kernville on the north end of Lake Isabella, drive north on Sierra Way/Road 99 for 27 miles to Johnsondale R-Ranch. Continue west (the road becomes Road 50), then in 5.5 miles, turn right on the Western Divide Highway. Drive eight miles to an unsigned parking pullout on the east (right) side of the road, and park there. (The pullout is exactly one mile north of the turnoff for Camp Whitsett and Lower Peppermint Camp, and a quarter mile south of the Crawford Road turnoff.)

Maps: For a map of Sequoia National Forest, send $4 to USDA-Forest Service, 630 Sansome

Street, San Francisco, CA 94111. To obtain a topographic map of the area, ask for Sentinel Peak from the USGS.

Contact: Sequoia National Forest, Hot Springs Ranger District, Route 4, Box 548, California Hot Springs, CA 93207; (805) 548-6503 or fax (805) 548-6236.

Trail notes: Nobe Young Falls is the secret waterfall of Sequoia National Forest, and now everyone is going to be mad at us for spilling the beans. There are no signs, no trail markers, and not even a trailhead to reach it. You need route-finding skills and some scrambling ability to visit the falls, but the rewards on the short path are definitely worth it. From the unmarked parking pullout, start hiking on the dirt road to your left. When it forks, bear right. Pass a makeshift camp as you draw close to Nobe Young Creek, which you will hear but not see. Listen carefully to its sound; in just a few minutes of walking beyond the trail fork, you should hear the pouring of a waterfall. Keep your eyes peeled on the left for spur trails leading down to the falls; there are several of them. Take any one and descend carefully down the steep and slippery dirt slope. When you reach the bottom, you're looking up at Nobe Young Falls, spilling and splashing 125 feet over three wide granite ledges. It's a great spot, with many small trout in the stream below the falls. Now don't go telling everybody.

🕙 Dome Rock

0.25 mi/0.5 hr

Location: In Sequoia National Forest near Quaking Aspen; map G5, grid e2.

User groups: Hikers, dogs, horses, and mountain bikes. No wheelchair facilities.

Permits: No permits are required. Parking and access are free.

Directions: From Kernville on the north end of Lake Isabella, drive north on Sierra Way/Road 99 for 27 miles to Johnsondale R-Ranch. Continue west (the road becomes Road 50), then in 5.5 miles, turn right on the Western Divide Highway. Drive 12 miles to the Dome Rock turnoff on the right (Road 21S69), across from Peppermint Work Center. Turn right and follow the dirt road for a few hundred yards; where it forks, bear left and continue to the trailhead, a half mile from the Western Divide Highway. (If you're traveling from the north, the turnoff is two miles south of Ponderosa Lodge.)

Maps: For a map of Sequoia National Forest, send $4 to USDA-Forest Service, 630 Sansome Street, San Francisco, CA 94111. To obtain a topographic map of the area, ask for Sentinel Peak from the USGS.

Contact: Sequoia National Forest, Tule River Ranger District, 32588 Highway 190, Springville, CA 93265; (209) 539-2607 or fax (209) 539-2067.

Trail notes: Dome Rock wins the prize for "Granite Dome with the Most Pedantic Name." But never mind. It also wins the prize for "Shortest Walk to an Incredible View." Trailhead elevation is 7,200 feet, and the trail is really just a route leading from the left side of the parking lot. Signs at the parking lot warn you not to drop or throw anything off the top of the dome, because there are rock climbers down below, on the dome's steep side. It's a mere five-minute walk to the top of Dome Rock, a huge cap of bare granite, where the views are incredible of Slate Mountain, Lake Isabella, and the Needles. If you look very carefully, you can just make out the fire lookout tower on top of the Needles. You'll want to hang around here for a while to ooh and aah. The only possible downer is if you show up during the few weeks of gnat season (the time varies from year to year), when little black flies hover around your face relentlessly. They don't bite, but they can be crazy-making.

⑥ Peppermint Creek Falls

0.25 mi/0.25 hr

Location: In Sequoia National Forest near Johnsondale; map G5, grid e2.

User groups: Hikers, dogs, horses, and mountain bikes. No wheelchair facilities.

Permits: No permits are required. Parking and access are free.

Directions: From Kernville on the north end of Lake Isabella, drive north on Sierra Way/Road 99 for 27 miles to Johnsondale R-Ranch. Turn right on Road 22S82 and drive 11.3 miles to Road 22S82F, signed for Camping Area 6. (It's on

the right, a quarter mile past Lower Peppermint Camp on the left.) Turn right on 22S82F, then drive three-quarters of a mile to a large clearing near the cliff edge.

Maps: For a map of Sequoia National Forest, send $4 to USDA-Forest Service, 630 Sansome Street, San Francisco, CA 94111. To obtain topographic maps of the area, ask for Sentinel Peak and Durrwood Creek from the USGS.

Contact: Sequoia National Forest, Hot Springs Ranger District, Route 4, Box 548, California Hot Springs, CA 93207; (805) 548-6503 or fax (805) 548-6236.

Trail notes: The trek to Peppermint Creek Falls is not so much a hike as a scramble, and should not be attempted by people who don't like climbing around on rough routes. However, if you watch your footing, it's a fairly easy descent to the base of the falls, and then a breathtaking climb back up the steep slope on your return. Since you park your car practically on top of the waterfall, you need only look over the cliff edge to spot the routes going down the side. Pick any one of the dirt trails, staying off the slippery granite as you descend. When you reach the bottom, you can watch Peppermint Creek plummeting 150 feet off the edge of a rounded granite dome, dropping into a wide pool that is deep enough for wading.

⑦ Alder Creek Trail

1.8 mi/1.0 hr

Location: In Sequoia National Forest near Johnsondale; map G5, grid e2.

User groups: Hikers and dogs. No horses or mountain bikes. No wheelchair facilities.

Permits: No permits are required. Parking and access are free.

Directions: From Kernville on the north end of Lake Isabella, drive north on Sierra Way/Road 99 for 27 miles to a half mile north of Johnsondale R-Ranch. Turn right on Road 22S82 and drive 5.7 miles to the day-use parking area on the right side of the road. Walk across Road 22S82 to the gated dirt road and the trailhead.

Maps: For a map of Sequoia National Forest, send $4 to USDA-Forest Service, 630 Sansome Street, San Francisco, CA 94111. To obtain a topographic map of the area, ask for Sentinel Peak from the USGS.

Contact: Sequoia National Forest, Hot Springs Ranger District, Route 4, Box 548, California Hot Springs, CA 93207; (805) 548-6503 or fax (805) 548-6236.

Trail notes: The granite slabs and pools on Alder Creek have gotten so popular with hikers, swimmers, and picnickers that the Forest Service has installed "No Parking Any Time" signs all over the road near the trailhead. But as long as you park where you're supposed to (off the road in the day-use parking area), you can still pay a visit to the tons-of-fun pools and slides along Alder Creek. To reach them, walk up the gated dirt road (Road 22S83), then turn right on the single-track trail. The path descends to the confluence of Alder Creek and Dry Meadow Creek, where there is a long length of swimming holes and rocky slides that pour into them. Make sure you wear denim or some other heavy material on your backside, so you can while away many happy hours pretending you are a river otter. It's exhilarating.

㊳ North Fork Kern River Trail

6.0 mi/3.0 hrs or 2.0 days

Location: In Sequoia National Forest north of Kernville; map G5, grid e3.

User groups: Hikers, dogs, and mountain bikes. No horses. No wheelchair facilities.

Permits: No permits are required. Parking and access are free.

Directions: From Kernville on the north end of Lake Isabella, drive north on Sierra Way/Road 99 for 22 miles to the Johnsondale highway bridge over the Kern River. Turn right and park in the large paved parking lot by the signboard at the bridge.

Maps: For a map of Sequoia National Forest, send $4 to USDA-Forest Service, 630 Sansome Street, San Francisco, CA 94111. To obtain a topographic map of the area, ask for Fairview from the USGS.

Contact: Sequoia National Forest, Cannell Meadow Ranger District, P.O. Box 6, Kernville, CA 93238; (760) 376-3781 or fax (760) 376-3795.

Trail notes: Sometimes you just want to walk alongside a beautiful river, and if that's what you're in the mood for, the Wild and Scenic North Fork Kern is a first-rate choice. From the giant parking lot, you walk across the hikers' bridge (separate from but next to the highway bridge) to reach the far side of the river, and then descend on stairsteps to reach the trail. The North Fork Kern River Trail winds along gently, heading deep into the dramatic Kern Canyon, sometimes under the shade of digger pines, live oaks, and incense cedars, and sometimes out in the bright sunshine. Spring wildflowers are stunning, especially in March and April. Spring river rafters are also entertaining to watch. Most people who walk this trail bring a fishing rod with them, and if you do, make sure you're up to date on the special fishing regulations. They're in effect for the first four miles of river, which is a wild trout area. Backpackers will find many campsites along the trail, even some that are under the cave-like canopy of big boulders.

㊴ Sherman Peak Trail

4.0 mi/2.0 hrs

Location: In Sequoia National Forest near Sherman Pass; map G5, grid e4.

User groups: Hikers, dogs, horses, and mountain bikes. No wheelchair facilities.

Permits: No permits are required. Parking and access are free.

Directions: From Kernville on the north end of Lake Isabella, drive north on Sierra Way/Road 99 for 22 miles to the right turnoff for Sherman Pass Road (22S05). Turn right and drive approximately 15 miles on Sherman Pass Road to the Sherman Pass Vista. The trailhead is across the road.

Maps: For a map of Sequoia National Forest, send $4 to USDA-Forest Service, 630 Sansome Street, San Francisco, CA 94111. To obtain topographic maps of the area, ask for Durrwood Creek and Sirretta Peak from the USGS.

Contact: Sequoia National Forest, Cannell Meadow Ranger District, P.O. Box 6, Kernville, CA 93238; (760) 376-3781 or fax (760) 376-3795.

Trail notes: From the Sherman Pass Vista along the highway, you can look to the north to Mount Whitney and the Great Western Divide.

After crossing the highway and hiking the Sherman Peak Trail to the top of Sherman Peak at 9,909 feet, you can pivot around and have a panoramic look at an even bigger chunk of the world. The trail is mostly forested with red firs and pines, and is gradual enough for children to climb. If you read the interpretive display at the Vista, you'll be able to identify the myriad of mountains you're looking at from the peak, including Split Rock and Dome Rock. It's only a 700-foot climb to the summit, mostly through a series of easy switchbacks.

⑩ Bald Mountain Lookout

0.25 mi/0.25 hr

Location: In Sequoia National Forest, on the north edge of the Dome Land Wilderness; map G5, grid e5.

User groups: Hikers, dogs, horses, and mountain bikes. No wheelchair facilities.

Permits: No permits are required. Parking and access are free.

Directions: From Kernville on the north end of Lake Isabella, drive north on Sierra Way/Road 99 for 22 miles to the right turnoff for Sherman Pass Road (22S05). Turn right and drive approximately 25 miles on Sherman Pass Road to Forest Service Road 22S77, signed for Bald Mountain Lookout. Turn east (right) on Road 22S77 and follow it for one mile to its end.

Maps: For a map of Sequoia National Forest, send $4 to USDA-Forest Service, 630 Sansome Street, San Francisco, CA 94111. To obtain a topographic map of the area, ask for Crag Peak from the USGS.

Contact: Sequoia National Forest, Cannell Meadow Ranger District, P.O. Box 6, Kernville, CA 93238; (760) 376-3781 or fax (760) 376-3795.

Trail notes: This short hike to the summit of 9,382-foot Bald Mountain is the easiest possible introduction to the Dome Land Wilderness. It's a brief stroll to the lookout, which is perched on the very northern edge of the wilderness. This wilderness region is famous for its many granite domes and monolithic rocks, the happy hunting ground of rock climbers from all over Southern California. Of the many big hunks of rock, Church Dome is perhaps the most outstanding,

and it can be seen from here, directly to the south. White Dome and Black Mountain are also visible, to the east of Church Dome, as well as a sweeping vista of the Kern Plateau, the Whitney Range, and the Great Western Divide.

⑪ Jackass Creek National Recreation Trail

5.0 mi/2.5 hrs

Location: In Sequoia National Forest near the South Sierra Wilderness; map G5, grid e6.

User groups: Hikers, dogs, horses, and mountain bikes. No wheelchair facilities.

Permits: No permits are required. Parking and access are free.

Directions: From Kernville on the north end of Lake Isabella, drive north on Sierra Way/Road 99 for 22 miles to the right turnoff for Sherman Pass Road (22S05). Turn right and drive approximately 35 miles on Sherman Pass Road to the four-way intersection with Road 21S03 near Blackrock Information Station. Turn right to continue on Road 22S05 and drive five miles to Fish Creek Campground and Road 21S01, where the trail begins.

Maps: For a map of Sequoia National Forest, send $4 to USDA-Forest Service, 630 Sansome Street, San Francisco, CA 94111. To obtain a topographic map of the area, ask for Crag Peak from the USGS.

Contact: Sequoia National Forest, Cannell Meadow Ranger District, P.O. Box 6, Kernville, CA 93238; (760) 376-3781 or fax (760) 376-3795.

Trail notes: The Jackass Creek Trail is way out there on the Kern Plateau. If you just want to be left alone, you have a decent chance of that here. The trailhead is at 8,000 feet, and the trail climbs 5.5 miles to Jackass Peak (elevation 9,245 feet), on the border of the South Sierra Wilderness. Most people don't bother traveling that far; instead they follow the trail along Jackass Creek for a couple of miles through red fir forest to the western edge of Jackass Meadow. In addition to the beautiful meadow, the trail offers a look at many handsome old-growth aspen trees. The trail is an old dirt road, wide enough for holding hands with your hiking partner. Our recommendation? Hike this trail in late September or early October, for the best of the golden aspen show.

㊷ Whiskey Flat Trail

5.0 mi/2.5 hrs

Location: In Sequoia National Forest near Fairview; map G5, grid f2.

User groups: Hikers, dogs, horses, and mountain bikes. No wheelchair facilities.

Permits: No permits are required. Parking and access are free.

Directions: From Kernville on the north end of Lake Isabella, drive north on Sierra Way/Road 99 for 17 miles to Fairview and the Fairview Lodge on the left side of the road. To the right of the lodge is a large parking area and a trailhead for the Whiskey Flat Trail.

Maps: For a map of Sequoia National Forest, send $4 to USDA-Forest Service, 630 Sansome Street, San Francisco, CA 94111. To obtain a topographic map of the area, ask for Fairview from the USGS.

Contact: Sequoia National Forest, Cannell Meadow Ranger District, P.O. Box 6, Kernville, CA 93238; (760) 376-3781 or fax (760) 376-3795.

Trail notes: The Whiskey Flat Trail is a 14.5-mile trail that parallels the Kern River from Fairview Lodge all the way south to Burlando Road in Kernville. Primarily used by anglers working the Kern River, it's also a good springtime stroll for river lovers. If you walk out and back for a few miles on the northern end of the trail by Fairview, you can end the day with a meal at Fairview Lodge's restaurant, where you can brag about the fish you did or didn't catch, like everybody else there. The Whiskey Flat Trail can be somewhat difficult to follow, especially in springtime when the numerous creeks you must cross are running full. (Early in the year, the creeks can sometimes be impassable.) The path begins on a suspension bridge, which is reminiscent of Huck Finn and his friends. You hike as far as you please; we suggest 2.5 miles, about an hour's walk each way. The terrain is grasslands and chaparral with occasional digger pines, which means no shade but plenty of spring wildflowers. Although the route is basically level, there are numerous steep stretches where you climb in and out of stream drainages running into the Kern. The trailhead elevation is 2,800 feet.

㊸ Packsaddle Cave Trail

4.6 mi/2.3 hrs

Location: In Sequoia National Forest near Fairview; map G5, grid f2.

User groups: Hikers, dogs, horses, and mountain bikes. No wheelchair facilities.

Permits: No permits are required. Parking and access are free.

Directions: From Kernville on the north end of Lake Isabella, drive north on Sierra Way/Road 99 for 18 miles to the Packsaddle Cave Trailhead on the right, a quarter mile beyond Fairview Campground. The parking area is across the road.

Maps: For a map of Sequoia National Forest, send $4 to USDA-Forest Service, 630 Sansome Street, San Francisco, CA 94111. To obtain a topographic map of the area, ask for Fairview from the USGS.

Contact: Sequoia National Forest, Cannell Meadow Ranger District, P.O. Box 6, Kernville, CA 93238; (760) 376-3781 or fax (760) 376-3795.

Trail notes: Everybody always enjoys the trip to Packsaddle Cave, even though the cave was long ago vandalized of its jewel-like stalactites and stalagmites. Nonetheless, the appeal of visiting the limestone cave keeps this trail well used and fairly well maintained. From the parking lot on Sierra Way, cross the highway and hike uphill on the path, huffing and puffing through some steep pitches. This is not a trail for summertime, because there is little shade among the manzanita, sagebrush, and deer brush, and the total climb is about 1,200 feet. At 1.8 miles, you cross Packsaddle Creek and see several campsites near it. Continue a short distance further; the cave is off to the left, a quarter mile before this trail's junction with the Rincon Trail. Don't forget your flashlight so you can take a peek inside.

㊹ Unal Trail

3.0 mi/1.5 hrs

Location: In Sequoia National Forest near Wofford Heights; map G5, grid g1.

User groups: Hikers, dogs, horses, and mountain bikes. No wheelchair facilities.

Permits: No permits are required. Parking and access are free.

Directions: From Wofford Heights on the west side of Lake Isabella, turn west on Highway 155 and drive eight miles to Greenhorn Summit. Turn left at the sign for Shirley Ski Meadows and drive 100 yards to the Greenhorn Fire Station and Unal Trailhead, on the right side of the road.

Maps: For a map of Sequoia National Forest, send $4 to USDA-Forest Service, 630 Sansome Street, San Francisco, CA 94111. To obtain a topographic map of the area, ask for Posey from the USGS.

Contact: Sequoia National Forest, Greenhorn Ranger District, c/o Lake Isabella Visitor Center, Lake Isabella, CA 93240; (760) 379-5646 or fax (760) 379-8597.

Trail notes: No doubt about it, this is a first-rate trail for families to hike, or for anybody who wants to have a good leg-stretching walk or run around a beautiful mountain. The Unal Trail is a three-mile loop which climbs gently for two miles to Unal Peak, then descends in one mile of switchbacks back down to the trailhead. (After the first 100 yards, where the trail forks, be sure you take the left fork and hike the trail clockwise.) The trail passes a Native American cultural site on the return of the loop, the homestead of the Tubatulabal Indians. With only a 700-foot climb and an excellent grade, even mountain bikers can manage this trail, although few bother with it. You'll likely see some deer on the hillsides, and the view from the top of Unal Peak makes the whole world seem peaceful and serene. Although most of the trail is lined with conifers, the top of the loop is a little exposed and catches a strong breeze.

---

④⑤ Sunday Peak Trail

3.4 mi/2.0 hrs

Location: In Sequoia National Forest near Wofford Heights; map G5, grid g1.

User groups: Hikers, dogs, horses, and mountain bikes. No wheelchair facilities.

Permits: No permits are required. Parking and access are free.

Directions: From Wofford Heights on the west side of Lake Isabella, turn west on Highway 155

and drive eight miles to Greenhorn Summit. Turn right on Road 24S15 (Forest Highway 90), signed for Portuguese Pass, and drive 6.5 miles north to the parking area for the Sunday Peak Trail, near the Girl Scout Camp.

Maps: For a map of Sequoia National Forest, send $4 to USDA-Forest Service, 630 Sansome Street, San Francisco, CA 94111. To obtain a topographic map of the area, ask for Posey from the USGS.

Contact: Sequoia National Forest, Greenhorn Ranger District, c/o Lake Isabella Visitor Center, Lake Isabella, CA 93240; (760) 379-5646 or fax (760) 379-8597.

Trail notes: From the Sunday Peak Trailhead at 7,200 feet in the Greenhorn Mountains, it's a 1,000-foot climb to the top of Sunday Peak, an excellent day hike for families. The grade is moderate and shaded by big conifers, and the destination is perfect on a day when the heat is sweltering down near Lake Isabella. From the top, you can look down at the Kern River Valley and feel sorry for all those people sweating it out down there. Although the peak's fire lookout tower was abandoned and then destroyed by the Forest Service in the 1950s, the wide-angle views remain—of the Kern Valley, Kern Plateau, and far-off high Sierra peaks. There are many good picnicking spots on the summit.

---

④⑥ Rincon Trail

4.0 mi/2.0 hrs

Location: In Sequoia National Forest near Fairview; map G5, grid g3.

User groups: Hikers, dogs, and mountain bikes. No horses. No wheelchair facilities.

Permits: No permits are required. Parking and access are free.

Directions: From Kernville on the north end of Lake Isabella, drive north on Sierra Way/Road 99 for 13 miles to the Rincon Trailhead on the right, across from the Ant Canyon dispersed camping area.

Maps: For a map of Sequoia National Forest, send $4 to USDA-Forest Service, 630 Sansome Street, San Francisco, CA 94111. To obtain a topographic map of the area, ask for Kernville from the USGS.

Contact: Sequoia National Forest, Cannell Meadow Ranger District, P.O. Box 6, Kernville, CA 93238; (760) 376-3781 or fax (760) 376-3795.

Trail notes: Let's say right away that this Rincon has absolutely nothing in common with the other Rincon, the classic surfing break on the Ventura coast. For one, there's no water here, and for two, there's no cool breeze. That means you should plan your hike for winter or spring, before the Kern Valley heats up. The trail leads first east and then steadily north along the Rincon Fault, heading for Forks of the Kern. It undulates up and down, in and out of the drainages of Salmon and other creeks. The destination on this trail is the long-distance view of Salmon Creek Falls, about two miles in, and the good fishing and camping prospects on the way along Salmon Creek. The trail crosses Salmon Creek on a bridge 1.7 miles in, but the waterfall view is about a quarter mile further. You might want to bring your binoculars to get a good look. (If you wish to hike further on the Rincon Trail, it intersects the route to Packsaddle Cave in another two miles, then crosses Sherman Pass Road in another 2.5 miles, and keeps going straight north all the way to Forks of the Kern. The total one-way trail length is a whopping 23 miles.)

47 Salmon Creek Falls

9.0 mi/5.0 hrs or 2.0 days

Location: In Sequoia National Forest near Big Meadow; map G5, grid g4.

User groups: Hikers, dogs, horses, and mountain bikes. No wheelchair facilities.

Permits: No permits are required. Parking and access are free.

Directions: From Kernville on the north end of Lake Isabella, drive north on Sierra Way/Road 99 for 22 miles to the right turnoff for Sherman Pass Road (22S05). Turn right and drive 6.1 miles on Sherman Pass Road, then turn right on Road 22S12, signed for Horse Meadow Campground. Drive 6.3 miles on Road 22S12 till you reach a fork; stay straight. At 8.0 miles, bear left. At 9.3 miles, turn right at the Horse Meadow Campground sign (Road 23S10). You'll reach the camp at 10.7 miles, but take the right turnoff just before the camp to reach the trailhead.

Maps: For a map of Sequoia National Forest, send $4 to USDA-Forest Service, 630 Sansome Street, San Francisco, CA 94111. To obtain topographic maps of the area, ask for Sirretta Peak and Fairview from the USGS.

Contact: Sequoia National Forest, Cannell Meadow Ranger District, P.O. Box 6, Kernville, CA 93238; (760) 376-3781 or fax (760) 376-3795.

Trail notes: The nine-mile round-trip to the brink of Salmon Creek Falls is a stellar walk through lodgepole pines and white fir, with a chance for fishing, skinny-dipping, and admiring a lot of beautiful scenery at 7,600 feet in elevation. Since there are campsites located along the trail, it's easy enough to turn the trip into an overnight excursion, but the trail also makes a good, long day hike. The trail is downhill all the way, dropping 600 feet over 4.5 miles, and follows granite-lined Salmon Creek. After skirting the edge of Horse Meadow, you simply follow the creek's meander. Trails run on both sides of the stream for the first two miles, so you can walk either side, but then they join as one. The path comes to an end above Salmon Creek Falls, where you can swim, fish, and camp, but don't expect to gaze out at the big waterfall—there's no way to get a good look at it from here, since you're perched on top of it.

48 Sirretta Peak

8.0 mi/5.0 hrs

Location: Near the Dome Land Wilderness; map G5, grid g4.

User groups: Hikers and dogs. No horses or mountain bikes. No wheelchair facilities.

Permits: No permits are required for day hiking. Parking and access are free.

Directions: From Kernville on the north end of Lake Isabella, drive north on Sierra Way/Road 99 for 22 miles to the right turnoff for Sherman Pass Road (22S05). Turn right and drive 6.1 miles on Sherman Pass Road, then turn right on Road 22S12, signed for Horse Meadow Campground. Drive 6.3 miles on Road 22S12 till you reach a fork; stay straight. At 8.0 miles, bear left, staying on Road 22S12. Continue four more miles, passing the Horse Meadow Campground turnoff, to Road 23S07 at the northern edge of Big

Meadow. Turn left on Road 23S07 and drive a half mile to the Cannell Trailhead.

Maps: For a map of Sequoia National Forest, send $4 to USDA-Forest Service, 630 Sansome Street, San Francisco, CA 94111. To obtain a topographic map of the area, ask for Sirretta Peak from the USGS.

Contact: Sequoia National Forest, Cannell Meadow Ranger District, P.O. Box 6, Kernville, CA 93238; (760) 376-3781 or fax (760) 376-3795.

Trail notes: Hey, what's that big meadow down there? It's Big Meadow, of course—that huge expanse of green you see from the top of Sirretta Peak. From Sirretta's summit, you get an eyeful of it, as well as long, lingering glances at the many granite domes of the Dome Land Wilderness Area, Sirretta and Deadwood Meadows, and the peaks of the High Sierra. The route to the peak starts at Big Meadow's northern edge, then travels north on the Cannell Trail for a half mile. Bear right (northeast) at the fork with the Sirretta Peak Trail and climb 2.5 miles to a spur trail which leads to the summit. There are many switchbacks and plenty of fine views along the way. Take the left spur (it's obvious) for a half mile to the rocky summit, then congratulate yourself on your fine mountaineering skills. The trail has an elevation gain of 1,200 feet, and if you decide to make the final summit climb, you'll add on another 700 feet. Sirretta Peak is just shy of 10,000 feet in elevation.

㊾ Manter Meadow Loop

10.0 mi/6.0 hrs

Location: In the Dome Land Wilderness; map G5, grid g4.

User groups: Hikers, dogs, and horses. No mountain bikes. No wheelchair facilities.

Permits: No permits are required for day hiking. Parking and access are free.

Directions: From Kernville on the north end of Lake Isabella, drive north on Sierra Way/Road 99 for 22 miles to the right turnoff for Sherman Pass Road (22S05). Turn right and drive 6.1 miles on Sherman Pass Road, then turn right on Road 22S12, signed for Horse Meadow Campground. Drive 6.3 miles on Road 22S12 till you reach a fork; stay straight. At 8.0 miles, bear left, stay-

ing on Road 22S12. Continue four more miles, passing the Horse Meadow Campground turn-off, to Road 23S07 at the northern edge of Big Meadow. Turn left on Road 23S07 and drive three miles to the southeast edge of Big Meadow and the South Manter Trailhead.

Maps: For a map of Sequoia National Forest, send $4 to USDA-Forest Service, 630 Sansome Street, San Francisco, CA 94111. To obtain a topographic map of the area, ask for Sirretta Peak from the USGS.

Contact: Sequoia National Forest, Cannell Meadow Ranger District, P.O. Box 6, Kernville, CA 93238; (760) 376-3781 or fax (760) 376-3795.

Trail notes: For people who love meadows, granite, and solitude, this loop trip is just about perfect. From the South Manter Trailhead at 7,800 feet, the trail goes uphill for four miles to Manter Meadow (bring your wildflower identification book and a map to identify surrounding peaks and domes). Along the way, several side trails branch off the main trail, leading to some of the granite domes of the Dome Land Wilderness, including spectacular Taylor Dome and Church Dome. A two-mile loop trail encircles the entire perimeter of the meadow, which you can add on to your trip if you wish. At the meadow's western edge, the South Manter Trail meets the North Manter Trail, and you follow the latter back to Forest Service Road 23S07 (the road you drove in on). Then it's a 1.5-mile walk on the dirt road back to your car. If you want to avoid the road, hike the South Manter Trail in both directions, and take the loop walk around the meadow. The mileage is about equal to the other trip.

㊿ Rockhouse Basin

4.0 mi/2.0 hrs

Location: On the eastern side of the Dome Land Wilderness; map G5, grid g6.

User groups: Hikers, dogs, and horses. No mountain bikes. No wheelchair facilities.

Permits: No permits are required for day hiking. Parking and access are free.

Directions: From the junction of Highway 14 and Highway 178 north of Mojave, drive west on Highway 178 for 18 miles to the right turnoff for Chimney Peak National Backcountry Byway, or Canebrake Road. Turn right and drive approximately nine miles. Turn left (west) on Long Valley Loop Road and drive 14 miles to the gate at the start of the Rockhouse Basin Trail. (You can also reach the trailhead by taking Ninemile Canyon Road west for 11 miles from the BLM administration site. Go past the BLM office, take the second dirt road on the left and drive eight miles to the trailhead. This road is much more rough.)

Maps: For a map of Sequoia National Forest, send $4 to USDA-Forest Service, 630 Sansome Street, San Francisco, CA 94111. To obtain a topographic map of the area, ask for Rockhouse Basin from the USGS.

Contact: Bureau of Land Management, Ridgecrest Resource Area, 300 South Richmond, Ridgecrest, CA 93555; (760) 384-5400 or fax (760) 384-5499. Or Sequoia National Forest, Cannell Meadow Ranger District, P.O. Box 6, Kernville, CA 93238; (760) 376-3781 or fax (760) 376-3795.

Trail notes: You're driving along in no-man's-land on Highway 178 between U.S. 395 and Lake Isabella, staring at thousands of those odd-looking pinyon pines. This is the transition zone between the Mojave Desert to the east and the Sierra Nevada to the west, and it doesn't look quite like either one of them. Want to see this strange land up close? This easy hike to Rockhouse Basin can take you there, and since it requires a long drive on dirt roads to reach the trailhead, you're likely to be free of the eastern Sierra hiking masses. A half mile from the trailhead, turn right and head north to Rockhouse Basin, where the noise of cicadas seranades you almost as loudly as the river. Explore the rocks, cool off in the river, and admire those pinyon pines. It can be as hot as Hades out here, so plan your trip for early in the year, when you can hike along the Kern River in relative comfort.

51 Fossil Falls

1.0 mi/0.5 hr

Location: Off U.S. 395 north of the Highway 178 and Highway 14 junction; map G5, grid g9.

User groups: Hikers, dogs, horses, and mountain bikes. No wheelchair facilities.

Permits: No permits are required. Parking and access are free.

Directions: From the junction of Highway 14 and U.S. 395 near Inyokern, drive north on U.S. 395 for 20 miles to just north of Little Lake and turn east on Cinder Road. Drive six-tenths of a mile, bear right at the fork, and drive another six-tenths of a mile to the Fossil Falls Trailhead.

Maps: To obtain a topographic map of the area, ask for Little Lake from the USGS.

Contact: Bureau of Land Management, Ridgecrest Resource Area, 300 South Richmond, Ridgecrest, CA 93555; (760) 384-5400 or fax (760) 384-5499.

Trail notes: Now don't get your hopes up and think you're going to find a waterfall way out here in the desert east of U.S. 395. There's no water to be found anywhere at Fossil Falls, but there's an excellent hike to an ancient lava field where you'll find polished and sculptured rock formations. The trail is well maintained, flat, and easy enough for children, although you don't want to hike it at high noon on a hot day. The falls look more like a giant pit or crevice in the ground, carved with beautiful windsculpted lava formations, which were polished in the last Ice Age. If you know what to look for, you'll also find Native American artifacts in the area, including petroglyphs and rock rings built by the Paiute Indians. If you're the kind of person who likes the weird-looking tufa formations at Mono Lake (we are), you'll enjoy this trail.

52 Cannell Meadow National Recreation Trail

18.0 mi/3.0 days

Location: In Sequoia National Forest north of Kernville; map G5, grid h3.

User groups: Hikers, dogs, horses, and mountain bikes. No wheelchair facilities.

Permits: No permits are required. Parking and access are free.

Directions: From Kernville on the north end of Lake Isabella, drive north on Sierra Way/Road 99 for 1.4 miles to the Cannell Meadow Trailhead on the right. Parking is available near the horse corrals.

Maps: For a map of Sequoia National Forest, send $4 to USDA-Forest Service, 630 Sansome Street, San Francisco, CA 94111. To obtain a topographic map of the area, ask for Kernville from the USGS.

Contact: Sequoia National Forest, Cannell Meadow Ranger District, P.O. Box 6, Kernville, CA 93238; (760) 376-3781 or fax (760) 376-3795.

Trail notes: The Cannell Meadow National Recreation Trail is the first trailhead you reach out of Kernville, and if it's summertime, you should start at the other end of this nine-mile trail. That's because the Kernville end is at 2,800 feet, set in rocky, chaparral and digger pine country, and, baby, it's hot out here. Still, if you can time your trip for late winter or spring, hiking this end of the Cannell Trail is a great adventure, watching the terrain and environment change as the elevation rises. The shadeless trail climbs right away, through sage and occasional live oaks, affording views of the Kern River Valley. The trail gets more and more steep as you near conifer country at Pine Flat, but then you also get some blessed shade. It crosses Cannell Creek twice and reaches the Cannell Meadow Forest Service Cabin, a log cabin that was built in 1904. Cannell Meadow is a beautiful spot on the western edge of the Kern Plateau, edged by Jeffrey and lodgepole pines. Elevation is 7,500 feet, which means a total climb of 4,700 feet. Spread it out over a couple of days.

Pacific Crest Trail (PCT) Section Overview

113.5 mi. one way/11.0 days

For PCT through-hikers, this section from Walker Pass north to the flank of Mount Whitney is a baptismal rite of passage. In the space of 113 miles, you go from hell to heaven, finally passing through the last of high desert, then to the Dome Land Wilderness and onward to the Golden Trout Wilderness and Whitney. You'll get your first look at the pristine high mountain meadows and streams, including South Fork Kern River, a gorgeous stream and memorable moment. Trail elevations within this section range from around 3,800 feet to more than 11,500 feet, and then topping out after the mandatory climb of the Whitney Summit, 14,494 feet. As you gain the higher elevations, the only downer can be heavy snow if you arrive too early in the hiking season.

PCT-19 Walker Pass to Kennedy Meadows

50.0 mi. one way/5.0 days

Location: From the Walker Pass Trailhead north to the trailhead parking area at Kennedy Meadows; map G5, grid i7.

User groups: Hikers, dogs, and horses. No mountain bikes. No wheelchair facilities.

Permits: A wilderness permit is required for traveling through various wilderness and special-use areas the trail traverses. Contact the Angeles National Forest at (805) 296-9710 for a permit that is good for the length of your trip.

Directions: To reach the Walker Pass Trailhead, from Highway 14 at Vincent, head west on Highway 178 toward Lake Isabella. Drive to Mill Creek Summit. The Walker Pass Trailhead is to the right of the parking area. To reach the Kennedy Meadows Trailhead, on Highway 395, drive north to the Kennedy Meadows turnoff. Turn left on Nine Mile Canyon Road. Drive on Nine Mile Canyon Road (it becomes Kennedy Meadows Road) to Kennedy Meadows Campground and the signed PCT Trailhead.

Maps: For an overall view of the trail route in this section, send $4 to the USDA-Forest Service, 630 Sansome Street, San Francisco, CA 94111, and ask for the Sequoia National Forest map. For topographic maps of the route, request Walker Pass, Lamont Peak, White Dome, Rockhouse Basin, and Crag Peak from the USGS.

Contact: Sequoia National Forest, Cannell Meadow Ranger District, P.O. Box 6, Kernville, CA 93238; (619) 376-3781 or fax (619) 376-3795.

Trail notes: As you take these first steps from Walker Pass, elevation 5,246 feet, you must again assess your water consumption, and how much water you're carrying, since the first 12 miles don't have a reliable water supply. "Ha!" you may even say, since in the weeks ahead water availability will become laughable as you enter the high Sierra. This initial 12 miles climbs into the Chimney Peak Wilderness, featuring long-distance views and a series of sparsely vegetated peaks. The latter include Mount Jenkins, named after the outdoors writer and PCT author, Jim Jenkins, who was hit and killed in a traffic accident on U.S. 395 when trying to assist a vehicle on the side of the road. The surrounding flora remains stark for the most part until entering the Dome Land Wilderness, a tromp of just over 30 miles from Walker Pass. From here, the surroundings undergo stunning changes over the next 20 miles. The Dome Land Wilderness features an awesome collection of rock formations, which attracts rock climbers from throughout the West. The trail skirts the east side of Rockhouse Basin, then is routed past a series of creeks, meadows, and, finally, high mountain forests. For long-distance hikers used to water rationing, seeing the South Fork Kern River will be like a trip into heaven. A final push will take you to the store at Kennedy Meadows, elevation 6,150 feet, where every PCT hiker will resupply.

PCT-20 Kennedy Meadows to Mount Whitney

63.5 mi. one way/6.0 days

Location: From the trailhead parking area at Kennedy Meadows Campground north to Mount Whitney; map G5, grid f6.

User groups: Hikers and horses. No dogs or mountain bikes. No wheelchair facilities.

Permits: A wilderness permit is required for traveling through various wilderness and special-use areas the trail traverses. Contact the Angeles National Forest at (805) 296-9710 for a permit that is good for the length of your trip.

Directions: To reach the Kennedy Meadows Trailhead, on Highway 395, drive north to the Kennedy Meadows turnoff. Turn left on Nine Mile Canyon Road. Drive on Nine Mile Canyon Road (it becomes Kennedy Meadows Road) to Kennedy Meadows Campground and the signed PCT Trailhead. To reach the Mount Whitney Trailhead, from Lone Pine and Highway 395, head west on Whitney Portal Road for approximately 13 miles to Whitney Portal and the trailhead for the Mount Whitney Trail.

Maps: For an overall view of the trail route in this section, send $4 for each map ordered to the USDA-Forest Service, 630 Sansome Street, San Francisco, CA 94111, and ask for the Sequoia National Forest and the Inyo National Forest maps. For topographic maps of the route,

request Crag Peak, Monache Mountain, Templeton Mountain, Cirque Peak, Mount Langley, and Mount Whitney from the USGS.

Contact: Sequoia National Forest, Cannell Meadow Ranger District, P.O. Box 6, Kernville, CA 93238; (619) 376-3781 or fax (619) 376-3795. Inyo National Forest, Mount Whitney Ranger District, P.O. Box 8, Lone Pine, CA 93545; (619) 876-6200 or fax (619) 876-6202.

Trail notes: Each step can seem like you're walking a little bit closer to heaven on this stretch of the PCT, and figuratively at least, you are. The surroundings not only become more enchanting as you forge onward, but you'll be gaining elevation—a lot of it. From Kennedy Meadows (not to be confused with the Kennedy Meadows in Stanislaus National Forest) at 6,150 feet, the PCT climbs nearly 9,000 feet to the Whitney Summit, a must-do side trip (see John Muir Trail-1 in chapter F5). Along the way, the views and scenery are dramatic, passing through the Golden Trout and Sierra Wildernesses, and arriving finally at the awesome Whitney, the highest point in the Lower 48. Often bordered by pinnacle-like granite formations, the trail is occasionally routed along the edges of meadows and forests, and sprinkled with small wildflowers, the dramatic granite ridges always looming in the distance. The Golden Trout Wilderness has few lakes, but is better known for its small, pristine streams that are native habitat for California's state fish. When you reach Trail Pass, elevation 10,740 feet, 40 miles from Kennedy Meadows, the surrounding grandeur of the pristine high country is astonishing. Untouched meadows, stunted pine forests, and small, pure streams become more common, a scene that draws hikers from all over the world to the high Sierra wilderness. The last 20 miles to the flank of Whitney feature unbelievable views, and it never stops, all the way to Whitney, when every mountaintop for hundreds of miles becomes visible. For PCT through-hikers, this wondrous vision makes the previous 600 miles from the Mexican border worth every step it took to get it.

PCT Continuation: To continue hiking along the Pacific Crest Trail, see chapter F5.

Map G6

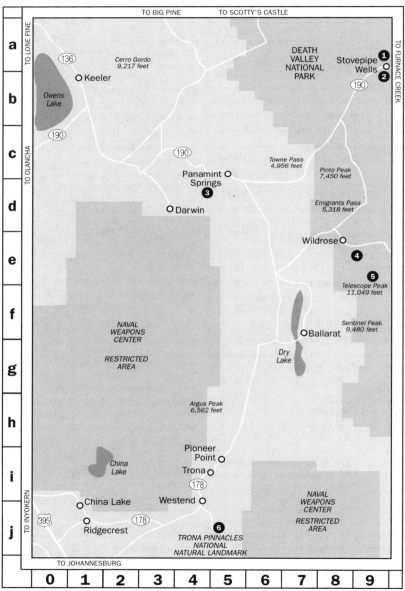

TO BIG PINE   TO SCOTTY'S CASTLE

TO LONE PINE

a

(136)   Cerro Gordo
9,217 feet

O Keeler

DEATH
VALLEY
NATIONAL
PARK

Stovepipe ❶
Wells O
❷

(190)

b

Owens
Lake

(190)

TO OLANCHA

c

(190)

Towne Pass
4,956 feet

Pinto Peak
7,450 feet

Panamint O
Springs
❸

d

O Darwin

Emigrants Pass
5,318 feet

e

Wildrose O

❹

❺

Telescope Peak
11,049 feet

f

NAVAL
WEAPONS
CENTER

Sentinel Peak
9,480 feet

O Ballarat

RESTRICTED
AREA

Dry
Lake

g

h

Argus Peak
6,562 feet

i

China
Lake

Pioneer
Point O

Trona O

(178)

NAVAL
WEAPONS
CENTER

TO INYOKERN

j

O China Lake

Westend O

RESTRICTED
AREA

(395)   (178)

O
Ridgecrest

❻

TRONA PINNACLES
NATIONAL
NATURAL LANDMARK

TO FURNACE CREEK

TO JOHANNESBURG

0 1 2 3 4 5 6 7 8 9

❶ Sand Dunes

3.0 mi/1.5 hrs

Location: In Death Valley National Park near Stovepipe Wells; map G6, grid a9.

User groups: Hikers only. No dogs, horses, or mountain bikes. No wheelchair facilities.

Permits: No permits are required. There is a $10 entrance fee at Death Valley National Park, good for seven days.

Directions: From Lone Pine on U.S. 395, drive east on Highway 136 for 18 miles, then continue driving east on Highway 190 for approximately 60 miles to Stovepipe Wells. Continue 2.2 miles east from Stovepipe Wells (still on Highway 190) to the entrance to the Sand Dunes Picnic Area.

Maps: Free park maps are available at park entrance stations or by contacting Death Valley National Park at the address below. A more detailed map is available for a fee from Tom Harrison Cartography at (415) 456-7940. To obtain a topographic map of the area, ask for Stovepipe Wells from the USGS.

Contact: Death Valley National Park, Death Valley, CA 92328; (760) 786-2331 or fax (760) 786-3283.

Trail notes: The Sand Dunes Picnic Area is the start of an excellent cross-country walk to 80-foot-tall sand dunes. If you've just driven in to Death Valley, this is the kind of hike that will convince your senses that you're really in the desert, a place that is like no place else. There's no marked trail, of course, because of the continually shifting desert sands, so you just make a straight beeline path from the picnic area to the dunes. Early in the morning (like 6 A.M.) or right about sunset are the best times, because of the incredible show of color and light in the ghostlike dunes. Full moon nights are also popular, and it's easy to imagine why. They'll have you dreaming of Arabian nights.

❷ Mosaic Canyon

2.4 mi/1.5 hrs

Location: In Death Valley National Park near Stovepipe Wells; map G6, grid b9.

User groups: Hikers only. No dogs, horses, or mountain bikes. No wheelchair facilities.

Permits: No permits are required. There is a $10 entrance fee at Death Valley National Park, good for seven days.

Directions: From Lone Pine on U.S. 395, drive east on Highway 136 for 18 miles, then continue driving east on Highway 190 for approximately 58 miles to a quarter mile west of Stovepipe Wells and the Mosaic Canyon turnoff on the right. (If you reach Stovepipe Wells Village, you missed the turnoff.) Turn right and drive 2.2 miles to the trailhead parking lot. The last two miles are rough dirt road, but usually passable by passenger cars.

Maps: Free park maps are available at park entrance stations or by contacting Death Valley National Park at the address below. A more detailed map is available for a fee from Tom Harrison Cartography at (415) 456-7940. To obtain a topographic map of the area, ask for Stovepipe Wells from the USGS.

Contact: Death Valley National Park, Death Valley, CA 92328; (760) 786-2331 or fax (760) 786-3283.

Trail notes: The Mosaic Canyon hike is one of the scenic highlights of Death Valley, accessible to most all kinds of hikers. The trail shows off plenty of colorful slickrock and polished marble as it winds its way up a narrow, high-walled canyon, which was formed by a fault zone. Mosaics of multi-colored rock fragments cemented together can be seen in the canyon walls, a gorgeous mix of red, white, black, and gray. In places, you must do a little easy scrambling over boulders and small dry waterfalls—the kind of scrambling that makes the trip seem like a real adventure, but in fact it's quite easy and safe. From the trailhead, the route enters the canyon almost immediately, and the smooth marble walls close in around you. In places, the fissure you're walking through opens wider into "rooms" lined with marble walls, then narrows again. The path ends at a dry waterfall, too high to be scaled. Note: Keep your eyes on the high cliffs around you for bighorn sheep—even if you don't see them, there's a good chance they've spotted you.

❸ Darwin Falls

1.5 mi/1.0 hr

Location: In Death Valley National Park near Panamint Springs; map G6, grid d4.

User groups: Hikers only. No dogs, horses, or mountain bikes. No wheelchair facilities.

Permits: No permits are required. Parking and access are free.

Directions: From Lone Pine on U.S. 395, drive east on Highway 136 for 18 miles, then continue straight on Highway 190 for 30 miles. The right (south) turnoff for Darwin Falls is exactly one mile before you reach the Panamint Springs Resort. Look for a small "Darwin Falls" sign and a dirt road. Turn right and drive 2.5 miles on the dirt road till you reach a fork, then bear right and drive three-tenths of a mile to the parking area. (Alternatively, you can exit Highway 395 at Olancha and Highway 190 and drive east on Highway 190 for 44 miles.)

Maps: To obtain a topographic map of the area, ask for Panamint Springs from the USGS.

Contact: Death Valley National Park, Death Valley, CA 92328; (760) 786-2331 or fax (760) 786-3283.

Trail notes: Darwin Falls is a must-do desert hike. A waterfall in the desert is a rare and precious thing, a miracle of life in a harsh world. The trip is easy enough for young children to accomplish, and although the temperatures in this area can become extreme in the summer, an early-morning start makes the short hike manageable almost year-round. (Of course, be sure to carry water with you.) From the trailhead, follow the jeep trail into the canyon, and soon you'll see a trickle of water on the ground which grows wider and more substantial the further you walk. The path is not always clearly defined, but you simply follow the stream, crossing it a few times, for about a mile. The canyon walls narrow, and the vegetation becomes much more lush as you travel. Just beyond a small stream-gauging station, you come to the waterfall, a 30-foot cascade tucked into a box canyon. A large cottonwood tree grows at its lip. In the spring, more than 80 species of resident and migrating birds have been sighted in this canyon.

❹ Wildrose Peak Trail

8.4 mi/5.0 hrs

Location: In Death Valley National Park; map G6, grid e8.

User groups: Hikers only. No dogs, horses, or mountain bikes. No wheelchair facilities.

Permits: No permits are required. There is a $10 entrance fee at Death Valley National Park, good for seven days.

Directions: From Stovepipe Wells, drive west on Highway 190 for eight miles to Emigrant Canyon Road, then turn left (south). Drive 21 miles to a junction with Wildrose Canyon Road. Turn left (east) and drive 6.5 miles to the parking area on the left for Charcoal Kilns and the Wildrose Peak Trailhead.

Maps: Free park maps are available at park entrance stations or by contacting Death Valley National Park at the address below. A more detailed map is available for a fee from Tom Harrison Cartography at (415) 456-7940. To obtain a topographic map of the area, ask for Wildrose Peak from the USGS.

Contact: Death Valley National Park, Death Valley, CA 92328; (760) 786-2331 or fax (760) 786-3283.

Trail notes: If it's boiling in Death Valley, you can always make the long drive out to Wildrose Canyon and begin your hike at a trailhead elevation of 6,800 feet. Get this—they even have trees here. Whew, what a relief, at least until you start climbing in earnest, heading for 9,064-foot Wildrose Peak. The hike begins at the 10 beehives, oops, make that 10 charcoal kilns (they look like beehives), that were built in the 1870s to make charcoal for the local mines. Walk to the north end of the kilns to find the signed trail, and start climbing through scattered pinyon pines and junipers. You can see far off to the Sierra, even Mount Whitney, and then as you climb higher, you can look down at Death Valley and Panamint Valley. Well-graded switchbacks make the 2,200-foot climb manageable, and the panoramic views make the energy expenditure completely worth it. If you tire out, at least try to hike the first 2.5 miles of trail, where you'll get a good dose of vistas. The last mile to the summit is the steepest, but no matter what, the climb is nowhere near as bad as on the Telescope Peak Trail (see the trail notes for hike number 5).

Special note: This trail can be snowed in any time between November and May. Check with the park before making the long drive.

❺ Telescope Peak Trail

14.0 mi/9.0 hrs

Location: In Death Valley National Park; map G6, grid e9.

User groups: Hikers only. No dogs, horses, or mountain bikes. No wheelchair facilities.

Permits: No permits are required. There is a $10 entrance fee at Death Valley National Park, good for seven days.

Directions: From Stovepipe Wells, drive west on Highway 190 for eight miles to Emigrant Canyon Road, then turn left (south). Drive 20 miles to a junction with Wildrose Canyon Road. Turn left (east) and drive nine miles to the end of Wildrose Canyon Road at Mahogany Flat Campground. The road gets very rough and steep after the Charcoal Kilns.

Maps: Free park maps are available at park entrance stations or by contacting Death Valley National Park at the address below. A more detailed map is available for a fee from Tom Harrison Cartography at (415) 456-7940. To obtain a topographic map of the area, ask for Telescope Peak from the USGS.

Contact: Death Valley National Park, Death Valley, CA 92328; (760) 786-2331 or fax (760) 786-3283.

Trail notes: The big deal about making the long hike to the summit of Telescope Peak is this: When you get there, you can pivot yourself around and in one long, sweeping glance take in Mount Whitney to the west and Badwater to the east. For the uninitiated, that means you're seeing the highest point in the contiguous United States and the lowest point in the Western Hemisphere from the same spot. (One is ahead of you and one is to your back.) The other big deal about the hike is that the trailhead is at 8,000 feet, so you don't have to worry about it being too hot in the summertime. The peak is the highest in Death Valley National Park at 11,049 feet, and the trail to reach it is well graded and well maintained. Nonetheless, the 3,000-foot climb and the long mileage takes its toll on you, so don't try it unless you're in good shape. In addition to passing pinyon pines and junipers, you'll also see some ancient bristlecone pine trees once you climb above 10,000 feet. Then, to supplement the vistas of Mount Whitney and Badwater, you are also witness to Death Valley and Panamint Valley and the White Mountains to the north. It's beyond spectacular. But the climb is one heck of a workout, so be prepared.

Special note: This trail can be snowed in any time between November and May. Check with the park before making the long drive.

❻ Trona Pinnacles

0.5 mi/0.5 hr

Location: East of Ridgecrest and south of Trona; map G6, grid j4.

User groups: Hikers, dogs, and horses. No mountain bikes. No wheelchair facilities.

Permits: No permits are required. Parking and access are free.

Directions: From Ridgecrest, drive east on Highway 178 for 12 miles to the right turnoff for Trona Pinnacles. Turn right on Pinnacles Road and drive seven miles to the signed trailhead. (High-clearance vehicles recommended.)

Maps: A free brochure on Trona Pinnacles is available from the Bureau of Land Management at the address below. To obtain a topographic map of the area, ask for Searles Lake from the USGS.

Contact: Bureau of Land Management, Ridgecrest Resource Area, 300 South Richmond Road, Ridgecrest, CA 93555; (760) 384-5400.

Trail notes: The Trona Pinnacles: If they were miniaturized, they'd look like little lumps of modeling clay, shaped into oblongs and ready to be turned on the potter's wheel. They're actually tufa spires, made of calcium carbonate, and the Trona Pinnacles National Natural Landmark features more than 500 of them, some as high as 140 feet. Like the tufa spires at Mono Lake, the Trona Pinnacles were formed underwater from calcium-rich springs, in the days when giant Searles Lake still had water in it— probably 50,000 years ago. Now the lakebed is dry, so the tufa spires jut upward from a flat, dry plain. Yes, they're weird looking, but in a good way. A half-mile loop trail leads from the parking lot through the pinnacles.

Leave No Trace Tips

Pack It In and Pack It Out

Take everything you bring into the wild back out with you.

Protect wildlife and your food by storing rations securely.
Pick up all spilled foods.

Use toilet paper or wipes sparingly; pack them out.

Inspect your campsite for trash and any evidence of your stay.
Pack out all trash—even if it's not yours!

Map G7

Adjoining Maps: West: G6 .. *page* 508
South: H7 552

Central California Map .... *page* 382

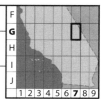

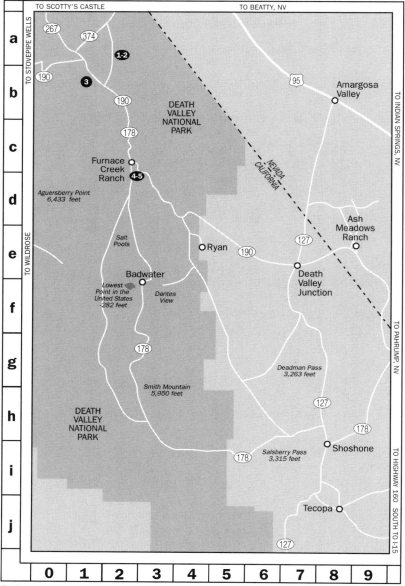

TO SCOTTY'S CASTLE

TO BEATTY, NV

TO STOVEPIPE WELLS

267

374

1-2

190

3

190

95

Amargosa
Valley

DEATH
VALLEY
NATIONAL
PARK

178

NEVADA
CALIFORNIA

TO INDIAN SPRINGS, NV

Furnace
Creek
Ranch

4-5

*Aguersberry Point
6,433 feet*

*Salt
Pools*

Ryan

190

127

Ash
Meadows
Ranch

Badwater

*Lowest
Point in the
United States
-282 feet*

*Dantes
View*

Death
Valley
Junction

TO WILDROSE

178

*Deadman Pass
3,263 feet*

127

*Smith Mountain
5,950 feet*

DEATH
VALLEY
NATIONAL
PARK

178

TO PAHRUMP, NV

178

178

*Salsberry Pass
3,315 feet*

Shoshone

TO HIGHWAY 160 SOUTH TO I-15

Tecopa

127

0 1 2 3 4 5 6 7 8 9

514

❶ Keane Wonder Mine Trail

2.0 mi/1.0 hr

Location: In Death Valley National Park; map G7, grid a2.

User groups: Hikers only. No dogs, horses, or mountain bikes. No wheelchair facilities.

Permits: No permits are required. There is a $10 entrance fee at Death Valley National Park, good for seven days.

Directions: From the Furnace Creek Visitor Center in Death Valley National Park, drive 10 miles north on Highway 190 to the Beatty Cut-off Road. Bear right (north) on Beatty Cutoff Road and drive 5.5 miles to the right turnoff for Keane Wonder Mine. Turn right and drive 2.4 miles to the parking area.

Maps: Free park maps are available at park entrance stations or by contacting Death Valley National Park at the address below. A more detailed map is available for a fee from Tom Harrison Cartography at (415) 456-7940. To obtain a topographic map of the area, ask for Chloride City from the USGS.

Contact: Death Valley National Park, Death Valley, CA 92328; (760) 786-2331 or fax (760) 786-3283.

Trail notes: You wouldn't think a two-mile round-trip trail could be this hard. But then again, most people don't usually climb 1,800 feet in one mile, and especially not this close to sea level in the desert. The million-dollar vistas on the Keane Wonder Mine Trail are worth the trek, though, and they're sure to pay off at least as well as the Wonder gold and silver mine did in the early 1900s. The mine had such promise, in fact, that ambitious miners built an aerial tramway to carry loads of rock down the mountainside to the mill. The vein of ore ran dry in 1915, but the mine's mill and tramway ruins still exist, and you'll see them on this steep trek into the Funeral Mountains. After only a half

mile of climbing, the views of Death Valley open wide; meanwhile the path steepens as it continues straight upward. As you pass mine shafts along the trail, remember to stay out of them—there are various potential dangers. The vistas, on the other hand, are perfectly safe and yours for the taking.

❷ Keane Wonder Springs

2.0 mi/1.0 hr

Location: In Death Valley National Park; map G7, grid a2.

User groups: Hikers only. No dogs, horses, or mountain bikes. No wheelchair facilities.

Permits: No permits are required. There is a $10 entrance fee at Death Valley National Park, good for seven days.

Directions: From the Furnace Creek Visitor Center in Death Valley National Park, drive 10 miles north on Highway 190 to the Beatty Cut-off Road. Bear right (north) on Beatty Cutoff Road and drive 5.5 miles to the right turnoff for Keane Wonder Mine. Turn right and drive 2.4 miles to the parking area.

Maps: Free park maps are available at park entrance stations or by contacting Death Valley National Park at the address below. A more detailed map is available for a fee from Tom Harrison Cartography at (415) 456-7940. To obtain a topographic map of the area, ask for Chloride City from the USGS.

Contact: Death Valley National Park, Death Valley, CA 92328; (760) 786-2331 or fax (760) 786-3283.

Trail notes: If you aren't up for the hot and steep climb to the top of the tramway at Keane Wonder Mine (see hike number 1), this easy and flat trail to Keane Wonder Springs provides a pleasant alternative. The mineral spring once provided water for the mining operation; now it provides a gathering place for birds and wildlife. From the trailhead, you walk toward the large metal water tank, then find the trail on the left side of it. Follow an old pipeline northward along the base of the mountains, cross a wash and pass mounds of travertine, a marble-like rock formed by the sulfur-rich spring water. The spring is just slightly off the trail three-quarters of a mile from the trailhead, and not really worth the scramble required to access it. Instead, follow the trail another quarter mile, beyond the spring, to the remains of an old stampmill and cabin.

---

❸ Salt Creek Interpretive Trail

1.0 mi/0.5 hr

Location: In Death Valley National Park; map G7, grid b1.

User groups: Hikers and wheelchairs. No dogs, horses, or mountain bikes.

Permits: No permits are required. There is a $10 entrance fee at Death Valley National Park, good for seven days.

Directions: From the Furnace Creek Visitor Center in Death Valley National Park, drive 12 miles north on Highway 190 to the left turnoff for Salt Creek. Turn left and drive one mile to the Salt Creek parking area.

Maps: Interpretive trail brochures are available for 50 cents at park visitor centers or at the trailhead. Free park maps are available at park entrance stations or by contacting Death Valley National Park at the address below. A more detailed map is available for a fee from Tom Harrison Cartography at (415) 456-7940. To obtain a topographic map of the area, ask for Beatty Junction from the USGS.

Contact: Death Valley National Park, Death Valley, CA 92328; (760) 786-2331 or fax (760) 786-3283.

Trail notes: Salt Creek is exactly what its name implies, a stream of saline water, and it's home to the Salt Creek pupfish, which lives nowhere else. The fish underwent an incredible evolutionary change in order to live in this saline creek, which was once a part of a much larger freshwater lake. The biological alteration would be about the same as if humans decided to drink gasoline instead of water. You can look down

into Salt Creek and easily spot the minnow-sized pupfish swimming about; late winter and spring is the best time to view them. The plants growing along the stream are typical of California coastal wetlands—salt grass and pickleweed. Birds congregate by the stream, including great blue herons. Because the trail is on a wooden boardwalk, it is accessible to all hikers, including wheelchair users.

---

❹ Golden Canyon Interpretive Trail

2.0 mi/1.0 hr

Location: In Death Valley National Park; map G7, grid d2.

User groups: Hikers only. No dogs, horses, or mountain bikes. No wheelchair facilities.

Permits: No permits are required. There is a $10 entrance fee at Death Valley National Park, good for seven days.

Directions: From the Furnace Creek Visitor Center in Death Valley National Park, drive southeast on Highway 190 for 1.2 miles to the right turnoff for Badwater. Bear right and drive south for two miles to the Golden Canyon parking area on the left side of the road.

Maps: Interpretive trail brochures are available for 50 cents at park visitor centers or at the trailhead. Free park maps are available at park entrance stations or by contacting Death Valley National Park at the address below. A more detailed map is available for a fee from Tom Harrison Cartography at (415) 456-7940. To obtain a topographic map of the area, ask for Furnace Creek from the USGS.

Contact: Death Valley National Park, Death Valley, CA 92328; (760) 786-2331 or fax (760) 786-3283.

Trail notes: The Golden Canyon Interpretive Trail is a perfect path for first-timers in Death Valley National Park. If you've been there, and done that, you can continue beyond the end of the self-guided trail, heading deeper into Golden Canyon to Red Cathedral, a third of a mile from the last numbered trail marker. The interpretive trail follows an old road through a flat alluvial fan exhibiting a colorful array of volcanic rocks, sand, and gravel; it then enters a badlands area. The badlands are deeply creased, eroded, and barren hillsides, great to photograph in black and white, especially as the shadows grow long later in the day. At the final interpretive post, you can turn around and head back, or take the left fork of the trail and continue to Red Cathedral, a huge red-colored cliff. Its lovely hue is caused by the weathering of rocks containing a large quantity of iron.

Zabriskie Point, which has a fine vista of the badlands and the Panamint Mountains. Be proud of yourself for walking to Zabriskie Point instead of driving, like everybody else. One thing to keep in mind: Be sure to carry enough water for the few hours you'll be out on the trail. The total elevation gain is only 700 feet, but it's pretty darn hot out here.

❺ Zabriskie Point

5.5 mi/3.0 hrs

Location: In Death Valley National Park; map G7, grid d2.

User groups: Hikers only. No dogs, horses, or mountain bikes. No wheelchair facilities.

Permits: No permits are required. There is a $10 entrance fee at Death Valley National Park, good for seven days.

Directions: From the Furnace Creek Visitor Center in Death Valley National Park, drive southeast on Highway 190 for 1.2 miles to the right turnoff for Badwater. Turn right and drive south for two miles to the Golden Canyon parking area on the left side of the road.

Maps: Free park maps are available at park entrance stations or by contacting Death Valley National Park at the address below. A more detailed map is available for a fee from Tom Harrison Cartography at (415) 456-7940. To obtain a topographic map of the area, ask for Furnace Creek from the USGS.

Contact: Death Valley National Park, Death Valley, CA 92328; (760) 786-2331 or fax (760) 786-3283.

Trail notes: This hike is an extension of the Golden Canyon Interpretive Trail for slightly more experienced hikers. See the trail notes for hike number 4, then when you reach the last interpretive trail marker, take the right fork for Zabriskie Point. The path is signed with small "hiker" symbols; watch for them as you continue your trek into the colorful badlands. You'll see white outcroppings in the rock, the *raison d'être* for the old borax mines that can still be found in the area. Climb to the top of Manly Beacon (a big sandstone hill and not particularly manly, but with lovely views), then continue to

Map H2

Adjoining Maps: East: H3 ... *page* 522
                      North: G2 466   South: I2 560

Central California Map .... *page* 382

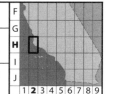

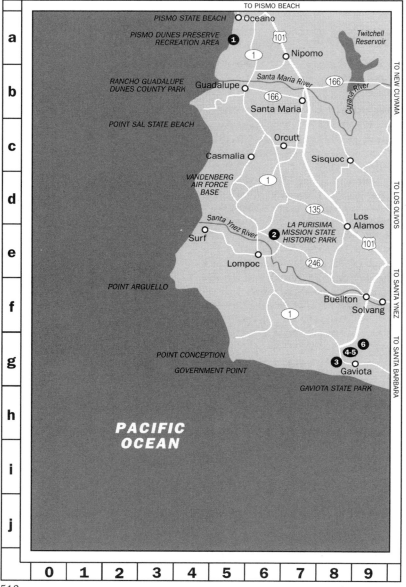

TO PISMO BEACH

PISMO STATE BEACH ○ Oceano

a

PISMO DUNES PRESERVE RECREATION AREA ❶
101

Twitchell Reservoir

1
○ Nipomo

RANCHO GUADALUPE DUNES COUNTY PARK   Guadalupe ○

Santa Maria River 166

Cuyama River

TO NEW CUYAMA

b

166
Santa Maria ○

POINT SAL STATE BEACH

c

Casmalia ○

Orcutt ○

Sisquoc ○

VANDENBERG AIR FORCE BASE

1

d

135

Los Alamos ○

Santa Ynez River
Surf ○

LA PURISIMA MISSION STATE HISTORIC PARK ❷

101

TO LOS OLIVOS

e

Lompoc ○

246

POINT ARGUELLO

f

1

Buellton ○
Solvang ○

TO SANTA YNEZ

g

POINT CONCEPTION

GOVERNMENT POINT

❻
4-5
❸ Gaviota ○

GAVIOTA STATE PARK

TO SANTA BARBARA

h

PACIFIC OCEAN

i

j

0   1   2   3   4   5   6   7   8   9

518

Chapter H2 features:

❶ Oso Flaco Lake

2.2 mi/1.0 hr

Location: Southwest of Arroyo Grande; map H2, grid a5.

User groups: Hikers and wheelchairs. No dogs, horses, or mountain bikes.

Permits: No permits are required. A $4 day-use fee is charged.

Directions: From Santa Maria on U.S. 101, take the Highway 166/Guadalupe exit and drive nine miles west, then turn north on Highway 1 at Guadalupe and drive 3.6 miles. Turn left on Oso Flaco Lake Road and drive three miles to the trailhead.

Maps: To obtain a topographic map of the area, ask for Oceano from the USGS.

Contact: Pismo Dunes State Vehicular Recreation Area, c/o Oceano Dunes District, 576 Camino Mercado, Arroyo Grande, CA 93420; (805) 473-7230.

Trail notes: A nature preserve in a state vehicular recreation area? Usually the two don't go together too well, but that's what you get here at Oso Flaco Lake, a part of the Pismo Dunes Natural Preserve, which is a part of the larger state vehicular recreation area. The trail to Oso Flaco Lake starts out paved for a third of a mile, but then you cut off to the left on a wooden walkway and footbridge that leads over the small lake. Immediately you are in the good company of shorebirds and waterfowl, including ducks that play hide-and-seek in the islands of reeds. The boardwalk extends beyond the lake's border and over a series of sand dunes, and serves the dual purpose of making the trail suitable for wheelchairs and also protecting the dunes' fragile plant life. Where the boardwalk ends, you can continue walking on the dunes, or head to the beach on your right. Only from the very end of the trail can you hear the occasional wail of off-road vehicles. Otherwise, all is peaceful here. By the way, what does "Oso Flaco" mean? Skinny bear. But it's been a long time since they've seen one of those around here.

Special note: Many sections of the boardwalk are under a few inches of water due to flooding. Most hikers will have no trouble with this, but wheelchair accessibility will be impaired until the boardwalk can be repaired. Call the park for an update.

❷ Las Zanjas and El Camino Loop

2.5 mi/1.25 hrs

Location: At La Purisima Mission north of Lompoc; map H2, grid e6.

User groups: Hikers, dogs, horses, and mountain bikes. No wheelchair facilities.

Permits: No permits are required. A $5 day-use fee is charged per vehicle.

Directions: From Buellton on U.S. 101, take the Solvang/Lompoc/Highway 246 exit and drive west for 13.2 miles, then turn right on Purisima Road. The park entrance is one mile down the road on the right. The trailhead is at the far end of the parking lot, near the visitor center.

Maps: A map of La Purisima Mission State Historic Park is available at the entrance station. To obtain a topographic map of the area, ask for Los Alamos from the USGS.

Contact: La Purisima Mission State Historic Park, 2295 Purisima Road, Lompoc, CA 93436; (805) 733-3713.

Trail notes: If you came to La Purisima Mission seeking heavenly sanctuary, but instead found a bunch of screaming school kids, you can still find your heaven in the hills surrounding the mission. There's a surprising number of good hiking trails here, considering this is a state historic park and not a recreation park. The best place to start is on a level loop trail around the mission. Set out on Las Zanjas Trail (also spelled Las Zonas on some signs), a wide ranch road that leads behind the mission buildings. If you like, take the short cutoff on the right to the large cross on the hill (the trail is signed as Vista de la Cruz). A steep climb gives you wide views of the mission area and the Pacific Coast. Then continue on Las Zanjas to the park boundary, where you can loop back on El Camino Real, an old paved ranch road. Along the way, you'll be accompanied by cool ocean breezes, blooming buckeye trees and bush monkeyflower, and green grasslands in springtime. Be sure to take a tour of the mission before or after your hike.

❸ Gaviota Overlook

3.0 mi/1.5 hrs

Location: In Gaviota State Park near Gaviota; map H2, grid g8.

User groups: Hikers, horses, and mountain bikes. No dogs. No wheelchair facilities.

Permits: No permits are required. Parking and access are free.

Directions: From Buellton, drive south on U.S. 101 for 10 miles to just north of Gaviota Pass, to the blue sign that reads: "Rest Area 1 Mile, Tourist Information." Immediately beyond it, you'll drive over a concrete bridge and must quickly turn right into the very small parking area, just beyond the bridge. It's easy to miss. If you reach the rest area, you've gone past it. (Coming from Santa Barbara and points south on U.S. 101, you must exit at Highway 1/Lompoc, then get back on the freeway heading south.)

Maps: To obtain topographic maps of the area, ask for Solvang and Gaviota from the USGS.

Contact: Gaviota State Park, c/o Refugio State Beach, 10 Refugio Beach Road, Goleta, CA 93117, (805) 968-3294.

Trail notes: If you don't mind a little climbing to get a great coastal view, the Gaviota Overlook Trail will suit you just fine. The trail (really a ranch road) is completely out in the open as it climbs from U.S. 101 to the top of the ridge above Gaviota Beach, but as long as the weather is cool, it's an easy ascent. There are two main trail forks; bear left at both. Since this is coastal grasslands territory, wildflowers are prolific in

springtime, but things get kind of arid-looking by late summer. No matter; the view from the top is priceless—miles of open ocean on the one side, including the Channel Islands, and miles of grasslands and chaparral on the other side. Hey, where are all the condominiums? Just kidding. The trail ends at some microwave towers below the highest point on the ridge, but the views are just fine from where you are. The only catch on this trail is that the trailhead is darn near impossible to find, so follow the directions above precisely.

❹ Gaviota Hot Springs

1.0 mi/0.5 hr

Location: In Gaviota State Park near Gaviota; map H2, grid g8.

User groups: Hikers, horses, and mountain bikes. No dogs. No wheelchair facilities.

Permits: No permits are required. A $2 day-use fee is charged per vehicle.

Directions: From Santa Barbara, drive north on U.S. 101 for 35 miles, pass through the tunnel at Gaviota Pass, then take the first exit after the tunnel which is signed as Highway 1/ Lompoc/Vandenberg Air Force Base. At the stop sign, turn right and head south on the frontage road that parallels the freeway. (Don't bear left on Highway 1.) The frontage road ends at the trailhead parking area.

Maps: To obtain a topographic map of the area, ask for Gaviota from the USGS.

Contact: Gaviota State Park, c/o Refugio State Beach, 10 Refugio Beach Road, Goleta, CA 93117, (805) 968-3294.

Trail notes: Gaviota State Park got smart and started charging a few bucks for people to park at this trailhead, since hot springs always draw a crowd. Still, if you show up first thing in the morning or anytime during the week, most likely you can soak all by yourself in one of the two small pools here. They're not very big, or very deep, or very hot, either, but hey—whaddya want for a couple bucks? The pools are a quick-to-reach destination, requiring a short but steep climb from the trailhead, mostly on a fire road. The smell of sulfur and the sway of the palm tree above the upper pool will lull you into believing you're at your own private spa. The upper pool is also the hotter of the two, nearly at bathtub temperature. If you look closely, you can see little bubbles coming up from the ground under the pool—geology in action. If you want to hike more, you can combine this trip with the trek to Gaviota Peak (see the trail notes for hike number 5).

❺ Gaviota Peak

6.4 mi/3.5 hrs

Location: In Gaviota State Park near Gaviota; map H2, grid g8.

User groups: Hikers, horses, and mountain bikes. No dogs. No wheelchair facilities.

Permits: No permits are required. A $2 day-use fee is charged per vehicle.

Directions: From Santa Barbara, drive north on U.S. 101 for 35 miles, pass through the tunnel at Gaviota Pass, then take the first exit after the tunnel which is signed as Highway 1/Lompoc/Vandenberg Air Force Base. At the stop sign, turn right and head south on the frontage road that parallels the freeway. (Don't bear left on to Highway 1.) The frontage road ends at the trailhead parking area.

Maps: To obtain a topographic map of the area, ask for Gaviota from the USGS.

Contact: Gaviota State Park, c/o Refugio State Beach, 10 Refugio Beach Road, Goleta, CA 93117, (805) 968-3294.

Trail notes: The best hike for a good workout in Gaviota State Park is the trail to Gaviota Peak. Start from the Gaviota Hot Springs Trailhead, but instead of taking the short spur trail to Gaviota Hot Springs (see hike number 4), head left on the Gaviota Peak Trail and begin your assault on Gaviota Hill, oops, that's Gaviota Peak, elevation 2,450 feet. The climb isn't too bad (2,000 feet in 3.2 miles), but, geez, it can get hot here without much shade. The trail is a dirt road (plus a few single-track sections) which climbs up a series of knolls on its way to Gaviota Peak. Technically, the peak is actually in Los Padres National Forest, not in the state park. Once you're there, you'll find the views are downright awesome. What can you see? Point Conception, the wide blue Pacific, the Channel Islands, Lompoc Val-

ley, and Gaviota Pass at your feet. Hope you picked a day when the fog wasn't visiting.

❻ Nojoqui Falls

0.5 mi/0.5 hr

Location: Near Gaviota; map H2, grid g9.

User groups: Hikers and dogs. No horses or mountain bikes. No wheelchair facilities.

Permits: No permits are required. Parking and access are free.

Directions: From Santa Barbara, drive 40 miles north on U.S. 101 to the signed turnoff for Nojoqui Park, north of Gaviota State Beach. Drive one mile on the Old Coast Highway, then turn east on Alisal Road. Drive eight-tenths of a mile, then turn right into the park entrance. Drive a quarter mile down the park access road to the parking lot and trailhead. The trail starts from the far end of the parking lot loop.

Maps: To obtain a topographic map of the area, ask for Solvang from the USGS.

Contact: Santa Barbara County Parks and Recreation, 300 North Goodwin Road, Santa Maria, CA 93455; (805) 934-6123.

Trail notes: A favorite spot of Santa Barbarans cruising upcoast on U.S. 101, Nojoqui County Park has plenty of picnic areas, sports fields, and the like, but only one hiking trail. It's a great, short stroll from the parking area to impressive Nojoqui Falls, which drop 80 feet over a sandstone cliff that is almost completely covered with delicate Venus maidenhair ferns. The hike is good no matter how much or how little the falls are running—it's a flat, easy walk that everyone in the family can do, under a cool canopy of oaks and laurels, with Nojoqui Creek babbling alongside the trail. Check out the interesting rocks along the route. They're made of shale, while the waterfall cliff is made of sandstone. You'll see the difference. There's a stair-stepped rock perch right by the waterfall's pool, where you can sit in the shade of big-leaf maples and admire the scene.

Map H3

Adjoining Maps:　East: H4 ... *page* 532　　West: H2 518
　　　　　　　　　　North: G3 .... 474　　South: I3 562

Central California Map .... *page* 382

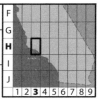

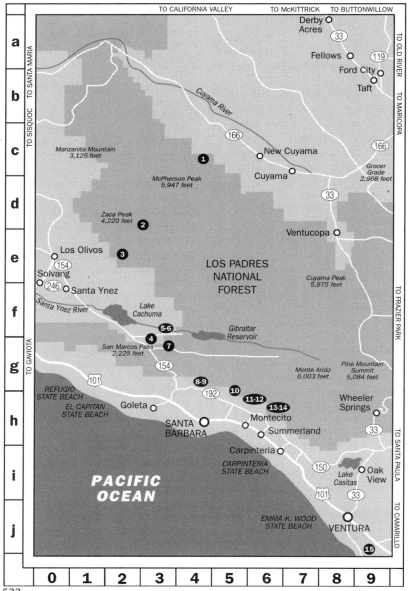

❶ McPherson Peak Trail

10.0 mi/2.0 days

Location: In the San Rafael Wilderness; map H3, grid c4.

User groups: Hikers, dogs, horses, and mountain bikes (mountain bikes may not go past the wilderness boundary). No wheelchair facilities.

Permits: No permits are required. A national forest recreation pass is required for each vehicle; fees are $5 for one day or $30 for a year.

Directions: From Santa Maria on U.S. 101, take Highway 166 east for 48 miles to just west of New Cuyama. Turn right (south) on Aliso Canyon Road and follow it for six miles to Aliso Park Campground. The dirt road can be very rough; high-clearance vehicles are recommended. (If you are coming from Ventura or Ojai, take Highway 33 north to Highway 166, then go west past New Cuyama.)

Maps: For a map of Los Padres National Forest, send $4 to USDA-Forest Service, 630 Sansome Street, San Francisco, CA 94111. To obtain a topographic map of the area, ask for Peak Mountain from the USGS.

Contact: Los Padres National Forest, Santa Lucia Ranger District, 1616 North Carlotti Drive, Santa Maria, CA 93454; (805) 925-9538, or fax (805) 349-0888.

Trail notes: McPherson Peak at elevation 5,747 feet is just on the edge of the spectacular San Rafael Wilderness, a land of condors and steep canyons. Although the trail is steep and can be hot in summer, it gives hikers outstanding views of the wilderness and the desert-like lands of Cuyama to the northeast. From Aliso Park Campground, you start hiking on the dirt road that is signed for Hog Pen Spring Campground, quickly saying good-bye to the shady canyon. Reach the camp in 1.5 miles (there's a spring nearby if you need water), then pick up a trail which continues climbing, now more steeply, to Sierra Madre Road, on the wilderness boundary. Turn right on the dirt road and hike another 2.5 miles through chaparral to McPherson Peak, passing McPherson Camp along the way. The camp has a spring, and is an excellent place to spend the night. You can watch the sun set from McPherson Peak, then crawl into your sleeping bag and watch the stars.

❷ Upper Manzana Creek Trail

13.0 mi/1–2 days

Location: In San Rafael Wilderness; map H3, grid d2.

User groups: Hikers, dogs, and horses. No mountain bikes. No wheelchair facilities.

Permits: No permits are required. A national forest recreation pass is required for each vehicle; fees are $5 for one day or $30 for a year.

Directions: From Santa Barbara on U.S. 101, take Highway 154 north and drive 23 miles, past Lake Cachuma, to Armour Ranch Road. Turn right and drive 1.5 miles to Happy Canyon Road (not suitable for trailers). Turn right and drive 14 miles to Cachuma Saddle and a junction with Figueroa Mountain Road, then continue straight on Sunset Valley Road and follow it for four miles to its end at Nira Campground. Park in the hikers' parking lot.

Maps: For a map of Los Padres National Forest, send $4 to USDA-Forest Service, 630 Sansome Street, San Francisco, CA 94111. To obtain a topographic map of the area, ask for Bald Mountain from the USGS.

Contact: Los Padres National Forest, Santa Lucia Ranger District, 1616 North Carlotti Drive, Santa Maria, CA 93454; (805) 925-9538, or fax (805) 349-0888.

Trail notes: From Nira Campground, a major entry point into the San Rafael Wilderness, you can hike east or west along Manzana Creek. In spring, the creek is popular with anglers, who come here to catch the resident trout in Manzana Creek. (Some trout are stocked by the campground.) Hikers and backpackers can take the Upper Manzana Creek Trail to the east and stop at any one of several excellent campsites, including Manzana (six miles out) and Manzana Narrows (seven miles out). Both have swimming holes. The trail climbs gently from the campground, sometimes switchbacking away from the creek but always returning. There is a modicum of shade from blue oaks and gray pines, mixed in among the low-lying chaparral and manzanita. Note that the creek gets low and is less attractive by mid summer, but that winter hiking can be dangerous if the stream level is too high. March to May is the best time to visit.

❸ Pino Alto Trail

0.5 mi/0.5 hr

Location: On Figueroa Mountain; map H3, grid e2.

User groups: Hikers, wheelchairs, and dogs. No horses or mountain bikes.

Permits: No permits are required. A national forest recreation pass is required for each vehicle; fees are $5 for one day or $30 for a year.

Directions: From Santa Barbara, drive north on U.S. 101, through Buellton, for 45 miles to the Highway 154 East turnoff. Turn east on Highway 154 and drive three miles to Los Olivos, then turn north (left) on Figueroa Mountain Road. Drive 13 miles to Figueroa Mountain Lookout Road and bear left for the Pino Alto Picnic Area.

Maps: For a map of Los Padres National Forest, send $4 to USDA-Forest Service, 630 Sansome Street, San Francisco, CA 94111. To obtain a topographic map of the area, ask for Figueroa Mountain from the USGS.

Contact: Los Padres National Forest, Santa Lucia Ranger District, 1616 North Carlotti Drive, Santa Maria, CA 93454; (805) 925-9538, or fax (805) 349-0888.

Trail notes: You just made the drive to Figueroa Mountain and you're wondering what in the heck this place is all about. The Pino Alto Interpretive Trail can spell it out for you, and, besides, the vistas will knock your socks off. Vistas? Try this: The Santa Ynez Valley is visible for some 20 miles from the northwest to the southeast. You can see Cuyama, Lake Cachuma, and the Santa Ynez Mountains, sometimes even the Channel Islands far off to sea. The trailhead is at 4,600 feet, situated among ponderosa and Jeffrey pines and big cone spruce. Conifers? In Santa Barbara? That's right. The trail is paved, which makes it suitable for wheelchairs. Make sure you go to the Figueroa lookout tower site for panoramic views of the mountains of the San Rafael Wilderness. If you like what you see on Figueroa Mountain, many longer day hikes are possible on the nearby Davy Brown/Fir Canyon Trail, starting at either Davy Brown Campground or at the trailhead on Figueroa Mountain Road.

❹ Snyder Trail

12.0 mi/7.0 hrs

Location: Near the Santa Ynez Recreation Area; map H3, grid f3.

User groups: Hikers, dogs, horses, and mountain bikes. No wheelchair facilities.

Permits: No permits are required. A national forest recreation pass is required for each vehicle; fees are $5 for one day or $30 for a year.

Directions: From U.S. 101 in Santa Barbara, take the Highway 154/State Street exit and drive north for about 12 miles. Turn right on Paradise Road and drive four miles to the trailhead for the Snyder Trail, which is at a locked gate on the right side of the road, a quarter mile west of the Los Prietos Ranger Station.

Maps: For a map of Los Padres National Forest, send $4 to USDA-Forest Service, 630 Sansome Street, San Francisco, CA 94111. To obtain a topographic map of the area, ask for San Marcos Pass from the USGS.

Contact: Los Padres National Forest, Santa

Barbara Ranger District, Los Prietos Station, Star Route, Santa Barbara, CA 93105; (805) 967-3481, or fax (805) 967-7312.

Trail notes: While Snyder Trail may start out looking like a plain old fire road at its lower end at Paradise Road, by the time it climbs six miles to East Camino Cielo it becomes a lovely single-track trail that is bordered by more wildflowers than you can count, and has more wide-reaching vistas than you can imagine. Don't bother twisting your neck to catch the views on your way up, because on your return trip downhill they will be laid out in front of you. The nice thing about the trail is that you start gaining vistas fairly quickly, so if you feel like you're tiring of the climb, you can simply find a knoll somewhere, have a seat, and pull out your sandwiches. If you decide to go all the way up the trail, just before you reach the top is a popular side trip to the ruins of Knapp's Castle (see hike number 7). Take the gated dirt road on the left, 5.5 miles up. If you hike the Snyder Trail's entire length, you'll be tired by the end of the day, but you'll have a whole storehouse of fine memories.

❺ Aliso Canyon Loop Trail

3.5 mi/2.0 hrs

Location: In the Santa Ynez Recreation Area; map H3, grid f3.

User groups: Hikers, dogs, horses, and mountain bikes. No wheelchair facilities.

Permits: No permits are required. A $3 day-use fee is charged per vehicle.

Directions: From U.S. 101 in Santa Barbara, take the Highway 154/State Street exit and drive north for about 12 miles. Turn right on Paradise Road and drive four miles to the ranger station. Turn left at the ranger station and drive one mile to Sage Hill Campground and the trailhead for the Aliso Canyon Trail.

Maps: For a map of Los Padres National Forest, send $4 to USDA-Forest Service, 630 Sansome Street, San Francisco, CA 94111. To obtain a topographic map of the area, ask for San Marcos Pass from the USGS.

Contact: Los Padres National Forest, Santa Barbara Ranger District, Los Prietos Station, Star

Route, Santa Barbara, CA 93105; (805) 967-3481, or fax (805) 967-7312.

Trail notes: From the east end of Sage Hill Campground, you can set off on the Aliso Canyon Trail and choose between a one-mile interpretive walk or a 3.5-mile loop trail. The former is the first mile of the latter, and follows Aliso Creek. Be sure to bring along a trail brochure so you can learn all about how the Chumash Indians lived in this area and what plants they used and ate. In the spring, a wildflower identification book also may be a good idea, as the variety of flowers along this short route is surprising. At the end of the interpretive trail, you can either turn around and hike back or continue on the longer loop trip. To do so, walk back a few feet to a trail junction, then ascend for a half mile to a meadow on a grassy plateau. From there, climb rather steeply to the top of the ridge that divides Aliso and Oso Canyons, where there are excellent views of the Santa Ynez Canyon and distant mountains. The loop trail takes you back by heading downhill all the way to the parking lot.

❻ Santa Cruz Trail

4.0 mi/2.0 hrs

Location: In the Santa Ynez Recreation Area; map H3, grid f3.

User groups: Hikers, dogs, horses, and mountain bikes. No wheelchair facilities.

Permits: No permits are required. A $3 day-use fee is charged per vehicle.

Directions: From U.S. 101 in Santa Barbara, take the Highway 154/State Street exit and drive north for about 12 miles. Turn right on Paradise Road and drive 5.5 miles, past the ranger station, to the left turnoff for Upper Oso Campground. Turn left and drive one mile to the campground.

Maps: For a map of Los Padres National Forest, send $4 to USDA-Forest Service, 630 Sansome Street, San Francisco, CA 94111. To obtain a topographic map of the area, ask for San Marcos Pass from the USGS.

Contact: Los Padres National Forest, Santa Barbara Ranger District, Los Prietos Station, Star Route, Santa Barbara, CA 93105; (805) 967-3481, or fax (805) 967-7312.

Trail notes: The Santa Cruz Trail is one of the most popular in the Santa Ynez Recreation Area, and it's no wonder. The hiking is easy and the swimming holes along Oso Creek are plentiful. (Cooling off in the water is the number one reason that people pay a visit to the Santa Ynez Recreation Area in summertime.) The destination on this trip is Nineteen Oaks Camp, a popular picnicking spot near the base of Little Pine Mountain. The trail follows an unattractive dirt road out of Upper Oso Campground, but it becomes lovely single-track as it continues into the shady canyon. The sandstone-carved creek pools are lovely to see even when the water level is low, and as you climb a bit, you get views of Little Pine Mountain. A spur trail on the right at 1.9 miles leads a few hundred yards to Nineteen Oaks Camp, with shady oaks and a few campsites and picnic tables. Most day hikers end their trip there, before the trail begins its hot, exposed switchbacks to the top of Little Pine Mountain, elevation 4,506 feet.

❼ Knapp's Castle

0.8 mi/0.5 hr

Location: North of Santa Barbara; map H3, grid g3.

User groups: Hikers and dogs. No horses or mountain bikes. No wheelchair facilities.

Permits: No permits are required. A national forest recreation pass is required for each vehicle; fees are $5 for one day or $30 for a year.

Directions: From U.S. 101 in Santa Barbara, take the Highway 154/State Street exit and drive north for 10.5 miles. Turn right on East Camino Cielo and drive 2.9 miles to the parking pullout on the right, across from a locked gate and dirt road on the left. The gate is signed "Private Property Ahead."

Maps: For a map of Los Padres National Forest, send $4 to USDA-Forest Service, 630 Sansome Street, San Francisco, CA 94111. To obtain a topographic map of the area, ask for San Marcos Pass from the USGS.

Contact: Los Padres National Forest, Santa Barbara Ranger District, Los Prietos Station, Star Route, Santa Barbara, CA 93105; (805) 967-3481, or fax (805) 967-7312.

Trail notes: Some hikes are just right for all kinds of hikers, no matter what their abilities or tastes, and the trail to Knapp's Castle is one of those. The tricky part is that Knapp's Castle, or actually the remains of Knapp's Castle, is on a chunk of private property within Los Padres National Forest, and it's only by the good graces of the landowner that the public is allowed to hike there. He's a very nice gentleman, and for years he has allowed Santa Barbara hikers to visit his land, which is well known not just for the castle ruins but also for its memorable vistas. (If we all mind our manners, hopefully we can keep this beautiful spot accessible for many years to come.) So who was the Knapp of Knapp's Castle? George Knapp was the former chairman of the board of Union Carbide, and he built a five-bedroom sandstone mansion on this site in 1916. Although the building burned down in a canyon fire in 1940, its foundation still stands, and it offers a fine spot to sit and look out over the Santa Ynez River Canyon and distant mountain ranges. You can even see far-off Lake Cachuma. The trail to reach Knapp's Castle is a well-graded dirt road, and you hike past the gate that says "Private Property Ahead." Pass through another gate, staying on the dirt road, and reach the castle remains and its fabulous lookout in less than a half mile of walking.

Special note: Because Knapp's Castle is on private property, its accessibility to the public is subject to change at any time. Phone the Santa Barbara Ranger District office for an update before visiting.

❽ Seven Falls

3.0 mi/1.5 hrs

Location: North of Santa Barbara; map H3, grid g4.

User groups: Hikers, dogs, horses, and mountain bikes. No wheelchair facilities.

Permits: No permits are required. Parking and access are free.

Directions: From U.S. 101 in Santa Barbara, take the Mission Street exit and follow it east for just over a mile, crossing State Street. When Mission Street ends, turn left on Laguna Street and drive past the Santa Barbara Mission, turning right on Los Olivos directly in front of the Mission. Passing the Mission, bear left on Mission Canyon Road for eight-tenths of a mile. Turn right on Foothill Boulevard. In one-tenth of a mile, turn left onto the continuation of Mission Canyon Road. Then bear left on Tunnel Road, and follow it for 1.1 miles until it ends. Park alongside the road, on the right.

Maps: For a map of Los Padres National Forest, send $4 to USDA-Forest Service, 630 Sansome Street, San Francisco, CA 94111. To obtain a topographic map of the area, ask for Santa Barbara from the USGS.

Contact: Los Padres National Forest, Santa Barbara Ranger District, Los Prietos Station, Star Route, Santa Barbara, CA 93105; (805) 967-3481, or fax (805) 967-7312.

Trail notes: Seven Falls is a perfect springtime day trip in Santa Barbara, best visited from February to April. It has a little bit of everything: waterfalls, swimming holes, vistas, wildflowers, and good trail. From the end of Tunnel Road, start hiking on the gated continuation of the road, passing a water tank and heading uphill on pavement for three-quarters of a mile. In a few minutes of climbing, you'll be able to see all the way out to the ocean. Cross a bridge over Mission Creek and continue hiking straight ahead on the road, which turns to dirt. In a few hundred feet you come to a junction; a sign on your left directs you to the Jesusita Trail. Follow it to the left, then bear left again as the path cuts down on single-track to Mission Creek, where you'll find many good swimming holes. Cross the creek, but instead of following the continuation of Jesusita Trail, head to your right, upstream, on a use trail. In a quarter mile of combined hiking and scrambling, you'll reach the first of the sandstone-carved cascades of Seven Falls. These falls flow with force only immediately after a period of rain, but the sandstone pools and canyon walls are pretty to look at even when the creek is nearly dry.

User groups: Hikers, dogs, horses, and mountain bikes. No wheelchair facilities.

Permits: No permits are required. Parking and access are free.

Directions: From U.S. 101 in Santa Barbara, take the Mission Street exit and follow it east for just over a mile, crossing State Street. When Mission Street ends, turn left on Laguna Street and drive past the Santa Barbara Mission, turning right on Los Olivos directly in front of the Mission. Passing the Mission, bear left on Mission Canyon Road for eight-tenths of a mile. Turn right on Foothill Boulevard. In one-tenth of a mile, turn left onto the continuation of Mission Canyon Road. Then bear left on Tunnel Road, and follow it for 1.1 miles until it ends. Park alongside the road, on the right.

Maps: For a map of Los Padres National Forest, send $4 to USDA-Forest Service, 630 Sansome Street, San Francisco, CA 94111. To obtain a topographic map of the area, ask for Santa Barbara from the USGS.

Contact: Los Padres National Forest, Santa Barbara Ranger District, Los Prietos Station, Star Route, Santa Barbara, CA 93105; (805) 967-3481, or fax (805) 967-7312.

Trail notes: The trail to Inspiration Point is sure to get you inspired, if only because it's a great path for year-round exercise in Santa Barbara. Follow the Tunnel Trail as described in the trail notes for hike number 8, but after crossing over Mission Creek, don't take the streamside use trails but instead keep following the main Jesusita Trail. Get ready for a switchbacking climb up to Inspiration Point, which is only one mile away. The tan-colored rock outcrops you see everywhere are coldwater sandstone; often you'll see hang gliders taking off from some of the highest rocks and gliding, seemingly effortlessly, overhead. When you reach Inspiration Point at 1,750 feet, you are rewarded with sweeping views of the Pacific Coast, Santa Barbara and Goleta, and the Channel Islands.

⑨ Inspiration Point

5.0 mi/2.5 hrs

Location: North of Santa Barbara; map H3, grid g4.

⑩ Rattlesnake Canyon

5.0 mi/2.5 hrs

Location: North of Santa Barbara; map H3, grid h5.

User groups: Hikers, dogs, horses, and mountain bikes. No wheelchair facilities.

Permits: No permits are required. Parking and access are free.

Directions: From U.S. 101 in Santa Barbara, take the Mission Street exit and follow it east for just over a mile, crossing State Street. When Mission Street ends, turn left on Laguna Street and drive past the Santa Barbara Mission, turning right on Los Olivos directly in front of the Mission. Passing the Mission, bear left on Mission Canyon Road for eight-tenths of a mile. Turn right on Foothill Boulevard. In one-tenth of a mile, turn left onto the continuation of Mission Canyon Road. Drive four-tenths of a mile and turn right on Las Conoas Road. Drive 1.2 miles and park on the right side of the road, across the road from the trailhead sign.

Maps: For a map of Los Padres National Forest, send $4 to USDA-Forest Service, 630 Sansome Street, San Francisco, CA 94111. To obtain a topographic map of the area, ask for Santa Barbara from the USGS.

Contact: Los Padres National Forest, Santa Barbara Ranger District, Los Prietos Station, Star Route, Santa Barbara, CA 93105; (805) 967-3481, or fax (805) 967-7312.

Trail notes: Rattlesnake Canyon Trail is considered by many to be the prettiest canyon trail in Santa Barbara, despite its menacing name. It is indeed pretty, and it's also tremendously popular, especially on weekends. The trail leads through a lush riparian environment around a year-round creek, a place where the plant life is so lavish that you may think you're in Mendocino or the North Coast. The trail crosses rocky Rattlesnake Creek many times, tunneling through a forest of oak, bay, and sycamore trees on the lower stretch of the trail. In the spring and summer months wildflowers are as good as you'll find anywhere in Santa Barbara. As you climb out of the canyon, you'll gain increasingly broad views of the Pacific Coast and the Channel Islands. At an intersection with a connector trail to Tunnel Trail, bear right to finish out the steep climb to Gibraltar Road. Suddenly, your surroundings aren't quite so lush any more, but the views—well, on a clear day, they don't get much better than this.

⓫ Montecito Overlook

3.0 mi/1.5 hrs

Location: In Montecito; map H3, grid h5.

User groups: Hikers, dogs, horses, and mountain bikes. No wheelchair facilities.

Permits: No permits are required. Parking and access are free.

Directions: From Santa Barbara, drive south on U.S. 101 for four miles and exit on Hot Springs Road. Turn left on Hot Springs Road and drive 2.5 miles to Mountain Drive. Turn left and continue 1.2 miles to the Cold Springs Trailhead. Park off the road, near where the creek runs across the road. The trail is marked by a rusty Forest Service sign.

Maps: For a map of Los Padres National Forest, send $4 to USDA-Forest Service, 630 Sansome Street, San Francisco, CA 94111. To obtain a topographic map of the area, ask for Santa Barbara from the USGS.

Contact: Los Padres National Forest, Santa Barbara Ranger District, Los Prietos Station, Star Route, Santa Barbara, CA 93105; (805) 967-3481, or fax (805) 967-7312.

Trail notes: The East Fork of Cold Springs is a perfect introductory hike to the Santa Barbara front country. For people who think the mountains in Santa Barbara are all chaparral-covered slopes, this trail is an eye-opener to the lush beauty of the mountain canyons. The climb to Montecito Overlook is a good aerobic workout, but not a killer, and affords great views of the Santa Barbara coast and Channel Islands. Many people don't go all the way to the overlook; they just hike through the shady forest to a bench that overlooks the confluence of the East Fork and Middle Fork of Cold Springs Creek, then find themselves a cool pool to soak their feet in. From the roadside pullout, follow the path through the alders alongside Cold Springs Creek, staying on the creek's right (east) side. After the first mile, you leave the creek and begin to switchback uphill to the overlook, where the views are clear and wide. (Of course, that's only if the famous Santa Barbara fog isn't paying a visit.) Hikers looking for more trail to cover can continue another two miles to Montecito Peak, elevation 3,214 feet, accessible via a right spur at 3.5 miles.

⑫ West Fork Cold Springs

4.0 mi/2.0 hrs

Location: In Montecito; map H3, grid h5.

User groups: Hikers, dogs, horses, and mountain bikes. No wheelchair facilities.

Permits: No permits are required. Parking and access are free.

Directions: From Santa Barbara, drive south on U.S. 101 for four miles and exit on Hot Springs Road. Turn left on Hot Springs Road and drive 2.5 miles to Mountain Drive. Turn left and continue 1.2 miles to the Cold Springs Trailhead. Park off the road, near where the creek crosses the road.

Maps: For a map of Los Padres National Forest, send $4 to USDA-Forest Service, 630 Sansome Street, San Francisco, CA 94111. To obtain a topographic map of the area, ask for Santa Barbara from the USGS.

Contact: Los Padres National Forest, Santa Barbara Ranger District, Los Prietos Station, Star Route, Santa Barbara, CA 93105; (805) 967-3481, or fax (805) 967-7312.

Trail notes: If you hike the West Fork of Cold Springs from its start—where it spurs off the East Fork Trail—to its end at Gibraltar Road, you get to see the wide range of terrain that is typical in Santa Barbara. Start hiking on the East Fork Cold Springs Trail (see trail notes for hike number 10), then turn left a half mile up the creek to join the West Fork Trail. (You'll cross the creek here; look carefully for the trail sign.) Soon you leave the dense, shady, fern-laden area surrounding Cold Springs Creek, and climb out of the canyon into a drier and more exposed landscape. In early spring, look for spectacular Tangerine Falls up ahead in the Middle Fork Canyon; the waterfall is clearly visible although distant from the West Fork Trail. (A use trail cuts off from the main trail to reach it, but it requires good scrambling abilities and an immunity to poison oak.) By the time you climb to the end of the West Fork Trail at Gibraltar Road, you'll be glad to turn around and head back down to the coolness below. The views are excellent from the road, however, and you'll get plenty more views as you walk back down the trail. Be careful going down—the West Fork Trail is not as well used as the East Fork Trail, and it's steep and eroded in places, especially when wet. But that's a small price to pay for the eyefuls of vistas out toward the Montecito coast.

⑬ San Ysidro Trail

8.0 mi/4.5 hrs

Location: In Montecito; map H3, grid h6.

User groups: Hikers, dogs, horses, and mountain bikes. No wheelchair facilities.

Permits: No permits are required. Parking and access are free.

Directions: From U.S. 101 in Montecito, take the San Ysidro Road exit and head east for one mile to East Valley Road/Highway 192. Turn right on East Valley Road/Highway 192 and travel nine-tenths of a mile, then turn left on Park Lane. Drive four-tenths of a mile on Park Lane, then bear left on East Mountain Drive. Drive to the end of East Mountain Drive in a quarter mile and park alongside the road. The trailhead is on the right side of the road.

Maps: For a map of Los Padres National Forest, send $4 to USDA-Forest Service, 630 Sansome Street, San Francisco, CA 94111. To obtain a topographic map of the area, ask for Carpinteria from the USGS.

Contact: Los Padres National Forest, Santa Barbara Ranger District, Los Prietos Station, Star Route, Santa Barbara, CA 93105; (805) 967-3481, or fax (805) 967-7312.

Trail notes: If you like running water, San Ysidro Canyon is your chance at seeing some, even long after the last rain. Other streams in the Santa Barbara area are often nearly dry by May, but San Ysidro keeps on flowing year-round. The trail up its canyon offers many possible destinations and stopping points; few hike all the way to its terminus at East Camino Cielo—it's four miles one way with a 3,000-foot elevation gain. The rewards are great no matter how far you go, beginning with swimming holes and waterfalls in the first two miles of trail, mostly under the shade of oaks and sycamores. After a rocky section, you climb out of the canyon into chaparral country, entering into a series of steep, exposed switchbacks. Most people give up somewhere along this stretch, but those who continue come out near Cold Spring Saddle on East Camino Cielo, elevation 3,480 feet. From there, you'll feel like you're on top of the world.

⑭ McMenemy Trail

2.5 mi/1.0 hr

Location: In Montecito; map H3, grid h6.

User groups: Hikers, dogs, horses, and mountain bikes. No wheelchair facilities.

Permits: No permits are required. Parking and access are free.

Directions: From U.S. 101 in Montecito, take the San Ysidro Road exit and head east for one mile to East Valley Road/Highway 192. Turn right on East Valley Road/Highway 192 and travel nine-tenths of a mile, then turn left on Park Lane. Drive four-tenths of a mile on Park Lane, then bear left on East Mountain Drive. Drive to the end of East Mountain Drive in a quarter mile and park alongside the road. The trailhead is on the right side of the road.

Maps: For a map of Los Padres National Forest, send $4 to USDA-Forest Service, 630 Sansome Street, San Francisco, CA 94111. To obtain a topographic map of the area, ask for Carpinteria from the USGS.

Contact: Los Padres National Forest, Santa Barbara Ranger District, Los Prietos Station, Star Route, Santa Barbara, CA 93105; (805) 967-3481, or fax (805) 967-7312.

Trail notes: If you only have time for a short hike, this lovely trip in San Ysidro Canyon includes a stint on the McMenemy Trail, a favorite of many Santa Barbara hikers. It has just enough of a climb to make you feel like you did your workout for the day, but enough pretty views to make you forget that hiking is actually exercise. Begin your trip on the San Ysidro Trail (see hike number 13), then bear left at the sign for the McMenemy Trail a half mile in. A series of switchbacks brings you to the Colonel's stone bench—Colonel McMenemy, that is—where you have a fine view down into Montecito and out to the coast. It's a good place to catch your breath. If you want to keep hiking, you can make a five-mile loop by continuing on McMenemy Trail to Saddle Rock Trail. Turn right, then right again on the Edison Catwalk, to return to San Ysidro Canyon Trail.

⑮ McGrath State Beach Nature Trail

0.75 mi/0.5 hr

Location: In Oxnard; map H3, grid j9.

User groups: Hikers only. No dogs, horses, or mountain bikes. No wheelchair facilities.

Permits: No permits are required. A $5 day-use fee is charged per vehicle.

Directions: From U.S. 101 in Ventura, take the Seaward Avenue exit to Harbor Boulevard. Turn south on Harbor Boulevard and drive four miles to the park entrance. The nature trail begins at the day-use parking lot, which is a quick right turn after the entrance kiosk. (If you are traveling north on U.S. 101, you must take the Victoria Avenue exit to reach Harbor Boulevard.)

Maps: To obtain a topographic map of the area, ask for Ventura from the USGS.

Contact: McGrath State Beach, 901 South San Pedro, Ventura, CA 93001; (805) 654-4610.

Trail notes: There's a great little nature trail at McGrath State Beach that makes for a far different hike than a walk along the sandy public beach. The trail runs along the Santa Clara Estuary, whih is designated as a natural preserve. It's the place where the Santa Clara River joins the Pacific Ocean. In that meeting space, freshwater and saltwater plants and animals intermingle, which means you have the chance to see migrating birds, resident shorebirds, and fish swimming in the estuary. The trail starts out in a shaded willow thicket, a secluded and peaceful change from the hustle and bustle of the beach campground. Watch for the endangered California least tern or Belding's savannah sparrow. When you reach the beach, you can continue hiking along the shoreline, or turn around and head back.

Leave No Trace Tips

Properly Dispose of What You Can't Pack Out

If no refuse facility is available, deposit human waste in catholes dug six to eight inches deep at least 200 feet from water, camps, or trails. Cover and disguise the catholes when you're finished.

To wash yourself or your dishes, carry the water 200 feet from streams or lakes and use small amounts of biodegradable soap. Scatter the strained dishwater.

Map H4

Adjoining Maps: East: H5 ... *page* 542   West: H3 522
North: G4 476   South: I4 564

Central California Map .... *page* 382

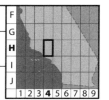

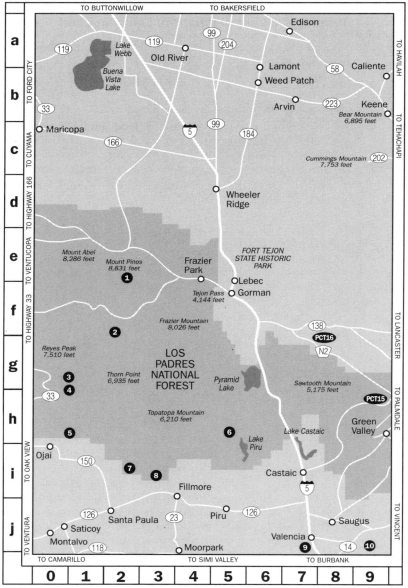

TO BUTTONWILLOW   TO BAKERSFILED

a

TO FORD CITY

119   Lake Webb   119   99   204   Edison

Buena Vista Lake   Old River   Lamont   58   Caliente

b

33   Weed Patch   Keene

TO TEHACHAPI

Arvin   223   Bear Mountain 6,895 feet

c

TO CUYAMA

Maricopa   166   99   184   Cummings Mountain 7,753 feet   202

d

TO HIGHWAY 166

5   Wheeler Ridge

e

TO VENTUCOPA

Mount Abel 8,286 feet   Mount Pinos 8,831 feet ❶   Frazier Park   FORT TEJON STATE HISTORIC PARK

Lebec

f

TO HIGHWAY 33

Tejon Pass 4,144 feet   Gorman

Frazier Mountain 8,026 feet ❷   138   PCT16   N2

g

Reyes Peak 7,510 feet   LOS PADRES NATIONAL FOREST

Thorn Point 6,935 feet ❸ ❹   Pyramid Lake   Sawtooth Mountain 5,175 feet   PCT15

33

h

TO OAK VIEW

❺   Topatopa Mountain 6,210 feet   ❻   Lake Piru   Lake Castaic   Green Valley

Ojai   150

i

❼   ❽   Castaic   5

Fillmore   TO PALMDALE

TO LANCASTER

j

TO VENTURA

126   Santa Paula   23   Piru   126   Saugus

Saticoy   Valencia ❾   14   ❿

Montalvo   118   Moorpark

TO CAMARILLO   TO SIMI VALLEY   TO BURBANK

| 0 | 1 | 2 | 3 | 4 | 5 | 6 | 7 | 8 | 9 |

❶ Vincent Tumamait Trail

5.0 mi/2.5 hrs

Location: In the Chumash Wilderness west of Frazier Park; map H4, grid e2.

User groups: Hikers, dogs, and horses. No mountain bikes. No wheelchair facilities.

Permits: No permits are required. A national forest recreation pass is required for each vehicle; fees are $5 for one day or $30 for a year.

Directions: From Interstate 5 near Lebec, take the Frazier Park exit and drive three miles west to Frazier Park, then continue west on Frazier Mountain Road for two miles to the Lake of the Woods fork. Bear right on Cuddy Valley Road, drive five miles, then bear left on Mount Pinos Highway for nine miles to the dirt road on the left signed for Condor Observation Point. Turn left and drive two miles to the point.

Maps: For a map of Los Padres National Forest, send $4 to USDA-Forest Service, 630 Sansome Street, San Francisco, CA 94111. To obtain a topographic map of the area, ask for Sawmill Mountain from the USGS.

Contact: Los Padres National Forest, Mount Pinos Ranger District, 34580 Lockwood Valley Road, Frazier Park, CA 93225; (805) 245-3731 or fax (805) 245-1526.

Trail notes: A day hike in the Chumash Wilderness means the possibility of seeing a magnificent condor fly overhead, and a visit to Mount Pinos, the highest point in Los Padres National Forest at 8,831 feet. This is conifer country, with the trail near the peak covered in snow a good part of the year, to the great delight of Southern California cross-country skiers. The Vincent Tumamait Trail runs five miles to Mount Abel, elevation 8,286 feet (also called Mount Cerro Noroeste). If you wish, you can leave a car at Mount Abel and take a one-way shuttle trip between the two impressive peaks. Otherwise, it's great fun just to wander a ways on the Vincent Tumamait Trail, heading out two miles, downhill at first and then up Sawmill Mountain, to the Sheep Camp Trail junction. You can bear left at the junction and walk a half mile to the camp, then open up your daypack and have lunch. After a rest, you'll be all fueled up for the return trip to the summit. As you hike, keep scanning the skies for those giant condors, many of whom nest in the nearby condor sanctuary. By the way, who was Vincent Tumamait? He was a Chumash elder and beloved storyteller who lived from 1919 to 1992.

❷ Cedar Creek and the Fishbowls

9.0 mi/4.5 hrs or 2.0 days

Location: In the Sespe Wilderness, southwest of Frazier Park; map H4, grid f2.

User groups: Hikers, dogs, and horses. No mountain bikes. No wheelchair facilities.

Permits: A California campfire permit is required for building a fire or using a backpacking stove; permits are available at any Southern California Forest Service ranger station. A national forest recreation pass is required for each vehicle; fees are $5 for one day or $30 for a year.

Directions: From Interstate 5 near Lebec, take the Frazier Park exit and drive three miles west to Frazier Park, then continue west on Frazier Mountain Road for two miles to the Lake of the

Woods fork. Bear left and drive 10.5 miles on Lockwood Valley Road. Turn left on Grade Valley Road/Road 7N03 (dirt) and drive 7.5 miles. Turn right on Thorn Meadows Road and drive a half mile to the Cedar Creek Trailhead.

Maps: For a map of Los Padres National Forest, send $4 to USDA-Forest Service, 630 Sansome Street, San Francisco, CA 94111. To obtain a topographic map of the area, ask for Lockwood Valley from the USGS.

Contact: Los Padres National Forest, Mount Pinos Ranger District, 34580 Lockwood Valley Road, Frazier Park, CA 93225; (805) 245-3731 or fax (805) 245-1526.

Trail notes: Despite the long mileage on this trail, the Fishbowls along Piru Creek are a popular and heavily visited spot, mostly because there is little that is finer in life than a creek with good swimming holes. That and the fact that the trail has a moderate elevation gain, so even with the nine-mile round-trip, it's a manageable day hike for most people. The Cedar Creek Trail leads uphill from Thorn Meadows Campground (elevation 5,050 feet), first through oaks and then a pretty conifer forest (including the trail's namesake incense cedars). It follows the South Fork of Piru Creek much of the way. What starts out as a wide dirt road eventually narrows to single-track. At 3.5 miles in, bear right on the Fishbowls Trail, hike along a ridgeline with lovely views of the forest below, then descend to Fishbowls Camp. Walk upstream from the camp for about 300 yards to reach the Fishbowls, a series of rounded sandstone pools on Piru Creek. Now strip down to your bathing suit, jump in, and shout, "I'm alive!"

❸ Piedra Blanca

2.0 mi/1.0 hr

Location: In the Rose Valley Recreation Area north of Ojai; map H4, grid g0.

User groups: Hikers, dogs, horses, and mountain bikes. No wheelchair facilities.

Permits: No permits are required. A national forest recreation pass is required for each vehicle; fees are $5 for one day or $30 for a year.

Directions: From Ojai, drive north on Highway 33 for 16 miles to Rose Valley Road and the sign

for Rose Valley Recreation Area. Turn right, drive 4.6 miles and take the left fork, then drive 1.1 miles further to Lion Campground. Park in the signed day-use area.

Maps: For a map of Los Padres National Forest, send $4 to USDA-Forest Service, 630 Sansome Street, San Francisco, CA 94111. To obtain a topographic map of the area, ask for Lion Canyon from the USGS.

Contact: Los Padres National Forest, Ojai Ranger District, 1190 East Ojai Avenue, Ojai, CA 93023; (805) 646-4348 or fax (805) 646-0484.

Trail notes: Sandstone lovers, this is your spot. Piedra Blanca is a series of huge, rounded sandstone boulders that are somewhat otherworldly-looking in appearance. If rocks can look sensual, these are. They're set in the Rose Valley Recreation Area, just a short stretch away from Sespe Creek, in what looks a lot like the desert—plenty of sand, desert scrub, and rocks. Hike from the day-use area at Lion Campground, crossing Sespe's often dry wash, then pick up the trail on the far side of the wash. The rocks of Piedra Blanca are clearly visible, so it's easy to see where you're going. Although the trail continues down the back side of the boulders and beyond, most people just climb to the top of the boulders, then spend some time wandering around and exploring. As you might guess, this is a first-class spot for watching sunsets.

❹ Rose Valley Falls

0.6 mi/0.5 hr

Location: In the Rose Valley Recreation Area north of Ojai; map H4, grid g0.

User groups: Hikers, dogs, horses, and mountain bikes. No wheelchair facilities.

Permits: No permits are required. A national forest recreation pass is required for each vehicle; fees are $5 for one day or $30 for a year.

Directions: From Ojai, drive north on Highway 33 for 16 miles to Rose Valley Road and the sign for Rose Valley Recreation Area. Turn right, drive three miles, then turn right again at the sign for Rose Valley Camp. Drive six-tenths of a mile to the campground. The trail leads from the far end of the camp, near site number 4.

Maps: For a map of Los Padres National Forest,

send $4 to USDA-Forest Service, 630 Sansome Street, San Francisco, CA 94111. To obtain a topographic map of the area, ask for Lion Canyon from the USGS.

Contact: Los Padres National Forest, Ojai Ranger District, 1190 East Ojai Avenue, Ojai, CA 93023; (805) 646-4348 or fax (805) 646-0484.

Trail notes: The trip to Rose Valley Falls is an easy walk in the woods to the base of a stunning and unusual limestone waterfall. If you're making the drive to Rose Valley Recreation Area to camp, fish, or hike, a side trip to Rose Valley Falls is just about mandatory. Start hiking on the signed trail in Rose Valley Campground. The path is bordered on both sides by oaks and fragrant bays, and it parallels Rose Creek. Cross the creek a few times, and as you walk into the canyon, keep looking ahead (up high) for your first glimpse of the 300-foot waterfall. If it has rained lately, you'll see it for sure. In 15 minutes you reach the base of the falls, which is glaringly different in appearance than the waterfall you were just looking at. That's because this is the bottom tier of huge Rose Valley Falls, and you were seeing the upper tier. The lower tier is layered with limestone and sandstone slabs, and oozing with wet moss. You can't resist touching it. Some daredevils attempt to climb up and over this lower tier to see more of the upper part of the waterfall, but this should only be attempted by experts with proper climbing equipment.

❺ Nordhoff Peak

12.0 mi/6.0 hrs

Location: East of Ojai; map H4, grid h1.

User groups: Hikers, dogs, horses, and mountain bikes. No wheelchair facilities.

Permits: No permits are required. A national forest recreation pass is required for each vehicle; fees are $5 for one day or $30 for a year.

Directions: From Ojai at the intersection of Highways 150 and 33, drive east on Highway 150 and turn left on Gridley Road, a half mile past the ranger station. Drive 1.5 miles north on Gridley Road to the trailhead on the left.

Maps: For a map of Los Padres National Forest, send $4 to USDA-Forest Service, 630 Sansome Street, San Francisco, CA 94111. To obtain a topographic map of the area, ask for Ojai from the USGS.

Contact: Los Padres National Forest, Ojai Ranger District, 1190 East Ojai Avenue, Ojai, CA 93023; (805) 646-4348 or fax (805) 646-0484.

Trail notes: The hike to Nordhoff Peak is a rite of passage for Ojai hikers. After all, journalist Charles Nordhoff was the guy who made Ojai famous. In the late 1800s, he wrote various magazine articles about Ojai Valley's many charms, which encouraged people to move here and start a new life. Nordhoff's summit is at 4,425 feet, high enough to get an occasional few inches of snow, and a hike to the top is a fine way to spend a spring day in Ojai. That's if you're up to the six-mile, 3,300-foot climb, of course. (Forget hiking in the heat of summer; much of the trail is on open fire roads, with no shade.) From the Gridley Trailhead, hike up to Gridley Fire Road and turn right, passing by seemingly endless avocado groves. Bear left at the next junction, then enter a shadier canyon and pass the primitive camp at Gridley Spring. This is the halfway point; take a breather. Prepare yourself for the next two miles—the steepest on the trip—then begin switchbacking your way up to Nordhoff Fire Road, where you turn left and hike one more mile to the peak. If you think that after all this climbing, you ought to get some good views, you won't be disappointed. You can see all the way to the Pacific Ocean and Channel Islands, plus Ojai Valley and Lake Casitas closer in, and miles of Los Padres National Forest and its wilderness areas.

❻ Pothole and Agua Blanca Loop

11.0 mi/1–2 days

Location: In the Sespe Wilderness near Lake Piru; map H4, grid h5.

User groups: Hikers, dogs, horses, and mountain bikes. No wheelchair facilities.

Permits: A free wilderness permit is required for overnight stays; they are available from the Ojai Ranger District or Lake Piru Recreation Area. A national forest recreation pass is required for each vehicle; fees are $5 for one day or $30 for a year.

Directions: From Fillmore, take Highway 126 east for eight miles to Piru Canyon Road, signed for Lake Piru. Turn left (north) on Piru Canyon Road and follow the signs through the town of Piru to Lake Piru's entrance station, then continue beyond the lake to Blue Point Campground. Continue past the camp, crossing a stream, to the day-use parking area. Total distance on Piru Canyon Road is 13.5 miles.

Maps: For a map of Los Padres National Forest, send $4 to USDA-Forest Service, 630 Sansome Street, San Francisco, CA 94111. To obtain a topographic map of the area, ask for Cobblestone Mountain from the USGS.

Contact: Los Padres National Forest, Ojai Ranger District, 1190 East Ojai Avenue, Ojai, CA 93023; (805) 646-4348 or fax (805) 646-0484. Or Lake Piru Recreation Area, (805) 521-1500.

Trail notes: Most people know to come to Lake Piru for waterskiing, sailing, and fishing, but not everybody knows to come here for hiking. An excellent trail begins from Blue Point Campground (beyond the north end of the lake), which can be hiked as a loop in either direction. Most people park at Blue Point Campground and hike up the Agua Blanca Trail from there, then return on the Pothole Trail, which brings you back to the road about a mile south of the campground. That makes the last mile an easy tromp on the road back to your car. Hiking the trail in this fashion, you set out on a dirt road out of Blue Point Camp for about a mile, following Piru Creek, then bear left on Agua Blanca Trail. Climb moderately along crystal-clear Agua Blanca Creek to Devil's Gateway, a rocky narrows area. The trail goes around the carved sandstone gorge, but when the water is low enough, some hikers wade through it instead, just for the fun of it. Reach Log Cabin Camp 4.5 miles in, a fine place to lay your sleeping bag. The next day is longer mileage, following the Pothole Trail for one mile to the Pothole, a huge, grassy depression in the ground. (It's just off the main trail; take the quarter-mile spur on your right to see it.) Climb from there, more gently now, with the gain spread out over a few miles. The final two miles of the trip are a steep descent to the campground road. Views are good all the way down, especially of Lake Piru and bluish-colored Blue

Point, a rock outcrop. At the road, turn left to return to Blue Point Camp.

❼ Santa Paula Canyon

6.0 mi/3.5 hrs or 2.0 days

Location: East of Ojai; map H4, grid i2.

User groups: Hikers, dogs, horses, and mountain bikes. No wheelchair facilities.

Permits: No permits are required. A national forest recreation pass is required for each vehicle; fees are $5 for one day or $30 for a year.

Directions: From Ojai, at the junction of Highways 33 and 150, drive east on Highway 150 for 11.5 miles to Thomas Aquinas College on the left (look for iron gates and stone buildings). Drive 100 yards further to the parking pullout on the right side of the road, just beyond the highway bridge over Santa Paula Creek. Park there and walk back across the bridge to the paved road on the right side of the college.

Maps: For a map of Los Padres National Forest, send $4 to USDA-Forest Service, 630 Sansome Street, San Francisco, CA 94111. To obtain a topographic map of the area, ask for Santa Paula Peak from the USGS.

Contact: Los Padres National Forest, Ojai Ranger District, 1190 East Ojai Avenue, Ojai, CA 93023; (805) 646-4348 or fax (805) 646-0484.

Trail notes: What starts out rather pedestrian gets much, much better on the Santa Paula Canyon Trail. That's because the first mile of the route is mostly on pavement, meandering around the grounds of Thomas Aquinas College and a private ranch and oil-drilling operation, before at last, you're on a real trail in the real outdoors. This slow start doesn't keep the Santa Paula Canyon Trail from being well loved and frequently used, especially by people looking for an easy overnight backpacking trip, or a place to jump in a swimming hole. You'll find a few people hiking the path even on weekdays. After following the well-signed route to the start of the "real" trail, you'll head deep into Santa Paula Canyon, following the creek and crossing it twice. The trees are dense and wildflowers are sublime. After the second creek crossing at two miles out, get ready for your first real climb on the trail, as you follow a wide dirt road up and around Hill 1989. Following the ascent, the trail drops down to a lovely campground in a grassy flat, surrounded by big cone spruce. There are six sites with fire rings there, at aptly named Big Cone Camp. The trail leads a short distance from the camp steeply down to Santa Paula Creek, where waterfalls and swimming holes await on a stretch of stream called "the Punchbowls." Here's a tip: If you can secure the campsite on the far left side of Big Cone Camp, it has its own little overlook on one of Santa Paula Creek's nicest waterfalls.

⑧ Santa Paula Peak

9.0 mi/5.0 hrs

Location: East of Ojai; map H4, grid i3.

User groups: Hikers, dogs, horses, and mountain bikes. No wheelchair facilities.

Permits: No permits are required. A national forest recreation pass is required for each vehicle; fees are $5 for one day or $30 for a year.

Directions: From Fillmore, take Highway 126 west for five miles. Turn right on Timber Canyon Road (dirt) and drive 4.5 miles to the gate and trailhead.

Maps: For a map of Los Padres National Forest, send $4 to USDA-Forest Service, 630 Sansome Street, San Francisco, CA 94111. To obtain a topographic map of the area, ask for Santa Paula Peak from the USGS.

Contact: Los Padres National Forest, Ojai Ranger District, 1190 East Ojai Avenue, Ojai, CA 93023; (805) 646-4348 or fax (805) 646-0484.

Trail notes: If you're looking for a good workout but the hike to Nordhoff Peak sounds a bit too long (see trail notes for hike number 5), the trail to Santa Paula Peak is a great alternative. The climb is the same—the trail gains 3,000 feet—but it's compressed into 4.5 miles and about a million switchbacks. The peak is actually higher than Nordhoff Peak—Santa Paula's summit is just shy of 5,000 feet—but the views are somewhat different, looking down into the Santa Clara Valley and out to the coast. There are no trail junctions to worry about until four miles up, when you reach the ridge just below the peak. Bear left (west) and finish out your climb, then pat yourself on the back for being such a fine mountaineer.

⑨ Canyon View Trail

2.0 mi/1.0 hr

Location: In Ed Davis Park in Towsley Canyon, south of Valencia; map H4, grid j7.

User groups: Hikers, dogs, horses, and mountain bikes. No wheelchair facilities.

Permits: No permits are required. Parking and access are free.

Directions: From the San Fernando Valley, drive north on Interstate 5 to Santa Clarita (five miles north of the Interstate 5 and Highway 14 junction). Take the Calgrove exit, turn left, drive a quarter mile and turn right onto the park entrance road. Park in the second parking lot.

Maps: To obtain topographic maps of the area, ask for Newhall and Oat Mountain from the USGS.

Contact: Santa Monica Mountains Conservancy, 5750 Ramirez Canyon Road, Malibu, CA 90265; (310) 589-3200.

Trail notes: Little Ed Davis Park is a part of larger Towsley Canyon, which is a part of the giant Santa Monica Mountains Conservancy parcel of lands. If you visit the park any time except during the sweltering heat of summer, you can walk the two-mile Canyon View Trail and pay a visit to all of Towsley Canyon's major plant communities—grasslands, sage and scrub, riparian, oak woodlands, and just about everything except old-growth redwood forest—in one short trip. How can a park this close to Interstate 5 be this wild looking? We can't figure it out, but it is. The trail begins near the creek, east of the nature center, and ends on the Wiley Canyon Trail. (You return via the dirt entrance road.) Despite the brevity of the trail, it has a surprisingly good climb to a ridge, where you have excellent views of the rock formations in Towsley Canyon and the Santa Clarita Valley.

⑩ Placerita Creek Waterfall

5.5 mi/2.5 hrs

Location: In Placerita Canyon County Park southeast of Valencia; map H4, grid j9.

User groups: Hikers, dogs, and horses. No mountain bikes. No wheelchair facilities.

Permits: No permits are required. A $3 day-use fee is charged per vehicle.

Directions: From the San Fernando Valley, drive north on Interstate 5 to Highway 14. Follow Highway 14 northeast for four miles to Newhall, then exit on Placerita Canyon Road. Turn right (east) and drive 1.5 miles to the park entrance on the right. Park in the nature center parking lot.

Maps: Free maps of Placerita Canyon County Park are available at the park nature center. To obtain topographic maps of the area, ask for San Fernando and Mint Canyon from the USGS.

Contact: Placerita Canyon County Park, 19152 Placerita Canyon Road, Newhall, CA 91321; (805) 259-7721.

Trail notes: Placerita Canyon County Park is a perfect destination for a family outing, being just far enough out of the Los Angeles basin to feel like someplace different, and with trails that are easy enough for hikers of almost any ability. Start your trip at the park nature center, where you should pay a visit to all the taxidermied animals and learn a thing or two about the flora and fauna of the area. Then start hiking on the Canyon Trail, which leads from the southeast side of the parking lot and crosses Placerita Creek. Hike through Placerita Canyon, often under the shade of sycamores and oaks, to Walker Ranch Picnic Area. At its far side, look for a trail on the right signed as Waterfall Trail, and get ready for the best part of the trip. (Make sure you don't take the Los Piñetos Trail, which is just before the Waterfall Trail, and doesn't go to the falls.) The canyon begins to narrow, and you twist and curve your way along the trail, crossing and recrossing the creek a few times. In the final 100 yards before the waterfall, the trail ends and you simply hike up the streambed. Although the waterfall is only 25 feet high, it forms a lovely little grotto, a perfect place to eat a Power Bar before heading back.

Pacific Crest Trail (PCT) Section Overview

65.0 mi. one way/7.0 days

While we have hiked all of the John Muir Trail and most of the Pacific Crest Trail, we took a pass on this section, which extends from the San Francisquito Canyon Road Trailhead north to the trailhead parking area on Tehachapi/Willow Springs Road. Unless inspired by a desire to hike the entire PCT after reaching Three Points, it makes no sense to hike beyond to Tehachapi Pass. The reason is that PCT through-hikers are forced to make a 45-mile excursion across the high-desert terrain of the Mojave Desert because the owners of megagiant Tejon Ranch wouldn't allow a true crest route to be built on their property. So hikers get dumped out on the desert, where 100-degree temperatures are common even in late spring. Water is always a critical factor here. If for some reason you decide to cross the Mojave, drink as much as possible when at a reliable source, and then carry as much as possible when hiking.

PCT-15 San Francisquito Canyon Road to Three Points

34.0 mi. one way/4.0 days

Location: From San Francisquito Canyon Road northwest to the trailhead parking area at Three Points; map H4, grid h9.

User groups: Hikers, dogs, and horses. No mountain bikes. No wheelchair facilities.

Permits: A wilderness permit is required for traveling through various wilderness and special-use areas the trail traverses. Contact the Angeles National Forest at (805) 296-9710 for a permit that is good for the length of your trip.

Directions: To reach the San Francisquito Canyon Trailhead, from Palmdale and Highway 14, drive west on County Road N2 (Elizabeth Lake Road) and turn left onto San Francisquito Canyon Road, just before reaching Elizabeth Lake. The trailhead is located near the San Francisquito Ranger Station and the campground. To reach the Three Points Trailhead, from Palmdale and Highway 14, drive west on County Road N2 (Elizabeth Lake Road) to the town of Three Points. Turn right (north) onto Oakdale Road. The PCT Trailhead is located near a small store at the junction of Oakdale Road and Pine Canyon Road. The PCT runs adjacent to Oakdale Road heading north.

Maps: For an overall view of the trail route in this section, send $4 for to the USDA-Forest Service, 630 Sansome Street, San Francisco, CA 94111, and ask for the Cleveland National Forest map. For topographic maps of the route, request Lake Hughes, Burnt Peak, and Liebre Mountain from the USGS. Two BLM surface maps cover the area as well and may be ordered from the Bureau of Land Management office listed below. Send $4.50 for each map ordered and ask for Tehachapi and Lancaster.

Contact: Angeles National Forest, Saugus Ranger District, 30800 Bouquet Canyon Road, Saugus, CA 91350; (805) 296-9710 or fax (805) 296-5847. Bureau of Land Management, Caliente Resource Area, 3801 Pegasus Drive, Bakersfield, CA 93308; (805) 391-6000 or fax (805) 391-6156.

Trail notes: During this 34-mile stint from San Francisquito Road to Three Points, you'll have lots of time to contemplate the awaiting trek across the Mojave Desert. The transition from Angeles National Forest, now well behind you, is complete as you head toward desert through scrub and sparsely vegetated canyons. The views are the lone highlight. From Liebre Mountain, where off-road vehicles have ruined the experience for many hikers, you can even see a piece of Hollywood and beyond to the Pacific Ocean, along with another view of the peaks in Angeles National Forest, and northeast across the Antelope Valley and the Mojave. From here it's a dry, downhill tromp to Pine Canyon, a drop of 2,000 feet, and then on to the Three Points Trailhead. Be absolutely certain to get information on water availability before heading out, then carefully plan your water stops and monitor supply and consumption.

PCT-16 Three Points to Tehachapi/Willow Springs Road

31.0 mi. one way/3.0 days

Location: From the trailhead parking area at Three Points northeast to Tehachapi/Willow Springs Road; map H4, grid g8.

User groups: Hikers, dogs, and horses. No mountain bikes. No wheelchair facilities.

Permits: A wilderness permit is required for traveling through various wilderness and special-use areas the trail traverses. Contact the Angeles National Forest at (805) 296-9710 for a permit that is good for the length of your trip.

Directions: To reach the Three Points Trailhead, from Palmdale and Highway 14, drive west on County Road N2 (Elizabeth Lake Road) to the town of Three Points. Turn right (north) onto Oakdale Road. The PCT Trailhead is located near a small store at the junction of Oakdale Road and Pine Canyon Road. The PCT runs adjacent to Oakdale Road heading north. To reach the Tehachapi/Willow Springs Road Trailhead, from Mojave and Highway 14, head west on Oak Creek Road to the intersection with Tehachapi/Willow Springs Road. The trailhead is located near the intersection.

Maps: For an overall view of the trail route in this section, send $4 for to the USDA-Forest Service, 630 Sansome Street, San Francisco, CA 94111, and ask for the Cleveland National Forest map. For topographic maps of the route, request Burnt Peak, Nenache School, Fairmont Butte, Tylerhorse Canyon, Tehachapi South, and Monolith from the USGS. Two BLM surface maps cover the area as well and may be ordered from the Bureau of Land Management office listed below. Send $4.50 for each map ordered and ask for Tehachapi and Lancaster.

Contact: Angeles National Forest, Valyermo Ranger District, 29835 Valyermo Road, P.O. Box 15, Valyermo, CA 93563; (805) 944-2187 or fax (805) 944-4698. Bureau of Land Management, Caliente Resource Area, 3801 Pegasus Drive, Bakersfield, CA 93308; (805) 391-6000 or fax (805) 391-6156.

Trail notes: This is a bizarre piece of trail, one that only PCT through-hikers would take the time to hike, and, even then, doing so only to keep the honor intact of having really hiked the entire route. After leaving Three Points, the Pacific Crest Trail follows no crest at all, but is routed across the high desert, up to the town of Mojave, then up into the Tehachapis. At times the trail parallels aqueducts and water pipelines, a terrible paradox, since the water is out of reach and other sources are near zero. The only features worth noting are occasional Joshua trees, and for those hiking at night with headlamps or under full moons, the chance of seeing desert wildlife that hides in shade during the day. The trail drops as low as 2,900 feet, then climbs out toward the Tehachapi Mountains, water scarce all the way. It's a rough go, always. From Cottonwood Canyon, which bottoms out at 2,915 feet, it's a 30-mile hike to Tehachapi Pass at 6,280 feet, surrounded by a barren landscape. The vision of the Sierra to the north and the forests, meadows, streams, lakes, and snow-laden passes could only seem like a mirage. From Tehachapi Pass, you then descend 2,000 feet down to Willow Springs Road and another PCT Trailhead.

PCT Continuation: To continue hiking along the Pacific Crest Trail, see chapter G5.

Leave No Trace Tips

Keep the Wilderness Wild

Treat our natural heritage with respect. Leave plants, rocks, and historical artifacts as you found them.

Good campsites are found, not made. Do not alter a campsite.

Let nature's sounds prevail; keep loud voices and noises to a minimum.

Do not build structures or furniture or dig trenches.

Map H5

Adjoining Maps: East: H6 ... *page* 550 West: H4 532
North: G5 .... 478 South: I5 578

Central California Map .... *page 382*

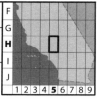

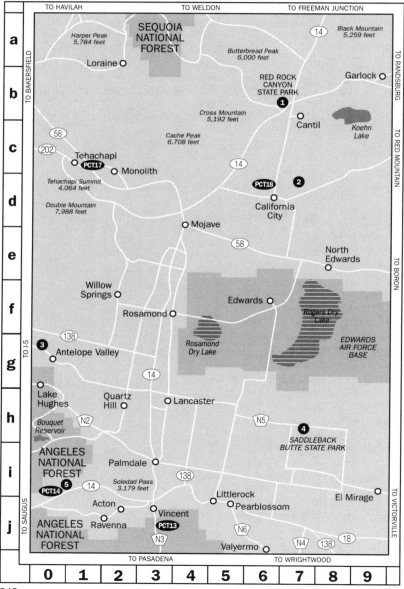

TO HAVILAH TO WELDON TO FREEMAN JUNCTION

a

TO BAKERSFIELD

Harper Peak
5,784 feet

**SEQUOIA
NATIONAL
FOREST**

Butterbread Peak
6,000 feet

14

Black Mountain
5,259 feet

Loraine

b

Garlock

TO RANDSBURG

RED ROCK
CANYON
STATE PARK

1

Cross Mountain
5,192 feet

Cantil

Koehn
Lake

c

58

202

Tehachapi

PCT17

Monolith

Cache Peak
6,708 feet

14

TO RED MOUNTAIN

d

Tehachapi Summit
4,064 feet

Double Mountain
7,988 feet

PCT18

2

California
City

Mojave

e

58

North
Edwards

TO BORON

f

Willow
Springs

Rosamond

Edwards

Rogers Dry
Lake

EDWARDS
AIR FORCE
BASE

g

TO I-5

138

3

Antelope Valley

Rosamond
Dry Lake

h

Lake
Hughes

Quartz
Hill

14

Lancaster

N5

Bouquet
Reservoir

N2

4

SADDLEBACK
BUTTE STATE PARK

i

ANGELES
NATIONAL
FOREST

Palmdale

138

El Mirage

TO VICTORVILLE

j

TO SAUGUS

PCT14

5

14

Soledad Pass
3,179 feet

Acton

Vincent

Littlerock

Pearblossom

Ravenna

PCT13

ANGELES
NATIONAL
FOREST

N3

N6

Valyermo

N4

138

18

TO PASADENA TO WRIGHTWOOD

0 1 2 3 4 5 6 7 8 9

❶ Red Cliffs

2.0 mi/1.0 hr

Location: In Red Rock Canyon State Park off Highway 14 north of Mojave; map H5, grid b6.

User groups: Hikers and horses. No dogs or mountain bikes. No wheelchair facilities.

Permits: No permits are required. A $5 day-use fee is charged per vehicle.

Directions: From Mojave, at the junction of Highways 58 and 14, drive northeast on Highway 14 for 25 miles to the Red Cliffs parking area on the right (east) side of the road.

Maps: To obtain a topographic map of the area, ask for Cantil from the USGS.

Contact: Red Rock Canyon State Park, c/o Mojave Desert Sector Office, 43779 15th Street West, Lancaster, CA 93534; (805) 942-0662.

Trail notes: Red Cliffs Natural Preserve is a hikers-only section of Red Rock Canyon State Park, where you can walk along and view close-up the reddish columns of 300-foot desert cliffs. The color is caused by iron oxide or rust, but the myriad of creases and folds in the cliffs have been formed by a combination of fire and water—volcanic action and the course of streams and rivers. You hike on old jeep tracks, not a formal trail, passing occasional Joshua trees as you go and gaining views of the El Paso Mountains. It's hard to believe that this wilderness-like desert is so close to urban Los Angeles, because when you're out here, you feel like you're really far away. At the preserve boundary, three-quarters of a mile from the trailhead, you can continue on the old jeep road into the Scenic Cliffs Preserve, or turn around and retrace your steps. The Scenic Cliffs area is closed each year from February to May, which is the nesting season for various birds of prey. If you really want to be wowed, take this hike at sunset, then spend the night in the state park campground, and see the stars like you've never seen them before.

❷ Desert Tortoise Discovery Loop

2.0 mi/1.0 hr

Location: Off Highway 14 near California City; map H5, grid c7.

User groups: Hikers and wheelchairs. No dogs, horses, or mountain bikes.

Permits: No permits are required. Parking and access are free.

Directions: From Mojave, at the junction of Highways 58 and 14, drive northeast on Highway 14 for 4.5 miles to California City Boulevard. Drive east on California City Boulevard for nine miles to 20 Mule Team Parkway. Go east on the parkway and continue driving 1.3 miles to Randsburg-Mojave Road. Turn left (northeast) on Randsburg-Mojave Road and drive four miles to the signed parking area.

Maps: A free trail map/guide to the Desert Tortoise Natural Area is available at the trailhead. To obtain topographic maps of the area, ask for California City North and Galileo Hill from the USGS.

Contact: Bureau of Land Management, Ridgecrest Resource Area, 300 South Richmond Road, Ridgecrest, CA 93555; (760) 384-5400.

Trail notes: The Desert Tortoise Natural Area features an easy interpretive trail that teaches visitors all about gopherus agassizi, better known as the desert tortoise, California's state reptile. Don't get your heart set on seeing one, though, as the creatures are rather shy. You have to look for them, and you have to get lucky. At the preserve, you can also learn all about other desert reptiles and desert plants. A few very short interpretive trails are worth taking a stroll around, but the two-mile Discovery Trail offers the best chance of seeing tortoises. Look for their burrows underneath creosote bushes, then keep your fingers crossed that one decides to pop his (or her) head out. Spring is the best time for tortoise sightings, usually from early March to late May, when the wildflowers are in bloom. The tortoises like to eat them. The best tortoise fact we learned on our trip? During a sudden rainstorm, a tortoise may emerge from its burrow and drink enough water to last a full year.

❸ Antelope Valley Poppy Preserve Loop

2.0 mi/1.0 hr

Location: West of Lancaster and Highway 14; map H5, grid g0.

User groups: Hikers and wheelchairs. No dogs, horses, or mountain bikes.

Permits: No permits are required. A $5 day-use fee is charged per vehicle.

Directions: From Lancaster on Highway 14, take the Avenue I exit and turn west on Avenue I, which becomes Lancaster Road. Drive 14 miles to the entrance to Antelope Valley California Poppy Preserve on the right. The trail begins by the visitor center.

Maps: To obtain a topographic map of the area, ask for Del Sur from the USGS.

Contact: Antelope Valley California Poppy Preserve, 15101 West Lancaster Road, Lancaster, CA 93536; (805) 724-1180 or (805) 942-0662.

Trail notes: Our first trip to the Antelope Valley California Poppy Preserve was a wee bit disappointing. We showed up in late March, expecting to see the hillsides completely covered in bright orange flowers, but only a few straggler poppies were left, dry and shriveled from the desert wind. It was our own darn fault for poor planning. If you want to see the magic

poppy show at Antelope Valley, you simply must time your trip perfectly. The best way to do it is to phone the park starting in late February; they'll tell you exactly when the bloom is at its best. It can be anywhere from late February to May, and it's different every year. (An updated "poppy hotline" is available every spring explaining how the flowers are doing; phone 805-724-1180.) Then, when the park says to come, do it—don't wait. There are several possible loop trips in the park, but the best one for poppy-watching is the North and South Poppy Loop, a combined two-mile loop that leads from the west side of the visitor center. Wheelchairs can access a short section of this trail. On either leg of the loop, be sure to take the cutoff trail that leads to the Tehachapi Vista Point, where you can get up high and take a look around.

❹ Saddleback and Little Butte Loop

5.0 mi/2.5 hrs

Location: East of Lancaster and Highway 14; map H5, grid h7.

User groups: Hikers only. No dogs, horses, or mountain bikes. No wheelchair facilities.

Permits: No permits are required. A $5 day-use fee is charged per vehicle.

Directions: From Lancaster on Highway 14, take the 20th Street exit. Drive north on 20th Street for less than a half mile, then turn right (east) on Avenue J. Drive 19 miles on Avenue J to the park entrance on the right. Turn right and drive to the park campground and trailhead.

Maps: To obtain a topographic map of the area, ask for Hi Vista from the USGS.

Contact: Saddleback Butte State Park, 17102 East Avenue J, Lancaster, CA 93535; (805) 727-1111 or (805) 942-0662.

Trail notes: Saddleback Butte State Park is a 3,000-acre Joshua tree woodland, but if that isn't enough to inspire you to make the trip, this loop hike to Saddleback Peak should do it. After a 1,000-foot climb to the 3,651-foot summit, you're rewarded with sweeping vistas of Antelope Valley, the San Gabriel Mountains, the Tehachapi Mountains, and the Mojave Desert. Start hiking from the park campground through sand and Joshua trees, heading directly for the clearly visible peak. At one mile out, a trail leads off to the left; this will be the return of your loop. For now, continue straight for the rocky peak, which you reach at two miles from the trailhead. After gazing around for a while, descend for a mile back to the junction, then bear right and continue on the Little Butte Trail. In a half mile, you reach an overlook on top of Little Butte, with views extending over much of the park. Continue onward for an easy return trip back to the park's picnic area. From there, you must walk up the park road a short distance to get back to your car.

⑤ Vasquez Rocks County Park

3.0 mi/1.5 hrs

Location: In Agua Dulce; map H5, grid i0.

User groups: Hikers, dogs, horses, and mountain bikes. No wheelchair facilities.

Permits: No permits are required. A $3 day-use fee is charged per vehicle.

Directions: From the junction of Interstate 5 and Highway 14, drive northeast on Highway 14 for 15 miles to Agua Dulce. Take the Vasquez Rocks/Escondido Canyon exit and drive north on Escondido Canyon Road for 2.2 miles to the park entrance. Continue down the dirt road to the large parking lot and picnic area, and begin hiking on the Foot Trail.

Maps: Free park trail maps are available at the visitor center. To obtain a topographic map of the area, ask for Agua Dulce from the USGS.

Contact: Vasquez Rocks County Park, 10700 West Escondido Canyon Road, Agua Dulce, CA 91350; (805) 268-0840.

Trail notes: In case you've started wondering whether there is any "country" left near the city of Los Angeles, the park office at Vasquez Rocks County Park should convince you. It's a barn, complete with hay and horses. After stopping by and picking up a trail map, take a walk on the Foot Trail at the park, and get a close-up look at the bizarre tilted rock slabs that have made this place famous. (The park has been used in various TV and movie productions.) The largest rock slabs are nearly 150 feet high, and they are tilted at as much as 50 degrees, jutting out at various angles toward the sky. The geologic wonders are a result of continuing earth movement along the Elkhorn Fault, which has compressed, folded, and tilted the underlying sandstone rock layers. If you think about it too much, you won't want to stand still in one place for too long. From the parking area, begin hiking on the Foot Trail through the colorful sandstone slabs, then loop back on the Pacific Crest Trail (a dirt road), which returns to the other side of the parking area. If this park interests you, you should also pay a visit to Devil's Punchbowl Natural Area, which shows off a more dramatic version of the same geologic action. See the trail notes for the Devil's Punchbowl in chapter I5.

Pacific Crest Trail (PCT) Section Overview

140.0 mi. one way/14.0 days

This section of the Pacific Crest Trail includes stretches from the Mill Creek Picnic Area to San Francisquito Canyon, and from Tehachapi to Walker Pass. (The stretch from San Francisquito Canyon to Tehachapi is covered in chapter H4.) Of the entire 2,700-mile PCT, this is the longest stretch of sustained hiking into a foreboding wasteland. After an initial tromp through Angeles National Forest, past Agua Dulce to Three Points, you face a 45-mile excursion across the high-desert terrain of the Mojave Desert, where 100-degree temperatures are common even in late spring. Some people time their trip here for a full moon and hike at night, wearing a head lamp to be used when necessary. Water is always a critical factor here. Drink as much as possible when at a reliable source, and then carry as much as possible when hiking.

PCT-13 Mill Creek Picnic Area to Vasquez Rocks

35.0 mi. one way/4.0 days

Location: From the Mill Creek Picnic Area northwest to the trailhead parking area at Vasquez Rocks; map H5, grid j3.

User groups: Hikers, dogs, and horses. No mountain bikes. No wheelchair facilities.

Permits: A wilderness permit is required for traveling through various wilderness and special-use areas that the trail traverses. Contact the Angeles National Forest at (805) 296-9710 for a permit that is good for the length of your trip.

Directions: To reach the Mill Creek Picnic Area Trailhead, from Highway 14 at Vincent, head south on the Angeles Forest Highway (Road N3) to the Mill Creek Summit and Picnic Area and the signed PCT Trailhead. To reach the Vasquez Rocks Trailhead, from San Fernando Valley, drive north on Interstate 5 to the Highway 14 exit. Drive north on Highway 14 to Agua Dulce Canyon Road and exit north. Drive up Agua Dulce Canyon Road to Escondido Canyon Road and the signed park entrance. Part of the PCT runs through the park.

Maps: For an overall view of the trail route in this section, send $4 to the USDA-Forest Service, 630 Sansome Street, San Francisco, CA 94111, and ask for the Angeles National Forest map. For topographic maps of the route, request Pacifico Mountain, Acton, and Agua Dulce from the USGS. Two BLM surface maps cover the area as well and may be ordered from the Bureau of Land Management office listed below. Send $4.50 for each map ordered and ask for Tehachapi and Lancaster.

Contact: Angeles National Forest, Saugus Ranger District, 30800 Bouquet Canyon Road, Saugus, CA 91350; (805) 296-9710 or fax (805) 296-5847. Bureau of Land Management, Caliente Resource Area, 3801 Pegasus Drive, Bakersfield, CA 93308; (805) 391-6000 or fax (805) 391-6156.

Trail notes: Your destination on this section of the PCT is Vasquez Rocks County Park. Well, at least the ending is good; along the way, there's not much to write home about, though the views from Mount Gleason are a true highlight. First off, after departing Mill Creek Ranger Station, you won't find a reliable water source on the trail for 12 miles, then after that, it's another five miles to the next water stop. The highlight of this section is the traverse near the summit of Mount Gleason at 6,502 feet. Fog often settles in the inland valleys, giving the appearance of a pearlescent sea, with bald mountaintops protruding like small islands, pro-

viding a dramatic view. We once did a live remote television show from this location, during which the host's microphone disconnected and we had to carry the show on our own for several minutes. No problem, eh? What *is* a problem is leaving this pretty setting, tromping downhill into a dry, once-burned section of brush to Messenger Flats Campground. Try to time your stay here for midweek, when it's quiet and lonely; on weekends this campground can turn into a nightmare scene with loud drunks on a binge. From here, it's 5.5 miles to Vasquez Rocks County Park, elevation 2,500 feet, a former hideout of an outlaw, and now known for its unique reddish-pink rocks, a geologic wonder. Reaching the rocks requires a significant descent.

PCT-14 Vasquez Rocks to San Francisquito Canyon

23.0 mi. one way/2.0 days

Location: From the trailhead parking area at Vasquez Rocks northwest to San Francisquito Canyon Road; map H5, grid i0.

User groups: Hikers, dogs, and horses. No mountain bikes. No wheelchair facilities.

Permits: A wilderness permit is required for traveling through various wilderness and special-use areas the trail traverses. Contact the Angeles National Forest at (805) 296-9710 for a permit that is good for the length of your trip.

Directions: To reach the Vasquez Rocks Trailhead, from San Fernando Valley, drive north on Interstate 5 to the Highway 14 exit. Drive north on Highway 14 to Agua Dulce Canyon Road and exit north. Drive on Agua Dulce Canyon Road to Escondido Canyon Road and the signed park entrance. Part of the PCT runs through the park. To reach the San Francisquito Canyon Trailhead, from Palmdale and Highway 14, drive west on County Road N2 (Elizabeth Lake Road) to a left turn onto San Francisquito Canyon Road, just before reaching Elizabeth Lake. The trailhead is located near the San Francisquito Ranger Station and the campground.

Maps: For an overall view of the trail route in this section, send $4 to the USDA-Forest Service, 630 Sansome Street, San Francisco, CA 94111, and ask for the Angeles National Forest map. For topographic maps of the route, request Agua Dulce, Sleepy Valley, Green Valley, and Lake Hughes from the USGS. Two BLM surface maps cover the area as well and may be ordered from the Bureau of Land Management office listed below. Send $4.50 for each map ordered and ask for Tehachapi and Lancaster.

Contact: Angeles National Forest, Saugus Ranger District, 30800 Bouquet Canyon Road, Saugus, CA 91350; (805) 296-9710 or fax (805) 296-5847. Bureau of Land Management, Caliente Resource Area, 3801 Pegasus Drive, Bakersfield, CA 93308; (805) 391-6000 or fax (805) 391-6156.

Trail notes: This 23-mile stretch of the Pacific Crest Trail starts at impressive Vasquez Rocks County Park (see previous hike), where you can take a great day hike. But for PCT hikers, it's onward you'll go, though it may be difficult to spark the inspiration for the next stretch of trail. The big highlight is the showers that are available in Agua Dulce, about a mile from Vasquez Rocks County Park. To put what awaits in perspective, the trail stretches 55 miles to Three Points, and from there, you'll face a 45-mile endurance test across the high Mojave Desert to Tehachapi Pass. On this stretch, after leaving Agua Dulce, you'll march up to a saddle on the Sierra Pelona Ridge, a 2,000-foot climb, where the reward is great views of Vasquez Rocks and the peaks of Angeles National Forest, dominated by Mount Gleason. The trail then drops more than 2,000 feet down to the road in San Francisquito Canyon, where in the process you'll walk the ridge above Bouquet Canyon, with a view of Bouquet Reservoir. Enjoy it; you'll dream of that water in the miles ahead.

PCT-17 Tehachapi to Jawbone Canyon Road

41.0 mi. one way/4.0 days

Location: From the trailhead parking area at Tehachapi northeast to Jawbone Canyon Road; map H5, grid c1.

User groups: Hikers, dogs, and horses. No mountain bikes. No wheelchair facilities.

Permits: A wilderness permit is required for traveling through various wilderness and special-use areas the trail traverses. Contact the Sequoia

National Forest at (805) 871-2223 for a permit that is good for the length of your trip.

Directions: To reach the Tehachapi/Willow Springs Road Trailhead, from Mojave and Highway 14, head west on Oak Creek Road to the intersection with Tehachapi/Willow Springs Road/Cameron Road. The trailhead is located near the intersection. To reach the Jawbone Canyon Road Trailhead, from Highways 58/14, head north on Highway 14, past California City Boulevard to Jawbone Canyon Road. Turn left onto Jawbone Canyon Road and drive past Kelso Valley Road. Continue driving on Jawbone Canyon Road for approximately eight miles, up a series of switchbacks to the signed Pacific Crest Trail crossing and parking area.

Maps: For an overall view of the trail route in this section, send $4 to the USDA-Forest Service, 630 Sansome Street, San Francisco, CA 94111, and ask for the Sequoia National Forest map. For topographic maps of the route, request Tehachapi South, Monolith, Tehachapi NE, Cache Peak, Cross Mountain, Pinyon Mountain, Claraville, and Emerald Mountain from the USGS. A BLM surface map covers the area as well and may be ordered from the Bureau of Land Management office listed below. Send $4.50 and ask for Tehachapi.

Contact: Sequoia National Forest, Greenhorn Ranger District, Lake Isabella Visitor Center, P.O. Box 3810, Lake Isabella, CA 93240; (760) 379-5646 or fax (760) 379-8597. Bureau of Land Management, Caliente Resource Area, 3801 Pegasus Drive, Bakersfield, CA 93308; (805) 391-6000 or fax (805) 391-6156.

Trail notes: PCT hikers in the midst of this scourge of a hike are acting on faith alone that, somehow, it will get better. Well, it doesn't, at least not for another 40 miles. The landscape is pig-ugly desert as you hike north from Tehachapi Pass, with water scarce and nobody else around. But again, remember that faith, because the first pine forest in weeks awaits relatively soon. In the meantime, the hike resembles a death march, especially if you hit it in a terrible hot spell. The positives are unobstructed views (unobstructed because there are hardly any trees anywhere), providing long-distance looks at distant ridgelines. The best view is from Cache

Peak, elevation 6,698 feet, the highest mountaintop in the region, from which you can see Mount Whitney looming to the north. The trail laterals about 600 feet beneath Cache Peak, then it's 20 miles to Jawbone Canyon, with one water stop on the way at Golden Oaks Spring.

PCT-18 Jawbone Canyon Road to Walker Pass

41.0 mi. one way/4.0 days

Location: From Jawbone Canyon Road to Walker Pass; map H5, grid d6.

User groups: Hikers, dogs, and horses. No mountain bikes. No wheelchair facilities.

Permits: A wilderness permit is required for traveling through various wilderness and special-use areas the trail traverses. Contact the Sequoia National Forest at (805) 871-2223 for a permit that is good for the length of your trip.

Directions: To reach the Jawbone Canyon Road Trailhead, from Highways 58/14, head north on Highway 14, past California City Boulevard and to Jawbone Canyon Road. Turn left onto Jawbone Canyon Road and drive past Kelso Valley Road. Continue driving on Jawbone Canyon Road for approximately eight miles, up a series of switchbacks to the signed Pacific Crest Trail crossing and parking area. To reach the Walker Pass Trailhead, from Highway 14, turn west onto Highway 178 and drive to the Walker Pass Trailhead Campground, built especially for Pacific Crest Trail hikers. The trailhead begins at the east end of the campground.

Maps: For an overall view of the trail route in this section, send $4 to the USDA-Forest Service, 630 Sansome Street, San Francisco, CA 94111, and ask for the Sequoia National Forest map. For topographic maps of the route, request Claraville, Pinyon Mountain, Cane Canyon, Horse Canyon, and Walker Pass from the USGS.

Contact: Sequoia National Forest, Cannell Meadow Ranger District, P.O. Box 6, Kernville, CA 93238; (619) 376-3781 or fax (619) 376-3795.

Trail notes: The mind-numbing walk continues here through high desert, surrounded by low scrub and catcus and whatever thoughts you can conjure to relieve you from the present. The one redemption is knowing that the south-ern Sierra awaits, with Mount Whitney just a little more than 100 miles distant. This section of trail starts by crossing desert foothill-like terrain, set at about the 6,500-foot level, with Joshua trees occasionally sprinkled along the way. This is a desolate patch of life, with no shade anywhere. Another common problem here are gale-force winds out of the east, quite possible if a storm (and low barometric pressure) moves into northern Arizona and New Mexico, while high barometric pressure dominates the Southern California coastal areas. The difference in barometric pressure causes horrendous winds out of the east, and it happens at least once every spring. After 30 miles of desert to Bird Spring Pass, elevation 5,355 feet, good things finally start to happen. You rise past the border of Sequoia National Forest, then shortly later, into the Kiavah Wilderness. The landscape is still desert, but after rising to nearly 7,000 feet, you start to see signs of forest, though interspersed with stretches of buckbrush. The trail rises again to nearly 7,000 feet, then descends to Walker Pass, 5,246 feet, where the Forest Service has constructed a trail for the express use of PCT hikers. Congratulations, better times are ahead.

PCT Continuation: To continue hiking along the Pacific Crest Trail, see chapters H4 and G5.

Leave No Trace Tips

Minimize Use and Impact of Fires

Campfires can have a lasting impact on the backcountry. Always carry a lightweight stove for cooking, and use a candle lantern instead of building a fire whenever possible.

Where fires are permitted, use established fire rings only.

Do not scar the natural setting by snapping the branches off live, dead, or downed trees.

Completely extinguish your campfire and make sure it is cold before departing. Remove all unburned trash from the fire ring and scatter the cold ashes over a large area well away from any camp.

Map H6

Adjoining Maps: East: H7 ... *page* 552   West: H5 542
North: G6 508   South: I6 600

Central California Map .... *page* 382

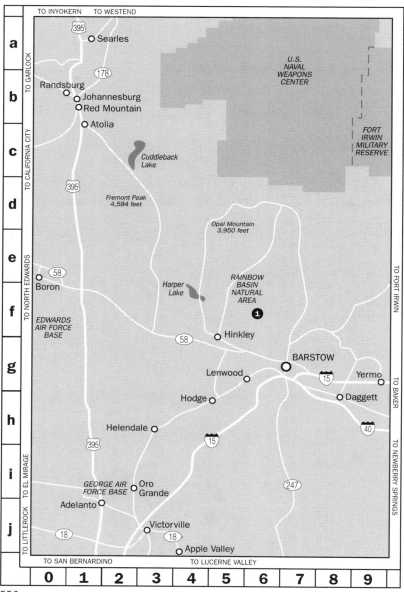

❶ Rainbow Basin

5.0 mi/2.5 hrs

Location: Northwest of Barstow; map H6, grid f5.

User groups: Hikers, dogs, horses, and mountain bikes. No wheelchair facilities.

Permits: No permits are required. Parking and access are free.

Directions: From Barstow, take Highway 58 northwest to Fort Irwin Road, then drive north on Fort Irwin Road for 5.5 miles. Turn northwest on Fossil Beds Road (a dirt road) and drive 2.8 miles to Owl Canyon Campground and Trailhead.

Maps: To obtain a topographic map of the area, ask for Mud Hills from the USGS.

Contact: Bureau of Land Management, Barstow Resource Area, 150 Coolwater Lane, Barstow, CA 92311; (760) 255-8700. Or California Desert Information Center, 831 Barstow Road, Barstow, CA 92311; (760) 255-8760.

Trail notes: You just never know what kind of good stuff you'll find when you travel around the state, and that's certainly true when you reach the Rainbow Basin area north of Barstow. From the BLM's Owl Canyon Campground, you can take a five-mile round-trip hike into some of the most colorful countryside around. You'll see nothing like the usual dull brown that colors so many desert landscapes; instead the well-named Rainbow Basin is made up of a cornucopia of colorful sediments—deposits that were formed in lakebeds 20 million years ago. Because of the ancient geologic history of the area, you may also find examples of ancient natural history, like fossilized remains from saber-toothed tigers, mastodons, and huge bear-dogs. The Owl Canyon Trail leads into Owl Canyon, which gets progressively narrow and rockier as you travel. There's so much to look at and photograph, you won't be moving very fast. In addition to all the colorful rocks, you might even get a peek at one of Owl Canyon's resident owls. The trail ends near the base of Velvet Peak, in a stunningly colorful rock bowl.

Map H7

Adjoining Maps: East: H8 ... *page* 554   West: H6 550
North: G7 514   South: I7 616

Central California Map .... *page* 382

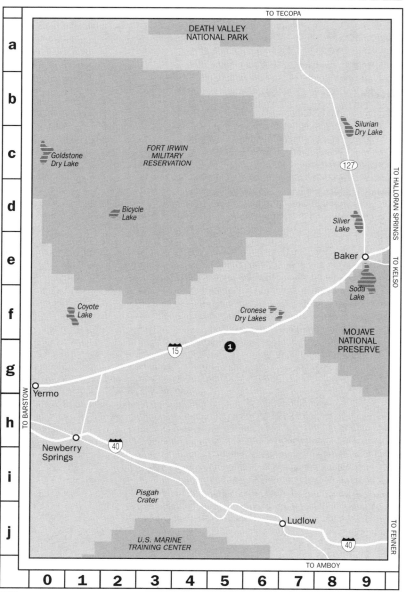

❶ Afton Canyon

3.0 mi/1.5 hrs

Location: East of Barstow; map H7, grid g5.

User groups: Hikers, dogs, horses, and mountain bikes. No wheelchair facilities.

Permits: No permits are required. Parking and access are free.

Directions: From Barstow, drive 33 miles east on Interstate 15 and take the Afton Canyon exit. Drive three miles southwest to Afton Campground (the dirt road is well graded). The trail begins at the campground.

Maps: To obtain topographic maps of the area, ask for Cave Mountain and Dunn from the USGS.

Contact: Bureau of Land Management, Barstow Resource Area, 150 Coolwater Lane, Barstow, CA 92311; (760) 255-8700.

Trail notes: They call Afton Canyon "the Grand Canyon of the Mojave," and although its proportions may be smaller than the other Grand Canyon, Afton is no slacker in terms of colorful desert drama. Sheer walls of pink and red rock rise straight up 300 feet above the Mojave River, where water flows almost year-round. From the campground, follow the trail east along the river, amid a surprising amount of foliage, considering this is the desert. Saltcedar trees thrive along the stream, as well as planted cottonwoods and willows, creating a protective habitat for birds and other wildlife. The canyon walls tower above you, beautifully carved and sculpted by the Mojave River in the days when it was a much bigger waterway—probably 50,000 years ago. Hike as far as you like into the canyon, then turn around and head back. A good side trip is a visit to Pyramid Canyon, one of Afton's side canyons. Start from the campground and cross the river under the first set of railroad trestles, then head south into Pyramid Canyon, a classic slot canyon. The canyon walls squeeze tighter and tighter around you as you walk, exhibiting a beautiful array of desert colors and fascinating water-sculpted shapes.

Map H8

Adjoining Maps: West: H7 552

Central California Map .... *page* 382

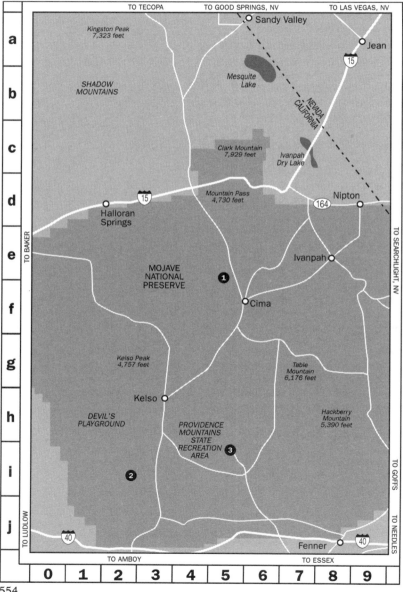

TO TECOPA

TO GOOD SPRINGS, NV

TO LAS VEGAS, NV

Sandy Valley

Jean

Kingston Peak
7,323 feet

SHADOW
MOUNTAINS

Mesquite
Lake

NEVADA
CALIFORNIA

Clark Mountain
7,929 feet

Ivanpah
Dry Lake

Mountain Pass
4,730 feet

Nipton

Halloran
Springs

164

TO BAKER

MOJAVE
NATIONAL
PRESERVE

Ivanpah

TO SEARCHLIGHT, NV

Cima

Kelso Peak
4,757 feet

Table
Mountain
6,176 feet

Kelso

DEVIL'S
PLAYGROUND

PROVIDENCE
MOUNTAINS
STATE
RECREATION
AREA

Hackberry
Mountain
5,390 feet

TO GOFFS

TO LUDLOW

40

TO NEEDLES

Fenner

40

TO AMBOY

TO ESSEX

0 1 2 3 4 5 6 7 8 9

Chapter H8 features:

desert views. If you choose, you can continue on and scramble the last short stretch to reach the summit, or just stay at this lookout, catch your breath, and enjoy the far-reaching vistas.

❶ Teutonia Peak

4.0 mi/2.0 hrs

Location: In the Mojave National Preserve east of Barstow; map H8, grid e5.

User groups: Hikers, dogs, and horses. No mountain bikes. No wheelchair facilities.

Permits: No permits are required. Parking and access are free.

Directions: From Barstow, take Interstate 15 east for approximately 85 miles to Cima Road. (Cima Road is about 25 miles east of Baker, near the town of Valley Wells on Interstate 15.) Turn south on Cima Road and drive 10 miles to the sign for the trailhead, on the west side of the road.

Maps: To obtain a topographic map of the area, ask for Cima Dome from the USGS.

Contact: Mojave National Preserve, P.O. Box 241, Baker, CA 92309; (760) 733-4040 or fax (760) 733-4027.

Trail notes: Cima Dome is the perfect summit for geometry enthusiasts. The huge granite dome's big claim to fame is that it's the most symmetrical dome of its type in the United States. It rises 1,500 feet above the surrounding landscape, and it's almost 70 miles square. In fact, it's so massive that when you're on it, it's hard to know that you're on it.

The summit of Cima Dome is Teutonia Peak, elevation 5,755 feet, and you can hike to it via a two-mile trail that leads up to head-swiveling desert vistas. The first mile is nearly flat and a little dull, leading through cacti and grazing lands, but as soon as you start to climb, things start to get more interesting. The dome is covered with Joshua trees, some as large as 25 feet tall. (They're a different variety than the kind found in Joshua Tree National Park.) Soon you can see your destination, Teutonia Peak, as well as the rugged-looking New York Mountains. At 1.9 miles, you reach a saddle just shy of Teutonia's summit, where you have panoramic

❷ Kelso Dunes

3.0 mi/1.5 hrs

Location: In the Mojave National Preserve southeast of Barstow; map H8, grid i2.

User groups: Hikers and dogs. No horses or mountain bikes. No wheelchair facilities.

Permits: No permits are required. Parking and access are free.

Directions: From Barstow, take Interstate 15 east for approximately 60 miles to Baker, then turn south on Kelbaker Road and drive 42 miles, past Kelso, to the signed road on the right for Kelso Dunes. Turn right (west) and drive three miles to the dunes parking area.

Maps: To obtain a topographic map of the area, ask for Kelso Dunes from the USGS.

Contact: Mojave National Preserve, P.O. Box 241, Baker, CA 92309; (760) 733-4040 or fax (760) 733-4027.

Trail notes: Kelso Dunes are the second highest sand dunes in California. (Eureka Dunes in Death Valley are the highest.) The dune complex is 50 miles square, and the dunes reach a height of 500 feet; they are a sandy pinkish color. In a wet spring, desert wildflowers bloom on and around them, adding even more color to the area. Make sure you read the interpretive signs at the Kelso Dunes Trailhead, walk a short distance on the dirt road, then just hike any which way toward the closest dunes, which are plainly visible. (Constantly moving sand makes a formal trail impossible.) If you climb high enough in the sand, you are rewarded with views of the surrounding desert mountains, including the Granite and Providence Mountains. Most people don't bother, though; they just plop themselves down and make sand angels, or roll around on the dunes' silky surface. Another popular activity is trying to cause small sand avalanches, which result in a harmonic booming sound. Some desert-lovers swear by the healing power of these vibrating noises.

❸ Crystal Springs Trail

1.0 mi/0.5 hr

Location: In the Providence Mountains State Recreation Area southeast of Barstow; map H8, grid i5.

User groups: Hikers only. No dogs, horses, or mountain bikes. No wheelchair facilities.

Permits: No permits are required. A $5 day-use fee is charged per vehicle.

Directions: From Barstow, take Interstate 40 east for approximately 85 miles to the exit for Essex Road, Mitchell Caverns, and Providence Mountains State Recreation Area (near the town of Essex). Turn north on Essex Road and drive 15.5 miles to the Providence Mountains visitor center.

Maps: To obtain a topographic map of the area, ask for Fountain Peak from the USGS.

Contact: Providence Mountains State Recreation Area, P.O. Box 1, Essex, CA 92332; (805) 942-0662.

Trail notes: The big draw at Providence Mountains State Recreation Area is touring Mitchell Caverns with a guide, so a lot of people miss out on the excellent do-it-yourself hiking trails in the area. Crystal Springs Trail is one of those, leading from the visitor center uphill to a rocky overlook in the Providence Mountains. The trailhead elevation is 4,300 feet. The hike is surprisingly steep and feels unusually remote for a state park trail. You hike through Crystal Canyon, where bighorn sheep are sometimes seen. Rocky outcrops shoot up from both sides of the trail as you walk between pinyon pines and junipers. Trailside cacti sometimes seem to reach out to grab you, but you're compensated by beautiful views in all directions. The trail ends near Crystal Springs, where you just turn around and head back, enjoying the vistas from a different perspective. A good side trip is to add on a jaunt in the opposite direction from the visitor center; this one follows the Nina Mora Overlook Trail from the park campground for a quarter mile to an overlook of the Marble Mountains and Clipper Valley. And, of course, if you've driven all the way out here, you should sign up for a tour of Mitchell Caverns. The limestone caverns with their stalagmites, stalactites, and helictites are fascinating to see.

Southern California

Featured Areas .... *pages* 558–559

Overall Rating									

Poor .... Fair .... Great

Difficulty				

A stroll .... Moderate ...... A real butt-kicker!

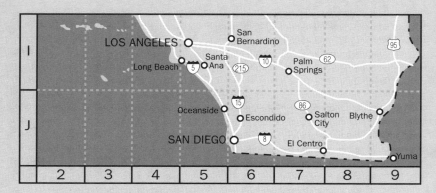

Featured Areas in Southern California

Map I2

Adjoining Maps: East: I3 ..... *page* 562
North: H2 518

Southern California Map .... *page* 558

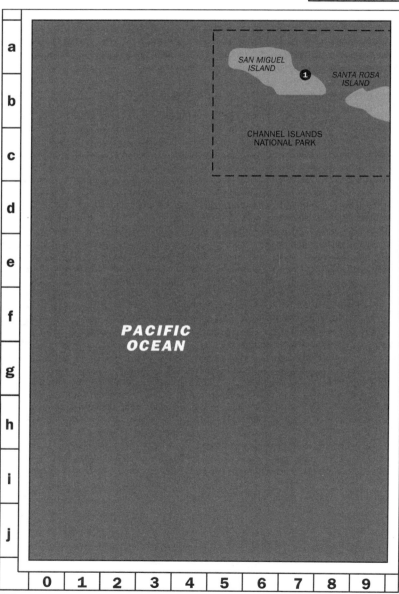

❶ San Miguel Island Trail

3.0 mi/2.0 days

Location: On San Miguel Island in Channel Islands National Park; map I2, grid b7.

User groups: Hikers only. No dogs, horses, or mountain bikes. No wheelchair facilities.

Permits: A free camping and hiking permit is required and is available from the Channel Islands Visitor Center in Ventura or by phoning (805) 658-5711. A fee is charged for transportation to the island via Island Packers, the authorized concessionaire to Channel Islands National Park. Phone Island Packers at the number below for rates and departure information. The current cost is $90 per person.

Directions: Island Packers provides boat transportation to San Miguel Island from Ventura Harbor. Advance reservations are required. Phone Island Packers at (805) 642-7688 or (805) 642-1393 for information and reservations.

Maps: A free map of Channel Islands National Park is available from park headquarters at the address below. To obtain topographic maps of the area, ask for San Miguel Island East and San Miguel Island West from the USGS.

Contact: Channel Islands National Park, 1901 Spinnaker Drive, Ventura, CA 93001; (805) 658-5700. Or Island Packers at (805) 642-7688 or (805) 642-1393 for information and reservations.

Trail notes: When some people find out there's an easy way and a hard way to do something, they immediately choose the hard way. If you're in that camp, you'll choose San Miguel Island as the Channel Island you want to visit, instead of Anacapa, Santa Cruz, or any of the other islands. San Miguel is the furthest island from the mainland, requiring a much-dreaded five-hour boat ride from Ventura. Once you get there, you stay there for a couple days; generally the boat schedule runs so that you get dropped off on one day and picked up a few days later. To add to the challenge, strong winds and fog are nearly constant on the island, so you must plan accordingly for both hiking and camping. Of course, if you're willing, your reward is having a spectacular island practically all to yourself. No more than 30 campers are allowed on San Miguel Island at one time, and during the week and off-season the campground is often not full. From Cuyler Harbor, where you are dropped off, you hike eastward along the beach for a half mile, then follow the path up Nidever Canyon. It's a steep stretch, especially if you're carrying a lot of camping gear. When you reach the ridge at the top, you can take a short left spur to see a stone monument to Juan Rodriguez Cabrillo, who claimed this island for the Spaniards in 1542 and may or may not be buried here—nobody's sure. (The monument wasn't erected until the 1930s.) The right fork continues to the campground, and then to the remains of the Lester Ranch. The Lester family lived on the island for 12 years and grazed sheep here. Outside of the Cuyler Harbor/Lester Ranch area, you may hike only in the company of a ranger, in order to protect the island's fragile resources. If you do so, you'll find that the main wildlife on and around the island are pinnipeds, or seals and sea lions. Up to six different species and more than 30,000 individuals can be seen at certain times of the year at Point Bennett. San Miguel Island has the largest sea lion rookery in California—basically, it's the entire south side of the island. Another interesting feature is the Caliche Forest, where the calcium carbonate sandcastings of dead plant roots and trunks stand like frozen statues. They're a bit like the tufa spires at Mono Lake or Trona Pinnacles, but more weird-looking.

Special note: Island Packers occasionally runs day trips to San Miguel Island for those who do not wish to camp, but this requires spending 10 hours in one day in a boat.

Map I3

Adjoining Maps: East: I4 ..... *page* 564   West: I2 .... *page* 560
                     North: H3 522

Southern California Map .... *page* 558

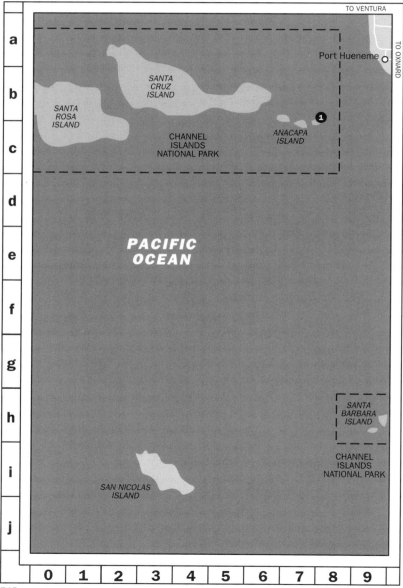

562

❶ East Anacapa Island Loop Trail

2.0 mi/1.0 hr

Location: On Anacapa Island in Channel Islands National Park; map 13, grid b7.

User groups: Hikers only. No dogs, horses, or mountain bikes. No wheelchair facilities.

Permits: No permits are required for day hiking. A fee is charged for transportation to the island via Island Packers, the authorized concessionaire to Channel Islands National Park. Phone Island Packers at the number below for rates and departure information. The current cost is $37 per person for a day trip, or $48 per person for an overnight trip.

Directions: Island Packers provides boat transportation to Anacapa Island from Ventura Harbor and Oxnard (Channel Island Harbor). Advance reservations are required. Phone Island Packers at (805) 642-7688 or (805) 642-1393 for information and reservations.

Maps: A free map of Channel Islands National Park is available from park headquarters at the address below. To obtain a topographic map of the area, ask for Anacapa Island from the USGS.

Contact: Channel Islands National Park, 1901 Spinnaker Drive, Ventura, CA 93001; (805) 658-5700. Or Island Packers at (805) 642-7688 or (805) 642-1393 for information and reservations.

Trail notes: Of all the Channel Islands to choose from, why do more people go to Anacapa Island than any other? Easy—because it's the closest to the mainland at only 12 miles from Port Hueneme, which means the boat ride doesn't take forever—only about an hour and a half. The island is actually three tiny islands, and the boat drops you off on the easternmost of the three. If you're feeling the slightest bit seasick, you'll quickly get over it when the boat pulls away and your first task is to climb up the 154 stair steps that cling to the island's cliffs. You'll get plenty of fresh air as you make your way to the island's visitor center, pick up some inter-pretive information, and set out on this loop trail, which tours the entire small island. The trail's main highlights are two overlooks at Inspiration Point and Cathedral Cove, where you can look down on seals and sea lions on the rocks below. There are also millions of opportunities for bird-watching, and where you can see over the edge of the rocky cliffs, you'll spot some of the island's 130 sea caves. Spring wildflowers are superb, including the giant coreopsis, which reportedly blooms so brightly that it can sometimes be seen from the mainland. Note that beaches on East Anacapa are not accessible, because the sea cliffs are hundreds of feet high, but on calm summer days you can swim at the landing cove.

Map I4

Adjoining Maps: East: I5 ..... *page* 578   West: I3 562
North: H4 532

Southern California Map .... *page* 558

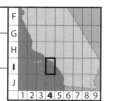

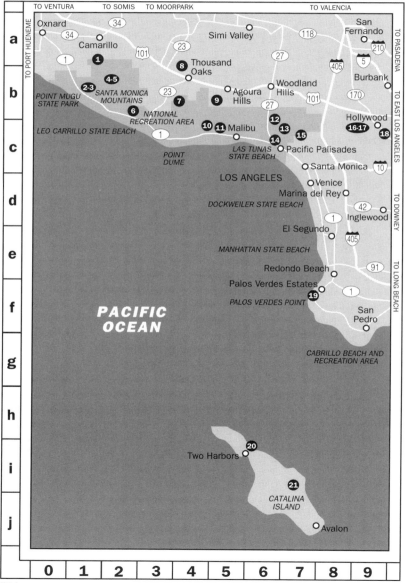

Chapter 14 features:

1 Satwiwa Loop Trail and Waterfall

3.0 mi/1.5 hrs

Location: In the Santa Monica Mountains National Recreation Area near Newbury Park; map 14, grid a1.

User groups: Hikers and dogs. (Dogs are not allowed past the border of Point Mugu State Park, only on the Satwiwa loop.) No horses or mountain bikes. No wheelchair facilities.

Permits: No permits are required. Parking and access are free.

Directions: From U.S. 101 in Newbury Park, exit on Wendy Drive and head south for 2.6 miles to Potrero Road. Turn right on Potrero Road and head west for 1.8 miles to the park entrance at the corner of West Potrero Road and Pine Hill Avenue. Turn left into the park and drive four-tenths of a mile to the main parking lot. Walk up the paved road that leads from the parking lot to a gate at the Big Sycamore Canyon Trail (also a road).

Maps: A free map of the Santa Monica Mountains National Recreation Area and a brochure on Rancho Sierra Vista/Satwiwa Site is available by contacting parking headquarters at the address below. A map of the Santa Monica Mountains is available for a fee from Tom Harrison Cartography, (415) 456-7940. To obtain a topographic map of the area, ask for Newbury Park from the USGS.

Contact: Santa Monica Mountains National Recreation Area, 30401 Agoura Road, Suite 100, Agoura Hills, CA 91301; (818) 597-9192 or fax (818) 597-8357.

Trail notes: You know the hike will be good when at the trailhead parking lot, you're greeted by two friendly roadrunners and half a dozen bunnies. That's how it is here at the Rancho Sierra Vista/Satwiwa Site, a part of the Santa Monica Mountains National Recreation Area near Newbury Park, just a couple miles off Highway 101. The park's proximity to millions of L.A. commuters makes it a perfect place to show up after work and hike or jog on the Satwiwa Loop Trail, and in the rainy season, take a side trip to see the waterfall just inside the border of Point Mugu State Park. From the parking lot, walk up the paved Sycamore Canyon Trail for a few hundred yards, then bear left on the Satwiwa Loop Trail by the Satwiwa Native American Indian Culture Center. Be sure to take a peek at the dome-shaped stick dwelling, which was reconstructed to show traditional Native American life. (But beware the sign that says "Caution—Rattlesnakes." It stops you from crawling inside the hut.) Follow the Satwiwa Loop for 1.5 miles, passing a small pond, a windmill, and grassy hillsides, then connect to the Old Boney Trail on the south side of the loop. Old Boney Trail leads downhill, and where it begins to make a sharp switchback up and out of the canyon, take the left spur up the creek that leads a few hundred feet to Sycamore Canyon Falls. The waterfall is a pretty, multi-tiered cascade over sandstone, with a surprising amount of foliage growing around it. Even when the fall is only a trickle, the big-leaf maples and ferns are a delight to visit.

❷ La Jolla Valley Loop

6.8 mi/3.5 hrs or 2.0 days

Location: In Point Mugu State Park south of Oxnard; map I4, grid b1.

User groups: Hikers only. No dogs, horses, or mountain bikes. No wheelchair facilities.

Permits: No day-hiking permits are necessary. Backpacking campsites are available on a first-come, first-served basis; backpackers must register at the Sycamore Canyon Campground. A $2 day-use fee is charged per vehicle at the Ray Miller Trailhead.

Directions: From U.S. 101 in Camarillo, take the Las Posas Road exit and drive south through Oxnard. Follow Las Posas Road for eight miles to Highway 1, then turn south on Highway 1. Drive five miles to the La Jolla Canyon Trailhead parking area on the left, across from Thornhill Broome State Beach.

(Alternatively, from Highway 1 in Malibu, drive west on Highway 1 for 22 miles to the La Jolla Canyon Trailhead parking area on the right.)

Maps: A park map is available for $1 from the ranger kiosk at Sycamore Canyon Campground, one mile south on Highway 1. A map of the Santa Monica Mountains is available for a fee from Tom Harrison Cartography, (415) 456-7940. To obtain a topographic map of the area, ask for Point Mugu from the USGS.

Contact: Point Mugu State Park, 9000 Pacific Coast Highway, Malibu, CA 90265; (805) 488-5223 or State Parks, Angeles District, 1925 Los Virgenes Road, Calabasas, CA 91302; (818) 880-0350.

Trail notes: We rate Point Mugu State Park as the best of all the parks in the Santa Monica Mountains, partly because of its more remote northern location, partly because of its proxim-

ity to the ocean, and partly because of its fine hiking trails. One of the best of the latter is this loop trip starting in La Jolla Canyon, which can be an excellent day hike or an easy two-day backpacking trip with an overnight at La Jolla Valley walk-in camp. Follow the La Jolla Canyon Trail from the Ray Miller Trailhead (that's the wide dirt trail on the left, not the single-track on the right) gently uphill. You hike through an open valley which is continually freshened by cool ocean breezes blowing up the canyon. Pass a small seasonal waterfall, then climb into a rocky area, where hidden among the chaparral are rock caves that were once used by Native Americans. Go right at the first fork, then take the left fork at 1.5 miles to La Jolla Valley walk-in camp, situated in a high meadow of native grasses. It's a half mile further, shortly beyond a cattail-bordered pond. From the camp, bear left on the dirt road, which narrows to single-track. Continue on the La Jolla Valley Loop Trail and circle around, through more native grasses, back to the La Jolla Canyon Trail. (If you like, you can add on a detour around Mugu Peak on the Mugu Peak Trail, which will add two more miles to your round-trip.) Turn right on La Jolla Canyon Trail to head down the canyon to your car. This trip is outstanding in winter or spring, when the hillside grasses are green and the wildflowers bloom.

❸ Big Sycamore Canyon Loop

9.5 mi/5.5 hrs

Location: In Point Mugu State Park south of Oxnard; map I4, grid b1.

User groups: Hikers, horses, and mountain bikes. No dogs. No wheelchair facilities.

Permits: No permits are required. A $6 day-use fee is charged per vehicle.

Directions: From U.S. 101 in Camarillo, take the Las Posas Road exit and drive south through Oxnard. Follow Las Posas Road for eight miles to Highway 1, then turn south on Highway 1. Drive seven miles to Sycamore Canyon Campground on the left. (Alternatively, from Highway 1 in Malibu, drive west on Highway 1 for 20 miles to Sycamore Canyon Campground on the right.)

Maps: A park map is available for $1 from the

entrance kiosk. A map of the Santa Monica Mountains is available for a fee from Tom Harrison Cartography, (415) 456-7940. To obtain a topographic map of the area, ask for Point Mugu from the USGS.

Contact: Point Mugu State Park, 9000 Pacific Coast Highway, Malibu, CA 90265; (805) 488-5223 or State Parks, Angeles District, 1925 Los Virgenes Road, Calabasas, CA 91302; (818) 880-0350.

Trail notes: If you don't mind hiking on fire roads and maybe sharing the trail with mountain bikers and horses, this loop trip in Point Mugu State Park offers a shady stroll in a sycamore-lined canyon, followed by miles and miles of unforgettable coastal views. Start from the gate at the far end of the campground and follow Big Sycamore Canyon Trail as it climbs very gently uphill, paralleling the creek. The sycamore trees here are large and old, and from October to February, you may spot monarch butterflies who cluster among them for the winter. At three miles, bear left on Wood Canyon Trail to reach Deer Camp Junction and picnic area. From there, pick up Overlook Trail for a long, rambling walk back to the trailhead. The Overlook Trail divides Point Mugu's two canyons, Big Sycamore and La Jolla, and is a ridgetop route that offers nonstop views of the coastline to the west and the canyons on either side of you. On a clear day, it's glorious. Note: When you near the end of the trail, you can take the single-track Scenic Trail to return to the trailhead. It shaves off a little distance, and it's more interesting than the final stretch of the Overlook Trail.

❹ Grotto Trail

3.5 mi/2.0 hrs

Location: In the Santa Monica Mountains National Recreation Area at Circle X Ranch; map I4, grid b1.

User groups: Hikers and dogs. No horses or mountain bikes. No wheelchair facilities.

Permits: No permits are required. Parking and access are free.

Directions: From Malibu, drive west on Highway 1 for 15 miles to Yerba Buena Road, 1.5 miles past Leo Carrillo State Beach. Turn right and drive 5.3 miles up Yerba Buena Road to the entrance to Circle X Ranch on the right. Park by the ranger station walk down the road to the group campground, where the Grotto Trail begins.

Maps: A free map of the Santa Monica Mountains National Recreation Area and a brochure on Circle X Ranch is available by contacting park headquarters at the address below. A map of the Santa Monica Mountains is available for a fee from Tom Harrison Cartography, (415) 456-7940. To obtain a topographic map of the area, ask for Triunfo Pass from the USGS.

Contact: Santa Monica Mountains National Recreation Area, 30401 Agoura Road, Suite 100, Agoura Hills, CA 91301; (818) 597-9192 or fax (818) 597-8357. Or contact Circle X Ranch Ranger Station at (310) 457-6408.

Trail notes: If you don't mind hiking downhill to your destination and then uphill on your return, the Grotto Trail is a fine route for a little excursion in the Santa Monica Mountains. The trail roughly follows the West Fork of the Arroyo Sequit on its downhill course to The Grotto, an area of jumbled volcanic boulders, many that are bigger than your average Volkswagen. Hidden among the giant rocks are small caves, pools, and waterfalls. The boulders are great fun to climb around, with millions of possible toe- and finger-holds in the porous rock. By the way, don't be bummed out when you arrive at The Grotto and see that other folks have only walked a few yards to get there; the Happy Hollow Campground is right next door and the park road leads right to it. You, on the other hand, must walk back uphill to the trailhead, covering a 600-foot elevation gain.

❺ Mishe Mokwa and Backbone Loop

6.0 mi/3.0 hrs

Location: In the Santa Monica Mountains National Recreation Area near Circle X Ranch; map I4, grid b1.

User groups: Hikers and dogs. No horses or mountain bikes. No wheelchair facilities.

Permits: No permits are required. Parking and access are free.

Directions: From Malibu, drive west on Highway 1 for 15 miles to Yerba Buena Road, 1.5 miles past Leo Carrillo State Beach. Turn right and drive 6.3 miles up Yerba Buena Road to the Backbone Trailhead parking area on the left side of the road, one mile beyond the entrance to Circle X Ranch on the right.

Maps: A free map of the Santa Monica Mountains National Recreation Area and a brochure on Circle X Ranch is available by contacting park headquarters at the address below. A map of the Santa Monica Mountains is available for a fee from Tom Harrison Cartography, (415) 456-7940. To obtain a topographic map of the area, ask for Triunfo Pass from the USGS.

Contact: Santa Monica Mountains National Recreation Area, 30401 Agoura Road, Suite 100, Agoura Hills, CA 91301; (818) 597-9192 or fax (818) 597-8357. Or contact Circle X Ranch Ranger Station at (310) 457-6408.

Trail notes: A great six-mile loop on the Santa Monica Mountains' Backbone Trail begins a short distance from the Circle X Ranch site on Yerba Buena Road. See all those wild-looking volcanic outcrops on the hillsides? That's where you're going. You can hike the loop in either direction, but most people start on the Mishe Mokwa Trail. From the Backbone Trailhead, hike uphill for a quarter mile and take the right fork to access Mishe Mokwa's single-track. Head uphill from there, gaining 1,100 feet over 1.7 miles to Split Rock, a big boulder with a split in the middle. It's an unspoken requirement to walk through the split. There's a picnic area at Split Rock among the oaks and sycamores, where you can catch some shade and your breath. From there, continue on the loop to the Backbone Trail, then begin to loop back. Be sure to take the short right spur to Inspiration Point (near Boney Peak) for inspiring views of the coast, and the short right spur to 3,111-foot Sandstone Peak, the highest point in the Santa Monica Mountains. Despite its name, the peak is not made of sandstone; rather it's volcanic rock. The views are outstanding—you'll think you're on top of the whole world.

❻ Nicholas Flat Trail

6.5 mi/3.0 hrs

Location: In Leo Carrillo State Beach near Malibu; map I4, grid b2.

User groups: Hikers and horses. No dogs or mountain bikes. No wheelchair facilities.

Permits: No permits are required. A $6 day-use fee is charged per vehicle.

Directions: From Malibu, drive west on Highway 1 for 13 miles to Leo Carrillo State Beach. Turn right into the park entrance. The Nicholas Flat/Willow Creek Trail begins by the entrance, on the inland side of the highway.

Maps: A map of Leo Carrillo State Beach is available for $1 at the park entrance station. A map of the Santa Monica Mountains is available for a fee from Tom Harrison Cartography, (415) 456-7940. To obtain a topographic map of the area, ask for Triunfo Pass from the USGS.

Contact: Leo Carrillo State Beach, 35000 Pacific Coast Highway, Malibu, CA 90265; (310) 706-1310. Or State Parks, Angeles District, 1925 Los Virgenes Road, Calabasas, CA 91302; (818) 880-0350.

Trail notes: Most Southern California state beaches are long stretches of sand with big campgrounds and lots of happy beach-goers, but few have any hiking trails worth writing home about. Leo Carrillo State Beach is the exception to the rule, with a couple excellent trails that are far more than just a stroll along the sand. The Nicholas Flat Trail is the park's best path, a fairly steep trail that climbs to a pond at Nicholas Flat, where redwing blackbirds and other songbirds like to spend their days. Start hiking from the Willow Creek/Nicholas Flat Trailhead, and at the first junction, bear left. A short but steep climb leads to immediate ocean vistas, and at three-quarters of a mile, a spur trail leads to Willow Creek Overlook, a fine viewpoint and an excellent spot to look for passing whales in winter. From the spur trail, you can call it a day and hike back downhill (a short loop is possible from this point—bear right to follow it), or continue uphill to Nicholas Flat. The climb gets steeper from here on, and you'll gain 1,000 feet more, but you are rewarded with two more spectacular vista points plus Nicholas Flat, with its man-made pond and high grasslands. You can loop around Nicholas Flat and choose from a myriad of good picnicking spots, then head back downhill. When you're finished hiking this trail, make sure you check out the beach across the road (take the pedestrian tunnel under the highway), where you'll find a sea-carved tunnel and many small caves and pocket beaches. Also pay a visit to the visitor center by the beach, open on weekends only, which is housed in a set of trailers painted with dolphins and whales.

❼ Meadow Trail and Ocean Vista Loop

3.0 mi/1.5 hrs

Location: In the Charmlee Natural Area near Zuma Beach; map I4, grid b3.

User groups: Hikers, dogs, horses, and mountain bikes. No wheelchair facilities.

Permits: No permits are required. A $3 day-use fee is charged per vehicle.

Directions: From Highway 1 in Zuma Beach, drive north on Encinal Canyon Road for four miles to the park entrance on the left. Turn left and drive four-tenths of a mile to the parking area near the park office and rest rooms.

Maps: A map of the Santa Monica Mountains is available for a fee from Tom Harrison Cartography, (415) 456-7940. To obtain topographic maps of the area, ask for Triunfo Pass and Point Dume from the USGS.

Contact: Charmlee Natural Area, City of Malibu Parks and Recreation Department, (310) 457-7247 or (310) 317-1364.

Trail notes: Maybe you need to change your perspective. If you've been hiking around in the lower canyons of the Santa Monica Mountains, it might be time to get up high and wander around where the wind blows and the vistas are wide. Charmlee County Park is the place to do it, located four miles up the hill from Zuma Beach. It's high enough so that you don't have to climb anywhere to gain a view; the vistas start right at the trailhead. The park's hiking trails are really fire roads, but that's okay. It just means you can hold hands with your hiking partner while you walk, or carry on a serious discussion about the coastal weather. Walk through the park's picnic area and follow the dirt road as it leads downhill to a meadow, filled with wildflower blooms in February, March, and April. Then follow the Meadow Trail to the Ocean Overlook, which is just one of many places where the

views of the Malibu coast are excellent. From several points, you have vistas in almost every direction, including up and down the Santa Monica Mountains to the east and west. When you're finished meditating on the scenery, loop back on the Meadow Trail to your starting point.

❽ Wildwood Park Loop

4.0 mi/2.0 hrs

Location: In Wildwood Park in Thousand Oaks; map I4, grid b3.

User groups: Hikers, dogs, horses, and mountain bikes. No wheelchair facilities.

Permits: No permits are required. Parking and access are free.

Directions: From U.S. 101 in Thousand Oaks, take the Lynn Road exit and head north. Drive 2.5 miles to Avenida de los Arboles, then turn left. Drive nine-tenths of a mile and make a U-turn into the Arboles parking lot on the left side of the road.

Maps: Park maps are available at the park visitor center. To obtain a topographic map of the area, ask for Thousand Oaks from the USGS.

Contact: Wildwood Park at (805) 492-3381 or Conejo Recreation and Park District, 155 East Wilbur Road, Thousand Oaks, CA 91360; (805) 495-6471.

Trail notes: Wildwood Park is one of the best-kept park secrets in Los Angeles, known mostly to the school kids who come here for outdoor field trips in the spring. But from the Arboles Trailhead in Thousand Oaks, you can hike downhill into Wildwood Canyon and then stroll along its year-round stream, which produces a stunningly beautiful waterfall when the stream flow is strong. Numerous trails cross and interconnect throughout the park, so you can put together a different loop trip or out-and-back hike every time you visit. For first-timers, a good tour is to hike due west on the Mesa Trail for a half mile to the North Tepee Trail, then turn left and drop down into the canyon. Once there, walk to your right and then bear left at the next fork, which puts you right at the base of the 70-foot waterfall. Hey, isn't Los Angeles supposed to be a semi-arid desert? Yes, but it's full of surprises. From the falls, you can continue walking downstream, then pick up the Lizard Rock Trail to loop back to the Mesa Trail. The presence of year-round water makes this canyon a haven for wildlife; look for mule deer, rabbits, coyotes, and numerous songbirds and raptors. Interpretive signs teach you to identify various plants and trees along the stream.

❾ Rock Pool and Century Lake

4.4 mi/2.0 hrs

Location: In Malibu Creek State Park; map I4, grid b4.

User groups: Hikers, horses, and mountain bikes. No dogs. No wheelchair facilities.

Permits: No permits are required. A $5 day-use fee is charged per vehicle.

Directions: From Agoura Hills on U.S. 101, take the Las Virgenes exit and drive 3.2 miles south to the entrance to Malibu Creek State Park on the right. Continue past the entrance kiosk to the day-use parking area. (Or from Malibu on Highway 1, drive north on Malibu Canyon Road/Las Virgenes Road for six miles to the park entrance on the left.)

Maps: A map of Malibu Creek State Park is available for $1 at the park entrance station. A map of the Santa Monica Mountains is available for a fee from Tom Harrison Cartography, (415) 456-7940. To obtain a topographic map of the area, ask for Point Dume from the USGS.

Contact: Malibu Creek State Park, 1925 Los Virgenes Road, Calabasas, CA 91302; (818) 880-0350.

Trail notes: The first time you lay eyes on the Rock Pool at Malibu Creek State Park, or cross the wide bridge over Malibu Creek, or visit pretty blue Century Lake, you may have to ask yourself the question: Where am I? Suddenly it's hard to believe you're in Los Angeles, and just a few miles off the freeway, but you are. Start hiking from the large main parking area on the flat fire road, called Crags Road, which heads for the visitor center. Continue past the visitor center on a wide bridge, then take the left spur to the Rock Pool, a startlingly beautiful pool in Malibu Creek that is dammed by huge volcanic boulders. Although the pool can nearly dry up in late

summer, during the rainy season and shortly thereafter it is quite dramatic. Retrace your steps back to Crags Road (you'll probably pass some rock climbers practicing their craft on an outcrop along the spur trail), then turn left and continue your park tour by visiting Century Lake, dammed in 1901 and now silting up and slowly becoming a marsh. From there, walk another half mile along Crags Road to the old set of the "M*A*S*H" television series, where you'll find a few obvious props from the show. From there, retrace your steps back through the park to the trailhead.

❿ Escondido Falls

4.2 mi/2.0 hrs

Location: In Escondido Canyon near Malibu; map I4, grid c4.

User groups: Hikers, dogs, horses, and mountain bikes. No wheelchair facilities.

Permits: No permits are required. Parking and access are free.

Directions: From Malibu, drive west on Highway 1 for 5.5 miles to Winding Way on the right, and the large sign for the Winding Way Trail. (If you reach Kanan Dume Road, you've gone 1.5 miles too far.) Turn right, then left immediately into the well-signed parking lot.

Maps: A map of the Santa Monica Mountains is available for a fee from Tom Harrison Cartography, (415) 456-7940. To obtain a topographic map of the area, ask for Point Dume from the USGS.

Contact: Santa Monica Mountains Conservancy, 5750 Ramirez Canyon Road, Malibu, CA 90265; (310) 589-3200.

Trail notes: We admit it: The first mile of this trail is pretty weird. That's because of an access problem; you have to park in the lot at the start of Winding Way and then walk up the paved road for a mile, past some mammoth Malibu homes, to the actual beginning of the Escondido Canyon Trail. Just do it and don't whine; when you finally reach the canyon, you'll be glad you came. When you finally reach the trailhead sign, head to the left, walking upstream. Cross the creek a few times on the flat path, which tunnels through shady sections and then opens out to grassy flats. In a half mile from the start of the "real" trail, you'll glimpse a big waterfall up ahead, and in a half mile more you're at its base. This is the lower tier of the huge limestone fall; the adventurous can take the side trail that leads up and over this 50-foot tier, and climb up to a higher, larger tier. Getting there requires some careful rock scrambling, so be cautious. The upper tier is 150 feet tall, with a deep pool at its base, perfect for wading.

⑪ Solstice Road and Rising Sun Loop Trail

2.8 mi/1.2 hrs

Location: In Solstice Canyon Park near Malibu; map I4, grid c4.

User groups: Hikers, dogs, horses, and mountain bikes. No wheelchair facilities.

Permits: No permits are required. A $5 day-use fee is charged per vehicle.

Directions: From Malibu, drive west on Highway 1 for three miles and turn right on Corral Canyon Road. Drive two-tenths of a mile to the park entrance on the left. Turn left, and drive to the Caballero Picnic Area and park office. Park there and continue walking up the paved road, past the office.

Maps: A free trail map is available at the park office. A map of the Santa Monica Mountains is available for a fee from Tom Harrison Cartography, (415) 456-7940. To obtain a topographic map of the area, ask for Malibu Beach from the USGS.

Contact: Solstice Canyon Park, (310) 456-7154. Or contact the Santa Monica Mountains Conservancy, 5750 Ramirez Canyon Road, Malibu, CA 90265; (310) 589-3200.

Trail notes: Solstice Canyon Park suffered from severe fire damage in the fall of 1996, but as is typical after a fire, the wildflowers are better than ever. The chaparral grows back so fast that in little time at all, it's difficult to tell that a fire ever occurred. This loop trip travels from the park office along the Old Solstice Road to the Roberts Ranch site, then returns via the winding Rising Sun Trail. Although the first mile on the Old Solstice Road is on pavement, it parallels Solstice Creek and is a pretty, pleasant stroll. Hike past the park office, turn right at the T junction, then simply walk up the canyon, enjoying the blooming mustard and monkeyflower. Pass by the 1865 Keller house, a lovely stone house that's the oldest in Malibu, then continue to the ruins of Tropical Terrace at the Roberts Ranch. This once-beautiful home burned in a fire in 1982, but its stone terraces and foundation remain. If you walk around to the far side of the foundation, you'll discover a pretty, 30-foot waterfall that drops on Solstice Creek. Enjoy its sweet music for a while, then hike back to the end of the Old Solstice Road and pick up the Rising Sun Trail, which undulates over the hillsides for 1.7 miles to the space-age-looking TRW building, now the staff building for the Santa Monica Mountains Conservancy. From there, you can take the left side of the TRW Loop Trail back to the parking lot.

⑫ Eagle Rock Loop

4.5 mi/2.5 hrs

Location: At Trippet Ranch in Topanga State Park; map I4, grid c6.

User groups: Hikers, horses, and mountain bikes. No dogs. No wheelchair facilities.

Permits: No permits are required. A $5 day-use fee is charged.

Directions: From Santa Monica, drive north on Highway 1 and turn right on Topanga Canyon Boulevard. Drive 4.7 miles to Entrada Road, then turn right and drive one mile to the park entrance at Trippet Ranch. The trailhead is at the far side of the parking lot.

Maps: A map of the Santa Monica Mountains is available for a fee from Tom Harrison Cartography, (415) 456-7940. To obtain a topographic map of the area, ask for Topanga from the USGS.

Contact: Topanga State Park, 20825 Entrada Road, Topanga, CA 90290; (310) 455-2465, (310) 454-8212, or (818) 880-0350.

Trail notes: Topanga State Park's most notable feature is sandstone Eagle Rock, and a loop hike from Trippet Ranch can take you to see it. Much of the route travels on a fire road, through grasslands and oaks, with vistas increasing as you ascend. At the main trailhead, a sign announces that Eagle Rock is two miles away. In a few hundred yards, bear left, and climb to a major intersection at 1.4 miles. Take the middle road, signed as North Loop Trail, and climb for a half mile to Eagle Rock. Leave the trail to explore the tiny caves, hollows, and holes in the smooth sandstone, and to enjoy the 360-degree views from the valley to the ocean. When you've had enough, retrace your steps to the junction, and take the single-track Musch Trail (on your right) for two miles back to the parking lot. You'll pass a walk-in camp along the way. Practice naming the chaparral plants as you hike: White sage, chamise, yucca, poison oak, elderberry, and chia, among others. Watch for roadrunners scurrying among them. (If you're in a hurry, you can return the way you came instead, following the fire road and shaving a half mile off the trip.)

⓭ Santa Ynez Canyon

2.4 mi/1.2 hrs

Location: In Topanga State Park in Pacific Palisades; map I4, grid c6.

User groups: Hikers only. No dogs, horses, or mountain bikes. No wheelchair facilities.

Permits: No permits are required. Parking and access are free.

Directions: From Santa Monica, drive north on Highway 1 and turn right on Sunset Boulevard in Pacific Palisades. Drive a half mile and turn left on Palisades Drive. Drive 2.4 miles, then turn left on to Vereda de la Montura. The trailhead is at the intersection of Camino de Yatasto, a private road, and Vereda de la Montura. Park alongside the road.

Maps: A map of the Santa Monica Mountains is available for a fee from Tom Harrison Cartography, (415) 456-7940. To obtain a topographic map of the area, ask for Topanga from the USGS.

Contact: Topanga State Park, 20825 Entrada Road, Topanga, CA 90290; (310) 455-2465, (310) 454-8212, or (818) 880-0350.

Trail notes: Topanga State Park is a park with nebulous borders, a patchwork of wilderness interspersed between continually growing housing developments. The park's Santa Ynez Canyon Trail, for instance, begins in a residential neighborhood, where you park your car right along the street. The surprising thing is that once you walk about 50 yards on the trail, you feel like you've gotten away from it all, especially

the sights and sounds of urban living. The canyon bottom makes for flat walking, and it's pleasantly shaded by oaks, willows, and sycamores. Five-foot-tall tiger lilies grow alongside the trail. A half mile in, cross the creek (don't take the spur trail up its right side), then shortly reach a trail junction, where you should head right. (The left fork continues for several miles all the way to Trippet Ranch and the main section of Topanga State Park.) A short walk and stream scramble brings you to the base of Santa Ynez Canyon's 15-foot limestone waterfall, a lovely spot that unfortunately has been defiled by graffiti. Even so, it's worth a look, and the canyon walk is pleasant whether or not the stream is flowing strong.

⓮ Temescal Canyon and Ridge Loop

3.8 mi/2.0 hrs

Location: In Temescal Gateway Park in Pacific Palisades; map I4, grid c6.

User groups: Hikers only. No dogs, horses, or mountain bikes. No wheelchair facilities.

Permits: No permits are required. A $5 day-use fee is charged per vehicle.

Directions: From Santa Monica, drive north on Highway 1 to Temescal Canyon Road in Pacific Palisades. Turn right and drive 1.1 miles to the entrance to Temescal Gateway Park. Cross Sunset Boulevard, then continue up the park road for a quarter mile to the park office and trail information kiosk.

Maps: A free trail map is available at the Temescal Gateway Park kiosk. A map of the Santa Monica Mountains is available for a fee from Tom Harrison Cartography, (415) 456-7940. To obtain a topographic map of the area, ask for Topanga from the USGS.

Contact: Temescal Gateway Park, 15601 Sunset Boulevard, Pacific Palisades, CA 90272; (310) 454-1395.

Trail notes: How about a nice loop hike in Temescal Gateway Park and Topanga State Park? Hey, good idea—throw some stuff in the daypack and let's go. The signed trail leads from the parking lot (it's to the left of the kiosk where you pay your fee), and heads north through a camp and conference center. In a quarter mile, you'll reach a junction of three trails. The Temescal Canyon Trail on the right is the start of the loop; the Temescal Ridge Trail in the middle is the return leg of the loop. The Temescal Canyon Trail leads you away from the camp and past a state park boundary sign, then the trail starts to climb. Although the route is bordered by rock walls and dry chaparral, leafy maples and sycamores grow along the stream beside you. At 1.2 miles you cross a footbridge over a small, seasonal waterfall, then cross over to the west side of the canyon to climb to an intersection with the Temescal Ridge Trail. If you like, you can take the right spur trail for a half mile to Skull Rock, a somewhat spooky-looking sandstone formation, then return to the junction. Finish out the loop by heading downhill on Temescal Ridge Trail, with fine views of the coast entertaining you as you walk.

⑮ Inspiration Point Trail

2.0 mi/1.0 hr

Location: In Will Rogers State Historic Park; map I4, grid c7.

User groups: Hikers and horses. No dogs or mountain bikes. No wheelchair facilities.

Permits: No permits are required. A $5 day-use fee is charged per vehicle.

Directions: From Santa Monica, drive north on Highway 1 to Sunset Boulevard in Pacific Palisades. Turn right on Sunset Boulevard and drive 4.5 miles to Will Rogers State Park Road, then turn left and drive one mile to the park entrance. The trail begins near the Rogers' mansion.

Maps: A map of Will Rogers State Historic Park is available for $1 at the park entrance station. To obtain a topographic map of the area, ask for Topanga from the USGS.

Contact: Will Rogers State Historic Park, 1501 Will Rogers State Park Road, Pacific Palisades, CA 90272; (310) 454-8212 or (818) 880-0350.

Trail notes: Most folks come to Will Rogers State Historic Park to visit the home of the "Cowboy Philosopher" and humorist Will Rogers. His humble abode was a gigantic 31-room ranch/mansion. But even if you never heard of the guy and have no interest in cowboy decorating style, the two-mile loop trip to Inspiration Point makes

a visit to the park worthwhile. The trail offers superb vistas of the Santa Monica Mountains and Pacific Ocean. Follow the well-signed fire road for three-quarters of a mile to the start of the short loop, then bear left for Inspiration Point. A few benches situated on the point are a great place to gaze out at the scene, which includes a wide view of the coast, the rugged Santa Monicas, the state park below you, and downtown Los Angeles to the southeast. It's kind of hard to believe that the big city is within view of this tranquil, natural place, but there it is. Considering the proportion of your view, it's also hard to believe you're only at 750 feet in elevation. On the clearest of days, you can see all the way to Catalina Island, 20-plus miles away.

⑯ Magic Forest Nature Trail

0.25 mi/0.25 hr

Location: In Coldwater Canyon Park; map I4, grid c8.

User groups: Hikers and dogs. No horses or mountain bikes. No wheelchair facilities.

Permits: No permits are required. Parking and access are free.

Directions: From U.S. 101 in Studio City, take the Coldwater Canyon exit and drive south for 2.3 miles, then turn left into the park entrance. The trail begins by the parking area.

Maps: A map/brochure of Coldwater Canyon Park is available for 25 cents at the park kiosk. To obtain a topographic map of the area, ask for Beverly Hills from the USGS.

Contact: Coldwater Canyon Park, c/o TreePeople, 12601 Mulholland Drive, Beverly Hills, CA 90210; (818) 753-4600.

Trail notes: If you have kids and you're anywhere in the vicinity of Coldwater Canyon, bring them to this park for a walk on the Magic Forest Nature Trail. The trail, like Coldwater Canyon Park itself, is a complete delight and a good source of inspiration for children who are growing up in an urban world. It's the perfect place for them to learn about the importance of planting trees in urban areas, which is what TreePeople, who run this park, do in Los Angeles neighborhoods. The trail begins at a small shrine to the rainforest, a coast live oak stump that has been carved into a wood nymph, and continues in an equally charming fashion. Soft wood chips line the path, and as you walk you learn all about toyon, coast live oak, chaparral, poison oak, periwinkle, and other common flora. The park isn't exactly wilderness, but it's a great example of how good a city park can be.

⑰ Hastain Trail

2.3 mi/1.5 hrs

Location: In Franklin Canyon in Santa Monica Mountains National Recreation Area; map I4, grid c8.

User groups: Hikers, dogs, and horses. No mountain bikes. No wheelchair facilities.

Permits: No permits are required. Parking and access are free.

Directions: From U.S. 101 in Studio City, take the Coldwater Canyon exit and drive south for 2.3 miles (the road becomes Mulholland Drive), then turn right on Franklin Canyon Drive. Drive 1.5 miles to the fork with Lake Drive, then bear left on Lake Drive. Just beyond the park entrance, look for a parking area and trailhead at a fire road on the left.

Maps: A free map of the Santa Monica Mountains National Recreation Area and a brochure on Franklin Canyon is available by contacting park headquarters at the address below. To obtain a topographic map of the area, ask for Beverly Hills from the USGS.

Contact: Santa Monica Mountains National Recreation Area, 30401 Agoura Road, Suite 100, Agoura Hills, CA 91301; (818) 597-9192 or fax (818) 597-8357.

Trail notes: Unlike at nearby Coldwater Canyon Park (see trail notes for hike number 16), here at Franklin Canyon Park you can't hear the noise of the freeway and the city, because you've dropped down into a canyon which is completed surrounded by open space. The park feels insulated from all the urban encroachment around it. (We were surprised to see a coyote right by the road as we drove in.) A hike on the park's Hastain Trail is an energetic climb on a fire road to an overlook with views of Franklin Canyon and its reservoir, west Los Angeles, and on

clear days all the way out to the ocean. After enjoying the view, you can return on a loop by taking the single-track trail on the right down to the Doheny House ranch and picnic area, then walk back on a trail alongside the park road. Before or after your hike, be sure to stop in at the park's Suki Goldman Nature Center, where you can learn all about the natural history of the Santa Monica Mountains. The center also features paintings of the mountains by local artists; we found them to be almost as inspiring as the hike.

⑱ Mount Hollywood

5.0 mi/2.5 hrs

Location: In Griffith Park; map I4, grid c9.

User groups: Hikers, dogs, and horses. No mountain bikes. No wheelchair facilities.

Permits: No permits are required. Parking and access are free.

Directions: From Interstate 5 in Hollywood, take the Los Feliz Boulevard exit and drive three miles to Ferndell Drive. Turn right and drive to the Ferndell Nature Museum. (Alternately, from U.S. 101 in Hollywood, take the Sunset Boulevard exit and drive east one block to Western Avenue. Turn left and go north on Western Avenue, then bear right on Los Feliz Boulevard. Turn left on Ferndell Drive and park near the Ferndell Nature Museum.)

Maps: A free park map is available at the park ranger station. To obtain a topographic map of the area, ask for Hollywood from the USGS.

Contact: Griffith Park Ranger Training Center, 4730 Crystal Springs, Los Angeles, CA 90027; (213) 665-5188.

Trail notes: Griffith Park is as much a part of Los Angeles legend as Mann's Chinese Theater or the Santa Monica Pier. In all of the park's many acres, no trail is more frequently hiked than the trail to the top of Mount Hollywood. Out-of-towners need to be told that this is not the peak that bears the famous "HOLLYWOOD" sign (that's Mount Lee), although you can see that sign from this peak. Actually, people hike to the top of Mount Hollywood for no other reason than because the view from its summit is unforgettable. To see it, start hiking across the street from the Ferndell Museum, heading uphill along the shady trail. A half mile out, bear right at the fork and keep climbing, soon leaving the shady, damp canyon and moving into chaparral. There are several well-signed junctions to negotiate, then all of a sudden, voila—you're at 1,625 feet in elevation on top of Mount Hollywood, the highest point in Hollywood. Check out the view that ranges from downtown all the way out to the ocean. Oh, and just in case you need to be reminded that you're not really in the wilderness, you'll find water fountains positioned at strategic locations along the trail.

⑲ Shipwreck Trail

4.0 mi/2.5 hrs

Location: On the Palos Verdes Peninsula; map I4, grid f7.

User groups: Hikers and dogs. No horses or mountain bikes. No wheelchair facilities.

Permits: No permits are required. Parking and access are free.

Directions: From Redondo Beach on Highway 1, drive south on Highway 1 to Palos Verdes Boulevard. Bear south on Palos Verdes Boulevard, which turns into Palos Verdes Drive West. Turn right on Via Corta, then in a half mile, turn right on Via Arroyo. In another half mile, turn left on Paseo del Mar and drive to Flat Rock Point. (If you reach Via Horcada, you've gone too far.) Park along the road.

Maps: To obtain a topographic map of the area, ask for Redondo Beach from the USGS.

Contact: Palos Verdes Estates City Hall, (310) 378-0383.

Trail notes: From Flat Rock Point on Paseo del Mar, you have access to the Palos Verdes Estates Shoreline Preserve and the Shipwreck Trail, a path that's sure to stimulate the imaginations of children and adults. The trail requires some scrambling over and around boulders, and running from incoming waves, but it's great fun. Note that the beach is extremely rocky so the going is slow, but that means tide-pooling is good, especially near Flat Rock Point. Check your tide table to make sure you're hiking at low tide. After dropping down to the beach, hike southward past Bluff Cove, enjoying views reaching all the way to Catalina Island. At about two miles out, just before Rocky Point, you'll see the remains of the freighter *Dominator,* a Greek ship which ran aground in 1961. The ship was never salvaged, but the years of rolling waves have taken their toll; little is left of her. If you have the energy to go a little further, just beyond the shipwreck is spectacular U-shaped Lunada Bay, with its sheer, terraced cliffs. Turn around wherever you please, and reverse your steps along the beach.

⑳ Two Harbors to Emerald Bay

9.0 mi/5.0 hrs

Location: On Catalina Island; map I4, grid i5.

User groups: Hikers only. No dogs, horses, or mountain bikes. No wheelchair facilities.

Permits: A free Santa Catalina Island hiking permit is required, and may be obtained from Visitor Services at Two Harbors; phone Santa Catalina Island Conservancy at (310) 510-2595 for more information. Fees are charged for the ferry from the mainland to Two Harbors. Phone the companies below for current rates and departure information. (Ferry fees are approximately $23 to $36 per adult, less for seniors and children under 12.)

Directions: Two companies provide ferry transportation to Two Harbors from San Pedro. Advance reservations are recommended. Phone Catalina Express at (310) 519-1212, or Catalina Cruises at (800) 228-2546.

Maps: A trail map of Catalina Island is available for 50 cents from the Santa Catalina Island Conservancy when you pick up your hiking permit. To obtain a topographic map of the area, ask for Santa Catalina West from the USGS.

Contact: Two Harbors Visitor Services, P.O. Box 5044, Two Harbors, CA 90704; (310) 510-1550. Or Santa Catalina Island Conservancy; (310) 510-2595.

Trail notes: If you want to take a hiking trip to Catalina Island, but you don't want anything on your trip to be complicated or crowded with people, there's only one key instruction to follow: Take the ferry to Two Harbors, not to Avalon. This applies whether you are going for the day or staying overnight. From where the ferry drops you off at the pier at Two Harbors, you can pick up your hiking permit and begin hiking right away on the West End Road, a dirt road that is nearly level and sticks close to the shoreline for its entire route. Head west, getting eyefuls of views of rocky outcrops, steep headlands, and beckoning coves, until at 1.25 miles you reach Cherry Valley and Cherry Cove. The area is named for the native Catalina cherry tree that grows there, which displays beautiful white flowers in the spring. Continue on the road/trail past Howlands Landing to Emerald Bay at 4.5 miles. Have a picnic, ponder how lucky we are to have this fabulous island so close to Los Angeles, then head back to Two Harbors. Although the excursion makes a fine day-trip getaway from the mainland, your best bet is to spend the night in Two Harbors (either camping or at more luxurious accommodations), then continue hiking and exploring the next day.

㉑ Empire Landing Road Trail

8.3 mi. one way/4.0 hrs

Location: On Catalina Island; map I4, grid i7.

User groups: Hikers only. No dogs, horses, or mountain bikes. No wheelchair facilities.

Permits: A free Santa Catalina Island hiking permit is required, and may be obtained from the Santa Catalina Island Conservancy at 125 Clarissa Avenue in Avalon, or at the Avalon airport. Phone (310) 510-2595 for more information. Fees are charged for the ferry from the mainland to Avalon, and for the shuttle bus from Avalon to Airport in the Sky. Phone the companies below for current rates and departure information. (Ferry fees are approximately $23 to $36 per adult, less for seniors and children under 12.)

Directions: Several companies provide ferry transportation to Avalon from San Pedro, Long Beach, Redondo Beach, and Newport Beach. Advance reservations are recommended. Phone Catalina Express at (310) 519-1212, Catalina Cruises at (800) 228-2546, or Catalina Passenger Service at (714) 673-5245. Transportation is also possible by plane or helicopter; phone

Island Express at (310) 510-2525. For information on shuttle bus service from Avalon to Airport in the Sky, phone (310) 510-0143.

Maps: A trail map of Catalina Island is available for 50 cents from the Santa Catalina Island Conservancy when you pick up your hiking permit. To obtain a topographic map of the area, ask for Santa Catalina North from the USGS.

Contact: Santa Catalina Island Conservancy; (310) 510-2595. Or Catalina Island Chamber of Commerce and Visitors Bureau, P.O. Box 217, #1 Green Pier, Avalon, CA 90704; (310) 510-1520.

Trail notes: This spectacular one-way hiking trip on Catalina Island requires a bare minimum of advance planning in exchange for tremendous rewards. First, you have to arrange to take the ferry from the mainland to Avalon, Catalina's "big city." Then when you arrive (after about a two-hour boat ride), you must pick up your free hiking permit in town at the Santa Catalina Island Conservancy, and take the shuttle bus from Avalon to Airport in the Sky. That's where your hike on the Empire Landing Road finally begins. Along its 8.3-mile length, you'll travel along the north side of the island on a curvy, up-and-down road that passes by a marble quarry, numerous coves and beaches, and fascinating rock formations. If you're lucky, you'll see island fox, huge bison, and maybe even a wild turkey.

When the trail ends at Two Harbors, you have three choices: Take the bus shuttle back to Avalon, camp or stay at the various lodgings in Two Harbors, or take the ferry from Two Harbors back to the mainland. For the latter two possibilities, you must plan in advance: Phone Two Harbors Visitor Services at (310) 510-1550 for lodgings and campground information in Two Harbors. If you want to take the ferry back to the mainland, you need to alert the ferry company that you're going in to Avalon but leaving from Two Harbors. There is no extra fee for this service, but you have to make sure you finish your hike in time to catch the last boat. One more thing to consider: When is the best time of year to visit Catalina? Unquestionably, it's spring or fall, when the weather is good and the summer crowds are nonexistent.

Leave No Trace Tips

Minimize Use and Impact of Fires

Campfires can have a lasting impact on the backcountry. Always carry a lightweight stove for cooking, and use a candle lantern instead of building a fire whenever possible.

Where fires are permitted, use established fire rings only.

Do not scar the natural setting by snapping the branches off live, dead, or downed trees.

Completely extinguish your campfire and make sure it is cold before departing. Remove all unburned trash from the fire ring and scatter the cold ashes over a large area well away from any camp.

Map I5

Adjoining Maps: East: I6 ..... *page* 600 West: I4 564
North: H5 .... 542 South: J5 622

Southern California Map .... *page* 558

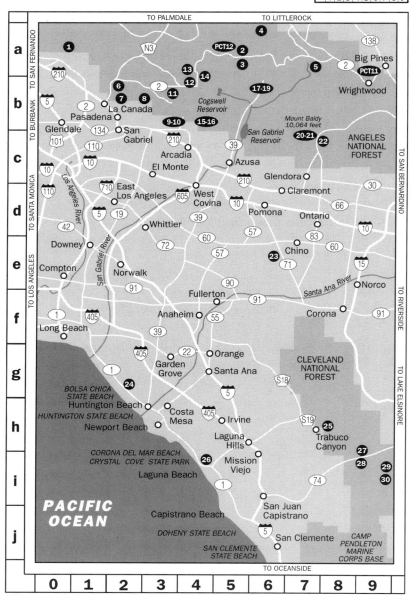

TO PALMDALE   TO LITTLEROCK

a
N3
1
PCT12 **2**
4
138
13
14
3
5
2
PCT11
Big Pines
210
12
Wrightwood
6
2
11
17-19

b
5
7 **8**
Cogswell
Reservoir
Mount Baldy
10,064 feet
ANGELES
NATIONAL
FOREST
2
La Canada
9-10
15-16
Pasadena
Glendale
134
San
Gabriel
210
San Gabriel
Reservoir
20-21 **22**
101
110

c
10
Arcadia
39
10
El Monte
Azusa
Glendora
30
210
Claremont
East
Los Angeles
605
West
Covina
66

d
710
10
Pomona
Ontario
710
605
Whittier
39
57
83
10
5
19
60
Downey

e
72
57
Chino
60
23
71
15
Compton
Norwalk
90
Santa Ana River
Norco
91
Fullerton
91

f
1
Anaheim
55
91
Corona
91
405
39
Long Beach

g
405
Orange
CLEVELAND
NATIONAL
FOREST
1
22
Garden
Grove
Santa Ana
S18
BOLSA CHICA
STATE BEACH
24
5
Huntington Beach

h
HUNTINGTON STATE BEACH
Costa
Mesa
405
Irvine
S19
25
Newport Beach
Laguna
Hills
Trabuco
Canyon
27
CORONA DEL MAR BEACH
CRYSTAL COVE STATE PARK
26
Mission
Viejo
28

i
Laguna Beach
74
29
1
30

j
**PACIFIC
OCEAN**
San Juan
Capistrano
Capistrano Beach
DOHENY STATE BEACH
5
San Clemente
CAMP
PENDLETON
MARINE
CORPS
BASE
SAN CLEMENTE
STATE BEACH

TO OCEANSIDE

TO SAN FERNANDO · TO BURBANK · TO SANTA MONICA · TO LOS ANGELES
TO SAN BERNARDINO · TO RIVERSIDE · TO LAKE ELSINORE

0 1 2 3 4 5 6 7 8 9

❶ Trail Canyon Trail

4.0 mi/2.0 hrs

Location: In Angeles National Forest near Sunland; map I5, grid a0.

User groups: Hikers, dogs, horses, and mountain bikes. No wheelchair facilities.

Permits: No permits are required. A national forest recreation pass is required for each vehicle; fees are $5 for one day or $30 for a year.

Directions: From Interstate 210 in Sunland, exit on Sunland Boulevard which becomes Foothill Boulevard. Drive east for one mile to Mount Gleason Avenue. Turn left (north), drive 1.3 miles, then turn right on Big Tujunga Canyon Road. Drive 3.4 miles on Big Tujunga Canyon Road to a sign for Trail Canyon Trail on the left. Drive a quarter mile to a fork, then bear right and drive a quarter mile on rough road to a large parking lot. The trailhead is on the left side of the lot as you drive in.

Maps: For a map of Angeles National Forest, send $4 to USDA-Forest Service, 630 Sansome Street, San Francisco, CA 94111. A map of the San Gabriel Mountains is available for a fee from Tom Harrison Cartography, (415) 456-7940. To obtain a topographic map of the area, ask for Sunland from the USGS.

Contact: Angeles National Forest, Tujunga Ranger District, 12371 North Little Tujunga Canyon Road, San Fernando, CA 91342; (818) 899-1900 of fax (818) 896-6727.

Trail notes: Trail Canyon is located on the western side of the San Gabriel Mountains, an area that is less visited than the more celebrated eastern side. The Trail Canyon Trail (as redundant as that sounds) leads through a shady, stream-carved canyon and up to open slopes, then curves its way to Trail Canyon Falls. The waterfall is so beautiful in winter and early spring that it can take your breath away. The trail begins with a ford and has several more stream crossings along the way, so be prepared for the possibility of wet feet. You walk on a dirt road past a community of cabins, then wind around the canyon until at three-quarters of a mile, you spy a single-track trail leading off on the right. Immediately you enter a densely shaded riparian area, thick with sycamores, alders, and cottonwoods. In another half mile, you climb out of this canyon and work your way up a slope among spring-blooming chaparral. The path is high above the creek now, and a sharp left curve suddenly reveals the waterfall, up ahead about a quarter mile. The trail leads to the top of it, where 50-foot Trail Canyon Falls spills over a smooth granite precipice. After admiring the falls, continue a little further to where the trail crosses the stream. Take a look at the beautiful colors in the rocky streambed. On your return trip downhill, you have lovely canyon vistas to look forward to.

❷ Cooper Canyon Falls

4.0 mi/2.0 hrs

Location: In Angeles National Forest near Mount Waterman; map I5, grid a5.

User groups: Hikers, dogs, horses, and mountain bikes. No wheelchair facilities.

Permits: No permits are required. A national forest recreation pass is required for each vehicle; fees are $5 for one day or $30 for a year.

Directions: From Interstate 210 in La Cañada, take Highway 2 north and drive 34 miles to Buckhorn Camp on the left. (It's 1.5 miles past the Mount Waterman ski lift, just beyond Cloudburst Summit.) The Burkhardt Trail starts at the far end of the camp near the rest rooms (bear left at site 18).

Maps: For a map of Angeles National Forest, send $4 to USDA-Forest Service, 630 Sansome Street, San Francisco, CA 94111. A map of the San Gabriel Mountains is available for a fee from Tom Harrison Cartography, (415) 456-7940. To obtain a topographic map of the area, ask for Waterman Mountain from the USGS.

Contact: Angeles National Forest, Arroyo Seco Ranger District, 4600 Oak Grove Drive, Flintridge, CA 91011; (818) 790-1151 or fax (818) 790-5392.

Trail notes: After the snow has melted, here's

a first-rate reason to make the 34-mile drive to the summit of Mount Waterman: A visit to Cooper Canyon Falls. The best thing about the waterfall, besides the fact that it's set in a gorgeous, 6,000-foot-elevation forest, is that it's just far enough away so that it doesn't get heavily visited. Start your hike at Buckhorn Campground at the trailhead for the Burkhardt Trail. Although there are small waterfalls and swimming holes along Buckhorn Creek within a quarter mile of the camp, the real treasure is two miles away at Cooper Canyon. The hike is a mostly downhill trip through a dense forest of big firs, cedars, and pines. There's almost no undergrowth in these woods—just conifers and big rocks. It feels like you're in the southern Sierra Nevada, but, no, this is the San Gabriels. The Burkhardt Trail laterals along the canyon slopes, high above Buckhorn Creek, then makes a left turn into Cooper Canyon, and traces a long switchback downhill. At 1.75 miles from the camp, you'll reach a junction with the Pacific Crest Trail and Silver Moccasin Trail. Turn right, toward Burkhardt Saddle and Eagle's Roost. It's only a tenth of a mile to the waterfall, which drops just below the trail's edge. A rope helps you down the steep cliff to its base, where you can stand on an island of boulders and enjoy the falls' noisy, 35-foot drop. Be sure to get here early in the year, when the stream flow is still strong. Trailhead elevation is 6,300 feet.

❸ Mount Waterman

7.0 mi/3.5 hrs

Location: In Angeles National Forest at Mount Waterman; map I5, grid a5.

User groups: Hikers, dogs, horses, and mountain bikes. No wheelchair facilities.

Permits: No permits are required. A national forest recreation pass is required for each vehicle; fees are $5 for one day or $30 for a year.

Directions: From Interstate 210 in La Cañada, take Highway 2 north and drive 33 miles to the trailhead for Mount Waterman on the right side of the road, just east of Cloudburst Summit and across from Buckhorn Campground.

Maps: For a map of Angeles National Forest, send $4 to USDA-Forest Service, 630 Sansome

Street, San Francisco, CA 94111. A map of the San Gabriel Mountains is available for a fee from Tom Harrison Cartography, (415) 456-7940. To obtain a topographic map of the area, ask for Waterman Mountain from the USGS.

Contact: Angeles National Forest, Arroyo Seco Ranger District, 4600 Oak Grove Drive, Flintridge, CA 91011; (818) 790-1151 or fax (818) 790-5392.

Trail notes: The peak of Mount Waterman at 8,038 feet is a fine destination for a moderate day hike in the San Gabriel Mountains. The only problem along the trail is figuring out which peak is really the peak, because the top of Mount Waterman is so wide that there are three summits. From the trailhead (elevation 6,700 feet) across from the entrance to Buckhorn Campground, head uphill on the well-graded single-track through a shady pine, cedar, and fir forest. At one mile out, you reach a saddle where your views open wide. Climb some more, through long switchbacks, to a junction at two miles out, where you go right for the summit. It's another 1.5 miles to the peak, with a total 1,300-foot elevation gain. Keep your eyes peeled for bighorn sheep, which are sometimes seen in the area. Also check out the huge sugar pine cones that can be found alongside the trail and hanging down from the pines. When you reach the U-shaped top of Mount Waterman, head off-trail for a quarter mile toward the southwest, where you'll find the highest of Waterman's summits and the one with the best view, looking out over the magnificent San Gabriel Mountains.

❹ Devil's Punchbowl

1.0 mi/0.5 hr

Location: In the Devil's Punchbowl Natural Area south of Pearblossom; map I5, grid a6.

User groups: Hikers, dogs, horses, and mountain bikes. No wheelchair facilities.

Permits: No permits are required. A $3 day-use fee is charged per vehicle.

Directions: From Highway 14 near Palmdale, take the Highway 138 exit east for 16 miles to Pearblossom. Turn right on County Road N-6 and drive south for 7.5 miles to the Devil's Punchbowl entrance. The trail begins behind the park nature center.

Maps: To obtain a topographic map of the area, ask for Valyermo from the USGS.

Contact: Devil's Punchbowl Natural Area, 28000 Devil's Punchbowl Road, Pearblossom, CA 93553; (805) 944-2743.

Trail notes: The Devil's Punchbowl is visual proof that you're in earthquake country, where faulting and erosion have made bizarre shapes out of ancient sedimentary rocks. They thrust and jut upward, creating vertical walls as high as 300 feet, which look like they're about to topple inward on each other. From the viewpoint behind the visitor center, you look down into the land of the devil—the Punchbowl—a giant abyss that is the working of the San Andreas Fault and the result of centuries of stream carving. Juniper, pinyon pine, and manzanita manage to eke out a meager living among all the sandstone. The park's one-mile loop trail offers fine views into the depths of the Punchbowl. It switchbacks gently downhill and then climbs back up, passing by some of the taller rock slabs in the park. Note that if this kind of geologic action fascinates you, you might want to pay a visit to nearby Vasquez Rocks County Park, which is detailed in chapter H5. Also, make sure you stop in at the nature center here at Devil's Punchbowl, a great place to get a geology lesson.

❺ Vincent Gap to Mount Baden-Powell

8.0 mi/4.0 hrs

Location: In Angeles National Forest near Big Pines; map I5, grid a7.

User groups: Hikers, dogs, and horses. No mountain bikes. No wheelchair facilities.

Permits: No permits are required. A national forest recreation pass is required for each vehicle; fees are $5 for one day or $30 for a year.

Directions: From Interstate 210 in La Cañada, take Highway 2 northeast and drive 53 miles to Vincent Gap. (If you are coming from Highway 138 near Phelan or Piñon Hills, take Highway 2 west for 15 miles to Vincent Gap, which is 5.5 miles west of Big Pines.)

Maps: For a map of Angeles National Forest, send $4 to USDA-Forest Service, 630 Sansome

Street, San Francisco, CA 94111. A map of the San Gabriel Mountains is available for a fee from Tom Harrison Cartography, (415) 456-7940. To obtain topographic maps of the area, ask for Mount San Antonio and Crystal Lake from the USGS.

Contact: Angeles National Forest, Valyermo Ranger District, 29835 Valyermo Road, Valyermo, CA 93563; (805) 944-2187 or fax (805) 944-4698.

Trail notes: Like the climb to the summit of Mount Baldy, the climb to the summit of Mount Baden-Powell is something of a requirement for Southern California hikers. Luckily, this requirement is a little easier to attain, because the trail up to Mount Baden-Powell is a mere eight-mile round-trip with a 2,800-foot elevation gain. The summit of Baden-Powell is at 9,399 feet, and it's directly across the San Gabriel Basin from, and slightly north of, Mount Baldy. As you might guess, the views from the summit are extraordinary. The summit area is also a botanist's delight, as 2,000-year-old limber pines can be found growing there. From the southwest edge of Vincent Gap, the trail leads through open forest—first oak, sugar pine, and Jeffrey pine, and, as you climb, mostly lodgepole pine and occasional limber pines. The trail is extremely well maintained, and it switchbacks on a moderate grade all the way up to the peak, where you can see more than a vertical mile below you, into the canyon of the East Fork San Gabriel River. In addition, your views extend north to the desert, and across the canyon to Mount Baldy. In case you haven't heard, the British Lord Baden-Powell, for whom this peak is named, founded the Boy Scouts organization. The scouts have placed a monument to him at the summit. While you're there, make a vow always to "Be Prepared," just like the Boy Scouts.

⑥ Gabrielino Trail to Bear Canyon

7.0 mi/4.0 hrs or 2.0 days

Location: In Angeles National Forest near La Cañada; map I5, grid b1.

User groups: Hikers, dogs, horses, and mountain bikes. No wheelchair facilities.

Permits: A free campfire permit is required only for hikers using a camp stove or building a campfire. A national forest recreation pass is required for each vehicle; fees are $5 for one day or $30 for a year.

Directions: From Interstate 210 in La Cañada, take Highway 2 north and drive 9.8 miles to Switzer Picnic Area on the right. (At 9.3 miles you reach Clear Creek Information Station; bear right and reach Switzer in a half mile.)

Maps: For a map of Angeles National Forest, send $4 to USDA-Forest Service, 630 Sansome Street, San Francisco, CA 94111. A map of the San Gabriel Mountains is available for a fee from Tom Harrison Cartography, (415) 456-7940. To obtain topographic maps of the area, ask for Condor Peak and Pasadena from the USGS.

Contact: Angeles National Forest, Arroyo Seco Ranger District, 4600 Oak Grove Drive, Flintridge, CA 91011; (818) 790-1151 or fax (818) 790-5392.

Trail notes: The Gabrielino National Recreation Trail is your ticket to visiting the waterslides, mini-cascades, and pools of spectacular Bear Canyon. Begin hiking into the canyon from the Switzer Picnic Area, which on summer weekends is usually packed with people. Head downstream on the smooth dirt trail through a shady canopy of willows, alders, oaks, and maples. A few creek crossings and one mile of trail brings you to Commodore Switzer Trail Camp, which is comprised of a few primitive sites along the creek—an excellent short and easy backpacking trip. Cross the stream by the camp and head uphill, still on the Gabrielino Trail. The trail passes 50-foot Switzer Falls, affording a decent view of it from across the canyon. The stone building ruins you see are the remains of the Switzer Chapel, where visitors at Switzer's Camp, a popular trail resort in the early 1900s, would attend Sunday services above the falls. A few steps further brings you to a junction where Gabrielino Trail heads right and uphill, and Bear Canyon Trail heads left and downhill. Bear left and descend steeply for a mile, being cautious of the steep dropoffs. When you reach the creek, continue downstream for another mile to Bear Canyon Trail Camp, passing many waterslides and crystal-clear pools along the way. Big cone spruce line the cool and shady trail. Trout fishing in the creek is good, best in spring.

❼ Millard Falls

1.0 mi/0.5 hr

Location: In Angeles National Forest near Pasadena; map I5, grid b1.

User groups: Hikers and dogs. No horses or mountain bikes. No wheelchair facilities.

Permits: No permits are required. A national forest recreation pass is required for each vehicle; fees are $5 for one day or $30 for a year.

Directions: From Interstate 210 in Pasadena, exit on Lake Avenue and drive north for 3.5 miles to Loma Alta Drive. Turn west (left) on Loma Alta Drive and drive one mile to Chaney Trail at the flashing yellow light. Turn right and drive 1.5 miles on Chaney Trail, keeping left at the fork, to Millard Campground. Park in the parking lot, then follow the fire road on the right (as you drove in) that leads into the campground.

Maps: For a map of Angeles National Forest, send $4 to USDA-Forest Service, 630 Sansome Street, San Francisco, CA 94111. A map of the San Gabriel Mountains is available for a fee from Tom Harrison Cartography, (415) 456-7940. To obtain a topographic map of the area, ask for Pasadena from the USGS.

Contact: Angeles National Forest, Arroyo Seco Ranger District, 4600 Oak Grove Drive, Flintridge, CA 91011; (818) 790-1151 or fax (818) 790-5392.

Trail notes: If you want to guarantee your kids (or adult friends) a good time, take them to Millard Campground for the short hike and scramble to Millard Falls. In springtime, make sure you're dressed to get wet, because you may have to spend more time in the stream than on a dry trail, especially if it has rained lately. This trip is a perfect easy adventure, suitable for hikers of all abilities. The only minus on the trail is the abundance of carvings found on the smooth-barked alder trees; the carvings desecrate almost every tree, as high as human hands can reach. (Take this opportunity to teach your children never, ever to carve anything on trees.) The route to the falls is a half-mile walk up the stream canyon, partly in the creek and partly on trail. Start walking at the edge of the camp, just beyond the camp host's site, where the trail leads to the right, past a couple of cabins. Simply head upstream, rock-hopping where necessary, until the canyon walls come together at 60-foot Millard Falls. The stream splits in two at the fall's lip, forced to detour around two boulders which are stuck in the waterfall's notch. The two streams rejoin about two-thirds of the way down, creating a tremendous rush of water in springtime. Trailhead elevation is 1,900 feet.

❽ Eaton Canyon

3.0 mi/1.5 hrs

Location: In Eaton Canyon County Park; map I5, grid b2.

User groups: Hikers, dogs, horses, and mountain bikes. No wheelchair facilities.

Permits: No permits are required. Parking and access are free.

Directions: From Interstate 210 in Pasadena heading east, take the Altadena Drive exit and drive north on Altadena Drive for 1.6 miles. Turn right into the entrance for Eaton Canyon County Park, which is one block north of New York Drive. (If you are heading west on Interstate 210, you must take the Rosemead Boulevard exit and drive north to New York Drive, then turn right on Altadena Drive and continue to the park entrance.)

Maps: A free map of Eaton Canyon County Park is available at the nature center. To obtain topographic maps of the area, ask for Pasadena and Mount Wilson from the USGS.

Contact: Eaton Canyon County Park, 1750 North Altadena Drive, Pasadena, CA 91107; (818) 398-5420.

Trail notes: Eaton Canyon County Park is the kind of place where elementary school groups come in the spring. The buses unload their cargoes of children, who then set off on what may be their first "real" hike, through Eaton Canyon's wash. And what a fine introduction to the outdoors—a hike along Eaton Canyon in the good company of cactus, chaparral plants, willows, oaks, and occasional bunnies and lizards. Start at the park nature center, where you can pick up a free map of the area, then walk to the far end of the parking lot and take the dirt road that leads to the right. Cross the wash and hike along the wide canyon trail, with the creek on your left. The stream attracts a large variety of wildlife, especially birds, who sing all day in this canyon. When you reach a bridge where your trail intersects with the Wilson Toll Road, cross the bridge and take the steep right cutoff on its far side down to the streambed. From there, hike upstream, crossing the creek several times as the canyon narrows on its way to Eaton Canyon Falls. Sadly, the waterfall's cliff has been desecrated by graffiti, but the falls remain a well-loved destination in Eaton Canyon. An odd side note: If you hear the sound of gunfire at the trailhead, don't panic, like we did. The local police have a shooting range nearby. As you walk into the canyon, you'll quickly get away from the noise.

❾ Big Santa Anita Canyon

6.0 mi/3.0 hrs

Location: In Angeles National Forest near Arcadia; map I5, grid b3.

User groups: Hikers, dogs, horses, and mountain bikes. No wheelchair facilities.

Permits: No permits are required. A national forest recreation pass is required for each vehicle; fees are $5 for one day or $30 for a year.

Directions: From Interstate 210 in Pasadena, drive seven miles east to Arcadia. Exit on Santa Anita Avenue and drive six miles north to the road's end at Chantry Flat. The trail begins across the road from the first parking area.

Maps: For a map of Angeles National Forest, send $4 to USDA-Forest Service, 630 Sansome Street, San Francisco, CA 94111. A map of the San Gabriel Mountains is available for a fee from Tom Harrison Cartography, (415) 456-7940. To obtain a topographic map of the area, ask for Mount Wilson from the USGS.

Contact: Angeles National Forest, Arroyo Seco Ranger District, 4600 Oak Grove Drive, Flintridge, CA 91011; (818) 790-1151 or fax (818) 790-5392.

Trail notes: Big Santa Anita Canyon is probably the top easy day-hike destination in all of the Arroyo Seco District of Angeles National Forest. It's easy to reach, and provides a short, simple, and sweet escape from urban life. The shady, overgrown, magical gulch is just a handful of miles from the Pasadena freeway. Day hikers can't help but covet the adorable summer cabins in the canyon, which you walk past on

your way to see 60-foot Sturtevant Falls, the canyon's showpiece. The cabins are what remains of Roberts Camp, a popular weekend resort from the early 1900s. The hike begins at Chantry Flat, elevation 2,200 feet, and you follow the Gabrielino National Recreation Trail downhill. It's paved for the first six-tenths of a mile heading down into the canyon, then when you reach the bottom, you cross Roberts Footbridge and head to the right on the dirt pathway. A one-mile upstream walk leads to Sturtevant Falls, traveling under the shade of oaks and alders and along Big Santa Anita Creek. The artificial waterfalls you see are small check dams, designed (poorly) to keep the creek from flooding. Where the Gabrielino Trail forks left and heads uphill, continue straight along the creek, admiring ferns and vines as you walk another quarter mile to Sturtevant Falls. It drops 60 feet over a granite cliff into a perfectly shaped rock bowl. Then retrace your steps to the junction, and follow the Gabrielino Trail uphill. Take the lower trail (the upper trail is safer for horses), which clings to the steep hillsides as it climbs above Sturtevant Falls to Cascade Picnic Area, a shady spot alongside the fern-lined creek. Take a break here before leaving Big Santa Anita Canyon and heading back uphill to the real world.

❿ First Water Trail

3.0 mi/1.5 hrs

Location: In Angeles National Forest near Arcadia; map I5, grid b3.

User groups: Hikers, dogs, horses, and mountain bikes. No wheelchair facilities.

Permits: No permits are required. A national forest recreation pass is required for each vehicle; fees are $5 for one day or $30 for a year.

Directions: From Interstate 210 in Pasadena, drive seven miles east to Arcadia. Exit on Santa Anita Avenue and drive six miles north to the road's end at Chantry Flat. The trail begins across the road from the first parking area.

Maps: For a map of Angeles National Forest, send $4 to USDA-Forest Service, 630 Sansome Street, San Francisco, CA 94111. To obtain a topographic map of the area, ask for Mount Wilson from the USGS.

Contact: Angeles National Forest, Arroyo Seco Ranger District, 4600 Oak Grove Drive, Flintridge, CA 91011; (818) 790-1151 or fax (818) 790-5392.

Trail notes: You say you flat out refuse to hike on pavement? Then the trip on the Gabrielino Trail to Sturtevant Falls might not be right for you (see trail notes for hike number 9), but don't bypass beautiful Big Santa Anita Canyon because of it. An alternate trail drops down into the canyon, but this one is on gorgeous single-track all the way, lined with tall oaks and alders, huge chain ferns, slender sword ferns, and half a dozen other fern varieties. The First Water Trail is mostly just a path used by cabin owners in the canyon to reach their homes. That means you'll see far less people than on the wide, paved Gabrielino Trail, the main trail into the canyon. You begin at the same trailhead and the first few hundred yards of the walk are the same, but then you cut off the Gabrielino Trail at the sign for the First Water Trail and Hermit Falls (on your right). The trail switchbacks gently down into the canyon, then heads south along the North Fork of Big Santa Anita Creek. The near-constant shade of the canyon, combined with the presence of a year-round stream, makes it possible for every inch of ground to spring forth plant life. As on the Gabrielino Trail, you pass many artificial waterfalls made by check dams on Santa Anita Creek, which are surprisingly beautiful. The First Water Trail crosses the creek a few times, which can be a little tricky early in the year, and follows the stream on its downstream course. The trail ends at the last cabin in the canyon, just above Hermit Falls. Pick a granite boulder, have a seat, and watch the water flow by.

⓫ Mount Wilson

8.0 mi/4.5 hrs

Location: In Angeles National Forest near Red Box; map I5, grid b3.

User groups: Hikers, dogs, horses, and mountain bikes. No wheelchair facilities.

Permits: No permits are required. A national forest recreation pass is required for each vehicle; fees are $5 for one day or $30 for a year.

Directions: From Interstate 210 in La Cañada, take Highway 2 north and drive 14 miles to Red

Box Divide. Turn right (east) on Red Box Road and drive five miles to the Rattlesnake Trailhead, about one mile west of West Fork Campground.

Maps: For a map of Angeles National Forest, send $4 to USDA-Forest Service, 630 Sansome Street, San Francisco, CA 94111. A map of the San Gabriel Mountains is available for a fee from Tom Harrison Cartography, (415) 456-7940. To obtain a topographic map of the area, ask for Mount Wilson from the USGS.

Contact: Angeles National Forest, Arroyo Seco Ranger District, 4600 Oak Grove Drive, Flintridge, CA 91011; (818) 790-1151 or fax (818) 790-5392.

Trail notes: There are many possible routes for climbing Mount Wilson, including the oldest of them all from Little Santa Anita Canyon, a trail built in 1864. But that's a long, 15-mile round-trip, and if you don't have the time or energy for it, the shorter Rattlesnake Trail to Mount Wilson is a fine alternative. Start from Red Box Road near West Fork Campground, where you get a head start on the climb from your trailhead elevation of 3,100 feet. The trail is a mix of chaparral and forest, but with many surprisingly cool sections in the shade along Strains Canyon. As you climb, you'll see progressively more big cone spruce, and near Mount Wilson's 5,710-foot summit, you'll hike among ponderosa, Jeffrey, and sugar pines. Views of the Mount Wilson Observatory and the high peaks of the San Gabriels are excellent. On the clearest of days, you can see all the way out to the ocean. When you get up here, you'll ask yourself the obvious question: Why would anyone drive to Mount Wilson when they could take this fine hike instead?

⓬ Vetter Mountain Lookout

1.5 mi/1.0 hr

Location: In Angeles National Forest near Charlton Flat; map I5, grid b3.

User groups: Hikers, dogs, horses, and mountain bikes. No wheelchair facilities.

Permits: No permits are required. A national forest recreation pass is required for each vehicle; fees are $5 for one day or $30 for a year.

Directions: From Interstate 210 in La Cañada, take Highway 2 northeast and drive 23 miles to

Charlton Flat. Turn left on the road to Charlton Flat Picnic Area, then turn right at the next junction. Continue down through Charlton Flat to the Forest Service pumphouse, across from the Wolf Tree Nature Trail. A trail sign on the left marks the start of the trail to Vetter Mountain.

Maps: For a map of Angeles National Forest, send $4 to USDA-Forest Service, 630 Sansome Street, San Francisco, CA 94111. To obtain a topographic map of the area, ask for Chilao Flat from the USGS.

Contact: Angeles National Forest, Arroyo Seco Ranger District, 4600 Oak Grove Drive, Flintridge, CA 91011; (818) 790-1151 or fax (818) 790-5392.

Trail notes: Vetter Mountain is a San Gabriel summit that even children can attain, via a trail that's less than a mile long and gains only 400 feet. The peak was named for Victor Vetter, a forest ranger during the 1920s and 1930s. From the trail sign, follow the path along a small ravine, crossing the Forest Service road in a half mile. The trail continues along the ravine and climbs to the ridgetop, where you turn left and head for the fire lookout on the summit, at elevation 5,908 feet. Views are extraordinary in all directions, with more than 20 named peaks visible. Bring a map so you can identify them. A historical note: Besides being used to spot fires, the Vetter Lookout was also used to spot enemy aircraft during World War II. Trailhead elevation is 5,500 feet.

⑬ Silver Moccasin Trail to Mount Hillyer

6.0 mi/3.0 hrs

Location: In Angeles National Forest near the Chilao Visitor Center; map I5, grid b4.

User groups: Hikers, dogs, horses, and mountain bikes. No wheelchair facilities.

Permits: No permits are required. A national forest recreation pass is required for each vehicle; fees are $5 for one day or $30 for a year.

Directions: From Interstate 210 in La Cañada, take Highway 2 north and drive 28 miles to the Chilao Visitor Center turnoff on the left. Turn left and drive past the Upper Chilao Picnic Area to a parking lot on the right for the Silver Moccasin Trailhead.

Maps: For a map of Angeles National Forest, send $4 to USDA-Forest Service, 630 Sansome Street, San Francisco, CA 94111. A map of the San Gabriel Mountains is available for a fee from Tom Harrison Cartography, (415) 456-7940. To obtain a topographic map of the area, ask for Chilao Flat from the USGS.

Contact: Angeles National Forest, Arroyo Seco Ranger District, 4600 Oak Grove Drive, Flintridge, CA 91011; (818) 790-1151 or fax (818) 790-5392.

Trail notes: The Silver Moccasin Trail is 53 miles long in its entirety, but not too many people hike the entire thing, except the Boy Scouts who have been doing it since 1942. When they finish, they get the Silver Moccasin Award, which is a much bigger deal than earning a badge for building a campfire. One of the best sections of the Silver Moccasin Trail is the route to Mount Hillyer, an 1,100-foot climb spread out over three miles. The trail starts in chaparral and occasional gray pines, interspersed with many tall, blooming yucca plants in the spring. Watch the terrain change as you climb into beautiful stands of Jeffrey pines and incense cedars. At one mile you near Horse Flats Campground, where you leave the Silver Moccasin Trail to join the Mount Hillyer Trail. The path bears left to go around the camp and continue up to the peak. A series of steep switchbacks brings you to Hillyer's summit, where there are many large granite boulders to climb around on and spread out your picnic lunch. Views of the surrounding mountains are only fair from the forested peak, but the air is clean and sweet, the crowds are nonexistent, and for a while, you'll want to stay right where you are and relax.

⑭ Devil's Canyon Trail

10.0 mi/6.0 hrs or 2.0 days

Location: In the San Gabriel Wilderness near Mount Waterman; map I5, grid b4.

User groups: Hikers, dogs, and horses. No mountain bikes. No wheelchair facilities.

Permits: A free campfire permit is required only for hikers using a camp stove or building a campfire. A national forest recreation pass is required for each vehicle; fees are $5 for one day or $30 for a year.

Directions: From Interstate 210 in La Cañada, take Highway 2 north and drive 27 miles to Chilao Campground on the left. Continue a quarter mile beyond the camp on Highway 2 to a parking lot on the left (west) side of the highway. Park there and walk across the road to the trailhead. (If you reach the Chilao Visitor Center, you've gone too far.)

Maps: For a map of Angeles National Forest, send $4 to USDA-Forest Service, 630 Sansome Street, San Francisco, CA 94111. A map of the San Gabriel Mountains is available for a fee from Tom Harrison Cartography, (415) 456-7940. To obtain topographic maps of the area, ask for Chilao Flat and Waterman Mountain from the USGS.

Contact: Angeles National Forest, Arroyo Seco Ranger District, 4600 Oak Grove Drive, Flintridge, CA 91011; (818) 790-1151 or fax (818) 790-5392.

Trail notes: When you've tired of the front country, it's time to make the trip to the rugged San Gabriel Wilderness. Just be prepared to pay for your pleasure, because this is an upside-down hike—down on the way in and up, up, up on the way out. It's a trail of extremes. There's chaparral on some slopes, then tall pines and big cone spruce on others. There's sun, then shade. It's dry for the first two miles, then you reach a tributary creek and follow its meander. The trip down to the Devil's Canyon Trail Camp, 3.5 miles in, is usually pretty quick—about an hour and a half for most people. From there, you can make your way downstream along Devil's Creek, partly on a trail and partly rock-hopping, wading, and scrambling. The canyon gets narrower as you go; willows and alders shade the stream. It's slow travel but immensely enjoyable. Fishing is surprisingly good along the creek, and the highlight of the trip is a 20-foot waterfall dropping over light-colored granite. The fall blocks any further travel downstream, so at this point turn around and head back to camp (or back to the trailhead) when you've had enough water play. Remember to save plenty of energy, and plenty of water, for the 3.5-mile trip from the camp back to the trailhead, which has a 2,000-foot elevation gain. We were convinced the miles on the way up were twice as long as they were on the trip down. Trailhead elevation is 5,200 feet.

⓯ Monrovia Canyon Falls

1.4 mi/1.0 hr

Location: In Monrovia Canyon Park; map I5, grid b4.

User groups: Hikers, dogs, horses, and mountain bikes. No wheelchair facilities.

Permits: No permits are required. A $2 day-use fee is charged per vehicle.

Directions: From Interstate 210 in Monrovia, take the Myrtle Avenue exit and drive north on Myrtle Avenue for 1.8 miles. Turn right on Scenic Drive, then drive 200 yards and turn right on Encinitas Drive, then turn left again immediately, back on Scenic Drive. Continue on Scenic Drive as it turns into Canyon Boulevard, then turn right at the sign for Monrovia Canyon Park. Park at the far end of the park road, near the picnic area and nature center.

Maps: A free park map is available at the nature center. To obtain a topographic map of the area, ask for Azusa from the USGS.

Contact: Monrovia Canyon Park, c/o City Hall, 415 South Ivy Avenue, Monrovia, CA 91016; (818) 359-4214 or (818) 357-5046.

Trail notes: Everything about Monrovia Canyon Park is a great experience, including the hike to the park's showpiece: Monrovia Canyon Falls. The trail is easy enough for families with small children, yet beautiful enough to keep seasoned hikers happy. It begins at the far edge of the picnic area at the clearly signed trailhead. At the first junction, bear right and walk upstream, passing several check dams along the creek. The canyon is lush and shaded, like a smaller version of nearby Big Santa Anita Canyon (see trail notes for hikes number 9 and 10), and crowded with oaks, alders, and ferns. The slightly uphill trail leads you quickly to the 50-foot waterfall. Many big rocks in front of it are perfectly situated for gazing in admiration. After visiting the falls, you can extend your hike by retracing your steps back down the canyon, then continuing beyond the picnic area junction, following the trail along the creek to its end at the park road. Turn left and walk up the road to return to your car. This will increase your round-trip to two miles instead of 1.4 miles.

Special note: Check your calendar before you go. Monrovia Canyon Park is closed on Tuesdays.

⑯ Ben Overturff Trail

7.0 mi/3.5 hrs

Location: In Monrovia Canyon Park; map I5, grid b4.

User groups: Hikers, dogs, and horses. No mountain bikes. No wheelchair facilities.

Permits: No permits are required. A $2 day-use fee is charged per vehicle.

Directions: From Interstate 210 in Monrovia, take the Myrtle Avenue exit and drive north on Myrtle Avenue for 1.8 miles. Turn right on Scenic Drive, then drive 200 yards and turn right on Encinitas Drive, then turn left again immediately, back on Scenic Drive. Continue on Scenic Drive as it turns into Canyon Boulevard, then turn right at the sign for Monrovia Canyon Park. Park at the first available parking lot near the entrance; the trail begins at the lower end of the park, by the park toll gate.

Maps: A free brochure on the Ben Overturff Trail is available at the nature center. To obtain a topographic map of the area, ask for Azusa from the USGS.

Contact: Monrovia Canyon Park, c/o City Hall, 415 South Ivy Avenue, Monrovia, CA 91016; (818) 359-4214 or (818) 357-5046.

Trail notes: Ben Overturff was the man who made Monrovia Canyon a popular recreation area early in this century. He ran a lodge at Deer Park from 1910 to 1945, a getaway for city dwellers which visitors would hike up the canyon to reach. This trail to the site of Deer Park Lodge was reconstructed in the 1990s and named in his honor. It's a gorgeous route that travels through a wonderland of streamside oaks, alders, and giant chain ferns. Foliage grows everywhere you look, with many diverse species of plants ranging from riparian ferns and vines to chaparral. Start your hike on the Sawpit Canyon Fire Road, passing Sawpit Dam almost immediately. The trail follows the fire road for 1.25 miles to Overturff Junction, where you bear left on the Ben Overturff Trail. Follow the well-built, single-track trail as it winds its way up the canyon, passing Twin Springs Junction at 2.5

miles. (A trail on the right connects to Sawpit Canyon Fire Road here, if you're getting tired and want to loop back.) Continue past the junction to the Deer Park Cabin site, where you can relax and pull your lunch out of your daypack. From here at trail's end, you have two options: Retrace your steps on the Ben Overturff Trail, or take the connector trail to Sawpit Canyon Fire Road, then follow the fire road all the way back to the trailhead. Our choice would be the Ben Overturff Trail, but loop-lovers will probably pick the fire road.

Special note: Check your calendar before you go. Although the entire park is closed on Tuesdays, the Ben Overturff Trail is closed on both Tuesdays and Wednesdays.

⑰ Soldier Creek/ Lewis Falls

1.25 mi/1.0 hr

Location: Near the Crystal Lake Recreation Area; map I5, grid b5.

User groups: Hikers and dogs. No horses or mountain bikes. No wheelchair facilities.

Permits: No permits are required. A national forest recreation pass is required for each vehicle; fees are $5 for one day or $30 for a year.

Directions: From Azusa on Interstate 210, drive north on Highway 39 for 18 miles to Coldbrook Camp on the left. From Coldbrook Camp, continue 2.4 miles up Highway 39 to a dirt pullout on the right, where Soldier Creek crosses under the highway. (If you reach the turnoff for Falling Springs Resort, you've gone two-tenths of a mile too far.) Park in the pullout and begin hiking from the far right side, heading up the right side of the creek.

Maps: For a map of Angeles National Forest, send $4 to USDA-Forest Service, 630 Sansome Street, San Francisco, CA 94111. A map of the San Gabriel Mountains is available for a fee from Tom Harrison Cartography, (415) 456-7940. To obtain a topographic map of the area, ask for Crystal Lake from the USGS.

Contact: Angeles National Forest, Mount Baldy Ranger District, 110 North Wabash Avenue, Glendora, CA 91740; (818) 335-1251 or fax (818) 914-3790.

Trail notes: The trip to Soldier Creek Falls, also

known as Lewis Falls, is the perfect kind of adventure for people who aren't really up for having an adventure. The hike is pure fun, more stream scramble than walk, especially in springtime when snowmelt and rain are making Soldier Creek flow strong and full. It's a short trip to the waterfall and the going is fairly easy. The trailhead is unmarked, so follow the directions above exactly, then walk up the canyon with the stream on your left side. The start of the trail has some graffiti and usually some litter (mutter a few curses at the perpetrators), but as you head back away from the road, conditions improve. Pass a few cabins as you wander under the shade of oaks and firs. When the trail vanishes, simply walk up the streambed, rock-hopping over small boulders and climbing over big ones. Just keep going until you can't go any further, where the canyon walls come together and Lewis Falls pours in from the left. The waterfall holds court in this narrow space, surrounded by high cliffs and verdant ferns and mosses.

⑱ Pinyon Ridge Nature Trail

1.0 mi/0.5 hr

Location: In the Crystal Lake Recreation Area; map I5, grid b5.

User groups: Hikers, dogs, and horses. No mountain bikes. No wheelchair facilities.

Permits: No permits are required. A $3 day-use fee is charged per vehicle.

Directions: From Azusa on Interstate 210, drive north on Highway 39 for 25 miles to the entrance station for Crystal Lake Recreation Area. Continue one mile to the visitor center and store, then bear right and drive a short distance to the parking area for the Yerba Santa Amphitheater. The Pinyon Ridge/Soldier Creek Trailhead is just to the left of the amphitheater.

Maps: For a map of Angeles National Forest, send $4 to USDA-Forest Service, 630 Sansome Street, San Francisco, CA 94111. A map of the San Gabriel Mountains is available for a fee from Tom Harrison Cartography, (415) 456-7940. To obtain a topographic map of the area, ask for Crystal Lake from the USGS.

Contact: Angeles National Forest, Mount Baldy Ranger District, 110 North Wabash Avenue, Glendora, CA 91740; (818) 335-1251 or fax (818) 914-3790.

Trail notes: The thing about the Crystal Lake Recreation Area is that you either know about it or you don't. Many Los Angeles families vacation here year after year, staying in the campground, hiking on the trails, and fishing in small Crystal Lake, the only natural lake in the San Gabriel Mountains. But if you take an informal poll on the streets of nearby Azusa or Glendora, at least half the people never will have heard of Crystal Lake Recreation Area. Nevertheless, it's a great outdoor destination, with high elevations, a dense forest of big cedars and pines, and clean, fresh air. The Pinyon Ridge Nature Trail is a perfect introduction to the area, beginning near the park amphitheater. Follow Soldier Creek Trail a short distance, then bear left for the beginning of the loop for Pinyon Ridge. We went clockwise on the loop, and although it makes the numbers on the interpretive markers read in reverse order, the views are better this way. As you walk among the pinyon pines, there's a remarkably steep canyon on your left, and a bench on top of the ridge that looks out over the valley. You can even see the very tip of the San Gabriel Reservoir, which you drove by on your way up Highway 39. If you hike this trail in the off-season, or any time that the park is quiet, you're almost guaranteed to see wildlife. On our trip, we saw five little black-tail deer and dozens of chipmunks.

⑲ Windy Gap Trail to Mount Islip

7.0 mi/3.5 hrs

Location: In the Crystal Lake Recreation Area; map I5, grid b5.

User groups: Hikers, dogs, and horses. No mountain bikes. No wheelchair facilities.

Permits: No permits are required. A $3 day-use fee is charged per vehicle.

Directions: From Azusa on Interstate 210, drive north on Highway 39 for 25 miles to the entrance station for Crystal Lake Recreation Area. Continue one mile to the visitor center and store, then bear left and drive six-tenths of a mile to the parking area for the Windy Gap Trailhead.

Maps: For a map of Angeles National Forest, send $4 to USDA-Forest Service, 630 Sansome Street, San Francisco, CA 94111. A map of the San Gabriel Mountains is available for a fee from Tom Harrison Cartography, (415) 456-7940. To obtain a topographic map of the area, ask for Crystal Lake from the USGS.

Contact: Angeles National Forest, Mount Baldy Ranger District, 110 North Wabash Avenue, Glendora, CA 91740; (818) 335-1251 or fax (818) 914-3790.

Trail notes: There are two ways to hike to 8,250-foot Mount Islip, and although the trailheads are close together as the crow flies, they're far apart as hikers drive. If you're somewhere on Highway 2, the Angeles Crest Highway, you'd hike to Mount Islip from near Islip Saddle, on the Little Jimmy Trail. But if you're spending some time in Crystal Lake Recreation Area, you'd hike to Mount Islip from this route on the Windy Gap Trail. Set off from the parking lot, leaving the busy Crystal Lake Campgrounds behind. You'll cross a paved camp road about three-quarters of a mile in, then a dirt road soon afterward. On the far side of the dirt road, take the Windy Gap Trail to the right, reaching the gap at 2.5 miles out, after grunting through some steep sections. Here, at a low pass on the ridge between Mount Islip and Mount Hawkins, take the far left trail for one more mile to Islip's bald summit. From way up high, you can see miles of national forest land, the Los Angeles basin, and even north to the Mojave. The stone foundation on the summit is remaining from the days when the Forest Service had a fire lookout here. By the way, when you get back, don't go telling everyone you climbed to the summit of "is-lip," or you'll get laughed at. It's pronounced "eye-slip."

⑳ San Antonio Falls

1.5 mi/1.0 hr

Location: On Mount Baldy; map I5, grid c7.

User groups: Hikers, dogs, horses, and mountain bikes. No wheelchair facilities.

Permits: No permits are required. A national forest recreation pass is required for each vehicle; fees are $5 for one day or $30 for a year.

Directions: From Interstate 10 near Upland

and Ontario, exit on Euclid Avenue (Highway 83) and drive north for six miles till Euclid Avenue joins Mount Baldy Road. Drive nine miles north on Mount Baldy Road to Manker Flats Camp, then continue three-tenths of a mile further to Falls Road on the left. Park in the dirt pullouts by Falls Road and begin walking on the gated, paved road.

Maps: For a map of Angeles National Forest, send $4 to USDA-Forest Service, 630 Sansome Street, San Francisco, CA 94111. A map of the San Gabriel Mountains is available for a fee from Tom Harrison Cartography, (415) 456-7940. To obtain a topographic map of the area, ask for Mount San Antonio from the USGS.

Contact: Angeles National Forest, Mount Baldy Ranger District, 110 North Wabash Avenue, Glendora, CA 91740; (818) 335-1251 or fax (818) 914-3790.

Trail notes: Mount Baldy is that big mountain that you can see from most everywhere in the Los Angeles basin (on a clear day), and if you hike the trail to San Antonio Falls, you'll be able to see most everywhere in the Los Angeles basin. Trailhead elevation is 6,160 feet, a fine elevation to be at if you like clean, fresh, mountain air. You've got to time your trip carefully for the first warm days after winter, sometimes as early as March, when the snow is melting off the mountain and causing 80-foot San Antonio Falls to put on its watery show. By summer, the show's over. The hike to the falls is easy, following the Mount Baldy ski lift maintenance road, which is paved and has only a slight uphill grade. At seven-tenths of a mile, you round a sharp curve and see the falls, which drop in three tiers. If you wish, you can carefully follow a well-worn path through loose gravel and talus to the waterfall's base, but be careful on the unstable slope. One of the best parts of this trip comes on your return walk back to the trailhead. You're witness to lofty views of the far away San Gabriel Basin as you stroll back down the road.

㉑ Mount Baldy

13.5 mi/8.0 hrs

Location: In Angeles National Forest near Upland; map I5, grid c7.

User groups: Hikers and dogs. No horses or mountain bikes. No wheelchair facilities.

Permits: A free campfire permit is required only for hikers using a camp stove or building a campfire. A national forest recreation pass is required for each vehicle; fees are $5 for one day or $30 for a year.

Directions: From Interstate 10 near Upland and Ontario, exit on Euclid Avenue (Highway 83) and drive north for six miles till Euclid Avenue joins Mount Baldy Road. Drive nine miles north on Mount Baldy Road to Manker Flats Camp, then continue three-tenths of a mile further to Falls Road on the left. Park in the dirt pullouts by Falls Road and begin walking on the gated, paved road.

Maps: For a map of Angeles National Forest, send $4 to USDA-Forest Service, 630 Sansome Street, San Francisco, CA 94111. A map of the San Gabriel Mountains is available for a fee from Tom Harrison Cartography, (415) 456-7940. To obtain topographic maps of the area, ask for Mount San Antonio and Telegraph Peak from the USGS.

Contact: Angeles National Forest, Mount Baldy Ranger District, 110 North Wabash Avenue, Glendora, CA 91740; (818) 335-1251 or fax (818) 914-3790.

Trail notes: You just can't call yourself a Southern California hiker until you've climbed to the top of Mount Baldy, the highest peak in the San Gabriel Mountains at 10,064 feet. The shortest and easiest route (which is not really short or easy, with a 13.5-mile round-trip and a 3,500-foot elevation gain) starts from San Antonio Falls Road. See the trail notes for the easy hike to San Antonio Falls (hike number 20), but from the waterfall, continue uphill on the road for another 2.5 miles to Mount Baldy Notch. From the top of the ski lift at Baldy Notch, you'll access the infamous Devil's Backbone, a sharp and jagged ridge. Prepare to act like a mountaineer, because the going gets a bit dicey on the well-named Devil's Backbone, with steep dropoffs on both sides. You've got three miles and a 2,200-foot elevation gain to go, and while some of it is in sparse pine and fir forest, most of it is exposed granite country. On your way, you'll pass the south side of Mount Harwood at 9,552 feet. When you finally reach Baldy's summit,

what can you see? Everything—desert, city, ocean, southern Sierras—it's a panoramic view like no other. Note that if you want to cut seven miles and 1,300 feet of elevation gain off your round-trip, you can ride the Mount Baldy ski lift up to Baldy Notch, rather than hiking 3.5 miles up (and then down) San Antonio Falls Road. The ski lift only operates on weekends and holidays during the hiking season, however. By the way, in case you were wondering, Mount Baldy's formal name is Mount San Antonio. "Baldy" has just been its nickname for as long as anybody can remember.

Special note: Don't try hiking to Baldy's summit in winter, as tempting as the peak looks when covered in snow, because the Devil's Backbone section is too treacherous. Try to hike the trail on a spring or early summer day when there is little visible air pollution in the Los Angeles basin, so the view from the summit is at its best.

㉒ Ice House Saddle

7.2 mi/4.0 hrs

Location: In the Cucamonga Wilderness; map I5, grid c7.

User groups: Hikers, dogs, and horses. No mountain bikes. No wheelchair facilities.

Permits: A free wilderness permit is required for both day hiking and backpacking in the Cucamonga Wilderness; they are available from the Mount Baldy Ranger Station in Glendora or the Mount Baldy Information Station (open weekends only). A national forest recreation pass is required for each vehicle; fees are $5 for one day or $30 for a year.

Directions: From Interstate 10 near Upland and Ontario, exit on Euclid Avenue (Highway 83) and drive north for six miles till Euclid Avenue joins Mount Baldy Road. Drive 9.3 miles north on Mount Baldy Road to Baldy Village, then continue straight for a quarter mile to Icehouse Canyon and the unsigned parking area where the road ends at an old stone foundation. (Don't take the left fork for Mount Baldy Ski Lift.) The trail begins at the road signed as "Private Road, Authorized Vehicles Only."

Maps: For a map of Angeles National Forest, send $4 to USDA-Forest Service, 630 Sansome

Street, San Francisco, CA 94111. A map of the San Gabriel Mountains is available for a fee from Tom Harrison Cartography, (415) 456-7940. To obtain topographic maps of the area, ask for Cucamonga Peak and Telegraph Peak from the USGS.

Contact: Angeles National Forest, Mount Baldy Ranger District, 110 North Wabash Avenue, Glendora, CA 91740; (818) 335-1251 or fax (818) 914-3790.

Trail notes: When it's wintertime in Southern California and you get the itch to throw a few snowballs, where do you go? Ice House Canyon on Mount Baldy, of course. But Ice House Canyon is good in the summer, too, especially if you want a hiking escape far from the smog of the Inland Empire. You can go for as long or as short as you like in the canyon—it's a great place to just set out from your car, climb till you're tired, then turn around and head back. If you hike only the first 1.8 miles of trail to the wilderness boundary sign, you don't even need a wilderness permit. (When the stream is running in the canyon, many people just go this far and find a spot to sit by the cold, clear water.)

But if you're looking for a destination, Ice House Saddle at 7,580 feet is a good one, perfect for picnicking with lovely views to the east and west. The saddle is also the site of a major trail junction, where routes lead in four directions, including the famous Three Ts Trail that leads to Timber Mountain, Telegraph Peak, and Thunder Mountain. The Ice House Canyon Trail begins by passing some summer cabins, some still in use and some in ruins, and paralleling the stunningly clear stream that runs all the way through the canyon. The path is well maintained, and the forest is a lovely mix of oak, big cone spruce, pine, fir, and cedar. At one mile in, you have a choice of taking either the Ice House Canyon Trail or the Chapman Trail. Both lead to Ice House Saddle, but the Ice House Canyon Trail stays along the creek and gets to Ice House Saddle sooner. It's 2.6 miles to the saddle, straight up the canyon, with a total 2,660-foot elevation gain. You'll be huffing and puffing for sure. If you like, you can take the longer Chapman Trail for your return trip, which will add 1.7 miles to the round-trip mileage listed above.

㉓ Telegraph Canyon and South Ridge Loop

4.0 mi/2.0 hrs

Location: In Chino Hills State Park near Pomona; map I5, grid e6.

User groups: Hikers, horses, and mountain bikes. No dogs. No wheelchair facilities.

Permits: No permits are required. A $5 day-use fee is charged per vehicle.

Directions: From the junction of Highway 71 and Highway 91 near Corona, drive north on Highway 71 to Butterfield Ranch Road. Turn left, then drive five miles on Butterfield Ranch Road. Turn left on Soquel Canyon Parkway and drive one mile to Elinvar Avenue. Turn left and drive to the end of Elinvar Avenue at its intersection with Sapphire Road. Turn left on Sapphire Road and then right immediately at the Chino Hills State Park sign. Continue down the park road to park headquarters, and turn into the parking area. The Telegraph Canyon Trail begins just below park headquarters.

Maps: A map of Chino Hills State Park is available at the entrance kiosk. To obtain topographic maps of the area, ask for Yorba Linda and Prado Dam from the USGS.

Contact: Chino Hills State Park, 1879 Jackson Street, Riverside, CA 92504; (909) 780-6222.

Trail notes: If you don't mind sharing your walk with equestrians and mountain bikers, this loop trail in Chino Hills State Park may be just what you need to revive yourself from the miles of surrounding freeways and rush-hour traffic. Start walking on the wide Telegraph Canyon Trail from near park headquarters, following a seasonal creek. You'll head out for about two miles and then loop back on the South Ridge Trail. If you're in the mood for some single-track hiking, you can always take the right fork one mile out on the Hills for Everyone Trail, then when it ends, turn left and return to park headquarters on the Telegraph Canyon Trail. The park is mostly grasslands and oaks, with a few wet canyon ravines providing homes for sycamore groves and wildlife. Native California walnut trees also grow here. Remember that the best time to visit the park is in winter or spring; if you come in summer, make it as early in the morning as possible. In addition to the heat, summer brings with it the infamous Inland Empire smog.

㉔ Bolsa Chica Ecological Reserve

1.5 mi/0.75 hr

Location: In Huntington Beach; map I5, grid g2.

User groups: Hikers only. No dogs, horses, or mountain bikes. No wheelchair facilities.

Permits: No permits are required. Parking and access are free.

Directions: From Interstate 405 in Seal Beach, exit at Seal Beach Boulevard and drive west to Highway 1. Turn south on Highway 1 and drive 4.5 miles to the entrance to Bolsa Chica Ecological Reserve on the inland side of the highway, across from Bolsa Chica State Beach.

Maps: To obtain a topographic map of the area, ask for Seal Beach from the USGS.

Contact: Amigos de Bolsa Chica, P.O. Box 3748, Huntington Beach, CA 92605; (714) 897-7003.

Trail notes: What a dichotomy. From the footbridge over the water at Bolsa Chica Ecological Reserve, you can see mussels, minnows, egrets, cordgrass, pickleweed, and huge flocks of shorebirds swirling in unison over the sparkling waters. But just a few hundred yards away, the state beach is lined with RVs, the oil-drilling grasshoppers are doing their monotonous job, and the traffic is crawling past on Highway 1. Where would you rather be? Right. The 1.5-mile loop trail at Bolsa Chica Ecological Reserve is the perfect opportunity to be reminded of what our coastline is supposed to look like, and who depends on it the most—the birds on the Pacific Flyway. The 530-acre reserve is a migratory rest stop, and the birds are plentiful and fascinating to watch. The trail runs along the top of a levee, providing a vantage point that's just a few feet above the water's edge. What birds will you see on your walk? Brown pelicans, widgeons, pie-billed grebes, mergansers, pintails, and terns. If you're lucky, you may even spot a few endangered species, like the Belding's savannah sparrow (an unusual bird because it can drink sea water and process it through its kidneys) or the

California least tern. Worth noting: For years, private developers have been trying to pave this place over and put up pricey homes and condominiums, but so far, the birds are winning. We're rooting for them.

㉕ Holy Jim Falls

2.5 mi/1.5 hrs

Location: In Trabuco Canyon in Cleveland National Forest; map I5, grid h7.

User groups: Hikers, dogs, horses, and mountain bikes. No wheelchair facilities.

Permits: No permits are required. A national forest recreation pass is required for each vehicle; fees are $5 for one day or $30 for a year.

Directions: From Laguna Hills (north of San Juan Capistrano) on Interstate 5, exit on El Toro Road and drive east for six miles. Turn right on Live Oak Canyon Road and drive for about four miles (two miles past the entrance to O'Neill Regional Park). Turn left on Trabuco Canyon Road, which is an often unsigned, rocky, dirt road, just past the paved Rose Canyon Road turnoff. Go five miles on the dirt road to the well-signed parking area for Holy Jim Trail. (The road is usually suitable for passenger cars.) The trail leads from the left side of the parking lot.

Maps: For a map of Cleveland National Forest, send $4 to USDA-Forest Service, 630 Sansome Street, San Francisco, CA 94111. To obtain a topographic map of the area, ask for Santiago Peak from the USGS.

Contact: Cleveland National Forest, Trabuco Ranger District, 1147 East Sixth Street, Corona, CA 91719; (909) 736-1811 or fax (909) 736-3002.

Trail notes: It seems that everybody in Orange County knows about, and likes to visit, Holy Jim Falls. The waterfall and its canyon were named for a beekeeper who lived here in the 1890s, James T. Smith, better known as "Cussin' Jim." Apparently he had a temper and a colorful way with language. But conservative mapmakers who plotted Trabuco Canyon in the early 1900s found Smith's nickname in bad taste, so they changed it to "Holy Jim," and it remains. Whether it's because of the interesting history of the area or the beauty that it still exhibits today, the trail to Holy Jim Falls is well known and frequently walked, especially in springtime. The 2.5-mile stroll is in the cool shade along Holy Jim Creek. Start by walking down the dirt road, past some leased cabins, to the signed trailhead. There the trail turns to single-track. You're surrounded by a lush canyon filled with oaks, vine maples, wildflowers, and even a few bracken ferns. The trail crosses the creek several times, and gently gains some elevation as it heads upstream. Where the trail steepens noticeably as you pass a large, old oak tree on your left, cross the creek one final time. Instead of following the main trail as it switchbacks uphill, you'll head to the right, continuing along the stream. An easy 300-yard stream scramble brings you to the waterfall's base, and if there isn't a troop of Boy Scouts there eating lunch (as there was on our trip), you'll be able to listen to the sweet music of the falls.

㉖ El Moro Canyon and Ridge Loop

4.5 mi/2.0 hrs

Location: In Crystal Cove State Park; map I5, grid i4.

User groups: Hikers, horses, and mountain bikes. No dogs. No wheelchair facilities.

Permits: No permits are required. A $6 day-use fee is charged per vehicle.

Directions: From Corona del Mar, drive south on Highway 1 for three miles to the entrance to Crystal Cove State Park on the inland side of the highway. Park near the park headquarters building; the El Moro Canyon Trail begins down the park road by the entrance kiosk.

Maps: A free backcountry user guide map of Crystal Cove State Park is available at the visitor center. To obtain a topographic map of the area, ask for Laguna Beach from the USGS.

Contact: Crystal Cove State Park, 8471 Pacific Coast Highway, Laguna Beach, CA 92651; (714) 494-3539. Or State Parks, Orange Coast District, (714) 848-1566.

Trail notes: El Moro Canyon is on the inland side of Crystal Cove State Park, and when you see how lush and overgrown it is, you'll have a hard time believing that only 12 inches of rain fall here each year. Although El Moro Creek flows

only in the wet season, its edges are lined with oaks, sycamores, and willows, and it attracts tons of birds, small mammals, and butterflies. We managed to identify the anise swallowtail butterfly (yellow and black) and the red admiral butterfly (brown, red, and black) on our trip. Unlike the other trails on the inland side of the park, the El Moro Canyon Trail is on a gentle grade, which makes it a fine route to take into the park's backcountry. The beginning of the trail is not so great, however, as it starts on a dirt road by the park entrance kiosk and winds behind the back of a trailer park. But in 10 minutes things start to look up, as you veer left on El Moro Canyon Trail and walk up the shady, tree-lined canyon. At 1.5 miles out, turn right on East Cut Across Trail, and make a switchbacking climb to El Moro Ridge. The ascent will get your heart pumping. Turn right on El Moro Ridge Trail and follow it as it rolls along the ridgetop, offering many excellent ocean views. The trail leads back down to a single-track trail on the right, which in turn heads back to the trailer park. From there, proceed straight to the park entrance kiosk.

㉗ San Juan Loop Trail

2.0 mi/1.0 hr

Location: In Cleveland National Forest near Lake Elsinore; map I5, grid i8.

User groups: Hikers, dogs, horses, and mountain bikes. No wheelchair facilities.

Permits: No permits are required. A national forest recreation pass is required for each vehicle; fees are $5 for one day or $30 for a year.

Directions: From Interstate 5 at San Juan Capistrano, take the Ortega Highway (Highway 74) exit and drive north. In 21 miles, you'll reach the Ortega Oaks store on the right (three-quarters of a mile past Upper San Juan Campground). The trailhead is across the road from the store; turn left and park in the large parking lot. Start the loop trail on the right (north) side of the parking lot.

Maps: For a map of Cleveland National Forest, send $4 to USDA-Forest Service, 630 Sansome Street, San Francisco, CA 94111. To obtain a topographic map of the area, ask for Sitton Peak from the USGS.

Contact: Cleveland National Forest, Trabuco Ranger District, 1147 East Sixth Street, Corona, CA 91719; (909) 736-1811 or fax (909) 736-3002.

Trail notes: The San Juan Loop Trail is an easy and informative walk that serves as a good introduction to the Santa Ana Mountains. The only factor you must consider: Don't try to hike here in summer, when these mountains can feel hotter than the desert. The trailhead features a rather negative sign, which explains in dooms-day-style terms the dangers of mountain lions, rattlesnakes, poison oak, and rugged terrain. If the sign doesn't convince you to get back in the car and go to Disneyland instead, start hiking on the loop trail, which parallels the road for its first half mile. You'll forget about the car noise as you start examining all the plant life along the trail, which includes deep red monkey-flowers, purple nightshade, and tall, spiky yuccas with their silky, milk-white flowers. Lizards dart here and there among the foliage. The terrain is dry and exposed, but thriving nonetheless. A half mile out, you'll pass a railing and overlook above a small seasonal waterfall on San Juan Creek, which has many clear, granite-lined pools. In another half mile, you'll pass the turnoff for the Chiquito Basin Trail (it's highly recommended for those seeking a longer trip), and then pass through a lovely grove of ancient oaks. The loop trail finishes out by bringing you back to the opposite side of the parking lot.

㉘ Bear Canyon Loop Trail

6.7 mi/3.5 hrs

Location: In the San Mateo Canyon Wilderness near Lake Elsinore; map I5, grid i8.

User groups: Hikers, dogs, and horses. No mountain bikes. No wheelchair facilities.

Permits: No permits are required. A national forest recreation pass is required for each vehicle; fees are $5 for one day or $30 for a year.

Directions: From Interstate 5 at San Juan Capistrano, take the Ortega Highway (Highway 74) exit and drive north. In 21 miles, you'll reach the Ortega Oaks store on the right (three-quarters of a mile past Upper San Juan Camp-ground). The parking area is across the road from the store; turn left and park in the large parking

lot. Cross the road to begin hiking on the Bear Canyon Trail, to the right of the store.

Maps: For a map of Cleveland National Forest, send $4 to USDA-Forest Service, 630 Sansome Street, San Francisco, CA 94111. To obtain a topographic map of the area, ask for Sitton Peak from the USGS.

Contact: Cleveland National Forest, Trabuco Ranger District, 1147 East Sixth Street, Corona, CA 91719; (909) 736-1811 or fax (909) 736-3002.

Trail notes: Is it winter or spring? Is the weather cool and clear? Good; this is a fine time to take a hike on the Bear Canyon Trail, either a little out-and-back trip for as far as you like, or the full 6.7-mile loop which circles around a junction called Four Corners. First, we suggest you stock up on some chocolate from the candy store at the trailhead (this is why it must be a cool day; otherwise carrying chocolate is out of the question). Then set off on the trail adjacent to the store, heading into the San Mateo Canyon Wilderness, climbing gently through chaparral-covered slopes. In spring, many yuccas bloom along this stretch. Take the right fork one mile in, then in another mile, you'll reach the start of the loop; take the right branch to start. The trail has a mere 700-foot elevation gain, and in places, it offers expansive views of the San Juan Canyon. Pigeon Springs is a popular resting point, where you can find some shade among the oaks. Four Corners is a half mile beyond Pigeon Springs, and there you'll turn sharply left to loop back.

㉙ Tenaja Falls

1.5 mi/1.0 hr

Location: In the San Mateo Canyon Wilderness near Murrieta; map I5, grid i9.

User groups: Hikers, dogs, and horses. No mountain bikes. No wheelchair facilities.

Permits: No permits are required. A national forest recreation pass is required for each vehicle; fees are $5 for one day or $30 for a year.

Directions: From Lake Elsinore, drive south on Interstate 15 for about 12 miles to the Clinton Keith Road exit in Murrieta. Drive south on Clinton Keith Road for five miles, which will become Tenaja Road, although you won't see any signs. At a signed intersection with Tenaja Road, turn right and drive west for 4.5 miles. Turn right on Rancho California Road; drive one mile to the Tenaja Trailhead. Reset your odometer here, and continue 4.4 miles on the dirt road (7S04) to a hairpin turn in the road and the parking area.

Maps: For a map of Cleveland National Forest, send $4 to USDA-Forest Service, 630 Sansome Street, San Francisco, CA 94111. To obtain a topographic map of the area, ask for Sitton Peak from the USGS.

Contact: Cleveland National Forest, Trabuco Ranger District, 1147 East Sixth Street, Corona, CA 91719; (909) 736-1811 or fax (909) 736-3002.

Trail notes: The only hard part about getting to Tenaja Falls is the long drive to the unmarked trailhead. But if you follow the directions above, even that shouldn't be a problem. Once you've parked, head for the fence that blocks the road into the San Mateo Canyon Wilderness to vehicles. Cross the creek on a concrete apron, or if the water is too deep, follow a use trail upstream and cross the creek where it's narrower. Just be sure to join up with the main road again; following the streamside use trails is a needlessly difficult way to the falls. (Guess how we know.) On the wide canyon road, you'll hike northward, rising out of the canyon alongside sage- and chaparral-covered hillsides. In a few minutes you'll round a curve and be treated to a partial view of the waterfall ahead. What a sight—Tenaja Falls is huge, compared to other waterfalls in Orange County, dropping 150 feet in five tiers. It's magnificent when flowing full, which is only after a period of rain, usually between December and March. Keep walking toward the waterfall; the trail deposits you at its lip. When the water is low enough, you can cross over the top of the falls to the other side of the creek, but be extremely cautious on the slippery granite if you choose to do so.

⑳ Santa Rosa Plateau Vernal Pools

4.8 mi/2.5 hrs

Location: In the Santa Rosa Plateau Ecological Reserve; map I5, grid i9.

User groups: Hikers only. No dogs, horses, or mountain bikes. (Horses and mountain bikes are allowed only on special docent-led trips.) No wheelchair facilities.

Permits: No permits are required. Parking and access are free.

Directions: From Lake Elsinore, drive south on Interstate 15 for about 12 miles to the Clinton Keith Road exit in Murrieta. Drive south on Clinton Keith Road for six miles to the preserve entrance on the left. Park along the side of the road. The trailhead is signed for the Oak Tree Trail and Vernal Pools.

Maps: To obtain a topographic map of the area, ask for Wildomar from the USGS.

Contact: Santa Rosa Plateau Ecological Reserve, 22115 Tenaja Road, Murrieta, CA 92562; (909) 677-6951.

Trail notes: Those volcanic-looking rocky mesas you've been seeing as you drive through the foothills along Clinton Keith Road are home to some of Southern California's last vernal pools, seasonal ponds which give life to endangered plants and wildflowers and provide a resting place for wintering birds. While these pools are more common in the San Joaquin Valley, here in Southern California they have all but vanished, which is one reason for the establishment of the Santa Rosa Plateau Ecological Reserve.

Another reason is the rare Engelmann oak, a semi-deciduous species of oak that only loses its leaves during times of drought. Several fine groves of Engelmann oaks are found within the reserve's border. To see them, start hiking on the Oak Tree Trail, a self-guided nature loop that is six-tenths of a mile in length. Take either side of the loop; once you've reached the far side of the loop, continue hiking on the Trans Preserve Trail, past Poppy Hill (beautiful in spring, if you time it right).

At 2.4 miles the trail intersects with the Vernal Pool Trail on top of Mesa de Colorado; turn left to see one of the preserve's vernal pools. The best time to visit, of course, is after a period of heavy rain, when the pool is filled to capacity and the grasslands are lush and green. Spring days at the preserve are often busy with docents leading school field trips.

Pacific Crest Trail (PCT) Section Overview

48.0 mi. one way/5.0 days

Dramatic ridge views, deep canyons with waterfalls, and tons of ravines can make this one of the stellar sections of the PCT in Southern California, with trail sections extending from the Angeles Crest Highway to the Mill Creek Picnic Area. Highlights are the side trip to the top of Mount Baden-Powell, where you can garner a view to the north all the way to Mount Whitney, and Cooper Canyon, where gorgeous Cooper Canyon Falls is a place you'll never want to leave. Trail elevations generally run in the 5,000- to 7,000-foot range. Water availability is decent enough, but always tank up at every opportunity.

PCT-11 Angeles Crest Highway to Three Points

32.0 mi. one way/3.0 days

Location: From the Angeles Crest Highway to Three Points; map I5, grid a8.

User groups: Hikers, dogs, and horses. No mountain bikes. No wheelchair facilities.

Permits: A wilderness permit is required for traveling through various wilderness and special-use areas the trail traverses. Contact the Angeles National Forest at (818) 574-5200 for permit information. For this section of the Pacific Crest Trail, no day-use permits are required.

Directions: To reach the Angeles Crest Trailhead, from Interstate 15 near Cajon, take Highway 138 east. Turn left (west) on the Angeles Crest Highway and drive five miles to Wrightwood. Continue for three miles to Big Pines. Bear left and continue on the Angeles Crest Highway for 1.5 miles to Inspiration Point, opposite Blue Ridge Road. To reach the Three Points Trailhead, from the Foothill Freeway (210) in La Cañada, exit onto the Angeles Crest Highway (2) and drive to Three Points Junction, approximately 2.5 miles north of Chilao. The exit to Three Points is marked by a sign indicating Horse Flats. Note: Do not confuse the Three Points Trailhead with the small town of Three Points, which is located near Tejon Ranch to the north.

Maps: For an overall view of the trail route in this section, send $4 to the USDA-Forest Service, 630 Sansome Street, San Francisco, CA 94111, and ask for the Angeles National Forest map. For topographic maps of the route, request Waterman Mountain, Crystal Lake, and Mount San Antonio from the USGS.

Contact: Angeles National Forest, 701 North Santa Anita Avenue, Arcadia, CA 91006; (818) 574-5200 or fax (818) 574-5233.

Trail notes: This particular stretch of the PCT is one of our favorites in Southern California. It starts with a great side trip to the top of Mount Baden-Powell (hike number 5), and with it, awesome views from the 9,399-foot summit, including all the way across the awaiting desert to the north for the first glimpse of Mount Whitney for PCT through-hikers. After this must-do trip, you'll be properly rejuvenated to forge on, and awaiting is the Sheep Mountain Wilderness, Crystal Lake Recreation Area, San Gabriel Wilderness, and several remote pieces of Angeles National Forest. The trip generally heads to the west, and after passing busy Crystal Lake, climbs up Kratka Ridge amid a sparse fir forest, providing distant views over and down canyons. Eventually, you continue to climb in and out of canyons, and drop into Cooper Canyon, a favorite. This is where we found Cooper Canyon Falls, a drop-dead gorgeous waterfall (hike number 2), a place we didn't want to leave, despite having run out of food (we later scored two treasured Baby Ruth candy bars before claiming dinner). From Cooper Canyon, it's a butt-kicking climb out of the canyon, back up to the Angeles Crest Highway, then to the Three Points Trailhead.

PCT-12 Three Points to Mill Creek Picnic Area

16.0 mi. one way/2.0 days

Location: From Three Points to Mill Creek; map I5, grid a4.

User groups: Hikers, dogs, and horses. No mountain bikes. No wheelchair facilities.

Permits: A wilderness permit is required for traveling through various wilderness and special-use areas the trail traverses. Contact the Angeles National Forest at (805) 296-9710 for a permit that is good for the length of your trip.

For this section of the Pacific Crest Trail, no day-use permits are required.

Directions: To reach the Three Points Trailhead, from the Foothill Freeway (210) in La Cañada, exit on the Angeles Crest Highway (2) and drive to Three Points Junction, approximately 2.5 miles north of Chilao. The exit to Three Points is marked by a sign indicating Horse Flats. To reach the Mill Creek Picnic Area Trailhead, from Highway 14 at Vincent, head south on the Angeles Forest Highway (County Road N3) to the Mill Creek Summit and Picnic Area and the signed PCT Trailhead.

Maps: For an overall view of the trail route in this section, send $4 to the USDA-Forest Service, 630 Sansome Street, San Francisco, CA 94111, and ask for the Angeles National Forest map. For topographic maps of the route, request Waterman Mountain, Chilao Flat, and Pacifico Mountain from the USGS.

Contact: Angeles National Forest, Saugus Ranger District, 30800 Bouquet Canyon Road, Saugus, CA 91350; (805) 296-9710 or fax (805) 296-5847.

Trail notes: This short section of the PCT features a series of ravines, draws, and short ridges, sprinkled with pines and sagebrush, with a few creeks to brighten up the trip. It's not an inspiring piece of trail work, but pleasant enough, and most PCT through-hikers make fast work of it. In the back of all minds the entire time, however, is what awaits: the butt-kicking desert tromp to the foot of the southern Sierra. This reality comes into view when you climb near the top of Mount Pacifico at 6,800 feet, and enjoy the view north of the sparse Antelope Valley and beyond. All PCT hikers stop at the Mill Creek Ranger Station, typically to resupply, get water, and prepare for the more serious adventure ahead.

PCT Continuation: To continue hiking along the Pacific Crest Trail, see chapter H5.

Leave No Trace Tips

Travel and Camp with Care

On the trail:

Stay on designated trails. Walk single file in the middle of the path.

Do not take shortcuts on switchbacks.

When traveling cross-country where there are no trails,
follow animal trails or spread out your group so no new routes are
created. Walk along the most durable surfaces available,
such as rock, gravel, dry grasses, or snow.

Use a map and compass to eliminate
the need for rock cairns, tree scars, or ribbons.

If you encounter pack animals, step to the downhill side
of the trail and speak softly to avoid startling them.

At camp:

Choose an established, legal site that will not be damaged by your stay.

Restrict activities to areas where vegetation is compacted or absent.

Keep pollutants out of the water by camping at least 200 feet
(about 70 adult steps) from lakes and streams.

Control pets at all times, or leave them at home
with a sitter. Remove dog feces.

Map I6

Adjoining Maps: East: I7 ..... *page* 616   West: I5 578
North: H6 550   South: J6 626

Southern California Map .... *page* 558

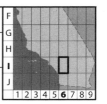

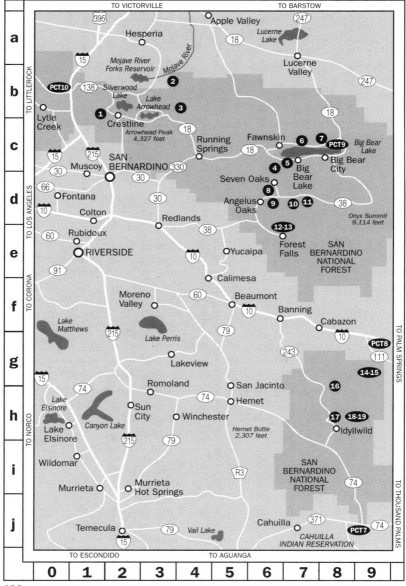

---

❶ Seeley Creek Trail

2.0 mi/1.0 hr

Location: In San Bernardino National Forest near Crestline; map I6, grid b1.

User groups: Hikers, dogs, horses, and mountain bikes. No wheelchair facilities.

Permits: No permits are required. A national forest recreation pass is required for each vehicle; fees are $5 for one day or $30 for a year.

Directions: From Crestline at the junction of Highways 18 and 138, turn north on Highway 138 and drive 2.5 miles to the sign for Camp Seeley, just past the town of Valley of Enchantment. Turn left at the camp sign on Road 2N03, then take the left fork in the road (don't park in the camp parking lot). Cross the creek, which usually flows over the road, then look for the double-track trail on the right, near a sewer pipeline sign. Park alongside the road. (You will be directly across the creek from the main parking lot for Camp Seeley, near the playground area.)

Maps: For a map of San Bernardino National Forest, send $4 to USDA-Forest Service, 630 Sansome Street, San Francisco, CA 94111. To obtain a topo-graphic map of the area, ask for San Bernardino North from the USGS.

Contact: San Bernardino National Forest, Arrowhead Ranger District, 28104 Highway 18, Skyforest, CA 92385; (909) 337-2444.

Trail notes: To reach the start of the Seeley Creek Trail, you have to drive through a town called Valley of Enchantment, and that should tell you just about all you need to know about the area and the trail. It's beautiful up here—no, let's say it's enchanting—and although the elevation is only 4,000 feet, the conifers grow so big you'll think you're in the southern Sierra. The Seeley Creek Trail is a short and easy walk to a destination called Heart Rock, which during periods of rain or after snowmelt becomes Heart Rock Falls. Heart Rock is a smooth giant boulder in which nature has carved a perfect, heart-shaped bowl, about three feet deep and five feet wide. When Seeley Creek is running strong, a 25-foot waterfall spills into the heart's crown, then flows out the bottom and freefalls downward. (The stream flows year-round, and Heart Rock is always fascinating to see, but it's most compelling when the waterfall is flowing strong.) The trail begins in a rather pedestrian fashion, along a road opposite the buildings of Seeley Camp, a Los Angeles Parks and Recreation Camp. But once you walk beyond the camp boundary, the enchantment begins.

❷ Deep Creek Hot Springs

3.0 mi/1.5 hrs

Location: In San Bernardino National Forest near Hesperia; map I6, grid b3.

User groups: Hikers and dogs. No horses or mountain bikes. No wheelchair facilities.

Permits: No permits are required. A toll is charged by Bowens Ranch for crossing over their private land.

Directions: From Cajon Pass at Interstate 15, drive north for six miles and take the Hesperia exit. Drive east through the town of Hesperia on Main Street, then turn left (east) on Rock Springs Road. Follow Rock Springs Road to its end. Turn left on Kiowa Road and drive a half mile, then turn right on Roundup Way. Follow Roundup Way for 4.4 miles (it turns to dirt), then turn right on Bowens Ranch Road (dirt). Drive 2.5 miles to a fork, bear right, and drive 3.3 miles further on Bowens Ranch Road. Stop and register at the ranch house (a toll is charged), then continue to the road's end and the parking area. The trail is signed as Goat Trail.

Maps: For a map of San Bernardino National Forest, send $4 to USDA-Forest Service, 630 Sansome Street, San Francisco, CA 94111. To obtain a topographic map of the area, ask for Lake Arrowhead from the USGS.

Contact: San Bernardino National Forest, Arrowhead Ranger District, 28104 Highway 18, Skyforest, CA 92385; (909) 337-2444.

Trail notes: This trail is not the highlight of this trip, but its destination is. Deep Creek's hot springs are well known, well loved, and heavily visited. Although there are a few ways to hike to them, this route is the most popular simply because it's the shortest. But remember, it's not called Goat Trail for no reason. This is a no-nonsense path that leads straight down from the trailhead to the creek, and straight up on the return. The total elevation change is only 700 feet, but on a hot day, it's . . . well, hot. Most people

visit on cool days in winter and spring. The hot springs consist of three pools alongside the creek; the hottest one is the furthest from the stream's edge. Note that Goat Trail ends on the north side of Deep Creek and you must ford the creek to reach the hot springs, then hike a short distance downstream. When Deep Creek is running high, this ford can be difficult, so check with the Arrowhead Ranger Station before planning an early spring visit.

❸ Deep Creek Fishermen's Trail

2.0 mi/1.0 hr

Location: In San Bernardino National Forest near Lake Arrowhead; map I6, grid b3.

User groups: Hikers and dogs. No horses or mountain bikes. No wheelchair facilities.

Permits: No permits are required. A national forest recreation pass is required for each vehicle; fees are $5 for one day or $30 for a year.

Directions: From Crestline at the junction of Highways 18 and 138, drive east on Highway 18 for 10 miles to the left turnoff for Highway 173. Drive north on Highway 173 to Lake Arrowhead, then continue for 1.5 miles to Hook Creek Road. Turn right on Hook Creek Road, and follow it until it turns to dirt and becomes Road 2N26Y. Continue on Road 2N26Y for one mile, then bear right on Road 3N34. In seven-tenths of a mile, you'll reach T-6 Crossing, where the road crosses Deep Creek. Park before the crossing and begin walking upstream on the fishermen's trail. (A high-clearance vehicle is recommended for the drive.)

Maps: For a map of San Bernardino National Forest, send $4 to USDA-Forest Service, 630 Sansome Street, San Francisco, CA 94111. To obtain a topographic map of the area, ask for Lake Arrowhead from the USGS.

Contact: San Bernardino National Forest, Arrowhead Ranger District, 28104 Highway 18, Skyforest, CA 92385; (909) 337-2444.

Trail notes: Deep Creek has many personalities. It's a geologically active creek sporting hot springs and pools, where warm-water lovers flock to bathe. It's a wild trout stream, filled with pockets of moss and algae, the start of a plentiful food chain for the fish. Technically, it's a branch of the Mojave River, and eventually it disappears in desert sand. Here at the T-6 Crossing, it's a secluded, quiet stream with many crystalline pools and small waterfalls. Few people hike this stretch, and the path here is just a fishermen's trail. You'll do a little more scrambling than walking, but the route is well worn and beautiful every step of the way. It passes granite boulders, small sandy beaches, leafy cottonwoods, and big conifers. As you walk, you'll see many small trout in the creek's pristine pools, but if you go fishing, be sure to follow the current regulations for wild trout. About one mile upstream, your progress gets blocked by a rocky waterfall. At times, a cable is in place here for crossing the stream and continuing your trek, but if you use it, proceed with great caution. The preferred option is to pick a smooth granite slab in the sun, or a good-sized wading pool, and spend the afternoon in streamside bliss.

Trail notes: Let's see now. The biggest giant Sequoia tree is the General Sherman Tree in Sequoia National Park, and the biggest coast redwood tree is the Giant Tree in Humboldt Redwoods State Park. So which is the biggest lodgepole pine tree? We're delighted you asked. It's the Champion Lodgepole, located only a few miles from Big Bear Lake. The big tree is growing in a grove of world champions, the largest lodgepole pines around. What's strange is that these big guys are growing at 7,500 feet in elevation, when usually in Southern California lodgepole pines won't grow at less than 8,000 feet. The Champion is about 400 years old, stands 112 feet tall, and has a circumference of 20 feet. The trail to reach it is flat and easy, following a small stream to a junction. Turn right and walk the last few yards to the big tree, which is surrounded by a fence and situated at the edge of a pretty meadow.

❹ Champion Lodgepole Pine

1.0 mi/0.5 hr

Location: Near Big Bear Lake; map I6, grid c6.

User groups: Hikers, dogs, horses, and mountain bikes. No wheelchair facilities.

Permits: No permits are required. A national forest recreation pass is required for each vehicle; fees are $5 for one day or $30 for a year.

Directions: From the dam on the west end of Big Bear Lake, drive 3.5 miles east on Highway 18 (Big Bear Boulevard) to Mill Creek Road. Turn right (south) on Mill Creek Road (Forest Service Road 2N10) and follow it for five miles, through several junctions. (The road turns to dirt.) At Forest Service Road 2N11, turn right and drive one mile to the parking area. The route is well signed for the Champion Lodgepole Pine.

Maps: For a map of San Bernardino National Forest, send $4 to USDA-Forest Service, 630 Sansome Street, San Francisco, CA 94111. To obtain a topographic map of the area, ask for Big Bear Lake from the USGS.

Contact: San Bernardino National Forest, Big Bear Ranger District, P.O. Box 290, North Shore Drive, Highway 18, Fawnskin, CA 92333; (909) 866-3437.

❺ Castle Rock Trail

2.0 mi/1.0 hr

Location: Near Big Bear Lake; map I6, grid c6.

User groups: Hikers, dogs, horses, and mountain bikes. No wheelchair facilities.

Permits: No permits are required. A national forest recreation pass is required for each vehicle; fees are $5 for one day or $30 for a year.

Directions: From the dam on the west end of Big Bear Lake, drive one mile east on Highway 18 (Big Bear Boulevard) to the signed Castle Rock Trailhead on the right (it's by the Big Bear City Limit sign). Park in the turnout on the lake side of Highway 18, about 50 yards further east, and then walk across the road to the trailhead.

Maps: For a map of San Bernardino National Forest, send $4 to USDA-Forest Service, 630 Sansome Street, San Francisco, CA 94111. To obtain a topographic map of the area, ask for Big Bear Lake from the USGS.

Contact: San Bernardino National Forest, Big Bear Ranger District, P.O. Box 290, North Shore Drive, Highway 18, Fawnskin, CA 92333; (909) 866-3437.

Trail notes: There are a couple tricky elements about this trail: There's no real parking area—just a pullout along the highway; and although the path to Castle Rock has a mere 700-foot elevation gain, it's compressed into one mile and climbs steeply right from the trailhead. The trail is smooth sand, surrounded by manzanita, big ponderosa pines, and a ton of rocks. It's located by the area of Big Bear Lake called Boulder Bay, a perfectly descriptive name. As you climb, you gain tremendous views of the lake, but you'll miss them completely unless you turn around. In about 20 minutes, you'll reach a rocky overlook, which is where many people stop and pull up a granite boulder to sit on. The main trail becomes a spider web of trails, as people have chosen all different routes around the rocks. If you continue upward, you'll reach a saddle and then start to descend slightly. Castle Rock, which is easily distinguishable by its shape, is just to the east, off the trail as you head downhill. If you tire out before the saddle, just pick any boulder that's easy to climb and get on top to enjoy the lovely views of the lake. When we did this in late March, we were treated to a lovely shower of snow flurries. Isn't Big Bear the greatest? Trailhead elevation is 6,700 feet.

❻ Cougar Crest Trail to Bertha Peak

6.0 mi/3.0 hrs

Location: Near Big Bear Lake; map I6, grid c6.

User groups: Hikers, dogs, horses, and mountain bikes. No wheelchair facilities.

Permits: No permits are required. A national forest recreation pass is required for each vehicle; fees are $5 for one day or $30 for a year.

Directions: From the town of Big Bear Lake on Highway 18, take the Stanfield cutoff to the north shore of the lake, where it junctions with Highway 38. Turn left and drive 1.3 miles on Highway 38 (a half mile past the Big Bear Ranger Station) to the Cougar Crest Trailhead, on the right side of the road. (If you are traveling from Fawnskin, the trailhead is 2.4 miles east of Fawnskin on Highway 38, on the left side of the road.)

Maps: For a map of San Bernardino National Forest, send $4 to USDA-Forest Service, 630 Sansome Street, San Francisco, CA 94111. To obtain a topographic map of the area, ask for Fawnskin from the USGS.

Contact: San Bernardino National Forest, Big Bear Ranger District, P.O. Box 290, North Shore Drive, Highway 18, Fawnskin, CA 92333; (909) 866-3437.

Trail notes: Put on your hiking boots and prepare to climb. That's what you have to do on the Cougar Crest Trail—gain 1,300 feet over three miles to reach Bertha Peak, elevation 8,201 feet. You can see the peak, capped with electronic relay equipment, from the trailhead parking lot. Views of the Big Bear area are spectacular along the route, and the trail is well built, making this an excellent day hike. The first mile is on dirt roads in a forest of pinyon and Jeffrey pines, but soon the path narrows to single-track. The more you climb upward, the more you can see; you should turn around every now and then to check out the lake and mountain views. Finally at two miles you reach the Pacific Crest Trail, where the grade eases considerably. Turn right and follow the PCT for a half mile to a dirt road, where you turn right and climb steeply once again to reach Bertha's Summit. Look for old, gnarled juniper trees along the route. The view from the peak includes Big Bear Lake, of course, plus Mount San Gorgonio and other high peaks and ridges, and green Holcomb Valley below you.

❼ Woodland Trail

1.5 mi/0.75 hr

Location: Near Big Bear Lake; map I6, grid c7.

User groups: Hikers, dogs, horses, and mountain bikes. No wheelchair facilities.

Permits: No permits are required. A national forest recreation pass is required for each vehicle; fees are $5 for one day or $30 for a year.

Directions: From the town of Big Bear Lake on Highway 18, take the Stanfield cutoff to the north shore of the lake, where it junctions with Highway 38. Turn left on Highway 38 and drive a half mile to the Woodland Trailhead, on the right side of the road. It's directly across the highway from the East Boat Ramp, near the ranger station.

Maps: For a map of San Bernardino National Forest, send $4 to USDA-Forest Service, 630 Sansome Street, San Francisco, CA 94111. To obtain a topographic map of the area, ask for Fawnskin from the USGS.

Contact: San Bernardino National Forest, Big Bear Ranger District, P.O. Box 290, North Shore Drive, Highway 18, Fawnskin, CA 92333; (909) 866-3437.

Trail notes: If you're spending the weekend or the week in Big Bear, you'd be well advised to pay a visit to the Forest Service Ranger Station in Fawnskin. You can get all the information you want about hiking, fishing, and exploring the area from the nice people there, then take this terrific short walk on the Woodland Trail, which starts near the ranger station. We picked up an interpretive brochure and learned all about serviceberry, yerba santa, Jeffrey and ponderosa pines, indigo bush, and pinyon pines. The only problem was that it seemed like somebody had moved the trail numbers around, because when the brochure said we were looking at a packrat's nest, instead we were looking at a pinyon pine tree. We're sure they'll get it all sorted out by the time you visit. A bonus is that on the return leg of the loop, you get great views of the lake, but you're far enough away from it that you don't get hit by the wind that often blows on the north side. You can see all the way across the lake to Big Bear City.

---

⑧ Ponderosa Vista Nature Trail

1.0 mi/0.5 hr

Location: In San Bernardino National Forest near Angelus Oaks; map I6, grid d6.

User groups: Hikers, dogs, horses, and mountain bikes. No wheelchair facilities.

Permits: No permits are required. A national forest recreation pass is required for each vehicle; fees are $5 for one day or $30 for a year.

Directions: From Interstate 10 at Redlands, take the Highway 38 exit and drive northeast for 25 miles to the trailhead for Ponderosa Vista Nature Trail on the left side of the road. (If you reach the Jenks Lake turnoff, you've passed it.) Park in the parking lot by the trailhead.

Maps: For a map of San Bernardino National Forest, send $4 to USDA-Forest Service, 630 Sansome Street, San Francisco, CA 94111. To obtain a topographic map of the area, ask for Big Bear Lake from the USGS.

Contact: San Bernardino National Forest, San Gorgonio Ranger District, 34701 Mill Creek Road, Mentone, CA 92359; (909) 794-1123.

Trail notes: The Ponderosa Vista Nature Trail wins hands down for the trail with the most corny interpretive plaques. When you visit, you'll see what we mean. But aside from the overdone prose, everything else on this trail is first-rate, making for a great introduction to the flora and fauna of San Bernardino National Forest. You can choose between the short loop (three-tenths of a mile) or the long loop (six-tenths of a mile), but we say, why not hike both? We learned about assorted birds of the forest (acorn woodpeckers, redbreasted sapsuckers, and yellow-rumped warblers) and various trees (ponderosa pine is the most common conifer in the area, but incense cedars, black oaks, white firs, and pinyon pines also grow). The highlight of the trail is an overlook point with a view across the Santa Ana River Canyon. An old photograph at the overlook shows what the canyon used to look like, and explains about the building of the Rim of the World Highway in 1935. That was the same year that black bears were introduced to the area. No wonder—with the new highway, they could just get in their RVs and drive in.

---

⑨ Whispering Pines Trail

0.5 mi/0.5 hr

Location: In San Bernardino National Forest near Angelus Oaks; map I6, grid d6.

User groups: Hikers, dogs, horses, and mountain bikes. No wheelchair facilities.

Permits: No permits are required. A national forest recreation pass is required for each vehicle; fees are $5 for one day or $30 for a year.

Directions: From Interstate 10 at Redlands, take the Highway 38 exit and drive northeast for 25 miles to the trailhead for Whispering Pines Trail on the right side of the road. (If you reach the Jenks Lake turnoff, you've passed it.) Park in the well-signed parking lot by the trailhead.

Maps: For a map of San Bernardino National Forest, send $4 to USDA-Forest Service, 630 Sansome Street, San Francisco, CA 94111. To obtain a topographic map of the area, ask for Big Bear Lake from the USGS.

Contact: San Bernardino National Forest, San Gorgonio Ranger District, 34701 Mill Creek Road, Mentone, CA 92359; (909) 794-1123.

Trail notes: Right across the road from the Ponderosa Vista Trail is the Whispering Pines Trail, another short, easy interpretive trail that is both fun and informative. Time to play Trivial Pursuit: This trail appeared on what television show, filmed in 1969, about a blind girl and a furry dog? If you guessed *Lassie,* you win. In the show, the girl walked this trail and read the braille interpretive displays. Anyway, this nature trail has less of a grade than the one across the highway, although it's not quite as scenic. You will see numerous pines with an incredible amount of holes drilled in them—the work of industrious acorn woodpeckers. A minus is the sound of nearby Highway 38, but the pluses are the sound of the wind in the pines and lots of squirrels and blue jays.

⑩ Jenks Lake

1.0 mi/0.5 hr

Location: In San Bernardino National Forest near Angelus Oaks; map I6, grid d6.

User groups: Hikers, dogs, horses, and mountain bikes. No wheelchair facilities.

Permits: No permits are required. A national forest recreation pass is required for each vehicle; fees are $5 for one day or $30 for a year.

Directions: From Interstate 10 at Redlands, take the Highway 38 exit and drive northeast for 27 miles to the Jenks Lake turnoff on the right. Turn right and follow Jenks Lake Road for two miles to the parking area for the lake. (Note that Jenks Lake Road continues and reconnects to Highway 38 a few miles to the east.)

Maps: For a map of San Bernardino National Forest, send $4 to USDA-Forest Service, 630 Sansome Street, San Francisco, CA 94111. To obtain a topographic map of the area, ask for Big Bear Lake from the USGS.

Contact: San Bernardino National Forest, San Gorgonio Ranger District, 34701 Mill Creek Road, Mentone, CA 92359; (909) 794-1123.

Trail notes: If you can get to Jenks Lake on a weekday, when nobody is around, you'll find it's a magical little spot of bright blue water, with Mount San Gorgonio looming in the background. When we visited in April, the peak was crested with snow, and the wind was whipping off the surface of the small lake, creating little whitecaps. If you visit Jenks Lake on a Saturday in July, however, it's another story. The place is likely to be packed with picnicking families, kids from nearby summer camps, and people fishing for largemouth bass, bluegill, and rainbow trout in the stocked lake. No matter when you arrive, you should take the short walk around the perimeter of the lake, then head off on the nature trail that leads behind the picnic area. The south shore of the lake is the quieter side, where no swimming is permitted. After looping around the lake, walk to the back side of the picnic area, where you're likely to be surprised by the view from the trail—the canyon drops off vertically, with sheer cliffs that fall hundreds of feet. Yes, this is the Rim of the World, just like the highway of the same name. Fortunately a railing is in place to keep you from leaning too far over the edge. Note that hikers looking for a longer adventure can set off from either the South Fork or Forsee Creek Trailheads (near Jenks Lake) and head into the San Gorgonio Wilderness. If you don't have a permit, you can always walk just to the wilderness boundary and turn around.

⑪ Aspen Grove Trail

5.0 mi/2.5 hrs

Location: In the San Gorgonio Wilderness near Angelus Oaks; map I6, grid d7.

User groups: Hikers, dogs, and horses. No mountain bikes. No wheelchair facilities.

Permits: A free wilderness permit is required for both day hiking and backpacking; they are available from the Mill Creek Ranger Station at the address below, the Barton Flats Visitor Center on Highway 38, or the Fawnskin Ranger Station in Big Bear. A national forest recreation pass is required for each vehicle; fees are $5 for one day or $30 for a year.

Directions: From Interstate 10 at Redlands, take the Highway 38 exit and drive northeast for 32 miles to Forest Service Road 1N02, signed for Heart Bar Campground, Coon Creek, and Fish Creek. Turn right (south) and drive 1.25 miles to

Road 1N05, then bear right. Drive 1.5 miles to the Aspen Grove Trailhead on the right.

Maps: For a map of San Bernardino National Forest or the San Gorgonio Wilderness, send $4 to USDA-Forest Service, 630 Sansome Street, San Francisco, CA 94111. To obtain a topographic map of the area, ask for Moonridge from the USGS.

Contact: San Bernardino National Forest, San Gorgonio Ranger District, 34701 Mill Creek Road, Mentone, CA 92359; (909) 794-1123.

Trail notes: From the Aspen Grove Trailhead, a short walk down a dirt road leads you into a cool and shady grove of aspen trees along Fish Creek, one of only two remaining in San Bernardino National Forest. The grove is small, and is continually threatened by non-native beavers who chew the aspens down to build dams in Fish Creek. The Department of Fish and Game introduced the beavers in the 1940s, thinking they'd be good for the ecosystem. Now they are trying to remove them, but the little guys with the big teeth are hard to catch. What a dilemma. Anyway, if you're accustomed to the aspen trees of the southern Sierra, you'll notice that these have smaller leaves—an adaptation to the dry climate. (One tip: Don't show up in April, like we did, when the aspens have no leaves at all. Autumn is the best time to see them, when they are bright gold in color.) If you want to do more than hike down the hill and wander among the aspens, you must have a wilderness permit. Once you cross Fish Creek, you're in the San Gorgonio Wilderness. The trail to the right leads to a few more aspens, then peters out. Follow the trail to your left (uphill), heading away from the creek. A pretty walk of less than two miles through a mixed conifer forest will deliver you to two meadows, first tiny Monkey Flower Flat and then, after crossing Fish Creek again, Lower Fish Creek Meadow. It's a fine place to lay out a picnic and count the wildflowers. A side note: The drive to and from the Aspen Grove Trailhead is awesome, with wide views at every turn in the road.

---

⑫ Big Falls

0.6 mi/0.5 hr

Location: In the Falls Recreation Area near Forest Falls; map I6, grid e6.

User groups: Hikers, dogs, horses, and mountain bikes. No wheelchair facilities.

Permits: No permits are required. A national forest recreation pass is required for each vehicle; fees are $5 for one day or $30 for a year.

Directions: From Interstate 10 at Redlands, take the Highway 38 exit and drive northeast for approximately 14 miles to the intersection with Forest Home Road. Bear right and continue for 4.5 miles to the Falls Recreation Area, past the town of Forest Falls. (The name of the road changes to Valley of the Falls Drive.) Park in the first parking lot on the left.

Maps: For a map of San Bernardino National Forest, send $4 to USDA-Forest Service, 630 Sansome Street, San Francisco, CA 94111. To obtain a topographic map of the area, ask for Forest Falls from the USGS.

Contact: San Bernardino National Forest, San Gorgonio Ranger District, 34701 Mill Creek Road, Mentone, CA 92359; (909) 794-1123.

Trail notes: Quick—what's the largest year-round waterfall in Southern California? Big Falls, of course. At 500 feet tall, Big Falls delivers on its name, but unfortunately it's difficult to see the waterfall's full height. That's okay, though, because the Falls Recreation Area is still a great destination, and the short hike to the overlook of Big Falls is a fun and easy walk. The elevation at the trailhead is just shy of 6,000 feet, which means the air is cool and clear. Begin hiking at the lower parking lot, below the picnic area, and set off on an unsigned path heading downstream along Mill Creek Wash. When you pass a private cabin alongside the wash, look for a good place to cross Mill Creek by rock-hopping, and then do so. On the far side of the stream, pick up the trail leading uphill on the right side of Falls Creek, which is a feeder stream to Mill Creek. Hike past a small cascade on the bottom of Falls Creek and head uphill for about five minutes to the overlook area for Big Falls. What you see is the top 40 to 50 feet of a very Yosemite-like freefall, and then some cascading water below. The huge middle part of the fall is hidden out of sight in the rocky canyon. Darn. So where can you get a better view of Big Falls? Actually, the best view is from your car window, as you drive past the last few houses along Valley of the Falls Drive, shortly before entering the Falls Recreation Area. Along this stretch, you can see (from a distance) the full-length vista of Big Falls that usually appears on postcards.

⑬ Vivian Creek Trail to Mount San Gorgonio

14.0 mi/1–2 days

Location: In the San Gorgonio Wilderness near Forest Falls; map I6, grid e6.

User groups: Hikers, dogs, and horses. No mountain bikes. No wheelchair facilities.

Permits: A free wilderness permit is required for both day hiking and backpacking; they are available from the Mill Creek Ranger Station at the address below, the Barton Flats Visitor Center on Highway 38, or the Fawnskin Ranger Station in Big Bear. A national forest recreation pass is required for each vehicle; fees are $5 for one day or $30 for a year.

Directions: From Interstate 10 at Redlands, take the Highway 38 exit and drive northeast for about 14 miles to the intersection with Forest Home Road. Bear right and continue for 4.5 miles to the Falls Recreation Area, past the town of Forest Falls. (The name of the road changes to Valley of the Falls Drive.) Drive to the parking area at the end of the road, then walk uphill through the picnic area on the dirt road to reach the trailhead.

Maps: For a map of San Bernardino National Forest or the San Gorgonio Wilderness, send $4 to USDA-Forest Service, 630 Sansome Street, San Francisco, CA 94111. To obtain topographic maps of the area, ask for Forest Falls and San Gorgonio Mountain from the USGS.

Contact: San Bernardino National Forest, San Gorgonio Ranger District, 34701 Mill Creek Road, Mentone, CA 92359; (909) 794-1123.

Trail notes: There are lots of ways to reach the summit of Mount San Gorgonio, the tallest mountain in Southern California, but the shortest way is on the Vivian Creek Trail. That's the good news. The bad news is that it's also the steepest way. The summit of San Gorgonio is at 11,490 feet, and the Vivian Creek Trailhead is at 6,100 feet, so you can see what you're in for. Luckily, there are several camps along the way: Vivian Creek Camp at 1.2 miles, Halfway Camp at 2.5 miles (halfway to

what? we wonder), and High Creek Camp at 4.8 miles. It's a seven-mile one-way trip to the summit, and although some people hike the round-trip in a day, it's much better to take two or more days so you can enjoy yourself and not have to rush back before dark.

The trail leaves the upper end of Big Falls Picnic Area and crosses Mill Creek Wash, then starts on a steep mile-long climb to the hanging valley of Vivian Creek, where Vivian Creek Falls sometimes falls. Vivian Creek Camp is located here, if you've gotten a late afternoon start. The trail continues along Vivian Creek, crossing it numerous times under the shade of a mixed conifer forest, to Halfway Camp. A few more switchbacks and you cross High Creek, arriving at High Creek Camp at 9,000 feet. High Creek Camp is famous for being a cold and windy place to spend the night. At this elevation, only lodgepole pines grow, and as you gain another 2,000 feet in elevation, even these stalwarts give way to granite. At the base of San Gorgonio's summit, you meet up with the trail from Dollar Lake. Turn right, then left at the next junction, and climb to the 11,490-foot summit of Old Greyback, as it's called. Are you exhausted? Join the party—so is everybody else who makes it this far. But what an achievement. Hope you brought a good map so you can identify all the major landmarks of Southern California.

⑭ Aerial Tramway to Desert View Trail

2.0 mi/1.0 hr

Location: In Mount San Jacinto State Park; map I6, grid g9.

User groups: Hikers only. No dogs, horses, or mountain bikes. No wheelchair facilities.

Permits: No permits are required. The Palm Springs Aerial Tramway charges $16.95 per adult and $10.95 per child under 12 for a round-trip ticket to Mountain Station. (Phone (760) 325-1391 for more information about schedules, fees, and special programs.)

Directions: From Banning, drive 12 miles east on Interstate 10 and take the Highway 111/Palm Springs exit. Drive nine miles south on Highway 111 to Tramway Road, then turn right and drive

3.5 miles to the tramway parking area. Walk to the tram station, buy your ticket, and ride the tram to its end at Mountain Station. Walk out the back side of Mountain Station, follow the paved path downhill, then walk to your left for the Desert View Trail.

Maps: A hiking trail map of the San Jacinto State Park and Wilderness is available for $1 at the state park and national forest offices listed below. For a map of San Bernardino National Forest or the San Jacinto Wilderness, send $4 to USDA-Forest Service, 630 Sansome Street, San Francisco, CA 94111. To obtain a topographic map of the area, ask for San Jacinto Peak from the USGS.

Contact: Mount San Jacinto State Park and Wilderness, P.O. Box 308, 25905 Highway 243, Idyllwild, CA 92549; (909) 659-2607. Or San Bernardino National Forest, San Jacinto Ranger District, P.O. Box 518, 54270 Pine Crest Avenue, Idyllwild, CA 92549; (909) 659-2117.

Trail notes: The first time you ride the Palm Springs Aerial Tramway, you realize that human beings are capable of creating miracles. In just a few minutes, which you spend gaping out the big windows at the view, you are whooshed from the desert floor at 2,643 feet in elevation to the San Jacinto State Park and Wilderness at 8,516 feet. From cactus to clouds, from palms to pines, and, in our case, from desert heat to snow flurries. There are dozens of possible hikes from the top of the tramway, but the easiest of them all is on the Desert View Trail. Since the trail is in the state park, but not in the state wilderness, you don't even need a permit—just get off the tram and start hiking. Where else, for so little effort, can you get expansive views of the desert and high mountain country? Not too many places.

To reach the Desert View Trail, follow the park's nature trail to the left from the back of the tram station; it joins Desert View. The vistas are awesome every step of the way, especially looking out over Palm Springs and the Indian Canyons. As you walk, be on the lookout for Cooper's hawks and yellow-rumped warblers. Here's an insider's tip for planning your trip: The best deal on the Palm Springs Aerial Tramway is to buy the Ride 'n' Dine ticket. For just a couple of extra bucks, you get a huge buffet dinner to go with

your tram ride and day of exploring on the mountain. It's an incredible experience to spend the day hiking, have dinner in the huge dining room as the sun goes down, then ride the tram back downhill in the darkness.

⓯ Aerial Tramway to San Jacinto Peak

11.6 mi/6.6 hrs

Location: In Mount San Jacinto State Park and Wilderness; map I6, grid g9.

User groups: Hikers only. No dogs, horses, or mountain bikes. No wheelchair facilities.

Permits: A free wilderness permit is required for day hiking or backpacking in the San Jacinto Wilderness; they are available from the ranger station at Mountain Station. The Palm Springs Aerial Tramway charges $16.95 per adult and $10.95 per child under 12 for a round-trip ticket to Mountain Station. (Phone (760) 325-1391 for more information about schedules, fees, and special programs.)

Directions: From Banning, drive 12 miles east on Interstate 10 and take the Highway 111/Palm Springs exit. Drive nine miles south on Highway 111 to Tramway Road, then turn right and drive 3.5 miles to the tramway parking area. Walk to the tram station, buy your ticket, and ride the tram to its end at Mountain Station. Walk out the back side of Mountain Station, follow the paved path downhill, then head west (right) for a few hundred yards to the ranger station. Get a day-hiking permit, then continue hiking on the well-signed trail heading for Round Valley.

Maps: A hiking trail map of the San Jacinto State Park and Wilderness is available for $1 at the state park and national forest offices listed below. For a map of San Bernardino National Forest or the San Jacinto Wilderness, send $4 to USDA-Forest Service, 630 Sansome Street, San Francisco, CA 94111. To obtain a topographic map of the area, ask for San Jacinto Peak from the USGS.

Contact: Mount San Jacinto State Park and Wilderness, P.O. Box 308, 25905 Highway 243, Idyllwild, CA 92549; (909) 659-2607. Or San Bernardino National Forest, San Jacinto Ranger District, P.O. Box 518, 54270 Pine Crest Avenue, Idyllwild, CA 92549; (909) 659-2117.

Trail notes: You could hike to 10,804-foot San Jacinto Peak the hard way, upward from Idyllwild on one of several possible trails, but then you'd miss out on the many delights of the Palm Springs Aerial Tramway, and hiking through Long and Round Valleys. (For information on the Palm Springs Aerial Tramway, see the trail notes for hike number 14.) So take the tram instead, then get your wilderness permit at the ranger station and begin hiking on the Round Valley Trail. It switchbacks gently uphill through the pines and firs, most of the time following a creek laden with corn lilies, to reach beautiful Round Valley at 9,100 feet. The left fork leads to a campground and backcountry ranger station, but you'll continue straight for Wellman Divide, with a short, steep climb just before you reach it. The views to the north and east are inspiring, including jagged Tahquitz Peak and Red Tahquitz—a bit of foreshadowing of things to come.

At the divide, turn right on the Deer Springs Trail. You have 2.6 miles to go, and the views stay with you the whole way. Climb northward on the granite slopes of Miller Peak, then make a sharp left switchback and head southwest to the spur trail for San Jacinto Peak, on the right. Once you're on the spur, it's only a few hundred yards to the peak, where the views are truly breathtaking. You can see just about all of Southern California, even into Mexico and Nevada, and out to the Pacific Ocean. John Muir said that the vista from San Jacinto was "one of the most sublime spectacles seen anywhere on earth," and he was a guy who saw a lot of vistas. Total elevation gain is 2,300 feet.

⑯ Seven Pines Trail

7.4 mi/4.0 hrs

Location: In the San Jacinto Wilderness near Idyllwild; map I6, grid g8.

User groups: Hikers and horses. No dogs or mountain bikes. No wheelchair facilities.

Permits: A free wilderness permit is required for day hiking or backpacking; they are available from the Idyllwild Ranger Station. A national forest recreation pass is required for each vehicle; fees are $5 for one day or $30 for a year.

Directions: From Idyllwild, drive northwest on

Highway 243 for 5.5 miles to the right turnoff for Stone Creek, Fern Basin, Marion Mountain, and Dark Canyon Campgrounds. Turn right and drive two-tenths of a mile, then bear left, following the signs for Dark Canyon Camp. Continue through the campground and up the hill to reach the Seven Pines Trailhead.

Maps: For a map of San Bernardino National Forest or the San Jacinto Wilderness, send $4 to USDA-Forest Service, 630 Sansome Street, San Francisco, CA 94111. To obtain a topographic map of the area, ask for San Jacinto Peak from the USGS.

Contact: San Bernardino National Forest, San Jacinto Ranger District, 54270 Pinecrest, Idyllwild, CA 92549; (909) 659-2117.

Trail notes: The best thing about the Seven Pines Trail is that you can just wander as far as you please and have a good time. The mileage above reflects hiking 3.7 miles, with a 2,300-foot elevation gain, to the junction with Deer Springs Trail, but even a mile or two on this path is enjoyable. The first mile climbs steeply through beautiful conifers and many granite boulders, then the trail joins the North Fork of the San Jacinto River. Where the path crosses the river, you enter a gorgeous forest of pines and incense cedars. Hanging out right here might suit you just fine, but if you want more exercise, continue uphill to Deer Springs Junction, which is also the headwaters for the North Fork. You'll cross the river twice more on your way. Trailhead elevation is 6,320 feet.

⑰ Deer Springs Trail to Suicide Rock

7.0 mi/4.0 hrs

Location: In the San Jacinto Wilderness near Idyllwild; map I6, grid h8.

User groups: Hikers and horses. No dogs or mountain bikes. No wheelchair facilities.

Permits: A free wilderness permit is required for both day hiking and backpacking; they are available from the Idyllwild Ranger Station. A national forest recreation pass is required for each vehicle; fees are $5 for one day or $30 for a year.

Directions: From Idyllwild, drive northwest on

Highway 243 for one mile to the Deer Springs Trailhead on the right side of the road (across the highway from the Idyllwild County Park visitor center parking area).

Maps: For a map of San Bernardino National Forest or the San Jacinto Wilderness, send $4 to USDA-Forest Service, 630 Sansome Street, San Francisco, CA 94111. To obtain topographic maps of the area, ask for Idyllwild and San Jacinto Peak from the USGS.

Contact: San Bernardino National Forest, San Jacinto Ranger District, 54270 Pinecrest, Idyllwild, CA 92549; (909) 659-2117.

Trail notes: If you're wondering how to spend a morning or an afternoon in Idyllwild, the hike to Suicide Rock will turn your visit into a trip you'll never forget. Pick up a wilderness permit and head for the trailhead, but be sure to pack some snacks and water for a little celebration at the top. Most of the work is in the first 2.4 miles to Suicide Junction, as you climb up through manzanita, ceanothus, and oaks, heading into the higher country of cedars and pines. At the junction, bear right and leave the Deer Creek Trail for the last mile to Suicide Rock, which contours on an easier grade. From the three-mile point onward, your views of Lily Rock and Tahquitz Peak are outstanding, and once you're on Suicide Rock at 7,528 feet in elevation, you are directly across from Lily Rock's Yosemite-like chunk of white granite. We watched a few clouds drift between us and the neighboring peaks, right at eye level. The view below is of the Idyllwild area—there's little in sight besides a few houses and water tanks, tucked in among a vast sea of conifers.

⑱ Ernie Maxwell Scenic Trail

5.2 mi/2.5 hrs

Location: In San Bernardino National Forest near Idyllwild; map I6, grid h8.

User groups: Hikers, dogs, horses, and mountain bikes. No wheelchair facilities.

Permits: No permits are required. A national forest recreation pass is required for each vehicle; fees are $5 for one day or $30 for a year.

Directions: From Idyllwild on Highway 243,

turn east on North Circle Drive in downtown, which becomes South Circle Drive, and then becomes Fern Valley Road. Follow Fern Valley Road to Humber Park. (You will drive a total of two miles from downtown.) The trailhead is on the right at the lower end of the parking lot.

Maps: For a map of San Bernardino National Forest, send $4 to USDA-Forest Service, 630 Sansome Street, San Francisco, CA 94111. To obtain a topographic map of the area, ask for Idyllwild from the USGS.

Contact: San Bernardino National Forest, San Jacinto Ranger District, 54270 Pinecrest, Idyllwild, CA 92549; (909) 659-2117.

Trail notes: The Ernie Maxwell Scenic Trail is the perfect route for hikers who aren't up to a lot of climbing, which is *de rigeur* for most trails in the Idyllwild area. With only a 300-foot elevation change on an undulating trail, even families with small children could manage this path, which leads through a lovely conifer forest. Keep in mind, however, that since you're not climbing, you will not get the spectacular views that are granted on most other trails in the area; this is a walk that is built for enjoying the close-up, rather than the far-off. The trail leads downhill from the start, contouring through a forest of Jeffrey, ponderosa, and coulter pines, with scattered firs and incense cedars among them. You can practice your tree identification. The trail's end is a bit of a disappointment; it simply reaches a dirt road where you turn around and hike back. Along the way, you'll see some good views of Suicide Rock and Tahquitz Peak.

⑲ Devil's Slide Trail to Tahquitz Peak

8.4 mi/4.0 hrs

Location: In the San Jacinto Wilderness near Idyllwild; map I6, grid h8.

User groups: Hikers, dogs, and horses. No mountain bikes. No wheelchair facilities.

Permits: A free wilderness permit is required for both day hiking and backpacking; they are available from the Idyllwild Ranger Station. Day-hiking permits are limited on weekends and holidays from Memorial Day weekend to Labor Day weekend. A national forest recreation pass is required for each vehicle; fees are $5 for one day or $30 for a year.

Directions: From Idyllwild on Highway 243, turn east on North Circle Drive in downtown, which becomes South Circle Drive, and then becomes Fern Valley Road. Follow Fern Valley Road to Humber Park. (You will drive a total of two miles from downtown.) The trailhead is on the right at the upper end of the parking lot.

Maps: For a map of San Bernardino National Forest or the San Jacinto Wilderness, send $4 to USDA-Forest Service, 630 Sansome Street, San Francisco, CA 94111. To obtain topographic maps of the area, ask for Idyllwild and San Jacinto Peak from the USGS.

Contact: San Bernardino National Forest, San Jacinto Ranger District, 54270 Pinecrest, Idyllwild, CA 92549; (909) 659-2117.

Trail notes: The Devil's Slide Trail is the premier hiking trail in the Idyllwild area, with 8,828-foot Tahquitz Peak as the favored destination, especially for hikers from out of town. The trail has gotten so popular that day-hiking permits are subject to a quota system on weekends and holidays in the summer months, so you must get to the ranger station early on those days or plan on hiking somewhere else. The best solution? Plan a trip for before Memorial Day, after Labor Day, or any time during the week. We hiked the trail in mid-May and saw almost nobody, but, then again, it snowed on our trip.

The trail leads from Idyllwild's Humber Park on a steady but manageable uphill climb through the forest to Saddle Junction, 2.5 miles up. Once you reach the junction, head right for Tahquitz Peak. The next mile is loaded with far-reaching views of the desert below and San Jacinto Mountains, seen from an increasingly open lodgepole pine forest. At the next junction, head right again, soon saying good-bye to the trees and hello to a stark landscape of granite. The summit is only a half mile away. Tahquitz Peak has the only operating fire lookout in the San Jacinto Ranger District, and it's staffed by nice folks in the summertime. From the lookout, which was constructed in 1938, you're offered a panoramic view of both the San Jacinto and Santa Rosa Mountains.

Special note: If you've got your heart set on hiking to Tahquitz Peak but can't get a wilderness permit on the day you want to go, you can always take the South Ridge Trail instead of the Devil's Slide Trail. There are no permit quotas for the South Ridge Trail, although you still need to pick up a free wilderness permit before hitting the trail. It's a 7.2-mile round-trip via South Ridge Trail from the vicinity of Saunders Meadow Road, but you should make sure to hike the route early in the day in the summer months—this trail is even more exposed than the Devil's Slide Trail.

Pacific Crest Trail (PCT) Section Overview

250.0 mi. one way/25.0 days

This giant swath of land—extending all the way from the Highway 74 Trailhead north to the Angeles Crest Highway—encompasses a diverse spectrum of terrain, flora, and fauna. The trail starts near the foot of the San Gorgonios at an elevation of about 5,000 feet, then climbs to nearly 9,000 feet high in the San Gorgonio Mountains, the highest the Pacific Crest Trail gets in Southern California. It then drops into semi-desert lowlands, as low as 1,200 feet elevation, the lowest the PCT gets anywhere. This represents special challenges to PCT through-hikers. The best scenario is to hike through the desert early enough in the year so that temperatures and water availability are ideal, yet not so early that you run into deep snow in the San Gorgonios. It's about a 50-50 split for hiking conditions between good years and bad. In bad years, deep snow and treacherous stream crossings from high water can delay embarking on this southern portion of the route until so late in the spring that it can jeopardize the ability to complete the entire route. Why? Because you get so far behind schedule that the fall weather window in the northern portion of the route closes down before you can traverse it. For hikers not attempting to complete the entire PCT, the high country here is best hiked from late April to early May on through June; to be on schedule, though, PCT through-hikers will need to make it through the San Gregonios well before that. Note that no campfires are permitted in most of the areas of this region.

Highway 74 to San Gorgonio Pass

60.0 mi. one way/6.0 days

Location: From the Highway 74 Trailhead north to the trailhead parking area at Interstate 10 near San Gorgonio; map I6, grid j9 .

User groups: Hikers, dogs (except in national parks), and horses. No mountain bikes. No wheelchair facilities.

Permits: A wilderness permit is required for traveling through various wilderness and special-use areas the trail traverses. Contact the San Bernardino National Forest at (909) 659-2117 for a permit that is good for the length of your trip.

Directions: To reach the Highway 74 Trailhead, from the town of Hemet, head east on Highway 74 to the junction of Highways 74 and 371 (Cahuilla Road). The trailhead for the PCT lies approximately one mile southeast on Highway 371, just west of the Santa Rosa Summit. To reach the Interstate 10 Trailhead, from Interstate 10 near the Palm Springs exit, take the Verbania Avenue exit and drive north to Tamarack Road. Turn left onto Tamarack Road and drive approximately a quarter of a mile to the signed PCT Trailhead, located just past Fremontia Road.

Maps: For an overall view of the trail route in this section, send $4 to the USDA-Forest Service, 630 Sansome Street, San Francisco, CA 94111, and ask for the San Bernardino National Forest map. For topographic maps of the route, request Butterfly Peak, Palm View Play, Idyllwild, San Jacinto Peak, and White Water from the USGS.

Contact: San Bernardino National Forest, San Jacinto Ranger District, P.O. Box 518, Idyllwild, CA 92549; (909) 659-2117 or fax (909) 659-2107.

Trail notes: This section of trail is either heaven or hell, depending on what kind of winter it has been here. In low snow years, it can be heaven, after making it past one of the most water-starved sections of trail, and most hikers are eager to reach the first real mountains of the trip in the traipse northward. Light snow in the San Gorgonio Mountains is a big plus because not only is the trail passable early in the year, but stream crossings are much easier as well. This section of the PCT has a ton of ups and downs, making the climbs much longer than you might think. The trail starts at an elevation of 5,000 feet, then climbs 2,000 feet (but not directly), then traverses up and down one canyon after another, and after about 25 miles from the trailhead, eventually reaches 8,570 feet and the base of Tahquitz Peak. Nearly everybody makes the short side trip to the top, where the setting is sparse but the expansive view of the valley below is reward enough. You forge onward, and in another half day, get your first view of Mount San Gorgonio, which at 11,499 feet is Southern California's highest point. Your traipse toward it passes through the San Jacinto Wilderness, with a mix of coulter pines and chaparral, laterals beneath San Jacinto Peak, then takes a mind-bending descent to San Gorgonio Pass, dropping all the way down to the desert again. This time you bottom out at 1,188 feet, the lowest point of the PCT in California, then a few miles later, reach Interstate 10 near the pass. A strange 60 miles? You bet.

PCT-8 ## San Gorgonio to Van Dusen Canyon Road

64.0 mi. one way/6.0 days

Location: From the trailhead parking area at Interstate 10 near San Gorgonio Pass north to Van Dusen Canyon Road near Big Bear; map I6, grid g9.

User groups: Hikers, dogs (except in national parks), and horses. No mountain bikes. No wheelchair facilities.

Permits: A wilderness permit is required for traveling through various wilderness and special-use areas the trail traverses. Contact the San Bernardino National Forest at (909) 794-1123 for a permit that is good for the length of your trip.

Directions: To reach the Interstate 10 Trailhead, from Interstate 10 near the Palm Springs exit, take the Verbania Avenue exit and drive north to Tamarack Road. Turn left onto Tamarack and go approximately a quarter of a mile to the signed PCT Trailhead located just past Fremontia Road. To reach the Van Dusen Road Trailhead, from Highway 18 in Big Bear City, head north on Van Dusen Canyon Road for three miles to the signed PCT Trailhead.

Maps: For an overall view of the trail route in this section, send $4 to the USDA-Forest Service, 630 Sansome Street, San Francisco, CA 94111, and ask for the San Bernardino National Forest map. For topographic maps of the route, request White Water, Catclaw Flat, Onyx Peak, Moonridge, and Big Bear City from the USGS.

Contact: San Bernardino National Forest, San Gorgonio Ranger District, Mill Creek Ranger Station, 34701 Mill Creek Road, Mentone, CA 92359; (909) 794-1123 or fax (909) 794-1125. Bureau of Land Management, Palm Springs-South Coast Resource Area, P.O. Box 2000, North Palm Springs, CA 92258; (619) 251-4800 fax at (619) 251-4899.

Trail notes: When you make your first steps from the trailhead near Interstate 10, your next serious destination, just above Big Bear Lake, may seem like the impossible dream. The trip starts at just 1,400 feet, then forces you through extremely stark desert, complete with cactus and not much else, as you face a rank climb, eventually rising all the way to 8,500 feet in San Bernardino National Forest, edging the San Gorgonio Wilderness. With water hard to come by over the first 25 miles of this part of the route, most day hikers stick exclusively to the high country, 7,000 feet and up. Admittedly, that's what we did, exhilarated by the mountain air (and a shared Baby Ruth candy bar), and enjoying the deep canyon views and mixed forest, sprinkled with pines and cedars.

Once you get above the desert, passing Mission Creek, you forge northward with renewed vigor. Hikers will top out at 8,750 feet in San Bernardino National Forest, then cross below Onyx Peak, after which the first views of Baldwin Lake, and later Big Bear Lake, come into view. The trail takes a general curving path counterclockwise around and just north of Big Bear Lake, and after taking in stellar views to the south of Big Bear and the peaks of the San Gorgonio Wilderness, you are routed to the Van Dusen Forest Service Campground. Note that in the spring and early summer, anything is possible here when it comes to weather. On our most recent visit, it was hot, then cold, then snowed lightly, cleared, then rained, was calm, then windy, then hot again, all in just a few days.

PCT-9 Van Dusen Canyon Road to Cajon Pass

99.0 mi. one way/10.0 days

Location: From the trailhead parking area at Van Dusen Canyon Road near Big Bear west to the trailhead parking area at Interstate 15 near Cajon Pass; map I6, grid c6.

User groups: Hikers, dogs (except in national parks), and horses. No mountain bikes. No wheelchair facilities.

Permits: A wilderness permit is required for traveling through various wilderness and special-use areas the trail traverses. Contact the San Bernardino National Forest at (909) 866-3437 for a permit that is good for the length of your trip.

Directions: To reach the Van Dusen Road Trailhead, from Highway 18 in Big Bear City, head north on Van Dusen Canyon Road for approximately three miles to the signed PCT Trailhead. To reach the Cajon Trailhead, from San Bernardino, take Interstate 15 north to Cajon Junction, where Highway 138 passes over the freeway. Exit here and follow the paved road branching off Highway 138, just east of the exit, to the trailhead.

Maps: For an overall view of the trail route in this section, send $4 for each map ordered to USDA-Forest Service, 630 Sansome Street, San Francisco, CA 94111, and ask for the San Bernardino National Forest and the San Gabriel National Forest maps. For topographic maps of the route, request Big Bear City, Fawnskin, Butler Peak, Lake Arrowhead, Silverwood Lake, and Cajon from the USGS.

Contact: San Bernardino National Forest, Big Bear Ranger District, P.O. Box 290, Fawnskin, CA 92333; (909) 866-3437 fax (909) 866-2867.

Trail notes: The PCT traces a line along the northern rim above Big Bear Lake, and while you're walking it, our suggestion is to take your time, soak in the views of the lake, and while you're at it, soak up as much drinking water as possible. In fact, you might want to pretend you're a camel, since after departing Big Bear at the Van Dusen Campground, the PCT suddenly veers off its northern course and instead heads to the west, bound eventually all the way to the

San Gabriel Wilderness. Highlights of the trail from Big Bear include Holcomb Creek and Deep Creek (a favorite of ours), in the process descending about 3,000 feet over the course of a little more than 23 miles. We suggest enjoying Deep Creek to your heart's content, because from here to Cajon, the trail once again becomes largely hot and dusty, even in the spring. After some 50 miles from Big Bear, Silverwood Lake provides a respite, and virtually everybody jumps in for a swim. From here, it's a day's walk (13 miles) to Interstate 15 near Cajon Pass.

PCT-10 Cajon Pass to Angeles Crest Highway

27.0 mi. one way/3.0 days

Location: From Interstate 15 near Cajon Pass to the Angeles Crest Highway; map I6, grid b0.

User groups: Hikers, dogs, and horses. No mountain bikes. No wheelchair facilities.

Permits: A wilderness permit is required for traveling through various wilderness and special-use areas the trail traverses. Contact the Angeles National Forest at (818) 574-5200 for a permit that is good for the length of your trip. No day-use permits are required for this section of trail.

Directions: To reach the Cajon Trailhead, from San Bernardino, take Interstate 15 north to Cajon Junction, where Highway 138 passes over the freeway. Exit here and follow a paved road branching off Highway 138, just east of the exit, to the trailhead. To reach the Angeles Crest Trailhead, from Interstate 15 near Cajon, take Highway 138 east. Turn left (west) on the Angeles Crest Highway and drive five miles to Wrightwood. Continue for three miles to Big Pines. Bear left and continue on Angeles Crest Highway for 1.5 miles to Inspiration Point, opposite Blue Ridge Road.

Maps: For an overall view of the trail route in this section, send $4 to the USDA-Forest Service, 630 Sansome Street, San Francisco, CA 94111, and ask for the Angeles National Forest map. For topographic maps of the route, request Telegraph Peak and Cajon from the USGS.

Contact: Angeles National Forest, 701 North Santa Anita Avenue, Arcadia, CA 91006; (818) 574-5200 or fax (818) 574-5233.

Trail notes: From the trailhead at Interstate 15 and Cajon Pass, the PCT is a real butt-kicker, climbing from just under 3,000 feet in elevation to 8,200 feet over the course of 23 miles to Guffy Campground, with no reliable water source anywhere in between. It's not only a long climb, but often hot as well, so drinking all of your water early in the affair can put you in danger of dehydration. Most PCT hikers take the side trip to Wrightwood instead of making it an endurance test to Guffy Campground (a campground that can be reached by car, and where water is hard to find anyway). From Guffy Camp, the PCT runs along the Sheep Mountain Wilderness until it hits the Angeles Crest Highway. The views of the canyons here are superb on clear days, and as a trailhead, it's an excellent jump-off point for those heading onward (see chapter I5).

PCT Continuation: To continue hiking along the Pacific Crest Trail, see chapter I5.

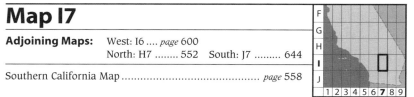

Map I7

Adjoining Maps: West: I6 .... *page* 600
North: H7 552   South: J7 644

Southern California Map .... *page* 558

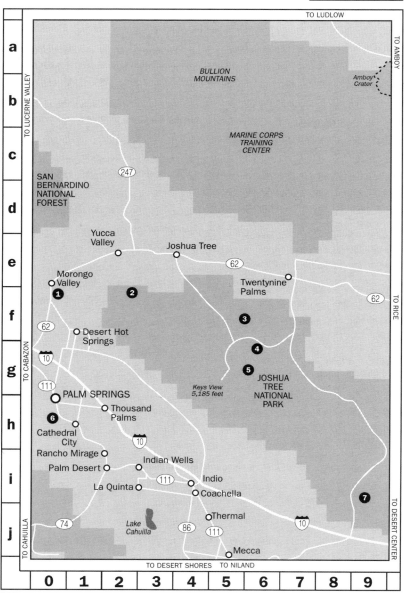

616

❶ Canyon Trail

3.0 mi/1.5 hrs

Location: In the Big Morongo Canyon Preserve north of Palm Springs; map 17, grid f0.

User groups: Hikers only. No dogs, horses, or mountain bikes. No wheelchair facilities.

Permits: No permits are required. Parking and access are free.

Directions: From Banning, drive east on Interstate 10 for 16 miles to the Highway 62 exit. Turn north on Highway 62 and drive 11 miles to Morongo Valley. Look for a sign on the right for the Big Morongo Canyon Preserve (at East Road); turn right and drive to the preserve entrance on the left.

Maps: To obtain a topographic map of the area, ask for Morongo Valley from the USGS.

Contact: Big Morongo Canyon Preserve, P.O. Box 780, Morongo Valley, CA 92256; (760) 363-7190 or fax (760) 363-1180.

Trail notes: The Canyon Trail at the Big Morongo Canyon Preserve is a birder's trail, plain and simple. More than 235 bird species have been identified in the preserve. In fact, if you're not carrying binoculars and a field book when you visit, you'll feel like a real outsider. Luckily, though, you don't have to know anything about birds to have a good time. We examined the interpretive exhibit at the trailhead kiosk, and in a few minutes of hiking we were able to spot and identify a pair of western tanagers. (And usually we can't tell a blue jay from a blue grouse.) Take the main trail out of the parking lot, then bear right and follow the ranch road to the Canyon Trail. Pass a few ranch buildings and before you know it, you're walking on a wooden boardwalk over a wet marsh, smelling the distinct scent of sulfur from underground springs. You exit the boardwalk onto a sandy trail in the canyon, where you can head back as far as you like. We startled a mule deer on this stretch, who acted like he hadn't seen any hikers for a long, long time. On your return trip, you can make a loop if you wish, by turning right on the Willow Trail just before the ranch house and following it to the Desert Wash Trail, which leads back to the parking lot.

❷ Eureka Peak

10.8 mi/6.0 hrs

Location: In Joshua Tree National Park near Yucca Valley; map 17, grid f2.

User groups: Hikers only. No dogs, horses, or mountain bikes. No wheelchair facilities.

Permits: No permits are required. There is a $5 entrance fee per vehicle at Joshua Tree National Park, good for seven days.

Directions: From Banning, drive east on Interstate 10 for 16 miles to the Highway 62 exit. Turn north on Highway 62 and drive 21 miles to Yucca Valley. Continue past Yucca Valley on Highway 62 for two more miles and turn right on Joshua Lane. Follow Joshua Lane for five miles to the Black Rock Canyon Visitor Center. The California Riding and Hiking Trail begins north of the visitor center at the campground.

Maps: Free park maps are available at park entrance stations. To obtain topographic maps of the area, ask for Yucca Valley South and Joshua Tree South from the USGS.

Contact: Joshua Tree National Park, 74485 National Park Drive, Twentynine Palms, CA 92277; (760) 367-7511.

Trail notes: The total elevation gain on this trip is only 1,500 feet to reach the summit of Eureka Peak at 5,518 feet, but it feels more difficult than that. The problem is sand and rocks—lots of them—and the fact that the trail is hard to discern in places. However, if you're willing to put in some effort, your reward is a commanding view of the western edge of Joshua Tree National Park, plus Mount San Jacinto and

Mount San Gorgonio. Sand and snow—you see it all from here. Begin hiking on the California Riding and Hiking Trail, which you'll follow for two miles until you come to a wash. This is where things start to get tricky; keep looking for trail markers to keep you on track. Take the right fork in the wash, then in another half mile, take the next right fork into another wash. Hike through this wash for two miles. A trail marker directs you to your left, heading up and over a ridge. At the top, turn right (south) and hike up to a saddle and then on to south side of Eureka Peak, where there's a short path to the summit. When you get to the top, what's the only downer? You find that plenty of people have driven their cars up to the peak, via a dirt road from Covington Flat. No fair. An option is to follow this road back downhill for one mile to the California Riding and Hiking Trail, then turn left and follow the trail back to your starting point. It makes a good loop trip without adding any extra miles.

❸ Barker Dam Loop

1.2 mi/1.0 hr

Location: In Joshua Tree National Park near Twentynine Palms; map I7, grid f5.

User groups: Hikers only. No dogs, horses, or mountain bikes. No wheelchair facilities.

Permits: No permits are required. There is a $5 entrance fee per vehicle at Joshua Tree National Park, good for seven days.

Directions: From Banning, drive east on Interstate 10 for 16 miles to the Highway 62 exit. Turn north on Highway 62 and drive 29 miles to the town of Joshua Tree and Park Boulevard. Turn right on Park Boulevard and drive 12 miles to Hidden Valley Campground on the left. Turn left and drive two miles to the signed trailhead for Barker Dam.

Maps: Free park maps are available at park entrance stations. To obtain a topographic map of the area, ask for Indian Cove from the USGS.

Contact: Joshua Tree National Park, 74485 National Park Drive, Twentynine Palms, CA 92277; (760) 367-7511.

Trail notes: There's a lake in the desert, and it's hidden in a magical place called the Wonderland of Rocks. You can't waterski or fish there,

but you can bird-watch and photograph the reflections of odd-shaped boulders in the water's surface. The lake is formed by Barker Dam, which was built at the turn of the century to improve upon the Wonderland of Rocks' natural dam, which captured rain runoff and contained it in this basin. The short loop trip takes you past many of the unique granite boulders of the Wonderland of Rocks, then around Barker Dam's small lake. It loops back past some petroglyphs (take the short right spur) and Indian grinding holes. If the petroglyphs seem remarkably visible and clear to you, it's because years ago a movie crew painted over them to make them more visible to the camera. For this tragic reason, the park calls these paintings the "Disney petroglyphs."

❹ Ryan Mountain Trail

3.0 mi/2.0 hrs

Location: In Joshua Tree National Park near Twentynine Palms; map I7, grid g5.

User groups: Hikers only. No dogs, horses, or mountain bikes. No wheelchair facilities.

Permits: No permits are required. There is a $5 entrance fee per vehicle at Joshua Tree National Park, good for seven days.

Directions: From Banning, drive east on Interstate 10 for 16 miles to the Highway 62 exit. Turn north on Highway 62 and drive 45 miles to Twentynine Palms and the park visitor center. Turn right on Utah Trail Road and drive eight miles to a Y junction. Bear right and continue for eight miles to Sheep Pass Campground on the left. You can begin hiking from the camp, or continue one mile further to the trailhead parking area, on the south side of the road. (You can also reach the trailhead via Park Road out of the town of Joshua Tree, turning left at Cap Rock Junction, then continuing 2.5 miles to the trailhead.)

Maps: Free park maps are available at park entrance stations. To obtain a topographic map of the area, ask for Keys View from the USGS.

Contact: Joshua Tree National Park, 74485 National Park Drive, Twentynine Palms, CA 92277; (760) 367-7511.

Trail notes: If you hike only one trail in Joshua Tree National Park, this should be the one. Ryan

Mountain at 5,470 feet provides what many insist is the best view in the park. You can see the Queen Valley, Wonderland of Rocks, Lost Horse Valley, Pleasant Valley, and the far-off mountains—San Gorgonio and San Jacinto. It's a complete 360-degree panorama. The route travels through boulders and Joshua trees—no surprises here—on a well-maintained and easy-to-follow trail. The ascent seems a bit steep, even though it's only a 700-foot elevation gain, but it's over with quickly, so just sweat it out. Be sure to sign the summit register, and then have a seat on one of the rocks of Ryan Mountain to enjoy the view. The peak's boulders are estimated to be several hundred million years old, which gives you something to think about while you admire the vista.

⑤ Lost Horse Mine

4.0 mi/2.0 hrs

Location: In Joshua Tree National Park near Twentynine Palms; map I7, grid g5.

User groups: Hikers only. No dogs, horses, or mountain bikes. No wheelchair facilities.

Permits: No permits are required. There is a $5 entrance fee per vehicle at Joshua Tree National Park, good for seven days.

Directions: From Banning, drive east on Interstate 10 for 16 miles to the Highway 62 exit. Turn north on Highway 62 and drive 29 miles to the town of Joshua Tree and Park Boulevard. Turn right on Park Boulevard and drive 14.5 miles to Cap Rock junction (Park Boulevard changes names to Quail Springs Road). Bear right and drive 2.7 miles to the dirt road on the left that is signed for Lost Horse Mine. Turn left and follow the dirt road to the trailhead parking area.

Maps: Free park maps are available at park entrance stations. To obtain a topographic map of the area, ask for Keys View from the USGS.

Contact: Joshua Tree National Park, 74485 National Park Drive, Twentynine Palms, CA 92277; (760) 367-7511.

Trail notes: You get the full "desert experience" on the Lost Horse Mine Loop, including spectacular mountain and valley vistas, high desert flora, and a visit to an old gold mine. The trail (really an old road) begins at an interpre-

tive exhibit describing the adventurous lives of this area's gold miners, then leads uphill for 1.8 miles to Lost Horse Mine. The mine produced a gold profit at the turn of the century—9,000 ounces of gold—and is the best preserved of all the mines in the national park. Still standing are the mine's stamp mill, old building foundations, and a few open mine shafts. From the mine, continue another quarter mile, climbing more steeply up the ridge to wide overlooks of the Queen Valley, Lost Horse Valley, Pleasant Valley, and the eastern stretch of the national park. Turn around and retrace your steps before the trail begins to descend.

⑥ Murray Canyon Trail

4.0 mi/2.0 hrs

Location: On the Agua Caliente Indian Reservation near Palm Springs; map I7, grid h0.

User groups: Hikers, dogs, and horses. No mountain bikes. No wheelchair facilities.

Permits: No permits are required. A $5 day-use fee is charged per adult; $1 for children 6 to 12.

Directions: From Palm Springs, drive south through the center of town on Highway 111/Palm Canyon Drive, and take the right fork signed for South Palm Canyon Drive. Drive 2.8 miles on South Palm Canyon Drive, bearing right at the sign for Palm Canyon/Andreas Canyon. Stop at the entrance kiosk, then drive about 200 yards, and turn right for Murray Canyon. Drive past the Andreas Canyon Trailhead, and continue to the Murray Canyon Picnic Area, one mile from the entrance kiosk.

Maps: A free map/brochure is available at the entrance kiosk. To obtain topographic maps of the area, ask for Palm Springs and Cathedral City from the USGS.

Contact: Agua Caliente Band of Cahuilla Indians, Tribal Council Office, at (760) 325-5673; or Indian Canyons Information at (760) 325-1053.

Trail notes: If you think Palm Springs is all tennis courts, golf courses, and beauty parlors, you haven't been to the Indian Canyons off South Palm Canyon Drive. The Indian Canyons—Palm, Andreas, and Murray—are what's left of the old Palm Springs. They're wide open stretches of desert with red rock, fan palms, sulfur streams, barrel cactus, and bighorn sheep, plus broad vistas of surprising color and beauty. The Murray Canyon Trail is an excellent exploration of this area, beginning at the picnic grounds between Murray and Andreas Canyons. The trail is well-packed sand and is clearly marked along the way. After an initial wide-open desert stretch, you enter Murray Canyon, which narrows and twists and turns, so you never see where you're going until you come around the next bend. The stream you've been following slowly begins to exhibit a stronger flow, and the streamside reeds, grasses, palm trees, and wild grape intensify their growth accordingly. If you're a fan of red rock, you'll love the 100-foot-tall slanted rock outcrops and cliffs. After passing a left fork for the Kaufmann Trail, climb up and over a small waterfall in Murray Canyon (stay on the left side of the stream). In another quarter mile, you'll reach a larger set of falls. These falls block any possible further progress, but provide many good pools for swimming, and granite shelves for picnicking.

❼ Cottonwood Spring Nature Trail

1.0 mi/0.5 hr

Location: In Joshua Tree National Park near Yucca Valley; map I7, grid i9.

User groups: Hikers only. No dogs, horses, or mountain bikes. No wheelchair facilities.

Permits: No permits are required. There is a $5 entrance fee per vehicle at Joshua Tree National Park, good for seven days.

Directions: From Indio, drive east on Interstate 10 for appproximately 25 miles. Turn north on Cottonwood Spring Road and drive eight miles north to Cottonwood Spring Campground and the trailhead, located near site number 13 at the end of the camp.

Maps: Free park maps are available at park entrance stations. To obtain a topographic map of the area, ask for Cottonwood Spring from the USGS.

Contact: Joshua Tree National Park, 74485 National Park Drive, Twentynine Palms, CA 92277; (760) 367-7511.

Trail notes: Some people say that there's nothing in the desert but sand, rocks, and Joshua trees, but a walk on the Cottonwood Spring Nature Trail will convince you otherwise. No interpretive brochures are necessary on this hike, because the park has placed plaques in front of every type of flora (mostly cactus at the start). The trail leads to Cottonwood Spring Oasis, a little slice of watery paradise for birds and wildlife, surrounded by a ton of greenery. It's not a completely natural paradise—the oasis was improved upon in the late 1800s, in order to make it a viable rest stop for travelers to and from the desert gold mines. In addition to sighting numerous birds flitting about the oasis, you'll also see evidence of the Native Americans who once lived here, in the form of bedrock mortars in the granite.

Leave No Trace Tips

Pack It In and Pack It Out

Take everything you bring into the wild back out with you.

Protect wildlife and your food by storing rations securely. Pick up all spilled foods.

Use toilet paper or wipes sparingly; pack them out.

Inspect your campsite for trash and any evidence of your stay. Pack out all trash—even if it's not yours!

Map J5

Adjoining Maps: East: J6 ..... *page* 626
North: I5 578

Southern California Map .... *page* 558

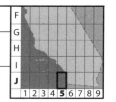

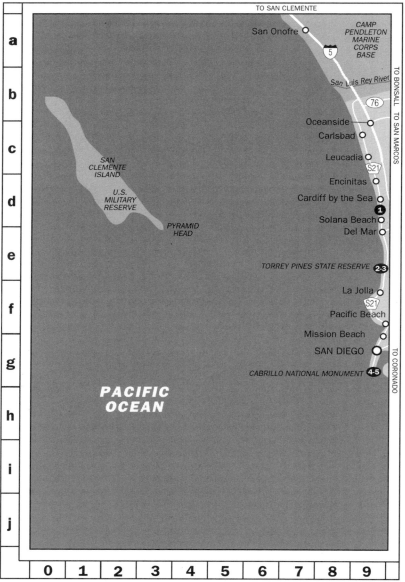

TO SAN CLEMENTE

San Onofre

CAMP PENDLETON MARINE CORPS BASE

San Luis Rey River

TO BONSALL
TO SAN MARCOS

76

Oceanside
Carlsbad
Leucadia
S21
Encinitas
Cardiff by the Sea
Solana Beach
Del Mar

SAN CLEMENTE ISLAND

U.S. MILITARY RESERVE

PYRAMID HEAD

TORREY PINES STATE RESERVE

La Jolla
S21
Pacific Beach
Mission Beach
SAN DIEGO

TO CORONADO

CABRILLO NATIONAL MONUMENT

PACIFIC OCEAN

❶ San Elijo Lagoon

2.5 mi/1.25 hrs

Location: In Solana Beach; map J5, grid d9.

User groups: Hikers and dogs. No horses or mountain bikes. No wheelchair facilities.

Permits: No permits are required. Parking and access are free.

Directions: From Interstate 5 in Solana Beach, take the Lomas Santa Fe Drive exit and drive west to North Rios Avenue. Turn right and go eight-tenths of a mile to the end of the road and the trailhead. Park alongside the road.

Maps: To obtain a topographic map of the area, ask for Encinitas from the USGS.

Contact: San Elijo Lagoon Ecological Reserve, San Diego County Parks and Recreation Department, 5201 Ruffin Road, Suite P, San Diego, CA 92123; (619) 694-3049. Or San Elijo Lagoon Conservancy at (760) 436-3944.

Trail notes: San Elijo Lagoon is bordered by Interstate 5, Highway 101, and a whole bunch of housing developments and shopping centers, but, amazingly, the birds don't seem to mind. The ecological preserve is sandwiched between Lomas Santa Fe Avenue and Manchester Avenue in Solana Beach, and when you first see it, it's hard to imagine hiking so close to the freeways and roads. But suspend your disbelief for a while and pay a vist to the lagoon, which is a mixture of freshwater from inland creeks and saltwater from the ocean. The Lomas Santa Fe side is a little more wild than the Manchester Avenue side, and the trails are longer, so it's the preferred side for hiking. A gated fire road leads down to the lagoon from the end of Lomas Sante Fe, and you can hike either right or left. There are tons of white egrets to be seen, as well as stilts, gulls, and godwits. Great blue herons occasionally make an appearance, and as you wander inland, you'll see many songbirds among the chaparral. Interpretive signs explain about saltwater and freshwater marshes, coastal sage scrub, and the wildlife who live in these communities. If you travel the east side of the trail, when you near Interstate 5 you'll reach a series of slot canyons in the sandstone, with cliffs that are 60 feet high. Hey, are you sure we're still in the city?

❷ Guy Fleming Loop Trail

0.75 mi/0.5 hr

Location: In Torrey Pines State Reserve near Del Mar; map J5, grid e9.

User groups: Hikers and wheelchairs. No dogs, horses, or mountain bikes.

Permits: No permits are required. A $4 day-use fee is charged per vehicle.

Directions: From Interstate 5 in Del Mar, take the Carmel Valley Road exit and drive west for 1.5 miles. Turn south on Torrey Pines Road and drive 1.7 miles to the reserve entrance. Drive up the hill and park at the first parking area on the right, signed for the Guy Fleming Trail. (If this lot is full, you can park further up the hill at the visitor center and walk back down the road.)

Maps: A free map of Torrey Pines State Reserve is available at the park visitor center. To obtain a topographic map of the area, ask for Del Mar from the USGS.

Contact: Torrey Pines State Reserve, 12000 North Torrey Pines Park Road, San Diego, CA 92008; (619) 755-2063.

Trail notes: Torrey Pines is one of the greatest hiking destinations in San Diego, with several short but sweet trails and enough spectacular scenery to keep you coming back for more. The Guy Fleming Loop Trail is the easiest of the trails in the park, with almost no elevation change, so it's suitable for all levels of hikers. The path has great views of the Pacific Ocean, La Jolla, Del Mar, and Los Peñasquitos Marsh. If you hike the right side of the loop first, you come to the North Overlook, where you can check out the vistas as well as San Diego's rare tree, the Torrey pine. The trail then loops around to the South Overlook, where you can sometimes see San Clemente and Catalina Islands. People frequently hold weddings at the South Overlook. If they're smart, they plan them for spring, when the wild-flowers bloom along the trail.

❸ Razor Point and Beach Trail Loop

3.5 mi/2.0 hrs

Location: In Torrey Pines State Reserve near Del Mar; map J5, grid e9.

User groups: Hikers only. No dogs, horses, or mountain bikes. No wheelchair facilities.

Permits: No permits are required. A $4 day-use fee is charged per vehicle.

Directions: From Interstate 5 in Del Mar, take the Carmel Valley Road exit and drive west for 1.5 miles. Turn south on Torrey Pines Road and drive 1.7 miles to the reserve entrance. Drive up the hill and park by the reserve office and visi-tor center. The trailhead is across the park road from the visitor center.

Maps: A free map of Torrey Pines State Reserve is available at the park visitor center. To obtain a topographic map of the area, ask for Del Mar from the USGS.

Contact: Torrey Pines State Reserve, 12000 North Torrey Pines Park Road, San Diego, CA 92008; (619) 755-2063.

Trail notes: If you can get a parking spot in the lot by the visitor center at Torrey Pines State Reserve (it's not easy on weekend afternoons), you can start hiking right away on the Razor Point Trail, then cut over to the Beach Trail from Razor Point and head to the beach. Razor Point Trail provides dramatic views of the reserve's eroded coastal badlands, which would look like something straight out of the desert if it wasn't for the ocean beyond. There's a spider web of paths, only some of which are signed, but it's fine to just wander around at random and visit as many of the overlooks as possible. Windswept Torrey pines grace the bluffs, and wildflowers

bloom in the sandy soil in springtime. When you're in the mood, head north from Razor Point (paralleling the ocean) until you hook up with the Beach Trail, then turn right and squeeze through the narrow, steep sandstone entrance to the beach. It's great fun. A return uphill on the Beach Trail makes an excellent loop.

❹ Bayside Trail

2.0 mi/1.0 hr

Location: In Cabrillo National Monument; map J5, grid g9.

User groups: Hikers only. No dogs, horses, or mountain bikes. No wheelchair facilities.

Permits: No permits are required. A $4 day-use fee is charged per vehicle.

Directions: From Interstate 5 in San Diego, take the Rosecrans Street exit (Highway 209) and drive south. Staying on Highway 209, you will turn right on Cannon Street, then left on Catalina Boulevard. The road ends at Cabrillo National Monument. The trail begins by the old lighthouse.

Maps: A free map/brochure of Cabrillo National Monument is available at the entrance kiosk or visitor center. To obtain a topographic map of the area, ask for Point Loma from the USGS.

Contact: Cabrillo National Monument, 1800 Cabrillo Memorial Drive, P.O. Box 6670, San Diego, CA 92106; (619) 557-5450.

Trail notes: While everybody else at Cabrillo National Monument is visiting the old Point Loma Lighthouse, or having their picture taken by the statue of Señor Cabrillo, or checking out the wonderful view of San Diego from the visi-tor center buildings, you can sneak off for a hike on the Bayside Trail and find a surprising amount of solitude. Luckily plenty of gorgeous coastal vistas come with the solitude, as well as an interesting lesson in native coastal vegetation.

Take the paved trail from the parking lot to the lighthouse, where you can peer inside at the pe-riod furniture and imagine what life was like for the lighthouse keeper and his family at the turn of the century. Then check out the great views from the overlooks on the far side of the light-house. After this short tour, pick up the paved road on the east side of the lighthouse, which is signed as Bayside Trail. Take the left fork, which is gravel, and wind gently downhill around Point Loma, occasionally tearing your eyes away from the view so you can read the interpretive signs. If you do, you'll learn all about coastal sage scrub and local and migrating birds. On every step of the trail, the whole of San Diego Bay and the Pacific Ocean are yours to survey. You'll see huge navy ships sailing out to sea, flocks of seagulls following the fishing boats back into harbor, sailboats, Jet skiers, and large offshore kelp beds. The trail ends directly below the statue of Cabrillo (about 400 feet below), where a sign says "Trail ends—Return by the same route." Darn. We had no interest in leaving.

pools, because the center has some great free handouts on how to explore the pools and identify the various creatures who live there. Even more importantly, you should check your tide table before you visit, or else your hike may be very, very short. A fenced trail leads along the blufftops for a few hundred feet, but then you descend to the rocky beach and walk as far as you please. What will you see? Most likely, you'll get a peek at mussels, crabs, abalones, barnacles, starfish, anemones, snails, and limpets. If you're lucky, you might see an octopus or a sea urchin. Is it wintertime? Why, we believe a passing gray whale just waved her flipper at you.

❺ Cabrillo Tide Pools

1.0 mi/0.5 hr

Location: In Cabrillo National Monument; map J5, grid g9.

User groups: Hikers and dogs. No horses or mountain bikes. No wheelchair facilities.

Permits: No permits are required. A $4 day-use fee is charged per vehicle.

Directions: From Interstate 5 in San Diego, take the Rosecrans Street exit (Highway 209) and drive south. Staying on Highway 209, you will turn right on Cannon Street, then left on Catalina Boulevard, and continue to the monument entrance. After paying the entrance fee at the kiosk, take the right fork (immediately following the kiosk) that is signed as "Tide pools Parking Area." Continue down the hill to the parking area.

Maps: A free map/brochure of Cabrillo National Monument is available at the entrance kiosk or visitor center. To obtain a topographic map of the area, ask for Point Loma from the USGS.

Contact: Cabrillo National Monument, 1800 Cabrillo Memorial Drive, P.O. Box 6670, San Diego, CA 92106; (619) 557-5450.

Trail notes: We love tide pools, and the ones at Cabrillo National Monument are some of the best in Southern California. You might want to stop in at the Cabrillo National Monument visitor center before you head straight for the tide

Map J6

Adjoining Maps: East: J7 ..... *page* 644   West: J5 622
North: I6 600

Southern California Map .... *page* 558

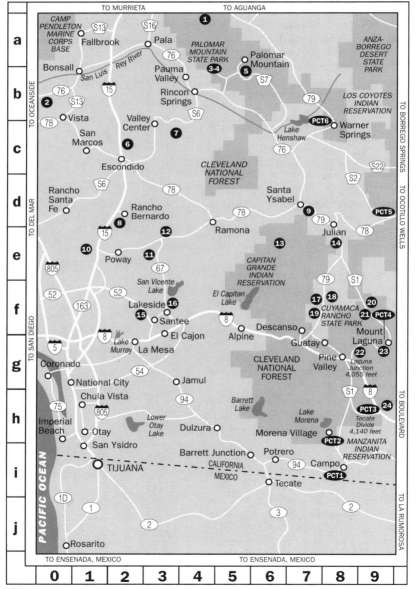

❶ Dripping Springs Trail

13.6 mi/2.0 days

Location: In the Aqua Tibia Wilderness; map J6, grid a4.

User groups: Hikers, dogs, and horses. No mountain bikes. No wheelchair facilities.

Permits: A free wilderness permit is required for overnight stays; you can obtain one at the Dripping Springs station near the campground or from the Palomar Ranger District at the address below. Day users should sign the register at the trailhead. A national forest recreation pass is required for each vehicle; fees are $5 for one day or $30 for a year.

Directions: From Interstate 15 in Temecula, take the Highway 79 east exit. Drive 10 miles east on Highway 79 to Dripping Springs Campground on the right. The trail begins at the south end of the campground.

Maps: For a map of Cleveland National Forest, send $4 to USDA-Forest Service, 630 Sansome Street, San Francisco, CA 94111. To obtain a topographic map of the area, ask for Vail Lake from the USGS.

Contact: Cleveland National Forest, Palomar Ranger District, 1634 Black Canyon Road, Ramona, CA 92065; (760) 788-0250.

Trail notes: At the very northern edge of San Diego County lies the Aqua Tibia Wilderness, a land of extreme summer heat, exposed slopes, no available water sources, and thick chaparral. The place appears suitable for only the most steadfast of hikers. Or so it seems. Actually, if you hike the Dripping Springs Trail in the spring, when the temperature is just right, the Aqua Tibia is a pastoral place with blooming shrubs and wildflowers, crystal-clear vistas, and flitting butterflies and bees. (Forget hiking in winter, though; these mountains are often covered in snow.) Trailhead elevation at Dripping Springs Campground is 1,600 feet, and the peak of Aqua Tibia Mountain is at 4,547 feet. The trail leaves the campground and crosses the rocky wash of

Arroyo Seco Creek, then starts to climb. In the first three miles of trail, you get views of Vail Lake to the north, then the big mountains of Southern California—San Jacinto, San Gorgonio, and San Antonio (Baldy). Another mile passes and you can see the white dome of Palomar Observatory to the south. The chaparral gets taller as you go, and the trail gets steeper and narrower. When you finally near the peak of Aqua Tibia Mountain, you've climbed out of the chaparral and into oak woodland with a few scattered pines, which means—yes!—shade.

❷ Guajome Lake Trail

2.0 mi/1.0 hr

Location: In Guajome Regional Park near Oceanside; map J6, grid b0.

User groups: Hikers, dogs, horses, and mountain bikes. No wheelchair facilities.

Permits: No permits are required. A $1 day-use fee is charged per vehicle.

Directions: From Interstate 5 in Oceanside, take the Mission Avenue and Highway 76 exit and drive east for seven miles to Guajome Lake Drive. Turn right (south) into the park entrance.

Maps: To obtain a topographic map of the area, ask for San Luis Rey from the USGS.

Contact: Guajome Regional Park, c/o San Diego County Parks and Recreation, 5201 Ruffin Road, Suite P, San Diego, CA 92123; (619) 694-3049.

Trail notes: As you drive into Guajome Regional Park, a prominent sign reads, "No piñatas." Geez, don't these guys have a sense of humor? Guess not. Anyway, Guajome Regional Park is home to one of the richest riparian areas of any of San Diego County's parks. The big draw is a spring-fed lake and marsh, which have enticed 144 species of birds to visit the park. The waterways also entice frogs, which you will hear but probably not see. In fact, "Guajome" means "home of the frog." The park's main hiking trail leads from the parking lot and goes around mid-sized Guajome Lake, up to the park's wedding gazebo, and alongside Guajome Marsh. Equestrian trails also lead into the drier grassland and chaparral areas of the park, but most hikers stay near the water. An out-and-back trip will cover about two miles, and along the way, you might

see a few red-winged blackbirds, or a white-faced ibis, or even the rare least bell's vireo. Fishing is also popular in Guajome Lake, for bullheads, crappie, catfish, and sunfish.

❸ Weir and Lower Doane Valley Loop

3.0 mi/1.5 hrs

Location: In Palomar Mountain State Park; map J6, grid b4.

User groups: Hikers only. No dogs, horses, or mountain bikes. No wheelchair facilities.

Permits: No permits are required. A $5 day-use fee is charged per vehicle.

Directions: From Interstate 15 north of Escondido, drive east on Highway 76 for 21 miles. Turn left (north) on Road S6 (South Grade Road) and drive 6.5 miles to where it junctions with Road S7. Turn left on Road S7 and drive three miles into the park. Drive past park headquarters, turn right and drive to the parking area by Doane Pond and the school camp.

Maps: A map of Palomar State Park is available for $1 at the entrance station or park headquarters. To obtain topographic maps of the area, ask for Boucher Hill and Palomar Observatory from the USGS.

Contact: Palomar Mountain State Park, P.O. Box 175, Palomar Mountain, CA 92060; (760) 742-3462.

Trail notes: If you've never visited before, Palomar Mountain State Park is like a shock to your system—a good shock. At 5,500 feet in elevation, the air is cool, the conifers are big, and suburban sprawl seems far, far away. We kept shaking our heads in disbelief at the Sierra Nevada-like feel of the place. A good introduction to the park is this loop hike on three trails: the Doane Valley Nature Trail, the Weir Trail, and the Lower Doane Valley Trail. From the parking area at Doane Pond (which is always busy with children learning to fish), head away from Doane Pond on the trail that crosses the park road. Start your walk on the Doane Valley Nature Trail, then veer left onto the Weir Trail, and follow pretty Doane Creek under the shade of big pines, firs, and cedars. Cross the creek about one mile out (shortly after the left fork for the Baptist Trail), then follow the Lower Doane Valley Trail as it loops back around a meadow. You'll probably see deer and mountain quail, and hear many bird calls. You'll certainly see the evidence of resident woodpeckers in the big old trees. When the trail nears Doane Valley Campground, cross the creek again and make a sharp switchback to the right on the Doane Valley Nature Trail. The nature trail will close out your trip, bringing you back to the trailhead in three-quarters of a mile. Along the way, as you pass the giant conifers and grassy meadows, you will ask yourself again and again, "Is this really San Diego?"

❹ Boucher Trail and Scott's Cabin Loop

4.0 mi/2.0 hrs

Location: In Palomar Mountain State Park; map J6, grid b4.

User groups: Hikers only. No dogs, horses, or mountain bikes. No wheelchair facilities.

Permits: No permits are required. A $5 day-use fee is charged per vehicle.

Directions: From Interstate 15 north of Escondido, drive east on Highway 76 for 21 miles. Turn left (north) on Road S6 (South Grade Road) and drive 6.5 miles to where it junctions with Road S7. Turn left on Road S7 and drive three miles into the park. Drive past park headquarters, then bear left at the sign for Boucher Lookout. Park at the lookout and begin hiking on the Boucher Trail.

Maps: A map of Palomar State Park is available for $1 at the entrance station or park headquarters. To obtain topographic maps of the area, ask for Boucher Hill and Palomar Observatory from the USGS.

Contact: Palomar Mountain State Park, P.O. Box 175, Palomar Mountain, CA 92060; (760) 742-3462.

Trail notes: You may be wowed by the view of Pauma Valley from the Boucher Lookout at elevation 5,438 feet, but start walking on the Boucher Trail and you'll be wowed even more. The trail descends from the lookout, passing meadows, oaks, dogwoods, and conifers, and dropping 600 feet as it crosses Nate Harrison Grade (a road) and heads for Cedar Grove Camp-

ground. The camp is well named; the cedars are huge and memorable here. Bear right at the fork by the campground, walk a brief stretch on the camp road, then cross the park road to pick up the Scott's Cabin Trail, which leads to the cabin site of an 1880s homesteader. Only the base of the cabin remains. From the site, take the right fork to head back to park headquarters and the Silver Crest Picnic Area, then walk to your right on the park road for a few hundred yards until you can pick up the Boucher Trail once more and walk back to the lookout. (Here the Boucher Trail is the narrow trail that runs between the legs of the driving loop to the lookout.) What? You say you forgot your troubles along the way? That's what happens here at Palomar Mountain.

❺ Observatory Trail

4.4 mi/2.5 hrs

Location: In Cleveland National Forest on Palomar Mountain; map J6, grid b5.

User groups: Hikers, dogs, horses, and mountain bikes. No wheelchair facilities.

Permits: No permits are required. A national forest recreation pass is required for each vehicle; fees are $5 for one day or $30 for a year.

Directions: From Interstate 15 north of Escondido, drive east on Highway 76 for 21 miles. Turn left (north) on Road S6 (South Grade Road) and drive 6.5 miles to where it junctions with Road S7, then continue north on Road S6 for three more miles to Observatory Campground on the right. Drive through the camp to the signed parking area for the amphitheater and trailhead.

Maps: For a map of Cleveland National Forest, send $4 to USDA-Forest Service, 630 Sansome Street, San Francisco, CA 94111. To obtain a topographic map of the area, ask for Palomar Observatory from the USGS.

Contact: Cleveland National Forest, Palomar Ranger District, 1634 Black Canyon Road, Ramona, CA 92065; (760) 788-0250.

Trail notes: The question: Is the Palomar Observatory as great as everybody says? The answer: Yes. And the hike to reach it is far better than the drive to reach it. Even if you have absolutely no interest in astronomy whatsoever, the National Recreation Trail to Palomar Observatory is just plain fun to hike. From Observatory Campground, the trail is an aerobic uphill climb, but on a well-graded, well-maintained trail with only a 600-foot elevation gain. The shade is dense from oaks and pines, and you'll find many giant-sized pine cones along the trail. A half mile up you reach an overlook platform with a lovely view of Mendenhall Valley, then head back into the forest to climb some more. The last stretch of trail brings you out to the observatory parking lot, where you turn right, walk through the lot and past the museum, and head straight for the big white golf ball which is the 200-inch Hale telescope. If you like, hike up the couple flights of stairs to the telescope viewing area, and learn all about how the thing works. Think about this: More than 100 billion galaxies like ours are within spotting range of the giant telescope.

❻ Jack Creek Nature Trail

1.0 mi/0.5 hr

Location: In the Dixon Lake Recreation Area near Escondido; map J6, grid c2.

User groups: Hikers and dogs. No horses or mountain bikes. No wheelchair facilities.

Permits: No permits are required. A $1 day-use fee is charged per vehicle on weekends only.

Directions: From Escondido, drive north on Interstate 15 and take the El Norte Parkway exit. Drive 3.1 miles east on El Norte Parkway, then turn left (north) on La Honda Drive, and drive 1.3 miles to the Dixon Lake entrance on the right. The trailhead is located directly across from the park entrance. Park by the playground/picnic area to the right of the park entrance, signed as Hilltop Picnic Area.

Maps: To obtain a topographic map of the area, ask for Valley Center from the USGS.

Contact: Dixon Lake Ranger Station, 201 North Broadway, Escondido, CA 92025; (760) 741-4680.

Trail notes: If you are exceptionally lucky, it will be a rainy year in San Diego and you can see the waterfall flow along Jack Creek at Dixon Lake Recreation Area. We've only seen it trickle, but we've seen pictures of the 20-foot fall at "flood," and it's quite beautiful. Nonetheless, a

stroll on the half-mile Jack Creek Nature Trail is good in any season, although best in winter and spring when the hills are green and the flowers in bloom. The trail begins by Dixon Lake's entrance station, and travels through a picnic area and along Jack Creek to the lake's edge. You can pick up an interpretive brochure at the trailhead or the park ranger station, or just march off boldly without one. Be on the alert: Many cute bunnies are likely to cross your path. (They are western cottontails, to be precise.) If the creek is flowing strong, be sure to take the right spur to the waterfall's base; otherwise just head straight for the lake. At the water's edge, the trail connects to the Shoreline Trail and Grand View Trail, which is useful if you're in the mood to hike more. Many people instead choose to plunk a line in the water, then see if they can catch a largemouth bass, rainbow trout, or catfish.

❼ Hellhole Canyon

3.0 mi/1.5 hrs

Location: In Hellhole Canyon Preserve; map J6, grid c2.

User groups: Hikers, dogs, horses, and mountain bikes. No wheelchair facilities.

Permits: No permits are required. Parking and access are free.

Directions: From Interstate 15 south of Temecula, take Highway 76 east for 15 miles, then turn right (south) on Road S6, Valley Center Road. Drive five miles, then turn left on North Lake Wohlford Road. Drive two miles, then turn left on Paradise Mountain Road. Drive 3.3 miles to a T-intersection, where you turn right on Los Hermanos Ranch Road and then immediately left on Kiavo Road. Drive a half mile on Kiavo Road to the park entrance. (Coming from Escondido and points south, take the Valley Parkway exit and drive northeast on Road S6 to Lake Wohlford Road. Take Lake Wohlford Road to Paradise Mountain Road and follow directions as above.)

Maps: To obtain a topographic map of the area, ask for Rodriguez Mountain from the USGS.

Contact: Hellhole Canyon Preserve, c/o San Diego County Parks and Recreation Department, 5201 Ruffin Road, Suite P, San Diego, CA 92123; (619) 694-3049.

Trail notes: Hellhole Canyon Preserve seems a bit misnamed. We didn't think there was anything hellish about it, except maybe the heat on an August afternoon. The preserve takes up 1,700 acres on the west flank of Rodriguez Mountain, and is bounded by Indian reservations to the north and south. The rocky land is covered in typical San Diego chaparral—redberry, manzanita, lilac, monkeyflower—which means no shade, of course. Only five miles of trail have so far been built in the preserve, although more are in the works. In the meantime, you can hike from the trailhead (behind the rest rooms at the parking lot) heading downhill into the canyon. The main trail branches off to three different viewpoints, with a loop connecting the two on the right and the left one off by itself, making an out-and-back trip necessary. Take the right loop. As you walk, you'll be surprised to find that the chaparral is often taller than you are, which creates a labyrinth effect. It's kind of fun, and the best part is the sense of solitude you get. One mile down the trail, you'll reach Hell Creek, which runs with vigor in the wet season.

❽ Blue Sky Ecological Preserve

4.0 mi/2.0 hrs

Location: In the Blue Sky Ecological Preserve near Poway; map J6, grid d2.

User groups: Hikers, dogs, and horses. No mountain bikes. No wheelchair facilities.

Permits: No permits are required. Parking and access are free.

Directions: From Interstate 15 near Poway, drive north to the Rancho Bernardo Road exit. Drive east for 3.3 miles on Rancho Bernardo Road; the reserve is on the left, at the junction of Rancho Bernardo Road and Espola Road.

Maps: To obtain a topographic map of the area, ask for Escondido from the USGS.

Contact: Blue Sky Ecological Preserve, P.O. Box 724, Poway, CA 92074; (619) 486-7238. Or the Department of Fish and Game, (310) 590-4808.

Trail notes: The Blue Sky Ecological Preserve provides habitat for several rare and threatened animal and plant species, including harried San Diego humans who desperately need a place to stop and smell the flowers. It's good for the San Diego horned lizard, it's good for the Engelmann oaks, it's good for people who live in the Poway area. From the trailhead, hike along the wide, flat fire road, ignoring the first two turnoffs. At the third junction, turn right to pay a visit to Lake Poway. The lake is a fine place to catch catfish and trout (they get planted every two weeks), or a fine place to rent a rowboat and row your hiking partner around the lake. You can also hike around the perimeter of the lake, which will add some climbing and descending to your basically flat route. Then retrace your steps back to the main preserve trail and head back to the trailhead for a four-mile round-trip. If you want to see more, continue on the main trail to the left fork for Lake Ramona. So, how do the flowers smell? Pretty good, we thought.

❾ Inaja Memorial Trail

0.5 mi/0.5 hr

Location: In Cleveland National Forest near Santa Ysabel; map J6, grid d7.

User groups: Hikers and dogs. No horses or mountain bikes. No wheelchair facilities (except at the picnic area).

Permits: No permits are required. A national forest recreation pass is required for each vehicle; fees are $5 for one day or $30 for a year.

Directions: From Julian, drive northwest on Highway 78/79 for six miles (to one mile south of Santa Ysabel). The Inaja Picnic Area and Trailhead is on the south (left) side of the road.

Maps: For a map of Cleveland National Forest, send $4 to USDA-Forest Service, 630 Sansome Street, San Francisco, CA 94111. To obtain a topographic map of the area, ask for Santa Ysabel from the USGS.

Contact: Cleveland National Forest, Palomar Ranger District, 1634 Black Canyon Road, Ramona, CA 92065; (760) 788-0250.

Trail notes: At 3,200 feet in elevation, you can look down a long way into the steep canyon of the San Diego River. That's what you get here on the Inaja Memorial National Recreation Trail, a short but interesting trail that begins at the Inaja Picnic Area. In places, there are steps built along the trail, as the path undulates up and down along the canyon edge, amid various types of chaparral. If you pick up an interpretive brochure at the trailhead, you can learn about live oaks, scrub oaks, wild lilac, toyon, manzanita, and chamise, as well as the granitic rocks of this area. The trail's highlights are the views of both the Santa Ysabel Valley and the Volcan Mountains near Julian. The picnic area and trail have an interesting history: They were named to honor the 11 firefighters who lost their lives in the 60,000-acre Inaja forest fire of 1956.

⑩ Los Peñasquitos Canyon

6.5 mi/3.0 hrs

Location: In Los Peñasquitos Canyon Preserve near Poway; map J6, grid e1.

User groups: Hikers, dogs, horses, and mountain bikes. No wheelchair facilities.

Permits: No permits are required. Parking and access are free.

Directions: From Escondido, drive south on Interstate 15 for 16 miles to the Mercy Road exit. Turn right (west) on Mercy Road and follow it for one mile, crossing Black Mountain Road, to the trailhead parking area.

Maps: To obtain a topographic map of the area, ask for Poway from the USGS.

Contact: Los Peñasquitos Canyon Preserve, c/o San Diego County Parks and Recreation Department, 5201 Ruffin Road, Suite P, San Diego, CA 92123; (619) 694-3049.

Trail notes: If it's winter or spring, and your thoughts are turning to love, there may be no better spot in San Diego for a first date than Los Peñasquitos Canyon Preserve. The trail that runs from one end of the canyon to the other is wide and flat, perfectly built for good conversation and maybe a little hand-holding. If the cascades along the creek are flowing, you can find a big volcanic boulder to sit on and watch the reflections of the sky in the water. If not, there are numerous places where you could lay out a picnic under a spreading oak tree, then sit and watch the birds fly past. Early in the year, the wildflowers bloom and the grasses become verdant. Can this much beauty be found so close to a large urban area? You bet. Although you can hike the trail through the canyon starting from either end, the eastern trailhead near Poway is preferred, because the path is more shaded. As you wander, keep watching for mileage marker 3.0, because soon after it you'll see a hitching post and bike rack on the right, where you can head off-trail and scramble down to the cascades on Los Peñasquitos Creek. Even when the stream is reduced to a trickle, the car-sized boulders in the creek are fascinating to look at.

⑪ Sycamore Canyon Preserve

2.5 mi/1.25 hrs

Location: In Sycamore Canyon Preserve; map J6, grid e2.

User groups: Hikers, dogs, horses, and mountain bikes. No wheelchair facilities.

Permits: No permits are required. Parking and access are free.

Directions: From Poway, drive east on Poway Road to Garden Road. Turn right and drive one mile on Garden Road, then turn right on Sycamore Canyon Road. Drive 2.5 miles to the road's end at a gate (the last 1.5 miles are dirt).

Maps: To obtain a topographic map of the area, ask for San Vicente Reservoir from the USGS.

Contact: Sycamore Canyon Preserve, c/o San Diego County Parks and Recreation Department, 5201 Ruffin Road, Suite P, San Diego, CA 92123; (619) 694-3049.

Trail notes: Are you looking for a good spot to watch the sun set, but you don't feel like braving the traffic to the beach? A trip to Sycamore Canyon Preserve could be just the ticket. The terrain is coastal sage scrub, chaparral, and oak woodland—no surprises here—but the path leads into beautiful canyons and offers wide vistas. The preserve's trails are well maintained, and even have hand-painted signs with maps at major intersections. From the parking lot, take the winding single-track trail through the chaparral, heading down through Martha's Grove (a group of old and lovely oak trees), and then head out into the grasslands. Turn right on the fire road, and then right again to loop back. Note that this is only one of many possible loops in the preserve, so if you want to hike longer, it's easy to add on a few miles. Also, although the preserve is extremely popular with mountain bikers, the ones we met were extremely courteous and friendly to hikers.

⑫ Mount Woodson

3.6 mi/2.0 hrs

Location: Near Poway; map J6, grid e3.

User groups: Hikers only. No dogs, horses, or mountain bikes. No wheelchair facilities.

Permits: No permits are required. Parking and access are free.

Directions: From Poway, drive east on Poway Road for 3.5 miles and turn north on Highway 67. Drive three miles to the Ramona CDF Fire Station on the left. The trail begins by the fire station, but you will have to park across the road.

Maps: To obtain a topographic map of the area, ask for San Pasqual from the USGS.

Contact: City of Poway, Lake Poway Recreation Area, (619) 679-4393.

Trail notes: Mount Woodson is the neighborhood summit to climb for the thousands of people who live in the Poway, Scripps Ranch, and Rancho Bernardo areas. The light-colored, rocky mountain is always there, in the background, looming over the suburbs below, a favorite playground of rock climbers from all over San Diego. If you've never seen Mount Woodson except from the bottom looking up, maybe it's time to lace up your hiking boots. The trail has a 1,500-foot elevation gain to reach the 2,894-foot peak, so you'll get in your workout for the day, but you won't be so wiped out that you can't enjoy the vistas, or the fascinating giant boulders you'll pass along the trail. Hike on the path south of the fire station and then follow the paved Mount Woodson Road. You'll reach the top at 1.8 miles, where a ton of electronic equipment is in place. Wander around a bit on the ridge till you find the best spot to look out over the wide blue Pacific, and congratulate yourself for having "bagged" Mount Woodson's peak.

⑬ Cedar Creek Falls

4.0 mi/2.0 hrs

Location: In Cleveland National Forest near Julian; map J6, grid e6.

User groups: Hikers, dogs, horses, and mountain bikes. No wheelchair facilities.

Permits: No permits are required. A national forest recreation pass is required for each vehicle; fees are $5 for one day or $30 for a year.

Directions: From Julian, drive two miles west on Highway 78/79, then turn left (south) on Pine Hills Road. In 1.5 miles, bear right on Eagle Peak Road. In 1.4 miles, bear right again, staying on Eagle Peak Road. Continue for eight miles on partly paved, partly dirt road to the signed Forest Service trailhead for the California Riding and Hiking Trail. (The road gets rough after the first four miles, but it's usually suitable for a passenger car.)

Maps: For a map of Cleveland National Forest, send $4 to USDA-Forest Service, 630 Sansome Street, San Francisco, CA 94111. To obtain a topographic map of the area, ask for Santa Ysabel from the USGS.

Contact: Cleveland National Forest, Palomar Ranger District, 1634 Black Canyon Road, Ramona, CA 92065; (760) 788-0250.

Trail notes: Cedar Creek Falls is no secret among San Diego hikers, since the trailhead is well signed and is an access point for the California Riding and Hiking Trail. But if you get up early on a winter or spring morning, you can probably be the first person at the waterfall and have it all to yourself for a while. Begin by hiking to the right and downhill on the wide fire road, enjoying good views of the far-off San Diego River Canyon, as well as colorful spring wildflowers on the slopes alongside the road. At 1.2 miles, you'll reach an unsigned left fork, where you should bear left and hike up and over a small hill. On the far side, you'll see three possible trail options; take the middle route for the most direct path to the falls. You'll come out upstream of the 100-foot freefall, at a series of clear pools under the shade of cottonwoods. Be very careful as you approach the lip of the waterfall; it has a sheer drop and the granite is deadly slick. You cannot descend to the falls' base (in addition to being too dangerous, it's private property), but you can cautiously make your way around the side of the falls for the best possible view. Then settle in at one of the upstream pools for sunning and swimming.

Note that although Cedar Creek flows year-round, the fall is most spectacular during San Diego's brief rainy season, so plan your trip accordingly.

⑭ Desert View and Canyon Oak Loop

3.5 mi/2.0 hrs

Location: In William Heise County Park near Julian; map J6, grid e7.

User groups: Hikers, horses, and mountain bikes. No dogs. No wheelchair facilities.

Permits: No permits are required. Parking and access are free.

Directions: From Julian, drive two miles west on Highway 78/79, then turn left (south) on Pine Hills Road. Drive two miles, then turn left on Frisius Drive and drive two more miles. Frisius Drive turns into Heise Park Road and enters the park. From the park entrance kiosk, continue straight on the park road and drive all the way to its end at the tent camping area, where the trailhead for the Desert View Trail is located.

Maps: A free map of William Heise County Park is available at the entrance station. To obtain a topographic map of the area, ask for Julian from the USGS.

Contact: William Heise County Park, c/o San Diego County Parks and Recreation Department, 5201 Ruffin Road, Suite P, San Diego, CA 92123; (619) 694-3049.

Trail notes: William Heise County Park is so pretty, so well run, and has such good hiking trails, we have to keep reminding ourselves that this is a county park and not a state park. We're not sure how they do it, but they really manage the park well, and it's clearly appreciated by the many campers and hikers who visit here regularly. The park is located near Julian at 4,000 feet in elevation, so the terrain is shady oak woodland with a few conifers mixed in—the transition zone between valley and mountains. The black oaks display gorgeous colors in the fall. From the tent camping area at the end of the park road, take the trail on the north side that is signed as "Nature Trail." Veer left almost immediately and head northeast to join the Canyon Oak Trail in a quarter mile. Bear left on the loop,

and circle around its 1.25-mile length through a lovely grove of oaks, then bear left on the Desert View Trail. Almost immediately you reach an overlook of the Anza-Borrego Desert and the Salton Sea, then continue along the ridge to Glen's View, where the vista includes not just the desert but also a sea of conifers and the Laguna Mountains. Wow? Yes, wow.

⑮ Cowles Mountain

3.0 mi/1.5 hrs

Location: In Mission Trails Regional Park; map J6, grid f3.

User groups: Hikers, dogs, and horses. No mountain bikes. No wheelchair facilities.

Permits: No permits are required. Parking and access are free.

Directions: From Interstate 15 south of Poway, take Highway 52 east for seven miles until it ends. Turn right on Mission Gorge Road and drive 2.5 miles, then turn left on Golfcrest Drive. Follow Golfcrest Drive to its intersection with Navajo Road, where the trailhead for Cowles Mountain Trailhead is located. (If you wish to go to the park visitor center first to get hiking information, continue past Golfcrest Drive on Mission Gorge Road and then turn right at the park entrance.)

Maps: To obtain a topographic map of the area, ask for La Mesa from the USGS.

Contact: Mission Trails Regional Park, One Father Junipero Serra Trail, San Diego, CA 92119; (619) 668-3275.

Trail notes: There are tons of trails to hike (and bike and horseback ride) in Mission Trails Regional Park. The visitor center alone provides enough entertainment to fill an entire afternoon—it's a huge, architecturally unique building with state-of-the-art displays, and it's better designed than many museums. But if you can only hike one trail in the park, you might as well go for the summit of Cowles Mountain, a 1,591-foot peak with a 360-degree view of the city. Cowles Mountain is the highest point in San Diego, they say, but they mean the city, not the county. Pick a cool day, because the trail is a wide, exposed fire road, with a 951-foot elevation gain to the summit. When you reach the top and you're looking out at the city below, think about the temporary state of all you survey, compared to the rock you're standing on, which is nearly 150 million years old. Hmm.

⑯ Silverwood Wildlife Sanctuary

1.5 mi/1.0 hr

Location: In the Silverwood Wildlife Sanctuary near Lakeside; map J6, grid f3.

User groups: Hikers only. No dogs, horses, or mountain bikes. No wheelchair facilities.

Permits: Hikers must sign in at the trailhead register. Parking and access are free.

Directions: From Interstate 8 in San Diego, drive east to Highway 67 near El Cajon. Drive north on Highway 67 to Lakeside, where you turn right on Mapleview Street. Drive a short distance, then turn left on Ashwood Street, which becomes Wildcat Canyon Road, and drive 4.8 miles to 13003 Wildcat Canyon Road.

Maps: To obtain a topographic map of the area, ask for San Vicente Reservoir from the USGS.

Contact: Silverwood Wildlife Sanctuary, 13003 Wildcat Canyon Road, Lakeside, CA 92040; (619) 443-2998.

Trail notes: The smartest thing you can do at the Silverwood Wildlife Sanctuary is show up on Sunday and take a guided walk with one of the Audubon Society's naturalists. These people really know their stuff, and they tailor the walk to the ability of the people who attend. On the other hand, if you want your sweet solitude, you can wander around Silverwood on your own, although there won't be anybody around to tell you the difference between a wrentit and a bushtit. Seven miles of hiking trails lace the preserve, which is home to over 240 plant species and 160 bird species. Start by heading straight from the parking lot to the bird observation area, where, in addition to watching birds, you can pick up a trail map. Then follow the Cienaga Trail to the Chaparral, Sunset, and Circuit Trails, making a short and easy 1.5-mile loop.

Special note: The Silverwood Wildlife Sanctuary is open to the public only on Sundays from 9 A.M. to 4 P.M. Guided walks are available every

Sunday at 10 A.M. and 1:30 P.M. The park is closed in August.

⑰ Cuyamaca Peak Trail

6.4 mi/3.5 hrs

Location: In Cuyamaca Rancho State Park; map J6, grid f7.

User groups: Hikers and horses. No dogs or mountain bikes. No wheelchair facilities.

Permits: No permits are required. A $5 day-use fee is charged per vehicle.

Directions: From San Diego, drive east on Interstate 8 for 40 miles to the Highway 79 exit. Drive north on Highway 79 for 11 miles, then turn left (west) at the sign for Paso Picacho Campground. The trail begins on the south end of the campground.

Maps: Various maps of Cuyamaca Rancho State Park are available for a fee at the park visitor center. To obtain a topographic map of the area, ask for Cuyamaca Peak from the USGS.

Contact: Cuyamaca Rancho State Park, 12551 Highway 79, Descanso, CA 91916; (760) 765-0755.

Trail notes: A 6,512-foot mountain in San Diego? Yup, here it is. Cuyamaca Peak is the undisputed king of the peaks in Cuyamaca Rancho State Park, and it's just shy of being the tallest summit in the county. (Hot Springs Mountain near Warner Springs stands at 6,533 feet.) The main trail to the summit is a paved road (closed to vehicle traffic). Luckily, many parts of the route are shaded by an assortment of hardwoods and conifers. Otherwise, the pavement would be brutal on a hot day. Halfway up, the trail passes Deer Spring, a popular spot for a rest and a drink. Catch your breath, then keep climbing. What do you see when you get to the top of Cuyamaca? Just about everything surrounding San Diego—the ocean, the desert, Mexico, and the Salton Sea. So what does Cuyamaca mean? Roughly, it's "place beyond the rain."

⑱ Stonewall Peak Trail

4.0 mi/2.0 hrs

Location: In Cuyamaca Rancho State Park; map J6, grid f7.

User groups: Hikers only. No dogs, horses, or mountain bikes. No wheelchair facilities.

Permits: No permits are required. A $5 day-use fee is charged per vehicle.

Directions: From San Diego, drive east on Interstate 8 for 40 miles to the Highway 79 exit. Drive north on Highway 79 for 11 miles, then look for Paso Picacho Campground on the left. The trail begins across the highway from the campground; park at the picnic area parking lot.

Maps: Various maps of Cuyamaca Rancho State Park are available for a fee at the park visitor center. To obtain a topographic map of the area, ask for Cuyamaca Peak from the USGS.

Contact: Cuyamaca Rancho State Park, 12551 Highway 79, Descanso, CA 91916; (760) 765-0755.

Trail notes: Although slightly dwarfed by neighboring Cuyamaca Peak, Stonewall Peak is no slouch in the summit department: Its peak stands at 5,730 feet in elevation. Stonewall Peak overlooks the site of the turn-of-the-century Stonewall Mine, as well as most of San Diego County, and has only a 900-foot elevation gain. About a million switchbacks whisk you to the summit, and about a million other hikers will likely join you on the trail, especially if it's a clear, not-too-warm day. But that's okay; everybody seems to be smiling as they ascend the well-graded path. Hike first through chaparral, then through oaks and incense cedars on the way to the rocky summit. (The oaks are gorgeous in the autumn.) The final 50-yard stretch is on an exposed stone ridge, with granite stair steps and a handrail keeping you from going over the edge. It makes you feel like you're climbing Half Dome. The view is grand, of course, taking in all the major peaks of the park as well as Lake Cuyamaca and the desert far to the east.

⑲ Green Valley Falls

1.5 mi/1.0 hr

Location: In Cuyamaca Rancho State Park; map J6, grid f7.

User groups: Hikers, horses, and mountain bikes. No dogs. No wheelchair facilities.

Permits: No permits are required. A $5 day-use fee is charged per vehicle.

Directions: From San Diego, drive east on Interstate 8 for 40 miles to the Highway 79 exit. Drive north on Highway 79 for seven miles, then turn left (west) at the sign for Green Valley Campground. Follow the signs to the picnic area. One sign points either straight ahead or to the left for the picnic area; continue straight to reach the trailhead.

Maps: Various maps of Cuyamaca Rancho State Park are available for a fee at the park visitor center. To obtain a topographic map of the area, ask for Cuyamaca Peak from the USGS.

Contact: Cuyamaca Rancho State Park, 12551 Highway 79, Descanso, CA 91916; (760) 765-0755.

Trail notes: If it's a hot afternoon in Cuyamaca Rancho State Park, chances are good that you won't be in the mood for climbing Cuyamaca or Stonewall Peaks (see trail notes for hikes 17 and 18). But if you're looking for a walk with a good payoff on a warm day, the trip to Green Valley Falls should do the trick. From the picnic area parking lot at Green Valley Campground, follow the wide fire road along the Sweetwater River to the cutoff for the falls, then hike downhill to your left. By summer, the river's cascades aren't terribly dramatic, but there are still many cool pools where you can soak your toes, and wide granite ledges where you can lay out a towel and lounge around on the rocks.

⑳ Garnet Peak

4.4 mi/2.5 hrs

Location: In the Laguna Mountain Recreation Area; map J6, grid f8.

User groups: Hikers, dogs, and horses. No mountain bikes. No wheelchair facilities.

Permits: No permits are required. A national forest recreation pass is required for each vehicle; fees are $5 for one day or $30 for a year.

Directions: From Julian, drive south on Highway 79 to the left fork for Road S1/Sunrise Scenic Byway. Bear left and drive south for about 12 miles to the Penny Pines Plantation, between mile markers 27.5 and 27.0. Park at the Penny Pines Plantation parking area.

Maps: For a map of Cleveland National Forest, send $4 to USDA-Forest Service, 630 Sansome

Street, San Francisco, CA 94111. To obtain a topographic map of the area, ask for Monument Peak from the USGS.

Contact: Cleveland National Forest, Descanso Ranger District, 3348 Alpine Boulevard, Alpine, CA 91901; (619) 445-6235.

Trail notes: The route to Garnet Peak begins on the Pacific Crest Trail at the Penny Pines Trailhead, where there is a picnic area for people who wish to explore the Penny Pines. (You can see the list of names of the good people who have donated funds to California's national forests for reforestation.) Follow the well-graded PCT to the north (left), heading through the pines. The trail has pleasantly little elevation gain, and it hugs the desert rim, offering views of the desert and Storm Canyon. When you turn right on the Garnet Peak Trail, the vistas really open wide. The path is rocky, but in less than a mile you reach the jagged, 5,900-foot summit, where you're rewarded with mind-boggling views of the Anza-Borrego Desert, Palomar Observatory, Mount San Jacinto and Mount San Gorgonio, the Laguna and Cuyamaca Mountains, and on and on. The desert floor is 5,000 feet below you, and it appears to be straight down. If you enjoyed the views from the Desert View Nature Trail (see trail notes for hike number 23), this summit vista will blow your mind. Total elevation gain on the trail? A mere 500 feet.

㉑ Lightning Ridge Trail

1.5 mi/1.0 hr

Location: In the Laguna Mountain Recreation Area; map J6, grid f8.

User groups: Hikers and dogs. No horses or mountain bikes. No wheelchair facilities.

Permits: No permits are required. A national forest recreation pass is required for each vehicle; fees are $5 for one day or $30 for a year.

Directions: From Julian, drive south on Highway 79 to the left fork for Road S1/Sunrise Scenic Byway. Bear left and drive south for approximately 13 miles to Laguna Campground on the right, between mile markers 26.5 and 26.0. Park at Laguna Campground near the amphitheater, where the trail begins.

Maps: For a map of Cleveland National Forest,

send $4 to USDA-Forest Service, 630 Sansome Street, San Francisco, CA 94111. To obtain a topographic map of the area, ask for Monument Peak from the USGS.

Contact: Cleveland National Forest, Descanso Ranger District, 3348 Alpine Boulevard, Alpine, CA 91901; (619) 445-6235.

Trail notes: The Lightning Ridge Trail is one of the show-and-tell trails of the Laguna Mountain Recreation Area, where you can get up high and get a clear view of how beautiful and unusual this high, cool mountain on the edge of the desert really is. The trail is easy enough for almost any hiker to accomplish, with only 250 feet of elevation gain. It begins at a stone monument and follows the edge of a meadow, then makes several long, sweeping switchbacks uphill through pines and oaks until it ends at a water tank at the top of the ridge. Laguna Meadows lies directly below, a beautiful sight in springtime. If you wander around on the ridge a bit, you'll find wide views of Anza-Borrego Desert and Storm Canyon. What's the best time to hike this trail? Unquestionably it's winter or spring—by Memorial Day the meadow grasses are often dry and brown. If you're lucky, you can walk this trail on a clear winter day when it's covered with a few inches of snow.

㉒ Cottonwood Creek Falls

2.0 mi/1.0 hr

Location: In the Laguna Mountain Recreation Area; map J6, grid g8.

User groups: Hikers, dogs, horses, and mountain bikes. No wheelchair facilities.

Permits: No permits are required. A national forest recreation pass is required for each vehicle; fees are $5 for one day or $30 for a year.

Directions: From San Diego, drive east on Interstate 8 for 47 miles to the Highway S1/Sunrise Scenic Byway turnoff. Drive north on Highway S1 for about two miles to the large pullout on the west side of the road, between mileposts 15.0 and 15.5. (It has an obvious, graffiti-covered rock wall.) Cross the road on foot, and locate the unmarked trail at the north end of the guardrail.

Maps: For a map of Cleveland National Forest, send $4 to USDA-Forest Service, 630 Sansome

Street, San Francisco, CA 94111. To obtain a topographic map of the area, ask for Mount Laguna from the USGS.

Contact: Cleveland National Forest, Descanso Ranger District, 3348 Alpine Boulevard, Alpine, CA 91901; (619) 445-6235.

Trail notes: If you don't have the time for the day hike to spectacular Kitchen Creek Falls (see hike number 24), this shorter trip to nearby Cottonwood Creek Falls is a close second choice for scenic beauty. With only a one-mile downhill walk, you'll quickly be exploring the many small waterfalls and big pools along Cottonwood Creek, or happily counting the bright pink flowers on the streamside cactus plants. The trail is unsigned at its start, and it usually appears overgrown with brush, but after about 100 yards of walking, the path widens and the downhill grade becomes less steep. When you reach the canyon bottom, which takes about 15 minutes, turn sharply left and walk alongside Cottonwood Creek, heading upstream. In just a few minutes you'll reach the first of several cascades, each about 12 feet high. Hike as far as you like, pick your favorite waterfall or pool, and have a seat alongside.

㉓ Desert View Nature Trail

1.2–3.0 mi/1–2 hrs

Location: In the Laguna Mountain Recreation Area; map J6, grid g9.

User groups: Hikers, dogs, horses, and mountain bikes. No wheelchair facilities.

Permits: No permits are required. A national forest recreation pass is required for each vehicle; fees are $5 for one day or $30 for a year.

Directions: From San Diego, drive east on Interstate 8 for 47 miles to the Highway S1/Sunrise Scenic Byway turnoff. Drive north on Highway S1 for about 10 miles to Burnt Rancheria Campground on the right, between mileposts 22.5 and 23.0. Park by the amphitheater at Burnt Rancheria Campground, where the trail begins.

Maps: For a map of Cleveland National Forest, send $4 to USDA-Forest Service, 630 Sansome Street, San Francisco, CA 94111. To obtain a topographic map of the area, ask for Mount Laguna from the USGS.

Contact: Cleveland National Forest, Descanso Ranger District, 3348 Alpine Boulevard, Alpine, CA 91901; (619) 445-6235.

Trail notes: Wow, what a view. If you've never stood on a conifer-covered mountain before and looked down on the vastness of the desert, your first time is something you'll always remember. That's what you get here on the Desert View Nature Trail, near the summit of Laguna Mountain. Start hiking from Burnt Rancheria Campground, heading east to the Pacific Crest Trail, then go north (left) along the mountain rim. The trail hugs the rim, which is perched on the edge of Anza-Borrego, providing awesome views of the desert floor 4,000 feet below you. On a clear day, you can see the Salton Sea shimmering in the distance. The trail makes a circle north to the Desert View Picnic Area, then returns through a shady forest of pines and oaks. If you hike the nature trail only, you'll have a 1.2-mile round-trip, but most people get so captivated by the views that they wind up walking a bit further on the Pacific Crest Trail to the north. It's so compelling, it's hard to stop.

㉔ Kitchen Creek Falls

4.5 mi/2.5 hrs

Location: In Cleveland National Forest near Pine Valley; map J6, grid h9.

User groups: Hikers, dogs, and horses. No mountain bikes. No wheelchair facilities.

Permits: No permits are required. A national forest recreation pass is required for each vehicle; fees are $5 for one day or $30 for a year.

Directions: From San Diego, drive east on Interstate 8 for 50 miles to the Buckman Springs Road turnoff. Drive south on the frontage road for 2.3 miles to the Boulder Oaks Store and Campground. (Stay on the frontage road; do not turn onto Buckman Springs Road.) Park across the road from the store, at the signed trailhead for the Pacific Crest Trail.

Maps: For a map of Cleveland National Forest, send $4 to USDA-Forest Service, 630 Sansome Street, San Francisco, CA 94111. To obtain a topographic map of the area, ask for Live Oak Springs from the USGS.

Contact: Cleveland National Forest, Descanso

Ranger District, 3348 Alpine Boulevard, Alpine, CA 91901; (619) 445-6235.

Trail notes: Kitchen Creek Falls is the most beautiful waterfall in San Diego, a visually stunning 150-foot drop that is hidden just a few hundred yards off the Pacific Crest Trail. Thousands of PCT hikers go right past it without even knowing it's there, although they may shake their heads and wonder where all those day hikers are heading to. The hike to reach the general vicinity of the falls is quite easy, since it follows the well-graded Pacific Crest Trail from Boulder Oaks, which crosses underneath Interstate 8 and then climbs uphill. The total gain is only about 500 feet. The tricky part comes in finding the unmarked cutoff for Kitchen Creek Falls, and then scrambling your way down steep slopes to reach its base. Here's how you do it: After 45 to 50 minutes of hiking, start looking carefully to your left for a narrow spur trail. You'll reach it at exactly two miles up, which for most people is about an hour of trail time. Turn left on the spur, and hike a short distance to see if you're looking down on Kitchen Creek—a fairly flat stream with many good-looking pools. If you are, you're also right above the waterfall, and to reach it, you must cut down the hillside on one of many use trails, heading downstream. (Keep the creek on your right; don't cross it.) Use great caution in getting to the waterfall's base—stay on the dirt trails and stay off the polished granite, even when it's dry. Get yourself safely to a spot where you can look up and admire the gorgeous falls, which are a series of tiered cascades that twist and turn over a rounded ledges in the bedrock. Plan on staying a while.

Pacific Crest Trail (PCT) Section Overview

156.0 mi. one way/15.0 days

Your heart will sound off like a bass drum on your first steps along this section of the Pacific Crest Trail—which extends from the Campo Border Station Trailhead north to the Highway 74 Trailhead—not from the terrain or grandeur, but rather from what these first steps along American's greatest hiking trail represent. It's an emotional impact that strikes nearly everybody. This is it, the PCT, from Mexico to Canada, 2,650

miles in all, traversing 37 wilderness areas and seven national parks, including some of the most breathtaking scenery anywhere in the world. The California section of the PCT spans 1,700 miles, and while only PCT through-hikers cover every mile, thousands of great day hikes and shorter backpacking expeditions are possible throughout much of the route. This first section features mountainous and high desert terrain that is both arid and hot. In summer, lack of water and 100-degree temperatures can make it virtually impassable. PCT through-hikers start their journeys from late winter to spring, sometime between late February and late March, in order to minimize these problems as much as possible. But instead of summer heat, they may find themselves stopping for two or three days at a time because of surprise rains, and in the higher elevations, snow. Regardless, this is better than setting out too late in the year and facing dried-up streams and springs, where you can go delirious wondering where your next drink of water will come from. For day hikes, the best conditions are from November through April. Trail elevations within this section range from 3,000 feet to more than 6,000 feet.

PCT-1 Campo Border Patrol to Lake Morena Park

20.0 mi. one way/2.0 days

Location: From the Campo Border Patrol north to the trailhead parking area at Lake Morena south of Interstate 8; map J6, grid i8.

User groups: Hikers, dogs (except in national parks), and horses. No mountain bikes. No wheelchair facilities.

Permits: A wilderness permit is required for traveling through various wilderness and special-use areas the trail traverses. Contact the Cleveland National Forest at (619) 445-6235 for a permit that is good for the length of your trip.

Directions: To reach the Campo Trailhead, from Highway 94, east of San Diego and south of Interstate 8, drive south on Forest Gate Road in the town of Campo to the U.S. Border Patrol Station; hikers are requested to check in here. The trailhead is located approximately 1.5 miles south of the station at the Mexican border. Specific directions will be given at the border patrol station. To reach the Lake Morena Trailhead, from San Diego, drive approximately 53 miles east on Interstate 8. Then drive south on County Road S1 (Buckman Springs Road) for five miles to Oak Drive. Turn right and follow the signs to the park. The PCT Trailhead is located at the corner of Lake Morena Road and Lakeshore Drive.

Maps: For an overall view of the trail route in this section, send $4 to the USDA-Forest Service, 630 Sansome Street, San Francisco, CA 94111; ask for the Cleveland National Forest map. For topographic maps of the route, request Campo, Potrero, and Morena Reservoir from the USGS.

Contact: Cleveland National Forest, Descanso Ranger District, 3348 Alpine Boulevard, Alpine, CA 91901; (619) 445-6235 or fax (619) 445-1753.

Trail notes: Your first steps on the Pacific Crest Trail can be a profound moment, when you realize you can walk all the way from Mexico to Canada. A small wooden monument at the trailhead reads: "Southern Terminus Pacific Crest National Scenic Trail. Established by act of Congress on October 2, 1968. Mexico to Canada 2627 miles. 1988 A.D. Elevation 2915." There is a small trail register, which everybody signs to mark the moment; then you take a deep breath, recognize what lies ahead, and start walking. You'll never forget it.

This first section is a good two-day pull, starting at the Mexico border and heading north 19 miles to your first supply point at a post office near Lake Morena County Park in Campo. Highlights include a climb up to Hauser Mountain, where you'll enter the Hauser Wilderness, California's smallest wilderness, and traverse one canyon after another, with the highest elevation at 3,400 feet. From here the trail drops down into Hauser Canyon, bottoming out at 2,320 feet. Most PCT hikers make their first night's camp in this area, then climb out of the canyon on the following day and head back up to the ridge. After enjoying sweeping views of the Laguna Mountain, you can push on to Lake Morena. A sidelight of this section, as well as others connecting to the north, is the adjacent mosaic of immigrant trails leading from Mexico into the U.S., and the occasional surveillance of them—as well as the PCT—by the Border Patrol.

PCT-2 Lake Morena Park to Boulder Oaks Camp

6.0 mi. one way/1.0 day

Location: From the trailhead parking area at Lake Morena south of Interstate 8 north to Boulder Oaks Camp near Interstate 8; map J6, grid h8.

User groups: Hikers, dogs (except in national parks), and horses. No mountain bikes. No wheelchair facilities.

Permits: A wilderness permit is required for traveling through various wilderness and special-use areas the trail traverses. Contact the Cleveland National Forest at (619) 445-6235 for a permit that is good for the length of your trip.

Directions: To reach the Lake Morena Trailhead, from San Diego, drive approximately 53 miles east on Interstate 8. Drive south on County Road S1 (Buckman Springs Road) for five miles to Oak Drive. Turn right and follow the signs to the park. The PCT Trailhead is located at the corner of Lake Morena Road and Lakeshore Drive. To reach the Boulder Campground Trailhead, from San Diego, drive approximately 53 miles east on Interstate 8. Drive south on County Road S1 (Buckman Springs Road) to Old Highway 80 and turn left. The Boulder Oaks Campground and the PCT Trailhead are located just off Old Highway 80.

Maps: For an overall view of the trail route in this section, send $4 to the USDA-Forest Service, 630 Sansome Street, San Francisco, CA 94111, and ask for the Cleveland National Forest map. For topographic maps of the route, request Morena Reservoir, Cameron Corners, and Mount Laguna from the USGS.

Contact: Cleveland National Forest, Descanso Ranger District, 3348 Alpine Boulevard, Alpine, CA 91901; (619) 445-6235 or fax (619) 445-1753.

Trail notes: This six-mile hike is an easy jaunt north toward the Laguna Mountains, tracing along a ridge primarily amid chaparral. Looming north are the Lagunas, the first mountains PCT hikers will encounter (though the first genuine mountains are the San Gorgonios), and most are eager to cross this high desert country, make the first climb, and start getting the gigantic panoramic views for which the PCT is famous.

The reason we included this short section as a separate segment is that it takes hikers near a Forest Service campground and the small Boulder Oaks Store, which is run by one of the nicest ladies on the planet; she let us fill up our canteens and sold us a few sodas before we set out for Kitchen Creek to see a hidden waterfall.

Boulder Oaks Camp to Sunrise Highway Trail

22.0 mi. one way/2.0 days

Location: From the trailhead parking area at Boulder Oaks Campground near Interstate 8 north to the Sunrise Highway Trailhead near Horse Heaven Campground; map J6, grid h9.

User groups: Hikers, dogs (except in national parks), and horses. No mountain bikes. No wheelchair facilities.

Permits: A wilderness permit is required for traveling through various wilderness and special-use areas the trail traverses. Contact the Cleveland National Forest at (619) 445-6235 for a permit that is good for the length of your trip.

Directions: To reach the Boulder Oaks Campground Trailhead, from San Diego, drive approximately 53 miles east on Interstate 8. Go south on County Road S1 (Buckman Springs Road) to Old Highway 80 and turn left. The Boulder Oaks Campground and the PCT Trailhead are located just off Old Highway 80. To reach the Sunrise Highway access from San Diego, drive approximately 50 miles east on Interstate 8 to the Laguna Junction exit. Go about 11 miles north on Sunrise Highway to the town of Mount Laguna. Drive two miles past Mount Laguna on Sunrise Highway/Laguna Mountain Road to the campground entrance and PCT access.

Maps: For an overall view of the trail route in this section, send $4 to the USDA-Forest Service, 630 Sansome Street, San Francisco, CA 94111, and ask for the Cleveland National Forest map. For topographic maps of the route, request Monument Peak, Cameron Corners, and Mount Laguna from the USGS.

Contact: Cleveland National Forest, Descanso Ranger District, 3348 Alpine Boulevard, Alpine, CA 91901; (619) 445-6235 or fax (619) 445-1753.

Trail notes: After paying your dues for a few days without being compensated with great views, you're ready to head up into the Laguna Mountains—and the beautiful panorama that comes with it. The trail departs from near the Boulder Oaks Campground, crosses beneath Highway 8 ("This is the PCT?" you'll wonder), then starts to climb, the first real climb of the hike, rising nearly 3,000 feet over the course of 14 miles high in the Lagunas. In the process, you'll hike above much of the scrub and be rewarded with long-distance views of the desert below. Sunsets can be stunningly dramatic and beautiful, with the colors changing minute by minute. In the spring, the ceanothus blooms provide a lot of color on the climb up, and once you hit the 6,000-foot elevation mark, you'll find a sprinkling of oaks and pines. You end this segment by hiking on the Desert View Nature Trail, highlighted by a breathtaking view of the Anza-Borrego Desert directly below. Most hikers time this section so they arrive at the campground to spend the night.

Sunrise Highway Trail to Highway 78 Trail

32.0 mi. one way/3.0 days

Location: From the trailhead parking area near the Sunrise Highway Trailhead and Horse Heaven Campground to the Highway 78 Trailhead; map J6, grid g9.

User groups: Hikers, dogs (except in national parks), and horses. No mountain bikes. No wheelchair facilities.

Permits: A wilderness permit is required for traveling through various wilderness and special-use areas the trail traverses. Contact the Cleveland National Forest at (619) 445-6235 for a permit that is good for the length of your trip.

Directions: To reach the Sunrise Highway access, from San Diego, drive approximately 50 miles east on Interstate 8 to the Laguna Junction exit. Go approximately 11 miles north on Sunrise Highway to the town of Mount Laguna. Then drive two miles past Mount Laguna on Sunrise Highway/Laguna Mountain Road to the campground entrance and PCT access. To reach the Highway 78 Trailhead, from Julian, head east on Highway 78 to the Highway 78/County Road S2 (Great Southern Overland Stage Route of 1849) junction. The PCT crosses here near the Butterfield Stage Line commemorative marker.

Maps: For an overall view of the trail route in this section, send $4 to the USDA-Forest Service, 630 Sansome Street, San Francisco, CA 94111, and ask for the Cleveland National Forest map. For topographic maps of the route, request Monument Peak, Cuyamaca Peak, Julian, and Earthquake Valley from the USGS.

Contact: Cleveland National Forest, Descanso Ranger District, 3348 Alpine Boulevard, Alpine, CA 91901; (619) 445-6235, or fax (619) 445-1753.

Trail notes: Water becomes sparse on this section of trail, so prior to leaving the campground/trailhead, make sure to contact the wilderness rangers to get updated on each of the most current reliable water supply points. That done, get ready to tromp, because this is where PCT hikers start to really move. The PCT enters Cuyamaca Rancho State Park, then drops and is routed into Oriflamme Canyon. When you rise out of the canyon and reach the rim, suddenly in front of you is 100 miles of high desert backed by the San Gorgonio Mountains. Here is where your wilderness skills, body condition, and knowledge of the land (and where the water is) become critical. Don't go on unless all three are first-rate. That done, plan a long-distance endurance test, with surroundings so meager that in summer, you'd be happy to drink water out of a hoof print.

PCT-5 Highway 78 Trailhead to Warner Springs

33.0 mi. one way/3.0 days

Location: From the Highway 78 Trailhead to the Warner Springs Trailhead; map J6, grid d9.

User groups: Hikers, dogs, and horses. No mountain bikes. No wheelchair facilities.

Permits: A wilderness permit is required for traveling through various wilderness and special-use areas the trail traverses. Contact the Cleveland National Forest at (619) 445-6235 for a permit that is good for the length of your trip.

Directions: To reach the Highway 78 Trailhead,

from Julian, head east on Highway 78 to the Highway 78/County Road S2 (Great Southern Overland Stage Route of 1849) junction. The PCT crosses here near the Butterfield Stage Line commemorative marker. To reach the Highway 79 Trailhead, from Warner Springs, head west on Highway 79 for approximately one mile to mile marker 36.7 and a turnout parking area next to the highway. Hike back to the bridge and mile marker 36.6 for the PCT Trailhead.

Maps: For an overall view of the trail route in this section, send $4 to the USDA-Forest Service, 630 Sansome Street, San Francisco, CA 94111, and ask for the Cleveland National Forest map. For topographic maps of the route, request Earthquake Valley, Julian, Ranchita, Hot Springs Mountain, and Warner Springs from the USGS.

Contact: Cleveland National Forest, Palomar Ranger District, 1634 Black Canyon Road, Ramona, CA 92065; (760) 788-0250 or fax (760) 788-6130.

Trail notes: Be done with it. That's the attitude most PCT through-hikers have about this section of trail. In late winter, it's tolerable when temperatures are relatively mild and you calculate your water stops perfectly. Highlights are Barrel Spring (water! water!), lonely canyons, and occasional ridges with endless views of miles and miles of desert valleys backed by dry mountain peaks. For many years, several sections of trail in this area were confusing, and many hikers either became lost or at least confused for a few hours. The new triangular PCT signs posted in the mid-1990s have done much to solve this frustration. As you near Warner Springs, you're rewarded with a view of Lake Henshaw (is that water in there?), real live trees (mainly oaks), and even a small stream (yes, it really is water) in the final miles to your resupply point at Warner Springs Post Office.

PCT-6 Warner Springs to Highway 74

43.0 mi. one way/4.0 days

Location: From the Warner Springs Trailhead to the Highway 74 Trailhead; map J6, grid c8.

User groups: Hikers, dogs, and horses. No mountain bikes. No wheelchair facilities.

Permits: A wilderness permit is required for traveling through various wilderness and special-use areas the trail traverses. Contact the Cleveland National Forest at (619) 445-6235 for a permit that is good for the length of your trip.

Directions: To reach the Highway 79 Trailhead, from Warner Springs, head west on Highway 79 for approximately one mile to mile marker 36.7 and a turnout parking area next to the highway. Hike back to the bridge and mile marker 36.6 for the PCT Trailhead. To reach the Highway 74 Trailhead, from the town of Hemet, head east on Highway 74 to the intersection of Highway 74 and Highway 371 (Cahuilla Road). The trailhead for the PCT is about one mile southeast on Highway 74 just west of the Santa Rosa Summit.

Maps: For an overall view of the trail route in this section, send $4 for each map to the USDA-Forest Service, 630 Sansome Street, San Francisco, CA 94111, and ask for the Cleveland National Forest and San Bernardino National Forest maps. For topographic maps of the route, request Hot Springs Mountain, Warner Springs, Bucksnort Mountain, and Butterfly Peak from the USGS.

Contact: Cleveland National Forest, Descanso Ranger District, 3348 Alpine Boulevard, Alpine, CA 91901; (619) 445-6235 or fax (619) 445-1753. San Bernardino National Forest, San Jacinto Ranger District, 54270 Pinecrest, Idyllwild, CA 92549; (909) 659-2117 or fax (909) 659-2107.

Trail notes: Here's the deal. We've met dozens of hikers en route from Mexico to Canada, and they all say the same thing: the most difficult sections of the PCT are the 30 miles out of Warner Springs, the Hat Creek Rim (in Lassen County), the Mojave, icy Forester Pass (north of Whitney), and Muir Pass (in high snow years). After leaving Warner Springs, you can face 28 miles without water. While we haven't hiked this particular section, PCT trail expert Ray Jardine says that in wet years, water can sometimes be discovered at about a half dozen spots along the way. Don't count on it, he also suggests. PCT through-hikers should have each of these spots mapped (location information is available from Forest Service wilderness experts). But we have also met expert hikers who made the entire 28 miles without a resupply, though they

resembled iguanas. The flora isn't much, mainly chaparral, cactus, and various scrub, the only plants that can live in such an inhospitable climate. The PCT is routed amid this, with a feature point being a 2,500-foot climb near the top of Combs Peak (6,000 feet), where there's a fantastic turn-your-head-around view of desert, dry peaks, and your eventual destination, the San Gorgonio Mountains to the north. From here, you drop into brush-beaten country, but then rise again to great lookouts over the course of a few days from Table, Bucksnort, and Lookout Mountains. If you have enough water, you might even enjoy it. Then again, maybe not.

PCT Continuation: To continue hiking along the Pacific Crest Trail, see chapter 16.

Map J7

Adjoining Maps: East: J8 ..... *page* 650   West: J6 626
North: I7 616

Southern California Map .... *page* 558

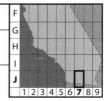

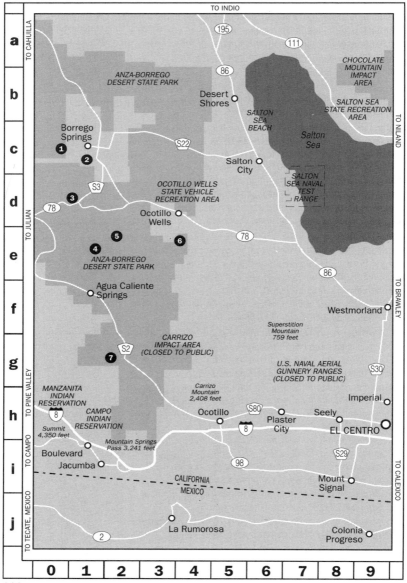

TO INDIO

a TO CAHUILLA

ANZA-BORREGO
DESERT STATE PARK

b

CHOCOLATE
MOUNTAIN
IMPACT
AREA

86

Desert
Shores

SALTON SEA
STATE RECREATION
AREA

SALTON
SEA
BEACH

TO NILAND

Borrego
Springs

c ❶

❷

S22

*Salton
Sea*

Salton
City

SALTON
SEA NAVAL
TEST
RANGE

d S3

❸

78

OCOTILLO WELLS
STATE VEHICLE
RECREATION AREA

TO JULIAN

Ocotillo
Wells

❺

❹

78

86

e ❻

ANZA-BORREGO
DESERT STATE PARK

Agua Caliente
Springs

Westmorland

TO BRAWLEY

f

Superstition
Mountain
759 feet

CARRIZO
IMPACT AREA
(CLOSED TO PUBLIC)

S2

g ❼

U.S. NAVAL AERIAL
GUNNERY RANGES
(CLOSED TO PUBLIC)

S30

TO PINE VALLEY

MANZANITA
INDIAN
RESERVATION

Carrizo
Mountain
2,408 feet

Imperial

h 8

CAMPO
INDIAN
RESERVATION

Ocotillo

S80

Seely

Summit
4,350 feet

Plaster
City

8

EL CENTRO

TO CAMPO

Mountain Springs
Pass 3,241 feet

Boulevard

Jacumba

S29

i

98

Mount
Signal

CALIFORNIA

MEXICO

TO CALEXICO

j TO TECATE, MEXICO

2

La Rumorosa

Colonia
Progreso

| 0 | 1 | 2 | 3 | 4 | 5 | 6 | 7 | 8 | 9 |

1 Borrego Palm Canyon Falls

3.0 mi/1.5 hrs

Location: In Anza-Borrego Desert State Park near Borrego Springs; map J7, grid c0.

User groups: Hikers only. No dogs, horses, or mountain bikes. No wheelchair facilities.

Permits: No permits are required. A $5 day-use fee is charged per vehicle.

Directions: From Julian, drive east on Highway 78 for approximately 19 miles to Highway S3/Yaqui Pass Road. Turn left (north) on Highway S3/Yaqui Pass Road and drive for 12 miles to Borrego Springs. Turn left on Highway S22/Palm Canyon Drive, and drive one mile to the signed junction just before the park visitor center. Turn right and drive one mile to Borrego Palm Canyon Campground. The trailhead is at the west end.

Maps: A free map of Anza-Borrego Desert State Park is available at the park visitor center. To obtain a topographic map of the area, ask for Borrego Palm Canyon from the USGS.

Contact: Anza-Borrego Desert State Park, 200 Palm Canyon Drive, Borrego Springs, CA 92004; (760) 767-5311.

Trail notes: The hike to Borrego Palm Canyon Falls is only 1.5 miles in length, but it feels like a trip from the desert to the tropics. You start out in a sandy, rocky, open plain, sweating it out with the cacti and ocotillo plants, and you end up in a shady oasis of fan palms, dipping your feet in the pool of a fern-covered waterfall. The trip begins on the Borrego Palm Canyon Trail from the state park campground, where you should top off your water bottles and start walking. If you pick up an interpretive brochure at the park visitor center, you can identify the array of desert plants that grow along the trail, including cheesebush, brittlebush, catclaw (ouch!), and chuparosa. In a half mile, when you pass in-

terpretive post 20, you're suddenly surprised by the sight of hundreds of bright green, leafy palm trees up ahead. Borrego Palm Canyon is home to more than 800 mature native palms, the largest of over 25 groves in the park. It's one of the largest oases in the United States. Head toward the palms, and in a few minutes you'll be nestled in their shade, listening to the desert wind rustle their fronds. Follow the trail a little further and you'll reach a 15-foot waterfall tucked in among the palms, which streams over giant boulders and forms a large, sandy pool. We saw many maidenhair ferns growing by the water's edge, and a tiny hummingbird flitted about the scene. Ah, paradise.

2 Maidenhair Falls

5.0 mi/3.0 hrs

Location: In Anza-Borrego Desert State Park near Hellhole Canyon; map J7, grid c1.

User groups: Hikers only. No dogs, horses, or mountain bikes. No wheelchair facilities.

Permits: No permits are required. A $5 day-use fee is charged per vehicle.

Directions: From Julian, drive east on Highway 78 for approximately 19 miles to Highway S3/Yaqui Pass Road. Turn left (north) on Highway S3/Yaqui Pass Road and drive for 12 miles to Borrego Springs. Turn left on Highway S22/Palm Canyon Drive, and drive one mile to the signed junction just before the park visitor center. Turn left and drive three-quarters of a mile to the large parking lot on the west side of the road.

Maps: A free map of Anza-Borrego Desert State Park is available at the park visitor center. To obtain a topographic map of the area, ask for Tubb Canyon from the USGS.

Contact: Anza-Borrego Desert State Park, 200 Palm Canyon Drive, Borrego Springs, CA 92004; (760) 767-5311.

Trail notes: If you have taken the hike to Borrego Palm Canyon Falls and found that it suited your taste for desert adventure, this trip to Maidenhair Falls is a more challenging path to a slightly bigger, and more dramatic, desert waterfall. Stop in at the park visitor center before you begin and pick up their photocopied handout with trail directions. Also, remember to be prepared for a longer excursion in the desert (bring tons of extra water, and cover your head with a light-colored hat). Your destination is a 20-foot waterfall with a walled backdrop of maidenhair ferns and mosses. The route to reach it travels from Highway S22 south of the visitor center into the mouth of Hellhole Canyon. Begin on the California Riding and Hiking Trail for the first 200 yards, then turn right. You'll pass a few fan palms, a myriad of cactus, some odd-shaped rocks, and Indian grinding holes along the route. Cottonwoods grow in places along the stream. Maidenhair Falls is a bit tricky to find, tucked into a narrow canyon corner, but, with luck, there will be enough water running in the stream to clue you in to its location.

❸ Cactus Loop and Yaqui Well

2.75 mi/1.5 hrs

Location: In Anza-Borrego Desert State Park near Tamarisk Grove; map J7, grid d1.

User groups: Hikers only. No dogs, horses, or mountain bikes. No wheelchair facilities.

Permits: No permits are required. A $5 day-use fee is charged per vehicle.

Directions: From Julian, drive east on Highway 78 for 19 miles to Tamarisk Grove Campground at Road S3. The trailheads for the Cactus Loop and Yaqui Well Trails are opposite the camp entrance off Road S3.

Maps: A free map of Anza-Borrego Desert State Park is available at the park visitor center. To obtain a topographic map of the area, ask for Borrego Sink from the USGS.

Contact: Anza-Borrego Desert State Park, 200 Palm Canyon Drive, Borrego Springs, CA 92004; (760) 767-5311.

Trail notes: The Cactus Loop and Yaqui Well Trails are two separate nature trails at Anza-Borrego Desert State Park, but since they're right beside each other, you might as well hike both. The Cactus Loop Trail is a three-quarter-mile loop, and more hilly than you might expect from a nature trail. It shows off seven kinds of cactus, including barrel, hedgehog, fishhook, beavertail, and cholla, some as tall as six feet. Visitors often spot chuckwallas and other lizards scurrying among the spiny plants. The Yaqui Well Trail climbs for one mile among cactus, ocotillo, and cholla to a mesquite grove, and then reaches sulphury-smelling Yaqui Well. In a small circle around this seep, a tremendous variety of greenery grows, including willows and mesquite, given life by the year-round presence of water. Desert birds show up here, particularly colorful hummingbirds. If you're in the mood for still more of a desert education, drive five miles east of Tamarisk Grove to the short little loop trail at the Narrows. It's packed with a lot of geologic punch; you'll get a big lesson in geological processes, from faulting and landslides to erosion and earthquakes.

❹ Ghost Mountain Trail

2.0 mi/1.0 hr

Location: In Anza-Borrego Desert State Park near Blair Valley; map J7, grid e1.

User groups: Hikers only. No dogs, horses, or mountain bikes. No wheelchair facilities.

Permits: No permits are required. A $5 day-use fee is charged per vehicle.

Directions: From Julian, drive east on Highway 78 for 12 miles to Road S2, then turn south and drive six miles to the left turnoff for Blair Valley Camp. Turn left (east) and drive 2.7 miles on dirt, then turn right and drive to the Ghost Mountain Trailhead.

Maps: A free map of Anza-Borrego Desert State Park is available at the park visitor center. To obtain a topographic map of the area, ask for Earthquake Valley from the USGS.

Contact: Anza-Borrego Desert State Park, 200 Palm Canyon Drive, Borrego Springs, CA 92004; (760) 767-5311.

Trail notes: Marshal South and his family lived way up here on Ghost Mountain in the 1930s, and this trail climbs steeply to his homesite. All that remains are the house foundation, a few partial walls, an old door frame, and some assorted junk, but the destination is worthwhile if only because it sparks the imagination. South was a writer and his wife was a poet, and they built this adobe home and lived there with their children for more than 15 years. Life in the desert was not easy, but they lived simply, trying to survive in the spartan style of early Native Americans. South called this place Yaquitepec, although no one is quite sure what that meant. The trail to reach it is switchbacked (thank goodness), but the rocky path makes the going slow. Although Blair Valley and Ghost Mountain is higher in elevation than other parts of the park, and hence somewhat cooler, the 400-foot elevation gain on this trail makes it strenuous on a hot day.

❺ Pictograph Trail

2.0 mi/1.0 hr

Location: In Anza-Borrego Desert State Park near Blair Valley; map J7, grid e1.

User groups: Hikers only. No dogs, horses, or mountain bikes. No wheelchair facilities.

Permits: No permits are required. A $5 day-use fee is charged per vehicle.

Directions: From Julian, drive east on Highway 78 for 12 miles to Road S2, then turn south and drive six miles to the left turnoff for Blair Valley Camp. Turn left (east) and drive 5.2 miles on dirt to the Pictographs Trailhead.

Maps: A free map of Anza-Borrego Desert State Park is available at the park visitor center. To obtain a topographic map of the area, ask for Earthquake Valley from the USGS.

Contact: Anza-Borrego Desert State Park, 200 Palm Canyon Drive, Borrego Springs, CA 92004; (760) 767-5311.

Trail notes: A Native American rock art site is the destination of this trip, but a bonus is an inspiring vista of the Vallecito Valley. The trail leads from the Pictograph Trailhead, wandering through huge granite boulders. First you head through a dry wash and then climb up a ridge, and at a half mile out, you begin to descend. At three-quarters of a mile, you'll find some pictographs, painted in red and yellow pigments by the Diegeño Indians. (Look for the pictographs on the right side of the canyon.) The faded geometric designs are on the side of a boulder, slightly protected by a rock overhang. Continue further on the trail, and the canyon narrows dramatically until its walls come together at the brink of a dry waterfall, more than 150 feet tall. From its edge, the panoramic view is stunning, both of the steep dropoff and the far-off mountains and valley.

❻ Elephant Trees

1.5 mi/1.0 hr

Location: In Anza-Borrego Desert State Park near Split Mountain; map J7, grid e3.

User groups: Hikers only. No dogs, horses, or mountain bikes. No wheelchair facilities.

Permits: No permits are required. A $5 day-use fee is charged per vehicle.

Directions: From Julian, drive east on Highway 78 for 35 miles to Ocotillo Wells. Turn south on Split Mountain Road and drive six miles to the right turnoff that is signed for Elephant Trees. Turn right and drive just under a mile to the trailhead.

Maps: A free map of Anza-Borrego Desert State Park is available at the park visitor center. To obtain a topographic map of the area, ask for Harper Canyon from the USGS.

Contact: Anza-Borrego Desert State Park, 200 Palm Canyon Drive, Borrego Springs, CA 92004; (760) 767-5311.

Trail notes: It's not just the fantastic-looking elephant tree that you get to see on this trail, but also many of the common flora of Anza-Borrego Desert—creosote bush, burroweed, indigo bush, barrel cactus, ocotillo, catclaw, cholla, smoke tree. . . . There's enough desert plant identification to do to keep you quizzing your hiking partner all day. But it's the elephant trees that steal the show, with the crinkled, folded "skin" on their trunks that looks somewhat elephant-like. The trees can grow to be 10 feet tall, which is huge by desert standards, and they are an odd patchwork of colors: yellowish bark, blue berries, and orange twigs. They have a very evocative odor in their bark, something like a spicy air freshener.

❼ Mountain Palm Springs Canyon

2.6 mi/2.0 hrs

Location: In Anza-Borrego Desert State Park near Bow Willow; map J7, grid g2.

User groups: Hikers only. No dogs, horses, or mountain bikes. No wheelchair facilities.

Permits: No permits are required. A $5 day-use fee is charged per vehicle.

Directions: From Julian, drive east on Highway 78 for 12 miles to Road S2, then turn south and drive 29 miles to the Mountain Palm Springs Campground entrance road on the right. Turn right and drive to the camp and trailhead.

Maps: A free map of Anza-Borrego Desert State Park is available at the park visitor center. To obtain a topographic map of the area, ask for Sweeney Pass from the USGS.

Contact: Anza-Borrego Desert State Park, 200 Palm Canyon Drive, Borrego Springs, CA 92004; (760) 767-5311.

Trail notes: Although the groves of fan palms in Mountain Palm Springs are not as large as in Borrego Palm Canyon (see trail notes for hike number 1), they're equally beautiful and popular with park visitors. The palm oases, fed by underground springs and shaded by the magnificent fan palms, create a haven for plants and wildlife, as well as for hikers looking for a cool and shady place to take a walk. Mountain Palm Springs is in close proximity to the Tierra Blanca foothills, which are lined with white granite. Six distinct palm groves grow in the area, as well as occasional elephant trees; you can visit all of the groves in one walk. From the trailhead, hike to the left on the main trail to Pygmy Grove, then head straight to Southwest Grove (the largest of the groves), with a possible side trip off the loop to Torote Bowl. Return to Southwest Grove and head left to Surprise Canyon, then turn left again to reach Palm Bowl Grove. Palm Bowl Grove is the most intriguing of them all—it's a natural bowl that is ringed with more than 100 palm trees.

Leave No Trace Tips

Properly Dispose of What You Can't Pack Out

If no refuse facility is available, deposit human waste in catholes dug six to eight inches deep at least 200 feet from water, camps, or trails. Cover and disguise the catholes when you're finished.

To wash yourself or your dishes, carry the water 200 feet from streams or lakes and use small amounts of biodegradable soap. Scatter the strained dishwater.

Map J8

Adjoining Maps: West: J7 .... *page* 644

Southern California Map .... *page* 558

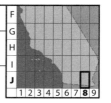

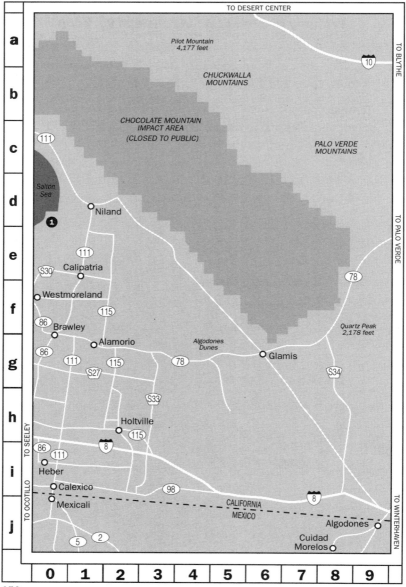

TO DESERT CENTER

a

Pilot Mountain
4,177 feet

TO BLYTHE

(10)

CHUCKWALLA
MOUNTAINS

b

CHOCOLATE MOUNTAIN
IMPACT AREA
(CLOSED TO PUBLIC)

PALO VERDE
MOUNTAINS

c

(111)

d

Salton
Sea

Niland

❶

TO PALO VERDE

e

(111)

(S30) Calipatria

(78)

f

Westmoreland

(115)

g

(86) Brawley

(86)

(111)

(S27)

(115)

Alamorio

(78)

Algodones
Dunes

Glamis

Quartz Peak
2,178 feet

(S34)

h

(S33)

Holtville

TO SEELEY

i

(86) (111)

Heber

(8)

(115)

TO OCOTILLO

Calexico

Mexicali

(98)

(8)

CALIFORNIA
MEXICO

TO WINTERHAVEN

j

(5)   (2)

Algodones

Cuidad
Morelos

| 0 | 1 | 2 | 3 | 4 | 5 | 6 | 7 | 8 | 9 |

Chapter J8 features:

❶ Salton Sea National Wildlife Refuge

3.0 mi/1.5 hrs

Location: On the east shore of the Salton Sea; map J8, grid d0.

User groups: Hikers only. No dogs, horses, or mountain bikes. No wheelchair facilities.

Permits: No permits are required. Parking and access are free.

Directions: From Indio, drive south on Highway 111 for approximately 50 miles to the turnoff for Sinclair Road, which is four miles south of Niland. (If you reach Calipatria, you've gone too far.) Turn right on Sinclair Road and drive six miles to the Salton Sea National Wildlife Refuge visitor center.

Maps: To obtain a topographic map of the area, ask for Niland from the USGS.

Contact: Salton Sea National Wildlife Refuge, 906 West Sinclair Road, Calipatria, CA 92233; (760) 348-5278.

Trail notes: If it's wintertime, anywhere from December to February, it's a good time to pay a visit to the Salton Sea National Wildlife Refuge, one of the lowest places in the United States at 228 feet below sea level. Winter is the only season when the area isn't blistering hot, and it's also the time that peak populations of birds are gathered at the refuge. The place has one hiking trail, which (believe it or not) gets hiked by approximately 35,000 bird-watchers a year. From the observation platform, the path heads out along a levee, then climbs gently to a hill above the Salton Sea. In addition to seeing the plentiful waterfowl who spend the winter in the saltwater and freshwater marshes—geese of many kinds, mergansers, wigeons, and teals—you might spot an endangered species such as the Yuma clapper rail or peregrine falcon.

Best Hikes

Can't decide where to hike this weekend?
Here are our picks for the best hikes in California in 19 different categories:

Waterfalls

Bridalveil Fall, Yosemite National Park, Chapter E4, page 357.

Lower Yosemite Fall, Yosemite National Park, Chapter E4, page 352.

Mist Trail and John Muir Loop to Nevada and Vernal Falls, Yosemite National Park, Chapter E4, pages 353-354.

Feather Falls National Recreation Trail, Plumas National Forest, Chapter C3, page 135.

Burney Falls Trail, McArthur-Burney Falls State Park, Chapter B3, page 88.

Grouse Falls, Tahoe National Forest, Chapter D3, page 177.

Illilouette Fall, Yosemite National Park, Chapter E4, page 362.

Chilnualna Falls, Yosemite National Park, Chapter E4, page 363.

Waterwheel Falls, Yosemite National Park, Chapter E4, page 345.

Rainbow Falls Trail, Devils Postpile National Monument, Chapter E5, page 376.

Tokopah Falls, Sequoia National Park, Chapter F5, page 451.

McWay Falls Overlook, Julia Pfeiffer Burns State Park, Chapter F1, page 399.

Hetch Hetchy Reservoir, Yosemite National Park, Chapter E4, page 337.

Wildflowers

Antelope Valley Poppy Preserve Loop, Chapter H5, page 544.

Vidette Meadow (PCT-21/JMT-1), John Muir Wilderness, Chapter F5, page 455.

Lundy Lake Trailhead, Hoover Wilderness, Chapter E5, page 371.

Hites Cove, Sierra National Forest, Chapter E4, page 356.

Path of the Padres, San Luis Reservoir State Recreation Area, Chapter F2, page 404.

Alamere Falls Trail, Point Reyes National Seashore, Chapter E1–Marin, page 228.

Grass Valley Loop, Anthony Chabot Regional Park, Chapter E1–East Bay, page 281.

Montana de Oro Bluffs Trail, Montana de Oro State Park, Chapter G2, page 469.

Butt-Kickers

Mount Whitney Trail, John Muir Wilderness, Chapter F5, page 453.

Shasta Summit Trail, Mount Shasta Wilderness, Chapter B2, page 70.

Muir Pass (PCT-21/JMT-1), John Muir Wilderness, Chapter F5, page 455.

Half Dome, Yosemite National Park, Chapter E4, page 355.

Rooster Comb Loop, Henry W. Coe State Park, Chapter E1–South Bay, page 318.

Beacoft Trail, Tahoe National Forest, Chapter D3, page 173.

Devil's Punchbowl, Siskiyou Wilderness, Chapter A1, page 18.

White Mountain Peak Trail, Inyo National Forest, Chapter E5, page 379.

Alta Peak, Sequoia National Park, Chapter F5, page 450.

Vivian Creek Trail to Mount San Gorgonio, San Gorgonio Wilderness, Chapter I6, page 608.

Mount Baldy, Angeles National Forest, Chapter I5, page 590.

Lookout Peak, Kings Canyon National Park, Chapter F5, page 433.

Views/Scenic Overlooks

Aerial Tramway to San Jacinto Peak, Mount San Jacinto State Park and Wilderness, Chapter I6, page 609.

Panorama Trail, Yosemite National Park, Chapter E4, page 361.

Mount Whitney Trail, John Muir Wilderness, Chapter F5, page 453.

Deadfall Lakes Trail (to Mount Eddy), Shasta-Trinity National Forest, Chapter B2, page 68.

High Sierra Trail to Hamilton Lake, Sequoia National Park, Chapter F5, page 447.

Moro Rock, Sequoia National Park, Chapter F5, page 445.

Upper Soda Springs Trailhead (Thousand Island Lake), Ansel Adams Wilderness, Chapter E5, page 375.

Lassen Summit Trail, Lassen Volcanic National Park, Chapter B3, page 92.

North Ridge/Sunset Trail, Angel Island State Park, Chapter E1–Marin, page 249.

Sentinel Dome, Yosemite National Park, Chapter E4, page 359.

Needles Lookout, Sequoia National Forest, Chapter G5, page 494.

Little Baldy, Sequoia National Park, Chapter F5, page 440.

Selden Pass (PCT-21/JMT-1), John Muir Wilderness, Chapter F5, page 456.

Fresno Dome, Sierra National Forest, Chapter F4, page 412.

Eagle Peak, Yosemite National Park, Chapter E4, page 351.

Rubicon Trail, D.L. Bliss State Park, Chapter D4, page 189.

Mount Baldy, Angeles National Forest, Chapter I5, page 590.

Devil's Slide Trail to Tahquitz Peak, San Jacinto Wilderness, Chapter I6, page 611.

Meadows

McGurk Meadow, Yosemite National Park, Chapter E4, page 357.

Vidette Meadow (PCT-21/JMT-1), John Muir Wilderness, Chapter F5, page 455.

Panther Meadows, Mount Shasta Wilderness, Chapter B2, page 72.

Grass Valley Loop, Anthony Chabot Regional Park, Chapter E1–East Bay, page 281.

Casa Vieja Meadow, Golden Trout Wilderness, Chapter G5, page 495.

Manter Meadow Loop, Dome Land Wilderness, Chapter G5, page 504.

Zumwalt Meadow Loop, Kings Canyon National Park, Chapter F5, page 434.

Swimming Holes

Toad Lake Trail, Shasta-Trinity National Forest, Chapter B2, page 74.

Lower McCloud Falls, Shasta-Trinity National Forest, Chapter B2, page 79.

Paradise Creek Trail, Sequoia National Park, Chapter F5, page 444.

Green Valley Falls, Cuyamaca Rancho State Park, Chapter J6, page 636.

Santa Paula Canyon, Los Padres National Forest, Chapter H4, page 536.

Indian Pools, Sierra National Forest, Chapter F4, page 416.

Alder Creek Trail, Sequoia National Forest, Chapter G5, page 498.

Big Falls and Little Falls, Santa Lucia Wilderness, Chapter G2, page 471.

Cedar Creek and the Fishbowls, Sespe Wilderness, Chapter H4, page 533.

Self-Guided Nature Walks

McCloud Nature Trail, Shasta-Trinity National Forest, Chapter B2, page 78.

Methuselah Trail, Inyo National Forest, Chapter E5, page 380.

Unal Trail, Sequoia National Forest, Chapter G5, page 501.

Shadow of the Giants, Sierra National Forest, Chapter F4, page 411.

Trail of the Gargoyles, Stanislaus National Forest, Chapter E4, page 331.

Cottonwood Creek, Tahoe National Forest, Chapter D4, page 182.

Rainbow and Lake of the Sky Trails, Lake Tahoe Basin, Chapter D4, page 193.

Pino Alto Trail, Los Padres National Forest, Chapter H3, page 524.

McGrath State Beach Nature Trail,
McGrath State Beach, Chapter H3, page 530.

Inaja Memorial Trail, Cleveland National Forest, Chapter J6, page 631.

Elephant Trees, Anza-Borrego Desert State Park, Chapter J7, page 647.

Ponderosa Vista Nature Trail, San Bernardino National Forest, Chapter I6, page 605.

Redwoods/Sequoia

Tall Trees Trail, Redwood National Park, Chapter AØ, page 13.

Redwood Creek Trail, Redwood National Park, Chapter AØ, page 13.

Boy Scout Tree Trail, Jedediah Smith Redwoods State Park, Chapter AØ, page 7.

Bull Creek Flats Trail, Humboldt Redwoods State Park, Chapter BØ, page 51.

Redwood Canyon, Kings Canyon National Park, Chapter F5, page 436.

Shadow of the Giants, Sierra National Forest, Chapter F4, page 411.

General Grant Tree, Kings Canyon National Park, Chapter F4, page 420.

Congress Trail Loop, Sequoia National Park, Chapter F5, page 449.

Trail of 100 Giants, Sequoia National Forest, Chapter G5, page 496.

Main Trail, Muir Woods National Monument, Chapter E1–Marin, page 239.

Short Backpack Trips

Ladybug Trail, Sequoia National Park, Chapter G5, page 479.

Gabrielino Trail to Bear Canyon, Angeles National Forest, Chapter I5, page 582.

Glen Aulin and Tuolumne Falls, Yosemite National Park, Chapter E4, page 346.

May Lake, Yosemite National Park, Chapter E4, page 339.

Toad Lake Trail, Shasta-Trinity National Forest, Chapter B2, page 74.

Winnemucca Lake Loop, Mokelumne Wilderness, Chapter D4, page 204.

Taylor Lake Trail, Russian Wilderness, Chapter A1, page 27.

Coast Trail, Point Reyes National Seashore, Chapter E1–Marin, page 223.

One-Way Hikes with Shuttle

John Muir Trail, begins in Chapter F5, page 455.

Panorama Trail, Yosemite National Park, Chapter E4, page 361.

Pohono Trail, Yosemite National Park, Chapter E4, page 360.

Skyline-to-Sea Trail, Big Basin Redwoods State Park, Chapter E1–South Bay, page 307.

Lost Coast Trail, Sinkyone Wilderness State Park, Chapter CØ, page 50.

Beach/Coast Walks

Lost Coast Trail, Sinkyone Wilderness State Park, Chapter CØ, page 110.

Lost Coast Trail, King Range National Conservation Area, Chapter BØ, page 50.

Coast Trail, Point Reyes National Seashore, Chapter E1-Marin, page 223.

Old Landing Cove Trail, Wilder Ranch State Park, Chapter F1, page 386.

Razor Point and Beach Trail Loop, Torrey Pines State Reserve, Chapter J5, page 624.

Rim Loop Trail, Patrick's Point State Park, Chapter BØ, page 47.

Montana de Oro Bluffs Trail, Montana de Oro State Park, Chapter G2, page 469.

Point Lobos Perimeter, Point Lobos State Reserve, Chapter F1, page 393.

Bayside Trail, Cabrillo National Monument, Chapter J5, page 624.

Cabrillo Tide Pools, Cabrillo National Monument, Chapter J5, page 625.

Wildlife

Note: Seeing wildlife is not guaranteed and is often seasonally influenced.

Tomales Point Trail, Point Reyes National Seashore, Chapter E1–Marin, page 217.

Año Nuevo Trail, Año Nuevo State Reserve, Chapter E1–South Bay, page 310.

Coastal Trail (Fern Canyon/Ossagon Section), Prairie Creek Redwoods State Park, Chapter AØ, page 11.

Desert Tortoise Discovery Loop, Desert Tortoise Natural Area, Chapter H5, page 543.

Tule Elk State Reserve, Chapter G4, page 477.

Timber Mountain, Modoc National Forest, Chapter A3, page 40.

Spirit Lake Trail, Marble Mountain Wilderness, Chapter A1, page 25.

Captain Jack's Stronghold, Lava Beds National Monument, Chapter A3, page 37.

Pescadero Marsh, south of Pescadero, Chapter E1–South Bay, page 297.

Bird-watching

Audubon Canyon Ranch Trail, near Bolinas Lagoon, Chapter E1–Marin, page 228.

South Tufa Trail, Mono Lake Tufa State Reserve, Chapter E5, page 372.

Sanctuary Trail, Arcata Marsh and Wildlife Sanctuary, Chapter BØ, page 48.

Abbotts Lagoon Trail, Point Reyes National Seashore, Chapter E1–Marin, page 218.

Elkhorn Slough South Marsh Loop, Elkhorn Slough National Estuarine Reserve, Chapter F1, page 390.

Chester and Winton Marsh Trails, San Luis National Wildlife Refuge, Chapter F2, page 403.

Silverwood Wildlife Sanctuary, Chapter J6, page 635.

Carrizo Plains and Painted Rock, Carrizo Plains Natural Area, Chapter G3, page 475.

Canyon Trail, Big Morongo Canyon Preserve, Chapter I7, page 617.

Arrowhead Marsh, Martin Luther King Regional Shoreline, Chapter E1–East Bay, page 279.

Summits

Shasta Summit Trail, Shasta-Trinity National Forest, Chapter B2, page 70.

Mount Whitney Trail, John Muir Wilderness, Chapter F5, page 453.

Aerial Tramway to San Jacinto Peak, Mount San Jacinto State Park, Chapter I6, page 609.

Mount Baldy, Angeles National Forest, Chapter I5, page 590.

Lassen Summit Trail, Lassen Volcanic National Park, Chapter B3, page 92.

Vivian Creek Trail to Mount San Gorgonio, San Gorgonio Wilderness, Chapter I6, page 608.

Grizzly Lake Trail (Thompson Peak), Trinity Alps Wilderness, Chapter B1, page 60.

White Mountain Peak Trail, Inyo National Forest, Chapter E5, page 379.

Preston Peak, Siskiyou Wilderness, Chapter A1, page 20.

East Peak Mount Tamalpais, Mount Tamalpais State Park, Chapter E1–Marin, page 236.

Island Walks

San Miguel Island Trail, Channel Islands National Park, Chapter I2, page 561.

East Anacapa Island Loop Trail, Channel Islands National Park, Chapter I3, page 563.

North Ridge/Sunset Trail, Angel Island State Park, Chapter E1–Marin, page 249.

Empire Landing Road Trail, Catalina Island, Chapter I4, page 576.

Two Harbors to Emerald Bay, Catalina Island, Chapter I4, page 575.

Wheelchair Accessible

South Yuba Independence Trail, near Nevada City, Chapter D3, page 167.

Kangaroo Lake, Klamath National Forest, Chapter B2, page 67.

Taylor Lake Trail, Russian Wilderness, Chapter A1, page 27.

Abbotts Lagoon Trail, Point Reyes National Seashore, Chapter E1–Marin, page 218.

Sierra Discovery Trail, PG&E Bear Valley Recreation Area, Chapter D3, page 170.

Salt Creek Interpretive Trail, Death Valley National Park, Chapter G7, page 516.

McWay Falls Overlook, Julia Pfeiffer Burns State Park, Chapter F1, page 399.

Lower Yosemite Fall, Yosemite National Park, Chapter E4, page 352.

Roaring River Falls, Kings Canyon National Park, Chapter F5, page 434.

Lake Cleone Trail, MacKerricher State Park, Chapter CØ, page 111.

Desert Terrain

Borrego Palm Canyon Falls, Anza-Borrego Desert State Park, Chapter J7, page 645.

Rainbow Basin, Rainbow Basin Natural Area, Chapter H6, page 551.

Afton Canyon, Afton Canyon Natural Area, Chapter H7, page 553.

Mosaic Canyon, Death Valley National Park, Chapter Chapter G6, page 509.

Wildrose Peak Trail, Death Valley National Park, Chapter Chapter G6, page 510.

Ubehebe Peak, Death Valley National Park, Chapter F6, page 459.

Ryan Mountain Trail, Joshua Tree National Park, Chapter I7, page 618.

For Kids

Angora Lakes Trail, Tahoe National Forest, Chapter D4, page 196.

Pinecrest Lake National Recreation Trail, Stanislaus National Forest, Chapter E4, page 333.

Desert Tortoise Discovery Loop, Desert Tortoise Natural Area, Chapter H5, page 543.

Rainbow and Lake of the Sky Trails, Lake Tahoe Basin, Chapter D4, page 193.

Bear Gulch Caves, Pinnacles National Monument, Chapter F2, page 407.

Rainbow Falls Trail, Devils Postpile National Monument, Chapter E5, page 376.

Tokopah Falls, Sequoia National Park, Chapter F5, page 451.

Año Nuevo Trail, Año Nuevo State Reserve, Chapter E1–South Bay, page 310.

Cabrillo Tide Pools, Cabrillo National Monument, Chapter J5, page 625.

Fitzgerald Marine Reserve, Moss Beach, Chapter E1–San Francisco Peninsula, page 259.

Tomales Point Trail, Point Reyes National Seashore, Chapter E1–Marin, page 217.

Fall Colors

Fallen Leaf Lake Trail, Tahoe National Forest, Chapter D4, page 194.

Farewell Gap Trail to Aspen Flat, Sequoia National Park, Chapter G5, page 482.

Desert View and Canyon Oak Loop, William Heise County Park, Chapter J6, page 634.

Boucher Trail and Scott's Cabin Loop, Palomar Mountain State Park, Chapter J6, page 629.

Stonewall Peak Trail, Cuyamaca Rancho State Park, Chapter J6, page 635.

Carlon Falls, Stanislaus National Forest, Chapter E4, page 338.

Lundy Lake Trailhead, Hoover Wilderness, Chapter E5, page 371.

McGee Creek to Steelhead Lake, John Muir Wilderness, Chapter F5, page 423.

Convict Lake Trailhead, Inyo National Forest, Chapter E5, page 379.

Index

667

BOLD PAGE NUMBERS INDICATE MAIN LISTINGS

BOLD PAGE NUMBERS INDICATE MAIN LISTINGS

Credits

Editor in Chief	Rebecca Poole Forée
Managing Editor	Donna Leverenz
Production Manager	Michele Thomas
Senior Editor	Jean Linsteadt
Associate Editor	Karin Mullen
Assistant Editor	Aimee Larsen
Production Coordinator	Alexander Lyon
Production Assistant	Leigh Anna Mendenhall
Acquisitions Editor	Judith Pynn
Research Editor	Janet Connaughton
Cover Photo	Twin Lakes, Hoover Wilderness by Ann Marie Brown

Tom and Ann Marie have shared many hikes and much information in the course of doing this book. Ultimately, Tom was responsible for the San Francisco Bay Area and Northern California (chapters A to E, except for D4 and E4), and for the entire length of the Pacific Crest Trail. Ann Marie was responsible for Lake Tahoe, Yosemite, and Southern California (chapters F to J, plus D4 and E4).

About the Authors

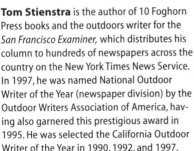

Tom Stienstra is the author of 10 Foghorn Press books and the outdoors writer for the *San Francisco Examiner,* which distributes his column to hundreds of newspapers across the country on the New York Times News Service. In 1997, he was named National Outdoor Writer of the Year (newspaper division) by the Outdoor Writers Association of America, having also garnered this prestigious award in 1995. He was selected the California Outdoor Writer of the Year in 1990, 1992, and 1997.

Ann Marie Brown is an outdoors writer and fitness instructor who lives in Marin County, California. She was raised in Southern California, where she attended Pomona College at the foot of the San Gabriel Mountains. Ann Marie has hiked Southern California trails extensively in the last few years, accumulating over 500 miles each summer. She is the author of three other Foghorn books: *Easy Hiking in Northern California, Easy Biking in Northern California,* and *California Waterfalls.*

California Hiking Chapter Reference Map

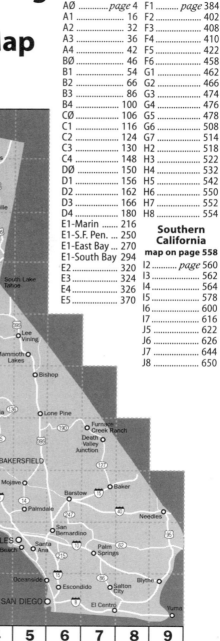